THE
Wartime Papers
of R. E. Lee

Confidential

Near Petersbg 2 Mar '65

Mr President

I enc a to day the letter from Genl Long
-street to which you refered in your note of the
28 Ulto — I have proposed to Genl Grant
an interview, in the hope that some good may
result, but I must confess that I am not
sanguine. My belief is that he will consent
to no terms, unless coupled with the condition
of an return to the Union; Whether this will
be acceptable to our people yet awhile I can
not say — I shall go to Richmond tomm
orrow next day to see you, & hope you will grant me
an hours conversation on the subject — Genl
Longstreet proposed that I should meet Genl
Grant at the point where he met Genl Ord, &
desired to have two or three days notice. I
have therefore appointed Monday next for the
interview with Genl Grant

With great respect your obt Servt
R E Lee
Genl

His Excy Jefferson Davis
Pres. C. States — Richmond

Courtesy of Duke University Library

A letter in General Lee's own hand to President Davis dated
March 2, 1865

(Letter 961 on Page 911)

THE
Wartime Papers
of R. E. Lee

CLIFFORD DOWDEY, *Editor*

LOUIS H. MANARIN, *Associate Editor*

with connective narratives by CLIFFORD DOWDEY

and maps by SAMUEL H. BRYANT

Virginia Civil War Commission
Bramhall House : New York

This edition published by Bramhall House,
a division of Clarkson N. Potter, Inc., by
arrangement with Little, Brown & Company.
h g f e d c b

Virginia Civil War Commission

Charles T. Moses
Chairman

Acknowledgments

The Virginia Civil War Commission extends its appreciation to the Virginia General Assembly and to Governor J. Lindsay Almond, Jr. for providing the substantial funds which made the editorial and research work on this project possible.

It is indebted to Mr. William J. Van Schreeven, Virginia State Archivist, for proposing the project and for his constant counsel during its publication.

It expresses its appreciation to the many individuals and institutions who provided information and assistance to the editors throughout the project.

The Editors wish to express their appreciation to the Editorial Advisory Committee, Mr. William J. Van Schreeven, Mr. William M. E. Rachal and Mr. James J. Geary for their assistance in the planning stages and in establishing procedures of operation. To the staff of the Virginia Civil War Commission, we express our gratitude for their invaluable assistance in providing facilities and in the preparation of the typed letters for the publisher. For his assistance in formulating the editorial procedure we are deeply grateful to Dr. Robert H. Woody, Duke University. To Dr. William G. Bean, Washington and Lee University, we are grateful for reading the narratives and for his interest and support.

For technical assistance in establishing procedure and arranging the final form of the book we are deeply indebted to Mr. John A. S. Cushman, of Little, Brown and Company.

The very helpful assistance received from the staffs of the numerous depositories containing Lee items cannot be adequately described here. To them we owe our appreciation for their co-operation and invaluable assistance in locating out-of-the-way manuscripts.

To Dr. Philip M. Hamer, Executive Director, National Historical Publications Commission, we would like to express our thanks for granting us permission to use the card catalogue on manuscript collections. We gratefully acknowledge Dr. David C. Mearns's assistance in lifting the restriction of the Lee collection at the Library of Congress and his general interest in our project. For his assistance in locating Lee items in private collections we are grateful to Mr. Van Dyk MacBride of Newark, New Jersey. To Miss Janet Fauntleroy Taylor, granddaughter of Colonel Walter H. Taylor, we express our gratitude for graciously granting us access to her grandfather's invaluable collection of Confederate and Lee material.

Along with the above-mentioned people and institutions, we would like to express our appreciation to the many people who volunteered information and assistance throughout this project.

Preface

The Virginia Civil War Commission accepted the proposal and program of the undersigned as State Archivist of Virginia to publish the war papers of R. E. Lee as a permanent contribution to the documentation of the war. Although the proposal advocated that all the war papers be published, it was found possible to publish only a single volume containing the most important letters, dispatches, orders and reports. The Commission recommended that a future project might include all the writings of R. E. Lee as part of the program to publish the papers of outstanding Americans.

In order to present the war papers in the best possible manner and to reduce to a minimum annotation of the documents, the proposal suggested that a series of connective narratives be prepared to introduce the reader to each division of the war papers. It was recommended that a noted authority on the Civil War be employed to write the connective narratives. The services of Mr. Clifford Dowdey were secured as Editor, and the reader will find in his connective narratives objective and careful appraisals of each division treated. Mr. Dowdey developed the narratives according to his interpretation of each period or campaign. The reader will find these narratives are no mere chronicle of dates and events.

The proposal to publish the war papers of R. E. Lee urged that the publication should be based upon original manuscripts and edited according to the highest scholarly standards. To this end the Commission employed Mr. Louis H. Manarin, a graduate student in the history of the Civil War period. He surveyed the various depositories holding R. E. Lee papers, selected material to be included, and edited the text from photocopies of the original manuscripts. Wherever possible he prepared for publication the first recorded manuscript when there was a choice between a recipient's copy and a file copy.

The introduction describes the Editors' method of final selection of the documents to be printed. This involved a careful reading of photocopies of all the manuscripts and the material to be included was chosen only after the most careful consideration. In many instances documents not included are summarized or used in the connective narratives.

The resulting publication presents for the first time in a single volume the most significant war papers of R. E. Lee that exist in manuscript or, if previously printed, are scattered through many separate volumes.

WILLIAM J. VAN SCHREEVEN
*State Archivist of Virginia and
Chairman of the Editorial Committee*

Introduction

FOR THE FOUR YEARS of the war, more than six thousand items of Lee's correspondence have been found, and others are known to exist, some of which were not made available to the editors of this volume. Outside of the strictly military letters in the *Official Records,* few of Lee's letters have been published in full, and most of his personal letters have never been published at all. Though his correspondence reveals the awesome consistency of the man, his completeness, there is a discernible difference between the man presented to the official Confederacy and to his family.

In his official correspondence, even in his most urgent messages on plans and needs, there is the guarded control of careful composition. In the letters he wrote to Mrs. Lee and his children, there is a casual candor about the larger events and the course of their fortunes in the simplicity of homey exchanges. Toward the end, when he wrote the War Department that "the result must be calamitous," he wrote his wife asking what she would do when Richmond was evacuated.

Because of the offhand revelations to his family, his personal letters complement his official letters in providing the mental background out of which his decisions were made. Through this, it is possible to trace the chart of his hopes and expectations, through the changes and decline of the Confederacy's lifespan; this chart reveals more dramatically than any descriptions or analyses of Lee's character the dominance of a sense of duty in his actions. This is not so much a sense of duty in the abstract as a duty to do the best he could. The point can clearly be seen when duty, as a sense of the pride of a professional in his craft, caused him to practice meticulously the techniques of command long after any military purpose could be achieved.

Because of the understanding offered by the interplay between his official and personal letters, the selections in this volume, about one sixth of General Lee's total correspondence during the four years, are concentrated largely on letters to his family and messages concerning his major military operations. The military operations of his own army were interrelated directly with the military actions throughout Virginia and in coastal North Carolina, indirectly with the Charleston area and middle Tennessee, and to some extent — at least as an element of consideration — with the entire Confederacy east of the Mississippi.

One glance at his correspondence will discredit forever the often repeated charge that Lee's interests were restricted to the Army of Northern Virginia. The enormous scope of his interests embraced, both in larger concepts and in minute details, all major Confederate operations east of the Mississippi. The false impression of his restricted range derives largely from the fact that all writers on Lee have stressed his actions with the Army of Northern Virginia. In turn, a fundamental reason for this was that his suggestions in other areas were seldom followed.

General Lee never possessed any authority beyond his own army and, as his letters show, it was not unrestricted even there. He was rarely able to field his complete army when and where he wanted it, or to effect cooperation with secondary forces scattered throughout Virginia and the Carolinas. While any general will fight to hold together the troops under his command, Lee recognized that constant dispersals from his army militated against the concentrations necessary for striking decisive strategic blows, as opposed, as he said repeatedly, to guarding all threatened points. In his struggle to maintain his own army, he never tried to obtain troops from another general's field command, and no point was ever seriously endangered from which he sought to draw troops—dispersed in garrisons—to his own army.

Though Lee never commanded more than one field army (except for the last two months when he received the then meaningless title of "general-in-chief"), President Davis regarded him throughout the war as a consultant, and his known consultations with Davis, the War Office, and sometimes with the Cabinet contributed to the impression of an authority he never possessed. The selected letters in this volume follow Lee's interchanges with the President and various secretaries of war where major decisions were involved.

The omissions from this book are chiefly in the areas of the detailed complexities of administration. Of the six thousand items, one sixth is devoted to special and general orders, the paper work passed on by his subordinates for Lee's signature, and reveal nothing of Lee as soldier or individual. Very few of these are used.

Of his total correspondence, approximately one half is devoted to the losing cause of maintaining his army physically in the field and in co-ordinating the actions of other forces not immediately under his control. This correspondence could be divided into separate categories: organization of the army; maintaining its numerical strength, with sizable subdivisions on the subjects of conscription and desertion; supplies, food for men and forage for the animals. With the limitations of the Confederacy and the inefficiency in its bureaus, Lee was forced throughout his command to double as commissary-general and quartermaster-general, and many of his letters to commanders of distant forces include instructions or pleas to discover sources of food and forage. This category would include a specific line on the shortage of animals, the poor condition of those on hand, and the stringent remedies used to prevent their collapse. The general section would also include the disposition of troops between Virginia and Charleston, those in the western mountains and in the southwestern part of the state. Many of the commanders in peripheral areas were, in one way or another, unsatisfactory, and it could be observed that the more often and the more at length Lee wrote a person the more he distrusted his ability.

Of the papers in these various categories, only illustrative examples have been used. Many of these were repetitious, as Lee not only wrote on the same subjects to different persons but, with passing time, only added some new detail or new shading of meaning to the flow of urgent solicitations for the support of his army. Also, either little action was taken or few results were obtained by his representations. Some of these eliminated letters contain sharp insights or a single passage revealing Lee's basic designs, but, in sacrificing these isolated fragments, we have not sacrificed any points not covered in following the lines of his major campaigns. The only unfortunate eliminations are those few which reflect his tact in divesting himself of subordinates who had proven unsatisfactory, but none of these concern major personalities. On the other hand, the letters detailing his relationships with Jackson and Longstreet, and to a lesser extent with other generals, have all been retained except where repetitious. Some of the letters to generals contain personal elements and at least one, to Stuart, is a personal letter.

The only personal letters eliminated were repetitions. In Lee's wide correspondence with members of his family, he frequently repeated the same sentiments, sometimes in the same words, and in such instances we have endeavored to select the single letter which best represents his views on a given subject. With the same exceptions of repetitions, all correspondence involving the development of his major campaigns has been reproduced.

The greatest lack in Lee's papers occurs in exchanges during battle, when most of his orders were verbal. He usually wrote fully, though charitably, in his battle reports, all of which have been reproduced except his preliminary report on Gettysburg, which was incorporated and expanded in his lengthy final report. There are no battle reports for 1864 and 1865, as these were burned in wagons on the way to Appomattox, though he wrote in considerable detail on the last actions in his April 12 letter to Davis. Toward the end, also, Lee burned considerable incoming correspondence and the copies of his answers.

Of his four daughters, Mildred, Agnes, Annie (who died on October 20, 1862), and Mary, Mary is the only one who did not preserve her father's letters, and there are none to her in this volume, though she is the "Daughter" of the letters. Of letters to his three sons, we have found none to R. E. Lee, Jr. The "Rob" of the letters, Lee's youngest son, left the University of Virginia to serve in an artillery battery and, except for a short stint on his brother Rooney's staff, remained a private to the end of the war. The middle son, W. H. F. Lee, the "Fitzhugh" of the letters, was called Rooney to distinguish him from his cousin Fitzhugh Lee, who is "Fitz" in Lee's letters. Called "too big to be a man and not big enough to be a horse," Rooney was a Harvard graduate who rose from command of the 9th Virginia cavalry to division command in Stuart's cavalry. The oldest son, Custis, the West Pointer of the boys, served as an aide on the President's staff and commanded Richmond's local defense troops, which were composed of companies of over-age men, under-age boys, workers from the Tredegar Iron Works and government arsenals, and the department clerks, many of whom were former soldiers invalided out of the army as unfit for active field service. The letters to Custis Lee are quite different in tone and subject matter from those to the other members of the family. Another facet of Lee is shown in the letters to his daughter-in-law Charlotte, Mrs. W. H. F. Lee, the "Chass" of the letters.

It was in a letter to Mildred that Lee wrote: "It has been said that our letters are good representatives of our minds. They certainly present a good criterion for judging of the character of the individual."

CLIFFORD DOWDEY, *Editor*
LOUIS H. MANARIN, *Associate Editor*

Richmond, Virginia

Contents

List of Maps

THE

Wartime Papers
of R. E. Lee

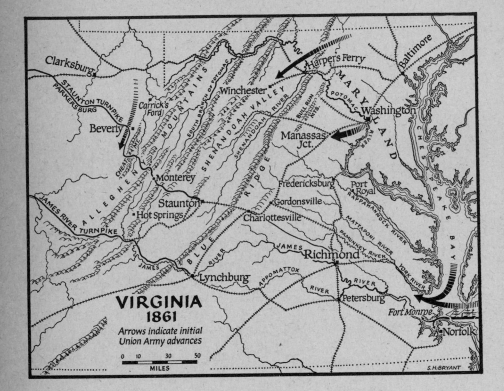

Clarksburg

STAUNTON TURNPIKE
PARKERSBURG

Carrick's
Ford

Beverly

A L L E G H E N Y   M O U N T A I N S

CHEAT

Monterey

JAMES RIVER
TURNPIKE

Hot Springs

Staunton

JAMES

RIVER

Lynchburg

SOUTH BRANCH OF POTOMAC

Winchester

S H E N A N D O A H   V A L L E Y

SHENANDOAH RIVER

B L U E   R I D G E

Harper's Ferry

Baltimore

M A R Y L A N D

BULL RUN
MTS.

POTOMAC

Washington

Manassas
Jct.

POTOMAC RIVER

Fredericksburg

Gordonsville

Charlottesville

Port
Royal

RAPPAHANNOCK RIVER

MATTAPONI RIVER

C H E S A P E A K E   B A Y

JAMES

RIVER

APPOMATTOX

RIVER

RIVER

PAMUNKEY RIVER

Richmond

Petersburg

YORK RIVER

Fort Monroe

Norfolk

VIRGINIA
1861

Arrows indicate initial
Union Army advances

0   10   30   50
MILES

S.H.BRYANT

CHAPTER ONE

Mobilizing Virginia

APRIL–JULY 1861

"Our policy is defense"

GENERAL LEE did not begin his Civil War career as a Confederate but as commander of Virginia's forces. This beginning largely contributed to the confusion which surrounded the employment of his gifts during the first year of the war, and which in turn led to his ambivalent status with President Davis throughout the war.

Lee was serving in the U. S. Cavalry in Texas when, on February 4, 1861, delegates from the six seceded states in the Lower South (subsequently joined by Texas) met at Montgomery, Alabama, to form an independent nation, and he felt no impulse to ally his state or offer his services to this movement. As with the majority of Virginians, he did not believe in secession nor, as a professional soldier, did he hold any stake in the institution of slavery. A number of slaves were included in the estate of his wife's father, George Washington Parke Custis (the grandson of Martha Washington and the adopted son of George Washington), who died in 1857, but by will these were to be manumitted. Before Lee effected the manumission, December 29, 1862, he wrote his son, Custis, of his distaste of involvement with chattel slaves, saying that Custis's grandfather "has left me an unpleasant legacy."

During February, 1861, when the tensions grew between the newly created Confederacy and the United States, with Fort Sumter as the symbol of disagreement, Lee was ordered to relinquish command of his regiment and report personally to General Winfield Scott, in Washington. Circumstantial evidence exists to indicate Scott's interest in retaining Lee in the U. S. Army, probably as commander of a new army to be raised to meet the emergency. Scott considered Lee "the very best soldier I ever saw in the field," and on March 16, 1861, promoted him to full colonel commanding the 1st Cavalry. (The commission was signed by President Lincoln on March 28.)

According to Lee, however, his only direct offer to command an army came from the powerfully connected Francis P. Blair. In a postwar letter to U. S. Senator Reverdy Johnson, February 25, 1868, Lee wrote:

I never intimated to any one that I desired the command of the United States Army; nor did I ever have a conversation with but one gentleman, Mr. Francis Preston Blair, on the subject, which was at his invitation, and, as I understood, at the instance of President Lincoln. After listening to his remarks, I declined the offer he made me, to take command of the army that was to be brought into the field; stating, as candidly and as courteously as I could, that, though opposed to secession and deprecating war, I could take no part in an invasion of the Southern States. I went directly from the interview [April 18, 1861] with Mr. Blair to the office of General Scott; told him of the proposition that had been made to me, and my decision. Upon reflection after returning to my home, I concluded that I ought no longer to retain the commission I held in the United States Army, and on the second morning thereafter I forwarded my resignation to General Scott. At the time, I hoped that peace would have been preserved; that some way would have been found to save the country from the calamities of war; and I then had no other intention than to pass the remainder of my life as a private citizen.

By the time Lee resigned on April 20, Virginia was, in effect, in a state of war with the United States. On April 15, the day after Sumter's evacuation, Lincoln had called for volunteers to "suppress" the "combination" formed by the Southern states; and though on April 4 a poll of the Virginia Convention had shown a two-to-one vote against secession, two days after Lincoln's call it voted to secede as an alternative to making war on sister states. In making this decision against participating in invasion, Virginia knew that her own soil would be invaded. On April 19, as Lee was struggling over his personal decision, the Virginia Convention passed an ordinance creating the post of major general to act as "the commander of the military and naval forces of Virginia," and the following day Governor Letcher accepted his advisory council's recommendation of Lee.

Ex-Colonel Lee enjoyed only one day as a private citizen, Sunday, April 21, while messengers from Richmond were on their way to the plantation mansion at Arlington. On Monday, he rode by train to Richmond, and, in an informal interview with the governor, accepted the command of Virginia's forces, under the control of the governor's constituted authority. The following day, April 23, the new major general went to the Capitol, designed by Jefferson, to receive his formal appointment from the Convention. Convention President John Janney

greeted Lee: "In the name of the people of your native State, here represented, I bid you a cordial and heartfelt welcome to this Hall, in which
we may almost yet hear the echo of the voices of the statesmen, the
soldiers and sages of by-gone days, who have borne your name, and
whose blood flows in your veins."

After stressing that Lee was the unanimous choice for the responsi-
ble assignment, Janney made a paraphrase on the famous eulogy which
Lee's father — Revolutionary cavalry leader, governor of Virginia and
United States Congressman — delivered on the death of his friend,
George Washington:

Sir, we have, by this unanimous vote, expressed our convictions that you are,
at this day, among the living citizens of Virginia, "first in war." We pray to
God most fervently that you may so conduct the operations committed to
your charge, that it will soon be said of you, that you are "first in peace," and
when that time comes you will have earned the still prouder distinction of being "first in the hearts of your countrymen."

Considering that Lee, at fifty-four, had spent the thirty-six years of
his adult life in the service of the United States Army and had relinquished the fruits of a career on which his family was dependent, he
responded to the call of his state with remarkably little to-do. Only his
personal letters reveal his extreme concern for the welfare of his semi-
invalid wife, four unmarried daughters, and three sons — one then in
college, who was to join the other two in the Confederate Army — for
his family faced not only loss of income but loss of their home and
Arlington plantation, which would fall to the enemy as soon as the
Potomac was crossed. In his unprecedented assignment of organizing a
state to defend itself against the invasion of a powerful nation, he faced
a situation for which chaotic would be an understatement, but he kept
to himself the multiple complex of problems to be solved and decisions to be made.

Two days after his formal appointment as commander of Virginia's
forces, the state formed a temporary alliance with the Confederacy.
This alliance placed all of Virginia's military organization under the
authority of the Confederate President, which meant that Lee, and all
of his and the governor's appointees, were operating on a temporary
basis. On May 21, 1861, the Confederate Congress decided to move the
capital to Richmond; by the end of May, Davis had come to the city, and
on June 8 the Virginia forces began to be transferred to the armies of
the Confederacy. Thus Major General Lee had little more than six weeks
to organize armed forces and a system of defense before shifting to the
uninspiring assignment of transferring units and positions to the new

arrivals from the original Confederacy. (North Carolina, Tennessee and Arkansas came in simultaneously with Virginia.)

During the first phase, in the relative obscurity of an office near Capitol Square, Lee revealed many of the assets that were to stand him in good stead during the coming years — an extraordinary gift for organization, his awesome patience, and a rare combination of conceiving in larger patterns with an "infinite capacity" for working in details. The paper work was mountainous; he operated with a small staff (of whom only Walter Taylor was to be permanent) and endured the usual solicitations from politicians who did not consider fitness a necessary qualification for appointment. Governor Letcher supported Lee in the policy of giving preferment to trained men and withholding posts of leadership from prominent civilians. Though "Honest John" made many appointments of his own, he won Lee's complete approval when he appointed to colonel a Lexington neighbor, Professor T. J. Jackson of the Virginia Military Institute, whom Lee remembered from the Mexican War days.

In creating regimental and brigade units where none had grown before, Lee had to contend with divisions between the militia companies (with which Virginia traditionally abounded), who came in as units and recruits who were divided between "volunteers" and soldiers in the "provisional" (regular) Virginia Army. With the briefest stays in "camps of instruction," where they were equipped and partially armed, the plantation grandees and the farm boys, the urban gallants and the village artisans, mostly all magnificently uniformed by themselves or their families, were hurried off to various danger spots.

Erecting an outline of defense required no particular brilliance but, though Lee planned to defend the obvious invasion approaches, he built soundly over the opposition of the hotbloods who urged the authorities to send off to battle the half-armed, gloriously caparisoned individuals like ancient knights against a robber baron.

Again with the support of Governor Letcher, Lee first fortified the tidewater rivers against the threat of the United States Navy, whose significance in the Virginia operations has never been sufficiently emphasized. The Potomac, the Rappahannock, the York and its subsidiary, the Pamunkey, and south of Richmond the James, all offered avenues of approach to armed vessels into the most populous sections of Virginia. Quickly built river forts were mounted with heavy guns and manned with hastily formed garrisons. Cannon of all caliber had fallen to the Virginians with the enforced evacuation of the Navy Yard at Norfolk, along with the hull of the scuttled frigate *Merrimac*, which was armored with iron plates manufactured by the Tredegar Iron Works in Richmond to become, as the *Virginia*, the first ironclad ship in the world used in combat.

But holding the port of Norfolk presented a problem as, three miles across Hampton Roads on the tip of the Virginia peninsula, the Federal-held Fort Monroe (where Lee's first son had been born when the young lieutenant was stationed there) dominated the area. By May 27, Union troops from Fort Monroe had occupied the city of Newport News and built land forts (or fortified camps) from which to invade straight west up the peninsula toward Richmond. Lee had men and guns on the peninsula, as well as in and around Norfolk, and on June 10, at what was then called the "Battle" of Big Bethel, the first Federal advance was repulsed with seventy-six casualties inflicted.

At the opposite side of the state, in the western mountains, which were soon to be severed from Virginia to form the new state of West Virginia, troops were sent for the dual purpose of holding the loyalist sections and preventing invasions from the west toward or into the Shenandoah Valley.

The great fertile Valley, which was to serve as the breadbasket of the Confederate forces in Virginia until near the very end, would obviously represent one of the most vital theaters of land operations. North of the Valley proper, at the juncture of the Shenandoah River and the Potomac, Harper's Ferry became an advance base and training camp of Colonel Thomas J. Jackson. There he began the molding of the tough Valley men into the First (later "Stonewall") Brigade which turned the battle tide and won him his sobriquet at First Manassas. There also Jackson established his military and personal intimacy with twenty-eight-year-old James Ewell Brown Stuart, the native-born cavalryman who had been a cadet at West Point when Lee served as superintendent.

The early seizure by Valley volunteers of the United States arsenal at Harper's Ferry had provided Virginians with the windfall of 16,000 modern rifles and, of more long-range importance, the machinery of manufacture. This was shipped to Richmond to form, with the Tredgar Iron Works and the Virginia Armory, the nucleus of the arms-producing center which made the capital the Ruhr of the Confederacy.

With these far-ranging and minute arrangements made by Lee, the most pressing point of danger was the plains of northern Virginia south of the Potomac in the neighborhood of Arlington. (Lee's letters reveal his acute awareness of his home throughout the war.) There the bulk of the uniformed civilians were concentrated on a defensive line drawn where Lee assumed, correctly, that the enemy would come. This straight-on drive southward across Virginia was the least promising approach to Richmond, but the Federal administration remained magnetized directly toward the enemy capital until the last and costliest failure, by Grant, four summers later.

As Lee was completing the groundwork of these inglorious assignments, the Confederate authorities arrived in Richmond to take over — especially Jefferson Davis, the commander-in-chief, and Confederate Brigadier General Beauregard, the hero of Fort Sumter. Beauregard was sent to Manassas, the line of importance, and Joseph E. Johnston, a Virginian who had offered his services directly to the Confederacy, superseded Jackson in the Valley. Lee occasionally conferred with Davis, and once he was permitted to consult with Beauregard, but, after he completed the transfer of the Virginia forces on June 15, officially he was in a vacuum, with no defined duties or authority.

Occupying himself as best he could, Lee supervised some of the garrisons and the movements of Virginia troops to points of greater concentration; many Virginia officers, like "Prince John" Magruder on the peninsula, continued to write him directly, and there was always the picayune paper work involving ordnance, equipment and the organization of troop units. However, as all eyes turned toward the approaching clash on the Virginia plains, Lee was a forgotten general without an army.

While he looked for a long war, the "fire-eaters" looked to the one battle that would send the invaders back home and convince the world that the sovereign people of the Confederate states could not be coerced by force. The one big battle came at Manassas on July 21st and — by the chance of action and no credit to Beauregard — the invaders did leave Virginia very unceremoniously, but the war was only beginning. The full impact of this reality seemed to be missed by the majority of the Southern leaders, and what Lee thought about it is unknown. In all the jubilation, "the very best soldier" whom Scott "ever saw in the field" was an unheeded spectator in his office in Richmond.

1   To GENERAL WINFIELD SCOTT
Commander-in-Chief, United States Army

Arlington, Washington City P.O.
April 20, 1861

General:
    Since my interview with you on the 18th instant I have felt that I ought not longer to retain my commission in the Army. I therefore tender my resignation, which I request you will recommend for acceptance.

It would have been presented at once, but for the struggle it has cost me to separate myself from a service to which I have devoted all the best years of my life & all the ability I possessed.

During the whole of that time, more than 30 years, I have experienced nothing but kindness from my superiors, & the most cordial friendship from my companions. To no one Genl have I been as much indebted as to yourself for uniform kindness & consideration, & it has always been my ardent desire to merit your approbation.

I shall carry with me to the grave the most grateful recollections of your kind consideration, & your name & fame will always be dear to me. Save in the defence of my native State, I never desire again to draw my sword.

Be pleased to accept my most earnest wishes for the continuance of your happiness & prosperity & believe me most truly yours

R. E. LEE

2 ## To SIMON CAMERON
Secretary of War

Arlington, Washington City P.O.
April 20, 1861

Sir:
I have the honour to tender the resignation of my commission as Colonel of the 1st Regt. of Cavalry.

Very resply your obt servt

R. E. LEE
Col. 1st Cavalry

3 ## To MRS. ANNE MARSHALL
Baltimore, Maryland

Arlington, Virginia
April 20, 1861

My Dear Sister:
I am grieved at my inability to see you. I have been waiting for a more convenient season, which has brought to many before me deep and lasting regret. Now we are in a state of war which will yield to nothing. The whole South is in a state of revolution, into which Virginia,

after a long struggle, has been drawn; and though I recognize no necessity for this state of things, and would have forborne and pleaded to the end for redress of grievances, real or supposed, yet in my own person I had to meet the question whether I should take part against my native State.

With all my devotion to the Union, and the feeling of loyalty and duty of an American citizen, I have not been able to make up my mind to raise my hand against my relatives, my children, my home. I have, therefore, resigned my commission in the Army, and save in defense of my native State (with the sincere hope that my poor services may never be needed) I hope I may never be called upon to draw my sword.

I know you will blame me, but you must think as kindly as you can, and believe that I have endeavored to do what I thought right. To show you the feeling and struggle it has cost me I send you a copy of my letter of resignation. I have no time for more. May God guard and protect you and yours and shower upon you everlasting blessings, is the prayer of

Your devoted brother,

R. E. LEE

4   To SYDNEY SMITH LEE
Washington, D. C.

Arlington, Virginia
April 20, 1861

My Dear Brother Smith:
The question which was the subject of my earnest consultation with you on the 18th instant has in my own mind been decided. After the most anxious inquiry as to the correct course for me to pursue, I concluded to resign, and sent in my resignation this morning. I wished to wait till the Ordinance of Secession should be acted on by the people of Virginia; but war seems to have commenced, and I am liable at any time to be ordered on duty which I could not conscientiously perform. To save me from such a position, and to prevent the necessity of resigning under orders, I had to act at once, and before I could see you again on the subject, as I had wished. I am now a private citizen, and have no other ambition than to remain at home. Save in defense of my native State, I have no desire ever again to draw my sword. I send you my warmest love.

Your affectionate brother,

R. E. LEE

5   SPEECH TO THE VIRGINIA CONVENTION UPON ACCEPTANCE OF COMMAND OF VIRGINIA FORCES

April 23, 1861

Mr. President and Gentlemen of the Convention:

Deeply impressed with the solemnity of the occasion on which I appear before you, & profoundly grateful for the honour conferred upon me, I accept the position your partiality has assigned me, though [I] would greatly have preferred your choice should have fallen on one more capable.

Trusting to Almighty God, an approving conscience & the aid of my fellow citizens, I will devote myself to the defence & service of my native State, in whose behalf alone would I have ever drawn my sword.

6   GENERAL ORDERS, NO. 1

Headquarters, Richmond, Virginia
April 23, 1861

In obedience to orders from his excellency John Letcher, governor of the State, Maj. Gen. Robert E. Lee assumes command of the military and naval forces of Virginia.

R. E. LEE
Major-General

7   To GENERAL DANIEL RUGGLES
Commanding Rappahannock River Defenses

Headquarters Forces of Virginia
April 24, 1861

General:

Your dispatch, of the 24th instant, requesting to know the policy and orders by which you are to be governed, is at hand. You will act on the defensive. Station your troops at suitable points to command the railroad; write and give assurance of protection to the inhabitants on the rivers; cause your troops to be instructed in the use of their several arms, and take immediate steps for provisioning them. If bacon cannot be procured, fresh meat must compose that part of your ration.

Two 8-inch howitzers have been sent you to-day; also ammunition for the same. I regret I cannot furnish you with carriages for these pieces, but I hope you will be able to have them constructed or made available for your purpose in Fredericksburg. You will endeavor to allay the popular excitement as far as possible. As soon as you can, send in a return of your troops, and where stationed.

I am, general, very respectfully,

R. E. LEE
Major-General, Commanding

8   To ————

Richmond
April 25, 1861

My Dear ————:

I have received your letter of 23d. I am sorry your nephew has left his college and become a soldier. It is necessary that persons on my staff should have a knowledge of their duties and an experience of the wants of the service to enable me to attend to other matters. It would otherwise give me great pleasure to take your nephew. I shall remember him if anything can be done. I am much obliged to you for Dr. M——'s letter. Express to him my gratitude for his sentiments, and tell him that no earthly act could give me so much pleasure as to restore peace to my country. But I fear it is now out of the power of man, and in God alone must be our trust. I think our policy should be purely on the defensive — to resist aggression and allow time to allay the passions and permit Reason to resume her sway. Virginia has to-day, I understand, joined the Confederate States. Her policy will doubtless, therefore, be shaped by united counsels. I cannot say what it will be, but trust that a merciful Providence will not dash us from the height to which his smiles have raised us. I wanted to say many things to you before I left home, but the event was rendered so imperatively speedy that I could not.

May God preserve you and yours! Very truly,

R. E. LEE

9   To HIS WIFE
Arlington

Richmond
April 26, 1861

My Dear Mary,

I return with my signature the pay accounts forwarded by Custis. I doubt the propriety of presenting them, & if presented I doubt whether they will be paid. I would therefore suppress them but for the probability, in the settlement of my accounts with the United States, some stoppage or disallowance, of which I am ignorant, may have been made against me for which they may be an off set to pay all charges against me. I wish if Custis or Lawrence Williams think proper they may be presented, otherwise destroy them & say nothing about it. I am very anxious about you. You have to move, & make arrangements to go to some point of safety which you must select. The Mt. Vernon plate & pictures ought to be secured. Keep quiet while you remain & in your preparations. War is inevitable & there is no telling when it will burst around you. Virginia yesterday I understand joined the Confederate States. What policy they may adopt I cannot conjecture. I send a check for $500., which you had better apply, tell Custis, in settling up matters. May God keep & preserve you & have mercy on all our people is the constant prayer of your affectionate husband.

R. E. LEE

10   To COLONEL THOMAS J. JACKSON
                    Camp Lee, Richmond

Headquarters Virginia Forces
Richmond, Virginia
April 27, 1861

Colonel:

You will proceed, without delay, to Harper's Ferry, Virginia, in execution of the orders of the governor of the State, and assume command of that post. After mustering into the service of the State such companies as may be accepted under your instructions, you will organize them into regiments or battalions, uniting, as far as possible, companies from the same section of the State. These will be placed under their senior captains, until the field officers can be appointed by the governor. It is desired that you expedite the transfer of the machinery to this place, ordered to the Richmond Armory, should it not have been done, and that you complete, as fast as possible, any guns or rifles partially constructed, should it be safe and practicable. Your attention will be particularly directed to the safety of such arms, machinery, parts of arms, raw material, &c., that may be useful, to insure which they must be at once sent into the interior, if in your judgment necessary. If any artillery companies offer their services, or are mustered into the service of the State, and are without batteries, report the facts.

I am, sir, very respectfully,

R. E. LEE
Major-General, Commanding

11   To JOHN LETCHER
                      Governor of Virginia

                                    Headquarters, Richmond, Virginia
                                                     April 27, 1861

I respectfully ask of the governor and council what arrangements have been made to enable the army of the State to take the field? Besides the necessary camp equipage, some means of transportation must be provided other than that furnished by the railroad companies. It will not always be possible to adhere to the railroad routes, and provision must be made for maneuvering in front of an enemy and for supplying troops with provisions, and at positions to be held or forced. Horses for the light batteries will be necessary, and wagons for local transportation. Are there any funds for these purposes, or how are they to be procured?

                                    Very respectfully,

                                              R. E. LEE
                                    Major-General, Commanding

12   To COLONEL ANDREW TALCOTT
               Engineers' Officer, Norfolk, Virginia

                                    Headquarters Virginia Forces
                                              Richmond, Virginia
                                                   April 29, 1861

Sir:
    You will proceed up James River, to the vicinity of Burwell's Bay, & select the most suitable point which, in your judgment, should be fortified, in order to prevent the ascent of the river by the enemy.
    Lay off the works & leave their construction to Lieut. C. Ap R. Jones, Virginia Navy, who will accompany you.
    You will then proceed to the mouth of the Appomattox, and there perform the same service, selecting some point below the mouth of that river, supposed to be old Fort Powhatan. Captain [Harrison H.] Cocke will take charge of the construction of this work.
    Be pleased to give the above mentioned officers such instructions as they may require in the construction of these works, and report what you shall have done.

                                    Respectfully, &c.,

                                              R. E. LEE
                                    Major-General, Commanding

13   To HIS WIFE
                               Arlington

                                                    Richmond
                                                 April 30, 1861
My Dear Mary,
    On going to my room last night I found my trunk & sword there &
opening it this morning discovered the package of letters, & was very
glad [to] learn you were all well & as yet, peaceful. I fear the latter state
will not continue long, not that I think Virginia is going to make war,
but if the Federal Government should be disposed to peace there is now
such a mass of [illegible] in Washington, such a pressure from the North,
& such fury manifested against the South that it may not be in the power
of the authorities to restrain them. Then again among such a mass of
all characters it might be considered a good smart thing to cross into
Virginia & rob, plunder, &c., especially when it is known to be the
residence of one of the Rebel leaders. I think therefore you had better
prepare all things for removal, that is the plate, pictures, &c., & be prepared at any moment. Where to go is the difficulty. When the war
commences no place will be exempt in my opinion, & indeed all the
avenues into the State will be the scene of military operations. Tell
Custis to consider the question. He is a discreet person & prudent & advise
what had better be done. I wrote to Robert that I could not consent to
take boys from their school & young men from their colleges & put them
in the ranks at the beginning of a war when they are not wanted & when
there were men enough for the purpose. The war may last 10 years.
Where are our ranks to be filled from then?
    I was willing for his company to continue at their studies, to keep
up its organization & to perfect themselves in their military exercises &
to perform duty at the College but not to be called into the field. I
therefore wished him to remain. If the exercises at the College are suspended he can then come home. I do not wish any more socks or shirts at
this time. I forgot to take from the old uniform coat I left for the servants
the eyes or hooks from the shoulders that confined the epaulettes. Will
you cut them out & also the loops at the collar. You will have to rip the
coat & take them out. If you will then wrap them up carefully & send
them to Mr. John G. or Mr. Daingerfield directed to the Spotswood
House, there are persons coming on every day by whom they can be
forwarded. I was much interested in Mary Childe's letter. My poor Anne
how she must have suffered. I have not time to write to her. There is no
prospect or intention of the government to propose a truce. Do not be

deceived by it. Custis must exercise his judgement about sending to the Arlington market. It is your only chance. Give much love to all my dear children & Helen. Tell them I want to see them very much. May God preserve you all & bring peace to our distracted country.

Truly yrs,

R. E. LEE

14   To MAJOR FRANCIS M. BOYKIN, JR.
Weston, Virginia

Headquarters Virginia Forces,
Richmond, Virginia
April 30, 1861

You are desired to take measures to muster into the service of the State such volunteer companies as may offer their services for the protection of the northwestern portion of the State. Assume the command, take post at or near Grafton, unless some other point should offer greater facilities for the command of the Baltimore & Ohio Railroad & the branch to Parkersburg.

It is not the object to interrupt peaceful travel on the road or to offer annoyance to citizens pursuing their usual avocations; but to hold the road for the benefit of Maryland & Virginia, and to prevent its being used against them. You will therefore endeavour to obtain the cooperation of the officers of the road, & afford them, on your part, every assistance in your power. You will also endeavour to give quiet & security to the inhabitants of the country.

Major A[lonzo] Loring, at Wheeling, has been directed, with the volunteer companies under his command, to give protection to the road, near its terminus at the Ohio River, and you will place yourself in communication with him, & cooperate with him if necessary.

Please state whether a force at Parkersburg will be necessary, & what number of companies can be furnished in that vicinity. You are requested to report the number of companies you may muster into the service of the State, their arms, condition, &c., and your views as to the best means for the accomplishment of the object in view.

To enable you to supply any deficiency in arms in the companies, 200 muskets, of the old pattern, flint-locks, will be forwarded by Col [Thomas J.] Jackson, the commanding officer at Harper's Ferry, to your order, from whence you must take measures to receive them & convey them in safety to their destination, under guard, if necessary. I regret that no other arms are at present for issue.

Very respectfully, &c.,

R. E. Lee
Major-Genl, Commanding

15   To COLONEL THOMAS J. JACKSON
Commanding at Harper's Ferry

Headquarters Virginia Forces
Richmond, Virginia
May 1, 1861

Colonel:

Under authority of the governor of the State, you are directed to call out volunteer companies from the counties in the valley adjacent to Harper's Ferry, viz, Morgan, Berkeley, Jefferson, Hampshire, Hardy, Frederick, & Clarke, not including the troops you may muster in at Harper's Ferry, five regiments of infantry, one regiment of cavalry, two batteries of light artillery, of four pieces each.

The average number of enlisted men in each company will be eighty-two, and the troops will be directed to rendezvous at Harper's Ferry. You will select, as far as possible, uniformed companies with arms, organize them into regiments under the senior captains, until proper field officers can be appointed. You will report the number of companies accepted in the service of the State under this authority, their description, arms, &c. Five hundred Louisiana troops, said to be en route for this place, will be directed to report to you, and you will make provision accordingly. You are desired to urge the transfer of all the machinery, materials, &c., from Harper's Ferry, as fast as possible, and have it prepared in Winchester for removal to Strasburg, whence it will be ordered to a place of safety. The machinery ordered to this place must be forwarded with dispatch, as has already been directed. The remainder will await at Strasburg further orders. All the machinery of the rifle factory, and everything of value therein, will be also removed as rapidly as your means will permit.

If the troops can be advantageously used in the removal of the machinery, they will be so employed. It is thought probable that some attack may be made upon your position from Pennsylvania, and you will keep yourself as well informed as possible of any movements against you. Should it become necessary to the defence of your position, you will destroy the bridge across the Potomac. You are particularly directed to keep your plans and operations secret, and endeavor to prevent their being published in the papers of the country.

I am, sir, &c.,

R. E. LEE
Major-Genl, Comdg

16   To HIS WIFE
"Ravensworth," Virginia

Richmond
May 2, 1861

My Dear Mary,

I received last night your letter of the 1st with the coat. It gave me great pleasure to learn that you were all well & in peace.

You know how pleased I should be to have you & my dear daughters with me. That I fear cannot be. There is no place that I can expect to be but in the field & there is no rest for me to look to. But I want you to be in a place of safety. To spare me that anxiety. Nor can any one say where safety can be found. I am very grateful to dear Cousin Anna for her invitation to you. She is always our friend in need. Ravensworth I suppose is as safe as any place, & if you could all be there comfortable together, my heart would have but the one place to leap to. I fear however it would add too much to Cousin Anna's anxiety & trouble. Of this you must judge, or where else you had better go. Do not go to Berkeley, or the Shenandoah Valley. Those points are much exposed, but you must not talk of what I write. Nor is Richmond perhaps more out of harms way. I take it for granted that our opponents will do us all the harm they can. They feel their power & they seem to have the desire to oppress & distress us. I assume therefore they will do it. We have only to be resigned to God's will & pleasure & do all we can for our protection.

Make your preparations quickly, to be ready for any emergency. Your arrangement of the servants I think good. I must have some one with me, & unless Perry can be of use somewhere will take him. Custis can take Billy or any one else he chooses. The plate, &c., will not be safe in Alexandria, as I suppose it will be occupied by troops of one side or the other & be enveloped in conflict. Ravensworth will be as safe as any place I presume, if they can be stored out of the way there.

Do keep yourselves quiet & out of harms way. I hope Mr. McGuire is able to prosecute work on the farm. Give love to all. I hope Helena is not alarmed & that she will when she wishes be able to return to her friends in safety.

I have just received Custis' letter of the 30th enclosing the acceptance of my resignation. It is stated it will take effect on the 25th April. I resigned on the 20th & wished it to take effect on that day. I cannot consent to its running on farther & he must receive no pay if they tender it beyond that day, but return the whole if need be. In answer to his question he had better I think, when he fully makes up his mind, tender his services formerly to the Governor.

Truly & affly

R. E. LEE

P.S. Mr. H. Daingerfield & all his family arrived here last night. Ask Custis to get & secure my package of private papers from the Br Farmers Bank of Alexandria where he placed it I think.

17   GENERAL ORDERS, NO. 10

Headquarters Virginia Forces
Richmond, Virginia
May 5, 1861

Troops called out under the proclamation of the Governor of the State of the 3d instant will be accepted and mustered into the service only by companies, and for the period of one year, unless sooner discharged. Companies offering themselves for service should address their applications, which should state their strength and the number, description, and caliber of their arms, to the mustering officer Virginia volunteers, at the place of rendezvous appointed for their county in the schedule appended to the Governor's proclamation. The instructions given to this officer will enable him to reply definitely to all such applications.

By order of Major-General Lee:

R. S. GARNETT
Adjutant-General

18   To COLONEL PHILIP ST. GEORGE COCKE
Commanding at Culpeper Court House

Headquarters Virginia Forces
Richmond, Virginia
May 6, 1861

Colonel:

You are desired to post at Manassas Gap Junction a force sufficient to defend that point against an attack likely to be made against it by troops from Washington. It will be necessary to give this point your personal attention.

Respectfully, &c.,

R. E. LEE
Maj Genl, Comdg

19   To COLONEL THOMAS J. JACKSON
Commanding at Harper's Ferry

Headquarters Virginia Forces
Richmond, Virginia
May 6, 1861

Colonel:

I consider it probable that the Government at Washington will make a movement against Harper's Ferry, and occupy the B[altimore] & O[hio] Railroad with that view, or use the Chesapeake & Ohio Canal for the transportation of troops.

You are desired to watch these avenues of approach, and endeavor to frustrate their designs. On receiving certain intelligence of the approach of troops it will become necessary to destroy the bridge at Harper's Ferry & obstruct their passage by the canal as much as possible. You might make some confidential arrangements with persons in Maryland to destroy the Monocacy railroad bridge and draw the water out of the canal, should there be assurances of the enemy's attempt to make use of either.

You are authorized to offer the payment of $5 a piece for each musket that may be returned of those taken possession of by the people in and about Harper's Ferry.

It is advisable that you establish some troops at Martinsburg, or other more advantageous point, if your force will permit.

I desire that you will report the amount of your present force & the number of volunteers that will probably respond to the call of the governor from the counties indicated in his proclamation.

Respecty, &c.,

R. E. LEE
Maj Genl, Comdg

20   To JEFFERSON DAVIS
                      Montgomery, Alabama
                          TELEGRAM

                                              Richmond, Virginia
                                                May 7, 1861

HONORABLE JEFFERSON DAVIS:

GENERAL JOHNSTON SICK. I CANNOT BE SPARED. SENATOR [R.M.T.]
HUNTER, ON THE WAY TO MONTGOMERY, IS FULLY INFORMED OF PLANS AND
WATER DEFENSES AT NORFOLK. SUFFICIENT LAND DEFENSES IN PROGRESS.
TROOPS SUFFICIENT, UNINSTRUCTED; OFFICERS NEW. MY COMMISSION IN
VIRGINIA SATISFACTORY TO ME.

                                                  R. E. LEE

21   To COLONEL WILLIAM B. TALIAFERRO
                    Commanding at Gloucester Point

                                        Headquarters Virginia Forces
                                              Richmond, Virginia
                                                May 8, 1861
Colonel:
     In reply to your letter of the 6th instant, asking instructions as to
the course to be pursued in the event of an attempt on the part of the
enemy to pass the battery at Gloucester Point, you are directed, on the
approach of a vessel of the enemy, & when she shall have gotten within
range, to fire a shot across her bows. Should this not deter her from
proceeding on, you will fire one over her; & if she still persist, you will
fire into her. Should the fire be returned, you will capture her, if possible.
Similar orders have been issued to the naval officer commanding battery.

                                        Respecty, &c.,

                                              R. E. LEE
                                              Maj Genl Comdg

22   To COLONEL THOMAS J. JACKSON
                 Commanding at Harper's Ferry

Headquarters Virginia Forces
Richmond, Virginia
May 9, 1861

Colonel:

I have received your letter of the 6th instant, & am gratified at the progress you have made in the organization of your command. I hope some of the field officers directed to report to you will have arrived & entered on their duties. In your preparation for the defence of your position it is considered advisable not to intrude upon the soil of Maryland, unless compelled by the necessities of war. The aid of its citizens might be obtained in that quarter. I regret I have no engineer of experience to send you. You will have to rely upon your judgment and the aid of the officers with you. I have directed that four 6-pounder guns be forwarded to you as soon as possible, and two 12-pounder howitzers, with a supply of ammunition and equipment for firing, will be sent to you at once. There are no caissons. Horses, wagons, & harness will be procured near you by an agent of the quartermaster's department, sent for the purpose.

Capt [William N.] Pendleton's company of artillery from Lexington will join you as soon as possible, with such field pieces as it has. Flour & provisions for use of the troops must be secured. In other respects it is not designed to embarrass the legitimate commerce of our citizens.

I have directed that one thousand muskets, obtained from North Carolina, be sent to you, to aid in arming your command and to respond to requisitions that may be made upon you by Col [George A.] Porterfield. Your requisitions upon the staff department at headquarters, as far as possible, will be filled.

Resp, &c.,

R. E. LEE
Maj Genl Comdg

23   To COLONEL PHILIP ST. GEORGE COCKE
               Commanding at Culpeper Court House

Headquarters Virginia Forces
Richmond, Virginia
May 10, 1861

Colonel:

It is very important that the volunteer troops be organized & instructed as rapidly as possible. I know you are doing all in your power
towards that object. It is desired that you attach to the battalions or
regiments, as formed, as soon as possible, the field officers who have been
or may be directed to report to you from the same region with the companies, place them at such point or points as you think best, with capable
instructors, & press forward their instruction & equipment. The regiments
under Colonels [Samuel] Garland & [James F.] Preston were designed
for Manassas Junction. You are requested to send them there, & as company & field officers are available which might properly be assigned to
them, to forward them to the respective regiments. That the troops may
be prepared for field service, it is desirable that they be removed from
the towns & placed in camp, where their instruction may be uninterrupted
& rigid discipline established. Officers & men will sooner become familiar
with the necessities of service, & make their preparations accordingly.

It is impossible at this time to furnish tents, but unoccupied buildings
might possibly be obtained or temporary plank huts established. I beg
you will adopt the best plan in your power to prepare the men for hard,
effective service.

Resp, &c.,

R. E. LEE
Maj Genl Comdg

24   To COLONEL THOMAS J. JACKSON
               Commanding at Harper's Ferry

Headquarters Virginia Forces
Richmond, Virginia
May 10, 1861

Colonel:

Your letter of the 9th May has just been received. The guns you
refer to, intended for Maryland, have, I understand, been stopped by the

governor. I wrote you today that two 32-pounders had been ordered to you. I fear you may have been premature in occupying the heights of Maryland with so strong a force near you. The true policy is to act on the defensive, & not invite an attack. If not too late, you might withdraw until the proper time.

I have already suggested to you the probability of the use of the canal as a means of carrying ordnance and munitions from Washington to use against you. In that event it would be well to cut the supply dams to prevent its use. Ten cadets have been ordered to report to you, in addition to the ten now there.

Very respy, &c.,

R. E. LEE
Maj Genl, Comdg

25   To COLONEL GEORGE H. TERRETT
Alexandria, Virginia

Headquarters Virginia Forces
Richmond, Virginia
May 10, 1861

Colonel:

In forwarding Special Orders, No. 39, I take occasion to say that, while pursuing a strictly defensive policy, it is necessary that you should be vigilant, have your troops at or near points where they may be needed, & urge forward their instruction & preparation with all the means in your power. For this purpose it will be necessary to remove them from the towns, if possible, & establish them in camps, where their constant instruction & discipline can be attended to. They will the sooner become familiar with the necessities of service, & be better prepared for its hardships. It will be impossible to furnish tents at this time, but it is hoped that unoccupied buildings or temporary plank huts might be obtained where needed. At Manassas Junction, where it will be necessary to establish a portion of your command to secure the road to Harper's Ferry, some preparation of this sort will be needed. Col Garland's & Col Preston's battalions, the first consisting of 4 & the second of 7 companies, have been ordered to that point, to report to you. These battalions will be increased to regiments as companies from their districts arrive, which will be forwarded to you by Col Cocke. You will give them the necessary orders & add such reinforcements as you think proper. The troops near Alexandria will be kept in readiness to move whenever necessary, will afford such protection to the town & neighborhood as their number will permit, & you will endeavor to take measures to allay unnecessary excitement, & not to provoke aggression.

An early report of the condition & resources of your command is desired. Requisitions upon the staff departments here will be filled as far as possible, &, for articles admitting of no delay you are authorized to call on Col Cocke.

Resp, &c.,

R. E. LEE
Maj Genl, Comdg

26   GENERAL ORDERS, NO. 14

Headquarters Virginia Forces
Richmond, Virginia
May 10, 1861

All officers in the military and naval service now on duty in Virginia are prohibited from granting free passes on railroads, steam-boats, or other public conveyances to any person, unless such person be traveling under orders or on duty of the State.

By order of Major-General Lee:

R. S. GARNETT
Adjutant-General

27   To HIS WIFE
Arlington

Richmond
May 11, 1861

I have received your letter of the 9th from Arlington. I had supposed you were at Ravensworth & directed my letter to Burke's Station, as advised by Cousin Anna. I also addressed my last letter to Custis there. My letter to you contained a check on Br Farmers Bank Alexandria in your favour for $500.

I told you of the safe arrival of the boxes &c. here. This morning I despatched them to Lexington except the box of my papers, which I retained. I advised in my letter to Custis, should he determine to come here as he proposed, to bring his horse, equipment &c., blankets, towels, knives, forks, spoons, if there are any at the house, for both of us, Perry & Billy. It will save their purchase & the supply here is meagre. He has been appointed Major of Engineers in the Provisional Army of

Virginia without any application on my part, as I had intended to have awaited his arrival. They were making some appointments in that corps & he was appointed at the same time. Tell him he is under no obligation to accept.

I am very sorry to hear of the case of our young friend. It is a high handed measure which will be justified by military necessity. Under the same stern law many enormities will be committed I fear on both sides.

I am glad to hear that you are at peace, & enjoying the sweet weather & beautiful flowers.

You had better complete your arrangements & retire further from the scene of war. It may burst upon you at any time. It is sad to think of the devastation, if not ruin it may bring upon a spot so endeared to us. But God's will be done. We must be resigned.

May He guard & keep you all is my constant prayer.

Truly & affectly

R. E. LEE

Give much love to all. I shall not want my dressing case, which you said Custis would bring on. If not too late, take to Ravensworth.

28   To GENERAL WALTER GWYNN
                      Commanding at Norfolk

Headquarters Virginia Forces
Richmond, Virginia
May 12, 1861

General:

I am gratified to learn that all your preparations for defence are so well advanced. It is important for you, now being prepared against any immediate attack, to review your lines of defence, strengthen, improve, & enlarge them, as necessity and opportunity may permit, and apply all your means & use every exertion to the instruction & discipline of your men, & prepare them for hard and active service. With this view, they should be placed at or near the points where their services will be required in case of an attack & be prepared and habituated to the necessities of service. Is the revetment of Fort Norfolk sufficiently protected by earthern-covered ways, & are the parapets of all your redoubts sufficiently thick & high to resist heavy shot & protect the men within? If not, they had better be strengthened & every measure taken to give confidence & security to the men.

In the fabrication of musket cartridges at this point we are now obliged to use coarse powder for want of musket powder. As you have a large amount of cartridges on hand, you are desired to send ten (10) barrels of musket powder, as soon as possible, to Col [Charles] Dimmock, at this place. Telegraphed to this effect today.

Very respectfully, &c.,

R. E. LEE
Major-General, Commanding

29   To COLONEL THOMAS J. JACKSON
Commanding at Harper's Ferry

Headquarters Virginia Forces
Richmond, Virginia
May 12, 1861

Colonel:

I have just received your letter of the 11th instant, by Col [Johnathan M.] Bennett. I am concerned at the feeling evinced in Maryland, & fear it may extend to other points, besides opposite Shepherdstown. It will be necessary, to allay it, if possible to confine yourself to a strictly defensive course. I presume the points occupied by you at Point of Rocks, Berlin, & Shepherdstown are on our side. I am glad to hear that volunteers are assembling; over 2000 arms have already been sent you, & 1000 more have been ordered this evening. If you only expect to receive sufficient volunteers to swell your force to 4500 men, I do not see how you can require 5000 arms, as you must now have nearly 3000 armed, besides 3000 arms, above mentioned, ordered to you. We have no rifles or cavalry equipments. The latter may use double-barreled shotguns & buck-shot, if no better arms can be procured.

I will see to the quartermaster. I fear no field battery can be sent you besides that now preparing. The 4th Regiment Alabama troops, from Lynchburg, have gone to you, & I have ordered two others from the same point. Ammunition has also been ordered to you. You know our limited resources, & must abstain from all provocation for attack as long as possible.

I am, &c.,

R. E. LEE
Maj Genl, Comdg

30   To GENERAL WALTER GWYNN
                    Commanding at Norfolk

Headquarters Virginia Forces
Richmond, Virginia
May 14, 1861

General:

I have understood that 200 mules were landed at Old Point Comfort on Saturday last, & some horses previously, with baggage wagons. I desire you, if you can, to ascertain the truth of this report, & whether any preparations are there being made for movements on land. I hope you are urging forward as fast as possible your land defences, securing a sufficient quantity of ammunition for all your arms, small as well as large, both for immediate action & for a protracted defence, & making every other needful arrangement in case of an attack. Your field batteries should be provided with horses and a full equipment for field service, & the men thoroughly instructed. The authority requested in your letter of the 10th instant, to call a cavalry company into service, in addition to the four now on hand, if you deem it necessary, is granted.

Very, &c.,

R. E. LEE
Maj Genl, Comdg

31   To COLONEL THOMAS J. JACKSON
                    Commanding at Harper's Ferry

Headquarters Virginia Forces
Richmond, Virginia
May 14, 1861

Colonel:

I am very much concerned at the condition of things & the failure to procure volunteers for the service of the State in the country west of you. One thousand stand of arms & some ammunition will be sent tomorrow, under the charge of a troop of cavalry, from Staunton to Beverly, Randolph County, for the use of Col Porterfield. This troop is to collect together volunteers from the well-affected portions of the country through which it passes. If your condition is such as to allow it, I would like you to send some aid to Col Porterfield; but I am unwilling for you to send a man, if by so doing you endanger yourself in the least. Reinforcements are being sent to you.

Very, &c.,

R. E. LEE
Maj Genl, Comdg

32   To COLONEL GEORGE H. TERRETT
Alexandria, Virginia

Headquarters Virginia Forces
Richmond, Virginia
May 15, 1861

Colonel:

I have requested Col Cocke to fill up Col Garland's regiment, stationed at Manassas Junction, from companies called by him into the service of the State, and, as soon as he can organize other regiments, to send such reinforcements to that point as he may deem necessary or you require. It will be necessary for you to give particular attention to the defence of that point, & to organize your force in front of it, to oppose, as far as your means will allow, any advance into the country from Washington. It is not expected possible, with the troops at present under your command, that you will be able to resist successfully an attempt to occupy Alexandria, but you may prevent the extension of marauders into the country & the advance of troops on the railroad. Should you discover an intention to seize the Manassas Junction, you will notify Col Cocke, who will advance to sustain you, & you will, with his & your whole force, oppose it. It will be necessary to watch the approaches on your right from the Potomac, as the distance from Occoquan, which point may be reached in boats, is not more than 18 or 20 miles from Manassas Junction. You are again requested to urge forward the organization and equipment of your troops, & to see that your officers labor diligently at the instruction & discipline, & be prepared to take the field at any moment.

Resp, &c.,

R. E. LEE
Maj Genl, Comdg

33   To COLONEL PHILIP ST. GEORGE COCKE
              Commanding at Culpeper Court House

Headquarters Virginia Forces
Richmond, Virginia
May 15, 1861

Colonel:

I have received your letter of the 14th instant, & am gratified at your arrangements for the defence of Manassas Junction, & the favorable account you give of the country towards the Potomac for defensive operations. I hope, by a judicious use of its natural obstacles, that the march of a hostile column will be much embarrassed. I have to request that you will endeavor to fill up Col Garland's & Col Preston's regiments from the companies that will report to you, as desired in my letter of the 10th instant, & as soon as you are able to form other regiments that you will send such reinforcements to Manassas Junction as in your judgment may be necessary or as may be requested by Col Terrett. Please direct the troops you may send to the Junction to report to Col Garland, & place them under Col Terrett's orders. I beg leave also to request that you will give to Col Terrett the benefit of your information & advice respecting the troops & country in which he is operating. It is desired to strengthen that whole line as rapidly as the organization of troops will admit, to resist any attack from the forces at Washington. Hitherto it was impossible to concentrate an adequate force for the defence of Alexandria, an abortive attempt at which would, in my opinion, have had no other effect than to hazard the destruction of the city. The posts at Norfolk & Harper's Ferry, which seemed to be first threatened, being in some measure fortified, our resources can now be applied to your line of operations. Should an advance be made on Col Terrett, or an intention be manifested to seize the Manassas Junction, you are desired to sustain Col Terrett with your whole force.

Resp, &c.,

R. E. LEE
Maj Genl, Comdg

34   To HIS WIFE
                        "Ravensworth," Virginia

                                                        Richmond
                                                        May 16, 1861
My Dear Mary:
    I am called down to Norfolk & leave this afternoon. I expect to
return Friday, but may be delayed. I write to advise you of my absence,
in case you should not receive answers to any letters that may arrive. I
have not heard from you since I last wrote; nor have I anything to relate.
I heard from my dear little Rob, who had an attack of chills & fever.
He hoped to escape the next paroxysm. Had seen the Daingerfields &
Fairfaxes. I witnessed the opening of the convention yesterday, & heard
the good Bishop's sermon, being the 50th anniversary of his ministry. It
was a most impressive [sermon], & more than once I felt the tears coming
down my cheek. It was from the text, "and Pharaoh said unto Jacob,
how old art thou?" It was full of humility and self-reproach. I saw Mr.
Walker, Bishop Johns, Bishop Atkinson, &c., &c. I have not been able to
attend any other services, & presume the session will not be prolonged. I
suppose it may be considered a small attendance. Should Custis arrive
during my absence, I will leave word for him to take my room at the
Spotswood till my return. Smith is well & enjoys a ride in the afternoon
with Mrs. Stannard. The charming women, you know, always find him
out. Give much love to Cousin Anna, Nannie, and dear daughters. When
Rob leaves the University take him with you.

                                                    Truly & affly,

                                                        R. E. Lee

35   To COLONEL WILLIAM B. TALIAFERRO
                      Commanding at Gloucester Point

                                            Headquarters Virginia Forces
                                                Richmond, Virginia
                                                    May 19, 1861
Colonel:
    Your letter of the 14th instant is in hand. I regret to learn that your
force is so small, & request you to use every exertion to increase it. Under
the authority of the governor, by his proclamation of the 3d instant, you
are authorized to extend your call for volunteers to the county of

Mathews. It is hoped that you will collect troops enough from the counties of Gloucester, King & Queen, & Mathews to form at least a regiment, to which your force should be extended. It is not desired to take private houses, unless the exigencies of the service imperatively require it. A proper hut can be erected for a hospital. There are no military engineers available for laying off the rear defences you desire, and it is hoped that the naval officers & others with you will be able to perform the duty. It is probable that the laboring force in the neighborhood will be sufficient to perform the work required on these lines of defence. Blank forms, &c., have been directed to be forwarded to you from the Quartermaster & Commissary Departments.

Very, &c.,

R. E. Lee
Maj Genl, Comdg

36   To JAMES M. MASON
            Winchester, Virginia

Headquarters Virginia Forces
Richmond, Virginia
May 21, 1861

Sir:

I have been gratified at the reception of your letter of the 15th instant, giving an account of your visit to Harper's Ferry. I had hoped that the Maryland people would relieve us of the necessity of occupying the Maryland Heights. Col Jackson was directed to give to their occupation the appearance of its being done by the people of that State, and not to take possession himself till necessary; but the time has been left to his discretion which I am sure will be wisely exercised. There is no doubt, under the circumstances, of our right to occupy these heights.

Measures have been taken, more than three weeks ago, for securing the control of both branches of the Baltimore & Ohio Railroad & for throwing a force into the disaffected region of the State. To carry out which Maj Loring has been sent to Wheeling to protect the terminus of the main road, and Col Porterfield has been sent to Grafton, with instructions to concentrate there three regiments, at Parkersburg one regiment, and at Moundsville one regiment. These measures having in part failed, several companies have been sent from Staunton to Beverly, with instructions to gather strength as they passed through the country for Col Porterfield's command. By these means it is hoped that a considerable force has been concentrated at Grafton by this time, and loyalty in some degree engendered in the disaffected region of which you speak.

Very resp, &c.,

R. E. LEE
Maj Genl, Comdg

37   To GENERAL MILLEDGE L. BONHAM
          Commanding at Manassas Junction

Headquarters Virginia Forces
Richmond, Virginia
May 22, 1861

General:

In the execution of the orders with which you have been furnished, relative to the command of the Alexandria line of operations, I need not call the attention of one as experienced as yourself to the necessity of preventing the troops from all interference with the rights and property of the citizens of the State, & of enforcing rigid discipline & obedience to orders. But it is proper for me to state to you that the policy of the State at present is strictly defensive. No attack, or provocation for attack will therefore be given, but every attack resisted to the extent of your means. Great reliance is placed on your discretion & judgment in the application of your force, and I must urge upon you the importance of organizing & instructing the troops as rapidly as possible and preparing them for active service. For this purpose it will be necessary to post them where their services may be needed & where they can be concentrated at the points threatened. The Manassas Junction is a very important point on your line, as it commands the communication with Harper's Ferry, & must be firmly held. Entrenchments at that point would add to its security, &, in connection with its defence, you must watch the approaches from either flank, particularly towards Occoquan. Alexandria in its front will, of course, claim your attention as the first point of attack, &, as soon as your force is sufficient, in your opinion, to resist successfully its occupation, you will so dispose it as to effect this object, if possible, without appearing to threaten Washington City. The navigation of the Potomac being closed to us, & the U. S. armed vessels being able to take a position in front of the town, you will perceive the hazard of its destruction, unless your measures are such as to prevent it. This subject, being one of great delicacy, is left to your judgment. The railroad communications must be secured, however, & their use by the enemy prevented. In the absence of tents or vacant houses, you will have to erect temporary plank sheds for the protection of your men.

Very, &c.,

R. E. LEE
Maj Genl, Comdg

38   To COLONEL GEORGE A. PORTERFIELD
Commanding at Grafton

Headquarters Virginia Forces
Richmond
May 24, 1861

Colonel:
I have just received your letter of the 18th, and regret that you have been unsuccessful in organizing the companies of volunteers that you expected. By this time the companies from Staunton must have reached you, as also one from Harper's Ferry; and I hope that the true men of that region have been encouraged to come out into the service of the State. I will write to the commanding officer of Harper's Ferry to give you all aid in his power, and I hope you will spare no pains to preserve the integrity of the State, and to prevent the occupation of the Baltimore & Ohio Railroad by its enemies. In answer to your inquiry as to the treatment of traitors, I cannot believe that any citizen of the State will betray its interests, and hope all will unite in supporting the policy she may adopt.

Very respectfully yr obt servt

R. E. LEE
Genl, Commdg

39   To GENERAL MILLEDGE L. BONHAM
Commanding at Manassas Junction

Richmond, Virginia
May 24, 1861

Send an express to Colonel [Eppa] Hunton, at Leesburg, to destroy all the bridges of the Loudoun and Hampshire Railroad as far down towards Alexandria as possible, and to keep you and General [Joseph E.] Johnston advised of the movements of the enemy towards Harper's Ferry.

R. E. LEE
Major-General, Commanding

40   To GENERAL BENJAMIN HUGER
Commanding at Norfolk

Headquarters Virginia Forces
Richmond, Virginia
May 25, 1861

General:

I wish to call your attention to the condition of Craney Island. It is the first point that will arrest the passage of a vessel to Norfolk; it is the most exposed & the least prepared for defense. I cannot urge upon you too strongly the necessity of putting it in good condition. More troops should be ordered there, & laborers, if practicable. If laborers cannot be obtained, the troops must work at the trenches at that point & all others within your lines of defense. A North Carolina regiment will leave here tomorrow for your post.

Very, &c.,

R. E. LEE
Genl, Comdg

41   To LEROY POPE WALKER
Secretary of War

Headquarters Virginia Forces
Richmond, Virginia
May 25, 1861

Sir:

Being very much embarrassed in furnishing the troops which have been called into service by the State of Virginia with arms, ammunition, & the necessary accoutrements, on account of the limited supply & the small size of our arsenal & workshops, I beg leave to suggest that the troops ordered to this State may come provided with arms, ammunition, cartridge-boxes, knapsacks, haversacks, & all other necessary equipments, & that their organization be as complete as practicable.

Very resp, &c.,

R. E. LEE
Genl, Comdg

42   To HIS WIFE
                        "Ravensworth," Virginia

Richmond
May 25, 1861

I have been trying, dearest Mary, ever since the reception of your letter by Custis to write to [you.] I sympathize deeply in your feelings at leaving your dear home. I have experienced them myself & they are constantly revived. I fear we have not been grateful enough for the happiness there within our reach, & our heavenly father has found it necessary to deprive us of what He had given us. I acknowledge my ingratitude, my transgressions & my unworthiness, & submit with resignation to what He thinks proper to inflict upon me.

We must trust all there to Him & I do not think it prudent or right for you to return there, while the U. S. troops occupy that country. I have gone over all this ground before & have just written to Cousin Anna on the subject.

While writing, I received a telegram from Cousin John G[oldsborough] urging your departure "South." I suppose he is impressed with the risk of your present position, & in addition to the possibility, or probability of personal annoyance to yourself, I fear your presence may provoke annoyance to Cousin Anna. But unless Cousin Anna goes with you, I shall be tortured about her being there alone. If the girls went to Kinlock or E[astern] V[iew] you & Cousin A[nna] might take care of yourselves because you could get in the carriage & go off in an emergency. But I really am afraid that you may prove of more harm than comfort to her.

Mr. William C. Rives has just been in to say that if you & Cousin A[nna] will go to his house, he will be very happy for you to stay as long as you please. That his son has a commodious house just opposite his, unoccupied, partially furnished, that you could if you prefer take that, bring up servants & what you desired, & remain there as independent as at home. It is 7 miles east of Charlottesville, Cobbrams station. That though is on the direct line to Staunton &c., & is objectionable unless we can shut them off below.

I must now leave the matter to you & pray that God may guard you. I have no time for more. I know & feel the discomfort of your position but it cannot be helped, & we must bear our trials like Christians.

Smith is well & Custis apparently so, Edward Butler is here. Perry & the horse has arrived. The former looking very badly.

If you & Cousin Anna choose to come here you know how happy we shall be to see you. I shall take the field as soon now as I can.

Give much love to the girls. Thank Cousin J[ohn] for his kindness. May God guard & bless you.

Ever yours truly & devotedly,

R. E. LEE

43   To JOSEPH E. BROWN
                Governor of Georgia

Headquarters Virginia Forces
Richmond, Virginia
May 26, 1861

Sir:

I deem it proper to call your attention to the fact that many of the volunteer companies from your State have arrived at Richmond without arms. The demand upon Virginia has been so great that all arms have been exhausted, except the old flint-lock muskets. It is apprehended that the troops thus provided will not do themselves justice, opposed to an enemy whose arms are so much superior. I thought it probable that you would like to provide the men of your State with such better arms as may be at your disposal, and therefore take the liberty of bringing this matter to your notice. The proximity of Virginia to the scene of action has induced the organization of a large force of cavalry, in consequence of which all the cavalry arms and equipments have been exhausted. If, then, you have to spare any pistols, carbines, or equipments for that arm, you would greatly further the common cause by sending them to Richmond. Allow me to express the hope that you will give these matters your early attention.

I am, &c.,

R. E. LEE
Genl, Comdg

44   To GENERAL BENJAMIN HUGER
                  Commanding at Norfolk

Headquarters Virginia Forces
Richmond, Virginia
May 27, 1861

Sir:

From the facts stated in your telegram received today I think it not improbable that the object of the troops which are landing at Newport News may be either to ascend Nausemond River to the town of Suffolk, or, if that river be too well protected for this, to cross James River to Burwell's Bay, and thence, by land, to Suffolk, or some point of the railroad. The effect of either of these movements will be to cut off your communication with Richmond, and I take the liberty of calling your attention to this, as I know the pressure of the duties now upon you. I would recommend that you telegraph the governor of North Carolina [John W. Ellis] to hasten the movements of those troops which are destined for Norfolk, Virginia, if they have not already arrived, and to recommend that he dispatch a sufficient force to Suffolk.

I am, general, with respect, yr obt servant,

R. E. LEE
Genl, Comdg

45   To COLONEL JOHN B. MAGRUDER
                  Commanding at Yorktown

Headquarters Virginia Forces
Richmond, Virginia
May 27, 1861

Sir:

I have received information, by telegraph, today from Norfolk that the Federal troops are landing at Newport News. I deem it proper to inform you of this, as it may be their intention to move on to Warwick Court House, and thence, by the road, to Yorktown. Captains [George B.] Cosby and [John B.] Hood, of the Confederate Army, have been ordered to report to you for the purpose of instructing the cavalry troop.

I am, sir, with great respect, yr obt sevt,

R. E. LEE
Genl, Comdg

46   To GENERAL JOSEPH E. JOHNSTON
        Commanding at Harper's Ferry

                                    Headquarters Virginia Forces
                                          Richmond, Virginia
                                            May 27, 1861

General:

In a letter from Colonel Jackson, of the 21st instant, lately received, he speaks of the want of an ordnance or artillery officer at your post. There is none at present available, but Major [Arnold] Elzey, of the Confederate Army, has been ordered here, and I will endeavor to place him on duty with you. Meantime I have thought that the services of Colonel Jackson might be applied to the mounting and preparing the batteries for service. The proper defence of the country west of you and the command of the railroad through that region is deemed very important to the safety of your position, and it is hoped you will be able to take measures to maintain it, or prevent the use of the road to invaders of the State. It is thought probable that you might add to the comfort of your command by procuring, or causing to be procured, at Winchester camp equipage for those companies said to be in want, and that arrangements might be made there for making cartridge-boxes, haversacks, &c.

            Very respectfully, yr obt servant,

                                            R. E. LEE
                                            Genl, Comdg

47   To HIS WIFE
                "Ravensworth," Virginia

                                              Manassas,
                                            May 28, 1861

I reached here dearest M[ary] this afternoon. I am very much occupied in examining matters & have to go out to examine the ground. Cousin J[ohn] tempts me strongly to go down, but I must resist for many reasons. If for no other, to prevent compromitting the house, for my visit would certainly be known.

I have written to you fully & to Cousin Anna. I am decidedly of opinion that it would be better for you to leave. On your account &

Cousin Anna's. My only objection is the leaving Cousin A[nna] alone, if she will not go with you.

If you prefer Richmond, go with Nannie. Otherwise, the upper country as John indicates. I fear I cannot be with you anywhere. I do not think Richmond will be permanent.

Love & kisses to all. God bless & preserve you all.

Truly,

R——

48   To BRIGADIER GENERAL JOSEPH E. JOHNSTON
Commanding at Harper's Ferry

Headquarters Virginia Forces
Richmond, Virginia
May 30, 1861

Sir:

While at Manassas I made the following arrangements of light troops: A corps of observation, of cavalry and infantry, has been established, under Col [Richard S.] Ewell, in advance of Fairfax Court House, the right extending towards Occoquan, the left to the Leesburg road. Col Eppa Hunton, commanding at Leesburg, has been ordered to have an advance post at Dranesville, and to extend his scouts down the Alexandria and Leesburg roads, to communicate with Col Ewell. He is to inform you of any movement of the U. S. troops, in the direction of Leesburg, tending to threaten your rear, through Capt [Turner] Ashby, at Point of Rocks. In the event of such a movement, should you deem it advisable, and should you be unable to hold your position, I would suggest a joint attack by you and Genl Bonham, commanding at Manassas, for the purpose of cutting them off. I have given full verbal explanations to Capt Thomas L. Preston, who leaves Richmond tomorrow, to join your command.

I am, sir, very respectfully, yr obt sevt,

R. E. Lee
General, Commanding

49   To GENERAL JOSEPH E. JOHNSTON
Commanding at Harper's Ferry

Headquarters Virginia Forces
Richmond, Virginia
June 1, 1861

General:

I received, on my return from Manassas Junction, your communications of the 26th and 28th ultimo, in reference to your position at Harper's Ferry. The difficulties which surround it have been felt from the beginning of its occupation, and I am aware of the obstacles to its maintenance with your present force. Every effort has been made to remove them and will be continued, but with similar necessities pressing on every side you need not be informed of the difficulty of providing against them.

The arrangements made and positions taken by the troops under your command are judicious, and it is hoped that sufficient reinforcements can be sent you to enable you to occupy your present point in force and carry out the plan of defence indicated in your communications. Great reliance is placed on your good judgment, the skill of your officers, and the ardor of your troops, and should you be attacked by a force which you may be unable to resist at all points and to keep beyond the frontier, you must move out of your present position, destroy all facilities for the approach or shelter of an enemy. Concentrate your troops and contest his approach step by step into the interior.

With a view of making your column movable, Quartermaster Department was ordered some weeks ago, to provide all the wagons they could, and I was informed that agents were sent to the country east & west of the Blue Ridge for the purpose. The little use for wagons, save for farming purposes, makes the collection difficult, but by the efforts of the Quartermaster Department and the means you have taken, it is hoped you may be provided. Ammunition has been sent you. The supply was necessarily limited in consequence of calls from other points. Can you make arrangements to provide an auxiliary amount for your command? I have informed you of the military arrangements east of the Blue Ridge. A large force is now collecting in front of Alexandria & Genl Beauregard has been sent to command those. Its presence will make the enemy cautious in approaching your rear south of the Potomac, and in that event I hope you will receive timely intelligence, through the light troops under Col Ewell, extending to the Leesburg road. Should such a movement be made, as was suggested in a previous letter, you are expected to use your discretion as to the best mode of meeting it.

Very respecty, yr obt sevt

R. E. Lee
Genl Commdg

50   To GENERAL JOSEPH E. JOHNSTON
            Commanding at Harper's Ferry

Headquarters Virginia Forces
Richmond, Virginia
June 1, 1861

General:

In answer to your letter of the 31st ultimo, received by Col H. A. Edmundson, I have to state that, since my letter to you of this morning, I have directed all the available companies at Staunton to proceed to Harper's Ferry and to report to you for duty. The First Tennessee Regiment, now at this place, Col [Peter] Turney, has also been directed to report to you as soon as practicable. With this reinforcement, and such as you may obtain from the valley, you may probably hold your position and prevent the passage of the Potomac by hostile troops until further troops can reach you. I think that no troops from Ohio have yet reached Grafton, as a special messenger from Colonel Porterfield reports the contrary, and that certain bridges on the Parkersburg road had been burned. Some little time must therefore elapse, in all probability, before a movement can be made against you from that direction. Information of the movements of troops in that direction might be obtained from friends in that region. Should you, however, be opposed by a force too large to resist, I can only repeat what is contained in my letter of this morning, viz, destroy everything that cannot be removed which may be of advantage to the enemy. Deprive them of the use of the railroad, take the field, and endeavor to arrest their advance up the valley.

I am, general, with great respect, yr obt sevt

R. E. Lee
Genl Comdg

51   To GENERAL JOSEPH E. JOHNSTON
                 Commanding at Harper's Ferry

                                    Headquarters Virginia Forces
                                         Richmond, Virginia
                                            June 7, 1861
General:
    I have had the honor to receive your letter of the 6th instant. The importance of the subject has induced me to lay it before the President, that he may be informed of your views. He places great value upon our retention of the command of the Shenandoah Valley and the position at Harper's Ferry. The evacuation of the latter would interrupt our communication with Maryland, and injure our cause in that State. He does not think it probable that there will be an immediate attack by troops from Ohio.

    Brigadier General R. S. Garnett, C. S. Army, with a command of 4000 men, has been directed to Beverly, to arrest the progress of troops towards the Shenandoah Valley. Col Angus W. McDonald has also been sent to interrupt the passage of troops over the Baltimore & Ohio Railroad. It is hoped by these means that you will be relieved from an attack in that direction, and will have merely to resist an attack in front from Pennsylvania.

    An effort will be made to send you cartridge-boxes and knapsacks for the two regiments that are without them, and also an additional supply of ammunition. Greater mobility might be given to your forces by directing their surplus baggage, trunks, valises, &c., to be returned home or sent to some place of safety. Another regiment from Georgia has been ordered to report to you, viz, Colonel [Lucius J.] Gartrell's. It is hoped that you will be able to be timely informed of the approach of troops against you, and retire, provided they cannot be successfully opposed. You must exercise your discretion and judgment in this respect, to insure, if possible, your safety. Precise instructions cannot be given you, but, being informed of the object of the campaign, you will be able to regulate its conduct to the best advantage.

                                       I am, sir, &c.,

                                          R. E. LEE
                                          Genl Commdg

52   GENERAL ORDERS, NO. 25

Headquarters Virginia Forces
Richmond, Virginia
June 8, 1861

By the Governor of Virginia

A PROCLAMATION

The delegates of the people of Virginia, in Convention assembled, having by their ordinance passed April 25, 1861, adopted and ratified the Constitution of the Provisional Government of the Confederate States of America, ordained and established at Montgomery, Alabama, on February 8, 1861, and the State of Virginia having been, by an act of the Confederate States, passed May 7, 1861, admitted as a State into the Confederate Government, and the President being, under the Constitution of the Provisional Government of the Confederate States, the Commander-in-Chief of the Army and Navy of the Confederate States and of the militia of the several states when called into the service of the Confederate States:

Now, therefore, I, John Letcher, governor of Virginia, by and with the advice and consent of the executive council, do hereby transfer to the authorities of the Confederate States, by regiments, all the volunteer forces which have been mustered into the service of Virginia, and do order a like transfer, by regiments, battalions, squadrons, and companies, of all volunteers or militia, as the same shall be formed, and their services may be required.

I further hereby transfer to the authorities of the Confederate States the command of all the officers, seamen, and marines of the Provisional Navy of Virginia, for service in the Confederate States.

I do further order that all officers of the Virginia service now on duty in any of the departments of the staff continue to discharge their respective functions, under the direction and control of the President, until otherwise ordered; and that all quartermaster, commissary, and medical stores belonging to the State and in charge of said officers, to be turned over for the use of the Confederate States, upon proper receipts for the articles turned over, to be forwarded to the accounting officer for settlement. All moneys in charge of any of the departments will be forthwith returned into the treasury of the State.

I do further order all the Provisional Army of Virginia to respect and obey all lawful orders emanating from the President, or those commanding under his authority, and that the same may be incorporated, in whole or in part, into the Provisional Army of the Confederate States, at the pleasure of the President.

I do hereby authorize the use of all public property, munitions of war, &c., captured from the United States, the machinery at Harper's Ferry excepted, by the President or those acting under his authority, for the common defense.

Given under my hand as governor, and under the seal of the State, at Richmond, this 6th day of June, A. D. 1861, and in the eighty-fifth year of the Commonwealth.

By the governor:
[Seal]

GEORGE W. MUNFORD
Secretary of the Commonwealth

In compliance with the foregoing proclamation, the command of the military and naval forces of the State of Virginia is transferred to the Confederate States. All officers of said forces will obey the orders they may receive from the heads of the War and Navy Departments, respectively. Officers of the staff will receive their instructions from the chiefs of the several branches of the Confederate States Government.

R. E. LEE
General, Commanding

53   To HIS WIFE
                    "Kinloch," Virginia

Richmond
June 9, 1861

Except through a letter to Nannie I have not heard of you dearest Mary for a long time. My letters it seems do not reach you & yours' perhaps to me share the same fate. I last wrote by Mr. F. S. Smith. He was returning to Manassas, near which he has his family, & he thought he could easily forward my letter by Cousin John. It contained a little money $100. & perhaps he has been over cautious for its safety & did not like to risk it by uncertain hands. I fear it has not reached you, as Daughter in her letter to Nannie said you would leave for Kinloch the day after she wrote, apparently Monday, & its contents may be convenient to you. How I can get funds to you now I do not know. I can transmit you a check, but how will you get it cashed?

I have just returned from a visit to the batteries & troops on James & York Rivers &c., where I was some days. I called a few hours at the

White House. Saw Charlotte & Annie. Fitzhugh was away but got out of the cars as I got in. Our little boy looked very sweet & seemed glad to kiss me a good bye. He seemed to be suffering from his teeth. Charlotte said she was going to prepare to leave home for the summer, but had not determined where to go. I could only see some of the servants about the house & stables. They were all well. The house was very nice & comfortable, & the corn looked well. Agnes is still here staying with Mrs. Dr. Conway. She talks of going down to the W[hite] H[ouse] Tuesday, 11th. I can rarely see her, & I believe I have seen Nannie but once since her arrival. Fitz. Lee is better. I heard of his walking down the street yesterday. Custis is also better than he was. He is a great comfort to me & if we have to separate I do not know what I shall do. You may be aware that the Confederate Government is established here. Yesterday I turned over to it the command of the military & naval forces of the State, in accordance with the proclamation of the governor & the agreement between the State & C[onfederate] States. I do not know what my position will be. I should like to retire to private life, if I could be with you & the children, but if I can be of any service to the State or her cause, I must continue. Mr. Davis & all his cabinet are here. Custis says he will write to you to day & I will leave to him the relation of local matters. On returning to my room last night I found Turksville & Arthur Stuart. The latter had arrived with a Louisiana regiment & both were to leave for Chantilly this morning at 6 a.m. It was then nearly 11 p.m. I wished to have written by them a few lines, but could not. Good bye. Give much love to kind friends. May God guard & bless you, them & our suffering country, & enable me to perform my duty. I think of you constantly. Write me what you will do. Direct here.

Always yours

R. E. Lee

I send a letter from Mrs. Cook, sent me from Louisville.

54   To GENERAL THEOPHILUS H. HOLMES
Commanding at Fredericksburg

Headquarters of Virginia Forces
Richmond
June 10, 1861

General:
   It is probable that realizing the inutility of cannonading the batteries at Aquia Creek with smooth bore guns, the naval force of the United

States, will hereafter employ rifled cannon, of large caliber, at long range. It is reported that such means will be employed.

It is therefore advisable that the batteries should be rendered as secure as possible, by the application of some such means as were so successfully employed at Charleston. Railroad iron laid at an angle of about 30 degrees with the horizon, on the exterior slope, the upper ends not projecting above the exterior crest, would probably answer the purpose. If such an arrangement can be made, you are authorized to procure the iron, and apply it where in your judgment it may be required.

It is not unlikely that for the attack of these batteries, the enemy will provide himself with iron plated vessels. In this event the shots from the batteries should be so directed as to strike the water short of but near the vessel, so that after the rebound, they may strike below any eave which may be presented, near the water line, and at right angles to her sides. The accompanying sketch expresses the idea herein contained.

Very respectfully, yr obt sevt

R. E. LEE
Genl Commdg

55   To HIS WIFE
"Kinloch," Virginia

Richmond
June 11, 1861

I have just received your letter of the 6th from Chantilly. I very much regret that my letters do not reach you. I know not what becomes of them. In a letter directed to Kinloch a few days since, I informed you of having written by Mr. F. S. Smith after my return from Manassas, which I hope has reached you. The letter contained $100. that I thought might be useful. My previous letters were directed to Burke's Station & though written after the regular passage of the cars to that point, I thought would be forwarded to that place from Manassas. I wrote to Cousin Anna, Mary, & yourself. The letters may have gone on to Alexandria in which case you will never get them. One contained a letter to you from little Helen, giving an account of her return home. I enclosed in my last a letter from Mrs. Cook. Both came to me from Louisville. You must be careful what you write to them now. All letters are opened. I am sorry to learn that you are so anxious & uneasy about passing events. We cannot change or hinder them, & it is not the part of wisdom to be annoyed by them. In this time of great suffering to the state & country, our private distresses we must bear with resignation like Christians & not aggrevate them by repining, trusting to a kind & merciful God to overrule them for our good. I hope you may secure a safe & quiet retreat & make yourself contented with our lot, which I feel as well as yourself, & which with my other anxieties press heavily upon me. You must all endeavor to take care of yourselves, do what is needful & necessary & not care whether it is agreable. I told you of my visit to the W[hite] H[ouse]. Our young people, as is natural I suppose, seem to look to what is agreable & I fear they will meet with disappointment. Agnes is still here. Thinks of going to the W[hite] H[ouse] tomorrow. She is going in the wrong direction & all of them ought to be away from there now. But procrastination & delay is the order of the day & may occasion the interruption of routes of travel & cut them off from where they wish to go. Events are not going to await our convenience.

I am glad to hear that some protection is afforded dear Arlington.

Robert arrived yesterday from the University [of Virginia] to know what he is to do. He has had chills & fevers & looks badly poor fellow. He goes back tomorrow to remain till the 4 July, when the term ends. He will then either remain there & go through a course of military instruction, or go to Lexington for the same purpose. Military course of instruction has been introduced at the U[niversity] but I think it probable it may be better conducted at Lex[ington]. Express my great gratitude to Edward [Turner, owner of Kinloch] for his kindness to you. I hope he can secure you in some quiet farmhouse, away from danger & anxiety, where your prayers may be offered for our distracted country. Hopewell is a retired spot. Give much love to Daughter. Mrs. Cooper & her party go to Abbeville in S[outh] C[arolina] & they wish Nannie to accompany them. She invites you also. Mrs. Rhett is there. Charlotte talks of N[orth] C[arolina] & want Annie to go with her. Write me of your plans. If Billy is useful to you keep him. It is probably too late to get him to Custis. I can take Meredith from the W[hite] H[ouse] after C[harlotte] leaves if wanted. I would rather you should have Billy if useful. I pray God to give you health & safety.

Faithfully,

R. E. LEE

56   To COLONEL GEORGE A. PORTERFIELD
                    Commanding at Huttonsville

Headquarters Virginia Forces
Richmond, Virginia
June 13, 1861

Colonel:

Your letter of the 9th has been received. I regret much the unfortunate circumstances with which you have been beset, and appreciate the difficulties you have had to encounter.

Genl R. S. Garnett, C. S. A., has been sent to take command in the Northwest with such a force as was disposable. It is hoped that he will soon reach the scene of action, that a more agreeable state of things will be inaugurated, and that loyal spirited citizens of the country will be encouraged and enabled to put down the revolution which you mention.

Your services will be very valuable to General Garnett, in giving him information as to the state of affairs in the country under his command, and in aiding him to achieve the object of his campaign.

Very respectfully, yr obt sevt

R. E. LEE
Genl Commdg

57   To COLONEL JOHN B. MAGRUDER
                    Commanding at Yorktown

Headquarters Virginia Forces
Richmond, Virginia
June 13, 1861

Colonel:

I have had the honor to receive your communication of the 10th instant, and I take pleasure in expressing my gratification at the gallant conduct of the troops under your command and my approbation of the dispositions made by you, resulting, as they did, in the route of the enemy.

I have referred your letter to the President of the Confederate States, that he may be fully informed of the operations so successfully conducted by you, and of the recommendations you have seen fit to make.

Respectfully, yr obt sevt

R. E. LEE
General Commanding

58   To JOHN LETCHER
                      Governor of Virginia

Headquarters of the Virginia Forces
Richmond, Virginia
June 14, 1861

Sir:

The defensive works about Richmond are progressing so slowly from the want of laborers, that I think it proper to call your attention to the subject, that you may submit it to the City Council for their consideration and action.

I beg leave also to suggest that all available persons in and about Richmond be organized for the defence of the city, that they provide themselves with such arms as each can procure, and that arrangements be made for the fabrication of suitable ammunition. These are intended as precautionary measures, which can better be made now, than upon the eve of the emergency, should it arise.

Very respectfully, &c.

R. E. LEE
Genl Commdg

59   To JOHN LETCHER
                      Governor of Virginia

Headquarters of the Virginia Forces
Richmond
June 15, 1861

Sir:

Agreeably to your request, I submit a statement of the military and naval preparations for the defence of Virginia, from the period of her separation from the United States Government to the date of transfer of the military operations of the State to the Confederate Government.

Arrangements were made for the establishment of batteries to prevent the ascent of our rivers by hostile vessels. As soon as an examination was made for the selection of sites, their construction was begun and their armament and defence committed to the Virginia Navy.

Preparations were also begun to receive into the service of the State volunteer companies, and for organizing, arming, and equipping them. Mustering officers were appointed, rendezvous established, and provision made for their subsistence and shelter.

The primary estimate of the number of troops of all arms required, based upon the points to be defended, amounted to 51,000 men. The estimated quota of each portion of the State has been furnished, except from the western section. Arrangements were made for calling out volunteers from the western section at the same time, and in the same manner as from the eastern section, but as yet it has been feebly responded to.

Complete returns from the troops in the field have not, and from the nature of things, cannot for some time be received. But from the best sources of information within my reach, the number of Virginia troops is about 35,000 men. This amount probably falls below the real number, for, referring to the report of the Colonel of Ordnance [Charles Dimmock], it will be seen that he has issued 2,054 rifles and carbines, and 41,604 muskets, in addition to pistols and sabers to the cavalry. Thirteen thousand arms have also been issued from Lexington, making a total of 56,658. Seven thousand of those from Lexington, and several thousand from the arsenal at Richmond have been issued to troops from other States, but as many of the Virginia companies, supposed to be about 5,000 men, were armed & equipped when received into the service of the State. Should the number of armed companies from other States not differ materially from the number of armed companies of the State, the number of Virginia troops in the field may be assumed to be about 40,000.

When it is remembered that this body of men was called from a state of profound peace to one of unexpected war, you will have reason to commend the alacrity with which they left their homes and families, and prepared themselves for the defence of the State. The assembling of the men, however, was not the most difficult operation. Provision for their instruction, subsistence, equipment, clothing, shelter, and transportation in the field, required more time and labor. Ammunition of every kind had to be manufactured. The carriages of the guns for river, land, & field service had to be made, with the necessary implements, caissons, battery wagons, &c.

One hundred and fifteen guns for field service have thus been provided, from which twenty light batteries of four guns each have been furnished with the requisite horses, harness, &c.

For the defence of James River, two batteries and two steamers have been provided, mounting altogether 40 guns, varying in calibre from 32-pounders to 8 & 9 inch columbiads. Arrangements are also in progress for mounting sixty guns, of different weights on the defences around Richmond, and a naval battery of six 12-pounder howitzers is in process of organization.

On York River three batteries have been constructed, mounting thirty guns of calibres similar to the guns on James River.

Sites for batteries on the Potomac have also been selected, and arrangements were in progress for their construction. But the entire command of that river being in possession of the United States Government, and a larger force required for their security than could be devoted to that purpose, the batteries at Aquia Creek have only been prepared. Twelve guns are in position there.

On the Rappahannock River a four gun battery of 32-pounders and 8 inch columbiads has been erected.

Six batteries have been erected on the Elizabeth River to guard the approaches to Norfolk and the Navy Yard. They mount 85 32-pounders and 8 & 9 inch columbiads.

To prevent the ascent of the Nansemond River & the occupation of the railroad from Norfolk to Richmond, three batteries have been constructed on that river which will mount 19 guns.

The frigate *United States* has been prepared for a school ship, and provided with a deck battery of 19 32-pounders and 9 inch columbiads, for habour defence.

The frigate *Merrimac* has been raised and is in the dry dock and arrangements are made for raising the *Germantown* and *Plymouth*.

In addition to the batteries already described, other works have been constructed for their land defence, exceeding in many instances the work on the batteries themselves. An extensive line of field works has been erected for the security of Norfolk, on the side towards the bay. Redoubts for the same purpose have been constructed at Jamestown Island, Gloucester Point, Yorktown and across the neck of land below Williamsburg.

I have confined myself to a general narrative of operations, and for the detail refer you to the reports of the several chiefs of staff.

I am, Governor,

Very Respectfully, your obt servt

R. E. LEE
Genl Comdg

60   To COLONEL JOHN B. MAGRUDER
            Commanding at Yorktown

Headquarters
Richmond, Virginia
June 16, 1861

Col D. H. Hill's letter of the 15th instant has been received. The advantage to the enemy of his possession of Yorktown will be sufficient to induce him to adopt every means to take it. It is hoped that every precaution will be adopted to prevent its being carried by surprise. Should it be besieged, measures will be taken for its relief. There are no siege guns at present available for your post. Re-enforcements will be sent to Yorktown as rapidly as the arrival of available troops at this point will permit. Should the works at Yorktown be too extensive for defense by the troops now there, it will be advisable, if possible, to contract the lines, so as to render them defensible by the force you can command for that purpose.

Respectfully, &c.

R. E. Lee
General Commanding

61   To HIS WIFE
            "Kinloch," Virginia

Richmond
June 24, 1861

I must take a few moments, dearest Mary, to write to you this morning though I have nothing to say, but to express the fervent hope that you are well & all with you. I heard the other day that Daughter was at Manassas, for some good object I trust. In times like these, the advancement of some praiseworthy object should be our only aim. The practice of self denial & self sacrifice even was never more urgently demanded.

I have not heard from you since I wrote last but cannot expect regularity in the mails, nor must you be surprised at not receiving intelligence from me.

Mildred, I hope is with you, & your future arrangements is the source of much anxiety to me. No one can say what is in the future, nor is it wise to anticipate evil. But it is well to prepare for what may reasonably happen & be provided for the worst. There is no saying when you can return to your home or what may be its condition when you do return. What, then, can you do in the mean time? To remain with friends may be inconvenient & where can you go? Agnes came up from the

W[hite] H[ouse] Saturday, 22nd & is staying with Mrs. Corbin War-wick's. Every one here is very kind & she has many invitations. Charlotte & Annie will be up tomorrow on their way to Hickory Hill where they expect to stay some weeks. What they will then do I know not. In the main Agnes thinks she had better remain here so as to lighten the party at Hickory Hill. Charlotte thinks she cannot get along at all without Annie at least & she may like both of the girls. I will see her I hope as she passes through Richmond & will try & have something decided on. These three might keep together & you, M[ildred], & M[ary] for the summer. How can I send you some money, of which I fear you will be in want. Is anything due Mrs. P[owell] for M[ildred]? My movements are very uncertain, & I wish to take the field as soon as certain arrangements can be made. I may go at any moment, & to any point where it may be neces-sary. I shall feel very anxious about you & the girls, & but for my firm re-liance upon our Heavenly Father would be miserable. I wrote you about Robert & sent you his letter which I hope has reached you. Custis I think is better, though frequently has to resort to medicine. He is engaged on the works around this city. Many of our old friends are dropping in. E. P. Alexander is here, Jimmy Hill, Alston, Jenifer, &c. &c., & I hear that my old colonel, A. S. Johnston, is crossing the plains from California. Smith & Nannie are still here, with Cherdie, John, Henry, & Robert C[arter]. Smith will go to Norfolk soon, Cherdie not well yet, John will go to the army, & Henry desires to enter some volunteer company. Carter was here Saturday. He wished Nannie & Agnes to return with him yesterday. But the former was unable & A[gnes] having just arrived thought she had better stay a few days. Your brother Carter seems to have become quite excited. I hope it is only due to the times. But the present occasion ought to tend to calm & determine men's conduct. Tell Life I received her letter & will try & mend my wardrobe. Give much love to all.

As ever

R. E. LEE

62   To MISS MILDRED LEE
                       "Kinloch," Virginia

Richmond
June 29, 1861

My Precious Life,

I have received your letter of the 8th instant & also your note of the 18th, announcing your arrival at Mr. Dulany's. I was very glad to receive both & am now pleased to learn by a letter from your mother that you are with her. You have finished your first year at school, & I hope have derived much benefit in every way. Whether you will be able to resume your studies or when, no one can now say. I am glad that you have had even a partial opportunity to improve yourself, & what ever may happen, hope that you will not consider your education, which has hardly been begun, completed. But that you will continue your studies, alone if necessary, & commence with them a system of reading which will be very beneficial. If you will also connect with it a system of work, you will acquire a fund of useful knowledge, which will make you useful & happy all your life. These are calamitous times, & we must conform to them & make the most of the opportunities afforded us. I hope you will find pleasure in assisting your mother, seeing your friends & aiding your neighbours. By so doing you will promote your own welfare.

I sent your letter to Agnes. They have left the White House now. Charlotte & Annie are in Hanover at Mr. Wickham's & Agnes is staying in Richmond at Mrs. Warwick's. She seems to be merry & content, though looks thin. Uncle Smith, Nannie, Cherdie, John & Robert C[arter] are also here, so with Custis we make quite a family party. Fitzhugh is with his company at Ashland & Henry has joined an artillery company at Yorktown. Your little nephew looked very sweet as he passed through Richmond but he would have little to do with his grandpapa. Indeed I only saw him once. Col [John A.] Washington brought his daughter Louisa down with him the other day, who is staying at a Mrs. Myers'. I think she & Agnes might enter into partnership & take care of their papas. I saw a beautiful yellow cat at Mr. Lyons' the other evening that reminded me of Tom. The latter no doubt lords it in a high manner over the British at Arlington. He will have strange things to tell when you next see him.

Give much love to your sister. Tell her I heard of her Aunt Anne the other day. She was at her own house & as well as usual. Kiss your mother for me & believe me always your affectionate father.

R. E. Lee

63   To HIS WIFE
                                       "Kinloch," Virginia

                                                            Richmond
                                                            July 2, 1861

I have received dear Mary your letter of the 25th announcing your return to Kinloch with Mildred, & I am glad you three are together. Charlotte & Annie are at Mr. Wickham's. Agnes in this city with Mrs. Warwick. The latter, little Agnes, is full of projected visits about the

State, Brandon, Cedar Grove &c., & of having "pleasant times," as if enjoyment was the order of the day. I hope no other times may befall her, but in my opinion these are serious times & our chief pleasure must be what is necessary & proper for the occasion. Agnes told me of the letters you sent her & of their contents. The other day a package was sent to me addressed by you to Mr. McGuinn at Arlington, which had been opened. The contents I suppose undisturbed. It contains a letter to Aunt Sally, Marcelena &c. I suppose seeing it directed within the enemy's lines, the postmasters considered it illicit. Why it was sent to me I do not know.

I shall be unable to forward them except by accident. Indeed should I meet persons going to that region or to Baltimore, they would be indisposed to carry letters that would indicate their associations, & that might compromit them. Travellers have to be very particular now. You will have to forego the indulgence of your correspondence at present.

I shall enclose ten dollars in small notes as you desire. They are all current here. I do not know whether they will pass with you. That reminds me that the note you sent me, of a Wheeling bank, will not pass. You must be careful in taking any of that city, or any point occupied by troops of the United States government. No one receives them here, nor will any of the banks. Wheeling is considered to have gone over to the enemy.

I am glad you are engaged working for the soldiers. They will want all they can get, & will particularly stand in need of the prayers of the good. May they be heard & answered.

I get many accounts of the number of troops & strength of positions of our opponents. I am prepared to find them as strong as they can make them. I trust a way through them will be opened to us when the time arrives.

[   ] you as to the dis [   ] from the tone of [   ] journals. They do not contribute to our self respect, or to a solution of the troubles of the country. They will change in time I hope. At present they are angered by the tone of the Northern Press.

You must give much love to every body. I pray for your happiness & welfare & that every blessing may be showered upon you. This letter has been before me all the morning & has been written line by line at intervals. I have kept the worst for the last. Custis is ordered to North Carolina to inspect the forts & works there. My greatest comfort is therefore taken from me. I do not know how long he will be absent.

Truly & affly

[R. E. Lee]

64   To GENERAL JOHN H. WINDER
                 Acting Inspector General

                                                    Headquarters
                                               Richmond, Virginia
                                                    July 5, 1861
General:
    The President has learned that the crew of the privateer *Savannah*
has been indicted by the grand jury of New York for treason and piracy,
which he views as indicating an intention of not considering them as
prisoners of war. I have consequently been directed to recall the paroles
granted to Lieutenant Colonel [Samuel] Bowman and Captains [Abram]
Kellog and [Edward] Chase, belonging to the Army of the United States
government, and to place them with the rest of the prisoners of war in
close confinement. You are therefore instructed to demand the written
paroles given to the officers named, and to express to them the regret
felt at depriving them of privileges which it would have been the pleasure of the President to have continued until they were regularly exchanged but for the necessity he is under of awarding to them the same
treatment extended the prisoners of the Confederate States.
    You will therefore take measures strictly to guard all the prisoners
of war under your charge, granting to them every kindness and attention
in your power compatible with their safe keeping. You are also at liberty
to explain to the prisoners the reason for the change in their treatment.

                                               Respectfully, &c.

                                                 R. E. LEE
                                               General Commanding

65   To COLONEL JOHN B. MAGRUDER
                  Commanding at Yorktown

                                                    Headquarters
                                               Richmond, Virginia
                                                    July 5, 1861
General:
    I have been gratified by your report of the 30th ultimo, of your ad-
vance with Lieutenant Colonel [Charles D.] Dreux's command to the
vicinity of Newport News, and of the measures taken by you to repress
the marauding parties of the enemy and to restrain them within their

limits. It is hoped that your letter to Colonel [John W.] Phelps will have the effect of preventing the barbarous treatment of our citizens, and it is believed that it cannot be in consonance with the feelings of the officers. In the expeditions sent to the neighborhood of the enemy you are desired to take every precaution to prevent being surprised or cut off.

Very respectfully, yours

R. E. LEE
General Commanding

CHAPTER TWO

Western Virginia

AUGUST–OCTOBER 1861

"It is a grievous disappointment"

LEE'S FIRST ASSIGNMENT with Confederate arms was the most inconclusive phase in his career as general (Congress confirmed his rank as full general on August 31, 1861). After the resounding repulse at First Manassas, both sides drew off, the Federals to prepare larger and better organized offensives, while the Confederates, as if overwhelmed by their success, merely prepared to receive another attack. The only fighting in Virginia was in the generally discouraging action in the Alleghenies, and there Lee was dispatched on July 28, though not as commanding general. In a policy which President Davis was to employ in all phases of his leadership, Lee was sent to western Virginia as "coordinator" without authority. In a letter written the following winter to Mrs. Lee, the general revealed that he recognized the hopelessness of the "expedition."

From the first, the Confederates underestimated three factors in relation to western Virginia—the organized action of the Unionists, the division of sentiment in the easterly state-loyal sections, and the extralegal pragmatism of the Federal government in using war powers to sever the Old Dominion and create a new Union state. While attention was concentrated on the Manassas-Valley sector, the forces sent to the mountains were small, the equipment generally poor and supplies precarious. Expectations of recruiting Confederates were not fully realized and the countryside was lean for provisions. In mid-July, Federal forces led by McClellan had broken the Confederates defending the approaches to Staunton, in the central Shenandoah Valley. In the rout, the only good general officer (Robert S. Garnett) among the Confederates was killed and command devolved on a glory-hunting troublemaker, W. W. Loring.

Farther south in the mountains, in the area of White Sulphur Springs and Hot Springs, two other Confederate forces were charged with defending the approaches along the Kanawha Valley. From this direction the enemy threatened the Virginia & Tennessee Railroad, and the Virginia Central, which connected Richmond with the Valley. The command situation in this section was something out of comic opera, though Lee doubtless failed to appreciate those aspects of this first, and last, command entrusted to political generals in Virginia.

Despite the efforts of Lee and Governor Letcher to withhold command from politicians, Jefferson Davis had rewarded a secessionist leader, John B. Floyd, former governor of Virginia and United States Secretary of War, with the authority to raise an independent brigade of riflemen. Another former Virginia governor, Henry A. Wise, had earlier raised a "legion" of nearly three thousand men of assorted arms, which he hoped to operate as a partisan force outside the regular channels of command, but Davis had also appointed him brigadier in the Confederate Army. It happened that these two militarily untrained gentlemen were passionately ambitious and ancient political rivals. By the time Lee arrived on the scene, the lines had already been drawn between the rival generals: Floyd was determined to exercise his seniority by assuming command of Wise's force and Wise was equally determined to remain in independent command. Wise appealed directly to Lee, whom he regarded as his defender, while Floyd wrote directly to Davis and the Secretary of War.

For gentle-natured Lee, without authority and a political innocent, the West Virginia campaign was a dismal experience. Cooperation between Floyd and Wise, and between their forces and Loring, was simply impossible. On the positive side, he did prevent any Federal advance and kept the railroads safe, but, in terms of the victory which Confederates expected in western Virginia, the expedition must be adjudged a failure. The saving of that area of western Virginia loomed much larger to Virginians at the time than it has in history. The people knew nothing of the demoralized condition of the poorly equipped Confederate forces, nor of the divided command situation, nor of Lee's ill-defined position as "co-ordinator." The people's pride was hurt at losing a part of their own state and Lee became the scapegoat. His letters show that he was not unmindful of attacks by the newspapers, but it was not in his character to explain or defend himself.

Except for revealing his unswerving policy, advanced through the war, of concentrating scattered troops to engage the enemy at points of his own selection, his military letters during this doleful period reveal little else about him as a soldier. However, his personal letters are among his most illuminating. As his duties were fewer than they were to become later, he had the time to write of his general interests and his letters contain some sharp pictures of camp life. He went to the mountains with a staff consisting only of Captain Walter Taylor and Lieutenant Colonel John A. Washington, who was killed on September 13th; at headquarters, he was attended only by a Negro body servant and a Negro cook. During the three rainy months he spent in the Alleghenies, the general allowed his beard to grow; though his hair was still dark, the beard came out gray, giving Lee the familiar appearance of the war period.

On the last day of October, with the campaign for all practical purposes dissolved, Lee was back in Richmond, still without a command.

66   To HIS WIFE
                           "Kinloch," Virginia

                                                  Huntersville, Virginia
                                                     August 4, 1861

I reached here yesterday dearest Mary to visit this portion of the army. The day after my arrival at Staunton I set off for Monterey, where the army of Genl [Robert S.] Garnett's command is stationed. Two regiments & a field-battery occupy the Alleghany Mountains in advance, about 30 miles, & this division guards the road to Staunton. The division here guard the road leading by the Warm Springs to Milboro & Covington. Two regiments are advanced about 28 miles to Middle Mountain. Fitzhugh [Lee] with his squadron is between that point & this & I have not yet seen him. I understand he is well.

South of here again is another column of our enemies, making their way up the Kanawha Valley & from Genl [Henry A.] Wise's report are not far from Lewisburg. Their object seems to be to get possession of the Virginia Central Railroad & the Virginia & Tennessee Railroad. By the first they can approach Richmond. By the last interrupt our reinforcements from the South. The points from which we can be attacked are numerous, & their means are unlimited. So we must always be on the alert. My uneasiness on these points brought me out here. It is so difficult to get our people, unaccustomed to the necessities of war, to comprehend & promptly execute the measures required for the occasion. Genl [Henry R.] Jackson of Georgia commands on the Monterey line. Genl [William W.] Loring on this line, & Genl Wise supported by Genl [John B.] Floyd on the Kanawha line. The soldiers everywhere are sick. The measles are prevalent throughout the whole army, & you know that disease leaves unpleasant results, attacks on the lungs, typhoid, &c., &c.,

especially in camp where accommodation for the sick is poor. I travelled from Staunton on horseback. A part of the road, as far as Buffalo Gap, I passed over in the summer of 1840, on my return to St. Louis, after bringing you home. If any one had then told me that the next time I travelled that road would have been on my present errand, I should have supposed him insane. I enjoyed the mountains as I rode along. The views were magnificent. The valleys so beautiful, the scenery so peaceful. What a glorious world Almighty God has given us. How thankless & ungrateful we are, & how we labour to mar His gifts. May He have mercy on us!

Col [John A.] Washington is with me. I hope you received my letters from Richmond. Give love to Daughter & Mildred. I did not see Rob as I passed through Charlottesville. He was at the University & I could not stop.

[R. E. LEE]

67   To GENERAL HENRY A. WISE
White Sulphur Springs, Virginia

Headquarters, Valley Mountain
August 8, 1861

General:

I have just received your letters of the 6th & 7th instant, & am glad to learn that Genl Floyd is moving on to Lewisburg.

In regard to the request to separate the commands of Genl Floyd & yourself, & to assign to each respective fields of action, it would, in my opinion, be contrary to the purpose of the President, & destroy the prospect of the success of the campaign in Kanawha District. Our enemy is so strong at all points that we can only hope to give him an effective blow by a concentration of our forces, & that this may be done surely & rapidly, their movements & actions must be controlled by one head. I hope, therefore, that as soon as your command can move forward, in the preparation for which I feel assured no time will be lost, that you will join Genl Floyd, & take that part in the campaign which may be assigned your brigade.

I am very resply your obt servt

R. E. LEE
Genl Commdg

68   To HIS WIFE
                         "Kinloch," Virginia

                                         Camp at Valley Mountain
                                         August 9, 1861

I have been here dear Mary three days. Coming from Monterey to
Huntersville & thence here. We are on the dividing ridge. Looking north
down the Tygart's river valley, whose waters flow into the Mononga-
hela, & south towards the Elk River & Greenbrier, flowing into the Kanawha. In the valley north of us lies Huttonsville & Beverly, occupied by
our invaders, & the Rich Mountains west, the scene of our former disaster,
& the Cheat Mountains east, their present stronghold, are in full view.
The mountains are beautiful, fertile to the tops, covered with the richest
sward of blue grass & white clover. The inclosed fields waving with the
natural growth of timothy. The habitations are few & population sparse.
This is a magnificent grazing country, & all it wants is labour to clear
the mountain-sides of its great growth of timber. There is surely no lack
of moisture at this time. It has rained I believe some portion of every day
since I left Staunton. Now it is pouring, & the wind, that has veered
around to every point of the compass, has settled down to the northeast.
What that portends in these regions I do not know. Col Washington,
Capt [Walter H.] Taylor and myself are in one tent, which as yet protects us. I have enjoyed the company of Fitzhugh since I have been
here. He is very well & very active, & as yet the war has not reduced
him much. He dined with me yesterday & preserves his fine appetite. Today he is out reconnoitering & has the full benefit of this fine rain. I fear
he is without his overcoat, as I do not recollect seeing it on his saddle.
I told you he had been promoted to a Major in cavalry, & is the commanding cavalry officer on this line at present. He is as sanguine, cheerful, &
hearty as ever. I sent him some cornmeal this morning & he sent me
some butter. A mutual interchange of good things. There are but few of
your acquaintances in this Army. I find here in the ranks of one company Henry Tiffany. The company is composed principally of Balti-
morians. George Lemon & Douglas Mercer are in it. It is a very fine company, well drilled & well instructed. Genl Daniel S. Donelson is in
command of a Tennessee regiment. I find that our old friend J[ohn] F.
Reynolds of West Point memory is in command of the troops immediately in front of us. He is a Brig-Genl. You may recollect him as the
assistant Professor of Philosophy & lived in the cottage beyond the west
gate, with his little palefaced wife, a great friend of Lawrence & Markie.

He resigned on being relieved from West Point, & was made Professor of some college in the West. Fitzhugh was the bearer of a flag the other day & he recognized him. Was very polite & made kind inquiries of us all. I am told they feel very safe & are very confident of success. Their numbers are said to be large, ranging from 12,000 to 30,000. But it is impossible for me to get correct information either as to their strength or position. Our citizens beyond this are all on their side. Our movements seem rapidly to be communicated to them while theirs come to us slowly & indistinctly. I have two regiments here, with others coming up. I think we shall shut up this road to the Central Railroad which they strongly threaten. Our means of transportation is limited & our supplies come up slowly. We have plenty of beef & can get some bread.

I hope you are well & content. I have heard nothing of you or the children since I left Richmond. You must write there. I received a letter at Monterey from Charlotte. She was well & mentioned having received a very comforting letter from you as regards Fitzhugh's departure to the wars.

I have no news. The men are suffering from the measles, &c. as elsewhere, but are cheerful & lighthearted. The atmosphere when not raining is delightful. The nights cool & water delicious. You must give much love to Daughter & Life. I want to see you all very much, but know not when that can be. May God guard & protect you all. In Him alone is our hope.

Remember me to Ned & all at Kinloch & Avenel. Send word to Miss Sue W[ashington] that her father is sitting on his blanket sewing the strap on his haversac. I think she ought to be here to do it.

[R. E. Lee]

69   To GENERAL HENRY A. WISE
Commanding Wise Legion, Sewell Mountain, Virginia

Headquarters
Valley Mountain, Virginia
August 21, 1861

General:

I have received your letter of the 18th instant, & according to your request, have issued the accompanying Special Orders, of this date, placing the 22nd & 23rd [36th] regiments Virginia Volunteers subject to the assignment of the commanding general of the Army of the Kanawha, & confining your immediate command to that of the "Wise Legion" as organized, by direction of the War Department.

It is proper, as well as necessary, for the commanding general to organize his troops in the field according to the exigencies of the service. It also becomes necessary to detach troops for special service from their appropriate brigades, & thus place them temporarily under other commanding officers. The rights of officers are not thereby violated, provided they are under their senior in rank, whose orders are always respected & obeyed in well-constituted armies.

The necessities of war require the organization of the forces to be adapted to the service to be performed, & sometimes brigades & separate commands have to be remodeled accordingly. This must be done in accordance with the judgment of the commanding officer. The transmission of orders to troops through their immediate commanders is in accordance with usage & propriety. Still, there are occasions when this can not be conformed to without detriment to the service. Obedience to all legal orders is nevertheless obligatory upon all officers & soldiers.

These remarks are not supposed necessary for your information, but to show why I have not considered orders on the subject necessary. Feeling assured of the patriotism & zeal of the officers & men composing the Army of the Kanawha, I have never apprehended any embarrassment or interference in the execution of their respective duties, believing they would make everything yield to the welfare of the republic.

I remain with high esteem, your obt servt

R. E. LEE
Genl Commdg

(INCLOSURE)

SPECIAL ORDERS, NO. 243

Headquarters
Valley Mountain, Virginia
August 21, 1861

I. The Twenty-second and Thirty-sixth Regiments Virginia Volunteers, under Colonels [Christopher Q.] Tompkins and [John] McCausland, will be formed into a distinct brigade, or be attached to other brigades of the Army of the Kanawha, as the commanding general of that army may determine.

II. The Wise Legion, as organized under the directions of the Secretary of War, will be under the immediate command of General H. A. Wise.

III.   The militia called into the service of the Confederate States, together with all the troops operating in the Kanawha Valley, will be subject to the orders and under the control of the commanding general of the Army of the Kanawha.

R. E. LEE
General Commanding

70   To GENERAL HENRY A. WISE
Commanding Wise Legion, Dogwood Gap, Virginia

Headquarters, Valley Mountain
August 27, 1861

General:
   I have just received your letter of the 24th instant, & am much concerned at the view you take of your position & its effect upon your Legion. I do not apprehend the consequences you suppose will follow from its being under the general orders of the commander of the Army of the Kanawha, or from its forming a part of that army. It will be under your immediate care & control, & though it may be occasionally detached from your command, it cannot suffer any harm under its regularly constituted officers. The Army of Kanawha is too small for active & successful operation to be divided at present. I beg, therefore, for the sake of the cause you have so much at heart, you will permit no division of sentiment or action to disturb its harmony or arrest its efficiency. In accordance with your request I will refer your application to be detached from Genl Floyd's command to the Secretary of War. At present I do not see how it can be done without injury to the service, and hope, therefore, you will not urge it.
   Your account of Genl Floyd's position makes me very anxious for his safety, & I would immediately despatch an infantry force to his support, the only character of troops that could reach him across the mountains, did I not suppose from the time that has already elapsed, & the distance they would have to march, about sixty miles, they could not possibly arrive in time to be of any avail. I think, therefore, he will either have retired up the Gauley & recrossed at the ferry, or that you will have built a flat & crossed to his support.
   I am with great respect, your obt servt

R. E. LEE
Genl Commdg

71   To MISSES ANNIE AND AGNES LEE
              Richmond, Virginia

                                          Valley Mountain
                                          August 29, 1861

My Precious Daughters:

I have just received your letters of the 24th & am rejoiced to hear that you are well & enjoying the company of your friends. You did not mention whether you had received a letter from me, written before my departure from Richmond & directed to Brandon. I do not know, therefore, whether you have funds for your projected visits. If not, you must call upon Custis. I am very sorry to hear that he is sick. I do not know what to do for him. Not having heard from him I supposed he might have left Richmond. Fitzhugh is very anxious to get his buffalo robe, which was directed to be sent to my care at the Spottswood, & which I wrote to Custis to forward, or rather to get Col [Abraham C.] Myers to forward to me at Huntersville. He fears it may be lost. He had come up to take his dinner with me. Sunset is the time of my banquet, & therefore received the latest intelligence of you & of Charlotte's departure for the White (Montgomery). I hope the mountains may restore her little boy & benefit her. It rains here all the time, literally. There has not been sunshine enough since my arrival to dry my clothes. Perry [a servant] is my washerman, & socks & towels suffer. But the worst of the rain is, that the ground has become so saturated with water that the constant travel on the roads have made them almost impassable, so that I cannot get up sufficient supplies for the troops to move. It is raining now. Has been all day, last night, day before & day before that, &c. But we must be patient. It is quite cool, too. I have on all my winter clothes & am writing in my overcoat. All the clouds seem to concentrate over this ridge of mountains, & by whatever wind they are driven, give us rain. The mountains are magnificent. The sugar maples are beginning to turn already, & the grass luxuriant. Richmond [Lee's horse] has not been accustomed to such fare or such treatment, but he gets along tolerably. Complains some, & has not much superfluous flesh. There has been much sickness among the men, measles, &c., & the weather has been unfavourable. I hope their attacks are nearly over, & that they will come out with the sun. Our party has kept well. I do not know whether this will find you in Richmond. But if it does, give my kind regards to all friends & warm thanks for their remembrances. Although we may be too weak to break through their lines, I feel well satisfied that the enemy cannot at present reach Richmond by either of the three routes leading to Staunton, Milboro, or Covington. He must find some other way.

I want to see you very much, your poor mother & all. I hope that day may come, but it is far off I fear. God bless you my children, & preserve you from all harm is the constant prayer of

Your devoted father

R. E. LEE

72   To HIS WIFE
                "Audley," Clarke County, Virginia

Valley Mountain
September 1, 1861

I have received, dearest Mary, your letter of 18th August from Audley, & am very glad to get news of your whereabouts. I wrote to you not long since & have but little to add to what I then related. I am very glad you are enabled to see so many of your friends, & to enjoy the cheering interchange of friendly association. I hope you have found all well in your tour, & I am very glad that our cousin Esther bears the separation from all her sons so bravely. I have no doubt they will do good service in our Southern cause, & wish they could be placed according to their fancies. I received a letter from Danger the other day, desiring the appointment of drillmaster to his regiment, an appointment I am not aware of & cannot attend to till I return to Richmond. I mentioned to the President shortly after his arrival in Richmond the desire of Edward Butler to serve the Southern cause, but the difficulty is to find places for all applicants unless they possess military knowledge & instruction. At this time our diplomatic relations require but few to look after them. I fear you have postponed your visit to the Hot [Springs] too late. It must be quite cold there now, judging from the temperature here, & it has been raining in these mountains since the 24 July. I heard from the girls in Richmond. They were meditating a visit to their Uncle Carter & to the Stuarts. I do not know when you will all get together again or where. Charlotte you will have heard has gone to the Montgomery White. Custis took her up. Fitzhugh has received a letter from her since her arrival, saying the baby was better. I hope both will be benefited. I see F[itzhugh] quite often, though he is encamped 4 miles from me. He is very well & not at all harmed by the campaign.

We have a great deal of sickness among the soldiers, & now those on the sick list would form an army. The measles is still among them, though I hope is dying out. But it is a disease which though light in childhood is severe in manhood, & prepares the system for other attacks. The constant cold rains, mud, &c., &c., with no shelter but tents, have aggravated it. All these drawbacks, with impassable roads, have paralysed our efforts. Still I think you will be safe at the Hot, for the present. We are right up to the enemy on the three lines, & in the Kanawha he has been pushed beyond the Gauley.

I had intended to write to Daughter by this opportunity, but have had so many letters & papers to despatch that I shall not be able. Tell her I was very glad to hear from her & hope to answer her letter soon. Custis is still in R[ichmond] or was on the 27 August when he wrote. He said nothing of his health so I hope he is well. My poor little Rob I never hear from scarcely. He is busy, I suppose, & knows not where to direct. Give much love to "Precious Life" & all with you & accept for yourself my love & prayers.

With much affection

R. E. LEE

73   To G. W. C. LEE
                Richmond, Virginia

Valley Mountain
September 3, 1861

My dear son:

I was very glad to receive your letter of the 27th ultimo, and to learn something of your whereabouts. I did not know what had become of you, and was very anxious to learn. You say nothing of your health, and I will hope you are well and able to do good service to the cause so dear to us all. I trust you may be able to get a position and field agreeable to you; and know that wherever you may be placed you will do your duty. That is all the pleasure, all the comfort, all the glory we can enjoy in this world. I have been able to do but little here. Still I hope I have been of some service. Things are better organized. I feel stronger, we are stronger. The three routes leading east are guarded. The men have more confidence, our people a feeling of security. The enemy has been driven back, and made to haul in his horns, and to find he cannot have everything his own way. This has been done without a battle, but by a steady advance of positions. Now to drive him farther a battle must come off, and I am anxious to begin it. Circumstances beyond human control delay it, I know for good, but I hope the Great Ruler of the Universe will continue to aid and prosper us, and crown at last our feeble efforts with success. Rain, rain, rain, there has been nothing but rain. So it has appeared to my anxious mind since I approached these mountains. It commenced before, but since has come down with a will. The cold too has been greater than I could have conceived. In my winter clothing and buttoned up in my overcoat, I have still been cold. This state of weather has aggravated the sickness that has attacked the whole army, measles and typhoid fever. Some regiments have not over 250 for duty, some 300, 500, or about half, according to its strength. This makes a terrible hole in our effectives. Do not mention this, I pray you. It will be in the papers next. The rains and constant travel have cut these dirt turnpikes so deep, the soil being rich mould in most parts, that wagons can only travel with double teams. But there is a change in the weather. The glorious sun has been shining these four days. The drowned earth is warming. The sick are improving, and the spirits of all are rising. F[itzhugh] is anxious to get his buffalo robe. Did you ever get my letter concerning it? It was directed to be sent to the Spotswood [Hotel] to me. I asked you to put it up securely, and get Colonel Myers to send it to me at Huntersville. I have heard nothing of it. F[itzhugh] feels the want of it every night. He is very well, hearty, and sanguine. I am glad to hear of Genl A. S. Johnston's approach and Captain [Richard B.] Garnett's arrival. The disaster at Cape Hatteras was a hard blow to us, but we must expect them, struggle against them, prepare for them. We cannot be always successful and reverses must come. May God give us courage, endurance, and faith to strive to the end. Good-by, my dear son. F[itzhugh] has just come in. He sends his love and Colonel W[ashington] and Captain T[aylor] their regards. Give my kind remembrances to everybody.

Your fond father

R. E. LEE

74   To HIS WIFE
"Audley," Virginia

Camp at Valley Mountain
September 9, 1861

I received last night, dearest Mary, your letter of 30 August, forwarded by Custis. I hope from the tone of your letter that you feel better & wish I could see you & be with you. I trust we may meet this fall somewhere if only for a little time. I have written to Robert telling him if, after considering what I had previously said to him on the subject of his joining the company he desires under Major Ross, he still thinks it best for him to do so, I will not withhold my consent. It seems he will be 18 (I thought 17). I am unable to judge for him, & he must decide for himself. In a reply to a recent letter from him to me on the same subject, I said to him all I could. I pray God to bring him to a correct conclusion!

As to the reports which you say are afloat about our separation I know nothing. Any one that can reason must see its necessity under present circumstances. They can only exist in the imaginations of a few. So give them no heed. We both know it cannot be otherwise, & must, therefore, be content. As to the vile slanders, too, with which you say the papers abound, why concern ourselves. I do not see them & would not mind them. They are inserted for no good intention you may be sure. The papers that publish them would not put in the refutation, so what good would be accomplished. I do not recollect the letter to you or even the part that you wish to publish. I only know I never write private letters for the public eye, & suppose what I said was for your own perusual. I am content to take no notice of the slanders you speak of but to let them die out.

Everybody is slandered, even the good. How should I escape?

You must do as you think best about Mildred. I am unable to help you, even about your own movements. All my time & attention is absorbed in my imperative duties, which are not confined to this division of the army, but extend to others in the State. What to advise you I really am at a loss. You must establish yourself somewhere this winter, & what place to propose I now do not know. Perhaps you had better make up your mind to board somewhere & let the girls do the same, & then you can move according to circumstances. Everything within the seat of war must be uncertain. Select some place, therefore, that will be agreable to you & where the expense will come within our means. Very little is necessary for me & you can have all the rest. Fitzhugh is quite well. Charlotte, poor child, has had to return to Richmond, the baby grew worse at the [Hot] Springs. She is going to Shirley. The baby has become better since she got back.

Custis is in R[ichmond] & I have heard has been appointed aid to the President (not however from him). The girls were in R[ichmond] when I last heard & going up with their Uncle Carter to Windsor.

For military news I must refer you to the papers. You will see there more than ever occurs, & what does occur, the relation must be taken with much allowance. Do not believe anything you see about me. There has been no battle, only skirmishing with the outposts, & nothing done [of] any moment. The weather is still unfavourable to us. The roads or rather tracks of mud almost impassable, & the number of sick large. I forgot to say that I have sent R[obert] $100. to get his equipment if he joins the army. Give much love to Daughter. I wrote to her the other day. Kiss Life for me too & remembrances to all friends.

Truly & devotedly your husband

R. E. LEE

75   To GENERAL HENRY A. WISE
Commanding Wise Legion, Hawk's Nest, Kanawha Valley, Virginia

Headquarters, Valley Mountain, Virginia
September 9, 1861

General:

I have just received your report of the 5th instant, & am very happy to again congratulate you on your success against the enemy. I am very sorry for the necessity under which Genl Floyd found it necessary to diminish your command, but you know how necessary it is to act upon reports touching the safety of troops, & that even rumors must not be neglected. Genl Floyd's position is an exposed one & inviting an attack. He is obliged, therefore, to be cautious, & there is no way of being secure against false information. Troops are consequently obliged to be subjected to wearisome marches. But it is not done intentionally. In my opinion it would be highly prejudicial to separate your Legion from Genl Floyd. It might be ruinous to our cause in the [Kanawha] Valley. United the force is not strong enough. It could effect nothing divided.

Great efforts have been made to get this force in marching order. Bad weather, impassable roads, sickness have paralyzed it for some time. There is a prospect now of being able to resume operations.

There must be a union of strength to drive back the invaders, & I beg you will act in concert.

I will forward your report to the Secretary of War, that he may be gratified at the account of the bravery of your troops & skill of your officers. But I must tell you, in candor, I cannot recommend the division of the Army of the Kanawha.

We must endure everything in the cause we maintain.

In pushing your movements against the enemy, I trust you will not allow your troops to hazard themselves unnecessarily or to jeopardize the accomplishment of the general operations.

I am with great respect, your obt servt

R. E. LEE
Genl Commdg

76   SPECIAL ORDERS, NO. ——

Headquarters of the Forces
Valley Mountain, Virginia
September 9, 1861

The forward movement announced to the Army of the Northwest in Special Orders, No. 28, from its headquarters, of this date, gives the general commanding the opportunity of exhorting the troops to keep steadily in view the great principles for which they contend and to manifest to the world their determination to maintain them. The eyes of the country are upon you. The safety of your homes and the lives of all you hold dear depend upon your courage and exertions. Let each man resolve to be victorious, and that the right of self-government, liberty, and peace shall in him find a defender. The progress of this army must be forward.

R. E. LEE
General Commanding

77   To HIS WIFE
Hot Springs, Virginia

Valley Mountain
September 17, 1861

I received, dear Mary, your letter of the 5th by Beverly T[urner], who is a nice young soldier. I am pained to see fine young men like him, of education & standing from all the old & respectable families in the State serving in the ranks. I hope in time they will receive their reward. I met him as I was returning from an expedition to the enemy's works, which I had hoped to have surprised on the morning of the 12th, both at Cheat Mountain and on [Tygart's] Valley-River. All the attacking parties with great labour had reached their destination, over mountains considered impassable to bodies of troops, notwithstanding a heavy storm that set in the day before & raged all night, in which they had to stand up till daylight. Their arms were then unserviceable & they in poor condition for a fierce assault against artillery & superior numbers. After waiting till 10 o'clock for the assault on Cheat Mountain which did not take place & which was to have been the signal for the rest, they were withdrawn, & after waiting three days in front of the enemy, hoping he would come out of his trenches, we returned to our position at this place.

I cannot tell you my regret & mortification at the untoward events that caused the failure of the plan. I had taken every precaution to ensure success & counted on it. But the Ruler of the Universe willed otherwise & sent a storm to disconcert a well laid plan, & to destroy my hopes. We are no worse off now than before, except the disclosure of our plan, against which they will guard.

We met with one heavy loss which grieves me deeply. Col [John A.] Washington accompanied Fitzhugh on a reconnoitering expedition, & I fear they were carried away by their zeal, & approached within the enemies pickets. The first they knew was a volley from a concealed party within a few yards of them. Their balls passed through the Col's body. Three struck F[itzhugh]'s horse, & the horse of one of the men was killed. F[itzhugh] mounted the Col's horse & brought him off. I am much grieved. He was always anxious to go on these expeditions. This was the first day I assented. Since I had been thrown in such intimate relations with him, I had learned to appreciate him very highly. Morning & evening have I seen him on his knees praying to his Maker.

"The righteous perisheth & no man layeth it to heart, and merciful men are taken away, none considering that the righteous is taken away from the evil to come." May God have mercy on us all!

I suppose you are at the Hot Springs & will direct to you there. Our poor sick I know suffer much. They bring it on themselves by not doing what they are told. They are worse than children, for the latter can be forced.

Custis writes the girls have gone to Carter's. They did not get your letter in time. I hope I may be able to get there before you leave. I may have to go to the Kanawha & if so will write to you from Lewisburg.

Fitzhugh is very well. Charlotte writes the baby is better.

Love to Daughter.

Truly yours

R. E. Lee

P.S. I am much obliged to you for your offer of socks. I should like to have ½ dozen good thick *cotton* socks if you could get them knit & have the cotton.

R. E. L.

78   To JOHN LETCHER
                            Governor of Virginia

                                                Valley Mountain
                                                September 17, 1861

My Dear Governor:

I received your very kind note of the 5th instant, just as I was about
to accompany General Loring's command on an expedition to the enemy's works in front, or I would have before thanked you for the interest
you take in my welfare, and your too flattering expressions of my ability.
Indeed, you overrate me much, and I feel humbled when I weigh myself by your standard. I am, however, very grateful for your confidence,
and I can answer for my sincerity in the earnest endeavour I make to advance the cause I have so much at heart, though conscious of the slow
progress I make.

I was very sanguine of taking the enemy's works on last Thursday
morning. I had considered the subject well. With great effort the troops
intended for the surprise had reached their destination, having traversed
twenty miles of steep, rugged mountain paths, and the last day through a
terrible storm, which lasted all night, and in which they had to stand
drenched to the skin in cold rain. Still, their spirits were good. When
morning broke, I could see the enemy's tents on Valley River, at the
point on the Huttonsville road just below me. It was a tempting sight.
We waited for the attack on Cheat Mountain, which was to be the signal,
till 10 A.M.; the men were cleaning their unserviceable arms. But the signal did not come. All chance for a surprise was gone. The provisions of
the men had been destroyed the preceding day by the storm. They had
nothing to eat that morning, could not hold out another day, and were
obliged to be withdrawn. The party sent to Cheat Mountain to take that
in rear had also to be withdrawn. The attack to come off from the east
side failed from the difficulties in the way; the opportunity was lost, and
our plan discovered.

It is a grievous disappointment to me, I assure you. But for the rain-
storm, I have no doubt it would have succeeded. This, Governor, is for
your own eye. Please do not speak of it; we must try again. Our greatest loss is the death of my dear friend, Colonel Washington. He and my
son were reconnoitering the front of the enemy. They came unawares
upon a concealed party, who fired upon them within twenty yards, and
the Colonel fell pierced by three balls. My son's horse received three

shots, but he escaped on the Colonel's horse. His zeal for the cause to which he had devoted himself carried him, I fear, too far.

We took some seventy prisoners, and killed some twenty-five or thirty of the enemy. Our loss was small besides what I have mentioned. Our greatest difficulty is the roads. It has been raining in these mountains about six weeks. It is impossible to get along. It is that which has paralysed all our efforts.

With sincere thanks for your good wishes,

I am very truly yours

R. E. LEE

79   To GENERAL HENRY A. WISE
Commanding Wise Legion, Sewell Mountain, Virginia

Camp at Meadow Bluff
September 21, 1861

General:

I have just arrived at this camp, and regret to find the forces not united. I know nothing of the relative advantages of the points occupied by yourself and Genl Floyd, but as far as I can judge our united forces are not more than one half of the strength of the enemy. Together they may not be able to withstand his assault.

It would be the height of imprudence to submit them separately to his attack. I am told by Genl Floyd that your position is a very strong one. This one I have not examined, but it seems to have the advantage of yours, in commanding the Wilderness road & the approach to Lewisburg, which I think is the aim of Genl [William S.] Rosecrans. I beg therefore, if not too late, that the troops be united and that we conquer or die together. You have spoken to me of want of consultation and concert, let that pass till the enemy is driven back, & then as far as I can, all shall be arranged. I expect this of your magnanimity; consult that and the interest of the cause, and all will go well.

With high respect, yr obt svt

R. E. LEE
Genl Comdg

80   To GENERAL HENRY A. WISE
        Commanding Wise Legion, Sewell Mountain, Virginia

                            Camp Defiance, Big Sewell, Virginia
                            September 25, 1861 — 5.5 o'clock

General R. E. Lee:

General:

By your aide (under the approach and fire of the enemy, at a stand, made under my orders, where the struggle will be severe, whatever be the result) I received the within order from the Acting Secretary of War. It is imperative, requiring "the least delay," but it could not have foreseen these circumstances — the most extremely embarrassing to me. I come to you for counsel, and will abide by it, because I have been under your eye, and you are competent to judge my act and its motive, whatever it may be. I desire to delay my report in person until after the fate of this battle. Dare I do so? On the other hand, can I, in honor, leave you at this moment, though the disobedience of the order may subject me to the severest penalties? Will you please advise and instruct me?

I am, with the highest respect and esteem, your obedient servant

                            HENRY A. WISE
                            Brigadier General

            [INDORSEMENT]

                                            [No date]
General:

I will briefly state, in answer to your inquiry, appreciating as I do the reluctance and embarrassment you feel at leaving your Legion at this time, what I should feel compelled to do, as a military man, under like circumstances. That is, to obey the President's order. The enemy is in our presence & testing the strength of our position. What may be the result, whether he will determine to attack or whether we may retire, cannot now be foreseen. I can conceive the desire your command would have for your presence, yet they will also do justice to your position.

With highest esteem, your obt servt

                            R. E. LEE
                            Genl Commdg

81   To HIS WIFE
                Hot Springs, Virginia

                                    Camp on Sewell's Mountain
                                    September 26, 1861

I have just received, dear Mary, your letters of the 17th & 19th instants, with one from Robert of the former date. I have but little time for writing tonight, & will, therefore, write to you. I infer from out of your letters that you have written for money. The letter I have not received, but send my check for $200, which I hope will answer your present purposes. As regards dear Robt I have said all I have to say. He must determine for himself. I cannot learn which of the institutions, Lexington [Virginia Military Institute] or the University [of Virginia], will be the most favourable for him, [or] what degree of instruction they will be able to afford. If they reach their former standard, I should incline to the University. He must ascertain & decide for himself. If he will say what amount of money he will require for his support at either I will try & furnish it. Having now disposed of the business matters, I will say how glad I am to hear from you, & to learn that you have reached the Hot in safety, with Daughter & Rob. I pray that its healing waters may benefit you all. I am glad to hear of Charlotte & the girls, & hope all will go well with them. I infer you received my letter written before leaving Valley Mountain, though you did not direct your letter "via Lewisburg, Greenbrier County," & hence its delay. I told you of the death of Colonel Washington. I grieve for his loss, though trust him to the mercy of our Heavenly Father. May He have mercy on us all. It is raining heavily. The men are all exposed on the mountains, with the enemy opposite to us. We are without tents, & for two nights I have laid buttoned up in my overcoat. Today my tent came up & I am in it. Yet I fear I shall not sleep for thinking of the poor men. I wrote about socks for myself. I have no doubt the yarn ones you mention will be very acceptable to the men here or elsewhere. If you can send them here, I will distribute [them] to the most needy. Tell Rob I could not write to him for want of time. My heart is always with you & my children. May God guard you & bless you all is the constant prayer of your devoted husband,

                                    R. E. LEE

82   To HIS WIFE
                         Hot Springs, Virginia

                                              Sewell's Mountain
                                              October 7, 1861

   I received, dear Mary, your letter by Doctor Quintard, with the
cotton socks. Both were very acceptable, though the latter I have not yet
tried. At the time of their reception the enemy was threatening an attack,
which was continued till Saturday night, when under cover of darkness
& our usual mountain mist he suddenly withdrew. Your letter of the 2nd,
with the yarn socks, 4 pairs, were handed to me when I was preparing to
follow, & I could not at the time attend to either. But I have since, &
as I found Perry in desperate need, I bestowed a couple of pairs on him
as a present from you. The others I have put in my trunk & suppose
they will fall to the lot of Meredith [Lee's cook], into the state of whose
hose I have not yet inquired. Should any sick man require them first, he
shall have them, but Meredith will have no one near to supply him but
me, & will naturally expect that attention.
   I hope, dear Mary, you & Daughter, as well as poor little Rob, have
derived some benefit from the sanitary baths of the Hot. What does
Daughter intend to do during the winter? And, indeed, what do you? It
is time you were determining. There is no prospect of your returning to
Arlington. I think you had better select some comfortable place in the
Carolinas or Georgia, & all board together. If Mildred goes to school at
Raleigh, why not go there? It is a good opportunity to try a warmer climate for your rheumatism. If I thought our enemies would not make a
vigorous move against Richmond, I would recommend to rent a house
there. But under these circumstances I would not feel as if you were
permanently located if there. I am ignorant where I shall be. In the field
somewhere, I suspect, so I have little hope of being with you, though I
hope to be able to see you. I am glad you will see dear Chass [Charlotte]
& am as delighted as grateful to the giver of all good that her little boy is
getting well. I hope you will all be happy together. I heard from Fitzhugh the other day. He is well, though his command is greatly reduced
by sickness. I wished much to bring him with me; but there is too much
cavalry on this line now, & I am dismounting them. I could not, therefore,
order more. The weather is almost as bad here as in the mountains I left.
There was a drenching rain yesterday, & as I had left my overcoat in
camp I was thoroughly wet from head to foot. It has been raining ever

since & is now coming down with a will. But I have my clothes out on the bushes & they will be well washed.

The force of the enemy, by a few prisoners captured yesterday and civilians on the road, is put down from 17,000 to 20,000. Some went as high as 22,000. General Floyd thinks 18,000. I do not think it exceeds 9 or 10,000, though it exceeds ours. I wish he had attacked us, as I believe he would have been repulsed with great loss. His plan was to have attacked us at all points at the same time. The rumbling of his wheels, &c., were heard by our pickets, but as that was customary at night in the moving & placing of his cannon, the officer of the day to whom it was reported paid no particular attention to it, supposing it to be a preparation for attack in the morning. When day appeared, the bird had flown, & the misfortune was that the reduced condition of our horses for want of provender, exposure to cold rains in these mountains, & want of provisions for the men prevented the vigorous pursuit & following up that was proper. We can only get up provisions from day to day, which paralyses our operations.

I am sorry, as you say, that the movements of the armies cannot keep pace with the expectations of the editors of papers. I know they can regulate matters satisfactorily to themselves on paper. I wish they could do so in the field. No one wishes them more success than I do & would be happy to see them have full swing. Genl Floyd has the benefit of three editors on his staff. I hope something will be done to please them.

Give much love to the children & everybody, & believe me always yours

R. E. Lee

CHAPTER THREE

Southern Coastal Defenses

NOVEMBER 1861–MARCH 1862

"Another forlorn hope expedition"

T HE NEXT ASSIGNMENT which Lee received from President
Davis, November 6, combined the duties and the unrewarding elements of the first two. He went to another emergency situation
without field command. Federal amphibious operations along the coasts
of South Carolina, Georgia and northern Florida threatened landings
which could expand into bases for inland operation into productive plantation areas and along the 100-mile course of the vital railroad from
Charleston to Savannah. This total area was suddenly formed into one
department, with Lee hurried southward as its commander.

Reorganizing the various state (and state-minded) units, scattered about
in garrisons, into a coherent system of defense, giving preferment to
strong, strategic positions, would in a measure duplicate his organization of Virginia's defenses. But he was determined that he would not
duplicate the gruesome West Virginia experience in trying to coordinate
prima donnas without the supporting authority. Jefferson Davis recorded
the interview in which Lee tactfully asked for a definition of his authority. "He [Lee] said that, while he was serving in Virginia, he had never
thought it needful to inquire about his rank; but now, when about to go
into other States and to meet officers with whom he had not previously
been connected, he would like to be informed upon that point." Davis
assured him that he possessed the authority of a full general.

Lee acted upon it. With Governor Pickens of South Carolina and
Governor Brown of Georgia, he operated with the same diplomacy that
had been so effective with Governor Letcher, and won their cooperation.
Despite the strong tendency of volunteers to fight only in their own states,
and the disruption caused by one-year enlistments ending in December

in South Carolina and in January in Georgia, Lee was able to bring 25,000 troops into the field. In dealing with subordinates, he abandoned the tactful efforts he had tried with Loring and the political generals, and acted with force as the commanding general. In doing this, he showed those gifts for eliminating the incompetents and advancing the able which were to characterize his later command of an army.

Also, in meeting the complex of problems presented by the enemy and a 300-mile coastal front, he displayed his strong bent toward concentration at points of strategic priority as opposed to the general policy of dispersing forces to meet all the threats of the enemy.

When Lee arrived in Georgia, small forts were manned on the sea islands that extended 300 miles from Georgetown, South Carolina, to the mouth of St. John's River in Florida. Many rivers in this area opened into the ocean, offering avenues of ascent for Federal gunboats, and only seven thousand troops, not all equipped with rifles and supported by little artillery, were somewhat frantically trying to cover all points of danger between Charleston and Savannah. The day before Lee arrived, two of the small sea island forts had been overwhelmed by fire from Federal gunboats, and there was little to impede a determined advance against the mainland (and the railroad) except the lack of coordination between the commander of the Federal land forces and the Navy.

Lee immediately ordered the abandonment of the scattered outlying positions. Then, instead of trying to protect the entire length of the railroad, he assembled Confederate forces at probable points of attack along the railroad beyond the range of the gunboats. To prevent the gunboats from ascending the rivers, he obstructed the waterways. On his interior lines, he stirred up considerable complaint by putting the would-be Prince Ruperts at the hard labor of digging fortifications. From the beginning Lee was extremely advanced in the use of fieldworks, which eventually became commonplace in both armies, and throughout the war his skill and training as an engineer were reflected in the powerful positions he fortified.

On the southern coast not only did Lee construct an impregnable work at Fort Pulaski, protecting Savannah from the sea, but in his three months in Georgia and South Carolina he built such a strong system of defense that neither Charleston nor Savannah was taken from the sea during the war. This solid achievement was made while he checked the enemy's offensive that had been mounted before his arrival.

Such contributions, of course, went largely unnoticed by a people thirsting for victories in the field, and added no color to Lee's reputation. While Confederate fortunes were tumbling in the West, and in Virginia the contestants were preparing for another decisive campaign, Lee passed inglorious hours on a treadmill of paper work involving recruiting, troop organization, details of ordnance and supply — arming and equipping — while keeping his hand in the delicate play of diplomacy to avoid arousing the antagonism of officials ever alert for encroachment on the rights of their states. Most of this repetitive and mundane correspondence, revealing little except his patience and capacity for detail, has been omitted in favor of the full personal letters which continued through this period.

In these letters the general revealed his anxiety over his wife's safety, but Mrs. Lee showed a will of her own and followed her preference for visiting among kinfolk. His first letter was written on November 5, just before he received the coastal assignment and when he was expecting to join his family. Lee had been particularly eager to join his wife at Shirley plantation, the magnificent house with its lawn on the tidal James, for that was his mother's home, where he had visited as a boy, and there his son Rooney had married Charlotte Wickham, the daughter-in-law of whom he was so fond.

On March 5, 1862, General Lee left Charleston for Richmond, after a full seven months away from the capital and his family on the two trying assignments. He probably would not have responded with such alacrity to Davis's request for him to return to Richmond had he known that the President had another desk job waiting for him.

83   To HIS WIFE
"Shirley," Virginia

Richmond
November 5, 1861

My Dear Mary:
    I received last night your letter of the 2nd & would have answered it at once but was detained with the Secretary till after 11 P.M. I fear now I may miss the mail. Saturday evening I tried to get down to you to spend Sunday, but could find no government boat going down & the passenger boats all go in the morning. I then went to the stable & got out my horse, but it was near night then & I was ignorant both of the road & distance & I gave it up.
    I was obliged to be here Monday &, as it would have consumed all Sunday to go & come, I have remained for better times. The President said I could not go today, so I must see what can be done tomorrow. I will come, however, wherever you are, either Shirley or the W[hite] H[ouse], as soon as possible, & if not sooner, Saturday at all events. If you wish to come to R[ichmond] come to the Spottswood. That is the only

place I can see you, & there but rarely, as I am occupied all the time &, in illustration, I commenced my letter to you the first thing this morning & now at 1 p.m. I have progressed thus far.

I am glad to hear you are well & the baby better.

I have sent the letter to F[itzhugh]. Custis is still in North Carolina. I have not got the letter enclosed to him. Hoping to see you very soon, with much love to C[harlotte] & all at S[hirley].

I am as ever yours

R. E. LEE

84 SPECIAL ORDERS, NO. 206

Adjutant and Inspector General's Office
Richmond
November 5, 1861

XII. The coasts of South Carolina, Georgia, and East Florida are constituted a military department, and General R. E. Lee, C. S. Army, is assigned to its command.

By command of the Secretary of War:

JOHN WITHERS
Assistant Adjutant-General

85 GENERAL ORDERS, NO. 1

Headquarters
Coosawhatchie, South Carolina
November 8, 1861

I. In pursuance of instructions from the War Department, General R. E. Lee, C. S. Army, assumes command of the military department composed of the coasts of South Carolina, Georgia, and East Florida.

II. Capt T. A. Washington, C. S. Army, is announced as adjutant general of the department; Capt Walter H. Taylor, Provisional Army, as assistant adjutant general; Capt Joseph C. Ives, C. S. Army, as chief engineer; Lt Col William G. Gill, Provisional Army, as ordnance officer, and Mr. Joseph Manigault as volunteer aide-de-camp to the commanding general.

By order of General Lee:

T. A. WASHINGTON
Captain, and Assistant Adjutant General, C. S. Army

86   To JUDAH P. BENJAMIN
Secretary of War

Headquarters, Coosawhatchie
November 9, 1861

Sir:

On the evening of the 7th, on my way to the entrance of Port Royal Harbor, I met General [Roswell S.] Ripley, returning from the battery at the north end of Hilton Head, called Fort Walker. He reported that the enemy's fleet had passed the batteries and entered the harbor. Nothing could then be done but to make arrangements to withdraw the troops from the batteries to prevent their capture and save the public property. The troops were got over during the night, but their tents, clothing, and provisions were mostly lost, and all the guns left in the batteries. General [Thomas F.] Drayton's command was transferred from Fort Walker to Bluffton; Colonel [Richard G. M.] Dunovant's from Bay Point to Saint Helena Island and thence to Beaufort. There are neither batteries nor guns for the defense of Beaufort, and Colonel Dunovant crossed Port Royal Ferry yesterday, and was halted at Garden's Corner. General Drayton reports he has but 955 men with him, and no field battery, the troops from Georgia that were on the island having returned to Savannah without orders. Colonel Dunovant's regiment is in as destitute a condition as General Drayton's command, as they were obliged to leave everything behind, and number between 600 and 700 men. I wrote to General [Alexander R.] Lawton to endeavor to withdraw the guns from the battery at the south end of Hilton Head. I have received as yet no report from him nor any official account from the commanders of the batteries. I fear every gun has been lost. At present I am endeavoring to collect troops to defend the line of the railroad and to push forward the defenses of Charleston and Savannah.

Colonel [Thomas L.] Clingman's regiment of North Carolina volunteers, six companies of Colonel [Oliver E.] Edwards' regiment of South Carolina volunteers, and Colonel [William E.] Martin's South Carolina cavalry compose the force now here. The enemy, having complete possession of the water and inland navigation, commands all the islands on this coast, and threatens both Savannah and Charleston, and can come in his boats within 4 miles of this place. His sloops of war and large steamers can come up Broad River to Mackay's Point, the mouth of the Pocotaligo, and his gunboats can ascend some distance up the Coosawhatchie and Tulifiny. We have no guns that can resist their batteries and have no resource but to prepare to meet them in the field. They have landed on Hilton Head. Their fleet is in Port Royal Harbor. Four of their gunboats are reported to be approaching Beaufort. I fear there are but few State troops ready for the field. The garrisons of the forts at Charleston and Savannah and on the coast cannot be removed from the batteries while ignorant of the designs of the enemy. I am endeavoring to bring into the field such light batteries as can be prepared.

I have the honor to be, your obedient servant

R. E. Lee
General Commanding

87   To MISS MILDRED LEE
Winchester, Virginia

Charleston
November 15, 1861

My Precious Daughter:

I have received your letter forwarded to Richmond by Mr. Powell, & I also got, while in the West, the letter sent by Beverly Turner. I can write but seldom, but your letters always give me great pleasure. I am glad you had such a pleasant visit at Kinloch. I have passed a great many pleasant days there myself in my young days. Now you must labour at your books & gain knowledge & wisdom. Do not mind what Rob says. I have a beautiful white beard. It is much admired. At least, much remarked on. You know I have told you not to believe what the young men tell you. I was unable to see your poor mother when in Richmond. Before I could get down I was sent off here. Another forlorn hope expedition. Worse than western Virginia. Fitzhugh has come in from the West on a little visit & is with Charlotte. She & your mother were at Shirley, & she wrote me of the death of Annie Leigh's little baby, which had just occurred there. Happy little creature to be spared the evil of this world. Charlotte's baby was improving, & they were all going to the White House.

I have much to do in this country. I have been to Savannah & have to go again. The enemy is quiet after his conquest of Port Royal Harbour & his whole fleet is lying there.

May God guard & protect you, my dear child, prays your

Affectionate father

R. E. Lee

88   To HIS WIFE
                         "Shirley," Virginia

                                                    Savannah
                                              November 18, 1861

My Dear Mary:
    This is the first moment I have had to write to you, & now am wait-
ing the call to breakfast, on my way to Brunswick [Georgia], Fernandina
[Florida], &c. This is my second visit to Savannah. Night before last, I
returned to Coosawhatchie, South Carolina, from Charleston, where I
have placed my headquarters, & last night came here, arriving after midnight. I received in Charleston your letter from Shirley. It was a grievous
disappointment to me not to have seen you, but better times will come
I hope. I am very glad Fitzhugh has got in to see his little wife & son &
hope the latter will soon be well now since he has seen his papa. Poor
little Annie [Leigh], I am sorry for her, but the child is happy.
    You probably have seen the operations of the enemy's fleet. Since
their first attack they have been quiescent, apparently confining themselves to Hilton Head, where they are apparently fortifying.
    I have no time for more. Love to all.

                                        Yours very affly & truly

                                                    R. E. LEE

89   To GENERAL SAMUEL COOPER
                     Adjutant and Inspector General

                                                    Savannah
                                              November 21, 1861

  General:
    I have the honor to report, for the information of the Secretary of
War, that I have just returned to this city after having inspected the batteries and posts along the coast from Charleston [South Carolina] to
Fernandina, Florida.
    The guns from the less important points have been removed, and are
employed in strengthening those considered of greater consequence. The
entrance to Cumberland Sound & Brunswick and the water approaches
to Savannah & Charleston are the only points which it is proposed to defend. At all of these places there is much yet to be done, but every
effort is being made to render them as strong as the nature of the posi-

tions and the means at hand will permit. They ought, after their completion, to make a good defence against any batteries that are likely to be
brought against them. More guns could be usefully employed if available
for this service. Those at hand have been placed in the best positions, and
the troops so distributed so as to work them to advantage, the batteries
are tolerably supplied with ammunition, having about 50 rounds to the
gun. This amount it would be well to have increased to 100 rounds. The
greatest difficulty to be contended with is the want of artillerists, and
proper officers as instructors. The naval officers directed to report to
me have been assigned to duty at the batteries in Charleston Harbor as
ordnance and artillery officers, with the exception of Capts [Franklin]
Buchanan & [Arthur] Sinclair, whom I have directed to return, having,
while uncertain as to any attack being in contemplation, no appropriate
duties for them to perform, and believing their services were important
at their former stations.

I have been able to learn nothing of any movements of the enemy's fleet along the coast of Georgia or Florida, and am inclined to believe that they have not yet made any further demonstrations of attack.

Very respectfully, your obt servt

R. E. LEE
Genl Comdg

90   To MISSES ANNIE AND AGNES LEE
"Clydale," Virginia

Savannah
November 22, 1861

My Darling Daughters:
I have received your joint letter of the 24th October from Clydale.
It was very cheering to me & the affection & sympathy you expressed
were very grateful to my feelings. I wish indeed I could see you, be
with you & never again part from you. God only can give me that happiness. I pray for it night & day. But my prayers I know are not worthy to be heard. I received your former letter in western Virginia, but
had no opportunity to reply to it. I enjoyed it nevertheless. I am glad you
do not wait to hear from me, as that would deprive me of the pleasure
of hearing from you often. I am so pressed with business. I am much
pleased at your description of Stratford & your visit. It is endeared to me
by many recollections & it has always been a great desire of my life to
be able to purchase it. Now that we have no other home, & the one we
so loved has been so foully polluted, the desire is stronger with me

than ever. The horse chestnut you mention in the garden was planted by my mother. I am sorry the vault is so dilapidated. You did not mention the spring, one of the objects of my earliest recollections. I am very glad my precious Agnes that you have become so early a riser. It is a good habit, & in these times for mighty works advantage should be taken of every hour.

I regretted much at being obliged to come from Richmond without seeing your poor mother. I hope she is well & happy with her grandchild. Fitzhugh, you may have heard has come in to see his little wife.

This is my second visit to Savannah. I have been down the coast as far as Amelia Island to examine the defences. They are poor indeed & I have laid off work enough to employ our people a month. I hope our enemy will be polite enough to wait for us. It is difficult to get our people to realize their position.

I have seen good old Mrs. Mackay, now 83, & her daughters Mrs. Joseph Stiles (the mother of your friends) & Mrs. Elliott. Mrs. Wm. H. Stiles is in Cass with her grandchildren. Henry & Robert Stiles are here. You may have heard that Mr. Lowe has been captured on his way from England and that Mrs. Lowe is with the Glens in Baltimore. She, I presume, will soon be here, but he will be detained by our yankee enemies. Give much love to all with you. Lucien Jones is here, corresponding I learn with sweet Margaret to win a place in Carrie's heart.

Good bye my dear daughters.

Your affectionate

R. E. Lee

91   To HIS WIFE
                    "White House," Virginia

Coosawhatchie, South Carolina
December 2, 1861

I received last night, dear Mary, your letter of the 12th, and am delighted to learn that you are all well and so many of you are together. I am much pleased that Fitzhugh has an opportunity to be with you all and will not be so far removed from his home in his new field of action. I hope to see him at the head of a fine regiment and that he will be able to do good service in the cause of his country. If Mary and Rob get to you Christmas, you will have quite a family party, especially if Fitzhugh is not obliged to leave his home and sweet wife before that time. I shall think of you all on that holy day more intensely than usual,

and shall pray to the great God of Heaven to shower His blessings upon
you in this world, and to unite you all in His courts in the world to come.
With a grateful heart I thank Him for His preservation thus far, and
trust to His mercy and kindness for the future. Oh, that I were more
worthy, more thankful for all He has done and continues to do for me!
Perry and Meredith [Lee's servants] send their respects to all. . . .

Truly and affectionately,

R. E. LEE

92   To MESSRS. WILLIAM ELLIOTT, EDMUND RHETT,
AND LEROY YOUMANS
Coosawhatchie, South Carolina

Headquarters, Coosawhatchie
December 3, 1861

Gentlemen:
I had the honor to receive the resolution passed by the citizens of
Beaufort District at their meeting at Coosawhatchie on the 1st instant,
requesting me to establish martial law on the sea coast of South Carolina
within prescribed limits.
The present condition of things, in my opinion, does not render such
a course advisable. There is as yet no operation of the enemy to justify
the interruption of the civil laws, & though many of the citizens of the
State are necessarily engaged in military duties, there must still be sufficient to attend to its civil service.
In no part of the Confederacy has it yet been found necessary to
arrest the due course of the laws of a State. It should only be resorted to
as a last extremity, which I do not see has yet arrived in South Carolina.
I am with great respect, your obt servant

R. E. LEE

93   To MISS ANNIE C. LEE
"White House," Virginia

Coosawhatchie, South Carolina
December 8, 1861

My Precious Annie:
I have taken the only quiet time I have been able to find on this
holy day to thank you for your letter of the 29th ultimo. One of the

miseries of war is that there is no Sabbath & the current of work & strife has no cessation. How can we be pardoned for all our offenses!

I am glad that you have joined your mama again & that some of you are together at least. It would be a great happiness to me were you all at some quiet place, remote from the vicissitudes of war where I could consider you safe. You must have had a pleasant time at Clydale. , hope indeed that Cedar Grove may be saved from the ruin & pillage that other places have received at the hands of our enemies, who are pursuing the same course here as they have practised elsewhere. Unfortunately too, the numerous deep estuaries all accessible to their ships, expose the multitude of islands to their predatory excursions, & what they leave is finished by the negroes whose masters have deserted their plantations subject to visitations of the enemy. I am afraid Cousin Julia [Stuart] will not be able to defend her home if attacked by the vandals, for they have little respect for anybody, & if they catch the Dr [Richard Stuart] they will certainly send him to Fort Warren or La Fayette. I fear too the yankees will bear off their pretty daughters. I am very glad you visited Chatham. I was there many years ago, when it was the residence of Judge Coulter, & some of the avenues of poplar, so dear to your grandmama, still existed. I presume they have all gone now. The letter that you & Agnes wrote from Clydale I replied to & sent to that place. You know I never have any news. I am trying to get a force to make head against our defenders, but it comes in very slow & the people do not seem to realize that there is war.

I am glad Custis is so well & tells you all his plans. He can explain them better than I & is besides at headquarters. Ask him to keep the dear Mim informed. It is very warm here if that is news, & as an evidence I enclose some violets I plucked in the yard of a deserted house I occupy. I wish I could see you & give them in person. There are other things I would give, & send some in this letter to the Mim, Chass, Agnes & the baby. If F[itzhugh] is there give him some too. I hope the poor little baby has revived at the sight of his papa. Who is Ella Campbell & Duncan? Poor little Life try & stop her from studying so hard. I fear it is not work that causes her hair to fall but its early luxuriance & want of cupping.

Goodbye my precious child. My feet are entirely neglected. Give much love to everybody & believe me your affectionate father,

[R. E. LEE]

94   To GENERAL STATES R. GIST
Adjutant and Inspector General of South Carolina

Charleston, South Carolina
December 16, 1861

General:

I have had the honor to receive today your letter of the 12th instant, & beg leave to express my thanks for the confidence & support promised me by His Excellency the Governor [Francis W. Pickens] & yourself. I did not need this fresh assurance of your kindness & consideration, & feel deeply obliged at your placing the troops of the State under my command. I hope you will allow me to call upon you for aid & assistance in all matters pertaining to the State defence. I will give orders to relieve the [troops] now on duty in guarding bridges, &c., as soon as their places can be supplied by the troops now in the field, & shall be happy to get into the field the batteries you mention. We have need of all the resources of the State. Eighty vessels of the enemy were counted at Port Royal on the 12th, & they appear to be in strength on Port Royal Island. I consider we have not an hour to lose. The land defences around the city are progressing, & if our men do our [their] duty at the batteries, which I feel certain they will do, the enemy ought not to be able to advance by the water approaches.

I am, &c.,

R. E. LEE
Genl Comdg

95   To JUDAH P. BENJAMIN
Secretary of War

Headquarters, Coosawhatchie
December 20, 1861

Sir:

It has been reported to me by Genl Ripley that the enemy brought his stone fleet to the entrance of Charleston Harbor today, & sunk between thirteen & seventeen vessels in the main ship channel. The North Channel & Maffit's Channel are still open.

This achievement, so unworthy any nation, is the abortive expression of the malice & revenge of a people which they wish to perpetuate by rendering more memorable a day hateful in their calendar. It is also indicative of their despair of ever capturing a city they design to ruin, for they can never expect to possess what they labor so hard to reduce to a condition not to be enjoyed.

I think, therefore, it is certain that an attack on the city of Charleston is not contemplated, & we must endeavour to be prepared against assaults elsewhere on the Southern coast.

I have the honor &c.,

R. E. LEE
Genl Commdg

96   To ANDREW G. MAGRATH
Charleston, South Carolina

Coosawhatchie
December 24, 1861

My Dear Sir:

I have just received your note announcing the meeting of the Convention about to take place at Columbia. The exposed condition of the State & the presence of a powerful enemy on her shores will naturally occupy the earnest consideration of that enlightened body. I do not think that any suggestion from me will be necessary or even useful, as I feel certain that every measure requisite for the protection of the State or her citizens will be adopted. In compliance, therefore, with your kind request to make to you any suggestions that seemed to me required by present circumstances, I think it only necessary to repeat more emphatically than perhaps I have been able to do in person, the urgent necessity of bringing out the military strength of the State, & putting it under the best and most permanent organization. The troops, in my opinion, should be organized for the war. We cannot stop short of its termination, be it long or short. No one, I presume, would desire to do so. No one, therefore, will continue in service longer than the war requires. The disbanding & reorganization of troops in time of peace is attended with loss & expense. What must it be in time of war, when it may occur at periods that might otherwise prove highly disastrous? I tremble to think of the consequences that may befall us next spring when all our twelve months' men may claim their discharge. At the opening of the campaign, when our enemies will take the field fresh & vigorous, after a year's preparation & winter's repose, we shall be in all the anxiety, excitement, & organization of new armies. In what different condition will be the opposing armies on the plains of Manassas at the resumption of active operations. I have thought that Genl [George B.] McClellan was waiting to seize the advantage he would then possess. I beg you will put a stop to this lamentable state of affairs. The Confederate States have now but one great object in view. The successful issue of their war of independence. Everything worth their possessing depends on that. Everything should yield to its accomplishment.

There is another point to which I would invite your attention. The best troops are ineffective without good officers. Our volunteers, more than any others, require officers whom they can respect and trust. The best men for that position should be selected, and it is important to consider how it can be effected. It would be safe to trust men of the intelligence & character of our volunteers to elect their officers, could they at the time of election realize their dependent condition in the day of battle. But this they cannot do, & I have known them in the hour of danger repudiate & disown officers of their choice & beg for others. Is it right, then, for a State to throw upon its citizens a responsibility which they do not feel and cannot properly exercise? The colonel of a regiment has an important trust, & is a guardian of the honor of the State as well as of the lives of her citizens. I think it better for the field officers of the regiments in State service to be appointed by the governor, with the advice & consent of its legislature, & those in the Confederate service by the President & Congress.

It would also, in my opinion, add to the simplicity & economy of our military establishment to conform to the same principle of organization. That adopted by Congress is formed by the united wisdom of the State representatives, & is followed in its army. It would be well for the State governments to adopt [it], as far as circumstances will permit. Special corps & separate commands are frequent causes of embarrassment.

It is useless for me to suggest that measures be taken to develop the military resources of the State; to advance the fabrication of powder, arms & all the necessaries of war, as well as the production of bountiful supplies for her troops & citizens. The strictest economy should be enforced in every department & the most rigid accountability required of its officers. I have not been able to get an accurate report of the troops under my command in the State. I hope it may be as large as you state, but I am sure those for duty fall far short of it. For instance, [Col. Wilmot G.] De Saussure's brigade is put down at three thousand four hundred & twenty men. When last in Charleston (the day I inquired) I was informed that in one regiment there were 110 men for duty in camp on the Race Course & in the other about 200. Col [John L.] Branch, I am told, had only about 200 men with him at Rockville, though I have had no official report of his retreat from there. The companies of mounted men in the service are very much reduced. The Charleston Light Dragoons & the Rutledge Mounted Rifles have about 45 men each. The companies of Col [William E.] Martin's regiment are very small. One of them, Capt [Thomas] Fripp's, reports 4 commissioned officers, 9 non-commissioned officers, & 19 privates. It is very expensive to retain in service companies of such strength, & I think all had better be reorganized.

I have only on this line for field operations [Col William C.] Heyward's, De Saussure's, [Col R. G. M.] Dunovant's, [Col James] Jones', & [Col Oliver E.] Edwards' regiments from South Carolina & [Col William E.] Martin's cavalry. Genl Ripley writes that [Col Charles J.] Elford's & [Col John H.] Means' regiments are poorly armed & equipped & at present ineffective, & that the organization of the troops thrown forward on James Island is so brittle that he fears it will break. The garrisons at Moultrie, Sumter, Johnson, & the fixed batteries, the best and most stable of our forces, cannot be removed from them. Neither can those at Georgetown, & should not be counted among those for operations in the field.

You must not understand that this is written in a complaining spirit. I know the difficulties in the way, & wish you to understand them, explain them to the governor, & if possible, remove them. Our enemy increases in strength faster than we do & is now enormous. Where he will strike I do not know, but the blow when it does fall will be hard.

I am, &c.

R. E. LEE

97   To HIS WIFE
"White House," Virginia

Coosawhatchie, South Carolina
December 25, 1861

I cannot let this day of greatful rejoicing pass, dear Mary, without some communion with you. I am thankful for the many among the past that I have passed with you, & the remembrance of them fills me with pleasure. For those on which we have been separated we must not repine. If it will make us more resigned & better prepared for what is in store for us, we should rejoice. Now we must be content with the many blessings we receive. If we can only become sensible of our transgressions, so as to be fully penitent & forgiven, that this heavy punishment under which we labour may with justice be removed from us & the whole nation, what a gracious consummation of all that we have endured it will be! I hope you had a pleasant visit to Richmond. So you do not like my invitation to Fayetteville? I thought I gave you the choice of Richmond too, as well as Charleston & Savannah, but for the threatening movements of the enemy. Well it shows the perverseness of human nature. To reject those agreable cities that were accessible & select a decrepid & deserted village because inaccessible. If you were to see the place, I think you would leave it too. I am here but little myself. The days I am not away, I visit some point exposed to the enemy & after our dinner at early candle light, am engaged in writing till 11 or 12 at night. But this place is too exposed to attack for the residence of a person as hard to move as you are. You would be captured while you were waiting "a moment." As to our old home, if not destroyed, it will be difficult ever to be recognized. Even if the enemy had wished to preserve it, it would almost have been impossible. With the number of troops encamped around it, the change of officers, &c., the want of fuel, shelter, &c., & all the dire necessities of war, it is vain to think of its being in a habitable condition. I fear too books, furniture, & the relics of Mount Vernon will be gone. It is better to make up our minds to a general loss. They cannot take away the remembrances of the spot, & the memories of those that to us rendered it sacred. That will remain to us as long as life will last, & that we can preserve. In the absence of a home, I wish I could purchase Stratford. That is the only other place that I could go to, now accessible to us, that would inspire me with feelings of pleasure & local love. You & the girls could remain there in quiet. It is a poor place, but we could make enough cornbread & bacon for our support, & the girls could weave us clothes. I wonder if it is for sale & at how much. Ask Fitzhugh to try & find out when he gets to Fredericksburg. You must not build your hopes on peace on account of the United States going into a war with England. She will be very loath to do that, notwithstanding the bluster of the Northern papers. Her rulers are not entirely mad, & if they find England is in earnest, & that war or a restitution of their captives must be the consequence, they will adopt the latter. We must make up our minds to fight our battles & win our independence alone. No one will help us. We require no extraneous aid, if true to ourselves. But we must be patient. It is not a light achievement & cannot be accomplished at once. I am very glad to hear of poor Anne. Her miseries are increased by the war too. I am also glad to hear of the kind sympathies & aid of Elianor Rodgers & Edmund. I had not heard of poor little Geary's sickness & do not know to what you allude when speaking of "Parke's affliction." We must expect Mrs. Bonaparte & our other put by friends to be opposed to us. They wish to save their demis[e]. It is necessary to them to preserve their good dinners. It will not last. I have received your letter enclosing Charlotte's &c. I cannot write to her [to] night. I wrote a few days since, giving you all the news, & have now therefore nothing to relate. The enemy is still quiet & increasing in strength. We grow in size slowly but are working hard. I have had a day of labour instead of rest & have written at intervals to some of the children. I hope they are with you & enclose my letters. Give much love to F[itzhugh], C[ustis], A[nnie], A[gnes], little Rob & all.

Affecty & truly yours

R. E. LEE

P.S. I recollect having seen that a Mr. Butler was killed in Kentucky, whom I supposed was Edward. I hoped it was not true as I have seen nothing of Lewis. It is that to which you doubtless allude in speaking of Parke &c. All must suffer.

R. E. L.

98   To G. W. C. LEE
Richmond, Virginia

Coosawhatchie, South Carolina
December 29, 1861

I have received my dear son your letter of the 21 & am happy that you have arranged with Mr. [John] Stewart about his house. I feel badly about not having paid rent for it all this time as I fear now I ought to have done. But was misled by what was told me at the time. I am willing to do it now if it can be arranged with propriety & if you can do so let me know. Not having had to pay for my quarters in Richmond I never charged for any or fuel either, & thought that the State would gain by Mr. Stewart's liberality if I did not. I find it would have been better for me & him too now, to have done so. If you can get pleasant people to join in taking the house, it would certainly be more agreable for you to live there than at a hotel, but I know how expensive a bachelor's mess is &c., unless there is someone who will attend to it & conduct it economically. If you can make the arrangement, however, do so, & I will pay my share. I feel extremely obliged to Mr. Stewart for his considerate kindness & for his more than kind sentiments & I hope when you see him you will make my acknowledgements. I heard recently from your mother & hope that you were able to get to spend Xmas with them all at the W[hite] H[ouse]. Mary, she thought, would be there, & if she gets to Richmond it will be a good opportunity for her to pay a visit to her Uncle Carter. I hope C[arter] will get into a good regiment & get

promoted too. His friend [Major A. L.] Long is with me as Chief of
Ordnance & Arthur Shaaff reported to me a few days since. I sent him
to Savannah to organize & instruct some regiments coming into the service there. I wish indeed I could have you with me if it was best for
you, but that no man can say & I am content to leave it to him who
orders all for the best. I have two officers of the old service as my aids
now, but may have to part with them as soon as I can do better for
them. I suppose it is in vain for me to expect to keep an instructed
officer, there is such demand for their services with troops. I have wished
to get one of our young relatives with me if I could find one to whom
it would be agreable & useful to me at the same time, for I have so
much to attend to, that I must have those with me who can be of
service. I have thought of Johnny Lee or Henry, Bev. Turner &c., &c., for
there are a host of our relatives in the army. Who can you recommend
to me? I have had numerous applications for the post of aid from citizens,
but do not want a retinue around me who seek nominal duty or an
excuse to get off of real service elsewhere. I have a great deal of work
to do & want men able & willing to do it. I received not long since, a
letter from Lewis Conrad applying for the appointment of aid to me. I
was unable to grant it, for as I have said I have two now. I should like
you to tell me, however, what sort of a youth he is & also your opinion
of other youths of our house. All that I have said I of course wish you
keep profoundly secret. If I had [one] of them in service with me I
could soon see whether they would suit me, or I them. I should dislike
to invite them & then for us to be obliged to part. The news from Europe
is indeed good, but I think the United States government, notwithstanding their moral & political commitment to [Capt Charles] Wilkes' act, if
it finds that England is in earnest & that it will have to fight or retract, will retract. We must make up our minds to fight our battles ourselves. Expect to receive aid from no one. Make every necessary sacrifice of comfort, money & labour to bring the war to a successful issue &
then we will succeed. The cry is too much for help. I am mortified to
hear it. We want no aid. We want to be true to ourselves, to be prudent,
just, fair, & bold. I am dreadfully disappointed at the spirit here. They
have all of a sudden realized the asperities of war, in what they must encounter, & do not seem to be prepared for it. If I only had some veteran troops to take the brunt, they would soon rally & be inspired with
the great principle for which we are contending. The enemy is quiet & safe
in his big boats. He is threatening every avenue. Pillaging, burning &
robbing where he can venture with impunity & alarming women & children. Every day I have reports of landing in force, marching &c. which
turns out to be some marauding party. The last was the North Edisto

[Inlet]. I yesterday went over the whole line in that region from the Ashepro to the Wadalaw & found everything quiet & could only see their big black ships lying down the Edisto where the water is too broad for anything we have to reach them. They will not venture as yet in the narrow waters. I went yesterday 115 miles but only 35 on horseback. I did not get back till 11 p.m. I took Greenbrier the whole distance. Take good care of Richmond. Draw his forage on my account. Send him to me if opportunity offers, if you do not want him. I have two horses now with me.

Good bye my dear son

R. E. Lee

99   To FRANCIS W. PICKENS
               Governor of South Carolina

Headquarters, Coosawhatchie
January 2, 1862

Governor:

I have had the honor to receive your communication of the 29th ultimo, enclosing a copy of the resolution adopted by the General Assembly at its recent meeting, relative to the employment of slaves on works for military defence. I have given instructions to Genl Ripley to make with Your Excellency the necessary arrangements, and to urge forward the works around Charleston as rapidly as possible. I hope that Your Excellency will see that his wants in the matter of laborers are complied with.

I beg leave again to submit to Your Excellency the great need of troops to defend this line. And would respectfully ask that you urge forward their organization with all possible dispatch.

I am very respy, your obt servant

R. E. Lee
Genl Comdg

100   To G. W. C. LEE
                Richmond, Virginia

Coosawhatchie
January 4, 1862

My Dear Son:

I have received your letter of the 30th ultimo enclosing decree of the Court of Appeals in reference to your grandfather's will. I am glad the matter is determined & hope it will give satisfaction to all parties. What more I can do than I have done in the execution of the will I do not know, nor how I can expedite its completion during the continuance of the war I cannot see. I must leave it to you & Fitzhugh to see to matters & to do justice to all parties. Unless the legacies are considered in the light of a debt of the estate, the people must be emancipated at the close of this year. If the legacies form a part of the debt of the estate then they must help to pay it by their work. This is the only part not clear to me & I will write to Mr. Smith on the subject. As the sooner the debts & legacies are paid the sooner the boys, F[itzhugh] & R[obert], will get their property & the people their freedom & cannot receive it before, if any of the people can by their hire pay more than by their labour on the White House & Romancoke tell F[itzhugh] I wish him to do so. All the hire of the Arlington people must go to this fund & I desire you so to apply it. If any account or return is necessary this year I wish you would make it out for me & hand it in. The war, condition of the estate, &c., makes it impossible to act regularly &c., & I hope will be considered by the court. The services of the people at A[rlington] if there, cannot be obtained now, & nothing I presume can be done with them. If you have not a copy of the decree of the court, I wish you would get one from the clerk of the court in Richmond for your guidance & also give one to F[itzhugh] for his. We must try, as well as the conditions of things will permit, to carry out your dear Grandfather's wishes, of which the decree is the legal & final construction & must, therefore, be received as his wishes & intentions.

I have also received your letter of the 31st ultimo, enclosing forage returns, which I have signed & return. I take up the black mare (Capt [Walter H.] Taylor's) as mine, being in my service & use. The dates I hope are right as I have no means of correcting them. As regards Richmond, unless you have your full number of horses you had better return for him as long as he is with you, as it will save trouble & be all the same to the government, in as much as I shall drop him. If you have your full number, I will send on returns for him. I am sorry to hear about his leg. Do not let him have too much grain. I fear he will be a great trouble to you, & if you cannot exercise him I do not know what will become of him. Give much love to every body. We are all well. No news. Enemy quiet & retired to his islands. The main[land] seemed too insecure for him & he never went 400 yards from his steamers, not even to the extent of the range of his guns. After burning some houses, three, on the river bank & feeling our proximity unpleasant, he retreated to Port Royal again. I hope we may always be able to keep him close. But he can move with great facility & rapidity & land any where he can bring his steamers, & burn, pillage & destroy, & we cannot prevent him. We lost one 12 pounder. It was drawn by mules with negro drivers, so hard are we pressed for men, who became alarmed at the firing, upset the gun in a ditch, broke the carriage & had to be abandoned. It was an old English gun, with G. R. on it & the carriage worthless. Do you hear of any more troops coming to me, or can any be sent? The Mississippi regiment, Col [Daniel R.] Russell, I understand, has gone to Tennessee & I hear of none coming in its place. The South Carolina troops come very slowly & Georgia has taken hers in the State service.

Your affectionate father

R. E. Lee

101   To GENERAL SAMUEL COOPER
Adjutant and Inspector General

Savannah

January 8, 1862

General:

From a paragraph in the Charleston & Savannah journals, to which my attention has been called, I fear I may have inadvertently misled the [War] Department as to my opinion of the strength of the defences of those cities and of my ability to prevent the enemy from penetrating into the interior of the country. In my letters describing the works & batteries in progress of construction, to which I cannot now refer, I intended to express the hope, rather than the confident assurance, that when completed, armed, & manned, if properly fought, the enemy's approach ought to be successfully resisted. I am aware that we must fight against great odds, & I always trust that the spirit of our soldiers will be an overmatch to the numbers of our opponents.

Our works are not yet finished. Their progress is slow. Guns are required for their armament, & I have not received as many troops from South Carolina & Georgia as I at first expected. The forces of the enemy are accumulating, & apparently increase faster than ours. I have feared, if handled with proportionate ability with his means of transportation & concentration, it would be impossible to gather troops, necessarily posted over a long line, in sufficient strength to oppose sudden movements. Wherever his fleet can be brought no opposition can be made to his landing, except within range of our fixed batteries. We have nothing to oppose his heavy guns, which sweep over the low banks of this country with irresistible force. The farther he can be withdrawn from his floating batteries the weaker he will become, & lines of defence, covering objects of attack, have been selected with this view.

I have thought his purpose would be to seize upon the Charleston & Savannah Railroad near the head of Broad River, sever the line of communication between those cities with one of his columns of land troops, and with the other two & his fleet by water envelope alternately each of those cities. This would be a difficult combination for us successfully to resist. I have been preparing to meet it with all the means in my power, & shall continue to the end. Any troops or guns that can be withdrawn from other points will greatly aid in this result.

I have the honor &c.

R. E. LEE
Genl Comdg

102   To CHARLES M. FURMAN
Charleston, South Carolina

Headquarters, Coosawhatchie
January 17, 1862

Sir:

I have had the honor to receive your letter of the 16th instant in reference to an ordinance of the State Convention to provide for the removal of property from portions of the State which may be invaded by the enemy, & to certain resolutions intended to carry its provisions into effect. Copies of the ordinance & resolutions have been furnished me, & I shall take great pleasure in doing all in my power to aid the commissioners in the performance of the duties required of them. As regards the probability of the occurrence of the contingencies in which you will be called to act, & of which you ask my opinion, I can only say, that seeing no reason now for apprehension, I think it an act of prudence to make provision in time of security for what would be required in time of danger, & that steps should be taken for the formation of depots, &c., & every arrangement made in anticipation of events which, should they happen, would mitigate their evil consequences. As regards the information which you may require from time to time to govern your action in relation to the city of Charleston, I suggest that you apply to the Confederate officer commanding in the city, should it not be convenient to refer to the commanding general of the department, as by so doing valuable time may be saved. I shall certainly apprize you of any danger I can foresee.

With great respect, &c.

R. E. LEE
Genl Comdg

103   To HIS WIFE
                            "White House," Virginia

                                            Coosawhatchie, South Carolina
                                                      January 18, 1862

On my return day before yesterday from Florida, dear Mary, I received your letter of the 1st. I am very glad to find that you had a pleasant family meeting Xmas & that it was so large. I am truly grateful for all the mercies we enjoy, notwithstanding the miseries of war, & join heartily in the wish that the next year may find us at peace with all the world. I am delighted to hear that our little grandson is improving so fast & is becoming such a perfect gentleman. May his path be strewn with flowers & his life with happiness. I am very glad to hear also that his dear papa is promoted. It will be gratifying to him & increase, I hope, his means of usefulness. Robert wrote he saw him on his way through Charlottesville with his squadron, & that he was well. While at Fernandina I went over to Cumberland Island [Georgia] & walked up to Dungeness, the former residence of Genl [Nathanael] Green[e]. It was my first visit to the house & I had the gratification at length of visiting my father's grave. He died there you may recollect on his way from the West Indies, & was interred in one corner of the family cemetery. The spot is marked by a plain marble slab, with his name, age, & date of his death. Mrs. Green[e] is also buried there, & her daughter Mrs. Shaw & her husband. The place is at present owned by Mr. Nightingale, nephew of Mrs. Shaw, who married a daughter of Mr. James King. The family have moved into the interior of Georgia, leaving only a few servants & a white gardener on the place. The garden was beautiful, enclosed by the finest hedge I have ever seen. It was of the wild olive. The orange trees were small, & the orange grove, which in Mrs. Shaw's lifetime, my tour of duty in Savannah in early life, was so productive, had been destroyed by an insect that has proved fatal to the orange on the coast of Georgia & Florida. There was a fine grove of olives, from which, I learn, Mr. N[ightingale] procures oil. The garden was filled with roses & beautiful vines, the names of which I do not know. Among them was the tomato vine in full bearing with the ripe fruit on it. There has as yet been no frost in that region of country this winter. I went in the dining room & parlour, in which the furniture still remained. In the latter room hung the portraits of Mr. John & James King, father & uncle of Mrs. N[ightingale] rabid abolitionists, with a bad likeness of Genl Green[e], & a handsome print of Florence Nightingale & some landscapes. There also hung

over the mantle a representation of Genl Green[e] & Mrs. Slute, presenting him the purse. The house has never been finished, but is a fine, large
one & beautifully located. A magnificent grove of live oaks envelops the
road from the landing to the house. I saw in Savannah good old Mrs.
Mackay with her two daughters, Misses Kate & Sarah, Mr. William H.
Stiles, now Lt Col & his sons Henry & Robert. Mrs. Stiles was in Cass with
Henry's wife & Mrs. Lowe's children. Robert is married also & he & his
wife seem to live with their Grandmother Mackay. I heard that Miss Sidney Stiles, Annie's friend, was engaged to her cousin, Dr. Elliott, son of
Mrs. Margaret Elliott, formerly Miss Mackay. Kitty, the elder sister,
takes care of her mother &c., as Phebe, eldest daughter of Mrs. Margaret
Elliott, takes care of that family. The three younger daughters of Mrs.
Elliott are married & their husbands are in the army. Mrs. Lowe, you
may have heard is in Baltimore with the Glens. Her husband a prisoner
at Fort Warren. I grieve over our dear Aunt Maria. How she can exist
I do not know. Rob says he has seen a Lt [Chiswell] Dabney in Charlottesville, aid to Genl [J. E. B.] Stuart, who has recently been at Ravensworth, who says the place looks lovely & has been undisturbed save by
carrying off the people &c. That is some comfort. I am glad also to hear
that dear Arlington is extant. In return for Aunt M[aria]'s letter I send
you one from Mrs. Dr. Kyh whom you will see, like every body else,
over estimates my ability & services. She sent me a beautiful pair of socks.
I do not know her, or how to thank her. I also enclose a letter from a
daughter of Mrs. Post as you like to hear from your relatives. Thank
Agnes for her letter. I forgot to mention I saw in S[avannah] Hugh
Mercer's children. My godson Robert is a handsome little boy & Miss
Mary a young lady with her beaux around her. Love to every body &
God bless you all.

Truly & faithfully yours

R. E. LEE

Perry & M[eredith] are well.

104   To G. W. C. LEE
                 Richmond, Virginia

Coosawhatchie, South Carolina
January 19, 1862

I have received my dear son your two letters of the 12th & 15th respectfully & seize this quiet hour to answer them. As regards paying
back rent for the house, you must do as you find best. Perhaps paying

for certain repairs will answer as well & if you will let me know the amount required I will remit it to you. I hope the arrangement you have made may be agreable as well as advantageous to you, & you must allow me to advise that you economize your funds, for I expect to be a pauper if I get through the war & you will want all your means. The bonds that I hold of the Northern railroads & cities will all be confiscated & those of the Southern states will be much depreciated & cannot pay interest so my revenue will be much reduced if not cut off. Everything at Arlington will I fear be lost & it will take all the land at the White House & Romancoke to pay the legacies to the girls with the interest. But if honour & independence is delt us I will be content. I am very glad that F[itzhugh] the fine fellow has been promoted & hope he will prove a good officer. If you can satisfy yourself about our young relatives let me know & you & F[itzhugh] must both, in your way, & as far as they deserve, try & aid them.

There is another matter that I wish to inquire about. My friend Genl Hugh Mercer has applied for information concerning Lt Col Henry H. Walker. I infer he is paying court to Miss Mary. Indeed I heard he was expected in Savannah. You may recollect him at W[est] P[oint]. (I believe it is the one). He graduated in 1853 & was commissioned in the 6th infantry. He is now Lt Col of the regiment commanded by Col Dabney Maury serving with Genl [T. H.] Holmes' division. As far as I recollect he was a fair officer & I think when I met him at the West was Adjutant of his regiment or on the staff of Genl Clarke. If his antecedents & surroundings are not objectionable & his family character, habits, &c., afford a reasonable guaranty for the lady's happiness, I suppose it is all a man can ask. But of these I know nothing &, cannot speak. You might ascertain from his acquaintances without being officious or obtrusive. It is a delicate & not agreable office I know, but I shall say nothing to implicate anyone & only wish to give him the means of inquiry. We must aid our friends all we can.

As Mr. Smith says the decision of the court is to liberate the people at the end of five years, that makes the decree all plain to me. I only wish I had opportunity to attend to the business of the estate to make it as profitable to the legatees as possible. If you & F[itzhugh] cannot attend to it I do not know what to do. I have written to F[itzhugh] to send you his accounts for 1861, & I wish if possible you would square them up & if there is any surplus invest in Virginia State bonds. I have some funds in the Farmers Bank in Richmond, which perhaps had better be invested anyhow, so that I may be prepared to make good any deficit. Ask Mr. McFarland what he could purchase $5000. Virginia State bonds for. If they are not higher than last quotation I saw, I can raise money to pay for them. Have the banks paid the January dividends, & there are certain coupons due which perhaps might be collected. The box containing them is in the Farmers Bank. If you require the box at Uncle Carter's at any time send for it. The papers could be returned, & the abstract & account current retained so as to continue the account. All the hire of the Arlington people must be payed to the estate, if it has not been, & I wish you could take steps to get that which is due. The hire of those about Alexandria I suppose can never be obtained. Perhaps Mr. Smith might secure some. I do not know where Mr. Scott is. Mr. William O. Winston may know. John Goldsborough knows where Harrison [a servant] is. Two years are due of his hire. He is hired to some gentleman on the Orange Railroad & is frequently in Richmond. Mr. Echo can attend to the people in R[ichmond].

I have just returned from a visit to the coast as far as Fernandina [Florida]. Our defences are growing stronger, but progress slowly. The volunteers dislike work & there is much sickness among them besides. Guns too are required, ammunition, & more men. Still on the whole matters are encouraging & if the enemy does not approach in overwhelming numbers we ought to hold our ground. He is quiescent still. What he is preparing for or where he will strike I cannot discover. His numerous boats cut off all communication with the islands, where he hides himself & his works. I saw in Fernandina Miss Matilda. I fear she is out with me. She had written me another tremendous long letter which I had never been able to read & it seems she wanted some companies placed near her at old Fort Carlos, & which I could not do. I was also at Dungeness. The garden was beautiful. Filled with roses &c., which had not so far been touched with frost this winter. The place is deserted. Mrs. N[ightingale] & her daughters occupy a log cabin in the pines near Tebeauville Junction on Brunswick [& Florida] & S[avannah], [Albany] & Gulf Railroads. Mr. N[ightingale] is on the St. Mary River. Every one on the coast has suffered, but they bear it manfully. No civilized nation within my knowledge has ever carried on war as the United States government has against us. I saw good old Mrs. Mackay, the young Stiles &c. in S[avannah]. Mrs. William H. Stiles is in Cass, with the Elliotts. Miss Sydney Stiles I understood was engaged to her cousin Dr. Elliot, son of Mrs. Ralph, who is said to be a fine young man. Everybody inquired kindly for you. [Captain Joseph C.] Ives is in Savannah helping [Captain William H.] Echols lay out entrenchments around the city.

Give much love to all friends, your mother &c., & believe me always

Your affectionate father

R. E. LEE

105   To HIS WIFE
                        "White House," Virginia

                                    Coosawhatchie, South Carolina
                                    January 28, 1862

I have just returned from Charleston, & received your letter of the 14th, dear Mary, enclosing one from dear Annie. I also found a letter from Mary who was then in Richmond but whom I suppose you will have seen before this reaches you. I am unable to write to the girls now & indeed have no time for such amusements. I think of them a great deal for my thoughts will be busy when I am busy about other things. I am glad to hear that poor little Life is well & hope nothing will interrupt her. It seems difficult for Robert to continue at his studies & I fear his time at college will yield him little profit. The times are unpropitious for labour of all kinds, & there are frequent interruptions at the University [of Virginia] at all times. I send you a letter from little Mary, for though Daughter may have told you the contents, you & the girls may still like to see it. She is a warm hearted true child & I am grieved to hear of her feeble health. I must let all my correspondents beyond our limits rest till after the war, should I see the end of it, for I cannot attend to them within our lines. I was called to Charleston by the appearance off the bar of a fleet of vessels the true character & intent of which could not be discerned during the continuance of the storm which obscured the view. Saturday, however, all doubt was dispelled, & from the beach on Sullivan's Island the preparations for sinking them were plainly seen. Twenty-one were visible the first day of my arrival, but at the end of the storm, Saturday, only 17 were seen. Five of these were vessels of war, what became of the other four is not known. The twelve old merchantmen were being stripped of their spars, masts, &c., & by sunset 7 were prepared apparently for sinking across the mouth of the Maffit Channel. They were placed in a line about 200 yards apart, & about 4 miles from Fort Moultrie. They will do but little harm to the channel, I think, but may deter vessels running out at night for fear of getting on them. There now seems to be indications of a movement against Savannah. The enemy's gunboats are pushing up the creeks to cut off communications between the city & Fort Pulaski on Cockspur Island. Unless I hear better news, I must go there today. There are so many points of attack, & so little means to meet them on water, that there is but little rest. I saw Shirley Turner & his family when in C[harleston]. He is a great sufferer from rhumatism & has been for some years. Miss Grace Totten that was, now Mrs. Stevens, is in C[harleston] but I did not see her. She married Lt Stevens of South Carolina who has now joined the Confederate Navy. I am very sorry to hear that Agnes suffers so from neuralgia. I had hoped she was relieved. Poor child, I wish something could be done for her. Perry & Meredith are well & send regards to every body. Give much love to Charlotte & the girls. To the boys when you see them. I have received the decree of the Court of Appeals in reference to your father's will. It has decided all the points. The people are to be emancipated at the end of the five years. So much of the legacies as may be unpaid must be raised out of the land of the White House & Romancoke, after devoting to them the proceeds of the sale of the lands at Smith's Island &c., & of all the personal property not otherwise devised at Arlington, White House, Romancoke, &c. The hire of the people at A[rlington] is also to be devoted to the payment of the legacies. I have requested Custis to get a copy of the decree for himself & Fitzhugh & to attend to all the business & to do what they can to advance the execution of the will. No sales of land can now be made. The enemy is in possession of Smith's Island & what I am to do with the negroes I do not know.

Very truly & sincerely yours

R. E. LEE

106   To GENERAL JOSEPH R. ANDERSON
Commanding District of Cape Fear, North Carolina

Coosawhatchie, South Carolina
January 28, 1862

General:

I have had the honor to receive your letter of the 24th instant, & can sympathize in your anxiety to make a successful resistance to the landing of the enemy on the coast of North Carolina. You may be assured that nothing will be wanting on my part to give you all the aid in my power, & I should be pleased to be able to send you my whole force if required. But I beg that you will not rely upon it, but endeavor to organize a sufficient force for your purpose independent of any reinforcement from this department. The enemy is in great strength on this coast. Has command of all the communications by water, & by means of his immense fleet & the network of sounds, rivers, & creeks spread over the Carolina & Georgia coast, a disembarkation of a large force can be made under cover of his floating batteries at any time. Scarcely a day passes that a demonstration is not made on some point which obliges us to keep troops always ready to oppose him. You will see, therefore, how impossible it may be for me to send you succors at the time you may most need them, as it may be expected that when an attack is made on a part of the coast the adjacent country will be imposingly threatened.

As regards the two North Carolina regiments & light battery, I understood they were to form a permanent part of the troops assigned to this department, & would be replaced in your district by receiving other regiments from the State into the service. This I had hoped had been done, as it is necessary to be prepared along the whole line. The want of arms has prevented my receiving troops that have offered their services from beyond the limits of the department, & has also prevented troops from the State coming into the service. I am sorry to say that I am not in a condition to spare any troops, but am using every means in my power to organize additional force for service in the department.

I am, &c.

R. E. LEE
Genl Comdg

107   To GENERAL THOMAS F. DRAYTON
Commanding at Hardeeville, South Carolina

Headquarters Department South Carolina &c.
February 4, 1862

General:

Mr. T. A. Reynolds, overseer of Capt John Screven, reports that on last Saturday night a party of Federal troops visited Capt Screven's Proctor plantation, and that on Sunday they made their appearance with negroes. After taking a view of Fort Jackson, &c., they retired without disturbing anything on the plantation. They reached Proctor's by way of Wright's Cut, which leads through the marsh from Savannah River to Wright's River. This information is derived from the watchman (negro) on the plantation, & is believed by Mr. Reynolds.

You are desired to advance a company, mounted or on foot, convenient to throw out pickets, to observe the approaches to the Savannah River, & to endeavor to catch or intercept reconnoitering parties of the enemy. I would suggest that they keep themselves concealed by day and take positions by night to accomplish their object effectively. Select a bold & intelligent officer for the service.

I am, &c.

R. E. LEE

108   To JUDAH P. BENJAMIN
                    Secretary of War

Headquarters Department of South Carolina &c.
Savannah
February 6, 1862

Sir:

The replacing the troops in the Confederate service in this State is a matter of serious consideration. The period of service of several companies, serving the batteries for the defence of the city of Savannah is about to expire. One that was mustered out of service a few days at Fort Pulaski declines to re-enter the service, & it is supposed that others will be equally averse. The loss of these companies at this time will be a serious injury to the defence of the city, as artillerists cannot be made on the eve of a battle. But the prospective injury to the service, I fear, will be equally great, as neither the sentiment of the people, or the policy of the State seems to favor the organization of troops for Confederate service. I have thought it probable that the influence of the [War] Department might be able to avert the evil I apprehend.

I have been very anxious to assign another general officer to duty with the troops in the State of Georgia. At the time the officers of that grade reported to me, an attack on the Carolina coast seemed so imminent, it was so unprovided, that all reinforcements were assigned to its defence, & every effort made to prepare the troops for their duty. The movements of the enemy for the last week indicate Savannah as the threatened point of attack, but I do not think it safe to withdraw troops from Carolina. I have no one to place in charge of the body of troops guarding the approaches from the Ogeechee [River] to Savannah. The troops are fresh, officers new in the service, & all require instruction. If some instructed officer could be spared me, I should be greatly relieved. I have already mentioned Genl [Henry] Heth & Col [Carter] Stevenson, but have been informed that they were wanted elsewhere, & I can name no one not disposed of. I therefore leave the matter to the Department.

I am &c.

R. E. LEE
Genl Comdg

109   To HIS WIFE
                    "White House," Virginia

                                        Savannah
                                    February 8, 1862

I wrote to you, dear Mary, the day I left Coosawhatchie for this
place. I have been here ever since, endeavouring to push forward the
works for the defence of the city, which has lagged terribly & which
ought to have been finished. But it is difficult to arouse ourselves from
ease & comfort to labour & self denial. Guns are scarce, as well as ammunition, & I shall have to break up batteries on the coast to provide, I
fear, for this city. Our enemies are endeavouring to work their way
through the creeks that traverse the impassable & soft marshes stretching along the interior of the coast & communicating with the sounds &
sea, through which the Savannah flows, & thus avoid the entrance of the
river commanded by Fort Pulaski. Their boats only require 7 feet water
to float them & the tide rises 7 feet, so that on high water they can work
their way & rest on the mud at low. They are also provided with dredges
& appliances for removing obstructions through the creeks in question,
which cannot be guarded by batteries. I hope, however, we shall be able
to stop them, & daily pray to the giver of all victory to enable us to do
so. I suppose if you have written, your letter is at Coosawhatchie & I
therefore have not heard from any one. I trust you are all well & doing
well, & wish I could do anything to promote either. I have more here
than I can do, & more, I fear, than I can well accomplish. It is so very
hard to get anything done, & while all wish well & mean well, it is so
difficult to get them to act energetically & promptly.

Mrs. Lowe is here with her grandmother. She brought her little
daughter Kate down who is very much like her & full of motion &
activity. Mrs. L[owe], herself, is much more quiet & sedate & perhaps
more pleasing though not so youthful in appearance. I have only seen
her for a short time in the evening, when her fingers have been more
busy with her knitting than her tongue in conversation. I see Mrs. Gilmer occasionally who remains here while her husband is in Kentucky.
Yesterday there was a report that he was captured on the Tennessee
River, but it was subsequently contradicted. The news from Kentucky &
Tennessee is not favourable, but we must make up our minds to meet
with reverses & to overcome them. I hope God will at last crown our
efforts with success. But the contest must be long & severe, & the whole
country has to go through much suffering. It is necessary we should be

humbled & taught to be less boastful, less selfish, & more devoted to right & justice to all the world. Give much love to every body — Charlotte & the girls & Custis, Fitzhugh & Robert when you write. Take good care of yourself & be resigned to what God ordains for us. I left Meredith at Coosawhatchie & have Perry with me. God bless you all & believe me always yours

R. E. LEE

110   To JUDAH P. BENJAMIN
                       Secretary of War

Headquarters Department South Carolina &c.
Savannah
February 10, 1862

Sir:

From the reports of Genl [Hugh W.] Mercer as to the inability of the batteries on Saint Simon's & Jekyl Islands to withstand an attack of the enemy's fleet, the isolated condition of those islands, & the impossibility of my reinforcing him with men or guns, I have given him authority, should he retain that opinion upon a calm review of the whole subject, to act according to his discretion, & if deemed advisable by him, to withdraw to the mainland, & take there a defensible position for the protection of the country. Should he adopt this course, the heavy guns at those batteries will be sent here for the defence of Savannah River, where they are much needed & cannot otherwise be obtained. The channel between Saint Simon's & Jekyl Islands leads into Brunswick Harbor. Brunswick is a summer resort for certain planters, & is the terminus of a railroad extending about 60 miles into the interior, where it intersects the Savannah, Albany & Gulf Railroad. There are no inhabitants now in Brunswick, & the planters on the islands have removed their property to the interior, nor is there any population in the vicinity of Brunswick that would seem to warrant jeopardizing the men & guns necessary elsewhere. I would not, therefore, originally have occupied Saint Simon's or Jekyl, but the batteries, though small, are well placed, & the guns well distributed, & I think would defend the channel against ordinary attacks, & I exceedingly dislike to yield an inch of territory to our enemies. They are, however, able to bring such large & powerful batteries to whatever point they please, that it becomes necessary for us to concentrate our strength. As this point may be selected by some of our forward bound vessels to run the blockade, I think proper to give you the earliest information of its probable relinquishment.

I am, &c.

R. E. LEE
Genl Comdg

111
To JOSEPH E. BROWN
Governor of Georgia

Headquarters, Department &c.
Savannah
February 10, 1862

Sir:

I have had the honor to receive your letter of the 8th instant in reference to the withdrawal of the batteries from Saint Simon's & Jekyl Islands. No one can regret the apparent necessity of such a measure more than I do, & so great is my repugnance to yield any point of our territory to our enemies, that I have endeavored from the time of my arrival to give strength to the defences of Brunswick. I find it impossible to obtain guns to secure it as I desire, & now everything is required to fortify this city. I have, therefore, given Genl Mercer discretionary authority to withdraw the troops & guns from the islands to the main[land], should he, upon a reconsideration of the subject, hold to his opinion as to the inability of the batteries to contend with the enemy's fleet.

I have sent Major Edward [C.] Anderson to assist in removing the guns, &c., and as soon as I know his determination will inform you. With the exception of the fact of opening another harbor on the coast to the enemy & receding from a point we have occupied, I do not know that any material interest is sacrificed, as the inhabitants of the islands & of Brunswick have removed their families & property, there is no trade or commerce with Brunswick, & no immediate back country to be injuriously affected.

I am, &c.

R. E. LEE
Genl Comdg

112   To GENERAL NATHAN G. EVANS
                Commanding at Adams Run, South Carolina

                                    Headquarters Department South Carolina &c.
                                                                    Savannah
                                                            February 15, 1862
General:
   I have had the honor to receive your letter of this day's date, &
have directed that a court martial be convened at Adams Run, for the
trial of the officers of the Lyles Rifles. As regards the reinforcements that
you request, I wrote you yesterday on the subject, which is all under
the circumstances that can be done. It will be impossible to find sufficient
troops to garrison the whole line of the coast, & all that can be done is
to ascertain the points of attack, concentrate the troops in the district to
meet the advance of the enemy, & if unable to drive him, to hold him
in check until reinforcements can be forwarded from other districts.

                                                            I am, &c.

                                                            R. E. LEE
                                                            Genl Comdg

113   To GENERAL HENRY C. WAYNE
                Adjutant and Inspector General of Georgia

                                    Headquarters Department South Carolina &c.
                                                                    Savannah
                                                            February 15, 1862
General:
   I have had the honor to receive your letter of the 14th instant, enclosing communications from the mayor of Augusta [Robert H. May]
& Col [W. B.] Griffin to His Excellency Governor Brown, in reference
to the propriety of obstructing the navigation of the Savannah River.
   This subject had already attracted my attention, &, in addition to
measures contemplated for closing the river above this city, I have authorized the adoption of a plan suggested by Major [George W.] Rains
for arresting its navigation below Augusta.
   To prevent the removal of obstacles, however, placed in the bed of
the stream, there should be a battery contiguous. For this I have no guns,
& cannot possibly obtain more than necessary for the defences of Savannah. I was, therefore, on the point of requesting the Governor to permit

me to apply any belonging to the State to the defence of the upper river, & am glad that the subject has been brought to his notice. May I ask you to inform me whether there are any State guns available for this purpose, whether they can be procured, their caliber, &c.

I am, &c.

R. E. LEE
Genl Comdg

114   To GENERAL SAMUEL COOPER
Adjutant and Inspector General

Savannah
February 18, 1862

General:

I have the honor to report, for the information of the honorable Secretary of War, that the guns have been withdrawn from the batteries on Saint Simon's & Jekyl Islands and the troops removed to Brunswick. The former are now in progress of transportation to this place, to be used in the defence of the city of Savannah, & the latter directed to occupy a position to command the [Charleston and Savannah] Railroad & protect the back country. The nature of the ground prevents the possibility of holding of Brunswick, as the gunboats of the enemy can unmolested ascend the river within four miles of the railroad at Waynesville & about 25 miles in the rear of Brunswick. Brunswick would prove a convenient & healthy position, if occupied by the enemy, affording shelter and comfort, quarters for the troops & hospitals for the sick. It is used as a summer resort, & is at this time mostly uninhabited. Should it fall into the possession of the enemy, its convenient harbor & salubrious climate, & comfortable buildings might tempt them to hold it for the continuance of the war, & rather than it should fall into his hands, I propose to destroy it. Before issuing orders to this effect, I desire that my views be known to the Secretary, so that if not approved by him I may be informed.

I am, &c.

R. E. LEE
Genl Comdg

115   To GENERAL ROSWELL S. RIPLEY
                Commanding at Charleston, South Carolina

Savannah, Georgia
February 19, 1862

General:

From the progress of the war it seems plain that the enemy, when ready to move against Charleston, should he select it as a point of attack, will advance in great force. We should, therefore, be prepared to concentrate rapidly in his front, on the lines that can be best defended, so as to be able to contend to the utmost of our strength. Beyond these lines, every preparation should be made to withdraw guns & munitions of war when it becomes necessary, or when the route of the enemy renders them valueless in the positions occupied. My object is to ascertain your opinion, whether, without weakening the plan of defence, our lines could be contracted, and exposed or distant points abandoned.

The batteries at Cole's Island, for instance, would not be available, provided the enemy should advance by the Edisto [River], and, unless arrangements are made to withdraw them, would be lost. If they can be reached in great force by the enemy's gunboats they might be suppressed, & the Stono [River] seized as an avenue of approach. If it is necessary to maintain these batteries, they should be made as strong as possible & their communications rendered practicable in case of a reverse. So at other exposed points.

I am in favor of abandoning all exposed points as far as possible, within reach of the enemy's fleet of gunboats & of taking interior positions, where we can meet on more equal terms. All our resources should be applied to those positions. I wish you therefore to review the whole subject, & see what changes or improvements can be made, both as to the importance & strength of the positions retained.

I am, &c.
R. E. LEE
Genl Comdg

116   To GENERAL JAMES H. TRAPIER
                Commanding District of Florida

Savannah, Georgia
February 19, 1862

General:

In looking at the whole defence of Florida, it becomes important to ascertain what points can probably be held, & what points had better be relinquished. The force that the enemy can bring against any position, where he can concentrate his floating batteries, renders it prudent & proper to withdraw from the islands to the main[land] & to prepare to contest his advance into the interior. Where an island offers the best point of defence, & is so connected with the main[land] that its communication cannot be cut off, it might be retained. Otherwise it should be abandoned. A dispatch was sent to you this morning on this subject, & I now wish you, in reviewing the defensive positions in your district, to see what changes & improvements can be made in the number & strength of the points occupied. I fear but little aid can be offered you from without the state of Florida, you must therefore use every exertion to make available the resources in it, & apply the means at your disposal to the best advantage. Whatever can be given from the means under my control will be cheerfully accorded. You must, however, prepare to concentrate your force at the point liable to be attacked, & make every arrangement to secure the troops, guns, & munitions of war, at such points as you may deem proper to relinquish.

I am, &c.

R. E. LEE
Genl Comdg

117   To JOSEPH E. BROWN
Governor of Georgia

Savannah, Georgia
February 22, 1862

Governor:
    In the present condition of affairs the connection between the cities of Charleston & Savannah by the Charleston & Savannah Railroad is very precarious. Should the force now on this coast be reinforced, an attempt will be made in all probability to cut the road between the two cities, &, in view of this contingency, I have the honor to call your attention to the importance to the defence of the cities of Charleston, Augusta, & Savannah, as well as to the states of Georgia & South Carolina, of connecting the Augusta & Savannah Railroad with the Georgia or South Carolina Railroad at Augusta. I am informed that the Augusta & Savannah Railroad Company is willing to build the connection at its own expense, provided they be allowed to take the route which they would prefer, & which the president of the road, Dr. [Francis T.] Willis, informs me is but ¼ of a mile in distance. And if permission was given at

once, the connection could be completed in one week. I am, moreover, informed by Dr. Willis that the railroad company will make the connection, taking the route selected by the City Council of Augusta, more than twice the distance however, if the State of Georgia will direct it & assume the expense.

In the latter case, no doubt the State would be reimbursed by the Confederate government, but all considerations of time & expense would seem to recommend that the former plan be adopted, and I earnestly request that, if there is no insurmountable objection to its being carried out, that Your Excellency lend your aid & influence to have it done immediately.

I am, &c.

R. E. LEE
Genl Comdg

118   To HIS WIFE
            "White House," Virginia

Savannah
February 23, 1862

I have been wishing dear Mary to write to you for more than a week, but every day & every hour seems so taken up that I have found it impossible. Your last letter was received a week ago & with it came one from Rooney & Rob & more recently one from Custis. To the former two I have replied as it was requisite for their guidance. I sent on by Col H. H. Walker an afghan or robe, knit for me by Miss Catharine Clinch, with a request that he give it to Custis to send to you. You must keep it for me & use it if you wish, as it is too handsome for camp life & my blankets more suitable. It was very kind in Miss C[linch] thus to occupy herself, but I feared I could not take care of it in the field. She is the daughter of Genl [D. L.] Clinch & sister of Mrs. Anderson, wife of Major [Robert] Anderson of Sumter renown. I am very glad to hear that you are all well & that your little sunbeam lightens up the house so brightly & cheerfully. I hope he will always give equal warmth & pleasure. The news from Tennessee & N[orth] Carolina is not all cheering, & disasters seem to be thickening around us. It calls for renewed energies & redoubled strength on our part, & I hope will produce it. I fear our soldiers have not realized the necessity of endurance & labour they are called upon to undergo, & that it is better to sacrifice themselves than our cause. God, I hope, will shield us & give us success. Here the enemy is progressing slowly in his designs, & does not seem prepared, or to have determined when or where to make his attack. His gunboats are pushing up all the creeks & marshes of the Savannah, & have attained a position so near the river as to shell the steamers navigating it. None have as yet been struck. I am engaged in constructing a line of defence at Fort Jackson which, if time permits & guns can be obtained, I hope will keep them out. They can bring such overwhelming force in all their movements that it has the effect to demoralize our new troops. The accounts given in the papers of the quantity of cotton shipped to New York is, of course, exaggerated. It is cotton in the seed & dirt, & has to be ginned & cleaned after its arrival. It is said that the negroes are employed in picking & collecting it, & are paid a certain amount. But all these things are gathered from rumour, & can only be believed as they appear probable, which this seems to be. You must give much love to the children. I hope Agnes is better of her neuralgia. Poor child she has suffered a great deal. I am very sorry to hear of Mrs. Barnes' condition. All must suffer it seems in this war. Mrs. W. H. Stiles has come down to see her mother. I have seen her once. She looks very well & is very anxious about her soldier husband. Mrs. Mackay seems to me very feeble, & is much reduced. Still her faculties seem quite clear. I went yesterday to church, being the day appointed for fasting & prayer. I wish I could have passed it more devoutly. The Bishop (Elliott) gave a most beautiful prayer for the President, which I trust may be heard & answered. It will give me great pleasure to do anything I can for Edward Turner's sons. What can it be? You know I cannot give appointments, & if I recommend, unless an occasion offers, it cannot be acted on. If either of them had sufficient experience to assist on my staff, when an opportunity offers I might give them an appointment. But I require efficient persons about me & I know nothing of any of our young relatives whom I should like to have about me. Give my love to Charlotte, I hope her trees & flowers are all prospering. Here the yellow jasmine, red bud, orange tree, &c., perfume the whole wood, & the japonicas & auzalias cover the gardens. Perry & Meredith are well. May God bless & keep you all is the constant prayer of your husband.

R. E. LEE

119   To JOHN MILTON
Governor of Florida

Savannah, Georgia
February 24, 1862

Governor:

I have had the honor to receive your letter of the 21st instant, handed to me by Col J. J. Williams of Florida. I regret very much to learn that the means for the defence of the capital of the state are so deficient. Not finding it possible to defend all the important points in the state, or to obtain guns to place Cumberland Harbor out of the reach of capture, I had previously authorized Genl Trapier to withdraw the troops & guns from that point, & to apply them to other vital portions of the state. This is the only course now left, to supply means for defending it. I have also authorized him to withdraw generally from the islands to the main[land], the only way, in my opinion, successfully to resist the large force that can be brought against us by the enemy, & to deprive him of the benefit derived from his fleet & heavy floating batteries.

In reference to the cargo landing from the steamer *Carolina*, its disposition has been made by the War Department at Richmond, which will go but a little way in supplying the urgent demands of the service. It is now impossible to arm troops entering the service for the war; I consider it therefore useless for troops entering the service for a less period to expect arms from the government. If regiments can be raised in Florida for the war, the only period, in my opinion, for which they ought to be accepted, I will endeavor to procure arms for them.

It will be necessary for the citizens of Florida to turn out to a man to defend their homes, and the sooner Your Excellency can impress upon them this fact, the easier will be its accomplishment. Troops cannot be now drawn from other states for this purpose. Every state is looking to the protection of her own borders & providing the regiments called for by the Secretary of War. The Governor of Georgia has been obliged to refuse my recent application to him for two regiments, to be placed under the command of Genl Trapier, for the purpose of preventing an advance of the enemy through Florida into the southwest portion of Georgia.

I am, &c.

R. E. LEE
Genl Comdg

120   To GENERAL JAMES H. TRAPIER
Commanding at Tallahassee, Florida

Headquarters Department South Carolina &c.
Savannah
March 1, 1862

General:

In pursuance of instructions from the War Department, you are directed to send the [Twenty-Fourth] Mississippi Regiment, Col [William F.] Dowd commanding, to Tennessee, by the most expeditious route, to report to Genl A. S. Johnston. He is reported to be at Murfreesboro, & it is presumed that the route by Chattanooga will be the most direct. I desire that no delay that you can possibly avoid will take place in forwarding these troops, as there is an immediate necessity of defending the road from Memphis to Richmond. The recent disasters to our arms in Tennessee [Forts Henry and Donelson] forces the government to withdraw forces employed in the defence of the seaboard. The only troops to be retained in Florida are such as may be necessary to defend the Apalachicola River, by which the enemy's gunboats may penetrate far into the State of Georgia. You are therefore desired to put that river & harbor in a satisfactory state of defence, & send forward all troops not necessary for that purpose to report to Genl A. S. Johnston. All the guns & munitions of war must be secured. Let me know what arrangements you can make, & whether all of the guns will be needed for local defence.

I am, &c.

R. E. LEE
Genl Comdg

121   To MISS ANNIE LEE
                    "Hickory Hill," Virginia

Savannah
March 2, 1862

My Precious Annie:

It has been a long time since I have written to you, but you have been constantly in my thoughts. I think of you all, separately & collectively, in the busy hours of the day & the silent hours of the night, & the recollection of each & every one whiles away the long nights, in which my anxious thoughts drive away sleep. But I always feel that you & Agnes at those times are sound & happy & that it is immaterial to either where the blockaders are or what their progress is in the river. I hope you are all well, & as happy as you can be in these perilous times to our country. They look dark at present, & it is plain we have not suffered enough, laboured enough, repented enough, to deserve success. But they will brighten after awhile, & I trust that a merciful God will arouse us to a sense of our danger, bless our honest efforts, & drive back our enemies to their homes. Our people have not been earnest enough, have thought too much of themselves & their ease, & instead of turning out to a man, have been content to nurse themselves & their dimes, & leave the protection of themselves & families to others. To satisfy their consciences, they have been clamorous in criticising what others have done, & endeavoured to prove that they ought to do nothing. This is not the way to accomplish our independence. I have been doing all I can, with our small means & slow workmen, to defend the cities & coast here. Against ordinary numbers we are pretty strong, but against the hosts our enemies seem able to bring everywhere, there is no calculation. But if our men will stand to their work, we shall give them trouble & damage them yet. They have worked their way across the marshes, with their dredges, under cover of their gunboats, to the Savannah River, above Fort Pulaski. I presume they will endeavour to reduce the fort & thus open the way for their heavier vessels up the river. But we have an interior line they must force before reaching the city. It is on this line we are working, slowly to my anxious mind, but as fast as I can drive them. I believe I mentioned to your mother that Mrs. William H. Stiles is here on a visit to her mother. I see them occasionally & they are as kind as they can be. Mrs. S[tiles] has undertaken to repair my shirts & necessity has compelled me to accept her offer, which I am ashamed to do, both on account of the trouble to her & the exhibition of my rags. But pride must have a fall. Her sisters & niece had offered before, but my pride objected. See how foolish I am. Mr. Edward Stiles is here on a leave of absence. His regiment is near Yorktown. He has seen his mother & sisters who are in the interior of G[eorgia] & who are well. The young people say here Miss Sidney is engaged to her cousin Dr. William Elliott. I know not how it is, but the doctor is a very clever gentleman, stands well in the army, in which he is an Assistant Surgeon. He was with the troops at Port Royal & remained with some wounded, three days after our troops left the island of Hilton Head, & got them off. He is the son of Dr. Ralph Elliott, who married Miss Margaret Mackay, sister of Mrs. Ben & William H. Stiles. His sister Carrie is in town, a sweet young lady. I believe I have nothing else to say, except to send love to everybody. Give much to your mother, Charlotte, Agnes, Mary, & the boys, among whom is included my grandson. I received a letter from Precious Life [Mildred] the other day. She is well but in a starving condition from her own account poor child, yet fattening. I hope it is not as bad as that, but you must tell her not to be too particular in her diet, but to eat everything before her. It is not necessary for young ladies to become etherial to grow wise. She moans after Tom [her cat, left at Arlington] & knows he is alive & that his precious heart will break if he does not see her soon. I shall have to get Genl Johnston to send in a flag of truce & make inquiries. I hope you girls are learning to be useful &

have entered into domestic manufactures. Take separate departments & prepare fabric, or it will end in destitution. Has my poor little Agnes recovered of her neuralgia. I will write to her as soon as I can. I hope her disease is not catching. Goodbye my dear child. May God bless you & our poor country.

Your devoted father

R. E. LEE

122   To JEFFERSON DAVIS
Richmond, Virginia
TELEGRAM

Savannah, Georgia
March 2, 1862

PRESIDENT DAVIS:

IF POSSIBLE, I WILL LEAVE TUESDAY MORNING; IF PREVENTED WILL INFORM YOU.

R. E. LEE

CHAPTER FOUR

Military Adviser to Jefferson Davis

MARCH–MAY 1862

"Under the direction of the President"

OF THE THIRD THANKLESS assignment the President had for him, Lee wrote frankly to his wife, "I do not see either pleasure or advantage in the duties." He was officially "charged with the conduct of military operations in the Army of the Confederacy . . . under the Direction of the President," though his position was usually referred to as "Military Adviser to the President." The grandiose official designation was almost meaningless and he was adviser in name only.

From the beginning, Davis apparently regarded Lee as something of an executive assistant — or, as we would say, an expediter. Davis assumed quite literally the full authority of commander-in-chief in the sincere conviction that he was the only Confederate qualified, and, as he surrounded himself by civilians, Lee was to serve as liaison between the President and the military establishment.

He remained at the President's beck and call for futile conferences, with little voice in policy and decisions, while the bulk of his time was spent in tedious tasks that belonged in the adjutant-general's and quartermaster's offices. This period, with its depressing sense of waste, represented the greatest strain on Lee's nerves and patience of probably any period in the war; but it is interesting in revealing the emergence of skill at diplomatic maneuver for military ends of his own conception, in which he found a way to execute behind the scenes the one strategic plan he knew to be necessary.

When Lee came to Richmond, on March 6th or 7th, Davis had already experienced considerable personality difficulties with civil officials and army generals. The first two Secretaries of State had resigned, the first Secretary of War had quit in a huff, and the second, an unwise choice, resigned to quiet public clamor; the third, Randolph (Thomas Jefferson's grandson), soon grew restive in his capacity as "The President's Clerk." Beauregard, early in Davis's black book, had been shifted to the West and would join the growing number of Davis's enemies. Ominously in Virginia, relations were strained between the commander-in-chief and the general commanding on the field, Joseph E. Johnston. Joe Johnston, who had disliked Davis since they were at West Point, felt a legitimate resentment at the interference with his army; for his part, he was rank-conscious, stiff-necked about his prerogatives and army protocol, and had grown secretive with Davis and the war office. Each was a man who would rather prove himself right than achieve effectiveness.

These were the unhealthy conditions under which Lee assumed his unenviable office chores at a time when the enemy, virtually enveloping Virginia, had prepared a spring campaign just to the point of mounting a multipronged offensive, without, however, revealing its main objective. The Confederate defensive alignment had contracted since Lee left Virginia, though retaining the general outlines he had established as commander of Virginia's forces. With the western Virginia campaign abandoned, only small forces remained in the Alleghenies to protect against quick thrusts into the Valley. Stonewall Jackson discontentedly patrolled the middle Valley with an infantry division, artillery, and some semiregular cavalry. In the Piedmont region, between the Blue Ridge and the Potomac, Johnston had abandoned the Manassas line and fallen back into central Virginia, with a defensive line extending from Culpeper to Fredericksburg. On the peninsula, Magruder had a small army in works at Yorktown.

Shortly after Lee took over his new duties, on March 17, McClellan began the shift of his army from the Manassas area by boat to Fort Monroe, completing the transfer on April 4. As McClellan left troops in the Manassas area, during these nineteen days the Confederates remained uncertain as to whether the main blow would come on the Culpeper-Fredericksburg line or on the peninsula, and, if on the peninsula, whether Richmond or Norfolk would be the objective. Norfolk's position, exposed to the United States Navy, had been changed by the appearance of the sea monster *Virginia-Merrimac*, which in effect nullified the gunboats supporting McClellan's transports. While the Confederates were puzzling over McClellan's intentions, General Lee was caught futilely between the conflicting strategic policies of Davis and Johnston.

General Johnston wished to concentrate their forces on the peninsula, which he believed to be the enemy's main objective, but the President characteristically preferred to balance the strength in the two primary defensive lines. As his wishes prevailed, the Confederate concentration was not completed on the peninsula when McClellan, with an army of 120,000 men, began his overland march from Fort Monroe toward Richmond on April 15. But, partly because of Magruder's convincing demonstrations and because of McClellan's caution, the Federal commander halted his advance at Yorktown and laid siege to Magruder's lines. When the bulk of the Confederate troops had been shifted to the peninsula, Johnston (who was formally given command of the peninsula and Department of Norfolk, along with the forces in northern Virginia) soon wanted to retreat westward up the peninsula to another position.

Davis, in opposition to this movement, called General Lee in a succession of conferences with Johnston, General G. W. Smith, second in command, and the new War Secretary, Randolph. Though Lee spoke for the majority decision to defend Yorktown, Johnston, more or less in defiance of the President's war council, evacuated the position and began a retrograde movement which continued to within seven miles of Richmond. There he was emphatically ordered to halt. McClellan, following cautiously, again prepared siege operations, within the sounds of the church bells of the capital. Johnston's unexpected withdrawal had uncovered Norfolk, causing the ironclad *Virginia-Merrimac* to be abandoned, which in turn opened the James River to the Federal gunboats all the way to Richmond. A river fort was hastily erected on Drewry's Bluff, eight miles southeast of Richmond; there a bend in the river gave the guns an angle on the gunboats which, with obstructions to narrow the channel, held enemy ships at bay throughout the war.

During these confused operations and quick improvisations, Lee's liaison work became hopeless as the relations between Johnston and Davis broke down completely. However, it was while these two antithetical gentlemen were preoccupied with the peninsula that General Lee devised and caused to be executed the first cause-and-effect strategy in the Virginia theater.

From Fredericksburg to the Alleghenies, the Federals had approximately 70,000 men, a large proportion of whom were designated for cooperative action with McClellan at Richmond. To counter this potential second army, and if possible prevent it from joining McClellan, the Confederates had a total of about 20,000 men scattered in small forces: at Fredericksburg Charles Field had one brigade, east of the Blue Ridge Ewell had one division, Jackson was in the Valley with his division and cavalry, in the Alleghenies Edward Johnson, Heth (pronounced "Heath") and Marshall each had a brigade. With Joe Johnston on the peninsula, no single commander was in immediate control of these separated units, each of which was daily confronted with defensive problems unrelated to the other units. As Lee began to handle much of the correspondence with these isolated commanders, he recognized that the soundest way of preventing the Federal forces from shifting from middle Virginia, for a concentration with McClellan, was to concentrate against their own scattered alignment and open a counteroffensive.

Winning the President's distracted approval and dexterously avoiding arousing Johnston's antagonism, Lee arranged a coordination of troops under Jackson to strike down the Valley (to the north). By playing on the fears of the Federal administration for Washington, he planned to immobilize the 70,000 enemy troops in middle Virginia by placing them on the defensive. The brilliantly executed maneuver, known as "Jackson's Valley Campaign," opened on April 29 and by June 14 its dramatic success had achieved all that Lee could have hoped for. Though Lee's part in this campaign passed unknown at the time, it represented his major positive accomplishment in the year of his desuetude, which ended on June 1, 1862.

123   GENERAL ORDERS, NO. 14

Adjutant and Inspector General's Office
Richmond
March 13, 1862

General Robert E. Lee is assigned to duty at the seat of government; and, under the direction of the President, is charged with the conduct of military operations in the armies of the Confederacy.

By command of the Secretary of War:

S. COOPER
Adjutant and Inspector General

124   To HIS WIFE
"White House," Virginia

Richmond
March 14, 1862

My Dear Mary:

I have been trying all the week to write to you, but have not been able. I have been placed on duty here to conduct operations under the direction of the President. It will give me great pleasure to do everything I can to relieve him & serve the country, but I do not see either advantage or pleasure in my duties. But I will not complain, but do my best. I do not see at present either that it will enable me to see much more of you. In the present condition of affairs no one can foresee what may happen, nor in my judgment is it advisable for any one to make any arrangements with a view to permanency or pleasure. We must all do what promises the most usefulness. The presence of some one at the W[hite] H[ouse] is necessary as long as practicable. How long it will be practicable for you & C[harlotte] to remain there I cannot say. The enemy is pushing us back in all directions, & how far he will be successful depends much upon our efforts & the mercy of Providence. I shall, in all human probability, soon have to take the field, so for the present I think things had better remain as they are. Write me your views. If you think it best for you to come to Richmond, I can soon make arrangements for your comfort & shall be very glad of your company & presence. We have experienced a great affliction, both in our private & public relations. Our good & noble Bishop Meade died last night. He was very anxious to see you, sent you his love & kindest remembrances, & had I known in time yesterday I would have sent expressly for you to come up. But I did not know of his wish or condition till after the departure of the cars yesterday. Between 6 & 7 P.M. yesterday he sent for me, said he wished to bid me good bye, & to give me his blessing, which he did in the most affecting manner. Called me Robert & reverted to the time I used to say the catechism to him. He invoked the blessing of God upon me & the country. He spoke with difficulty & pain, but perfectly calm & clear. His hand was then cold & pulseless, yet he shook mine warmly. I ne'er shall look upon his like again. He died during the night. I presume the papers of tomorrow will tell you all. Mary is still sick & confined to her room, but better. Your basket of eggs arrived safely. You had better if possible repeat it. Annie & Agnes are well & enjoying themselves at Mr. Warwick's. We were all invited last night to Mrs. Lyons'. I could not go & Agnes was the only one of the family that went. Tell Robert the Secretary of War has exempted from military service the professors & students of the University. But as he has now left he must judge whether it would be well for him to return. Charlotte did not go to F[itzhugh]. He telegraphed for her not to come. She is at Mrs. Lyons'. I send a letter received from Mrs. R.

Very truly & sincerely

R. E. LEE

125   To HIS WIFE
                      "White House," Virginia

                                                    Richmond
                                                March 15, 1862
My Dear Mary:
    I wrote to you yesterday by mail. On returning to my quarters last
night after 11 p.m. Custis informed me Robert had arrived & had made
up his mind to go into the army. He staid at the Spottswood, & this
morning I went with him to get his overcoat, blankets, &c. There is
great difficulty in procuring what is good. They all have to be made, &
he has gone to the Adjutant General's office of Virginia to engage in the
service. God grant it may be for his good. As He has permitted it I must
be resigned. I told him of the exemption granted by the Secretary of
War to the professors & students of the University, but he expressed no
desire to take advantage of it. It would be useless for him to go, if he
did not improve himself, nor would I wish him to go, merely for exemption. As I have done all in the matter that seems proper & right, I must
now leave the rest in the hands of our merciful God. I hope our son will
do his duty & make a good soldier. I have not seen the children since I
wrote yesterday. Rob will see them & tell you about them. I had expected yesterday to go to N[orth] C[arolina] this morning, but the
President changed his mind. I should like to go to see you tomorrow, but
in the present condition of things I do not feel that I ought to be absent.
If I remain here after Charlotte returns I think you had better come up
for a little while. I may have to go to N[orth] C[arolina] or Norfolk
yet. New Berne, N[orth] C[arolina] has fallen into the hands of the
enemy. In Arkansas our troops under [General Earl] Van Dorn have had
a hard battle [Elkhorn (Pea Ridge)], but nothing decisive gained. Four
generals killed — [James McQ.] McIntosh, [Ben] McCullogh, [Colo-
nel Louis] Hébert [taken prisoner — not killed], & [William Y.] Slack.
Genl [Sterling] Price wounded. Loss on both sides said to be heavy.
Many of our best colonels &c. reported killed. Our army had fallen back
& the enemy claim a victory. I send Mrs. Powell's bill which I paid Mr.
P[owell]. Custis can find nothing of your letter enclosing to him your
check. How did you send it & did you put other enclosures in the letter.
When you send money in a letter, it should be as unattractive as possible. Kiss Life for me & the baby.

                                        Very truly yours,
                                            R. E. LEE

126   To GENERAL THEOPHILUS H. HOLMES
            Commanding, Fredericksburg, Virginia

Richmond, Virginia
March 16, 1862

General:

I have had the honor to receive your letter of the 13th [15th] & 16th instant, by the hands of Lt [John W.] Hinsdale. The enemy has naturally occupied the ground from which we have withdrawn, & seems to have taken a line approaching parallelism to the position of our army. What route of approach to Richmond he will adopt does not now seem certain. His land transportation would be shortened by coming up the Rappahannock, though the route from the Potomac through Fredericksburg offers other advantages.

I do not think his advance from Dumfries, &c., can be immediate, from what I learn of the condition of the roads, but that he will advance upon our line as soon as he can, I have no doubt. To retard his movements, cut him up in detail if possible, attack him at disadvantage, and if practicable drive him back, will of course be your effort and study. It is not the plan of the government to abandon any country that can be held, and it is only the necessity of the case, I presume, that has caused the withdrawal of the troops to the Rappahannock. I trust there will be no necessity of retrograding further. The position of the main body of the army of the Potomac seems to have been taken in reference to the reported advance of the enemy up the Shenandoah Valley. A report from Genl [Joseph E.] Johnston of his plans and intentions has not yet been received. His movements are doubtless regulated by those of the enemy, and he alone can say whether it is practicable to reinforce you, to enable you to make the attack you propose, or not. As advised by my dispatch of today, he has been informed of the contents of your letter, and as he must also have received your communication to him, he will doubtless give such directions as the case admits of. In the uncertainty of the position of our own troops, that of the enemy, the condition of the roads, &c., the measures you propose could not safely be directed from here. A blow at the enemy at the crossing of the Chopawamsic might, it seems to me, come within the scope of your forces, provided it meets with the concurrence of Genl Johnston, whose directions in the matter must of course be had. I very much regret to learn from your letter of the 14th that it is the opinion of yourself & officers, that Fredericksburg is in itself untenable. Can it be maintained by occupying a position on the left bank of the river or in advance of the hills on that side? I request that you will cause an examination of the country to be made, should you not be sufficiently acquainted with it, both in your front and rear, with a view to take the best position the case admits of. I would also suggest that arrangements be made to break up the railroad to Aquia Creek & remove the iron as soon as in your judgment it can be done without detriment to the service. I think it certain the enemy will press his advance on Richmond in every direction. Our troops are coming in spiritedly, & if we can gain time, I trust we shall be able to drive him back.

I am, &c.

R. E. LEE
Genl Comdg

127   To GENERAL JOSEPH E. JOHNSTON
Commanding at Culpeper Court House, Virginia

Richmond, Virginia
March 17, 1862

General:
   I received yesterday from Genl Holmes a letter dated 14th instant, of which the accompanying is a copy. I presume he has already communicated with you on the subject, but as the matter is briefly & distinctly stated, I have thought it might be convenient to you to consider it in the manner presented. In a letter of the 16th Genl Holmes also reports that [General Joseph] Hooker's division had crossed the Potomac at Evansport, & that a column of five or six thousand of the enemy had reached Brentsville from the direction of Manassas. Dumfries was occupied in force, but whether from Evansport or via Occoquan he did not know. He states that the enemy landed a part of his force below Chopawamsic, & marched up that creek to where it is crossed by the telegraphic road. He considers these movements indicate a purpose of the enemy to concentrate his forces for an attack on Fredericksburg, & that unless he can be defeated before reaching it, the town could not be held an hour after the occupation of the hills on the opposite bank of the river. From what is stated of the condition of the roads, I hardly think an immediate movement against Fredericksburg can be made, nor am I aware of anything that indicates with any degree of certainty what route the enemy will adopt in his march towards Richmond.
   You have doubtless considered the subject with reference to your

operations, & made your arrangements as to the points to be held & defended.

I am, &c.

R. E. LEE
Genl Comdg

128 To GENERAL JOHN B. MAGRUDER
Commanding Army of Peninsula
Yorktown, Virginia

Richmond, Virginia
March 18, 1862

General:

Notwithstanding the demonstrations of the enemy in your front, I see nothing to prove that he intends immediately to attempt your line. He is feeling your strength and desires to prevent your occupying other points. If strong enough, his feint may be converted into a real attack. I hope you will so maneuver as to deceive and thwart him.

The roads are hardly firm enough yet to invite his advance by land, and I discover nothing at present indicating co-operation with his column from Newport News. You can therefore only prevent his accumulating information and reserve your men. Should the *Monitor* appear before your batteries, it has occurred to me that by reserving your fire until she arrives near and discharging by word of command or simultaneously your heavy guns at her turret at the time when her gun was protruded for delivering fire, if the gun was struck it would be disabled, or if the turret was hit by a number of shot it would be deranged or capsized from its center.

Wrought-iron shot are being forged with a view to penetrate her armor. Some will be sent you. I do not think she will enter York River and leave the *Virginia* in her rear.

Directions have been given in reference to the completion of the battery at Harden's Bluff, and General [Benjamin] Huger's attention called to all the points referred to in Colonel [Henry C.] Cabell's letter. It would be better in some respects if the battery formed part of your command, but its supporting force, &c., must be drawn from the command of General Huger. I can learn nothing of "the two Mississippi companies promised," mentioned in your postscript to telegram of 17th.

Very respectfully, &c.

R. E. LEE
Genl Comdg

129   To GENERAL EDWARD JOHNSON
                Commanding at Monterey, Virginia

                                    Headquarters, Richmond, Virginia
                                                March 21, 1862
General:
    Your letter of the 18th has been received. I regret to learn that the prospect of calling volunteers to your aid from the country in which you are operating is so unfavorable. It is important that you call out the militia, as authorized by the proclamation of the Governor, to fill up your companies of Virginia regiments to 100 each, concerning which you will receive instructions. I also desire that you send a competent officer to examine the Shenandoah Mountain, with a view of ascertaining its capacity for defence, accommodation of the troops, &c., in case you may deem it advisable, or be forced to take a position secure from being turned, on the one side through Franklin, & on the other through Huntersville. The object of this examination must be concealed, so as not to excite either alarm or apprehension, and be viewed on your part as merely precautionary. Should you ascertain that the Shenandoah affords the best position in your rear for defending the approaches to Staunton, and preparations can be made for its occupation by your troops, without disclosing your views to the enemy, it will be well for you to do so.
    I need not urge upon you the necessity of keeping yourself advised of the movements of the enemy, of using every means in your power to thwart and defeat him, of increasing your own forces, & putting your army in the best condition possible for the opening campaign.

                                    I am, very res, your obt servt

                                                R. E. LEE
                                                Genl Comdg

130   To HIS WIFE
                    "White House," Virginia

                                                Richmond
                                                March 22, 1862

    I have received, dear Mary, your letter by Rob & had hoped to have been with you tomorrow. The President, who is at Fredericksburg, has telegraphed me to go to N[orth] C[arolina] & I go in the morning. I shall not, therefore, be able to go to the W[hite] H[ouse], which I very much regret. When I shall be back I cannot say, & therefore cannot urge you to come up. I had requested Annie & Agnes to look out for rooms for you as I have not had time. Tell Charlotte & Mildred I am so sorry not to see them. I think they had better come up with you. Our enemies are pressing us everywhere & our army is in the fermentation of reorganization. I pray that the great God may aid us & am endeavouring by every means in my power to bring out the troops & hasten them to their destination. This call away will retard the operations. I send a note from Cousin Ann & Mrs. Stiles. The shirts she speaks of have arrived & look very nice. I have not tried them, but three new shirts are as many as a man requires these wartimes. Those I sent down I am in no hurry for & you can take your time. I would only use those bodies for re-equipment that promise good service. Otherwise they will soon be all collars & ristbands. You will see that the present collars & ristbands are of different size. The smallest of each are too small. Take the large size. The collars are too high especially the bands. Some of them you may recollect you altered at A[rlington]. I will tell Annie to cut a pattern of some I have here. Or you can guess at it. Do not let the points of the collars project so much. I have no time for more. Our dear Rob went off this morning in good spirits with two of his comrades. He got all his things & said he had all he wanted. I think he ought to have had another pair of pants.

Love to Charlotte, Mildred & little Rob. Mary is better & walking out. The others well.

Very truly

R. E. Lee

P.S. Billy has come down from Kinloch — is well.

131 To GENERAL JOSEPH E. JOHNSTON
Commanding Army in Northern Virginia

Headquarters, Richmond
March 25, 1862

General:

The President desires to know with what force you can march to reinforce the Army of the Peninsula or Norfolk. Both armies are now threatened by the enemy assembling in great numbers, according to the reports received at Old Point Comfort. It seems probable that the troops assembling there are drawn from the army of Genl [George B.] McClellan. Whether it is intended to move against Norfolk or Richmond there is as yet nothing to determine. But from the accounts received nothing less than twenty or thirty thousand men with the troops already in position, will be sufficient successfully to oppose them. It will be necessary, therefore, for you to organize a part of your troops to hold your present line, & to prepare the remainder to move to this city, to be thrown on the point attacked. The object of the President is to prepare you for a movement which now appears imperative, as no troops are available but those of your army to meet the enemy concentrating on the coast. As soon as something more definite can be learned you will be informed, & should you receive a despatch saying *move at once*, you will understand that you are to repair immediately to this city, where you will be informed to what point you are to direct your course. Such arrangements as you deem necessary for the transportation & subsistence of your troops on their march, you are desired to make. Every facility that can be given here to the same end will be prepared. This is sent by a special messenger, to insure secrecy & despatch.

I have the honour to be, your obt servt

R. E. LEE
Genl

132   To GENERAL BENJAMIN HUGER
Commanding at Norfolk, Virginia

Headquarters, Richmond, Virginia
March 25, 1862

General:

It seems certain from the reports received that the enemy is assembling in great force at Old Point Comfort. Whether he will move against Norfolk or Richmond nothing is yet disclosed. Should the former be his point of attack, reinforcements from the Army of the Peninsula and from troops concentrating here, will be dispatched to your support. You must therefore prepare to receive them and determine the points to which they will be directed. Watch vigilantly the movements of the enemy and endeavor to discover his plans. On the contrary, should Richmond be the object of his attack, and his route be by the Peninsula, you must throw across James River at a point to reach his front as large a force as can be safely withdrawn from the defence of Norfolk. It is probable a feint will be made against one city, while the attack will be against the other, and great care and judgment must be exercised not to be deceived. You must, therefore, immediately look to all your defences, organize the troops to hold them, mobilize the remainder to move at a moment's warning, should they not be required to oppose the enemy in the lines around Norfolk. You will have also to arrange means of transportation, should it be necessary to cross your troops over James River. The infantry it is suggested might be sent by railroad to City Point and ferried over by steamers. Artillery could be crossed lower down, from Carter's Wharf to Grove's Wharf unless the enemy's gunboats prevent it. But as to the best points and means, you must judge, and make such preparations under both contingencies as are necessary.

Keep me advised of the preparations and movements of the enemy as far as you can discover. And also of your opinion as to the object he has in view.

I have the honor to be, your obt servt

R. E. LEE
Genl Comdg &c.

133   To GENERAL JOHN B. MAGRUDER
Commanding at Yorktown, Virginia

Headquarters, Richmond, Virginia
March 26, 1862

General:
Your several telegrams of yesterday and previous dates were received. The information forwarded by you, derived from the signal office at Norfolk, was transmitted by General Huger. It is unnecessary for you to repeat in detail such dispatches; the substance will be sufficient, or your opinion of the facts related.

It seems certain that a large force of the enemy is accumulating at Old Point Comfort, no doubt with a purpose of attacking either Norfolk or Richmond, but which of these points he may select, or what line of approach he may choose, I have as yet heard nothing to enable me to decide. Until some conclusion can be drawn as to his point of attack it would be manifestly improper to accumulate at either the army to oppose him. Measures, however, have been taken to throw into the Peninsula the available troops from Norfolk in case the enemy move against your line, and it will be necessary for you to be prepared to re-enforce Norfolk in the event of the attack being upon that city. All the boats on James River are ordered to be prepared to ferry across the troops, and troops are being concentrated in this city to be moved to either point that may be threatened.

It will no doubt be the policy of the enemy to disguise his intention by threatening one point while preparing to attack the other, and the utmost care and judgment should be exercised to ascertain his real design. You will use every means in your power to obtain information on this point, and communicate every material fact tending in your opinion to throw light upon the subject, with your own inferences from such facts.

Assuming that the enemy will advance up the Peninsula to Richmond, and supposing that their boats may be able to force a passage by the batteries on York and James Rivers, they will be in a position, should they land on the Pamunkey on one side and about the Chickahominy on the other, to intercept your retreat, and will have turned the line of your land defenses. You must take measures to guard against such a catastrophe, and be prepared in such event to throw your whole force behind the Chickahominy, where a stand must be made. For this purpose you will cause examinations to be made of suitable positions on the lines of the Pamunkey and James Rivers above the water batteries, to be occupied by you in such force as to delay the landing and advance of the enemy while you are withdrawing the body of your army behind the Chickahominy. In selecting these positions you will ascertain the best wharves and landings on each river above your river batteries, and take measures in the event of the enemy's passing those batteries to destroy those wharves and impede the landing of the enemy in every way, and to display such a force opposite the wharves and landings which the enemy may approach as to delay his advance while the body of your army is being withdrawn behind the proposed new line. Of course you will understand that these positions to cover the withdrawal of your army are only to be occupied by you in the event of the danger of the enemy's passing the river batteries becoming so imminent as in your judgment to render it necessary.

In the mean time you will only select suitable places to be occupied by you in the happening of the contingency above mentioned, and make such preparations as may be necessary to accomplish the purposes above indicated. All the information received here leads me to believe that the troops of the enemy now being concentrated at Old Point are drawn from the army that has heretofore been threatening the lines lately occupied by the Army of the Potomac under General Johnston.

I am, general, with great respect, your obedient servant

R. E. LEE
General Commanding

134   To GENERAL JOSEPH E. JOHNSTON
Commanding Army of Northern Virginia

Headquarters, Richmond, Virginia
March 28, 1862
1 o'clock a.m.

General:

Your letter by Mr. Turner of the 26th has been received, together with the reports of Mr. [W.] Stoddert & Genl [J. E. B.] Stuart.

In consequence of the information conveyed by your telegraphic dispatch (No. 50) that the enemy was reported in force in front of your line beyond Rappahannock Bridge, coupled with his reported strength in the above named reports, you have been desired in a dispatch just sent to use your discretion in complying with the requisition for troops, as it was feared your line could not be weakened and held, and no stronger ground is known to me between your position and Richmond than that you occupy.

Since then your dispatch (No. 55) has been received, recommending that you repair here with the largest number of troops named in my letter of the 25th, viz, 30,000, from which it is inferred that you apprehend no attack upon your line. If this inference is correct you can commence the movement of your troops to this place. The reason the President desired, in my first telegraphic dispatch, that only about half the troops you might designate for reinforcing our right flank should be sent, was to have a portion in position here to throw where required, while the balance might follow if necessary. For although the enemy is menacing both Norfolk & Portsmouth, he has not yet disclosed his real design further than by advancing up the Peninsula as far as Bethel, but in what force is not yet known. You can, therefore, with this understanding of the case, proceed to forward the desired reinforcements in part or whole, as in your judgment they can be spared from the defence of your line. It is unnecessary to observe that the baggage of the detachment should be as light as possible.

I have the honor to be, your obt sev't

R. E. LEE
Genl Comdg

135   To GENERAL JOSEPH E. JOHNSTON
            Commanding Army of Northern Virginia

Headquarters, Richmond, Virginia
March 28, 1862

General:

Your letter of the 27th, by Lt [J. Barroll] Washington, your aide-de-camp, has been received. The reports of Generals [T. J.] Jackson & Stuart indicate a large force in your front. Should the enemy seize Gordonsville & Charlottesville and advance his right wing to Staunton the whole of western Virginia, our lines of communication through Tennessee, and the armies of Genls Edward Johnson, [Henry] Heth, and [Humphrey] Marshall will be cut off. The enemy is apparently advancing to your present position, and if your force is weakened so as to entail the loss of the line of the Rapidan, it will carry with it the consequences above stated.

When the proposition was made to you to co-operate with a large part of your forces in the defence of the Peninsula or Norfolk, as the case might be, it was under the supposition that the enemy could not advance, which would therefore require in your present line, for the period during which you were expected to be absent but little more than an army of observation. If such be the fact, then you will move with all the force you think it safe to withdraw. But as a mode of expressing to you the limit which it is intended to affix I will cite the remark of the President, that the loss of the [Virginia] Central road & communication with the Valley at Staunton would be more injurious than the withdrawal from the Peninsula and the evacuation of Norfolk. You are aware that between your present position and Richmond there is no defensive line so strong as that you now hold, and this consideration gives to that line an additional value.

The President is not at all reluctant to take the responsibility of any movement of the propriety of which he is confident, and it is only designed to ask of you that judgment which your better information enables you more safely to render. He desires you to exercise that judgment and give him the benefit of your views. In the mean time, if doubtful of the course to be pursued, he invites you to a full conference at this place, where the latest intelligence is collected.

I have the honor to be, your obt servt

R. E. LEE
Genl Comdg

136   To GENERAL JOHN B. MAGRUDER
                Commanding at Yorktown, Virginia

                                        Headquarters, Richmond, Virginia
                                                        March 29, 1862

General:
    Your letter of the 28th, relative to the promise of the Secretary of
War to send you an unarmed regiment of 1,000 men and the arrival at
Yorktown of the two Alabama regiments, has been received. These were
the only troops which were here and available. I am fully alive to the
importance of increasing your command, and all that is possible is being
done in this way. Genl [Cadmus M.] Wilcox's brigade leaves City Point
today for the Peninsula to join you. As regards the brigade of Genl
[Raleigh E.] Colston, it was not intended that he should move until
there was positive evidence that the intention of the enemy was to attack
you in force. Full instructions to that effect have been forwarded to him.
You are desired to keep him fully advised as to the movements and
probable designs of the enemy. A steamer for the necessary transportation has been placed at Stone House Wharf, subject to the orders of
Genl Colston.
    The enemy is pressing us on all sides, and a call for reinforcements
comes from every department. It is impossible to place at every point
which is threatened a force which shall prove equal to every emergency.
As yet the design of the enemy in your front is somewhat vague and
undecided. The movement against you may be a feint, and the real attack may be on Norfolk. When it is unmistakably ascertained that he shall
attempt to force his way up the Peninsula every exertion shall be made
to enable you successfully to resist and drive him.

                        I am, very respy, your obt servt

                                                R. E. LEE
                                                Genl Comdg

137   To GENERAL JOHN B. MAGRUDER
                Commanding at Yorktown, Virginia

                                        Headquarters, Richmond, Virginia
                                                        March 31, 1862

General:
    I have the honor to acknowledge your telegram asking that [Major
Stephen D.] Ramseur's battery be sent you. There is already under your

command on the Peninsula double the amount of the artillery in the Department of Norfolk. It was not intended that Genl [Raleigh E.] Colston should cross the river unless there was positive evidence of an attack against you in force. The instructions were to this effect. Nor was it contemplated that Ramseur's battery or the cavalry should accompany him, until it was ascertained that no attack was threatened on Norfolk. From present indications, I think that Norfolk is quite as seriously threatened as the Peninsula, and more probably the object of attack. Should the latter prove the case, it is expected, as intimated to you by letter on 26th instant, that you will render all the assistance in your power compatible with the security of your own line.

I am very respy, your obt servt

R. E. Lee
Genl Comdg

138   To GENERAL THEOPHILUS H. HOLMES
Commanding Department of North Carolina

Headquarters, Richmond, Virginia
April 1, 1862

General:

From your telegraphic dispatches I learn that the enemy apparently is making no forward movements, nor do you appear to be able to discover that he is making any preparations with that view. That leads me to fear that while making demonstrations in that quarter and on the Peninsula against Genl Magruder, his real object is to attack Norfolk from both sides, with the force now collecting at Hampton and neighborhood on one side, and that under General Burnside on the other. I desire you, therefore, to watch the movements of the enemy vigilantly, and at the same time so to post your troops that while restraining his operations you may readily reinforce any point attacked. If Wilmington should be the point, you must concentrate there. If Norfolk, it will be necessary to move all your disposable force there. With this view it might be well to hold a portion of your troops at Weldon. This will depend upon your facilities for moving, and of this you may judge.

I am with high respect, your obt servt

R. E. Lee
General Comdg

139   To HIS WIFE
              "White House," Virginia

Richmond
April 4, 1862

I enclose two letters, dear Mary, that have come for you. The one from Charlotte I opened thinking she had written for something. But the only thing I can do for her is to send some stamps for general use. I will send & see if I can get some envelopes as she desires. I hope you all got down safe & are making preparations for a summer home. I hear troops are still arriving at Old Point & that great activity prevails there. I do not pretend to know what they will attempt or what they can accomplish. I believe they will make a great effort to take Norfolk & Richmond, for I cannot conceive what other use they can put their vast army to. One of the probable routes to the latter city is up the Pamunkey. Should they select that, their whole army &c. will land at the White House. To be enveloped in it would be extremely annoying & embarassing, as I believe hundreds would delight in persecuting you all for my & F[itzhugh]'s sake. I do not think their respectable officers would authorize such proceedings, but believe they would not be able to prevent them. I think it better, therefore, that you should all get out of the way. No one can say what place will be perfectly safe or even quiet, but I think a locality within the route of the invading army will be least so. All that lower country is subject to invasion & molestation, for there is no telling from what quarter the enemy will proceed. It seems to me that Gloucester or Westmoreland would be less exposed than where you are, or some where in King William even towards the Berkley's or Pampatike. Charlotte's effects would be safer at Hickory Hill or North Wales than at the White House, though what place may be considered safe I do not know. I hope you are all well. Mary is better. I took her a ride on my roan yesterday & she is charmed with him. Thinks she never rode a more pleasant goer. He not very easy in his gaites save his walk & canter, but steady & tolerably well trained to his duty. There is nothing new. All are anxious & expectant. God I hope will give us his countenance & blessing then all will go well. I have nothing to send but love. I saw one of Fitzhugh's captains the other day. He reports him well & a great favourite. I send you a letter from Rob.

May God bless you my dear Mary & preserve you & all with you.

Truly & afft your husband

R. E. LEE

P.S. I fear I shall not be able to get to see you tomorrow & therefore write. Everything is so unsettled & there is such constant demands from all quarters & no telling what a day may bring forth, that I do not feel I ought to be out of the way.

R. E. L.

140   To STEPHEN R. MALLORY
Secretary of Navy

Headquarters, Richmond, Virginia
April 8, 1862

Sir:

I have the honor to inform you that, from recent developments of the intentions of the enemy in the Peninsula, it is my opinion that they are endeavoring to change their base of operations from James to York River. This change has no doubt been occasioned by their fear of the effect of the *Virginia* upon their shipping in the James. General Magruder informs me that their gunboats & transports have appeared off Shipping Point, on the Poquosin, near the mouth of the York, where they intend apparently to establish a landing for stores, preparatory to moving against our lines at Yorktown. They could easily ascend York and the Pamunkey River with their gunboats & transports as high as the railroad bridge over the latter if they succeed in passing the defences at Yorktown. I respectfully suggest for your consideration the practicability of the *Virginia* passing Fort Monroe in the night to York River. She could, by destroying the enemy's gunboats and transports, thwart this design. After effecting this object, she could again return to Hampton Roads under cover of night. I would, however, recommend that the *Virginia*, previously to an attempt against the enemy in York River, should strike a blow at their transports and shipping in Hampton Roads and the bay outside of Forts Monroe and Calhoun, so as to prevent the possibility of an attack on Norfolk. In this manner she could so cripple their means of supplying their army, as to prevent its moving against Richmond, while she would deter any movement against Norfolk.

Coal could be sent by railroad & York River to Yorktown for her use.

I am very respectfully, your obt servt

R. E. LEE
General

141 To GENERAL JOHN B. MAGRUDER
Commanding at Yorktown, Virginia

Headquarters, Richmond, Virginia
April 9, 1862

General:

Col [Hill] Carter reported to me yesterday, in conformity to orders from you. I find that my letter of 26th March was not sufficiently explicit. I intended to call your attention to the possibility of the enemy's forcing a passage by the batteries on the York and James Rivers, below your lines at Yorktown, and effecting a landing in your rear above your lines at Yorktown & Williamsburg. It was not my intention to advise an abandonment of the Williamsburg lines, even should you be compelled to fall back from Yorktown, unless the movements of the enemy by water should place him in the rear of the former as well as the latter position. In that event, you would be compelled to place the Chickahominy between you and the enemy. At what point you can cross that river will depend on the course of the enemy. Should you find it necessary to fall back, the public roads leading up the Peninsula along the north side of the Chickahominy, and the present bridges over the upper part of that river, are considered the best, and in this connection, I would suggest that those roads and bridges be put in good order for use. I did not intend to advise the passage of the lower Chickahominy, in the contingency named, except in the event of your march by the upper route along the north side of that river being prevented by the enemy. Should such a state of things occur, you would be compelled to cross the river lower down, and I advised on that account an examination of the lower crossings and of the roads leading to them with a view to putting them in good condition, and also that you make the best preparation you can to enable your army to pass at these crossings, if necessary. In case the enemy succeed in passing your lower river batteries so as to threaten your line of march across the Chickahominy, as above indicated, I further advise that you should take measures to keep the road open as long as might be necessary to enable you to withdraw. For this purpose, I advise that you should prepare to destroy such wharves on the York & James Rivers in the rear of your present lines, as the enemy would be likely to use for landing their troops. Of course it would not be necessary to extend these preparations to other wharves higher up the river than those which the enemy would probably employ for that purpose, nor would it be necessary to destroy any wharves until in your judgment the danger becomes imminent. I further advised, with the same object of keeping open your line of march across the Chickahominy, that you should prepare to make such display of force in front of the landings which the enemy may approach, as will retard their advance from the rivers to the interior of the country in your rear. The object of all the precautions advised by me, is to secure and keep open the best practicable route by which you can retire behind the Chickahominy, in the event of the enemy getting in the rear of your lines at Williamsburg in the manner indicated, and forcing you to withdraw behind that river.

I am General very respy, your obt serv't

R. E. LEE
General Commdg

142   To GENERAL JOHN C. PEMBERTON
Commanding Department of South Carolina, Georgia, and Florida
TELEGRAM

Richmond
April 10, 1862

BEAUREGARD IS PRESSED FOR TROOPS. SEND, IF POSSIBLE, [GENERAL DANIEL S.] DONELSON'S BRIGADE OF TWO REGIMENTS TO CORINTH. IF MISSISSIPPI VALLEY IS LOST ATLANTIC STATES WILL BE RUINED.

VERY RESPECTFULLY,

R. E. LEE

143   SPECIAL ORDERS, NO. 6

Headquarters, Richmond, Virginia
April 12, 1862

The Departments of Norfolk and the Peninsula are embraced for the present within the limits of the operations of the Army of Northern Virginia. General J. E. Johnston will direct the military and naval operations in these departments. The commanders of the departments and navy-yards, while conforming to his instructions, will make their reports and requisitions, as heretofore, to the proper departments in Richmond until further orders.

By order of the President:

R. E. LEE
General Commanding

144   To GENERAL RICHARD S. EWELL
Rappahannock, Virginia

Headquarters, Richmond
April 17, 1862

General:

Your letter of the 16th has been received. Genl Johnston telegraphed his views to you on the subject. Should they not conflict with your proposition, & you feel reasonably assured that you can strike a successful blow at the enemy in your front, you are authorized to do so. Communicate with Genls Jackson [Commanding Valley District] & [Charles W.] Field [Commanding at Fredericksburg], that the former may be advised & the latter push forward a light corps on your right. The more active the troops on the Rappahannock, the more on the defensive will the enemy be kept.

I need not caution you to be watchful & prudent & not to compromit your command. The safety of your line depends on it.

I have the honour to be, your obt servt

R. E. LEE
Genl

145   To GENERAL HENRY HETH
Commanding at Lewisburg, Virginia

Headquarters, Richmond, Virginia
April 18, 1862

General:

The report of the strength of the enemy in Shenandoah Valley renders it probable that he may succeed in occupying Staunton. Your communication by that route will in that event be cut, and you must rely on the Virginia & Tennessee Railroad. It will depend upon the ability of the enemy and his further movements whether you may not be obliged to fall back toward Lynchburg. In that event you must endeavor to hold the passage of the Blue Ridge. To this end have your army in a movable condition, and keep in communication with Genl Edward Johnson, who, if compelled, will retire through Waynesboro to the Blue Ridge. All surplus ammunition and stores should be sent to Lynchburg, the movements of the enemy carefully watched, and every preparation made to make your army effective and formidable. You must also keep Genl

H. Marshall advised of your movements, and of the necessities which govern them, who, under similar contingencies, will move to Abingdon, and, if unable to form a junction with you, will retire east of the Blue Ridge into N[orth] C[arolina], probably through Taylorsville. Should you have any suggestions tó make as to the proposed movements under the necessity supposed, I shall be pleased to receive them.

I am very respectfully, your obt servt

R. E. Lee
General

146   To GENERAL HUMPHREY MARSHALL
Commanding at Lebanon, Virginia

Headquarters, Richmond, Virginia
April 18, 1862

General:

Should the enemy in the Shenandoah Valley be able to reach Staunton, Genl Heth will be compelled to retire upon Lynchburg. In that event you may not be able to maintain your position, but be obliged to fall back upon Abingdon, and, should circumstances require, to join Genl Heth, and unite in the endeavor to hold the line of the Blue Ridge. With this view I have to request that you prepare yourself and command for the execution of any movements that may be necessary, and satisfy yourself as to the best routes, & should you be unable to form a junction with Genl Heth, to ascertain the best route into North Carolina from Abingdon, or other point on the road at which your march may be interrupted. Genl Heth has been directed to keep you advised of his movements and their necessity. Place your army in as movable and effective a condition as possible.

I am very respy, your obt sev't

R. E. Lee
General

147   To GENERAL EDWARD JOHNSON
Commanding at Shenandoah Mountain, Virginia

Headquarters, Richmond, Virginia
April 18, 1862

General:

I have received information that Genl Jackson has fallen back to Big Spring, some 9 miles from New Market, and that the enemy is still pressing him in the direction of Staunton. If he is forced to continue to retire, he will do so by the way of Swift Run Gap, in order to form a junction with the forces of General Ewell, and hold the Blue Ridge Mountains at that place. You are directed to keep yourself in communication with General Jackson, and regulate your movements by those he may be forced to make. If he is compelled to retire to Swift Run Gap it will be necessary for you to move to Staunton; and should you find the enemy marching in too strong force, for you to resist, upon that place, you must retire towards Waynesboro & endeavor to hold the passage through the Blue Ridge Mountains. In view of these contingencies, it is advisable that you send all your heavy baggage and surplus stores at once to Charlottesville, keeping your force light and movable, so that if the necessity to retire should arise you could do so without incumbrance and preserve a firm face to the enemy. You might keep a small, active force at your present position, as long as you deem prudent, in order to make [mask] the movement of your army from the enemy in your front.

I am very respect'y, your obt serv't

R. E. LEE
General

148   To GENERAL CHARLES W. FIELD
Commanding near Fredericksburg, Virginia

Headquarters, Richmond, Virginia
April 19, 1862

General:
Your letter of the 17th instant is received. I desire that you shall do everything in your power to prevent the enemy from advancing from Fredericksburg or making that place a base. I shall order to Hanover Junction to support you, in such manner as you may direct, two local regiments of artillery, armed and serving as infantry, a field battery, and a body of horse. I have received information, obtained from a wounded prisoner, that the enemy's force at Fredericksburg consisted of one regiment of cavalry, about five hundred strong, one regiment of infantry, and two batteries of artillery, and that their entire force on the lower Potomac is less than five thousand. You will use every exertion to ascertain the strength and movements of the enemy, and keep me informed of the same. You will also communicate with General Ewell as to the movements of the enemy, in order that in case of necessity, that officer

may send you reinforcements if it be in his power. I desire also that you will render all the assistance you can in obstructing the Rappahannock River below Fredericksburg, to prevent the ascent of the enemy's boats. I am informed by the Secretary of the Navy that some naval officers have been sent to the Rappahannock for that purpose, and also to provide fire ships to oppose the enemy. You will also watch closely any movements of the enemy from Urbana or Tappahannock in the direction of West Point or the Pamunkey River. Should such an attempt be made, you will do everything in your power to prevent it.

I call your attention particularly to the importance of exercising the utmost caution in destroying the railroad & bridges. This should not be done except as a measure of extreme necessity, as great injury may result from our advance being retarded or prevented. In connection with the subject of preventing the enemy's boats from ascending the Rappahannock, I am informed to day that there are six tug boats off Urbana, two very large, moving up the river.

I am very respy, your obt sev't

R. E. LEE
General

149   To GENERAL CHARLES W. FIELD
Commanding near Fredericksburg, Virginia

Headquarters, Richmond, Virginia
April 19, 1862

General:

Since my letter of this morning I have received verbal reports of the evacuation of Fredericksburg, which have caused me regret. I wish you to give an official account, that I may have a true state of the case on record. The number of the enemy, manner of approach, and when first discovered.

In securing the stores, those most valuable ought to be first removed, and it is necessary to give particular attention to all kinds of ammunition.

I have the honor to be, your obt servt

R. E. LEE
General

150   To GENERAL JOHN C. PEMBERTON
Pocotaligo, South Carolina

Headquarters, Richmond, Virginia
April 20, 1862

General:

I regret very much to be obliged to reduce the force in your department, & would rather increase it if possible. But from present appearances it will be necessary to collect additional troops to oppose the advance of the enemy, who has now reached the Rappahannock, & may move upon Richmond from that direction as well as from the coast, where he is assembling large bodies of troops. I fear therefore to be obliged to draw further detachments from your department & desire you to consider where they can best be spared, & to make every exertion to arm the new regiments still remaining in Georgia & South Carolina. I have no arms to send from here but pikes, which you might place in the hands of the men at the batteries, & give their guns to troops in the field, by a proper distribution of guns & pikes in this way, the troops that are now unarmed might become effective. Can you not send on a good brigade for operations on the Rappahannock?

I am very resp, yr obt svt

R. E. LEE
Genl

151   To GENERAL CHARLES W. FIELD
Commanding near Fredericksburg, Virginia

Headquarters, Richmond, Virginia
April 21, 1862
6 a.m.

General:

I am directed by Genl Lee to acknowledge the receipt of your letter of 20th instant, with its enclosures, reporting the supposed strength and intentions of the enemy in your front, and to say that no efforts will be spared to reinforce you as soon as possible. He wishes you to preserve a firm front to the enemy, to keep yourself accurately advised of his strength and movements, and to communicate anything of importance that may occur, at once to this office. The telegraphic operator with his instruments will be sent you to day. Several regiments from the

South are expected to day or to night and will be forwarded without delay to your support. The general instructs me to add that he desires you to keep your force as near the enemy as is prudent, and not to retire further than is positively necessary.

I am very respecty, your obt sevt

W. H. TAYLOR
A. A. G.

152   To GENERAL THOMAS J. JACKSON
Commanding Valley District

Headquarters, Richmond, Virginia
April 21, 1862

General:

General Field reports the occupation of Falmouth by about 5,000 of the enemy, under Genl [Christopher C.] Augur, and that it is stated that Genl [Irwin] McDowell with a large force is landing at Aquia. Five of the enemy's gunboats have ascended the Rappahannock as far as Spotswood Bar five miles below Fredericksburg. I have no doubt an attempt will be made to occupy Fredericksburg and use it as a base of operations against Richmond. Our present force there is very small and cannot be reinforced except by weakening other corps. If you can use Genl Ewell's division in an attack on Genl [N. P.] Banks and to drive him back, it will prove a great relief to the pressure on Fredericksburg, but if you should find Genl Banks too strong to be approached and your object is to hold Genl Ewell in supporting distance to your column, he may be of more importance at this time between Fredericksburg and Richmond. I do not know whether your column alone will be able to hold Banks in check and prevent his advance up the Valley, but if it will, and there is no immediate use for Genl Ewell's command with yours, I would suggest the propriety of its being held in readiness to reinforce General Field. Please communicate with me on this subject, should I get further information from Fredericksburg of importance I will transmit it to you.

Genl Field has abandoned Fredericksburg, burned the bridges over the Rappahannock and retired fourteen miles south of the town.

I have the honor to be, your obt servt

R. E. LEE
Genl

153   To GENERAL RICHARD S. EWELL
Commanding Third Division

Headquarters, Richmond
April 21, 1862

General:

Your letter of the 20th has been received. When I wrote to you in reference to your proposition to advance against the enemy in your front I was under the impression that General Johnston had communicated with you by telegraph. It seems it was by letter, and I therefore see no reason for doubting the fidelity of the telegraph line, which you think may be involved. I am ignorant of the strength of the enemy east of the Rappahannock in your late front. General Field has been compelled to abandon Fredericksburg. General Augur's division (reported 5,000 strong) is said to occupy Falmouth, and General McDowell, with a large force, to be landing at Aquia. General Field thinks that an attempt will be made to advance on Richmond from that direction. If it is practicable to strike a speedy blow at General Banks and drive him back it will tend to relieve the pressure on Fredericksburg.

I do not know where the forces said to be approaching Fredericksburg are drawn from, unless from those attributed to Banks' column.

I have the honor to be, your obedient servant

R. E. LEE
General

154   To GENERAL JOSEPH E. JOHNSTON
Commanding Army of Northern Virginia

Headquarters, Richmond, Virginia
April 21, 1862

General:

I have just received your letter of the 20th instant giving the result of your examination of the lines occupied by your army. I regret the defects they exhibit, and trust it may be in your power to remedy them, or to assume a position better calculated for your purpose. Having no knowledge of their character or condition except from report, I can offer no suggestions for their improvement, but should be glad to receive your views as to what can best be done under all the circumstances that surround your position that I may lay them before the President.

The *Virginia* has not been returned to dock, I am informed, since her last visit to Hampton Roads, but is at the Navy Yard having her port shutters adjusted in their places. She is ready for service at any moment. Her commander is Flag Officer [Josiah] Tatnall.

The steamers *Patrick Henry, Jamestown, Beaufort, Raleigh* and *Teazer*, under command of Captain [John R.] Tucker, are in the mouth of James River. I have written to night that my letter may be ready for your courier in the morning.

I am very respectfully, your obt serv't

R. E. LEE
General

155   To HIS WIFE
               "White House," Virginia

Richmond
April 22, 1862

I received this morning dear Mary your letter of 20th & will give to Custis & Mary their enclosures. I send a letter from Fitzhugh whom I understand is very well & has been active in front of the enemy. I got a report of a reconnaissance he made of the enemy's position in Stafford, giving their numbers &c., which was very good. I will ask Custis to give you all the news, as he circulates with the young people & thus collects it. I saw Mary Sunday. Not so well. As usual at this time among the women, bothered what to do. I fear she may become burdensome to her kind hosts. I sent to you Saturday a letter from Rob. He had a wretched cold & was then at New Castle guarding some prisoners. He no doubt is with Jackson's army in the Blue Ridge near Swift Run Gap. The enemy is pressing us on all sides. I hope a kind Providence will protect us & drive them back. I trust your new position will be agreable. As before stated it is more retired from the line of the enemy than the W[hite] H[ouse], though by no means removed. Should they be able to advance up York River their boats can ascend the Pamunkey to the Piping Tree [Road], the road from which to Richmond passes immediately by Mrs. Braxton's, the Old Church &c., & I think in sight of Mr. Layre's. There is another consideration, for it is always well to look at the worst phaze of a subject, suppose the army is driven south of James River & you are encompassed in the enemy's lines. How are you to live? The Confederate money would be valueless & the Virginia money perhaps not very cur-

rent if I could get it to you. But there is the difficulty & it has been in
view of these sad reverses, which God in his mercy forbid may ever
happen, that I have recommended a more distant move to Carolina or
even Georgia. This is for your own consideration & not for public discussion which would only be mischievous. The corn ought to be sold as
I wrote Charlotte & the wheat too. She will have to manage for her husband now. I want to see you all very much but do not know when that
can be. Tell Chass I hope she is not more sick than she wishes to be.
Perhaps she just wants to see her papa. If so she must come up & bring
Life & stay with him. I will tell her all about Fitzhugh. There is to be a
wedding to night. A poor young girl, Miss Addie Deans to Dr. Lyons,
son of the James'. Did you ever hear of such a thing! In such times to
think of such trivial amusements! The news from N[ew] Orleans is
encouraging. It is reported but not confirmed that the forts below the
city still hold out, that two of the enemy's boats are sunk & that the
Louisiana (iron clad) went down last night to the assistance of the forts,
the fire of which had slacked. Neither is the enemy at Fredericksburg as
strong as reported. Give much love to all & many kisses. For yourself
know always that I am truly

R. E. Lee

156   To GENERAL JOSEPH E. JOHNSTON
Commanding Army of Northern Virginia

Headquarters, Richmond, Virginia
April 23, 1862

General:
    A dispatch from Genl Field to day reports all quiet in his front.
The enemy has not crossed the Rappahannock and the gunboats that
were arrested in their ascent by the obstructions at Spotswood Bar have
left the river. I presume his numbers are much exaggerated for if Genl
Augur had the force attributed to him, or if Genl McDowell had reached
Aquia, I think they would have occupied Fredericksburg. I think it
probable, that finding our weakness in that quarter the enemy will now
endeavor to seize upon Fredericksburg and make use of the Rappahannock as a means of approach. In addition to the force under Genl Field
left by you, I have ordered to him two regiments and a light battery
from this city, probably over 1,000 men, [Colonel William E.] Starke's
Virginia and [Colonel James L.] Orr's South Carolina regiments, over
2,000 men, [General Maxcy] Gregg's South Carolina brigade, and
J. R. Anderson's brigade from North Carolina. I hope this may enable

him to occupy his former position or at least to preserve a strong front against any advance of the enemy. In my dispatch to you on this subject I had not intended to propose a division of your army, but thought it possible some regiments might in your opinion be better applied towards the Rappahannock, as among the reports furnished us was one that the enemy was sending back troops to the Potomac. Should the force now sent to the Rappahannock not be sufficient to arrest a forward movement from that river, I will inform you, and then you must consider how far it will involve the necessity of a retrograde movement on your part. But in the meantime, referring to your letter of the 20th, should there be reason in your opinion for a withdrawal from the Peninsula, I beg you will state them with your recommendation that I may submit them to the President. You can best judge of the difficulties before you, and know the interests involved in the question.

I have the honor to be, your obedient sev't

R. E. Lee
General

157   To GENERAL RICHARD S. EWELL
      Commanding Third Division

Richmond, Virginia
April 25, 1862

General:

I had the honor to receive your letter of the 23d instant. Your intelligence of the movements of the enemy from the direction of Warrenton toward Fredericksburg corresponds with what I have received from other sources. I think the enemy is establishing a strong force at that point, with a view perhaps of making a diversion or a real attack against Richmond. It has occurred to me as probable that for this purpose he has stripped his line between the Rappahannock Bridge and Manassas; if not, it must be so weakened that I hope a blow from the combined forces of yourself and General [T. J.] Jackson can destroy him. Should he have evacuated that region, and you are not required to oppose General Banks' column, by uniting such part of your force as can be spared with General Field, a successful blow might be struck at the enemy in front of Fredericksburg. At last accounts he had not crossed the Rappahannock nor repaired the bridges.

Several steamers, containing men and towing barges and flat boats, probably with the view of bridging the river, were ascending the Rappahannock.

In addition to Field's brigade, about 5,000 troops, including two field batteries, under Brig Gen J. R. Anderson, have reached Fredericksburg; 3,000 more are on the way, but have not reached this city.

I have written to General Jackson on this subject. Please forward the letter without delay, and gain all information of the position and movements of the enemy near you that you can.

Your obedient servant

R. E. LEE
General

158   To GENERAL THOMAS J. JACKSON
Commanding Valley District

Richmond
April 25, 1862

General:

I have received your letter written on the evening of the 23rd referring to a communication from Genl Field to Genl Ewell.

I have hoped in the present divided condition of the enemy's forces that a successful blow may be dealt them by rapid combination of our troops, before they can strengthen themselves either in their position, or by reinforcements. I do not know what strength Genl Banks shows in your front. As far as I can learn, Genl Augur's division now opposite Fredericksburg has been drawn from the neighborhood of Warrenton. A second division, with which Genl McDowell is said to be, is reported as being directed upon Fredericksburg from the same point. It is certain that the enemy have not yet occupied Fredericksburg, but that several steamers containing troops and towing canal boats laden probably with provisions, and flat boats for the purpose perhaps of forming a bridge across the river, have ascended the Rappahannock, and I think from all indications they are collecting a strong force at that point.

For this purpose, they must weaken other points, and now is the time to concentrate on any that may be exposed within our reach. If Banks is too strong in numbers and position to attempt, cannot a blow be struck at the enemy in the direction of Warrenton, by a combination of your own and Ewell's command? With this view Genl Edward Johnson might be brought nearer to you. The dispersion of the enemy in that quarter would relieve Fredericksburg. But if neither of these movements be advisable, then a combination of Ewell and Field might be advisable, and a direct blow be given to the enemy at Fredericksburg. That you may judge of the practicability of this step I will mention, that in addition to Field's brigade, about 5,000 troops under Genl J. R. Anderson, including two field batteries, have joined him, and 3,000 on their way to him are yet to pass through this city. The blow wherever struck, must, to be successful, be sudden and heavy.

The troops used, must be efficient and light. I cannot pretend at this distance to direct operations depending on circumstances unknown to me and requiring the exercise of discretion and judgment as to time and execution, but submit these suggestions for your consideration.

I am general very respy, your obt servt

R. E. Lee
Genl Comdg

159   To GENERAL JOSEPH R. ANDERSON
Richmond, Virginia

Headquarters, Richmond, Virginia
April 25, 1862

General:

You will proceed with your brigade to the vicinity of Fredericksburg, where Brig Genl C. W. Field now is with the troops which have preceded you, and assume command of the operations of our army in that quarter, being the senior general officer. If it be impossible to drive the enemy from his present position, I desire you to lose no effort to keep him confined to the smallest possible margin. Particularly is your attention called to the importance of preventing the navigation of the Rappahannock by the enemy's boats so as to forbid their using the river as an avenue of supply. Instructions were given sometime since to obstruct the river at Holmes' Hole, a little above Tappahannock. This however was reported by Genl Field to be impracticable and you are desired to confer with him as to the best place and mode of effecting the obstruction. The means of land transportation at your command will be limited, and your attention is called to the importance of reducing the baggage of the troops to the smallest quantity necessary, limiting that of the regiments to the regimental cooking utensils and tents, and that of the officers to the regulation allowance. For all the information concerning the movements, strength and probable intentions of the enemy, and also of the means at our command for opposing him in his advance from Fredericksburg, you are referred to Genl Field, who will also afford you valuable assistance in becoming acquainted with the topographical features of the country in which you are to operate.

I am very respy, your obt sev't

R. E. LEE
General

160   To MISS AGNES LEE
"Hickory Hill," Virginia

Richmond
April 26, 1862

My Precious Daughter:

I received your note of the 24th this morning by mail. I will reply by the same mode as I presume Mr. W[ickham] has not come to R[ichmond]. I am delighted to hear from you & hope you are well. I had learned from your mother that you & Charlotte had gone to Hickory Hill & that she & Annie expected to leave for Mr. Layre's house on Monday. The rain will however have made the roads very bad & streams high & I doubt whether will be able to do so. I am glad you have the opportunity of visiting Hickory Hill & its sweet occupants. You must give my love to them singly & collectively. I hope the Federals will not have an opportunity to pay them a visit, though they seem now to have the ability to go where they choose. They will have a pleasant time if they get there any how. I wish I had pleasant tidings to give but there are none & we must struggle along as we can & hope for the best. I have not seen Mary for some days. She is still at Mrs. Caskie's & does not yet to tire of Richmond. I will deliver your message when I see her. I have written to Charlotte & will place this under cover to her. Mrs. Phebe Warwick has gone to join Miss Sallie within a day or two. I met her riding out with Spouse the other evening. Cupid is very active & weddings are abundant. The Smoking Club in Franklin Street, concealed in a cloud of its own raising, is untouched by his arrows. The Macfarlands & others are about leaving I understand.

God bless you my dear child.

Affy your father

R. E. LEE

161   To GENERAL RICHARD S. EWELL
               Commanding Third Division

Headquarters
Richmond, Virginia
April 27, 1862

General:

I have just received by the hands of Lt Alexander your letter of the 26th instant. It was my object in my letter of the 25th to explain briefly the position of the enemy north of the Rappahannock, and to suggest the practicability of a combination of your army with Genl Jackson, to strike at Genl Banks, or should that be not advisable, & your force not required to hold Banks in check, that with the available part of it for other operations, you should unite yourself with the forces under Genls Anderson & Field, & drive back the enemy attempting the occupation of Fredericksburg. My views were more fully set forth in my communication to Genl Jackson, & my desire was that you should possess yourself of the necessary information for any movement that might be determined on.

I am very resp, yr obt svt

R. E. LEE
Genl

162   To GENERAL THEOPHILUS H. HOLMES
               Goldsboro, North Carolina

Headquarters, Richmond, Virginia
April 28, 1862

General:

I have had the honor to receive your letter of the 25th instant relative to the removal of a brigade from your command, and giving your objections to a further decrease of your force. You will have learned since the date of your letter, as I informed you in mine of the 26th, of the arrival of arms at Wilmington, and the assignment of a portion of them, to your order, for the purpose of arming the new troops within your department. The number turned over to you together with those collected by your agents and those of the State, will enable you to arm, it is hoped, six new regiments. The need for troops in the vicinity of Fredericksburg is very urgent, and they can contribute to the defence of

North Carolina as materially at that point, as they would in assisting to prevent an advance from the enemy now occupying the eastern waters of the State. In view of the pressing necessity for reinforcing the army operating in Northern Virginia, and of the assignment of arms to troops in your department, I determined to order a brigade of your forces to the vicinity of Fredericksburg, as you were advised on the 26th. You will please forward the command you may select without unnecessary delay, and lose no efforts to supply their places by some of the new regiments at Raleigh. I would also request that if it can possibly be spared, you will forward some of the land transportation heretofore used by the troops which have been withdrawn from North Carolina. Wagons & teams are much needed by the army collecting near Fredericksburg.

I am very respectfully, your obt serv't

R. E. Lee
General

163   To GENERAL THOMAS J. JACKSON
Commanding Valley District

Headquarters, Richmond, Virginia
April 29, 1862

General:

I have had the honour to receive your letter of yesterday's date. From the reports entitled to credit which have reached me, the force of the enemy opposite Fredericksburg is too large to admit of a reduction of our army in that quarter. By so doing it would not only open an attack upon Richmond, but might jeopardize the safety of the army in the Peninsula by threatening its rear. I very much regret my inability to send you the reinforcements you desire & which might enable you to make an advantageous movement. Unless a sufficient force can be obtained by a union of the command of Genls Edward Johnson, Ewell & your own, there is no other way of obtaining one. Should this not enable you to move against Genl Banks, I think you would at least be able to dispense such troops as may be in the vicinity of Warrenton. Should however the enemy have evacuated that region, then a portion of Genl Ewell's force could be detached to Fredericksburg where he might be able to strike a successful blow at the enemy still north of the Rappahannock. It may be necessary to detach Genl Ewell with one of his brigades in any event from his present position & assign him to the command of the troops in the Aquia district. The enemy seems to have concentrated his force on his two flanks, leaving his center open, & we shall have to do the same to oppose him. Please inform me whether Genl Ewell with one of his brigades can be spared for this service, & whether with the remaining force you could hold the upper country against Banks.

I am very respy, your obt servt

R. E. Lee
Genl

164   To GENERAL JOSEPH E. JOHNSTON
              Commanding Army of Northern Virginia

Headquarters, Richmond, Virginia
April 30, 1862

General:

Your letter of the 27th reporting the condition of affairs on the Peninsula has been received. The preparation of Batteaux by the enemy indicates, I think, an attack on Gloucester Point, in conjunction with his general attack upon your lines. The presence of the *Virginia* in York River would disconcert that part of his plan, as well as the ascent of York River. I have conversed with the Secretary of the Navy, who thinks the *Virginia* should repair to Yorktown, and that it might be accomplished at night. Should you, after hearing from Flag Officer Tatnall, determine upon this measure, could you arrange a signal to call the steamer to you, should you not be able to designate the precise time. Coal will have to be prepared for her at Yorktown. Do you wish any sent? I trust you may be able to retain command of York River, but we must make every preparation for a disaster which may occur, and I will write to Genl Huger to prepare him for the contingency apprehended. Operations for obstructing the channel of the James River at a point eight miles below the city have been in progress ever since my arrival. I regret to state it is not completed, and the work has been much retarded by freshets and the want of means of transportation, all of the latter being in requisition for troops and provisions for your army. The quartermaster says that the bridges across the Chickahominy in this vicinity are repaired, except one which will be finished to morrow. Bottom's, Long & Forge Bridges below required much work. Workmen are now engaged on them and they are directed to use every exertion to complete them.

Most respecty, your obt serv't

R. E. Lee
General

165   To GENERAL BENJAMIN HUGER
Norfolk, Virginia

Headquarters, Richmond, Virginia
April 30, 1862

General:

The movements of the enemy near Elizabeth City do not seem to indicate a real attack, and is probably intended to distract attention from other points, or to watch that entrance into the sound by which they seem to apprehend the introduction of our gunboats. It will be necessary for your scouts to be vigilant and your troops prepared. The subject of Genl Johnston's letter is of a more serious nature. If he is obliged to retire from the Peninsula and thus liberate the enemy's gunboats, &c., his attention will naturally be turned to Norfolk. His possession of James River would render the evacuation of Norfolk in time necessary. Its possibility as well as practicability had better therefore be considered now, in order that it be executed at the most opportune moment. I need hardly suggest to you that the troops be put in as movable condition as possible. That all surplus stores, &c., be sent to a place of safety, and that without evacuating any place that you consider important, what is not deemed essential for its defence be withdrawn. Your knowledge of what would be required in the event of the necessity contemplated will point out the proper course to be pursued, and I feel every assurance that it will be pursued with discretion, judgment, and energy. It will be necessary for you to see the means of transportation, routes, &c. Being disembarrassed of surplus stores and other articles the troops can be withdrawn in the presence of the enemy with order and celerity. The safety of all ammunition must require your particular attention. Whatever arrangements you find it necessary to make, will of course be preparatory and be done quietly.

I have the honor to be, your obt servt

R. E. LEE
Genl

166   To GENERAL THOMAS J. JACKSON
Commanding Valley District

Headquarters, Richmond
May 1, 1862

General:

Your letter of the 29th ultimo is received, and I have carefully considered the three plans of operation proposed by you. I must leave the selection of the one to be adopted to your judgment. So far as rein-forcements at this time are concerned, I have already informed you of the state of affairs that prevents me from sending them. You will there-fore use your discretion in employing the forces now available so as to accomplish the best result you can attain. If you can strike an effective blow against the enemy west of Staunton it will be very advantageous. You might then avail yourself of your success, to bring with you Genl Johnson's command, leaving a guard on the road beyond Staunton, and move your army thus reinforced back to the Blue Ridge. Should your combined forces, with those of Genl Ewell prove strong enough to war-rant an attack on Genl Banks, it might then be made. But if this should not be the case, as my information of Banks' strength leads me to sup-pose, you would by this combination be enabled to leave a force sufficient to mask your movement, and send a strong column to attack the enemy at White Plains or Salem. This would threaten Banks' communication at Winchester and probably cause him to fall back. It might also relieve the pressure at Fredericksburg. You must use your judgment and discretion in these matters, and be careful to husband the strength of your com-mand as much as possible. Two signal men have been ordered to you. They can readily instruct as many as you may require.

I am general very respy, your obt servt

R. E. Lee
Genl Comdg

167   To GENERAL RICHARD S. EWELL
                 Commanding Third Division

Headquarters, Richmond, Virginia
May 1, 1862

General:

Your letter of the 30th ultimo, with the enclosures, is received. A letter from Genl Jackson of the 29th ultimo apprised me of a movement towards Staunton which he had in contemplation, and which is doubtless that referred to by you. This explains the necessity of your occupying the place of Genl Jackson until his return. All information I have re-ceived confirms your intelligence with regard to the force of the enemy in front of the Rappahannock towards Manassas. It is desirable to remove the supplies in the country referred to by you, but I do not know how it can be done. The cattle, horses, &c., might be driven off, and I advise that you continue to accumulate stores at Gordonsville for your command. You will keep your command in readiness to move towards Fredericksburg, or to co-operate with Genl Jackson in any movement he may make against the enemy at the White Plains, or Salem, as occasion may require.

I am genl very respy, your obt serv't

R. E. LEE
Genl Comndg

168   To GENERAL JOSEPH E. JOHNSTON
Commanding Army of Northern Virginia

Headquarters, Richmond, Virginia
May 2, 1862

General:

Your letter of the 1st instant has been received and your directions to Genl Huger, Capt [S. Smith] Lee, & Flag Officer Tatnall forwarded to Norfolk. The Secretary of War went to Norfolk this morning to make arrangements preparatory to the evacuation of that department and for securing the public property at the forts and Navy Yard and to endeavor to send the unfinished gunboats to this city. All the time that can be gained will facilitate these operations. It is not known under what necessity you are acting, or how far you can delay the movements of the enemy, whom it is presumed will move up York River as soon as opened to him to annoy your flank. His advance on land can be retarded, and he might be delayed in effecting a landing on York River until your stores are withdrawn. The safety of all your ammunition is of the highest importance and I feel every assurance that everything that can be accomplished by forethought, energy, and skill on your part will be done. If it is possible for the *Virginia*, which upon the fall of Norfolk must be destroyed, to run into Yorktown at the last moment, and destroy the enemy's gunboats and transports, it would greatly cripple his present and future movements, relieve your army from pursuit, and prevent its meeting the same army in Northern Virginia.

I have the honor to be, your obt serv't

R. E. LEE
Genl

169   To GENERAL RICHARD S. EWELL
                    Commanding Third Division
                            TELEGRAM

                                    From Richmond
                    (Received at Gordonsville May 6, 1862)

IF ENEMY HAVE WITHDRAWN FROM HARRISONBURG I SEE NO NECESSITY
FOR YOUR DIVISION AT SWIFT RUN GAP. OBJECT MAY BE CONCENTRATION AT
FREDERICKSBURG. TRY AND ASCERTAIN. CAN YOU CUT OFF PARTY AT CULPEPER
COURT HOUSE?

                                                R. E. LEE
                                                General

170   To GENERAL BENJAMIN HUGER
                    Norfolk, Virginia

                                Headquarters, Richmond, Virginia
                                                May 8, 1862
General:
    I have received your letter of the 6th instant. With regard to the
movements of the steamer *Virginia*, it is deemed of the utmost importance that she guard the entrance to James River, to prevent its ascent
by the gunboats of the enemy. I am aware of the aid she can render in
the evacuation of the batteries at Sewell's Point & Craney Island, but it
is believed that she will as effectually cover this movement while stationed at the mouth of James River, as if in Hampton Roads. The enemy
would not be likely to attempt to cross from the opposite side, while she
was within so short a distance, and she would moreover in this position
prevent any movement to cut you off by landing a force above. It is
desired that you send the Blakely gun to this city. Such troops as you
may find expedient to send by the way of Garysburg will continue to
Petersburg. It is intended to hold the line of railroad from the latter place
to Weldon, but no points east of it not necessary for its security. It will
be necessary therefore to station a force sufficient for the purpose at
convenient points near the road, the remainder of the troops of your department to move to this city, except the regiment of Col [William J.]
Clarke, as previously advised.

                    I am very respecty, your obt serv't

                                                R. E. LEE
                                                General

171   To GENERAL JOSEPH E. JOHNSTON
            Commanding Army of Northern Virginia

Headquarters, Richmond, Virginia
May 8, 1862

Your letter of the 8th has just been received. Those to which you allude as having received yesterday were prepared for my signature and being unexpectedly called away and not wishing to detain the messenger, I directed Major [Walter H.] Taylor to affix my signature and send to you. The one referring to the telegram of Genl Loring was merely intended to advise you of the progress of the evacuation of Norfolk, and what had been done to maintain the posts guarding the communication to that place until the evacuation was completed, and which was supposed to be in accordance with your general instructions on the subject. Nothing was done to interrupt the portion of Genl [Raleigh E.] Colston's brigade joining him. I consider your authority to extend over the troops on both sides of James River, and have transmitted as rapidly as I could all the orders sent to me. I do not recollect your having requested information relating to the other departments of your command to be forwarded by any other means than the usual course of the mails, and supposed the commanders were in direct correspondence with you. I advised you on the 23rd of April of certain troops having been ordered to report to Genl Field, viz, two regiments from this city raised for local defence, 2 light batteries, a brigade from South Carolina, & a brigade from North Carolina, making in all about 8,000 men, in addition to those previously there. The brigade of Genl J. R. Anderson, having been sent from North Carolina by Genl Holmes, places Genl Anderson in command of the troops, he being the senior officer present. He has taken position about Massaponax, south of Fredericksburg, extending his pickets towards Port Royal. I understand that the enemy has built a bridge of boats across the Rappahannock opposite Fredericksburg, but has not yet occupied the town. His troops occupying the hills in Stafford, his left being opposite Port Royal, his strength estimated at from 15 to 20,-000. Genl Ewell at last reports was at Swift Run Gap, a portion of his division being at Stanardsville. General Jackson was at Staunton, with a view of uniting with Genl Edward Johnson and attacking Genl [Robert H.] Milroy, who was not far from Buffalo Gap. Genl Banks was reported as having evacuated Harrisonburg and passed down the Valley, his main body being beyond New Market. It has occurred to me that his object may be to form a junction with Genl McDowell on the Rappahannock. I have telegraphed my apprehension to both Genls Jackson & Ewell to place them on their guard. Two brigades, one from North Carolina and one from Norfolk have been directed under the orders of the President to proceed to Gordonsville, to reinforce that line, which at onetime was threatened by a column from Warrenton, the advance of which entered Culpeper Court House. The obstructions of James River are progressing as rapidly as possible, and batteries in process of erection for their defence. I know of no one more competent to direct the construction of these works than Major [Walter H.] Stevens, if not wanted with your army.

In reference to the obstruction of the Pamunkey, before it was commenced the subject was referred to you, and directions were given for the preparation of material, procuring of pile driver, &c. The river had been previously examined for that purpose and the best position stated to be about 8 miles below the railroad bridge. Capt [Charles S.] Carrington, who understood the work, was directed to report to you for instructions and any aid he might require. But from the difficulty of communicating with you and the necessity of the case, and being only able to use the boats in the river, the work I fear has been imperfectly done, all the transports however were carried above the obstructions and their cargoes I understand are at present secure. The quartermaster and commissary departments will be informed as to the point to which to send you provisions. The President has heard with much pleasure of the handsome manner in which the enemy was dislodged on the afternoon of the 6th by a portion of your command, and your commendatory remarks on the officers engaged have been reported to him.

Most respy, your obt serv't

R. E. LEE
General

172   To GENERAL RICHARD S. EWELL
Commanding Third Division, beyond Gordonsville

Headquarters, Richmond, Virginia
May 8, 1862

General:

I have had the honor to receive your letter of the 6th instant reporting the movement of the enemy down the Valley & the condition of affairs east of the Blue Ridge. As I telegraphed you on the same day as the date of your letter, I see no necessity for retaining your division at

Swift Run Gap, if it is ascertained that the intention of the enemy is to retire from the Valley and that he no longer meditates an advance towards Staunton. From present indications it is thought that the column under Genl Banks will attempt to form a junction with that opposite Fredericksburg under Genl McDowell. If you ascertain this to be the fact, an opportunity might be presented for intercepting Banks' march & striking him a blow while en route for Fredericksburg, & with this view it is suggested that you move the bulk of your command to Gordonsville on the line of the Rappahannock, so as to have it available for this purpose, & moreover to enable you more readily to form a junction with the force this side of Fredericksburg under Genl Anderson, if necessary. A small force could be left to watch the pass through Swift Run Gap if the above course is adopted. I have today written to Genl Jackson advising him of the contents of this letter. Should you move you will report the fact to him.

In addition to the brigade of General [L. O'Bryan] Branch, that of Genl [William] Mahone from the Department of Norfolk, has been ordered to Gordonsville to report to you for duty. Two regiments of the latter have already left this city for that place.

I am very respecty, your obt servt

R. E. Lee
Genl

173   To GENERAL THOMAS J. JACKSON
              Commanding Valley District

Headquarters, Richmond, Virginia
May 8, 1862

General:
Your letter of the 5th instant reporting your presence at Staunton and the movement of the troops en route to that place, has been received. I have not seen Capt [John D.] Imboden, if I can find him I will urge him to join you with such men as he can at once, as you desired. From the retrograde movement of the enemy down the Valley, and their apparent intention to leave it, it is presumed that Genl Banks contemplates a move in the direction of Fredericksburg for the purpose of forming a junction with the column of Genl McDowell in front of that city. Should it be ascertained that this is his intention, there will be no necessity for retaining the division of Genl Ewell at Swift Run Gap, and I have already so advised Genl Ewell by telegraph on the 6th, and again by letter to day,

at the same time suggesting to him the practicability of striking Banks a
blow while en route to Fredericksburg. With this view it was recommended that he move the bulk of his command to Gordonsville or the
line of the Rappahannock, leaving a sufficient force to watch the pass
through Swift Run Gap. Moreover in this latter position he would be
enabled the more readily to reinforce Genl Anderson, who is this side of
Fredericksburg, if necessary. Of course the above course would only
be pursued when it was positively ascertained that the enemy intended
leaving the Valley. Genl Ewell states in his letter of the 6th instant that
he will not leave his position at Swift Run Gap until the enemy have entirely left the Valley or until he has orders to that effect from you.

I am very respectfully, your obt serv't

R. E. Lee
Genl

174   To GENERAL JOSEPH E. JOHNSTON
           Commanding Army of Northern Virginia

Headquarters, Richmond, Virginia
May 10, 1862

General:
Your two letters of the 9th have been received. The object of the
President in obtaining a general for the portion of your army on the
Rappahannock was with a view that operations of its several divisions
might be combined to attack the enemy, who seemed to have exposed
himself and his lines of communication, and to prevent any movement
that might threaten your rear. He still thinks such a commander very desirable, but as the condition of things is now changed, and the branches
of your army are brought nearer, it may not be so important, as it was
while you were occupied in front of Yorktown. Your command still
includes the Department of Northern Virginia and the Army of the Rappahannock is under your control. In addition to the three guns originally
at Drewry's Bluff several navy guns have been mounted and every exertion is being made to render the obstructions effective and the battery
commanding it as formidable as possible. It would appear from your letter (9th) that you had not received mine of the 8th giving you detailed
information as regards the strength and position of our army near Fredericksburg. I presume it has subsequently reached you. In a letter this
morning received from Genl Anderson he reports that the enemy have
crossed over one regiment perhaps more. Genl [Marsena R.] Patrick

[U. S. Army], brigade commander, has headquarters in Fredericksburg. He [General Anderson] states the strength of enemy at nearly 40,000 and increasing.

I am very respecty, your obt serv't

R. E. LEE
General

175   To GENERAL JOSEPH R. ANDERSON
Commanding near Fredericksburg, Virginia

Headquarters, Richmond, Virginia
May 11, 1862

General:

I had the honor to receive your letter of yesterday's date. You are correct in your conjectures relative to the force sent to Gordonsville and the object in collecting it in that quarter. It was hoped that a favorable opportunity would have been presented for penetrating the country and cutting Banks' communication with Alexandria and relieving the pressure on Fredericksburg. Genl Ewell, in the event of a forward movement, would have communicated with you. He is now at Swift Run Gap and may yet be detained there some days as Genl Jackson has united with Genl Edward Johnson and is driving the enemy back towards Cheat Mountains. As regards the force of the enemy opposite Fredericksburg, I have good reason to believe that it has been much exaggerated. From a secret agent who has been through their lines I learn that the force immediately opposite the town is not more than 36 or 3700 and from 10,000 to 15,000 between that and the Potomac. It is stated that there is no intention of an advance by this column in this direction, but it is merely to divert our attention and withdraw troops from other sections. The agent also reports that this is the object of Banks' column. I think if McDowell was as strong as reported to you he would have crossed the Rappahannock before this. You must not however relax your watchfulness or fail to take advantage of any false step of the enemy, and will of course conform all your movements to the direction of Genl Johnston.

I am very respectfully, your obt serv't

R. E. LEE
General

176   To GENERAL JOSEPH E. JOHNSTON
          Commanding Army of Northern Virginia

Richmond, Virginia
May 12, 1862
4 A.M.

General:

Your letter of 10:30 p.m. May 10, 1862, has just been received. I must suppose that some of my letters to you have miscarried.

The army on the Rappahannock is located on the line on which you placed it. General Jackson in the Valley, General Ewell in the direction of Gordonsville, and General J. R. Anderson, senior officer, with the troops near Fredericksburg, in the vicinity of that city. General Jackson has been moved to General Edward Johnson, and General Ewell has been called by him to Swift Run Gap. General Anderson is on the Massaponax Hills, south of Fredericksburg.

The enemy is in front of each of these divisions, and reported to be in greater strength than either. That opposite Fredericksburg, by last accounts from General Anderson, approaches 40,000. Probably it is the whole of McDowell's column, and I hope exaggerated.

As our troops recede the enemy will naturally follow. Toward what point in the vicinity of Richmond do you desire them to concentrate?

General Huger has left Norfolk, and I presume the enemy is in it. General Holmes at Goldsboro. A brigade from Generals Holmes and Huger has been drawn into Virginia to strengthen the army on the Rappahannock. It is in this way that General Anderson becomes the commanding general at Fredericksburg. I will forward him any directions you may have for his guidance and for the other divisions of your army. If General Anderson retires south of the junction of the Central and Fredericksburg Railroad it will interrupt the railroad communication with Generals Jackson and Ewell, and from the tenor of your letter it may be necessary for him to come nearer this city.

Very respectfully, your obedient servant

R. E. LEE
General

177   To HIS WIFE
                            "White House," Virginia

                                                        Richmond
                                                        May 13, 1862

My Dear Mary:
    I can only write a few lines to you. It is very late & I got but little
sleep last night & have been much occupied all day. But the loss of the
Virginia has produced such profound sensation that all personal considerations are smothered. I fear Agnes will not be able to get up. I will leave
with Mr. Caskie funds for you. All I have in bank. Tell Annie & the girls
it will be necessary for them to take the bonds &c. The thing is done &
cannot be undone. I desired to make some arrangement to provide for
them as well as I could. I wish it was better, but I hope it may be sufficient for their wants. It is better it should be so. I have considered
the matter maturely. I had intended writing a letter to them all, explain-
ing the matter & my reasons. I wish it to stand & hope it may serve their
convenience & comfort. As for yourself I will leave the bonds either
with Mr. Caskie or Mr. John Stewart (whose house we occupy). They
are coupon bonds & if lost are gone. The girls' [bonds] are registered,
& can be renewed.
    Custis will write & tell you everything.
    God bless you my dear wife & children.

                                                        Truly & affec

                                                        R. E. LEE

178   To GENERAL JOSEPH E. JOHNSTON
             Commanding Army of Northern Virginia

                                                Headquarters, Richmond
                                                        May 15, 1862

General:
    I have the honor to forward for your information the following
copy of a dispatch just received from Maj Genl Ewell, dated Swift Run
Gap, May 14, 1862: "Under instructions from Genl Jackson I am moving
down the Valley. I have ordered a part of the forces to cross the ridge
via Madison Court House & Fisher's Gap."

Genl Mahone who is in command at Drewry's Bluff where he has most of his brigade, reports that the enemy's gunboats opened on the batteries on the river this morning at eight o'clock. Only the two iron boats engaged, no one exposed and no chance for sharp shooters. No signs of landing.

I am very respy, your obt serv't

R. E. LEE
General

179   To GENERAL BENJAMIN HUGER
Petersburg, Virginia

Headquarters, Richmond, Virginia
May 16, 1862

General:

I have received your letter of this morning. As regards the future movements of the enemy, it is impossible to divine which plan of attack he will adopt. I presume however he will avail himself of the river as far up as possible. He may come beyond City Point, he may go to Port Walthall. It would appear advisable therefore that you keep your command light and movable, so as to move with celerity to any point he may select. The river should be well picketed by trusty men to keep you advised of any movement up the river by the boats and transports of the enemy. I think the Blackwater [River] too far removed for you to keep a force stationed there, it would be in constant danger of being cut off and too remote to be relieved. I expect the reports in Col [Harrison B.] Tomlin's letter are much exaggerated. They cannot have the tremendous force which they are represented to have everywhere. If they are in such strength along the Norfolk road they cannot come in the same strength up the river. Any considerable force that may advance from Norfolk must diminish the army on the Peninsula, this McClellan is not likely to do for he is even now calling for reinforcements. In retiring along the Norfolk and P[etersburg] Railroad it should be so destroyed as to prevent its use by the enemy. So far as I can learn the road is almost intact. The stone piers of the bridges should be destroyed as well as the bridges themselves.

If you find that the enemy is coming up the river it may be necessary for you to retire in this direction, so as to take a part in the contest which must take place near Richmond. It is advisable that you make all arrangements in view of this contingency.

Very respectfully, your obt serv't

R. E. LEE
Genl

180   To GENERAL THOMAS J. JACKSON
Commanding Valley District

Headquarters, Richmond, Virginia
May 16, 1862

General:

Your letter of the 14th instant is received. Genl Ewell has no doubt informed you that on the 14th the brigades of Genls [James] Shields and [Nathan] Kimball, about 7,000 strong with 36 pieces of artillery and two companies of cavalry, were reported as marching on Front Royal from New Market. Banks has fallen back on Strasburg, and the Manassas Gap Railroad is in running order from the latter point to Alexandria. Banks may intend to move his army to the Manassas Junction and march thence to Fredericksburg, or he may design going to Alexandria, and proceeding thence by water either to Fredericksburg, or as I think more probable, to the Peninsula to reinforce McClellan, who is calling for reinforcements as I learn. Whatever may be Banks' intention it is very desirable to prevent him from going either to Fredericksburg or to the Peninsula, and also to destroy the Manassas road. A successful blow struck at him would delay, if it does not prevent, his moving to either place, and might also lead to the recall of the reinforcements sent to [General John C.] Frémont from Winchester, as reported by you. Genl Ewell telegraphed yesterday that in pursuance of instructions from you, he was moving down the Valley, and had ordered part of the troops at Gordonsville to cross the ridge by way of Madison Court House & Fisher's Gap. The troops sent to Gordonsville were ordered to report to Genl Ewell, and can be employed in making the movement on Banks.

But you will not, in any demonstration you may make in that direction, lose sight of the fact that it may become necessary for you to come to the support of Genl Johnston, and hold yourself in readiness to do so if required. There are indications of an intention on the part of McClellan to move his army to the James River. The gunboats attacked our battery on that river about 8 miles below the city yesterday and retired after a cannonade of two hours and a half, having sustained some damage, as is reported. The two signal men ordered to you, and a third subsequently sent, were directed to proceed to Swift Run Gap, and may be with Genl Ewell. Whatever movements you make against Banks do it speedily, and if successful, drive him back towards the Potomac, and create the impression as far as practicable that you design threatening that line.

I am general very respecty, your obt serv't

R. E. Lee
General

181   To GENERAL JOSEPH E. JOHNSTON
Commanding Army of Northern Virginia

Headquarters, Richmond, Virginia
May 17, 1862

General:

I had the honor to reply yesterday to that portion of your letter of the 15th instant relating to the works and obstructions for the defence of James River. In relation to the information brought by your scouts of the position of the Federal Army and your impression that Genl McClellan may place his troops in communication with the fleet on James River, I think there can be little doubt as to the correctness of your views on this latter point. It is evidently now his best policy to do so, and it is fair for us to conclude that his operations in front of Yorktown will be re-enacted in front of the obstructions on James River, unless you can prevent it. Will it be possible for you to strike him a successful blow in the passage of his army to James River and before he can have the co-operation of his gunboats? Should his course to James River be below the mouth of the Chickahominy, this will be difficult. But should his march be across the Chickahominy his passage between that river and the James may furnish you the opportunity. Although I have little doubt but that you have already considered this subject, your attention is now invited to it by direction of the President. I am endeavoring to organize and arm the companies of heavy artillery that have been serving at the different batteries on the Peninsula and at Norfolk, and expect to form two regiments: the companies of one are now with Genl Huger, of the other, in this city. The latter with all the other companies that can be armed will be ordered down to you as soon as possible.

I am very respecty, your obt serv't

R. E. Lee

182   To GENERAL JOSEPH E. JOHNSTON
          Commanding Army of Northern Virginia

                                        Headquarters, Richmond
                                        May 18, 1862

General:

I am directed by the President to say that, in locating your troops in the neighborhood of Richmond, he requests you will give strict orders that the residences, inclosures, gardens, &c., shall be strictly respected. Besides the individual injury that will otherwise result, the feelings of the people, now thoroughly enlisted in aid of the operations of the army, may be alienated from it.

He desires also that private houses be not taken for the use of the army without the consent of the owners and to their discomfort, as it has been stated to him in some instances has been done, no doubt without your knowledge.

As you are now so convenient to the city the President wishes you to confer with him upon your future plans, and for that purpose desires you to see him at his office.

Please say when it will be convenient for you to come in.

                    I have the honor to be, your obedient servant

                                        R. E. LEE
                                        General

183   To GENERAL JOSEPH E. JOHNSTON
          Commanding Army of Northern Virginia

                                        Headquarters, Richmond, Virginia
                                        May 21, 1862

General:

The President desires to know the number of troops around Richmond, how they are posted, and the organization of the divisions and brigades; also the programme of operations which you propose. The information relative to the composition and position of your army can readily be furnished, but your plan of operations dependent upon circumstances perhaps yet to be developed, may not be so easily explained, nor may it be prudent to commit it to paper.

I would therefore respectfully suggest that you communicate your views on this subject personally to the President, which perhaps would be more convenient to you and satisfactory to him.

I am very respy, your obt serv't

R. E. LEE
General

184   To GENERAL JOSEPH E. JOHNSTON
          Commanding Army of Northern Virginia

Headquarters, Richmond
May 22, 1862

General:

Your letter of this morning by Major [Jasper S.] Whiting has been received and I can only assure you that there is no question as to the extent of your authority or command. The troops at and around Drewry's Bluff are commanded by Genl Mahone and are a part of Genl Huger's division, whose operations you of course control. As regards the work at Drewry's Bluff it was commenced under the general plan and superintendence of Captain [Alfred L.] Rives and subsequently has been placed in immediate charge of the Navy. The system adopted is so far advanced, as to render it hazardous to change it, and the only thing to be done is to strengthen and complete it as fast as possible. Capt [John J.] Clarke is considered the constructing engineer and I see no objection to Major Stevens having the general control if his other duties will permit, or at least to his giving Capt Clarke and the naval officers in charge the benefit of his experience and knowledge. But the President is unwilling to disturb the arrangement with the Navy Department now existing, further than is necessary to insure the general control of the military operations now exercised by Genl Mahone, who is of course subject to your orders.

I am general most respy, your obt serv't

R. E. LEE
General

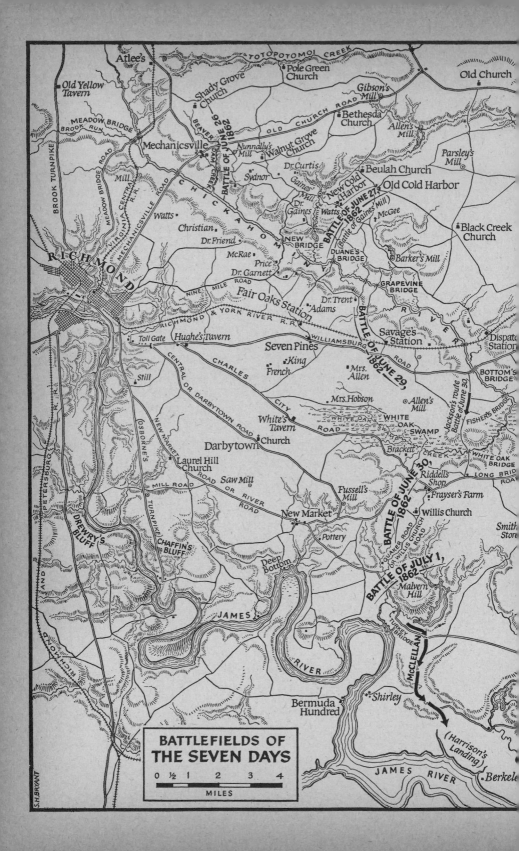

BATTLEFIELDS OF
THE SEVEN DAYS

0 ½ 1   2   3   4
MILES

CHAPTER FIVE

The Seven Days

"Soldiers, the country will thank you"

BEFORE THE VALLEY CAMPAIGN was completed, Lee, by the chance of a stray bullet, was finally given field command. On May 31, President Davis forced General Johnston to leave his entrenchments and attack McClellan at Seven Pines (today a part of a Richmond suburb). During the "phenomenally mismanaged battle," Joe Johnston rode toward the front — some say to avoid Davis's approaching entourage — where he took a heavy wound. The army devolved on the second in command, Gustavus W. Smith, and on the second day of the fighting he suffered a mental or nervous collapse. After the inconclusive action was over, Lee, who had been "available" since the war began, was given command of the heterogeneous collection of troops assembled in front of Richmond.

Given this force in an emergency, when his reputation was low with the public, Lee was soon to mold it into the Army of Northern Virginia. From his assumption of command, the character of the war changed in Virginia and he changed from the long-suffering "expediter." To the end, to all ends, he continued his tactful deference to the President, under whose authority he remained, but he made his own decisions and he made the army in the field his army. There were certain restrictions imposed by Davis and certain interferences, especially concerning the shuttling about of troop units, but the hodgepodge of divisions and brigades, battalions, legions and what-not, assumed the single character impressed upon the body of men and units by Lee's leadership.

When Lee took command, his first purpose was to put into practice his long-suppressed strategy of counteroffensive — to concentrate for attack at a point of *his* selection rather than to wait on the enemy's initiative. In twenty-five days after he assumed command, June 26, he opened the boldest and most ambitious action hitherto attempted in the war.

During the weeks of Lee's preparation for his counterstroke, McClellan's army lay in an arc from due east of Richmond to northeast, with his naval-supported base on the Pamunkey at the White House (the former home of Martha Washington, which had been inherited by General Lee's son, Rooney). The arc of McClellan's position was sliced by the swampy Chickahominy, and Fitz-John Porter's large corps, north of the water barrier, was separated from the rest of the army. McClellan made this unsound arrangement in the expectation of McDowell's bringing 50,000 men down from Fredericksburg to join Porter in a huge pincer movement on Richmond. Had McClellan been permitted to execute this movement, the Confederates would have had no choice except to evacuate the capital. In the city the citizens, with only little-regarded Lee as their protector, feared the worst, and their apprehensions were excited by Professor Lowe's observation balloon, from which their daily rounds were watched.

General Lee's plan depended on the *threat* of Jackson's Valley campaign holding McDowell at Fredericksburg, while Jackson slipped to Richmond and cooperated in a counter-pincer on Porter's separated corps. To accomplish this, Lee shifted the bulk of the army — the divisions of Longstreet, A. P. Hill and D. H. Hill — to the north of Richmond, across the Chickahominy and mostly hidden from Porter. Jackson, making a forced march from the Valley, was to come in on Porter's flank and rear. In design it was a flawless trap, accompanied by the large hazard of leaving Richmond defended from the east against McClellan's main army only by the indifferently organized forces under Magruder and Huger. However, Lee had forced the soldiers — over complaints and criticisms — to the digging of heavy fieldworks. With some assurance from these breastworks, Lee audaciously took his risk chiefly on the calculation that McClellan would not attack until McDowell came.

As has often been pointed out, Lee's strategy was a little grand for that stage of development of the collection of units he had inherited. Then, his personal staff, which had grown to seven (as large as he was ever to have during the war), was relatively inexperienced. The three who were to evolve into the nucleus of his permanent personal staff were civilians: young Walter Taylor was a businessman, Venable a mathematics professor, and Marshall, a kinsman of the chief justice, a lawyer. Inevitably tactics were not up to supporting the strategy.

However, Lee seized the initiative, McClellan went on the defensive, and, despite breakdowns in detail and brutal casualties, Lee kept pressing

him. From June 26 through July 1, the Confederates won only one
clear-cut victory, at Gaines' Mill on the second day. But this was a key
battle, sending Porter's forces back across the Chickahominy — with
heavy losses in men, guns and supplies — and precipitating the general
retreat of McClellan's army. Lee attempted another trap, at Frayser's
Farm (or Glendale), and then in desperation made a disjointed assault at
Malvern Hill on July 1. The Seven Days Battle lasted actually six days;
the seventh day was McClellan's retreat to a new base on the James
River at Berkeley plantation, called in Federal dispatches Harrison's
Landing, from the private wharf of the historic builders of the great
plantation.

In seven days the military situation was changed from a two-armed
siege threatening Richmond into a defeated Federal army huddling
under the protection of gunboats in the miasmic lowlands twenty-odd
miles from the capital. Basically, the change went much deeper. After
one year of successive losses through a defensive policy, Lee's initiative
had disrupted the enemy's plan and for the first time in the war the Confederacy was on the offensive.

Lee's battle report (at the end of the chapter) is a charitable account
of the running action, and places no blame on the subordinates who, in
one way and another, caused collapses in the details of Lee's plan.
Measured by his intentions, Lee's success was incomplete (as he con-
fessed to his wife), but measured by its effects on the war it was incal-
culable. Personally in that one week General Lee emerged from obscurity into world-wide fame and founded the prestige in the Confederacy that was to make him its greatest figure. After thirteen frustrating
months, he emerged quite suddenly as the General Lee of the legend.

185   SPECIAL ORDERS, NO. 22

Headquarters, Richmond, Virginia
June 1, 1862

I. In pursuance of the orders of the President, General R. E. Lee
assumes command of the armies of Eastern Virginia and North Carolina.

The unfortunate casualty that has deprived the army in front of
Richmond of the valuable services of its able general is not more deeply
deplored by any member of his command than by its present commander. He hopes his absence will be but temporary, and while he will
endeavor to the best of his ability to perform his duties, he feels he will
be totally inadequate to the task unless he shall receive the cordial support of every officer and man.

The presence of the enemy in front of the capital, the great interests involved, and the existence of all that is dear to us appeal in terms too strong to be unheard, and he feels assured that every man has resolved to maintain the ancient fame of the Army of Northern Virginia and the reputation of its general and to conquer or die in the approaching contest.

II. Commanders of divisions and brigades will take every precaution and use every means in their power to have their commands in readiness at all times for immediate action. They will be careful to preserve their men as much as possible, that they may be fresh when called upon for active service. All surplus baggage, broken down wagons, horses, and mules, and everything that may embarrass the prompt and speedy movement of the army will be turned into depot. Only sufficient transportation will be retained for carrying the necessary cooking utensils and such tents or tent flies as are indispensable to the comfort and protection of the troops.

By order of General Lee:

W. H. Taylor
Assistant Adjutant General

186   To MAJOR WALTER H. STEVENS
            Chief Engineer, Army of Northern Virginia

Headquarters
Dabb's House
June 3, 1862

Major:
I desire you to make an examination of the country in the vicinity of the line which our army now occupies, with a view of ascertaining the best position in which we may fight a battle or resist the advance of the enemy. The commanding points on this line I desire to be prepared for occupation by our field guns and the whole line strengthened by such artificial defences as time and opportunity may permit. My object is to make use of every means in our power to strengthen ourselves, and enable us to fight the enemy to the best advantage. It is not intended to construct a continuous line of defence or to erect extensive works. Having selected the line and put the works in progress of construction, I desire you to resume the examination and see what other positions can be taken nearer Richmond in case of necessity. You will please make requisitions upon the commanders of divisions in the vicinity of the works to be constructed for such working parties as may be necessary. You must also make arrangements to collect such tools as may be with the

army, and I have to request that you will push forward the work with the utmost diligence.

I am very resp'y, your obt servt

R. E. LEE
General

187   To MAJOR WALTER H. STEVENS
Chief Engineer

Headquarters, Dabb's House
June 4, 1862

Major:

I am much gratified to learn by your letter of today that you have commenced a line for the occupation of our troops and hope you may be able to obtain a satisfactory one. Strengthen its natural positions by artificial defences. The plan you propose for doing this is approved, and I hope you will be able to prosecute the work with vigor. I last evening directed Capt [Alfred L.] Rives to send 200 spades, and shovels & picks in proportion, & 50 axes to you. Should Maj [Alfred M.] Barbour have a sufficient quantity of tools to enable you to dispense with these, please have them returned. I have also directed him to send you such engineer officers as are available. I enclose you a copy of a general order issued today relative to the establishment of a pioneer corps.

I am very resply, yr obt servt

R. E. LEE
General

P.S. I wish you particularly to cause an examination to be made of the nature of the ground along the York River Railroad, to see whether or not some heavier guns might be placed there, as I think the only way the enemy can get his heavy guns up that way will be by the railroad.

R. E. L.

188   To JEFFERSON DAVIS
Richmond, Virginia

Headquarters near Richmond
June 5, 1862

After much reflection I think if it was possible to reinforce Jackson strongly, it would change the character of the war. This can only be done by the troops in Georgia, South Carolina & North Carolina. Jackson could in that event cross Maryland into Pennsylvania. It would call all the enemy from our Southern coast & liberate those states. If these states will give up their troops I think it can be done. McClellan will make this a battle of posts. He will take position from position, under cover of his heavy guns, & we cannot get at him without storming his works, which with our new troops is extremely hazardous. You witnessed the experiment Saturday. It will require 100,000 men to resist the regular siege of Richmond, which perhaps would only prolong not save it. I am preparing a line that I can hold with part of our forces in front, while with the rest I will endeavour to make a diversion to bring McClellan out. He sticks under his batteries & is working day & night. He is obliged to adhere to the railroad unless he can reach James River to provision his army. I am endeavouring to block his progress on the railroad & have written up to see if I can get made an iron battery on trucks with a heavy gun, to sweep the country in our front. The enemy cannot move his heavy guns except on the railroad. You have seen nothing like the roads on the Chickahominy bottom. Our people are opposed to work. Our troops, officers, community & press. All ridicule & resist it. It is the very means by which McClellan has & is advancing. Why should we leave to him the whole advantage of labour. Combined with valour, fortitude & boldness, of which we have our fair proportion, it should lead us to success. What carried the Roman soldiers into all countries, but this happy combination. The evidences of their labour last to this day. There is nothing so military as labour, & nothing so important to an army as to save the lives of its soldiers.

I enclose a letter I have received from Genl D. H. Hill, for your own perusal. Please return it to me. I had taken means to arrest stragglers. I hope he is mistaken about his Brigadiers. I fear not in [General Gabriel J.] Rains' case. Of [General Winfield S.] Featherston I know nothing. I thought you ought to know it. Our position requires you should know everything & you must excuse my troubling you. The firing in our front has ceased. I believe it was the enemy's shell practice. Col Long [*illegible*] went down early this morning to keep me advised, but as I hear nothing from them I assume it is unimportant.

Very respy & truly

R. E. LEE

189   To COLONEL JOSIAH GORGAS
                    Chief of Ordnance

                                                        Headquarters
                                                        June 5, 1862
Colonel:
    Is there a possibility of constructing an iron plated battery, mount-
ing a heavy gun, on trucks, the whole covered with iron, to move along
the York River Railroad? Please see what can be done. See the Navy
Department & officers. If a proper one can be got up at once it will be of
immense advantage to us. Have you any mortars that we could put at
some point on the railroad?

                                                        Very respy

                                                            R. E. Lee
                                                            General

190   To GEORGE W. RANDOLPH
                         Secretary of War

                                            Headquarters, Near Richmond
                                                        June 5, 1862
Sir:
    I wrote to His Excellency the President this morning about re-en-
forcements for General Jackson. The troops from Georgia you propose
sending him I believe form a part of General Lawton's brigade. I wish
they were mine; but with the North Carolina Battalion, if they can join
him, will fill up his ranks. He ought to have more or these will not
materially aid him. His plan is to march to Front Royal and crush Shields.
It is his only course, and as he is a good soldier I expect him to do it.
    I telegraphed yesterday to Major [A. W.] Harman at Staunton to
collect all the troops in that vicinity, raise the community, magnify
their numbers, and march down the Valley and communicate with Jackson. It will shake Shields and make him pause.

                                                        Very respectfully

                                                            R. E. Lee
                                                            General

191   To GENERAL JOHN B. MAGRUDER
             Commanding, Thorne's House, Virginia

                                        Headquarters, Dabb's House
                                                      June 5, 1862
General:
     General Lee directs me to acknowledge the receipt of your letter
of this evening and to express his gratification at the handsome conduct
of our troops during the day. He only regrets that the working parties of
the enemy were not driven off this morning, as this would have rendered
our advantages greater. His object in directing the withdrawal of the
troops and the establishment of a picket only at Mr. James Garnett's
was to save the men the unnecessary exposure and fatigue which they
would incur if kept constantly drawn up in line of battle. He thought
the picket would give you such timely notice of the movements of the
enemy as to enable you to make the necessary disposition to resist and
repulse him should he attempt to occupy the position. At this distance he
cannot judge of the effect of the several combinations of the enemy
upon the positions we now hold to which you allude, nor does he intend
to give definite instructions in the case. He is unwilling however to
recede from a position when only threatened, and thinks our artillery
could as effectually damage the enemy as his would injure us. Mr. James
Garnett's place would be so important to him that it is highly desirable
to prevent his possession of it if we can do so without unnecessary or
unwarrantable sacrifice, and he wishes you under these circumstances to
resist him should he attempt to gain the position. As you are on the
ground he leaves the matter to your judgment and discretion, but suggests that the men be allowed to rest tonight if possible, and that the
necessary dispositions be made early in the morning should you determine to contest the occupancy of the place.

     I am general very respectfully, your obedient servant

                                        W. H. TAYLOR
                                        Major and Aide-de-Camp

192   To GENERAL THOMAS J. JACKSON
            Commanding Valley District

Headquarters, Department of Northern Virginia
June 8, 1862

General:

Your letter of the 6th has been received. I congratulate you upon defeating & then avoiding your enemy. Your march to Winchester has been of great advantage & has been conducted with your accustomed skill & boldness. I hope you will be able to rest & refresh your troops for a few days before compelled to enter upon active service. I desire you to report the probable intentions of the enemy & what steps you can take to thwart them. Should there be nothing requiring your attention in the Valley so as to prevent your leaving it a few days, & you can make arrangements to deceive the enemy & impress him with the idea of your presence, please let me know, that you may unite at the decisive moment with the army near Richmond. Make your arrangements accordingly, but should an opportunity occur for striking the enemy a successful blow do not let it escape you.

I am very resply, your obt servt

R. E. LEE

193   To GENERAL ROBERT RANSOM
            Petersburg, Virginia

Headquarters, Department of Northern Virginia
June 8, 1862

General:

Your letter of June 4th is received. I desire to reunite the regiments of your brigade, but I think the probability is there will be more need of your whole command at Drewry's Bluff than at Petersburg. I am now expecting Genl Holmes to reach Petersburg with a part of his command, when the troops with you can be ordered to Drewry's Bluff to join those now at that place, where they will be nearer the probable scene of action.

I am general very respy, your obt serv't

R. E. LEE
Genl Comdg

194   TO GEORGE W. RANDOLPH
                        Secretary of War
                           TELEGRAM
                                                    Headquarters
SIR: June 9, 1862

    I RECEIVED THIS MORNING A TELEGRAM FROM STAUNTON ANNOUNCING
A GLORIOUS VICTORY ACHIEVED BY THE GALLANT JACKSON AND HIS TROOPS.
IF CONFIRMED IT WILL ENABLE HIM TO TAKE THE OFFENSIVE AGAIN. RE-
ENFORCEMENTS WILL THEREFORE BE IMPORTANT TO HIM. THOSE YOU ORDERED
SHOULD GO ON IN THAT EVENT.
    VERY RESPECTFULLY, YOUR OBEDIENT SERVANT

                                                    R. E. LEE

195   To JEFFERSON DAVIS
                        Richmond, Virginia

                                                    Headquarters
                                                    June 10, 1862
Mr. President:
    I propose for your consideration sending two good brigades from
this army to re-enforce General Jackson. These, with the Georgia regiments now on the way, and [General Alexander R.] Lawton's brigade,
ordered to take the Lynchburg Railroad at Petersburg, will make him
strong enough to wipe out Frémont. With his whole force Jackson can
then be directed to move rapidly to Ashland, where I will re-enforce
him with fresh troops, with directions to sweep down north of the
Chickahominy, cut up McClellan's communications and rear, while I
attack in front. I can hold McClellan in his present position for a week
or ten days during this movement, and be getting our troops from the
south. I think this is our surest move. McClellan will not move out of his
intrenchments unless forced, which this must accomplish, and it will
hazard too much, with our inferior numbers, to attack him in them.
Please consider this immediately and decide. It must be commenced to
night. If you decide in favor, direct railroad transportation. Officer must
be sent to hasten Lawton along, who will require aid. I am reconnoitering
on our right and have sent cavalry in McClellan's rear to cut up foraging parties and wagon trains.

    Very respectfully, with high esteem, your obedient servant

                                                    R. E. LEE
                                                    General

196   To COLONEL ABRAHAM C. MYERS
                    Quartermaster General

                                        Headquarters, Dabb's House
                                                June 10, 1862
Colonel:
    This army has with it in the field little or no protection from the
weather. Tents seem to have been abandoned, and the men cover themselves by means of their blankets & other contrivances. The shelter tent
seems to be preferred by them, and I have thought that something could
be manufactured out of the tents now on hand better than what they
have in use. A simple fly or cloth of that shape would answer the purpose. This continued inclement weather I fear will produce great sickness & I desire to see what can be done for the protection and comfort
of the men. Please give me your views and the capabilities of the department to afford relief.

                            I am most respy, your obt servt

                                                R. E. LEE
                                                General

197   To HIS WIFE
                      Richmond, Virginia

                                                June 10, 1862
My Dear Mary:
    I only received yesterday your letter of the 6th announcing the
death of our little grandson. I cannot help grieving at his loss & know
what a void it will occasion in the hearts of his parents. But when I reflect
upon his great gain by his merciful transition from earth to Heaven, I
think we ought to rejoice. God grant that we may all join him around
the throne of our Maker to unite in praise & adoration of the Most High
forever. Write to Charlotte for me. When I left F[itzhugh] day before
yesterday he had not heard it.
    I have directed my trunk to be brought to Custis' room & now send
the key that he may get out the key of the box of papers he desires. It is
on a bunch which I think is in the drawer of the tray. He will know it. It
is cuniform & there is one on the bunch that resembles it but will not
fit. He had better take both. There are duplicates of the proper key. The
other key that resembles them is larger. Perry says Custis packed up his

flannel pants in his trunk. I hope he may find them there, but P[erry] is not entirely reliable. I wish you would place in my trunk the blue coat I return. It is of no use to me here & send me one of the linen coats in it. The thick linen I prefer. Though old it will answer for me to wear in the house. You must not think I am sick. I have taken cold this excessively hot weather, from being too thickly clad. I am better I hope to day. At any rate have not time to be sick. Give much love to everybody.

Truly & aft

R. E. Lee

198   To HIS WIFE
Richmond, Virginia

Near Richmond
June 10, 1862

My Dear Mary:
I have heard with great delight of your arrival in Richmond. I am strongly tempted to go in to see you. My constant duties here alone prevent, & preparations for the anticipated movement of troops will detain me. I will go up to see you as soon as I can. Where do you intend to locate yourself? Let me know. I hope your arrival will restore my dear Custis, about whom I have been very uneasy. Give much love to Annie & Life & tell them I want to see them badly.

Very truly & affectly

R. E. Lee

199   To GENERAL JOHN B. MAGRUDER
Commanding Division, Thorne's House, Virginia

Headquarters
June 11, 1862

General:
Two brigades of Genl [G. W.] Smith's division under Genl [W. H. C.] Whiting have been selected to reinforce temporarily Genl Jackson. This will render some change in the disposition of the troops in front of the enemy necessary. I desire you to extend your command to the York River Railroad. The brigades of Genls [William Dorsey] Pender & [James J.] Archer will as soon as relieved by you join the portion of Genl Smith's command under Genl A. P. Hill who has been directed to take position nearer to your left. If you find it necessary for the occupa-

tion of the ground between the Nine Mile road & railroad you can withdraw from your left such portion of your troops as may be requisite as
Genl A. P. Hill closes upon you. Make the movement quietly if practicable, consulting the comfort of the troops as well as the good of the
service, which I know your good judgment will insure.

I am general with great esteem, your obt serv't

R. E. LEE
General

200   To GENERAL AMBROSE P. HILL
Brooke Road, Virginia
TELEGRAM

Headquarters
June 11, 1862

GENL MAGRUDER HAS BEEN DIRECTED TO CLOSE BY THE RIGHT TO THE
YORK RIVER RAILROAD. HE WILL PROBABLY BE OBLIGED TO VACATE A PORTION
OF THE GROUND ON HIS LEFT, WHICH YOU MUST OCCUPY. THE BRIGADES OF
GENLS [WADE] HAMPTON, PENDER, & ARCHER HAVE BEEN DIRECTED TO REPORT
TO YOU. AS THEY ARE SUFFERING FROM SICKNESS I SUGGEST THEY BE PLACED
IN RESERVE.

R. E. LEE

201   To GEORGE W. RANDOLPH
Secretary of War
TELEGRAM

Headquarters, Dabb's House
June 11, 1862

SIR:

IT IS VERY DESIRABLE AND IMPORTANT THAT THE ACQUISITION OF TROOPS
TO THE COMMAND OF MAJ GENL T. J. JACKSON SHOULD BE KEPT SECRET.
WITH THIS VIEW I HAVE THE HONOR TO REQUEST THAT YOU WILL USE YOUR
INFLUENCE WITH THE RICHMOND NEWSPAPERS TO PREVENT ANY MENTION
OF THE SAME IN THE PUBLIC PRINTS.

I AM MOST RESPECTFULLY, YOUR OBEDIENT SERVANT

R. E. LEE
General

202   To GENERAL J. E. B. STUART
                  Commanding Cavalry

                                    Headquarters, Dabb's Farm
                                    June 11, 1862
General:
    You are desired to make a secret movement to the rear of the enemy
now posted on the Chickahominy with a view of gaining intelligence of
his operations, communications, &c., of driving in his foraging parties &
securing such grain, cattle, &c. for ourselves as you can make arrangements to have driven in. Another object is to destroy his wagon trains,
said to be daily passing from the Piping Tree road to his camp on the
Chickahominy.
    The utmost vigilance on your part will be necessary to prevent any
surprise to yourself & the greatest caution must be practiced in keeping
well in your front & flanks reliable scouts to give you information.
    You will return as soon as the object of your expedition is accom-
plished & you must bear constantly in mind while endeavoring to execute
the general purpose of your mission not to hazard, unnecessarily, your
command or to attempt what your judgment may not approve; but be
content to accomplish all the good you can, without feeling it necessary
to obtain all that might be desired.
    I recommend that you only take such men & horses as can stand the
expedition & that you take every means in your power to save & cherish
those you do take. You must leave sufficient cavalry here for the service
of this army, & remember that one of the chief objects of your expedition is to gain intelligence for the guidance of future operations.
    Information received last evening, the points of which I sent you,
lead me to infer that there is a stronger force on the enemy's right than
was previously reported. A large body of infantry as well as cavalry was
reported near the Central Railroad. Should you find upon investigation
that the enemy is moving to his right, or is so strongly posted as to
render your expedition inopportune, as its success in my opinion depends
upon its secrecy, you will, after gaining all the information you can,
resume your former position.

                I am with great respect, your obt serv't

                                    R. E. LEE
                                    General

203   GENERAL THOMAS J. JACKSON TO GENERAL LEE

Headquarters Valley District
Near Mount Meridian
June 13, 1862

General:

Your letter of the 8th instant was not received until this morning. From a letter received from [General James] Shields on the 11th, he was about ten miles above Luray in Pope county. From a letter received this morning from Frémont he was at Mount Jackson yesterday. Our cavalry have been upwards of (12) twelve miles beyond Harrisonburg. So circumstances greatly favor my moving to Richmond in accordance with your plan.

I will remain if practicable in this neighborhood until I hear from you, and rest the troops who are greatly fatigued.

You can halt the reenforcements coming here if you so desire, without interfering with my plans provided the movement to Richmond takes place. So far as I am concerned my opinion is that we should not attempt another march down the Valley to Winchester until we are in a condition under the blessing of Providence to hold the country. Gratefully appreciating your kind expression,

I remain general your obdt servt

T. J. JACKSON
Maj Genl

(INDORSEMENT)

Respectfully referred for the information of the President. I think the sooner Jackson can move this way, the better. The first object now is to defeat McClellan. The enemy in the Valley seem at a pause. We may strike them here before they are ready there to move up the Valley. They will naturally be cautious & we must be secret & quick. Will you ask the Secretary to make arrangements for moving Jackson down if you agree with me, as soon as his troops are refreshed a little. They must rest in the journey. Please return me this letter that I may reply.

R. E. LEE
Genl

(INDORSEMENT)

Views concurred in.

J[EFFERSON] D[AVIS]

204   To GENERAL THOMAS J. JACKSON
                    Commanding Valley District

                                Headquarters, Near Richmond, Virginia
                                                    June 16, 1862
General:

I have received your letter by the Honorable Mr. [A. R.] Boteler [Confederate Congressman]. I hope you will be able to recruit and refresh your troops sufficiently for the movement proposed in my letter of the 11th. You have only acknowledged my letter of the 8th. I am therefore ignorant whether that of the 11th has reached you. From your account of the position of the enemy, I think it would be difficult for you to engage him in time to unite with this army in the battle for Richmond. Frémont and Shields are apparently retrograding, their troops shaken and disorganized, and some time will be required to set them again in the field. If this is so the sooner you unite with this army the better. McClellan is being strengthened, Burnside is with him and some of McDowell's troops are also reported to have joined him. There is much sickness in his ranks but his reinforcements by far exceed his losses.

The present therefore seems to be favorable for a junction of your army and this. If you agree with me the sooner you can make arrangements to do so the better. In moving your troops you could let it be understood that it was to pursue the enemy in your front. Dispose those to hold the Valley so as to deceive the enemy, keeping your cavalry well in their front and at the proper time suddenly descending upon the Pamunkey. To be efficacious the movement must be secret. Let me know the force you can bring and be careful to guard from friends and foes your purpose and your intention of personally leaving the Valley. The country is full of spies and our plans are immediately carried to the enemy. Please inform me what arrangements you can make for subsisting your troops. Beef cattle could at least be driven and if necessary we can subsist on meat alone. Unless McClellan can be driven out of his entrenchments he will move by positions under cover of his heavy guns within shelling distance of Richmond. I know of no surer way of thwarting him than that proposed. I should like to have the advantage of your views and be able to confer with you. Will meet you at some point on your approach to the Chickahominy.

I enclose a copy of my letter of the 11th lest the original should not have reached you.

                    I am with great respect, your obt servant

                                                    R. E. LEE
                                                    General

205   To GENERAL THEOPHILUS H. HOLMES
          Commanding, Goldsboro, North Carolina

Headquarters, Dabb's House
June 18, 1862

General:

By information received direct from Norfolk it is ascertained that at a "council of war" held at Fort Monroe a short time since, Genl McClellan expressed an inability to take Richmond without the cooperation of Genl Burnside, and that the force of the latter should advance by way of James River, landing and taking the batteries at Drewry's Bluff in rear, the gunboats being unable to reduce them. It is also ascertained that Genl Burnside has reinforced McClellan with 14,000 men. This is reported from several different sources; in one instance the language is, "embarked at Norfolk with 14,000 men" and proceeded to join McClellan. It may be that his troops were transported to Norfolk through the canal. All reports however agree that he has formed a junction with the army under McClellan. In event of Burnside's ascending James River it will be necessary for you to oppose him with your whole force, and it was with this view that I desired you to concentrate at or near Petersburg, so as to have your command available to move speedily to the threatened point.

I am very respectfully, your obt serv't

R. E. LEE
General

206   To GENERAL THEOPHILUS H. HOLMES
        Commanding Department between James and Cape Fear Rivers
                    Petersburg, Virginia

Headquarters
June 21, 1862

General:

I congratulate you upon the arrival of your troops at Petersburg. Your command has been extended from the Cape Fear to the James River & I desire you to take charge of the military operations in the whole department. Your headquarters will be established where most convenient. It is difficult to say what may be the course adopted by the enemy, but I think he will endeavor to break up the batteries at Drewry's & Chaffin's Bluffs to let his gunboats up to Richmond. Should he attempt this on the south side you will of course resist it with all the force in your department. Should he attempt it on the north side of James River, you may be able to reinforce the army on this side.

I am very anxious to get the assistance of [General Robert] Ransom's brigade in the operations of next week. Could you prepare it, & should there be no movement on your side of the river send it with light baggage for temporary service? I will telegraph you as to the time & think it will be about Tuesday. It can either come by rail, or if you place it near Drewry's, it might cross on the pontoon bridge.

I have explained to Genl Ransom, Burnside's movements & probable intentions, & have requested him to give you the information.

I am with high esteem, your obt servt

R. E. LEE
Genl

207   To STEPHEN R. MALLORY
Secretary of Navy

Headquarters, Dabb's House
June 21, 1862

Sir:

I have been informed by Col Gorgas that the railroad battery will be ready for service tomorrow. Inasmuch as this battery has been constructed by the Navy, I would be pleased if you assigned an officer and a requisite number of men to take charge of and operate it. If you desire to do so, I request that you will designate the officer at once, as I wish to place the battery in position tomorrow.

I am very much obliged to you for your kindness as well as promptness in its construction.

I am very respy, your obt serv't

R. E. LEE

208   To MRS. W. H. F. LEE
White Sulphur, North Carolina

Dabb's
June 22, 1862

I must take a part of this holy day, my dearest Chass, to thank you for your letter of the 14th. I am very glad that my communication after the battle reached you so opportunely and relieved your anxiety about your Fitzhugh. He has, since that, made a hazardous scout, and been protected by that Divine Providence which, I trust and pray, may always smile on, as I know it will ever watch over you and yours. I sent you some account of this expedition in a former letter, as well as the order of General Stuart, on the subject. It was badly printed, but may serve to show you that he conducted himself well. The General deals in the flowering style, as you will perceive if you ever see his report in detail; but he is a good soldier, and speaks highly of the conduct of the two Lees, who, as far as I can learn, deserve his encomiums. Your mama is very zealous in her attentions to your sick brother. He is reported better. I think he was a few evenings since, when I saw him, and a note this morning from her states that he slowly improves. I hope he will soon be well again. He is much reduced, and looks very feeble. I suppose he will be obliged to go to the "N. C. White Sulphur" to keep you young women company. How will you like that? And now I must answer your inquiries about myself. My habiliments are not as comfortable as yours, nor so suited to this hot weather, but they are the best I have. My coat is of gray, of the regulation style and pattern, and my pants of dark blue, as is also prescribed, partly hid by my long boots. I have the same handsome hat which surmounts my gray head (the latter is not prescribed in the regulations) and shields my ugly face, which is masked by a white beard as stiff and wiry as the teeth of a card. In fact, an uglier person you have never seen, and so unattractive is it to our enemies that they shoot at it whenever visible to them, but though age with its snow has whitened my head, and its frosts have stiffened my limbs, my heart, you well know, is not frozen to you, and summer returns when I see you. Having now answered your questions, I have little more to say. Our enemy is quietly working within his lines, and collecting additional forces to drive us from our Capital. I hope we shall be able yet to disappoint him, and drive him back to his own country. I saw Fitzhugh the other day. He was looking very well in a new suit of gray. . . .

And now I must bid you farewell. Kiss your sweet boy for me, and love always,

Your devoted papa

R. E. Lee

209   GENERAL ORDERS, NO. 74

Headquarters Department of Northern Virginia

June 23, 1862

The general commanding announces with great satisfaction to the Army the brilliant exploit of Brig Genl J. E. B. Stuart with part of the troops under his command. This gallant officer, with portions of the First, Fourth, and Ninth Virginia Cavalry, a part of the Jeff Davis Legion, with whom were the Boykin Rangers and a section of the Stuart Horse Artillery, on June 13, 14, and 15, made a reconnaissance between the Pamunkey and Chickahominy Rivers, and succeeded in passing around the rear of the whole Federal army, routing the enemy in a series of skirmishes, taking a number of prisoners, and destroying and capturing stores to a large amount. Having most successfully accomplished its object, the expedition recrossed the Chickahominy almost in the presence of the enemy with the same coolness and address that marked every step of its progress, and with the loss of but one man, the lamented Captain [William] Latane, of the Ninth Virginia Cavalry, who fell bravely leading a successful charge against a superior force of the enemy.

In announcing this signal success to the Army the general commanding takes great pleasure in expressing his admiration of the courage and skill so conspicuously exhibited throughout by the general and the officers and men under his command.

In addition to the officers honorably mentioned in the report of the expedition, the conduct of the following privates has received the special commendation of their respective commanders: Privates Thomas P. Clapp, Company D, First Virginia Cavalry, and J. S. Mosby, serving with the same regiment; Privates [Lewis] Ashton, [J. R. A.] Brent, R. Herring, F. S. Herring, and H. F. Coleman, Company E, Ninth Virginia Cavalry.

By command of General Lee:

R. H. CHILTON
Assistant Adjutant General

210   GENERAL ORDERS, NO. 75

Headquarters, Department of Northern Virginia
June 24, 1862

I. Genl Jackson's command will proceed tomorrow from Ashland towards the Slash Church and encamp at some convenient point west of the Central Railroad. [General L. O'Bryan] Branch's brigade, of A. P. Hill's division, will also tomorrow evening take position on the Chickahominy near Half Sink. At 3 o'clock Thursday morning, 26th instant, Genl Jackson will advance on the road leading to Pole Green Church, communicating his march to Genl Branch, who will immediately cross the Chickahominy, and take the road leading to Mechanicsville. As soon as the movements of these columns are discovered, Genl A. P. Hill will cross the Chickahominy near Meadow Bridge and move direct upon Mechanicsville. To aid his advance the heavy batteries on the Chickahominy will at the proper time open upon the batteries at Mechanicsville. The enemy being driven from Mechanicsville, and the passage across the bridge opened, Genl Longstreet with his division and that of Genl D. H. Hill will cross the Chickahominy at or near that point, Genl D. H. Hill moving to the support of Genl Jackson, and Genl Longstreet supporting Genl A. P. Hill. The four divisions keeping in communication with each other and moving in echelon, on separate roads, if practicable, the left division in advance, with skirmishers and sharpshooters extended in their front, will sweep down the Chickahominy, and endeavor to drive the enemy from his positions above New Bridge, Genl Jackson bearing well to his left, turning Beaver Dam Creek and taking the direction toward Cold Harbor. They will then press forward towards the York River Railroad, closing upon the enemy's rear and forcing him down the Chickahominy. Any advance of the enemy towards Richmond will be prevented by vigorously following his rear and crippling and arresting his progress.

II. The divisions under Genls Huger and Magruder will hold their positions in front of the enemy against attack, and make such demonstrations Thursday as to discover his operations. Should opportunity offer, the feint will be converted into a real attack, and should abandonment of his entrenchments by the enemy be discovered, he will be closely pursued.

III. The 3rd Virginia Cavalry will observe the Charles City road. The 5th Virginia, the 1st North Carolina, and the Hampton Legion Cavalry will observe the Darbytown, Varina, and Osborne roads. Should a movement of the enemy down the Chickahominy be discovered, they will close upon his flank and endeavor to arrest his march.

IV. Genl Stuart with the 1st, 4th, & 9th Virginia Cavalry, the cavalry of Cobb's Legion, and the Jeff Davis Legion, will cross the Chickahominy tomorrow and take position to the left of Genl Jackson's line of march. The main body will be held in reserve, with scouts well extended to the front and left. Genl Stuart will keep Genl Jackson informed of the movements of the enemy on his left and will cooperate with him in his advance. The 10th Virginia Cavalry, Col [James L.] Davis, will remain in reserve on the 9 Mile road.

V. Genl Ransom's brigade of Genl Holmes' command will be placed in reserve on the Williamsburg road by Genl Huger to whom he will report for orders.

VI. Commanders of divisions will cause their commands to be provided with three days' cooked rations. The necessary ambulance and ordnance trains will be ready to accompany the divisions and receive orders from the respective commanders. Officers in charge of all trains will invariably remain with them. Batteries and wagons will keep on the right of the road. The chief engineer, Maj Stevens, will assign engineer officers to each division whose duty it will be to make provision for overcoming all difficulties to the progress of the troops. The staff departments will give the necessary instructions to facilitate the movements herein directed.

By command of Genl Lee:

R. H. CHILTON
A. A. G.

211   To JEFFERSON DAVIS
Richmond, Virginia

Headquarters, Department of Northern Virginia
June 24, 1862

Sir:

I regret that I did not see you when you called this afternoon. I was called to the Williamsburg road where some heavy skirmishing was going on most of the day. One of the brigades, (Genl Ransom's) was new which rendered me more anxious of the result. The general behaviour of the troops was good, but the affair on the whole was not well managed. This has caused me some anxiety. The enemy however was driven back from his advanced position. I have determined to make no change in the plan. I have ordered Genl Huger to hold his lines at all hazards, and to advance if possible, making to night every preparation to meet any attack of the enemy in the morning should he move against him.

I have the honour to be, very respectfully yours

R. E. LEE
Genl

212   To HIS WIFE
Richmond, Virginia

June 25, 1862

My Dear Mary:

I have been on our lines on the Williamsburg road since noon, dear Mary, & having finished my dinner find it near 10 p.m. with a great deal to do to night. It is therefore impossible for me to see you. Indeed I should have to wake you up to do so. I therefore must deny myself the pleasure & hope we may meet many happy days yet. I know your prayers & well wishes are constantly with me, & my trust is that a Merciful Providence may hear & answer them. Give much love to Custis & all the girls. I am very glad to learn the former is improving.

God guard & preserve you all.

Very truly & afft

R. E. LEE

213   To JEFFERSON DAVIS
Richmond, Virginia

Headquarters Dabb's House
June 26, 1862

Sir:

A note just received from General Jackson this morning states that in consequence of the high water & mud, his command only reached Ashland last night. It was his purpose to resume his march this morning at 2:30. I fear from the operations of the enemy yesterday that our plan of operations has been discovered to them. It seemed to be his purpose, by his advance on our right yesterday, to discover whether our force on that front had been diminished. General Jackson writes that there was a movement on our extreme left beyond the Chickahominy. Our cavalry pickets were driven in that direction, & the telegraph wire near Ashland was cut.

I am most respy, your obt servant

R. E. LEE
Genl

214   To GENERAL BENJAMIN HUGER
Commanding Division, Williamsburg Road

Headquarters
June 26, 1862

General:

Hold your trenches to night at the point of the bayonet if necessary. If you discover demonstrations against you and do not feel strong enough call upon Colonel [Thomas S.] Rhett for his battalion of infantry armed with muskets. Should there be no indications of the enemy on James River, call on General [Henry A.] Wise for such as he can spare. If the enemy should press you and this does not give you force enough, send to the Secretary of War to order Walker's brigade from Drewry's Bluff to join you, if only for to night.

I am most respectfully, your obedient servant

R. E. LEE
General

215　　COLONEL R. H. CHILTON TO JEFFERSON DAVIS
Richmond, Virginia
TELEGRAM

Headquarters, Army Northern Virginia
June 26, 1862

SIR:

THE HEADQUARTERS OF THE COMMANDING GENERAL TO DAY WILL BE ON THE MECHANICSVILLE TURNPIKE.

I HAVE THE HONOUR TO BE VERY RESPECTFULLY, YOUR OBT SERVT

R. H. CHILTON
A. A. G.

216　　　　　　To JEFFERSON DAVIS
Richmond, Virginia

Headquarters
June 27, 1862

Mr. President:

Profoundly grateful to Almighty God for the signal victory granted to us, it is my pleasing task to announce to you the success achieved by this army today. The enemy was this morning driven from his strong position behind Beaver Dam Creek and pursued to that behind Powhite Creek, and finally, after a severe contest of five hours, entirely repulsed from the field. Night put an end to the contest. I grieve to state that our loss in officers and men is great. We sleep on the field, and shall renew the contest in the morning.

I have the honor to be, very respectfully

R. E. LEE
General

217   To GENERAL BENJAMIN HUGER
Commanding Division, Williamsburg Road
TELEGRAM

Hogan's House
June 27, 1862

GENL LONGSTREET'S BRIGADE [DIVISION] IS ON THE ROAD FROM HOGAN'S HOUSE TO DR. GAINES'. GENL A. P. HILL IS ON THE ROAD FROM WALNUT GROVE CHURCH TO COLD HARBOR VIA GAINES' MILL. GENL JACKSON'S COMMAND SUPPORT BY D. H. HILL IS ON THE ROAD TO COLD HARBOR TURNING PO-WHITE CREEK. I THINK IT PROBABLE THAT THE ENEMY IS IN FORCE BEHIND POWHITE CREEK, CROSSING THE CHICKAHOMINY ON HIS LINE TO GOLDING'S BY FAIR OAKS STATION ALONG YOUR FRONT. IF HE SHOULD DIMINISH HIS FORCES IN FRONT OF YOU OR SHOW A DISPOSITION TO ABANDON HIS WORKS YOU MUST PRESS HIM, CAUTIOUSLY & HOLD YOUR LINE AT ALL HAZARDS. THE NEW BRIDGE ROAD IS OPEN TO US & WE MUST CONNECT WITH GENL MA-GRUDER.

R. E. LEE

PLEASE SEND THIS TO THE PRESIDENT.

218   To GENERAL JOHN B. MAGRUDER
Commanding Division, Williamsburg Road

Headquarters Department of Northern Virginia
[June 28], 1862

Major-General Magruder:
I have joined General Longstreet at the intersection of the New Market, Charles City, and Quaker roads, and wish to know how far you have progressed en route to this point.

I am respectfully, your obedient servant

R. E. LEE

219   To GENERAL JOHN B. MAGRUDER
Commanding Division, Williamsburg Road

Headquarters &c.
Dr. Gaines' House
June 28, 1862

General:

The indications on this side of the Chickahominy go to show that the enemy is projecting an abandonment of his intrenched camp & it may possibly even have been commenced to day. Wagons have been seen descending the river within his lines. None going up; conflagrations have been observed as if property was being destroyed. No cannon has been exhibited in the works about Goldings, nor have they responded to any of our batteries from this side. Genl Longstreet will tonight make practicable a ford between New Bridge & the enemy's bridge at Goldings (which latter has been destroyed by the enemy) so that if any of your parties hear work progressing in that position they will know that it is our left & friends. Genl Longstreet will endeavor to test the presence of the enemy at daylight in the morning & should he be discovered to have moved & gone towards James River, he will cross & pass immediately through their camp. I desire you & Genl Huger to ascertain on your part the intention & movement of the enemy, & should he move towards James River you must oppose him, & should he cross the Chickahominy you must follow him.

Very respy, yr obt svt

R. E. LEE
Genl

220   To GENERAL JOHN B. MAGRUDER
Commanding Division, Williamsburg Road

June 28, 1862

Major General Magruder:

My second note. Seems first was error, the men turning out to be your own. The possession of that point would seem to liberate all the forces to his left, guarding Garnett's plateau. They can be used in driving the enemy from his other positions. We shall proceed on this side. How far [does] his right extend up the Chickahominy? Jackson's division is at Grapevine Bridge; Ewell sent to Dispatch Station. I will communicate whenever I can discover anything of importance; you do the same, and operate on the principle before established — to hold your lines at all hazards, defending the approaches to Richmond, moving against the enemy whenever you can do so to advantage.

By order of General Lee:

R. H. CHILTON
Assistant Adjutant General

221   To GENERAL JOHN B. MAGRUDER
Commanding Division, Williamsburg Road

Headquarters, Department of Northern Virginia
June 29, 1862

General:

I regret much that you have made so little progress today in the pursuit of the enemy. In order to reap the fruits of our victory the pursuit should be most vigorous. I must urge you, then, again to press on his rear rapidly and steadily. We must lose no more time or he will escape us entirely.

Very respectfully yours, &c.

R. E. LEE
General

P.S. Since the above was written I learn from Major Taylor that you are under the impression that General Jackson has been ordered not to support you. On the contrary, he has been directed to do so, and to push the pursuit vigorously.

222   To JEFFERSON DAVIS
Richmond, Virginia

Headquarters &c.
Williamsburg Road
June 29, 1862

Mr. President:

I have the honor to report for your information that after the enemy had been driven from the left bank of the Chickahominy on the 27th instant, he seemed to have determined to abandon his position on the right bank & commenced promptly & quietly his arrangements for its evacuation. His intention was discovered but his proposed route could not be ascertained, though efforts were made all day yesterday with that view.

Having however discovered that no movements were made on his part to maintain or recover his communications with York River, which were entirely severed by our occupation of the York River Railroad & the Williamsburg road; his only course seemed to me was to make for James River & thus open communications with his gunboats and fleet. Though not yet certain of his route, the whole army has been put in motion upon this supposition. It is certain that he is south of the Chickahominy and can only cross it at or below Long Bridge. Genl Stuart is on the left bank watching his movements in that direction. General Jackson will cross to the right bank at Grapevine Bridge. Genl Magruder is pursuing down the Williamsburg road. Genl Huger on the Charles City, & Genl Longstreet on the Darbytown. The cavalry on the several roads south of the Chickahominy have not yet reported any of his forces in their front. I have directed the staff departments to send over to the battle ground north of the Chickahominy & secure all the public property left there of every description, & also that which has been abandoned by the enemy in his camp on the south side, where their tents are now still standing. I request that these orders may be repeated by the Secretary of War. Col [George W.] Lay & Col [Edwin J.] Harvie have been charged with the execution of my directions in this matter on the north side of the Chickahominy.

I am with high respect, your obt servt

R. E. LEE

223   To JEFFERSON DAVIS
                    Richmond, Virginia

Headquarters
July 2, 1862

Mr. President:

The enemy this morning was found to have abandoned his position which he held yesterday. The heavy rain, his extended cavalry, & some infantry, succeeded in keeping from us this information until arrangements could be made to collect our troops in some force, which owing to the battle of yesterday reaching into the night & the unfavorable day, required some time. The cavalry is in pursuit. Genls Longstreet's & Jackson's commands will be formed to follow him rapidly, while the main body of the army will maintain its position today, to take care of the wounded, bury the dead & collect stragglers. Owing to the conflicting reports as to the course the enemy has taken, I have determined to send Genls Holmes' & Wise's commands back to Drewry's & Chaffin's Bluffs respectively. Some reports state that a part of the enemy has crossed to the south side of James River with a view of joining Genl Burnside. While from others it appears he is fleeing down the north bank of the river, covered by his gunboats, to connect with his transports. I enclose you a note just received from Genl Holmes. Can a good commander be procured for Walker's brigade?

I have the honor to be, yr obt svt

R. E. LEE
Genl

224   To JEFFERSON DAVIS
Richmond, Virginia

Headquarters
Dr. Poindexter's House
July 3, 1862

Mr. President:

I enclose you recent dispatches received from Genl Stuart. They leave little doubt in my mind even as to the possibility of the truth of Genl McClellan's grand movement across the James River to Richmond. Such a movement on his part is hardly possible, but in the uncertainty as to whether they will be required in advance, I have determined to retain for the present in their present positions the commands of Magruder, Huger, D. H. Hill & Ransom. I shall probably myself go farther down the river in the course of the day, unless other information detains me here.

I have the honor to be, your obt servt

R. E. LEE
Genl

225   To GENERAL DANIEL H. HILL
Malvern Hill, Virginia

Headquarters
Dr. Poindexter's
July 4, 1862

General:

I desire you today to continue the work of burying the dead, collecting the wounded & sending them to the hospitals, & gathering up all arms and other property left on the field. I understand that many of the enemy's wounded of Monday's fight are still on the field, they must have suffered greatly, & every effort should be made to remove all of them where they will be comfortable. The enemy's dead (particularly at the scene of Monday's fight) must be buried, & any prisoners that may be in your hands can be devoted to this work.

Lose no exertion to collect your command, & in every way prepare it for immediate service. Send a strong detail under efficient officers & finish the work at once.

I shall proceed to join the advance of the army under Genl Longstreet, where you can communicate with me.

I am most respy, yr obt svt

R. E. LEE
Genl

226   To JEFFERSON DAVIS
               Richmond, Virginia

Headquarters &c.
Phillips' House
July 4, 1862

Mr. President:

I have just returned from examining the ground at Westover occupied by the enemy. I enclose a rough sketch. The enemy is strongly posted in the neck formed by Herring Creek & James River. The creek is not fordable, below where the road crosses it, except for a few hundred yards, the rest is marshy & deep. Above it is fordable for infantry for about the same distance. The enemy's batteries occupy the ridge along which the Charles City road runs, north of the creek, and his gunboats lying below the mouth of the creek sweep the ground in front of his batteries. Above his encampments which lie on the river, his gunboats also extend, where the ground is more favorable to be searched by their cannon. As far as I can now see, there is no way to attack him to advantage, nor do I wish to expose the men to the destructive missiles of his gunboats. Our troops are posted in line in his front & closer examinations of the ground are being made.

I fear he is too secure under cover of his boats to be driven from his position. I discover no intention of either ascending or crossing the river at present. Reinforcements have joined him & his sick, wounded and demoralized troops have been sent down the river.

I am most respecty, your obt servt

R. E. LEE
General

227   To JEFFERSON DAVIS
                                    Richmond, Virginia

                                    Headquarters, Department of Northern Virginia
                                                                Phillips' House
                                                                July 6, 1862

Mr. President:

From the conflicting & exaggerated reports of the movements of
the enemy I conclude that he has been reinforced, and there are besides
indications that it may be his purpose to make a lodgment on the James
River as a base for further operations. Seven large steamers were reported
to have come up Wednesday, said to be of the large size New York
Sound steamers, crowded with soldiers; other steamers with troops are
also reported to have arrived at Westover. Many sail transports with supplies, some of which contained bales of hay on their decks. Steamers
going back are also said to contain men, but they appear to be sick,
wounded, & demoralized, do not exhibit themselves on the decks &c. A
large New York ferry boat is also reported at the Westover Landing,
where wharves have been prepared by means of their pontoon bridges.
This boat may be nothing more than any other transport, but it would
prove very convenient should he meditate a transfer of his troops to the
other side of the river. The great obstacle to operations here is the presence of the enemy's gunboats, which protect our approaches to him &
should we even force him from his positions on his land front, would
prevent us from reaping any of the fruits of victory & expose our men
to great destruction. These considerations induce the opinion that it may
be better to leave a small light force with the cavalry here & retire the
army near Richmond where it can be better refreshed and strengthened,
and be prepared for a renewal of the contest, which must take place at
some quarter soon. I beg that you will take every practicable means to
reinforce our ranks, which [are] much reduced and which will require
to be strengthened to their full extent to be able to compete with the
reinvigorated force of the enemy. I enclose a report from Capt Wingfield, stationed on the opposite side of the river, which corroborates the
reports that I have received from this side.

                              I have the honor to be, your obt svt

                                                        R. E. Lee
                                                        Genl

228   GENERAL ORDERS, NO. 75

Headquarters in the Field
July 7, 1862

The general commanding, profoundly grateful to the only Giver of all victory for the signal success with which He has blessed our arms, tenders his warmest thanks and congratulations to the army, by whose valor such splendid results have been achieved.

On Thursday, June 26th, the powerful and thoroughly equipped army of the enemy was entrenched in works vast in extent and most formidable in character within sight of our capital.

Today the remains of that confident and threatening host lie upon the banks of James River, thirty miles from Richmond, seeking to recover, under the protection of his gunboats, from the effects of a series of disastrous defeats.

The battle, beginning on the afternoon of the 26th of June, above Mechanicsville, continued until the night of July 1st, with only such intervals as were necessary to pursue and overtake the flying foe. His strong entrenchments and obstinate resistance were overcome, and our army swept resistlessly down the north side of the Chickahominy until it reached the rear of the enemy and broke his communication with the York, capturing or causing the destruction of many valuable stores, and by the decisive battle of Friday forcing the enemy from his line of powerful fortifications on the south side of the Chickahominy and driving him to a precipitate retreat. This victorious army pursued as rapidly as the obstructions placed by the enemy in his rear would permit, three times overtaking his flying column and as often driving him with slaughter from the field, leaving his numerous dead and wounded in our hands in every conflict.

The immediate fruits of our success are the relief of Richmond from a state of siege; the rout of the great army that so long menaced its safety, many thousand prisoners including officers of high rank, the capture or destruction of stores to the value of millions, and the acquisition of thousands of arms and forty pieces of superior artillery.

The service rendered to the country in this short but eventful period can scarcely be estimated, and the general commanding cannot adequately express his admiration of the courage, endurance, and soldierly conduct of the officers and men engaged.

These brilliant results have cost us many brave men, but while we mourn the loss of our gallant dead let us not forget that they died nobly in defence of their country's freedom, and have linked their memory with an event that will live forever in the hearts of a grateful people.

Soldiers, your country will thank you for the heroic conduct you have displayed — conduct worthy of men engaged in a cause so just and sacred, and deserving a nation's gratitude and praise.

By command of General Lee:

R. H. CHILTON
A. A. General

229   To GENERAL SAMUEL COOPER
Adjutant and Inspector General

BATTLE REPORT ON THE SEVEN DAYS

Headquarters Army of Northern Virginia
March 6, 1863

Sir:

After the battle of Seven Pines the Federal Army under General McClellan preparatory to an advance upon Richmond, proceeded to fortify its position on the Chickahominy, and to perfect the communications with its base of supplies near the head of York River.

Its left was established south of the Chickahominy, between White Oak Swamp and New Bridge, defended by a line of strong works, access to which except by a few narrow roads, was obstructed by felling the dense forests in front. These roads were commanded for a great distance by the heavy guns in the fortifications.

The right wing lay north of the Chickahominy, extending beyond Mechanicsville, and the approaches from the south side were strongly defended by entrenchments.

Our army was around Richmond, the divisions of Huger and Magruder, supported by those of Longstreet and D. H. Hill, in front of the enemy's left, and that of A. P. Hill extending from Magruder's left beyond Meadow Bridge. The command of Genl Jackson, including Ewell's division, operating in the Shenandoah Valley, succeeded in diverting the army of McDowell at Fredericksburg from uniting with that of McClellan.

To render this diversion more decided, and effectually mask his withdrawal from the Valley at the proper time, Jackson after the defeat of Frémont and Shields was reinforced by [General William H. C.] Whiting's division, composed of Hood's Texas brigade, and his own under Col [Evander M.] Law, from Richmond, and that of [General Alexander R.] Lawton from the south.

The intention of the enemy seemed to be to attack Richmond by regular approaches. The strength of his left wing rendered a direct assault injudicious, if not impracticable. It was therefore determined to construct defensive lines so as to enable a part of the army to defend the city, and leave the other part free to cross the Chickahominy and operate on the north bank. By sweeping down the river on that side, and threatening his communications with York River it was thought that the enemy would be compelled to retreat or give battle out of his entrenchments. The plan was submitted to His Excellency the President, who was repeatedly on the field in the course of its execution.

While preparations were in progress, a cavalry expedition under General Stuart, was made around the rear of the Federal Army, to ascertain its position and movements. This was executed with great address and daring by that accomplished officer.

As soon as the defensive works were sufficiently advanced General Jackson was directed to move rapidly and secretly from the Valley, so as to arrive in the vicinity of Ashland by the 24th June. The enemy appeared to be unaware of our purpose, and on the 25th attacked Genl Huger on the Williamsburg road, with the intention, as appeared by a dispatch from Genl McClellan, of securing his advance towards Richmond.

The effort was successfully resisted, and our line maintained.

BATTLE OF MECHANICSVILLE

According to the general order of battle [General Order No. 75], a copy of which is annexed, General Jackson was to march from Ashland on the 25th in the direction of Slash Church, encamping for the night west of the Central Railroad, and to advance at 3 a.m. on the 26th and turn Beaver Dam. A. P. Hill was to cross the Chickahominy at Meadow Bridge when Jackson's advance beyond that point should be known, and move directly upon Mechanicsville. As soon as the Mechanicsville Bridge should be uncovered Longstreet and D. H. Hill were to cross, the latter to proceed to the support of Jackson, and the former to that of A. P. Hill. The four commands were directed to sweep down the north side of the Chickahominy towards the York River Railroad, Jackson on the left and in advance, Longstreet nearest the river and in the rear. Huger and Magruder were ordered to hold their positions against any assault of the enemy, to observe his movements, and follow him closely should he retreat.

General Stuart with the cavalry was thrown out on Jackson's left to guard his flank and give notice of the enemy's movements. Brig General [William N.] Pendleton was directed to employ the Reserve Artillery so as to resist any approach of the enemy towards Richmond, to superintend that portion of it posted to aid in the operations of the north bank, and hold the remainder ready for use when it might be required.

In consequence of unavoidable delays, the whole of Genl Jackson's command did not arrive at Ashland in time to enable him to reach the point designated on the 25th. His march on the 26th was consequently longer than had been anticipated, and his progress being also retarded by the enemy, A. P. Hill did not begin his movement until 3 p.m. when he crossed the river and advanced upon Mechanicsville. After a sharp conflict he drove the enemy from his entrenchments, and forced him to take refuge in his works on the left bank of Beaver Dam about a mile distant.

This position was a strong one, the banks of the creek in front being high and almost perpendicular, and the approach to it over open fields, commanded by the fire of artillery and infantry entrenched on the opposite side. The difficulty of crossing the stream had been increased by felling the woods on its banks and destroying the bridges. Jackson being expected to pass Beaver Dam above and turn the enemy's right, a direct attack was not made by Genl Hill. One of his regiments on the left of his line crossed the creek to communicate with Jackson and remained until after dark, when it was withdrawn. Longstreet and D. H. Hill's crossed the Mechanicsville Bridge as soon as it was uncovered and could be repaired, but it was late before they reached the north bank of the Chickahominy. D. H. Hill's leading brigade under [General Roswell S.] Ripley advanced to the support of the troops engaged, and at a late hour united with [General William Dorsey] Pender's brigade of A. P. Hill's division in an effort to turn the enemy's left, but the troops were unable in the growing darkness to overcome the obstructions, and after sustaining a destructive fire of musketry and artillery at short range, were withdrawn.

The fire was continued until about 9 p.m. when the engagement ceased. Our troops retained the ground on the right bank from which the enemy had been driven. Ripley was relieved at 3 a.m. on the 27th by two of Longstreet's brigades which were subsequently reinforced. In expectation of Jackson's arrival on the enemy's right, the battle was renewed at dawn, and continued with animation for about two hours, during which the passage of the creek was attempted, and our troops forced their way to its banks, where their progress was arrested by the nature of the stream.

They maintained their position while preparations were being made to cross at another point nearer the Chickahominy. Before they were completed, Jackson crossed Beaver Dam above and the enemy abandoned his entrenchments and retired rapidly down the river, destroying a great deal of property, but leaving much in his deserted camps.

BATTLE OF THE CHICKAHOMINY
[Gaines' Mill]

After repairing the bridges over Beaver Dam the several columns resumed their march as nearly as possible as prescribed in the order. Jackson with whom D. H. Hill had united, bore to the left, in order to cut off reinforcements to the enemy or intercept his retreat in that direction. Longstreet and A. P. Hill moved nearer the Chickahominy. Many prisoners were taken in their progress and the conflagration of wagons and stores marked the way of the retreating army. Longstreet and Hill reached the vicinity of New Bridge about noon. It was ascertained that the enemy had taken a position behind Powhite Creek, prepared to dispute our progress. He occupied a range of hills, with his right resting in the vicinity of McGehee's house and his left near that of Dr. Gaines', on a wooded bluff, which rose abruptly from a deep ravine. The ravine was filled with sharpshooters, to whom its banks gave protection. A second line of infantry was stationed on the side of the hill behind a breastwork of trees above the first. A third occupied the crest, strengthened with rifle trenches and crowned with artillery. The approach to this position was over an open plain, about a quarter of a mile wide, commanded by this triple line of fire and swept by the heavy batteries south of the Chickahominy. In front of his center and right the ground was generally open, bounded on the side of our approach by a wood, with dense and tangled undergrowth, and traversed by a sluggish stream which converted the soil into a deep morass. The woods on the further side of the swamp were occupied by sharpshooters, and trees had been felled to increase the difficulty of its passage and detain our advancing columns under the fire of infantry massed on the slopes of the opposite hills and of the batteries on their crests.

Pressing on towards the York River Railroad, A. P. Hill who was in advance, reached the vicinity of New Cold Harbor about 2 p.m., where he encountered the enemy. He immediately formed his line nearly parallel to the road leading from that place towards McGehee's house, and soon became hotly engaged. The arrival of Jackson on our left was momentarily expected, and it was supposed that his approach would cause the extension of the enemy's line in that direction. Under this impression Longstreet was held back until this movement should commence.

The principal part of the Federal Army was now on the north side of the Chickahominy. Hill's single division met this large force with the impetuous courage for which that officer and his troops are distinguished. They drove the enemy back and assailed him in his strong position on the ridge. The battle raged fiercely and with varying fortune more than two hours. Three regiments pierced the enemy's line and forced their way to the crest of the hill on his left, but were compelled to fall back before overwhelming numbers. The superior force of the enemy, assisted by the fire of his batteries south of the Chickahominy, which played incessantly on our columns as they pressed through the difficulties that obstructed their way, caused them to recoil. Though most of the men had never been under fire until the day before, they were rallied and in turn repelled the advance of the enemy. Some brigades were broken, others stubbornly maintained their positions, but it became apparent that the enemy was gradually gaining ground.

The attack on our left being delayed by the length of Jackson's march and the obstacles he encountered, Longstreet was ordered to make a diversion in Hill's favor by a feint on the enemy's left. In making this demonstration the great strength of the position already described was discovered, and General Longstreet perceived that to render the diversion effectual the feint must be converted into an attack. He resolved with characteristic promptness to carry the heights by assault. His column was quickly formed near the open ground. As his preparations were completed Jackson arrived, and his right division, that of Whiting, took position on the left of Longstreet. At the same time D. H. Hill formed on our extreme left, and after a short but bloody conflict forced his way through the morass and obstructions and drove the enemy from the woods on the opposite side. Ewell advanced on Hill's right and engaged the enemy furiously. The first and fourth brigades of Jackson's own division filled the interval between Ewell and A. P. Hill. The second and third were sent to the right. The arrival of these fresh troops enabled A. P. Hill to withdraw some of his brigades, wearied and reduced by their long and arduous conflict. The line being now complete, a general advance from right to left was ordered. On the right the troops moved forward with steadiness, unchecked by the terrible fire from the triple lines of infantry on the hill, and the cannon on both sides of the river, which burst upon them as they emerged upon the plain. The dead and wounded marked the way of their intrepid advance, the brave Texans leading, closely followed by their no less daring comrades. The enemy were driven from the ravine to the first line of breastworks, over which our impetuous column dashed up to the entrenchments on the crest. These were quickly stormed, fourteen pieces of artillery captured, and the enemy driven into the field beyond. Fresh troops came to his support and he endeavored repeatedly to rally, but in vain. He was forced back with great slaughter until he reached the woods on the banks of the Chickahominy, and night put an end to the pursuit.

Long lines of dead and wounded marked each stand made by the enemy in his stubborn resistance, and the field over which he retreated was strewn with the slain. On the left the attack was no less vigorous and successful. D. H. Hill charged across the open ground in his front, one of his regiments having first bravely carried a battery whose fire enfiladed his advance. Gallantly supported by the troops on his right, who pressed forward with unfaltering resolution, he reached the crest of the ridge, and after a sanguinary struggle broke the enemy's line, captured several of his batteries, and drove him in confusion towards the Chickahominy until darkness rendered further pursuit impossible. Our troops remained in undisturbed possession of the field, covered with the Federal dead and wounded, and their broken forces fled to the river or wandered through the woods.

Owing to the nature of the country the cavalry was unable to participate in the general engagement. It rendered valuable service in guarding Jackson's flank and took a large number of prisoners.

On the morning of the 28th it was ascertained that none of the enemy remained in our front north of the Chickahominy. As he might yet intend to give battle to preserve his communications, the 9th Cavalry, supported by Ewell's division, was ordered to seize the York River Railroad, and Genl Stuart with his main body to cooperate.

When the cavalry reached Dispatch Station the enemy retreated to the south bank of the river and burned the railroad bridge. Ewell, coming up shortly afterwards, destroyed a portion of the track. During the forenoon columns of dust south of the Chickahominy showed that the Federal Army was in motion. The abandonment of the railroad and destruction of the bridge proved that no further attempt would be made to hold that line; but from the position it occupied, the roads which led towards James River, would also enable it to reach the lower bridges over the Chickahominy and retreat down the Peninsula. In the latter event it was necessary that our troops should continue on the north bank of the river, and until the intention of Genl McClellan was discovered it was deemed injudicious to change their disposition. Ewell was therefore ordered to proceed to Bottom's Bridge to guard that point, and the cavalry to watch the bridges below. No certain indications of a retreat to James River were discovered by our forces on the south side of the Chickahominy, and late in the afternoon the enemy's works were reported to be fully manned. The strength of these fortifications prevented Generals Huger and Magruder from discovering what was passing in their front. Below the enemy's works the country was densely wooded and intersected by impassable swamps, at once concealing his movements and precluding reconnaissances except by the regular roads, all of which were strongly guarded. The bridges over the Chickahominy in rear of the enemy were destroyed, and their reconstruction impracticable in the presence of his whole army and powerful batteries. We were therefore compelled to wait until his purpose should be developed.

Generals Huger and Magruder were again directed to use the utmost vigilance and pursue the enemy vigorously should they discover that he was retreating. During the afternoon and night of the 28th the signs of a general movement were apparent, and no indications of his approach to the lower bridges of the Chickahominy having been discovered by the troops in observation at those points, it became manifest that General McClellan was retreating to the James River.

BATTLE OF SAVAGE STATION

Early on the 29th Longstreet and A. P. Hill were ordered to recross the Chickahominy at New Bridge, and move by the Darbytown to the Long Bridge road. Major R. K. Meade and Lieutenant S. R. Johnston of the Engineers, attached to General Longstreet's division, who had been sent to reconnoiter, found about sunrise, the work on the upper extremity of the enemy's line of entrenchments abandoned. Generals Huger and Magruder were immediately ordered in pursuit, the former by the Charles City road, so as to take the Federal Army in flank, and the latter by the Williamsburg road, to attack its rear.

Jackson was directed to cross at Grapevine Bridge and move down the south side of the Chickahominy. Magruder and Huger found the whole line of works deserted and large quantities of military stores of every description abandoned or destroyed. The former reached the vicinity of Savage Station about noon, where he came upon the rear guard of the retreating army. Being informed that the enemy was advancing, he halted and sent for reinforcements. Two brigades of Huger's division were ordered to his support, but subsequently withdrawn, it being apparent that the force in Magruder's front was covering the retreat of the main body. Jackson's route led to the flank and rear of Savage Station, but he was delayed by the necessity of reconstructing Grapevine Bridge. Late in the afternoon Magruder attacked the enemy with one of his divisions and two regiments of another. A severe action ensued and continued about two hours, when it was terminated by night. The troops displayed great gallantry and inflicted heavy loss upon the enemy, but owing to the lateness of the hour and the small force employed, the result was not decisive and the enemy continued his retreat under cover of darkness, leaving several hundred prisoners, with his dead and wounded, in our hands. At Savage Station were found about twenty-five hundred men in hospital and a large amount of property. Stores of much value had been destroyed, including the necessary medical supplies for the sick and wounded. But the time gained enabled the retreating column to cross White Oak Swamp without interruption and destroy the bridge.

BATTLE OF FRAYSER'S FARM
[Glendale]

Jackson reached Savage Station early on the 30th. He was directed to pursue the enemy on the road he had taken and Magruder to follow Longstreet by the Darbytown road. As Jackson advanced he captured such numbers of prisoners and collected so many arms that two regiments had to be detached for their security. His progress was arrested at White Oak Swamp. The enemy occupied the opposite side and obstinately resisted the reconstruction of the bridge. Longstreet and A. P. Hill, continuing their advance on the 30th, soon came upon the enemy strongly posted across the Long Bridge road about a mile from its intersection with the Charles City road. Huger's route led to the right of this position, Jackson's to the rear, and the arrival of their commands was awaited to begin the attack.

On the 29th Genl Holmes had crossed from the south side of James River with part of his division. On the 30th, reinforced by General Wise with a detachment of his brigade, he moved down the River road and came upon the line of the retreating army near Malvern Hill. Perceiving indications of confusion, Genl Holmes was ordered to open upon the column with artillery. He soon discovered that a number of batteries, advantageously posted, supported by an infantry force superior to his own and assisted by the fire of the gunboats in the James River, guarded this part of the line. Magruder, who had reached the Darbytown road, was ordered to reinforce Holmes, but being at a greater distance than had been supposed, he did not reach the position of the latter in time for an attack.

Huger reported that his progress was obstructed, but about 4 p.m. firing was heard in the direction of the Charles City road, which was supposed to indicate his approach. Longstreet immediately opened with one of his batteries to give notice of his presence. This brought on the engagement, but Huger not coming up, and Jackson having been unable to force the passage of White Oak Swamp, Longstreet and Hill were without the expected support. The superiority of numbers and advantage of position were on the side of the enemy. The battle raged furiously until 9 p.m. By that time the enemy had been driven with great slaughter from every position but one, which he maintained until he was enabled to withdraw under cover of darkness. At the close of the struggle nearly the entire field remained in our possession, covered with the enemy's dead and wounded. Many prisoners, including a general of division, were captured, and [*blank*] pieces of artillery with some thousands of small arms taken. Could the other commands have cooperated in the action the result would have proved most diastrous to the enemy. After the engagement Magruder was recalled to relieve the troops of Longstreet and Hill. His men, much fatigued by their long, hot march, arrived during the night.

BATTLE OF MALVERN HILL

Early on the 1st July Jackson reached the battle field of the previous day, having succeeded in crossing White Oak Swamp, where he captured a part of the enemy's artillery and a number of prisoners. He was directed to continue the pursuit down the Willis Church road, and soon found the enemy occupying a high range, extending obliquely across the road, in front of Malvern Hill. On this position of great natural strength he had concentrated his powerful artillery, supported by masses of infantry, partially protected by earthworks. His left rested near Crew's house and his right near Binford's. Immediately in his front the ground was open, varying in width from a quarter to half a mile, and sloping gradually from the crest, was completely swept by the fire of his infantry and artillery. To reach this open ground our troops had to advance through a broken and thickly wooded country, traversed nearly throughout its whole extent by a swamp passable at but few places and difficult at those. The whole was within range of the batteries on the heights and the gunboats in the river, under whose incessant fire our movements had to be executed.

Jackson formed his line with Whiting's division on his left and D. H. Hill's on his right, one of Ewell's brigades occupying the interval. The rest of Ewell's and Jackson's own divisions were held in reserve. Magruder was directed to take position on Jackson's right, but before his arrival two of Huger's brigades came up and were placed next to Hill. Magruder subsequently formed on the right of these brigades, which with a third of Huger's, were placed under his command. Longstreet and A. P. Hill were held in reserve and took no part in the engagement. Owing to ignorance of the country, the dense forests impeding necessary communication, and the extreme difficulty of the ground, the whole line was not formed until a late hour in the afternoon. The obstacles presented by the woods and swamp made it impracticable to bring up a sufficient amount of artillery to oppose successfully the extraordinary force of that arm employed by the enemy, while the field itself afforded us few positions favorable for its use and none for its proper concentration. Orders were issued for a general advance at a given signal, but the causes referred to prevented the proper concert of action among the troops. D. H. Hill pressed forward across the open field and engaged the enemy gallantly, breaking and driving back his first line, but a simultaneous advance of the other troops not taking place, he found himself unable to maintain the ground he had gained against the overwhelming numbers and numerous batteries of the enemy. Jackson sent to his support his own division and that part of Ewell's which was in reserve, but owing to the increasing darkness and intricacy of the forest and swamp they did not arrive in time to render the desired assistance. Hill was therefore compelled to abandon part of the ground he had gained after suffering severe loss and inflicting heavy damage upon the enemy. On the right the attack was gallantly made by Huger's and Magruder's commands. Two brigades of the former commenced the action, the other two were subsequently sent to the support of Magruder and Hill. Several determined efforts were made to storm the hill at Crew's house. The brigades advanced bravely across the open field, raked by the fire of a hundred cannon and the musketry of large bodies of infantry. Some were broken and gave way, others approached close to the guns, driving back the infantry, compelling the advanced batteries to retire to escape capture, and mingling their dead with those of the enemy. For want of concert among the attacking columns their assaults were too weak to break the Federal lines, and after struggling gallantly, sustaining and inflicting great loss, they were compelled successively to retire. Night was approaching when the attack began, and it soon became difficult to distinguish friend from foe. The firing continued until after 9 p.m., but no decided result was gained. Part of the troops were withdrawn to their original positions, others remained on the open field, and some rested within a hundred yards of the batteries that had been so bravely but vainly assailed.

The general conduct of the troops was excellent, in some instances heroic. The lateness of the hour at which the attack necessarily began gave the enemy the full advantage of his superior position and augmented the natural difficulties of our own.

After seizing the York River Railroad on the 28th June and driving the enemy across the Chickahominy, as already narrated, the cavalry under General Stuart proceeded down the railroad to ascertain if there was any movement of the enemy in that direction. He encountered but little opposition and reached the vicinity of the White House on the 29th.

At his approach the enemy destroyed the greater part of the immense stores accumulated at that depot and retreated towards Fortress Monroe.

With one gun and some dismounted men Genl Stuart drove off a gunboat which lay near the White House and secured a large amount of property, including more than ten thousand stand of small arms, partially burned. Leaving one squadron at the White House, in compliance with his orders he returned to guard the lower bridges of the Chickahominy. On the 30th he was directed to recross and cooperate with General Jackson. After a long march he reached the rear of the enemy at Malvern Hill on the night of the 1st July at the close of the engagement.

On the 2nd July it was discovered that the enemy had withdrawn during the night, leaving the ground covered with his dead and wounded, and his route exhibiting abundant evidence of precipitate retreat. The pursuit was commenced, General Stuart with his cavalry in advance, but a violent storm which prevailed throughout the day, greatly retarded our progress. The enemy, harassed and closely followed by the cavalry, succeeded in gaining Westover on James River, and the protection of his gunboats. He immediately began to fortify his position, which was one of great natural strength, flanked on each side by a creek, and the approach to his front commanded by the heavy guns of his shipping in addition to those mounted in his entrenchments.

It was deemed inexpedient to attack him, and in view of the condition of our troops, who had been marching and fighting almost incessantly for seven days under the most trying circumstances, it was determined to withdraw in order to afford them the repose of which they stood so much in need. Several days were spent in collecting arms and other property abandoned by the enemy, and in the mean time some artillery and cavalry were sent below Westover to annoy his transports.

On the 8th July the army returned to the vicinity of Richmond. Under ordinary circumstances the Federal Army should have been destroyed. Its escape was due to the causes already stated. Prominent among these is the want of correct and timely information. This fact, attributable chiefly to the character of the country, enabled Genl McClellan skillfully to conceal his retreat and to add much to the obstructions with which nature had beset the way of our pursing columns.

But regret that more was not accomplished gives way to gratitude to the Sovereign Ruler of the Universe for the results achieved. The siege of Richmond was raised, and the object of a campaign, which had been prosecuted after months of preparation at an enormous expenditure of men and money, completely frustrated. More than ten thousand prisoners, including officers of rank, fifty-two pieces of artillery, and upwards of thirty-five thousand stand of small arms were captured. The stores and supplies of every description which fell into our hands were great in amount and value, but small in comparison with those destroyed by the enemy. His losses in battle exceeded our own, as attested by the thousands of dead and wounded left on every field, while his subsequent inaction shows in what condition the survivors reached the protection to which they fled.

The accompanying tables contain the lists of our casualties in the series of engagements. Among the dead will be found many whose names will ever be associated with the great events in which they all bore so honorable a part. For these, as well as for the names of their no less distinguished surviving comrades, who earned for themselves the high honor of special commendation, where all so well discharged their duty, reference must necessarily be made to the accompanying reports. But I cannot forbear expressing my admiration of the noble qualities displayed, with rare exceptions, by officers and men, under circumstances which demanded the exercise of every soldierly virtue.

To the officers commanding divisions and brigades belongs the credit for the management of their troops in action. The extent of the fields of battle, the nature of the ground, and the denseness of the forests rendered more than general directions impracticable.

To the officers of my staff I am indebted for constant aid during the entire period. Colonels [Robert H.] Chilton and [Armistead L.] Long, Majors [Walter H.] Taylor, [Charles S.] Venable, [Thomas M. R.] Talcott, and [Charles] Marshall, and Captain [A. P.] Mason were continuously with me in the field. General Pendleton, Chief of Artillery; Lieut Col [James L.] Corley, Chief Quartermaster; Lieut Col [Roger G.] Cole, Chief Commissary; Lieut Col [Edward P.] Alexander, Chief of Ordnance; Surgeon [Lafayette] Guild, Medical Director; Col [George W.] Lay and Lieut Col [Edwin J.] Harvie, Inspectors General, and Lieut Col [Walter H.] Stevens, Chief Engineer, attended unceasingly to their several departments. To the whole medical corps of the army I return my thanks for the care and attention bestowed on the wounded.

I am very respectfully, your obt servt

R. E. LEE
General

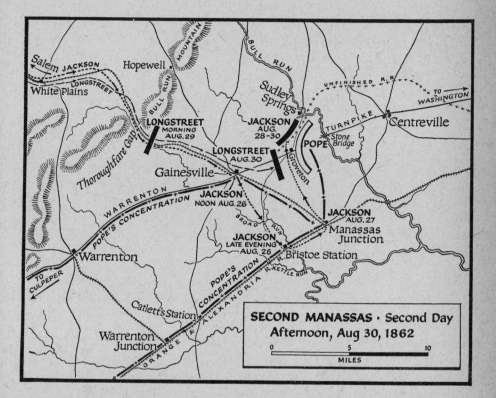

Salem JACKSON
White Plains LONGSTREET
Hopewell
Sudley Springs
UNFINISHED R.R.
TO WASHINGTON
BULL RUN
BULL RUN MOUNTAIN
LONGSTREET MORNING AUG. 29
JACKSON AUG. 28-30
TURNPIKE
Centreville
Thoroughfare Gap
LONGSTREET AUG. 30
POPE
Stone Bridge
Groveton
Gainesville
WARRENTON
POPE'S CONCENTRATION
JACKSON NOON AUG. 26
BROAD RUN
JACKSON AUG. 27
Manassas Junction
JACKSON LATE EVENING AUG. 26
Bristoe Station
Warrenton
TO CULPEPER
POPE'S CONCENTRATION
ORANGE & ALEXANDRIA R.R. KETTLE RUN
Catlett's Station
Warrenton Junction

SECOND MANASSAS · Second Day
Afternoon, Aug 30, 1862

0   5   10
MILES

CHAPTER SIX

Second Manassas

"Change the theater of war"

AFTER THE DECISIVE VICTORY of the Seven Days, the new army commander was confronted with a military dilemma similar to that which existed during his first days as Military Adviser. McClellan was on the Peninsula, and in middle Virginia the forces that had been immobilized — McDowell, Banks and Frémont — were united under General Pope and started moving in the direction of the vital Virginia Central Railroad. This Pope was a snorting, pawing sort of general who had won some success in the West and, coming to Virginia with boastful proclamations and threats, he introduced extremely harsh measures against civilians. Though Lee deeply resented the wanton destructiveness of the enemy's forces in Virginia, Pope seems to be the only Federal general who aroused his personal dislike. (Lee respected McClellan. During the Peninsula Campaign, Mrs. Lee was twice caught within Federal lines, and each time ceremoniously escorted to safety; the second time, she was delivered from McClellan's own headquarters to a Confederate officer.)

The fundamental difference between Lee and the previous Confederate policies was revealed in his approach to the problem of contending with two Federal armies. Under the Johnston-Davis combine, plans were made for defense against the threats; Lee plotted ways of getting at the enemy. Of course, Lee must obtain the President's approval. But where Johnston had never tried to get along with the authoritarian commander-in-chief, Lee, in submitting his plans, continued the skillful use of the tact that sustained him in Davis's graces. Also, his plans were supported by the prestige of the only significant victory won since First Manassas.

In preparing to assume the offensive, Lee had not yet organized his forces into the structure of the Army of Northern Virginia, though the general outlines appeared and he began using the name. To operate against Pope, Stonewall Jackson was sent with a semi-independent command composed of his division, Ewell's division, and A. P. Hill's large and inversely called Light Division — the force perhaps 30,000, including artillery and a brigade of Stuart's newly organized cavalry division. For discovering what Pope was up to and in taking such measures as seemed indicated, Lee gave Old Jack the discretionary orders under which, Lee had discovered, he functioned best.

Against McClellan at Berkeley plantation (Harrison's Landing), Longstreet was placed in command of a "wing" composed of five comparatively loosely formed divisions. When the organization was completed, a division would consist usually of four brigades. The divisions with Longstreet's wing were composed of two, three and four brigades, several not truly divisions as they were later to become. While the men were refitted and re-equipped with the bountiful supplies left by the enemy, and units were re-formed, Lee started the building of the powerful fortifications around Richmond which, continued under Colonel Gilmer after he took the army northward, were to remain impregnable throughout the war. The men no longer complained of digging works.

On the south side of the James River, Generals French and D. H. Hill commanded forces charged with guarding against a shift of McClellan's army to the south side and, against such a shift, strengthening the hastily improvised river fort at Drewry's Bluff and building fortifications outside Petersburg, a railroad junction city twenty-two miles south of Richmond. (Drewry's Bluff was also to stand throughout the war and Petersburg until the end.)

All during the summer of 1862, a heavy proportion of Lee's correspondence was devoted to the south side of the James, a vulnerable approach to Richmond's connections with the South and a back-door approach to Richmond which was never fully exploited by the Federals. At one period, from the night of July 31 through early August, Lee directed D. H. Hill to try cross-river artillery bombardments of the Federal camp in order to force McClellan to move, but this only annoyed McClellan into driving them away.

McClellan was not to be hurried into making a move. He sent out limited forays and once led his army back to Malvern Hill, only to retire again. In Lee's eagerness to get at Pope, he was restrained in diminishing the force between McClellan and Richmond by the uncertainty of where Burnside, then at Fort Monroe, would move his army. Lee had at his

disposal in Virginia at that stage more than 85,000 troops, but the various
Federal armies more than doubled that number.

On August 5 or 6, Lee learned that Burnside was landing his force
at Fredericksburg, obviously to swell Pope's army. On the 9th, before
Burnside's landing was completed, Hood's division was sent to Hanover
Junction, to cooperate with Jackson, and on the 13th Longstreet with
three divisions went to join Jackson. On the day that Longstreet left,
Lee learned that McClellan was at last moving: he was beginning to
break up his force. Two days later, August 15, Lee left for Gordonsville
(by train, on the Virginia Central) while McClellan's main army was
still in the stage of preparing to leave Harrison's Landing. Only Lee's
diplomacy and aura of success could have induced Davis to permit Lee
to join the bulk of his command in middle Virginia, leaving only four
divisions in the entire Richmond area, when a Federal army was still encamped twenty miles away. Nothing more vividly illustrates Lee's principle of acting in anticipation of the enemy, with concentration for a
single major stroke, and his audacity in the execution based on faith in
his appraisal of the enemy's intention.

When General Lee went to assume command of operations in middle Virginia, he left the Richmond forces — both north and south of the
James — in the command of Gustavus W. Smith, who had recovered from
his strange collapse on June 1. At that period Lee was responsible for
the operations south of the James, and the command situation immediately
around Richmond was one of those departmentalized affairs that exerted
such crippling effects throughout the Confederacy. D. H. Hill was commander of a department from south of the James to Cape Fear River, at
Wilmington, and this department's forces, attached to Lee's army by organization, in turn came under Smith, as commander of the Department
of Richmond. Because of history's concentration on Lee's major campaigns, attention has not been directed to his concern for other areas,
but (though little of the correspondence is reproduced) Lee wrote to
General Smith more often and more fully than to any other Confederate,
while directing operations away from Richmond.

Before Jackson had been reinforced he had attacked the advances of
Pope's army at Cedar Mountain (August 9) and this small-scale Confederate victory dampened Pope's fiery aggressiveness. By the time Lee
arrived at Gordonsville, Pope was halted between the Rapidan and Rappahannock Rivers, with his numbers swelled by the arrival of Burnside.
Lee immediately tried to get at him, to cut his army off from the Rappahannock. A heavy rain delayed Lee for two days and when he moved
again on the 20th, Pope, then alerted, retreated across the Rappahannock.
On the defense of the fords, Pope showed himself to be diligent, able

and determined, and Lee then tried, on the 22nd, to turn his right flank and to disrupt his communication with Stuart's cavalry. Again rain intervened. Rising waters cut Jackson's command in half and, though the cavalry got on Pope's communications at Catlett's Station, wet timbers saved the bridge. However, at Catlett's Station, directly in the rear of the Federal army, Stuart made the sizable accomplishment of capturing Pope's papers.

From these papers Lee learned that Fitz-John Porter's corps, the advance of McClellan's northward shifting army, was to march from Fredericksburg to strengthen Pope's left, and that Pope's plan was to hold Lee at the Rappahannock until all of McClellan came up. Lee's hurry had been for the purpose of falling upon Pope before the two Federal armies made juncture and grew into a force too large for Lee to contend with. At the same time Lee was experiencing his first difficulty in persuading Davis to release troops from guarding possible points of danger until the last enemy soldier was proven to have actually vanished. With troops held at Richmond and five brigades at Hanover Junction, Lee could field only 55,000 infantry for his desired concentration.

Making do with what he had, Lee boldly divided his force and sent Jackson on a forced march in a sweep around Pope's right flank to his rear. On the 25th and 26th, Jackson's men made the most famous march of the war. Covering fifty-four miles in two days in the dusty heat, the total force of not more than 25,000 swung in an arc around Pope's army and came out thirteen miles behind him at Bristoe Station. Jackson was between Pope and Washington, but he was also in the midst of 100,000 of the enemy, with 50,000 more coming up. Setting up a rear guard at Bristoe, Jackson marched the rest of his exhausted men seven miles farther through the night to Manassas Junction, where they fell upon the grand capture of the Federal supply base.

On the 27th and 28th, Pope put all of his army and parts of McClellan's in motion toward Manassas Junction and Centreville, with the plan of interposing between Jackson and Longstreet. However, Jackson slipped northwest to Groveton during the night, and on the 28th, while his men rested in woods, was totally lost to Pope. Late in the day of the 28th Jackson, in order to draw the scattered Federals toward him, attacked a passing enemy column of King's division. Jackson's men ran into one of the toughest fights of the war and darkness fell on a field on which the Confederates had gained no tactical advantage whatever. (Ewell went out with a wound that caused a leg amputation.) But the engagement did serve Jackson's purpose of concentrating the Federals in his front.

On the 29th, while Jackson stood off repeated attacks across his slim front, extending southward from Sudley's Ford at Bull Run, Longstreet's units began to come up in support of Jackson's right. Lee had moved out with Longstreet on the afternoon of the 26th, marching west of the Bull Run Mountains to the eastern passageway at Thoroughfare Gap. There a Federal force had delayed the eastward passage until night of the 28th. Longstreet's first troops reached the field late in the morning of the 29th.

Where Jackson's units were then formed in the divisional organization which they would maintain, Longstreet's more loosely organized units operated partly by brigade movement. However, in response to a second, more urgent message from Lee to Davis (August 25), the President had released more troops to Longstreet's wing (later the First Corps), and these brigades had reached the field on the 29th. It was Lee's intent to attack with Longstreet while Jackson was holding off enemy assaults, before more of McClellan's troops arrived.

Here Lee first encountered the dangerous obstinacy in Longstreet when he was consulted about a movement in which he was to participate. It was Lee's habit, after he planned an action, to trust the execution to subordinates; and, as he wished to encourage initiative in a people's army, he preferred discretionary rather than direct orders to high-ranking subordinates. Though it is not mentioned in his letters to Davis nor in his Battle Report — the only existing correspondence on the battle, during which he gave verbal orders — Lee withheld the counterattack on the 29th rather than override Longstreet's stubborn objections.

Longstreet did not like to commit his troops until everything was just so. The ideal situation presented itself on the afternoon of the 30th when, with Jackson's force almost wrecked by its resistance to continued heavy attacks — and with the luck of reinforcements to the Federal left being late — the enemy's left flank was exposed to counterattack. When Lee's order came then, Longstreet was ready. In a curious rerun of First Manassas, Pope was driven from what had been the Confederate position on the old battlefield, back across Bull Run. Due more to Pope's than the soldiers' demoralization, much of the army was in rout.

On the 1st of September, Lee's pursuit was hampered by a violent storm and downpour, and Jackson's men, fought out and marched out, having suffered heavily in the loss of general officers, were in poor condition for vigorous, concerted action. On September 2, Pope withdrew the army into the defenses of Washington.

Yet, though the defeated enemy had escaped, Lee, in exactly three months, had cleared the invading forces from Virginia. Federal units were scattered in the northern end of the Valley, but they offered no menace, and militarily Lee shifted the theater of war from the interior to the border. In returning the war in Virginia to where it was at the beginning, he inflicted a severe blow to Union morale and gave substance in world opinion to the Confederacy's claim of its right to independence.

Personally, Lee ended the Second Manassas campaign as a minor casualty. On August 31 his horse Traveler was startled while Lee, dismounted, was standing at his head, and the general, tripping over the reins, fell heavily to the ground. A small bone was broken in one hand, the other hand was sprained, and, with both in splints, Lee was forced to ride in an ambulance.

230   To JEFFERSON DAVIS
Richmond, Virginia

Headquarters, Army Northern Virginia
July 9, 1862

Sir:

    After a thorough reconnaissance of the position taken up by the enemy on James River, I found him strongly posted and effectually flanked by his gunboats. In the present condition of our troops I did not think proper to risk an attack, on the results of which so much depended. I caused field batteries to play on his forces, and on his transports, from points on the river below. But they were too light to accomplish much, and were always attacked with superior force by the gunboats. I have caused the army to fall back to a position higher up the river, in order to meet the enemy should he again advance on Richmond, leaving the cavalry to watch his movements below. I have returned to my old quarters at Dabb's house, & will proceed at once to reorganize our forces for active operations. We have lost many valuable officers whose places must be supplied, and our thinned ranks must be filled as rapidly as possible.

    I have the honour to be very respectfully, your obt servt

R. E. LEE
Genl

231   To HIS WIFE
Richmond, Virginia

Dabb's Farm
June [July] 9, 1862

    I have returned to my old quarters dear Mary & am filled with gratitude to our Heavenly Father for all the mercies He has extended to us.

Our success has not been as great or complete as I could have desired, but God knows what is best for us. Our enemy has met with a heavy loss from which he must take some time to recover & then recommence his operations.

I hope you are all well & that Custis is recovering. I send in some clothes, please have them washed for me. I also want my trunk, left in Custis' room, to see if I have not some thinner clothes. I have also a pair of spectacles in it which I wish to get. Having lost my other pair. I shall come in when I can but I have much to do & do not know when that will be.

In the meantime I am with much love to all.

Always & as ever, yours

R. E. LEE

232   To GEORGE W. RANDOLPH
Secretary of War

Headquarters, Army of Northern Virginia
July 11, 1862

General:
Special Orders, Nos. 158 and 159, issued from the Adjutant and Inspector General's Office, July 10, announce six transfers of privates in different regiments of this army, two of these being to the Signal Corps, which is already sufficiently large. By the same orders 23 privates are detailed for duty in commissary, ordnance, and medical departments, and on special duty not named. In accordance with the Regulations, applications for details, furloughs, and transfers should pass through the headquarters of this army, that I may pronounce upon their propriety. If it is the desire of the Department, however, to adopt a different rule, I would be glad to have it so stated, that no confusion may arise and I may be relieved from the responsibility now resting on me. I fear that both officers and men are assigned to special duty on individual applications, in which the public service is not sufficiently considered. Efforts are constantly made to release men from the ranks where they are most needed. Many will be discharged on July 17 by the conscript law, and who could no doubt be employed in the different offices. I would recommend also that these be employed in the development of the niter caves, instead of making details for this purpose from the ranks under General Orders, No. 41, of which 20 have been requested from this army. I hope,

general, you will aid me to prevent as far as possible the diminution of our ranks by these various details.

I have the honor to be, yours, with high respect

R. E. LEE
General

233   To GEORGE W. RANDOLPH
                              Secretary of War

Headquarters Army of Northern Virginia
July 12, 1862

General:

I am compelled again to call your attention to details, transfers, &c., of soldiers in this army. By Special Orders, No. 160, from the Adjutant and Inspector General's Office, six privates are detailed for special duty — two to report to the Governor of Alabama; two privates are transferred from this army (one to forces in Georgia, the other to the Southwest), and a leave of absence is granted to an officer for thirty days. There are, no doubt, good reasons for these details, but unless the applications pass through the headquarters of this army I am unable to judge of their propriety. I have been obliged to issue an order that no application for furloughs will be considered except on a surgeon's certificate of disability. If this order can be evaded by application to the War Department dissatisfaction will be created among those who have been refused. I know you understand the condition of the army, and believe it is only necessary to call your attention to the injurious effects of this course to have it remedied. I regard the subject as one of immediate importance to the efficiency of the army.

I have the honor to be, with high respect, your obedient servant

R. E. LEE
General

234   To GENERAL FITZHUGH LEE
                              Reserve Camp, Near Richmond

Headquarters
July 15, 1862

My Dear Fitz:

I have just received your letter of the 13th. I am very sorry to hear of the sufferings of the wounded prisoners, and wish I could relieve them. I proposed to General McClellan on Tuesday, before the battle of that day, to parole and send to him all his wounded if he would receive them. Since that the arrangement has been made, and the sick and wounded are now being conveyed to him. This will relieve them very much, and enable us to devote our attention to those retained. In addition, the enemy has at last agreed to a general exchange of all prisoners of war and Generals [John A.] Dix and D. H. Hill are to meet tomorrow to commence the negotiations. I hope in this way much relief will be afforded; at first the hospitals were overtaxed, men could not be had to bury the dead, and the sufferings of all were increased. Friend Clitz ought to recollect that this is a matter of his own seeking, and he has only to blame himself. I will still be happy to do for him all I can, and will refer your letter to the director of the hospital if I can find him.

Your loving uncle

R. E. LEE

235   To JEFFERSON DAVIS
              Richmond, Virginia

Headquarters, Near Richmond
July 18, 1862

Mr. President:
    I have the honor to inclose a note just received from General Stuart. I have directed General Jackson, in the uncertainty of the enemy's intentions and in the hope of striking a blow at him, to take position from Beaver Dam Station to Frederick's Hall, so as to be on his flank should he move from Fredericksburg to Richmond or make an attempt toward Charlottesville from Culpeper. He writes me, under date of 17th, that from the reports received he was under the impression that Fredericksburg was being evacuated and the enemy was moving to Orange Court House. He was therefore drawing nearer Gordonsville and collecting his troops at Louisa Court House. This information from General Stuart would indicate a large force assembling at Winchester, which I do not credit. But it may be the enemy's intention to secure possession of the Valley, for which purpose they would seize the Central Railroad at Staunton and advance toward Charlottesville to cut off that communication with Lynchburg. The reports are so conflicting and sometimes opposing, and our people take up so readily all alarming accounts, which swell in their progress, that it is difficult to learn the truth till too late to profit by it. I think it is certain that heavy re-enforcements are reaching

McClellan, and that they will leave no stone unturned to capture Richmond. I fear they will draw upon their Western army, leaving a force to mask ours, and thus render it unavailable to us. I hear nothing of [General John C.] Pemberton's troops or of the conscripts from the south. We must endeavor to arouse our people. This army is improving, increasing, reorganizing, and undergoing daily instruction. When we get the new officers in their places, I mean the present vacancies filled, their improvement will be more apparent. I need not tell you that the whole division takes tone from its commander. The brigade receives its share in addition to what is imparted from the brigadiers.

I am with great esteem, your obedient servant

R. E. LEE
General

236   To GENERAL J. E. B. STUART
Commanding Cavalry

Headquarters
July 18, 1862

General:

A letter just received from Genl Jackson states that from information received he inclines to the belief that the enemy is withdrawing from Fredericksburg, and his destination is Gordonsville and that quarter. He is therefore moving nearer that point and has been obliged to withdraw his cavalry from Hanover Junction and the protection of the railroad.

Former accounts indicate a large force of the enemy concentrated at Fredericksburg. But whether it was his intention to move by water to reinforce McClellan or to march by land upon Richmond was not so clear.

I wish you to send some cavalry at least as far north as Hanover Junction or North Anna to watch the movements of the enemy and give protection to the railroad & country, and endeavour to get information of the enemy at Fredericksburg if possible, his intention, strength, &c. It is also an object to encourage our people to bring up from the Rappahannock Valley corn and grain of all kinds. Endeavour to spare your horses as much as possible & charge your officers to look to their comfort and that of the men.

Very respectfully, your obt serv't

R. E. LEE
General

237   To GENERAL GEORGE B. McCLELLAN
                     Commanding Army of the Potomac

                                              Headquarters, Near Richmond
                                                         July 21, 1862

General:

It has come to my knowledge that many of our citizens engaged in peaceful avocations have been arrested and imprisoned because they refused to take the oath of allegiance to the United States, while others by hard and harsh treatment have been compelled to take an oath not to bear arms against that Government.

I have learned that about one hundred of the latter class have recently been released from Fortress Monroe.

This Government refuses to admit the right of the authorities of the United States to arrest our citizens and extort from them their parole not to render military service to their country under the penalty of incurring punishment in case they fall into the hands of your forces.

I am directed by the Secretary of War to inform you that such oaths will not be regarded as obligatory, and persons who take them will be required to render military service.

Should your Government treat the rendition of such service by these persons as a breach of parole and punish it accordingly this Government will resort to retaliatory measures as the only means of compelling the observance of the rules of civilized warfare.

I have the honor to be very respectfully, your obt serv't

                                                         R. E. LEE
                                                         Genl Comndg

238   To GENERAL JAMES LONGSTREET
                     Commanding Division, Near Richmond

                                                         Headquarters
                                                         July 23, 1862

General:

Your note of this morning is received. If you can find suitable positions you can locate a brigade on the Darbytown & River roads and give them the necessary directions. They will serve in addition to what was proposed to prevent alarms and thus prevent annoyance to the troops. I have directed Genl Wise's brigade to be attached to your command. He is in your front and I desire you to take charge of the operations of that wing of the army.

General McClellan's demonstrations may be to deceive, test our strength, or preparatory to real movements. He will require to be watched and restrained. I have directed Genl D. H. Hill from the right bank of the river to endeavor by movable batteries, sharpshooters, &c., to annoy and arrest if possible the transport of his supplies.

Very respectfully

R. E. Lee
General

239   To GENERAL THOMAS J. JACKSON
            Commanding Valley District

Headquarters
July 23, 1862

General:

I have received your letter of the 21st with enclosures. I am in doubt as to the position and numbers of the enemy in your front and on the Rappahannock, and can get no clue as to his intentions. I am inclined to the belief that General McClellan is being reinforced to the extent of the means of his government and that he will continue to be so. A force will be kept in front of Washington to guard its approach and Genl [John] Pope I presume is charged with this duty. His main body I suspect is not far from Manassas, that being his best front, and his scouts and skirmishers are sent out for plunder, provisions, and devastation.

I have not been as yet able to send you reinforcements. Indeed, unless Genl Pope was within striking distance or you were prepared with transportation, provisions, &c., for a further aggressive movement I saw no object. I have not heard your strength or condition, or what favorable prospect you saw for a blow. The troops have not yet arrived from the south. Genl McClellan is feeling stronger, is uneasy in his position, and no doubt feels the necessity to advance upon his Richmond. He is making daily demonstrations to deceive or test our strength. Under these circumstances I am reluctant to weaken the force around Richmond without seeing a prospect of striking a blow elsewhere. I am however ready to reinforce you as soon as that prospect is apparent.

I am most resply & truly, yours

R. E. Lee
Genl

240   To GENERAL THOMAS J. JACKSON
Commanding Valley District

Headquarters, Department of Northern Virginia
July 25, 1862

General:

Your letter of the 24th is received. I hope you will be able to get definite information on Pope, his numbers, &c. You must keep your troops well in hand and your cavalry close upon him so that he cannot strike you an unexpected blow should you not be strong enough to strike at him. I wrote you on the subject of sending you reinforcements and the difficulty. Since then I have heard of [General Isaac I.] Stevens' division, from S[outh] C[arolina] joining McClellan. All Burnside's is said to have been withdrawn from N[orth] C[arolina]. I am extremely anxious to reinforce you, and would send Genl A. P. Hill's division but he is now in arrest. Genl D. H. Hill I have been obliged to send south of James River to take Holmes' place, who has gone to Arkansas, &c., instead of Magruder. D. H. Hill's division at present is without a commander in consequence of confusion among the major genls. Although feeling weak, uncertain which side of the James River the enemy will advance, and being obliged to watch both, I could send you a force to suppress Pope could I see a chance of your hitting him which did not involve its too long absence. Keep me advised and yourself prepared. They will be constantly annoying the railroad unless we can find their main body and drive it.

If Pope goes far enough could you swoop down north of the Rappahannock suddenly uniting with Stuart and clear the left bank opposite Fredericksburg? Wishing you all health and success.

I am very truly

R. E. LEE

241   To JEFFERSON DAVIS
Richmond, Virginia

Headquarters
July 25, 1862

Sir:

In reply to the letter of Col P. F. Liddell, 11th Mississippi Regiment applying for a transfer of his regiment & the 2nd Mississippi Col [J. M.]

Stone to one of the Mississippi brigades in Virginia, which you have referred to me for my remarks. I have the honour to state that I consider
the brigade to which they are now attached a Mississippi brigade. Two
of the four regiments which compose it are from Mississippi, & it is
commanded by a Mississippian. It is my intention as soon as the 42nd
Mississippi Regiment, lately arrived in Richmond, Col [Hugh R.] Miller,
can be withdrawn from the city, to assign it to that brigade, & to attach
the 6th N[orth] C[arolina] now with it to Col [J. A.] Walker's brigade.
I should like to obtain a fourth Mississippi regiment to replace the 4th
Alabama, it would then be entirely composed of Mississippi regiments.

If the 11th & 2nd are now withdrawn from it, it will break up a veteran brigade, distinguished for good service from the beginning of the war
in Virginia, & will leave Genl [W. H. C.] Whiting, an officer from Mississippi, without a brigade.

I have the honour to be, your obt servt

R. E. LEE
Genl

242   To JEFFERSON DAVIS
Richmond, Virginia

Headquarters, Army of Northern Virginia
July 25, [1862]

Mr. President:
I have read with care the telegram signed J. Walker from Hanover
Junction. His statements differ from those of two spies (Texans) who
arrived from Washington today. These say that Pope with the greater
portion of his forces is at Warrenton; that there are but three regiments
of infantry about Fredericksburg (at Falmouth), the cavalry being on
this side the river. They estimate Pope's force at about thirty-five thousand men, and report about eight thousand men in Washington and Alexandria, and further that seven heavy guns of the fourteen commanding
the approaches to the Long Bridge have been sent to McClellan since he
reached James River.

I have the honour to be with the highest respect, your obt servant

R. E. LEE
Genl

3 SECOND MANASSAS

243 To JEFFERSON DAVIS
Richmond, Virginia

Headquarters
July 26, 1862

Mr. President:

I enclose for your information a letter from Genl Jackson. He seems to be of the opinion that he is too weak to encounter Pope & I fear Pope is too strong to be allowed to remain so near our communications. He ought to be suppressed if possible. I would have sent A. P. Hill's division as I stated to you, but have no one to command it. Branch is the senior brigadier & I cannot trust the division to him. I feel that it will be necessary to reinforce him before he can do anything & yet I fear to jeopardize the division of this army, upon which so much depends.

If the impression made by [General John H.] Morgan in Kentucky could be confirmed by a strong infantry force, it would have the happiest effect. If he is obliged to fall back, the reaction may produce the same result as in Missouri: Where is Genl [Humphrey] Marshall? Now is the time for him to go in. But if Bragg could make a move, or with E. K. Smith & Loring, it would produce a great effect. Do you think anything can be done. I go to Drewry's Bluff today.

Very respy

R. E. Lee
Genl

244 To GENERAL THOMAS J. JACKSON
Commanding Valley District

Headquarters
July 26, 1862

General:

I have received your letter of the 23d instant giving the report of your scout concerning the position of Genl Pope's forces. I am glad to hear that you have sufficient transportation for your present purposes. I did not desire you to purchase more in reference to your future movements, but to collect and prepare what you had so as to have it at your command at a safe and convenient position. I have written to you on the subject of reinforcements. It is a difficult question. I am sorry you feel yourself so weak. I was in hopes your stragglers were coming to you. It has been determined to brigade the Louisiana regiments. The regiments assigned to you are those that will be first filled up with recruits from Louisiana. That is the reason for the change. I send you two & a battery and take away one regiment. Genl [Richard] Taylor, still an invalid, will go to Louisiana to hurry on the men. I will endeavour to send you a division in addition. Can you not take a strong position & resist the advance of Pope? Let me know your strength. Have field returns every ten days.

Very respectfully

R. E. LEE
General

245   To GENERAL THOMAS J. JACKSON
              Commanding Valley District

Headquarters, Army of Northern Virginia
July 27, 1862

General:

I have received your dispatch of 26th instant. I will send A. P. Hill's division and the 2nd Brigade of Louisiana Volunteers to you. [Colonel L. A.] Stafford's regiment 9th Louisiana need not therefore be sent here as directed in Special Orders, No. 163. These troops will exceed 18,000 men. Your command ought certainly to number that amount. What has become of them? I heard they were coming to you from the Valley. Do not let your troops run down if it can possibly be avoided by attention to their wants, comforts, &c., by their respective commanders. This will require your personal attention, also consideration and preparation in your movements.

I want Pope to be suppressed. The course indicated in his orders if the newspapers report them correctly cannot be permitted and will lead to retaliation on our part. You had better notify him the first opportunity. The order of [General Adolph von] Steinwehr must be disavowed or you must hold the first captains from his army for retaliation. They will not be exchanged. A. P. Hill you will find I think a good officer with whom you can consult and by advising with your division commanders as to your movements much trouble will be saved you in arranging details as they can act more intelligently. I wish to save you trouble from my increasing your command. Cache your troops as much

as possible till you can strike your blow and be prepared to return to me
when done if necessary. I will endeavour to keep Genl McClellan quiet
till it is over if rapidly executed.

Very respectfully and truly

R. E. LEE
Genl

246   To MISS MILDRED LEE
                     Richmond, Virginia

Headquarters, Near Richmond
July 28, 1862

My Precious Life:
    I have just received in a letter from your mother your note of the
20th. It is as you state very short & little. But in that it is like you. And
like you it is very sweet, & like you it has given me much pleasure. But
I cannot see what you are proud of & advise you against all such feelings for you know what is said in that good book about a proud spirit
going before a fall. I can join you in your gratitude to our Heavenly Father for preserving the members of our immediate family, when so many
others have suffered. I hope you are all well & happy. How are my Annie & Agnes? I wrote a letter to you all some time since, which probably
has not reached you. Your mama & Charlotte are at Hickory Hill &
quite well. I do not know how long they will remain. They seem to enjoy
the quiet & affection they experience. Custis & your sister are at your
Uncle Carter's. I have only heard once of the former since he left. He
was getting along very slowly but I hope surely. Rob is off with Jackson
& I hope will catch Pope & his cousin Louis Marshall. I could forgive
the latter for fighting against us, if he had not have joined such a miscreant as Pope. Love & kisses to you all from your father.

R. E. LEE

247   To GEORGE W. RANDOLPH
                     Secretary of War

Headquarters, Army of Northern Virginia
July 28, 1862

Sir:
    Genl D. H. Hill has been directed to proceed with picked troops to
old Fort Powhatan and about 50 pieces of artillery to endeavor to cut off

Genl McClellan's communications by the river. I have ordered Genl [William N.] Pendleton with five of his reserve batteries, the two 32-pounders, the long 32-pounder (Long Tom) and the 18-pounder, all on siege carriages on the same expedition. I know of no heavier blow that could be dealt Genl McClellan's army than to cut off his communication. It would oblige him to break up from his position and retire at least to the broad part of the river. But if this cannot be done the attempt if partially successful will anchor him in his present position from which he would not dare to advance, so that I can reinforce Jackson without hazard to Richmond, and thus enable him to drive if not destroy the miscreant Pope.

I am particularly anxious that our newspapers may not give the enemy notice of our intentions and have directed Genl [D. H.] Hill in order to cover his movement to say he was moving against Suffolk and Norfolk, so as to satisfy the curiosity of our countrymen. I leave it for you to judge whether an enigmatical paragraph in the *Dispatch* to that effect or entire silence may be most advisable.

I have the honor to be, &c., &c.

R. E. LEE
Genl

248   To SYDNEY SMITH LEE
               Richmond, Virginia

July 31, 1862

My Dear Smith:

I send by General Martin your overcoat. It was a great comfort to me and kept me very warm, but it is not waterproof. I was out till 12 that night. Upon my return I found Fitzhugh's promotion, which I had applied for some days before. I consider him one of our best cavalry officers. He, of course, knew nothing of my application, and when his promotion was announced to him he could find but one objection, viz., his fear he might be mistaken for the other General Lee, and that they would be so mixed up, together they would not be able to tell one from the other. I pity him if he is mistaken for me. With much love and affection.

Your brother

R. E. LEE

249   To GENERAL DANIEL H. HILL
                 Commanding Department South of James River

                                                        Headquarters
                                                        August 2, 1862
General:
    I am glad to learn by your dispatch that your attack upon the ene-
my's shipping was successful, and that they were driven from their moor-
ings. Any positive damage inflicted upon their vessels, &c., was of course
a positive gain to us. But this does not satisfy the object I had in view.
My desire was for you to cut off their communication by the river if
practicable, or should this be impossible, to render it so insecure and
precarious as to oblige General McClellan to abandon his position, or at
least to prevent any advance or attack on his part. This will require continuous and systematic effort and a well digested plan. To form the latter
the river bank below Coggins Point should be examined and the best
modes of approach and retreat ascertained. The artillery officers and
others that will have to operate can be used for this purpose, and the
enemy's vessels should be driven from every position we can reach. If the
site of old Fort Powhatan can be held, the passage of his transports will
be arrested. If it cannot, there are points below and above that can be
temporarily occupied, and by seizing several at the same and different
times, the enemy will be annoyed and harassed and will lose confidence and security in their position. I wish you would see what can be
done in this way. A sufficient force of infantry in my opinion will be
necessary for the guns, which could be at hand in covered spots to be used
if required.
    Cavalry will also be required to give you information of the move-
ments of the enemy.

                        I have the honor to be, your obt servt

                                                        R. E. LEE
                                                        Genl

250   To HIS WIFE
                         "Hickory Hill," Virginia

                                                        Dabbs'
                                                        August 3, 1862

    I have received dear Mary your letter of the 1st & am glad to learn
that you are well & are enjoying the society of such dear friends. You

must thank them for their kind remembrances of me & say how delighted I should be could I get to see them. I feel very grateful for their prayers & am sure that they are heard in heaven, & tend to the merciful protection so constantly extended to me by the great God of all. How I wish I was in any way worthy of his blessing! Tell aunt Judy Nelson I beg she will always remember me in her devotions, & that I hope she will enjoy many years of peace & quiet of the country. I have forwarded your letters to Mrs. Caskie. I was called in by the President eight or ten days ago & called to see her. They were as kind as ever but I could only remain a few moments. Custis & Mary had not returned when I last heard from the house, but it was said C[ustis] would be back yesterday. Mrs. Mary Stevenson has arrived in Richmond & drove up to the house prepared to stay, supposing you were there. Her sister Anne is dead & she is extremely anxious to return to Georgetown & has come on that mission. I do not know what I can do for her except give my consent to her marrying Major Hutter which may reconcile her to remaining in the Confederacy. I have heard nothing from the girls. Poor little things. I am afraid they are all astray. Fitzhugh passed up to Hanover Friday & I hope you will see him. I am told he is very well. I went down one day to visit the cavalry pickets, but he was at the other end of the line & I could not get to him. I have heard of Grace [Darling]. She was seen bestrode by some yankee with her colt by her side. I could be better resigned to many things than that. I must try & be resigned to that too. I have also lost my horse Richmond. He died Thursday. I had ridden him the day before. He seemed in the morning as well as ever, but I discovered in the evening he was not well, but thought he was merely distressed by the heat & brought him along very slowly. Finding at bed time he had not recuperated & was breathing heavily I had him bled which seemed to relieve him & in the morning he was pronounced better. I however administered a purgative, & at noon he was reported dead. But his labours are over & he is at rest. He carried me very faithfully & I shall never have so beautiful an animal again. His fate is different from Grace's & to his loss I can easily be resigned. I shall want but few horses more, & have as many as I require.

Give much love to all with you & believe me always yours

R. E. LEE

P.S. I send a letter from Mrs. Stiles, which you must answer for me & say everything that is kind for me.

R. E. L.

251   To GENERAL DANIEL H. HILL
           Commanding Department of North Carolina

Headquarters, Army of Northern Virginia
August 3, 1862
8 p.m.

General:

Your letter of 9½ a.m. has been received. The landing of the force opposite Westover may be to prevent annoyance from our artillery, or it may be, as you suppose, the commencement of the advance on the south side of the river. If the former, they can be driven away, and if the latter they can be resisted as well on that side of the river as on this. The news from Norfolk may or may not be true, but we must set to work vigorously to prepare to arrest their progress. I wish you to examine the ground and see how this can best be done. I will send Lt Col [Walter H.] Stevens to make an examination of the country, and I wish you to ascertain what force of labourers can be drawn from that country and from North Carolina. In regard to harassing the enemy by cutting off his communications, his occupancy of the south side will render it more difficult, but even the attempt seems to have caused him to divide his forces, and I hope that on one side or the other of the river may be demolished. The removal of Genl [Richard H.] Anderson from his present position would stop the construction of the defences of Drewry's Bluff, which it will be imprudent to do at this time. The stand for riflemen at City Point which you recommended to be intrenched could surely be accomplished by the troops at Petersburg. Genl Pendleton can remain for the present if he is needed.

Very respectfully, your obt servt

R. E. LEE
Genl

252   To GENERAL DANIEL H. HILL
           Commanding Department of North Carolina

Headquarters, Army of Northern Virginia
August 4, 1862

General:

It is reported that the enemy are seizing wood on the banks of the James and Appomattox Rivers. Please cause all the wood in the wood-yards accessible to their boats to be burned where it is possible to do so, unless it can be removed and appropriated to the benefit of its owners or of our army.

Very respectfully, your obt servant

R. E. LEE
General

253   To GENERAL THOMAS J. JACKSON
Commanding Valley District

Headquarters, Army of Northern Virginia
August 4, 1862

General:

I have just received your letter of this date. The letter of Mr. R. T. Scott which I have read with much interest I return. It carries with it an air of probability and truth. I have heard nothing further from Fredericksburg. General Stuart was yesterday to move with all his cavalry in that direction with a view of penetrating the interdicted limits and ascertaining if possible the veiled movements of the enemy. I have not had time to hear. I cannot think their force there large and believe it is concentrated in your front. You are right in not attacking them in their strong and chosen positions. They ought always to be turned as you propose and thus force them on more favorable ground. I do not know that the central position you refer to will accomplish this. But you ought to know. I should think passing their left flank would. It is important the strength of the enemy at Fredericksburg should be ascertained, or your communication might be cut.

The enemy on the James River seem unsettled in his plans. Yesterday he crossed the river with infantry, artillery, and cavalry, and seem to threaten an advance on Petersburg with a view of seizing that road. To-day some of his gunboats have moved up to Malvern Hill and have taken position as if to sweep the ground preparatory to its occupation by a land force. In a day or two their object may be disclosed. They still too threaten Goldsboro from New Berne.

General A. P. Hill carried with him an excess of transportation. The order for its return probably did not reach him in time for him to send it back. If so and it reaches your army you can retain it as it will be required for other troops which I hope to send. But have it turned over to your quartermaster.

I am very respectfully & truly

R. E. LEE
General

254   To GENERAL DANIEL H. HILL
Commanding Department of North Carolina

Headquarters, New Market
August 7, 1862

General:

Your letter of the 5th was received this morning. I regret to hear of the feeble conduct of your cavalry. Who is its commander & what is its strength? I hope you will see to its organization & instruction. The gunboat ought to have been destroyed. It may be too late to attack it now, but if not try it with incendiary shells. You must endeavor to make your present division superior to your former & I have great confidence of your accomplishing it.

I hope you will lose no opportunity of damaging the enemy in every way. I fear I shall have to recall Pendleton soon. His command requires his presence & his guns are wanted here now. His batteries may also be wanted around Richmond. The enemy appear extremely active & are making their appearance at all points bearing on the city. Push on your defenses at Petersburg & around Drewry's Bluff. I wish to have Anderson's division liberated. It is wanted now. Get all the free black & slave labour you can, & if you can accomplish anything against the enemy at Coggins Point, or his communications by the river, do so at the earliest favourable moment.

Most resply, your obt servt

R. E. LEE
Genl

255   To JEFFERSON DAVIS
Richmond, Virginia

Headquarters, New Market
August 7, 1862

Mr. President:

It having been reported to me Tuesday evening that the enemy in considerable force had occupied Malvern Hill, and that it looked like a general advance of McClellan's army, I directed the divisions of Genls Longstreet & McLaws & the brigades under Genl Ripley to advance next morning to the Long Bridge road. On reaching that road the enemy appeared in considerable strength & to occupy the ground on which the battle was fought on Tuesday the 31st June [July 1]. His troops were drawn up in line of battle, his artillery in position, & he apparently was prepared to deliver battle in as strong force as he did on that day. Genls McLaws' & Ripley's divisions, reinforced by that of Genl D. R. Jones' formed our left, while Genl Longstreet's formed the right. The day was intensely hot and the progress of the troops necessarily slow. Before the Long Bridge & Charles City roads were clear of his pickets and his line of battle disclosed the sun had nearly set. Orders were then given for our left wing to advance to Willis' Church, extending well to the left & threatening the enemy's communications with Westover. Two brigades of Genl Longstreet's division were ordered to advance upon Malvern Hill and drive in his parties extending over Curl's [Curles] Neck. This latter operation was handsomely done by Genl Evans with his own & Cobb's brigades, and the enemy's parties were driven under their guns at Malvern Hill.

From the prisoners captured during the day it was ascertained that the enemy was in strong force — infantry, artillery, & cavalry. [Generals Joseph E.] Hooker's, [John] Sedgwick's, [Philip] Kearny's, and [David B.] Birney's divisions were mentioned as being present, [also] [William H.] Emory's cavalry and [Samuel P.] Heintzelman's and [Edwin V.] Sumner's corps.

This morning upon the advance of the troops it was ascertained that the enemy had disappeared during the night, & has now apparently retired within his former lines.

I have directed the reestablishment of our pickets & the return of our troops to their former positions & duties. The number of the killed & captured of the enemy I do not exactly know, but they are few. Our casualties small.

I have the honor to be, your obt svt

R. E. LEE
Genl

256   To GENERAL THOMAS J. JACKSON
Commanding Valley District

Headquarters, Near New Market
August 7, 1862
9 a.m.

General:

Your dispatch of yesterday is received. I am here in consequence of the reported advance of McClellan's army. I have no idea that he will ad-

vance on Richmond now. But it may be premonitory to get a new position, reconnoiter, &c. I think it more probable to cover other movements.
Probably that of Burnside's from Fredericksburg, of which I wrote you
last night. [Admiral David D.] Porter's mortar fleet is in Hampton
Roads. His gunboats at City Point and Curles Neck. I hope to determine
today what it means. But at present it seems to me too hazardous to
diminish the forces here, until something more is ascertained. I therefore
cannot promise to send you the reinforcements I intended and still desire. As the expectation of reinforcements may delay your operations and
otherwise embarrass you and prevent your making an advantageous
movement you had better not calculate on them. If I can send them
I will. If I cannot and you think it proper and advantageous act without them. Being on the spot you must determine what force to operate
against. I agree with you in believing that if you advance into Fauquier
that the force at Fredericksburg, if it be Pope's, would in all probability follow. But if it be Burnside's, and Pope in your front is strong
enough to resist you, it might operate injuriously on your rear, also to
the railroad, your communications, &c. If you were strong enough to
bear down all opposition in your front the force at Fredericksburg
might be neglected, for it would be sure to fall if that in your front
was suppressed. It was to save you the abundance of hard fighting that I
ventured to suggest for your consideration not to attack the enemy's
strong points, but to turn his position at Warrenton, &c., so as to draw
him out of them. I would rather you should have easy fighting and heavy
victories. I must now leave the matter to your reflection and good judgment. Make up your mind what is best to be done under all the circumstances which surround us and let me hear the result at which you
arrive. I will inform you if any change takes place here that bears on the
subject.

I am very respy, &c., &c.

R. E. Lee
Genl Comdg

257   To HENRY T. CLARK
                 Governor of North Carolina

Headquarters, Department of Northern Virginia
August 8, 1862

Sir:
    I have the honor to acknowledge the receipt of your letter of the
4th instant.

I have been an eye witness of the outrages and depredations upon private property committed by the enemy in this State and can fully appreciate what you say of the injuries sustained by the people of North Carolina; nor am I unmindful of the importance of protecting the line of railroad, and as far as practicable the valuable private interests in the section of country to which you refer. But it is impossible with the means at our command, to pursue the policy of concentrating our forces to protect important points and baffle the principal efforts of the enemy, and at the same time extend all the protection we desire to give to every district. The safety of the whole State of North Carolina, as well as of Virginia, depends in a measure upon the result of the enemy's efforts in this quarter, which if successful, would make your State the theater of hostilities far more injurious and destructive to your citizens than anything they have yet been called upon to suffer.

To prevent effectually the enemy's gunboats from ascending navigable rivers would require not only batteries, but adequate land forces to defend them, which would lead to a subdivision of our forces from which we could anticipate nothing but disaster. The selection of the troops to be withdrawn from North Carolina was made by Genl Holmes, who brought the most serviceable because there was most probability of their being used, the enemy being known to be here in great force, and it being believed that most of his troops had been withdrawn from North Carolina. The raw troops were left for the additional reason that it was thought they would stand the usual camp diseases better at home than if removed.

General Holmes and part of his army left N[orth] Carolina before the late battles, and participated in them. He brought the brigades of Genls [James G.] Martin & [Samuel G.] French because the enemy being in and upon James River, it was thought proper to provide against any attempt he might make to penetrate North Carolina and cut the railroad from the north, which might have been among his designs. With this view Genl Holmes was ordered back to the south side of the river immediately after the battles, where he was joined by Genls Martin & French.

The information received by General Holmes led him to believe, as I do, that the principal part of Genl Burnside's command had been transferred to Virginia, where I believe they now are.

Major Genl D. H. Hill is in command of the district lately commanded by General Holmes, as you will perceive from the enclosed copy of the order assigning him to it. He will no doubt be very glad to confer with you as to the best means of protecting the country you refer to, and I should be most happy if your plan of retaking the places on

the coast now held by the enemy can be carried out. I am most anxious to
do all in our power to accomplish so desirable a result and extend the best
protection to the people our means will permit. I regret to hear what you
say of the character of the officers appointed to command the troops in
North Carolina.

I have the honor to be very respectfully, your obt servt

R. E. LEE
General

258   To MISSES ANNIE AND AGNES LEE
             Warren County, North Carolina

Near Richmond
August 9, 1862

I can only write you a short letter my dear daughters & it must
therefore be a joint one. On my return night before last from Malvern
Hill I found your sweet affectionate letters my dear Annie & Agnes
which made me wish to see you more than ever. I am glad you are all
well & have determined to write to me sometimes without waiting for
replies. I have but little time for such recreation & I feel after they are
written they are not worth reading, so it gives but little encouragement.
I was called to Malvern Hill by its occupation by the enemy. On reaching there Wednesday afternoon after a dreadful hot march for our
men, I found the enemy in position & in the same lines they occupied
Tuesday the 1st July & apparently in the same strength, drawn up, infantry, cavalry & artillery in battle array. I thought they were going to
fight the battle over again. We got in position by dark & rested till 3
next morning. On moving up we found they had slipped through our
fingers during the night leaving in our hands some forty or fifty prisoners
& a few dead on the field, the result of the skirmish the previous evening.
They took refuge within their lines & we took another hot march to
our camp. Your mother is at Hickory Hill. Charlotte also. She says she
is going to join you soon.

Mrs. Mary Stevenson & little M. are in Richmond & return to
Georgetown on Tuesday with Genl S. Thomas. Markie's friend. I received a note from Annette the other day by an unknown hand. From
what she said I supposed it was one of her sweethearts coming to the wars.
All were well & all at Goodwood. Mary Hoffman & her spouse had been
to see them. The former in full health again, looking very well. I send

you her letter & card. Preserve the latter for me & if you ever write express my thanks &c. Miss Kittie Stiles came on for her brother. He left the morning of the evening of her arrival in Richmond. Your mother' saw her. He was slightly wounded. Your sister is at Mrs. C[askie]'s. Custis is at his castle with his bachelors, looking quite well but reporting weak. I will send him your letters that he may read your messages. Rob is with Jackson. It will be difficult for a letter to find him. Fitzhugh near Hanover Court House.

No time for more. Love & kisses to you all.

Your devoted father

R. E. LEE

259   To GENERAL THOMAS J. JACKSON
Commanding Valley District

Headquarters, Department of Northern Virginia
August 12, 1862

General:

I congratulate you most heartily on the victory which God has granted you over our enemies at Cedar Run. The country owes to you and your brave officers and soldiers a deep debt of gratitude.

I hope your victory is but the precursor of others over our foe in that quarter which will entirely break up and scatter his army. I mourn with you the loss of many gallant officers and men, and chief among them that noble and accomplished officer and patriot Genl C. S. Winder.

I am most respectfully, your obt svt

R. E. LEE
Genl

260   To GENERAL DANIEL H. HILL
Commanding Department of North Carolina

Headquarters, Department of Northern Virginia
August 13, 1862

General:

I desire you to select from the troops under your command some of your most reliable & intelligent men and send them down the south side of James River to watch the movements of the enemy, & ascertain the truthfulness of the report made by the English deserter of the embarkation of a part of McClellan's army.

It is of the first importance that I should be advised positively on this point, as our own movements must be in a measure regulated by those of that army.

The scouts that you send should remain in the vicinity of the enemy, watch their movements narrowly and unceasingly and report immediately anything of importance that should occur.

R. E. LEE
Genl .

261   To GEORGE W. RANDOLPH
Secretary of War

Headquarters, Near Richmond
August 14, 1862

General:
Your letter of this date is received. From every indication it appears that McClellan's forces on James River are being withdrawn and sent to reinforce Pope. Under these circumstances I think it will be necessary to withdraw R. H. Anderson's division from Drewry's Bluff and send it in the direction of Gordonsville. Colonel [George C.] Gibbs' regiment [Forty-second North Carolina Regiment] and the Fifty-seventh North Carolina Regiment (Colonel H. C. Jones) had better be ordered for the present to that point. In case Anderson is removed these troops will serve for the defense of Drewry's Bluff, and since they are new they can be drilled and accustomed to camp, &c.

I am very respectfully, your obedient servant

R. E. LEE
General

262   To GENERAL JAMES LONGSTREET
Commanding Division, Gordonsville, Virginia

Headquarters
August 14, 1862
9 a.m.

General:
Your note of 6½ p.m. yesterday is just received. At this distance without knowing the position or strength of the enemy, it is impossible

for me to decide the question you propose. I incline however to the right flank movement, the easiest way of accomplishing that I should prefer. You being on the spot, with all information before you and the benefit of consultation with officers acquainted with the ground and circumstances, must use your own judgment and determine. As soon as I learned yesterday that Burnside had left Fredericksburg I ordered [General John B.] Hood to march and report to you. Send him word to what point to direct his march. You can stop the troops in transit from here at Louisa if you think fit and direct them to move towards the Rappahannock. I have directed Stuart to get ready his cavalry to move on. I have proposed as I informed you when here to send Stuart by the right to sweep round by the enemy's rear and cut his communications when we get ready to move, keeping Jackson's cavalry on our left and in the enemy's front to disguise the movement. Is there any objection to this? If so Stuart must be directed otherwise.

I mention this because in your letter after speaking of the movement forward, you say "the cavalry will be necessary on the other flank," by which I infer you mean the left. It is all important that our movement in what ever direction it is determined should be as quick as possible. I fear Genl Pope can be reinforced quicker than ourselves, prepare accordingly. Order the transportation of the respective brigades to the point on the railroad you wish the troops to halt. I had arranged to leave in the cars tomorrow morning at 4 o'clock to join you. Let me know where I shall find you. I should like if convenient to see Jackson too.

Most resply and truly yours

R. E. LEE

263   To JEFFERSON DAVIS
                    Richmond, Virginia

Headquarters
August 14, 1862

Mr. President:

I have made all arrangements for the well being of the troops around Richmond. I have given instructions to Genl [G. W.] Smith, & Col [J. F.] Gilmer in reference to the defences & have placed the former in command of the troops on both sides of the river. The aggregate of the four divisions, present & absent, amounts to 72,047 men.

From every account that reaches me the enemy is accumulating a large force in Culpeper. Three deserters from Burnside came in today, &

report that he reached Fredericksburg with 12000, & received 21 regiments after his arrival there. They were old troops & came via Aquia Creek. They did not know where from. What do you think of the propriety of withdrawing R. H. Anderson's division from here to Gordonsville? It amounts to 13,142 aggregate. This would leave an aggregate here of about 60,000. In addition to the four divisions above stated, the two N[orth] C[arolina] regiments from Salisbury & Lynchburg are ordered to D. H. Hill. This will add about 1300 men to his strength. I thought they would do better there, having not yet been in the field & give them a better opportunity for instruction & to pass through the camp diseases. I did this in anticipation of the necessity of withdrawing Hill or [General Lafayette] McLaws. Unless I hear from you to the contrary I shall leave for G[ordonsville] at 4 a.m. tomorrow. The troops are accumulating there & I must see that arrangements are made for the field. I received a letter from Longstreet today requesting my presence. I will keep you informed of everything of importance that transpires. When you do not hear from me, you may feel sure that I do not think it necessary to trouble you. I shall feel obliged to you for any directions you may think proper to give. I learn that Genl Johnston will soon return to Richmond. He is riding on horseback every day & is gaining his strength rapidly.

Wishing you every happiness & prosperity I am with high esteem, your obt servt

R. E. LEE
Genl

P.S. A note just received from Genl D. H. Hill says he has sent reliable scouts to ascertain McL—s [McClellan's] condition, & that there can be no doubt but that [General Fitz John] Porter's corps has left.

R. E. L.

264   To GENERAL GUSTAVUS W. SMITH
Commanding Division, Richmond, Virginia

Headquarters, Army of Northern Virginia
August 14, 1862

General:
I propose joining that portion of the Army of Northern Virginia now under Genl Longstreet and expect to leave here tomorrow. In my absence you will be the senior officer with this wing of the army and I

request you to direct its operations. For all purpose connected with the defence of Richmond, James River, its approaches and &c., you will give directions to Genls D. H. Hill and R. H. Anderson stationed on the south side of James River. Genl D. H. Hill is in command of the Department of N[orth] C[arolina] which has been extended from the Cape Fear to the James River, and that army has been united to this. From your general knowledge of the affairs of this army, its objects & position, I deem no instructions necessary beyond the necessity of holding Richmond to the last extremity should any attack be made upon it. The lines of defence on both sides of the river must be completed as soon as possible and every attention given to the organization, instruction, and discipline of the troops. Trimonthly returns of the troops are required by existing orders, and I wish you would cause a consolidated return of the four divisions with you to be forwarded to me. Should you be able to ascertain whether General McClellan is diminishing his force at his present position, please let me know, and to what points they are being sent. It may be necessary in that event to reduce our own force correspondingly or to withdraw it entirely. I wish you to keep this contingency constantly in view. Genls D. H. Hill & Hampton have instructions to keep out scouts and to use every means in their power to ascertain Genl McClellan's movements. Lieut Col E. P. Alexander has undertaken measures to the same end.

I am with high respect, your obt servant

R. E. Lee
General

P.S. My headquarters will first be at Gordonsville.

R. E. L.

265

To G. W. C. LEE
Richmond, Virginia

[August 14, 1862]

My Dear Custis:
I write a line to say good-bye to you & Mary. I had hoped to have been able to have come in & see you both to night, but I find it impossible to enjoy that pleasure. I have had much to do which with preparation for my departure renders it impossible.
Good bye my dear children. May God bless & guard you both. Tell your mother when she arrives that I was unable to stop to see her. I

go to Gordonsville. My after movements depends on circumstances that I cannot foresee.

Truly & affly your father

R. E. LEE

P.S. I send in my straw hat which please give house room to. Also a summer under-jacket which I find out of my trunk. If you have the key put it in, or ask your mother to mend it & keep it for me.

R. E. L.

266   To JEFFERSON DAVIS
                Richmond, Virginia
                TELEGRAM

Gordonsville, Virginia
August 15, 1862

HIS EXCELLENCY JEFFERSON DAVIS:
  PLEASE PUT GENERAL R. H. ANDERSON'S DIVISION IN MOTION TOMORROW. DIRECT HIM TO HALT AT LOUISA COURT HOUSE; ORDERS WILL MEET HIM THERE. I MOVE TOMORROW TOWARD RAPIDAN.

R. E. LEE

267   To JEFFERSON DAVIS
                Richmond, Virginia

Gordonsville
August 16, 1862

Mr. President:
  I think it certain that Genls Burnside & [Rufus] King with their troops from Fredericksburg have joined Genl Pope at Culpeper Court House. Their numbers are variously estimated, reaching as high as 40,000. Putting them at 20,000, Pope's force according to Genl Jackson's estimate will be between 65,000 & 70,000. This corresponds with accounts of intelligent men from Culpeper. Two citizens who had been taken prisoner made their escape from Culpeper Court House yesterday & say from overheard conversations the Federals estimate themselves at 92,000. They report nothing but provisions coming by railroad from Alexandria which is constantly arriving. No troops, unless they are drawing men from

McClellan. I do not see where they will get them at present. I hope to hear every day of Imboden's success in his attempt on the Baltimore & Ohio Railroad. He started from Staunton sometime since with about 600 men & by his own calculations would have reached the trestle work four or five days since. We must make allowance for delays & difficulties. I hope he will be in time to arrest troops from the West. Reports from Genl [Samuel G.] French today say McClellan is still sending off troops, & I see a letter published in the *Philadelphia Enquirer* of the 13th from its Fort Monroe correspondent, stating that the mail boat from Harrison's Landing had reached Old Point 11 August, & that the indications were that a movement of the whole or a large part of the army was about taking place. If it was going up the river, I suppose it would have been discovered before this. If down, they must again be about to change their base of operations. It may be that this part of the country is to be the scene of operations. In that event the war will for a season at least be removed from Richmond & I would recommend that the troops be removed too. The garrisons can be kept up & the defences in every particular perfected. The completion of the *Richmond* should be pushed forward with all vigour & in a short time she would clear the river. I think the health as well as discipline of the army will be benefited by a change to the country from the town & the city itself receive a more healthy atmosphere. If it can be ascertained that McClellan is moving, unless his quarters can be beaten up, I would recommend that another division follow Anderson's.

> I am with great respect, your obt servt
> R. E. Lee
> Genl

268   To HIS WIFE
                           "Hickory Hill," Virginia

> Camp Near Orange Court House
> August 17, 1862

My Dear Mary:

I passed by you Friday morning when you were asleep. I looked very hard but could see no body. I should have liked so much to stop to have waked you all up. I was afraid at such an hour I should not have been welcome. But welcome or not I was obliged to go on & here I am in a tent, instead of my comfortable quarters at Dabb's. The tent however is very comfortable & of that I have nothing to complain.

Genl Pope says he is very strong & seems to feel so, for he is moving apparently up to the Rapidan. I hope he will not prove stronger than we are. I learn since I have left that Genl McClellan has moved down the river with his whole army, I suppose he is coming here too, so we shall have a busy time. I do not know that it is true, but such are the despatches I get this morning. Burnside & King from Fredericksburg have joined Pope, which from their own report has swelled Pope to 92,000. I do not believe it, though I believe he is very big. Johnny Lee saw Louis M[arshall] after Jackson's last battle, who asked kindly after his old uncle & said his mother &c. were well. Johnny said he looked wretchedly himself. I am sorry he is in such bad company. But I suppose he could not help it. I have not seen my precious Rob yet. I hear he is well. I presume he does not know I am here, & I have not had time to go to him. Give much love to every body & plenty of kisses to Chass, Cousin Anne &c.

Truly & devotedly yours

R. E. Lee

269   To JEFFERSON DAVIS
Richmond, Virginia

Headquarters East of Orange Court House
August 17, 1862

Mr. President:

From dispatches just received from General French it appears certain that General McClellan's force has escaped us. I feel greatly mortified, for though the material damage dealt him in the battles of the Chickahominy was not as great as I could have wished, he must have been so morally shattered as to have induced the belief that the safety of his army required his retreat and to have caused his abandonment of his present attack on Richmond. This of itself I feel as a great relief, but he ought not to have got off so easily. This induces me to say what I have had on my mind for some time. I fear General [D. H.] Hill is not entirely equal to his present position. An excellent executive officer, he does not appear to have much administrative ability. Left to himself he seems embarrassed and backward to act. If the people would think so, I really believe French would make the better commander of the department. This is only for you to think about, but I fear all was not done that might have been done to harass and destroy our enemies, but I blame nobody but myself. General Hampton may have picked up some stragglers, but that is all I can now hope for. I can only conjecture two positions that he will now assume: To ascend the Rappahannock, occupy Fredericksburg, and threaten Richmond from there, or to unite with General Pope. It is possible that hearing of the advance of our army in this direction it may have been taken advantage of to extricate him from his dilemma under the pretense of defending Washington. We shall, however, see, but we must lose no time in preparing to meet him wherever he may appear. I wrote you on this subject yesterday, and will not repeat. The troops had better march, beginning at once, using the railroad as far as it goes, and as a help to transport the feeble of all the divisions. By the time they reach Hanover Junction we shall probably hear where the new base is assumed. Colonel Northrop must make arrangements for their provisions, and his arrangements must precede the movement of the troops. I beg you will excuse my troubling you with my opinions, and especially these details, but your kindness had led you to receive them without objection so often that I know I am tempted to trespass. I am getting the troops in position near the fords of Somerville Mills and Raccoon Ford of the Rapidan. They have preceded their transportation and the process is slow and tedious. I hope to succeed by tomorrow, all except Anderson's.

With high respect, your obedient servant

R. E. LEE
General

270   SPECIAL ORDERS, NO. 185

Headquarters, Army of Northern Virginia
August 19, 1862

I.   Genl Longstreet's command constituting the right wing of the army, will cross the Rapidan at Raccoon Ford, and move in the direction of Culpeper Court House.

Genl Jackson's command constituting the left wing, will cross at Summerville Ford, and move in the same direction, keeping on the left of Genl Longstreet.

Genl Anderson's division will cross at Somerville Ford, follow the route of Genl Jackson & act in reserve. The battalion of light artillery under Col S. D. Lee will take the same route. The cavalry under Genl Stuart will cross at Morton's Ford, pursue the route by Stevensburg to Rappahannock Station, destroy the railroad bridge, cut the enemy's communication, telegraph line, and, operating towards Culpeper Court House, will take position on Genl Longstreet's right.

II.   The commanders of each wing will designate the reserve for their commands. Medical & ammunition wagons will alone follow the troops across the Rapidan. The baggage & supply trains will be parked under their respective officers in secure positions, on the south side, so as not to embarrass the different roads.

III.   Cooked rations for three days will be carried in the haversacks of the men, and provision must be made for foraging the animals. Straggling from the ranks is strictly prohibited, & commanders will make arrangements to secure & punish offenders.

IV.   The movements herein directed will commence tomorrow 20th instant at dawn of day.

By command of Genl R. E. Lee:

R. H. CHILTON
A A Genl

271   To GENERAL J. E. B. STUART
                        Commanding Cavalry

August 19, 1862

General:

I desire you to rest your men today, refresh your horses, prepare rations & everything for the march tomorrow. Get what information you can of fords, roads, & position of enemy, so that your march can be made understandingly & with vigour. I sent to you Capt Mason an experienced bridge builder, &c., whom I think will be able to aid you in the destruction of the bridge, &c. When that is accomplished, or while in train of execution, as circumstances permit, I wish you to operate back towards Culpeper Court House, creating such confusion & consternation as you can without unnecessarily exposing your men till you feel Longstreet's right. Take position then on his right & hold yourself in reserve, & act as circumstances may require. I wish to know during the day how you proceed in your preparations. They will require the personal attention of all your officers. The last reports from the signal stations yesterday evening were that the enemy was breaking up his principal encampments & moving in direction of Culpeper Court House.

Very resply, &c.

R. E. LEE
Genl

272   To GEORGE W. RANDOLPH
                              Secretary of War
                                 TELEGRAM

                                        Headquarters, Crenshaw's [Farm]
                                                     August 19, 1862

IT IS REPORTED A BODY OF ENEMY IS MOVING FROM FREDERICKSBURG
TOWARDS HANOVER JUNCTION. TROOPS FROM RICHMOND COULD MARCH AT
ONCE TO NORTH ANNA, ASSEMBLE THERE, PROTECT RAILROAD, & THEN BE
MOVED ACCORDING TO CIRCUMSTANCES.

                                                        R. E. LEE

273   To JEFFERSON DAVIS
                              Richmond, Virginia
                                 TELEGRAM

                                                   Headquarters, &c.
                                                     August 21, 1862

CROSSED RAPIDAN LAST NIGHT AND THIS MORNING AT SOMERVILLE, RAC-
COON, AND MORTON'S FORDS. ENEMY COMMENCED RETREATING YESTERDAY.
GOT BEYOND RAPPAHANNOCK, EXCEPT A PORTION OF HIS CAVALRY, WHICH
WERE DRIVEN. BURNSIDE, [ISAAC I.] STEVENS, AND KING APPEAR TO HAVE
GONE TOWARD FREDERICKSBURG. POPE, BANKS, [FRANZ] SIGEL, &C., TOWARD
WARRENTON. CAN RICHMOND BE HELD IF FOLLOWED?

                                                        R. E. LEE
                                                 General Commanding

274   To JEFFERSON DAVIS
                              Richmond, Virginia

                                        Headquarters, Rappahannock River
                                                     August 23, 1862
His Excellency President Davis:
    I appointed Monday last 18th instant as the day for crossing the
Rapidan, but the troops could not be got into position or provisioned.
Monday it was hoped we should cross, but the cavalry had not got up

and the order was changed for Wednesday, 20th. This delay proved fatal to our success, for the enemy through the instrumentality of a spy got information of our plans & concentration on his left flank while threatening his right, & commenced Sunday night to retire his stores, &c., behind the Rappahannock. The atmosphere was unfavorable for observation & fear of creating alarms kept reconnaissances quiet until Tuesday when their withdrawal was discovered. By the time the army had crossed Wednesday everything but their cavalry had retired behind the Rappahannock, the fords which were strongly guarded. Upon examination it was deemed best to turn their right flank and Genl Jackson in command of our left wing was put in motion Thursday for the purpose, while Genl Longstreet threatened their left with our right. The ground on the left bank of the Rappahannock commands that on the right & as the examination presented it was found necessary to extend as high up as the road leading to Warrenton Springs. Yesterday Genl Stuart with the cavalry crossed above the road & proceeded to cut the enemy's communication at Catlett's Station, on the Orange & Alexandria Railroad. On account of a violent storm he could not burn the bridge over Cedar Run and was unable to cut it down. He accomplished some minor advantages, destroyed some wagons & captured some prisoners. In the mean time Jackson was crossing his force near the Warrenton Springs until interrupted by high water, occasioned by the rain, which has also put a stop to the movement in that direction from this point, as Hazel or Eastham River is in swimming condition today. There appears to be a heavy rain in the mountains at this time which will no doubt continue the high water & give the enemy ample time to reinforce Genl Pope with McClellan's army if desired. I can get no news from our troops on the North Anna. If McClellan has not halted at Fredericksburg the troops there will be required here. If we are able to change the theater of the war from James River to north of the Rappahannock we shall be able to consume provisions and forage now being used in supporting the enemy. This will be some advantage & prevent so great a draft upon other parts of the country. General Pope's chief quartermaster was captured last night by Genl Stuart, & he is reported to state that Genl [Jacob D.] Cox's forces are being withdrawn from the Kanawha Valley by way of Wheeling. If the campaign could be pushed in this direction it would have the effect of relieving other parts of the country. To do this all available reinforcements should be sent here.

I am with high respect, your obt servant

R. E. LEE
Genl

275   To JEFFERSON DAVIS
                          Richmond, Virginia

                                    Headquarters, Jefferson
                                    August 24, 1862

Mr. President:

The enemy is in force before us occupying the left bank of the Rappahannock & has greatly the advantage of us in artillery. I send you an autograph letter from Genl Pope to Genl McClellan. It is of old date 4 July, but interesting as exhibiting his plan of campaign when you compare it with its failure. I have another letter from Genl Pope to Genl [Henry W.] Halleck, dated 20th instant, placing his whole force for duty at 45,000 independent of Burnside, & stating his plan to be to hold us in check until McClellan can join him from the lower Rappahannock. Genl Fitz John Porter is to march from Falmouth & is the advance of McClellan. I think I can feed the whole army here if Col Northrop will give the necessary directions about collecting beef & if we can secure this country the millers will give us flour. At first there will be difficulties, but they will be softened as we advance & we shall relieve other parts of the country & employ what would be consumed & destroyed by the enemy. The theatre of war will thus be changed for a season at least, unless we are overpowered. This last letter of Pope's I think makes it certain that McClellan's destination is to join Pope. The whole army I think should be united here as soon as possible. I have ordered up Ripley, whom I had advanced to Culpeper & will direct Genl G. W. Smith to send on McLaws, D. H. Hill, & other available troops. Should you not agree with me in the propriety of this step please countermand the order & let me know. Genl Loring should also be directed to operate northward & descend the Valley of Shenandoah, so as to threaten their possession of the Valley, in the event of the information I sent you about the withdrawal of Cox proving true. Hampton's cavalry I particularly require. The defences around Richmond must be perfected & completed with hired labour & held by the field batteries. I shall require Genl Pendleton's reserve batteries.

I have the honour to be with, your obt servt

                                    R. E. LEE
                                    Genl

P.S. I advanced the troops here last night & this morning in consequence of ascertaining that the enemy feeling secure on their left from the high water of the Rappahannock was concentrating his force upon Genl Jackson.

R. E. L.

276   To JEFFERSON DAVIS
              Richmond, Virginia
                  TELEGRAM

August 25, 1862

I BELIEVE A PORTION OF MCCLELLAN'S ARMY HAS JOINED POPE, EXPEDITE THE ADVANCE OF OUR TROOPS.

R. E. LEE

277   To HIS WIFE
              "Hickory Hill," Virginia

Jefferson (Near Warrenton)
August 25, 1862

You see I am getting farther & farther from you dear Mary. The high water of the Rappahannock prevented our crossing lower down & I have been obliged to ascend the river. I hope we shall find practicable fords in this region & be able to throw the army across. The enemy follows us on the opposite bank & is prepared to oppose the passage. The rains have however ceased now & I trust the river will soon fall. I think we shall at least change the theater of war from James River to north of the Rappahannock. That is part of the advantage I contemplated. If it is effected at least for a season, it will be a great gain. In the contest at Rappahannock Bridge Saturday, I regret to inform you that my aid Major [Charles] Marshall lost his brother. He was killed by the bursting of one of our own guns. We easily drove the enemy but the river had been swelled by the rains to swimming stage & we could not cross. The bridge was burned by the enemy & all the fine houses on the north side (in revenge I suppose) before they retreated. Fitzhugh is well & is doing good service. Rob too, but I have seen neither of them. I saw the latter Sunday week on the Rapidan. We are all too busy for visiting. If I can only think of them, it is as much as I can do.

Give much love to every body. Kiss Chass for her papa. Tell Cousin Anne & pretty Luce that Williams is very well & is improved by a little shooting. Remember me to dear old Uncle & Mr. Wickham. Tell Chass that Genl Stuart says Fitzhugh made a beautiful charge the other night at Catlett's Station. He has no doubt written her all about it, several long letters, but I fear the couriers have been at fault & not delivered them at their destination. But she will hear at last.

Very truly & affly

R. E. LEE

278 To COLONEL JEREMY F. GILMER
Chief Engineer, Army of Northern Virginia

Headquarters, Army of Northern Virginia
Jefferson
August 25, 1862

Colonel:

I desire you to use every exertion to perfect and complete the defences around and to the approaches of Richmond by land and water. I wish to place them in such a condition that troops can be withdrawn from them with safety to the city, leaving a proper guard, and again restored when necessary. Your services as well as those of the engineers with you, are necessary to this army, and I am only willing to dispense with them to insure the safety of Richmond. I beg you will employ every means in your power for this purpose, and if they are not sufficient, create them.

The Secretary of War and President will give you every assistance. As soon as you can leave Richmond I desire you to join me.

I am very respectfully, your obt servt

R. E. LEE
Genl

279 To JEFFERSON DAVIS
Richmond, Virginia
TELEGRAM

By Telegraph from 2½ miles of Salem
August 27, 1862
Via Rapidan 28th

THE ADVANCE UNDER GENL JACKSON LAST NIGHT BROKE UP THE ORANGE AND ALEXANDRIA RAILROAD AT BRISTOE STATION CAPTURING THREE (3) TRAINS

OF CARS AND PRISONERS. THIS WAS GENL [ISAAC R.] TRIMBLE'S BRIGADE, CAPTURED MANASSAS TAKING EIGHT GUNS, PROVISIONS AND PRISONERS.

PARTS OF HOOKER'S AND [DANIEL E.] SICKLES' BRIGADES HAVE JOINED POPE AT WARRENTON FROM ALEXANDRIA. OTHER TROOPS FROM AQUIA.

I PARTICULARLY REQUIRE HAMPTON'S CAVALRY, EXPEDITE THE REINFORCEMENTS ORDERED.

R. E. LEE
General

280   To JEFFERSON DAVIS
                    Richmond, Virginia
                    TELEGRAM

Headquarters, Manassas Junction
August 29, 1862
9 o'clock p.m.
Via Rapidan 30

SO FAR THIS ARMY HAS STEADILY ADVANCED AND REPULSED THE FREQUENT ATTACKS OF THE ENEMY. THE LINE OF THE RAPPAHANNOCK AND WARRENTON HAS BEEN RELIEVED. MANY PRISONERS ARE CAPTURED AND I REGRET QUANTITIES OF STORES TO BE DESTROYED FOR WANT OF TRANSPORTATION. ANDERSON NOT YET UP AND I HEAR NOTHING OF THOSE BEHIND. WE HAVE [GENERALS] EWELL, TRIMBLE AND [WILLIAM B.] TALIAFERRO WOUNDED. THE LATTER SLIGHTLY, THE OTHERS NOT MORTAL.

R. E. LEE

281   To JEFFERSON DAVIS
                    Richmond, Virginia

Headquarters, Department of Northern Virginia
Near Groveton, Virginia
August 30, 1862

Mr. President:
My despatches will have informed you of the march of this portion of the army. Its progress has been necessarily slow, having a large and superior force on its flank, narrow & rough roads to travel, and the difficulties of obtaining forage & provisions to contend with. It has so far advanced in safety and has succeeded in deceiving the enemy as to its object. The movement has, as far as I am able to judge, drawn the enemy from the Rappahannock frontier and caused him to concentrate his

troops between Manassas & Centreville. My desire has been to avoid a general engagement, being the weaker force, & by manoeuvring to relieve the portion of the country referred to. I think if not overpowered we shall be able to relieve other portions of the country, as it seems to be the purpose of the enemy to collect his strength here. This morning General [R. H.] Anderson's division arrived and Col [Stephen D.] Lee's reserve batteries. The partial contests in which both wings of the army have been obliged to engage has reduced our ammunition, & the reinforcements seem to be advancing slowly. I have heard of none on the road except Genl [R. S.] Ripley, one mile south of Amissville on yesterday evening. In order that we may obtain the advantages I hope for, we must be in larger force; and I hope every exertion will be made to create troops & to increase our strength & supplies. Beef, flour & forage may be obtained in the back country by proper exertions in the different departments; & it will be far better for us to consume them than to leave them for the enemy. We have no time to lose & must make every exertion if we expect to reap advantage.

I have the honor to be with high respect, your obt servant

R. E. LEE
Genl

282 REPORT OF CAPTAIN JOSEPH L. BARTLETT
Signal Officer, Confederate States Army

Manassas Battle Ground, Virginia
Saturday, August 30, 1862

I signaled from General Lee's headquarters on the Warrenton pike to General Jackson's position across the pike near some wheat stacks, bearing nearly north, distant about 2 miles, as follows:

General Jackson:
What is result of movements on your left?

LEE

ANSWER.
General Lee:
So far, enemy appear to be trying to get possession of a piece of woods to withdraw out of our sight.

JACKSON

Terrific fighting now commences on the left and General Jackson sends for a division of Longstreet's command.

General Jackson:
Do you still want re-enforcements?

LEE

Some half hour elapses and General Jackson replies:

No; the enemy are giving way.

JACKSON

General Lee now prepares to move and sends the following:

General Jackson:
General Longstreet is advancing; look out for and protect his left flank.

LEE

General Lee having moved his headquarters, I also removed the signal station.

J. L. BARTLETT

283   To JEFFERSON DAVIS
                    Richmond, Virginia
                       TELEGRAM

Headquarters, Army of Northern Virginia
Groveton
August 30, 1862
10 o'clock P.M.

THIS ARMY ACHIEVED TODAY ON THE PLAINS OF MANASSAS A SIGNAL VICTORY OVER COMBINED FORCES OF GENLS MCCLELLAN AND POPE. ON THE 28TH AND 29TH EACH WING UNDER GENLS LONGSTREET AND JACKSON REPULSED WITH VALOUR ATTACKS MADE ON THEM SEPARATELY. WE MOURN THE LOSS OF OUR GALLANT DEAD, IN EVERY CONFLICT YET OUR GRATITUDE TO ALMIGHTY GOD FOR HIS MERCIES RISES HIGHER AND HIGHER EACH DAY, TO HIM AND TO THE VALOUR OF OUR TROOPS A NATION'S GRATITUDE IS DUE.

R. E. LEE

284   To JEFFERSON DAVIS
Richmond, Virginia

Headquarters, Army of Northern Virginia
Chantilly
September 3, 1862

Mr. President:

My letter of the 30th ultimo will have informed Your Excellency of the progress of this army to that date. Genl Longstreet's division having arrived the day previous was formed in order of battle on the right of Genl Jackson, who had been engaged with the enemy since morning, resisting an attack commenced on the 28th. The enemy on the latter day was vigorously repulsed, leaving his numerous dead & wounded on the field. His attack on the morning of the 29th was feeble, but became warmer in the afternoon when he was again repulsed by both wings of the army. His loss on this day, as stated in his published report herewith enclosed, amounted to 8,000 in killed & wounded.

The enemy, being reinforced, renewed the attack on the afternoon of the 30th, when a general advance of both wings of the army was ordered, & after a fierce combat which raged till after 9 o'clock, he was completely defeated & driven beyond Bull Run. The darkness of the night, his destruction of the Stone Bridge after crossing, and the uncertainty of the fords stopped the pursuit. The next morning the enemy was discovered in the strong position of Centreville, & the army was put in motion towards the Little River turnpike to turn his right. Upon reaching Ox Hill, on the 1st September he was again discovered in our front on the heights of Germantown, & about 5 p.m. made a spirited attack on the front & right of our column with a view apparently of covering the withdrawal of his trains on the Centreville road, & masking his retreat. Our position was maintained with but slight loss on both sides. Maj Genl [Philip] Kearny was left by the enemy, dead on the field. During the night the enemy fell back to Fairfax Court House & abandoned his position at Centreville. Yesterday about noon he evacuated Fairfax Court House, taking the roads as reported to me, to Alexandria & Washington.

I have as yet been unable to get official reports of our loss or captures in these various engagements. Many gallant officers have been killed or wounded. Of the General officers Ewell, Trimble, Taliaferro, Field, [Micah] Jenkins, & Mahone have been reported wounded. Cols [John H.] Means, [J. Foster] Marshall, [William S. H.] Baylor, [John F.] Neff, and [James M.] Gadberry killed. About 7,000 prisoners have already been paroled, about the same number of small arms collected from the field, & 30 pieces of cannon captured, besides a number of wagons, ambulances, &c. A large number of arms still remain on the ground. For want of transportation valuable stores had to be destroyed as captured, while the enemy at their various depots are reported to have burned many millions of property in their retreat.

The great advantage of the advance of the army is the withdrawal of the enemy from our territory, & the hurling back upon their capital their two great armies from the banks of the James & Rappahannock Rivers.

The divisions of Genls Hill & McLaws have now arrived within supporting distance, & the ordnance & other trains are not far behind. The progress & protection of our trains have caused our greatest difficulties. Nothing could surpass the gallantry & endurance of the troops, who have cheerfully borne every danger & hardship, both on the battle field & march.

I have the honor to be very respecty, your mo obt svt

R. E. Lee
Genl

285   To GENERAL SAMUEL COOPER
Adjutant and Inspector General

BATTLE REPORT OF CEDAR MOUNTAIN

Headquarters, Army of Northern Virginia
April 18, 1863

General:
I respectfully submit herewith my report of the operations of this army from the battles before Richmond to and including the battle of Cedar Mountain. The accompanying documents comprising reports of subordinate commanders, &c., are designated in the schedule attached to my report.

I have the honor to be with much respect, &c.

R. E. Lee
General

BATTLE REPORT OF CEDAR MOUNTAIN

After the retreat of General McClellan to Westover, his army remained inactive for about a month.

His front was closely watched by a brigade of cavalry, and preparations made to resist a renewal of his attempt upon Richmond from his new base.

In the meantime another Federal army under Major General Pope, advanced southward from Washington and crossed the Rappahannock, as if to seize Gordonsville and move thence upon Richmond.

The enemy also appeared in force at Fredericksburg and threatened the railroad from Gordonsville to Richmond, apparently for the purpose of cooperating with the movements of General Pope.

To meet the advance of the latter and restrain, as far as possible, the atrocities which he threatened to perpetrate upon our defenceless citizens, Genl Jackson with his own and Ewell's division was ordered to proceed towards Gordonsville on the 13th July. Upon reaching that vicinity he ascertained that the force under General Pope was superior to his own, but the uncertainty that then surrounded the designs of General McClellan rendered it inexpedient to reinforce him from the army at Richmond. He was directed to observe the enemy's movements closely, to avail himself of any opportunity to attack that might arise, and assistance was promised should the progress of Pope put in our power to strike an effectual blow without withdrawing the troops too long from the defence of the capital.

The army at Westover continuing to manifest no intention of resuming active operations, and General Pope's advance having reached the Rapidan, General A. P. Hill with his division was ordered on the 27th July to join General Jackson. At the same time, in order to keep McClellan stationary, or if possible, to cause him to withdraw, General D. H. Hill commanding south of James River, was directed to threaten his communications by seizing favorable positions below Westover from which to attack the transports in the river. That officer selected Coggins Point, opposite Westover, and the conduct of the expedition was committed to Brigadier General French.

On the night of the 31st General French accompanied by Brigadier General Pendleton, Chief of Artillery, placed forty-three guns in position within range of the enemy's shipping in the river and of the camps on the north side, upon both of which fire was opened, causing consternation and inflicting serious damage. The guns were withdrawn before daybreak, with the loss of one killed and two wounded by the gunboats and batteries of the enemy. The attack caused General McClellan to send a strong force to the south bank of the river which entrenched itself on Coggins Point.

In the latter part of July the enemy's cavalry from Fredericksburg attempted to cut Jackson's communications by destroying the Central

Railroad at Beaver Dam. This force did no serious damage, but to prevent the repetition of the attempt and to ascertain the strength and designs of the enemy General Stuart was directed to proceed from Hanover Court House, where he was posted, towards Fredericksburg.

His progress was delayed by high water until the 4th August, when he advanced with Fitzhugh Lee's brigade and the Stuart Horse Artillery upon Port Royal. Arriving at that place on the 5th without opposition he proceeded in the direction of Fredericksburg, and the next day came into the Telegraph road at Massaponax Church just after two brigades of the enemy had passed that point on the way to the Central Railroad. His vigorous attack caused the expedition to return in haste to Fredericksburg, and General Stuart retired with a loss of only two men, bringing off eighty-five prisoners and a number of horses, wagons and arms. No further attempt was made upon the railroad.

On the 5th August our cavalry reported that the enemy had advanced in large force from Westover to Malvern Hill, and the next day the divisions of Generals Longstreet and McLaws and that commanded by General Ripley were moved down to the Long Bridge road. The enemy was found occupying the ground on which the action of July 1st was fought, and seemed ready to deliver battle in as great force as on that day. McLaws' and Ripley's divisions reinforced by D. R. Jones' division formed our left, Longstreet the right. The heat was intense, and the progress of the troops necessarily slow. Before the road was cleared of the enemy's pickets and his line of battle disclosed the sun had almost set. Orders were given for our left wing to advance to Willis' Church, threatening the communication with Westover by extending well to the left, while two brigades of Longstreet's division were directed to advance upon Malvern Hill and drive in the enemy on Curles Neck. The latter operation was handsomely executed by General Evans with his own and Cobb's brigade, forcing the enemy back to his guns on Malvern Hill.

The next morning, upon advancing it was found that he had withdrawn during the night and retired to Westover. Our pickets were reestablished, and the troops returned to their former positions.

This expedition, which was the last undertaken by General McClellan on James River, was attended with small loss on either side. General Hampton with his brigade of cavalry, kept the enemy closely confined within his lines until his final withdrawal.

BATTLE OF CEDAR RUN
[Cedar Mountain]

While the main body of the army awaited the development of McClellan's intentions, General Jackson, now reinforced by A. P. Hill, determined to assume the offensive against General Pope, whose army, still superior in numbers, lay north of the Rapidan.

On the 2d August, Colonel now Brigadier General W. E. Jones, of the 7th Virginia Cavalry of [General Beverly H.] Robertson's brigade, was sent to take charge of the outposts on the Rapidan. Arriving near Orange Court House, he found it occupied by a large cavalry force, which by a bold and vigorous charge he drove from the town. The enemy rallied, and Col Jones was in turn compelled to fall back before superior numbers to the place where the engagement began. The enemy soon after withdrew. Learning that only a portion of General Pope's army was at Culpeper Court House Genl Jackson resolved to attack it before the arrival of the remainder, and on the 7th August moved from Gordonsville for that purpose. The next day the Federal cavalry on the north side of the Rapidan was driven back by General Robertson, and on the 9th Jackson's command arrived within eight miles of Culpeper Court House, when the enemy was found near Cedar Run, a short distance northwest of Slaughter Mountain. Early's brigade of Ewell's division, was thrown forward on the road to Culpeper Court House, the remaining two brigades, those of Trimble and [Harry T.] Hays, the latter under Col [Henry] Forno, diverging to the right, took position on the western slope of Slaughter Mountain. Jackson's own division under Brig General [Charles S.] Winder was placed on the left of the road, [General John A.] Campbell's brigade, Lt Col [Thomas S.] Garnett commanding being on the left, Taliaferro's parallel to the road, supporting the batteries, and Winder's own brigade under Col [Charles A.] Ronald in reserve. [General A. R.] Lawton's brigade having been detached by General Jackson to guard the train, was prevented from taking part in the engagement.

The battle was opened with a fierce fire of artillery, which continued for about two hours, during which Brigadier General Charles S. Winder, while directing the movements of his batteries, received a wound from the effects of which he expired in a few hours.

I can add nothing to the well deserved tribute paid to the courage, capacity and conspicuous merit of this lamented officer by General Jackson, in whose brilliant campaign in the Valley and on the Chickahominy he bore a distinguished part.

The enemy's infantry advanced about 5 o'clock p.m. and attacked General Early in front, while another body concealed by the irregularity of the ground, moved upon his right. [General Edward L.] Thomas' brigade of A. P. Hill's division which had now arrived was sent to his support, and the contest soon became animated.

In the mean time, the main body of the Federal infantry, under cover of a wood and the undulations of the field, gained the left of Jackson's division, now commanded by Brig General Taliaferro, and poured a destructive fire into its flank and rear. Campbell's brigade fell back in confusion, exposing the flank of Taliaferro's, which also gave way, as did the left of Early's. The rest of his brigade however firmly held its ground. Winder's brigade, with Branch's of A. P. Hill's division on its right, advanced promptly to the support of Jackson's division, and after a sanguinary struggle the enemy was repulsed with loss.

Pender's and Archer's brigades also of Hill's division came up on the left of Winder's, and by a general charge the enemy was driven back in confusion, leaving the ground covered with his dead and wounded.

General Ewell with two brigades on the extreme right had been prevented from advancing by the fire of our own artillery, which swept his approach to the enemy's left. This obstacle being now removed, he pressed forward under a hot fire and came gallantly into action. Repulsed and vigorously followed on our left and center, and now hotly pressed on our right, the enemy gave way, and his whole line was soon in full retreat. Night had now set in, but General Jackson desiring to enter Culpeper Court House before morning, determined to pursue. Hill's division led the advance but owing to the darkness it was compelled to move slowly and with caution.

The enemy was found about a mile and a half in rear of the field of battle, and information was received that reinforcements had arrived. General Jackson thereupon halted for the night, and the next day becoming satisfied that the enemy's strength had been so largely increased as to render a further advance on his part imprudent, he sent his wounded to the rear, and proceeded to bury the dead and collect the arms from the battle field.

On the 11th the enemy asked and received permission to bury those of his dead not already interred. General Jackson remained in position during the day, and at night retired to the vicinity of Gordonsville.

In this engagement four hundred prisoners, including a Brigadier General [Henry Prince], were captured, and five thousand three hundred stands of small arms, one piece of artillery, several caissons, and three colors fell into our hands.

Our casualties will appear from the report of the Medical Director. For a more detailed account of the action, reference must be made to the clear report of General Jackson herewith transmitted, and the accompanying reports of his officers.

The conduct of his troops is commended in terms of well deserved praise by their distinguished leader, and the success achieved was worthy of the skillful management and bold and vigorous prosecution of the whole enterprise.

I am very respecty, your obt serv't

R. E. LEE
General

286   To GENERAL SAMUEL COOPER
Adjutant and Inspector General
BATTLE REPORT OF SECOND MANASSAS CAMPAIGN

Headquarters, Army of Northern Virginia
June 8, 1863

General:

I have the honor to transmit herewith the report of the operations of this army from the time it crossed the Rappahannock through the battle of Manassas. Many of the sub-reports of these operations I have been obliged to retain, because they contain the narrative in part of the latter operations of the campaign. Of those operations succeeding the battle of Manassas I have not yet made a report, as I have not yet received full reports from Jackson's corps.

I am with the greatest respect, your obedient servant

R. E. LEE
General

Headquarters, Army of Northern Virginia
June 5, 1863

General:

The victory at Cedar Run effectually checked the progress of the enemy for the time, but it soon became apparent that his army was being largely increased.

The corps of Major General Burnside from North Carolina which had reached Fredericksburg, was reported to have moved up the Rappahannock a few days after the battle to unite with General Pope, and a part of General McClellan's army was believed to have left Westover for the same purpose. It therefore seemed that active operations on the James were no longer contemplated and that the most effectual way to relieve Richmond from any danger of attack from that quarter would be to reinforce General Jackson and advance upon General Pope.

Accordingly on the 13th August Major General Longstreet with his division, and the two brigades under General Hood were ordered to proceed to Gordonsville. At the same time General Stuart was directed to move with the main body of his cavalry to that point, leaving a sufficient force to observe the enemy still remaining in Fredericksburg, and to guard the railroad. General R. H. Anderson was also directed to leave his position on James River and to follow Longstreet.

On the 16th the troops began to move from the vicinity of Gordonsville towards the Rapidan on the north side of which, extending along the Orange and Alexandria Railroad in the direction of Culpeper Court House, the Federal Army lay in great force.

It was determined with the cavalry to destroy the railroad bridge over the Rappahannock in rear of the enemy while Longstreet and Jackson crossed the Rapidan and attacked his left flank.

The movement as explained in the following order was appointed for the 18th August, but the necessary preparations not having been completed, its execution was postponed to the 20th. In the interval the enemy, being apprised of our design, hastily retired beyond the Rappahannock.

General Longstreet crossed the Rapidan at Raccoon Ford, and preceded by Fitzhugh Lee's cavalry brigade arrived early in the afternoon near Kelly's Ford on the Rappahannock where Lee had a sharp and successful skirmish with the rear guard of the enemy, who held the north side of the river in strong force.

Jackson passed the Rapidan at Somerville Ford and moved towards Brandy Station, Robertson's brigade of cavalry, accompanied by General Stuart in person leading the advance. Near Brandy Station a large body of the enemy's cavalry was encountered, which was gallantly attacked and driven across the Rappahannock by Robertson's command. General Jackson halted for the night near Stevensburg, and on the morning of the 21st moved upon Beverly's Ford on the Rappahannock.

The 5th Virginia Cavalry under Colonel [Thomas L.] Rosser, was sent forward by General Stuart to seize the north bank of the river at this point and gallantly accomplished the object, capturing a number of prisoners and arms. General Stuart subsequently arrived and being furnished by General Jackson with a section of artillery, maintained his position for several hours, skirmishing warmly with the enemy.

General Robertson who had crossed the river above Beverly's Ford, reported that the enemy was advancing in large force upon the position held by General Stuart, and as it had been determined in the mean time not to attempt the passage of the river at that point with the army, that officer withdrew to the south side. The enemy soon afterwards appeared in great strength on the opposite bank, and an animated fire was kept up during the rest of the day between his artillery and the batteries attached to Jackson's leading division under Brigadier General Taliaferro.

As our positions on the south bank of the Rappahannock were commanded by those of the enemy who guarded all the fords, it was determined to seek a more favorable place to cross higher up the river, and thus gain the enemy's right.

Accordingly General Longstreet was directed to leave Kelly's Ford on the 21st and take the position in front of the enemy in the vicinity of Beverly's Ford and the Orange and Alexandria Railroad bridge, then held by Jackson, in order to mask the movement of the latter, who was instructed to ascend the river.

On the 22d Jackson crossed Hazel River at Welford's Mill and proceeded up the Rappahannock, leaving Trimble's brigade near Freeman's Ford to protect his trains. In the afternoon Longstreet sent General Hood with his own and Whiting's brigade under Colonel [Evander M.] Law to relieve Trimble. Hood had just reached the position when he and Trimble were attacked by a considerable force which had crossed at Freeman's Ford. After a short but spirited engagement the enemy was driven precipitately over the river with heavy loss.

General Jackson arrived at Warrenton Springs Ford in the afternoon and immediately began to cross his troops to the north side, occupying the Springs and the adjacent heights. He was interrupted by a heavy rain, which caused the river to rise so rapidly that the ford soon became impassable for infantry and artillery. Under these circumstances it was deemed advisable to withdraw the troops who had reached the opposite side, and they recrossed during the night of the 23d on a temporary bridge constructed for the purpose.

General Stuart who had been directed to cut the railroad in rear of General Pope's army, crossed the Rappahannock on the morning of the 22d, about six miles above the Springs, with parts of Lee's and Robertson's brigades. Passing through Warrenton, he reached Catlett's Station at night, but was prevented from destroying the railroad bridge at that point by the same storm that had arrested Jackson's movements. He captured more than three hundred prisoners, including a number of officers. Becoming apprehensive of the effect of the rain upon the streams which separated him from the main body of the army, he retired firing the enemy's camp and recrossed the Rappahannock at Warrenton Springs.

On the 23d General Longstreet directed Colonel [John B.] Walton with part of the Washington Artillery and other batteries of his command to drive back a force of the enemy that had crossed to the south bank of the Rappahannock near the railroad bridge upon the withdrawal of

General Jackson on the previous day. Fire was opened about sunrise and continued with great vigor for several hours, the enemy being compelled to withdraw with loss. Some of the batteries of Colonel S. D. Lee's battalion were ordered to aid those of Colonel Walton, and under their united fire the enemy was forced to abandon his position on the north side of the river, burning in his retreat the railroad bridge and the neighboring dwellings.

The rise of the river rendering the lower fords impassable, enabled the enemy to concentrate his main body opposite General Jackson, and on the 24th Longstreet was ordered to proceed to his support. Although retarded by the swollen condition of Hazel River and other tributaries of the Rappahannock he reached Jeffersonton in the afternoon.

General Jackson's command lay between that place and the [Warrenton] Springs Ford, and a warm cannonade was progressing between the batteries of General A. P. Hill's division and those of the enemy.

The enemy was massed between Warrenton and the Springs, and guarded the fords of the Rappahannock as far above as Waterloo.

The army of General McClellan had left Westover. Part of it had already marched to join General Pope, and it was reported that the rest would soon follow. The captured correspondence of General Pope confirmed this information, and also disclosed the fact that the greater part of the army of General [Jacob D.] Cox had been withdrawn from the Kanawha Valley for the same purpose.

Two brigades of D. H. Hill's division under General Ripley had already been ordered from Richmond, and the remainder under General D. H. Hill in person, with the division of General McLaws, two brigades under General Walker, and Hampton's cavalry brigade, were now directed to join this army and were approaching.

BATTLE OF MANASSAS

In pursuance of the plan of operations determined upon, Jackson was directed on the 25th to cross above Waterloo and move around the enemy's right so as to strike the Orange and Alexandria Railroad in his rear.

Longstreet in the mean time was to divert his attention by threatening him in front, and to follow Jackson as soon as the latter should be sufficiently advanced.

General Jackson crossed the Rappahannock at Hinson's Mill about four miles above Waterloo, and passing through Orleans encamped on the night of the 25th near Salem, after a long and fatiguing march. The next morning, continuing his route with his accustomed vigor and celerity, he passed the Bull Run Mountains at Thoroughfare Gap, and proceeding by way of Gainesville, reached the railroad at Bristoe Station after sunset. At Gainesville he was joined by General Stuart with the brigades of Robertson and Fitzhugh Lee who continued with him during the rest of his operations, vigilantly and effectually guarding both his flanks. General Jackson was now between the large army of General Pope and the Federal capital. Thus far no considerable force of the enemy had been encountered, and he did not appear to be aware of his situation.

Upon arriving at Bristoe the greater part of the guard at that point fled. Two trains of cars coming from the direction of Warrenton were captured and a few prisoners were taken. Notwithstanding the darkness of the night and the long and arduous march of the day, General Jackson determined to lose no time in capturing the depot of the enemy at Manassas Junction, about seven miles distant on the road to Alexandria. General Trimble volunteered to proceed at once to that place with the 21st North Carolina and the 21st Georgia Regiments. The offer was accepted and to render success more certain General Jackson directed General Stuart to accompany the expedition with part of his cavalry, and as ranking officer, to assume the command. Upon arriving near the Junction, General Stuart sent Colonel [Williams C.] Wickham with his regiment, the 4th Virginia Cavalry, to get in rear of the enemy, who opened with musketry and artillery upon our troops as they approached. The darkness of the night and ignorance of the enemy's position and numbers made it necessary to move cautiously, but about midnight the place was taken with little difficulty, those that defended it being captured or dispersed. Eight pieces of artillery, with their horses, ammunition and equipments, were taken. More than three hundred prisoners, one hundred and seventy-five horses besides those belonging to the artillery, two hundred new tents, and immense quantities of commissary and quartermaster's stores fell into our hands.

General Jackson left Ewell's division, with the 5th Virginia Cavalry under Colonel Rosser at Bristoe Station, and with the rest of his command proceeded to the Junction where he arrived early in the morning. Soon afterwards a considerable force of the enemy under Brigadier General [George W.] Taylor approached from the direction of Alexandria and pushed forward boldly to recapture the stores that had been lost.

After a sharp engagement the enemy was routed and driven back, leaving his killed and wounded on the field, General Taylor himself being mortally wounded during the pursuit.

The troops remained at Manassas Junction during the rest of the day, supplying themselves with everything they required from the captured stores.

In the afternoon the enemy advanced upon General Ewell at Bristoe from the direction of Warrenton Junction. They were attacked by three regiments and the batteries of Ewell's division, and two columns of not less than a brigade each were broken and repulsed. Their places were soon supplied by fresh troops, and it was apparent that the Federal commander had now become aware of the situation of affairs, and had turned upon General Jackson with his whole force.

In pursuance of instructions to that effect, General Ewell upon perceiving the strength of the enemy, withdrew his command, part of which was at the time engaged, and rejoined General Jackson at Manassas Junction, having first destroyed the railroad bridge over Broad Run. The enemy halted at Bristoe.

General Jackson's force being much inferior to that of General Pope, it became necessary for him to withdraw from Manassas and take a position west of the turnpike road from Warrenton to Alexandria, where he could more readily unite with the approaching column of Longstreet. Having fully supplied the wants of his troops, he was compelled for want of transportation, to destroy the rest of the captured property. This was done during the night of the 27th, and fifty thousand pounds of bacon, one thousand barrels of corned beef, two thousand barrels of salt pork, and two thousand barrels of flour, besides other property of great value were burned. Taliaferro's division moved during the night by the road to Sudley, and crossing the turnpike near Groveton, halted on the west side near the battle field of July 21st, 1861, where it was joined on the 28th by the divisions of Hill and Ewell.

Perceiving during the afternoon that the enemy approaching from the direction of Warrenton, was moving down the turnpike towards Alexandria, thus exposing his left flank, General Jackson advanced to attack him. A fierce and sanguinary conflict ensued which continued until about 9 o'clock p.m. when the enemy slowly fell back and left us in possession of the field. The loss on both sides was heavy, and among our wounded were Major General Ewell and Brig General Taliaferro, the former severely.

The next morning the 29th the enemy had taken a position to interpose his army between General Jackson and Alexandria, and about 10 a.m. opened with artillery upon the right of Jackson's line. The troops of the latter were disposed in rear of Groveton along the line of the unfinished branch of the Manassas Gap Railroad and extended from a point a short distance west of the turnpike.

Jackson's division under Brig General [William E.] Starke being on the right, Ewell's under Brigadier General Lawton in the center, and A. P. Hill's on the left.

The Federal Army was evidently concentrating upon Jackson with the design of overwhelming him before the arrival of Longstreet.

The latter officer left his position opposite Warrenton Springs on the 26th, being relieved by General R. H. Anderson's division, and marched to join Jackson. He crossed at Hinson's Mill in the afternoon and encamped near Orleans that night. The next day he reached the White Plains, his march being retarded by the want of cavalry to ascertain the meaning of certain movements of the enemy from the direction of Warrenton, which seemed to menace the right flank of his column.

On the 28th, arriving at Thoroughfare Gap he found the enemy prepared to dispute his progress. General D. R. Jones' division being ordered to force the passage of the mountain, quickly dislodged the enemy's sharpshooters from the trees and rocks, and advanced into the gorge. The enemy held the eastern extremity of the pass in large force, and directed a heavy fire of artillery upon the road leading through it and upon the sides of the mountain. The ground occupied by Jones afforded no opportunity for the employment of artillery.

Hood, with his two brigades, and Wilcox with three, were ordered to turn the enemy's right, the former moving over the mountain by a narrow path to the left of the pass and the latter further to the north by Hopewell Gap. Before these troops reached their destinations the enemy advanced and attacked Jones' left under Brigadier General G. T. Anderson. Being vigorously repulsed he withdrew to his position at the eastern end of the Gap, from which he kept up an active fire of artillery until dark and then retreated.

Generals Jones and Wilcox bivouacked that night east of the mountain, and on the morning of the 29th the whole command resumed the march, the sound of cannon at Manassas announcing that Jackson was already engaged.

Longstreet entered the turnpike near Gainesville, and moving down towards Groveton, the head of his column came upon the field in rear of the enemy's left, which had already opened with artillery upon Jackson's right as previously described. He immediately placed some of his batteries in position, but before he could complete his dispositions to attack the enemy withdrew, not however without loss from our artillery.

Longstreet took position on the right of Jackson, Hood's two brigades supported by [Nathan G.] Evans being deployed across the turnpike and at right angles to it. These troops were supported on the left by three brigades under General Wilcox and by a like force on the right under General [James L.] Kemper. D. R. Jones' division formed the extreme right of the line, resting on the Manassas Gap Railroad.

The cavalry guarded our right and left flanks, that on the right being under General Stuart in person.

After the arrival of Longstreet, the enemy changed his position and began to concentrate opposite Jackson's left, opening a brisk fire of artillery, which was responded to with effect by some of General A. P. Hill's batteries.

Colonel Walton placed a part of his artillery upon a commanding position between the lines of Generals Jackson and Longstreet, by order of the latter, and engaged the enemy vigorously for several hours. Soon afterwards General Stuart reported the approach of a large force of the enemy from the direction of Bristoe Station, threatening Longstreet's right. The brigades under General Wilcox were sent to reinforce General Jones, but no serious attack was made, and after firing a few shots the enemy withdrew. While this demonstration was being made on our right a large force advanced to assail the left of Jackson's position, occupied by the division of General A. P. Hill. The attack was received by his troops with their accustomed steadiness, and the battle raged with great fury. The enemy was repeatedly repulsed, but again pressed on to the attack with fresh troops.

Once he succeeded in penetrating an interval between General Gregg's brigade on the extreme left and that of General Thomas, but was quickly driven back with great slaughter by the 14th South Carolina Regiment, then in reserve, and the 44th [49th] Georgia of Thomas' brigade. The contest was close and obstinate, the combatants sometimes delivering their fire at ten paces. General Gregg, who was most exposed, was reinforced by Hays' brigade under Colonel Forno and successfully and gallantly resisted the attacks of the enemy until the ammunition of his brigade being exhausted and all its field officers but two killed or wounded it was relieved after several hours of severe fighting, by Early's brigade and the 8th Louisiana Regiment.

General Early drove the enemy back with heavy loss and pursued about two hundred yards beyond the line of battle when he was recalled to the position on the railroad where Thomas, Pender and Archer had firmly held their ground against every attack.

While the battle was raging on the left, General Longstreet ordered Hood and Evans to advance, but before the order could be obeyed, Hood was himself attacked and his command at once became warmly engaged. General Wilcox was recalled from the right and ordered to advance on Hood's left, and one of Kemper's brigades under Colonel [Eppa] Hunton moved forward on his right. The enemy was repulsed by Hood after a severe contest and fell back closely followed by our troops.

The battle continued until 9 p.m., the enemy retreating until he reached a strong position, which he held with a large force. The darkness of the night put a stop to the engagement, and our troops remained in their advanced position until early next morning when they were withdrawn to their first position.

One piece of artillery, several stands of colors, and a number of prisoners were captured.

Our loss was severe in this engagement. Brigadier Generals Field and Trimble, and Colonel Forno commanding Hays' brigade, were severely wounded, and several other valuable officers killed or disabled, whose names are mentioned in the accompanying reports.

On the morning of the 30th the enemy again advanced and skirmishing began along the line. The troops of Jackson and Longstreet maintained their positions of the previous day. Fitzhugh Lee with three regiments of his cavalry was posted on Jackson's left, and R. H. Anderson's division which arrived during the forenoon was held in reserve near the turnpike.

The batteries of Colonel S. D. Lee took the position occupied the day before by Colonel Walton, and engaged the enemy actively until noon, when firing ceased, and all was quiet for several hours. About 3 p.m. the enemy having massed his troops in front of General Jackson, advanced against his position in strong force. His front line pushed forward until engaged at close quarters by Jackson's troops, when its progress was checked and a fierce and bloody struggle ensued.

A second and third line of great strength moved up to support the first, but in doing so came within easy range of a position a little in advance of Longstreet's left. He immediately ordered up two batteries, and two others being thrown forward about the same time by Colonel S. D. Lee, under their well directed and destructive fire the supporting lines were broken and fell back in confusion. Their repeated efforts to rally were unavailing, and Jackson's troops being thus relieved from the pressure of overwhelming numbers, began to press steadily forward, driving the enemy before them. He retreated in confusion, suffering severely from our artillery which advanced as he retired.

General Longstreet, anticipating the order for a general advance, now threw his whole command against the Federal center and left. Hood's two brigades closely followed by Evans' led the attack. R. H. Anderson's division came gallantly to the support of Hood, while the three brigades under Wilcox moved forward on his left and those of Kemper on his right. D. R. Jones advanced on the extreme right, and the whole line swept steadily on, driving the enemy with great carnage from each successive position until 10 p.m. when darkness put an end to the battle and the pursuit.

During the latter part of the engagement General Wilcox with his own brigade was ordered to the right, where the resistance of the enemy was most obstinate, and rendered efficient assistance to the troops engaged on that part of the line. His other two brigades acted with General Jackson's command, maintaining their position in line.

The obscurity of night and the uncertainty of the fords of Bull Run rendered it necessary to suspend operations until morning, when the cavalry, being pushed forward, discovered that the enemy had escaped to the strong position of Centreville, about four miles beyond Bull Run.

The prevalence of a heavy rain which began during the night threatened to render Bull Run impassable and impeded our movements. Longstreet remained on the battle field to engage the attention of the enemy and cover the burial of the dead and the removal of the wounded, while Jackson proceeded by Sudley Ford to the Little River turnpike to turn the enemy's right and intercept his retreat to Washington.

Jackson's progress was retarded by the inclemency of the weather and the fatigue of his troops, who, in addition to their arduous marches, had fought three severe engagements in as many days.

He reached Little River turnpike in the evening, and the next day, September 1st, advanced by that road towards Fairfax Court House.

The enemy in the meantime was falling back rapidly towards Washington, and had thrown out a strong force to Germantown on the Little River turnpike, to cover his line of retreat from Centreville. The advance of Jackson's column encountered the enemy at Ox Hill near Germantown about 5 p.m. Line of battle was at once formed, and two brigades of A. P. Hill's division, those of Branch and Field under Colonel [John M.] Brockenbrough, were thrown forward to attack the enemy and ascertain his strength and position. A cold and drenching rain storm drove in the faces of our troops as they advanced and gallantly engaged the enemy. They were subsequently supported by the brigades of Gregg, Thomas, and Pender, also of Hill's division, which with part of Ewell's became engaged. The conflict was obstinately maintained by the enemy until dark, when he retreated, having lost two general officers, one of whom Major General Kearny was left dead on the field.

Longstreet's command arrived after the action was over, and the next morning it was found that the enemy had conducted his retreat so rapidly that the attempt to intercept him was abandoned.

The proximity of the fortifications around Alexandria and Washington rendered further pursuit useless, and our army rested during the 2d near Chantilly, the enemy being followed only by the cavalry, who continued to harass him until he reached the shelter of his entrenchments.

In the series of engagements on the plains of Manassas more than seven thousand prisoners were taken, in addition to about two thousand wounded left in our hands. Thirty pieces of artillery, upwards of twenty thousand stand of small arms, numerous colors, and a large amount of stores, besides those taken by General Jackson at Manassas Junction, were captured.

The history of the achievements of the army from the time it advanced from Gordonsville leaves nothing to be said in commendation of the courage, fortitude and good conduct of both officers and men.

The accompanying report of the Medical Director will show the number of our killed and wounded. Among them will be found the names of many valuable and distinguished officers, who bravely and faithfully discharged their duty, and with the gallant soldiers who fell with them, have nobly deserved the love and gratitude of their countrymen.

The reports of the several commanding officers must necessarily be referred to for the names of those whose services were most conspicuous. The list is too long for enumeration here.

During all these operations the cavalry under General Stuart, consisting of the brigades of Generals Robertson and Fitzhugh Lee, rendered most important and valuable service. It guarded the flanks of the army, protected its trains, and gave information of the enemy's movements.

Besides engaging the cavalry of the enemy on several occasions, with uniform success, a detachment under the gallant and lamented Major [William] Patrick, assisted by Stuart's horse artillery under Major [John] Pelham, effectually protected General Jackson's trains against a body of the enemy who penetrated to his rear on the 29th, before the arrival of General Longstreet.

Towards the close of the action on the 30th, General Robertson, with the 2d Virginia Regiment under Colonel [Thomas T.] Munford, supported by the 7th and 12th made a brilliant charge upon a brigade of the enemy's cavalry, Colonel Munford leading with great gallantry, and completely routed it. Many of the enemy were killed and wounded, more than three hundred prisoners were captured, and the remainder pursued beyond Bull Run.

The reports of General Stuart and the officers under his command, as well as that of General Jackson, are referred to for more complete details of these and other services of the cavalry.

Respectfully submitted

R. E. LEE
General

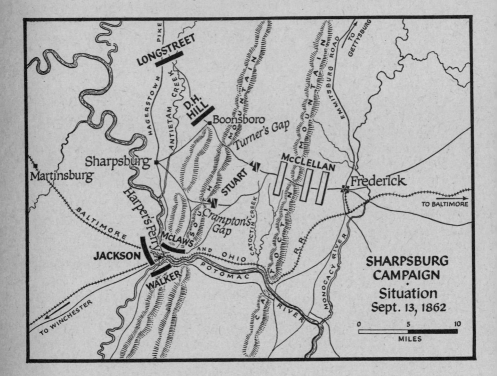

LONGSTREET

HAGERSTOWN PIKE

ANTIETAM CREEK

D.H. HILL

Boonsboro

Turner's Gap

Sharpsburg

Martinsburg

Harper's Ferry

STUART

MOUNTAIN

Crampton's Gap

CATOCTIN CREEK

McCLELLAN

EMMITSBURG ROAD

TO GETTYSBURG

Frederick

TO BALTIMORE

BALTIMORE

McLAWS

AND OHIO

POTOMAC

MONOCACY RIVER

B. & O. R.R.

JACKSON

WALKER

RIVER

TO WINCHESTER

SHARPSBURG
CAMPAIGN
·
Situation
Sept. 13, 1862

0   5   10

MILES

CHAPTER SEVEN

Maryland Campaign

"Special orders, #191"

HAVING SHIFTED THE THEATER of war to the border, with the invasion forces retired into their own forts, for a variety of reasons the next logical movement for Lee was to take the war into the enemy's country. These reasons are fully developed in his letters to Davis, which provide a rare revelation of Lee's thinking processes as a general. With his bandaged hands, he obviously dictated the letters and they read almost as if he were thinking aloud.

The fundamental reason behind Lee's plans was food. The army was in a devastated part of Virginia and a long way from Richmond to be supplied by breaking-down wagons. A move to the Valley to supply the army and its animals would either bring the enemy into the Valley or, by clearing his path, encourage him to strike toward Richmond. By moving into Maryland and Pennsylvania, Lee's army could subsist out of Virginia, the Valley farmers would have the opportunity to get in their fall harvest, and the enemy must follow Lee northward. Lee definitely did not cross the Potomac to seek battles.

A secondary element was the mistaken estimate, which Lee shared with all Confederates, of the strength of Southern sympathies in Maryland. There was a strain of intense Southern sympathizers in Maryland (who gave fine volunteers to the Army of Northern Virginia) but, as the state was under Federal control, the majority of its citizens were rather coldly neutral; in western Maryland, many were Unionists. However, in the psychological area, Lee's crossing of the Potomac, accompanied by an upsurge in Confederate fortunes in the West, profoundly influenced Britain in its consideration of recognizing the Confederacy among the society of nations.

Lee's decision was made and acted upon very quickly — as it turned out, too quickly. On September 2d, Pope retired into the Washington forts, on the 3rd Lee wrote Davis of his suddenly formed plan and, without waiting for an answer, put his army in motion on the 4th. On the 7th, with the Potomac behind, Lee and his army camped at Frederick, Maryland (where old, bedridden Barbara Frietchie did *not* wave a flag at Stonewall Jackson — who was in his tent, recovering from the effects of a fall from a new horse). It was at Frederick, despite the enthusiasm of young ladies who crowded around their camp, that the Confederates first encountered a chilly reception. In all truth, the men's appearance was not likely to win any volunteers to their ranks. They were in hard case: their clothes were in rags, their bearded faces streaked with mud and dust, their bodies attenuated, and their shoes in tatters. Thousands were barefooted. Lee had not considered the physical effects of the grueling campaign on the men, nor the punishment to their feet in shifting to the hard-surfaced roads of Maryland. Of the 55,000 infantry he took into Maryland, less than 40,000 were to be available for combat when needed, as the army suffered the heaviest losses from straggling in its history.

Lee also miscalculated in assuming that the Federal garrisons at Harper's Ferry and Martinsburg would be evacuated when his army crossed the Potomac. Since they were not, and these forces lay across his line of communications via the Shenandoah Valley, these two positions had to be taken before Lee swung northwest into Pennsylvania. By then McClellan had resumed command of the combined Federal army at Washington and, as he was known for his caution, Lee felt no qualms in dividing his forces while maintaining his course toward Pennsylvania. Jackson, with three of Longstreet's divisions, was to march southwest from Frederick, dispose of the Martinsburg garrison, and close in on three sides on Harper's Ferry at the bottom of a cup of mountains on the south bank of the Potomac. Longstreet, with only two divisions, and the unattached division of D. H. Hill (which had come up to the army on September 2), were to march with the wagon train and the cavalry northwest across the South Mountain range and on to Hagerstown.

The order of march was sent on September 10, and this "Special Orders, #191" became one of the most fateful pieces of paper in the history of war. Colonel Chilton, of Lee's staff, sent a copy to Longstreet, Jackson and D. H. Hill; because Harvey Hill, Jackson's brother-in-law, had formerly been attached to his command, Old Jack meticulously sent him a copy of the order. Jackson's copy was destroyed after Hill absorbed its contents, but some staff officer (an unconfessed culprit) used Chilton's copy as a wrapper for three cigars and then, when the army

broke camp at Frederick, lost the package. On September 13, when Mc-
Clellan brought his army into Frederick, an Indiana private found the
famous "lost order," and his sergeant sent the paper through the channels
of command until it reached Colonel Pittman, General Williams's adjutant-general. To compound the ill luck — and the unlikely odds of
such a coincidence — Pittman was an acquaintance of Chilton and, recognizing the signature, was able to assure McClellan that the order
was genuine.

Knowing nothing of this turn of fortune, General Lee was surprised
and unsettled when McClellan, the timorous slowpoke, was galvanized
into bold movement that unaccountably struck at the precise point which
led between Lee's divided forces. Except for the vigilance and quick
action of Jeb Stuart, McClellan would probably have made it. Due to
his prompt warning of D. H. Hill, who hurried on the intelligence to
Lee at Hagerstown, Hill's rear guard returned to the pass across South
Mountain at Turner's Gap, and Longstreet was ordered to march his
men back from Hagerstown on the morning of the 14th to support
Harvey Hill.

Having imposed his will on Lee at Second Manassas, Longstreet protested against holding South Mountain in favor of a concentration at
Sharpsburg. However, in the realm of strategy Lee made his decisions
alone and those decisions were final. Lee showed his cold nerve in elect-
ing to fight a delaying action against McClellan's whole army with less
than a corps, in order to give Jackson more time to capture Harper's
Ferry.

On the 14th, while Jackson completed the investment of the garrison
in the mountain pocket, so that it could be taken with minimal loss of
life, D. H. Hill, with the later support of Longstreet, fought one of the
war's hardest actions in holding the Turner's Gap pass until night fell.
At the same time, farther south, Crampton's Gap, which was defended
only by cavalry, was forced late in the afternoon; this placed Federal
infantry on the rear of McLaws' division, then attacking Harper's Ferry
from the north side of the Potomac. On the 15th, while Longstreet and
Hill fell back with Lee to Sharpsburg, and while McLaws faced about
some of his regiments, Jackson completed the capture of Harper's
Ferry (where the garrison from Martinsburg had taken refuge). The
booty was worth Lee's risk: 73 guns, 13,000 small arms, military stores,
and 11,000 prisoners who would be useful in restoring captured Confederates through the prisoner exchange.

Just west of Harper's Ferry, the Potomac bends into a north-south
line. By proceeding northward up the western bank, two divisions of
Jackson and two of Longstreet crossed the river just west of Sharpsburg

and began joining Lee during the 16th. A. P. Hill, whose division had
borne the brunt of the fighting, was left at Harper's Ferry as rear guard —
to parole the prisoners and collect the stores for passage south. McLaws,
with the road blocked behind him, had first to cross to the south bank
at Harper's Ferry before following Jackson's route, and did not reach Lee
until during the day of the 17th.

Fortunately, from the Confederate viewpoint, McClellan lost some of
his boldness when he confronted his old enemy standing steadily on
defense, as if his whole army was assembled, and let the day of the 16th
get away from him. Longstreet's and D. H. Hill's men used the day for
rest, and Jackson's men, getting into position to receive attack during the
day, had some hours of repose. When the assaults came on the 17th,
McLaws and R. H. Anderson's divisions were on or near the field, to be
thrown in at critical spots. All of these mostly exhausted troops totaled
scarcely half the number McClellan commanded, and his longer-range
guns made the day, as the cannoneers said, "an artillerist's hell."

The little town of Sharpsburg was situated on a low ridge along the
Hagerstown road. Directly in front of the town, Antietam Creek was
barely one mile to the east, but to the north the creek was more than
two miles to the east at a ford by which McClellan crossed a large
portion of his army to the same side as Lee's army. The Confederate
line faced partly east, partly northeast, and Jackson about due north,
with Stuart's cavalry and Pelham's horse-guns out on the flank to the
west.

The first heavy attacks came against Jackson from the north, in the
East Woods and West Woods. Though his units were hurled about and
all but shattered, they refused to break and Lee rushed in the late-arrivals
in a series of last-ditch stands. After the offense was drained out of that
segment of McClellan's army, he then sent new waves at the left center,
where D. H. Hill's then slim division occupied a sunken road — called
since that day the "bloody lane." Hill's units were fragmented and, in
effect, defeated, but he refused to admit it. Himself placing one available
battery and personally rounding up a couple of hundred men to rush
forward, he hung onto the field until Lee moved some last-minute supports over from the right. When the center had withstood McClellan's
second waves, Burnside was then sent against the depleted Confederate
right. Here a Confederate brigade fought behind Antietam Creek, guarding a bridge (which became known as Burnside's Bridge), and this
stubborn line held up Burnside until midafternoon. By the time his troops
stormed over, threatening Lee's flank and rear, A. P. Hill came on the
field, having marched his men in the hot dust from Harper's Ferry

seventeen miles in seven hours. Only about three thousand of his division made it, but under Powell Hill they were enough to roll Burnside back across the bridge.

McClellan, employing less than three fourths of his available force, mounted three separate attacks and not one concerted assault along the whole line. Lee, directing his first battle on the field (in contrast to planning the strategy and relinquishing the tactics to subordinates), revealed himself to be as great a combat general as he had already shown himself a strategist. It was entirely his fight, as he moved brigade units and even gun batteries about with no regard to army organization. His men stood up to 25 per cent casualties, 10,000 men, inflicted 13,000 on the heavily weighted enemy, and permanently cooled off McClellan's battle ardor.

Yet Lee had no choice except to abandon the terrible field. Presenting a defiant front during the 18th, while his wounded and wagons were prepared for movement, he slipped across the Potomac that night. Without encountering vigorous pursuit, he withdrew southward into the fat country around Martinsburg and went into camp.

McClellan followed him west of the Blue Ridge. With no enemy to threaten Richmond from east of the mountains, across the plains of northern Virginia, Lee's men rested and refitted during all of a fine month of October. The only action of any importance was Stuart's Chambersburg raid which, aside from stirring things up, added 1200 horses to the gaunt animals with Lee. There is nothing revealing in Lee's correspondence during this period, as most of his attention was directed to doubling as commissary-general and quartermaster-general. He fed his army well by Confederate standards and, except for the chronic shoe shortage, improved the soldiers' outfits. (The men's families helped considerably, as they could send packages of clothes while the army remained in one place.) With time and rest, most of the 15,000 stragglers returned, recuperated wounded and exchanged prisoners rejoined their units, and by the end of the month Lee fielded about the most powerful army physically he was ever to command.

Except for failing in his larger intention of maintaining his army in the North, Lee had accomplished his fundamental purposes: he had victualed his army in a fertile region without drawing a destructive enemy into the Valley or exposing Richmond. Completely recovered from the rigors of evicting Pope and McClellan from Virginia during July and August, his army was more than ready to encounter the enemy's next move. But, though Lee's correspondence does not reveal an awareness of it, his greatest chance for winning the Confederacy's independence had come and gone.

He could not know that Lord John Russell, on the point of recognizing the Confederacy, had permanently closed the door on Britain's recognition — which also guided France's course. Nor, since he and the large majority of his men were not slaveholders (some, like A. P. Hill, were intensely anti-slavery), did he read the significance in Lincoln's Emancipation Proclamation — which, contrary to general impression, applied only to the regions in rebellion. (Slavery was legally abolished by Act of Congress after Lincoln's death.) Lincoln had written the war measure as a means of putting heart into the flagging efforts to subdue the Southern states and, with masterful timing, waited to deliver the proclamation until Lee's army was retiring to Virginia (September 22). This happened to coincide with the acute shortage of cotton which the English mills were suffering as a result of the blockaded Confederate ports, and the injection of an anti-slavery crusade gave the British mill workers a moral cause to support their loss of wages. It was the larger forces, beyond Lee's control, which were affected by the brevity of his campaign north of the Potomac — accompanied by the inconclusive end of the promising campaign in the West.

According to Lee's appraisal as a soldier, though he had failed to win a victory, his army had acquitted itself superbly against great odds in a drawn battle, and the men's physical condition and fighting potential were brought to a peak. But in history's measure, Lee needed to win. Time was against the Confederacy and it is truly said that Sharpsburg was "the high tide" in the South's struggle for independence.

287   To JEFFERSON DAVIS
                            Richmond, Virginia

                            Headquarters Alexandria & Leesburg Road
                                                    Near Dranesville
                                                September 3, 1862

Mr. President:
    The present seems to be the most propitious time since the commencement of the war for the Confederate Army to enter Maryland. The two grand armies of the United States that have been operating in Virginia, though now united, are much weakened and demoralized. Their new levies, of which I understand sixty thousand men have already been posted in Washington, are not yet organized, and will take some time to prepare for the field. If it is ever desired to give material aid to Maryland and afford her an opportunity of throwing off the op-

pression to which she is now subject, this would seem the most favorable. After the enemy had disappeared from the vicinity of Fairfax Court House and taken the road to Alexandria & Washington, I did not think it would be advantageous to follow him farther. I had no intention of attacking him in his fortifications, and am not prepared to invest them. If I possessed the necessary munitions, I should be unable to supply provisions for the troops. I therefore determined while threatening the approaches to Washington, to draw the troops into Loudoun, where forage and some provisions can be obtained, menace their possession of the Shenandoah Valley, and if found practicable, to cross into Maryland.

The purpose, if discovered, will have the effect of carrying the enemy north of the Potomac, and if prevented, will not result in much evil. The army is not properly equipped for an invasion of an enemy's territory. It lacks much of the material of war, is feeble in transportation, the animals being much reduced, and the men are poorly provided with clothes, and in thousands of instances are destitute of shoes. Still we cannot afford to be idle, and though weaker than our opponents in men and military equipments, must endeavor to harass, if we cannot destroy them. I am aware that the movement is attended with much risk, yet I do not consider success impossible, and shall endeavor to guard it from loss. As long as the army of the enemy are employed on this frontier I have no fears for the safety of Richmond, yet I earnestly recommend that advantage be taken of this period of comparative safety to place its defence, both by land and water, in the most perfect condition. A respectable force can be collected to defend its approaches by land, and the steamer *Richmond* I hope is now ready to clear the river of hostile vessels. Should Genl [Braxton] Bragg find it impracticable to operate to advantage on his present frontier, his army, after leaving sufficient garrisons, could be advantageously employed in opposing the overwhelming numbers which it seems to be the intention of the enemy now to concentrate in Virginia. I have already been told by prisoners that some of [General Don Carlos] Buell's cavalry have been joined to Genl Pope's army, and have reason to believe that the whole of McClellan's, the larger portions of Burnside's & Cox's and a portion of [General David] Hunter's, are united to it. What occasions me most concern is the fear of getting out of ammunition. I beg you will instruct the Ordnance Department to spare no pains in manufacturing a sufficient amount of the best kind, & to be particular in preparing that for the artillery, to provide three times as much of the long range ammunition as of that for smooth bore or short range guns.

The points to which I desire the ammunition to be forwarded will be made known to the Department in time. If the Quartermaster Department can furnish any shoes, it would be the greatest relief.

We have entered upon September, and the nights are becoming cool.

I have the honor to be with high respect, your ob't servant

R. E. LEE
Genl

288   To JEFFERSON DAVIS
Richmond, Virginia

Headquarters, Leesburg
September 4, 1862

Mr. President:

I am extremely indebted to Your Excellency for your letter of the 30th ultimo, and the letter from Washington which you enclosed to me. You will already have learned all that I have ascertained subsequently of the movements of McClellan's army, a large part, if not the whole of which participated in the battle of Saturday last, as I have good reason to believe.

Since my last communication to you with reference to the movements I propose to make with this army, I am more fully persuaded of the benefits that will result from an expedition into Maryland, and I shall proceed to make the movement at once, unless you should signify your disapprobation. The only two subjects that give me any uneasiness are my supplies of ammunition and subsistence. Of the former, I have enough for present use, and must await results before deciding to what point I will have additional supplies forwarded.

Of subsistence, I am taking measures to obtain all that this region will afford, but to be able to collect supplies to advantage in Maryland, I think it important to have the services of some one known to the people and acquainted with the resources of the country.

I wish therefore that if ex-Governor [Enoch L.] Lowe can make it convenient, he would come to me at once, as I have already requested by telegram. As I contemplate entering a part of the State with which Governor Lowe is well acquainted, I think he could be of much service to me in many ways.

Should the results of the expedition justify it, I propose to enter Pennsylvania, unless you should deem it unadvisable upon political or other grounds.

As to the movements of the enemy, my latest intelligence shows that the army of Pope is concentrating around Washington and Alexandria in their fortifications. Citizens of this county report that Winchester has been evacuated, which is confirmed by the *Baltimore Sun* of this morning, containing extracts from the *Washington Star* of yesterday. This will still further relieve our country, and I think leaves the Valley entirely free. They will probably concentrate behind the Potomac.

I have the honor to be with high respect, your obt servt

R. E. LEE
Genl

289   To JEFFERSON DAVIS
                    Richmond, Virginia

Headquarters, Army of Northern Virginia
Leesburg
September 5, 1862

Mr. President:

As I have already had the honor to inform you, this army is about entering Maryland, with a view of affording the people of that State an opportunity of liberating themselves. Whatever success may attend that effort, I hope at any rate to annoy and harass the enemy.

The army being transferred to this section, the road to Richmond through Warrenton, has been abandoned as far back as Culpeper Court House and all trains are directed to proceed by way of Luray & Front Royal from Culpeper Court House to Winchester. I desire that everything coming from Richmond may take that route, or any nearer one turning off before reaching Culpeper Court House. Notwithstanding the abandonment of the line as above mentioned, I deem it important that as soon as the bridge over the Rapidan shall be completed, that over the Rappahannock should be constructed as soon as possible, and I have requested the president of the road to have timber prepared for that purpose. My reason for desiring that this bridge shall be repaired is, that in the event of falling back, it is my intention to take a position about Warrenton, where should the enemy attempt an advance on Richmond, I should be on his flank, or, should he attack me, I should have a favorable country to operate in, and the bridges being repaired, should be in full communication with Richmond. I have had all the arms taken in the late battles collected as far as possible, and am informed that about ten thousand are now at Gainesville. All empty trains returning to Rapidan are ordered to take in arms at Gainesville to transport to Rapidan. They should be sent at once to Richmond to be put in order, as arms may be needed in Maryland.

I desire that Col Gorgas will send some one to take charge of these arms at once, as the cavalry regiment now on duty in the vicinity of Gainesville will have to be withdrawn. We shall supply ourselves with provisions and forage in the country in which we operate, but ammunition must be sent from Richmond.

I hope that the Secretary of War will see that the Ordnance Department provides ample supplies of all kinds. In forwarding the ammunition it can be sent in the way above designated for the other trains, or it can be sent to Staunton, and thence by the Valley road to Winchester, which will be my depot. It is not yet certain that the enemy have evacuated the Valley, but there are reports to that effect, and I have no doubt that they will leave that section as soon as they learn of the movement across the Potomac. Any officer however proceeding towards Winchester with a train will of course not move without first ascertaining that the way is clear. I am now more desirous that my suggestion as to General [William W.] Loring's movements shall be carried into effect as soon as possible so that with the least delay he may move to the lower end of the valley about Martinsburg, and guard the approach in that direction. He should first drive the enemy from the Kanawha Valley, if he can, and afterwards, or if he finds he cannot accomplish that result, I wish him to move by way of Romney towards Martinsburg and take position in that vicinity.

I have the honor to be with high respect, your obt servt

R. E. LEE
Genl

290   To JEFFERSON DAVIS
Richmond, Virginia
TELEGRAM

13 miles from Fredericktown, Maryland
September 6, 1862

TWO DIVISIONS OF THE ARMY HAVE CROSSED THE POTOMAC. I HOPE ALL WILL CROSS TO DAY. NAVIGATION OF THE CANAL HAS BEEN INTERRUPTED AND EFFORTS WILL BE MADE TO BREAK UP THE USE OF THE BALTIMORE AND OHIO RAILROAD.

R. E. LEE

291   To GENERAL GUSTAVUS W. SMITH
                    Richmond, Virginia

Headquarters, two miles from Fredericktown, Maryland
September 7, 1862

General:

I have received your letter of the 1st instant reporting the condition of affairs at Suffolk, New Kent, Fredericksburg, &c. I do not think the enemy will be able to maintain a large force south of James River, and unless prevented by the enemy's gunboats you will be able to retake Norfolk. I feel convinced that their land force at that point will be small. I have thought of suggesting to you the advantages of strengthening and reoccupying old Fort Powhatan, as opportunity may offer. It will extend your command of James River, and stop the ascent of the enemy's boats and depredations upon the river banks, &c. It could be held by the Navy, and as soon as the *Richmond* is completed will enable her to clear out the river. Every effort should now be made to complete the *Richmond* immediately, and heavy guns could now be prepared for Powhatan at the Tredegar Works. We must leave no stone unturned to expel the enemy from our borders. I have seen official accounts of the complete evacuation of Fredericksburg, and official reports from the Valley state that Winchester was abandoned on the night of September 2d. Genl [Julius] White commanding at that place is stated to have retired into Pennsylvania. I think the enemy will concentrate about Washington. I hope you will make every effort to collect available troops on the James River and Rappahannock, so as to protect Richmond and cover the country. You must expect to be annoyed by the fleet of the enemy.

I am with high respect, your obt servt

R. E. LEE
Genl

292   To JEFFERSON DAVIS
                    Richmond, Virginia

Headquarters, two miles from Fredericktown, Maryland
September 7, 1862

Mr. President:

I have the honor to inform you that all the divisions of the army have crossed the Potomac, unless it may be Genl [John G.] Walker's from whom I have had no report since his arrival at Leesburg on the evening of the 5th instant. They occupy the line of the Monocacy. I find there is plenty of provisions and forage in this country, and the community have received us with kindness. There may be some embarrassment in paying for necessaries for the army, as it is probable that many individuals will hesitate to receive Confederate currency. I shall in all cases endeavor to purchase what is wanted, and if unable to pay upon the spot, will give certificates of indebtedness of the Confederate States, for future adjustment.

It is very desirable that the Chief Quartermaster and Commissary should be provided with funds, and that some general arrangement should be made for liquidating the debts that may be incurred to the satisfaction of the people of Maryland, in order that they may willingly furnish us with what is wanted. I shall endeavor to purchase horses, clothing, shoes, and medical stores for our present use, and you will see the facility that would arise from being provided with the means of paying for them. I hope it may be convenient for ex-Governor Lowe, or some prominent citizen of Maryland to join me, with a view of expediting these and other arrangements necessary to the success of our army in this State. Notwithstanding individual expressions of kindness that have been given, and the general sympathy in the success of the Confederate States, situated as Maryland is, I do not anticipate any general rising of the people in our behalf. Some additions to our ranks will no doubt be received, and I hope to procure subsistence for our troops. As yet we have had no encounter with the enemy on this side of the river, except a detachment of cavalry at Poolesville, which resulted in slight loss on both sides, thirty-one of the enemy being captured. As far as I can learn, the enemy are in their entrenchments around Washington. Genl Banks with his division, has advanced to Darnestown. The Shenandoah Valley has been evacuated, and their stores at Winchester &c., are stated to have been destroyed. By the enclosed unfinished note from an officer of the Federal Army, dated at Poolesville, you will perceive that the enemy are withdrawing troops from Hilton Head.

I have the honor to be with high respect, your obt servt

R. E. LEE
Genl

293   To THE PEOPLE OF MARYLAND

Headquarters, Army of Northern Virginia
Near Fredericktown
September 8, 1862

It is right that you should know the purpose that has brought the army under my command within the limits of your State, so far as that purpose concerns yourselves.

The people of the Confederate States have long watched with the deepest sympathy the wrongs and outrages that have been inflicted upon the citizens of a commonwealth allied to the States of the South by the strongest social, political and commercial ties.

They have seen with profound indignation their sister State deprived of every right and reduced to the condition of a conquered province.

Under the pretense of supporting the Constitution, but in violation of its most valuable provisions, your citizens have been arrested and imprisoned upon no charge and contrary to all forms of law; the faithful and manly protest against this outrage made by the venerable and illustrious Marylander, to whom in better days no citizen appealed for right in vain, was treated with scorn and contempt; the government of your chief city has been usurped by armed strangers; your legislature has been dissolved by the unlawful arrest of its members; freedom of the press and of speech has been suppressed; words have been declared offences by an arbitrary decree of the Federal Executive, and citizens ordered to be tried by a military commission for what they may dare to speak.

Believing that the people of Maryland possessed a spirit too lofty to submit to such a government, the people of the South have long wished to aid you in throwing off this foreign yoke, to enable you again to enjoy the inalienable rights of freemen, and restore independence and sovereignty to your State.

In obedience to this wish, our army has come among you, and is prepared to assist you with the power of its arms in regaining the rights of which you have been despoiled.

This, citizens of Maryland, is our mission, so far as you are concerned.

No constraint upon your free will is intended, no intimidation will be allowed.

Within the limits of this army, at least, Marylanders shall once more enjoy their ancient freedom of thought and speech.

We know no enemies among you, and will protect all of every opinion.

It is for you to decide your destiny, freely and without constraint.

This army will respect your choice whatever it may be, and while the Southern people will rejoice to welcome you to your natural position among them, they will only welcome you when you come of your own free will.

R. E. LEE
General Commanding

294   To JEFFERSON DAVIS
Richmond, Virginia

Headquarters, Near Fredericktown, Maryland
September 8, 1862

Mr. President:

Since my letter to you of the 7th instant nothing of interest in a military point of view has transpired. As far as I can learn the enemy are not moving in this direction, but continue to concentrate about Washington.

I am endeavoring to break up the line of communication as far back as Culpeper Court House and turn everything into the Valley of Virginia, in accordance with the plan which I have heretofore made known to you. I fear that the arms captured on the plains of Manassas, of which some ten or twelve thousand were collected at Gainesville, will all be lost for want of transportation to remove them. I made the best arrangement in my power, being compelled to move the army away, and the wagons ordered to go by Gainesville to take arms back were taken to transport sick and wounded back to Warrenton. I can get no satisfactory account of these arms. The last I heard of them they were still at Gainesville.

So far we have had no difficulty in procuring provisions in the country, though we have not relied exclusively upon them for our subsistence.

I have the honor to be with high respect, your obt servt

R. E. LEE
Genl

295   To JEFFERSON DAVIS
                          Richmond, Virginia

                                    Headquarters, Near Fredericktown, Maryland
                                                    September 8, 1862
Mr. President:
    The present posture of affairs, in my opinion, places it in the power
of the Government of the Confederate States to propose with propriety
to that of the United States the recognition of our independence.
    For more than a year both sections of the country have been dev-
astated by hostilities which have brought sorrow and suffering upon
thousands of homes, without advancing the objects which our enemies
proposed to themselves in beginning the contest.
    Such a proposition coming from us at this time, could in no way be
regarded as suing for peace, but being made when it is in our power to
inflict injury upon our adversary, would show conclusively to the world
that our sole object is the establishment of our independence, and the
attainment of an honorable peace. The rejection of this offer would
prove to the country that the responsibility of the continuance of the
war does not rest upon us, but that the party in power in the United
States elect to prosecute it for purposes of their own. The proposal of
peace would enable the people of the United States to determine at their
coming elections whether they will support those who favor a pro-
longation of the war, or those who wish to bring it to a termination,
which can but be productive of good to both parties without affecting
the honor of either.

        I have the honor to be with high respect, your obt servt

                                            R. E. Lee
                                            Genl Comdg

296   SPECIAL ORDERS, NO. 191

                                    Headquarters, Army of Northern Virginia
                                                    September 9, 1862

    I. The citizens of Fredericktown being unwilling, while overrun
by members of this army, to open their stores, in order to give them confidence, and to secure to officers and men purchasing supplies for benefit
of this command, all officers and men of this army are strictly prohibited

from visiting Fredericktown except on business, in which case they will bear evidence of this in writing from division commanders. The provost marshal in Fredericktown will see that his guard rigidly enforces this order.

II. Major Taylor will proceed to Leesburg, Virginia, and arrange for transportation of the sick and those unable to walk to Winchester, securing the transportation of the country for this purpose. The route between this and Culpeper Court House east of the mountains being unsafe will no longer be traveled. Those on the way to this army already across the river will move up promptly; all others will proceed to Winchester collectively and under command of officers, at which point, being the general depot of this army, its movements will be known and instructions given by commanding officer regulating further movements.

III. The army will resume its march tomorrow taking the Hagerstown road. Genl Jackson's command will form the advance and after passing Middletown, with such portion as he may select take the route towards Sharpsburg cross the Potomac at the most convenient point and by Friday morning take possession of the Baltimore & Ohio Railroad, capture such of the enemy as may be at Martinsburg and intercept such as may attempt to escape from Harper's Ferry.

IV. Genl Longstreet's command will pursue the main road as far as Boonsboro, where it will halt, with reserve, supply, and baggage trains of the army.

V. Genl McLaws with his own division and that of Genl R. H. Anderson will follow Genl Longstreet. On reaching Middletown will take the route to Harper's Ferry and by Friday morning possess himself of the Maryland Heights and endeavor to capture the enemy at Harper's Ferry and vicinity.

VI. Genl Walker with his division after accomplishing the object in which he is now engaged, will cross the Potomac at Cheek's Ford ascend its right bank to Lovettsville take possession of Loudoun Heights if practicable by Friday morning, Keys' Ford on his left and the road between the end of the mountain and the Potomac on his right. He will as far as practicable co-operate with Genls McLaws & Jackson & intercept retreat of the enemy.

VII. Genl D. H. Hill's division will form the rear guard of the army pursuing the road taken by the main body. The reserve artillery, ordnance and supply trains, &c., will precede Genl Hill.

VIII. Genl Stuart will detach a squadron of cavalry to accompany the commands of Genls Longstreet, Jackson, and McLaws, and with the main body of the cavalry will cover the route of the army, bring up all stragglers that may have been left behind.

IX. The commands of Genls Jackson, McLaws, & Walker after accomplishing the objects for which they have been detached will join the main body of the army at Boonsboro or Hagerstown.

X. Each regiment on the march will habitually carry its axes in the regimental ordnance wagons for use of the men at their encampments to procure wood, &c.

By command of Genl R. E. Lee:

R. H. CHILTON
A A General

297   To JEFFERSON DAVIS
                      Richmond, Virginia

Headquarters, Near Fredericktown
September 9, 1862

Mr. President:

I have just received your letter of the 7th instant from Rapidan, informing me of your intention to come on to Leesburg. While I should feel the greatest satisfaction in having an interview with you and consulting upon all subjects of interest, I cannot but feel great uneasiness for your safety should you undertake to reach me. You will not only encounter the hardships and fatigue of a very disagreeable journey, but also run the risk of capture by the enemy. I send my aide-de-camp, Maj [W. H.] Taylor back to explain to you the difficulties and dangers of the journey, which I cannot recommend you to undertake. I am endeavoring to break up the line through Leesburg, which is no longer safe, and turn everything off from Culpeper Court House towards Winchester. I shall move in the direction I originally intended, towards Hagerstown and Chambersburg, for the purpose of opening our line of communication through the Valley, in order to procure sufficient supplies of flour. I shall not move until tomorrow, or perhaps next day, but when I do move, the line of communication in this direction will be entirely broken up. I must therefore advise that you do not make an attempt that I cannot but regard as hazardous.

I have the honor to be with high resepect, your obt servt

R. E. LEE
Genl

298   To JEFFERSON DAVIS
                           Richmond, Virginia

                              Headquarters, Near Fredericktown, Maryland
                                                September 9, 1862
Mr. President:
    Nothing of interest in a military point of view has transpired since
my last communication. We are able to obtain forage for our animals,
and some provisions, but there is more difficulty about the latter. Many
of the farmers have not yet gotten out their wheat, and there is a reluctance on the part of millers and others to commit themselves in our favor.
I shall now open our communication with the Valley, so that we can obtain more supplies. Some cattle, but not in any great numbers, are obtained in this country, the inhabitants are said to have driven many off to
Pennsylvania.
    From reports that have reached me, I believe that the enemy are
pushing a strong column up the River (Potomac) by Rockville and
Darnestown, and by Poolesville towards Seneca Mills. I hear that the
commands of Sumner, Sigel, Burnside and Hooker are advancing in the
direction above mentioned.

            I have the honor to be with high respect, your obt servt

                                                R. E. LEE
                                                Genl

299   To JEFFERSON DAVIS
                           Richmond, Virginia

                              Headquarters, Army of Northern Virginia
                                            Hagerstown, Maryland
                                                September 12, 1862
Mr. President:
    Before crossing the Potomac I considered the advantages of entering
Maryland east or west of the Blue Ridge. In either case it was my inten-
tion to march upon this town. By crossing east of the Blue Ridge, both
Washington and Baltimore would be threatened, which I believed would
insure the withdrawal of the mass of the enemy's troops north of the
Potomac. I think this has been accomplished.
    I had also supposed that as soon as it was known that the army had
reached Fredericktown, the enemy's forces in the Valley of Virginia,

which had retired to Harper's Ferry and Martinsburg, would retreat altogether from the State. In this I was disappointed, and you will preceive from the accompanying order [Special Orders, No. 191] of the 9th instant that Genls Jackson and McLaws have been detached with a view of capturing their forces at each place, should they not have retired. The army has been received in this region with sympathy and kindness. We have found in this city about fifteen hundred barrels of flour, and I am led to hope that a supply can be gathered from the mills in the country, though I fear we shall have to haul from the Valley of Virginia. The supply of beef has been very small, and we have been able to procure no bacon. A thousand pairs of shoes and some clothing were obtained in Fredericktown, two hundred & fifty pairs in Williamsport, and about four hundred pairs in this city. They will not be sufficient to cover the bare feet of the army. Our advance pickets are at Middleburg on the Pennsylvania line. I await here the result of the movements upon Harper's Ferry and Martinsburg.

I have the honor to enclose to you a copy of a proclamation which I issued to the people of Maryland. I waited on entering the State for the arrival of ex-Governor Lowe, but finding that he did not come up, and that the citizens were embarrassed as to the intentions of the army, I determined to delay no longer in making known our purpose.

I have the honor to be with high respect, your obt servt

R. E. LEE
Genl Comdg

300   COLONEL A. L. LONG TO GENERAL LAFAYETTE McLAWS
Commanding Division, Maryland Heights, Maryland

Headquarters, Army of Northern Virginia
Hagerstown, Maryland
September 13, 1862

General:
General Lee desires me to say that he has not heard from you since you left the main body of the army. He hopes that you have been able to reach your destined position [Maryland Heights]. He is anxious that the object of your expedition be speedily accomplished. The enemy have doubtless occupied Frederick since our troops have abandoned it, and are following our rear. The enemy have abandoned Martinsburg and retreated to Harper's Ferry, about 2,500 or 3,000 strong. General Jackson

will be at Harper's Ferry by noon today to cooperate with you. General Stuart, with his cavalry, occupies the Middletown Valley. General D. H. Hill is a mile or two west of Boonsboro at the junction of the Sharpsburg and Hagerstown roads, and General Longstreet is at Hagerstown. You are particularly desired to watch well the main road from Frederick to Harper's Ferry, so as to prevent the enemy from turning your position. The commanding general hopes that the enemy about Harper's Ferry will be speedily disposed of, and the various detachments returned to the main body of the army. You are also desired to communicate as frequently as you can with headquarters.

I am very respectfully, your obedient servant

A. L. Long
Colonel and Military Secretary

301   To JEFFERSON DAVIS
Richmond, Virginia

Headquarters, Army of Northern Virginia
Hagerstown Maryland
September 13, 1862

Mr. President:

I regret that you should have exposed yourself while indisposed, to the fatigue of travel, though I should have been highly gratified at an opportunity of conferring with you on many points. You will perceive by the printed address to the people of Maryland which has been sent you, that I have not gone contrary to the views expressed by you on the subject. Should there be anything in it to correct, please let me know. I have received as yet no official list of the casualties in the late battles, and from the number of absentees from the army, and the vice of straggling, a correct list cannot now be obtained. The army has been so constantly in motion, its attention has been so unremittingly devoted to what was necessary, that little opportunity has been afforded for attention to this subject. I wish your views of its operations could be realized, but so much depends upon circumstances beyond its control, and the aid that we may receive, that it is difficult for me to conjecture the result.

To look to the safety of our own frontier, and to operate untrammeled in an enemy's territory, you need not be told, is very difficult. Every effort however will be made to acquire every advantage which our position and means may warrant.

One great embarrassment is the reduction of our ranks by straggling, which it seems impossible to prevent with our present regimental officers. Our ranks are very much diminished, I fear from a third to a half of the original numbers, though I have reason to hope that our casualties in battle will not exceed five thousand men.

I am glad to hear that the railroad bridge over the Rapidan is in a fair way to completion. I fear all the locomotives and cars captured at Bristoe & Manassas have been destroyed either by the enemy or ourselves. As I before stated, having only Jackson's & Longstreet's corps in the battle of Manassas, I was unable to spare men to save property, though I knew and felt its value.

I fear there was much suffering among the wounded, but it was impossible to prevent it. Dr. [Lafayette] Guild, the Medical Director, with detachments from each brigade, was left upon the field, and all the wounded committed to their care. All the means of transportation at our command were given to him, including the wagons, with directions that they must receive the first attention and be sent to Warrenton. They were ordered to be forwarded thence to Gordonsville, as fast as possible, and as they were able to bear the transportation. Only one regiment of cavalry is in front of Warrenton, and that I fear my necessities will oblige me to withdraw. Unless Genl [G. W.] Smith can organize a force and advance it, of sufficient strength to cover that section of country, it will be liable to raids from Washington and Alexandria by the enemy's cavalry. It is a risk we must necessarily run to use the troops elsewhere.

With sincere wishes for your health and prosperity,

I am most respectfully & truly yours

R. E. LEE
Genl Comdg

302   COLONEL R. H. CHILTON TO GENERAL
LAFAYETTE McLAWS
Commanding Division, Weverton, Maryland

Headquarters, Army of Northern Virginia
September 14, 1862
8 p.m.

General:

The day has gone against us [reverses at Crampton's Gap and South Mountain] and this army will go by Sharpsburg and cross the river. It is necessary for you to abandon your position tonight. Send your trains not required on the road to cross the river. Your troops you must have well in hand to unite with this command, which will retire by Sharpsburg. Send forward officers to explore the way, ascertain the best crossing of the Potomac, and if you can find any between you and Shepherdstown leave Shepherdstown Ford for this command. Send an officer to report to me on the Sharpsburg road, where you are and what crossing you will take. You will of course bring Anderson's division with you.

I am sir respectfully, your obedient servant

R. H. CHILTON
Assistant Adjutant General

303   To GENERAL LAFAYETTE McLAWS
Commanding Division, Weverton, Maryland

Headquarters, Army of Northern Virginia
Hagerstown
September 14, 1862

General:
    Genl Longstreet moves down this morning to occupy the Boonsboro Valley so as to protect your flank from forces coming from Frederick, until the operations at Harper's Ferry are finished. I desire your operations there to be pushed on as rapidly as possible, and, if the point is not ultimately taken to arrange it that your forces may be brought up the Boonsboro Valley. Genl Stuart with a portion of Genl D. H. Hill's forces holds the gap between Boonsboro and Middletown, & Hampton's & Munford's brigades of cavalry occupy Burkittsville & the pass through the mountains there. Should Harper's Ferry be taken, the road will be open to you at Sharpsburg, around the mountains. From Sharpsburg the road communicates with Boonsboro and Hagerstown.

Very respectfully, your obt servt

R. E. LEE
General

304   COLONEL A. L. LONG TO GENERAL
                      LAFAYETTE McLAWS
                   Maryland Heights, Maryland

                                              Headquarters
                            Centreville, [Keedysville,] Maryland
                                         September 15, 1862
General:
    General Lee desires me to say that he sent several dispatches to you
last night; he is in doubt that they have been received. We have fallen
back to this place to enable you more readily to join us. You are desired
to withdraw immediately from your position on Maryland Heights, and
join us here. If you can't get off any other way, you must cross the
mountain. The utmost dispatch is required. Should you be able to cross
over to Harper's Ferry, do so and report immediately.

        I am very respectfully, your obedient servant

                                           A. L. LONG
                            Colonel and Military Secretary

305   To JEFFERSON DAVIS
                         Richmond, Virginia

                          Headquarters, Sharpsburg, Maryland
                                         September 16, 1862
Mr. President:
    My letter to you of the 13th instant informed you of the positions of
the different divisions of this army. Learning that night that Harper's
Ferry had not surrendered, and that the enemy was advancing more
rapidly than convenient from Fredericktown, I determined to return with Longstreet's command to the Blue Ridge to strengthen
D. H. Hill's and Stuart's divisions engaged in holding the passes of the
mountains lest the enemy should fall upon McLaws' rear, drive him
from the Maryland Heights, and thus relieve the garrison at Harper's
Ferry. On approaching Boonsboro I received information from Genl
D. H. Hill [at Turner's Gap] that the enemy in strong force was at the
main pass on the Frederick and Hagerstown road, pressing him so
heavily as to require immediate reinforcements. Longstreet advanced
rapidly to his support, and immediately placed his troops in position. By
this time Hill's right had been forced back, the gallant [General Samuel]

Garland having fallen in rallying his brigade. Under Genl Longstreet's directions, our right was soon restored, and firmly resisted the attacks of the enemy to the last. His superior numbers enabled him to extend beyond both of our flanks, and his right was able to reach the summit of the mountain to our left, and press us heavily in that direction. The battle raged until after night, the enemy's efforts to force a passage were resisted, but we had been unable to repulse him. Learning later in the evening that Crampton's Gap on the direct road from Fredericktown to Sharpsburg had been forced, and McLaws' rear thus threatened, and believing from a report from Genl Jackson that Harper's Ferry would fall next morning, I determined to withdraw Longstreet and D. H. Hill from their positions and retire to the vicinity of Sharpsburg, where the army could be more readily united. Before abandoning the position, indications led me to believe that the enemy was withdrawing, but learning from a prisoner that Sumner's corps, which had not been engaged, was being put in position to relieve their wearied troops while the most of ours were exhausted by a fatiguing march and a hard conflict and I feared would be unable to renew the fight successfully in the morning, confirmed me in my determination. Accordingly the troops were withdrawn preceded by the trains without molestation by the enemy, and about daybreak took position in front of this place. The enemy did not pass through the gap until about 8 o'clock of the morning after the battle, and their advance reached a position in front of us about 2 p.m. Before their arrival, I received intelligence from Genl Jackson that Harper's Ferry had surrendered early in the morning. I enclose his report. From a more detailed statement furnished by Genl Jackson's adjutant general it appears that forty-nine pieces of artillery, twenty-four mountain howitzers and seventeen revolving guns, eleven thousand men fit for duty, consisting of twelve regiments of infantry, three companies of cavalry, and six companies of artillery, together with eleven thousand small arms, were the fruits of this victory.

Part of Genl Jackson's corps has reached us, and the rest are approaching, except Genl A. P. Hill's division left at Harper's Ferry to guard the place and take care of public property. The enemy have made no attack up to this afternoon, but are in force in our front.

This victory of the indomitable Jackson and his troops gives us renewed occasion for gratitude to Almighty God for His guidance and protection.

I am with high respect, your obt servt

R. E. LEE
General

306   To JEFFERSON DAVIS
                          Richmond, Virginia

                                        Headquarters, Sharpsburg, Maryland
                                                      September 18, 1862
                                                            6½ a. m.

Mr. President:

On the afternoon of the 16th instant the enemy, who, you were informed on that day, was in our front, opened a light fire of artillery upon
our line.

Early next morning it was renewed in earnest, and large masses of
the Federal troops that had crossed the Antietam above our position
assembled on our left and threatened to overwhelm us. They advanced in
three compact lines. The divisions of Genls McLaws, R. H. Anderson,
A. P. Hill, and Walker had not arrived the previous night, as I had hoped,
and were still beyond the Potomac.

Genl Jackson's and Genl Ewell's divisions were thrown to the left of
Generals D. H. Hill and Longstreet. The enemy advanced between the
Antietam and the Sharpsburg and Hagerstown turnpike and was met
by Genl Hill's and the left of Genl Longstreet's divisions, where the
contest raged fiercely, extending to our entire left. The enemy was
driven back and held in check, but before the divisions of McLaws,
Anderson, and Walker, who, upon their arrival on the morning of the
17th, were advanced to support the left wing and center, could be
brought into action, that portion of our lines was forced back by superior numbers. The line after a severe conflict was restored and the enemy
driven back, and our position maintained during the rest of the day. In
the afternoon the enemy advanced on our right, where Genl Jones' division was posted, who handsomely maintained his position. Genl
[Robert A.] Toombs' brigade, guarding the bridge over Antietam Creek,
gallantly resisted the approach of the enemy, but his superior numbers
enabling him to extend his left, he crossed below the bridge, and assumed a threatening attitude on our right, which fell back in confusion.
By this time, between three and four o'clock p.m., Genl A. P. Hill with
five of his brigades had reached the scene of action, drove the enemy
immediately from the position they had taken, and continued the contest until dark, restoring our right, and maintaining our ground.

                                                      R. E. LEE
                                                      Genl Comdg

307   To GENERAL SAMUEL COOPER
Richmond, Virginia

BATTLE REPORT OF SHARPSBURG CAMPAIGN

Headquarters
August 19, 1863

General:

I have the honour to forward a report of the capture of Harper's Ferry & the operations of the army in Maryland (1862). The official reports of Lt Genl Jackson & the officers of his corps have only been recently received, which prevented its earlier transmittal. This finishes the reports of the operations of the campaign of 1862. They were designed to form a continuous narrative, though for reasons given were written at intervals. May I ask you to cause the several reports to be united, & to append the tabular statements accompanying each. Should this be inconvenient, if you could return the reports to me, I would have them properly arranged.

With great respect, your obt servt

R. E. LEE
Genl

CAPTURE OF HARPER'S FERRY AND OPERATIONS IN MARYLAND

The enemy having retired to the protection of the fortifications around Washington and Alexandria, the army marched on the 3d September towards Leesburg.

The armies of Generals McClellan and Pope had now been brought back to the point from which they set out on the campaigns of the spring and summer. The objects of those campaigns had been frustrated and the designs of the enemy on the coast of North Carolina and in western Virginia thwarted by the withdrawal of the main body of his forces from those regions.

Northeastern Virginia was freed from the presence of Federal soldiers up to the entrenchments of Washington, and soon after the arrival of the army at Leesburg information was received that the troops which had occupied Winchester had retired to Harper's Ferry and Martinsburg.

The war was thus transferred from the interior to the frontier and the supplies of rich and productive districts made accessible to our army.

To prolong a state of affairs in every way desirable, and not to permit the season for active operations to pass without endeavoring to inflict further injury upon the enemy, the best course appeared to be the transfer of the army into Maryland.

Although not properly equipped for invasion, lacking much of the material of war, and feeble in transportation, the troops poorly provided with clothing, and thousands of them destitute of shoes, it was yet believed to be strong enough to detain the enemy upon the northern frontier until the approach of winter should render his advance into Virginia difficult, if not impracticable.

The condition of Maryland encouraged the belief that the presence of our army, however inferior to that of the enemy, would induce the Washington Government to retain all its available force to provide against contingencies which its course towards the people of that State gave it reason to apprehend.

At the same time it was hoped that military success might afford us an opportunity to aid the citizens of Maryland in any efforts they might be disposed to make to recover their liberties.

The difficulties that surrounded them were fully appreciated, and we expected to derive more assistance in the attainment of our object from the just fears of the Washington Government, than from any active demonstration on the part of the people, unless success should enable us to give them assurance of continued protection.

Influenced by these considerations, the army was put in motion, D. H. Hill's division which had joined us on the 2nd being in advance, and between the 4th and 7th of September crossed the Potomac at the fords near Leesburg, and encamped in the vicinity of Fredericktown.

It was decided to cross the Potomac east of the Blue Ridge, in order, by threatening Washington and Baltimore, to cause the enemy to withdraw from the south bank, where his presence endangered our communications and the safety of those engaged in the removal of our wounded and the captured property from the late battlefields.

Having accomplished this result, it was proposed to move the army into western Maryland, establish our communications with Richmond through the Valley of the Shenandoah, and by threatening Pennsylvania, induce the enemy to follow, and thus draw him from his base of supplies.

It had been supposed that the advance upon Fredericktown would lead to the evacuation of Martinsburg and Harper's Ferry, thus opening the line of communication through the Valley. This not having occurred, it became necessary to dislodge the enemy from those positions before concentrating the army west of the mountains.

To accomplish this with the least delay, General Jackson was directed to proceed with his command to Martinsburg, and after driving the enemy from that place, to move down the south side of the Potomac upon Harper's Ferry. General McLaws with his own and R. H. Anderson's division was ordered to seize Maryland Heights on the north side of the Potomac opposite Harper's Ferry, and Brigadier General Walker, to take possession of Loudoun Heights, on the east side of the Shenandoah where it unites with the Potomac. These several commands were directed, after reducing Harper's Ferry and clearing the Valley of the enemy, to join the rest of the army at Boonsboro or Hagerstown.

The march of these troops began on the 10th, and at the same time the remainder of Longstreet's command and the division of D. H. Hill crossed the South Mountain and moved towards Boonsboro.

General Stuart with the cavalry remained east of the mountains, to observe the enemy and retard his advance.

A report having been received that a Federal force was approaching Hagerstown from the direction of Chambersburg, Longstreet continued his march to the former place, in order to secure the road leading thence to Williamsport, and also to prevent the removal of stores which were said to be in Hagerstown. He arrived at that place on the 11th, General Hill halting near Boonsboro to prevent the enemy at Harper's Ferry from escaping through Pleasant Valley, and at the same time to support the cavalry.

The advance of the Federal Army was so slow at the time we left Fredericktown as to justify the belief that the reduction of Harper's Ferry would be accomplished and our troops concentrated before they would be called upon to meet it. In that event it had not been intended to oppose its passage through the South Mountains, as it was desired to engage it as far as possible from its base.

General Jackson marched very rapidly, and crossing the Potomac near Williamsport on the 11th, sent A. P. Hill's division directly to Martinsburg, and disposed the rest of his command to cut off the retreat of the enemy westward. On his approach the Federal troops evacuated Martinsburg, retiring to Harper's Ferry on the night of the 11th, and Jackson entered the former place on the 12th capturing some prisoners and abandoned stores. In the forenoon of the following day his leading division under General A. P. Hill came in sight of the enemy strongly entrenched on Bolivar Heights in rear of Harper's Ferry. Before beginning the attack, General Jackson proceeded to put himself in communication with the cooperating forces under Generals McLaws and Walker, from the former of whom he was separated by the Potomac, and from the latter by the Shenandoah. General Walker took possession of Loudoun Heights on the 13th and the next day was in readiness to open upon Harper's Ferry. General McLaws encountered more opposition. He entered Pleasant Valley on the 11th. On the 12th he directed General Kershaw with his own and [William] Barksdale's brigade to ascend the ridge whose southern extremity is known as Maryland Heights, and attack the enemy who occupied that position with infantry and artillery protected by entrenchments. He disposed the rest of his command to hold the roads leading from Harper's Ferry eastward through Weverton, and northward from Sandy Hook, guarding the pass in his rear through which he had entered Pleasant Valley, with the brigades of [Paul W.] Semmes and Mahone.

Owing to the rugged nature of the ground on which Kershaw had to operate and the want of roads, he was compelled to use infantry alone.

Driving in the advance parties of the enemy on the summit of the ridge on the 12th he assailed the works the next day. After a spirited contest they were carried, the troops engaged in their defence spiking their heavy guns and retreating to Harper's Ferry. By 4½ p.m. Kershaw was in possession of Maryland Heights. On the 14th a road for artillery was cut along the ridge, and at 2 p.m. four guns opened upon the enemy on the opposite side of the river, and the investment of Harper's Ferry was complete.

In the meantime events transpired in another quarter which threatened to interfere with the reduction of the place.

A copy of the order directing the movement of the army from Fredericktown had fallen into the hands of General McClellan, and disclosed to him the disposition of our forces. He immediately began to push forward rapidly, and on the afternoon of the 13th was reported approaching the pass in South Mountain on the Boonsboro and Fredericktown road. The cavalry under General Stuart fell back before him, materially impeding his progress by its gallant resistance, and gaining time for preparations to oppose his advance.

By penetrating the mountains at this point he would reach the rear of McLaws and be enabled to relieve the garrison at Harper's Ferry. To prevent this, General D. H. Hill was directed to guard the Boonsboro Gap, and Longstreet ordered to march from Hagerstown to his support. On the 13th General Hill sent back the brigades of Garland and [Alfred H.] Colquitt to hold the pass, but subsequently ascertaining that the enemy was near in heavy force, he ordered up the rest of his division. Early on the 14th a large body of the enemy attempted to force its way to the rear of the position held by Hill, by a road south of the Boonsboro and Fredericktown turnpike. The attack was repulsed by Garland's brigade after a severe conflict, in which that brave and accomplished young officer was killed. The remainder of the division arriving shortly afterwards, Colquitt's brigade was disposed across the turnpike road, that of G. B. Anderson supported by [Roswell S.] Ripley, was placed on the right, and [Robert E.] Rodes' occupied an important position on the left. Garland's brigade which had suffered heavily in the first attack, was withdrawn, and the defence of the road occupied by it entrusted to Colonel Rosser of the 5th Virginia Cavalry, who reported to General Hill with his regiment and some artillery.

The small command of General Hill repelled the repeated assaults of the Federal Army and held it in check for five hours. Several attacks on the center were gallantly repulsed by Colquitt's brigade, and Rodes maintained his position against heavy odds with the utmost tenacity. Longstreet, leaving one brigade at Hagerstown had hurried to the assistance of Hill, and reached the scene of action between 3 and 4 p.m. His troops much exhausted by a long rapid march, and the heat of the day, were disposed on both sides of the turnpike.

General D. R. Jones with three of his brigades, those of [George E.] Pickett (under General [Richard B.] Garnett), Kemper, and Jenkins (under Colonel [R. Lindsay] Walker) together with Evans' brigade, was posted along the mountain on the left, General Hood with his own and Whiting's brigade under Colonel [Evander M.] Law, [Thomas F.] Drayton's, and D. R. Jones' under Colonel G. T. Anderson, on the right. Batteries had been placed by General Hill in such positions as could be found, but the ground was unfavorable for the use of artillery. The battle continued with great animation until night. On the south of the turnpike the enemy was driven back some distance, and his attack on the center repulsed with loss.

His great superiority of numbers enabled him to extend beyond both of our flanks. By this means he succeeded in reaching the summit of the mountain beyond our left, and, pressing upon us heavily from that direction, gradually forced our troops back, after an obstinate resistance. Darkness put an end to the contest. The effort to force the passage of the mountains had failed, but it was manifest that without reinforcements we could not hazard a renewal of the engagement, as the enemy could easily turn either flank. Information was also received that another large body of Federal troops had during the afternoon forced their way through Crampton's Gap, only five miles in rear of McLaws. Under these circumstances, it was determined to retire to Sharpsburg, where we would be upon the flank and rear of the enemy should he move against McLaws, and where we could more readily unite with the rest of the army.

This movement was efficiently and skillfully covered by the cavalry brigade of General Fitzhugh Lee and was accomplished without interruption by the enemy, who did not appear on the west side of the pass at Boonsboro until about 8 a.m. on the following morning.

The resistance that had been offered to the enemy at Boonsboro secured sufficient time to enable General Jackson to complete the reduction of Harper's Ferry.

On the afternoon of the 14th, when he found that the troops of Walker and McLaws were in position to cooperate in the attack, he ordered General A. P. Hill to turn the enemy's left flank and enter Harper's Ferry. Ewell's division under General [Alexander R.] Lawton was ordered to support Hill, while Winder's brigade of Jackson's division under Colonel [A. J.] Grigsby with a battery of artillery made a demonstration on the enemy's right near the Potomac. The rest of the division was held in reserve. The cavalry under Major [T. B.] Massie was placed on the extreme left to prevent the escape of the enemy. Colonel Grigsby succeeded in getting possession of an eminence on the left, upon which two batteries were advantageously posted. General A. P. Hill observing a hill on the enemy's extreme left, occupied by infantry without artillery, and protected only by an abatis of felled timber, directed General Pender with his own brigade and those of General Archer and Colonel Brockenbrough to seize the crest which was done with slight resistance. At the same time he ordered Generals Branch and Gregg to march along the Shenandoah, and, taking advantage of the ravines intersecting its steep banks, to establish themselves on the plain to the left and rear of the enemy's works. This was accomplished during the night. Lieut Colonel Walker, Chief of Artillery, of A. P. Hill's division placed several batteries on the eminence taken by General Pender, and, under the directions of Colonel [Stapleton] Crutchfield, General Jackson's Chief of Artillery, ten guns belonging to Ewell's division were posted on the east side of the Shenandoah, so as to enfilade the enemy's entrenchments on Bolivar Heights, and take his nearest and most formidable works in reverse.

General McLaws in the meantime made his preparations to prevent the force which had penetrated at Crampton's Gap from coming to the relief of the garrison.

This pass had been defended by the brigade of General [Howell] Cobb supported by those of Semmes and Mahone, but unable to oppose successfully the superior numbers brought against them, they had been compelled to retire with loss. The enemy halted at the gap, and during the night General McLaws formed his command in line of battle across Pleasant Valley, about a mile and a half below Crampton's [Gap] leaving one regiment to support the artillery on Maryland Heights, and two brigades on each of the roads from Harper's Ferry.

The attack on the garrison began at dawn. A rapid and vigorous fire was opened from the batteries of General Jackson and those on Maryland and Loudoun Heights. In about two hours the garrison consisting of more than eleven thousand men, surrendered. Seventy-three pieces of artillery, about thirteen thousand small arms, and a large quantity of military stores fell into our hands.

Leaving General A. P. Hill to receive the surrender of the Federal troops and secure the captured property, General Jackson with his two other divisions, set out at once for Sharpsburg, ordering Generals McLaws and Walker to follow without delay.

Official information of the fall of Harper's Ferry and the approach of General Jackson was received soon after the commands of Longstreet and D. H. Hill reached Sharpsburg on the morning of the 15th, and reanimated the courage of the troops. General Jackson arrived early on the 16th, and General Walker came up in the afternoon.

The presence of the enemy at Crampton's Gap embarrassed the movements of General McLaws. He retained the position taken during the night of the 14th to oppose an advance towards Harper's Ferry, until the capitulation of that place, when finding the enemy indisposed to attack, he gradually withdrew his command towards the Potomac. Deeming the roads to Sharpsburg on the north side of the river impracticable, he resolved to cross at Harper's Ferry and march by way of Shepherdstown. Owing to the condition of his troops and other circumstances, his progress was slow, and he did not reach the battlefield at Sharpsburg until some time after the engagement of the 17th began.

The commands of Longstreet and D. H. Hill on their arrival at Sharpsburg were placed in position along the range of hills between the town and the Antietam, nearly parallel to the course of that stream, Longstreet on the right of the road to Boonsboro and Hill on the left. The advance of the enemy was delayed by the brave opposition he encountered from Fitzhugh Lee's cavalry, and he did not appear on the opposite side of the Antietam until about 2 p.m. During the afternoon the batteries on each side were slightly engaged.

On the 16th the artillery fire became warmer, and continued throughout the day. The enemy crossed the Antietam beyond the reach of our batteries and menaced our left. In anticipation of this movement, Hood's two brigades had been transferred from the right and posted between D. H. Hill and the Hagerstown road.

General Jackson was now directed to take position on Hood's left, and formed his line with his right resting upon the Hagerstown road and his left extending towards the Potomac, protected by General Stuart with the cavalry and horse artillery. General Walker with his two brigades was stationed on Longstreet's right.

As evening approached, the enemy opened more vigorously with his artillery, and bore down heavily with his infantry upon Hood, but the attack was gallantly repulsed. At 10 p.m. Hood's troops were relieved by the brigades of Lawton and Trimble, of Ewell's division, commanded by General Lawton. Jackson's own division under General J. R. Jones was on Lawton's left, supported by the remaining brigades of Ewell's.

At early dawn on the 17th the enemy's artillery opened vigorously from both sides of the Antietam, the heaviest fire being directed against our left. Under cover of this fire a large force of infantry attacked General Jackson. They were met by his troops with the utmost resolution, and for several hours the conflict raged with great fury and alternate success. General J. R. Jones was compelled to leave the field and the command of Jackson's division devolved on General [William E.] Starke. The troops advanced with great spirit and the enemy's lines were repeatedly broken and forced to retire. Fresh troops however soon replaced those that were beaten, and Jackson's men were in turn compelled to fall back. The brave General Starke was killed, General Lawton was wounded, and nearly all the field officers with a large proportion of the men, killed or disabled. Our troops slowly yielded to overwhelming numbers and fell back, obstinately disputing the progress of the enemy. Hood returned to the field, and relieved the brigades of Trimble, Lawton, and Hays, which had suffered severely.

General Early who succeeded General Lawton in the command of Ewell's division, was ordered by General Jackson to move with his brigade to take the place of Jackson's division, most of which was withdrawn, its ammunition being nearly exhausted and its numbers much reduced. A small part of the division under Colonels Grigsby and [Leroy A.] Stafford, united with Early's brigade, as did portions of the brigades of Trimble, Lawton, and Hays.

The battle now raged with great violence, the small commands under Hood and Early holding their ground against many times their own numbers of the enemy, and under a tremendous fire of artillery. Hood was reinforced by the brigades of Ripley, Colquitt, and Garland (under Colonel [Duncan K.] McRae), of D. H. Hill's division and afterward by D. R. Jones' brigade, under Colonel G. T. Anderson.

The enemy's lines were broken and forced back, but fresh numbers advanced to their support and they began to gain ground. The desperate resistance they encountered however delayed their progress until the troops of General McLaws arrived and those of General Walker could be brought from the right. Hood's brigade, greatly diminished in numbers, withdrew to replenish their ammunition, their supply being entirely exhausted. They were relieved by Walker's command who immediately attacked the enemy vigorously, driving him back with great slaughter. Colonel [Van H.] Manning commanding Walker's brigade pursued until he was stopped by a strong fence, behind which was posted a large force of infantry with several batteries.

The gallant colonel was severely wounded, and his brigade retired to the line on which the rest of Walker's command had halted.

Upon the arrival of the reinforcements under General McLaws, General Early attacked with great resolution the large force opposed to him. McLaws advanced at the same time and the enemy were driven back in confusion, closely followed by our troops beyond the position occupied at the beginning of the engagement.

The enemy renewed the assault on our left several times, but was repulsed with loss. He finally ceased to advance his infantry and for several hours kept up a furious fire from his numerous batteries, under which our troops held their position with great coolness and courage. The attack on our left was speedily followed by one in heavy force on the center. This was met by part of Walker's division and the brigades of G. B. Anderson and Rodes of D. H. Hill's command assisted by a few pieces of artillery. The enemy was repulsed and retired behind the crest of a hill from which they kept up a desultory fire.

General R. H. Anderson's division came to Hill's support and formed in rear of his line. At this time by a mistake of orders, General Rodes' brigade was withdrawn from its position during the temporary absence of that officer at another part of the field. The enemy immediately pressed through the gap thus created and G. B. Anderson's brigade was broken and retired, General Anderson himself being mortally wounded. Major General R. H. Anderson and Brigadier General [Ambrose R.] Wright were also wounded and borne from the field.

The heavy masses of the enemy again moved forward, being opposed only by four pieces of artillery, supported by a few hundreds of men belonging to different brigades, rallied by General D. H. Hill and other officers, and parts of Walker's and R. H. Anderson's commands, Colonel [John R.] Cooke, with the 27th North Carolina Regiment of Walker's brigade, standing boldly in line without a cartridge. The firm front presented by this small force and the well directed fire of the artillery under Captain [Merritt B.] Miller of the Washington Artillery, and Captain [Robert] Boyce's South Carolina battery, checked the progress of the enemy, and in about an hour and a half he retired. Another attack was made soon afterwards a little farther to the right, but was repulsed by Miller's guns, which continued to hold the ground until the close of the engagement, supported by a part of R. H. Anderson's troops.

While the attack on the center and left was in progress, the enemy made repeated efforts to force the passage of the bridge over the Antietam, opposite the right wing of General Longstreet, commanded by Brigadier General D. R. Jones. This bridge was defended by General [Robert] Toombs with two regiments of his brigade, the 2d and 20th Georgia, and the batteries of General Jones. General Toombs' small command repulsed five different assaults made by a greatly superior force and maintained its position with distinguished gallantry.

In the afternoon the enemy began to extend his line as if to cross the Antietam below the bridge, and at 4 p.m. Toombs' regiments retired from the position they had so bravely held.

The enemy immediately crossed the bridge in large numbers and advanced against General Jones, who held the crest with less than two thousand men. After a determined and brave resistance, he was forced to give way, and the enemy gained the summit.

General A. P. Hill had arrived from Harper's Ferry, having left that place at 7½ a.m. He was now ordered to reinforce General Jones, and moved to his support with the brigades of Archer, Branch, Gregg, and Pender, the last of whom was placed on the right of the line, and the other three advanced and attacked the enemy now flushed with success. Hill's batteries were thrown forward and united their fire with those of General Jones, and one of General D. H. Hill's also opened with good effect from the left of the Boonsboro road. The progress of the enemy was immediately arrested and his lines began to waver. At this moment General Jones ordered Toombs' to charge the flank, while Archer supported by Branch and Gregg, moved upon the front of the Federal line. The enemy made a brief resistance, then broke and retreated in confusion towards the Antietam, pursued by the troops of Hill and Jones, until he reached the protection of his batteries on the opposite side of the river.

In this attack the brave and lamented Brigadier General L. O'B. Branch was killed, gallantly leading his brigade.

It was now nearly dark and the enemy had massed a number of batteries to sweep the approaches to the Antietam, on the opposite side of which the corps of General [Fitz John] Porter, which had not been engaged, now appeared to dispute our advance.

Our troops were much exhausted and greatly reduced in numbers by fatigue and the casualties of battle. Under these circumstances it was deemed injudicious to push our advantage further in the face of fresh troops of the enemy, much exceeding the number of our own. They were accordingly recalled and formed on the line originally held by General Jones.

While the attack on our center was progressing, General Jackson had been directed to endeavor to turn the enemy's right, but found it extending nearly to the Potomac, and so strongly defended with artillery that the attempt had to be abandoned.

The repulse on the right ended the engagement, and after a protracted and sanguinary conflict, every effort of the enemy to dislodge us from our position had been defeated with severe loss.

The arduous service in which our troops had been engaged, their great privations of rest and food, and the long marches without shoes over mountain roads, had greatly reduced our ranks before the action began. These causes had compelled thousands of brave men to absent themselves, and many more had done so from unworthy motives. This great battle was fought by less than forty thousand men on our side, all of whom had undergone the greatest labors and hardships in the field and on the march. Nothing could surpass the determined valor with which they met the large army of the enemy, fully supplied and equipped, and the result reflects the highest credit on the officers and men engaged. Our artillery, though much inferior to that of the enemy in the number of guns and weight of metal, rendered most efficient and gallant service throughout the day, and contributed greatly to the repulse of the attacks on every part of the line.

General Stuart, with the cavalry and horse artillery, performed the duty entrusted to him of guarding our left wing with great energy and courage, and rendered valuable assistance in defeating the attack on that part of our line.

On the 18th we occupied the position of the preceding day, except in the center, where our line was drawn in about two hundred yards.

Our ranks were increased by the arrival of a number of troops who had not been engaged the day before, and though still too weak to assume the offensive, we awaited without apprehension the renewal of the attack.

The day passed without any demonstration on the part of the enemy, who from the reports received, was expecting the arrival of reinforcements. As we could not look for a material increase in strength, and the enemy's force could be largely and rapidly augmented, it was not thought prudent to wait until he should be ready again to offer battle.

During the night of the 18th the army was accordingly withdrawn to the south side of the Potomac crossing near Shepherdstown, without loss or molestation.

The enemy advanced the next morning, but was held in check by

General Fitzhugh Lee with his cavalry, who covered our movement with boldness and success.

General Stuart with the main body, crossed the Potomac above Shepherdstown and moved up the river. The next day he recrossed at Williamsport and took position to operate upon the right and rear of the enemy should he attempt to follow us.

After the army had safely reached the Virginia shore with such of the wounded as could be removed, and all its trains, General Porter's corps with a number of batteries and some cavalry appeared on the opposite side.

General Pendleton was left to guard the ford with the reserve artillery and about six hundred infantry. That night the enemy crossed the river above General Pendleton's position, and his infantry support giving way, four of his guns were taken. A considerable force took position on the right bank under cover of their artillery on the commanding hills on the opposite side. The next morning General A. P. Hill was ordered to return with his division and dislodge them. Advancing under a heavy fire of artillery, the three brigades of Gregg, Pender, and Archer attacked the enemy vigorously, and drove him over the river with heavy loss.

The condition of our troops now demanded repose, and the army marched to the Opequon near Martinsburg, where it remained several days, and then moved to the vicinity of Bunker Hill and Winchester.

The enemy seemed to be concentrating in and near Harper's Ferry, but made no forward movement. During this time the Baltimore and Ohio Railroad was destroyed for several miles, and that from Winchester to Harper's Ferry broken up to within a short distance of the latter place, in order to render the occupation of the Valley by the enemy after our withdrawal more difficult.

On the 8th October General Stuart was ordered to cross the Potomac above Williamsport with twelve or fifteen hundred cavalry, and endeavor to ascertain the position and designs of the enemy. He was directed if practicable, to enter Pennsylvania, and do all in his power to impede and embarrass the military operations of the enemy. This order was executed with skill, address, and courage. General Stuart passed through Maryland, occupied Chambersburg, and destroyed a large amount of public property. Making the entire circuit of General McClellan's army, he recrossed the Potomac below Harper's Ferry without loss.

The enemy soon afterward crossed the Potomac east of the Blue Ridge, and advanced southward, seizing the passes of the mountains as he progressed.

General Jackson's corps was ordered to take position on the road between Berryville and Charlestown, to be prepared to oppose an advance from Harper's Ferry, or a movement into the Shenandoah Valley from the east side of the mountains, while at the same time he would threaten the flank of the enemy should he continue his march along the eastern base of the Blue Ridge.

One division of Longstreet's corps was sent to the vicinity of Upperville to observe the enemy's movements in front.

About the last of October the Federal Army began to incline eastwardly from the mountains, moving in the direction of Warrenton. As soon as this intention developed itself, Longstreet's corps was moved across the Blue Ridge and about the 3d November took position at Culpeper Court House, while Jackson advanced one of his divisions to the east side of the Blue Ridge.

The enemy gradually concentrated about Warrenton, his cavalry being thrown forward beyond the Rappahannock in the direction of Culpeper Court House and occasionally skirmishing with our own, which was closely observing his movements.

This situation of affairs continued without material change until about the middle of November, when the movements began which resulted in the winter campaign on the lower Rappahannock.

The accompanying return of the Medical Director will show the extent of our losses in the engagements mentioned.

The reports of the different commanding officers must of necessity be referred to for the details of these operations.

I desire to call the attention of the Department to the names of those brave officers and men who are particularly mentioned for courage and good conduct by their commanders. The limits of this report will not permit me to do more than renew the expression of my admiration for the valor that shrunk from no peril and the fortitude that endured every privation without a murmur.

I must also refer to the report of General Stuart for the particulars of the services rendered by the cavalry, besides those to which I have alluded.

Its vigilance, activity and courage were conspicuous, and to its assistance is due, in a great measure the success of some of the most important and delicate operations of the campaign.

Respectfully submitted

R. E. LEE
General

CHAPTER EIGHT

Fredericksburg

"The columns were broken and fled"

THE REHABILITATION CAMP at Martinsburg was broken on October 28, two days after McClellan was prodded by the Administration into making a move. McClellan crossed the Potomac and moved southward in the general direction of Gordonsville, where the Orange & Alexandria connected with the Virginia Central. It was the Federal commander's purpose to operate against Lee's communications with Richmond and, in anticipation of this, Lee divided his army. Longstreet was moved east of the Blue Ridge to Culpeper, and Jackson was left in the Valley — either to guard against a thrust of McClellan's over the mountain passes or to threaten McClellan's communications.

By then Lee had completed his army's organization into two corps of four divisions each, with Longstreet and Jackson promoted (November 6) to the newly created rank of lieutenant-general. In Longstreet's corps, the divisions of McLaws and Hood consisted of four brigades each, Pickett's and R. H. Anderson's five each (one of Anderson's quite small). Counting a two-brigade division under Ransom, which was soon to be detached, Longstreet fielded twenty-two brigades of about 31,-000 infantry by the end of November. With Jackson, Ewell's division, then commanded by Jubal Early, and Jackson's old division, then commanded by Taliaferro (pronounced "Tolliver"), numbered four brigades each; D. H. Hill had five brigades and A. P. Hill six. The nineteen brigades totaled about 34,000 men. At this time, the artillery was not organized into the otherwise tightly administered corps units. Batteries, without standard size, remained attached to divisions, and a reserve artillery, commanded by Brigadier General Pendleton, carried twenty-two batteries.

While the two armies were maneuvering, McClellan was removed from

command on November 7 and two days later superseded by Burnside. As
Lee expected, Burnside changed McClellan's plans. He shifted to the
favorite overland route to Richmond, with Fredericksburg as his first
objective on the way to Hanover Junction — the crossing of the Virginia
Central and Richmond, Fredericksburg & Potomac near the main highway (present Route 1) between Washington and Richmond. On November 9, with Burnside commanding the Federal army at Warrenton —
though Lee did not know of the change until the next day — Lee was
with Longstreet at Culpeper. Here began the maneuvers that led to the
Battle of Fredericksburg.

From the beginning Lee inclined toward Fredericksburg as Burnside's
immediate objective, but he was slow to make a positive commitment.
Fredericksburg was near the naval-supported supply base at Aquia Creek,
and Lee was concerned over the possibility of the Federal army being
transported to the south side of the James or even North Carolina, as
the season was growing late for fighting in Virginia. Burnside had at his
disposal an army of 150,000 troops, supported by almost 100,000 (many
second-line troops) in the environs of Washington, and this was a large
force for Lee to keep track of and to account for. With the disparity of
numbers, an offensive was out of the question, though Jackson remained
in the Valley with a semi-independent command to exploit any opportunity for a quick thrust.

Lee's letters to Jackson, to Davis and the war office reveal his delibera-
tions in studying all available information, balancing all factors, while
trying always to maneuver for his advantage. He preferred giving battle
near Hanover Junction on the North Anna, with maneuvering room,
but another consideration was preventing the enemy's entry into the as
yet undevastated country south of the Rappahannock. The rapidity with
which Burnside moved more or less decided for Lee. By night of November 17, Sumner's corps reached Falmouth, across the Rappahannock and
slightly upriver from Fredericksburg.

On the same day, Lee dispatched one division of Longstreet's to support the small observation force at Fredericksburg and another division
on the North Anna. By the 19th, Lee left Culpeper and began the concentration of all of Longstreet's corps at Fredericksburg. Burnside's full
force began to assemble across the Rappahannock, while the weather
turned "tempestuous" (as General Lee described it).

Lee did not intend to defend the city itself. Founded in the seventeenth
century, Fredericksburg was one of Virginia's loveliest and most charming small cities; though a manufacturing plant was situated there, it was
essentially residential and served as a trading center for the surrounding
plantations. Its red-brick houses were built on a hillside which sloped to

a plain along the river, across from which the palisades of Stafford Heights and Falmouth gave the enemy's artillery complete domination of the city. Lee's lines were drawn on hills south of town and, hence, the approaching battle was not *for* Fredericksburg but *at* Fredericksburg.

On November 21, General Sumner gave the citizens of Fredericksburg the alternative of surrendering the city or evacuating. The women, children and old men left their homes, with a few hastily gathered belongings, in a snowstorm on the night of the 21st to 22nd. After the city was evacuated, with the bad weather continuing, Burnside delayed making his move, and Lee, extending Jackson the extreme limits of discretion, did not give him the direct order to join Longstreet until November 27. Jackson moved into line on December 1.

Burnside's crossing of the river began before daylight on December 11. The laying of the pontoon bridges was delayed most of the day by a famous stand of the 17th and part of the 18th Mississippi, of Barksdale's brigade, acting as sharpshooters in the riverfront buildings under shelling by 181 Federal guns, which half demolished the old city. Crossing his army over the river under cover of a fog that night and the next day, Burnside opened a frontal assault on December 13. After all his fine marching and great preparations, Burnside's actual assault was a dull and stupid affair.

Jackson, in the wooded, partly swampy region on Lee's right, experienced some local trouble in throwing back the enemy, but on the left Longstreet's men fought their easiest battle. With the infantry in a sunken road, supported by gun batteries on Marye's Heights, the fire power they discharged into the repeatedly advancing masses produced one of the heaviest casualty lists of the war: out of the 12,653 total lost by Burnside, 9000 Federal soldiers fell trying to storm Marye's Heights. Of the 5039 Confederate casualties, many were wounded so slightly as to be soon ready again for duty.

As a most decisive repulse of the enemy's fall campaign, the victory accomplished nothing positive for the Confederates. Burnside withdrew across the river and Lee had no way of getting at him. The first year of Lee's command, 1862, ended with the Federal forces stalemated far away from Richmond in a war-desolated countryside, but, as Jackson had said before the battle opened, "We will whip the enemy but gain no fruits of victory."

For Lee personally the period which ended with the battle was a time of deep sorrow. On October 20 his twenty-three-year-old daughter Annie died of a sudden illness, and December brought the death of Lee's grandchild — the infant of Rooney and Charlotte Wickham Lee.

308   To GEORGE W. RANDOLPH
                              Secretary of War

                                    Headquarters, Army of Northern Virginia
                                                       November 7, 1862

Sir:
    The enemy today occupied Warrenton, and his cavalry have reached
the Rappahannock. The latter is reported to be at Rappahannock Station,
White Sulphur Springs Ford, & Hart's Ford. Two brigades of infantry
reached Orleans yesterday. The last reports from our cavalry scouts indicated an intention on the part of their cavalry to cross the Rappahannock,
though I have not heard whether it was accomplished. They are apparently advancing on the general route pursued by this army last summer, holding the gaps through the Blue Ridge as they progress. If they
advance tomorrow with the same speed, they will reach Hazel River,
about ten miles from this point. I have ordered back all surplus articles
from Culpeper Court House and shall be prepared to move towards
Madison Court House tomorrow if circumstances require it. I yesterday
directed Genl Jackson to ascend the Shenandoah Valley in order to make
a junction with Genl Longstreet. He will probably cross the Blue Ridge
at Swift Run Gap should the enemy press forward, as I shall not resist
his occupation of Thornton's Gap, where his large army would have
great advantage, as the country there is flat and open. The enemy apparently is in very strong force, especially in cavalry, in which we are
greatly outnumbered. Our cavalry diminished by the casualties of battle
and hard service, is now reduced by disease among the horses, sore
tongue and soft hoof. I will tomorrow begin to send back from Gordonsville all surplus articles that may have accumulated there, and I wish
you would instruct the staff officers accordingly. I think such articles
had better be removed towards Lynchburg. It has been snowing all day,
and I fear that our men with insufficient clothing, blankets and shoes,
will suffer much, and our ranks be proportionably diminished. The
enemy's strength will however decrease the farther he removes from his
base, and I hope an opportunity will offer for us to strike a successful
blow. I beg that you will urge forward the defences and preparations at
Richmond, and collect all the force you can.

            I have the honor to be very respectfully, your obt servt

                                                       R. E. LEE
                                                       Genl

309   To GENERAL J. E. B. STUART
                        Commanding Cavalry

                    Headquarters, Department of Northern Virginia
                        Camp near Culpeper Court House
                                November 7, 1862
                                        9 A.M.

Your note of yesterday evening has been received. I am much
pleased at the adroitness with which Col Rosser extricated himself from
Warrenton & hope that none of his men were seriously injured. I very
much regret to learn of the injury to your horses by scratches & sore
tongue. The former I think by proper attention on the part of your men
can be easily remedied, & the latter is probably occasioned or aggravated
by feeding on the ground. I need not recommend to you to urge upon
your officers & men strict attention to this matter. As soon as you can
get exact information of the strength & movements of the enemy, let me
know. As far as I can now see, he seems either to be operating by his
right flank entirely, or is moving his whole army along the Blue Ridge.
In neither case does it seem to me prudent to interpose his army between Jackson's and Longstreet's corps, which would be the case, if the
movement you suggested was made. If Longstreet's corps be strong
enough to contend with this force about Warrenton then it might answer
for him to move upon them by Warrenton Junction. But if weaker, it
might be crushed, if separated from Jackson by the Blue Ridge. Should we
be pressed back from here my design is to retire through Madison, while
Jackson ascends the Valley, so that a junction can be made through
Swift Run Gap, & we hold ourselves on the enemy's right flank if he
attempts to proceed southward. As soon as I can learn something more
of Jackson's movements and position, I will ride forward to see you,
somewhere about Aestham River. I will send forward to let you know
where. It will be a great thing if you can establish communication with
Jackson with your signal corps, & thus with Longstreet. I have had no
notice from Jackson of a want of ammunition, & presume he is supplying
himself from Staunton. I will however attend to the matter. Try & husband your horses & men while watching the enemy as closely as you can.

                                            Very respecty

                                                R. E. LEE
                                                Genl

310   To GENERAL THOMAS J. JACKSON
                    Commanding Left Wing

Headquarters, Army of Northern Virginia
November 9, 1862
1 P.M.

General:

Your letter of the 7th is at hand. The enemy seems to be massing his troops along the Manassas Railroad in the vicinity of Piedmont, which gives him great facilities of bringing up supplies from Alexandria. It has occurred to me that his object may be to seize upon Strasburg with his main force to intercept your ascent of the Valley. This would oblige you to cross into the Lost River Valley, or west of it, unless you could force a passage through the Blue Ridge. Hence my anxiety for your safety. If you can prevent such a movement of the enemy, & operate strongly upon his flank & rear through the gaps of the Blue Ridge, you would certainly in my opinion, effect the object you propose. A demonstration of crossing into Maryland would serve the same purpose & might call him back to the Potomac. As my object is to retard & baffle his designs, if it can be accomplished by maneuvering your corps as you propose, it will serve my purpose as well as if effected in any other way. With this understanding you can use your discretion, which I know I can rely upon, in remaining or advancing up the Valley. But I desire you will take precautions to prevent the enemy occupying the roads west of the Massanutten Mountains, & your demonstration upon his flank might probably be as well made from a position nearer to Strasburg as from that you now occupy. If the enemy should move into the Valley through Thornton's Gap, you must seize the pass through the Massanutten Mountains as soon as you can, while Longstreet will advance through Milman's, which you term Fisher's Gap (on the direct road from Madison Court House to New Market). But I think his movement upon Front Royal the more probable of the two.

Keep me advised of your movements & intentions. And you must keep always in view the probability of an attack upon Richmond from either north or south, when a concentration of forces will become necessary.

The enemy has made no advance south of the Rappahannock line since I last wrote you.

Colonel [James L.] Corley has just returned from Staunton & says that he has sent you shoes & blankets, which I hope you will soon receive & find sufficient for the necessities of your command. They may have been stopped at New Market with the expectation of your advancing up the Valley; if so, send & get them & use every exertion to ensure the health & comfort of your men. I am much gratified at the conduct of Maj [Elijah V.] White & I desire you to express to Genl A. P. Hill my appreciation of his conduct.

The non-occupation of Martinsburg by the enemy & his not marching into the Valley from his former base on the Potomac, shows I think that his whole force has been drawn from Maryland into Virginia east of the Blue Ridge. His retirement from Snicker's & Ashby's Gaps, & concentration of his force on the railroad in the vicinity of Manassas Gap must either be for the purpose of supplying it, or for making a descent upon Front Royal & Strasburg. I hope therefore you will be on your guard.

I am, &c.

R. E. Lee
Genl

311   To GENERAL J. E. B. STUART
Commanding Cavalry

Headquarters, Army of Northern Virginia
November 9, 1862
10 P.M.

General:

I find from dispatches from Genl Jackson that the enemy has abandoned Snicker's and Ashby's Gaps & concentrated his main force along the Manassas Gap Railroad, in the vicinity of Piedmont, Genl McClellan's headquarters being at Rectortown. This may be for obtaining supplies by the railroad, or it may be with the view of making a descent upon Front Royal or Strasburg, to intercept Genl Jackson in his egress from the Valley. Can you ascertain what he is doing in your front? If he is stationary or what he is about? If he moves into the Valley, I will advance Longstreet's corps to cut off his communication with the railroad. You will see the necessity therefore of watching him closely. You will be pleased to learn that upon the abandonment of Snicker's Gap, Genl A. P. Hill pushed his pickets to Snickersville, & that Maj White with his battalion of cavalry took 104 prisoners & captured some wagons & ambulances.

I am, &c.

R. E. Lee
Genl

312　　　　　To GEORGE W. RANDOLPH
　　　　　　　　　　Secretary of War

　　　　　　　　　　　　　Headquarters, Army of Northern Virginia
　　　　　　　　　　　　　　　　　　　　November 10, 1862
Sir:

　　From my last report it appears that Genl McClellan has massed his army on the Manassas Gap Railroad in the vicinity of Piedmont. He withdrew his force from Snicker's Gap and moved it towards Middleburg. The force at Paris and Upperville was likewise withdrawn to the Manassas Railroad.

　　His cavalry is advanced to the line of the Rappahannock. Genl A. P. Hill finding Snicker's Gap open, advanced his pickets to Snickersville where they were by last reports, and on that occasion Maj White with his battalion of cavalry, captured one hundred & four prisoners and some ambulances and wagons loaded with stores. Genl D. H. Hill's division is in the forks of the Shenandoah guarding the passes in that direction.

　　As long as Genl Jackson can operate with safety, and secure his retirement west of the Massanutten Mountains, I think it advantageous that he should be in position to threaten the enemy's flank and rear, and thus prevent his advance southward on the east side of the Blue Ridge. Genl Jackson has been directed accordingly, and should the enemy descend into the Valley, Genl Longstreet will attack his rear and cut off his communications. The enemy apparently is so strong in numbers that I think it preferable to attempt to baffle his designs by maneuvering, rather than to resist his advance by main force. To accomplish the latter without too great risk and loss, would require more than double our present numbers.

　　I beg if possible that shoes and blankets be sent to me at Gordonsville. Those sent to Staunton will not be more than are required by Genl Jackson.

　　　　　　I have the honor to be with great respect, your obt servt

　　　　　　　　　　　　　　　　　　　　　　　　R. E. LEE
　　　　　　　　　　　　　　　　　　　　　　　　Genl

313   To G. W. C. LEE
              Richmond, Virginia

                                    Camp, Culpeper Court House
                                       November 10, 1862
My Dear Custis:
    I have received a letter from Mr. William F. Taylor, cashier Bank
of Virginia, saying he had sold the Hudson River Railroad coupons
@ 150 per cent premium — City of Pittsburg Railroad coupons @ 100
per cent premium — City of St. Louis Railroad coupons @ 40 per cent
premium, & if he had the others now due he could sell them at the same
rate. I have written to him that you would hand them to him. If convenient please do so & tell him he can sell them now or when practicable
to advantage.
    F[itzhugh] reached here yesterday from the Valley & joined his
brigade now in my front. I have nothing new to relate beyond my
public despatches. I am operating to baffle the advance of the enemy &
retain him among the mountains until I can get him separated that I
can strike at him to advantage. His force will be thus diminished & dis-
heartened. His sick & stragglers must be going back. He is along the
Manassas Railroad near Piedmont. His advance cavalry along the line of
the Rappahannock.
    Give much love to your dear mother, Agnes & Charlotte, not for-
getting my granddaughter. I wish you were with me.

                                    Truly & affly your father

                                         R. E. LEE

314   To GENERAL THOMAS J. JACKSON
           Commanding Left Wing

                          Headquarters, Department of Northern Virginia
                                          November 12, 1862
                                               8 A.M.
General:
    Your letter of the 10th by special courier has been received. In my
letter of yesterday in reply to yours of first date, I discussed the question of your further delay in the Valley. I cannot add more to what has
been said & it must depend upon the advantages you can effect by
operating against the communications of the enemy. He has given as

yet no indications of his further movement or direction southward. Whether he will cross the Rappahannock or proceed to Fredericksburg I cannot tell. It is easier for you to determine what damage you can inflict upon him where you are. If you can accomplish nothing but to retain occupation of the Valley, in the apparent & probable need of all our forces southward, the force under you is too far from the scene of action. If an advance towards Fredericksburg is discovered it is plain that you cannot delay longer and you must be prepared to move at any time. Make your arrangements accordingly, & be prepared to move at any moment. Genl Stuart has been directed to watch the enemy closely, but you know the difficulty of determining the first movements. You may learn more from the rear than we can in front. It would be grievous for the Valley & its supplies to fall into the hands of the enemy unnecessarily, but we can only act upon probabilities and endeavor to avoid greater evils. Col [Henry B.] Davidson at Staunton telegraphs that the enemy is within 35 miles of that place. One column at McDowell & one at Rawley Springs. The two columns estimated at from four to six thousand men. He asks for reinforcements. I have none to send him. Have you a disposable force? The Marylanders if unable to remain at Winchester might be stationed there.

I am, &c.

R. E. LEE
General

315   To GENERAL THOMAS J. JACKSON
Commanding Left Wing

Headquarters, Army of Northern Virginia
November 14, 1862

General:
Your letter of the 13th is received. I regret that the shoes and blankets forwarded by Colonel Corley fell short of your wants. More will be forwarded as soon as they can be obtained. The next supply must be distributed to Longstreet's corps.

I have advised you of the information received from the scouts north of the Rappahannock. I can learn of no movement on any of the roads from Warrenton or Brentsville toward Fredericksburg. A scout is now on the road from Fredericksburg to Occoquan. [General Daniel] Sickles' corps is reported to be on the Orange and Alexandria Railroad, advanced toward the Rappahannock as far as Bealeton, his own headquarters at Dr. Shumate's. I think [General Fitz John] Porter's corps is in Virginia, inasmuch as the Washington papers state [General Joseph] Hooker's departure for Virginia to relieve Porter, who is to be court martialed on charges by General Pope. Your demonstrations through the gaps of the mountains have probably embarrassed and retarded the enemy's movements, and if you were in condition to push them vigorously I have no doubt you would arrest his advance. We will however endeavor to confuse and confound him as much as our circumstances will permit. As one mode of embarrassing him, I should have commenced breaking up the Orange and Alexandria Railroad from the Rappahannock to Gordonsville as well as that from Fredericksburg to Hanover Junction but for my reluctance to perpetuate what might prove an unnecessary injury to the community. If I could ascertain that he would pursue either of these routes, I should commence at once. I have ordered the destruction of the road from Fredericksburg to Aquia Creek. No depots of forage have been placed on the road between Front Royal and Culpeper Court House, nor can they be until the enemy is farther removed from the route as they would be as likely to benefit him as us.

I am with great respect, your obedient servant

R. E. LEE
General

316   To GENERAL THOMAS J. JACKSON
Commanding Left Wing

Headquarters, Army of Northern Virginia
November 14, 1862

General:

Your letter of the 10th instant, by courier, and telegraphic dispatch of today have been received. The withdrawal of the enemy from the Blue Ridge, and concentration at Warrenton and Waterloo, show I think, that he has abandoned his former base, and assumed that of the Alexandria and Warrenton Railroad.

Your presence then in the Valley seems to be too distant from his line of operations to affect his movements should you remain quiescent. If you were able by a movement through Snicker's Gap to threaten his communication north of Manassas Junction, it would have the effect of recalling him. This, in your condition would be a hazardous movement, as he could bring a force against you too strong for you to resist, and might intercept your return into the Valley. I do not see then what good your continuance in the Valley will effect beyond the support of your troops.

It is true it may prevent the occupation of Winchester by a portion of the enemy's forces, but in a military point of view, that would accomplish but little beyond the annoyance of the inhabitants, which is much to be lamented. Your detention there until the occurrence of bad weather and deep roads, might so break down your command as to render it inefficient for further operations, should they become requisite elsewhere. Your remaining in the Valley was based upon the supposition that by operating upon the flank and rear of the enemy, you might prevent his progress southward, and so long as you found that this could be effected, I considered it advantageous. But when this cannot be accomplished, the sooner you make a junction with Longstreet's corps the better. The question now is, whether you can, in the present condition of things, affect the movements of the enemy. He is in a position to move upon Culpeper, using the Orange and Alexandria Railroad as a line of communication, or to march upon Fredericksburg, and establish his base on the Potomac. As you are the best judge of your ability to operate advantageously against him, I leave you to determine the question whether you will continue in your present position or march at once to join Longstreet. I have heard of no movement of the enemy as yet below Kelly's Ford, except a visit of a small party of his cavalry to Fredericksburg on the 8th, when they charged through the town, but were immediately driven back across the river by our cavalry. Genl Stuart reports this evening that two brigades of the enemy's infantry are at Jeffersonton. Our cavalry still hold the line of Aestham River to Sperryville. The position of Longstreet's corps remains unchanged since you were last informed.

I am with great respect, your obt servt

R. E. LEE
Genl

317   To GENERAL W. H. F. LEE
                 Commanding Cavalry

Headquarters, Department of Northern Virginia
Culpeper Court House
November 15, 1862
7 P.M.

General:
    I request you to order the Sixty-first Virginia Volunteers, Colonel [Virginius D.] Groner commanding, and the Norfolk Light Artillery

Blues, Captain [Charles R.] Grandy commanding, to proceed at once to Fredericksburg. They will take the route by Stevensburg crossing the Rapidan at Raccoon Ford till they intersect the Plank road from Orange Court House to Fredericksburg. Should they learn that Fredericksburg is unoccupied by the enemy they will pursue the Plank road to that city; but should they learn of its occupation they will fall back through Spotsylvania Court House, and take position on the Fredericksburg and Richmond Railroad, where it crosses the North Anna. After crossing the Rapidan Colonel Groner must send forward his staff officers to ascertain the best roads, prepare forage for his command, &c., at points where it will be needed. He will be careful on the march to permit no straggling, depredation upon the citizens, country, &c., and be careful to pay for all articles consumed by his command, or to give proper receipts for the same.

I have the honor to be with great respect, &c.

R. E. Lee
General

318   To GEORGE W. RANDOLPH
                     Secretary of War

Headquarters, Department of Northern Virginia
Camp near Culpeper Court House
November 17, 1862

Sir:

From the general reports received from the scouts yesterday, it is plain that the enemy is abandoning his position around Warrenton, and does not intend to advance in the direction first assumed. His troops and trains, as far as can be discovered, are moving towards the Orange & Alexandria Railroad; but whether with a view of massing them on that line of communication, to threaten Gordonsville, or to fall down upon Fredericksburg, or to retire towards Alexandria, to be transferred by water south of the James River, I cannot yet discover. The railroad trains are kept in active operation, but it is not known whether they are employed in carrying troops towards Alexandria, or in bringing them in this direction. Knowing the difficulties of his pursuing his former route along the Blue Ridge, I have supposed from the halt that has taken place, that he intended to march upon Fredericksburg, but have learned of no preparations to rebuild the wharves, &c., at Aquia, or to subsist his army, which would naturally precede such a movement. I think it therefore probable that the movement in execution is with a view of transferring the army south of James River. And the appointment of Genl Burnside to the command favors this supposition. I will give you further information as soon as anything reliable can be ascertained. But in the mean time, I beg that every preparation that can possibly be made, with a view of opposing his progress in North Carolina, may be urged forward.

In the condition in which both corps of this army now are, I do not think it advisable to advance upon the enemy, as it might injure their efficiency in future operations, which I think are threatening us. Partial operations however have been & are being made, tending to embarrass and damage the enemy.

I learn that Col [John D.] Imboden was unable to destroy the bridging at Cheat River in consequence of the strength of the enemy in that quarter, & is in position on the Shenandoah Mountains. He captured one company of the enemy, paroled the men & brought off their arms & equipments. Col [Henry B.] Davidson reports that the force which has been threatening Staunton has retired beyond the Alleghanies.

I am most respy, yr obt svt

R. E. LEE
Genl

319   To JEFFERSON DAVIS
Richmond, Virginia

Camp near Culpeper
November 17, 1862

Mr. President:
There is a general movement of the enemy from Warrenton, & he is falling down to the O[range] & A[lexandria] R[ailroad]. I am not certain as to his destination. There are indications of his retiring towards Alexandria, but I have apprehended that he would transfer himself to Fredericksburg & establish his base on the Potomac & Rappahannock, but there is nothing to show his purpose in that direction beyond the guards established on the roads leading to Fredericksburg, which would naturally be done, to cut off information of his movements towards Alexandria. I have heard of no preparation to rebuild the wharves, &c., &c., at Aquia Creek. Col [William B.] Ball is engaged in breaking up the railroad to that point. I should think some provision would be made for subsisting a large army if a movement upon Fredericksburg was designed. The enemy's trains from Warrenton move in the direction of the

O[range] and A[lexandria] R[ailroad]. The cars on said road are in active operation, I cannot tell whether they are carrying back or bringing forward troops.

I am with great respect, yr obdt servt

R. E. LEE
Genl

320   To GENERAL SAMUEL COOPER
Adjutant and Inspector General

Headquarters, Army of Northern Virginia
November 18, 1862
7.30 P.M.

General:

The force of the enemy reported yesterday to be moving towards Fredericksburg is stated by one of my scouts to be [General Edwin J.] Sumner's corps. His cavalry with one battery of horse artillery reached Falmouth about 3 p.m., but was baffled in his attempt to cross the river by the force under Col Ball, 15th Virginia Cavalry, 4 companies of Mississippi infantry & Lewis' battery of field artillery.

The 61st Virginia & the Norfolk Light Artillery Blues arrived at Fredericksburg this morning, and I have not heard of the occupation of the town by the enemy. I hope his advance has been successfully resisted.

McLaws' & Ransom's divisions of Longstreet's corps and Genl W. H. F. Lee's cavalry brigade marched this morning for Fredericksburg. Also Lane's "long range" battery.

Should the enemy's force only consist of Sumner's corps, I think it will be held in check until his object is developed.

General Jackson reports that the enemy's force at Harper's Ferry is being increased largely, and our scouts in Loudoun state that a large Federal force has returned to Middleburg, said to be [General Franz] Sigel's corps, fearing that Jackson was advancing on their rear.

Lt Col [Richard H.] Dulany, 7th Virginia Cavalry, while scouting in Loudoun on the 16th instant, captured 22 of the enemy. The passes in the Catoctin Mountains are guarded.

I have at this point of my letter received a dispatch from Genl J. E. B. Stuart (dated 3 p.m. today), whom I directed to cross the Rappahannock this morning to ascertain the position of the enemy. He forced a passage at Warrenton Springs in the face of a regiment of cav-

alry & three pieces of artillery. When driven, they retired toward Bealeton. One of our scouts, who joined him north of the Rappahannock, informed him that the enemy on Sunday moved from Bealeton back to
Warrenton Junction. Thence their main body marched towards Fredericksburg. At the date of his note he had ascertained nothing further.

I have the honor to be with great respect, your obt servt

R. E. LEE
Genl

321   To GENERAL THOMAS J. JACKSON
        Commanding Left Wing, near Winchester

Headquarters, Department of Northern Virginia
Camp near Culpeper Court House
November 19, 1862
9 A.M.

General:
Your letter of the 18th has been received. It is certainly important
to deceive the enemy as long as possible as to our position & intention,
provided it is rendered certain that a junction can be made before a battle; and this latter point we must always keep in view as necessary to
enable us to resist the large force now on the Rappahannock. As to the
place where it may be necessary or best to fight, I cannot now state, as
this must be determined by circumstances which may arise. I now do
not anticipate making a determined stand north of the North Anna.
Longstreet's corps is moving to Fredericksburg, opposite to which place
Sumner's corps has arrived. As before stated you can remain in the Valley as long as you see that your presence there cripples & embarrasses
the general movement of the enemy, and yet leaves you free to unite
with Longstreet for a battle. I will advise you from time to time of the
movements of the enemy and of mine, as far as they can be discovered,
& with as little delay as possible, but you must make allowances for the
inaccuracy of the first & the delay of the second, & predicate your movements so as to be on the safe side. Col Corley has placed 1,000 bushels
(I think he stated) of corn at Madison Court House, but at any rate
enough in his opinion to fill up your wagons after reaching that point,
until you can get further supplies. [Colonel William] Phillips' Legion
was left by Stuart with Genl D. H. Hill. I wish you would direct it to
join Hampton's brigade.
Genl Stuart wrote from Warrenton at 6½ p.m. yesterday that Hooker's, Sumner's, [General John F.] Reynolds', and Burnside's (old) corps

had passed through Warrenton in the direction of the Orange & Alexandria Railroad. The last of the infantry & artillery passed through yesterday at 2 p.m., the last of the cavalry at 3 p.m. Part of Sigel's corps had been there under [General Julius] Stahel. Sumner's corps marched on Sunday from Catlett's Station towards Fredericksburg. He considers the information he received as conclusive that Burnside's whole army had marched for Fredericksburg. Genl [Henry W.] Halleck had been to Warrenton on a visit. I shall wait to hear again from Stuart today & will then start for Fredericksburg if circumstances warrant.

I am most respecty

R. E. LEE
Genl

322   To JEFFERSON DAVIS
Richmond, Virginia
TELEGRAM

Fredericksburg
November 20, 1862

I THINK BURNSIDE IS CONCENTRATING HIS WHOLE ARMY OPPOSITE FREDERICKSBURG.

R. E. LEE

323   To GENERAL SAMUEL COOPER
Adjutant and Inspector General

Headquarters, Army of Northern Virginia
Camp, Fredericksburg
November 22, 1862
8 P.M.

General:

I have the honor to report for the information of the President and Department that General Burnside's army, apparently in full force, is on the other side of the Rappahannock, opposite this place, stretching from the banks of the river towards Aquia Creek. I have learned from our scouts sent towards the Potomac, but who were unable to reach Aquia, that it is reported by citizens that the enemy were making preparations to reconstruct the wharves at that place by means of their pontoon trains. I have not heard of a commencement being made to rebuild the railroad. Their immense wagon train is actively engaged apparently in provisioning their army, which during the last three days of rain and cold, I know has been a difficult operation, and must have been attended with suffering among their troops.

I have with me two brigades of Stuart's cavalry, Pendleton's reserve artillery, and four divisions of Longstreet's corps. The fifth will be here tomorrow. If the enemy attempt to cross the river I shall resist it, though the ground is favorable for him. Yesterday he summoned the corporate authorities of Fredericksburg to surrender the city by 5 p.m. and threatened in the event of its not being delivered up, to commence to shell the town at 9 a.m. today. Upon the reference of this communication to me, as I was unable to prevent the city from being cannonaded, I requested General Longstreet to inform the authorities that they might say that I would not occupy or use the city for military purposes, but that I would resist its occupation by the enemy, and recommended that the women and children be at once removed. Our wagons and ambulances have been employed all last night and today in accomplishing this object. This morning the authorities were informed that the bombardment would not commence at the hour threatened, but that a definite answer would be returned in a short time. I have not learned whether it has yet been received.

General Stuart reports as the result of his reconnaissance north of the Rappahannock, that Fauquier and Loudoun counties have been abandoned by the enemy, except the force retained at Harper's Ferry, under Generals [Henry W.] Slocum and [John W.] Geary; that the bridges on the Orange and Alexandria Railroad, from the Rappahannock to Bull Run inclusive, have been destroyed, and the stores at Warrenton Junction and Manassas burned. Two divisions of Sigel's corps, those of Stahel and Carl Schurz passed through Centreville to Washington. The rest of his corps is with Burnside.

I have the honor to be with great respect, your obt servt

R. E. LEE
Genl

324   To HIS WIFE
                          Richmond, Virginia

Camp, Fredericksburg
November 22, 1862

I have received dearest Mary your letter of the 18th with the letters of Marshall & Markie enclosed. I was much gratified at their perusal &

particularly glad to hear of my poor sister's improved condition. I do not know when I shall be able to thank him for his sympathy. I return Markie's as you desire & place with it a letter from Mrs. Elliott, sister of Mrs. Stiles. I have also received the package of drawers you sent me. I have not yet been able to open it, but I have no doubt the garments are excellent & fit perfect. The morning I left Culpeper Rob walked into my camp, so I put him on one of my horses & brought him along in the evening. He had a rainy ride but we reached here next morning. Fortunately his upper garments were good & he had picked up on the last battle field a soldiers overcoat (yankee) which kept him tolerably dry. But he had nothing but what he stood in, & never has when I see him. I must try & get him something. He did not have a blanket, so I had to share mine with him. I wish Miss Norvell [Caskie] would marry him & take care of him. I have given him a horse, saddle & bridle to begin with. I have not received Mr. Kipler's letter but no doubt will in time & will attend to it. I do not now know what I can do. We have had wretched weather since I have been here & I fear our men have suffered much. It has been very cold & still is. But it has been dry today. I have been out ever since my arrival surveying the enemy & preparing for them. I hope we shall give a good account of them if they cross. They seem to be hesitating, but are very numerous. They demanded the surrender of Fredericksburg yesterday & said if it was not yielded by 5 p.m. they would shell the town at 9 a.m. today. They however did not commence. I was moving out the women & children all last night & today. It was a pitious sight. But they have brave hearts. What is to become of them God only knows. I pray he may have mercy on them. Fitzhugh is well, tell Chass. He dined with me yesterday. Rob will join him now. Give much love to her & the baby. Also to Agnes. Remember me to all friends.

Very truly & affly

R. E. LEE

325 To GENERAL THOMAS J. JACKSON
Commanding Left Wing

Headquarters, Army of Northern Virginia
Camp, Fredericksburg
November 23, 1862

General:
Should my former dispatches have been received, you will have been informed of the position of the enemy and of that portion of the

army with me. I will however repeat that Genl Burnside's whole army is apparently opposite Fredericksburg, stretching from the Rappahannock to the Potomac. Since my last dispatch Genl Stuart has reported that Warrenton Junction and Manassas have been abandoned, and the stores collected there burned. The bridges on the Orange and Alexandria Railroad from the Rappahannock to Bull Run inclusive have been destroyed, and the indications are that hostile operations in that country have ceased for the winter. Genl Stuart also reports that two divisions of Sigel's corps, those of Stahel and Carl Schurz have passed through Centreville on the way to Washington; and that but three brigades under Genls Slocum and Geary were left at Harper's Ferry, and one brigade in Maryland. Under this view of things, if correct, I do not see at this distance, what military effect can be produced by the continuance of your corps in the Valley. If it was east of the Blue Ridge, either in Loudoun, Fauquier, or Culpeper, its influence would be felt by the enemy, whose rear would be threatened, though they might feel safe with regard to their communications. Another advantage would be, provided you were at Culpeper, that you would be in railroad communication with several points, so that the transfer of your troops would be rendered certain without regard to the state of the weather or the condition of the roads. If therefore you see no way of making an impression on the enemy from where you are, and concur with me in the views I have expressed, I wish you would move east of the Blue Ridge and take such a position as you may find best. There is forage and subsistence in Rappahannock, Culpeper, Madison, and Greene, and I believe in upper Fauquier and Loudoun, all of which ought to be collected and secured. I am as yet unable to discover what may be the plan of the enemy. He is certainly making no forward movement, though he may be preparing to do so. I am apprehensive that while keeping a force in our front, he may be transferring his troops to some other quarter, and the march of a portion of Sigel's corps to Alexandria would favor this view of the subject. Should this be the case, the position of your corps at Culpeper would be advantageous. Genl Longstreet's corps is now here with two brigades of cavalry and the reserve artillery. One brigade of cavalry, Genl Hampton's, occupies the forks of the Rappahannock, headquarters at Stevensburg.

I am with great respect, your obt servt

R. E. Lee
Genl

326   To JEFFERSON DAVIS
Richmond, Virginia

Headquarters, Army of Northern Virginia
November 25, 1862

Mr. President:
I have endeavoured in my official communications to the Adjutant and Inspector General of the Army to keep you apprised of the military condition of affairs on this frontier. For the first two days after my arrival the enemy's forces were being massed on the heights of Stafford opposite to Fredericksburg. But on the evening of the 22nd, which was the 2nd day after my arrival, his camps and trains commenced to move to the rear, and on the morning of the 23rd his parks of artillery had all disappeared save four batteries posted on the plateau just opposite the town. Now their force in view is very small. It was generally supposed that this retrograde movement indicated another transfer of operations, but I believe it was made to secure their camps from our fire, and for the convenience of obtaining subsistence. I think from the tone of the Northern papers it is intended that Genl Burnside shall advance from Fredericksburg to Richmond, and that he is obliged to wait until he can reconstruct proper landings on the Potomac and rebuild the railroad to the Rappahannock. All their movements that I have been able to discover look to a concentration at this point, and it appears to me that should Genl Burnside change his base of operations the effect produced in the United States would be almost equivalent to a defeat. I think therefore he will persevere in his present course, and the longer we can delay him and throw him into the winter, the more difficult will be his undertaking. It is for this reason that I have determined to resist him at the outset, and to throw every obstacle in the way of his advance. I propose to commence breaking up the railroad as one of the means of retarding him, so as to oblige him to move with a large wagon train. I fear this measure will produce opposition on the part of the citizens, and may be viewed by this community as an abandonment of their country. I therefore do not wish to undertake it without due consideration, and should you think it preferable to concentrate the troops nearer to Richmond, I should be glad if you would advise me. I have waited to draw Jackson's corps to me to the last moment, as I have seen that his presence on their flank has embarrassed their plans, and defeated their first purpose of advancing upon Gordonsville and Charlottesville. I think they will now endeavour to get possession of Hanover Junction. I need not express to you the importance of urging forward all preparations about Richmond,

and of uniting all our efforts to resist the great attempt now being made to reach our capital, which if defeated, may prove the last. I should like to get some long range guns from Richmond if any can be obtained, on traveling carriages, and will write to Col Gorgas on the subject. I need not say how glad I should be if your convenience would permit you to visit the army, that I might have the benefit of your views and directions.

I have the honour to be with great respect, your obt servt

R. E. LEE
Genl

327   To GENERAL THOMAS J. JACKSON
Commanding Left Wing

Headquarters, Department of Northern Virginia
Near Fredericksburg, Virginia
November 25, 1862

General:

From your letter of the 21st which with its enclosures I received last night, I infer that your command is in motion up the Valley. I wrote to you on the 23d instant suggesting that you should cross the Blue Ridge, & stated my reasons for believing that by taking position at Culpeper, &c., it would be advantageous. I do not now see any reason for hastening your march if it has been commenced, but I wish you would advise me of your line of approach from point to point, that I may notify you should any necessity exist. I will send this to Madison in hopes that it will meet you there, as I infer that you will cross the mountains at Millan's Gap. Should you think it advisable to halt at Culpeper or to make any demonstration on the enemy's rear, I request you to do so. In the mean time should any movement of the enemy make it desirable that you should join me at once, I will advise you. Genl Burnside has thrown back from view the force he so ostentatiously displayed on his first arrival, but I believe his object has been to secure his camps & facilitate his attainment of supplies. Only a small force is now visible from this side, & I anticipate no forward movement until the wharves on the Potomac are constructed, & the railroad to the Rappahannock repaired. As far as I can judge his plan is to advance on Richmond from this base; & to delay him as long as practicable & throw him into the winter, I have determined to resist him from the beginning. Your corps may therefore be needed here, & if from the circumstances which surround you, you see that no good can be obtained by a flank movement on Culpeper or Warrenton, you can march directly to this point.

I am most respy, &c.

R. E. LEE
Genl

328   To GENERAL THOMAS J. JACKSON
          Commanding Left Wing

Headquarters, Army of Northern Virginia
November 27, 1862

General:

Your letter of the 26th instant from Madison Court House has been received. I presume your letter of the 23rd to which you refer, was the one written from near Strasburg, to which I replied on the 25th instant. In a letter to you of the 26th instant I suggested the probability that it was too late to make the movement projected to threaten the enemy's rear, as another storm, which may be anticipated at any time at this season, would render the roads impassable and subject your troops to labor and suffering, to which I am unwilling to expose them upon a doubtful issue. Should therefore in your judgment, nothing be probably gained by such a demonstration, I desire you to continue your route, without fatigue to your men, to this place, taking position on the Massaponax in easy distance from the railroad, by which your subsistence will have to be drawn.

The orders for the general courts martial in your brigade, I am informed by the Adjutant General have been issued and forwarded to you. I concur with you entirely in the advantages of speedy trials and prompt punishment. The proceedings of the general courts martial in your corps about Winchester were acted upon before my departure for Richmond, and placed in the hands of the printer for publication. Genl George H. Steuart was desired to expedite their completion, and to send half of the copies to you and half to my headquarters. The whole however were sent to me at Culpeper Court House whence one hundred & fifty copies were sent back to you. I hope they have reached you before this.

Reports from the scouts received today show that the enemy's forces are concentrated on the railroad between Aquia and Fredericksburg. They are encamped on the Telegraph road, and extend from

Chopawamsic Creek to Stafford Court House. The wharf at Aquia is finished, and the cars and locomotive on the track. Four war steamers, seven gunboats, and six steamers were seen in the river, also fifteen sail vessels and tug boats towing barges loaded with stores. There were no signs of embarkation. They were opening a road from Evansport to Brooke's Water Station on the railroad. A small force was at Dumfries and Occoquan constructing telegraph line to Alexandria. There is said to be a small cavalry force at Brentsville. All accounts agree that general dissatisfaction prevails in the army.

I am with great respect, your obt sevt

R. E. Lee
Genl

P.S. — Your letter of the 20th from Winchester is only just received.

329   To JEFFERSON DAVIS
               Richmond, Virginia

Headquarters, Army of Northern Virginia
November 27, 1862

Mr. President:

The reports of the scouts received today state that the whole force of the enemy is concentrated between Fredericksburg and Aquia Creek. Their camps extend along the Telegraph road from Chopawamsic Creek to south of Stafford Court House. A small force is stationed at Dumfries, Occoquan, and Brentsville. The wharf at Aquia Creek is finished, and a locomotive and cars were seen on the track. They are opening a broad road from Evansport to Brooke's Water Station on the railroad, and reconstructing the telegraph line to Alexandria. No transports were seen on the river, but four war steamers and seven gunboats were lying off the creek. There were also six steamers, fifteen sail vessels, and some tugs towing barges loaded with stores. Everything seems to indicate a purpose of occupying their present position. No preparation has yet been discovered of an attempt to cross the river, but I have learned of a large pontoon train having reached Genl Burnside's headquarters on the Stafford road. Their object may be to make a winter campaign, under the belief that our troops will not be sufficiently guarded against the cold for operations in the field.

Our army at present is in good health, and I think capable of making a strong resistance. Genl Jackson's corps is halted at Orange Court House, and but for the uncertainty of the weather, I should advance it in Culpeper [County] as far as the Rappahannock. The last two storms have produced a great effect upon the roads in this country, and I feel unwilling to expose the men to the labor and suffering they might have to undergo should it become necessary to unite the army. We are procuring abundance of forage in the Rappahannock Valley for our animals, but no flour or meat. Genl Jackson's corps is supplying itself with flour from the mills in the neighborhood, and is also able to procure plenty of forage. From my present position I am unable to ascertain the purpose of the enemy in North Carolina. I am aware of the frequent demonstrations he is making upon several points, but cannot help thinking that it is with a view of distracting us, for it is plain that his whole fighting force is now posted between the Rappahannock and Potomac.

I have the honor to be with great respect, your obt servt

R. E. Lee
Genl

P.S. — Since writing the above three gunboats are reported to have arrived at Port Royal last evening, November 28th.

330   To GENERAL THOMAS J. JACKSON
Commanding Left Wing

Headquarters, Army of Northern Virginia
November 28, 1862

General:

Your dispatches of the 26th and 27th have been received. My letter of the 27th will have advised you of the position which I think it best for you to assume, namely on Massaponax Creek at a convenient distance from the railroad. I recommend that you send forward a staff officer to select an encampment convenient to wood and water, and to collect forage for your animals upon their arrival. I have nothing new to state as regards the enemy, except the appearance at Port Royal about sunset of five of their gunboats. One of them descended the river this morning, and the rest I believe are still there. I am of the opinion that the enemy will not attempt to cross the Rappahannock in front of Fredericksburg, but at some point below, if he crosses at all. I have examined the river some ten or twelve miles down, and find the banks generally abrupt and requiring work to make a practicable ingress and egress for their pontoon bridges. I understand that at Port Royal the access to the river is easier, and as their large class gunboats can reach that point, I think it possible that he may select a bend in the river which can be flanked by his gunboats, so as to give him an undisturbed passage. The road from Port Royal to Bowling Green I am told is good, and will give him an easy access to the railroad. Should I discern any indications that my supposition is correct, I think it may be well to place your corps within reach of the road from Bowling Green to Port Royal.

I am very respectfully, your obt servt

R. E. LEE
Genl

331   To G. W. C. LEE
            Richmond, Virginia

Camp near Fredericksburg
November 28, 1862

My Dear son:

I have received your note of the 25th & am much obliged to you for attending to the business at the bank. The dividend coupons due in January you can give to Mr. Taylor if he can dispose of them to advantage. I hope you will be able to arrange for the people whom I wish to liberate the 31 December. See if Mr. Eacho can not propose & prepare the papers. The expenses can be paid from the hire. Give him the names of all those hired in Richmond. Perry, Billy & such of those as are at the White House as wish it or who can support themselves, must be included. Indeed I should like to include the whole list at Arlington, White House &c., if it can be done so as to finish the business. It is possible that during the winter though hardly before Xmas I might get to R[ichmond] to attend to it, or the papers could be brought to me. I send down some summer drawers & socks. Please put them in my trunk. It will relieve my valise here. If you are not using that Mexican bit, I should like to try it on my grey horse. If you are, do not send it, as it is only an experiment & may not prove good. The bit I use is probably equally severe. But my hands are weaker now. I send a passport for Ella [Carter] & Mrs. [Robert] Haxall, but do not recommend the trip. It is hazardous & dangerous. It is all I can do. The enemy's gunboats appeared at Port Royal last evening & their pickets extend to King George Court House. The route from Warrenton is more open now. Give much love to your mother, Chass & Agnes. I hope all will continue well. Remember me to all friends.

God grant that our armies may sustain the confidence reposed in them by our people & I trust that the prayers offered up in their behalf may be answered. But the people must help themselves, or Providence will not help them. If you can have me a vest made, of blue, black or grey cassimere or cloth, rolling collar & army buttons, I shall be obliged to you. It can be made on your measure a size larger, or they have my measure at the Clothing Bureau if made there. All here send their regards. F[itzhugh] is well. I was with him yesterday. Johnny [Lee] too.

Very truly & affly your father

R. E. LEE

332   To GENERAL THOMAS J. JACKSON
             Commanding Left Wing

Headquarters, Army of Northern Virginia
December 2, 1862
7 P.M.

General:

I send you a note just received from Genl Stuart. Not knowing whether you met with him in your ride today. In addition I will state that information was sent us today from the other side of the Rappahannock, that President Lincoln was at Aquia Creek yesterday and stated to Genl Burnside that he must advance within two days. A citizen doctor who came from the other side of the river yesterday also reports that the forces of the enemy are divided, a large body in King George nearly opposite Port Royal, another part above Fredericksburg in the neighborhood of Ellise's Ford. Where Burnside's headquarters are said to be. And but a small force is opposite Fredericksburg. They have been very industrious all day in throwing up intrenchments. This division of the enemy's force seems to me very strange, but so many reports may indicate some movement of the enemy and I send them to you that you may be prepared.

I am very respy, your obt servt

R. E. LEE
General

P.S. Maj [Thomas M. R.] Talcott has just returned from a reconnaissance as far as the mouth of the Rapidan and he reports that there are no favorable points for throwing over a pontoon bridge.

R. E. L.

333   To JEFFERSON DAVIS
                            Richmond, Virginia

                            Headquarters, Army of Northern Virginia
                                          December 6, 1862

Mr. President:
    The enemy still maintains his position north of the Rappahannock. I
can discover no indications of his advancing, or of transferring his
troops to other positions. Scouts on both of his flanks north of the Rappahannock report no movements, nor have those stationed on the Potomac discovered the collection of transports or the passage of troops
down that river. General Burnside's whole army appears to be encamped
between the Rappahannock and Potomac. His apparent inaction suggests
the probability that he is waiting for expected operations elsewhere, and
I fear troops may be collecting south of James River. Yet I get no reliable
information of organized or tried troops being sent to that quarter, nor
am I aware of any of their general officers in whom confidence is
placed being there in command. There is an evident concentration of
troops hitherto disposed in other parts of Virginia, but whether for the
purpose of augmenting General Burnside's army or any other I cannot
tell. Colonel Imboden reports that the Federal forces in Northwestern
Virginia have retired towards New Creek, leaving a guard of some two
hundred at Beverly. There are now none at Moorefield, or in the Valley
of the South Branch of the Potomac. There is but one company at
Springfield, one at Paw Paw, one at the mouth of Little Cacapon, and
three at Oldtown in Maryland, just opposite. General Jones reports on
the 4th instant that Generals [Jacob D.] Cox and [Robert H.] Milroy
were marching from New Creek towards Martinsburg, Col Imboden
having previously reported the rumor of Cox's withdrawal from the
Kanawha Valley. Genl Geary I fear is in possession of Winchester, as on
the evening of the 3rd he was reported with his division within four
miles of that place. Cox's, Milroy's, & Geary's forces may be intended
to occupy the Valley and reconstruct the railroads in that section, but
I have thought it more probable that the greater portion were intended
for operations elsewhere. I have heard that on the 30th ultimo ten regiments from Virginia had reached the Baltimore depot in Washington,
their destination unknown. Should General Cox have withdrawn from
the Kanawha Valley, I should think the State troops under General
[John B.] Floyd could protect that country, and would recommend that
the Confederate troops be brought at once to Staunton, to operate in the
Shenandoah Valley, if necessary, or south of James River. I think the

strength of the enemy south of James River is greatly exaggerated, but have no means of ascertaining the fact. From the reports forwarded to me by General G. W. Smith, the officers serving there seem to be impressed with its magnitude. If I felt sure of our ability to resist the advance of the enemy south of that river, it would relieve me of great embarrassment, and I should feel better able to oppose the operations which may be contemplated by General Burnside. I presume that the operations in the departments of the west and south will require all the troops in each, but should there be a lull of the war in those departments, it might be advantageous to leave a sufficient covering force to conceal the movements, and draw an active force, when the exigency arrives, to the vicinity of Richmond. Provisions and forage in the mean time could be collected in Richmond. When the crisis shall have passed, these troops could be returned to their departments with reinforcements. I need not state to you the advantages of a combination of our troops for a battle, if it can be accomplished, and unless it can be done, we must make up our minds to fight with great odds against us. I hope Your Excellency will cause me to be advised when in your judgment it may become necessary for this army to move nearer Richmond. It was never in better health or in better condition for battle than now. Some shoes, blankets, arms, and accouterments are still wanting, but we are occasionally receiving small supplies, and I hope all will be provided in time. There was quite a fall of snow yesterday, which will produce some temporary discomfort.

I have the honor to be with great respect, your obt servt

R. E. Lee
Genl

334   To HIS WIFE
Richmond, Virginia

Camp near Fredericksburg
December 7, 1862

I have received dear Mary your letter of the 1st instant by Major Taylor. When he went to Richmond I supposed you were in Hanover, & as his departure was sudden I did not write. I am very sorry to hear of Rob's attack. I hope it has been slight & that he is now well. I have not seen Fitzhugh since I last wrote. He has moved his camp to the vicinity of Port Royal & is some 20 miles from me. I hear he is well & his command has been active. Sixty of his old regiment under Major [Thomas] Waller, dismounted & crossed the Rappahannock a few nights since, & captured 49 of the enemy's cavalry picket, & brought them over with their horses, &c. A bold expedition & well planned by Col [Richard L. T.] Beale of the 9th [Virginia Cavalry], F[itzhugh]'s old regiment. His horse artillery too aided the other day in driving away the gunboats that had been lying opposite P[ort] R[oyal] very much to my dissatisfaction. I fear though they were not as much damaged as I could wish. We had quite a snow day before yesterday & last night was very cold. It is thawing a little this morning though the water was freezing as I washed. I fear it will bring much discomfort to those of our men who are bare-footed & poorly clad. I can take but little pleasure in my comforts for thinking of them. A kind lady, Mrs. Sally Braxton Slaughter of Fredericksburg (who is she?) sent me a mattress, some catsup & preserves, during the snowstorm. I was quite warm last night. You must thank Miss Norvell for her nice cake which I enjoyed very much. But tell her I preserve kisses to cake. I had it (the cake) set out under the pines the day after its arrival & assembled all the young gentlemen around it, & though I told them it was a present from a beautiful young lady, they did not leave a crumb. I want a good servant badly but I do not think it is worth while to commence with Fleming at this late day. He would have to learn a good deal before he would be useful, & on the 31st of December I wish to liberate all of them. Those in Richmond & those at the W[hite] H[ouse]. I have asked Custis to have the papers prepared for my signature, as I cannot attend to it myself. The greatest trouble will be to get at those hired on the railroad. I wish you would ask C[ustis] if he has found out where they are. Perry is very willing & I believe does as well as he can. You know he is slow & inefficient & moves much like his father Lawrence, whom he resembles very much. He is also very fond of his blankets in the morning. The time I most require him out. He is not very strong either. I hope he will do well when he leaves me & get in the service of some good person who will take care of him. I sent F[itzhugh] word that Rob was sick. You must give much love to Chass & Agnes for me & give my granddaughter a kiss. I am sorry I cannot give it myself. I hope her sweet mother is well now, but she must be very careful this winter & take all the exercise & breathe all the fresh air she can. Present my kind regards to Mr. & Mrs. [James M.] Caskie & all friends.

Very truly & affly yours

R. E. LEE

P.S. I send you a letter from Mr. Butler, that you may hear his story. I have answered it.

R. E. L.

335   To JEFFERSON DAVIS
                                Richmond, Virginia

Headquarters, Army of Northern Virginia
December 8, 1862

Mr. President:

A scout who has been absent several weeks returned last night. He has visited the cities from Washington to New York inclusive. The former city he left on the night of the 2nd instant, coming through Stafford County. He reports vast preparations for our suppression, and the expression of great confidence on the part of the North. Reinforcements are still coming to General Burnside's army. Two regiments left Alexandria while he was there, and four were waiting for transportation to Aquia Creek. Three regiments of cavalry were also marching by land, and a large pontoon train was moving through Dumfries when he was in that vicinity. He visited Staten Island where the troops said to be for [General Nathaniel P.] Banks' expedition were assembled. He thought there were about seven thousand troops there, though it was stated that the expedition consisted of about thirty-five thousand. He was shown at Brooklyn Navy Yard some iron clad steamers said to be preparing for the expedition, and among them was the *Monitor*. From all that he saw and heard, he is convinced that the expedition is not for Texas. If he is correct in the opinion that they are providing iron clad vessels for the expedition, it certainly cannot be intended for Texas, and the report has been circulated to conceal its real object. I noticed in some of the intercepted private correspondence of the enemy, that many stated they had signed a paper to accompany Banks' expedition to Texas. Not supposing that he would be assigned to a command of much importance, I attached some credit to these letters. I see from the Northern papers that his troops are principally from Massachusetts, Connecticut, New York and Pennsylvania, and must be new, nor am I aware that he has with him any officer of prominence in their army. I also see it stated that his troops embarked in sea-going vessels, and I believe the fleet of steamers now in Hampton Roads is part of that expedition. It would seem that they were not intended to operate in that quarter, or they would not be conveyed in steamers of that character. A telegram of the

30th ultimo from Fortress Monroe states that the ocean steamers with troops still remain there, that they are drilled on shore daily, and reports rough weather. It would seem therefore that they are destined for some other port. The indications from the Northern papers are, that the expedition is intended to operate in the Southwest, it may be in the Mississippi River, or against Mobile.

The scout above referred to was told in Washington, by a person in the Coast Survey Office, that it was intended for Brunswick Harbor, with the design of taking Mobile in reverse, and another person told him that it was intended for James River. He is of the opinion that Burnside's army is intended to force a passage to Richmond by this route, and he heard great anxiety expressed at his delay. The impression seemed general at the North, that if Richmond was taken the war would be ended, and that every effort would be made this winter to accomplish that object.

Burnside's army is represented by him to be two hundred and twenty thousand strong and increasing.

It is difficult to say from this statement what is the actual plan of the enemy, but I think that Burnside's army is much magnified, and that Banks' expedition is more probably designed for some point south of James River. The *Monitor* and four other iron clad boats are now in Hampton Roads, and they are probably intended to operate in those waters. If the troops in North Carolina and around Richmond can keep back attacks directed from south of the river, this army, if not able to resist Genl Burnside's advance, can retire upon the capital, and then operate as circumstances may dictate, but if the operations of the enemy south of James River cannot be resisted, it had better at once approach nearer Richmond. In this latter event I would leave a covering force here to embarrass Genl Burnside's advance.

Genl Geary on the 4th instant entered Winchester, but evacuated it in less than an hour, as he stated, for prudential reasons, and retired to Harper's Ferry. Our troops there hold their old positions. One of my objects in destroying the railroads in that region was to prevent the occupation of Winchester by the enemy, this winter at least. I am reluctant to trouble Your Excellency with my wants, but unless the Richmond and Fredericksburg Railroad is more energetically operated, it will be impossible to supply this army with provisions, and oblige its retirement to Hanover Junction.

I have the honor to be with great respect, Your Excellency's obt servt

R. E. LEE
Genl

336   To MRS. W. H. F. LEE
                                 Richmond, Virginia

                                              Camp Fredericksburg
                                              December 10, 1862

   I heard yesterday, by dear daughter, with the deepest sorrow, of the
death of your infant. I was so grateful at her birth. I felt that she would
be such a comfort to you, such a pleasure to my dear Fitzhugh, and
would fill so full the void still aching in your hearts. But you have now
two sweet angels in heaven. What joy there is in the thought! I can
say nothing to soften the anguish you must feel, and I know you are
assured of my deep and affectionate sympathy. May God give you
strength to bear the affliction He has imposed, and produce future joy
out of your present misery, is my earnest prayer.
   I saw Fitzhugh yesterday. He is well, and wants much to see you.
When you are strong enough, cannot you come up to Hickory Hill, or
your grandpa's, on a little visit, when he can come down and see you?
My horse is waiting at my tent door, but I could not refrain from sending these few lines to recall to you the thought and love of

                                      Your devoted father

                                      R. E. LEE

337   To HIS WIFE
                                 Richmond, Virginia

                                              Camp Fredericksburg
                                              December 11, 1862

My Dear Mary:
   I return a bit sent up by Custis. It is not the one I wished. He misunderstood me. But I do not want the one I wrote for now, as I have
one that will answer as well. I have no way of carrying this & therefore return it. Custis is gone, but you can give it to Charlotte as I believe
it is the one I gave F[itzhugh] some time since. The enemy succeeded
after bombarding the town of Fredericksburg, setting fire to many
houses & knocking down nearly all those along the river, to cross over a
large force about dark & now occupies the town. We hold the hills com-

manding it & hope we shall be able to damage them yet. Their positions
& heavy guns command the town entirely.

With much love to all I remain

As always truly & affly yours

R. E. LEE

338   To JAMES A. SEDDON
Secretary of War
TELEGRAM

Near Fredericksburg
December 11, 1862
Half past 12 P.M.

AT FIVE A.M. ENEMY COMMENCED THROWING THREE (3) BRIDGES ACROSS
RIVER. ONE AT RAILROAD BRIDGE, ONE AT FORD ABOVE, & ONE BELOW MOUTH
OF DEEP RUN. THEY WERE SOON DRIVEN FROM FIRST TWO, BUT AT THIRD (3)
THEIR GUNS, SWEEPING THE PLAIN IN ALL DIRECTIONS, HAVE DRIVEN BACK OUR
SHARPSHOOTERS, & THEIR MEN CANNOT BE MOLESTED. BRIDGE IS REPORTED
NEARLY COMPLETED. OUR GUNS COMMAND PLAINS SHOULD THEY CROSS. NO
ATTEMPT TO CROSS YET. GENL W. E. JONES REPORTS SLOCUM'S WHOLE FORCE
LEFT HARPER'S FERRY YESTERDAY IN CARS FOR WASHINGTON. MILROY REACHED
PETERSBURG, NORTHWEST VIRGINIA, SUNDAY NIGHT. FORCES AT NEW CREEK
MOVED DOWN THE B[ALTIMORE] & O[HIO] RAILROAD & ENTERED MARTINSBURG
AT SUNDOWN YESTERDAY.

R. E. LEE

339   To GENERAL SAMUEL COOPER
Adjutant and Inspector General
TELEGRAM

Near Fredericksburg
December 11, 1862

ENEMY, AFTER CANNONADING FREDERICKSBURG, AND DEMOLISHING MANY
HOUSES NEXT THE RIVER, SUCCEEDED IN DRIVING BACK OUR SHARPSHOOTERS
AND OCCUPYING FREDERICKSBURG. THEY CROSSED ALSO ON THEIR BRIDGE BELOW
DEEP RUN ABOUT DUSK. WE HOLD THE HILLS AROUND THE CITY.

R. E. LEE

340   To GENERAL SAMUEL COOPER
Adjutant and Inspector General
TELEGRAM

Fredericksburg
December 12, 1862

THE ENEMY PASSING OVER ALL OF LAST NIGHT & TODAY THEIR TROOPS BY
THE DIFFERENT BRIDGES. THEY ARE MASSED UNDER PROTECTION OF THEIR
GUNS ON THE NORTH BANK OF THE RIVER, BEYOND THE REACH OF WHICH THEY
HAVE NOT YET VENTURED. THEY HOLD FREDERICKSBURG WITH THEIR PICKETS.
HOUSES ARE BEING CONTINUALLY BURNED IN THE TOWN.

R. E. LEE

341   To JAMES A. SEDDON
Secretary of War
TELEGRAM

Fredericksburg
December 13 [1862]
9 P.M.

ABOUT 9 A.M. THE ENEMY ATTACKED OUR RIGHT, AND AS THE FOG LIFTED
THE BATTLE RAN FROM RIGHT TO LEFT. RAGED TILL 6 P.M. BUT THANKS TO
ALMIGHTY GOD, THE DAY CLOSED REPULSED ALONG OUR WHOLE FRONT. OUR
TROOPS BEHAVED ADMIRABLE, BUT AS USUAL WE HAVE TO MOURN THE LOSS
OF MANY BRAVE MEN. I EXPECT THE BATTLE TO BE RENEWED AT DAYLIGHT.
PLEASE SEND THIS TO THE PRESIDENT.

R. E. LEE

342   To GENERAL SAMUEL COOPER
Adjutant and Inspector General
TELEGRAM

Headquarters, Army of Northern Virginia
December 13, 1862

GENERAL:

YOUR DESPATCH OF YESTERDAY HAS BEEN RECEIVED. IT WILL BE IMPOS-
SIBLE TO REINFORCE WILMINGTON [NORTH CAROLINA] FROM THIS ARMY. I
WOULD WISH IT TO BE DOUBLE ITS PRESENT STRENGTH FOR THE WORK BEFORE
IT IF PRACTICABLE. DETACHMENTS FROM IT TO THAT DISTANCE LAYS OPEN
RICHMOND TO GENL BURNSIDE. REINFORCEMENTS FOR WILMINGTON & THE

COAST OF NORTH CAROLINA GENERALLY, MUST BE DRAWN FROM THAT STATE. IN THE EVENT OF NO ATTACK UPON SOUTH CAROLINA OR GEORGIA, GENL BEAUREGARD COULD REINFORCE WILMINGTON, & I RECOMMEND THAT THAT COURSE BE ADOPTED. THE PEOPLE MUST TURN OUT TO DEFEND THEIR HOMES, OR THEY WILL BE TAKEN FROM THEM.

I AM, &C., &C.

R. E. LEE
Genl

343   To GENERAL SAMUEL COOPER
                Adjutant and Inspector General
                        TELEGRAM

Fredericksburg
December 13, 1862

I REQUEST NO ONE TO BE SENT TO THE ARMY EXCEPT THOSE ATTACHED TO IT ON DUTY. ALL OTHERS ARE HINDERANCES.

R. E. LEE
Genl Comdg

344   To JAMES A. SEDDON
                   Secretary of War
                        TELEGRAM

Fredericksburg
December 14, 1862

I AM INFORMED BY CHIEF OF ORDNANCE OF THIS ARMY THAT THE TRAIN NOW ON THE ROAD CONTAINS ALL THE AMMUNITION PREPARED IN RICHMOND. I BEG THAT EVERY EXERTION BE MADE TO PROVIDE ADDITIONAL SUPPLIES AS THERE IS EVERY INDICATION THAT IT WILL BE NEEDED.

R. E. LEE
Genl Comndg

345   To JAMES A. SEDDON
                   Secretary of War

Headquarters, Army of Northern Virginia
December 14, 1862

Sir:
    On the night of the 10th instant the enemy commenced to throw three bridges over the Rappahannock, two at Fredericksburg, and the

third about a mile and a quarter below, near the mouth of Deep Run.

The plain on which Fredericksburg stands is so completely commanded by the hills of Stafford, in possession of the enemy, that no effectual opposition could be offered to the construction of the bridges or the passage of the river, without exposing our troops to the destructive fire of his numerous batteries. Positions were therefore selected to oppose his advance after crossing. The narrowness of the Rappahannock, its winding course, and deep bed, afforded opportunity for the construction of bridges at points beyond the reach of our artillery, and the banks had to be watched by skirmishers.

The latter, sheltering themselves behind the houses, drove back the working parties of the enemy at the bridges opposite the city, but at the lowest point of crossing, where no shelter could be had, our sharpshooters were themselves driven off, and the completion of that bridge was effected about noon on the 11th. In the afternoon of that day, the enemy's batteries opened upon the city, and by dark had so demolished the houses on the river bank, as to deprive our skirmishers of shelter, and under cover of his guns he effected a lodgment in the town. The troops which had so gallantly held their position in the city under the severe cannonade during the day, resisting the advance of the enemy at every step, were withdrawn during the night, as were also those who with equal tenacity, had maintained their post at the lowest bridge. Under cover of darkness and of a dense fog on the 12th, a large force passed the river and took position on the right bank, protected by their heavy guns on the left.

The morning of the 13th, his arrangements for attack being completed, about 9 o'clock, the movement veiled by a fog, he advanced boldly in large force against our right wing. General Jackson's corps occupied the right of our line, which rested on the railroad; General Longstreet's the left, extending along the heights to the Rappahannock above Fredericksburg. General Stuart with two brigades of cavalry, was posted in the extensive plain on our extreme right.

As soon as the advance of the enemy was discovered through the fog, Genl Stuart with his accustomed promptness, moved up a section of his horse artillery, which opened with effect upon his flank and drew upon the gallant [Major John] Pelham a heavy fire, which he sustained unflinchingly for about two hours. In the mean time the enemy was fiercely encountered by Genl A. P. Hill's division, forming Genl Jackson's right, and after an obstinate combat, repulsed. During this attack, which was protracted and hotly contested, two of Genl Hill's brigades were driven back upon our second line. General Early with part of his division being ordered to his support, drove the enemy back from the point of woods he had seized, and pursued him into the plain until arrested by his artillery. The right of the enemy's column extending beyond Hill's front, encountered the right of General Hood of Longstreet's corps. The enemy took possession of a small copse in front of Hood, but were quickly dispossessed and repulsed with loss.

During the attack on our right, the enemy was crossing troops over his bridges at Fredericksburg and massing them in front of Longstreet's line. Soon after his repulse on our right, he commenced a series of attacks on our left with a view of obtaining possession of the heights immediately overlooking the town. These repeated attacks were repulsed in gallant style by the Washington Artillery, under Colonel [James B.] Walton, and a portion of McLaws' division, which occupied these heights.

The last assault was made after dark, when Colonel [Edward Porter] Alexander's battalion had relieved the Washington Artillery (whose ammunition had been exhausted), and ended the contest for the day. The enemy was supported in his attacks by the fire of strong batteries of artillery on the right bank of the river, as well as by his numerous heavy batteries on the Stafford Heights. Our loss during the operations since the movements of the enemy began amounts to about eighteen hundred killed and wounded. Among the former I regret to report the death of the patriotic soldier and statesman, Brig General Thomas R. R. Cobb, who fell upon our left, and among the latter that brave soldier and accomplished gentleman, Brig General Maxcy Gregg, who was very seriously, and it is feared, mortally wounded during the attack on our right.

The enemy today has been apparently engaged in caring for his wounded and burying his dead. His troops are visible in their first position in line of battle, but, with the exception of some desultory cannonading and firing between skirmishers, he has not attempted to renew the attack. About five hundred and fifty prisoners were taken during the engagement, but the full extent of his loss in unknown.

I have the honor to be very respectfully, your obt servt

R. E. LEE
Genl

346   To JAMES A. SEDDON
                            Secretary of War
                               TELEGRAM

                                                    Headquarters
                                                 December 15, 1862

YESTERDAY WAS SPENT BY THE ENEMY IN CARING FOR HIS WOUNDED,
BURYING HIS DEAD. HE RETAINS HIS POSITION UNDER COVER OF HIS GUNS ON
THE NORTH BANK OF THE RAPPAHANNOCK.

                                                    R. E. LEE
                                                    Genl Comdg

347   To JAMES A. SEDDON
                            Secretary of War

                           Headquarters, Army of Northern Virginia
                                          Near Fredericksburg
                                          December 16, 1862
Sir:
    I have the honor to report that the army of Genl Burnside recrossed
the Rappahannock last night, leaving a number of his dead & some of
his wounded on this side. Our skirmishers again occupy Fredericksburg
& the south bank of the river. Large camps and wagon trains are visible
on the hills of Stafford, & his heavy guns occupy their former positions
on that bank. There is nothing to indicate his future purpose. I have
sent one brigade of cavalry down the Rappahannock & have put Jackson's corps in motion in the same direction. I think it probable an attempt will be made to cross at Port Royal. Another brigade of cavalry
has been sent up the Rappahannock with orders, if opportunity offers,
to cross and penetrate the enemy's rear & endeavor to ascertain his
intention. I learn from prisoners that the three grand divisions of Genl
Burnside's army, viz, Hooker's, [Edwin V.] Sumner's, & [William B.]
Franklin's, crossed this side, & were engaged in the battle of the 13th.
They also state that the corps of Genls [Samuel P.] Heintzelman &
[Franz] Sigel reached Fredericksburg Sunday evening. Should the enemy cross at Port Royal in force before I can get this army in position to
meet him, I think it more advantageous to retire to the Annas & give battle than on the banks of the Rappahannock. My design was to have done
so in the first instance. My purpose was changed not from any advantage

in this position, but from an unwillingness to open more of our country to depredation than possible, & also with a view of collecting such forage & provisions as could be obtained in the Rappahannock Valley.

With the numerous army opposed to me, and the bridges & transportation at its command, the crossing of the Rappahannock, where it is as narrow & winding as in the vicinity of Fredericksburg, can be made at almost any point without molestation. It will therefore be more advantageous to us, to draw him farther away from his base of operations.

The loss of the enemy in the battle of the 13th seems to have been heavy, though I have no means of computing it accurately. An intelligent prisoner says he heard it stated in the army to have amounted to 19,000, though a citizen of Fredericksburg who remained in the city computes it at 10,000. I think the latter number nearer the truth than the former.

I hope that there will be no relaxation in making every preparation for the contest which will have to be renewed, but at what point I cannot now state.

I have learned that on the side of the enemy Generals [George D.] Bayard & [Conrad F.] Jackson were killed, and Generals Hooker & [John] Gibbon wounded, the former said to be severely so.

I am most respecty, your obdt servt

R. E. Lee
General

348　　　　　　　To HIS WIFE
　　　　　　　　　Richmond, Virginia

Camp, Fredericksburg
December 16, 1862

I have not had time dear Mary before to day to reply to your letter of the 8th. I have grieved over the death of that little child of so many hopes & so much affection, & in whose life so much of the future was centered. But God's will be done. It is a bright angel in Heaven, free from the pains & sorrows of this world. I feel much for the father & mother but hope they will bear their great loss as Christians. God has been so merciful to us in so many ways, that I cannot repine at whatever he does. His discomfiture of our numerous foes & obliging them to recross the river was a signal interference in our behalf for which I feel I cannot be sufficiently grateful. I had supposed they were just preparing for battle, & was saving our men for the conflict. Their hosts covered the plain & hills beyond the river, & their numbers to me are unknown. Still I felt a confidence we could stand the shock & was anxious for the blow that has to fall on some point, & was prepared to meet it here. Yesterday evening I had my suspicions that they might retire during the night, but could not believe they would relinquish their purpose after all their boasting & preparations, & when I say that the latter is equal to the former, you will have some idea of its magnitude. This morning they were all safe on the north side of the Rappahannock. They went as they came, in the night. They suffered heavily as far as the battle went, but it did not go far enough to satisfy me. Our loss was comparatively slight, & I think will not exceed 2000. The contest will have now to be renewed, but on what field I cannot say. As regards the liberation of the people, I wish to progress in it as far as I can. Those hired in Richmond can still find employment there if they choose. Those in the country can do the same or remain on the farms. I hope they will all do well & behave themselves. I should like if I could to attend to their wants & see them placed to the best advantage. But that is impossible. All that choose can leave the State before the war closes. I wish you would see Mr. Echo & ascertain what can be done. The quartermaster informs me he has received the things you sent. The mits will be very serviceable. Make as many as you obtain good material for. I have everything I want. Fitzhugh & Rob are well. I saw both on the battlefield, once only. Nephew Fitz I saw this morning on his way up the Rappahannock. Give much love to all. Chass & Agnes specially. I send the last letter from M[ary]. No letters can reach her. Yours & mine I have retaken from the scouts. They add to their danger. I saw a scout to day who saw her a few days since. All were well.

Truly & in haste

R. E. Lee

349 To JAMES A. SEDDON
Secretary of War
TELEGRAM

Headquarters
December 16, 1862

AS FAR AS CAN BE ASCERTAINED THIS STORMY MORNING, THE ENEMY HAS DISAPPEARED IN OUR IMMEDIATE FRONT, AND HAS RECROSSED THE RAPPAHANNOCK. I PRESUME HE IS MEDITATING A PASSAGE AT SOME OTHER POINT.

R. E. Lee
Genl

350   To GENERAL SAMUEL COOPER
             Adjutant and Inspector General

BATTLE REPORT OF FREDERICKSBURG CAMPAIGN

Headquarters, Army of Northern Virginia
April 10, 1863

General:

I have the honor to submit herewith my report of the operations of this army from the time that it moved from Culpeper Court House in November, 1862, and including the battle of Fredericksburg. This report is sent in prior to reports of some of the preceding operations in consequence of the subordinate reports of this period having been first received.

I have not yet received all the reports of the division & corps commanders for the intervening period, but hope soon to be able to furnish to the Department complete records of our operations during the last campaign.

I have the honor to be with great respect, your obt servt

R. E. LEE
Genl

FREDERICKSBURG

On the 15th November it was known that the enemy was in motion towards the Orange and Alexandria Railroad, and one regiment of infantry with a battery of light artillery was sent to reinforce the garrison at Fredericksburg.

On the 17th it was ascertained that Sumner's corps had marched from Catlett's Station in the direction of Falmouth, and information was also received that on the 15th some Federal gunboats and transports had entered Aquia Creek. This looked as if Fredericksburg was again to be occupied, and McLaws' and Ransom's divisions accompanied by W. H. F. Lee's brigade of cavalry and Lane's battery, were ordered to proceed to that city. To ascertain more fully the movements of the enemy, Genl Stuart was directed to cross the Rappahannock. On the morning of the 18th he forced a passage at Warrenton Springs in the face of a regiment of cavalry and three pieces of artillery, guarding the ford, and reached Warrenton soon after the last of the enemy's column had left. The information he obtained confirmed the previous reports and it was clear that the whole Federal Army under Major Genl Burnside was moving towards Fredericksburg.

On the morning of the 19th therefore, the remainder of Longstreet's corps was put in motion for that point.

The advance of General Sumner reached Falmouth on the afternoon of the 17th and attempted to cross the Rappahannock, but was driven back by Col [William B.] Ball with the 15th Virginia Cavalry, four companies of Mississippi infantry, and [Captain J. W.] Lewis' light battery. On the 21st it became apparent that General Burnside was concentrating his whole army on the north side of the Rappahannock. On the same day General Sumner summoned the corporate authorities of Fredericksburg to surrender the place by 5 p.m., and threatened in case of refusal, to bombard the city at 9 o'clock next morning.

The weather had been tempestuous for two days, and a storm was raging at the time of the summons. It was impossible to prevent the execution of the threat to shell the city, as it was completely exposed to the batteries on the Stafford hills, which were beyond our reach.

The city authorities were informed that while our forces would not use the place for military purposes, its occupation by the enemy would be resisted, and directions were given for the removal of the women and children as rapidly as possible. The threatened bombardment did not take place, but in view of the imminence of a collision between the two armies, the inhabitants were advised to leave the city, and almost the entire population, without a murmur, abandoned their homes.

History presents no instance of a people exhibiting a purer and more unselfish patriotism or a higher spirit of fortitude and courage than was evinced by the citizens of Fredericksburg. They cheerfully incurred great hardships and privations, and surrendered their homes and property to destruction rather than yield them into the hands of the enemies of their country.

General Burnside now commenced his preparations to force the passage of the Rappahannock and advance upon Richmond. When his army first began to move towards Fredericksburg General Jackson, in pursuance of instructions, crossed the Blue Ridge, and placed his corps in the vicinity of Orange Court House, to enable him more promptly to cooperate with Longstreet. About the 26th November he was directed to advance towards Fredericksburg, and as some Federal gunboats had appeared in the river at Port Royal, and it was possible that an attempt might be made to cross in that vicinity, D. H. Hill's division was stationed near that place, and the rest of Jackson's corps so disposed as to support Hill or Longstreet as occasion might require.

The fords of the Rappahannock above Fredericksburg were closely guarded by our cavalry, and the brigade of General W. H. F. Lee was stationed near Port Royal to watch the river above and below. On the 28th General Hampton, guarding the upper Rappahannock, crossed to make a reconnaissance on the enemy's right, and proceeding as far as Dumfries and Occoquan, encountered and dispersed his cavalry, capturing two squadrons and a number of wagons.

About the same time some dismounted men of Beale's regiment, Lee's brigade, crossed in boats below Port Royal to observe the enemy's left, and took a number of prisoners.

On the 5th December, General D. H. Hill with some of his field guns assisted by Major Pelham of Stuart's horse artillery, attacked the gunboats at Port Royal, and caused them to retire.

With these exceptions, no important movement took place, but it became evident that the advance of the enemy would not be long delayed. The interval was employed in strengthening our lines, extending from the river about a mile and a half above Fredericksburg along the range of hills in the rear of the city to the Richmond railroad. As these hills were commanded by the opposite heights in possession of the enemy, earthworks were constructed upon their crest at the most eligible positions for artillery. These positions were judiciously chosen and fortified under the direction of Brig General Pendleton, Chief of Artillery; Col [Henry C.] Cabell of McLaws' division; Col E. P. Alexander, and Capt S. R. Johnston of the engineers. To prevent gunboats from ascending the river, a battery protected by entrenchments was placed on the bank, about four miles below the city in an excellent position selected by my aide-de-camp, Major [Thomas M. R.] Talcott.

The plain of Fredericksburg is so completely commanded by the Stafford Heights that no effectual opposition could be made to the construction of bridges or the passage of the river without exposing our troops to the destructive fire of the numerous batteries of the enemy.

At the same time the narrowness of the Rappahannock, its winding course and deep bed presented opportunities for laying down bridges at points secure from the fire of our artillery. Our position was therefore selected with a view to resist the enemy's advance after crossing, and the river was guarded only by a force sufficient to impede his movements until the army could be concentrated.

Before dawn on the 11th December, our signal guns announced that the enemy was in motion.

About 2 a.m. he commenced preparations to throw two bridges over the Rappahannock, opposite Fredericksburg, and one about a mile and a quarter below near the mouth of Deep Run.

Two regiments of [General William] Barksdale's brigade, McLaws' division, the 17th and 18th Mississippi, guarded these points, the former, assisted by the 8th Florida of [General Richard H.] Anderson's division being at the upper. The rest of the brigade, with the 3rd Georgia Regiment also of Anderson's division was held in reserve in the city. From daybreak until 4 p.m. the troops, sheltered behind the houses on the river bank, repelled the repeated efforts of the enemy to lay his bridges opposite the town, driving back his working parties and their supports with great slaughter. At the lower point where there was no such protection, the enemy was successfully resisted until nearly noon, when being greatly exposed to the fire of the batteries on the opposite heights and a superior force of infantry on the river bank, our troops were withdrawn, and about 1 p.m. the bridge was completed.

Soon afterwards, one hundred and fifty pieces of artillery opened a furious fire upon the city, causing our troops to retire from the river bank about 4 p.m. The enemy then crossed in boats and proceeded rapidly to lay down the bridges. His advance into the town was bravely resisted until dark, when our troops were recalled, the necessary time for concentration having been gained.

During the night and the succeeding day the enemy crossed in large numbers at and below the town, secured from material interruption by a dense fog. Our artillery could only be used with effect when the occasional clearing of the mist rendered his columns visible. His batteries on the Stafford Heights fired at intervals upon our position.

Longstreet's corps constituted our left, with Anderson's division resting upon the river, and those of McLaws, Pickett, and Hood extending to the right in the order named. Ransom's division supported the batteries of Marye's [Heights] and Willis' Hills, at the foot of which Cobb's brigade, of McLaws' division, and the 24th North Carolina of Ransom's brigade were stationed protected by a stone wall. The immediate care of this point was committed to General Ransom.

The Washington Artillery under Col [James B.] Walton occupied the redoubts on the crest of Marye's Hill, and those on the heights to the right and left were held by part of the reserve artillery, Col. E. P. Alexander's battalion, and the division batteries of Anderson, Ransom, and McLaws.

A. P. Hill of Jackson's corps was posted between Hood's right and Hamilton's Crossing on the railroad. His front line, consisting of the brigades of [Generals William D.] Pender, [James H.] Lane, and [James J.] Archer, occupied the edge of a wood. Lieut Co [R. Lindsay] Walker, with fourteen pieces of artillery, was posted near the right, supported by the 40th and 55th Virginia Regiments, of Field's brigade, commanded by Col [John M.] Brockenbrough. Lane's brigade, thrown forward in advance of the general line, held the woods which here projected into the open ground. [General Edward L.] Thomas' brigade was stationed behind the interval between Lane and Pender, [General Maxcy] Gregg's in rear of that, between Lane and Archer. These two brigades with the 47th Virginia Regiment and 22d Virginia Battalion of Field's brigade, constituted General Hill's reserve. Early's and Taliaferro's divisions composed Jackson's second line. D. H. Hill's division his reserve.

His artillery was distributed along his line in the most eligible positions so as to command the open ground in front.

General Stuart with two brigades of cavalry and his horse artillery, occupied the plain on Jackson's right, extending to Massaponax Creek.

On the morning of the 13th the plain on which the Federal army lay was still enveloped in fog, making it impossible to discern its operations.

At an early hour the batteries on the heights of Stafford began to play upon Longstreet's position. Shortly after 9 a.m. the partial rising of the mist disclosed a large force moving in line of battle against Jackson. Dense masses appeared in front of A. P. Hill, stretching far up the river in the direction of Fredericksburg. As they advanced, Major Pelham of Stuart's horse artillery, who was stationed near the Port Royal road with one section, opened a rapid and well directed enfilade fire, which arrested their progress. Four batteries immediately turned upon him, but he sustained their heavy fire with the unflinching courage that ever distinguished him.

Upon his withdrawal, the enemy extended his left down the Port Royal road and his numerous batteries opened with vigor upon Jackson's line. Eliciting no response, his infantry moved forward to seize the position occupied by Lieut Col Walker. The latter, reserving his fire until their line had approached within less than eight hundred yards, opened upon it with such destructive effect as to cause it to waver and soon to retreat in confusion.

About 1 p.m. the main attack on our right began by a furious cannonade, under cover of which three compact lines of infantry advanced against Hill's front. They were received as before by our batteries, by whose fire they were momentarily checked, but soon recovering, they pressed forward until, coming within range of our infantry, the contest became fierce and bloody. Archer and Lane repulsed those portions of the line immediately in front of them, but before the interval between these commands could be closed, the enemy pressed through in overwhelming numbers and turned the left of Archer and the right of Lane. Attacked in front and flank, two regiments of the former and the brigade of the latter, after a brave and obstinate resistance, gave way. Archer held his line with the 1st Tennessee, and with the 5th Alabama Battalion, assisted by the 47th Virginia Regiment and the 22d Virginia Battalion, continued the struggle until the arrival of reinforcements. Thomas came gallantly to the relief of Lane, and joined by the 7th and part of the 18th North Carolina of that brigade, repulsed the column that had broken Lane's line and drove it back to the railroad. In the meantime a large force had penetrated the wood as far as Hill's reserve and encountered Gregg's brigade. The attack was so sudden and unexpected that Orr's Rifles, mistaking the enemy for our own troops retiring, were thrown into confusion. While in the act of rallying them, that brave soldier and true patriot, Brigadier General Maxcy Gregg fell mortally wounded. Col [Daniel H.] Hamilton upon whom the command devolved, with the four remaining regiments of the brigade and one company of the Rifles, met the enemy firmly and checked his further progress. The second line was advancing to the support of the first. Lawton's brigade of Early's division under Col [Edmund N.] Atkinson first encountered the enemy, quickly followed on the right and left by the brigades of Trimble, under Col [Robert F.] Hoke, and Early, under Col [James A.] Walker. Taliaferro's division moved forward at the same time on Early's left, and his right regiment, the 2d Virginia belonging to [General Elisha F.] Paxton's brigade, joined in the attack. The contest in the woods was short and decisive. The enemy was quickly routed and driven out with loss, and though largely reinforced, he was forced back and pursued to the shelter of the railroad embankment. Here he was gallantly charged by the brigades of Hoke and Atkinson, and driven across the plain to his batteries.

Atkinson continuing the pursuit too far, his flank became exposed, and at the same time a heavy fire of musketry and artillery was directed against his front. Its ammunition becoming exhausted, and Col Atkinson being severely, and Capt [Edward P.] Lawton, [assistant] adjutant-general, mortally wounded, the brigade was compelled to fall back to the main body, now occupying our original line of battle, with detachments thrown forward to the railroad.

The attack on Hill's left was repulsed by the artillery on that part of the line, against which the enemy directed a hot fire from twenty-four guns. One brigade advanced up Deep Run, sheltered by its banks from our batteries, but was charged and put to flight by the 16th North Carolina of Pender's brigade, assisted by the 54th and 57th North Carolina of [General Evander M.] Law's brigade, Hood's division.

The repulse of the enemy on our right was decisive, and the attack was not renewed, but his batteries kept up an active fire at intervals and sharpshooters skirmished along the front during the rest of the afternoon.

While these events were transpiring on our right, the enemy in formidable numbers, made repeated and desperate assaults upon the left of our line. About 11 a.m., having massed his troops under cover of the houses of Fredericksburg, he moved forward in strong columns to seize Marye's and Willis' Hills. General Ransom advanced [General Joseph R.] Cooke's brigade to the top of the hill, and placed his own with the exception of the 24th North Carolina a short distance in the rear. All the batteries on the Stafford Heights directed their fire upon the positions occupied by our artillery with a view to silence it and cover the movement of the infantry. Without replying to this furious cannonade, our batteries poured a rapid and destructive fire into the dense lines of the enemy as they advanced to the attack, frequently breaking their ranks and forcing them to retreat to the shelter of the houses. Six times did the enemy, notwithstanding the havoc caused by our batteries, press on with great determination to within one hundred yards of the foot of the hill, but here encountering the deadly fire of our infantry, his columns were broken and fled in confusion to the town.

In the third assault, the brave and lamented Brigadier General Thomas R. R. Cobb fell at the head of his gallant troops, and almost at the same moment, Brigadier General Cooke was borne from the field severely wounded.

Fearing that Cobb's brigade might exhaust its ammunition, General Longstreet had directed General Kershaw to take two regiments to its support. Arriving after the fall of General Cobb, he assumed command, his troops taking position on the crest and at the foot of the hill, to which point General Ransom also advanced three other regiments. The Washington Artillery, which had sustained the heavy fire of artillery and infantry with unshaken steadiness and contributed much to the repulse of the enemy, having exhausted its ammunition was relieved about 4 p.m. by Col Alexander's battalion. The latter occupied the position during the rest of the engagement, and by its well directed fire, rendered great assistance in repelling the assaults made in the afternoon, the last of which occurred shortly before dark. This effort met the fate of those that preceded it, and when night closed in the shattered masses of the enemy had disappeared in the town, leaving the field covered with dead and wounded. Anderson's division supported the batteries on Longstreet's left, and though not engaged was exposed throughout the day to a hot artillery fire which it sustained with steady courage.

During the night our lines were strengthened by the construction of earthworks at exposed points, and preparations made to receive the enemy next day. The 14th, however, passed without a renewal of the attack. The enemy's batteries on both sides of the river played upon our lines at intervals, our own firing but little. The sharpshooters on each side skirmished occasionally along the front. On the 15th the enemy still retained his position, apparently ready for battle, but the day passed as the preceding.

The attack on the 13th had been so easily repulsed and by so small a part of our army, that it was not supposed the enemy would limit his efforts to an attempt which, in view of the magnitude of his preparations and the extent of his force, seemed to be comparatively insignificant.

Believing therefore that he would attack us, it was not deemed expedient to lose the advantages of our position and expose the troops to the fire of his inaccessible batteries beyond the river, by advancing against him. But we were necessarily ignorant of the extent to which he had suffered, and only became aware of it when, on the morning of the 16th it was discovered that he had availed himself of the darkness of night, and the prevalence of a violent storm of wind and rain, to recross the river. The town was immediately reoccupied and our positions on the river bank resumed.

In the engagement more than nine hundred prisoners and nine thousand stand of arms were taken. A large quantity of ammunition was found at Fredericksburg.

The extent of our casualties will appear from the accompanying report of the Medical Director. We have again to deplore the loss of valuable lives.

In Brigadier Generals Gregg and Cobb, the Confederacy has lost two of its noblest citizens, and the army two of its bravest and most distinguished officers.

The country consents to the sacrifice of such men as these and the gallant soldiers who fell with them, only to secure the inestimable blessing they died to obtain.

The troops displayed at Fredericksburg, in a high degree, the spirit and courage that distinguished them throughout the campaign, while the calmness and steadiness with which orders were obeyed and maneuvers executed in the midst of battle, evinced the discipline of a veteran army.

The artillery rendered efficient service on every part of the field, and greatly assisted in the defeat of the enemy. The batteries were exposed to an unusually heavy fire of artillery and infantry, which officers and men sustained with a coolness and courage worthy of the highest praise. Those on our right being without defensive works suffered more severely. Among those who fell was Lieut Col [Lewis M.] Coleman, 1st Regiment Virginia Artillery, who was mortally wounded while bravely discharging his duty.

To the vigilance, boldness, and energy of General Stuart and his cavalry is chiefly due the early and valuable information of the movements of the enemy. His reconnaissances frequently extended within the Federal lines, resulting in skirmishes and engagements in which the cavalry was greatly distinguished.

In the battle of Fredericksburg the cavalry effectually guarded our right, annoying the enemy and embarrassing his movements by hanging on his flank, and attacking when opportunity occurred. The nature of the ground and the relative positions of the armies prevented them from doing more.

To Generals Longstreet and Jackson great praise is due for the disposition and management of their respective corps. Their quick perception enabled them to discover the projected assaults upon their positions, and their ready skill to devise the best means to resist them. Besides their services in the field, which every battle of the campaign from Richmond to Fredericksburg has served to illustrate, I am also indebted to them for valuable counsel, both as regards the general operations of the army and the execution of the particular measures adopted. To division and brigade commanders I must also express my thanks for the prompt, intelligent, and determined manner in which they executed their several parts.

To the officers of the General Staff, Brig Genl Robert H. Chilton, Adjutant & Inspector General, assisted by Major [Henry E.] Peyton; Lieut Col [James L.] Corley, Chief Quartermaster; Lieut Col [Robert G.] Cole, Chief Commissary; Surgeon [Lafayette] Guild, Medical Director, and Lieut Col Briscoe G. Baldwin, Chief of Ordnance, were committed the care of their respective departments, and the charge of supplying the demands upon each. They were always in the field, anticipating as far as possible the wants of the troops.

My personal staff were unremittingly engaged in conveying and bringing information from all parts of the field. Col [Armistead L.] Long was particularly useful before and during the battle in posting and securing the artillery, in which he was untiringly aided by Captain Samuel R. Johnston of the Provisional Engineers; Majors [Thomas M. R.] Talcott and [Charles S.] Venable in examining the ground and the approaches of the enemy; Majors [Walter H.] Taylor and [Charles] Marshall in communicating orders and intelligence.

I have the honor to be, very respectfully, your obt serv't

R. E. LEE
General

CHAPTER NINE

Prelude to Chancellorsville

DECEMBER 1862 – MARCH 1863

"Our men and animals have suffered much"

AFTER THE BATTLE of Fredericksburg, the bitter weather continued into an extremely hard winter. With the army put into winter headquarters, General Lee was occupied with the dual problems of physically maintaining his forces and of countering threatening actions south of Richmond and in the supply areas of coastal North Carolina.

As the shortage of food and clothes for men and of forage for the animals grew acute during the winter, Lee devoted more time, thought and, most of all, concern, to the specter of hunger than to the enemy in his front — or all fronts. In addition to his usual stratagems, he wrote strong, lengthy letters to the war office. Though his communications accomplished nothing, he also wrote very strongly on the subject of getting able-bodied men into the army, especially those on special details. With a clear vision of the deadliness of the enemy's intentions, Lee was trying, in vain, to arouse the Richmond authorities to prepare for the magnitude of the struggle.

In order to tighten further the organization of the Army of Northern Virginia, he attached artillery battalions (averaging about twenty guns, mostly in uniform four-gun batteries) directly to the corps, to be administered by corps artillery commanders, and reduced Pendleton's reserve to six batteries.

Though he remained constantly alert against the enemy across the Rappahannock, and built powerful lines to the east of Fredericksburg, nothing serious developed. On January 20, poor luckless Burnside tried a wide flanking movement to turn Lee's left upriver, but rain poured on the bottomless roads (and the wretched troops), and the humiliatingly abortive maneuver entered history as the "Mud March." On January 26, Burnside was replaced by "Fighting Joe" Hooker — the fourth opponent to be given a try at Lee in seven months — and he made some violently threatening motions, which failed to convince the case-hardened Confederates.

In the western part of the state, where W. E. ("Grumble") Jones had been left with a brigade of cavalry when Jackson moved east of the mountains, the arsonist Milroy became troublesome against civilians and private property, and Fitz Lee was sent with his brigade to support Jones in suppressing him. But with all the little-recorded actions radiating from his front — skirmishes and feints and alarums — most of Lee's thinking was directed to those more distant actions which he supervised without controlling.

The dangers in North Carolina began in December, when General Foster thrust his Federal force inland from New Bern and, doing some damage along the way, wrecked a bridge and destroyed four miles of track of the railroad that led from Wilmington through Weldon to Petersburg. The threat was made the more alarming by the gross ineptitude displayed by the Confederates in North Carolina, and general apprehension was aroused when, on February 14, transports crowded with Federal troops sailed south down the Potomac for a destination unknown to the Confederates. They could reinforce Federal units for a strike anywhere from south of the James River to Charleston (where Beauregard commanded), and from the James to Wilmington inclusive the command situation was little short of chaotic.

Fundamentally the division of authority reflected the bureaucratic departmentalization of Davis's military bureau and the President's inability to allocate clearly defined authority with complete control. The city of Richmond had become a sub-department under Elzey; French still commanded the forces in southeastern Virginia and Whiting the defenses of Wilmington. D. H. Hill, ill and contumacious, had been sent by Lee to rally and organize the forces in North Carolina, his home state. Vaguely floating about over the whole grand department was Gustavus W. Smith, under Lee's authority. Having grown bitter at not being promoted to lieutenant-general, Smith was effective nowhere. In January, when Harvey Hill was sent personally to North Carolina, Lee also sent Robert Ransom with his two-brigade division of good Tarheel veterans. Ransom immediately wrote a personal letter to Colonel Chilton, describing Smith's incompetence, and, as Ransom intended, the letter went unofficially to Lee and on to Davis. General Smith, recalled to Richmond, was placed in a vacuum where he could do no harm, and, seeing the way things were, resigned on February 7. Contemporaneously

War Secretary Randolph resigned, to be replaced by Seddon, who was not immediately conversant with the nuances of the Confederate military establishment.

Into this fantasia went Longstreet. When the Federal transports, which were to land the IX Corps at Newport News, sailed southward, Lee sent Pickett's and Hood's divisions south of the James, and then on February 17 Longstreet to assume command, under Lee, of the total department vacated by Smith. Though Longstreet's two divisions numbered barely 16,000, the total force he commanded (in the Department of Virginia and of North Carolina), including Robertson's cavalry brigade detached from Stuart, numbered 41,530 present for duty in the March 10th returns. The size of this force, the area of command and the discretion allowed by Lee evidently incited in Longstreet an ambition for independent command. He immediately began to make plans for his department which not only committed Hood and Pickett to continued detachment but suggested the strategy that General Lee might adopt for the army in order that more of the First Corps troops be sent to him.

Longstreet distantly supervised two ill-directed and futile operations in North Carolina (New Bern and Washington), and then advanced the idea of gathering the food supplies in southeastern Virginia which General French had discovered and exploited some time previously.

At this point the employment of Longstreet's detached operations and the urgent need for food blended into one problem. Before Longstreet's supply expedition was suggested, Lee's plan was to hold Pickett and Hood near the railroad south of Richmond where they could move either against any Federal advance south of the James or quickly return to Lee in the event the weather opened sufficiently for Hooker to advance. Because the Federals neglected the southside avenue, history has neglected it also, but it was a constant concern of Lee's. In addition to the Federal corps newly poised at Newport News across Hampton Roads from Norfolk, about fifteen miles west of Norfolk a sizable Federal force occupied the gracious small city of Suffolk. As long as the forces at Newport News and Suffolk remained separated, there was little to fear from a Federal advance. However, if Longstreet moved south of Suffolk for provisions, he claimed this would precipitate action from the enemy.

General Lee, of course, wanted the provisions. However, he did not want Longstreet's First Corps troops involved in an action which would prevent their quick return to the army. Lee seemed personally committed to continue the wide latitude of discretion he extended Longstreet, as he had Jackson before the Fredericksburg concentration, for he was willing to take any risks with his army that offered opportunities for disrupting the enemy's plans. He continually studied all reports of enemy troop movements, in order to appraise the balance of strength in Hooker's army, on the Southern coast, and in the West, and to judge the enemy's intentions accordingly. During this period Davis and new War Secretary, Seddon were considering possibilities of reinforcing Bragg in middle Tennessee and/or preventing reinforcements from going to Bragg's opponent, Rosecrans.

With the approach of spring and conditions favorable to the enemy's movement, General Lee's correspondence indicates that he held some private reservations about Longstreet's use of discretion. There is a revealing sentence in his March 21 letter to Longstreet: "I am confident that at all times and in all places you will do all that can be done for the defense of the country and advancement of the service, and are ready to cooperate or act singly as circumstances dictate."

On his last communication to Longstreet in March, Lee gave a strong hint as to his preferences, when he asked Longstreet to verify the report that Burnside personally and the Federal troops in Newport News had been shifted to the West. If the report was correct, the original reason for Longstreet's detachment would have ceased to exist. The report was correct but Longstreet did not take the hint. Thus, for all of General Lee's preparation of his army for what he recognized as a crucial campaign, he ended the winter with one fourth of his veterans and his senior corps commander absent.

351   To HIS WIFE
Richmond, Virginia

Camp, Fredericksburg
December 21, 1862

My Dear Mary:
I have just received your letters of the 11th & 19. The former written before your visit to Hickory Hill & the latter on your return to Richmond. I am glad dear Chass is out of Richmond. I hope she will soon recover now. Tell her she must be very prudent & whenever she eats think of her papa & his military family at sunrise & at dusk in the evenings, with their tin plates & cups freezing to their fingers out of doors enjoying their sup & tough biscuit, & restrain herself. I have not the same opinion of her judgment that she has. It only wants proper exercise. As regards the servants. Those that are hired out can soon be settled. They can be furnished with their free papers & hire themselves out. Those on the farms I will issue free papers to as soon as I can see that they can get a support. As long as they remain on the farms they

must continue as they are. Any who wish to leave can do so. The men could no doubt find homes, but what are the women & children to do? As regards Mr. Collins he must remain & take care of the people till I can dispose of them some way. I desire to do what is right & best for the people. The estate is only indebted to me now. The legacies & debts are paid, & I wish to close the whole affair, but whether I can do so during the war I cannot say, nor do I know that I shall live to the end of it. I cannot give the date of your father's will. The papers are not with me. Perhaps Custis can get at them. The will was probated before the county court of Alexandria. Custis has also the bonds of the men who hired Reuben, &c. When he returns see him about it. He will return with the President who will be back before New Year's day. I shall not issue any free passes to the people while they are on the farms. As long as they remain there they must work as usual. I will be willing to devote the net proceeds of their labour for the year to their future establishment. Those at Arlington & Alexandria I cannot now reach. They are already free & when I can get to them I will give them their papers. Thank Mr. C[askie] for his kindness & give love to Agnes & kind remembrances to all friends. Tell Mrs. Conway I am very grateful for the prayers of her house. I feel that I require them all. That boy for Rob has arrived. Carter left this morning. Give love to Smith. Tell him he must not concern himself about me. I have no time to think of my private affairs. I expect to die a pauper, & I see no way of preventing it. So that I can get enough for you & the girls I am content.

Truly & affly

R. E. Lee

352   To HIS WIFE
Richmond, Virginia

Camp, Fredericksburg
December 25, 1862

I will commence this holy day dearest Mary by writing to you. My heart is filled with gratitude to Almighty God for His unspeakable mercies with which He has blessed us in this day, for those He has granted us from the beginning of life, & particularly for those He has vouchsafed us during the past year. What should have become of us without His crowning help & protection? I have seen His hand in all the events of the war. Oh if our people would only recognize it & cease from their

vain self boasting & adulation, how strong would be my belief in final
success & happiness to our country. For in Him alone I know is our trust
& safety. Cut off from all communication with you & my children, my
greatest pleasure is to write to you & them. Yet I have no time to indulge
in it. You must tell them so, & say that I constantly think of them &
love them fervently with all my heart. They must write to me without
waiting for replies. I shall endeavour to write to Mildred from whom I
have not heard for a long time. Tell dear Charlotte I have received her
letter & feel greatly for her. I saw her Fitzhugh this morning with his
young aid, riding at the head of his brigade on his way up the Rappahannock. I regret so he could not get to see her. He only got her letter
I enclosed him last evening. She ought not to have married a young
soldier, but an old "exempt" like her papa, who would have loved her as
much as he does. F[itzhugh] & R[obert] were very well. But what a
cruel thing is war. To separate & separate & destroy families & friends &
mar the purest joys & happiness God has granted us in this world. To
fill our hearts with hatred instead of love for our neighbours & to devas-
tate the fair face of this beautiful world. I pray that on this day when
"peace & good will" are preached to all mankind, that better thoughts
will fill the hearts of our enemies & turn them to peace. The confusion
that now exists in their counsels will thus result in good. Our army was
never in such good health & condition since I have been attached to it
& I believe they share with me my disappointment that the enemy did
not renew the combat of the 13th. I was holding back all that day, &
husbanding our strength & ammunition for the great struggle for which
I thought he was preparing. Had I devined that was to have been his
only effort, he would have had more of it. But I am content. We might
have gained more but we would have lost more, & perhaps our relative
condition would not have been improved. My heart bleeds at the death
of every one of our gallant men. Give much love to every one. Kiss
Chass & Agnes for me, & believe me with true affection

Yours

R. E. LEE

[P.S.] I send a note that has reached me from a Mrs. Cook. You had
better not respond. I do not wish your letters to get into the papers,
any more than mine. I heard from Col [Williams C.] Wickham yesterday.
He was well.

353   To MISS MILDRED LEE
                 Raleigh, North Carolina

Camp, Fredericksburg
December 25, 1862

My darling little daughter:

I have pleased myself in reminiscences to day, of the many happy Xmas' we have enjoyed together at our once happy home. Notwithstanding its present desecrated & pillaged condition, I trust that a just & merciful God may yet gather all that He may spare under its beloved roof. How filled with thanks & gratitude will our hearts then be! But in the meantime let us not forget how abundantly He has blessed us in our condition, & should it please Him eventually to establish our independence & spare our lives, all will be well. I cannot tell you how I long to see you. When a little quiet occurs & my thoughts revert to you, your sisters & mother, my heart aches for our reunion. Your brothers I see occasionally. This morning Fitzhugh rode by with his young aid de camp (Rob) at the head of his brigade on his way up the Rappahannock. They were both very well & I hope will be back soon. Custis I expect will return to Richmond early next week. I hear from your sister [Mary] occasionally through our scouts in King George [County]. She is still at Dr. [Richard] Stuarts & being within the enemy's lines, cannot write. I hope you are well my precious child. You must study hard. Gain knowledge & virtue & learn your duty to God & your neighbour. That is the great object of life. I suppose your mother & Agnes write to you regularly. Charlotte is now at Hickory Hill & has been quite sick. She was better than I last heard of her. I have no news. Confined constantly to camp & my thoughts occupied with its necessities & duties, I learn little of what is occurring beyond its confines. I am however happy in the knowledge that Genl Burnside & his army will not eat their promised Xmas dinner in Richmond to day. I trust they never will. You must write to me sometimes you precious child, without waiting for me to reply. I have little time for writing to my children. But you must be sure that I am always thinking of you, always wishing to see you. I have only received two letters from you & replied to both.

I am with true affection, your devoted father

R. E. LEE

354   To MISS AGNES LEE
                Richmond, Virginia

Camp, Fredericksburg
December 26, 1862

My precious little Agnes:

I have not heard of you for a long time. I do not know where you are, or how to address you. I hope you are well & enjoying the happiness of doing all the good you can. I wish you were with me, for always solitary, I am sometimes weary, & long for the reunion of my family once again. But I will not speak of myself but of you. I hope your old enemy, neuralgia, has left you at peace this winter, & that you take a great deal of exercise in the open air. I have a fine trotting horse that would agitate you much in a small space, that delights in a lofty head, & would feel proud to bear your gossamer weight. Come up & try him & tell Miss Sallie I have a smooth ambler for her. But I shall not let the young men look at her. I have only seen the ladies in this vicinity when flying from the enemy, & it caused me acute grief to witness their exposure & suffering. But a more noble spirit was never displayed anywhere. The faces of old & young were wreathed with smiles & glowed with happiness at their sacrifices for the good of their country. Many have lost every thing. What the fire & shells of the enemy spared, their pillagers destroyed. But a kind Providence will shelter them I know. So much virtue will not be unregarded. I can only hold oral communication with your sister [Mary]. I have received one letter from her, but have forbidden the scouts to bring any writing, & have taken back some that I had given them for her. If caught, it would compromise them. They only convey messages. I learn in that way she is well & is profuse in speech. All the family are likewise reported in good condition, & Carrie as being uncommonly pretty. I fear she caused the capture of a tall youth a week or two since. He left with such a heavy heart that on being discovered by the enemy's patrols, he could not keep up with his party & was overtaken. I have therefore forbidden them going to the house.

I must stop now. You always have my prayers for your health & happiness my dear daughter, & I now wish you many returns of the New Year, each more freighted with happiness than the other. With kind regards to all friends

I remain always your father

R. E. LEE

355   To JAMES A. SEDDON
                                   Secretary of War

                              Headquarters, Army of Northern Virginia
                                                    December 29, 1862

Sir:

I have the honor to transmit herewith two letters from Brig Genl
W. E. Jones, of the 26th instant. General Jones, by my direction, was
left in command of the troops in the Valley by General Jackson, when
his corps was withdrawn. As soon as I heard of the movement of the
enemy to Moorefield, I instructed him to concentrate the troops in that
region if necessary, cut off the enemy's communication with the Baltimore and Ohio Railroad and endeavor to drive him across the Potomac.

You will perceive from one of his letters that Colonel [Henry B.]
Davidson, and the troops under him, are considered under the command
of General [Arnold] Elzey, who I understand is on duty in Richmond.
I think it better that all the troops in the Valley should be under one
commander, and have therefore so ordered it. I have repeated my orders
to General Jones to endeavor to drive back the enemy, and to endeavor
to rally around him all the citizens of the west, for their protection and
defense.

I am with great respect, your obedient servant

                                                          R. E. LEE
                                                          General

P.S. I inclose the copies of orders issued by authority of General
Milroy, and the oath of allegiance demanded of our citizens, by which
it will be seen what a system of oppression is inaugurated against them.
I would recommend that the major of the Tenth [West] Virginia, reported by General Jones, be not paroled, but that he be detained as
hostage.

356   To GENERAL GUSTAVUS W. SMITH
                         Commanding, Richmond, Virginia

                              Headquarters, Army of Northern Virginia
                                           Camp near Fredericksburg
                                                      January 4, 1863

General:

Your letter of the 1st instant has been received. As you seem to be
certain that the enemy are reinforcing Suffolk and passing troops from

that point to New Berne, I would recommend that you collect a force at Goldsboro, and within supporting distance of it, adequate to oppose them. I do not think that the enemy can bring into the field in that region at present a large or stable force. Their troops must be new and not very reliable, nor have they an officer there that I am aware of in whom much confidence is reposed by his Government. It is as impossible for him to have a large operating army at every assailable point in our territory as it is for us to keep one to defend it. We must move our troops from point to point as required, & by close observation and accurate information the true point of attack can generally be ascertained. I may be mistaken, but I have thought that the troops at your disposal would be sufficient to drive back the threatened incursions of the enemy south of James River until he is reinforced from some of his armies now in the field.

Genl Burnside has all his army between Fredericksburg and Aquia Creek, with the addition of Sigel's corps. His own headquarters are near Brooke's Station, nor is there any indication of an embarkation or retrograde movement or going into winter quarters. I think it dangerous to diminish this army until something can be ascertained of the intentions of that opposed to it, and I hope you will be able by judicious arrangements and concentration of the troops under your command, to protect the frontier line of North Carolina. Partial encroachments of the enemy we must expect, but they can always be recovered, and any defeat of their large army will reinstate everything. From information received from the Secretary of War, I yesterday put Ransom's division in motion to Hanover Junction, and will continue him to Richmond unless I receive other information. You will find it necessary in North Carolina to dispose your troops so that they can march to the points required instead of trusting to the railroads, otherwise it will be impossible to collect your troops as speedily as necessary. The railroads must be reserved for transporting munitions of war. I would recommend that you take the field in person and endeavor to get out troops from the State of North Carolina for her defense. Wilmington should be defended at all hazards.

I have the honor to be with great repect, your obt svt

R. E. LEE
Genl

357   To G. W. C. LEE
                       Richmond, Virginia

                                    Camp, Fredericksburg
                                       January 5, 1863

My Dear Custis:

Col [James L.] Corley informs me that Major [Richard P.] Waller has received some good cloth, a part of which is to be applied to the necessities of this army. All that I want at present is a pair of pantaloons. Will you get them for me? They have my measure at the Clothing Bureau, or any one can measure you, encreasing all the horizontal measures, around girth, hips, &c. I like the legs full, & so cut as to spring over the boot. Please have them made at once & sent to me with or without stripes on seams as circumstances may render convenient. I requested your mother to inform you that I had sent power of attorney to Mr. Eacho. Liberate Harrison, Reuben & Parks as soon as you can. Give to them any wages earned this year. We have another snow storm this morning which promises to be deep. Our men & animals have suffered much from scarcity of food & I fear they are destined to more. I am doubtful whether I shall be able to retain my position & may be at last obliged to yield to a greater force than that under command of Genl Hooker. We shall lose the moral advantages we have gained & our men may become discouraged. Give much love to your mother, Agnes, if in R[ichmond], & all friends. Present me particularly to the gentlemen of the President's staff, & believe me always

                                        Your father

                                        R. E. LEE

358   To JAMES A. SEDDON
                         Secretary of War

                          Headquarters, Army of Northern Virginia
                                       January 5, 1863

Sir:

I have to thank you for your long explanatory letter of the 3d instant in relation to operations in North Carolina. Owing to the position of the enemy, the features of the country, and the strength of our army in that State, we can only at present expect to act upon the defensive. I hope we shall be able to obtain troops for that purpose. I have relied much on the troops of that State turning out for its defense, and have heretofore found that they have cheerfully and promptly done so when necessity required. If you think any benefit will be derived by sending an officer to Raleigh to inspirit or encourage the people I will send from this army Maj Genl D. H. Hill, a native of North Carolina, and a most valuable officer, for the purpose. By cooperating with the Governor and State authorities great advantage might be gained. At this distance I do not see how offensive operations could be undertaken with advantage, as the most we could hope for would be to drive the enemy to his gunboats, where he would be safe. The assignment therefore of any of our active forces to North Carolina would be to withdraw them from the field of operations, where as far as I can yet discover they may be much needed. Genl Burnside's army is increasing rather than diminishing. The troops from the front of Washington and the upper Potomac that have not made a junction with him have been moved down towards Stafford. Genl Slocum's division is at Occoquan and Dumfries. Genl Sigel's corps is at Stafford Court House. Genl Milroy has moved down as far as Martinsburg. From the letter of Mr. Jones, which you sent me, it seems that reinforcements from Yorktown and Gloucester are being forwarded to him. I have not however yet heard of their arrival. It is very clear that Genl Burnside will not advance towards Richmond unless he is reinforced. If he determines to go into winter quarters I think it probable that a part of his force may be sent south of James River, but if he does not he must be strengthened rather than weakened. Before the battle of the 13th I think his force could not have been less than one hundred & twenty thousand men. It may have been more. Since then Genls Sigel's, Slocum's, and Geary's forces have joined him. Taking the lowest number, his force is double that of this army. You can judge then of the propriety of weakening it if it is to keep the field. I have always believed that Genl [John G.] Foster's force [all the Union troops in North Carolina which constituted the Eighteenth Army Corps] has been much overrated. The reports from citizens however intelligent and honest cannot be relied on. Had Genl Foster received all the reinforcements that have been reported since this army recrossed the Potomac he ought to have the largest Federal army now in the field. I am not certain that he will attempt any expeditions except those of a predatory character. I think he will rather be deterred than encouraged by the result of his late expedition, especially when he considers the probability of reinforcements being sent to North Carolina. It is as natural that he should be preparing for defence as offence. It is proper however that we should be prepared, & we ought to concentrate there as large a force as possible, & to be successful in our operations our officers must be bold

& energetic. Information should be obtained by our own scouts, men accustomed to see things as they are, & not liable to excitement or exaggeration. After receiving your dispatch of the 2d instant I put Genl Ransom's division in march for Richmond on the morning of the 3rd. He has orders to report to Genl Smith. I hope it may not be necessary to advance him beyond Drewry's Bluff. I think it very hazardous to divide this army. Much labor has been expended in its organization. It is now in excellent condition, physically & morally, & I wish to maintain it so if possible. If I get further intelligence today, rendering it advisable, I will place another division near Hanover Junction, but until I can learn something definite of Genl Burnside's intentions I do not think it advisable to send it farther. I think it very certain that Genl Burnside's whole army is between this place and the Potomac, & that as yet he has made no movement to put it into winter quarters or to transfer it elsewhere. The glorious victory obtained by Genl Bragg [at Stone's River, Tennessee] will I think produce a pause in the military operations of the Federal Army everywhere. New organizations and new combinations will have to be made before much of importance can be attempted. In the mean time we should prosecute our preparations with the greatest energy & vigor.

I am, &c.

R. E. LEE
General

359   To JEFFERSON DAVIS
                Richmond, Virginia

Camp, Fredericksburg
January 6, 1863

Mr. President:

Allow me to congratulate you & the country upon your safe return to Richmond. I trust your health has been invigorated, & that you have enjoyed great satisfaction as well as comfort from the condition of affairs in the great West. I know that your visit has inspired the people with confidence, & encouraged them to renewed exertions & greater sacrifices in the defence of the country, & I attribute mainly the great victory of Genl Bragg to the courage diffused by your cheering words & presence. I hope it will result in driving the enemy beyond the Ohio. We have also much to do in the East. My letters to the [War] Department will inform you of the condition of affairs here. I am more uneasy at the state of affairs in North Carolina. Wilmington which I think is the real point of attack ought to be defended to the last extremity. It can be reinforced by Beauregard, & North Carolina ought to turn out every man in the State for its defence & the protection of its eastern frontier. Genl. D. H. Hill is suffering greatly in health, & seems depressed in spirits. Do you think he could be of service in arousing his people & in calming conflicting political views, which the Secretary of War & Genl G. W. Smith seems to think threaten disastrous consequences? If so I will detach him from this army. I know you will have much to occupy your attention. I will not trespass farther on your time, but wishing you all happiness & prosperity, & many returns of the New Year, remain with great esteem, your obt servt

R. E. LEE

360   To GENERAL SAMUEL COOPER
Adjutant and Inspector General
TELEGRAM

Culpeper
January 9, 1863

THE ENEMY CROSSED THE RAPPAHANNOCK THIS MORNING AT 5 A.M. AT THE VARIOUS FORDS FROM BEVERLY TO KELLY'S WITH LARGE FORCE OF CAVALRY, ACCOMPANIED BY INFANTRY AND ARTILLERY. AFTER A SEVERE CONTEST TILL 5 P.M., GENL STUART DROVE THEM ACROSS THE RIVER.

R. E. LEE

361   To JAMES A. SEDDON
Secretary of War

Headquarters, Army of Northern Virginia
January 10, 1863

Sir:
I have the honor to represent to you the absolute necessity that exists, in my opinion, to increase our armies, if we desire to oppose effectual resistance to the vast numbers that the enemy is now precipitating upon us. It has occurred to me that the people are not fully aware of their danger, nor of the importance of making every exertion to put

fresh troops in the field at once, and that if the facts were presented by those whose position best enables them to know the urgency of the case, they and the State authorities would be stimulated to make greater efforts. I trust therefore that it may not be deemed improper by the Department to communicate these facts to the Governors of the several States, that they may give efficient aid to the enrolling officers within their limits, and arouse the people to a sense of the vital importance of the subject.

The success with which our efforts have been crowned, under the blessing of God, should not betray our people into the dangerous delusion that the armies now in the field are sufficient to bring this war to a successful and speedy termination.

While the spirit of our soldiers is unabated, their ranks have been greatly thinned by the casualties of battle and the diseases of the camp. Losses in battle are rendered much heavier by reason of our being compelled to encounter the enemy with inferior numbers, so that every man who remains out of service increases the dangers to which the brave men, who have so well borne the burden of the war, are exposed. The great increase of the enemy's forces will augment the disparity of numbers to such a degree that victory, if attained, can only be achieved by a terrible expenditure of the most precious blood of the country.

This blood will be upon the hands of the thousands of able bodied men who remain at home in safety and ease, while their fellow citizens are bravely confronting the enemy in the field, or enduring with noble fortitude the hardships and privations of the march and camp.

Justice to these brave men, as well as the most urgent considerations of public safety, imperatively demands that the ranks of our army should be immediately filled.

The country has yet to learn how often advantages, secured at the expense of many valuable lives, have failed to produce their legitimate results by reason of our inability to prosecute them against the reinforcements which the superior numbers of the enemy enabled him to interpose between the defeat of an army and its ruin.

More than once have most promising opportunities been lost for want of men to take advantage of them, and victory itself has been made to put on the appearance of defeat, because our diminished and exhausted troops have been unable to renew a successful struggle against fresh numbers of the enemy. The lives of our soldiers are too precious to be sacrificed in the attainment of successes that inflict no loss upon the enemy beyond the actual loss in battle. Every victory should bring us nearer to the great end which it is the object of this war to reach.

The people of the Confederate States have it in their power to prevent a recurrence of these misfortunes, and render less remote the termination of this desolating war, at much smaller expense of treasure, suffering and blood, than must attend its prosecution with inadequate numbers.

They must put forth their full strength at once. Let them hear the appeal of their defenders for help, and drive into the ranks, from very shame, those who will not heed the dictates of honor and of patriotism. Let the State authorities take the matter in hand, and see that no man able to bear arms be allowed to evade his duty.

In view of the vast increase of the forces of the enemy, of the savage and brutal policy he has proclaimed, which leaves us no alternative but success or degradation worse than death, if we would save the honor of our families from pollution, our social system from destruction, let every effort be made, every means be employed, to fill and maintain the ranks of our armies, until God, in His mercy, shall bless us with the establishment of our independence.

I have the honor to be very respectfully, your obt servt

R. E. LEE
Genl

362 To JEFFERSON DAVIS
Richmond, Virginia

Headquarters, Camp near Fredericksburg
January 13, 1863

Mr. President:
I have had the honor to receive your dispatch of yesterday. For several days past there have been general indications of some movement by the army of Burnside, but nothing sufficiently definite to designate it if true. Rumors are abundant, but whether it is intended to retire, advance, or transfer it elsewhere I cannot ascertain. I am pretty sure that the whole army is between the Rappahannock and Potomac. No considerable portion ought to have been able to leave without my knowing it. Reinforcements of infantry & artillery have reached it from Washington. Wharves are still being constructed at Potomac Creek. The army has recently been more concentrated, its land communications with Alexandria more strongly guarded, and its right flank more extended towards the Orange & Alexandria Railroad. Cattle are being driven down on the Maryland side and crossed over on steamers to Aquia. No winter quarters are being erected, but the men are covering themselves, constructing

chimneys to tents, &c. There are a great many vessels of all sorts in the Potomac, but not more than enough to supply so large a force. It is said by their army that their transports were sent off with Genl Banks, and that there are not enough now to move it. Citizens in Stafford and King George Counties are not allowed to leave their dwellings. Persons even going to mill are guarded. You may have remarked that recent Northern papers are silent as to its movements. It is said this is by order. I have hoped from day to day to have been able to discover what is contemplated, and to be guided in my movements accordingly. I think by spring if not before they will move upon James River. In the mean time they will endeavor to damage our railroads, &c., in North Carolina and get possession of Wilmington and Charleston. Should Genl Burnside retire from his present position, I have intended to throw part of this army into North Carolina, and with another endeavor to clear the Valley of the Shenandoah. I did not wish to move until the designs of the enemy were developed. I have hoped that Genl Smith with the troops at his disposal could keep the enemy in North Carolina in check in the mean time. I still hope so. Since you seem to think my presence there would be of service I will endeavor to go on as soon as I can. All the troops in that State should be concentrated as near as possible to the threatened points. Charleston will not be attacked until Wilmington is captured. Genl Beauregard can therefore fight them at both points. As far as I have been able to judge, I have apprehended the movements in North Carolina were intended more as a feint to withdraw troops from this point, when Genl Burnside could move at once upon Richmond. Telegraph to me your wishes.

> With great respect, your obt servant
>
> R. E. Lee
> General

363   To JEFFERSON DAVIS
                    Richmond, Virginia

> Headquarters, Army of Northern Virginia
> January 19, 1863

Mr. President:

I go down this morning to examine the preparations which the enemy seem to be making on the banks of the Rappahannock. I understand that a redoubt has been built on the hill overlooking the river where their causeway has been constructed. Since my arrival I have learned nothing more of the designs of the enemy than what had been previously received, except the enclosed notes from two of our scouts on their right & left flank. Everything combined seems to indicate a movement, and I believe that their army, instead of being diminished by detachments to North Carolina, has been reinforced since the battle of the 13th December. I therefore have suspended the march of the brigades ordered to North Carolina until I can ascertain something more definitely. If in your opinion the necessity there is more urgent than here, I will despatch them immediately; they are ready for the march.

I have directed the Chief Quartermaster of this army to take fifty wagons belonging to its transportation, and apply them exclusively to convey the wheat that may be purchased by the agents of the Commissary Department, at Richmond, in the counties lying between the Rappahannock & Pamunkey, to the Central Railroad at Hanover Court House. I think this a more convenient point than any on the Fredericksburg Railroad, and one from which transportation to Richmond can be more readily obtained. I would suggest that the Quartermaster General in Richmond, collect all the wagons that can be spared from the posts at Gordonsville, Charlottesville, Staunton, Lynchburg, Richmond, &c., which may probably amount to fifty, & apply them to the transportation of the wheat in Greene, Madison & Culpeper Counties, &c., to the railroad for conveyance to Richmond. Our necessities make it imperative that every exertion be made to supply the army with bread.

As the Commissary Department proposes to issue sugar to the army in lieu of part of its meat ration, it has occurred to me that if its supply will warrant it, that by offering to exchange sugar for salt meat in the counties where grain is being collected, many persons might be tempted to part with bacon now retained for their own use. A few thousand pounds collected in this way would be of assistance to the army.

I have the honor to be with great respect, your obt servt

R. E. LEE
General

364   To GENERAL WADE HAMPTON
                 Commanding Cavalry Brigade

Headquarters, Army of Northern Virginia
January 20, 1863

General:

From the reports of the scouts from both flanks of the enemy, he appears to be on the eve of making an advance. Sigel's corps, which is stationed at Stafford and Dumfries, I understand, has marching orders, and the impression among the men is that they will go in the direction of Warrenton. I think it probable that he will attempt to cross the Rappahannock at Kelly's Ford, or at Rappahannock Station. He will hardly go higher at this inclement season, I think. Infantry is said to be collecting near Richmond Ford. The infantry pickets in front of Fredericksburg have been withdrawn this evening, and columns of infantry are reported to have been seen marching up the river.

I think it probable that the enemy will cross the upper Rappahannock, with a view to turn our left flank. Make such resistance as you can to retard or defeat him, and should he cross with a force too large for you to encounter, concentrate your troops; hang upon his flank and rear; cut up his communications; cause him embarrassment, and report all that you can discover of his movements and designs. A scout just in from Maryland reports that the Fourth and Fifth U. S. Regular Cavalry marched through Piscataway to Liverpool Point, and then across to Aquia Creek. A thousand head of mules, sutlers' wagons, &c., are taking the same route, and it is said that a number of old mules have been sent down there for the purpose of parking. Direct your picket to be on the alert everywhere, and be in readiness for whatever may occur.

I am very respectfully, your obedient servant

R. E. LEE
General

365 To COLONEL JOSIAH GORGAS
Chief of Ordnance

Headquarters, Fredericksburg, Virginia
January 22, 1863

Colonel:

I have had the honor to receive your letter of the 20 instant, and beg leave to thank you for your attention to my requests. I hope you will be able to get the carriages for the Whitworth guns made without delay, and the ten Napoleons now in progress finished at once. I assure you both kinds of guns are wanted with this army this very day. The enemy is moving to the line of the Rappahannock above and below Fredericksburg and from his preparations it would seem to be his intention to cross. The guns in question would add materially to our ability to resist him.

I am with great respect, your obt svt

R. E. LEE
Genl

366   To JEFFERSON DAVIS
Richmond, Virginia

Headquarters, Army of Northern Virginia
January 23, 1863

Mr. President:

Appearances now indicate that the enemy intend to advance. They seem to be moving to the line of the Rappahannock. They have shown themselves opposite Port Royal. Our scouts also report the preparation of bridges on Mr. I. Seddon's farm, to which point they are conveying their pontoons and artillery. In addition to the force reported near the mouth of the Rapidan, consisting of cavalry, artillery, and infantry, with their wagon trains, Capt [Robert] Randolph reports, on the 20th, a force of cavalry with 12 pieces of artillery, marching up the White Ridge road. No infantry was seen. This last named force may be intended to join hands with Genl Milroy in the Shenandoah Valley, who has abandoned Moorefield and the south branch of the Potomac, and has his advance at Front Royal.

Lieut [William R.] Smith of the Black Horse Cavalry, also reports that the portion of the Federal Army near Alexandria, presumed to be Genl Slocum's command, crossed the Wolf Run Shoals on the 19th and resumed its march on the 20th in the direction of Dumfries or Fredericksburg, moving as rapidly as possible, with a large train of wagons.

It looks as if they intended to concentrate all their forces, and make a vigorous effort to drive us from our position. The storm of yesterday and the day before will prove unfavorable for their advance, as the roads have become heavy and the streams swollen. It will also operate unfavorably to our rapid concentration to oppose them at the point they may select.

I have requested General Cooper to direct all men and officers belonging to this army, now in Richmond without authority, to return to their posts. I have also directed Genl W. E. Jones, should Genl Milroy cross the Blue Ridge, to follow with his whole force and unite with Genl Hampton.

If there are any available troops about Staunton or Richmond, it will be well to advance them towards this line.

I have the honor to be with great respect, your most obt servt

R. E. LEE
Genl

367   To GENERAL SAMUEL COOPER
            Adjutant and Inspector General

                        Headquarters, Army of Northern Virginia
                        January 26, 1863

General:
    I have had the honour to receive your letter of the 24th instant
forwarding a resolution of the House of Representatives calling upon the
President for copies of the official reports of all battles not already presented to that body.
    I have endeavored to keep the Department advised of the result of
all battles in which this army has been engaged, as well as its movements
and operations, but so great has been the labour of the troops during
the campaign, so constant their occupation in the march & field, and so
great the change of officers from wounds and death, that it has been impossible for the various commanders to make out the required detailed
reports. I have not yet received all the reports of the commanders of
the battles around Richmond, nor of those subsequent. As soon as received, I shall endeavor to give a brief narrative of events.

            I am with great respect, your obt servant

                        R. E. LEE
                        General

368   To HIS WIFE
                Richmond, Virginia

                        Camp, Fredericksburg
                        January 29, 1863

My Dear Mary:
    I am grieved to hear of your sufferings. I trust now that the storm
has passed, you are relieved. It has terminated here in a deep snow which
does not improve our comfort. But as long as we can retain our health
we can stand anything. It came however peculiarly hard on some of our
troops whom I was obliged to send some 11 miles up the Rappahannock
to meet the recent movement of Genl Burnside. Their bivouac in the
rain & snow was less comfortable than at their former stations where
they had constructed some shelter. Genl Burnside's designs have apparently been frustrated either by the storm or other causes & he last

Saturday took a special steamer to Washington to consult the military oracles at the Federal seat of Government. Sunday I heard of his being closeted with President Lincoln, Secretary [Edwin M.] Stanton & Genl [Henry W.] Halleck. I suppose we shall have a new move, around next week. You had better finish all the gloves you intend making at once & send them to the army. Next month they will be much needed. After that, no use for this winter. Why did you not bring a lot for the young party to enjoy with their peanuts. The young beaux would have worked powerfully under the inspiration of Misses Norvell & Silby, nor would their labours have impeded the flow of their "sweet nonsense." I have heard nothing of F[itzhugh] or Charlotte since I wrote. The mail facilities from that region I suspect are poor. She can hardly therefore write to you. My attention has been directed up the river, & I have not been below at all. Tell my poor Agnes I am sorry I cannot see her. But I trust she is well & free from pains in her dear face. As she is so small, if she thinks she can make her bed on three stools in the corner of my tent, she had better come on to see me. I will lend her some warm blankets. I have got the snow removed from the top & from around my tent & will be dry in a day or two. I am glad you have seen Smith. I got a long affectionate letter from him the other day, to which I have replied, tell him. Say also to Custis I have sent the power of attorney to Mr. Eacho. Tell Mr. Caskie I am delighted the turkey was so good. I was that day up at U. S. Mine Ford on the Rappahannock. Did not get back till late at night, after our nocturnal repast was over. Having been on horse back from early breakfast he can imagine how I would have enjoyed it. I was however thinking so much of Genl Burnside's playing us such a shabby trick, running off to Washington while we were waiting for him, that I did not then miss my dinner. I confess I should like to have had some peanuts with some of Miss N[orvell]'s & Silbie's consomitants. I send some copies of the verses of Mrs. Clarke on dear Annie. They have been published in the Petersburg paper & some one sent me five copies. I will send a copy to Fitzhugh & one to Mary if I can. Remember me kindly to all with you. I do not know what my movements will be. They depend upon circumstances beyond my control. I hope I shall see you soon. You must endeavour to enjoy the pleasure of doing good. That is all that makes life valuable. When I measure my own by that standard I am filled with confusion & despair. You are always present with me in my prayers & thoughts.

Truly yours

R. E. LEE

369   To JAMES A. SEDDON
Secretary of War

Headquarters, Fredericksburg
January 29, 1863

Sir:

On the 19th instant, being satisfied that Genl Burnside was massing the larger portion of his army in the vicinity of Hartwood Church, that his artillery & pontoon trains were moving in the same direction, & that Genl Slocum's command was advancing from the vicinity of Fairfax towards the Rappahannock, our positions at Banks' & United States Mine Fords were strengthened & reinforced. These being the points apparently threatened. The movements of the enemy on the 20th confirmed the belief that an effort would be made to turn our left flank & that Franklin's & Hooker's corps were the troops selected for that purpose. About dark that evening the rain which had been threatening during the day commenced to fall & continued all night & the two following days. Whether the storm or other causes frustrated the designs of the enemy I do not know but no attempt as yet has been made to cross the Rappahannock, & some of the enemy's forces have apparently resumed their former positions. A second storm commenced before day on the 27th & continued till this morning. The ground is covered with at least six inches of snow, the probabilities are that the roads will be impracticable for some time.

I have the honour to be with great respect, your obt servt

R. E. LEE
Genl

370   To JAMES A. SEDDON
Secretary of War

Headquarters, Fredericksburg
January [February] 4, 1863.

Sir:

I have received your dispatch of yesterday in reference to the propriety of sending reinforcements from this army to North Carolina to replace those recalled to Charleston. I will do so if you deem the exigency requires it and should like to be informed as to the number of troops withdrawn to Charleston. As far as I can judge I think it probable that an attempt will be made on Charleston. Demonstrations have been made on Genesis Point & North Carolina, apparently with a view of attracting attention elsewhere, and I notice that the new ironsides, *Montauk* & *Passaic* are in Beaufort Harbor. A fourth ironclad is also mentioned to have been in the attack on Genesis Point, Ogeechee River, Georgia. I do not know what are the indications of an attack upon Wilmington. The ironclads seem to have passed south of the Cape Fear, & the last reports I saw of the sailing of Genl [John G.] Foster left me in doubt as to whether he was bound for the Cape Fear River or further south. I see it stated too in the Northern papers that 75,000 troops from this army have reached North Carolina, & that reinforcements were being sent from it to Genl [Braxton] Bragg.

These are made use of as arguments why Genl Hooker can move upon Richmond. Genl Hooker has many strong reasons to induce him to take this step, and if he believes that but a feeble resistance can be made to his advance he will more likely do so. I think this was one of the main causes that impelled Genl Burnside to make his last attempt on the 20th ultimo, in which as far as I can see, it was fortunate for him that he was balked by the storm. I am trying to be prepared for any movement that may be made by Genl Hooker. But if the pressure on Wilmington is the more urgent it should be reinforced. I would suggest that the troops now in North Carolina should be concentrated as near as possible to Wilmington, leaving their places to be supplied if necessary from here. I beg leave also to suggest that your directions by telegraph for the movement of troops which you desire to conceal be sent in cypher, as I have found that otherwise they invariably become known. There are persons who frequent the telegraph office with no evil purpose but from curiosity to learn the news, & others are near to catch what transpires, and thus information is spread and reaches wrong ears.

I have the honor to be with great esteem, &c.

R. E. LEE
Genl

371   To JEFFERSON DAVIS
Richmond, Virginia

Headquarters, Army of Northern Virginia
February 5, 1863

Mr. President:
Your Excellency's letter of the 4th instant has just been received. I yesterday addressed a communication to the Secretary of War giving the

reasons which rendered it possible that an attack would be made upon Charleston. In addition I will state that the fall of Savannah will not carry with it the advantages to the United States Government which would result from the possession of Charleston. It is to be expected then that demonstrations will be made against the former city to attract there reinforcements. As soon as the point of attack is ascertained I would recommend that all the troops which can be spared from the city not in danger should be rapidly thrown to the other, as it is clear that both cities cannot be attacked at the same time. Attempts will be made to deceive by advancing against the point not intended for the real attack such gunboats, vessels and troops as will not be required against the other, and care and discrimination will be required to discover the feint. As far as I can learn at this distance it seems that the ironclad gunboats of the enemy are south of the Cape Fear River, and that Genl Foster, with his troops, has gone south too. I do not think therefore that Wilmington is at present in danger of being attacked, though no doubt efforts will be made to detain all of our troops there. They can however, I think with safety, be detached to Charleston.

Should a sufficient force not be left in North Carolina to guard our lines, which cannot under the circumstances be seriously threatened, some regiments of Genl Wise's brigade might be temporarily ordered to take their place. In case of necessity troops from this army can be sent to Richmond, and if you think the exigencies of the South more pressing than here I will send them at once. In my letter of yesterday to the Secretary of War I stated the reasons why I thought we might expect the advance of Genl Hooker. The weather today is unfavorable for his movement, & it may prove so for some time. It appears to me that if either Charleston or Savannah is attacked the rest of the coast may be stripped pretty bare of troops without imprudence. The troops of this army are ready to move at a moment's warning, and all I require is notice where they are wanted. I presume but few of the enemy's troops are left in North Carolina, perhaps not more than enough to guard his positions.

I have the honor to be with great respect, your obt servt

R. E. LEE
Genl

372   To MISS AGNES LEE
                Richmond, Virginia

                                        Camp, Fredericksburg
                                        February 6, 1863

I received yesterday my precious daughter your letter of the 3rd. I grieved very much when last in Richmond at not seeing you. You did right however in not coming down from H[ickory] H[ill] on Saturday under the circumstances. I was obliged to leave Sunday morning myself. My movements are so uncertain & time so occupied that I cannot be relied on for anything. The only place I am to be found is in camp, & I am so cross now that I am not worth seeing anywhere. Here you will have to take me with the three stools, the snow, the rain & the mud. The storm of the last 24 hours has added to our stock of all, & we are now in a floating condition. But the sun & wind will carry all off in time, & then we shall appreciate our relief. Our horses & mules suffer the most. They have to bear the cold & rain, tug through the mud, & suffer all the time with hunger. The roads are wretched, almost impassable. I heard of Mary lately. One of our scouts brought me a card of Margaret Stuart's, with a pair of gauntlets directed to "Cousin Robert." All were well. Fitzhugh, Charlotte & Robt are a long way from me. I hear nothing from them. I hope they are all well. Give much love to your poor mother. I fear she will suffer this weather. Tell Miss Sallie to kiss you on your poor little face for me & keep away the pain. Remember me to Mrs. Warwick, Mr. Warwick & Douglass. I have no news. Genl Hooker is obliged to do something. I do not know what it will be. He is playing the Chinese game. Trying what frightening will do. He runs out his guns, starts his wagons & troops up & down the river, & creates an excitement generally. Our men look on in wonder, give a cheer, & all again subsides "in statu quo ante bellum." I wish you were here with me today. You would have to sit by this little stove, look out at the rain, & keep yourself dry. But here comes in all their wet the Adjutant Generals with the papers. I must stop & go to work. See how kind God is, we have plenty to do in good weather & bad. Kiss Custis for me. I hope Miss Sallie takes him some flowers sometime. She can carry him nothing so sweet as her smiles.

                                        Your devoted father

                                        R. E. LEE

373   To HIS WIFE
                            Richmond, Virginia

                                                          Camp
                                                February 8, 1863

I have just received dear Mary your letter of the 7th. I am distressed
to hear of your suffering. I fear you are very imprudent, & that unless
you are careful, you will reduce yourself to confinement altogether. You
ought not to go out in bad weather, or to expose yourself at any time. I
beg you will be careful. I send the passport for Mrs. Murdock, &c. I presume they intend returning the way they came, by Leesburg. Inform
them they cannot pass through Fredericksburg. Genl Hooker has refused to permit passage through his lines here. I see in the Washington
papers orders from Genl Halleck forbidding transportation of any
citizens on the steamers plying between that city & Aquia Creek. All
the boats &c. are reserved for the military. There is therefore no chance
for them by this route. They can take the cars to Culpeper Court
House & must thence find their way to Warrenton & Leesburg by private conveyance. Their best route is by flag of truce boat from City
Point to Baltimore if that is permitted. But when they get home, my
advice is to stay there & to let their sons & brothers alone. The men can
do very well & soldiers must learn to take care of themselves. I have
done however all I can. If this passport does not answer, it is useless to
apply to me for another. It will take them anywhere through my lines.
I know the yankees will get out of them all they know. I hope they
know nothing to injure us. Not that I believe they will intentionally say
or do ought to injure us, but the yankees have a very coaxing & insidious
manner, that our Southern women in their artlessness cannot resist, no
matter how favourable they may be to our cause or how full of good
works for our men. I have not seen any of your gloves on the men, &
therefore cannot say how they answer. I should think well, if they fit, &
you know all your garments are warranted to do that. I advise you however to send up all you have made at once & then stop for this winter.
After about a month they will be of no use. The men cannot preserve
them & will throw them away. Remember me kindly to the Caskies. I
cannot get down to R[ichmond] now. Nor can I expect any pleasure,
during this war. We are in a liquid state at present. Up to our knees in
mud & what is worse on short rations for men & beasts. This keeps me
miserable. I am willing to starve myself, but cannot bear my men or
horses to be pinched. I fear many of the latter will die. Give my love to
Agnes. I wrote to her the other day. Where is she staying? As you both

seem to prefer Richmond to anywhere else, you had better take a house there. Be careful of the small pox & other diseases. Tell Miss N[orvell] that I told Major Talcott, after he had seen his sweetheart, he must go up & look at her for me. So she must give him a sweet look. Present me very kindly to Mrs. Jones. I sympathize with her deeply in the death of her husband [General David R. Jones]. He was always a great favorite with me. Fitzhugh is still low down the Rappahannock, I believe Charlotte is with him still. But have not heard. He is 40 miles from me.

With great affection, yours

R. E. LEE

P.S. I have George as cook now. He is quite subdued but has only been here a day. I give him & Perry each 8.20 per month. I hope they will be able to lay up something for themselves.

R. E. L.

374   To GENERAL J. E. B. STUART
Commanding Cavalry

Headquarters, Fredericksburg
February 13, 1863

General:

The present seems favourable for an attempt to limit the operations of Genl Milroy in the Shenandoah Valley, if he cannot be dislodged. Not deeming it prudent to detach any infantry for the expedition, I desire you to select from Genl Fitz Lee's brigade of cavalry such men and horses as may be fit for the service, & to direct their commander to proceed to Upperville, & thence into the Valley by Snickersville unless circumstances should determine otherwise. If you think it advisable, & the condition of his horses will permit, you can also form a detachment from Genl Hampton's brigade, either to watch the enemy east of the Blue Ridge or to join you as you may deem best. Genl W. E. Jones, commanding the Valley District, will be directed with all his available force to report to you, & it is suggested that you proceed to New Market or such other point in the Valley as you may prefer where he can join you. With the infantry in the Valley you can threaten Winchester in front, while with the cavalry it is advised you cut off its communication with Martinsburg, threaten the latter place, if you cannot drive the enemy from it, destroy as much of the railroad as possible & damage the enemy otherwise to the extent of your ability. It is probable that Fitz Lee's brigade, by seizing the railroad near Kearneysville & destroying the bridge over the Opequon might with caution capture a train of cars. You must endeavour to learn the periods of the arrival of the cars at Martinsburg & of the passage of the wagon trains to Winchester. Your particular attention must be given to the comfort of your men & horses, & should circumstances now unforeseen render it inexpedient in your judgment with a due regard to their future usefulness & service, upon your reaching the Valley, to carry out the object of the expedition, you are desired to limit or abandon it at your discretion. It is desirable that you gain all information you can of the general plans of the enemy, & especially whether any troops have been sent west over the Baltimore & Ohio Railroad, & all intelligence bearing upon the future movements of the Federal Army of the Potomac.

Commending you to a kind Providence, & your own good judgment,

I am with high respect, your obt servt

R. E. LEE
Genl

375   To GENERAL J. E. B. STUART
                 Commanding Cavalry

Headquarters
February 15, 1863

General:

That you may be advised of what is transpiring within the enemy's lines, I send you the last reports of scouts. A large body of troops have been reported to have landed at Newport News on the 11th. I think there is but little doubt that a corps of the enemy has gone down the river. It is said in the Northern papers that it is Genl W. F. Smith's. It may be for some special purpose, or it may be the beginning of a general move & change of base. If you find on your arrival at Culpeper that such is the case & that the opportunity of striking a damaging blow at the enemy is greater on the Potomac than in the Valley, you are desired to give precedence to the former & take measures accordingly. In that event you must notify Genl W. E. Jones, and keep me advised of your designs & operations & how I can facilitate them. I do not enclose Genl Hampton's letter reporting enemy's movements on their right as he can inform you & can probably give you later intelligence.

Very respectfully & truly yours

R. E. LEE

376   To JEFFERSON DAVIS
                    Richmond, Virginia

                                    Headquarters, Camp near Fredericksburg
                                                    February 16, 1863
Mr. President:
    On the 14th I advised the Secretary of War that Pickett's division
was ordered to Richmond. On the reception last night of his despatch of
the 15th, conveying your wishes, I directed Hood's division to be put in
motion this morning for Hanover Junction. I will halt it there or continue its march as circumstances may require. I have heard as yet of the
embarkation of but one corps of Genl Hooker's army, the 9th formerly
commanded by Genl Burnside. It reached Hampton Roads Wednesday
the 11th. Whether it is intended for operations there or further south
ought to be ascertained at once. The concentration of a large force of the
enemy at Aquia Creek, with other indications, renders it probable that a
general movement is in progress. I learn from Baltimore that all transports of every description are ordered from there to Aquia, & deserters
report that their army is going either to Tennessee or North Carolina. I
think more probably the latter. Their exterior line of pickets is as extended as before their recent advance to the Rappahannock, but the most
lamentable part of the present condition of things is the impossibility of
attacking them with any prospect of advantage. The rivers & streams are
all swollen beyond fording. We have no bridges, & the roads are in a
liquid state & nearly impracticable. In addition our horses & mules are in
that reduced state that the labor & exposure incident to an attack would
result in their destruction, & leave us destitute of the means of transportation. By making a circuit by Culpeper & making use of the Orange &
Alexandria Railroad it would still leave us such a long line to haul over
that in the present condition of the country I fear it would result in failure & the discouragement of our troops, even provided we could get
the provisions & forage to Rappahannock Station.

                        I am with great respect, your obt servt

                                                    R. E. LEE
                                                    Genl

377   To JEFFERSON DAVIS
                           Richmond, Virginia

Headquarters, Fredericksburg
February 18, 1863

Mr. President:

From the information I daily receive it appears that the Federal Army under Genl Hooker is abandoning its present position between the Rappahannock & the Potomac. The greater portion which has so far left has descended the Potomac. Some infantry & cavalry have gone towards Washington City. Two corps have gone down the river, a third was reported to be embarking Sunday. I have not heard its destination.

The portion rendezvousing in Hampton Roads may be for the purpose of reorganization or for operations in North Carolina. Pickett's & Hood's divisions are in march for the Chickahominy. I have directed them to halt near Atlee's Station on the Central Railroad, where their supplies will be placed. I did not wish them to approach near Richmond unless necessary. Should the movements of the enemy render it necessary for them to proceed south of Richmond, they can continue their march. To be prepared for any emergency I have directed Genl Longstreet to join these divisions. If necessary, the rest of his corps will follow. Accurate information ought to be obtained of the enemy's movements & intentions in Hampton Roads, and it should be ascertained whether he is preparing to re-embark his troops for a more southern port, or place them in camp, or advance them to Suffolk or into North Carolina. The present storm is more favourable for the enemy's movements than ours, as his communication is by water. I fear our men will suffer and many of our animals perish. Unless circumstances render it necessary, I shall put no other troops in motion at present.

I am with great respect, your obt servt

R. E. LEE
Genl

378   To GENERAL JAMES LONGSTREET
                 Commanding Corps

Headquarters, Army of Northern Virginia
February 18, 1863

General:

The transfer of a portion of the Federal Army of the Potomac to Hampton Roads has rendered it necessary to move two divisions of your corps towards James River. I desire you to join them and to place them in position where their comfort will be secured and whence they can be readily moved to resist an advance upon Richmond by the enemy from his new base. It is reported that he has been largely reinforced at Suffolk. It will therefore be prudent for you to change the present order for General Pickett to halt on the Chickahominy, and let him proceed to Falling Creek on the south side of James River, or to some better point from which you can readily defend Petersburg, &c. Should the movement of the enemy from the Potomac render it expedient, your other divisions will be ordered to join you. I desire therefore you be prepared to receive them and to select encampments for their comfortable accommodation. You will be advised of their approach.

I need not remind you of the importance of selecting sheltered positions, where there is plenty of wood, and which may be convenient to supplies. It is also desirable that these positions be, as far as possible, not liable to prove injurious to the agricultural interests of the country. You will require at least two battalions of your artillery and probably one of your reserve corps. The horses are in such a reduced state, & the country so saturated with water, that it will be almost impossible for them to drag the guns. They might be transported by railroad, by which route all heavy baggage if possible should also be conveyed, & the battery horses be led.

I wish you to inform me where I can communicate with you. To inform yourself of the movements of the enemy in your front, and to keep me advised. I suggest that you report to the Secretary of War on your arrival in Richmond, as he will have information and possibly some orders to communicate.

It will be well to have Lane's battery at some favorable point on the James River, to destroy the enemy's transports, if they should ascend.

I am with much respect, your obt servt

R. E. Lee

379   To MISS AGNES LEE
Richmond, Virginia

Camp, Fredericksburg
February 20, 1863

My precious little Agnes:

Genl Jones arrived yesterday with your letter. He brought some mud with him too, but that is a drug at present. If you see him he can tell you of the delights of our camp & you will regret more than ever that you did not come. It is true we have had a heavy storm of three days, snow, sleet & rain. Though Perry had entrenched me, the water night before last broke through my tent. But I did not know it till morning & had a quiet night. This morning the glorious sun is out, & will soon warm & dry us. How good is God! I am distressed at the continued indisposition of your mother. I trust this bright sun will dissipate her pains. Give much love to her & take care of her. I am sorry for the poor brides. Tell Miss Gurby & Mary Mercer, this is the best tour for them. The ruins of Fredericksburg. Nobody wants to see them as much as I do. Thank Mrs. & Miss Rives for the beautiful blanket you describe. I fear it is too beautiful for me, but is worthy of them. You & Miss Sallie must weave fabrics for soldiers' garments. They are much wanted now. Kiss Douglass for General E. & remember me to his mother & Mr. Warwick. I am called to the good breakfast.

Very truly your father

R. E. Lee

380 To HIS WIFE
Richmond, Virginia

Camp, Fredericksburg
February 23, 1863

I have received your letter of the 20th dear Mary & am very sorry that your suffering continues. I wish I could relieve it, but can only pray that our Heavenly Father will guard & comfort you. The weather now is very hard upon we poor bushmen. This morning the whole country is covered with a mantle of snow full a foot deep. It was nearly up to my knees as I stepped out this morning & our poor horses were enveloped. We have dug them out & opened our avenues a little, but it will be terrible & the roads impassable. No cars from Richmond yesterday, & I fear our short rations for man & horse will have to be curtailed. Our enemies have their troubles too. They are very strong immediately in front of us but have withdrawn their troops above & below us back towards Aquia Creek, where they can be better provisioned, or be disposed of. They keep very close & we cannot get within their lines to discover their movements. They have sent to Newport News a portion of their force, about three corps, enough to form an army for Burnside. I do not know what more they will do but am waiting on them. I enclose an answer to Mrs. Rives according to your request. I have only time for few words now for everybody. You must make up for my deficiencies in all things. I believe she is a cousin of my mothers & consequently a relative of mine. You had better keep the blanket if Mrs. C[askie] can give it houseroom. I have heard nothing of the titled ladies of England. That is evidently fancy. From Charlotte I hear nothing, nor do I know where she is. I hope she is well. From F[itzhugh] & R[obert] I have received nothing since my return from Richmond. I saw them at the cavalry review. They are down in Essex or Middlesex & I expect F[itzhugh] is exercised to get forage for his horses, &c. That is a great labour now, & I fear this hard weather will kill a great many. I owe Mr. F[ighting] J[oe] Hooker no thanks for keeping me here in this state of expectancy. He ought to have made up his mind long ago what to do. The men can do very well but our animals suffer terribly. I am very sorry to hear of the resignation of Genl [Gustavus W.] Smith. No one ought to resign now, from any cause, if able to do duty. Nor do I know what he is going to do.

24th. We had no mail yesterday & I could not send my letter. To day the cars have arrived & has brought me a young french officer, full of vivacity & no english, ardent for service with me. I think the appearance of things will cool him, if they do not, the night will, for he brought no blankets. Tell Mr. Caskie I have received his letter & have sent Mr. Moore's letter to Lord Lyons to be passed over the river if Genl H[ooker] will receive it. The courier with his mail was sent over yesterday. Give love to all.

Truly yours

R. E. LEE

P.S. I have just received the package brought by Miss Judy Gordon & sent by you on the 16th. It contains the sermon of Bishop Elliott, preached on Thanksgiving Day on September last, & copies of extracts relative to the privates of the army, justly eulogizing them.

R. E. L.

381   To JEFFERSON DAVIS
Richmond, Virginia

Headquarters, Army of Northern Virginia
February 26, 1863

Mr. President:

I was very glad to learn by your letter of the 18th that your health had been reestablished & that you were again able to take the open air. I hope now you will soon regain your strength & be long preserved to the Republic. I have for some time been doubtful of the intentions of the enemy. His movements could be accounted for on several suppositions. The weather for the last eight or ten days has been so unfavourable for observation that it has prevented the scouts from acquiring information. I have only learned positively of three army corps of the enemy having descended the Potomac. Some troops have been sent up the river. Probably Sigel's corps, but reports are contradictory on that subject. Slocum's division is at Dumfries. Three thousand infantry are reported at Centreville. Three regiments cavalry at Chantilly, scouting as high as Upperville & Paris, and probably connecting with Milroy at Winchester. Franklin's former grand division, detached to Newport News, is probably intended for Burnside, & I see it announced in Northern papers that he is to repair immediately to his new command, without stating where. I think the scene of his operations will be south of James River. The army of Genl Hooker is now located along the line of railroad from Falmouth to Aquia. The infantry formerly thrown out on its flanks has been drawn in & retired towards the Potomac. A line of cavalry on either flank in proximity to the railroad extends from river to river. I believe for the present the purpose of crossing the Rappahannock is abandoned & that the late storms or other causes have suspended the movements recently in progress. The disposition I have described may be intended to continue the remainder of the winter or until their conscript law becomes operative. Around Falmouth there is apparently a large force. During the late storm their pickets on the upper Rappahannock were withdrawn, & not being able to hear from the outlying scouts, I directed a reconnoitering party of [Colonel Williams C.] Wickham's cavalry to cross at the U. S. Mine Ford, to descend the left bank of the river and ascertain its meaning. The river was at swimming stage. Within about five miles of the ford the enemy's cavalry was found in too great force to drive in. Capt [Robert] Randolph of the Black Horse Company, having reported his inability to penetrate their lines farther north, Genl Fitz Lee was ordered with his brigade from Culpeper to break through their outposts & ascertain what was occurring. He yesterday penetrated their lines five miles in rear of Falmouth, found the enemy in strong force, fell upon their camps, & brought off about 150 prisoners, killing thirty-six, & losing six of his own men. I have received no official report, but this is the account given by a lieutenant, who left him at Hartwood Church, on his return to the Rappahannock, which he probably recrossed last night. Genl Wm. F. Lee reports that he engaged two gunboats near Tappahannock, that had ascended the river, and drove them off with a Napoleon & Blakely gun without loss to us. Genl Imboden reports that Capts [John H.] McNeill & [George W.] Stump of his cavalry with 23 men attacked a supply train of the enemy on the evening of the 16th, on the Northwestern turnpike, 5 miles west of Romney, guarded by 150 infantry & cavalry. After a brisk skirmish the guard was driven off, 72 taken prisoners, 106 horses with harness, some saddles, bridles, pistols, & sabers captured. Though hotly pursued to the south branch of the Potomac, Capt McNeill, by marching all night, succeeded in bringing his prisoners, &c., into Hardy, 12 miles south of Moorefield, where for want of subsistence he had to parole the former. No loss on his side is reported. These successes show the vigilance of the cavalry & do credit to their officers. The weather & condition of the country forbid any military operations. The last fall of snow was fully a foot deep. The rain of last night & today will add to the discomfort of the troops & the hardships of our horses. I had hoped that the latter would have been in good condition for the Spring campaign. The prospect in the beginning of the winter was good, and continued so until recently. Now, when their labours are much increased, it is impossible to procure sufficient forage. As soon as I can ascertain what is the probable intention of the enemy, & feel that I can leave here with propriety, I will visit Richmond & consult with you on the condition of things in North Carolina, &c. Charleston ought to be very strong. There will be but little time now to strengthen it, if it is to be attacked, as I see Genl Foster left Old Point on the 19th on his return to Port Royal. There is yet time to do much at Wilmington if improved. Genl Whiting is a good engineer & hard labourer. If he has the means he will make a good defence. I do not think Burnside will be able to move immediately, but every preparation should be energetically pushed forward. With the additional divisions under Longstreet, I consider that line safe.

I am with great respect, very truly yours,

R. E. LEE
Genl

382   To G. W. C. LEE
Richmond, Virginia

Camp, Fredericksburg
February 28, 1863

My Dear Son:
    I have received your note of the 23rd & am very much obliged to you for getting the cloth. As soon as you can have the pants made I

will be obliged to you if you will send them up, provided you do not hear I am coming down. Upon reflection keep the pants till you hear from me, but have them made as soon as you can. The rest of the cloth retain. I am very much obliged to Capt [William G.] Ferguson for his offer to have an overcoat made for me. But my old Blue will serve me yet awhile. I think you had better have yourself one made. For as far as I recollect yours is lost. I owe you now $28 for cloth & $25 for vest — $53. If you have not been able to collect any money of Mr. Eacho, I will send you a check for amount. Have you heard anything of Harrison, Reuben or Parks?

I have no news. We have mud up to our eyes. River very high. Enemy seems very strong in our front. Cannot ascertain yet what he is going to do, unless it is to remain as he is, till better weather, then push his columns now at Newport News up James River, thus cause us to fall back, & to move his army now in the Rappahannock across the river. Seems to be his best plan. Must try & defeat it. To do this, will require our regiments to be filled up. Can you devise any plan to get the laggards out? Give much love to your mother & Agnes. Have not heard from my Precious Life since January. I wrote to the President account of Fitz Lee's & Fitzhugh's handsome conduct. I am very glad to learn that he is able to attend his office again. You see the Federal Congress has put the whole power of their country into the hands of their President. Nine hundred millions of dollars & three millions of men. Nothing now can arrest during the present administration the most desolating war that was ever practiced, except a revolution among their people. Nothing can produce a revolution except systematic success on our part. What has our Congress done to meet the exigency? I may say extremity, in which we are placed! As far as I know, concocted bills to excuse a certain class of men from taking service, & to transfer another class in service, out of active service, where they hope never to do service. Among the thousand applications of Kentuckians, Missourians, Marylanders, Alabamians, Georgians, South Carolinians, &c., &c., to join native regiments out of this army, who ever heard of their applying to enter regiments in it when in face of the enemy? I hope Congress will define what makes a man a citizen of a State. For some apply for regiments of States in which they were born, when it suits their purpose, while others apply for regiments of States in which they live, or have married, or visited, or where they have relatives when it suits their purpose, but never when the regiments of these States are in active service. Genl Fitz Lee has reached his camp in Culpeper with 150 prisoners, including 5 commissioned & 10 non-commissioned officers, taken in his recent fight. Had to leave behind his wounded, six or eight (one, Sergeant [Surgeon W. B.] Davis, 2nd Regiment, mortally). Genl W. E. Jones reports that 2 regiments Federal cavalry drove in his pickets on the 26th. He fell upon them with small force, cut them up badly, captured 200 prisoners with horses & equipments. His loss, 4 wounded (2 mortally). Please read to the President these items. Have not time to write another letter before mail closes.

Cannot Genl [Louis T.] Wigfall do something for us with Congress?

Your father

R. E. LEE

383   To G. W. C. LEE
                    Richmond, Virginia

Camp
March 3, 1863

My Dear Custis:

Will you send the enclosed note to Mr. Taylor? Our mails are very uncertain now. It contains a draft. If my pants are done, will you give them to Mr. Thomas, the bearer, who will bring them up tomorrow. If they are not, keep them. I am in my last pair, and very sensitive, fearful of an accident. Our Federal neighbors are quiet. Their balloons are up during the day watching our movements, and remain up half the night observing our camp fires. They seem to be expecting us to move and are quite vigilant. They appear in great numbers in our front, and no manifestations yet of their intentions. Give much love to your mother and Agnes, and present me to all friends.

Very truly your father

R. E. LEE

384   To HIS WIFE
                    Richmond, Virginia

Camp, Fredericksburg
March 9, 1863

Bryan [Lee's mess steward] arrived yesterday my dear Mary with your letters. The one to Charlotte with the *Churchman* will go by the first courier in that direction, indeed has already gone. I am glad to hear that you are even a little better. I hope you may continue to improve &

soon recover your accustomed health. It would give me great pleasure to go to Richmond that I might see you even for a little while, & I must try & do so before you leave, but I cannot now say when. There is a constant demand for my presence. The Spring is opening upon us & the enemy may break out at any time. As for my health I suppose I shall never be better. Old age & sorrow is wearing me away, & constant anxiety & labour, day & night, leaves me but little repose. You forget how much writing, talking & thinking I have to do, when you complain of the interval between my letters. You lose sight also of the letters you receive. I wrote one but a short time before that sent by Bryan. It contained a note of thanks to Mrs. Rives. I hope it reached you, or she may think me negligent of her kindness. I am glad to hear Agnes is not a great sufferer & is able to take a little enjoyment. Remember me to the two young brides & wish for them for me every happiness. I am glad to hear of so many weddings. The young people have a great deal to do in the present exhausted state of the country. I wish them all success & happiness. The scarcity & high price of provisions are distressing. We must eat less. We can live on very little. Tell Mrs. Caskie she will have to bring her household down to our fare. It is very wholesome & nutritious. I will refer you to Custis for more detailed accounts. He returns this morning. I do not know that anything can be done to my summer apparel. You know it is very limited. Only a change of under garments. I dare say some of the socks are broken, but I have a good number of them & some are perfect. There are but two pairs left of my thinnest drawers, & I doubt whether anything can be done for them as far as I can recollect their condition. My apparel gives me but little trouble. I may be so soon cast off. Do pray do not let the papers get hold of the sash, &c. I forgot that when I sent them to Richmond. I am overwhelmed with confusion when I hear of my name in the papers. Tell Mr. Caskie that I yesterday received a letter from Genl Hooker saying that my application for permission for Mr. Dumas the messenger of the French Consulate to pass through his lines to Washington had been referred to the Secretary of War & been refused. On the arrival here of Mr. Dumas, I sent him down under flag of truce & passed him over the river. He never returned & I presume went on to Washington. Give love to everybody & believe me always yours

R. E. Lee

P.S. I get the *Churchman* regularly now. Have you paid the subscription?

R. E. L.

385   To GENERAL JAMES LONGSTREET
Commanding Department of Virginia and North Carolina
Petersburg, Virginia

Headquarters, Army of Northern Virginia
March 19, 1863

General:

On my arrival here yesterday I learned that the cavalry force of the enemy which crossed at Kelly's Ford had subsequently retired, and that the reported attempt to force a passage at the U. S. [Mine] Ford had not been made. I therefore sent a telegram to General Cooper, requesting that the divisions ordered up here might be stopped and returned to their former positions. I need not remind you that it will be necessary to maintain great vigilance in your front as well as here, and to hold the troops at both points ready to cooperate whenever it is correctly ascertained where the attack of the enemy will fall. I hope you will be able to act on the suggestions contained in my letter from Richmond relative to obtaining all the supplies possible of forage and subsistence from North Carolina and turn all the energies of your Department in that direction.

With great respect, your ob'dt servt

R. E. LEE
Genl

386   To HIS WIFE
Richmond, Virginia

Camp, Fredericksburg
March 19, 1863

My Dear Mary:

On arriving yesterday I learned that the enemy's cavalry had recrossed the Rappahannock, & that the report of their infantry crossing the river was not as threatening as stated. I therefore countermanded all my orders for concentration & we stand as before. Genl [George] Stoneman's attempt seems to have proved a failure. His whole corps of cavalry was driven back by Fitz Lee's small brigade. If he could restore to us our gallant dead I should be content. I grieve over the loss of Major [John] Pelham. He had been stricken down in the midst of his career of usefulness & honour, which in its progress I had hoped would have expanded in brightness. Fitz had his horse shot under him but is safe. I enclose the latest accounts from Fitzhugh. It shows he has his brigade in hand &

is prompt. I trust he will make a good soldier & serve his country well. Tell Miss N[orvell] she had better take Robert, though not of the "fighting Lee's" she might bring him out of the kinks. While that gallant young artillery man is waiting on her, his sisters are busy in moving their mother's furniture from Fredericksburg. I took two of them in at Ashland yesterday morning. I hope they may be able to carry back with them the piano, that he may not be troubled even with that. She & Miss Silby must be kind to him. I am glad I was able to see you even for a short time. I do not know when I shall have that pleasure again.

I can write but seldom, so you must not expect letters too often. I hope you will soon be relieved of your pains. Give much love to Agnes. I am sorry she had such a hard ride from Shirley & fear it may bring back the pains in her poor little face. She had better come up & stay with her papa. You must express my heartfelt thanks to your kind friends for the trouble & attention they give to your wants, & for their continued kindness to you in your suffering, I pray God may spare them all distress & enable them to continue their charities to the poor & needy. Tell Mr. Caskie he can say to Mrs. Lucy A. Govan, that her wishes have been anticipated in regard to her son, & that his transfer was made on the 15th instant by Paragraph VIII, General Orders, No. 74, on his former application. So that she troubled him uselessly. Miss Silby never came over to explain to me her brother's papers. So I am left to my natural dullness to penetrate them. She & Miss N[orvell] will have to come up to enlighten me.

With much love I am very truly yours

R. E. LEE

P.S. You can give Fitzhugh's autograph to those persons desiring mine. It is worth more.

R. E. L.

387   To GENERAL JAMES LONGSTREET
Petersburg, Virginia

Headquarters, Army of Northern Virginia
March 21, 1863

General:

I have received your letter of the 19th instant. I had hoped that you would have been able with the troops in North Carolina to have accomplished the object proposed in my letter of the 17th and did not suppose that you would have required Pickett's and Hood's divisions. As from information I received, the enemy between the Roanoke and Tar is feeble. I still think if you can retain them in reserve, to be thrown on any point attacked or where a blow can be struck, it will be the best disposition of them. If however you see an opportunity of dealing a damaging blow, or of driving him from any important positions, do not be idle, but act promptly. If circumstances render it impossible or disadvantageous for you to rejoin this army when attacked, we must withdraw towards you, if we cannot resist alone. In operating against any point accessible to the enemy's gunboats be prepared for them.

I am confident that at all times and in all places you will do all that can be done for the defence of the country and advancement of the service, and are ready to cooperate or act singly as circumstances dictate. I only wish you therefore to keep me advised of your movements that I may shape mine accordingly, and not to feel trammeled in your operations, other than is required by the general plan of operations, when an opportunity offers for you to advance the object of the campaign.

I am with great respect, very truly yours

R. E. LEE.

388 To HIS WIFE
Richmond, Virginia

Camp, Fredericksburg
March 21, 1863

I send you Mrs. Lee a likeness of your husband that has come from beyond the big water. He is a hard favoured man & has a very rickety position on his pins. I hope his beard will please you, for the artist seems to have laid himself out on that. We are poor judges of ourselves & I cannot therefore pronounce as to his success. But I can say that in his portrait of Genl Jackson he has failed to give his fine candid & frank expression, so charming to see & so attractive to the beholder. Tell Miss Norvell I did not recognize the likeness she sent me by Capt Taylor. She must send me her own. Mrs. Chilton proposed to return to day, but may be detained by the storm. The weather is extremely harsh & unfavourable for outsiders. Genl Hooker seems to have postponed his movements till the next fair day. Give much love to Agnes & kind regards to all with you.

Truly & affly yours

R. E. LEE

389   To GENERAL JAMES LONGSTREET
                    Petersburg, Virginia

Headquarters, Fredericksburg
March 27, 1863

General:

I received by the last mail your letter of the 24th instant accompanying the report of Major [R. J.] Moses on the subject of subsistence to be obtained in North Carolina. I do not know whether the supplies in that State are necessary for the subsistence of our armies, but I consider it of the first importance to draw from the invaded districts every pound of provision & forage we can. It will lighten the draft from other sections & give relief to our citizens. As to the force necessary for this purpose I cannot so well decide. As far as I am informed the force of the enemy south of James River & north of the Cape Fear is small. It can be reinforced speedily from the troops encamped at Newport News, but if you operate discreetly, concealing your movements & only occupying the country from which you are drawing, I think much may be done before your purpose is discovered & time be gained to develop the plans of the enemy, when we can act more understandingly. You have about 40,000 effective men. The enemy can bring out no more. I feel assured that with equal numbers you can go where you choose. If this army is further weakened we must retire to the line of the Annas & trust to a battle nearer Richmond for the defense of the capital. It throws open a broad margin of our frontier & renders our railroad communications more hazardous & more difficult to secure. Unless therefore a retrograde movement becomes necessary I deem it advantageous to keep the enemy at a distance & trust to striking him on his line of advance. A sudden & vigorous attack on Suffolk would doubtless give you that place. Of the propriety of this step you can best judge. To hold it you must control the navigation of the Nansemond or the troops from Newport News could soon be thrown upon you. There is a point about six miles below Suffolk where we once had a four gun battery that was said to be a good position, & other points lower down. A battery I should think would also have to be just below Smithfield & one at Manny's Neck, unless there is some better point at the head of the Chowan. If operations in that quarter should draw reinforcements from Genl Hooker, more troops could be spared from this army; but I hope you now have available troops in North Carolina sufficient for the purpose. Should you find it advisable to have a personal conference with me at any time I will be happy to see you here, or it may be that I could meet you in Richmond.

                    I am with great esteem, very truly yours

                                                    R. E. LEE
                                                      Genl

390   To JAMES A. SEDDON
                      Secretary of War

                              Headquarters, Army of Northern Virginia
                                                 March 27, 1863

Sir:
    About the last of January I directed Genl W. E. Jones to send an escort of cavalry with Maj W. J. Johnson, commissary of the cavalry division, into Hardy County, for the purpose of collecting beef cattle, &c. Genl Jones was also directed to send parties into the counties west for the same purpose. Maj Johnson has returned from his expedition, and reports that he obtained in Hardy County 500 beef cattle, 200 sheep & 4,200 pounds of bacon. He also obtained from Loudoun & Culpeper 200 head of cattle, & from Rockingham 3,000 pounds of bacon. I have not yet learned what amount of subsistence the parties sent by Genl Jones obtained. I have endeavored during the past campaign to draw subsistence from the country occupied by the troops, wherever it was possible, and I believe by that means much relief has been afforded to the Commissary Department. At this time but few supplies can be procured from the country we now occupy.
    Genl Longstreet has been directed to employ the troops south of James River, when not required for military operations, to collect supplies in that quarter, and penetrate, if practicable, the district held by the enemy.
    The troops of this portion of the army have for some time been confined to reduced rations, consisting of 18 ounces of flour, 4 ounces of bacon of indifferent quality, with occasionally supplies of rice, sugar, or molasses. The men are cheerful, and I receive but few complaints; still I do not think it is enough to continue them in health & vigor, and I fear they will be unable to endure the hardships of the approaching campaign. Symptoms of scurvy are appearing among them, and to supply the place of vegetables each regiment is directed to send a daily detail to gather sassafras buds, wild onions, lamb's quarter, & poke sprouts. But for so large an army the supply obtained is very small.

I have understood, I do not know with what truth, that the Army of the West & that in the Department of South Carolina & Georgia are more bountifully supplied with provisions. I have also heard that the troops in North Carolina receive one half of a pound of bacon per day. I think this army deserves as much consideration as either of those named, and if it can be supplied, respectfully ask that it be similarly provided.

I have the honor to be with great respect, your obt servt

R. E. LEE
Genl

391   To HIS WIFE
Richmond, Virginia

Headquarters, Fredericksburg
March 27, 1863

My Dear Mary:

I will not let pass the day devoted to thanksgiving to Almighty God for His mercies without holding communion with you. I know you will unite with me in fervent prayers for His manifold individual & national blessings. I wish I could be sufficiently thankful for all He has done for us, & felt that we deserved a continuance of the protection & guidance He has heretofore vouchsafed to us. I know that in Him is our only salvation. He alone can give us peace & freedom & I humbly submit to His holy will. I have been able to take no part in the services of the day. My poor prayers have been offered in the solitude of my tent. Too feeble I fear to be heard or answered. I enclose the order for the day. The troops are not encamped near me & I have felt so unwell since my return as not to be able to go anywhere. I have been suffering from a heavy cold which I hope is passing away. The weather has been wretched. More unpleasant than any other part of the winter. The earth has been almost fluid & my tent even muddy. But the storm has passed & the glorious sun is warming & drying us. We have our blankets out & tents up & a wonderful change has occurred in the ground & atmosphere since morning. I have received your letter of the 20th & have distributed the socks & gloves accompanying it. I send you a letter from Miss Kitty Stiles which has come to me. I should have liked to have read what she said, but her hand is so pale & fine that I will not make the effort. I send you also a pair of gloves. They were knit by a pretty little lady at the South & I think you who have given so many to the army are entitled to one pair. I also send

Mr. Caskie an English paper, & a speech at a convention of coloured gentlemen by Mr. Cole to show what a sensible view was taken of their interest in the present war. The commencement of the proceedings was torn off, but they appear in a Baltimore paper. I am very sorry for poor little Agnes' attack. I fear it originated in her ride that stormy night. See what suffering her papa brings on everybody. I am glad Mildred is alive & hope she will derive the pleasure I enjoyed in the study of Astronomy. I think it afforded me more pleasure than any other branch of study. I am glad that Parks has been heard from. Harrison is on a farm of Maline to whom he was hired. I have written for him to be sent to Mr. Eacho. Please inform Custis. I am sorry to hear of Reuben's death. Seanthe & Jim can remain with Mrs. D. this year if they choose & receive their wages. I do not send the pillow case for it is pretty good. Broken but a little & answers well. The other is a great comfort to me. Genl Hooker sent me yesterday the account of the death of Genl [Edwin V.] Sumner. He died at Syracuse after a week's sickness from a cold. Col Long is now with Mrs. L[ong] & I sent it to him.

You must give much love to everybody & believe me always yours

R. E. LEE

392   To GENERAL JAMES LONGSTREET
Petersburg, Virginia

Headquarters, Army of Northern Virginia
March 30, 1863

General:

One of our scouts reports under date of 29th instant that he was in Washington and Baltimore the first of last week and that Burnside's corps left Newport News at that time for the West. He does not state whether the information was derived from his own observation or from others. The *New York Times* of the 25th and the *Washington Chronicle* of the 26th state that Burnside was in Cincinnati on the 24th and is charged with the defence of Kentucky, but do not mention his troops.

Can you not ascertain definitely whether these statements are correct?

I am general very respectfully, & truly yours

R. E. LEE
General

CHAPTER TEN

Chancellorsville

APRIL–MAY 1863

"I should have chosen . . . to be disabled in your stead"

EE BEGAN APRIL, the month of the enemy's offensives, seriously ill. Though not so diagnosed at the time, later medical studies indicate that, along with his heavy cold, he suffered an attack of acute pericarditis. Before he completely recovered, General Lee was confronted with decisions involving the employment of Confederate troops across their whole front, from the Atlantic to the Mississippi.

Longstreet wanted to draw more troops from Lee to support his proposed expedition across the Blackwater River, for an attack on Suffolk by way of getting at the provisions in southeastern Virginia; the War Department considered reinforcing Bragg in middle Tennessee, or Pemberton at Vicksburg, with troops drawn from Lee's army. Already outnumbered more than two-to-one by Hooker, Lee refused more troops to Longstreet's peripheral operation, and suggested to the War Department that the best method of relieving the pressure on Bragg and Pemberton was another invasion of the North. On April 9 he wrote that he preferred to make this venture provided that Longstreet returned with provisions before Hooker moved on the offensive.

Instead, Longstreet settled down on April 11 to a pointless, futile siege of Suffolk, and on April 27 Hooker began his offensive. Perhaps influenced by his need of the provisions, Lee showed a curious reluctance to giving Longstreet a direct order, and an oblique approach he tried through the President availed nothing. He was also experiencing what became the chronic difficulties of getting the return of troops detached from his army (like Ransom's two brigades) and of the transfer to Virginia of troops in inactive areas. The result was that he faced Hooker's movement with something over 50,000 infantry against Hooker's 122,000

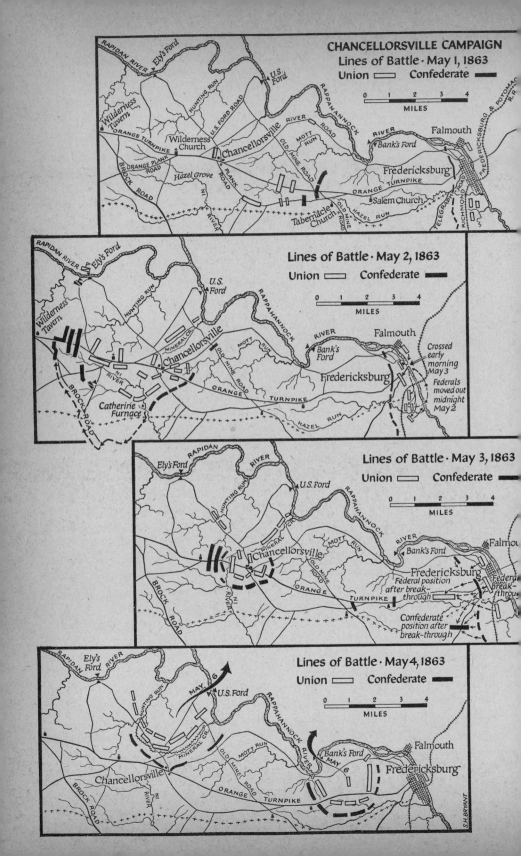

CHANCELLORSVILLE CAMPAIGN
Lines of Battle · May 1, 1863
Union ▭ Confederate ▬

0 1 2 3 4
MILES

RAPIDAN RIVER
Ely's Ford
Wilderness Tavern
HUNTING RUN
U.S. Ford
ORANGE TURNPIKE
Wilderness Church
U.S. FORD ROAD
Chancellorsville
RAPPAHANNOCK
RIVER
Falmouth
Bank's Ford
ORANGE PLANK ROAD
MOTT RUN
RIVER ROAD
Fredericksburg
Hazel Grove
PLANK ROAD
OLD MINE ROAD
FREDERICKSBURG & POTOMAC R.R.
BROCK ROAD
NI RIVER
ORANGE TURNPIKE
Salem Church
TELEGRAPH ROAD
RICHMOND
Tabernacle Church
OLD ROAD
HAZEL RUN

Lines of Battle · May 2, 1863
Union ▭ Confederate ▬

0 1 2 3 4
MILES

RAPIDAN RIVER
Ely's Ford
Wilderness Tavern
HUNTING RUN
MINERAL CR.
U.S. Ford
RAPPAHANNOCK
Chancellorsville
RIVER
Bank's Ford
Falmouth
NI RIVER
OLD MINE ROAD
MOTT RUN
Fredericksburg
BROCK ROAD
Catherine Furnace
ORANGE TURNPIKE
HAZEL RUN
Crossed early morning May 3
Federals moved out midnight May 2

Lines of Battle · May 3, 1863
Union ▭ Confederate ▬

0 1 2 3 4
MILES

RAPIDAN RIVER
Ely's Ford
HUNTING RUN
U.S. Ford
RAPPAHANNOCK
MINERAL CR.
Chancellorsville
RIVER
Bank's Ford
Falmou
NI RIVER
OLD MINE ROAD
MOTT RUN
Fredericksburg
Federal position after break-through
BROCK ROAD
ORANGE TURNPIKE
Federa break-throu
Confederate position after break-through

Lines of Battle · May 4, 1863
Union ▭ Confederate ▬

0 1 2 3 4
MILES

RAPIDAN RIVER
Ely's Ford
MAY 6
U.S. Ford
HUNTING RUN
MINERAL CR.
RAPPAHANNOCK RIVER
Bank's Ford
MAY 6
Falmouth
Chancellorsville
OLD MINE ROAD
MOTT RUN
Fredericksburg
BROCK ROAD
NI RIVER
ORANGE TURNPIKE

S.H. BRYANT

infantry, and less than 5000 cavalry present against Hooker's 12,000 cavalry.

Before the Federal infantry was put in motion, Hooker somewhat eased the disparity of numbers by sending off all his cavalry, with the exception of Pleasonton's small brigade, on a raid under Stoneman. Though Stoneman levied heavily on civilian property, his military damage was inconsequential, and Lee sent off only two regiments of his horsemen to observe the course of the raid and to prevent the Federals from settling down too comfortably to the work of destruction.

However, the raid suggested to Lee the possibility that Hooker might swing wide around his left toward the objective of the Virginia Central. Lee was certain that Hooker would not move to the Confederate right, as east of Fredericksburg the river widened, and the country was generally open and marshy. To the left, Hooker could either turn his flank at Fredericksburg or swing west against the railroad. Because severing Lee's army and Richmond from the Valley is what Lee himself would have done, throughout his command of the army he was sensitive about the Virginia Central.

On the 27th, with half of his army remaining across from Fredericksburg, Hooker sent roughly the other half westward along the north bank of the Rappahannock. About fifteen straight miles west of Fredericksburg the looping Rappahannock divided and formed a widening angle, with the Rappahannock along the northwest and the Rapidan along the southwest. On the 29th three Federal corps under Slocum crossed the Rappahannock at Kelly's Ford and pushed — not southwest toward the railroad, as Lee expected — southeast toward the crossing of the Rapidan at Ely's Ford on Lee's exposed flank. Simultaneously Sedgwick crossed two corps over the river at Fredericksburg and made demonstrations toward an assault over the ground of Burnside's charges. A third Federal corps remained at Stafford Heights, ready to move either way, and the last of Hooker's seven corps (the Second) was divided between Falmouth and the north bank of the Rappahannock at Banks' Ford.

Against this somewhat wasteful dispersion of strength, Lee, with his smaller numbers and the poor condition of his men and animals, was forced to wait for the enemy's move to be developed before committing his army. Because of this and his uncertainty of Hooker's objective until late in the day of the 29th, the three Federal corps under Slocum arrived squarely on Lee's flank at Chancellorsville by dark of the 30th, where they were joined by the two Second Corps divisions which crossed at the United States Ford. Fourteen miles west of Fredericksburg, where the Plank Road divided from the Orange Turnpike, Chancellorsville was the nondescriptive place name given a clearing in the Wilderness on which was situated the large house, and its appendages, owned by Mr. Chancellor. Ten miles from north to south and fourteen from east to west, the Wilderness was a dense forest of second-growth timber and stands of saplings made almost impenetrable by the screens of briary vines and creepers which rose from the matted earth to the treetops. Chancellorsville was one of the few large clearings in this maze, and it was so near the eastern edge of the Wilderness that Hooker camped there during the night of the 30th instead of pushing on through.

On the 30th the only Confederates in front of him were those of Anderson's division, whom Lee had hurried out at midnight of the 29th. On the day of the 30th, when Sedgwick, with an available force about the size of Lee's army, demonstrated fiercely on the plains below Fredericksburg, General Lee made perhaps his boldest battle decision in a career marked by audacity. Instead of retreating between the two jaws of Hooker's offensive, he determined to attack those Federal troops moving along the narrow, shrouded roads of the Wilderness. The jungle would reduce the effectiveness of their numbers and nullify their superior artillery.

To counter Sedgwick, he left at Fredericksburg only Early's division (approximately 8000) of Jackson's corps, well supported by artillery, with another brigade to the west of the city at Banks' Ford. McLaws's division was hurried forward to support Anderson, placing together the 17,000 infantry of the First Corps, minus the brigade at the ford. Before daylight of May 1st, Jackson moved out to join the assault with three divisions of about 26,000 men — A. P. Hill, Robert Rodes on D. H. Hill's former division, and Colston on Jackson's former division. Their left flank was supported by Fitz Lee's brigade of the cavalry which, in the absence of Stoneman's troopers, had done a superlative job in keeping Lee informed of the enemy's troop dispositions.

Until the Confederates moved forward during the morning of May 1st, Hooker had skillfully executed a superior strategic plan, and by all reason Lee should be retreating to escape entrapment. When, instead, the Confederates advanced, something went out of Hooker's nerve that did not come back. Various stories to account for the failure of his courage have gone the rounds, but the fact is that his fine forward movement turned into a slow withdrawal. Under the circumstances, any falling back was so strange that Lee suspected a trap. Then, at the end of the day, the vigilance of Stuart's cavalry discovered that Hooker's right flank was unanchored, "in the air." With this information, Lee resolved — whatever Hooker might be up to — to turn his flank and catch him in the rear.

Lee conferred with Jackson that night in the woods around a fire, in a scene immortalized in old lithographs and etchings as "The Last Meeting Between Lee and Jackson." Their conference was a perfect illustration of the intuitive collaboration between Lee and his great subordinate. Lee suggested the strategy, Jackson filled in the tactics, and the next morning Lee redivided his already divided army in implicit confidence in Jackson's execution of the hazardous plan.

Jackson marched his three divisions, minus a small rear guard, south and southwest, until he turned north behind Hooker's army on the Brock Road. His movement was observed by the Federals, but Hooker convinced himself that Lee was retreating and, by the confusion in his command, Jackson was permitted to form two divisions in line of battle across the Orange Turnpike, attacking to the east into Howard's XI Corps. The assault began at six in the evening and rolled up most of the XI Corps in disorder back on the other units. Making a personal reconnaissance after dark, Jackson's party was fired upon by their own men as they returned toward the Confederate lines. Jackson, with three shots in his left arm, was removed under artillery fire through the black woods.

At 2:30 in the morning of the 3rd, Lee was awakened by Captain Wilbourn, of Jackson's staff, and given the information that Jackson was wounded. With A. P. Hill, senior division commander, also wounded, Jackson had turned over the Second Corps to Jeb Stuart. Not knowing then the seriousness of Jackson's wound, Lee returned to the battle at daylight of the 3rd. The two First Corps divisions attacked from the east and southeast, and, across a gap, Stuart led the Second Corps from the west. By virtue of rattled Hooker's abandoning Hazel Grove, Stuart placed thirty guns in that commanding position, and the Federals fell back at all points. By noon, the Anderson-McLaws wing united with the Second Corps and pressed the enemy back toward the river in a victory which represented one of the military masterpieces in the history of warfare.

At that stage Lee hoped to destroy the part of the Federal Army with Hooker, but it was not to be. Sedgwick, who had been held up by Early's small force at Fredericksburg, had finally overrun the thin lines and was marching westward along the Orange Turnpike to Lee's rear. There was nothing for it save to pull McLaws out of line and hurry him back to check Sedgwick.

On the next day, the 4th, there was another turnabout. Early, having retreated out of Sedgwick's path on the 3rd, returned on the 4th behind *him*. Lee sent out Anderson to support McLaws, at Salem Church, and

Sedgwick, from threatening Lee's rear, found himself enclosed by Confederates on three sides and the river on the fourth. He escaped across the river, with his command having suffered heavy losses.

On the 5th, Lee at last assembled his whole army against Hooker, fortified along the riverbank, and prepared for the penultimate effort on the following day. (It was the first large-scale battle of the war in which both sides built field fortifications.) On the 6th, however, Hooker was also back on the other side of the river, his army, in comparative terms, little the worse for wear. Though he had suffered a decisive repulse, his campaign wrecked before it started, his 14,000 casualties represented little more than 10 per cent of his army. Lee, sustaining 10,000 casualties, mostly in his infantry, suffered nearly a 20 per cent loss in his veteran foot soldiers. This was the high cost of performing miracles with an undermanned army, to which no significant replacements were coming.

Most grievous of all was the loss of Stonewall Jackson. General Lee learned during the day of the 3rd that Jackson's arm was amputated, and he was profoundly shaken even by the prospect of Jackson's absence for an indefinite period. When the news came on the 10th that Jackson had succumbed to pneumonia, Lee's personal grief was equaled by the recognition that the rare combination was forever gone. As he later wrote his son, Custis, "Any victory is dear at such a price."

393   To HIS WIFE
Richmond, Virginia

Camp, Fredericksburg
April 3, 1863

I have received dear Mary your two letters, the last by Genl Chilton, since I last wrote. I am very sorry to find that you have been such a sufferer. Though your attendance upon church is no doubt very agreable to you, I fear it is not beneficial to your health. I hope the cheering weather of Spring which seems now to have commenced may restore you to your usual comfort. I am glad to hear Agnes has recovered & hope she may have a pleasant visit to the Braxtons. I wish I could assist you in establishing yourself for the summer, that you might have around you such of your children as are free to join you. The southwest part of Virginia (south of James River & east of the mountains) is the only portion of the State that has escaped the ravages of war & I hope retains some of its comforts & abundance. I do not know that I can recommend any better location. I hope you will be able to find some agreable habitation where you can enjoy yourself as much as possible under present circumstances. I am getting better I trust though apparently very slowly & have suffered a great deal since I last wrote. I have had to call upon the doctors who are very kind & attentive & do every thing for me that is possible. I have taken a violent cold, either from going in or coming out of a warm house, perhaps both, which is very difficult to get rid of & very distressing to have. Since the subsidence of the storm of last Tuesday the weather has moderated very much. The snow has entirely disappeared & the sun & wind has dried the ground amazingly. If Genl Hooker is going to do anything we shall hear from him soon. He is reported to be all ready & only waiting upon the weather. I wish I could say the same for ourselves. We are scattered, without forage & provisions, & could not remain long together if united for want of food. But God I hope will take care of us. I will see if I can spare Rob some socks & if so send them. Could I get into my trunks I know I could find him some, but those you allude to I fear he will scorn. I am glad to see he is making such advancements towards Miss N[orvell]. Present me kindly to all the family & tell Mr. C[askie] that I congratulate the city of Richmond at his retention as Alderman of Madison Ward. Give much love to Agnes & Precious Life when you write & believe me always

Affectly & truly yours

R. E. Lee

P.S. I send two pairs of socks, not on the grounds you put it, "if I wish to get rid of them," but on the principle that ought to actuate me, a willingness to share any thing with a friend in distress.

R. E. L.

394   TO HIS WIFE
                          "White House," Virginia

Near Fredericksburg
April 5, 1863

Genl Stuart brought me this morning your letter of yesterday dear Mary. I am much better I think, in fact when the weather becomes so that I can ride out, I shall get quite well again. I am suffering with a bad cold as I told you, & was threatened the doctors thought with some malady which must be dreadful if it resembles its name, but which I have forgotten. So they bundled me up on Monday last & brought me over to Mr. Yuby's where I have a comfortable room with Perry to attend to me. I have not been so very sick, though have suffered a good deal of pain in my chest, back, & arms. It came on in paroxysms, was quite sharp & seemed to me to be a mixture of your's & Agnes' diseases, from which I infer they are catching & that I fell a victim while in R[ichmond]. But they have passed off I hope, some fever remains, & I am enjoying the sensation of a complete saturation of my system with quinine. The doctors are very attentive & kind & have examined my lungs, my heart, circulation, &c. I believe they pronounce me tolerable sound. They have been tapping me all over like an old steam boiler before condemning it. I am about a mile from my camp & my handsome aids ride over with the papers after breakfast which I labour through by 3 p.m., when Mrs. Neal sends me some good soup or something else which is more to my taste than the doctors pills. I am in need of nothing. I have tea & sugar & all that I want. My brother officers too have been very kind. Some have sent me apples, some butter from the Valley, others turkey, tongue, hams, sweet potatoes, &c. So it seems to me I had better remain sick. But I should enjoy your company very much & should much prefer my little Agnes to Perry. I am not however altogether destitute. Mr. Yuby is very kind & is a perfect Sir Charles Grandison in manner. He has a married son living with him & the young wife of course has a baby. Then there is Mrs. Neal & a Capt & Mrs. McIntyre & their two daughters, relatives, refugees from Fredericksburg. The whole family came in one day to see me. The baby & black George besides. They expressed great sympathy for my condition, & Mrs. N[eal] thought she could make me a cotton shirt, that would extract all the pain out of me. But the doctor lacked confidence, & I was wanting in faith so the scheme fell through. Thank Mr. and Mrs. Caskie for their kind invitation. My thoughts have reverted very often to their pleasant house, & I have imagined how comfortable I should be in the sick room, with Miss Nannie & Norvell running in to enquire my wants. But then I thought they might not run in as often as they did when it was previously occupied, & that would be dreadfully mortifying. I shall therefore have to remain where I am as long as I can attend to my duty. When I cannot I must then give it up to others. But I think I shall be well soon & in the meantime must suffer, & I do not see how you can relieve me. Soldiers you know are born to suffer & they cannot escape it. I am still confined to my room. I am very glad to hear you are better, & trust you will go on to improve. We had a terrible snow storm last night which continued this morning. It caught Fitzhugh's brigade on the march, I fear, & I apprehend both men & horses suffered last night, as they were probably without tents, &c. I thought the late fine weather might bring Mr.

Hooker over, as he has been so anxious, but he stands fast yet awhile. I am glad Mary is well, but grieve for our poor people who have been so plundered. There is a just God in Heaven, who will make all things right in time. To Him we must trust & for that we must wait.

Remember me very kindly to all with you. Give much love to Agnes & believe me

Always yours

R. E. LEE

395   To GENERAL ARNOLD ELZEY
                    Commanding at Richmond, Virginia

Headquarters, Army of Northern Virginia
April 6, 1863

General:
Genl Longstreet contemplates a move across the Blackwater [River] and thinks he may require more infantry & artillery than he now has. In that event, can you spare him either Wise's brigade or your artillery battalion, armed as infantry, with a light battery or two? As he will be in front of Richmond, & as there are now no Federal troops on the James River except those in his front I think you could reinforce him with advantage. Please see the Secretary on the subject and communicate with Genl Longstreet.

I am with great respect, your obt servt

R. E. LEE
Genl

396   To JAMES A. SEDDON
                    Secretary of War

Headquarters, Army of Northern Virginia
April 9, 1863

Sir:
I have had the honor to receive your letter of the 6th instant. I do not know that I can add anything to what I have already said on the subject of reinforcing the Army of the West. If a division has been taken from Memphis to reinforce [General William S.] Rosecrans, it diminishes the force opposed to our troops in that quarter, & may enable them to

take the aggressive & to call them back. The enemy is reported to have abandoned his operations on the Tallahatchee River, which releases Genl [William W.] Loring's force also.

I have thought it probable that the enemy may have determined to confine for the present the operations of the Army of the Potomac & of his army south of James River, to the defensive, while with a portion of his troops from the east he should operate in Kentucky or elsewhere in the west. When the season shall suspend operations on the Mississippi, to return with an increased force to the east. There is, however, nothing as yet to indicate this determination except the transfer of Burnside's corps to Kentucky.

The most natural way to reinforce Genl [Joseph E.] Johnston would seem to be to transfer a portion of the troops from this department to oppose those sent west, but it is not as easy for us to change troops from one department to another as it is for the enemy, and if we rely on that method we may be always too late.

Should Genl Hooker's army assume the defensive, the readiest method of relieving the pressure upon Genl Johnston & Genl Beauregard would be for this army to cross into Maryland. This cannot be done, however, in the present condition of the roads, nor unless I can obtain a certain amount of provisions and suitable transportation. But this is what I would recommend if practicable.

Genl Longstreet is now engaged on an extended line, endeavoring to withdraw supplies from the invaded districts south of James River. He does not think that he has troops enough for the purpose, & has applied for more of his corps to be sent him, which I have not thought advisable to do. If any of his troops are taken from him, I fear it will arrest his operations & deprive us of the benefit anticipated from increasing the supplies of the army. I must therefore submit your proposition to the determination of yourself & the President. If you think it will be advisable at present to send a part of the troops operating in North Carolina to Genl Johnston, General Longstreet will designate such as ought to go.

If Genls [John] Pegram, [Humphrey] Marshall, & Sam Jones can by judicious operations occupy Genl Burnside in Kentucky, it will relieve Genl Johnston more than by sending their troops to him.

I have the honor to be with much respect, your obt servt

R. E. LEE
Genl

397   To MISS AGNES LEE
                        Richmond, Virginia

                                          Near Fredericksburg
                                          April 11, 1863

My precious little Agnes:

I was very glad to receive your note of the 5th & should have been
still more pleased to have seen you, had you & Custis come up as proposed. I could have given you better accommodation than I could in
camp, seeing that I have a large room with three beds in it. The smallest
I occupy, so that you & Custis could each have had a large high post
double bed, with canopy & valence [lace]. You would have slept magnificently, & I should have enjoyed "the balmy" by double proxy. For
you know what confidence I have in the powers of my children. You
would have soon made me well, for you could have taken all my pills,
&c., & kept the doctors off me. But when you come you must leave your
troops behind. I am too weak to stand the knocks & bruises they occasion.
My pins are remarkably unsteady at this time, & the vigour & violent
movements of young women might knock them from under me. But you
are such a little gad Agnes, always flitting about, how do you ever
expect to see me, or to be stationary anywhere? I do not see how you
can tear yourself from Miss Sallie. Still I am glad you can visit your
friends. Keep in the open air. Take all the exercise you can, & throw off
the neuralgia if possible. If you would ask Mrs. B[raxton] to give you
a hoe & let you go into the cornfield, she will be doing you a great
service, & you might make a few bushels of corn, & thereby benefit
your country. I am very glad to hear that Mrs. Tucker has been so kind
as to give you a balmoral. I hope it will be of great service to you & ward
off all harm until peace is restored when I hope I can have you with me
again. If you have an opportunity tell Miss Hattie Powell that I duly
received her pretty present, & acknowledged it at the earliest opportunity
& directed the letter according to her address. I am much better. I am
able to ride out every day, & now that the weather has become good, I
hope I shall recover my strength. My pulse is still about 90 the doctors
say, too quick for an old man, but I hope the fresh air & exercise will
reduce it soon. Mr. & Mrs. Gerby are very kind & their house is a fair
type of the Virginia mansion. There are two or three families residing
here at present & there are two young ladies in the establishment who
attract the beaux. I am very much in my room. Perry brings me my meals
so I am prevented from scaring off the young men & only show myself in
passing out & in the house. I am longing to get back to my camp but the

doctors prohibit it yet awhile. You know how pleased I am at the presence of strangers. What a cheerful mood their company produces. Imagine then the expression of my face & the merry times I have. Give much love to your mother, & remember me to all friends. If you get to Shirley tell Cousin N[annie] [Mrs. Sidney Smith Lee] I wish I could get there. I should soon be well.

Very truly your father

R. E. LEE

398   To HIS WIFE
                          Richmond, Virginia

Fredericksburg
April 12, 1863

My Dear Mary:
    I received your note of the 7th by Capt Caskie enclosing Mildred's. The report of her studies is very gratifying, & embraces a large area. I hope she may understand them all. But poor little Life's wardrobe seems to be very scant. What can be done for her? I have some socks & other garments with which I can supply her & can lend her a long pair of boots that cover up a great deal of space. She could hang over them some drapery which would make her comfortable. I think she will have to come up to the army where we are accustomed to short commons every way, & scant wardrobes are fashionable. She had better set to work I think & make something for I suppose that is the only way it can be obtained. I am much better, my cough is not annoying, pulse declining, & I am free of pain. I hope in a few days I shall be as well as ever, though that I fear will not be a very elevated standard. Still I am very thankful for the condition I have attained. I hope you are better & that you will be able to pay your visit to Hickory Hill, though I fear you are hardly in a condition to travel. We shall now have to leave those things to the young Mrs. Lee & you & I will have to find some spot, if that is possible, from which we shall only be required to make one more journey. The Reverend Mr. [B. Tucker] Lacy held service within about a mile of me to day, but I was unable to attend, fearing to stand out in the open air, though the day was mild & bright. I had my solitary prayers in my own room & enjoyed a sermon sent me from Hampden-Sydney College, preached by the Reverend Mr. [Robert Lewis] Dabney in commemoration of the death of Lt [A. C.] Carrington. It was a beautiful discourse, & the character he drew of Lt C[arrington] was delightful to see. He was killed in the battles around Richmond — Frazier's farm. How many

noble martyrs have laid down their lives on the altar of their country. I received a letter from Charlotte the other day & am glad to find she was so well & cheerful. She was so full of telling me of Fitzhugh, that she told me nothing of herself, or even where she was & where she was going to be. I cannot therefore write to her. I enclose a letter to Agnes, whom I suppose has gone to Mrs. Braxton's. You must keep it till her return. As to the gondolier coat, I do not know what to do with it. I cannot afford to carry about a coat to sleep in & another to wear. I have to make one do for both purposes. If you can find some one that is in actual need you had better give it to them. I hope Mr. Caskie will soon be able to take the field & perhaps it may suit his purposes. Spring seems at last to have opened upon us. The ground has dried amazingly. The grass is springing. I suppose I shall soon hear from Genl Hooker. Give much love to every body & believe me always yours

R. E. Lee

399   To GENERAL SAMUEL COOPER
Adjutant and Inspector General

Headquarters, Army of Northern Virginia
April 16, 1863

General:

I have had the honour to receive your letter of the 14th instant on the subject of reinforcing the army in middle Tennessee. I consider it of vital importance that we maintain our possession of the Mississippi River, to do which it will be necessary to hold Rosecrans' army in check. I regret to learn that it so much exceeds our army in strength. I have reflected with great anxiety upon the condition of affairs in that region, but can arrive at no satisfactory conclusion with regard to reinforcing the troops in that department. I believe the enemy in every department outnumbers us, and it is difficult to say from which troops can with safety be spared. If it is determined to be best that the army here should remain inactive, I doubt whether Genl Hooker will be quiescent. There is some movement in agitation now not yet developed. By the last reports he was drawing rations for ninety thousand men. This does not include the troops in front of Alexandria, or in and about Washington. Making a liberal deduction, I should think this would give from sixty-five to seventy thousand effectives. By the last returns, the effectives in this army, excluding Hood's & Pickett's divisions [with Longstreet], were thirty-eight thousand. A report from Genl Longstreet of the 13th instant states that Genl Hill had been ordered to reduce the force with which he was operating at Washington, North Carolina, to reinforce Genl Beauregard. If Pickett's division is withdrawn from him, I fear he will be unable to obtain the supplies we hoped to draw from the eastern portion of the department, which as far as I am able to judge, are essential for the support of the troops. I had expected to recall Genl Longstreet as soon as he had secured all the subsistence which could be obtained in that region, to hold Genl Hooker in check, while Milroy could be driven out of the Valley. If however it is decided that it will be more advantageous to reinforce Genl Johnston, these operations will have to be arrested. The repulse of the enemy's iron clads at Charleston may have the effect of deranging his projected plans of attack, and he can accomplish nothing in the interior after May. If such be the case troops might be spared from that department to Genl Johnston. But I think his great reliance is to concentrate the troops in his own department and use them where they can be most effectively employed. The troops in the vicinity of Charleston, Savannah, Mobile, & Vicksburg will not be called in requisition at these places, and no more will be necessary than to man the batteries. If the statements which I see in the papers are true, Genl Grant is withdrawing from Vicksburg, and will hardly return to his former position there this summer. The President from his position, being able to survey all the scenes of action, can better decide than any one else, and I recommend that he follow the dictates of his good judgment. I am anxious for nothing but our success, and will cheerfully concur in any arrangement which may be decided on.

I am with great respect, your obt servt

R. E. LEE
Genl

400 To JEFFERSON DAVIS
Richmond, Virginia

Headquarters, Army of Northern Virginia
April 16, 1863

Mr. President:
Information derived from our scouts has shown that a movement on the part of the enemy's cavalry was in contemplation. They have been kept massed and rationed for several days past. On Monday evening they were seen moving up the Rappahannock, and on Tuesday morning they appeared at Kelly's Ford with an intention to cross. They were

however repulsed by our dismounted skirmishers, but forced a passage at the Rappahannock Bridge where they were soon driven back. From information which I received I was led to believe that their destination was the Shenandoah Valley. Genl Stuart was apprised of this suspected movement and Genl W. E. Jones was placed upon his guard. The last despatches from Genl Stuart dated yesterday report the enemy's cavalry north of the Rappahannock, massed opposite Kelly's, Rappahannock Bridge and Beverly Fords. Prisoners report they were rationed for eight days. The cavalry were accompanied by artillery and wagons. Genl Stuart thinks the movement a feint to cover other operations. He can learn of no force moving towards the Blue Ridge, but thinks from the reports of his scouts that Genl Hooker intends to transfer his army to the White House on the Pamunkey or to the south side of James River. My own impression has been that the movement was intended to draw us to the upper Rappahannock that Fredericksburg might be seized and the bridges across the river rebuilt. I do not think that Genl Hooker will venture to uncover Washington by transferring his army to James River unless the force in front of Alexandria is greater than I suppose, or unless he believes this army incapable of advancing to the Potomac. My only anxiety arises from the present immobility of the army, owing to the condition of our horses and the scarcity of forage and provisions. I think it all important that we should assume the aggressive by the first of May, when we may expect Genl Hooker's army to be weakened by the expiration of the term of service of many of his regiments, and before new recruits can be received. If we could be placed in a condition to make a vigorous advance at that time I think the Valley could be swept of Milroy and the army opposite me be thrown north of the Potomac. I believe greater relief would in this way be afforded to the armies in middle Tennessee and on the Carolina coast than by any other method. I had hoped by Genl Longstreet's operations in North Carolina to obtain sufficient subsistence to commence the movement, and by the operations in north west Virginia to continue the supplies. It must depend therefore upon the success of these operations unless other means can be devised for procuring subsistence. I therefore submit the matter to Your Excellency for consideration in the hope that some plan may be formed to attain this object. At present we are very much scattered and I am unable to bring the army together for want of proper subsistence & forage.

I am with great respect, your obt servt

R. E. LEE
Genl

P.S. — A despatch from Genl Stuart dated 9 p.m. yesterday, just received, states that the heavy rains and swollen streams have entirely arrested military operations on the upper Rappahannock. The contest terminated yesterday with the capture of about forty of the enemy's cavalry at Beverly's Ford. Several were killed and drowned in crossing the river. Our loss, one killed & four wounded. Genl Wm. H. F. Lee's brigade was engaged, two regiments being absent. Genl Fitz Lee's brigade was held at Amissville.

R. E. L.

401   To GENERAL JAMES LONGSTREET
Commanding near Suffolk

Headquarters, Army of Northern Virginia
April 17, 1863

General:
Your letter of the 13th has been received. I am glad that you are steadily progressing in your operations. I wish I could give you any aid, but I feel every confidence that you will do all that can be done. I wrote to Richmond to ask assistance for you, from the Navy if possible. I have had no reply. Should you know of any assistance which could be given, you had better write direct to Richmond for it and state that it is at my request. The enemy's cavalry are again on our left. They presented themselves Tuesday evening at Kelly's Ford, Rappahannock Bridge, & Beverly's Ford in large force. Their attempts to cross the river have been so far repulsed. Stuart thinks the movement is intended to cover a change of base or some other operation of the grand army. Nothing however has been ascertained. Yesterday three gunboats appeared in the Rappahannock below Port Royal, and are reported to be ascending the river. Their character, description, and intentions are not yet known.

I am very respectfully & truly yours

R. E. Lee
Genl

402   To GENERAL WILLIAM E. JONES
                    Commanding Valley District

                              Headquarters, Army of Northern Virginia
                                              April 18, 1863

Sir:
    I wish you to keep General J. E. B. Stuart informed of all move-
ments of importance of the enemy in the Valley, while he is operating
on your right flank. He is now near Culpeper Court House.

                    Very respectfully, your obedient servant

                                              R. E. Lee
                                              General

403   To HIS WIFE
                        "Shirley," Virginia

                                          Camp, Fredericksburg
                                              April 19, 1863

    I received dear Mary your letter of the 15th contained in the box
sent by Col Corley & a subsequent letter from you without date reached
me to day enveloped in the *Churchman*. I am very glad to hear you are
better & hope your visit to Shirley may restore you. I am very much
obliged to you for the contents of the box. You must thank Mrs. Caskie,
Mrs. Booker & dear Cousin Anne for their contributions to my comfort.
They are very nice & I believe I enjoy the thought of their kindness
even more than the good things they have sent. The jars I fear will be
irrevocably lost, as it will be almost impossible to send them back. But I
will try. Tell Miss Norvell & Sallie that I was afraid they would be so
absorbed in their beaux that I should never get a sight of them, which
would be so mortifying as to increase my disease & that I had better
keep at a distance. The sight of them would have been very cheering to
me I confess, but they are no longer school girls, & I cannot impose on
them any more. Tell Miss Nannie she will have to suffer. I am sorry Mr.
Caskie thinks I was jesting at his debility. I was hoping he would become stronger & was thinking of adding to his protection. The war will
terminate some of these days & we shall all then be at peace. I send you a
letter from Mrs. Coderise. Bev[erly Coderise?] is a fine boy & I wish I
could do something for him. His mother has tried before to get him out
of the service in various ways, but he has so far remained firm. If you
see him tell him to write to me & say what I can do for him. I do not

think our enemies are so confident of success as they used to be. If we
can baffle them in their various designs this year & our people are true
to our cause & not so devoted to themselves & their own aggrandisement,
I think our success will be certain. We will have to suffer & must suffer
to the end. But it will all come right. This year I hope will establish our
supplies on a firm basis. On every other point we are strong. If successful this year, next fall there will be a great change in public opinion at
the North. The Republicans will be destroyed & I think the friends of
peace will become so strong as that the next administration will go in on
that basis. We have only therefore to resist manfully. I think you had
better not answer Mrs. C[oderise]. Do what you can for Bev, but be
silent. You see their feelings & temper. I am better & returned to my
camp three days since. I am feeble & worthless & can do but little. Kiss
Chass & Agnes for me. Tell the former F[itzhugh] is working hard & is
doing nobly. Kind love to all.

Very truly & affly

R. E. LEE

P.S. You appear to forget that the *Churchman* is sent me regularly
by the Publisher. One number is as much as I can dispose of. Love to
Smith, Nannie & all at Shirley.

R. E. L.

404   To GENERAL THOMAS J. JACKSON
Commanding Right Wing

Headquarters, Army of Northern Virginia
April 23, 1863

General:
I have received General [Raleigh E.] Colston's letter of 8.30 o'clock
today which you forwarded to me. I think from the account given me
by Lieutenant Colonel [W. Proctor] Smith of the Engineers, who was at
Port Royal yesterday, of the enemy's operations there the day and night
previous, that his present purpose is to draw our troops in that direction,
while he attempts a passage elsewhere. I would not then send down more
troops than are actually necessary. I will notify General [Lafayette]
McLaws and [Richard H.] Anderson to be on the alert for I think that if
a real attempt is made to cross the river it will be above Fredericksburg.

Very respectfully

R. E. LEE
General

405   To JAMES A. SEDDON
                                Secretary of War

                                    Headquarters, Army of Northern Virginia
                                                    April 24, 1863
Sir:
    The enemy on crossing over to Port Royal as reported to you
yesterday, remained in the village long enough to take from the inhabitants what they could get, consisting of horses, mules, &c., & recrossed before our troops could reach them.

                            I am very respectfully, your obt servt

                                                    R. E. LEE
                                                    Genl

406   To HIS WIFE
                                Richmond, Virginia

                                            Camp, Fredericksburg
                                                    April 24, 1863

    I have received dear Mary your's & Agnes' joint letter of the 21st.
I hope you were enabled to get to Shirley as I am sure you will derive
benefit as well as pleasure from the pure air & sweet society you will
find there. I hope too that Chass & Agnes will receive equal benefit from
rural scenes & rural friends. As usual I have nothing to relate. The
weather has been very changeable & unpleasant. The health of the army
is pretty good & my own health is improving. The enemy is making
various demonstrations either to amuse themselves or deceive us, but so
far they have done us little harm. Last week they infested all the fords
on the upper Rappahannock as far as Warrenton Springs. Tuesday they
abandoned them. Sent down the river their infantry & artillery & with
their cavalry swept around by Warrenton towards the Blue Ridge as if
intending to visit the Valley. Day before yesterday they made their appearance on the lower Rappahannock. Formed in line of battle, threw
out skirmishers, advanced their artillery, brought up their wagons,
built up large fires, & after dark commenced chopping, cutting, & sawing
as if working for life till midnight, when the noise ceased & at day light
all had disappeared but 8 or 10 men keeping up the fires. I suppose they
thought we were frightened out of all propriety & required refreshment.

Yesterday morning at daylight a party crossed at Port Royal in their pontoon boats, stole from our citizens all they could get and recrossed before we could get to them. Their expeditions will serve for texts to the writers for the *Herald, Tribune* & *Times* for brilliant accounts of grand Union victories & great rejoicings of the saints of the party. I hope God in His own time will give us more substantial cause for rejoicing & thankfulness. Liberty is in a healthy & beautiful section of country. I have passed through it, but cannot distinguish it in my memory from other villages on the route. The only objection I know to it is its being directly on the railroad & subject to all the false & exciting rumours floating through the country & borne on the thousand tongues of passengers. But it is in the vicinity of Fincastle & I have no doubt quiet farm houses can be found in the neighborhood. You must let me know what funds you require & where I must send them. Tell Chass & Agnes I send them a great deal of love, but cannot write to them now. Indeed I can write to no one & feel oppressed by what I have to undergo for the first time in my life. Mr. Carole has made his appearance. But I doubt whether he can accomplish anything. It has been raining ever since his arrival. My portrait I think can give pleasure to no one, & should it resemble the original would not be worth having. Get the portraits of the young, the happy, the gay. Take Miss Hettie & her lover for instance. F[itzhugh] & R[obert] were well when last heard from. They are on the upper Rappahannock. Love to all at Shirley.

Mrs. Hattie Harrison has been recently to Baltimore, said Anne was fatter & looking younger than when she last saw her. I heard yesterday of Mrs. Knapp & Selden in Middleburg. All well. I regret very much to hear that the President continues unwell.

Truly & affly yours

R. E. Lee

407   To GENERAL JAMES LONGSTREET
            Commanding near Suffolk

Headquarters, Army of Northern Virginia
April 27, 1863

General:

I received last night a dispatch from Major [William] Norris, Chief of Signal Corps in Richmond, stating that a special scout to Washington City had returned Saturday night. After giving the strength of Genl Hooker's army, which he had put down very heavy, between 150 & 160,000, and that he had been reinforced from Baltimore, Washington,

Alexandria, and Harper's Ferry; he says that ten or twelve thousand men had been sent to Suffolk which were not taken from Hooker's army. Although I think his statement very much exaggerated, yet all accounts agree that Hooker has been reinforced, and that troops from the rear have been brought forward to the Rappahannock. This looks as if he intended to make an aggressive movement, but by what route I cannot ascertain. A despatch from Stuart of the 26th, received last night, states that Stoneman is in force in the neighborhood of Warrenton. That a brigade of infantry is guarding the Rappahannock Bridge and the fords each side; that the trains are running regularly over the Orange & Alexandria Railroad to Bealeton, but that he does not learn that they bring up any troops.

I am glad to learn by your letter received yesterday by special courier that you are getting everything out of North Carolina as rapidly as possible. Can you give me any idea when your operations will be completed and whether any of the troops you have in Carolina can be spared from there? As regards your aggressive movement upon Suffolk, you must act according to your good judgment. If a damaging blow could be struck there or elsewhere of course it would be advantageous, but if the place was taken I doubt whether we could spare a garrison to hold it, and storming of his works might cost us very dear.

I am very respectfully, yours

R. E. LEE
Genl

P.S. Is not the Eighth Corps, which you mention in your front, [General Erasmus D.] Keyes', from Yorktown?

R. E. LEE

408   To GENERAL SAMUEL COOPER
Adjutant and Inspector General
TELEGRAM

Fredericksburg, Virginia
April 29, 1863

THE ENEMY IS IN LARGE FORCE ON NORTH BANK OF RAPPAHANNOCK OPPOSITE THE RAILROAD AT HAMILTON'S CROSSING. HE IS CROSSING TROOPS BELOW THE POINT AT WHICH HE CROSSED IN DECEMBER AND EXTENDS LOWER DOWN THE RIVER. I HAVE DISCOVERED NOTHING LOWER THAN THE MOUTH OF MASSAPONAX CREEK. HE IS CERTAINLY CROSSING IN LARGE FORCE HERE, AND IT LOOKS AS IF HE WAS IN EARNEST. I HEAR OF NO OTHER POINT AT WHICH HE

IS CROSSING EXCEPT BELOW KELLY'S FORD, WHERE GENL [OLIVER O.] HOWARD HAS CROSSED WITH HIS DIVISION, SAID TO BE 14,000, SIX PIECES OF ARTILLERY, AND SOME CAVALRY. STONEMAN WILL PROBABLY CROSS ABOUT THE WARRENTON SPRINGS, AND I FEAR WILL MAKE FOR GORDONSVILLE AND MAY DESTROY OUR ROADS. I HAVE NOTHING TO OPPOSE TO ALL THAT FORCE UP THERE EXCEPT THE TWO BRIGADES OF CAVALRY UNDER GENL STUART. ALL AVAILABLE TROOPS HAD BETTER BE SENT FORWARD AS RAPIDLY AS POSSIBLE BY RAIL AND OTHERWISE.

R. E. LEE

409   To JEFFERSON DAVIS
                Richmond, Virginia
                   TELEGRAM

Fredericksburg
April 29, 1863

HIS EXCELLENCY JEFFERSON DAVIS:

THE ENEMY CROSSED THE RAPPAHANNOCK TODAY IN LARGE NUMBERS & HAVE TAKEN POSITION UNDER THE BANK OF THE RIVER, UNDER COVER OF THEIR HEAVY GUNS ON THE OPPOSITE SIDE. THE DAY HAS BEEN FAVORABLE FOR HIS OPERATIONS, & TONIGHT HE WILL PROBABLY GET OVER THE REMAINDER OF HIS FORCES. BESIDES THE FORCE WHICH WAS REPORTED BY GENL STUART TO HAVE CROSSED ON THE PONTOON BRIDGES LAID BELOW KELLY'S FORD, I HAVE LEARNED THIS EVENING BY COURIERS FROM GERMANNA & ELY'S FORDS THAT THE ENEMY'S CAVALRY CROSSED THE RAPIDAN AT THOSE POINTS ABOUT TWO (2) P.M. TODAY. I COULD NOT LEARN THEIR STRENGTH, BUT INFANTRY WAS SAID TO HAVE CROSSED WITH THE CAVALRY AT THE FORMER POINT. THEIR INTENTION I PRESUME IS TO TURN OUR LEFT & PROBABLY TO GET INTO OUR REAR. OUR SCATTERED CONDITION FAVORS THEIR OPERATIONS. I HOPE IF ANY REINFORCEMENTS CAN BE SENT THEY MAY BE FORWARDED IMMEDIATELY. THE BRIDGES OVER THE ANNAS OUGHT TO BE GUARDED, IF POSSIBLE.

R. E. LEE

410   To GENERAL SAMUEL COOPER
              Adjutant and Inspector General
                   TELEGRAM

[Fredericksburg]
[April 29, 1863]

THE ENEMY IS CROSSING BELOW DEEP RUN ABOUT THE SAME PLACE AS BEFORE. THE FOG HAS BEEN SO THICK DURING THE NIGHT AND MORNING THAT

WE CAN ONLY SEE A FEW YARDS. TAKEN WITH THE REPORTS RECEIVED FROM
OUR LEFT IT LOOKS LIKE A GENERAL ADVANCE, BUT WHERE HIS MAIN EFFORT
WILL BE MADE CANNOT SAY. TROOPS NOT WANTED SOUTH OF JAMES RIVER
HAD BETTER BE MOVED IN THIS DIRECTION AND ALL OTHER NECESSARY PREPA-
RATIONS MADE.

R. E. LEE

411   To JEFFERSON DAVIS
                  Richmond, Virginia
                      TELEGRAM

                                        Fredericksburg
                                        April 29, 1863

TO HIS EXCELLENCY JEFF DAVIS:

   IF ANY TROOPS CAN BE SENT BY RAIL TO GORDONSVILLE UNDER A GOOD
OFFICER I RECOMMEND IT. LONGSTREET'S DIVISION, IF AVAILABLE, HAD BETTER
COME TO ME, AND THE TROOPS FOR GORDONSVILLE AND PROTECTION OF RAIL-
ROAD FROM RICHMOND AND NORTH CAROLINA, IF PRACTICABLE. GENL HOWARD
HAS SIX (6) BATTERIES WITH HIM. PLEASE ORDER THE FORWARDING OF OUR
SUPPLIES.

R. E. LEE

412   MAJOR CHARLES MARSHALL TO COLONEL
                  JOHN CRITCHER
          Commanding Fifteenth Virginia Regiment

                          Headquarters, Army of Northern Virginia
                                        April 29, 1863
Colonel:
    General Jackson's troops have been withdrawn from the vicinity of
Port Royal and will join the army near Fredericksburg. General Lee
directs me to say that he desires you to move up at the same time with
the other troops and take position on our right, leaving some vedettes to
watch the river between here and report any movements they may observe.

            Respectfully, your obedient servant

                          CHARLES MARSHALL
                          Major and Aide-de-Camp

413   To GENERAL LAFAYETTE McLAWS
                    Commanding Division

                              Headquarters, Army of Northern Virginia
                                                    April 29, 1863
                                                         6½ P.M.
General:

As arranged today, I wish you to draw your troops out of Fredericksburg, leaving your sharpshooters, and take a position in the rifle pits, so as to maintain the heights back of the town as in December. Extend your right to Deep Run, and the troops not necessary on the front hold in reserve to throw where they may be required. You should have all your men in position by daylight in the morning, with rations for the day.

Caution your officers to be vigilant & energetic; repair your line of defenses when you may find it necessary, & pay every attention to the comfort of your men & the support of your horses. Communicate to General Jackson & Genl Anderson all movements of the enemy affecting them, and, if they ask for reinforcements, furnish what you can. I have just heard that the enemy's cavalry, accompanied by infantry, has crossed at Germanna Ford (the Rapidan).

                    I am very respectfully, your obt servt

                                             R. E. LEE
                                                Genl

P.S. I have just heard that a regiment of cavalry crossed at Ely's Ford. We may be obliged to change our position in consequence of the enemy's having come in between us & Genl Stuart. Make your preparatory arrangements tonight to secure all your property. Leave no more sharpshooters on the river & in Fredericksburg than are absolutely necessary, so as to have as strong a force as possible to strengthen our left.

                                             R. E. L.

414   To GENERAL RICHARD H. ANDERSON
Commanding Division

Headquarters, Army of Northern Virginia
April 29, 1863
6-3/4 P.M.

General:

I have just heard that a portion of the enemy's cavalry accompanied by infantry, crossed the Rapidan at Germanna Ford about 1 o'clock. Draw in your brigades at U. S. Ford, & throw your left back so as to cover the road leading from Chancellorsville down the river, taking the strongest line you can, & holding it to the best advantage. I wish you to go forward yourself & attend to this matter. Let me know where communications will reach you, & inform me of the condition of things. See if you can find where Col [J. L.] Davis' cavalry is, & collect all the mounted men which you can in your front. See to the provisions & forage of your men & animals.

Very respectfully, your obt servt

R. E. LEE
Genl

P.S. I have just heard that a regiment of cavalry crossed at Ely's Ford. We may be obliged to change our position in consequence of the enemy having come in between us and Genl Stuart. Make your preparatory arrangements tonight to secure all your property. Leave no more sharpshooters on the river than are absolutely necessary, so as to have as strong a force as possible to strengthen our left.

R. E. L.

415   To JEFFERSON DAVIS
Richmond, Virginia
TELEGRAM

Fredericksburg
April 30, 1863

HIS EXCELLENCY PRESIDENT DAVIS:

DISPATCH OF 11.30 P.M. YESTERDAY RECEIVED. GENL STUART IS SUPPOSED TO HAVE CROSSED RAPIDAN LAST NIGHT TO INTERRUPT ENEMY'S COLUMN AT

GERMANNA. HE CUT IT IN THE AFTERNOON NEAR MADDEN'S, NORTH OF RAP-
IDAN. HE CAPTURED PRISONERS FROM 5TH, 11TH & 12TH CORPS. ENEMY WAS
STILL CROSSING THE RAPPAHANNOCK AT 5 P.M. YESTERDAY. WAGONS, BEEF
CATTLE STILL ON NORTH SIDE. [GENERALS GEORGE G.] MEADE, [HENRY W.]
SLOCUM, AND [OLIVER O.] HOWARD COMMANDED CORPS. OBJECT EVIDENTLY
TO TURN OUR LEFT. IF HAD LONGSTREET'S DIVISION, WOULD FEEL SAFE.

R. E. LEE

416   To GENERAL RICHARD H. ANDERSON
          Commanding Division, Tabernacle Church

Headquarters, Army of Northern Virginia
April 30, 1863
2 ½ P.M.

General:

I have received your note of this morning. I will write to Genl
McLaws in relation to [General Paul J.] Semmes' brigade. I hope you
have been able to select a good line and can fortify it strongly. At what
point will your right rest? Will it include Wilcox's position, and can you
draw him on the line? Set all your spades to work as vigorously as possible. I hope to send you additional troops if I can learn in time; so hold
your position firmly, and prepare your line for them. Send me word this
evening what additional guns you will require to those you have. Keep
two days' rations cooked that the men can carry on their persons, and
give orders that everything be prepared to pack your trains and move off
at any moment when ordered. All your baggage, camp equipage, including your headquarters, &c., must be immediately reduced in order to
accomplish this. General Stuart writes that the 3rd Virginia Cavalry, Col
[Thomas H.] Owen, and 2d North Carolina, Col [W. H.] Payne [of the
Fourth Virginia Cavalry, temporarily in command], have been ordered
to report to me. They are probably on the Plank road. Direct them to
keep in your front and keep you advised of all movements of the enemy,
and to delay his progress as much as possible.

I am very respectfully, your obt servt

R. E. LEE
Genl

417   SPECIAL ORDERS, NO. 121

Headquarters, Army of Northern Virginia
April 30, 1863

I.   Maj Genl McLaws will designate a brigade of his division to hold the lines in rear of Fredericksburg, the commander of which will report to the Maj Genl left in charge. With the rest of his division, Genl McLaws will move as soon as possible to reinforce Genl Anderson at the Tabernacle Church, on the Plank road to Orange Court House.

II.   General Jackson will designate a division to hold the lines in front of the enemy on Pratt's and Bernard's farms. The commander of the division will establish such pickets as may be necessary. With the remainder of his corps Genl Jackson at daylight tomorrow morning will proceed to Tabernacle Church and make arrangements to repulse the enemy.

III.   The troops will be provided with two days' cooked provisions. The trains of all the divisions will be packed with all their equipage, and move to the rear under the direction of the Chief Quartermaster of the Army. The reserve ammunition trains will be under the charge of the Chief of Ordnance. The regimental ordnance wagons, ambulances, and medical wagons will accompany the troops.

IV.   The Chief of Artillery will superintend the service of the batteries in position on the lines and take charge of those not required to operate with the troops.

By command of General R. E. Lee:

W. H. TAYLOR
A. A. General

418   To GENERAL LAFAYETTE McLAWS
Commanding Division

Headquarters, Army of Northern Virginia
April 30, 1863

General:
Major Taylor has returned and says you want positive orders as to who is to relieve your pickets. In my previous note, I intended you to leave one of your brigades to report to Genl Early, the commander of which would arrange with him how to dispose of the pickets. I suggested Genl Barksdale as the officer to be left, believing from his quali-

fications and knowledge that he would be able to render valuable service, and that by his remaining, the trouble of withdrawing pickets from the front would be diminished. You can designate any brigade to remain that you think best, and I wish you to direct the commanding officer to report to Genl Early at once that he may receive directions as to the disposition of the pickets to be established. Withdraw the pickets of the brigades that go with you as soon as they are relieved, and get the brigades in motion as soon as possible. Take with you your regimental ordnance wagons, the reserve ordnance can be sent to the rear, and parked where you can call upon it tomorrow night if necessary. Col [Briscoe G.] Baldwin will have charge of all the ordnance trains not with the troops, and the officer in charge of your reserve train will report to him.

From the report of Col [William P.] Smith of the Engineers just from Genl Anderson's position, the country appears to be unfavorable for the use of artillery, and Col Smith thinks that there is as much artillery there now as is necessary. I would not therefore take all your artillery. Select therefore your best guns & horses. The rest may be either left in position or sent back to Massaponax Church to report to Genl Pendleton.

I am with great respect, your obt servt

R. E. LEE
Genl

P.S. I think there is a mistake in the report of your courier of the enemy having the intersection of the Mine road & Plank roads, for that is just where Genl Anderson is, according to my understanding. When Major Talcott left at 6½ p.m. he came by the Mine road. The intersection was then held by Genl Anderson, and the enemy that appeared in his front, had been driven back by his artillery.

R. E. L.

419   To GENERAL THOMAS J. JACKSON
Commanding Division

Headquarters, Army of Northern Virginia
April 30, 1863

General:

Genl [Paul J.] Semmes reached Genl Anderson about 7 this evening. The 3rd Virginia Cavalry has also joined him. I expect Genl Stuart from a dispatch dated 4 p.m. will be on his left by morning. Genl

Anderson now thinks that it was dismounted cavalry that moved against his front line. Genl McLaws I hope will get two other of his brigades in motion by 1 a.m. to join Genl Anderson. He is in some difficulty about who is to relieve his pickets. Will you instruct Genl Early to attend to it.

Lt Col Smith, Engineers, who returned this evening from Genl Anderson's position, reports the country unfavorable for the use of artillery, and thinks that Alexander's battalion with the batteries attached to Anderson's division sufficient. I would not therefore encumber myself with artillery, but would take the best guns and horses. Use, however, your judgment.

Very respectfully, your obt servt

R. E. LEE
Genl

420   WAR DEPARTMENT
TELEGRAM

Headquarters, Fredericksburg
[April 30, 1863]
12 o'clock

LEARNING YESTERDAY AFTERNOON THAT THE ENEMY'S RIGHT WING HAD CROSSED THE RAPIDAN, AND ITS HEAD HAD REACHED THE POSITION ASSUMED ON OUR EXTREME LEFT TO ARREST THEIR PROGRESS, I DETERMINED TO HOLD OUR LINES IN REAR OF FREDERICKSBURG WITH PART OF THE FORCE AND ENDEAVOR WITH THE REST TO DRIVE THE ENEMY BACK TO THE RAPIDAN. TROOPS WERE PUT IN MOTION LAST NIGHT AND WILL SOON BE IN POSITION.

I HEAR NOTHING OF THE EXPECTED REINFORCEMENTS.

R. E. LEE
Genl

421   To GENERAL J. E. B. STUART
Commanding Cavalry

Plank Road, 2 Miles from Chancellorsville
May 1, 1863
4 o'clock

General:

The captured prisoners agree in stating that this is Meade's corps with which we are now engaged, and that Howard's corps preceded them across the Rapidan, and has taken some other road. This is the only column that we can find in this direction. What has become of the other two?

Meade appears to be falling back.

I am very respectfully yours, &c.

R. E. LEE
General

422   To JEFFERSON DAVIS
Richmond, Virginia

Headquarters, Near Chancellorsville, Virginia
May 2, 1863

Mr. President:

I find the enemy in a strong position at Chancellorsville and in large force; his communications extend to the Rapidan at Germanna and Ely's Fords, and to the Rappahannock at U. S. Mine Ford. He seems determined to make the fight here, and from what I learn from Genl Early, has sent up troops from his position opposite Fredericksburg. Anticipating such a movement on his part, I directed General Early last evening, if it occurred, to leave a guard at his position, and join me with the rest of the forces. I have repeated the orders this morning. It is plain that if the enemy is too strong for me here I shall have to fall back and Fredericksburg must be abandoned. If successful here Fredericksburg will be saved and our communications retained. I may be forced back to the Orange and Alexandria or the Virginia Central road, but in either case I will be in position to contest the enemy's advance upon Richmond. I have no expectation that any reinforcements from Longstreet or North Carolina will join me in time to aid in the contest at this point, but they may be in time for a subsequent occasion. We succeeded yesterday in driving the enemy from in front of our position at Tabernacle Church, on all the roads back to Chancellorsville, where he concentrated in a position remarkably favorable for him. We were unable last evening to dislodge him. I am now swinging around to my left to come up in his rear. I learn from prisoners taken that [General Samuel P.] Heintzelman's troops from Washington are here, and the enemy seems to have concentrated his strength for this effort. If I had with me all my command, and could keep it supplied with provisions and forage, I should feel easy, but as far as I can judge, the advantage of numbers and position is greatly in favor of the enemy.

I have received a despatch from General Imboden dated 28th April. On the 26th he had penetrated the country midway between Philippi and Buckhannon. Genl [James A.] Mulligan who occupied Philippi, and Genl [Benjamin S.] Roberts who occupied Buckhannon, both fled, burning their stores. I have had no report from Genl W. E. Jones, but Genl Imboden states upon reliable authority that he has been entirely successful in destroying the railroad as far as Rowlesburg. General Imboden was to advance on the day of his report to Grafton and Clarksburg, of both of which he hoped to be in possession within three days. His horses have been much reduced by hard work, bad roads, and scant forage. His men are in excellent condition.

Very respectfully, your obt servt

R. E. LEE
Genl

423   To GENERAL J. E. B. STUART
Commanding Left Wing

May 3, 1863
3 A.M.

General:

It is necessary that the glorious victory thus far achieved be prosecuted with the utmost vigor and the enemy given no time to rally. As soon therefore as it is possible they must be pressed, so that we can unite the two wings of the army.

Endeavor therefore to dispossess them of Chancellorsville, which will permit the union of the whole army.

I shall myself proceed to join you as soon as I can make arrangements on this side, but let nothing delay the completion of the plan of driving the enemy from his rear and from his positions.

I shall give orders that every effort be made on this side at daylight to aid in the junction.

Very respectfully

R. E. LEE
General

424   To GENERAL J. E. B. STUART
Commanding Left Wing

May 3, 1863
3.30 A.M.

General:

I repeat what I have said half an hour since. It is all-important that you still continue pressing to the right, turning if possible all the fortified points in order that we can unite both wings of the army. Keep the troops well together and press on, on the general plan, which is to work by the right wing, turning the positions of the enemy so as to drive him from Chancellorsville, which will again unite us. Everything will be done on this side to accomplish the same object. Try and keep the troops provisioned and together, and proceed vigorously.

Very respectfully

R. E. LEE
General

425   To JEFFERSON DAVIS
Richmond, Virginia
TELEGRAM

Milford
May 3, 1863

YESTERDAY GENL JACKSON WITH THREE (3) OF HIS DIVISIONS PENE-
TRATED TO THE REAR OF THE ENEMY & DROVE HIM FROM ALL HIS POSITIONS
FROM THE WILDERNESS TO WITHIN ONE (1) MILE OF CHANCELLORSVILLE. HE
WAS ENGAGED AT THE SAME TIME IN FRONT BY TWO (2) OF LONGSTREET'S
DIVISIONS. THIS MORNING THE BATTLE WAS RENEWED. HE WAS DISLODGED
FROM ALL HIS POSITIONS AROUND CHANCELLORSVILLE & DRIVEN BACK TOWARDS
THE RAPPAHANNOCK, OVER WHICH HE IS NOW RETREATING. MANY PRISONERS
WERE TAKEN, & THE ENEMY'S LOSS KILLED & WOUNDED LARGE. WE HAVE
AGAIN TO THANK ALMIGHTY GOD FOR A GREAT VICTORY. I REGRET TO STATE
THAT GENL [ELISHA F.] PAXTON WAS KILLED. GENL JACKSON SEVERELY AND
GENERALS HETH, A. P. HILL SLIGHTLY WOUNDED.

R. E. LEE
Genl

426   To GENERAL THOMAS J. JACKSON
Field Hospital near Old Wilderness Tavern

Chancellorsville
May 4 [3]

General:
    I have just received your note informing me that you were wounded.
I cannot express my regret at the occurrence. Could I have directed

events, I should have chosen for the good of the country to have been disabled in your stead.

I congratulate you upon the victory which is due to your skill and energy.

Most truly yours

R. E. LEE
Genl

427   To JAMES A. SEDDON
Secretary of War
TELEGRAM

Milford
May 3, 1863

I REQUEST THAT [GENERALS ROBERT] RANSOM'S AND [JAMES J.] PETTI-GREW'S BRIGADES BE STOPPED AT HANOVER JUNCTION WITH ORDERS TO PROTECT THE RAILROADS FROM THE ENEMY'S CAVALRY. IT IS REPORTED THAT THE ENEMY HAS CROSSED AT FREDERICKSBURG AND DRIVEN BACK OUR FORCE THAT WAS LEFT THERE. I HAVE SENT BACK REINFORCEMENTS.

R. E. LEE
Genl Comdg

428   To GENERAL JUBAL A. EARLY
Commanding Division, near Fredericksburg

Headquarters, Battle Field
May 3, 1863
7 P.M.

General:

I have received your note of this date. I very much regret the possession of Fredericksburg by the enemy. I heard today of their taking the hills in rear of the city, and sent down General McLaws with two brigades of Anderson's division and three of his own to unite with the forces under you and endeavor to drive them back. I heard this afternoon that he had halted at Tabernacle Church, on hearing that the enemy was advancing up the Plank road. I hear firing in that direction at this time and presume that an engagement is going on. If they are attacking him there, and you could come upon their left flank, and communicate with Genl McLaws, I think you would demolish them. See if you cannot unite with him and together destroy him. With his five brigades, and you with your division and the remnant of Barksdale's brigade, I think you ought to be more than a match for the enemy.

Respectfully, &c.

R. E. LEE
Genl

P.S. I understand Genl Wilcox is with him also.

R. E. L.

429   To GENERAL LAFAYETTE McLAWS
                    Tabernacle Church

[May 3, 1863]
7 P.M.

General:
   I presume from the firing which I hear in your direction that you are engaged with the enemy. Upon the receipt of your note, I sent Col Alexander with his battalion of artillery to report to you. I hope he reached you in time. I have just written to Early, who informs me that he is on the Telegraph road, near Mrs. Smith's house, to endeavor to unite with you to attack the enemy on their left flank. Communicate with him, & arrange the junction, if necessary & practicable. It is necessary that you beat the enemy, & I hope you will do it.

Very resply

R. E. LEE
Genl

430   To GENERAL LAFAYETTE McLAWS
                    Tabernacle Church

Downman's House
May 4, [1863]
10 P.M.

General:
   Genls Anderson & Early drove the enemy handsomely from the positions on Downman's Hill beyond the Plank road. General Anderson's

left is now on Plank road opposite to Mr. Guest's house, & his line perpendicular to road. Genl Early is on his right. I do not yet know how far he has advanced. We can't find any of the enemy south of the Plank road. But if we let them alone until morning we will find them again intrenched, so I wish to push them over the river tonight. I understand that Kershaw's left is at the toll gate on the Plank road. [General William T.] Wofford on the right, not up to the road. I want them to advance the right of their line so as to occupy the Plank road & you to communicate with the left of their line. Direct Col Alexander to endeavour to arrest all movements across Banks' Ford, or up the River road. Anderson & Early are north of the Plank road.

I am very respectfully, yours

R. E. LEE
Genl

431   To JEFFERSON DAVIS
Richmond, Virginia
TELEGRAM

Headquarters, Guiney's
May 5, 1863

AT THE CLOSE OF THE BATTLE OF CHANCELLORSVILLE ON SUNDAY THE ENEMY WAS REPORTED ADVANCING FROM FREDERICKSBURG IN OUR REAR. GENL MCLAWS WAS SENT BACK TO ARREST HIS PROGRESS, AND REPULSED HIM HANDSOMELY THAT AFTERNOON AT TABERNACLE CHURCH. LEARNING THAT THIS FORCE CONSISTED OF TWO CORPS UNDER GENL SEDGWICK, I DETERMINED TO ATTACK IT. LEAVING A SUFFICIENT FORCE TO HOLD GENL HOOKER IN CHECK, WHO HAD NOT RECROSSED THE RAPPAHANNOCK, AS WAS REPORTED, BUT OCCUPIED A STRONG POSITION IN FRONT OF THE U. S. FORD, I MARCHED BACK YESTERDAY WITH GENL ANDERSON, & UNITING WITH MCLAWS & EARLY IN THE AFTERNOON, SUCCEEDED BY THE BLESSING OF HEAVEN IN DRIVING GENL SEDGWICK OVER THE RIVER. WE HAVE REOCCUPIED FREDERICKSBURG AND NO ENEMY REMAINS SOUTH THE RAPPAHANNOCK IN ITS VICINITY.

R. E. LEE
Genl

432

To JAMES A. SEDDON
Secretary of War
TELEGRAM

Near Chancellorsville
May 6, 1863

SIR:

GENL HOOKER DID NOT RECROSS THE RAPPAHANNOCK AFTER HIS DEFEAT ON SUNDAY, BUT RETREATED TO A STRONG POSITION IN FRONT OF THE UNITED STATES FORD, WHERE HE IS NOW FORTIFYING HIMSELF WITH A VIEW I PRESUME OF HOLDING A POSITION THIS SIDE OF THE RAPPAHANNOCK. I UNDERSTAND FROM PRISONERS THAT HE IS AWAITING REINFORCEMENTS, & THAT AMONG OTHERS GENL [SAMUEL P.] HEINTZELMAN IS EXPECTED. I HAVE RECEIVED NONE OF THE TROOPS ORDERED FROM SOUTH OF THE JAMES RIVER.

I PARTICULARLY REQUESTED RANSOM'S DIVISION. HALF OF IT, GENERAL [JOHN R.] COOKE'S BRIGADE, [IS] IN SOUTH CAROLINA WHERE IT IS NOT WANTED. NOR ARE MORE TROOPS REQUIRED THERE THAN ARE SUFFICIENT TO SUPPORT THE BATTERIES. I HAD HOPED THAT LONGSTREET WOULD HAVE BEEN HERE BEFORE THIS TIME. GENL D. H. HILL HAS ORDERED UP PETTIGREW'S BRIGADE. IF IT IS SENT UP IN PLACE OF RANSOM'S, I DO NOT WANT IT. I HOPE EVERY EFFORT WILL BE MADE TO RESTORE THE RAILROADS, ELSE WE SHALL HAVE TO ABANDON THIS COUNTRY.

VERY RESPY

R. E. LEE
Genl

433

To JAMES A. SEDDON
Secretary of War
TELEGRAM

Headquarters, Army of Northern Virginia
May 6, 1863

SIR:

I HAVE THE HONOR TO STATE THAT TWO DISPATCHES HAVE JUST BEEN RECEIVED, ONE FROM LAKE, A TEXAS SCOUT, & ONE FROM J. W. GREGORY, SCOUT, 5TH VIRGINIA CAVALRY, STATING THAT GENL STONEMAN'S DIVISION OF CAVALRY, 5,000 STRONG, WITH 8 OR 11 PIECES OF ARTILLERY, WAS MOVING IN THE DIRECTION OF CARTERSVILLE ON JAMES RIVER, APPARENTLY WITH THE INTENTION OF CROSSING & PROCEEDING TO THE SOUTH SIDE RAILROAD.

UNLESS SOME OF THE CAVALRY IN NORTH CAROLINA & THE SOUTH IS SENT
HERE, IT WILL BE IMPOSSIBLE TO ARREST THESE RAIDS, AND THEY WILL ROAM
THROUGH THIS ENTIRE SECTION OF COUNTRY WITH LITTLE OR NO MOLESTA-
TION.

I AM VERY RESPECTLY, &C., &C.

R. E. LEE
Genl

434   To JEFFERSON DAVIS
Richmond, Virginia
TELEGRAM

Fredericksburg
May 7, 1863

AFTER DRIVING GENL SEDGWICK ACROSS THE RAPPAHANNOCK ON THE
NIGHT OF THE FOURTH (4TH) INSTANT I RETURNED ON THE 5TH TO CHAN-
CELLORSVILLE WITH THE DIVISIONS OF GENLS MCLAWS & ANDERSON. THEIR
MARCH WAS DELAYED BY A STORM WHICH CONTINUED ALL NIGHT & THE
FOLLOWING DAY. IN PLACING THE TROOPS IN POSITION ON THE MORNING OF
THE SIXTH (6TH) TO ATTACK GENL HOOKER, IT WAS ASCERTAINED HE HAD
ABANDONED HIS FORTIFIED POSITION. THE LINE OF SKIRMISHERS WAS PRESSED
FORWARD UNTIL THEY CAME WITHIN RANGE OF THE ENEMY'S BATTERIES
PLANTED NORTH OF THE RAPPAHANNOCK WHICH FROM THE CONFIGURATION
OF THE GROUND COMPLETELY COMMANDED THIS SIDE. HIS ARMY THEREFORE
ESCAPED WITH THE LOSS OF A FEW ADDITIONAL PRISONERS.

R. E. LEE
Genl

435   To JAMES A. SEDDON
Secretary of War
TELEGRAM

Fredericksburg
May 7, 1863

GENL FITZ LEE REPORTS FROM INFORMATION RECEIVED THAT ENEMY'S
CAVALRY IN LARGE FORCE WITH ARTILLERY REACHED ORANGE SPRINGS ABOUT
NOON YESTERDAY FROM THE DIRECTION OF CENTRAL RAILROAD. THEY CROSSED

PLANK ROAD LAST NIGHT ABOUT ELEVEN (11) O'CLOCK. IT IS PROBABLY STONE-
MAN ON HIS WAY TO THE RAPPAHANNOCK. GENL STUART WITH FITZ LEE'S
BRIGADE WILL ENDEAVOR TO STRIKE THEM.

R. E. LEE
Genl

436   To GENERAL JAMES LONGSTREET
Richmond, Virginia

Headquarters, Army of Northern Virginia
May 7, 1863

General:

I have just received yours of 2d instant upon my return to my
former camp. My letter of the 1st instant to which you refer was intended to apprise you of my intended movement and to express the wish
rather than the expectation that one of your divisions could cooperate
in it. I did not intend to express the opinion that you could reach me in
time, as I did not think it practicable. The emergency that made your
presence so desirable has passed for the present so far as I can see, and I
desire that you will not distress your troops by a forced movement to
join me, or sacrifice for that purpose any public interest that your sudden departure might make it necessary to abandon. The only immediate
service that your troops could render would be to protect our communications from the enemy's cavalry, and assist in punishing them for
the damage they have done us.

Very respy, your obt sev't

R. E. LEE
Genl

437   To GENERAL SAMUEL COOPER
Adjutant and Inspector General

BATTLE REPORT OF CHANCELLORSVILLE CAMPAIGN

Headquarters, Army of Northern Virginia
September 23, 1863

General:

I have the honor to transmit herewith my report of the operations
of this army from the time the enemy crossed the Rappahannock on the

28th April last to his retreat over that river on the night of May 5th, embracing the battles of Chancellorsville, Salem Church, &c. I also forward the reports of the several commanding officers of corps, divisions, brigades, & regiments, and the returns of the Medical and Ordnance Departments, together with a map of the scene of operations. The accompanying reports and other documents are enumerated in a schedule annexed to my report.

Very respectfully, your obt servt

R. E. LEE
Genl

BATTLE OF CHANCELLORSVILLE

After the battle of Fredericksburg the army remained encamped on the south side of the Rappahannock until the latter part of April.

The Federal Army occupied the north side of the river opposite Fredericksburg, extending to the Potomac.

Two brigades of [General Richard H.] Anderson's division, those of Generals [William] Mahone and [Carnot] Posey, were stationed near the United States Mine or Bark Mill Ford, and a third, under General [Cadmus M.] Wilcox, guarded Banks' Ford.

The cavalry was distributed on both flanks, Fitzhugh Lee's brigade picketing the Rappahannock above the mouth of the Rapidan, and W. H. F. Lee's near Port Royal. [General Wade] Hampton's brigade had been sent into the interior to recruit.

General [James] Longstreet, with two divisions of his corps, was detached for service south of James River in February, and did not rejoin the army until after the battle of Chancellorsville.

With the exception of the engagement between Fitz Lee's brigade and the enemy's cavalry near Kelly's Ford on the 17th of March, of which a brief report has been already forwarded to the Department, nothing of interest transpired during this period of inactivity.

On the 14th of April intelligence was received that the enemy's cavalry was concentrating on the upper Rappahannock. Their efforts to establish themselves on the south side of the river were successfully resisted by Fitz Lee's brigade and two regiments of W. H. F. Lee's, the whole under the immediate command of Genl Stuart.

About the 21st small bodies of infantry appeared at Kelly's Ford and the Rappahannock Bridge, and almost at the same time a demonstration was made opposite Port Royal, where a party of infantry crossed the river about the 23d. These movements were evidently intended to conceal the designs of the enemy, but taken in connection with the reports of scouts, indicated that the Federal Army, now commanded by Major General [Joseph E.] Hooker, was about to resume active operations.

At 5½ a.m. on the 28th April the enemy crossed the Rappahannock in boats near Fredericksburg, and driving off the pickets on the river proceeded to lay down a pontoon bridge a short distance below the mouth of Deep Run. Later in the forenoon another bridge was constructed about a mile below the first. A considerable force crossed on these bridges during the day, and was massed out of view under the high banks of the river. The bridges as well as the troops were effectually protected from our artillery by the depth of the river's bed and the narrowness of the stream, while the batteries on the opposite heights completely commanded the wide plain between our lines and the river. As in the first battle of Fredericksburg it was thought best to select positions with a view to resist the advance of the enemy rather than incur the heavy loss that would attend any attempt to prevent his crossing. Our dispositions were accordingly made as on the former occasion.

No demonstration was made opposite any other point of our lines at Fredericksburg, and the strength of the force that had crossed and its apparent indisposition to attack indicated that the principal effort of the enemy would be made in some other quarter. This impression was confirmed by intelligence received from General Stuart that a large body of infantry and artillery was passing up the river. During the forenoon of the 29th that officer reported that the enemy had crossed in force near Kelly's Ford on the preceding evening. Later in the day he announced that a heavy column was moving from Kelly's towards Germanna Ford on the Rapidan, and another toward Ely's Ford on that river. The routes they were pursuing after crossing the Rapidan converge near Chancellorsville, whence several roads lead to the rear of our position at Fredericksburg.

On the night of the 29th General Anderson was directed to proceed towards Chancellorsville, and dispose Wright's brigade and the troops from the Bark Mill Ford to cover these roads. Arriving at Chancellorsville about midnight, he found the commands of Generals Mahone and Posey already there, having been withdrawn from the Bark Mill Ford, with the exception of a small guard. Learning that the enemy had crossed the Rapidan and were approaching in strong force, General Anderson retired early on the morning of the 30th to the intersection of the Mine and Plank roads near Tabernacle Church, and began to intrench himself. The enemy's cavalry skirmished with his rear guard as he left Chancellorsville, but being vigorously repulsed by Mahone's brigade offered no further opposition to his march. Mahone was placed on the old Turnpike, [Ambrose R.] Wright and Posey on the Plank road. In the meantime General Stuart had been directed to endeavor to impede the progress of the column marching by way of Germanna Ford. Detaching W. H. F. Lee with his two regiments, the 9th and 13th Virginia, to oppose the main body of the enemy's cavalry, General Stuart crossed the Rapidan at Raccoon Ford with Fitz Lee's brigade on the night of the 29th. Halting to give his men a few hours' repose, he ordered Colonel [Thomas H.] Owen with the 3d Virginia Cavalry to throw himself in front of the enemy, while the rest of the brigade attacked his right flank at the Wilderness Tavern between Germanna Ford and Chancellorsville.

By this means the march of this column was delayed until 12 m., when learning that the one from Ely's Ford had already reached Chancellorsville, General Stuart marched by Todd's Tavern towards Spotsylvania Court House to put himself in communication with the main body of the army, and Colonel Owen fell back upon General Anderson.

The enemy in our front near Fredericksburg continued inactive, and it was now apparent that the main attack would be made upon our flank and rear. It was therefore determined to leave sufficient troops to hold our lines, and with the main body of the army to give battle to the approaching column.

[General Jubal A.] Early's division of Jackson's corps, and [General William] Barkesdale's brigade, of [General Lafayette] McLaws' division, with part of the reserve artillery under General [William N.] Pendleton, were entrusted with the defence of our position at Fredericksburg, and at midnight on the 30th General McLaws marched with the rest of his command towards Chancellorsville. General Jackson followed at dawn next morning with the remaining divisions of his corps. He reached the position occupied by General Anderson at 8 a.m. and immediately began preparations to advance. At 11 a.m. the troops moved forward upon the Plank and old Turnpike roads, Anderson with the brigades of Wright and Posey leading on the former, McLaws with his three brigades preceded by Mahone's on the latter. Generals Wilcox and [Edward A.] Perry of Anderson's division, cooperated with McLaws. Jackson's troops followed Anderson on the Plank road. Colonel Alexander's battalion of artillery accompanied the advance. The enemy was soon encountered on both roads and heavy skirmishing with infantry and artillery ensued, our troops pressing steadily forward. A strong attack upon General McLaws was repulsed with spirit by [General Paul J.] Semmes' brigade, and General Wright by direction of General Anderson diverging to the left of the Plank road marched by way of the unfinished railroad from Fredericksburg to Gordonsville and turned the enemy's right. His whole line thereupon retreated rapidly, vigorously pursued by our troops until they arrived within about one mile of Chancellorsville. Here the enemy had assumed a position of great natural strength surrounded on all sides by a dense forest filled with a tangled undergrowth, in the midst of which breastworks of logs had been constructed with trees felled in front so as to form an almost impenetrable abatis.

His artillery swept the few narrow roads by which his position could be approached from the front, and commanded the adjacent woods. The left of his line extended from Chancellorsville towards the Rappahannock, covering the Bark Mill Ford, where he communicated with the north bank of the river by a pontoon bridge.

His right stretched westwards along the Germanna Ford road more than two miles. Darkness was approaching before the strength and extent of his line could be ascertained, and as the nature of the country rendered it hazardous to attack by night, our troops were halted and formed in line of battle in front of Chancellorsville at right angles to the Plank road extending on the right to the Mine road and to the left in the direction of the Catharine Furnace. Colonel [Williams C.] Wickham with the 4th Virginia Cavalry and Colonel Owen's regiment was stationed between the Mine road and the Rappahannock. The rest of the cavalry was upon our left flank.

It was evident that a direct attack upon the enemy would be attended with great difficulty and loss, in view of the strength of his position and his superiority of numbers. It was therefore resolved to endeavor to turn his right flank and gain his rear, leaving a force in front to hold him in check and conceal the movement. The execution of this plan was entrusted to Lieut General Jackson with his three divisions. The commands of Generals McLaws and Anderson, with the exception of Wilcox's brigade, which during the night had been ordered back to Banks' Ford, remained in front of the enemy.

Early on the morning of the 2d, General Jackson marched by the Furnace and Brock roads, his movement being effectually covered by Fitz Lee's cavalry under General Stuart in person.

As the rear of the train was passing the furnace a large force of the enemy advanced from Chancellorsville and attempted its capture. General Jackson had left the 23d Georgia Regiment under Colonel [Emory F.] Best at this point to guard his flank, and upon the approach of the enemy Lieut Colonel John T. Brown, whose artillery was passing at the time, placed a battery in position to aid in checking his advance. A small number of men who were marching to join their commands, including Captain [William S.] Moore with two companies of the 14th Tennessee Regiment of [James J.] Archer's brigade, reported to Colonel Brown and supported his guns. The enemy was kept back by this small force until the train had passed, but his superior numbers enabled him subsequently to surround and capture the greater part of the 23d Georgia Regiment. General Anderson was directed to send a brigade to resist the further progress of this column, and detached General Posey for that purpose. General Posey became warmly engaged with a superior force, but being reinforced by General Wright, the enemy's advance was arrested.

After a long and fatiguing march General Jackson's leading division under General [Robert E.] Rodes reached the old Turnpike about three miles in rear of Chancellorsville at 4 p.m. As the different divisions arrived they were formed at right angles to the road, Rodes in front, [Isaac R.] Trimble's division under Brig General [Raleigh E.] Colston in the second, and A. P. Hill's in the third line.

At 6 p.m. the advance was ordered. The enemy were taken by surprise and fled after a brief resistance. General Rodes' men pushed forward with great vigor and enthusiasm, followed closely by the second and third lines. Position after position was carried, the guns captured, and every effort of the enemy to rally defeated by the impetuous rush of our troops. In the ardor of pursuit through the thick and tangled woods the first and second lines at last became mingled and moved on together as one. The enemy made a stand at a line of breastworks across the road at the house of Melzie Chancellor, but the troops of Rodes and Colston dashed over the entrenchments together, and the flight and pursuit were resumed, and continued until our advance was arrested by the abatis in front of the line of works near the central position at Chancellorsville. It was now dark and General Jackson ordered the third line under General Hill to advance to the front and relieve the troops of Rodes and Colston, who were completely blended and in such disorder from their rapid advance through intricate woods and over broken ground that it was necessary to reform them.

As Hill's men moved forward, General Jackson with his staff and escort returning from the extreme front met his skirmishers advancing, and in the obscurity of the night were mistaken for the enemy and fired upon. Captain [James K.] Boswell, Chief Engineer of the corps and several others were killed, and a number wounded. General Jackson himself received a severe injury, and was borne from the field. The command devolved upon Major General Hill, whose division under General [Henry] Heth was advanced to the line of entrenchments which had been reached by Rodes and Colston.

A furious fire of artillery was opened upon them by the enemy, under cover of which his infantry advanced to the attack. They were handsomely repulsed by the 55th Virginia Regiment under Colonel [Francis] Mallory, who was killed while bravely leading his men. General Hill was soon afterwards disabled, and Major General Stuart, who had been directed by General Jackson to seize the road to Ely's Ford in rear of the enemy, was sent for to take command.

At this time the right of Hill's division was attacked by the column of the enemy already mentioned as having penetrated to the furnace, which had been recalled to Chancellorsville to avoid being cut off by the advance of Jackson. This attack was gallantly met and repulsed by the 18th and 28th and a portion of the 33d North Carolina Regiments, [James H.] Lane's brigade.

Upon General Stuart's arrival soon afterwards, the command was turned over to him by General Hill. He immediately proceeded to reconnoiter the ground and make himself acquainted with the disposition of the troops. The darkness of the night and the difficulty of moving through the woods and undergrowth rendered it advisable to defer further operations until morning, and the troops rested on their arms in line of battle. Colonel Stapleton Crutchfield, Chief of Artillery of the corps, was severely wounded, and Colonel Edward P. Alexander, senior artillery officer present, was engaged during the entire night in selecting positions for our batteries.

As soon as the sound of cannon gave notice of Jackson's attack on the enemy's right, our troops in front of Chancellorsville were ordered to press him strongly on the left to prevent reinforcements being sent to the point assailed. They were directed not to attack in force unless a favorable opportunity should present itself, and while continuing to cover the roads leading from their respective positions towards Chancellorsville, to incline to the left so as to connect with Jackson's right as he closed in upon the center. These orders were well executed, our troops advancing up to the enemy's entrenchments, while several batteries played with good effect upon his lines until prevented by the increasing darkness.

Early on the morning of the 3d General Stuart renewed the attack upon the enemy, who had strengthened his right during the night with additional breastworks, while a large number of guns, protected by entrenchments, were posted so as to sweep the woods through which our troops had to advance. Hill's division was in front, with Colston in the second line and Rodes in the third.

The second and third lines soon advanced to the support of the first, and the whole became hotly engaged. The breastworks at which the attack was suspended the preceding evening were carried by assault under a terrible fire of musketry and artillery. In rear of these breastworks was a barricade from which the enemy was quickly driven.

The troops on the left of the Plank road, pressing through the woods, attacked and broke the next line, while those on the right bravely assailed the extensive earthworks behind which the enemy's artillery was posted. Three times were these works carried, and as often were the brave assailants compelled to abandon them, twice by the retirement of the troops on their left, who fell back after a gallant struggle with superior numbers, and once by a movement of the enemy on their right, caused by the advance of General Anderson. The left being reinforced finally succeeded in driving back the enemy, and the artillery under Lieut-Colonels [Thomas H.] Carter and [Hilary P.] Jones being thrown forward to occupy favorable positions secured by the advance of the infantry, began to play with great precision and effect.

Anderson in the meantime pressed gallantly forward directly upon Chancellorsville, his right resting upon the Plank road and his left extending around towards the furnace, while McLaws made a strong demonstration to the right of the road. As the troops advancing upon the enemy's front and right converged upon his central position Anderson effected a junction with Jackson's corps, and the whole line pressed irresistibly on. The enemy was driven from all his fortified positions with heavy loss in killed, wounded, and prisoners, and retreated towards the Rappahannock. By 10 a.m. we were in full possession of the field.

The troops having become somewhat scattered by the difficulties of the ground and the ardor of the contest were immediately reformed preparatory to renewing the attack. The enemy had withdrawn to a strong position nearer to the Rappahannock, which he had previously fortified. His superiority of numbers, the unfavorable nature of the ground, which was densely wooded, and the condition of our troops after the arduous and sanguinary conflict in which they had been engaged rendered great caution necessary. Our preparations were just completed when further operations were arrested by intelligence received from Fredericksburg.

General Early had been instructed, in the event of the enemy withdrawing from his front and moving up the river, to join the main body of the army with so much of his command as could be spared from the defence of his lines. This order was repeated on the 2d, but by a misapprehension on the part of the officer conveying it, General Early was directed to move unconditionally. Leaving [General Harry T.] Hays' brigade and one regiment of Barksdale's at Fredericksburg, and directing a part of General Pendleton's artillery to be sent to the rear, in compliance with the order delivered to him General Early moved with the rest of his command towards Chancellorsville. As soon as his withdrawal was perceived the enemy began to give evidence of an intention to advance, but the mistake in the transmission of the order being corrected General Early returned to his original position.

The line to be defended by Barksdale's brigade extended from the Rappahannock above Fredericksburg, to the rear of Howison's house, a distance of more than two miles. The artillery was posted along the heights in rear of the town. Before dawn on the morning of the 3d General Barksdale reported to General Early that the enemy had occupied Fredericksburg in large force and laid down a bridge at the town. Hays' brigade was sent to his support and placed on his extreme left, with the exception of one regiment stationed on the right of his line behind Howison's house. Seven companies of the 21st Mississippi Regiment were posted by General Barksdale between the Marye house and the Plank road, the 18th and the three other companies of the 21st occupied the Telegraph road at the foot of Marye's Hill, the two remaining regiments of the brigade being further to the right on the hills near Howison's house. The enemy made a demonstration against the extreme right which was easily repulsed by General Early. Soon afterwards a column moved from Fredericksburg along the river bank as if to gain the heights on the extreme left which commanded those immediately in rear of the town. This attempt was foiled by General Hays and the arrival of General Wilcox from Banks' Ford, who deployed a few skirmishers on the hill near Taylor's house, and opened on the enemy with a section of artillery. Very soon the enemy advanced in large force against Marye's and the hills to the right and left of it. Two assaults were gallantly repulsed by Barksdale's men and the artillery. After the second, a flag of truce was sent from the town to obtain permission to provide for the wounded.

Three heavy lines advanced immediately upon the return of the flag and renewed the attack. They were bravely repulsed on the right and left, but the small force at the foot of Marye's Hill, overpowered by more than ten times their numbers, was captured after a heroic resistance, and the hill carried. Eight pieces of artillery were taken on Marye's and the adjacent heights. The remainder of Barksdale's brigade together with that of General Hays and the artillery on the right retired down the Telegraph road.

The success of the enemy enabled him to threaten our communications by moving down the Telegraph road, or to come upon our rear at Chancellorsville by the Plank road. He at first advanced on the former, but was checked by General Early, who had halted the commands of

Barksdale and Hays with the artillery about two miles from Marye's Hill, and reinforced them with three regiments of [General John B.] Gordon's brigade.

The enemy then began to advance up the Plank road, his progress being gallantly disputed by the brigade of General Wilcox, who had moved from Banks' Ford as rapidly as possible to the assistance of General Barksdale, but arrived too late to take part in the action. General Wilcox fell back slowly until he reached Salem Church on the Plank road about five miles from Fredericksburg.

Information of the state of affairs in our rear having reached Chancellorsville, as already stated, General McLaws, with his three brigades and one of General Anderson's was ordered to reinforce General Wilcox. He arrived at Salem Church early in the afternoon, where he found General Wilcox in line of battle, with a large force of the enemy, consisting, as was reported, of one army corps and part of another under Major General [John] Sedgwick, in his front. The brigades of [Generals Joseph B.] Kershaw and [William T.] Wofford were placed on the right of Wilcox, those of Semmes and Mahone on his left. The enemy's artillery played vigorously upon our position for some time, when his infantry advanced in three strong lines, the attack being directed mainly against General Wilcox, but partially involving the brigades on his left.

The assault was met with the utmost firmness, and after a fierce struggle the first line was repulsed with great slaughter. The second then came forward, but immediately broke under the close and deadly fire which it encountered, and the whole mass fled in confusion to the rear.

They were pursued by the brigades of Wilcox and Semmes, which advanced nearly a mile, when they were halted to reform in the presence of the enemy's reserve, which now appeared in large force. It being quite dark, General Wilcox deemed it imprudent to push the attack with his small numbers, and retired to his original position, the enemy making no attempt to follow. The next morning General Early advanced along the Telegraph road and recaptured Marye's and the adjacent hills without difficulty, thus gaining the rear of the enemy's left. He then proposed to General McLaws that a simultaneous attack should be made by their respective commands, but the latter officer not deeming his force adequate to assail the enemy in front, the proposition was not carried into effect.

In the meantime the enemy had so strengthened his position near Chancellorsville that it was deemed inexpedient to assail it with less than our whole force, which could not be concentrated until we were relieved from the danger that menaced our rear. It was accordingly resolved still further to reinforce the troops in front of General Sedgwick, in order, if possible, to drive him across the Rappahannock. Accordingly, on the 4th, General Anderson was directed to proceed with his remaining three brigades to join General McLaws, the three divisions of Jackson's corps holding our position at Chancellorsville. Anderson reached Salem Church about noon, and was directed to gain the left flank of the enemy and effect a junction with Early. McLaws' troops were disposed as on the previous day, with orders to hold the enemy in front, and to push forward his right brigades as soon as the advance of Anderson and Early should be perceived, so as to connect with them and complete the continuity of our line.

Some delay occurred in getting the troops into position, owing to the broken and irregular nature of the ground and the difficulty of ascertaining the disposition of the enemy's forces. The attack did not begin until 6 p.m., when Anderson and Early moved forward and drove General Sedgwick's troops rapidly before them across the Plank road in the direction of the Rappahannock. The speedy approach of darkness prevented General McLaws from perceiving the success of the attack until the enemy began to recross the river a short distance below Banks' Ford, where he had laid one of his pontoon bridges. His right brigades, under Kershaw and Wofford, advanced through the woods in the direction of the firing, but the retreat was so rapid that they could only join in the pursuit. A dense fog settled over the field increasing the obscurity, and rendering great caution necessary to avoid collision between our own troops. Their movements were consequently slow. General Wilcox, with Kershaw's brigade and two regiments of his own, accompanied by a battery, proceeded nearly to the river, capturing a number of prisoners and inflicting great damage upon the enemy. General McLaws also directed Colonel Alexander's artillery to fire upon the locality of the enemy's bridge, which was done with good effect. The next morning it was found that General Sedgwick had made good his escape and removed his bridges. Fredericksburg was also evacuated, and our rear no longer threatened. But as General Sedgwick had it in his power to recross, it was deemed best to leave General Early with his division and Barksdale's brigade to hold our lines as before, McLaws and Anderson being directed to return to Chancellorsville. They reached their destination during the afternoon, in the midst of a violent storm, which continued throughout the night and most of the following day.

Preparations were made to assail the enemy's works at daylight on the 6th, but on advancing our skirmishers it was found that under cover of the storm and darkness of the night he had retreated over the river.

A detachment was left to guard the battle field while the wounded were being removed and the captured property collected. The rest of the army returned to its former position.

The particulars of these operations will be found in the reports of the several commanding officers which are herewith transmitted. They will show more fully than my limits will suffer me to do the dangers and difficulties which, under God's blessing, were surmounted by the fortitude and valor of our army. The conduct of the troops cannot be too highly praised.

Attacking largely superior numbers in strongly entrenched positions their heroic courage overcame every obstacle of nature and art, and achieved a triumph most honorable to our arms.

I commend to the particular notice of the Department the brave officers and men mentioned by their superiors for extraordinary daring and merit, whose names I am unable to enumerate here. Among them will be found some who have passed by a glorious death beyond the reach of praise, but the memory of whose virtues and devoted patriotism will ever be cherished by their grateful countrymen.

The returns of the Medical Director will show the extent of our loss, which from the nature of the circumstances attending the engagements could not be otherwise than severe. Many valuable officers and men were killed or wounded in the faithful discharge of duty. Among the former, Brigadier General [Elisha F.] Paxton fell while leading his brigade with conspicuous courage in the assault on the enemy's works at Chancellorsville. The gallant Brigadier General [Francis R. T.] Nicholls lost a leg. Brigadier General [Samuel] McGowan was severely and Brigadier Generals Heth and [W. Dorsey] Pender were slightly wounded in the same engagement. The latter officer led his brigade to the attack under a destructive fire bearing the colors of a regiment in his own hands up to and over the entrenchments with the most distinguished gallantry. General [Robert F.] Hoke received a painful wound in the action near Fredericksburg.

The movement by which the enemy's position was turned and the fortune of the day decided was conducted by the lamented Lieutenant General Jackson, who, as has already been stated, was severely wounded near the close of the engagement on Saturday evening. I do not propose here to speak of the character of this illustrious man, since removed from the scene of his eminent usefulness by the hand of an inscrutable but all wise Providence. I nevertheless desire to pay the tribute of my admiration to the matchless energy and skill that marked this last act of his life, forming as it did, a worthy conclusion of that long series of splendid achievements which won for him the lasting love and gratitude of his country.

Major General A. P. Hill was disabled soon after assuming command, but did not leave the field until the arrival of Major General Stuart. The latter officer ably discharged the difficult and responsible duties which he was thus unexpectedly called to perform. Assuming the command late in the night, at the close of a fierce engagement, and in the immediate presence of the enemy, necessarily ignorant in a great measure of the disposition of the troops and of the plans of those who had preceded him, General Stuart exhibited great energy, promptness, and intelligence. During the continuance of the engagement the next day, he conducted the operations on the left with distinguished capacity and vigor, stimulating and cheering the troops by the example of his own coolness and daring.

While it is impossible to mention all who were conspicuous in the several engagements, it will not be considered an invidious distinction to say that General Jackson, after he was wounded, in expressing the satisfaction he derived from the conduct of his whole command, commended to my particular attention the services of Brigadier General (now Major General) Rodes and his gallant division.

Major General Early performed the important and responsible duty entrusted to him in a manner which reflected credit upon himself and his command. Major General R. H. Anderson was also distinguished for the promptness, courage, and skill with which he and his division executed every order, and Brigadier General (now Major General) Wilcox is entitled to especial praise for the judgment and bravery displayed in impeding the advance of General Sedgwick towards Chancellorsville, and for the gallant and successful stand at Salem Church.

To the skillful and efficient management of the artillery the successful issue of the contest is in great measure due. The ground was not favorable for its employment, but every suitable position was taken with alacrity, and the operations of the infantry supported and assisted with a spirit and courage not second to their own. It bore a prominent part in the final assault which ended in driving the enemy from the field at Chancellorsville, silencing his batteries, and by a destructive enfilade fire upon his works opened the way for the advance of our troops.

Colonels Crutchfield, Alexander, and [R. Lindsay] Walker, and Lieutenant Colonels Brown, Carter, and [R. Snowden] Andrews, with the officers and men of their commands, are mentioned as deserving especial commendation. The batteries under General Pendleton also acted with great gallantry.

The cavalry of the army at the time of these operations was much reduced. To its vigilance and energy we were indebted for timely information of the enemy's movements before the battle, and for impeding his march to Chancellorsville. It guarded both flanks of the army during the battle at that place, and a portion of it, as has been already stated, rendered valuable service in covering the march of Jackson to the enemy's rear. The Horse Artillery accompanied the infantry, and participated with credit to itself in the engagement. The nature of the country rendered it impossible for the cavalry to do more.

When the enemy's infantry passed the Rappahannock at Kelly's Ford, his cavalry under Genl [George] Stoneman also crossed in large force, and proceeded through Culpeper County towards Gordonsville for the purpose of cutting the railroads to Richmond.

General Stuart had nothing to oppose to this movement but two regiments of Brigadier General W. H. F. Lee's brigade, the 9th and 13th Virginia Cavalry.

General Lee fell back before the overwhelming numbers of the enemy, and after holding the railroad bridge over the Rapidan during the 1st May, burned the bridge, and retired to Gordonsville at night.

The enemy avoided Gordonsville and reached Louisa Court House, on the Central Railroad, which he proceeded to break up. Dividing his force, a part of it also cut the Richmond and Fredericksburg Railroad, and a part proceeded to Columbia, on the James River and Kanawha Canal, with the design of destroying the aqueduct at that place. The small command of General Lee exerted itself vigorously to defeat this purpose. The damage done to the railroads was small and soon repaired, and the canal was saved from injury. The details of his operations will be found in the accompanying memorandum, and are creditable to officers and men.

The loss of the enemy in the battle of Chancellorsville and the other engagements was severe. His dead, and a large number of wounded, were left on the field. About five thousand prisoners, exclusive of the wounded, were taken, and thirteen pieces of artillery, nineteen thousand five hundred stand of arms, seventeen colors, and a large quantity of ammunition fell into our hands.

To the members of my staff I am greatly indebted for assistance in observing the movements of the enemy, posting troops, and conveying orders.

On so extended and varied a field all were called into requisition, and all evinced the greatest energy and zeal.

The Medical Director of the army, Surgeon [Lafayette] Guild, with the officers of his department, were untiring in their attention to the wounded. Lieutenant Colonel [James L.] Corley, Chief Quartermaster, took charge of the disposition and safety of the trains of the army. Lieutenant Colonel [Robert G.] Cole, Chief Commissary of its subsistence, and Lieutenant Colonel [Briscoe G.] Baldwin, Chief of Ordnance, were everywhere on the field attending to the wants of their departments. General [Richard H.] Chilton, Chief of Staff, Lieutenant Colonel [Edward] Murray, Major [Henry E.] Peyton, and Captain [Henry E.] Young, of the Adjutant and Inspector General's Department, were active in seeing to the execution of orders. Lieutenant Colonel [William P.] Smith and Captain [Samuel R.] Johnston, of the Engineers, in reconnoitering the enemy and constructing batteries. Colonel [Armistead L.] Long in posting troops and artillery. Majors [Walter H.] Taylor, [Thomas M. R.] Talcott, [Charles] Marshall, and [Charles S.] Venable were engaged night and day in watching the operations, carrying orders, &c.

Respectfully submitted

R. E. LEE
Genl

CHAPTER ELEVEN

Gettysburg Campaign

"I do not know how to replace him"

THE ARMY OF NORTHERN VIRGINIA was still recovering from the shock of Chancellorsville when Lee was called upon to make the decision involving the Confederate West. The major force along the Mississippi, under Pemberton, was divided from potential supports under Joe Johnston, the Department commander, and, with Johnston's scratch force useless, Pemberton was forced back into Vicksburg. There on May 18 his army and the citizens began to withstand a siege conducted by the United States Navy from the river and Grant from land.

The considerable postwar analyses would give the impression that Lee chose to sacrifice Vicksburg, by withholding troops from his own army, in preference to making a doomed invasion. The fact was — as Lee pointed out in the elaborate circumlocutions of his diplomacy — that one or two of his largest divisions sent to Vicksburg would hardly save the situation there, while their removal would make maneuver impossible for the Army of Northern Virginia. With his veteran infantry reduced to little more than 40,000 after Chancellorsville, to withhold the detached troops of Longstreet from Lee's army would leave Lee little choice except to retire into the works around Richmond. Then there would have been two sieges instead of one. Beneath all of Lee's elaborations and secondary points, this theme ran clearly through his communications.

Because of Lee's successes, a tendency had grown in various quarters to regard his defensive line across the middle of the state as impregnable: his admirers, like Davis, attributed this to his invincibility; those jealous of him, like Johnston and Beauregard, attributed it to an exaggerated estimate of his manpower. Both camps, however, wanted the use of units

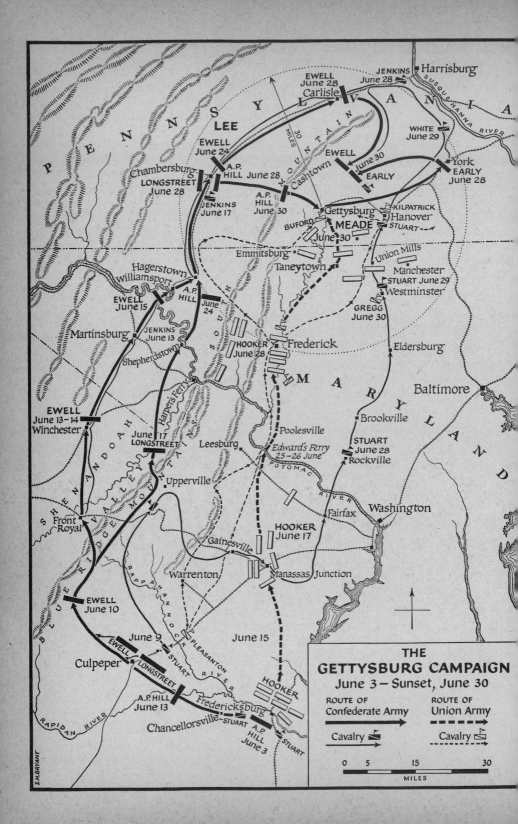

THE
GETTYSBURG CAMPAIGN
June 3 – Sunset, June 30

ROUTE OF
Confederate Army

ROUTE OF
Union Army

Cavalry

Cavalry

0   5   15   30
MILES

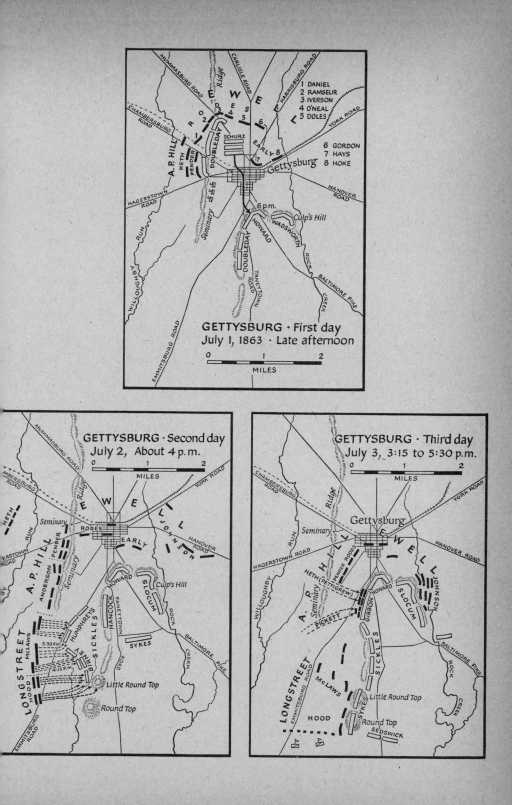

GETTYSBURG · First day
July 1, 1863 · Late afternoon

0   1   2
MILES

1 DANIEL
2 RAMSEUR
3 IVERSON
4 O'NEAL
5 DOLES

6 GORDON
7 HAYS
8 HOKE

GETTYSBURG · Second day
July 2, About 4 p.m.

0   1   2
MILES

GETTYSBURG · Third day
July 3, 3:15 to 5:30 p.m.

0   1   2
MILES

from a winning combination. Lee recognized that the combination sustained the maneuver on which his defense was founded, and fought to prevent the breakup of a successful organization.

Though he argued that an invasion would provide the most effective use of his troops in relation to the West, primarily it represented the most effective use he could make of the one successful army in the Confederacy. Mere numbers would not swing the balance of a military decision and, though Lee could not bring himself to say this outright, he did write in reference to Pickett's division of "the uncertainty of its employment" in the West. Lee recognized then, what history recognizes in perspective, that a further decline in the manpower in his army and in physical support of its men would bring defeat to the Confederacy. In a significant letter to Davis on June 10, Lee predicted the ultimate consequences of inferiority in manpower and supply.

When Lee won Davis's support of the Northern invasion, the President's support was halfhearted and he gave preferment to defensive garrisons over returning veteran units for the completion of the Army of Northern Virginia. Davis did not announce this policy: he simply refused to cooperate in returning detached units and, in effect, countermanded Lee's orders for bringing up his troops to the army.

Lee received Hood's division of Longstreet's corps and, after many exchanges, three brigades of Pickett's division. The last two of Pickett's brigades, Jenkins and Corse, never came, though Lee did not know this when he started north. The brigades of Ransom, Cooke and "Shanks" Evans also never reached him, though he had ordered them forward. All through his increasingly urgent letters, as he moved out, run the names of "Jenkins" and "Cooke" and "Ransom." These were proven commands led by good men, especially the brilliant young Micah Jenkins. Instead, Lee was sent the brigades of Pettigrew and Joseph Davis, the latter, the President's nephew, an amiable lawyer with little more battle experience than the green regiments which formed part of his command. In summary, instead of five veteran brigades, the equivalent of a full division, Lee received two untried brigades — a numerical loss of three brigades (Jenkins's was large), in addition to the substitution of comparative strangers for units of the working combination.

Veteran units were particularly important to Lee at that time because of the necessity of reorganizing the army after Stonewall Jackson's death. The loss of the unequaled tactician represented the loss of Lee's mobile striking force, along with the one commander who had been intuitive in his use of the discretionary orders by which Lee functioned at his best. General Lee did not try to replace "the great and good Jackson."

He divided his army into three corps of three divisions each, and abolished the reserve artillery. Longstreet retained his corps, minus Anderson's division; Ewell (recovered from his leg amputation) returned and assumed command of the old Second Corps, minus A. P. Hill's division; and Powell Hill was given a new Third Corps, originally designed to be formed of his Light Division, Anderson's division, and Ransom's detached half-division augmented by other brigades. As Ransom was withheld by Davis, Hill's third division became a makeshift affair, formed by detaching two brigades from Hill's old division and adding the two new brigades from North Carolina. Heth became commander of this new division and Dorsey Pender succeeded to command of the reduced Light Division.

In the Second Corps, Rodes was given permanent command of D. H. Hill's former division and Edward ("Allegheny") Johnson of Jackson's old, frequently orphaned division. Early remained in command of Ewell's former division.

Jeb Stuart, with all his cavalry assembled (including Jones from the Valley and Robertson from North Carolina), fielded a five-brigade division of about 9500 troopers, the most he had ever or was ever to command. In addition, for the movement north, Lee obtained the use of Imboden's and Albert Jenkins's cavalry brigades, poorly disciplined raiders who had operated in western Virginia and were undependable for orthodox work.

While Lee was preparing his army to move out, command trouble rose in another quarter. D. H. Hill who, on Lee's recommendation, succeeded Longstreet in command of the Department of Virginia and North Carolina, proved uncooperative, and Lee wrote an irritated letter to Davis asking to be relieved of command of that area under the existing conditions. In an unwise move, which was to have vast future consequences, the President accepted what amounted to Lee's ultimatum and relieved him of official command of the area south of the James — though never of the responsibility.

With the return of Longstreet's two divisions and the two new brigades palmed off on him, Lee started his movement north with 60,000 infantry on June 3. Leaving Hill's new Third Corps, with about 75 guns, on guard along the Rappahannock in the Fredericksburg area, Lee moved Ewell and Longstreet and the cavalry to Culpeper. There the main force tarried until June 10, when Ewell's corps moved west to the Blue Ridge. Gobbling up scattered garrisons along the way, Ewell captured Milroy's force at Winchester — with welcome acquisitions in guns, horses, wagons and food — and cleared the Valley route to the North.

When Ewell took Winchester on June 15, Hooker withdrew from the Rappahannock line, shifting his army northward between Washington and the Blue Ridge. With the enemy gone from his front, Hill followed Longstreet by way of Culpeper into the Valley, and they both followed Ewell northward across the Potomac. Reunited at Hagerstown, the full army reached Chambersburg, Pennsylvania, on June 27. The army had moved slowly, gathering provisions along the way, for the commissary aspects of the movement were as important to sustaining the troops as in the Maryland invasion the summer before.

From Chambersburg, Ewell moved with two of his divisions north to Carlisle, with the destination of Harrisburg, the state capital. The third division, Early's, moved to the east side of South Mountain (an extension of the Blue Ridge range), then, by way of Gettysburg, to York. This was the leisurely disposition of the foraging army when a repeat of the Maryland campaign occurred. This time it was not a lost order, but the lost cavalry.

The vigilant Jeb Stuart, of all people, used little discretion (actually violating one of Lee's provisions) in executing a discretionary order, and indulged himself in the vainglorious adventure of riding around Hooker's army. Though Stuart's way of going had been discretionary, Lee's last order to Stuart (5 p.m., June 23) was very specific about his assignment: "after crossing the river [Potomac], you must move on and feel the right of Ewell's troops, collecting information." Instead of Stuart covering Lee's flank on the east of the mountains, and providing the commanding general with information about the enemy, Stuart's men were sleep-riding on jaded horses east of the Federal army, which was spread out between Lee and his own cavalry.

Lee heard no more from his cavalry chief after dispatching the order back in Virginia. His first news from east of the mountains came from a spy who, reaching Lee at Chambersburg, warned him that the Federal army was approaching the low mountains from the east. Lee also learned that Hooker, whom he lightly regarded, had been replaced in command by General Meade, whom Lee respected both as a soldier and as a person. Once again in enemy country, Lee was forced to order (June 28) a hasty convergence of his scattered forces: this time the enemy did not know where Lee's army was, but neither did Lee know where the enemy was.

A. P. Hill's corps led the way over the pass at South Mountain, reaching the eastern side at the village of Cashtown, and on June 30 his van pushed east to the thriving market place and county seat of Gettysburg. Late in the day, Pettigrew's brigade (of the newly formed division under Heth) encountered Federal cavalry outside the town. After learning there were some shoes in Gettysburg, Pettigrew fell back on the rest of the corps. The next day, July 1, Lee ordered two divisions of Hill's corps forward to develop the situation.

While Buford's cavalry fell back before Hill's infantry, Federal infantry formed behind the cavalry screen and, against Lee's order to bring on a general engagement, Heth's division blundered into the enemy infantry and found itself in the midst of a battle it could not break off. Lee hurried up supports and Meade, who knew little more than Lee, also rushed forward reinforcements, with the result that a collision fight developed into a major battle along the road about two miles west of Gettysburg.

The only importance of Gettysburg was its location as a hub of roads leading in all directions. Down one of these marched Ewell's corps, coming up during the afternoon from the northwest on the Federal flank. Though a newly arriving Federal corps (Howard's XI, of the Chancellorsville break) came up to meet Ewell, the Confederates drove them, and the whole Federal line fell back into and beyond Gettysburg.

The routed Federals, giving up several thousand prisoners, retired to Cemetery Hill, a strong position south of town on the L-shaped rise of Cemetery Ridge. Federal generals have supported those Confederates who claimed that the natural bastion could have been taken before sundown, but Ewell, newly in command of the old Second Corps, grew irresolute and failed to push the pursuit of the beaten enemy.

The next day, July 2, two of Longstreet's divisions (Hood and McLaws) assaulted the southern end of the Cemetery Ridge line, supposedly in conjunction with an attack by Ewell on Culp's Hill, where the ridge bent back to the east with its front to the north. As Longstreet was late in mounting his assault, Ewell attacked separately. Longstreet, in a rebellious humor, directed a badly managed attack, sending his men in by brigades and exercising no coherent control over the action. Despite this, his men failed by yards and minutes of taking Little Round Top, the rocky column at the end of the bastion, and, breaking through Federal divisions on the flats in the western front of Cemetery Ridge, stormed to the top of the ridge, in the heart of the Federal position. No supports were sent up by Longstreet, and the most advanced units were forced to fall back to the floor of the shallow valley between Cemetery Ridge and Seminary Ridge.

This was the crucial action at Gettysburg. Lee's army suffered more casualties than on the first and third days together, shook the enemy and were the nearest to victory. The drama of what went into history as "Pickett's charge" was an anticlimax on the third day, July 3.

Lee had no real chance after the July 2nd failure in concert of action.

On July 3, having shaken both flanks and pinned down Federal troops at ends of a line stretching for nearly three miles, he tried a frontal attack toward the center with the three fresh brigades Pickett brought up, six somewhat battered brigades of Hill's corps and the heaviest concentration of guns up to that time. Longstreet was ordered to direct the assault, with Wilcox's brigade supporting on the right flank, two other brigades to move out as immediate supports, and supporting artillery to move out behind the infantry. Still recalcitrant, Longstreet gave little personal attention to the assaulting force. The artillery barrage was not effective, the three supporting brigades did not move out and the artillery supports were out of ammunition. The charge was gallantly made by the doomed men but, with all the latter-day sentimentalizing about the "high tide of the Confederacy," it was hopeless from the beginning.

The so-called "Longstreet controversy" was an entirely postwar development between former comrades who became bitter enemies, and it grew in vehemence as Longstreet justified his poor performance by claiming that Lee failed because he refused to be guided by Longstreet's strategy. Longstreet was an opinionated subordinate, who had imposed his will on Lee at Second Manassas, tried again at Sharpsburg and misused the discretion extended when he was on detached command in southeastern Virginia. Coming onto the field at Gettysburg late on the first day, in which he had taken no part, he wanted immediately to go on defense. Because the offensive failed, he was able to make a strong after-the-fact case for his strategy, naturally omitting his own contributions to the failure, especially on the second day. In his many writings about Gettysburg, from five to thirty years after the war, as his case grew stronger in retrospect, his contradictions and distortions grew more numerous.

He even went so far as to claim that he had opposed the invasion from the first and he (a subordinate recently returned to the army) had "agreed" only because Lee promised him to adopt defensive tactics on the invasion. This claim was made while Lee was still alive, and Lee flatly denied it, saying, "I would never have dreamed of such a thing." There was also a letter which Longstreet had forgotten he wrote his friend Wigfall, Senator from Texas. "When I agreed with the Sect. [War Secretary Seddon] & yourself about sending troops west [to Vicksburg], it was under the impression that we would be obliged to remain on the defensive here. But the prospect of an advance changes the aspect of affairs to us entirely." He wrote that he anticipated the "fair prospect of a forward movement."

None of this unpleasant aftermath was even hinted at the battle. At the time, the general officers' heaviest censure fell upon Stuart, whose absence precipitated the collision-engagement and forced the army to operate "as a blinded giant." Then, after the action was joined, the battle was the first fought without Stonewall Jackson. A foreign military observer pointed out that Lee had not then adjusted himself to fighting without his "right arm," and after the war Lee is reported to have said that with Jackson he would have won. The failures of Ewell and Longstreet, largely caused by their personalities, were the most outstanding and costliest examples in a general breakdown in command in the new organization which had not then become another working combination.

General Lee's official report of the battle was, on the whole, unrevealing, and his only implied censure — and this indirect — was of General Stuart. Of the crucial second day action on the Federal left, he wrote only a single, undetailed paragraph. Most of the action was beyond his range of vision and the details of Longstreet's erratic mismanagement of the Confederate assault were not supplied until years later by Hood, McLaws, Kershaw, Wilcox, Law and Colonel Oates. As Longstreet's official report was vague, General Lee was unaware of the actions of the poorly directed units when he wrote his report, if, indeed, he ever was.

In bringing his bleeding army back to Virginia, Lee had to overcome the unexpected hazard of rising waters at the Potomac crossings and an insufficiency of pontoons. As Meade's army, itself severely crippled, followed slowly and pressed with little vigor, Lee was able to make a last-minute crossing over a shaky, improvised bridge at Falling Waters.

Back in Virginia, in the northern extension of the Valley, Lee was permitted little time to rest his exhausted men, whose ranks were being drained by stragglers. Meade crossed the Potomac to the east of the Blue Ridge, forcing Lee to move his army back to middle Virginia to interpose between the Federals and Richmond. The movements were made without urgency and on August 4, two months after he had started his northward movement, Lee's army returned to camp south of the Rapidan River.

In those two months, Lee's army in all arms suffered approximately 23,000 casualties. Many listed as "missing" were stragglers who would show up in time, many were lightly wounded who would soon return to duty, and all prisoners would return in the exchange. Federal casualties over the same period had been somewhat higher, even at Gettysburg, but proportionately to numbers engaged they were lower and they would all be replaced. For the second summer, Lee had maneuvered the Federal forces out of Virginia, victualed his own men on the move and kept the enemy out of the Valley breadbasket. But much less had been accomplished than he had hoped for, and the people of the Confederacy had illogically expected more than was in the potential of Lee's army to achieve. Newspapers were critical and, though he made no public acknowledgment of the criticisms, his letters reveal a scornful resentment of armchair generals. From isolated phrases and the tone of his correspondence, his hope for independence was obviously waning.

438   To JAMES A. SEDDON
                         Secretary of War

                              Headquarters, Army of Northern Virginia
                                                  May 10, 1863

Sir:

Your telegraph of the 9th instant was received last night, but so many errors occurred in its transmission that it was not until noon today that it could be rendered intelligibly. I have replied to it by telegraph, but think it proper to go more into detail than in my dispatch. If you determine to send Pickett's division to Genl [John C.] Pemberton, I presume it could not reach him until the last of this month. If anything is done in that quarter, it will be over by that time, as the climate in June will force the enemy to retire. The uncertainty of its arrival and the uncertainty of its application cause me to doubt the policy of sending it. Its removal from this army will be sensibly felt. Unless we can obtain some reinforcements, we may be obliged to withdraw into the defences around Richmond. We are greatly outnumbered by the enemy now. Taking the report of Surgeon [Jonathan] Letterman, Medical Director of Genl Hooker's army, the number of sick reported by him and the ratio of the sick to the whole number, his aggregate force by calculation amounts to more than 159,000 men. I see by the *Herald* of the 7th instant that Heintzelman with thirty thousand men had marched to reinforce him. You can therefore see the odds against us and decide whether the line of Virginia is more in danger than the line of the Mississippi. If Pickett's division is ordered to the west, Pettigrew's brigade had better be ordered to the Blackwater [River]. I think troops ordered from Virginia to the Mississippi at this season would be greatly endangered by the climate. The strength of this army has been reduced by the casualties in the late battles.

                    I am with great respect, your obt servt

                                          R. E. LEE
                                          Genl

439   To JAMES A. SEDDON
                                    Secretary of War
                                      TELEGRAM

                                                            Fredericksburg
                                                            May 10, 1863

IT BECOMES MY MELANCHOLY DUTY TO ANNOUNCE TO YOU THE DEATH
OF GENL JACKSON. HE EXPIRED AT THREE AND A QUARTER (3¼) P.M. TODAY.
HIS BODY WILL BE CONVEYED TO RICHMOND IN THE TRAIN TOMORROW, UNDER
CHARGE OF MAJOR [ALEXANDER S.] PENDLETON, ASSISTANT ADJUTANT GEN-
ERAL. PLEASE DIRECT AN ESCORT OF HONOR TO MEET IT AT THE DEPOT, AND
THAT SUITABLE ARRANGEMENTS BE MADE FOR ITS DISPOSITION.

                                                            R. E. LEE
                                                            Genl

440   To JEFFERSON DAVIS
                                    Richmond, Virginia

                                 Headquarters, Army of Northern Virginia
                                                            May 11, 1863

Mr. President:
    I judge from the tone of the Northern papers that it is the intention
of the administration at Washington to reinforce the army of Genl
Hooker. The *Chronicle*, the *Herald*, and the *World* state this positively.
The latter represents that Genl Heintzelman is ordered to reinforce it
with 30,000 men, and that 18,000 are ordered to it from other quarters. A
scout from Old Point reports that the whole of the force at Fort Monroe, except four hundred men have left that place. Only eight thousand
are at Suffolk. The rest of the force there have been sent to reinforce
Genl Hooker. Genl D. H. Hill forwards reports of May 9th from which
I judge that troops are being sent from New Berne, and Genl Longstreet thinks it probable from what he has heard that some of Genl
[David] Hunter's army will be brought on from South Carolina. I suppose these are the sources from which the 18,000 men mentioned in the
New York papers are to be obtained. It would seem therefore that Virginia is to be the theater of action, and this army, if possible, ought to be
strengthened. If I could get in a position to advance beyond the Rappahannock I should certainly draw their troops from the Southern coasts
and give some respite in that quarter.
    I propose for your consideration to place Genl D. H. Hill in com-

mand of the department between James River and Cape Fear, and to draw from it, [Generals Robert] Ransom's and [Micah] Jenkins' brigades. I do not know what force has been left in the Department of South Carolina, Georgia, and Florida, since troops have been sent thence to Vicksburg. But I believe no more force is required there than sufficient to maintain the water batteries. A vigorous movement here would certainly draw the enemy from there, and the two brigades which went originally from this army [Generals John R.] Cooke's & [Nathan G.] Evans' could be returned. I think you will agree with me that every effort should be made to reinforce this army in order to oppose the large force which the enemy seems to be concentrating against it.

I am with great respect, your obt servt

R. E. Lee
Genl

441   To G. W. C. LEE
Richmond, Virginia

Camp
May 11, 1863

My Dear Custis:
These hot days remind me I must prepare to lighten my clothing. Will you send me, by Thomas, the messenger of the Adjutant and Inspector General, my gray sack, cotton drawers, and some cotton socks that I sent down last fall. Upon their arrival, I will send my flannels and will get you to put them in my trunk. You must excuse all the trouble I give you. I have no one else to aid me, and cannot leave here.

If the President cannot visit the army, I must go to him for a day at least. In that event, I could make these exchanges myself. I found Ham in this army, and requested his employer to send him down to Mr. Eacho to get his free papers.

I have not heard whether he obtained them. I heard from your mother yesterday. She was at Shirley, but did not seem satisfied. I fear she is no better. I wish I could do something for her relief. You will have heard of the death of General Jackson. It is a terrible loss. I do not know how to replace him. Any victory would be dear at such a cost. But God's will be done. His body goes to R[ichmond] today. Give love to all.

Truly and aff your father

R. E. Lee

442   GENERAL ORDERS, NO. 61

Headquarters, Army of Northern Virginia
May 11, 1863

With deep grief the commanding general announces to the army the death of Lieut Genl T. J. Jackson, who expired on the 10th instant, at 3.15 p.m. The daring, skill, and energy of this great and good soldier, by the decree of an all wise Providence, are now lost to us. But while we mourn his death, we feel that his spirit still lives, and will inspire the whole army with his indomitable courage and unshaken confidence in God as our hope and our strength. Let his name be a watchword to his corps who have followed him to victory on so many fields. Let officers and soldiers emulate his invincible determination to do everything in the defense of our beloved country.

R. E. LEE
General

443   To GENERAL DANIEL H. HILL
Commanding Department South of James River

Richmond
May 16, 1863

General:
In reply to your letter of the 14th, I will state that the extent of the reinforcements you can send to the Army of Northern Virginia must necessarily depend upon the strength of the enemy in your front. The plan you propose of exchanging your full for its reduced brigades I fear will add but little to its real strength. It would increase it numerically but weaken it intrinsically by taking away tried troops under experienced officers & replacing them with fresh men & uninstructed commanders. I should therefore have more to feed but less to depend on. I can exchange Daniel's brigade with one of those you propose, but cannot designate which until I return to camp, as I am not sufficiently acquainted with their condition to make the selection. You can therefore put Daniel's in motion at once. Ransom & Cooke I consider as belonging to the Army of Northern Virginia & have relied upon their return. As far as I am able to judge, the plan of the enemy is to concentrate as large a force as possible to operate in Virginia. Whether he will unite the whole under General H[ooker] on the Rappahannock or operate with

different columns I cannot say, but from the information I receive he is withdrawing troops from South Carolina & the country south of James River. It is of course our best policy to do the same & to endeavour to repel his advance into Virginia. If he weakens his force in North Carolina I think you will be able, by using all your local troops, such portion of your regular cavalry & regular brigades as may be necessary, to repulse & restrain his marauding expeditions, protect the railroads & farming interests of the country you now hold. Every man not required for this purpose I desire you to send to me & rely upon your good judgment to proportion the means to the object in view. I think it is now too late for any important expedition to be undertaken by the enemy in the Carolinas. They will, I think, place themselves on the defensive in those States, endeavour to deceive us by threatening our communications, &c., & send their available troops where they can operate to more advantage. I have no fear that they will be able to mislead you. I hope you will be able to collect & secure for the use of the army all the provisions & forage in the districts in which you are operating.

I am with great respect, your obt servt

R. E. LEE
Genl

444   To HIS WIFE
                Richmond, Virginia

Camp, Fredericksburg
May 20, 1863

I felt very sad dear Mary at leaving you in so helpless & suffering a state. I pray that our merciful Father in Heaven may in his own time & own way give you relief. I hope you will make use of all the means at your disposal to attain it. If you cannot get to the Hot Springs suppose you try the Bath Alum. It may suit your case. But wherever you go, you must be careful not to go to extremes, but take care of yourself. Take your daughters with you that they may aid & take care of you. I found on my return a letter from Mary which I enclose. Also some kind notes from the Stuarts. I send also a letter from Fitzhugh, & one from Mrs. Atkinson, so you will have plenty of reading & I hope it will assuage your pains. As usual I have no news. I learn that our poor wounded are doing well. Genl Hooker is agitating himself north of the Rappahannock & again threatens us with a crossing. It was reported last night that he had brought his pontoons to the river, but I hear nothing of him this morning. I think he will consider it a few days. He has published a congratulatory order to his troops, telling them they have covered themselves with new laurels, have destroyed our stores, communications, thousands of our choice troops, captured prisoners within the fortifications of the capital & filled the country with fear & consternation. "Profoundly loyal & conscious of its own strength, the Army of the Potomac will give or decline battle whenever its interest or honour may demand. It will also be the guardian of its own history & its own honour." All of which is signed by our old friend "S[eth] Williams, A. A. G." It shows at least he is unhurt & is so far good, but as to the truth of history I will not speak. You must give much love to my poor little Agnes. She ought to be here with her papa. The nights are warm & she would not require many blankets, & perhaps bacon & black eyed peas would cure her neuralgia. I despair of Miss Norvell & Silby Booker's coming up, for though I could give them thousands of beaux, I could give them no marine officer. Remember me very kindly to Mr. & Mrs. Caskie & thank them for all their kindness to me & to you. May the great God have you all in His holy keeping & soon unite us again.

Truly & sincerely yours

R. E. LEE

445 To JEFFERSON DAVIS
Richmond, Virginia

Camp, Fredericksburg
May 20, 1863

Mr. President:

I cannot express the concern I felt at leaving you in such feeble health, with so many anxious thoughts for the welfare of the whole Confederacy weighing upon your mind. I pray that a kind Providence will give you strength to bear the weight of care it has thought good to impose upon you, & that you may soon have the gratification of seeing the country liberated from its enemies, & all your labours crowned with success. In the matters I propose now to submit to the consideration of Your Excellency I shall endeavour to be brief.

[Generals Elisha] Paxton's & J. R. Jones' places have been filled by [Generals James A.] Walker & John M. Jones. Should the latter officer fail in his duty he will instantly resign. I have not yet been able to fill [General Francis T.] Nicholls' place. I have not seen Col [James B.]

Walton, but Longstreet thinks he would not like the exchange, & I am doubtful whether he would answer. The misfortune is that the brigade is at present commanded by Col [Edmund] Pendleton, who is not highly considered, & its services I fear will be lost to the army. I have determined to place [General John B.] Gordon in command of Rodes' (former) brigade. That will leave [General Alexander P.] Lawton's vacant. If the latter is not wanted elsewhere, he can be returned to it. But I believe Col Edward Willis, of the 12th Georgia, or Col John T. Mercer, of the 21st would answer better for the field. Both have been educated at West Point. The latter served several years in the army. I think it better to relieve [General Raleigh E.] Colston from duty, & to place Genl George [H.] Steuart in command of his brigade. The brigade is composed of 2 North Carolina & 3 Virginia regiments. The former have complained of being commanded by a Virginia brigadier, & I presume the latter would complain if commanded by a North Carolinian. Genl Steuart being of the old army, no one has a right to complain. I shall write to Genl Cooper for Genl Steuart. I shall also write to Genl Trimble to know whether he can not take general control of affairs in the Valley. He will have Col Davidson at Staunton & Genl Jenkins with the cavalry below.

I have for the past year felt that the corps of this army were too large for one commander. Nothing prevented my proposing to you to reduce their size & increase their number, but my inability to recommend commanders. Each corps contains when in fighting condition about 30,000 men. These are more than one man can properly handle & keep under his eye in battle in the country that we have to operate in. They are always beyond the range of his vision, & frequently beyond his reach. The loss of Jackson from the command of one half the army seems to me a good opportunity to remedy this evil. If therefore you think Ewell is able to do field duty, I submit to your better judgment whether the most advantageous arrangement would not be to put him in command of three divisions of Jackson's corps. To take one of Longstreet's divisions [R. H. Anderson's], [and] A. P. Hill's division, & form a division of Ransom's, Cooke's, & Pettigrew's brigades, & give the corps thus formed to A. P. Hill. This would make three corps of three divisions each, under Longstreet, Ewell & A. P. Hill. In this event I also submit to you whether it would not be well to promote Ewell & A. P. Hill. The former is an honest, brave soldier, who has always done his duty well. The latter I think upon the whole is the best soldier of his grade with me. Inasmuch as this army has done hard work, & there is still harder before it, I wish to take advantage of every circumstance to inspire & encourage them, & induce the officers & men to believe that their labours are appreciated,

& when vacancies occur that they will receive the advantages of promotion if they deserve it. I believe the efficiency of the corps would be promoted by being commanded by lt genls, & I do not know where to get better men than those I have named. R. H. Anderson & J. B. Hood are also capital officers. They are improving too, & will make good corps commanders if necessary. I think it is better to take officers from each corps respectively for promotion in the respective corps as far as practicable, consideration being always given to the best man in the particular army. If A. P. Hill is promoted, a major genl will be wanted for his division. [General Henry] Heth is the senior brigadier in the division. I think him a good officer. He has lately joined this army, was in the last battle, & did well. His nomination having been once declined by the Senate, I do not know whether it would be proper to promote him. [General W. Dorsey] Pender is an excellent officer, attentive, industrious, & brave. Has been conspicuous in every battle, & I believe wounded in almost all of them. I must now ask you to do in all this matter as seems best to you from your point of view. I have frankly given you my opinions from mine. I hope you will be able to give me your conclusions at your earliest convenience, as it is time I was in motion. With earnest wishes for your health & happiness, & with great respect,

I am your obt servt

R. E. Lee
Genl

446   To JAMES A. SEDDON
                          Secretary of War

Headquarters, Army of Northern Virginia
May 20, 1863

Sir:

The services of Genl Longstreet will be required with this army. Upon his leaving the department south of James River, I had supposed its command would have devolved upon Genl D. H. Hill, as the senior major genl. He informed me this morning that he directed the three major genls in command of the several districts to report directly to the War Department. I would recommend therefore that Genl D. H. Hill be assigned to the command of the department between the James River & the Cape Fear. The battery at Drewry's Bluff, if considered more convenient, could be embraced within the command of Genl Elzey. I wish Genl Hill to make such disposition of his troops as to give me all the force that can be spared from North Carolina. Jenkins' brigade, belonging to Pickett's division, is still on the Blackwater, & I do not like to order it up until I hear whether proper dispositions are made to relieve it. It is much wanted with its division.

Our scouts report that Genl Heintzelman with his corps from Washington has joined Genl Hooker, Governor [Andrew G.] Curtin [of Pennsylvania] having promised to defend Washington City with 20,000 State troops. I have not heard yet of any fleet of transports ascending the Potomac. Single transports are frequently seen coming up the river. Yesterday 40 transports were counted at Aquia Creek. Regiments of the two years' men are being discharged I learn as their time expires, & it is thought are sent off at night.

I am with great respect, your obt servt

R. E. Lee
Genl

447   To GENERAL JOHN B. HOOD
Commanding Division

Camp, Fredericksburg
May 21, 1863

My Dear General:

Upon my return from Richmond I found your letter of the 13th awaiting me. Although separated from me, I have always had you in my eye and thoughts. I wished for you much in the last battle, and believe had I had the whole army with me, General Hooker would have been demolished. But God ordered otherwise.

I grieve much over the death of General Jackson. For our sakes not for his. He is happy and at peace. But his spirit lives with us. I hope it will raise up many Jacksons in our ranks. . . . I rely much upon you. You must so inspire and lead your brave division as that it may accomplish the work of a corps. . . . I agree with you in believing that our army would be invincible if it could be properly organized and officered. There never were such men in an army before. They will go anywhere and do anything if properly led. But there is the difficulty — proper commanders. Where can they be obtained? . . . . Wishing you every health and happiness, and commending you to the care of a kind Providence, I am, now and always your friend

R. E. Lee

448   To HIS WIFE
                        Richmond, Virginia

                                              Camp, Fredericksburg
                                              May 23, 1863

My Dear Mary:

   I received yesterday your letter of the 21st with the socks & am
much obliged to you for their reparation. I see though you are relapsing
into your old error, supposing that I have a superabundance of time &
have only my own pleasures to attend to. You do not recollect that after
an absence of some days, that matters accumulate formidably, & that my
attention is entirely engrossed in public business. I am unable therefore
even to write to you, though my thoughts are always with you. You
must not therefore be always expecting letters from me, for I repeat
that I am able to write but seldom, & at long intervals. I send down the
pillow case as you request. It is in worse condition than I supposed & I
do not think you will be able to do anything with it. I can do very well
with out it, & I may have to dispence with the pillow, so the case will be
of little service. I also return a letter of poor little Laura. The death of
Washington [Stuart] was a heavy blow to them all & I truly sympathize
in their grief. I am glad you heard from F[itzhugh] & R[obert] & that
Charlotte is so well accomodated. I hope she will be able to spend a
little time with F[itzhugh] though that is problematical. I hope indeed
the doctor's prescriptions under the blessing of Heaven may relieve you
of your painful affliction for I can do nothing but offer my poor feeble
prayers to almighty God for your relief, & which ascend night & morning to his throne of grace! I am glad to hear that the President has given
his permission to C[ustis] to join the army. I hope his inclinations
prompt him to join this, & tell him I send a formal invitation for him to
join me. You must give much love to Mr. & Mrs. Caskie & my heartfelt
thanks for all their kindness to you in your great necessity. God alone
can reward them for their charity & benevolence & I pray that his blessings may be showered upon them in this world & the next. Tell Miss
N[orvell] I suspect Capt Smith Lee has her beaux, & that he would like to
capture her & Miss Silby too. Col Withers would not interfere with them
for he knows how highly I value them. They will all return though tell
her, when they find I have gone. She shall have a plenty if she will come
up here. Thank my poor little Agnes for her affectionate note. I hope
her little propellers are not becoming afflicted too. She must exercise
them more. She had better take my advice & ask some of her friends to
employ her in their corn fields. Give much love to my "precious life." I

am very sorry I could not see her, & God only knows when we shall meet again. She must write to her papa, & not eat plum cakes.

With great affection very truly yours

R. E. LEE

P.S. I send a kind note from Mr. Rives. It may distract your thoughts from your pains a moment. I do not think that I take any of his commendation to myself. I know I am entitled to none. But he does not over estimate this brave army. It is for your perusal alone. After which destroy it.

R. E. L.

449   To MISS AGNES LEE
Richmond, Virginia

Camp, Fredericksburg
May 25, 1863

My precious little Agnes:

I have received your "little note" by Major Venable, & heartily thank you for your affectionate remembrances & regrets at my departure. I sincerely join in your wish that the war was over & that we could all be once more united, though it may be for a short time. Then too what calamity would be spared the country! What pain & anguish would be turned from many a household! I trust that a merciful God in His own good time will accomplish His holy will & give us peace & happiness. I hope you are not going to be afflicted with rheumatism too. You must take regular exercise, be much out in the open air, & be careful not to expose yourself to the sudden alternation of heat & cold. You girls have no time to be sick. You have a sacred charge, the care of your poor mother. You must endeavour to get her to some of the healing waters this summer & I hope you may find relief in your own person. She has tried the Hot Springs twice, without permanent relief, though I believe with some benefit. It may be the best for her. But I have heard of the Rockbridge Alum proving advantageous in many cases, & I think she had better give that a trial. She might go to the Hot, before or after as might be judged best. Tell Miss Sallie I am very grateful for her love, but I wish she had not ran away from Richmond before my last visit. I do not know when I shall be there again, but I shall think of her very often. You must also give my kind regards to Mrs. Phoebe & Mr. Warwick. I do not believe I told you that our old friend Charlie

Turnbull was engaged against us in the battle at Chancellorsville. He commands the old sapper & miner company I understand, of which he is captain. He is married to some rich Boston lady, & I suppose she has turned him. The train which brought me up Monday stopped at Ashland for breakfast & I went in to see Bishop Johns, &c. I saw Laura & Bella. They were very sad but composed. I did not see Cousin Cornelia. Perhaps she had not left her room as it was early. Tell Miss Sallie if I had hair like hers, "whose glossy hue to shame might bring, the plumage of the ravens wing" I would send her some, but she must not laugh at my grey hairs. Good-bye my precious child. Kiss your mother for me & take good care of her. You know I can do nothing for her now. Remember me in your sweet prayers & supplicate the throne of grace for mercy & forgiveness towards me.

May God guard & protect you, prays your devoted father

R. E. LEE

450   To GENERAL DANIEL H. HILL
          Commanding Department South of James River

Headquarters, Fredericksburg
May 25, 1863

General:
    I have received by courier your letter of the 21st. I am much gratified to learn that the enemy has been so harassed & punished during the past months, & wish that your force was sufficient to drive them from the State. If your information is correct that their troops are moving from the State I hope you will be able to spare the brigades belonging to this army. They are very essential to aid in the effort to turn back the tide of war that is now pressing South. Since the battle of Chancellorsville the enemy has made a lodgment at West Point, the confluence of the Pamunkey & Mattapony Rivers, & are fortifying that neck. Whether it is a feint or preparation for a new base of operations I do not know. I have thought it probable that the troops from your department may be in process of transference to that point. I therefore desire that you direct Br Genl Jenkins to join his division, Pickett's, at Hanover Junction, & Br Genl Ransom to repair to Richmond. Should it be necessary to move him farther he will receive orders from Genl Elzey, to whom he will report. You can retain Br Genl Cooke for the present, or until you can more fully ascertain the intentions of the enemy, & see what dispositions you can best make for the protection of your department. I think if

necessary troops may be drawn from South Carolina & Georgia to reinforce you, as I can hardly suppose that the enemy contemplates any
serious invasion of that department this summer. I think too the season
has passed for making any movement in North Carolina more than raids
of devastation or attempts to retain there our troops in idleness. I hope
you will be able to frustrate & punish all such efforts.

I am very much in need of cavalry, & if you can spare another regiment as you suggest, I will be much obliged to you to order it to repair
to Orange Court House & report to Genl Stuart. I am told there is a regiment on the Blackwater, whose horses are in good condition, which if
you could replace by another, it might be well to send. If you require
Genl Robertson to command or organize the cavalry in your department
I will return him to you.

I am with great respect, your obt servt

R. E. LEE
Genl

451   To GENERAL ARNOLD ELZEY
Commanding at Richmond

Headquarters, Army of Northern Virginia
May 27, 1863

General:
From the reports of scouts, it is very probable that a large force of
Federal cavalry is about to set out on an expedition to the interior of the
State. A large body of cavalry has moved up from Aquia Creek towards
Warrenton. Among the Federal soldiers two cavalry raids are spoken of,
having in view the capture of Richmond. There are indications of a
movement on the part of Hooker's army in front also. The number of
tents is much diminished, the wagon trains coming from the depot are
much smaller, & the camp fires on the hills in the rear much lessened.
Citizens & others across the Rappahannock speak of a change of base to
the James River. From all that I can judge Foster has left North Carolina
and I suspect that his forces are at West Point. I have ordered Ransom's
brigade to report to you in Richmond and await further orders. Jenkins'
brigade I have ordered up to Genl Pickett, at Hanover Junction. I wish
you to have the defences of Richmond put in proper condition immediately, your guns & magazines ready for use, and your garrison in readiness for any emergency. Make available all the cavalry which you have
at your disposal, and, in short, make every arrangement to protect the

city against insult from a cavalry inroad, or from a sudden attack from any quarter. If you can take care of Richmond with the force which you now have, I will order Pickett's division up to join Hood, on the Rapidan, so as to have a force in the rear of the enemy should he cross that stream.

I am very respectfully, your obt servt

R. E. LEE
Genl

452   To JEFFERSON DAVIS
Richmond, Virginia
TELEGRAM

Fredericksburg
May 29, 1863

I GAVE GENL [D. H.] HILL DISCRETIONARY ORDERS FROM RICHMOND TO APPORTION HIS FORCE TO THE STRENGTH OF ENEMY AND SEND WHAT COULD BE SPARED. HE DECLINED TO ACT AND REQUESTED POSITIVE ORDERS. I GAVE SUCH ORDERS AS I COULD AT THIS DISTANCE. NOW HE OBJECTS. I CANNOT OPERATE IN THIS MANNER. I REQUEST YOU TO CAUSE SUCH ORDERS TO BE GIVEN HIM AS YOUR JUDGMENT DICTATES. PICKETT HAS NO BRIGADE IN PLACE OF JENKINS' SO GENL LONGSTREET REPORTS. GENL HILL HAS RETAINED ONE REGIMENT FROM PETTIGREW AND ONE FROM DANIELS.

R. E. LEE

453   To JEFFERSON DAVIS
Richmond, Virginia

Headquarters, Fredericksburg
May 30, 1863

Mr. President:

I hope you received my reply to your dispatch of yesterday. When in Richmond, I gave Genl D. H. Hill discretionary instructions, stating my belief that the contest of the summer would take place in Virginia, to apportion his force to the strength of the enemy, and send me every man he could spare. He declined to act under those instructions, and requested positive instructions. He now offers objections, which if previously presented, I should not have issued the latter. You will see that I am unable to operate under these circumstances, and request to be re-

lieved from any control of the department from the James to the Cape
Fear River. I have for nearly a month been endeavoring to get this army
in a condition to move, to anticipate an expected blow from the enemy.
I fear I shall have to receive it here at a disadvantage, or to retreat. The
enemy will either make a combined movement to force me back, or
transfer his army to the James River. If I was stronger, I think I could
prevent either, and force him back. You will perceive by the return of
the 20th, forwarded to the Adjutant and Inspector General, the effective
strength of the army. If I could use it altogether, or had only to oppose
Genl Hooker's army, I should be content. But my wish has been to organize a force to defend Richmond against the army apparently collecting on the York River. I can get no positive information as to its
strength. I have no knowledge of the scouts sent in that direction. Genl
Longstreet, when on the Blackwater, sent a person to Washington. He
could get no farther than Baltimore. No one but the military were allowed on the cars from Baltimore to Washington. He said while in B[alti-
more] troops were constantly passing to W[ashington], said to be
[Robert B.] Mitchell's from the west, going to Genl Hooker. At Old
Point, on his return, he saw some of Foster's troops, and was informed
that Genls Dix, Keyes, and Foster were at West Point. There were only
three companies at Fort Monroe. I received this information with some
allowance. But it may be taken as evidence that troops are being thrown
into Virginia. I only directed Ransom's brigade to be sent to Richmond;
Jenkins' to Hanover Junction; Cooke's to wait till movements of the enemy could be further ascertained. Genl Longstreet says Pickett has no
brigade in the place of Jenkins'. He had temporarily a brigade formed
of two regiments from Genl Sam Jones & two from Genl Marshall. It
was first under Pryor and afterwards under Colston. Three of the regiments were sent back to the west, one is still in Petersburg, or rather
one that was exchanged for it. This army has been diminished since last
fall by the brigades of Jenkins, Ransom, Cooke, & Evans. It has been increased by Pettigrew's. I consider Colquitt's exchanged for Daniel's.
General Hill has retained in North Carolina a regiment from Pettigrew
and Daniel. Genl Hooker's army, as far as I can form an opinion, has
been increased. I have given Your Excellency all the facts in my possession to enable you to form an opinion as to what is best to be done. I fear
the time has passed when I could have taken the offensive with advantage.
From the indications that reach me, the enemy is contemplating another
movement. I have not discovered what it is. There may be nothing left
for me to do but fall back. Genl Hill has in North Carolina Jenkins',
[Joseph R.] Davis', Cooke's, Ransom's, [Thomas L.] Clingman's, &
[James G.] Martin's brigades, a large amount of field artillery, & three

regiments of cavalry; one of the latter, in addition to the two sent, he has offered to send me. I have directed him to suspend the execution of the orders from me, & await orders from the Adjutant and Inspector General.

I am with great respect, your obt servt

R. E. LEE
Genl

454   To GENERAL DANIEL H. HILL
        Commanding Department South of James River

Headquarters, Army of Northern Virginia
May 30, 1863

General:
     Your letter of May 27th has been received. I telegraphed to you this morning to suspend the execution of my order of the 25th instant. The President will give you such orders as he may see fit. I know nothing of the force in your front, but I attach no importance to the estimate of the enemy's forces in New Berne, based on the captured mail. These letters only go to show that the writers thought these regiments were in New Berne at the time they wrote. One of Longstreet's scouts, in whom he places some confidence, has just returned from Fortress Monroe. He reports some of [General John G.] Foster's forces at that point, & that Foster, [John A.] Dix, & [Erasmus D.] Keyes are at Yorktown & West Point. From the returns of Pettigrew's & Daniel's brigades, the effective force of the two is 5,844. Two cavalry regiments give 1,068 effectives. Estimating the third regiment of cavalry at 500, this will give a total effective of 7,500 sent from your department. Each of the two brigades is reported to have left one regiment in North Carolina.

I am very respectfully, your obt servt

R. E. LEE
Genl

455   To JAMES A. SEDDON
              Secretary of War

Headquarters, Army of Northern Virginia
May 30, 1863

Sir:
     I have the honor to recommend that you expedite as much as possible the organization of the citizens of Richmond as a local force for the

defence of the city. All the citizens capable of doing duty should be encouraged to take up arms for the defence of their homes. I also recommend that such troops as can be spared from the Departments of South Carolina, Georgia, and Florida, and from the James to the Cape Fear Rivers, should be advanced to Virginia. The brigades ordered by me from the latter department to Virginia I have directed to await your further orders, & I request to be relieved from the control of that department. I think it probable from information received that Genl Hooker will endeavour to turn the left of my present position and hold me in check, while an effort is made by the forces collected on York River, by forced marches and with the aid of their cavalry under Genl Stoneman to gain possession of Richmond. Two scouts from within the enemy's lines have brought me this report. It may be a rumor propagated to cause me to abandon my present position, but I think preparations had better be made to guard against any such attempt. But movements of the enemy on the upper Rappahannock now in progress indicate an advance from him in that direction. I need not express to you the hope that the arrangements you may think proper to make will not be of a character to excite alarm or useless apprehension in the community.

I have the honor to be with much respect, your obt servt

R. E. LEE
Genl

456   To HIS WIFE
Richmond, Virginia

Camp, Fredericksburg
May 31, 1863

I have been trying all the week my dear Mary to write to you. But have been unable. You must always remember when you do not hear from me that I have no time to write, & have nothing particular to say. I am very glad to hear that you are even a little better. I trust your improvement will continue & that you will attain your usual comfortable condition. That will be a great relief for which I shall be fervently thankful to our Heavenly Father. I told you you would not be satisfied with the photographs. I should indeed like very much to see Mildred on her return from school, both for the pleasure it would give me, & also that I might better form an opinion as to her future course. But where I may be then, or what may be the condition of things, I cannot say. I shall leave it therefore to you & Custis. I think I can trust the discretion of the latter in this case. I enclose a very complimentary letter from Dr. Smedes. I have been extremely gratified at his account of her progress & deportment. As far as I can now judge I think she had better return for I do not see what better she can do in the present unsettled state of affairs. I am sorry indeed that Mr. Caskie is deprived of the services of Arthur. He has doubtless gone to the enemy. Young Toler is very well. I have seen him since the last battle, on the battlefield. Beverly Coderise I can hear nothing of. I should like to know where he is. I have received a letter from Charlotte. She was at Culpeper Court House very comfortable & happy. Had seen the review & all the Genls & had much to say about Fitzhugh. It was written in pencil so I suppose ink is scarce. Fitzhugh & Robert were both well & according to Charlotte looked uncommonly handsome at the review. Tell Miss Norvell about Robert. Give my kindest regards to Mr. & Mrs. Caskie. I hope they are all well & Miss Nannie Hutchinson also. Genl Hooker has been very busy the past week & equally active. He has not said what he intended to do, but has given out by his movements that he designs crossing the Rappahannock. I think we shall hear from Genl Stoneman next week also. I hope we may be able to frustrate their plans in part if not in whole. He has Genl [Samuel P.] Heintzelman with him now on whom the Northern papers seem to place great reliance & his corps of veterans of 30,000 men. I pray that our merciful Father in Heaven may protect & direct us. In that case I fear no odds & no numbers. Kiss Agnes for me & Custis. I hope the President's health is improving, though I suppose he cannot feel better as long as this uncertainty hangs over Vicksburg. May God bless us with a victory there too! Genl Ewell came up day before yesterday with his wife, son & daughter. He looks very well & is very stout of heart. Mrs. Ewell & daughter I think returned to Richmond yesterday. God bless you my dear Mary.

Truly yours

R. E. LEE

457   To JAMES A. SEDDON
                             Secretary of War

                                        Headquarters, Army of Northern Virginia
                                        June 2, 1863

Sir:

I had the honour to receive your letter of the 29th ultimo. I have subsequently received a communication from His Excellency the President on the same subject, and I believe he has determined the question as to the disposition of the troops in North Carolina. I think you are under a misapprehension in regard to a brigade having been attached to Pickett's division in the place of Jenkins'. Genl Longstreet states that Colston's brigade, formed of the regiments of Genls Sam Jones' & Marshall's commands, was temporarily assigned to Pickett's division at the time that Jenkins was detached. Colston's brigade was subsequently broken up when these regiments were returned by you to their former commands. Pickett's division is now at Hanover Junction, with no brigades with it except those taken from this army, Jenkins being still detached. I regret to be deprived of Ransom & Jenkins, upon whom, as well as their troops, I greatly relied. I replied to Genl D. H. Hill's proposition when I was in Richmond, in reference to the exchange of brigades in North Carolina with certain brigades in this army. I believe it would add to my numerical strength & give me more men to subsist, but I doubt whether it would add to my fighting force. I should like much to have the thinned ranks of the brigades he mentions filled up, but dislike to part with officers & men who have been tried in battle and seasoned to the hardships of the campaign in exchange for wholly untried troops.

I am with great respect, your obt servt

R. E. Lee
Genl

458   To HIS WIFE
Richmond, Virginia

Camp, Fredericksburg
June 3, 1863

Although I have written to you quite recently dear Mary, I take advantage of Major Venable being called to Richmond to say that I am well. I have nothing new to relate, & am thankful that our enemy has not been able as yet to capture Vicksburg, or to do us all the harm he meditates. I trust that a kind Providence will watch over us, & notwithstanding our weakness & sins will yet give us a name & place among the nations of the earth. I have heard nothing from Fitzhugh or Charlotte since I last wrote. From the enclosed note of Fitz, my nephew, I presume they are all well. I fear I shall not be able to attend the review on Friday. I hope Smith will be able to visit his sons. He is an iron clad, he is safe in his position & can go about & enjoy himself. I had a nice basket of strawberries sent me last evening & this evening I am invited out to eat ice cream. See what enjoyments we have. The first I did my part to demolish, the second I had to decline. When do you expect Mildred? I hear the two Ellens of the Macfarland house arrived from Columbia a few days since. Probably the wedding of last night brought them on. Remember me very kindly to Mr. & Mrs. Caskie. Tell Miss Norvell to send up all her beaux now. I want them. Kiss Agnes for me & believe me

Always yours

R. E. LEE

459 To GENERAL SAMUEL COOPER
Adjutant and Inspector General
TELEGRAM

Headquarters, Army of Northern Virginia
June 4, 1863

I HAVE THE HONOR TO REQUEST THAT UPON THE RECEIPT OF THIS LETTER, INSTRUCTIONS BE ISSUED DIRECTING THAT CONVALESCENTS AND OTHERS BELONGING TO THE DIVISIONS OF HOOD & MCLAWS, OF LONGSTREET'S CORPS, AND THOSE RETURNING TO THE DIVISIONS OF EARLY AND JOHNSON AND RODES, OF EWELL'S CORPS, BE FORWARDED TO CULPEPER COURT HOUSE INSTEAD OF THIS PLACE AS HERETOFORE.

VERY RESPECTFULLY, YOUR OBT SERVT

R. E. LEE
Genl

460 To GENERAL AMBROSE P. HILL
Commanding Third Corps

Headquarters, Army of Northern Virginia
June 5, 1863

I desire you to occupy the position of Fredericksburg with the troops under your command, making such disposition as will be best calculated to deceive the enemy, and keep him in ignorance of any change in the disposition of the army.

Should the enemy make an advance upon you, you will endeavor to repel him, and, if not able to do so, or hold him in check, you must fall back along the line of the [Richmond,] Fredericksburg [and Potomac] Railroad, protecting your communications, and offering such resistance as you can to his advance towards Richmond. If you find it necessary, you can call up Pickett and Pettigrew, now at Hanover Junction.

Should you find that the enemy has evacuated his position opposite, you will, after informing yourself of the fact by your scouts, &c., if practicable and in your opinion advantageous, cross the river and pursue him, inflicting all the damage you can upon his rear.

I request that you will keep me informed of everything material relative to yourself, position, and of the enemy. Col [Williams C.] Wickham with his cavalry is on your left, and Major [Charles R.] Collins, commanding 15th Virginia Cavalry, is on your right. Capt [Richard E.] Frayser, signal officer, is at Port Royal. These officers have been instructed to report to you. There is a line of couriers to Culpeper Court House. My headquarters will be there for the present.

You are desired to open any official communications sent to me, and if necessary act upon them according to the dictates of your good judgment.

Very respectfully, your obt svt

R. E. LEE
General

461 To JEFFERSON DAVIS
Richmond, Virginia

Headquarters, Army of Northern Virginia
Culpeper
June 7, 1863

Mr. President:

I commenced to draw the army from the vicinity of Fredericksburg on Wednesday morning (June 3rd). McLaws' division of Longstreet's corps marched that day. It was followed Thursday morning by Rodes' division and on Friday by Early's & [Edward] Johnson's of Ewell's corps. Hood's division of Longstreet's corps, which had previously been advanced to the Rapidan was directed on the 3rd instant to move to Culpeper Court House. On the afternoon of Friday the 5th instant the enemy made open preparations to cross the Rappahannock at the old position at the mouth of Deep Run. After driving back our sharpshooters, under a furious cannonade from their batteries, by a force of skirmishers, they crossed a small body of troops and occupied the bank of the river.

It was so devoid of concealment, that I supposed the intention was to ascertain what force occupied the position at Fredericksburg, or to fix our attention upon that point while they should accomplish some other object. I thought it prudent to send that night to Genl Ewell to halt his march until I could see what the next day would develop, and placed A. P. Hill's corps in position to meet any attack that might be made the next morning. After watching the enemy's operations Saturday, and being unable to discover more troops than could be attended to by Hill, and no advance having been made by them, I sent forward to Genl Ewell to resume his march, and left Fredericksburg myself in the evening. My conclusion was that the enemy had discovered the withdrawal of our troops from Fredericksburg and wished to detain us until he could make corresponding changes. I have with me two divisions of Longstreet's & the three divisions of Ewell's. I desire to bring up the remaining division of Longstreet's (Pickett's), and sent you a dispatch this morning, requesting that Cooke should be advanced to his place [Hanover Junction], & that Jenkins should be brought from the Blackwater to replace Cooke. If it is true as reported by Genl Elzey that only 1,500 of the enemy remain in Suffolk, Ransom's brigade will be more than sufficient for that line. West Point being evacuated and the force at Yorktown reduced, there is nothing to be apprehended from that quarter, and Cooke & Jenkins should be directed to follow me as soon as you think it safe for them to do so. As far as I can learn, the enemy appears to be extending up the Rappahannock from Fredericksburg. The whole line of the Rappahannock is closely guarded, every ford defended and closely picketed to Beverly's, above the railroad bridge. His cavalry is massed along the line of the railway from Catlett's to Bealeton. Stoneman's headquarters being at Shumate's on Cedar Run (Fauquier). I think if I can create an apprehension for the safety of their right flank & the Potomac, more troops will be brought from their line of operations in the south. But to gain any material advantage, I should if possible have a large force, as their army by all accounts is represented as very large. If it is true, as stated in the Northern papers that Genl Hunter's forces have been reduced by reinforcements sent to the Gulf, it would be well for Genl Beauregard with the force made available by this withdrawal to be sent to reinforce Johnston in the west, or be ordered to reinforce this army. If these troops remain where they are, their services will be lost to the country and they will become a prey to disease.

I am with great respect, your obt servant

R. E. Lee
Genl

462   To COLONEL JOSIAH GORGAS
Chief of Ordnance

Headquarters, Army of Northern Virginia
June 8, 1863

Colonel:

I reviewed today the five brigades of cavalry in this army forming the division commanded by General Stuart. My attention was thus called to a subject which I have previously brought to your notice, viz, the saddles and carbines manufactured in Richmond. I could not examine them myself, but was assured by officers that the former ruined the horses' backs, and the latter were so defective as to be demoralizing to the men. I am aware of the difficulties attending the manufacture of arms and equipments, but I suggest that you have the matter inquired into by your ordnance officers, and see if they cannot rectify the evils complained of. It would be better I think to make fewer articles and have them serviceable. The English saddles which you import are said to be good. It is the tree of the Richmond saddle that is complained of.

I am most respecty, your obt servt

R. E. Lee
Genl

463   To JAMES A. SEDDON
Secretary of War

Headquarters, Army of Northern Virginia
June 8, 1863

Sir:

I have had the honour to receive your letter of the 5th instant, transmitting copies of two letters from Genl Whiting, at the suggestion of the President. I can understand the anxiety felt by Genl Whiting for the safety of Wilmington and its railroad communications. I have no means of knowing the force of the enemy in North Carolina and the extent of his operations excepting from the reports of the officers. He does not seem to have projected much, and has accomplished less. This is no doubt partly owing to the judicious dispositions of our troops by the commanding officers in that department. But I think if the force of the enemy was as strong as supposed by Genls D. H. Hill & Whiting, at least more would have been attempted. There is always hazard in military movements, but we must decide between the positive loss of inactivity and the risk of action. I think the letters mailed to New Berne only show that the writers supposed their correspondents were in North Carolina. Many of them may have been there at one time, but it is known that a large force was withdrawn from there to South Carolina, and that they have not been returned. Genl Hill, at his last visit to New Berne with two brigades, drove the enemy within his entrenchments and kept him there all day. I cannot suppose that so large a force as is estimated by Genls Whiting & Hill could have been thus cooped up by so small a body of men. As far as I can judge there is nothing to be gained by this army remaining quietly on the defensive, which it must do unless it can be reinforced. I am aware that there is difficulty & hazard in taking the aggressive with so large an army in its front, entrenched behind a river where it cannot be advantageously attacked. Unless it can be drawn out in a position to be assailed, it will take its own time to prepare and strengthen itself to renew its advance upon Richmond, and force this army back within the intrenchments of that city. This may be the result in any event, still I think it is worth a trial to prevent such a catastrophe. Still, if the Department thinks it better to remain on the defensive, and guard as far as possible all the avenues of approach and await the time of the enemy, I am ready to adopt this course. You have therefore only to inform me. I think our southern coast might be held during the sickly season by local troops aided by a small organized force, and the predatory excursions of the enemy be repressed. This would give us an active force in the field with which we might hope to make some impression on the enemy, both on our northern & western frontiers. Unless this can be done, I see little hope of accomplishing anything of importance. All our military preparations and organizations should now be pressed forward with the greatest vigor, and every exertion made to obtain some material advantage in this campaign.

I am with great respect, your obt ser

R. E. LEE
Genl

464   MAJOR C. S. VENABLE TO GENERAL
J. E. B. STUART
Commanding Cavalry

Headquarters, Army of Northern Virginia
June 9, 1863

General:
    Genl Lee desires me to say that he has received your dispatches by the couriers & from signal station. Genl Longstreet has a division looking

to Stevensburg, & Genl Ewell on the other side looking to Brandy Station.

He desires you not to expose your men too much, but to do the enemy damage when possible. As the whole thing seems to be a reconnaissance to determine our force & position, he wishes these concealed as much as possible, & the infantry not to be seen, if it is possible to avoid it.

I am very respectfully, your obt servt

C. S. Venable
Major, & Aide-de-Camp

465   To JEFFERSON DAVIS
Richmond, Virginia
TELEGRAM

Culpeper
June 9, 1863 .

COOKE HAD BETTER BE ADVANCED TO HANOVER JUNCTION, & JENKINS TO CHICKAHOMINY. [GENERAL MONTGOMERY D.] CORSE IS ORDERED TO JOIN PICKETT. ENEMY CROSSED RAPPAHANNOCK AT BEVERLY FORD, CAVALRY, INFANTRY, & ARTILLERY, IN LARGE FORCE THIS MORNING. PRISONERS FROM TWO CORPS HAVE BEEN CAPTURED THIS SIDE OF THE RIVER. TWO (2) OTHER CORPS ARE REPORTED TO BE ADVANCING NORTH OF THE RAPPAHANNOCK.

R. E. Lee

466   To HIS WIFE
Richmond, Virginia

Culpepeɪ
June 9, 1863

It has been a long time dear Mary since I have been able to write to you. I have received two letters from you since I last wrote, & the pillow case also. The latter is very nice & will answer as well as a new one. It is now on my pillow. I was glad to see by Maret's letter that she was well, & still retained her warm affection for you. I have heard that Beverly Coderise is at Staunton, as assistant in the hospital there. I wish I could do something for him, for he seems to be a fine boy. It is very difficult to get places for young men, there are so many of them in the like situation. The only chance is for them to make it for themselves. I think he had better remain there for the present. I reviewed the cavalry in this section yesterday. It was a splendid sight. The men & horses looked well. They had recuperated since last fall. Stuart was in all his glory. Your sons & nephews well & flourishing. Fitz Lee was on the ground not in the saddle tell Sis Nannie, but sitting by some pretty girls in a carriage. He says he is afflicted by an attack of rheumatism in his knee. I fear it is so, but he is getting over it & expects to be on duty in a few days. Fitzhugh was on his black charger tell Charlotte & Rob by his side. John, Henry, &c., were in their places. I am very sorry Charlotte had left. But understand from Fitzhugh she was very well. The country here looks very green & pretty notwithstanding the ravages of war. What a beautiful world God in His loving kindness to His creatures has given us. What a shame that man endowed with reason & a knowledge of right should mar His gifts. May He soon change the hearts of men, shew them their sins & enable them to repent & be forgiven! I hope dear Mary you are better. Rob says you are as well as usual. I trust that is better than when I was with you. I spend many anxious hours reflecting on your suffering condition & my inability to aid or tend you & my dear daughters. May God in His mercy take you all under His protection! I hope you may be able to reach some of the healing waters this summer & that they may under the blessing of our merciful Father in Heaven effect a cure. Remember me very kindly to Mr. & Mrs. Caskie, Miss Norvell & all friends. Kiss my daughters for me, & you must all remember me in your prayers, & implore the Lord of Hosts for the removal of the terrible scourge with which He has thought best to afflict our bleeding country.

Truly & affly yours

R. E. LEE

467   To JEFFERSON DAVIS
                 Richmond, Virginia

Headquarters, Army of Northern Virginia
June 10, 1863

Mr. President:

I beg leave to bring to your attention a subject with reference to which I have thought that the course pursued by writers and speakers among us has had a tendency to interfere with our success. I refer to the manner in which the demonstration of a desire for peace at the North has been received in our country.

I think there can be no doubt that journalists and others at the South, to whom the Northern people naturally look for a reflection of our opinions, have met these indications in such wise as to weaken the hands of the advocates of a pacific policy on the part of the Federal Government, and give much encouragement to those who urge a continuance of the war.

Recent political movements in the United States, and the comments of influential newspapers upon them, have attracted my attention particularly to this subject, which I deem not unworthy of the consideration of Your Excellency, nor inappropriate to be adverted to by me in view of its connection with the situation of military affairs.

Conceding to our enemies the superiority claimed by them in numbers, resources, and all the means and appliances for carrying on the war, we have no right to look for exemptions from the military consequences of a vigorous use of these advantages, excepting by such deliverance as the mercy of Heaven may accord to the courage of our soldiers, the justice of our cause, and the constancy and prayers of our people. While making the most we can of the means of resistance we possess, and gratefully accepting the measure of success with which God has blessed our efforts as an earnest of His approval and favor, it is nevertheless the part of wisdom to carefully measure and husband our strength, and not to expect from it more than in the ordinary course of affairs it is capable of accomplishing. We should not therefore conceal from ourselves that our resources in men are constantly diminishing, and the disproportion in this respect between us and our enemies, if they continue united in their efforts to subjugate us, is steadily augmenting. The decrease of the aggregate of this army as disclosed by the returns affords an illustration of this fact. Its effective strength varies from time to time, but the falling off in its aggregate shows that its ranks are growing weaker and that its losses are not supplied by recruits.

Under these circumstances we should neglect no honorable means of dividing and weakening our enemies that they may feel some of the difficulties experienced by ourselves. It seems to me that the most effectual mode of accomplishing this object, now within our reach, is to give all the encouragement we can, consistently with truth, to the rising peace party of the North.

Nor do I think we should in this connection make nice distinctions between those who declare for peace unconditionally and those who advocate it as a means of restoring the Union however much we may prefer the former.

We should bear in mind that the friends of peace at the North must make concessions to the earnest desire that exists in the minds of their countrymen for a restoration of the Union, and that to hold out such a result as an inducement is essential to the success of their party.

Should the belief that peace will bring back the Union become general, the war would no longer be supported, and that after all is what we are interested in bringing about. When peace is proposed to us it will be time enough to discuss its terms, and it is not the part of prudence to spurn the proposition in advance, merely because those who wish to make it believe, or affect to believe, that it will result in bringing us back to the Union. We entertain no such apprehensions, nor doubt that the desire of our people for a distinct and independent national existence will prove as steadfast under the influence of peaceful measures as it has shown itself in the midst of war.

If the views I have indicated meet the approval of Your Excellency you will best know how to give effect to them. Should you deem them inexpedient or impracticable, I think you will nevertheless agree with me that we should at least carefully abstain from measures or expressions that tend to discourage any party whose purpose is peace.

With the statement of my own opinion on the subject, the length of which you will excuse, I leave to your better judgment to determine the proper course to be pursued.

I am with great respect, your obt servt

R. E. LEE
Genl

468   To W. H. F. LEE
                   Culpeper, Virginia

[June 10, 1863]

My Dear Son:
I send you a dispatch received from Custis last night. I hope you are comfortable this morning. I wish I could see you, but I cannot. Take care of yourself and make haste and get well and return. Though I scarcely ever saw you, it was a great comfort to know that you were near and with me. I could think of you and hope to see you. May we yet meet in peace and happiness! Kiss Chass for me. Tell her she must not tease you while you are sick, and let me know how you are. God bless you both, my children.

Truly your father,

R. E. LEE

469   To GENERAL ALBERT G. JENKINS
                    Commanding near Strasburg

                              Headquarters, Army of Northern Virginia
                                                    June 10, 1863
General:
    I have received your letter of the 8th instant, and am glad to find
your command is already at a point convenient for future operations. I
desire you to keep it prepared for active service, see to its subsistence,
forage, and ammunition, and when you receive notice from Genl Ewell
of his arrival in the Valley, to report to him for duty. In the meantime,
I request that you will keep your scouts out and collect all information
of the strength & position of the enemy's forces at Winchester, Berryville, Martinsburg & Harper's Ferry, so that you may give Genl Ewell
the benefit of the latest intelligence.

                    I am very respectfully, your obt servt

                                                    R. E. LEE
                                                    Genl

470   To GENERAL JOHN D. IMBODEN
                    Commanding Northwestern Brigade

                              Headquarters, Army of Northern Virginia
                                                    June 10, 1863
General:
    I was glad to learn by your telegraphic dispatch that you had so
promptly moved towards the Potomac. I hope you will be able to effect
a diversion favourable to operations in the Valley, increase the ranks of
your brigade, & collect horses and cattle for the army. The latter had
better be sent back promptly to the upper part of the Shenandoah Valley, and turned over to the agents of the Quartermaster's & Commissary
Departments. Genl Ewell will be in command in the lower Valley, and I
desire you to communicate to him any intelligence which may aid him
in his operations and to carry out any instructions he may give. Wishing
you all success, I remain,

                    Very respectfully, your obt servt

                                                    R. E. LEE
                                                    Genl

471   To HIS WIFE
                             Richmond, Virginia

                                                        Culpeper
                                                   June 11, 1863

I received yesterday dear Mary your letter of the 7th. I am grieved
to learn that you are confined to your room. I would that my prayers,
or anything else I could do could bring you relief! My trust is in our
Heavenly Father to whom my supplications continually ascend for you,
my children & my country! I know if uttered in faith & truth they will
be heard, & oh I pray they may be answered. I do not know where
Willy Deas' battery may be now. If at Guiney's as stated by Burnie, he
has probably received her note to him. He is so far from me I can do
nothing now. When I last wrote I did not suppose that Fitzhugh would
so soon be sent to the rear disabled. I hope it will be but for a short
time. I saw him the night after the battle. Indeed met him on the field
as they were bringing him from the front. At night he appeared comfortable & cheerful. Neither the bone or artery of the leg I am informed
is injured. He is young & healthy & I trust will soon be up again. He
seemed to be more concerned about his brave men & officers who had
fallen in the battle than himself. God takes care of us all & calls to him
those he prefers. Fitzhugh was sent to the rear yesterday with the other
wounded. He thought of stopping at Hickory Hill if the doctors thought
well of it. He had better not go to Richmond. I wish to separate the
sick, not to congregate them at any one place. I send you a note received from Dr. Smedes in reply to one I had written him. I agree with
the Dr. in the importance of Mildred's continuing her studies, believing
it best for her morally & intellectually. If there is any thing better she
can do, I am willing, you & she must judge. I am sorry I cannot see her.
I grieve I fear too much over my separation from you, my children &
friends. Tell Mr. Caskie I gave directions for the man he wrote about
to be sent under guard, & to be delivered to the Sheriff of Richmond.
I hope it was done. I sent a message to him to that effect in a letter to
you. I fear it has miscarried. The hat you speak of was sent me by an
aunt of Major Venable, & forwarded to him to have it done up. It
reached him just as he was leaving Richmond & he could do nothing
with it. If it is a handsome one have it done up to fit Mr. Caskie & present it to him. I cannot use it now. I requested Curtis to settle with the
artist for the photographs. A dozen were to be sent to you. I spoke to
Mr. Mennes myself on the subject. A note to him will set it right. I

want none myself. Kiss Agnes & Mildred for me. Love to the Caskies & kind regards to all.

Truly & affectly yours

R. E. LEE

472   To MRS. W. H. F. LEE
                        "Hickory Hill," Virginia

Culpeper
June 11, 1863

I am so grieved, my dear daughter, to send Fitzhugh to you wounded. But I am so grateful that his wound is of a character to give us full hope of a speedy recovery. With his youth and strength to aid him, and your tender care to nurse him, I trust he will soon be well again. I know that you will unite with me in thanks to Almighty God, who has so often shielded him in the hour of danger, for this recent deliverance, and lift up your whole heart in praise to Him for sparing a life so dear to us, while enabling him to do his duty in the station in which He had placed him. Ask him to join us in supplication that He may always cover him with the shadow of His almighty arm, and teach him that his only refuge is in Him, the greatness of whose mercy reacheth unto the heavens, and His truth unto the clouds. As some good is always mixed with the evil in this world, you will now have him with you for a time, and I shall look to you to cure him very soon and send him back to me, for though I saw him seldom, I knew he was near and always hoped to see him. I went today to thank Mrs. Hill for her attention to him and kindness to you. She desired me to give her regards to you both. I must now thank you for the letter you wrote to me while at Fredericksburg. I kept it by me till preparing for the battlefield, when fearing it might reach the eyes of General Hooker I destroyed it. We can carry with us only our recollections. I must leave F[itzhugh] to tell you about the battle, the army, and the country . . . Tell Cousin A[nne] I am rejoiced that [Colonel] Williams [C. Wickham] is unhurt, though pretty Sue might like to see the ambulance driving up again. I want all the husbands in the field, and their wives at home encouraging them, loving them, and praying for them. We have a great work to accomplish, which requires the cordial and united strength of all . . . Give much love to Cousin A., Mrs. L. and her sweet children,

Mr. W[ickham], and my dear Uncle W[illiams]. Tell Fitzhugh he must make haste and get well, that I am sad without him. You and Rob must let me know how he gets on.

Truly and affectionately yours

R. E. LEE

473   To JAMES A. SEDDON
                 Secretary of War

Headquarters, Army of Northern Virginia
June 13, 1863

I had the honor to receive yesterday your letters of the 9th & 10th instant. You can realize the difficulty of operating in any offensive movement with this army if it has to be divided to cover Richmond. It seems to me useless to attempt it with the force against it. You will have seen its effective strength by the last returns. I grieve over the desolation of the country & the distress to innocent women & children occasioned by spiteful excursions of the enemy, unworthy of a civilized nation. It can only be prevented by local organizations & bold measures. As regards cavalry, I have not half as much as I require to keep back the enemy's mounted force in my front. If I weaken it I fear a heavier calamity may befall us than that we wish to avoid. I have not yet heard of Col R. [H.] Anderson's regiment of cavalry leaving Georgia, or Col [James H.] Clanton's from Alabama, which I understood had been ordered by the President some time since. Genl D. H. Hill offered to send me a North Carolina regiment. It had better be ordered to Richmond. I believe the expedition reported to Genl Elzey as marching up the Peninsula is one of those raids. All accounts agree that the Federal forces at Suffolk, Yorktown, & Gloucester, &c., have been reduced, & Genl Hooker reinforced. Some of Genl Dix's men were captured on the 11th at Fredericksburg. I think the enemy had been mystified as to our movements until the publication of my dispatch to the Department of the cavalry fight on the 9th, & the comments & assertions of some of our Richmond papers. The day after the fight everything subsided to their former lines. Yesterday movements were discovered up the Rappahannock, & pickets report they continued all night. I send down Col [Armistead L.] Long to give an exact account of the reported movements of the enemy up the Peninsula. He will inform you of the condition of affairs here.

I am very respectfully, your obt servt

R. E. LEE
Genl

474
To G. W. C. LEE
Richmond, Virginia

June 13, 1863

My Dear Custis:
I find my blue flannel pants yielding to the wear & tear of the road. I have another blue pair in my trunk of summer cloth, which I wish you would send me. They are plain without cords on the seams. I send down Col Long to see if possible what this move of the enemy is up the Peninsula. I believe it to be a raid to destroy our crops & lay waste our country. All the accounts I get agree in stating that the enemy has sent off his troops from Suffolk, Yorktown, Gloucester, &c., to reinforce Genl Hooker. He can only have a small force in that region, which he has probably collected for this expedition. We must do the same & beat him back at all hazards. Genl Hooker's army has not moved in that direction as far as I can be certain of anything in war. It is extending now up the Rappahannock.
I hope Fitzhugh is doing well. Let me know how he gets on. Give much love to your mother & sisters & remember me to all friends.

God bless you all

R. E. LEE

475
To JEFFERSON DAVIS
Richmond, Virginia

Headquarters, Army of Northern Virginia
June 15, 1863
7 A.M.

Mr. President:
On the 10th I put Ewell's corps in motion for the Valley. He reports, under date of the 13th, that with Rodes' division he drove the enemy out of Berryville, & with Early's & Johnson's drove him within his entrenchments at Winchester, where it seems he is more strongly fortified than supposed. According to our understanding I presume he

has advanced towards the Potomac, leaving a division in front of Winchester. Genl A. P. Hill reported yesterday that the Federal force in front of him withdrew from the south side of the Rappahannock on the night of the 13th, & by morning had nearly all disappeared, leaving strong pickets on the river. One division was seen going over the Stafford Hills in the direction of Aquia, & he supposes the main body to have taken that route. Our scouts report a general movement of the enemy up the Rappahannock, but I have got no certain information on that point. I know a large force has been thrown towards Warrenton. The uncertainty of the reports as to threatened expeditions of the enemy along the coast of North Carolina, & between the Rappahannock & James Rivers in Virginia, has caused delay in the movements of this army, & it may now be too late to accomplish all that was desired. I still am ignorant as to the extent of the expedition said to be moving up the Peninsula, & hesitate to draw the whole of A. P. Hill's corps to me. Two of Pickett's brigades are at Hanover Junction & Richmond, so that I am quite weak.

I am with great respect, your obt servt

R. E. LEE
Genl

476   To JEFFERSON DAVIS
Richmond, Virginia
TELEGRAM

June [15], 1863

GOD HAS AGAIN CROWNED THE VALOR OF OUR TROOPS WITH SUCCESS. EARLY'S DIVISION STORMED THE ENEMY'S ENTRENCHMENTS AT WINCHESTER CAPTURING THEIR ARTILLERY &C.

R. E. LEE
Genl

477   To GENERAL SAMUEL COOPER
Adjutant and Inspector General

Headquarters, Army of Northern Virginia
June 15, 1863

General:

I have the honor to request that after the receipt of this letter all mail and other communications which may be sent me, may be forwarded by way of Gordonsville and Staunton. Also that instructions may be given to forward all convalescents and other soldiers returning to the army by the same route, sending them in detachments, properly rationed, and under charge of such officers as may be available.

I am most respecty, your obt svt

R. E. LEE
Genl

478 To GENERAL JAMES LONGSTREET
Commanding First Corps

Headquarters, Army of Northern Virginia
June 15, 1863
8½ P.M.

General:
A dispatch from Ewell dated 5 a.m. today, states that Early's division stormed the enemy's works at Winchester, capturing their cannon, &c., with little loss on our side. He was pushing on. I have as yet received no particulars.

I have been waiting for the arrival of Stuart, or of information from him, but as yet have received none. If anything of importance is received, I will write again. Should nothing render it inadvisable within your knowledge, I wish you would advance Hood on the road by Barbee's Crossroads, &c., to Markham, as arranged today. Your reserve artillery, trains, &c., may be sent, if you think proper, by Chester Gap. Let McLaws & Pickett follow you as rapidly as they can & should the roads or other circumstances make it advantageous that they should proceed by Front Royal, give them the proper directions accordingly. You can threaten as much as you please an attack upon the enemy's right flank, so as to throw them back upon the Potomac, but advance as rapidly as you can with propriety. Anderson encamped this evening two miles this side of Germanna, & will pass beyond this place tomorrow evening. Heth left Fredericksburg today. Hill wrote that Pender was ready & would move as soon as he heard from his scouts that he had sent north of the Rappahannock. As far as heard from, the enemy had all gone.

I am, &c.

R. E. LEE
Genl

479   To GENERAL AMBROSE P. HILL
                   Commanding Third Corps

                              Headquarters, Army of Northern Virginia
                                                    June 16, 1863
General:

I have received your two dispatches of yesterday & conclude that the enemy has entirely disappeared from your front. Genl Anderson's division arrived here this morning. It will be supplied with provisions & forage, & will resume its march tomorrow. Heth I hope will reach here tomorrow, & as I have not yet heard of Pender being in motion, I presume he will not reach here until the next day. I wish your corps to follow Longstreet as closely as you can, &, keeping your divisions within supporting distance, your reserve artillery, heavy batteries, and reserve trains might advantageously take the Sperryville road as far as Woodville, and there turn off for Chester Gap to Front Royal, and so down the Valley. Longstreet's troops have taken the Winchester road as far as Gaines' Crossroads, or some point in that vicinity, where he will turn off to Rocks Ford, across Hedgeman's River, and thence by Edgeworth and Barbee's Crossroads to Markham. He will then either pursue the route by Paris or fall down into the Valley by the Manassas Gap road according to circumstances. This road is said to furnish good grazing and some dry forage, and will tend to deceive the enemy as to our ultimate destination, at least for a time. Should the route not prove a favorable one, Longstreet will send back word to the marching columns, & they will be turned back on the Chester Gap road. Govern yourself accordingly. Your divisions as they come up will be furnished with all the provisions & forage which they can take from this place. This being the last point where we will be in railroad communication with Richmond, I recommend that everything which may be found surplus in the baggage of your troops should be sent back from this place. If not here, I will be found in the advance with Genl Longstreet. Genl Ewell reported, under date of the 15th instant, that Early's division stormed the enemy's works at Winchester, capturing their cannon, &c., with very little loss on our side, and that everything was pushing on.

                    I am very respectfully, your obt servt

                                                    R. E. LEE
                                                    Genl

480   To GENERAL RICHARD S. EWELL
Commanding Second Corps

Headquarters, Army of Northern Virginia
Markham
June 17, 1863
3 ½ P.M.

General:

I have just received your letter, the first from you since your dispatch announcing fall of Winchester. I think the reports which you have of the forces in Harper's Ferry must be exaggerated. I wish you to move Rodes' division on as far as Hagerstown, and operate in the enemy's country according to the plan proposed. Give out that your movement is for the purpose of enveloping Harper's Ferry. Repress marauding. Take what is necessary for the army & give citizens of Maryland Confederate money or certificates. Do not expose yourself. Keep your own scouts.

Very respectfully, your obt servt

R. E. LEE
Genl

481   To GENERAL JAMES LONGSTREET
Commanding First Corps

Headquarters, Army of Northern Virginia
Markham
June 17, 1863
3 ½ P.M.

General:

Your note of 10 a.m. today just received. I have heard nothing of the movements of Genl Hooker either from Genl Stuart or yourself, & therefore can form no opinion of the best move against him. If a part of our force could have operated east of the mountains it would have served more to confuse him, but as you have turned off to the Valley, & I understand all the trains have taken that route, I hope it is for the best. At any rate it is too late to change from any information I have. You had better therefore push on, relieve Ewell's division as soon as you can, & let him advance into Maryland, at least as far as Hagerstown. Give out it is against Harper's Ferry. I will send back for A. P. Hill to move by Chester Gap. I wrote to you today & yesterday. I shall go from here to the Valley.

> Very respectfully
> R. E. Lee
> Genl

482　To GENERAL SAMUEL COOPER
Adjutant and Inspector General
TELEGRAM

> Culpeper Court House
> June 18, 1863

GENERAL:

ON THE AFTERNOON OF THE 14TH, GENL RODES TOOK POSSESSION OF MARTINSBURG, CAPTURING SEVERAL PIECES OF ARTILLERY, MORE THAN TWO HUNDRED (200) PRISONERS, A SUPPLY OF AMMUNITION & GRAIN. OUR LOSS, ONE KILLED & TWO (2) WOUNDED.

> R. E. Lee
> Genl

483　To JEFFERSON DAVIS
Richmond, Virginia

> Headquarters, Army of Northern Virginia
> June 18, 1863

Mr. President:

The enemy has been thrown back from the line of the Rappahannock, & is concentrating, as far as I can learn, in the vicinity of Centreville. The last reports from the scouts indicate that he is moving over towards the upper Potomac, whether with a view of proceeding to Harper's Ferry, crossing the Potomac River into Maryland, or advancing through the mountains into the Valley, I cannot yet decide. Longstreet's corps has moved east of the Blue Ridge with the view of creating embarrassment as to our plans, while Ewell, having driven the enemy from Winchester & Martinsburg, has seized upon the Potomac so as to enable Genl Hill's corps to move up from Fredericksburg. In the meantime Genl Stuart has held with his cavalry the approaches to the Blue Ridge, & has in various conflicts with the enemy's cavalry punished them severely, having captured more than 400 prisoners with their arms & horses & several standards. I have received no official returns, but learn from Genl Ewell's reports that he has captured in the Valley more than 4,000 prisoners, about 30 pieces of artillery, 250 wagons, 20 ambulances, 400 horses, a lot of ammunition, &c. Genl Milroy with a small body of organized troops and some stragglers escaped into Harper's Ferry. The whole number who escaped will not reach a thousand. Our loss small; it is stated that it will not exceed 175 killed, wounded, & missing.

Very respectfully, &c.

R. E. LEE
Genl

484   To JEFFERSON DAVIS
Richmond, Virginia

Headquarters, near Millwood, Virginia
June 19, 1863

Mr. President:

Genl Ewell with two divisions has advanced from the Potomac towards Pennsylvania. His third division is retained near Shepherdstown for the present to guard his flank & rear. Genl Longstreet's corps on the Ashby's & Snicker's Gaps roads threatens the enemy, who is massed between him & Washington. Genl Stuart's cavalry is operating in his front. I hope the first division of A. P. Hill's corps will reach here today so that Early may be relieved & follow Ewell. All attempts of the enemy to penetrate the mountains have been repulsed by Stuart's cavalry, who yesterday again drove him from Middleburg, & by reports received last evening the enemy's infantry have evacuated Aldie. Indications seem to be that his main body is proceeding towards the Potomac, whether upon Harper's Ferry or to cross the river east of it is not yet known. The difficulty of procuring supplies retards & renders more uncertain our future movements.

I am with great respect, your obt servt

R. E. LEE
Genl

485   To GENERAL RICHARD S. EWELL
Commanding Second Corps

Headquarters, Army of Northern Virginia
June 19, 1863
7 A.M.

General:

Your two letters of the 18th instant (one from 4 miles north of Winchester & one from 4 miles north of Martinsburg) have been received. Hood's division was sent yesterday from Upperville to replace

Early's in order that you might have with you your whole corps to operate with in Maryland & Pennsylvania, but later in the day the reports from Genl Stuart indicated that the enemy were moving up the roads concentrating at Snickersville with the view of forcing a passage through the mountains to get into your rear, and Hood was directed to cross Snicker's Ferry & hold Snicker's Gap as we had only cavalry on that route. Longstreet's corps has been operating with a view to embarrass the enemy as to our movements, so as to detain his forces east of the mountains, until A. P. Hill could get up to your support. But should the enemy force a passage through the mountains you would be separated, which it is the object of Longstreet to prevent if possible. Anderson's division ought to be within reach today, & I will move him towards Berryville so as either to relieve Early or support Hood as circumstances may require. I very much regret that you have not the benefit of your whole corps, for, with that north of the Potomac, should we be able to detain Genl Hooker's army from following you, you would be able to accomplish as much, unmolested, as the whole army could perform with Genl Hooker in its front. Not knowing what force there is at Harper's Ferry, or what can be collected to oppose your progress, I cannot give definite instructions, especially as the movements of Genl Hooker's army are not yet ascertained. You must therefore be guided in your movements by controlling circumstances around you, endeavor to keep yourself supplied with provisions, send back any surplus, and carry out the plan you proposed so far as in your judgment may seem fit. If your advance causes Hooker to cross the Potomac or separate his army in any way Longstreet can follow you. The last of Hill's divisions had, on the evening of the 18th, advanced a few miles this side of Culpeper Court House en route to the Valley. I hope all are now well on their way. As soon as I can get definite information as to the movements of Genl Hooker and the approach of Genl Hill I will write to you again.

I am very respectfully & truly

R. E. LEE
Genl

486   To GENERAL JOHN D. IMBODEN
Commanding in Hampshire County, West Virginia

Headquarters, Army of Northern Virginia
June 20, 1863

General:
    Your letter of the 18th from French's Depot, reporting the destruction of the important bridges on the Baltimore & Ohio Railroad over

Evitt's Creek, Patterson's Creek, North & South Branches of the Potomac, with the depots, water tanks, & engines between Little Cacapon & Cumberland, has been received. I am very much gratified at the thorough manner in which your work in that line has been done. Genl [Benjamin F.] Kelley's force at New Creek, I hope, is exaggerated, or that at any rate you will be able to disperse it in some way. I am also gratified at the cattle and horses that you have already captured for the use of the army, and hope that your expectations of obtaining similar supplies will be realized. They are not only important but essential, and I request that you will do all in your power to obtain all you can. At this time it is impossible to send a mounted brigade to your assistance, as the whole of the cavalry are required to watch the enemy and guard our movements east of the Blue Ridge & in Maryland. Should you find an opportunity you can yourself advance north of the Potomac and keep on the left of this army in its advance into Pennsylvania. But you must repress all marauding, take only the supplies necessary for your army, animals & provisions through your regular staff officers, who will account for the same, and give receipts to the owners, stating the kind, quantity, and estimated value of the articles received, the valuation to be made according to the market price in the country where the property is taken. I desire you will destroy all my letters to you after perusal (having impressed on your memory their main points), to prevent the possibility of their falling into the hands of the enemy.

Very respectfully, &c.

R. E. LEE
Genl

487   To GENERAL SAMUEL JONES
Commanding, Dublin, Virginia

Berryville
June 20, 1863

General:

General Milroy has been driven out of Winchester and Martinsburg with the loss of about 4,000 prisoners, 30 pieces of cannon, a large wagon train, &c., and has crossed the Potomac, occupying with the rest of his troops Maryland Heights, retaining a mere picket in Harper's Ferry. The Baltimore & Ohio Railroad has been cut by our cavalry east of the Point of Rocks, and General Imboden has destroyed the important bridges over the Little Cacapon, Patterson's Creek, North &

South Branches of the Potomac, &c., &c., and the tanks, depots, engines, &c., from Cacapon to Cumberland included. Genl Hooker has abandoned the line of the Rappahannock and fallen back towards the Potomac. General Ewell's corps is in Maryland, and his advance cavalry occupies Chambersburg. I think the present offers to you a favorable time to threaten western Virginia, and if circumstances favor, you might convert the threat into a real attack. A more favorable opportunity will probably not occur during the war, and if you can accomplish nothing else, you may at least prevent the troops in that region from being sent to reinforce other points. I would recommend therefore that you unite all your available forces, and strike at some vulnerable point. Wishing you great success,

I am general with great respect, your obt servt

R. E. LEE
Genl

488   To GENERAL J. E. B. STUART
Commanding Cavalry

Headquarters
June 22, 1863

General:

I have just received your note of 7.45 this morning to Genl Longstreet. I judge the efforts of the enemy yesterday were to arrest our progress and ascertain our whereabouts. Perhaps he is satisfied. Do you know where he is and what he is doing? I fear he will steal a march on us and get across the Potomac before we are aware. If you find that he is moving northward, and that two brigades can guard the Blue Ridge & take care of your rear, you can move with the other three into Maryland & take position on General Ewell's right, place yourself in communication with him, guard his flank, keep him informed of the enemy's movements, & collect all the supplies you can for the use of the army. One column of Genl Ewell's army will probably move towards the Susquehanna by the Emmitsburg route; another by Chambersburg. Accounts from him last night state that there was no enemy west of Fredericktown. A cavalry force (about 100) guarded the Monocacy Bridge, which was barricaded. You will of course take charge of Jenkins' brigade, and give him necessary instructions.

All supplies taken in Maryland must be by authorized staff officers for their respective departments, by no one else. They will be paid for, or receipts for the same given to the owners. I will send you a general order on this subject, which I wish you to see is strictly complied with.

I am very respectfully, your obt servt

R. E. LEE
Genl

489   To GENERAL RICHARD S. EWELL
          Commanding Second Corps

Headquarters
June 22, 1863

General:

Your letter of 6 p.m. yesterday has been received. If you are ready to move, you can do so. I think your best course will be towards the Susquehanna, taking the routes by Emmitsburg, Chambersburg, McConnellsburg. Your trains had better be, as far as possible, kept on the center route. You must get command of your cavalry, & use it in gathering supplies, obtaining information, & protecting your flanks. If necessary, send a staff officer to remain with Genl [Albert G.] Jenkins. It will depend upon the quantity of supplies obtained in that country whether the rest of the army can follow. There may be enough for your command, but none for the others. Every exertion should therefore be made to locate and secure them. Beef we can drive with us, but bread we cannot carry, and must secure it in the country. I send you copies of a general order [No. 72] on this subject, which I think is based on rectitude and sound policy, and the spirit of which I wish you to see enforced in your command. I am much gratified at the success which has attended your movements, and feel assured, if they are conducted with the same energy and circumspection, it will continue. Your progress and direction will of course depend upon development of circumstances. If Harrisburg comes within your means, capture it. Genl A. P. Hill arrived yesterday in the vicinity of Berryville. I shall move him on today if possible. Saturday Longstreet withdrew from the Blue Ridge. Yesterday the enemy pressed our cavalry so hard with infantry & cavalry on the Upperville road that McLaws' division had to be sent back to hold Ashby's Gap. I have not yet heard from there this morning. Genl Stuart could not ascertain whether it was intended as a real advance towards the Valley or to ascertain our position. The pontoons will reach Martinsburg today, and will be laid at the point you suggest, four or five miles below Williamsport, if found suitable. I have not countermanded your order withdrawing the cavalry from Charlestown. I will write you again if I receive information affecting your movements. Trusting in the guidance of a merciful God, and invoking His protection for your corps.

I am with great respect, your obt servt

R. E. LEE
Genl

490   To GENERAL RICHARD S. EWELL
              Commanding Second Corps

Headquarters
June 22, 1863
3.30 P.M.

General:

I have just received your letter of this morning from opposite Shepherdstown. Mine of today, authorizing you to move towards the Susquehanna, I hope has reached you ere this. After dispatching my letter, learning that the enemy had not renewed his attempts of yesterday to break through the Blue Ridge, I directed Genl R. H. Anderson's division to commence its march towards Shepherdstown. It will reach there tomorrow. I also directed Genl Stuart, should the enemy have so far retired from his front as to permit of the departure of a portion of the cavalry, to march with three brigades across the Potomac, and place himself on your right, & in communication with you, keep you advised of the movements of the enemy, and assist in collecting supplies for the army. I have not heard from him since. I also directed Imboden, if opportunity offered, to cross the Potomac, and perform the same offices on your left. I shall endeavor to get Genl Early's regiments to him as soon as possible. I do not know what has become of the infantry of the Maryland Line. I had intended that to guard Winchester.

I am most respy yours

R. E. LEE
Genl

491   To GENERAL JAMES LONGSTREET
              Commanding First Corps

Headquarters, &c.
June 23, 1863
11 A.M.

General:

Your last note acknowledging receipt of mine of this morning is received. I wish you to get your corps ready to move in the morning. Let your ordnance officers see Colonel [Briscoe G.] Baldwin and make arrangements to turn in the damaged ammunition and have it replaced by a fresh supply, as it would be useless to take the former along. I have wished to ride over to see you, but thus far it has been impossible. If I am unable to do so this morning, cannot you come over this afternoon to my camp?

I am respectfully and truly, yours

R. E. LEE

General Hill's two divisions (the remaining ones) have been ordered to move.

R. E. L.

492   To GENERAL J. E. B. STUART
Commanding Cavalry

Headquarters, Army of Northern Virginia
June 23, 1863
5 P.M.

General:

Your notes of 9 & 10½ a.m. today have just been received. As regards the purchase of tobacco for your men, supposing that Confederate money not be taken, I am willing for your commissaries or quartermasters to purchase this tobacco and let the men get it from them, but I can have nothing seized by the men.

If Genl Hooker's army remains inactive you can leave two brigades to watch him & withdraw with the three others, but should he not appear to be moving northward I think you had better withdraw this side of the mountain tomorrow night, cross at Shepherdstown next day, & move over to Fredericktown.

You will however be able to judge whether you can pass around their army without hinderance, doing them all the damage you can, & cross the river east of the mountains. In either case, after crossing the river, you must move on & feel the right of Ewell's troops, collecting information, provisions, &c.

Give instructions to the commander of the brigades left behind to watch the flank & rear of the army, & (in event of the enemy leaving their front) retire from the mountains west of the Shenandoah, leaving sufficient pickets to guard the passes, & bringing everything clean along the Valley, closing upon the rear of the army.

As regards the movements of the two brigades of the enemy moving towards Warrenton, the commander of the brigades to be left in the mountains must do what he can to counteract them, but I think the sooner you cross into Maryland after tomorrow the better.

The movements of Ewell's corps are as stated in my former letter. Hill's first division will reach the Potomac today and Longstreet will follow tomorrow.

Be watchful & circumspect in all your movements.

I am very respy & truly, yours

R. E. LEE
Genl

493   To JEFFERSON DAVIS
Richmond, Virginia

Headquarters, Army of Northern Virginia
June 23, 1863

Mr. President:

The season is now so far advanced as to render it improbable that the enemy will undertake active operations on the Carolina and Georgia coast before the return of frost.

This impression is confirmed by the statements contained in Northern papers, that part of Genl [David D.] Hunter's command has gone to reinforce Genl [Nathaniel P.] Banks, and that Admiral [Andrew H.] Foote, the successor of Admiral [Samuel F.] DuPont in the command of the South Atlantic fleet, lies dangerously ill, a circumstance that will tend further to embarrass any designs the enemy may entertain of operating against the cities of the seaboard.

Federal papers of the 19th allude to the frequent arrival or departure of troops and munitions of war at Fortress Monroe, and those of the 20th announce the arrival in Washington of Genl [John J.] Peck & staff, without indicating the object of his visit, further than it may be connected with the movements just referred to.

At this distance, I can see no benefit to be derived from maintaining a large force on the southern coast during the unhealthy months of the summer and autumn, and I think that a part at least, of the troops in North Carolina, and of those under Genl Beauregard, can be employed at this time with great advantage in Virginia. If an army could be organized under the command of Genl Beauregard, and pushed forward to Culpeper Court House, threatening Washington from that direction, it would not only effect a diversion most favorable for this army, but would I think, relieve us of any apprehension of an attack upon Richmond during our absence. The well known anxiety of the Northern Government for the safety of its capital would induce it to retain a large force for its defence, and thus sensibly relieve the opposition to our advance. Last summer you will remember that troops were recalled from Hilton Head, North Carolina, and western Virginia for the protection of Washington, and there can be little doubt that if our present movements northward are accompanied by a demonstration on the south side of the Potomac, the coast would be again relieved, and the troops now in the Peninsula and south of James River withdrawn. If success should attend the operations of this army, and what I now suggest would greatly increase the probability of that result, we might even hope to compel the recall of some of the enemy's troops from the west.

I think it most important that whatever forces be used for the purpose I have named, General Beauregard be placed in command, and that his department be extended over North Carolina and Virginia. His presence would give magnitude to even a small demonstration, and tend greatly to perplex and confound the enemy.

Of course the larger the force we can employ the better, but should you think it imprudent to withdraw a part of Genl Beauregard's army for the purpose indicated I think good results would follow from sending forward, under Genl Beauregard, such of the troops about Richmond and in North Carolina as could be spared for a short time.

The good effects of beginning to assemble an army at Culpeper Court House would I think soon become apparent, and the movement might be increased in importance as the result might appear to justify. Should you agree with me, I need not say that it is desirable that the execution of the plan proposed should immediately begin. The enemy will hear of it soon enough, and a proper reticence on the part of our papers will cause them to attribute greater importance to it. I need not mention the benefit that the troops themselves would derive from being transferred to a more healthy climate.

Very respectfully, your obt servt

R. E. Lee
Genl

494   To GENERAL SAMUEL COOPER
Adjutant and Inspector General

Headquarters, Army of Northern Virginia
June 23, 1863

General:

Upon leaving Fredericksburg, a regiment of General Pettigrew's brigade was sent to relieve Genl Corse's brigade, at Hanover Junction, to enable the latter to rejoin his division.

General Corse was subsequently ordered to remain at the Junction, and I have not heard whether he has yet been sent forward. If not, I think the regiment will suffice for a guard at that point, and wish Corse's brigade to be ordered to rejoin its division under Genl Pickett as soon as possible.

He will march by Culpeper Court House, and thence through Chester Gap to Winchester, where he will be instructed by what route to proceed. I wish to have every man that can be spared, and desire that Cooke's brigade may be sent forward by the same route, if it is not needed at Richmond. I think there will be no necessity for keeping a large number of troops at that place, especially if the plan of assembling an army at Culpeper Court House under General Beauregard be adopted.

Very respectfully, your obt servt

R. E. LEE
Genl

495   To JEFFERSON DAVIS
Richmond, Virginia

Headquarters, Army of Northern Virginia
June 23, 1863

Mr. President:

Reports of movements of the enemy east of the Blue Ridge cause me to believe that he is preparing to cross the Potomac. A pontoon bridge is stated to be laid at Edward's Ferry, and his army corps that he has advanced to Leesburg and the foot of the mountains, appear to be withdrawing. Their attempts to penetrate the mountains have been successfully repelled by Genl Stuart with the cavalry. Genl Stuart last night was within a few miles of Aldie, to which point the enemy had retired.

Genl Ewell's corps is in motion towards the Susquehanna. Genl A. P. Hill's corps is moving towards the Potomac, his leading division will reach Shepherdstown today. I have withdrawn Longstreet west of the Shenandoah, and if nothing prevents, he will follow tomorrow.

In addition to the supplies that we have been able to gather in Fauquier & Loudoun Counties, in the Shenandoah Valley, and west of the Alleghany, we have collected sufficient north of the Potomac for the support of Ewell's corps to the 30th instant, and 1,700 barrels of flour are on hand in Maryland for the rest of the army. I hope we shall get enough for the subsistence of our men. Forage is very scarce, and we have mainly to rely on grass for the animals. From the reports I receive, I believe we shall obtain enough salt for our purposes while north of the Potomac, for which we are paying 75 cents a bushel. The flour that we have purchased in Maryland costs $6.50 per barrel, beef $5 per hundred gross. We use Confederate money for all payments. I shall continue to purchase all the supplies that are furnished me while north of the Potomac, impressing only when necessary.

With great respect, your obt servt

R. E. Lee
Genl

496   To JEFFERSON DAVIS
Richmond, Virginia

Opposite Williamsport
June 25, 1863

Mr. President:

I have received today your letter of the 19th instant, and am much gratified by your views in relation to the peace party at the North. It is plain to my understanding that everything that will tend to repress the war feeling in the Federal States will inure to our benefit. I do not know that we can do anything to promote the pacific feeling, but our course ought to be so shaped as not to discourage it.

I am sorry to hear that any controversy has arisen in relation to the exchange of prisoners. That is a matter in which our enemies have an advantage over us. Although we may have more prisoners than they, theirs are maintained at less expense than ours. Moreover, our citizens are much more accessible to them than theirs to us, so that the system of retaliation if commenced will not be on an equal basis. Besides, I am not in favor of retaliation except in very extreme cases, and I think it would be better for us to suffer, and be right in our own eyes and in the eyes of the world. We will gain more by it in the end. I hope therefore some plan may be adopted to prevent a course so repugnant to the feelings of humanity and the sense of right, and that the one you propose may be crowned with success.

You will see that apprehension for the safety of Washington and their own territory has aroused the Federal Government and people to great exertions, and it is incumbent upon us to call forth all our energies. In addition to the hundred thousand troops called for by President Lincoln to defend the frontier of Pennsylvania, you will see that he is concentrating other organized forces in Maryland. It is stated in the papers that they are all being withdrawn from Suffolk, and according to Genl [Simon B.] Buckner's report, Burnside and his corps are recalled from Kentucky. It is reasonable to suppose that this would be the case if their apprehensions were once aroused.

I think this should liberate the troops in the Carolinas, and enable Genls Buckner & Bragg to accomplish something in Ohio. It is plain that if all the Federal Army is concentrated upon this, it will result in our accomplishing nothing, and being compelled to return to Virginia. If the plan that I suggested the other day, of organizing an army, even in effigy, under Genl Beauregard at Culpeper Court House, can be carried into effect, much relief will be afforded. If even the brigades in Virginia & North Carolina, which Genls Hill & Elzey think cannot be spared, were ordered there at once, and Genl Beauregard were sent there, if he had to return to South Carolina, it would do more to protect both States from marauding expeditions of the enemy than anything else.

I have not sufficient troops to maintain my communications, and therefore have to abandon them. I think I can throw Genl Hooker's army across the Potomac and draw troops from the south, embarrassing their plan of campaign in a measure, if I can do nothing more and have to return.

I still hope that all things will end well for us at Vicksburg. At any rate every effort should be made to bring about that result.

With great respect, your obt servt

R. E. LEE
Genl

497   To JEFFERSON DAVIS
                          Richmond, Virginia

                                                   Williamsport
                                                   June 25, 1863

Mr. President:

So strong is my conviction of the necessity of activity on our part in military affairs, that you will excuse my adverting to the subject again, notwithstanding what I have said in my previous letter of today.

It seems to me that we cannot afford to keep our troops awaiting possible movements of the enemy, but that our true policy is, as far as we can, so to employ our own forces as to give occupation to his at points of our selection.

I have observed that extracts from Northern journals contained in Richmond papers of the 22nd instant, state that the yellow fever has appeared at New Berne, and that in consequence the Federal troops are being moved back to Morehead City. If in fact the fever is in New Berne, it would tend of itself to prevent active operations from that point. But as I have never heard of the disease being in that city, and as it does not generally break out so early in the season, even in localities which are subject to it, I am disposed to doubt the truth of the statement, and regard it as a cover for the withdrawal of the enemy's forces for some other field. The attempt to conceal their movements, as in the case of the withdrawal of the troops from Suffolk, coupled with the fact that nothing has up to this time been undertaken on the North Carolina coast, convinces me that the enemy contemplates nothing important in that region, and that it is unnecessary to keep our troops to watch him.

If he has been waiting until this time for reinforcements, the probability of their being furnished is greatly diminished by the movements now in progress on our part, and they must at least await the result of our operations. The same course of reasoning is applicable to the question of the probability of the enemy assuming the offensive against Richmond, either on the Peninsula or south of the James. I feel sure therefore that the best use that can be made of the troops in Carolina, and those in Virginia now guarding Richmond, would be the prompt assembling of the main body of them, leaving sufficient to prevent raids, together with as many as can be drawn from the army of Genl Beauregard at Culpeper Court House under the command of that officer. I do not think they could more effectually prevent aggressive movements on the part of the enemy in any other way, while their assistance to this army in its operations would be very great.

If the report received from Genl Buckner of the withdrawal of Genl Burnside from Kentucky be correct, I think there is nothing to prevent a united movement of the commands of Genls Buckner and Sam Jones into that State. They could render valuable service by collecting and bringing out supplies, if they did no more, and would embarrass the enemy and prevent troops now there from being sent to other points. If they are too weak to attempt this object, they need not be idle, and I think that if the enemy's forces have in fact been so far weakened as to render present active operations on his part against them improbable, they should go where they can be of immediate service, leaving only a sufficient guard to watch the lines they now hold. They might be sent with benefit to reinforce Genl Johnston or Genl Bragg, to constitute a part of the proposed army of Genl Beauregard at Culpeper Court House, or they might accomplish good results by going into northwestern Virginia. It should never be forgotten that our concentration at any point compels that of the enemy, and his numbers being limited, tends to relieve all other threatened localities.

I earnestly commend these considerations to the attention of Your Excellency, and trust that you will be at liberty, in your better judgment, and with the superior means of information you possess as to our own necessities and the enemy's movements in the distant regions I have mentioned, to give effect to them, either in the way I have suggested, or in such other manner as may seem to you more judicious.

I am with great respect, your obt servt

R. E. Lee
Genl

498   GENERAL ORDERS, NO. 73

Headquarters, Army of Northern Virginia
Chambersburg, Pennsylvania
June 27, 1863

The commanding general has observed with marked satisfaction the conduct of the troops on the march, and confidently anticipates results commensurate with the high spirit they have manifested.

No troops could have displayed greater fortitude or better performed the arduous marches of the past ten days.

Their conduct in other respects has with few exceptions been in keeping with their character as soldiers, and entitles them to approbation and praise.

There have however been instances of forgetfulness on the part of some, that they have in keeping the yet unsullied reputation of the army, and that the duties exacted of us by civilization and Christianity are not less obligatory in the country of the enemy than in our own.

The commanding general considers that no greater disgrace could befall the army, and through it our whole people, than the perpetration of the barbarous outrages upon the unarmed, and defenceless and the wanton destruction of private property that have marked the course of the enemy in our own country.

Such proceedings not only degrade the perpetrators and all connected with them, but are subversive of the discipline and efficiency of the army, and destructive of the ends of our present movement.

It must be remembered that we make war only upon armed men, and that we cannot take vengeance for the wrongs our people have suffered without lowering ourselves in the eyes of all whose abhorrence has been excited by the atrocities of our enemies, and offending against Him to whom vengeance belongeth, without whose favor and support our efforts must all prove in vain.

The commanding general therefore earnestly exhorts the troops to abstain with most scrupulous care from unnecessary or wanton injury to private property, and he enjoins upon all officers to arrest and bring to summary punishment all who shall in any way offend against the orders on this subject.

R. E. Lee
General

499   To GENERAL RICHARD S. EWELL
Commanding Second Corps

Headquarters, Army of Northern Virginia
Chambersburg
June 28, 1863
7½ A.M.

General:
I wrote you last night stating that Genl Hooker was reported to have crossed the Potomac & is advancing by way of Middletown, the head of his column being at that point in Frederick County. I directed you in that letter to move your forces to this point. If you have not already progressed on the road, and if you have no good reason against it, I desire you to move in the direction of Gettysburg, via Heidlersburg, where you will have turnpike most of the way, & you can thus join your

other divisions to Early's which is east of the mountains. I think it preferable to keep on the east side of the mountains. When you come to
Heidlersburg you can either move directly on Gettysburg or turn down
to Cashtown. Your trains & heavy artillery you can send, if you think
proper, on the road to Chambersburg. But if the roads which your troops
take are good, they had better follow you.

R. E. LEE
Genl

500   COLONEL W. H. TAYLOR TO GENERAL GEORGE E. PICKETT
Commanding Division

Headquarters, Army of Northern Virginia
June 29, 1863

General:
    Your letter of the 21st instant in reference to the condition and
strength of your division has been received, and in reply I am directed
by the commanding general to say that he has repeatedly requested that
the two brigades be returned, and had hoped that at least one of them
(Corse's) would have been sent to the division ere this. There is no other
brigade in the army which could be assigned to the division at this time.
Though Corse's may not be expected immediately, he hopes that ere long
it will be enabled to rejoin its division.

    I am general very respectfully, your obt servt

W. H. TAYLOR
A. A. G.

501   To HIS WIFE
"Hickory Hill," Virginia

Greenwood
June 30, 1863

    I have received dear M[ary] your letter from Richmond announcing
Mildred's arrival, & that of the 21st from Hickory Hill. I am glad you
found F[itzhugh] doing well & all happy there. Tell Mildred I am much
obliged to her for her letter, which I will answer when I can. I grieve that
I cannot see her, but I trust the time will come yet. I saw in Smithfield

some of her schoolmates, in Winchester Miss Fanny Mc——ia. All inquired kindly after her & sent much love. I hope you will get to the Hot. Perhaps you can take Rob with you, or rather he can take you. Give much love to F[itzhugh], Chass, the girls & all at Hickory Hill. All must remember us in their prayers. I think constantly of you & pray for your welfare & happiness. It is doubtful whether this gets through. Therefore I say nothing more.

Truly, &c.

502   To GENERAL JOHN D. IMBODEN
Commanding Cavalry, Chambersburg, Pennsylvania

Greenwood
July 1, 1863

General:

I have received your letter of 7 a.m. yesterday from near Mercersburg. I regret the capture of Capt Irwin and part of his company at McConnellsburg, especially as it appears to have been the result of want of proper caution on his part. I hope it will have the effect of teaching proper circumspection in future.

Upon arriving at Chambersburg today, I desire you to relieve Genl Pickett, who will then move forward to this place. You will of course establish guards on the roads leading to your position, and take every precaution for the safety of your command. Obtain all the flour that you can load in your wagons from the mills in your vicinity, and if you cannot get sufficient, I believe there are seven or eight hundred barrels at Shippensburg, about 10 miles north of Chambersburg on the Carlisle road. You must turn off everybody belonging to the army on the road to Gettysburg. The reserve trains of the army are parked between Greenwood & Cashtown, on said road, and tomorrow I desire you to move up to this place, establish yourself so as to command the crossroads & roads leading into town, throw out pickets on the roads to Shippensburg, New Guilford, Chambersburg, & Greencastle, and establish a separate picket at Greencastle to turn off all persons seeking the army by the direct road from Greencastle to Greenwood. It will be necessary for you to have your men well together and always on the alert, and to pay strict attention to the safety of the trains, which are for the present placed under your charge, and upon the safety of which the operations of this army depend.

You will at the same time have an opportunity of organizing your troops, refreshing them for a day or two, and getting everything prepared for active operations in the field, for which you will be speedily wanted.

Send word to Genl Pickett at this place tomorrow, which is eight miles from Chambersburg, the hour when you will arrive here, in order that he may be prepared to move on your arrival. My headquarters for the present will be at Cashtown, east of the mountains.

Very respy, your obt servt

R. E. LEE
Genl

503   To GENERAL JOHN D. IMBODEN
Commanding Cavalry

Headquarters, Army of Northern Virginia
July 4, 1863

General:

In pursuance of verbal directions given you last night, I desire you to take charge of the train belonging to this army, which I have directed to be assembled in the vicinity of Cashtown this afternoon. I advise that you start the train at least by 5 p.m. today, and endeavor to push it through to Greencastle by tomorrow morning by the road turning off at Greenwood. Thence you can follow the direct road to Williamsport, where the train must be put across the Potomac at once, and advance beyond Falling Waters, whence it can proceed more leisurely to Winchester. It will be necessary to escort it beyond Martinsburg, at least as far as Bunker Hill. I have directed two batteries to report to you this afternoon, to accompany the train, so that you may have sufficient artillery to guard the front & rear, and distribute along at intervals, in order to repel any attack that may be made along the line by parties of the enemy. I advise that in turning off at Greenwood you have your scouts out on the Chambersburg road until the rear of your train has passed it, and that you also keep scouts out on your left towards Waynesborough. From Greencastle you had better send a scouting party through Hagerstown and hold that place until the train shall have crossed the river. At the river you can post your artillery to hold the ford, keeping out your scouts towards Hagerstown, Boonsboro, &c., until further orders. After the train has reached a place of safety you can return to the Maryland side, taking position in front of Hagerstown so as to keep open communications. I need not caution you as to preserving quiet & order in your train, secrecy of your movements, promptness and energy, and increasing vigilance on the part of yourself & officers. I enclose a letter to the commanding officer at Winchester, which I wish you would forward to him immediately upon crossing the river, unless you can find opportunity to send it securely before.

Very respectfully, your obt servt

R. E. LEE
Genl

P.S. I desire you to turn back everybody you may meet on the road coming to join this army, to Falling Waters.

R. E. L.

504　To COMMANDING OFFICER, WINCHESTER

Headquarters, Army of Northern Virginia
July 4, 1863

Sir:

I wish you to convey to the commanding officers of the regiments of Ewell's corps instructions from me to proceed to Falling Waters, where they will take position and guard the pontoon bridge at that place, and also the ford at Williamsport, holding there all persons belonging to this army, and collecting all stragglers from it. Any sick of course will be forwarded to Winchester. The senior officer present will take command. Should it be necessary that a part of that force remain in Winchester, you have my authority for retaining it there. Upon the arrival of the sick & wounded at Winchester, they will be forwarded to Staunton as rapidly as possible, as also any surplus articles not needed for the army in the field.

Very respectfully, your obt servt

R. E. LEE
Genl

505　To JEFFERSON DAVIS
Richmond, Virginia

Headquarters, Army of Northern Virginia
Near Gettysburg, Pennsylvania
July 4, 1863

Mr. President:

After the rear of the army had crossed the Potomac, the leading corps under General Ewell pushed on to Carlisle & York, passing through Chambersburg. The other two corps closed up at the latter place, and soon afterward intelligence was received that the army of Genl Hooker was advancing. Our whole force was directed to concentrate at Gettysburg, and the corps of Generals Ewell & A. P. Hill reached that place on the 1st July, the former advancing from Carlisle and the latter from Chambersburg. The two leading divisions of these corps, upon reaching the vicinity of Gettysburg, found the enemy and attacked him, driving him from the town, which was occupied by our troops. The enemy's loss was heavy, including more than four thousand prisoners. He took up a strong position in rear of the town which he immediately began to fortify, and where his reinforcements joined him.

On the 2nd July, Longstreet's corps with the exception of one division having arrived, we attempted to dislodge the enemy, and though we gained some ground, we were unable to get possession of his position. The next day, the third division of Genl Longstreet having come up, a more extensive attack was made. The works on the enemy's extreme right & left were taken, but his numbers were so great and his position so commanding, that our troops were compelled to relinquish their advantage and retire.

It is believed that the enemy suffered severely in these operations, but our own loss has not been light.

Genl [William] Barksdale is killed. Genls [Richard B.] Garnett & [Lewis A.] Armistead are missing, & it is feared that the former is killed and the latter wounded and a prisoner. Generals [W. Dorsey] Pender & [Isaac R.] Trimble are wounded in the leg, Genl [John B.] Hood in the arm, and Genl [Henry] Heth slightly in the head. Genl [James L.] Kemper it is feared is mortally wounded. Our losses embrace many other valuable officers and men.

Genl Wade Hampton was severely wounded in a different action in which the cavalry was engaged yesterday.

Very respectfully, your obt servt

R. E. LEE
Genl

506   GENERAL ORDERS, NO. 74

Headquarters, Army of Northern Virginia
July 4, 1863

I.   The army will vacate its position this evening. General A. P. Hill's corps will commence the movement, withdrawing from its position after dark, and proceed on the Fairfield road to the pass in the mountains, which it will occupy, selecting the strongest ground for defense toward the east; General Longstreet's corps will follow, and General Ewell's corps bring up the rear. These two latter corps will proceed through and go into camp. General Longstreet's corps will be charged with the escort of the prisoners, and will habitually occupy the center of the line of march. General Ewell's and General Hill's corps will alternately take the front and rear on the march.

II.   The trains which accompany the army will habitually move between the leading and the rear corps, each under the charge of their respective chief quartermasters. Lieutenant Colonel [James L.] Corley, chief quartermaster of the army, will regulate the order in which they shall move. Corps commanders will see that the officers remain with their trains, and that they move steadily and quietly, and that the animals are properly cared for.

III.   The artillery of each corps will move under the charge of their respective chiefs of artillery, the whole under the general superintendence of the commander of the artillery of the army.

IV.   General Stuart will designate a cavalry command, not exceeding two squadrons, to precede and follow the army in its line of march, the commander of the advance reporting to the commander of the leading corps, the commander of the rear to the commander of the rear corps. He will direct one or two brigades, as he may think proper, to proceed to Cashtown this afternoon, and hold that place until the rear of the army has passed Fairfield, and occupy the gorge in the mountains; after crossing which, to proceed in the direction of Greencastle, guarding the right and rear of the army on its march to Hagerstown and Williamsport. General Stuart with the rest of the cavalry will this evening take the route to Emmitsburg and proceed thence toward Cavetown and Boonsboro, guarding the left and rear of the army.

V.   The commanding general earnestly exhorts each corps commander to see that every officer exerts the utmost vigilance, steadiness, and boldness during the whole march.

R. E. LEE
General

507   To JEFFERSON DAVIS
Richmond, Virginia

Hagerstown
July 7, 1863

Mr. President:
My letter of the 4th instant will have informed you of the unsuccessful issue of our final attack on the enemy in the rear of Gettysburg. Find-

ing the position too strong to be carried, and being much hindered in collecting necessary supplies for the army by the numerous bodies of local and other troops which watched the passes, I determined to withdraw to the west side of the mountains. This has been safely accomplished with great labor, and the army is now in the vicinity of this place. One of my reasons for moving in this direction after crossing the mountains, was to protect our trains with the sick and wounded, which had been sent back to Williamsport, and which were threatened by the enemy's cavalry. Our advance reached here yesterday afternoon in time to support our cavalry in repulsing an attempt of the enemy to reach our trains.

Before leaving Gettysburg, such of the sick and wounded as could be removed were sent back to Williamsport, but the rains that have interfered so much with our general movements have so swollen the Potomac as to render it unfordable, and they are still on the north side. Arrangements are being made to ferry them over today. We captured at Gettysburg about six thousand prisoners, besides the wounded that remained in our hands after the engagements of the 1st & 2d. Fifteen hundred of these prisoners and the wounded were paroled, but I suppose that under the late arrangements these paroles will not be regarded. The rest have been sent to Williamsport where they will cross. We were obliged to leave a large number of our wounded who were unable to travel, and many arms that had been collected on the field at Gettysburg. In addition to the general officers killed or wounded, of whom I sent you a list in my former letter, I have to mention General [Paul J.] Semmes, General G. T. Anderson, General [James J.] Pettigrew, and General J. M. Jones, wounded; General [James J.] Archer was made prisoner. General Heth is again in command.

In sending back our trains in advance, that of General Ewell was cut by the enemy's cavalry, and a number of wagons, said to be about forty were captured. The enemy's cavalry force which attempted to reach our trains yesterday afternoon was a large one. They came as far as Hagerstown where they were attacked by General Stuart and driven back rapidly towards Sharpsburg.

Very respectfully, your obt servt

R. E. LEE
General

508   To HIS WIFE
Richmond, Virginia

Williamsport
July 7, 1863

I have heard with great grief my dear Mary that Fitzhugh has been captured by the enemy. I had not expected that he would have been taken from his bed & carried off. But we must bear this additional affliction with fortitude & resignation & not repine at the will of God. It will eventuate in some good that we know not of now. I am particularly grieved on your account & Charlotte's. Tell the latter it will all come to good in the end. I fear I will not be able to write to her. But say for me all I feel & would say if opportunity offered. Tell dear Cousin Anne I am grateful for her sympathy. But I must bear this as I have to bear other things. I have sent a check for $1000 to Mr. Caskie for you. Thank Agnes for her affectionate letter, & say I will write when I can. Kiss my Precious Life for me. We are all well & bear our labours & hardships manfully. Our noble men are cheerful & confident. May God in His mercy bless our efforts to serve our country! I constantly remember you in my thoughts & in my prayers. May God bless you all is my constant prayer.

With true affection

R. E. LEE

509   To GENERAL GEORGE E. PICKETT
Commanding Division

Headquarters, Army of Northern Virginia
July 8, 1863

General:
I have received your letter of the 7th instant, and hope the arrangements you have made may secure the safety of the trains on the other side of the river. The present storm will place the Potomac beyond fording stage, and I fear you will have to rely upon the boats to pass over the wounded and prisoners. In sending forward the officers, send with them such a guard as will secure their safety, and Garnett's brigade might not be too large to take them to Winchester, but from that point to Staunton I should think a smaller guard would be sufficient. You can

use the rest of your division in guarding the remaining prisoners to Winchester with one of the batteries, unless you think both necessary. But I do not wish the division to go further than Winchester. You must halt there, collect all your stragglers, convalescents, &c., and use every exertion to resuscitate the command. You will assume command at Winchester. I wish you to make every exertion to aid this army, by protecting its trains and coming to its assistance, if necessary. I do not think Corse can be spared at this time from his present position, and for the present you must rely for recruits upon your convalescents and absentees, which I hope you will gather in.

After reaching Winchester with the prisoners you can arrange a guard to take them to Staunton, and to Richmond if necessary.

Establish your headquarters at Winchester for the present, and get together your men as soon as practicable.

Very respectfully, your obt servant

R. E. LEE
General

510   To JEFFERSON DAVIS
Richmond, Virginia

Headquarters, Army of Northern Virginia
Near Hagerstown, Maryland
July 8, 1863

Mr. President:

My letter of yesterday will have informed you of the position of this army. Though reduced in numbers by the hardships & battles through which it has passed since leaving the Rappahannock, its condition is good and its confidence unimpaired. Upon crossing the Potomac into Maryland, I had calculated upon the river remaining fordable during the summer, so as to enable me to recross at my pleasure, but a series of storms commencing the day after our entrance into Maryland has placed the river beyond fording stage, and the present storm will keep it so for at least a week. I shall therefore have to accept battle if the enemy offers it, whether I wish to or not, and as the result is in the hands of the Sovereign Ruler of the Universe, and known to Him only, I deem it prudent to make every arrangement in our power to meet any emergency that may arise. From information gathered from the papers, I believe that the troops from North Carolina and the coast of Virginia under Genls Foster & Dix have been ordered to the Potomac and that recently

additional reinforcements have been sent from the coast of South Carolina to Genl Banks. If I am correct in my opinion this will liberate most
of the troops in those regions, & should Your Excellency have not already
done so, I earnestly recommend that all that can be spared be concentrated on the upper Rappahannock under Genl Beauregard, with directions to cross that river and make a demonstration upon Washington.
This command will answer the double purpose of affording protection
to the capital at Richmond & relieving the pressure upon this army.

I hope Your Excellency will understand that I am not in the least
discouraged, or that my faith in the protection of an all merciful Providence, or in the fortitude of this army, is at all shaken. But, though conscious that the enemy has been much shattered in the recent battle, I
am aware that he can be easily reinforced, while no addition can be
made to our numbers. The measure therefore that I have recommended is
altogether one of a prudential nature.

I am, most respectfully, your obedient servant

R. E. LEE
Genl

P.S. I see it stated in a letter from the special correspondent of the
New York Times that a bearer of despatches from Your Excellency to
myself was captured at Hagerstown on the 2d July, & the despatches are
said to be of the greatest importance, & to have a great bearing on "coming events." I have thought proper to mention this, that you may know
whether it is so.

R. E. L.

511   To GENERAL J. E. B. STUART
Commanding Cavalry

Headquarters
July 9, 1863
4.30 P.M.

General:

I have received your note of today and regret very much to learn
your loss was so great yesterday. I hope your parties that you have sent
out may gain us information of the enemy. It is much needed. I hope you
will secure all the flour and forage on Beaver Creek. It is very scarce
and the enemy in the Clear Spring Valley are attacking all our wagon
trains. Yesterday they captured 11 wagons and today I have heard of 1.

Imboden's cavalry is on that side. They are unsteady and I fear inefficient. I think it more important to clear them away than to take Chambersburg. I doubt whether a shoe could be found there. They are all hidden or carried off.

Very respectfully

R. E. LEE
General

512   To JEFFERSON DAVIS
                               Richmond, Virginia

Headquarters, Army of Northern Virginia
Hagerstown
July 10, 1863

Mr. President:

Since my letter of the 8th instant nothing of importance in a military point of view has transpired.

The Potomac continues to be past fording, and owing to the rapidity of the stream and the limited facilities we have for crossing, the prisoners and wounded are not yet over. I hope they will all be across today.

I have not received any definite intelligence of the movements or designs of the enemy. A scout reports that a column which followed us across the mountains has reached Waynesboro in Pennsylvania and other bodies are reported as moving by way of Frederick from Emmitsburg, as if approaching in this direction.

If these reports be correct, it would appear to be the intention of the enemy to deliver battle, and we have no alternative but to accept it if offered. The army is in good condition, and we have a good supply of ammunition.

The chief difficulty is to procure subsistence. The supply of flour is affected by the high waters, which interfere with the working of the mills.

With the blessing of Heaven, I trust that the courage and fortitude of the army will be found sufficient to relieve us from the embarrassment caused by the unlooked for natural difficulties of our situation, if not to secure more valuable and substantial results.

I am with great respect, your obt servt

R. E. LEE
Genl

513   To JEFFERSON DAVIS
                    Richmond, Virginia
                    TELEGRAM

Near Hagerstown
July 10, 1863

YOUR TELEGRAM OF JULY 9TH HAS BEEN RECEIVED. I THANK YOU FOR THE
TROOPS SENT. MY LETTER WILL INFORM YOU THE STATE OF THINGS. THE
ARMY IS IN GOOD HEALTH AND CONDITION AND HOLD A POSITION BETWEEN
HAGERSTOWN AND WILLIAMSPORT. THE ENEMY IS GRADUALLY MAKING AP-
PEARANCE AGAINST US. I HAVE SENT ALL THE PRISONERS AND MOST OF THE
WOUNDED ACROSS THE RIVER.

R. E. LEE

514   MAJOR C. S. VENABLE TO GENERAL
             J. E. B. STUART
             Commanding Cavalry

Headquarters, Army of Northern Virginia
July 11, 1863

General:
    General Lee desires me to acknowlege your letter of this evening.
He desires you to keep in Longstreet's front as long as possible, awaiting
the developments of the enemy, and if forced back to take position on
the left of the army.
    Uniting with you in earnest hopes of a great victory, and new luster
to our arms,

        I am very respectfully, your obedient servant

C. S. VENABLE
Major and Aide-de-Camp

515   To GENERAL J. E. B. STUART
                    Commanding Cavalry

Headquarters, Army of Northern Virginia
July 12, 1863
9 P.M.

General:
    Your letter of 7.35 received. I this afternoon sent you a letter re-
questing you to have your cavalry in hand on our left to prevent any

attempt of the enemy on that quarter, and should an opportunity occur to advance upon the enemy's right and rear with your horse artillery to shake him in his position or attack. Should we be fortunate enough to break him you will then have an opportunity to pursue. I understood Fitz Lee to say that General Longstreet said he only wanted a few vedettes from his brigade, and in that event you had better have him with you. I shall write to General Longstreet if his brigade can be of no service there and has not joined you to order it accordingly.

Keep your eye over the field, use your good judgment, and give assistance where necessary.

I am most respectfully, your obedient servant

R. E. LEE
General

516   To HIS WIFE
                                        Richmond, Virginia

Camp near Hagerstown
July 12, 1863

I have received dear Mary your letter of the 7th. I have written once or twice since my arrival here, but do not know whether my letters have reached you. I am very glad to hear that Fitzhugh suffered but little by his removal. I trust he will soon be well. We must expect to endure every injury that our enemies can inflict upon us & be resigned to it. Their conduct is not dictated by kindness or love, & therefore we should not expect them to behave otherwise than they do. But I do not think we should follow their example. The consequences of war is horrid enough at best, surrounded by all the amelioration of civilization & Christianity. Why should we aggravate them? I am very sorry for the injuries done the family at Hickory Hill & particularly that our dear old Uncle Williams in his 80th year should be subjected to such treatment. But we cannot help it & must endure it. You will have learned before this reaches you that our success at Gettysburg was not as great as reported. In fact, that we failed to drive the enemy from his position & that our army withdrew to the Potomac. Had the river not unexpectedly risen, all would have been well with us. But God in His all wise Providence willed otherwise, & our communications have been interrupted & almost cut off. The waters have subsided to about 4 feet & if they continue, by tomorrow I hope our communications will be open. I trust that our merciful God, our only help & refuge, will not desert us in this our hour of need, but will deliver us by His almighty hand, that the whole world may recognize His power & all hearts be lifted up in adoration & praise of His unbounded loving kindness. We must however submit to His almighty will, whatever that may be. Give much love to my dear children. You & they are never out of my thoughts. May God guide & protect us all is the constant prayer of yours

Vry truly & affly

R

517
To JEFFERSON DAVIS
Richmond, Virginia

Headquarters, Army of Northern Virginia
Near Williamsport
July 12, 1863

Mr. President:

I have nothing of moment to add to what I have said in my letter of the 10th. So far everything goes well. The army is in good condition, and occupies a strong position covering the Potomac from Williamsport to Falling Waters. The enemy seems to be collecting his forces in the Valley of the Antietam, his main body stretching from Boonsboro to Sharpsburg. But for the power he possesses of accumulating troops, I should be willing to await his attack, except that in our restricted limits the means of obtaining subsistence is becoming precarious. The river has now fallen to four feet, and a bridge which is being constructed I hope will be passable by tomorrow morning. Should the river continue to subside, our communications with the south bank will be open by tomorrow. Had the late unexpected rise not occurred, there would have been no cause for anxiety, as it would then have been in my power to recross the Potomac on my first reaching it without molestation. Everything would have been accomplished that could have been reasonably expected. The Army of the Potomac had been thrown north of that river, the forces invading the coasts of North Carolina and Virginia had been diminished, their plan of the present campaign broken up, and, before new arrangements could have been made for its resumption, the summer would have been ended.

I still trust that a kind Providence will cause all things to work together for our good.

I am with great respect, your obt servt

R. E. LEE
Genl

518   COLONEL W. H. TAYLOR TO GENERAL
SAMUEL JONES
Commanding at Dublin Depot

Headquarters, Army of Northern Virginia
Near Hagerstown, Maryland
July 12, 1863

General:

I am directed by General Lee to say that he has received information from the War Department that you had been ordered with a force of infantry and artillery to Winchester, and that you would there receive orders from him. He wishes you on reaching Winchester to assume command there, and make all possible arrangements for the protection of Government property and the communications of this army. He also desires that you will cause all men improperly absent from this army who may be arrested, together with all convalescents and other soldiers en route to join the army, to be organized into parties under charge of such officers and with such arms as are available and sent on to Williamsport, that they may rejoin their respective commands.

I am most respectfully, your obt servt

W. H. TAYLOR
A. A. G.

519   To GENERAL J. E. B. STUART
Commanding Cavalry

July 13, 1863
4.15 P.M.

General:

As arranged this afternoon I wish you to place your cavalry in position before night so as to relieve the infantry along the whole extent of their lines when they retire, and take the place of their sharpshooters when withdrawn. They will be withdrawn about 12 o'clock tonight. Direct your men to be very vigilant and bold and not let the enemy discover that our lines have been vacated. At daylight withdraw your skirmishers and retire with all your force to cross the river. Have officers stationed at the fords so as to direct your men immediately upon arrival, and make every arrangement to get your command over in safety. The cavalry that occupies Longstreet's line might cross at the bridge if the officer in command will take measures to see that the bridge is clear at daylight. The rest had better cross at the ford I think but you may take any course that you may think best. I know it to be a difficult as well as delicate operation to cover this army and then withdraw your command with safety, but I rely upon your good judgment, energy, and boldness to accomplish it, and trust you may be as successful as you have been on former occasions. After crossing continue to cover the rear of the army with part of your force, and with the rest move forward to our front where you will receive further orders.

Very respectfully, &c.

R. E. Lee
General

520   To JEFFERSON DAVIS
Richmond, Virginia
TELEGRAM

Near Martinsburg
July 14, 1863

AFTER REMAINING AT HAGERSTOWN LONG ENOUGH TO CAUSE THE ENEMY TO CONCENTRATE HIS FORCES IN THAT VICINITY & FINDING HE WAS FORTIFYING HIMSELF IN HIS POSITION I THOUGHT IT ADVISABLE IN THE PRESENT UNCERTAIN STAGE OF THE RIVER TO WITHDRAW THE ARMY TO THE SOUTH SIDE OF THE POTOMAC WHICH WAS DONE LAST NIGHT WITHOUT MOLESTATION. WE SHOULD HAVE NOTHING TO REGRET HAD NOT GENL [JAMES J.] PETTIGREW RECEIVED A SEVERE WOUND IN A FEEBLE ATTACK OF THE ENEMY'S CAVALRY UPON OUR REAR GUARD AS HE WAS BEING WITHDRAWN THIS MORNING ACROSS THE RIVER.

R. E. Lee

521   CIRCULAR

Headquarters, Army of Northern Virginia
July 14, 1863

I.   The army will continue its march tomorrow. A. P. Hill's corps will start at 5 a.m. and camp on the waters of Mill Creek west of Bunker Hill. Longstreet will follow at 6.30 a.m. and encamp on the waters of Mill Creek east of Bunker Hill. Ewell's corps will march at 8 a.m. and camp on the stream passing through Darkesville. The trains will follow their respective corps. The ordnance and supply trains will move at 3.30 p.m. and camp on the branch of Mill Run south of Bunker Hill. The following day the army will rest in camp should circumstances permit.

II.   An officer will be sent by each corps commander to Winchester to collect men returning from hospitals, absentees, &c.

III.   Headquarters of the army will be at Bunker Hill.

IV.   The movement of Pickett's division will be regulated by Longstreet.

By order of General R. E. Lee:

R. H. CHILTON
Assistant Adjutant and Inspector General

522   To HIS WIFE
Richmond, Virginia

Bunker Hill
July 15, 1863

The army has returned to Virginia dear Mary. Its return is rather sooner than I had originally contemplated, but having accomplished what I purposed on leaving the Rappahannock, viz., relieving the Valley of the presence of the enemy & drawing his army north of the Potomac, I determined to recross the latter river. The enemy after concentrating his forces in our front began to fortify himself in his position, bring up his local troops, militia, &c., & all those around Washington & Alexandria. This gave him enormous odds. It also circumscribed our limits for procuring subsistence for men & animals, which with the uncertain stage of the river rendered it too hazardous for us to continue on the north side. It has been raining ever since we first crossed the Potomac. Making the roads horrid & embarrassing our operations. The night we recrossed it rained terribly. Had been raining during that day & previous days. Yet we got all over safe. Save such vehicles as broke down on the road from the mud, rocks, &c. We are all well. I hope will yet be able to damage our adversaries when they meet us, & that all will go right with us. That it should be so, we must implore the forgiveness of God for our sins, & the continuance of His blessings. There is nothing but His almighty power that can sustain us. I hear that Mary has found you. I hope she is well. Give love to all. I have no time to write, & my pen or ink, or both, forbids my attempting more. God bless you all.

Truly & affly
R. E. LEE

To JEFFERSON DAVIS
                            Richmond, Virginia

                                          Headquarters, Army of Northern Virginia
                                          Bunker Hill, Virginia
                                          July 16, 1863

Mr. President:

I have received your letter of the 12th instant and thank you for the kind terms in which you speak of the army, and for your consideration of myself.

I enclose a copy of my letter of the 7th instant which failed to reach you.

The army is encamped around this place, where we shall rest today. The men are in good health and spirits, but want shoes and clothing badly. I have sent back to endeavor to procure a supply of both, and also horseshoes, for want of which nearly half our cavalry is unserviceable. As soon as these necessary articles are obtained we shall be prepared to resume operations.

I shall not need the pontoon train now, as the boats used at Falling Waters have been brought away, excepting the new ones constructed by us, which were too heavy and too large for transportation. I have accordingly ordered the train of which you speak to come no farther.

The attacks on the coast may have been caused by the information contained in the captured letter. I think that all these demonstrations of the enemy are designed to retain troops from the field, and while he must be resisted and a force kept at threatened points sufficient to secure them, we should endeavour to avoid being misled as to his numbers and real intentions, and thus enable him to accomplish his purpose. I do not know that I shall need any more troops here, and they had better be kept in front of Richmond to secure it from attack and protect our railroads.

I learn that the enemy has thrown a pontoon bridge over the Potomac at Harper's Ferry. Should he follow us in this direction, I shall lead him up the Valley and endeavor to attack him as far from his base as possible.

I share in Your Excellency's regret for the fall of Vicksburg. It will be necessary for us to endeavor to select some point on the Mississippi and fortify it strongly, so that it may be held by a small garrison, which could be supplied with ammunition and provisions to enable it to stand a siege, thus leaving as many troops as possible free to operate against the enemy. I think that in this way a land attack against such position as we may select can be prevented.

I am with great respect, Your Excellency's obt servant

R. E. LEE
General

524   To JAMES A. SEDDON
                   Secretary of War

Headquarters, Bunker Hill
July 16, 1863

Sir:
I have received the communication sent me by your brother, Major [John] Seddon, & shall endeavour to carry out your views. He will inform you of the arrival of the army at this point. It is a little foot sore, & in much need of shoes for men & horses. Otherwise well. I expect a supply of shoes of both kinds today, which will afford some relief, but not enough. Clothing is also required. The labours of the march have been increased by the constant rains, muddy roads, &c.

I am with great respect, your obt servt

R. E. LEE
Genl

525   To GENERAL J. E. B. STUART
                   Commanding Cavalry

Headquarters, Army of Northern Virginia
July 18, 1863

General:
Your note of this date is received.
Let me know as soon as you can the truth of the report that the enemy has occupied Snicker's Gap in force and is advancing upon Ashby's Gap. This may oblige us to move up the Valley. I do not understand where Jones' pickets are, but the Sixth [Virginia Cavalry] Regiment, which you state are at Ashby's Gap and cannot recross the river, will have to retire southward along the mountain if pressed, checking the enemy all they can. I wish you to endeavor to ascertain the exact condi-

tion of things, whether this force is simply cavalry, or whether the enemy's infantry is moving in that direction.

I am respectfully and truly, your obedient servant

R. E. LEE
General

526   To GENERAL JAMES LONGSTREET
Commanding First Corps

Headquarters, Army of Northern Virginia
July 19, 1863

General:

On reaching Millwood, should nothing occur to arrest your progress or render it advisable for you to cross Berry's Ferry and occupy Ashby's Gap, I request you to proceed next day to Front Royal, cross the mountains at Chester Gap and take some position at the headwaters of the Rappahannock in Fauquier or Rappahannock Counties as you may select. Should you be able to subsist your army in that position by drawing flour in that region of country and not hear that the enemy is pushing on on the route to Richmond I desire you will halt there. Should you hear that the enemy is advancing on to Richmond you will proceed by the most direct route and place yourself behind the Rapidan. You had better send forward and see what flour you can obtain on your route until you can come within the reach of the railroad. I have heard that the railroad bridge over the Rapidan has been carried away by the freshet. It was immediately ordered to be rebuilt, but it is probable that you can get nothing by railroad north of the Rapidan Station. Col [Robert G.] Cole has sent an officer up to New Market and Harrisonburg to load some empty wagons in that region with flour and take them across to the Sperryville Valley. These may reach there in time to supply you provided you cannot obtain enough elsewhere. I need not suggest to you the importance of causing every attention to be paid to your artillery and wagon horses, for as little or no grain can be procured it will be impossible for them to stand hard work without the utmost care and relief from all superfluous weight. I have advised Genl [Samuel] Jones and Genl [Beverly H.] Robertson, who are picketing on the Shenandoah, to give you all information which may be of importance to you. Should I receive information which may render it necessary, A. P. Hill will follow you on Tuesday morning. Please give instructions to keep all the mills going in your route, so as to supply flour to the other troops. I have directed a pontoon bridge to be laid at Front Royal, and you had better send an officer forward to see its progress.

Should you determine to cross at Ashby's Gap you must order it to you.

I am very respectfully, your obt servt

R. E. Lee
General

527   To GENERAL SAMUEL COOPER
               Adjutant and Inspector General

Headquarters, Army of Northern Virginia
July 20, 1863

General:

At the time the army left Fredericksburg, I directed a package of battle reports to be sent to Richmond to be kept in your office until I should call for them. The endorsement on the envelope of the package is to that effect. I now desire that they may be sent to me, as they are necessary to enable me to complete my report of the operations embraced by them.

Very respectfully, your obt servt

R. E. Lee
Genl

528   To GENERAL RICHARD S. EWELL
               Commanding Second Corps

Headquarters, Army of Northern Virginia
July 20, 1863

General:

Unless I receive contrary information to what I now possess Genl A. P. Hill's corps will move in the morning for Rappahannock County. General Stuart has been directed with his cavalry to continue in the Valley until he finds the forces of the enemy sufficiently reduced then to withdraw and interpose his forces between the enemy and the portion of the army east of the Blue Ridge. He will notify you of all movements of the enemy of any importance. I have directed General [John D.] Imboden to return to Winchester with his troops from Staunton. Colonel [George W.] Imboden with his cavalry will remain with you until you leave the Valley, and you must give directions to all the other troops. I think it probable that you will be required to follow me in a few days, so be prepared with provisions, &c., to move at short notice. I have directed Colonel [Gabriel C.] Wharton, who commands such troops from Genl Sam Jones as have arrived, to occupy Winchester and to receive your instructions. Should you not require Colonel [James B.] Terrill (now in Winchester, belonging to Early's division), I suggest that he be directed to move to Front Royal to guard the pontoon bridge which I will leave there for you. I suggest that you move higher up the Valley in the direction of Berryville or Milwood so as to be prepared to vacate the Valley if pressed by superior numbers or to join me as circumstances may require. Should your line of march by Chester Gap be cut off, you can proceed west of the Massanutten Mountain and go by Thornton's or Swift Run Gap. I will march with A. P. Hill's corps. Please send me any information of the enemy's movements which you may deem important.

I am very respectfully, your obt servt

R. E. LEE
General

529   To GENERAL JOHN D. IMBODEN
Staunton, Virginia

Headquarters, Hollingsworth's Mills
1 Mile South of Winchester
July 21, 1863

General:

I am obliged to withdraw the army east of the Blue Ridge. A portion of General Sam Jones' troops under Colonel Wharton have reached the Valley, but General Jones himself has not arrived and circumstances may prevent his coming altogether. In his absence I desire you to take command of the Valley District and so dispose of your troops as to operate to the best advantage, covering from the depredations of the enemy, giving protection to the inhabitants, and damaging the enemy all in your power. The forces of Generals [James A.] Mulligan, [Benjamin F.] Kelley, and [William W.] Averell were said to be in the neighborhood of Cherry Run and Back Creek, and General Ewell with his corps moved down last evening to attack them this morning, but they escaped from him during the night. It has been reported by scouts that all the troops have been withdrawn from northwestern Virginia, leaving only a small guard at Grafton and New Creek, the rest being in the vicinity of Cherry Run. If this is true, this is a fine opportunity of damaging the road and destroying the workshops at Piedmont, which I hope you will take advantage of.

I desire Colonel Wharton to remain in command of all of General Jones' troops that are here or may arrive, until the arrival of General Jones himself.

I am most respectfully, your obt servt

R. E. LEE
General

530   To GENERAL SAMUEL COOPER
Adjutant and Inspector General

Headquarters, Army of Northern Virginia
July 21, 1863

General:

I have seen in the Northern papers what purported to be an official dispatch of General Meade, stating that he had captured a brigade of infantry, two pieces of artillery, two caissons, and a large number of small arms, as this army retired to the south bank of the Potomac on the 13th and 14th instant.

This dispatch has been copied into the Richmond papers, and as its official character may cause it to be believed, I desire to state that it is incorrect. The enemy did not capture any organized body of men on that occasion, but only stragglers and such as were left asleep on the road, exhausted by the fatigue and exposure of one of the most inclement nights I have ever known at this season of the year. It rained without cessation, rendering the road by which our troops marched to the bridge at Falling Waters very difficult to pass, and causing so much delay that the last of the troops did not cross the river at the bridge until 1 p.m. on the 14th. While the column was thus detained on the road, a number of men, worn down with fatigue, lay down in barns and by the roadside, and though officers were sent back to arouse them as the troops moved on, the darkness and rain prevented them from finding all, and many were in this way left behind.

Two guns were left in the road. The horses that drew them became exhausted and the officers went forward to procure others. When they returned, the rear of the column had passed the guns so far that it was deemed unsafe to send back for them and they were thus lost. No arms, cannon, or prisoners were taken by the enemy in battle, but only such as were left behind under the circumstances I have described. The number of stragglers thus lost I am unable to state with accuracy, but it is greatly exaggerated in the dispatch referred to.

I am with great respect, your obt servt

R. E. Lee
Genl

531　　　　　To JEFFERSON DAVIS
Richmond, Virginia

Headquarters, Army of Northern Virginia
Culpeper Court House
July 24, 1863

Mr. President:

After the army recrossed the Potomac from Maryland I had determined to move it into Loudoun, but the rains that had swelled the Potomac placed the Shenandoah six feet above fording stage, and before arrangements could be made to use the pontoon bridge, so thoughtfully forwarded by you, the enemy crossed into Loudoun County and occupied the passes of the Blue Ridge through which I had intended to advance. The difficulty of ascertaining his plans, the delay that would have been occasioned by forcing a passage in his front, and the ease with which he could have thrown himself upon Richmond, induced me to move up to Chester Gap and take position at this place. General Longstreet's corps reached here today, Genl A. P. Hill's is expected to arrive within ten miles, and Genl Ewell's corps which was to pass through Thornton's Gap will probably be here day after tomorrow. My intention is, if practicable, to give the army a few days' rest, and refresh our weary animals, which having been obliged to subsist chiefly on grass, are much reduced. I desire also to draw to me as rapidly as possible all the convalescents and absentees, and to strengthen our ranks. We are in great need of horseshoes having been able to procure none on our expedition, and our constant motion preventing their manufacture from iron that fell into our possession, more than half the cavalry is dismounted, and the artillery horses and wagon teams have suffered equally.

I learn that the enemy is massing a large army between Centreville and Manassas Junction. A portion of General Meade's army crossed the Potomac as low down as the Chain Bridge, and I understand embraces the commands of Generals Dix and Foster. General [Michael] Corcoran advanced on the road from Alexandria. Since crossing the mountain, I have learned that the Manassas Gap Railroad is in operation as high as Salem, and I hear that they are carrying up timber with the view probably of extending it beyond. It would seem to have been the intention of the enemy to penetrate the Shenandoah Valley above Winchester, for in addition to these preparations I am informed that last evening he advanced three corps into Manassas Gap.

Very respectfully, your obt servt

R. E. Lee
Genl

532   To HIS WIFE
                        Hot Springs, Virginia

Camp, Culpeper
July 26, 1863

I received last night dear Mary your letter commenced at Hickory Hill on the 18th enclosing one from Charlotte of the same date. I also got a kind note from Margaret Stuart dated 22nd at Ashland giving me an account of your journey that far & of your departure for the Hot Springs. I am extremely grateful to our kind friends for their considerate attentions to you & wish it was in my power even to thank them for it. I hope the car prepared for you may alleviate as far as possible the pain & fatigue I fear you will suffer in your journey. But if a merciful God will only bless the means it seems alone open to you to attain relief, we must bear all else in the effort to accomplish it. I pray this may be His holy pleasure, & that you may be again restored to a comfortable state of health should a perfect cure not be vouchsafed you. I am glad too you have Mary & Agnes with you, but who will go to the Alum with Charlotte? Poor child I am too sorry she is suffering in health as well as from her separation from Fitzhugh. She writes as if in distress & sadness. You must try & cheer her. It now cannot be avoided & we have only to submit. I hope his exchange may be soon effected. But nothing can be done to hasten it. The more anxiety shewn on our part, the more it will be procrastinated by our enemies, whose pleasure seems to be to injure, harass, & annoy us as much as their extensive means enable them. I am glad Mary's health is so good. I hope my poor little Agnes will be able to throw off her neuralgia & that you will all return full of health & thankfulness to our Heavenly Father for the mercies bestowed upon us. Tell Mary I received her (two) letters from Dr. Stuart's, but was unable to reply for fear of compromitting our scouts, on whom if my letters had been found extreme punishment would have been inflicted. For the same reason I had to discourage her writing to me. Now I have no time, but I think of her constantly & I cannot express how I long & pray that God in His mercy may pardon my many & long standing sins & once more gather around me you & my dear children & grant me a little time with you all before I go hence & be no more seen. How great is my remorse at having thrown away my time & abused the opportunities afforded me. Now I am unable to benefit either myself or others, & am receiving in this world the punishment due to my sins & follies. I regret so not seeing Mildred & am saddened by the thought that the opportunity may never recur. But God's will be done! I am glad you have my Rob for your escort. I trust all will go well with you & him. After crossing the Potomac, finding that the Shenandoah was six feet above fording stage, & having waited a week for it to fall so that I might cross into Loudoun; fearing that the enemy might take advantage of our position to move upon Richmond, I determined to ascend the Valley & come into Culpeper. Two corps are here with me. The third passed up to Thorton's Gap & I hope will be in striking distance tomorrow. The army has laboured hard, endured much & behaved nobly. It has accomplished all that could have been reasonably expected. It ought not to have been expected to have performed impossibilities or to have fulfilled the anticipations of the thoughtless & unreasonable. You must give a great deal of love to Daughter & Agnes. Also to Charlotte & Mildred when you write. Tell Charlotte my affection for Fitzhugh, my sympathy for her, & distress at their forcible separation, is not the less because their expression is restrained. I am accustomed to bear my sorrows in silence. My prayers for her & Fitzhugh are fervent & constant & my trust is in God for their relief from their distress.

　　May God in his infinite mercy guard, guide & protect you all, & once more give peace & rest to our distracted country!

Truly & affcly yours

R. E. LEE

P.S. I do not recollect whether I told you of the death of Mary Lowe. She died at Savannah in June in premature child birth, leaving four little children. Her mother was in Bartow & her little grandchildren have all been taken up to her by their good aunt, Miss Kate Mackay. I have written a short note of condolence to Mrs. Lowe.

R. E. L.

533   To MISS MARGARET STUART
"Clydale," Virginia

Camp, Culpeper
July 26, 1863

I am so much obliged to you, my dear Cousin Margaret, for your kind note of the 22d. It adds to my gratitude for your former note, your welcome messages, and acceptable present of the gloves. Having had no opportunity to acknowledge them I now thank you for all with my whole heart. I cannot tell you how often and much I have thought of you the past winter, how I have grieved over your restraint and ill usage by our enemies, and how I have regretted my inability to relieve you. Your father, mother, Ada, and Carrie have been constantly in my thoughts. I have longed to see you all. I knew that crossing the Potomac would draw them off, and if we could only have been strong enough we should have detained them. But God willed otherwise, & I fear we shall soon have them all back. The army did all it could. I fear I required of it impossibilities. But it responded to the call nobly and cheerfully, and though it did not win a victory it conquered a success. We must now prepare for harder blows and harder work. But my trust is in Him who favors the weak and relieves the oppressed, and my hourly prayer is that He will "fight for us once again." I know we shall have your sweet prayers, and I am cheered by the belief that your dear father and mother will not forget us, but that their pious supplications will be offered up in our behalf night and morning. Give much love to them. Tell Ada if she will join the Army, I will give my consent, but Carrie need not think of that other one. I shall let no one have you Maggie till the war is over. I have one in reserve for you. I must now bid you good-bye. May God guard and protect you all, is the earnest prayer of,

Your affectionate cousin

R. E. LEE

534   To MISS MILDRED LEE
Raleigh, North Carolina

Camp, Culpeper
July 27, 1863

I have heard my precious daughter that you have returned to your school. I cannot tell you how I regret not having seen you. I had looked

forward to your vacation with so much pleasure this summer in the hope
of seeing you a little while at least. But it is past & I am disappointed. I
wanted to see how you were, how you looked, & whom you resembled.
Have you no photograph of yourself that you could send me. I am glad
however that you have returned to school for your sake. I think it is the
best course you could have pursued. I hope you will be able to learn a
great deal this year & by the next that there will be peace over the land &
that we shall all be together when I can enjoy the happiness of being
once more with you. I long for that time very much & pray that we
may all be long united in this world & forever in the next. I heard from
your mother on her way to the Hot Springs the day she started from
Ashland. She had got that far very well & her prospects for a comfortable
journey were good. I trust she may be relieved from her great affliction
& at last find ease. I hope indeed all may be benefited & especially that
Charlotte & Agnes may be cured, the one of dibility & the other of
neuralgia. I suppose sister had a great [torn] sufferings of our poor
[torn] extends pretty much [torn] make up our minds to bear it. I saw
some of your acquaintances in the Valley who enquired particularly after
you, particularly Miss Sally Dandrige & Miss Fanny Mc—— of Smithfield. I have forgotten her name but her mother was a Miss Nelson. She
said she was a great friend of yours & that you had once accompanied
her home during some holy day. I saw her mother also & Dr. Nelson,
&c., &c. Poor Winchester has been terribly devastated & the inhabitants
plundered of all they possessed. Mr. James Mason's residence has been
torn down to the ground. Scarcely one brick stands upon another & a
pile of rubbish rests upon the hill on which it stood. I hope you will have
time to write to me sometimes, for though I have little time to reply, I
shall enjoy the perusal of your letters very much. You must tell me how
you found your mother, Charlotte, sisters & Rob. I suppose Rob thinks
himself almost a man now. I hope you had a pleasant visit to Virginia &
that you have carried back with you pleasant thoughts & reflections. My
only pleasure is to think of your mother & my children. May God bless
you my dear daughter, strew your path in this world with every happiness, & finally gather you & all of us to His mansions of bliss in heaven,
is my daily & hourly prayer! Tell me of your companions, your room-
mate, studies, occupations, &c. All that concerns you will be interesting
to me.

[R. E. LEE]

535   To JEFFERSON DAVIS
                          Richmond, Virginia

                              Headquarters, Army of Northern Virginia
                                                July 29, 1863
Mr. President:
    Your letter of the 21st instant has been received, and I am much obliged to you for the suggestions it contains. As soon as I receive an official account of the casualties in the army it will be forwarded. The list of our wounded and missing I know will be large. Many of the first could not be moved and had to be left behind. The latter will be swelled by the stragglers who commenced on crossing the Potomac to stray from the line of march and were intercepted by the enemy's cavalry and armed citizens, notwithstanding every effort which was made to prevent it. Our people are so little liable to control that it is difficult to get them to follow any course not in accordance with their inclinations. The day after the last battle at Gettysburg, on sending back the train with the wounded, it was reported that about 5,000 well men started back at night to overtake it. I fear most of these were captured by the enemy's cavalry and armed citizens who beset their route. These added to other stragglers, men captured in battle, and those of the wounded unfit to be transported, will swell our list of missing. And as far as I can judge the killed, wounded, and missing from the time we left the Rappahannock until our return will not fall short of twenty thousand. This comprises however the slightly wounded and those who straggled from the ranks who are now rejoining us. After recrossing the Potomac, I commenced to consolidate the troops, considering the cases individually, and united Archer's and Heth's (Field's) former brigade under General Henry H. Walker, and Pender's and Heth's divisions under General Heth. The accession of convalescents and stragglers is enlarging these divisions so much that I shall have to separate them again. As regards General [Joseph R.] Davis' brigade, I think it will be better to attach the three Mississippi regiments to [General Carnot] Posey's brigade in [General Richard H.] Anderson's division, where I hope they will soon be increased in numbers. The North Carolina regiment of this brigade I suggest be attached to Pettigrew's old brigade.
    The only objection to this plan is that it breaks up General Davis' command, but if his indisposition will detain him long from the field, it will be best to do it for the present at least. Although our loss has been so heavy, which is a source of constant grief to me, I believe the damage to the enemy has been as great in proportion. This is shown by their

feeble operations since. Their army is now massed in the vicinity of Warrenton, along the Orange and Alexandria Railroad, collecting reinforcements. Unfortunately their means are greater than ours and I fear when they move again they will much outnumber us. Their future plans I cannot discover and think it doubtful with their experience of last year whether they will assume the Fredericksburg line again or not, though it is very probable. Should they do so, I doubt the policy of our resuming our former position in rear of Fredericksburg, as any battle fought there excepting to resist a front attack would be on disadvantageous terms, and I therefore think it better to take a position farther back. I should like your views upon this point. The enemy now seems to be content to remain quiescent, prepared to oppose any offensive movement on our part. General Meade's headquarters are at Warrenton. I learn by our scouts that the seven corps are between that point and the Orange and Alexandria Railroad. They are all much reduced in numbers. From the observation of some corps, the report of citizens and their prisoners, the reduction is general, and the corps do not exceed from six to eight thousand men. I have halted Ewell's corps on Robertson River, about three miles in front of Madison Court House where grazing is represented to be very fine, and in the vicinity of which sufficient flour can be obtained. We have experienced no trouble from the enemy in crossing the Blue Ridge. Except the attempt at Manassas Gap upon Ewell and of a cavalry force on the Gourd Vine road on A. P. Hill our march has been nearly unmolested. Our cavalry is in our front along the Rappahannock. I am endeavouring to collect all the provisions I can in this part of the country, which was also done in the Valley. While there, in order to obtain sufficient flour we were obliged to send men and horses, thresh the wheat, carry it to the mills, and have it ground. There is little or no grain in that vicinity, and I cannot learn of more in Madison than sufficient for Ewell's corps.

Very respectfully, your obt servt

R. E. LEE
General

536 To JEFFERSON DAVIS
Richmond, Virginia

Camp, Culpeper
July 31, 1863

Mr. President:

Your note of the 27 enclosing a slip from the *Charleston Mercury* relative to the battle of Gettysburg is received. I much regret its general censure upon the operations of the army, as it is calculated to do us no good either at home or abroad. But I am prepared for similar criticism & as far as I am concerned the remarks fall harmless. I am particularly sorry however that from partial information & mere assumption of facts that injustice should be done any officer, & that occasion should be taken to asperse your conduct, who of all others are most free of blame. I do not fear that your position in the confidence of the people, can be injured by such attacks, & I hope the official reports will protect the reputation of every officer. These cannot be made at once, & in the meantime as you state much falsehood may be promulgated. But truth is mighty & will eventually prevail. As regards the article in question I think it contains its own contradiction. Although charging Heth with the failure of the battle, it expressly states he was absent wounded. The object of the writer & publisher is evidently to cast discredit upon the operations of the Government & those connected with it & thus gratify feelings more to be pitied than envied. To take notice of such attacks would I think do more harm than good, & would be just what is desired. The delay that will necessarily occur in receiving official reports has induced me to make for the information of the Department a brief outline of operations of the army, in which however I have been unable to state the conduct of troops or officers. It is sufficient to show what was done & what was not done. No blame can be attached to the army for its failure to accomplish what was projected by me, nor should it be censured for the unreasonable expectations of the public. I am alone to blame, in perhaps expecting too much of its prowess & valour. It however in my opinion achieved under the guidance of the Most High a general success, though it did not win a victory. I thought at the time that the latter was practicable. I still think if all things could have worked together it would have been accomplished. But with the knowledge I then had, & in the circumstances I was then placed, I do not know what better course I could have pursued. With my present knowledge, & could I have foreseen that the attack on the last day would have failed to drive the enemy from his position, I should certainly have tried some other course. What the ultimate result would have been is not so clear to me. Our loss has been very heavy, that of the enemy's is proportionally so. His crippled condition enabled us to retire from the country comparatively unmolested. The unexpected state of the Potomac was our only embarrassment. I will not trespass upon Your Excellency's time more. With prayers for your health & happiness, & the recognition by your grateful country of your great services

I remain truly & sincerely yours

R. E. LEE

537   To JEFFERSON DAVIS
Richmond, Virginia
TELEGRAM

Culpeper Court House
July 31, 1863

REPORTS FROM SCOUTS INDICATE MOVEMENTS OF ENEMY TO FREDERICKS-
BURG. I AM MAKING CORRESPONDING MOVEMENTS.

R. E. LEE
Genl

538   To JEFFERSON DAVIS
Richmond, Virginia
TELEGRAM

Culpeper Court House
August 1, 1863

REPORTS OF ENEMY MOVING TO FREDERICKSBURG ARE NOT CONFIRMED
TODAY. ON THE CONTRARY THEY APPEAR TO BE ADVANCING ON THIS ROUTE.
HAVE CROSSED COLUMNS OF INFANTRY ON PONTOON BRIDGES AT ELLIS' &
KELLY'S FORDS & RAPPAHANNOCK BRIDGE. THEIR CAVALRY HAVE PRESSED
OURS THIS SIDE OF BRANDY STATION. THEIR CAMP SEEMS TO BE IN MOTION. I
SHALL NOT FIGHT A BATTLE NORTH OF THE RAPIDAN, BUT WILL ENDEAVOR TO
CONCENTRATE EVERYTHING BEHIND IT. IT WOULD BE WELL TO SEND ALL RE-
INFORCEMENTS IN RICHMOND TO ORANGE COURT HOUSE.

R. E. LEE

539   To HIS WIFE
Hot Springs, Virginia

Camp, Culpeper
August 2, 1863

I have received dear Mary your letter of the 26th from the Hot
Springs & am truly grateful to the kindness of our friends for their care
& attention of you, & to Almighty God for His help & support. I fervently pray that He may bless the means He has provided you for your
relief, & should He not grant you a perfect restoration, that you may at
least obtain ease & comfort. You must not mind the trouble or even
suffering of your journey or sojourn, provided you attain the benefit we

much desire. You must thank for me all the kind friends that have aided
in alleviating the pain of your journey as I am unable to do so. I am
glad at least you have with you so pleasant a party. I wish I was along.
Tell Chass never mind the face. It is very temporary in its effects &
the plainer it is the more healthy. I have heard of some doctor having
reached Richmond that had seen our dear Fitzhugh at Fort Monroe. He
said his wound was improving & that he himself was well & walking
about on crutches. The exchange of prisoners that had been going on,
has for some cause been suspended, owing to some crotchet or other,
but I hope will soon be resumed & that we shall have him soon back.
Tell Chass I think it very doubtful whether they would allow her to
visit him. The only way of accomplishing it is to get permission from
Mr. Secretary Stanton in Washington through Mr. [Robert] Ould to
take the flag of truce boat to Old Point. I do not think he would give
it in her case. It having been refused in others, which they would not
feel as much objection in obliging, & I believe their permission is always
coupled with the obligation to take the oath of allegiance to the U. S. I
think an application therefore would be useless. Our only course is to
be patient & pray God for his preservation & speedy restoration. I grieve
much at his position, but know no way of mending it. Any expression
on my part would injure matters. I can therefore do nothing but sorrow. We are all as well here as usual. The armies are in such close
proximity that frequent collisions are common along the outposts. Yesterday the enemy laid down two or three pontoon bridges over the
Rappahannock & crossed his cavalry & a large force of his infantry. It
looked at first as if it was the advance of his army & as I had not intended to deliver battle I directed the cavalry to retire slowly before
them, but to check their too rapid progress. Finding later in the day
that their army was not following I ordered out the infantry & drove
them back to the river. Hampton's brigade was the portion of our cavalry
opposed to them, & it behaved very handsomely. Hampton himself is
absent wounded, & the brigade was under Col [Lawrence S.] Baker, who
acquitted himself well. He is wounded in the arm. Cols [John L.] Black
& [Pierce M. B.] Young also wounded. Our loss in numbers was small.
I suppose they intend to push on towards Richmond by this or some
other route. I trust they will never reach there. Give much love to all
with you. I wrote to you a week since from this camp enclosing a letter
to Chass. I hope it reached you. Kiss my daughters for me & Annie
Leigh. God bless & preserve you all!

Truly

R. E. LEE

540　　　　　　To GENERAL SAMUEL COOPER
　　　　　　　　　Adjutant and Inspector General

Headquarters, Army of Northern Virginia
August 4, 1863

General:

The movements of the enemy north of the Rappahannock, rendering it difficult for me to ascertain whether he intended to advance through Culpeper or fall down the river to Fredericksburg, determined me to unite the army south of the Rapidan. Genl Ewell's corps, which after crossing the Blue Ridge had been posted in Madison, had been previously ordered to Orange Court House. Longstreet's & Hill's corps were yesterday ordered to the Rapidan. I could find no field in Culpeper offering advantages for battle, and any taken could be so easily avoided should the enemy wish to reach the south bank of the Rapidan, that I thought it advisable at once to retire to that bank. Should he advance by this route I shall endeavour to resist him and if he falls down to Fredericksburg, will oppose him on that line.

I am very respectfully, your obt servt

R. E. LEE
Genl

541　　　　　　To GENERAL J. E. B. STUART
　　　　　　　　　Commanding Cavalry

Headquarters, Army of Northern Virginia
August 4, 1863

General:

Your note inclosing one from Fitz Lee was received. The corps of Longstreet and Hill will cross the Rapidan today and the army will be concentrated south of the Rapidan. If we leave Culpeper the enemy will enter it. If you can hold it without sacrificing your men it will be well. So long as you remain your supplies can be forwarded by rail to the Court House, and you can inform Colonel [James L.] Corley whether it will be safe. If you are forced back it will be best to come back to the rivers where you can get good grazing.

I am very respectfully, your obedient servant

R. E. LEE
General

542   To GENERAL SAMUEL COOPER
              Adjutant and Inspector General

BATTLE REPORT OF GETTYSBURG CAMPAIGN

Headquarters, Army of Northern Virginia
January 20, 1864

General:

I forward today my report of the late campaign of this army in Maryland & Pennsylvania, together with those of the corps and other commanders so far as they have been received. Genl Longstreet's list of casualties and the reports of his subordinate officers shall be sent as soon as they can be obtained from him.

I also forward the report of the Medical Director, and some other documents mentioned in the accompanying schedule. With reference to the former I would remark that it is necessarily imperfect for reasons stated in my report. The actual casualties & the number of missing can only be learned from the reports of the commanding officers, and it should be borne in mind that they usually embrace all the slightly wounded, even such as remain on duty, under the impression commonly entertained that the loss sustained is a measure of the service performed and the danger incurred. I also enclose a map of the routes of the army, and one of the lines at Hagerstown & Williamsport. That of the battlefield of Gettysburg shall be forwarded as soon as completed.

Very respectfully, your obt servt

R. E. LEE
Genl

I have the honor to submit a detailed report of the operations of this army from the time it left the vicinity of Fredericksburg early in June to its occupation of the line of the Rapidan in August.

Upon the retreat of the Federal Army commanded by Major General Hooker from Chancellorsville, it reoccupied the ground north of the Rappahannock opposite Fredericksburg, where it could not be attacked except at a disadvantage.

It was determined to draw it from this position, and if practicable to transfer the scene of hostilities beyond the Potomac. The execution of this purpose also embraced the expulsion of the force under General Milroy which had infested the lower Shenandoah Valley during the preceding winter & spring. If unable to attain the valuable results which might be expected to follow a decided advantage gained over the enemy in Maryland or Pennsylvania, it was hoped that we should at least so far disturb the plan for the summer campaign as to prevent its execution during the season of active operations.

The commands of Longstreet and Ewell were put in motion and encamped around Culpeper Court House on the 7th June. As soon as their march was discovered by the enemy, he threw a force across the Rappahannock about two miles below Fredericksburg, apparently for the purpose of observation. Hill's corps was left to watch these troops, with instructions to follow the movements of the army as soon as they should retire.

The cavalry under General Stuart, which had been concentrated near Culpeper Court House, was attacked on the 9th June by a large force of Federal cavalry supported by infantry, which crossed the Rappahannock at Beverly's and Kelly's Fords. After a severe engagement, which continued from early in the morning until late in the afternoon, the enemy was compelled to recross the river with heavy loss, leaving about five hundred prisoners, three pieces of artillery and several colors in our hands.

General Imboden and General Jenkins had been ordered to cooperate in the projected expedition into the Valley, General Imboden by moving toward Romney with his command, to prevent the troops guarding the Baltimore and Ohio Railroad from reinforcing those at Winchester, while General Jenkins advanced directly towards the latter place with his cavalry brigade, supported by a battalion of infantry & a battery of the Maryland Line.

General Ewell left Culpeper Court House on the 10th June. He crossed the branches of the Shenandoah near Front Royal, and reached Cedarville on the 12th, where he was joined by General Jenkins. Detaching General [Robert E.] Rodes with his division and the greater part of Jenkins' brigade to dislodge a force of the enemy stationed at Berryville, General Ewell with the rest of his command moved upon Winchester, [Edward] Johnson's division advancing by the Front Royal road, Early's by the Valley turnpike, which it entered at Newtown, where it was joined by the Maryland troops.

BATTLE OF WINCHESTER

The enemy was driven in on both roads, and our troops halted in line of battle near the town on the evening of the 13th. The same day the force which had occupied Berryville retreated to Winchester on the approach of General Rodes. The following morning General Ewell ordered General Early to carry an entrenched position northwest of Winchester, near the Pughtown road, which the latter officer upon examining the ground discovered would command the principal fortifications.

To cover the movement of General Early, General Johnson took position between the road to Millwood and that to Berryville, and advanced his skirmishers towards the town. General Early, leaving a portion of his command to engage the enemy's attention, with the remainder gained a favorable position without being perceived, and about 5 p.m. twenty pieces of artillery under Lieut Col Hilary P. Jones opened suddenly upon the entrenchments. The enemy's guns were soon silenced. [General Henry T.] Hays' brigade then advanced to the assault & carried the works by storm, capturing six rifled pieces, two of which were turned upon and dispersed a column which was forming to retake the position.

The enemy immediately abandoned the works on the left of those taken by Hays, and retired into his main fortifications which General Early prepared to assail in the morning. The loss of the advanced works however rendered the others untenable, and the enemy retreated in the night, abandoning his sick and wounded, together with his artillery, wagons, and stores. Anticipating such a movement as soon as he heard of Early's success, General Ewell directed General Johnson to occupy with part of his command a point on the Martinsburg road about two and a half miles from Winchester, where he could either intercept the enemy's retreat, or aid in an attack should further resistance be offered in the morning. General Johnson marched with [Francis T.] Nicholls' and part of [George H.] Steuart's brigades, accompanied by Lieut Col [R. Snowden] Andrews with a detachment of his artillery, the Stonewall Brigade being ordered to follow. Finding the road to the place indicated by General Ewell difficult of passage in the darkness, General Johnson pursued that leading by Jordan's Springs to Stephenson's Depot, where he took a favorable position on the Martinsburg road, about five miles from Winchester. Just as his line was formed, the retreating column consisting of the main body of General Milroy's army arrived and immediately attacked him.

The enemy though in superior force, consisting of both infantry and cavalry, was gallantly repulsed, and finding all efforts to cut his way unavailing, he sent strong flanking parties simultaneously to the right and left, still keeping up a heavy fire in front. The party on the right was driven back and pursued by the Stonewall Brigade, which opportunely arrived. That on the left was broken and dispersed by the 2d and 10th Louisiana Regiments aided by the artillery, and in a short time nearly the whole infantry force, amounting to more than twenty three hundred men with eleven stand of colors, surrendered, the cavalry alone escaping.

General Milroy with a small party of fugitives fled to Harper's Ferry.

The number of prisoners taken in this action exceeded the force engaged under General Johnson, who speaks in terms of well deserved praise of the conduct of the officers and men of his command.

In the meantime General Rodes marched from Berryville to Martinsburg, reaching the latter place in the afternoon of the 14th. The enemy made a show of resistance but soon gave way, the cavalry and artillery retreating towards Williamsport, the infantry towards Shepherdstown, under cover of night. The route taken by the latter was not known until it was too late to follow but the former were pursued so rapidly, Jenkins' troops leading, that they were forced to abandon five of their six pieces of artillery. About two hundred prisoners were taken, but the enemy destroyed most of his stores.

These operations resulted in the expulsion of the enemy from the Valley, the capture of four thousand prisoners, with a corresponding number of small arms, twenty-eight pieces of superior artillery, including those taken by General Rodes and General Hays, about three hundred wagons and as many horses, together with a considerable quantity of ordnance, commissary, and quartermaster's stores. Our entire loss was 47 killed, 219 wounded, and three missing.

MARCH INTO PENNSYLVANIA

On the night of Ewell's appearance at Winchester, the enemy in front of A. P. Hill at Fredericksburg recrossed the Rappahannock, and the whole army of General Hooker withdrew from the north side of the river. In order to mislead him as to our intentions, and at the same time protect Hill's corps in its march up the Rappahannock, Longstreet left Culpeper Court House on the 15th, and advancing along the eastern side of the Blue Ridge, occupied Ashby's and Snicker's Gaps. He had been joined, while at Culpeper, by General Pickett, with three brigades of his division.

General Stuart with three brigades of cavalry moved on Longstreet's right, and took position in front of the gaps.

Hampton's and [William E.] Jones' brigades remained along the Rappahannock and Hazel Rivers in front of Culpeper Court House with instructions to follow the main body as soon as Hill's corps had passed that point.

On the 17th Fitz Lee's brigade under Colonel [Thomas T.] Munford, which was on the road to Snicker's Gap, was attacked near Aldie by the Federal cavalry. The attack was repulsed with loss, and the brigade held its ground until ordered to fall back, its right being threatened by another body coming from Hopewell towards Middleburg. The latter force was driven from Middleburg and pursued towards Hopewell by [Beverly H.] Robertson's brigade, which arrived about dark. Its retreat was intercepted by W. H. F. Lee's brigade under Colonel [John R.] Chambliss, Jr., and the greater part of a regiment captured.

During the three succeeding days there was much skirmishing, General Stuart taking a position west of Middleburg where he awaited the rest of his command.

General Jones arrived on the 19th, and General Hampton in the afternoon of the following day, having repulsed on his march a cavalry force sent to reconnoiter in the direction of Warrenton. On the 21st the enemy attacked with infantry and cavalry, and obliged Genl Stuart, after a brave resistance, to fall back to the gaps of the mountains. The enemy retired the next day, having advanced only a short distance beyond Upperville.

In these engagements the cavalry sustained a loss of five hundred and ten killed, wounded, and missing. Among them were several valuable officers whose names are mentioned in Genl Stuart's report. One piece of artillery was disabled and left on the field.

The enemy's loss was heavy. About four hundred prisoners were taken and several stand of colors.

The Federal Army was apparently guarding the approaches to Washington, and manifested no disposition to resume the offensive. In the meantime the progress of Ewell, who was already in Maryland, with Jenkins' cavalry advanced into Pennsylvania as far as Chambersburg, rendered it necessary that the rest of the army should be within supporting distance, and Hill having reached the Valley, Longstreet was withdrawn to the west side of the Shenandoah, and the two corps encamped near Berryville.

General Stuart was directed to hold the mountain passes with part of his command as long as the enemy remained south of the Potomac, and with the remainder to cross into Maryland and place himself on the right of General Ewell. Upon the suggestion of the former officer that he could damage the enemy and delay his passage of the river by getting in his rear, he was authorized to do so, and it was left to his discretion whether to enter Maryland east or west of the Blue Ridge, but he was instructed to lose no time in placing his command on the right of our column as soon as he should perceive the enemy moving northward.

On the 22d General Ewell marched into Pennsylvania with Rodes' and Johnson's divisions preceded by Jenkins' cavalry, taking the road from Hagerstown through Chambersburg to Carlisle, where he arrived on the 27th. Early's division, which had occupied Boonsboro, moved by a parallel road to Greenwood, and in pursuance of instructions previously given to General Ewell marched towards York. On the 24th Longstreet and Hill were put in motion to follow Ewell, and on the 27th encamped near Chambersburg.

General Imboden, under the orders before referred to, had been operating on Ewell's left while the latter was advancing into Maryland. He drove off the troops guarding the Baltimore and Ohio Railroad, and destroyed all the important bridges on that route from Martinsburg to Cumberland, besides inflicting serious damage upon the Chesapeake and Ohio Canal. He was at Hancock when Longstreet and Hill reached Chambersburg, and was directed to proceed to the latter place by way of McConnellsburg, collecting supplies for the army on his route.

The cavalry force at this time with the army, consisting of Jenkins' brigade and [Elijah V.] White's battalion, was not greater than was required to accompany the advance of General Ewell and General Early with whom it performed valuable service as appears from their reports. It was expected that as soon as the Federal Army should cross the Potomac, General Stuart would give notice of its movements, and nothing having been heard from him since our entrance into Maryland, it was inferred that the enemy had not yet left Virginia. Orders were therefore issued to move upon Harrisburg. The expedition of General Early to York was designed in part to prepare for this undertaking by breaking the railroad between Baltimore and Harrisburg, and seizing the bridge over the Susquehanna at Wrightsville. General Early succeeded in the first object, destroying a number of bridges above and below York, but on the approach of the troops sent by him to Wrightsville, a body of militia stationed at that place fled across the river and burned the bridge in their retreat. General Early then marched to rejoin his corps. The advance against Harrisburg was arrested by intelligence received from a scout on the night of the 28th to the effect that the army of General Hooker had crossed the Potomac and was approaching the South Mountains. In the absence of the cavalry it was impossible to ascertain his intentions, but to deter him from advancing farther west and intercepting our communications with Virginia, it was determined to concentrate the army east of the mountains.

BATTLE OF GETTYSBURG

Hill's corps was accordingly ordered to move towards Cashtown on the 29th, and Longstreet to follow the next day, leaving Pickett's division at Chambersburg to guard the rear until relieved by Imboden.

General Ewell was recalled from Carlisle and directed to join the army at Cashtown or Gettysburg as circumstances might require.

The advance of the enemy to the latter place was unknown, and the weather being inclement, the march was conducted with a view to the comfort of the troops.

[General Henry] Heth's division reached Cashtown on the 29th, and the following morning [General James J.] Pettigrew's brigade, sent by Genl Heth to procure supplies at Gettysburg, found it occupied by the enemy. Being ignorant of the extent of his force General Pettigrew was unwilling to hazard an attack with his single brigade and returned to Cashtown. General Hill arrived with [General W. Dorsey] Pender's division in the evening, and the following morning, July 1st, advanced with these two divisions, accompanied by [William J.] Pegram's and [David G.] McIntosh's battalions of artillery, to ascertain the strength of the enemy, whose force was supposed to consist chiefly of cavalry.

The leading division under General Heth found the enemy's vedettes about three miles west of Gettysburg, and continued to advance until within a mile of the town, when two brigades were sent forward to reconnoiter. They drove in the advance of the enemy very gallantly, but subsequently encountered largely superior numbers, and were compelled to retire with loss, Brigadier General [James J.] Archer, commanding one of the brigades, being taken prisoner.

General Heth then prepared for action, and as soon as Pender arrived to support him, was ordered by General Hill to advance. The artillery was placed in position and the engagement opened with vigor. General Heth pressed the enemy steadily back, breaking his first and second lines, and attacking his third with great resolution. About 2½ p.m. the advance of Ewell's corps, consisting of Rodes' division, with [Thomas H.] Carter's battalion of artillery, arrived by the Middletown road, and forming on Heth's left, nearly at right angles with his line, became warmly engaged with fresh numbers of the enemy. Heth's troops having suffered heavily in their protracted contest with a superior force were relieved by Pender's and Early coming up by the Heidlersburg road soon afterward took position on the left of Rodes, when a general advance was made.

The enemy gave way on all sides and was driven through Gettysburg with great loss. Major General [John F.] Reynolds, who was in command, was killed. More than five thousand prisoners, exclusive of a large number of wounded, three pieces of artillery, and several colors were captured. Among the prisoners were two brigadier generals, one of whom was wounded.

Our own loss was heavy, including a number of officers, among whom were Major General Heth, slightly, and Brigadier General [Alfred M.] Scales, of Pender's division, severely, wounded.

The enemy retired to a range of hills south of Gettysburg, where he displayed a strong force of infantry and artillery.

It was ascertained from the prisoners that we had been engaged with two corps of the army formerly commanded by General [Joseph] Hooker, and that the remainder of that army under General [George G.] Meade was approaching Gettysburg. Without information as to its proximity, the strong position which the enemy had assumed could not be attacked without danger of exposing the four divisions present, already weakened and exhausted by a long and bloody struggle, to overwhelming numbers of fresh troops.

General Ewell was therefore instructed to carry the hill occupied by the enemy if he found it practicable, but to avoid a general engagement until the arrival of the other divisions of the army which were ordered to hasten forward. He decided to await Johnson's division, which had marched from Carlisle by the road west of the mountains to guard the trains of his corps, and consequently did not reach Gettysburg until a late hour. In the meantime the enemy occupied the point which General Ewell designed to seize, but in what force could not be ascertained owing to the darkness. An intercepted dispatch showed that another corps had halted that afternoon four miles from Gettysburg.

Under these circumstances it was decided not to attack until the arrival of Longstreet, two of whose divisions, those of [John B.] Hood and [Lafayette] McLaws encamped about four miles in the rear during the night. Anderson's division of Hill's corps came up after the engagement.

It had not been intended to deliver a general battle so far from our base unless attacked, but coming unexpectedly upon the whole Federal Army, to withdraw through the mountains with our extensive trains would have been difficult and dangerous. At the same time we were unable to await an attack, as the country was unfavorable for collecting supplies in the presence of the enemy who could restrain our foraging parties by holding the mountain passes with local and other troops. A battle had therefore become in a measure unavoidable, and the success already gained gave hope of a favorable issue.

The enemy occupied a strong position, with his right upon two commanding elevations adjacent to each other, one southeast and the other known as Cemetery Hill immediately south of the town, which lay at its base. His line extended thence upon the high ground along the Emmitsburg road, with a steep ridge in rear, which was also occupied. This ridge was difficult of ascent, particularly the two hills above mentioned as forming its northern extremity, and a third at the other end on which the enemy's left rested. Numerous stone and rail fences along the slope served to afford protection to his troops and impede our advance. In his front the ground was undulating and generally open for about three quarters of a mile.

General Ewell's corps constituted our left, [Edward] Johnson's division being opposite the height adjoining Cemetery Hill, Early's in the center, in front of the north face of the latter, and Rodes upon his right. Hill's corps faced the west side of Cemetery Hill, and extended nearly parallel to the Emmitsburg road, making an angle with Ewell's. Pender's division formed his left, [Richard H.] Anderson's his right, Heth's, under Brigadier General Pettigrew, being in reserve. His artillery under Colonel [R. Lindsay] Walker, was posted in eligible position along his line.

It was determined to make the principal attack upon the enemy's left and endeavor to gain a position from which it was thought that our artillery could be brought to bear with effect. Longstreet was directed to place the divisions of McLaws and Hood on the right of Hill, partially enveloping the enemy's left, which he was to drive in. General Hill was ordered to threaten the enemy's center, to prevent reinforcements being drawn to either wing, and cooperate with his right division in Longstreet's attack.

General Ewell was instructed to make a simultaneous demonstration upon the enemy's right, to be converted into a real attack should opportunity offer.

About four p.m. Longstreet's batteries opened, and soon afterwards Hood's division on the extreme right moved to the attack. McLaws followed somewhat later, four of Anderson's brigades, those of [Cadmus M.] Wilcox, [Edward A.] Perry, [Ambrose R.] Wright, and [Carnot] Posey supporting him on the left in the order named. The enemy was soon driven from his position on the Emmitsburg road to the cover of a ravine and a line of stone fences at the foot of the ridge in his rear. He was dislodged from these after a severe struggle, and retired up the ridge, leaving a number of his batteries in our possession. Wilcox's and Wright's brigades advanced with great gallantry, breaking successive lines of the enemy's infantry, and compelling him to abandon much of his artillery. Wilcox reached the foot and Wright gained the crest of the ridge itself, driving the enemy down the opposite side. But having become separated from McLaws and gone beyond the other two brigades of the division they were attacked in front and on both flanks and compelled to retire, being unable to bring off any of the captured artillery. McLaws' left also fell back, and it being now nearly dark General Longstreet determined to await the arrival of General Pickett.

He disposed his command to hold the ground gained on the right, withdrawing his left to the first position from which the enemy had been driven.

Four pieces of artillery, several hundred prisoners, and two regimental flags were taken. As soon as the engagement began on our right, General Johnson opened with his artillery, and about two hours later advanced up the hill next to Cemetery Hill with three brigades, the fourth being detained by a demonstration on his left. Soon afterwards General Early attacked Cemetery Hill with two brigades, supported by a third, the fourth having been previously detached. The enemy had greatly increased the strength of the positions assailed by Johnson and Early by earthworks.

The troops of the former moved steadily up the steep and rugged ascent under a heavy fire, driving the enemy into his entrenchments, part of which was carried by Steuart's brigade, and a number of prisoners taken. The contest was continued to a late hour, but without further advantage. On Cemetery Hill the attack by Early's leading brigades, those of Hays and [Robert F.] Hoke, under Colonel [Isaac E.] Avery, was made with vigor. Two lines of the enemy's infantry were dislodged from the cover of some stone and board fences on the side of the ascent and driven back into the works on the crest into which our troops forced their way and seized several pieces of artillery.

A heavy force advanced against their right which was without support and they were compelled to retire, bringing with them about a hundred prisoners and four stand of colors. General Ewell had directed General Rodes to attack in concert with Early, covering his right, and had requested Brigadier General [James H.] Lane, then commanding Pender's division, to cooperate on the right of Rodes. When the time to attack arrived, General Rodes, not having his troops in position, was unprepared to cooperate with General Early, and before he could get in readiness the latter had been obliged to retire for want of the expected support on his right. General Lane was prepared to give the assistance required of him, and so informed General Rodes, but the latter deemed it useless to advance after the failure of Early's attack.

In this engagement our loss in men and officers was large. Major Generals Hood and Pender, Brigadier Generals [John M.] Jones, [Paul J.] Semmes, George T. Anderson, and [William] Barksdale, and Colonel Avery commanding Hoke's brigade, were wounded, the last two mortally. Generals Pender and Semmes died after their removal to Virginia.

The result of this day's operations induced the belief that with proper concert of action, and with the increased support that the positions gained on the right would enable the artillery to render the assaulting columns, we should ultimately succeed, and it was accordingly determined to continue the attack.

The general plan was unchanged. Longstreet, reinforced by Pickett's three brigades, which arrived near the battle field during the afternoon of the 2d, was ordered to attack the next morning, and General Ewell was directed to assail the enemy's right at the same time. The latter, during the night, reinforced General Johnson with two brigades from Rodes' and one from Early's division.

General Longstreet's dispositions were not completed as early as was expected, but before notice could be sent to General Ewell, General Johnson had already become engaged, and it was too late to recall him. The enemy attempted to recover the works taken the preceding evening but was repulsed, and General Johnson attacked in turn. After a gallant and prolonged struggle, in which the enemy was forced to abandon part of his entrenchments, General Johnson found himself unable to carry the strongly fortified crest of the hill. The projected attack on the enemy's left not having been made he was enabled to hold his right with a force largely superior to that of General Johnson, and finally to threaten his flank and rear, rendering it necessary for him to retire to his original position about one p.m.

General Longstreet was delayed by a force occupying the high rocky hills on the enemy's extreme left, from which his troops could be attacked in reverse as they advanced. His operations had been embarrassed the day previous by the same cause, and he now deemed it necessary to defend his flank and rear with the divisions of Hood and McLaws. He was therefore reinforced by Heth's division and two brigades of Pender's, to the command of which Major General [Isaac R.] Trimble was assigned. General Hill was directed to hold his line with the rest of his command, afford General Longstreet further assistance if required, and avail himself of any success that might be gained.

A careful examination was made of the ground secured by Longstreet, and his batteries placed in positions which it was believed would enable them to silence those of the enemy.

Hill's artillery and part of Ewell's was ordered to open simultaneously, and the assaulting column to advance under cover of the combined fire of the three. The batteries were directed to be pushed forward as the infantry progressed, protect their flanks, and support their attacks closely.

About 1 p.m. at a given signal a heavy cannonade was opened, and continued for about two hours with marked effect upon the enemy. His batteries replied vigorously at first, but towards the close their fire slackened perceptibly, and General Longstreet ordered forward the column of attack, consisting of Pickett's and Heth's division in two lines, Pickett on the right. Wilcox's brigade marched in rear of Pickett's right to guard that flank, and Heth's was supported by Lane's and Scales' brigades, under General Trimble.

The troops moved steadily on under a heavy fire of musketry and artillery, the main attack being directed against the enemy's left center. His batteries reopened as soon as they appeared. Our own having nearly exhausted their ammunition in the protracted cannonade that preceded the advance of the infantry were unable to reply or render the necessary support to the attacking party. Owing to this fact, which was unknown to me when the assault took place, the enemy was enabled to throw a strong force of infantry against our left, already wavering under a concentrated fire of artillery from the ridge in front, and from Cemetery Hill on the left. It finally gave way, and the right, after penetrating the enemy's lines, entering his advance works, and capturing some of his artillery, was attacked simultaneously in front and on both flanks, and driven back with heavy loss. The troops were rallied and reformed, but the enemy did not pursue.

A large number of brave officers and men fell or were captured on this occasion. Of Pickett's three brigade commanders, Generals [Lewis A.] Armistead and [Richard B.] Garnett were killed, and General [James L.] Kemper dangerously wounded. Major General Trimble and Brigadier General Pettigrew were also wounded, the former severely.

The movements of the army preceding the battle of Gettysburg had been much embarrassed by the absence of the cavalry. As soon as it was known that the enemy had crossed into Maryland, orders were sent to the brigades of [Beverly H.] Robertson and [William E.] Jones, which had been left to guard the passes of the Blue Ridge, to rejoin the army without delay, and it was expected that General Stuart with the remainder of his command would soon arrive. In the exercise of the discretion given him when Longstreet and Hill marched into Maryland, General Stuart determined to pass around the rear of the Federal Army with three brigades and cross the Potomac between it and Washington, believing that he would be able by that route to place himself on our right flank in time to keep us properly advised of the enemy's movements.

He marched from Salem on the night of the 24th June intending to pass west of Centreville, but found the enemy's forces so distributed as to render that route impracticable. Adhering to his original plan, he was forced to make a wide *detour* through Buckland and Brentsville, and crossed the Occoquan at Wolf Run Shoals on the morning of the 27th. Continuing his march through Fairfax Court House and Dranesville, he arrived at the Potomac below the mouth of Seneca Creek in the evening. He found the river much swollen by the recent rains, but after great exertion gained the Maryland shore before midnight with his whole command. He now ascertained that the Federal Army, which he had discovered to be drawing towards the Potomac, had crossed the day before, and was moving towards Fredericktown, thus interposing itself between him and our forces.

He accordingly marched northward, through Rockville and Westminster, to Hanover, Pennsylvania, where he arrived on the 30th, but the enemy advanced with equal rapidity on his left and continued to obstruct communication with our main body.

Supposing from such information as he could obtain that part of the army was at Carlisle, he left Hanover that night and proceeded thither by way of Dover. He reached Carlisle on the 1st July, where he received orders to proceed to Gettysburg. He arrived in the afternoon of the following day and took position on General Ewell's left. His leading brigade under General [Wade] Hampton encountered and repulsed a body of the enemy's cavalry at Hunterstown endeavoring to reach our rear.

General Stuart had several skirmishes during his march, and at Hanover quite a severe engagement took place with a strong force of cavalry, which was finally compelled to withdraw from the town.

The prisoners taken by the cavalry and paroled at various places amounted to about eight hundred, and at Rockville a large train of wagons coming from Washington was intercepted and captured. Many of them were destroyed, but one hundred and twenty-five, with all the animals of the train, were secured.

The ranks of the cavalry were much reduced by its long and arduous march, repeated conflicts, and insufficient supplies of food and forage, but the day after its arrival at Gettysburg it engaged the enemy's cavalry with unabated spirit, and effectually protected our left. In this action Brigadier General Hampton was seriously wounded while acting with his accustomed gallantry.

Robertson's and Jones' brigades arrived on the 3d July and were stationed upon our right flank. The severe loss sustained by the army and the reduction of its ammunition, rendered another attempt to dislodge the enemy unadvisable, and it was therefore determined to withdraw.

The trains with such of the wounded as could bear removal were ordered to Williamsport on the 4th July, part moving through Cashtown and Greencastle, escorted by General Imboden, and the remainder by the Fairfield road. The army retained its position until dark, when it was put in motion for the Potomac by the last named route. A heavy rain continued throughout the night, and so much impeded its progress that

Ewell's corps, which brought up the rear, did not leave Gettysburg until late in the forenoon of the following day. The enemy offered no serious interruption, and after an arduous march we arrived at Hagerstown in the afternoon of the 6th and morning of the 7th July.

The great length of our trains made it difficult to guard them effectually in passing through the mountains, and a number of wagons and ambulances were captured. They succeeded in reaching Williamsport on the 6th, but were unable to cross the Potomac on account of the high stage of water. Here they were attacked by a strong force of cavalry and artillery, which was gallantly repulsed by General Imboden, whose command had been strengthened by several batteries and by two regiments of infantry which had been detached at Winchester to guard prisoners and were returning to the army. While the enemy were being held in check, General Stuart arrived with the cavalry, which had performed valuable service in guarding the flanks of the army during the retrograde movement, and after a short engagement drove him from the field.

The rains that had prevailed almost without intermission since our entrance into Maryland, and greatly interfered with our movements, had made the Potomac unfordable, and the pontoon bridge left at Falling Waters had been partially destroyed by the enemy. The wounded and prisoners were sent over the river as rapidly as possible in a few ferry boats, while the trains awaited the subsiding of the waters and the construction of a new pontoon bridge.

On the 8th July, the enemy's cavalry advanced towards Hagerstown, but was repulsed by General Stuart, and pursued as far as Boonsboro. With this exception nothing but occasional skirmishing occurred until the 12th, when the main body of the enemy arrived. The army then took a position previously selected, covering the Potomac from Williamsport to Falling Waters, where it remained for two days, with the enemy immediately in front, manifesting no disposition to attack, but throwing up entrenchments along his whole line.

By the 13th the river at Williamsport though still deep was fordable, and a good bridge was completed at Falling Waters, new boats having been constructed and some of the old recovered. As further delay would enable the enemy to obtain reinforcements, and as it was found difficult to procure a sufficient supply of flour for the troops, the working of the mills being interrupted by high water, it was determined to await an attack no longer. Orders were accordingly given to cross the Potomac that night, Ewell's corps by the ford at Williamsport, and those of Longstreet and Hill on the bridge. The cavalry was directed to relieve the infantry skirmishers and bring up the rear.

The movement was much retarded by a severe rain storm and the darkness of the night. Ewell's corps, having the advantage of a turnpike road, marched with less difficulty, and crossed the river by 8 o'clock the following morning.

The condition of the road to the bridge and the time consumed in the passage of the artillery, ammunition wagons, and ambulances, which could not ford the river, so much delayed the progress of Longstreet and Hill, that it was daylight before their troops began to cross. Heth's division was halted about a mile and a half from the bridge to protect the passage of the column. No interruption was offered by the enemy until about 11 a.m., when his cavalry supported by artillery appeared in front of General Heth. A small number in advance of the main body was mistaken for our own cavalry retiring, no notice having been given of the withdrawal of the latter, and was suffered to approach our lines. They were immediately destroyed or captured, with the exception of two or three, but Brigadier General Pettigrew, an officer of great merit and promise, was mortally wounded in the encounter. He survived his removal to Virginia only a few days. The bridge being clear, General Heth began to withdraw. The enemy advanced but his efforts to break our lines were repulsed, and the passage of the river was completed by one p.m. Owing to the extent of General Heth's line, some of his men most remote from the bridge were cut off before they could reach it, but the greater part of those taken by the enemy during the movement, supposed to amount in all to about five hundred, consisted of men from various commands who lingered behind, overcome by previous labors and hardships, and the fatigue of a most trying night march. There was no loss of *matériel* except a few broken wagons and two pieces of artillery, which the horses were unable to draw through the deep mud. Other horses were sent back for them, but the rear of the column had passed before their arrival.

The army proceeded to the vicinity of Bunker Hill and Darkesville, where it halted to afford the troops repose.

The enemy made no effort to follow except with his cavalry, which crossed the Potomac at Harper's Ferry and advanced towards Martinsburg on the 16th July. They were attacked by General Fitz Lee with his own and Chambliss' brigades and driven back with loss.

When the army returned to Virginia, it was intended to move into Loudoun, but the Shenandoah was found to be impassable. While waiting for it to subside, the enemy crossed the Potomac east of the Blue Ridge, and seized the passes we designed to use. As he continued to advance along the eastern slope, apparently with the purpose of cutting us off from the railroad to Richmond, General Longstreet was ordered on the 19th July to proceed to Culpeper Court House by the way of Front

Royal. He succeeded in passing part of his command over the Shenandoah in time to prevent the occupation of Manassas and Chester Gaps by the enemy, whose cavalry had already made its appearance. As soon as a pontoon bridge could be laid down the rest of his corps crossed the river and marched through Chester Gap to Culpeper Court House, where it arrived on the 24th. He was followed by General A. P. Hill without serious opposition.

General Ewell having been detained in the Valley by an effort to capture a force of the enemy guarding the Baltimore and Ohio Railroad west of Martinsburg, Wright's brigade was left to hold Manassas Gap until his arrival. He reached Front Royal on the 23d with Johnson's and Rodes' divisions, Early's being near Winchester, and found General Wright skirmishing with the enemy's infantry which had already appeared in Manassas Gap. General Ewell supported Wright with Rodes' division and some artillery, and the enemy was held in check.

Finding that the Federal force greatly exceeded his own, General Ewell marched through Thornton's Gap and ordered Early to move up the Valley by Strasburg and New Market. He encamped near Madison Court House on the 29th July.

The enemy massed his army in the vicinity of Warrenton, and, on the night of the 31st July, his cavalry with a large supporting force of infantry crossed the Rappahannock at Rappahannock Station and Kelly's Ford. The next day they advanced towards Brandy Station, their progress being gallantly resisted by General Stuart with Hampton's brigade commanded by Colonel [Lawrence S.] Baker, who fell back gradually to our lines about two miles south of Brandy. Our infantry skirmishers advanced and drove the enemy beyond Brandy Station.

It was now determined to place the army in a position to enable it more readily to oppose the enemy should he attempt to move southward, that near Culpeper Court House being one that he could easily avoid.

Longstreet and Hill were put in motion the 3d August, leaving the cavalry at Culpeper. Ewell had been previously ordered from Madison, and by the 4th the army occupied the line of the Rapidan.

The highest praise is due to both officers and men for their conduct during the campaign.

The privations and hardships of the march and camp were cheerfully encountered, and borne with fortitude unsurpassed by our ancestors in their struggle for independence, while their courage in battle entitles them to rank with the soldiers of any army and of any time. Their forbearance and discipline, under strong provocation to retaliate for the cruelty of the enemy to our own citizens, is not their least claim to the respect and admiration of their countrymen and of the world.

I forward returns of our loss in killed, wounded, and missing. Many of the latter were killed or wounded in the several assaults at Gettysburg, and necessarily left in the hands of the enemy.

I cannot speak of these brave men as their merits and exploits deserve. Some of them are appropriately mentioned in the accompanying reports, and the memory of all will be gratefully and affectionately cherished by the people in whose defence they fell.

The loss of Major General Pender is severely felt by the army and the country. He served with this army from the beginning of the war, and took a distinguished part in all its engagements. Wounded on several occasions, he never left his command in action until he received the injury that resulted in his death. His promise and usefulness as an officer were only equaled by the purity and excellence of his private life.

Brigadier Generals Armistead, Barksdale, Garnett, and Semmes died as they had lived, discharging the highest duty of patriots with devotion that never faltered and courage that shrank from no danger.

I earnestly commend to the attention of the Government those gallant officers and men whose conduct merited the special commendation of their superiors, but whose names I am unable to mention in this report.

The officers of the General Staff of the army were unremittingly engaged in the duties of their respective departments. Much depended on their management and exertion. The labors of the Quartermaster's, Commissary, and Medical Departments were more than usually severe. The Inspectors-General were also laboriously occupied in their attention to the troops, both on the march and in camp, and the officers of engineers showed skill and judgment in expediting the passage of rivers and streams, the swollen condition of which by almost continuous rains, called for extraordinary exertion. The Chief of Ordnance and his assistants are entitled to praise for their care and watchfulness given to the ordnance trains and ammunition of the army, which in a long march and in many conflicts, were always at hand and accessible to the troops. My thanks are due to my personal staff for the constant aid afforded me at all times on the march and in the field, and their willing discharge of every duty.

There were captured at Gettysburg nearly seven thousand prisoners, of whom about fifteen hundred were paroled, and the remainder brought to Virginia. Seven pieces of artillery were also secured.

I forward herewith the reports of the corps, division, and other commanders mentioned in the accompanying schedule, together with maps of the scene of operations, and one showing the routes pursued by the army.

Respectfully submitted

R. E. LEE
General

CHAPTER TWELVE

Aftermath of Gettysburg

AUGUST–DECEMBER 1863

"The number of desertions . . . is so great"

WHILE LEE (after offering to resign) was patching up his worn army south of the Rapidan, and resuming his struggle to obtain subsistence from the malfunctioning commissary, the general and his troops were called upon to support areas of the collapsing Confederacy. After Vicksburg surrendered on July 4, though the Federals incomprehensibly dispersed their victorious army on the Mississippi, in middle Tennessee the Federals under Rosecrans were threatening to evict Bragg from Chattanooga and open the gateway to Atlanta. At the same time the Administration grew frightened over Charleston, which was withstanding a formal siege from the harbor. Lee was called down to Richmond in late August to return temporarily and informally to his role of "Military Adviser."

On September 3, during his extended conferences with the President, Knoxville fell to the Federals, severing Virginia from Tennessee by railroad and foreshadowing the advance on Chattanooga. With no alternatives between the West and an offensive in Virginia, Lee agreed to the decision of sending Longstreet and two divisions temporarily to Bragg. To replace losses at Gettysburg, Micah Jenkins's big brigade, which had been kept behind in the invasion, was transferred to Hood's division in Longstreet's expedition. The remaining four of Pickett's brigades were variously scattered, some going to North Carolina in the shifting about of troops which needlessly strengthened the garrison at Charleston.

When Lee returned on September 4 to his camp, it was to dispatch one third of his veteran infantry to other sectors. Before Longstreet reached the West, Bragg had been maneuvered out of Chattanooga, but on September 19-20, with decisive help from Longstreet and his Army of Northern Virginia troops, Rosecrans was defeated at the battle of Chickamauga and driven back into Chattanooga. At the moment of victory, neurotic Bragg suffered a collapse of will and gained nothing from the battle. The result was an intra-army controversy, which involved Longstreet, and the final military effect of Longstreet's emergency detachment was his retention in the Tennessee mountains, on another of his semi-independent operations, while Lee faced the enemy without the old dependables of the First Corps.

During the Chickamauga operations, Lee fell ill again. He suffered acute rheumatic pains, and various other aches believed by later medical studies to be symptoms of angina pectoris. Lee was very florid and was probably also suffering from hypertension. When he was recovering again in late September, General Lee learned that two corps (something over 16,000 men) had been drawn off from Meade to be sent to Rosecrans, and he determined to pry the Federals out of their favorable position for maneuver at Culpeper.

He tried a limited version of his 1862 turning of Pope's flank. The movement maneuvered Meade into falling back toward Centreville, and at Bristoe Station, on October 14, the army caught Meade's rear guard in a vulnerable position. But the same failure in concert of action as at Gettysburg, this time involving A. P. Hill, permitted the enemy to escape while inflicting relatively heavy casualties in Hill's corps. Technically a victory, this inconclusive minor operation left the debilitated army in the war-made barrens of the Virginia plains, and Lee could only retire to the region of the upper Rappahannock where he was closer to the dubious supply lines with Richmond.

Here he confronted the growing problem of desertions among the underfed men. The demoralizing effects of continued debility began to become manifest, especially after any untoward exertion. He corresponded frequently from late summer on with Imboden in the West, directing small raids with the dual purpose of distracting the enemy and gathering supplies, but little came of these peripheral actions. Supporters joined Davis in wishing Lee to assume command of the disorganized Army of Tennessee, and on October 26 he wrote General Polk, the bishop who had been with him at West Point, giving tactful reasons for declining the command. Essentially his mind was on rebuilding his own army, as he seemed alone in realizing that the Army of Northern Virginia was past its peak, and without a change in the administration's policy its proficiency would continue to decline. On November 4 he wrote Adjutant General Cooper very candidly on this point:

I believe the troops of this army have been called upon in winter, spring, and summer to do almost as active service as those of any other department, and I do not see that the good of the service will be promoted by scattering its brigades and regiments along all the threatened points of the Confederacy. It is only by the concentration of our troops that we can hope to win any decisive advantage.

When Lee retired to the upper Rappahannock, he destroyed the Orange & Alexandria Railroad behind him. As the heavily supplied Federal army could not move in the devastated country without support from trains or naval bases, Meade's following movement after Lee was paced to the rebuilding of the railroad — a speedy operation to the mobile construction force attached to the Army of the Potomac. On November 7, Meade thrust at a crossing at Rappahannock Bridge, where Lee had built fortified points on both the north and south banks of the river, connected by pontoons. Here another melancholy failure in command lost both points, along with several guns and a bag of prisoners.

Lee withdrew his army south across the upper Rapidan, toward Orange Court House on the railroad. On November 26, from Culpeper (which had become something of a permanent Federal base in Virginia), Meade thrust across the lower Rapidan over the Ely and Germanna fords, into the region around Chancellorsville. Lee determined to strike him in flank in the type of limited offensive of which his army was still capable. However, it developed on the 27th that Meade was not moving south across Lee's front, but west toward Lee's army. It suited Lee even better for the enemy to attack him, and on the 28th he formed a solid front along the little creek, Mine Run, which ran south from the Rapidan, and quickly dug in. When the Federals came up, Meade crossed Lee for the second time, and began to dig in his own army. During November 29th and 30th, in the bitter cold in the desolate Wilderness, Meade built works as fast and as strong as Lee's.

In concentrating on outbuilding Lee, Meade neglected to secure his left flank, and Wade Hampton discovered that Meade's position was "in the air." During the frigid 1st of December, Lee planned in careful detail a flanking movement to exploit the first big opportunity the enemy had offered him since Hooker, in these same woods. During December 1st, Meade also learned that his flank was in the air, and when Lee's ragged men prepared to burst out of the woods at daylight on the 2nd, the Federals were gone. In one of the greatest anticlimaxes of any battle in the war, Mine Run concluded the discouraging operations which followed Gettysburg. The army went into winter headquarters.

543   To JEFFERSON DAVIS
                         Richmond, Virginia

Camp Orange
August 8, 1863

Mr. President:

Your letters of July 28 and August 2 have been received, and I have waited for a leisure hour to reply, but I fear that will never come. I am extremely obliged to you for the attention given to the wants of this army, and the efforts made to supply them. Our absentees are returning, and I hope the earnest and beautiful appeal made to the country in your proclamation may stir up the virtue of the whole people, and that they may see their duty and perform it. Nothing is wanted but that their fortitude should equal their bravery to insure the success of our cause. We must expect reverses, even defeats. They are sent to teach us wisdom and prudence, to call forth greater energies, and to prevent our falling into greater disasters. Our people have only to be true and united, to bear manfully the misfortunes incident to war, and all will come right in the end.

I know how prone we are to censure and how ready to blame others for the non-fulfillment of our expectations. This is unbecoming in a generous people, and I grieve to see its expression. The general remedy for the want of success in a military commander is his removal. This is natural, and in many instances proper. For no matter what may be the ability of the officer, if he loses the confidence of his troops disaster must sooner or later ensue.

I have been prompted by these reflections more than once since my return from Pennsylvania to propose to Your Excellency the propriety of selecting another commander for this army. I have seen and heard of expression of discontent in the public journals at the result of the expedition. I do not know how far this feeling extends in the army. My brother officers have been too kind to report it, and so far the troops have been too generous to exhibit it. It is fair, however, to suppose that it does exist, and success is so necessary to us that nothing should be risked to secure it. I therefore, in all sincerity, request Your Excellency to take measures to supply my place. I do this with the more earnestness because no one is more aware than myself of my inability for the duties of my position. I cannot even accomplish what I myself desire. How can I fulfill the expectations of others? In addition I sensibly feel the growing failure of my bodily strength. I have not yet recovered from the attack I experienced the past spring. I am becoming more and more incapable of exertion, and am thus prevented from making the personal examinations and giving the personal supervision to the operations in the field which I feel to be necessary. I am so dull that in making use of the eyes of others I am frequently misled. Everything, therefore, points to the advantages to be derived from a new commander, and I the more anxiously urge the matter upon Your Excellency from my belief that a younger and abler man than myself can readily be attained. I know that he will have as gallant and brave an army as ever existed to second his efforts, and it would be the happiest day of my life to see at its head a worthy leader, one that would accomplish more than I could perform and all that I have wished. I hope Your Excellency will attribute my request to the true reason, the desire to serve my country, and to do all in my power to insure the success of her righteous cause.

I have no complaints to make of any one but myself. I have received nothing but kindness from those above me, and the most considerate attention from my comrades and companions in arms. To Your Excellency I am specially indebted for uniform kindness and consideration. You have done everything in your power to aid me in the work committed to my charge, without omitting anything to promote the general welfare. I pray that your efforts may at length be crowned with success, and that you may long live to enjoy the thanks of a grateful people.

With sentiments of great esteem,

I am very respectfully and truly yours

R. E. LEE
General

544   To COLONEL JOSIAH GORGAS
Chief of Ordnance

Headquarters, Army of Northern Virginia
August 15, 1863

Colonel:

I send Lieut Col [Briscoe G.] Baldwin down this morning to consult with you on the subject of arms for this army. We are in especial need of good arms for the cavalry division, and as you will see from this report there is a considerable deficiency of arms in the infantry, which deficiency will become greater as the number of returning convalescents increases. I have heard from several sources that there are arms in Charleston, S. C., held in reserve for troops, which are still to be reserved. If this is so, I think that they should be distributed to troops in the field. In fact I should think in the present condition of things, that no ordnance, arms, or other supplies should be kept in Charleston excepting such as are necessary for the troops engaged in its defence. I hope you will be able to make some arrangements by which the deficiencies in this army may be speedily supplied.

I am very respectfully, your obt servt

R. E. LEE
General

545   To JEFFERSON DAVIS
Richmond, Virginia

Headquarters, Army of Northern Virginia
August 17, 1863

Mr. President:

The number of desertions from this army is so great and still continues to such an extent, that unless some cessation of them can be caused, I fear success in the field will be seriously endangered. Immediately on the publication of the amnesty, which I thought would be beneficial in its effects, many presumed on it and absented themselves from their commands, choosing to place on it a wrong interpretation. In one corps the desertions of North Carolinians and to some extent of Virginians has grown to be a very serious matter. The Virginians go off in many cases to join the various partisan corps in the State. General [John D.] Imboden writes that there are great numbers of deserters in the Valley who conceal themselves successfully from the small squads sent to arrest them. Many cross the James River near Balcony Falls *en route* for the south along the mountain ridges. Night before last thirty went from one regiment and eighteen from another. Great dissatisfaction is reported among the good men in the army at the apparent impunity of deserters.

In order to remove all palliation from the offense of desertion, and as a reward to merit, I have instituted in the army a system of furloughs which are to be granted to the most meritorious and urgent cases at the rate of one for every hundred men present for duty. I would now respectfully submit to Your Excellency the opinion that all has been done which forbearance and mercy call for, and that nothing will remedy this great evil which so much endangers our cause except the rigid enforcement of the death penalty in future in cases of conviction.

I am with great respect, your obt serv't

R. E. LEE
General

546   To G. W. C. LEE
                              Richmond, Virginia

                                                        Camp Orange
                                                        August 18, 1863
My Dear Custis:
    I have received your letter of the 15th, and thank you for the infor-
mation of your mother and Fitzhugh, &c.
    I have been much exercised as to how I can pay my taxes. I have
looked out for assessors and gatherers in vain. I have sent to find col-
lectors in the counties where I have been without success. I wish to pay
the amount as a matter of right and conscience and for the benefit of
the State, but cannot accomplish it. I see too by the papers that unless a
man pays by the 9th of September he is charged double. That will come
hard on those who have always been anxious to meet the requirements
of law. Can you pay for me in Richmond? I do not know what I am
chargeable for or how much I am to pay. I have nothing now not in the
hands of the enemy, except $5,000 in Confederate States bonds, which
are not taxable I believe, and $5,000 or $8,000 in N. C. bonds, I forget
which, that you may recollect have not been issued to me for want of a
receipt that cannot be found. Perhaps there is a memorandum in my private box. Mr. MacFarland knows. I do not know how those coupon
bonds I hold of the State, &c., within the U. S. that are beyond my reach,
and some you know not available, and which do not pay, are considered.
    In addition, I own three horses, a watch, my apparel and camp
equipage. You know the condition of the estates of your grandfather.
They are either in the hands of the enemy or beyond my reach. The
negroes have been liberated, everything swept off of them, houses,
fences, &c., all gone. The land alone remains a waste. See if you can find
some one that can enlighten you as to what I am to pay, both for myself
and as executor of your grandfather's estates, and pay for me. I will
send a check for the amount if you will inform me. Give much love
to all friends, and accept my warm love and prayers for your health and
happiness.

                                          Very truly and affly

                                               R. E. LEE

547   To JEFFERSON DAVIS
                              Richmond, Virginia

Headquarters
Camp, Orange Court House
August 22, 1863

Mr. President:
   I have read with attention your letter of the 11th instant, and am
grateful for your kind and partial consideration of my feeble services. I
confess I am disappointed at your determination, but since you have so
directed, I shall not continue the subject, but beg that whenever in
your opinion the public service will be advanced, no matter from what
cause, that you will act upon the application before you. I am as willing
to serve now as in the beginning in any capacity and at any post where I
can do good. The lower the position, the more suitable to my ability,
and the more agreeable to my feelings. Beyond such assistance as I can
give to an invalid wife and three houseless daughters I have no object
in life but to devote myself to the defense of our violated country's
rights.

With great respect, your obedient servant

R. E. LEE
General

548   To JEFFERSON DAVIS
                              Richmond, Virginia

Headquarters
Orange Court House
August 24, 1863

Mr. President:
   The information from the signal officer in Maryland telegraphed
me by Genl Cooper is confirmed by the scouts on the Potomac. They
report that on the 17th three steamers passed down the river loaded with
troops. On the 18th, one, on the 19th, two, on the 20th, a very large
steamer with two smoke stacks, crowded, & on the 21st, one large
steamer filled with troops. These troops may belong to the 11th Army
Corps on their way to Charleston, mentioned in my previous letter, or
those said to have passed through Maryland from the west on their way
to Washington. A scout from north of the Rappahannock states, on Sunday, 16th instant, the 12th Army Corps went back to Alexandria.

Whether he confounded the 11th with the 12th, or that an additional corps has gone back, I do not know yet. The enemy's lines are so closely watched & our scouts have to make so wide a circuit, that their information is frequently late reaching me. I can discover no change of importance in the enemy's position on the Rappahannock. Nothing prevents my advancing now but the fear of killing our artillery horses. They are much reduced, & the hot weather & scarce forage keeps them so. The cavalry also suffer, & I fear to set them at work. Some days we get a pound of corn per horse & some days more, some none. Our limit is 5 pounds per day per horse. You can judge of our prospects. Genl Fitz Lee is getting from north of the Rappahannock, below Fredericksburg, about 1,000 pounds per day, which is a considerable relief on that wing. Everything is being done by me that can be to recruit the horses. I have been obliged to diminish the number of guns in the artillery, & fear I shall have to lose more.

> I am with great respect, your obt servt
>
> R. E. Lee
> Genl

549   To GENERAL JAMES LONGSTREET
Headquarters, Army of Northern Virginia

> Richmond, Virginia
> August 31, 1863

General:

I have wished for several days past to return to the army but have been detained by the President. He will not listen to my proposition to leave tomorrow. I hope you will use every exertion to prepare the army for offensive operations and improve the condition of men and animals. I can see nothing better to be done than to endeavor to bring General Meade out and use our efforts to crush his army while in its present condition. The Quartermaster Department promises to send up 3,000 bushels of corn per day, provided the cars can be unloaded and returned without delay. I hope you will be able to arrange so that the cars will not be detained. With this supply of corn, if it can be maintained, the condition of our animals should improve.

> Very respectfully and truly yours
>
> R. E. Lee
> General

550   To HIS WIFE
                          Buford's Depot, Virginia

                                              Camp, Orange Court House
                                                  September 4, 1863

You see I am still here dear Mary. When I last wrote the indications
were that the enemy would move against us any day, but this past week
he has been very quiet & seems at present disposed to continue so. I was
out looking at him yesterday from Clarke's Mountain. He has spread
himself over a large surface & looks immense, but I hope will not prove
as formidable as he looks. He has I believe been sending off some of his
troops to reinforce Rosecrans, but has been getting up others, among
them several negro regiments are reported, & I can discover no diminution. I am glad you have procured a house & I hope you will all be con-
tented & happy. I shall be very glad to visit you when I can, but when
that will be I cannot say. I have been suffering ever since my last visit
to Richmond from a heavy cold taken in the hot & badly ventilated
rooms in the various departments which resulted in an attack of rheumatism in my back, which has given me great pain & anxiety, for if I cannot
get relief I do not see what is to become of me. I had at one time to go
about a great deal & the motion of my horse was extremely painful, so
much so that I took to a spring wagon, but the stony roads I had to
traverse made the motion of the wagon almost as bad. I think today I
am better. I rode to church this morning on horse back & was surprized
to experience so little pain & mounted & dismounted with comparative
ease. The doctor gave me some lotion, which I applied faithfully a week
to the almost excoriation of the back without apparent benefit. I hope
though it is passing away. I wish I had Daughter's back here to apply it
to, it might do it service. How are those poor little girls? I am so sorry
to hear of Charlotte's suffering. I suspect she only thinks herself sick, & it
is merely the desire to [see] her Fitzhugh or her papa. Tell her to cheer
up, we shall get her Fitzhugh back soon. Mr. Ould says they are better disposed now for exchange of prisoners than they have ever been. I hope
Genl Bragg has taken some officers of note, which will help the matter
amazingly. Genl Wickham still continues in the service, but I fear is
getting tired of it. I am sorry that the approach of cold weather increases
your pain. Bryan comforts me with the assurance that October is the
worst month in the year for rheumatism, so I am in hope that both of
us may improve. I saw Rob day before yesterday. He was well. I sent him
your letter which was enclosed in the one to me. I have not a word of
news. The army is pretty well. We are getting some new corn for our

horses, which helps us amazingly, & we still have bread & meat for the men. The latter are sadly in need of clothes, shoes & blankets. I am [in] hopes they will be somewhat relieved by the contributions of Miss Buford & my daughters. Remember me very kindly to the Capt & all the family. Give much love to the girls & Charlotte,

                      & believe me always yours,

                               R. E. LEE

551   To JEFFERSON DAVIS
                      Richmond, Virginia

                             Richmond, Virginia
                           September 6, 1863

Mr. President:

I have arranged with the Quartermaster General for the transportation of Longstreet's Corps, and have given the necessary orders for the movement of the troops and their subsistence on the road. I go to the Army of Northern Virginia tomorrow morning to assist in carrying out what has been directed, and to make whatever other arrangements may be necessary.

As regards myself, should you think that the service will be benefited by my repairing to the Army of Tennessee, I will of course submit to your judgment. From your knowledge of all the circumstances attending the operations of both armies, you can come to a more correct conclusion than I can from my point of view. In my conversation with you on this subject when the question was proposed, I did not intend to decline the service if desired that I should undertake it, but merely to express the opinion that the duty could be better performed by the officers already in that department.

                 I am with great esteem, your obt svt

                               R. E. LEE
                               Genl

552   To JEFFERSON DAVIS
                      Richmond, Virginia

                     Camp at Orange Court House
                           September 9, 1863

Mr. President:

I have placed the troops on march towards Richmond. Two divisions will reach Hanover Junction this morning. The third will reach or pass beyond Louisa Court House today. Genl Longstreet proposes that [General George E.] Pickett's division take the place of [Generals Henry A.] Wise's & [Micah] Jenkins' brigades about Richmond, & that they accompany him. Pickett's division wants many officers, owing to the number wounded & captured, which cannot now be replaced. He also thinks it might increase its ranks in that locality. Wise's & Jenkins' brigades will probably exceed Pickett's division in numbers, though they will not give the Virginia troops you desire for the south. I know no other objection. Genl Longstreet has selected two Georgia brigades for Charleston, one from McLaws' & one from Hood's division. He does not want to take them into Georgia for fear of desertion. If he takes Wise's & Jenkins' instead of Pickett's, he will [assign] them to McLaws & Hood, respectively, in their stead. The division of Pickett, according to the arrangement of the Quartermaster General, will be moved last. It is in march to Richmond. You can therefore decide. The two Georgia brigades are also directed to march to Richmond, & can be sent to Charleston whenever transportation can be furnished. Your dispatch of yesterday is not very clear in reference to Burnside's movement. But I understand it to mean that he is approaching [General William S.] Rosecrans. I think Rosecrans is maneuvering to cause the evacuation of Chattanooga, & for Burnside to form a junction with him. He ought to be attacked as soon as possible. I think it probable [General Quincy A.] Gillmore will now seize upon Sullivan's Island to cause the evacuation of Fort Moultrie, & thus close the entrance to Charleston.

With great respect, your obt servt

R. E. LEE
Genl

553   To MISS MILDRED LEE
Raleigh, North Carolina

Camp, Orange Court House
September 10, 1863

I have received my precious daughter your letter of 23rd August. It must have arrived here shortly after I was called to Richmond where I was detained more than a week. I am glad to hear of the progress made in your studies & feel assured that you will continue to improve by diligent application. The struggle which you describe you experience between doing what you ought & what you desire, is common to all. You have only always to do what is right. It will become easier by practice,

& you will always enjoy in the midst of your trials, the pleasure of an approving conscience. That will be worth every thing else. You say rightly, the more you learn the more you are conscious of your ignorance. Because the more you know, the more you find there is to know in this grand & beautiful world. It is only the ignorant who suppose themselves omniscient. You will find all the days of your life that there is much to learn & much to do. As regards the length of time to continue at school I am now willing to leave that to you. You can leave at the end of the present session or continue as you think best. While there, endeavor to learn all you can. You will find in after life you cannot know too much. I found on my return from Richmond Monday (7th) letters from your mother, Agnes & Charlotte. The former I hope is better. She does not experience so much pain, but I fear cannot move with more ease. She is comfortably located in a beautiful healthy country among kind friends. Mary & Agnes are with her. Charlotte & Annie Leigh are in Charlottesville. They were detained there by Charlotte's indisposition. She is better now poor child & will either return to the Bath Alum or go to the Yellow Sulphur, which is not far from where your mother is. I suppose you know she is at Capt Buford's (Buford's Depot, Bedford County, Virginia) at the foot of the Peaks of Otter, who for many years has been in the habit of accommodating wayfarers. I left Custis well & busy as usual. Fitzhugh is still a prisoner at Fort Monroe. His wound is nearly healed & he is able to walk about, though his leg is still stiff. His keepers are kind to him & give him all that is necessary. I understand some ladies have obtained the privilege of sending him a basket of supplies once a week, & that they are very bountiful in their provision. I see no prospect yet of his exchange. Rob is in advance with the cavalry. I have not seen him since his first arrival. I saw Miss Norvell when in Richmond. She says she wishes to join you at St. Marys. So does Miss Champe Conway. Evelyn Carter of Annefield I understand is going there this fall. I am very glad you have such a kind friend in Mrs. Evans. You must exhibit to her your appreciation & express to her my thanks for her kindness. I want to see you very much "my precious life" & long for the time to come when we may all be together again. God grant in his mercy, that time may soon come. I have been obliged to write in great haste amid many interruptions & have not said half I wish. Margaret & Carrie Stuart, whom you know have been pent up in King George [County] for so long by the enemy, came up with me to see the army. They are staying at the Court House with Mrs. Ewell, under whose charge I placed them, but as they are two miles from me I fear I shall scarcely ever see them. Mrs. Randolph was to have come up with them, but could not leave the morning I did. Good bye my dear daughter. May God bless you now & forever is the constant prayer of your devoted father.

R. E. LEE

554   To JEFFERSON DAVIS
Richmond, Virginia

Camp Near Orange Court House
September 11, 1863

Mr. President:

I replied by telegraph to your dispatch of the 10th instant. I think if Pickett's division is retained it had better be kept entire. Its brigades are small, should if possible be recruited, & it will be more efficient united. It will require some days for it to march to Richmond, & in the meantime Wise can be made ready. Longstreet should have reached Richmond last evening, & can make all necessary arrangements.

The defences around Richmond should now be completed as soon as possible. I did not see any connection or communication between the redoubts for the defence of Drewry's Bluff from a land attack, & the defensive line around Manchester. This is important, and also that there should be obstructions in the river connecting this intermediate line (as it was termed) on both sides of the river. Should the enemy's land forces drive us from Drewry's Bluff, they would remove the obstructions at that point, and although we might be able to hold the intermediate line, his gunboats could ascend the river and destroy Richmond. I think, too, Colonel Gorgas should commence at once to enlarge his manufacturing arsenals, &c., in the interior, so that if Richmond should fall we would not be destitute. These are only recommended as prudential measures, & such as should the necessity for them ever arise, we will then wish had been taken.

Scouts on the Potomac report four large schooners crowded with troops, passing up the river on the 8th instant. I think they must have come from south of James River. Scouts should be sent to Suffolk and elsewhere to ascertain what points have been evacuated.

If I was a little stronger, I think I could drive Meade's army under cover of the fortifications of Washington before he gathers more reinforcements. When he gets all his reinforcements I may be forced back to Richmond. The blow at Rosecrans should be made promptly and Longstreet returned.

I am with great respect, your obt servt

R. E. LEE
Genl

555 To JEFFERSON DAVIS
Richmond, Virginia

Headquarters, Army of Northern Virginia
September 14, 1863

Mr. President:

My letter of this morning will have informed you of the crossing of the Rappahannock by the cavalry of Genl Meade's army, and of the retirement of ours to the Rapidan.

The enemy's cavalry so greatly outnumbers ours, and is generally accompanied by so large a force of infantry in its operations, that it must always force ours back. I advanced last night to the Rapidan a portion of Early's and Anderson's divisions and arrested the farther progress of the enemy.

I have just returned from an examination of the enemy's cavalry on the Rapidan. It seems to consist of their entire force, three divisions, with horse artillery, and as far as I can judge is the advance of Genl Meade's army. All the cavalry have been withdrawn from the lower Rappahannock, except some reduced pickets from Richards' Ford to Fredericksburg. Our scouts report that their whole army is under marching orders and that two corps have already crossed the Rappahannock. The 11th Corps, which has been guarding the line of the railroad, marched through Manassas on the 12th instant, for the Rappahannock. Three steamers heavily loaded with troops reached Alexandria on the 9th, and the troops were forwarded in trains on the 10th to the same destination.

Everything looks like a concentration of their forces, and it is stated by our scouts that they have learned of the large reduction of this army. I begin to fear that we have lost the use of troops here where they are much needed, and that they have gone where they will do no good. I learn by the papers of today that Genl Rosecrans' army entered Chattanooga on the 9th, and that Genl Bragg has retired still farther into the interior. It also appears that Genl Burnside did not move to make a junction with Rosecrans, but marched upon Knoxville. Genl Bragg must therefore either have been misinformed of his movements, or he subsequently changed them. Had I been aware that Knoxville was the destination of Genl Burnside, I should have recommended that Genl Longstreet be sent to oppose him instead of to Atlanta. If Genl Bragg is unable to bring Genl Rosecrans to battle, I think it would be better to return Genl Longstreet to this army to enable me to oppose the advance of Genl Meade with a greater prospect of success. And it is a matter worthy of consideration whether Genl Longstreet's corps will reach Genl Bragg in time and condition to be of any advantage to him. If the report sent me by Genl Cooper since my return from Richmond is correct, Genl Bragg had on the 20th August last, 51,101 effective men, Genl [Simon B.] Buckner, 16,118 effective men. He was to receive from Genl [Joseph E.] Johnston 9,000 effective men. His total force will therefore be 76,219 effective men, as large a number as I presume he can operate with. This is independent of the local troops, which you may recollect he reported as exceeding his expectations. Should Genl Longstreet reach Genl Bragg in time to aid him in winning a victory and return to this army, it will be well, but should he be detained there without being able to do any good, it will result in evil. I hope you will have the means of judging of this matter and of deciding correctly. There seems to be no prospect now of Genl Burnside effecting a junction with Genl Rosecrans, but it is to be apprehended that he will force Genl [Samuel] Jones back and thus aid the advance of Genl Meade.

I am with great respect, your obt servt

R. E. LEE
Genl

556   To JEFFERSON DAVIS
Richmond, Virginia

Headquarters, Army of Northern Virginia
September 18, 1863

Mr. President:

I have had the honor to receive your letter of the 16th instant. Should Generals Rosecrans and Burnside unite at Chattanooga as now seems to be probable, and there fortify themselves, they will have as you say such vast means at their disposal as to render an attack upon that position by us extremely hazardous. I can see no other way at this distance of causing them to abandon that strong position than that which you suggest, of attacking their line of communication. For this purpose their position will be favorable. For although from Stevenson two routes are open to the enemy, one to Memphis and the other to Nashville, from Stevenson to Chattanooga there is but a single route. General Bragg by concentrating his cavalry and sending it to cut the lines of communication beyond Stevenson, will cause General Rosecrans to detach largely for its maintenance. Then by moving with his whole force upon a vulnerable point, according to the nature of the ground he will in all human probability break up his position.

From the reports of our scouts General Meade's whole army is this side of the Rappahannock, and it is stated that he is preparing to march against us. The route he will take is not certain, though a deserter who came in last night reported he was to force a passage across the Rapidan at Morton's Ford today. The heavy rains of this morning may interfere with his plans. It has also been reported by our scouts that on the 10th instant two very large steamers passed up the Potomac loaded with troops. On the 12th a very large ocean steamer passed up heavily laden, and on the 14th another steamer passed up, also loaded with troops. They have been forwarding troops on the Orange & A[lexandria] Railroad for the last few days, which I think are those I have mentioned as having ascended the Potomac. I think it also probable that these troops are conscripts, as the deserter referred to stated that the party he came with was shipped at Philadelphia to prevent their desertion. I also see it stated in the Northern papers that General Meade has been promised that his army shall be filled up to its full organization by conscripts as fast as obtained. The only reinforcements for this army that I can now obtain is [General John R.] Cooke's brigade, stationed at Hanover Junction. If a portion of Pickett's division could be sent there for the occasion, I should like to draw it to me.

Very respectfully, your obt servt

R. E. LEE
General

557   To JEFFERSON DAVIS
Richmond, Virginia

Camp, Orange Court House
September 23, 1863

Mr. President:

I have had the honour to receive your letter of the 21st instant. I was rejoiced yesterday to learn by a despatch from the War Department of the complete victory gained by Genl Bragg. I hope he will be able to follow it up, to concentrate his troops & operate on the enemy's rear. I infer from the accounts I have seen that Buckner had not joined him. Unless he is occupying a superior force to his own, he ought at once to unite with Bragg, that he may push the advantage gained. If that can be done, Longstreet can successfully move to E[ast] Tennessee, open that country, where [General] Sam Jones can unite with him, & thence rejoin me. No time ought now to be lost or wasted. Everything should be done that can be done at once, so that the troops may be speedily returned to this department. As far as I can judge they will not get here too soon. The enemy is aware of Longstreet's departure. They report in their papers the day he passed through Augusta, & give the positions of Ewell's & Hill's corps. Genl Meade is strengthening himself daily. Our last scouts report the return of the troops sent north to enforce the draft. Nine trains loaded with troops reached Culpeper Thursday night. Three trains arrived on Monday & three on Tuesday last, in addition to between four & five thousand by marching. It was apparently expected by the enemy that we would abandon the line of the Rapidan on his approach. His advance seems to be delayed by doubts as to our strength from the maintenance of our position. His reconnoitering parties & cavalry are busy in observation. During Monday & Tuesday he quietly massed his cavalry on his right & moved through Madison to turn our left. [General David] Gregg came down the road to Orange Court House by Barnett's Ford, [General Judson] Kilpatrick the road by Liberty Mills, & [General John] Buford the road by Barboursville leading to Gordonsville. Genl Stuart, with one division of cavalry guarding our left flank, opposed so obstinately the progress of these three divisions of the enemy that he brought them to a halt last night at the Rapidan. By that time Genl Fitz Lee had hastened from the right & joined him. During the night the enemy commenced to retire & Genl Stuart is now pursuing him on his route back to Culpeper. I presume his next attempt will be on our right, unless he determines to move his whole army around our left to Gordonsville. Genl Stuart shewed his usual energy, promptness, & boldness in his operations yesterday. Keeping with the front line of his troops, his horse was shot under him. Citizens report the enemy's loss heavy. I hope ours is not large. I have only heard of the death of Col [H. A.] Rogers of N. C., [General Alfred M.] Scales' brigade, who was killed by a shell at Barnett's Ford, & of Lt Col [William G.] Delony of the cavalry wounded.

I am with great respect, your obt servt

R. E. LEE
Genl

P.S. From the details brought by the train today of the battle of Chickamauga, I see that Buckner had united with Bragg. I am grieved to learn the death of Genl [John B.] Hood. I fear also from the accounts that Genl [William T.] Wofford is dead. He was one of Georgia's best soldiers. I am gradually losing my best men. [Generals Thomas J.] Jackson, [W. Dorsey] Pender, [John B.] Hood! There was no braver soldier in the Confederacy than [General James] Deshler. I see he is numbered among the dead.

R. E. L.

558   To GENERAL ARNOLD ELZEY
Commanding, Richmond, Virginia

Headquarters, Army of Northern Virginia
September 25, 1863

General:

I judge from the enemy's movements in front and the reports of my scouts in his rear that he is preparing to move against me with all the strength he can gather. The troops sent to New York have returned and pontoon trains are being brought up. I wish every man who can possibly be sent to reinforce me, and therefore would be glad for you to make your arrangements so as to send me all you can spare at the proper moment. Please let me know whether Pickett has yet gone to Hanover Junction, so that I can draw Cooke up at once.

Very respectfully, your obt svt

R. E. LEE
Genl

P.S. I have delayed sending the Maryland troops down until after the battle.

559   To GENERAL JAMES LONGSTREET
Near Chattanooga, Tennessee

Headquarters
Orange
September 25, 1863

General:

If it gives you as much pleasure to receive my warmest congratulations as it does me to convey them, this letter will not have been written in vain. My whole heart and soul have been with you and your brave corps in your late battle. It was natural to hear of Longstreet and [Daniel H.] Hill charging side by side, and pleasing to find the armies of the east and west vying with each other in valour and devotion to their country. A complete and glorious victory must ensue under such circumstances. I hope the result will equal the beginning and that General Bragg will be able to reoccupy Tennessee. I grieve for the gallant dead and mourn for our brave Hood. The names of others have reached me, but I hope the report of their fall may not prove true. Finish the work before you, my dear general, and return to me. I want you badly and you cannot get back too soon. Your departure was known to the enemy as soon as it occurred. General Meade has been actively engaged collecting his forces and is now up to the Rapidan. All his troops that were sent north have returned and reinforcements are daily arriving. His cavalry and engineers are constantly reconnoitering, and a vigorous effort was made Monday and Tuesday to turn our left. We are endeavoring to maintain a bold front, and shall endeavor to delay them all we can till you return. Present my sincere compliments and admiration to the officers around you and accept for yourself and command my ardent wishes for the welfare and happiness of all.

Very truly yours

R. E. LEE
General

560   To JEFFERSON DAVIS
Richmond, Virginia

Camp, Orange Court House
September 27, 1863

Mr. President:

The enemy has made no serious advance yet. All his preparations indicate that intention. The troops in his rear have been closed up on the Rapidan. Genl [Rufus] King's division, that has been stationed for some time at Centreville watching the passes through the Bull Run Mountains, has been brought forward to Culpeper. Our scouts also report that the troops from about Washington under Genl [Samuel P.] Heintzelman have joined Genl Meade. The report that the former officer had taken command at Harper's Ferry I find is not correct. He visited that post and inspected the troops along the line of the Baltimore & Ohio Railroad, probably with a view to withdrawing all that could be spared, which gave rise to the report. The pontoon trains have again been brought up from Centreville, & a Confederate soldier that escaped from Point Lookout & crossed the Potomac on the 9th instant, brings the report that some of the troops lately landed at Alexandria came from Charleston. Every effort seems to be making to collect a large army under Genl Meade, & I fear as usual he will come in overwhelming numbers. I have brought Cooke's brigade to Gordonsville to have him as near as possible, while retaining him on the line of the railroad. The N. C. companies of [General James J.] Pettigrew's and [Junius] Daniel's brigades left last spring in Richmond, which I have several times requested might be returned to their regiments, have not yet been sent to me. I know of no other troops that I could get, unless [General Montgomery D.] Corse's brigade could be withdrawn from Genl Sam Jones. The enemy will now send from E[ast] Tennessee to Genl Rosecrans all the regular troops in that quarter, and if Genl Sam Jones could reoccupy Knoxville he could materially assist Genl Bragg. If he cannot, the troops with him will be in a measure idle. I am much obliged to Your Excellency for the information contained in your dispatch of last evening in reference to Genls Hood & Wofford. It has given me great relief.

I am with great respect, your obt servt

R. E. LEE
Genl

561   To JEFFERSON DAVIS
Richmond, Virginia

Camp, Orange Court House
September 30, 1863

Mr. President:

Reports are coming in corroborating the statement that two corps, 11th & 12th, of Genl Meade's army, will proceed to Genl Rosecrans. A scout in whom I have not entire confidence, sends me information to that effect from Washington City, under date of 26th September, & adds that Genl Meade's army will be transferred to the Peninsula. The latter I do not believe. Another scout in Prince William County, under date of 27th, states that "it is currently reported" that one division of 11th Corps, & 1st & 3rd of 12th Corps, have passed through Alexandria to reinforce Rosecrans. None of the scouts have yet seen the troops in motion, nor can any material change be observed in their camps in our front. If sent, their most probable route would be down the Ohio & up the Tennessee to Clarksburg, & thence by rail to Stevenson. It would be well to advise Genl Bragg that his cavalry if possible might break the line. No indications this morning of a movement on the part of Genl Meade. His army occupies the ridge north of Culpeper Court House, extending some miles east & west. His cavalry massed in front of his right & our left.

His position answers as well for defence as attack. Genl [Samuel] Jones writes that he does not believe there is any enemy between him & Knoxville. I presume he does not intend to advance, as he says he has ordered back Corse's brigade.

With great respect, your obt servt

R. E. Lee
Genl

562   To GENERAL JOHN D. IMBODEN
Commanding, Staunton, Virginia

Headquarters Army of Northern Virginia
October 9, 1863

General:

It is a matter of great importance in my judgment that our troops should advance upon the enemy in all quarters, for the purpose of preventing him from reinforcing points more seriously threatened, if nothing better can be accomplished. I desire you to move some part of your force to Strasburg and scout over towards Manassas and Thornton's Gaps, to prevent anything from coming in rear of those of our troops which will now be operating in the direction of Woodville and Sperryville. Should you find no opposition, or such as you can overcome, you may continue your advance farther down the Valley, taking care to observe closely the points above indicated.

Very respecty, your obt svt

R. E. Lee
Genl

563   To JAMES A. SEDDON
Secretary of War

Headquarters, Army of Northern Virginia
Near Madison Court House
October 11, 1863

Sir:

Yesterday I moved the army into this position with the hope of getting an opportunity to strike a blow at the enemy. I regretted to hear that it was announced in one of the Richmond papers of yesterday that this army was in motion and had crossed the Rapidan. All such publications are injurious to us. We have difficulties enough to overcome interposed by our enemies without having them augmented by our friends. I wish you could impress upon the editors the importance of rejecting from their papers all mention of military movements until the result has been obtained. The announcement was erroneous, but still that information received by the enemy would serve to place him upon his guard.

I am very respectfully, your obedient servant

R. E. LEE
General

564   To JAMES A. SEDDON
Secretary of War

Headquarters
Near Warrenton Springs
October 13, 1863

Sir:
I have the honor to inform you that Genl Meade's army has been compelled to retire north of the Rappahannock by the movements of this army upon his right flank. I am still moving with the view of throwing him further back towards Washington. Two divisions have already crossed the Rappahannock at this place and the remainder are now following. The enemy were apprised of our movements and withdrew so rapidly that we have not been able to come up with his main body, but there have been a number of encounters between his cavalry and that of Genl Stuart, in which the latter has been uniformly successful, capturing more than six hundred prisoners, and inflicting serious damage upon the enemy.

Very respectfully, your obt servt

R. E. LEE
Genl

565   To JEFFERSON DAVIS
Richmond, Virginia

Headquarters, Army of Northern Virginia
Bristoe Station
October 17, 1863

Mr. President:
I have the honor to inform you that with the view of bringing on an engagement with the army of Genl Meade, which lay around Cul-

peper Court House, extending thence to the Rapidan, this army marched on the 9th instant by way of Madison Court House and arrived near Culpeper on the 11th. The enemy retired towards the Rappahannock at the railroad bridge, declining battle, and removing all his stores.

I determined to make another effort to reach him, and moved through Warrenton towards the railroad north of the Rappahannock. The enemy had several direct roads by which he retired, while we were compelled to march by a more circuitous route. We only succeeded in coming up with a portion of his rear guard at this place on the 15th [14th] instant, with which a severe skirmish ensued, but without any decisive or satisfactory result. During the night of the 15th [14th] the enemy continued his retreat, and is now reported to be fortifying at Centreville. I do not deem it advisable to attack him in his entrenchments, or to force him further back by turning his present position, as he could quickly reach the fortifications around Washington and Alexandria, which we are not prepared to invest. Should I advance further, I should be compelled to go to Loudoun for subsistence for the army, this region being entirely destitute, and the enemy having made the railroad useless to us by the complete destruction of the Rappahannock bridge. Such a movement would take us too far from other points where the army might be needed, and the want of clothing, shoes, blankets, and overcoats would entail great suffering upon our men. I can see no benefit to be derived from remaining where we are, and shall consequently return to the line of the Rappahannock. The railroad bridges over Cub Run, Broad Run, and Cedar Run have been destroyed, and the track torn up from the first named point back towards the Rappahannock, the ties burned, and the rails bent. The destruction will be continued as far as the river, and may prevent another advance of the enemy in this direction this season.

We have captured about sixteen hundred prisoners, and inflicted some additional loss upon the enemy in the various skirmishes that have occurred since the movement began. Our own loss was slight, except in the action at this place, where it was quite severe, and I regret to add that five pieces of artillery belonging to [General Ambrose P.] Hill's corps were captured. The particulars have not yet been officially reported to me, but shall be communicated as soon as received.

Very respectfully, your obt servt

R. E. LEE
Genl

566   To GENERAL ALEXANDER R. LAWTON
Quartermaster General, Richmond, Virginia

Headquarters, Army of Northern Virginia
October 19, 1863

General:

I have received your letter of the 12th instant and am very glad to find that your exertions to supply the army have been so successful. The want of the supplies of shoes, clothing, overcoats, and blankets is very great. Nothing but my unwillingness to expose the men to the hardships that would have resulted from moving them into Loudoun in their present condition induced me to return to the Rappahannock. But I was averse to marching them over the rough roads of that region, at a season, too, when frosts are certain and snows probable, unless they were better provided to encounter them without suffering.

I should otherwise have endeavored to detain General Meade near the Potomac, if I could not throw him to the north side.

The supplies you now have at your disposal for this army will be most welcome, and I trust that your exertions to increase them will meet with full success.

Very respectfully, your obt servt

R. E. LEE
Genl

567   To HIS WIFE
Buford's Depot, Virginia

Rappahannock River
October 19, 1863

I have received dear Mary your letter of the 10th. I am very glad to hear that you are better, though your improvement may be slight, if progressive, your comfort & mine may be materially benefited. I hope it may be & that our merciful Father in Heaven may grant us yet the days He has allotted us on earth, much health & peace. I am glad to hear that you have had so pleasant a visit at Liberty though you did not state who were the friends that caused it. I hope you will find your house in Richmond comfortable & your sojourn pleasant. As regards your obtaining supplies from the Commissary I presume that will be impracticable. If the arrangement you speak of is extended to the families of officers, it

must be to those who are on duty there. I am not & have no ground
for having my family there, except their convenience. Everything abstracted from the Commissary diminishes the supply for the army which
I endeavour to increase as much as possible. I hope though you will be
able to buy enough for your comfortable maintenance. As soon as I
learn of your arrival in Richmond I will send you a check for some
money which in spite of Capt Buford's generosity you must stand in
need of. I am sorry that he would not accept compensation, for though
I feel very grateful for his kindness, I do not wish to burden my friends.
I am sorry I have no nice silk handkerchiefs, all that I have are in use, &
have not been improved by Perry's washing. A year ago I could have
given him three beautiful ones that I purchased in New York some years
since. See if you cannot buy him a dozen beauties. I have received a letter from Mildred, who was well & studying hard. When is her term up?
I have returned to the Rappahannock. I did not proceed with the main
army beyond Bristoe or Broad Run. Our advance went as far as Bull
Run. Where the enemy was entrenching, extending his right as far as
Chantilly, in the yard of which he was building a redoubt. I could have
thrown him further back, but I saw no chance of bringing him to battle,
& it would have only served to fatigue our troops by advancing further.
If they had have been properly provided with clothes I would certainly
have endeavoured to have thrown them north of the Potomac. But thousands were barefooted, thousands with fragments of shoes, & all without
overcoats, blankets or warm clothing. I could not bear to expose them to
certain suffering, on an uncertain issue. We could only come up with
their rear, punished them a little & captured altogether over 1700 prisoners. Give much love to the girls & all friends. I have no time for more.
I think my rheumatism is a little better. Yet I still suffer. The first two
days of our march I had to be hauled in a wagon. I can now ride.

Truly & affly

R. E. Lee

568   To GENERAL SAMUEL COOPER
Adjutant and Inspector General
TELEGRAM

Rappahannock River
October 20, 1863

GENL STUART YESTERDAY OPPOSED AT BUCKLAND THE ADVANCE OF GENL
[JUDSON] KILPATRICK'S DIVISION OF CAVALRY, WHILST GENL FITZ LEE AT-

TACKED HIS FLANK AND REAR. THE ENEMY WAS ROUTED AND PURSUED UNTIL
HE REACHED HIS INFANTRY SUPPORT AT HAY MARKET AND GAINESVILLE. TWO
HUNDRED PRISONERS, WITH HORSES, ARMS, AND EQUIPMENTS, EIGHT WAGONS
AND AMBULANCES, WERE CAPTURED.

R. E. LEE

569   To GENERAL SAMUEL COOPER
               Adjutant and Inspector General

Headquarters, Army of Northern Virginia
October 23, 1863

General:

In advance of a detailed report, I have the honor to submit for the information of the Department the following outline of the recent operations of this army.

With the design of bringing on an engagement with the Federal Army, which was encamped around Culpeper Court House, extending thence to the Rapidan, this army crossed that river on the 9th instant and advanced by way of Madison Court House. Our progress was necessarily slow, as the march was by circuitous and concealed roads, in order to avoid the observation of the enemy.

General Fitz Lee with his cavalry division and a detachment of infantry remained to hold our lines south of the Rapidan. General Stuart with Hampton's division moved on the right of the column. With a portion of his command he attacked the advance of the enemy near James City on the 10th, and drove them back towards Culpeper. Our main body arrived near that place on the 11th instant and discovered that the enemy had retreated towards the Rappahannock, removing or destroying his stores. We were compelled to halt during the rest of the day to provision the troops, but the cavalry under General Stuart continued to press the enemy's rear guard towards the Rappahannock. A large force of Federal cavalry in the meantime had crossed the Rapidan after our movement began, but was repulsed by General Fitz Lee and pursued towards Brandy Station.

Near that place the commands of Stuart and Lee united on the afternoon of the 11th, and after a severe engagement drove the enemy's cavalry across the Rappahannock with heavy loss.

On the morning of the 12th, the army marched in two columns with the design of reaching the Orange and Alexandria Railroad north of the river, and intercepting the retreat of the enemy.

After a skirmish with some of the Federal cavalry at Jeffersonton, we reached the Rappahannock at Warrenton Springs in the afternoon, where the passage of the river was disputed by cavalry and artillery.

The enemy was quickly driven off by a detachment of our cavalry, aided by a small force of infantry and a battery. Early next morning (13th) the march was resumed, and the two columns reunited at Warrenton in the afternoon, where another halt was made to supply the troops with provisions.

The enemy fell back rapidly along the line of the railroad, and early on the 14th the pursuit was continued, a portion of the army moving by way of New Baltimore towards Bristoe Station, and the rest, accompanied by the main body of the cavalry, proceeding to the same point by Auburn Mills and Greenwich. Near the former place a skirmish took place between General Ewell's advance and the rear guard of the enemy, which was forced back and rapidly pursued.

The retreat of the enemy was conducted by several direct parallel roads, while our troops were compelled to march by difficult and circuitous routes. We were consequently unable to intercept him. General Hill arrived first at Bristoe, where his advance, consisting of two brigades, became engaged with a force largely superior in numbers, posted behind the railroad embankment. The particulars of the action have not been officially reported, but the brigades were repulsed with some loss, and five pieces of artillery, with a number of prisoners, captured. Before the rest of the troops could be brought up and the position of the enemy ascertained, he retreated across Broad Run.

The next morning he was reported to be fortifying beyond Bull Run, extending his line towards the Little River turnpike.

The vicinity of the entrenchments around Washington and Alexandria rendered it useless to turn his new position, as it was apparent that he could readily retire to them, and would decline an engagement unless attacked in his fortifications. A further advance was therefore deemed unnecessary, and after destroying the railroad from Cub Run southwardly to the Rappahannock the army returned on the 18th to the line of that river, leaving the cavalry in the enemy's front.

The cavalry of the latter advanced on the following day, and some skirmishing occurred at Buckland. General Stuart, with Hampton's division, retired slowly towards Warrenton, in order to draw the enemy in that direction, thus exposing his flank and rear to General Lee, who moved from Auburn and attacked him near Buckland. As soon as General Stuart heard the sound of Lee's guns he turned upon the enemy, who after a stubborn resistance broke and fled in confusion pursued by General Stuart nearly to Hay Market, and by General Lee to Gainesville. Here the Federal infantry was encountered, and after capturing a number of them during the night the cavalry slowly retired before their advance on the following day.

When the movement of the army from the Rapidan commenced, General Imboden was instructed to advance down the Valley and guard the gaps of the mountains on our left. This duty was well performed by that officer, and on the 18th instant he marched upon Charlestown and succeeded, by a well concerted plan, in surrounding the place and capturing nearly the whole force stationed there, with all their stores and transportation. Only a few escaped to Harper's Ferry. The enemy advanced from that place in superior numbers to attack General Imboden, who retired, bringing off his prisoners and captured property, his command suffering very little loss and inflicting some damage upon the pursuing columns.

In the course of these operations, two thousand four hundred and thirty-six prisoners were captured, including forty-one commissioned officers. Of the above number, four hundred and thirty-four taken by General Imboden.

A more complete account with a statement of our loss in killed, wounded, and prisoners, will be forwarded as soon as the necessary official reports shall have been received.

Very respectfully, your obt servt

R. E. Lee
General

570   To GENERAL LEONIDAS POLK
Atlanta, Georgia

Camp Rappahannock
October 26, 1863

My Dear General:

I received your letter of the 27th ultimo, the day I was about to make a move upon General Meade to prevent his further reinforcing General Rosecrans. I have been unable to reply until now. I have rejoiced exceedingly at your great victory, and heartily wished that the advantages gained could be pursued and confirmed. I am indebted, I know, entirely to your kind feelings for the proposition made to me. I wish I could be of any service in the west, but I do not feel that I could do much anywhere. In addition to other infirmities, I have been for more than a month a great sufferer from rheumatism in my back, so that I can hardly get about. I hope the President has been able to rectify all difficulties in your army, and that Rosecrans will at last be obliged to abandon his position. I trust you are again with your command, and that a merciful God will continue His blessings to us and shield us from any danger. That He may have you and your brave army under His care is my earnest prayer.

I am general with great respect, your obedient servant

R. E. LEE

571   To HIS WIFE
Richmond, Virginia

Camp, Rappahannock
October 28, 1863

I received last night dear Mary your letter from Richmond. It was without date, but I presume was written on Saturday, as that was the day of rain here. I answered your letter from Liberty, but as the railroad bridges were carried away by the freshet, & great irregularity in the trains existed, it was probably delayed in transmission. I hope it has reached you before this. It was directed to Mr. Caskie's care. I am glad you are so pleased with your house & am truly grateful to the kind friends who have aided you in procuring & furnishing it. I am very sorry that it is too small to accomodate Charlotte. It takes from me half the pleasure of your accomodation, as I wish to think of you all together, & in her feeble condition & separation from her Fitzhugh, no one can sympathize or attend to her as yourself & her sisters. Tell her she had better come up & take my tent. I moved yesterday in a nice pine thicket, & Perry is today engaged in constructing a chimney in front, which will make it warm & comfortable. I have no idea when Fitzhugh will be exchanged. The Federal authorities still resist all exchanges because they think it is to our interest to make them. Any desire expressed on our part, for an exchange of any individual, magnifies the difficulty, as they at once think some great benefit is to result to us from it. If you want a person exchanged, the best course is to keep quiet about it. His detention is very grievous to me, & I besides want his services. But I know no way of shortening it, & must make up my mind to bear it. As regards the flannel, I do not wish to take the girls' provision or break into their arrangements. Perhaps you can find some in Richmond, coarser & heavier than they require. If you could take the four pairs you made for me last year & convert them into two, I think they would be large enough. They may be too small as they are even for Rob's kilder legs. But of that I do not know. My flannel jackets of which I hoped to derive much comfort this winter, have shrunk to such a degree, that they are very uncomfortable. If you can get flannel enough for two jackets & two pairs of drawers, please do so. I do not know what I shall do when the winter really comes, I have suffered so from cold already. I hope I shall get used to it. But I have felt very differently since my attack of last spring, from which I have never recovered. Two of each garment is sufficient, as the rule in camp is for one to be on & the other in the wash. It saves transportation. I shall wear my yarn socks this winter & have a plenty. As soon as Custis returns he can get into my trunk & send what is necessary. I am glad you have some socks for the army. Send them to me or Col Corley. They will come safe. Tell the girls to send all they can. I wish they could make some shoes too. We have thousands of barefooted men. I have not seen Rob since I last wrote. I hope he is well. He is serving with Col [John R.] Chambliss who is in command of Fitzhugh's brigade. You must remember me to all the kind people who take the trouble to inquire after me & thank them for me for their attentions to you. I see no prospect of ever repaying them. I do not now know when I shall be in Richmond. I want to see you very much, but as I always return with an attack of sickness, it is best for me to keep away. My rheumatism is better, though I still suffer. I hope in time it will pass away. I have read Mrs. Cocke's letter with much pleasure. Our people are too kind. There is no news. Genl Meade I believe is repairing the railroad & I presume will come on again. If I could only get some shoes & clothes for the army, I would save him the trouble. I hope Custis will return soon, as he will be a great comfort to you. Give much love to the girls & Mildred when you write. Tell her I received her letter. I hope Charlotte will now get well. Tell her it is no time for her to be sick, she is young. Only old people can be allowed to be sick.

With true affection, yours

R. E. LEE

572   To JAMES A. SEDDON
Secretary of War

Headquarters, Army of Northern Virginia
October 28, 1863

Sir:

I have seen a statement in the Richmond papers that the Federal Government has definitely declined any further exchange of prisoners.

If this is true I think we should commence at once to make thorough and effective arrangements to keep our prisoners of war during the period of hostilities between the two Governments.

I would respectfully suggest that the city of Richmond is not a suitable place for the accommodation and safe keeping of these prisoners. I think the presence of a large number there is, for many reasons, very injurious. It increases largely the amount of supplies to be transported to the city, and thus employs transportation which might be used for the benefit of the citizens. This has a tendency to increase high prices and cause distress among the poorer classes. Then they are supplied at much greater cost and trouble to the Government in Richmond than they would be at some point or points in the interior. Our capital is the great point of attack of the enemy in the eastern portion of the Confederacy, and the emergency might arise in which it would be exceedingly inconvenient to have Federal prisoners within its limits. I have no doubt that even now they add much to the sources of information of the enemy with regard to the movements of troops and the disposition of our forces, as it is exceedingly difficult to prevent all communication with persons outside or to remove all means of escape. The Federal Government seems to have made permanent arrangements to keep their prisoners during the war. I think that like dispositions on our part would manifest our indifference on the subject and would bring them to terms of exchange sooner than anything else we could do. I hardly know what points in the interior to suggest, but one on the extension of the Danville Railroad near the border of North Carolina has been named, where wood is cheap and provisions are in abundance, where there is little danger of any raid or attack from the enemy, and whence they could be easily and rapidly transported to City Point in case exchange should be resumed.

I am very respectfully, your obt servt

R. E. Lee
General

573   To GENERAL SAMUEL JONES
Commanding, Abingdon, Virginia

Headquarters, Army of Northern Virginia
November 2, 1863

General:

I have received your letter of the 22d ultimo and regret that I cannot at this time spare any troops from this army to reinforce you. General Meade is again advancing on this line, repairing the railroad as he moves forward. I had desired to take advantage of any lull in his operations and the good weather of this fall to drive General [Benjamin F.] Kelley's forces out of Hardy and Hampshire, and make another attempt to interrupt transportation on the Baltimore & Ohio Railroad, but in the present condition of affairs, I am unable to reinforce General Imboden, who thinks himself too weak to accomplish it.

Your movement upon East Tennessee may attract the attention of the enemy in northwestern Virginia, so as to prevent a combination of his forces upon General Imboden. I hope you will be able to occupy Knoxville. It is the best manner of securing the line of the Virginia & Tennessee Railroad, and preventing the constant and annoying demonstrations against you, and I suggest that you unite your whole force, leaving detachments out only to observe the enemy and keep up appearances, while you strike rapid and strong blows upon the force in Tennessee. Should you not be able to do this, a movement upon northwestern Virginia, combined with a movement of Imboden upon the railroad, might enable both detachments to injure the enemy. As far as I can learn, I believe there is little probability of the threatened movement of Averell from Beverly, of which you advise me, nor have I any reason to believe that an advance will be made by him in that direction this fall. It behooves us to be active, to give the enemy no rest, and to prevent his reinforcing his army about Chattanooga, which now seems to be the important point of his operations.

Very respectfully, your obt servt

R. E. LEE
General

574   To HIS WIFE
Richmond, Virginia

Camp, Rappahannock
November 5, 1863

I received last night dear Mary your letter of the 2nd with the pair of drawers. The flannel seems to be very nice & they fit me very well now, but I fear when washed they will shrink up like the others. Ought not the lining of the waist band to be of the same material, or of something warmer than that thin cotton? However I am content with them. I think you had better not make the jackets until you can get some pattern. However large sized men's jackets, long in the body will suit. But I thought if I could ever get these I now have to you, so that you might insert in the back & arms a wide piece, they might last for the winter, so as flannel is so scarce I think you had better not make the jackets yet awhile. I am glad to hear that Charlotte is better, I hope she will get strong & well poor child. The visit of her grandpa will cheer her up I trust & I know he gave her plenty of good advice. Tell Mrs. Atkinson that her son Nelson is a very good scout & good soldier. I wish I had some way of promoting him. I received the bucket of butter she was so kind as to send me, but have had no opportunity of returning the vessel, which I hope to be able to do. The messenger has just brought me your letter of Tuesday or Wednesday I presume, but it is without date. I am sorry Smith does not like your house. I have told you my only objection to it & wish it was large enough to hold Charlotte. It must have reminded you of old times to have your brother Carter & Uncle Williams to see you. I think my rheumatism is better today. I have been through a great deal with comparatively little suffering. I have been wanting to review the cavalry for some time, & appointed today with fear & trembling. I had not been on horse back for five days previously & feared I would not get through. But to my surprize I got along very well. The Governor was here, & told me Mrs. Letcher had seen you recently. I saw all my nephews looking very handsome, & Rob too. The latter says he has written to you three times since he crossed the river. Tell Chass I think Fitzhugh's old regiment, the 9th, made the best appearance on review. While on the ground a man rode up to me & said he was just from Alexandria & had been requested to give me a box which he handed to me, but did not know who sent it. It contained a handsome pair of gilt spurs. Good night. I pray a kind Heaven guard you all.

Truly & affly

R. E. LEE

575   To JAMES A. SEDDON
               Secretary of War

Headquarters, Army of Northern Virginia
November 7, 1863

Sir:

The enemy advanced today to the Rappahannock and made an attack at Kelly's Ford, followed soon after by a demonstration in large force at Rappahannock Station. He forced a passage at the former place, and has laid down a pontoon bridge on which a considerable force has crossed, to be followed I presume by his main body.

After some skirmishing and quite a heavy cannonade at the station, he advanced after sunset in overwhelming numbers on the troops on the north side of the river guarding our *tête-de-pont*, and succeeded in capturing the greater part of the two brigades there stationed (those of [Generals Robert F.] Hoke & [Harry T.] Hays) and four pieces of artillery.

Very respectfully, your obt servt

R. E. LEE
Genl

576 To JEFFERSON DAVIS
Richmond, Virginia

Headquarters, Army of Northern Virginia
November 10, 1863

Mr. President:

I have seen with pleasure the announcement of your return to Richmond, after a journey which I hope has proved as beneficial to yourself as I am persuaded it has been to the country.

After my letter written from Bristoe Station, in pursuance of the purpose therein indicated, the army returned to the line of the Rappahannock, having destroyed the Orange & Alexandria Railroad from Cub Run to the river. The enemy immediately began to repair the railroad, advancing his army as the work progressed, until he reached Warrenton Junction, where he halted for a short time. His movement from that point towards Rappahannock Station and Kelly's Ford was subsequently reported. With the view of deterring him if possible from advancing further into the interior this winter, I caused the works he had constructed on the north side of the river near the bridge to be converted into a *tête-de-pont* to defend a pontoon bridge, which we had laid down at this point, constructing at the same time lines of rifle pits on each side of the stream.

Four pieces of artillery were placed in the redoubt on the north bank and eight others in a similar work on the south side, the rest having been sent further back to obtain pasturage for the animals. Hays' brigade was in the rifle pits on the north side of the river, and upon learning the approach of the enemy on Saturday, the 7th instant, Hoke's, with the exception of one regiment, previously detached, was ordered to reinforce it. The rest of Early's division was brought down to occupy the south bank east of the railroad, and Anderson's the line of hills along the river on the same side, west of the road. Rodes' division was stationed at Kelly's Ford. The enemy began by a demonstration with two corps at the latter place, where he effected a passage, the ground being unfavorable for us, much resembling the country at Fredericksburg. A line was selected however further back, on which it had been supposed that we would be able to check his advance in that direction. In the afternoon the enemy's artillery opened upon our lines at the bridge and a force estimated to be three army corps was deployed in our front, massing behind a range of hills parallel to the river, and out of reach of our guns. After dark this force advanced and succeeded in overcoming the troops that held the rifle pits and captured the four pieces of artillery in the redoubt on that side. I have called for an official report of the affair, which I will forward to you as soon as received. I am unable at this time to give further particulars. General Hays and some of his officers with about six hundred men escaped.

Finding that we would not be able to maintain our position with the enemy in possession of the works on the north side, the troops were withdrawn at night to the only tenable line north of Culpeper between that place and Brandy Station, which they continued to hold without molestation during Sunday, the trains being sent back towards the Rapidan. The position was not however a good one, and I accordingly withdrew on Sunday night to the south bank of the Rapidan, where a general battle can be delivered on more favorable terms. The army now occupies about the same position as before the recent advance.

I have the honor to be with great respect, your obt servt

R. E. LEE
General

577   To HIS WIFE
                           Richmond, Virginia

Camp, Rapidan
November 11, 1863

I have received dear Mary your notes by Col Cole & Bryan. I am very glad that you & Charlotte are better & that Fitzhugh has been heard from. I had heard nothing of the latter for a long time. In my previous letters I told you all about the jackets & drawers. I want two of each.

The doctor thinks garments made of flannel are better than the knit or woven. Let them be of flannel then. The pair you sent me fit well now. The flannel does not appear to have been shrunk & I therefore fear when washed will shrink as small as the others. Please have all the flannel well shrunk before being made up, or the material will probably be lost. I have been afraid to wear the pair sent, as I have no change. As regards the people at the White House & Romancoke I directed Mr. Collins as soon as he could get in the small crop this fall, to obtain from the county courts their free papers & to emancipate them. They can then hire themselves out & support themselves. Their families if they choose or until they can do better can remain at their present homes. I do not know what to do better for them. The enemy has carried off all the teams, &c., & there is no certainty if they remain of making enough to live on. I wish this done. Custis is apprised of it & will see to it as far as possible. I am distressed to hear of our dear little Mary Childe. Bryan got up last night with the fur robe & letters. Thank Agnes for hers, I will write when I can. Give love to Mary & all friends. I have not time for more now. I am better than I was. Col Cole brought up the socks & gloves. They will be very acceptable this cold weather. We had a snow storm day before yesterday. The mountains are covered & last night ice made in my tent. I withdrew the army Monday to the line of the Rapidan. I held the Rappahannock in hope of deterring the enemy from advancing this winter. As he seems disposed to come on, the ground is more favourable for us here than there & I hope a kind Providence will prosper us & give us victory. Our only trust is in [Him].

Truly & affly

R. E. LEE

578   To JAMES A. SEDDON
             Secretary of War

Headquarters, Army of Northern Virginia
November 12, 1863

Sir:

The condition of the Virginia Central Railroad, on which we depend almost entirely for our supplies, seems to become worse every day. Col Corley reports the frequent accidents of cars running off the track, and that the track in many places is very bad. I beg you to consult with the President and Superintendent of the road as to what measures can be taken for its repair before the winter fairly sets in. To make details from this army for the purpose in the present reduced condition of our regiments is next to impossible. I hope, however, something may be done to put it in good repair so that it may be relied on for the regular transportation of our supplies. If this cannot be done, the only alternative will be to fall back nearer to Richmond. This would leave not only the railroad, but the richest portion of the State of Virginia at the mercy of the enemy. If the Engineer Department can do the work and the railroad company cannot, I think they might set a portion of the force employed on the defences of Richmond at work at once and charge the work done to the company, to be deducted from the tolls on supplies transported to the army. It is of great importance that the work should be done while the good weather lasts.

I am sir respectfully, your obt servt

R. E. LEE
General

579   To MISS AGNES LEE
                  Richmond, Virginia

Camp, Rapidan
November 13, 1863

My precious little Agnes:

I have been wishing to reply to your letter of the 4th for some days, but like yourself cannot always find time to write. I have not failed however to enjoy it & have read it more than once. I am very much obliged to you for the flannel, but do not wish to absorb your little importations. I hope your mother will be able to manufacture the garments out of the sets of last year. You must help her & then you will learn to manufacture for the soldiers. As to the jackets, they may be of silk if good thick English ones can be obtained. Otherwise they will not be warm enough. The price is nothing now a days. Everything has become so enormous, that I stickle at nothing & go in without consideration of cost. But then I buy nothing but what is necessary. I wish indeed I could see you & would gladly visit Richmond for that purpose for I want to see you all very much. But when I shall be able to do so, have no idea. I must therefore be patient. I hope however you are all well & happy. I see the papers are calling upon persons that have no business in the city to leave it. I hope that does not include you all. But I was afraid you would be in the way. If they send you off you must come to your papa & I will give you a fair opportunity to cure my rheumatic pains. I am better now & have been riding a great deal lately. Still I have some twinges & general stiffness to remind me of the grip they have upon me. I do not know when you will be able to see the army, though wish you could have done so earlier. The days of reviews are passed for the present. The enemy seems to be emboldened by his successes on the Rappahannock River, has received & is still receiving reinforcements, & threatens dreadful things. I hope we shall be able to stand up under them. You must pray to the great God who rideth in the heavens, to give us strength & courage to do the work He has set before us, & to Him be all the praise! I am glad you think Charlotte is better. I hope she will get well now. I received a letter from her to night, in which she says she feels better, but cannot walk yet. It is very grievous to me to have you all sick & I unable to do anything for you. How are your poor little pains now? All gone I hope. I am so sorry to hear of Mary Childe's afflictions. You must give her much love & sincere sympathy for me when you write. I fear I may never be able to write to her again. Major Gilmore who was a prisoner in Baltimore some time since, told me he saw her when there. She has never been well he says since the birth of her last child. Give a great deal of love to your poor mama, Daughter & Charlotte. Daughter seems to have forgotten to write to her papa. How is little Sallie? She had better learn to spin, to weave, & to make up all kinds of clothes, or I shall not let her marry Shirley. Remember me to all friends & believe me

Your affectionate father

R. E. LEE

580   To HIS WIFE
Richmond, Virginia

Camp
November 21, 1863

I have received dear Mary your letter of the 15th with the drawers. The latter fit very well & I hope will not shrink by washing. The weather has been so warm that I have not required them. As to the jackets you had better not make them until you get some measure. I could send one of these I have, but you would have to add two or three inches to all their dimensions. The elbows have burst out from over tension. The pattern is good enough if it contained more material. I think you had better retain the gloves until you accumulate more &

the weather becomes colder; socks if you have them are very desirable. We have been getting more shoes, but cannot keep all the bare feet covered. Some shoes are all the time giving out, & as you cover some feet others become destitute. I told Mr. Collins my wishes & gave him his instructions in person. I hope he has been able to carry them out, & that he will be able to close up his stewardship this fall. I told him to sell all that was in the place, pay all debts & deposit the remainder to my credit in the bank at Richmond. If he has been able to get the wheat to market, he will have surplus funds. Mr. Laroby has visited me several times. He is very friendly to our cause & a strong well wisher of our success. I do not know that he can do much more for us. I see by the papers that Fitzhugh has been sent to Fort Lafayette. Any place would be better than Fort Monroe with [General Benjamin] Butler in command. It is probable he will be sent to Johnson's Island, where the rest of our officers are. From what Mrs. Stevens says, I hope he has recovered of his wound. His long confinement is very grievous to me. Yet it may all turn out for the best. Mr. Chapman Leigh has been remarkably kind. You must thank him for all his kindness to you & Charlotte. I hope Mary will have a pleasant visit to Shirley, & that Genl Butler may never reach that point. I am very glad to hear that Charlotte is well enough to spend the day with you & that she is getting so fat. I hope she will soon be strong again. Scott must be a good marketman. I send you a check for $1000. I hope you are able to procure what you want. You must not mind the price of necessary articles, but get them. I fear the community consider us very poor. They are constantly making me little presents, butter, eggs, chickens, potatoes, cabbage, &c., which I am unable to make any return for. I wish I could get some to you. I am content to be poor, & to live on corn bread the rest of my life if a gracious God will give us our independence. I expect the President here today. It is however raining hard & I fear he will have an uncomfortable time. The mud here is dreadful after a rain. Custis you know is with me. All the Lees have been to see him. Fitz, John, Henry & Rob, also little Dainger. What is Miss Norvell writing to him about? Tell her I don't like that, she ought to write to Rob. Remember me to the Caskies, &c., & give much love to Mary, Agnes & Chass.

Truly & affly

R. E. LEE

581   To JEFFERSON DAVIS
                        Richmond, Virginia
                        TELEGRAM

                                              Orange Court House
                                              November 26, 1863

YOUR DISPATCH RECEIVED. I SHOULD LIKE THE ASSISTANCE OF COL
[HENRY C.] LEE IF CONVENIENT. THE ENEMY'S WHOLE FORCE IS MOVING TO
OUR RIGHT & WILL REACH THE LOWER FORD OF THE RAPIDAN TONIGHT. I AM
MAKING A CORRESPONDING MOVEMENT. PREPARE THE TROOPS ABOUT RICH-
MOND. ALL SHOULD BE ADVANCED TOWARDS HANOVER JUNCTION THAT CAN.
FORAGE SHOULD BE PARTICULARLY FORWARDED TO US.

                                                        R. E. LEE

582   To GENERAL SAMUEL COOPER
                   Adjutant and Inspector General
                        TELEGRAM

                                              Orange Court House
                                              November 26, 1863

GENL MEADE'S WHOLE ARMY WAS DISCOVERED TODAY IN MOTION TO-
WARDS THE LOWER FORDS OF RAPIDAN. THIS ARMY WILL MOVE TOWARDS
SPOTSYLVANIA COURT HOUSE TO OPPOSE IT.

                                                        R. E. LEE

583   To JEFFERSON DAVIS
                        Richmond, Virginia
                        TELEGRAM

                                              Orange Court House
                                              November 27, 1863

GENERAL MEADE'S ARMY CROSSING THE RAPIDAN AT GERMANNA, ELY'S
FORD, &C., AND MOVING ON CHANCELLORSVILLE. I AM CONCENTRATING THIS
ARMY UPON ITS RIGHT FLANK WITH A VIEW TO BRING HIM TO BATTLE.

                                                        R. E. LEE

584   To GENERAL SAMUEL COOPER
                    Adjutant and Inspector General
                          TELEGRAM

                                        Orange Court House
                                        November 28, 1863

THE ENEMY'S WHOLE FORCE IS ON THE ROADS TO ORANGE COURT HOUSE.
NO ADVANCE TOWARDS SPOTSYLVANIA. HIS PROGRESS YESTERDAY WAS SUCCESS-
FULLY RESISTED.

                                        R. E. LEE

585   To GENERAL SAMUEL COOPER
                    Adjutant and Inspector General
                          TELEGRAM

                          Headquarters, Army of Northern Virginia
                                        November 29, 1863
                                                9 A.M.

A RAIN STORM PREVAILED ALL DAY YESTERDAY. NO MOVEMENTS OF ANY
IMPORTANCE BY EITHER ARMY. THIS MORNING ENEMY IS DEPLOYING IN LINE
OF BATTLE IN OUR FRONT.

                                        R. E. LEE
                                        Genl

586   To GENERAL SAMUEL COOPER
                    Adjutant and Inspector General
                          TELEGRAM

                                        Orange Court House
                                        November 30, 1863

NO MOVEMENT OF IMPORTANCE BY EITHER ARMY YESTERDAY. THE EN-
EMY IS IN LINE ON THE EAST SIDE OF MINE RUN. THIS ARMY IS IN POSITION
ON THE WEST SIDE.

                                        R. E. LEE

587   To GENERAL SAMUEL COOPER
            Adjutant and Inspector General
                    TELEGRAM

                                    Orange Court House
                                    December 1, 1863

THE ENEMY OPENED THEIR BATTERIES ON OUR LINES YESTERDAY. SOME
SKIRMISHING TOOK PLACE, BUT NO ATTACK.

                                    R. E. LEE
                                    Genl

588   To GENERAL SAMUEL COOPER
            Adjutant and Inspector General
                    TELEGRAM

                                    Orange Court House
                                    December 2, 1863

YESTERDAY ENEMY APPEARED TO BE CLOSING UP HIS FORCES ON PLANK
ROAD. NO OTHER MOVEMENT DISCOVERED.

                                    R. E. LEE
                                    Genl

589   To GENERAL SAMUEL COOPER
            Adjutant and Inspector General
                    TELEGRAM

                                    Orange Court House
                                    December 2, 1863

THE ENEMY RETREATED DURING THE NIGHT. PURSUIT WAS MADE THIS
MORNING, BUT HE HAD RECROSSED RAPIDAN BEFORE WE REACHED IT. A FEW
PRISONERS WERE CAPTURED.

                                    R. E. LEE
                                    General

590   To GENERAL SAMUEL COOPER
                  Adjutant and Inspector General

                                    Headquarters, Army of Northern Virginia
                                                        December 2, 1863

General:

On Thursday, 26th ultimo, it became known that the army of General Meade was in motion for Germanna & Ely's Fords, on the Rapidan. Supposing that his design was either to draw us from our position by a flank movement or to occupy Fredericksburg, the army was withdrawn from the line of the upper Rapidan the same night and marched eastward to strike the enemy while moving, or accept battle if offered.

Ewell's corps under General Early was directed to proceed to the old turnpike near Locust Grove and Hill's to move down the Plank road.

During the march on the 27th, intelligence was received that the enemy was advancing towards Orange Court House by both roads.

It was at first supposed that this force was only intended to cover the movement of the main body, and the army continued its march. Hampton's division of cavalry which was in advance encountered the enemy near New Hope Church on the Plank road, and some skirmishing ensued which was participated in by the advance of Hill's corps, and the progress of the enemy was checked. General Johnson's division of Ewell's corps met a corps of the enemy under General [William H.] French moving up the river on our left, and after a spirited engagement repulsed it. General Early continued to advance until he discovered a large force near Locust Grove. In the meantime intelligence was received from General [Thomas L.] Rosser, whose brigade had been stationed to guard the roads leading from Ely's and Germanna Fords to Fredericksburg, that the whole army of General Meade, after crossing the Rapidan, had taken roads leading up the river to Orange Court House. General Rosser attacked their train near Wilderness Tavern and burned a considerable number of wagons, bringing off eighteen, together with 280 mules and 150 prisoners. As soon as this movement of the enemy was reported, preparations were made to meet the expected attack, but none being made that day the army was withdrawn that night to a better position on the west side of Mine Run, where it has since remained. The enemy advanced on the 28th to the east side of the creek immediately in our front, but has made no effort to attack. He has thrown up earth works along his line and makes a great display of artillery, but I have not been able to discover his purpose.

General Fitz Lee, with his division was left to guard the upper fords of the Rapidan after the withdrawal of our army, and on Friday drove back Kilpatrick's cavalry which crossed at Morton's and Raccoon Fords and attacked him.

The same day Major [John S.] Mosby fell upon a train of wagons at Brandy Station and destroyed a number of them, bringing off 112 mules and a few prisoners.

On Saturday the enemy still remaining quiet, General Stuart with Hampton's division of cavalry endeavored to penetrate to his rear. He met a body of cavalry near Parker's Shop, where he had a sharp skirmish, but was recalled by a report that the enemy was moving on our right.

Very respectfully, your obt svt

R. E. LEE
General

591   To GENERAL SAMUEL COOPER
Adjutant and Inspector General

Headquarters, Army of Northern Virginia
December 3, 1863

General:

My letter of the 2d instant will have informed you of the condition of affairs up to the preceding night. Preferring to receive an attack rather than assume the offensive, our army remained in its position all day on the 1st instant. During the day information was received that the 6th Army Corps under General [John] Sedgwick had advanced on the Plank road, and appearances indicated that the enemy was massing to our right. This was rendered more probable by the withdrawal of some batteries and the retiring of his pickets in front of our extreme left.

Anderson's and Wilcox's divisions were withdrawn from the trenches at 3 a.m. on the 2d and moved to our right with a view to make an attack in that quarter. As soon as it became light enough to distinguish objects, it was discovered that the enemy's pickets along our entire line had retired, and our skirmishers were sent forward to ascertain his position. Finding that he had retired from our front, the army was put in motion, Hill's corps on the Plank road and Early's on the old turnpike. General Stuart, with Hampton's division of cavalry, was directed to sweep around on our right as far as Chancellorsville, and should he not find the enemy pursuing the roads leading to Spotsylvania to press down to the Rapidan.

It was soon discovered that a portion of the enemy's force had taken the road to Germanna and the other portion towards Ely's Ford. Genl Hill's corps was halted after advancing eight miles on the Plank road. General Early and General Stuart proceeded as far as Germanna Ford, and discovered that the enemy's whole force had recrossed the Rapidan and proceeded to their former position on the Rappahannock. The army was then returned to its former lines on the Rapidan.

The movement of General Meade, and all the reports received as to his intention, led me to believe that he would attack, and I desired to have the advantage that such an attempt on his part would afford.

After awaiting his advance until Tuesday evening, preparations were made to attack him on Wednesday morning. This was prevented by his retreat. The dense forest which covers the scene of operations prevented our discovering his withdrawal until he was beyond pursuit.

Very respectfully, your obt servt

R. E. Lee
General

592   To HIS WIFE
Richmond, Virginia

Camp, Rapidan
December 4, 1863

My Dear Mary:
I received when the army was in line of battle your letter of the 28th ultimo & as Custis proposes to return to Richmond tomorrow I must endeavour to write a few lines in reply. You will probably have seen that Genl Meade has retired to his old position on the Rappahannock without giving us battle. I had expected from his movements & all that I had heard that it was his intention to do so, & after the first day, when I thought it necessary to skirmish pretty sharply with him on both flanks to ascertain his views, I waited patiently his attack. Tuesday however I thought he had changed his mind & that night made preparations to move around his left next morning & attack him. But when day dawned he was no where to be seen. He had commenced to withdraw at dark Tuesday evening. We pursued to the Rapidan, but he was over. Owing to the nature of the ground it was to our advantage to receive rather than to make the attack, & as he about doubled us in numbers, I wished to have that advantage. I am greatly disappointed at his getting off with so little damage, but we do not know what is best for us, & I believe a kind God has ordered all things for our good. I must leave to Custis to tell you

of all events. I send you a letter from Judge Field, which I also received when in line of battle. I have kept the salve & will try it, but you will see the prescription & can have it made & try it. I hope it will relieve us both. I am much better, though still stiff & painful. I fear I will never be better & must be content. I received the box from Mrs. Heiskell when we returned to Culpeper. It was very acceptable & contained all things a man might want in the field. It was sent to Col Corley for whom half the box was intended & Bryan divided it with him. I hope it was done fairly. Col Corley promised to return all the clothes, &c., with my thanks for her kind consideration. Mr. Heiskell was in western Virginia with Col Corley, & it was on that account I suppose I came in for part of his favours. Do ask Mrs. Atkinson to express my gratitude to Mrs. H. I am glad to hear there is a prospect of getting socks & gloves for the soldiers. Tell all the young girls to set to work industriously, knit night & day. None of them shall see their sweethearts till they are forth coming. So Misses Norvell & Silby must listen themselves. Send Beverly Coderise's coat, &c., to me through Col Corley, as you send the socks. They will come safely. I have not seen him for sometime. As to my jackets get any pattern to fit a big old man & cut them large. Measure Custis & give an extra size or two. Good bye with love to the girls & Charlotte.

I am most truly & affly yours

R. E. LEE

593   To GENERAL SAMUEL COOPER
Adjutant and Inspector General

BATTLE REPORT OF MINE RUN

Headquarters, Army of Northern Virginia
April 27, 1864

General:

I have the honor to submit a report of the operations of this army on the occasion of the advance of the Federal forces under Major General Meade in November, 1863.

After its return from Culpeper as previously reported, the army occupied the line of the Rapidan without interruption until the 26th November. The enemy was encamped in the vicinity of Culpeper Court House and between that place and the Rappahannock.

On the day last mentioned, large bodies of troops were observed moving towards the lower fords of the Rapidan, and at a later hour intelligence was received that the enemy had crossed that river in force at

Ely's, Culpeper Mine, Germanna, and Jacobs' Fords. The country in that vicinity was unfavorable for observation, being almost an unbroken forest, and it could not be discovered whether it was the design of the Federal commander to advance towards Richmond or move up the Rapidan upon our right flank. The army was withdrawn from its lines during the night of the 26th and put in motion with the intention of falling upon his flank and rear should he attempt the first mentioned movement, or giving battle should he essay the execution of the second.

Lieut General Ewell being absent on account of sickness, his corps was placed under the command of Major General Early, who was directed to move by the old Turnpike and Raccoon Ford roads to Locust Grove. Hill's corps marched down the Plank road. Hampton's division of cavalry accompanied by General Stuart preceded the advance of the main body.

The defence of our line on the Rapidan was entrusted to Fitz Lee's cavalry division.

During the forenoon of the 27th, the cavalry in front reported the enemy advancing up the Turnpike and Plank road, but as it was supposed that it might be only a force thrown out to cover the movement of the main body towards Fredericksburg, the march of the troops was continued.

About a mile and a half east of Mine Run, General Hill's leading division, under General Heth, met the cavalry slowly retiring before the enemy. A brigade of infantry was deployed to support the cavalry, and after a brisk skirmish the progress of the enemy was arrested.

In the meantime Early's division under General [Harry T.] Hays advanced on the old Turnpike to within less than a mile of Locust Grove, and discovered that the enemy's infantry already occupied that place. General Rodes who had marched by Zoar Church into the Raccoon Ford road, came up soon afterwards and took position on the left of Hays. Sharp skirmishing ensued, but as the enemy had an advantageous position, and the density of the woods rendered it impossible to ascertain his strength, it was deemed best to defer the attack until the arrival of General [Edward] Johnson's division.

General Johnson marched on the Raccoon Ford road by Bartlett's Mill, and the head of his column had nearly reached General Rodes when, at a point less than two miles from the mill, his ambulance train moving in advance of the rear brigade, under General G. H. Steuart, was fired into from the left of the road. General Steuart immediately formed his command and took measures to protect the train. Upon advancing his skirmishers it was discovered that the attacking party consisted of infantry, apparently in considerable force.

General Johnson countermarched the other brigades of his division and formed them on the right of General Steuart. After skirmishing for some time, about 4 p.m. he ordered a general advance, and after a sharp engagement the enemy was driven back through the woods and pursued into an open field beyond.

The density of the forest rendered it impossible for the troops to preserve their line unbroken in the advance and prevented the proper concert of action. General Johnson was therefore unable to follow up his success, the numbers of the enemy greatly exceeding his own, and reformed his troops on the edge of the open ground, which position they continued to hold until dark.

The force of the enemy encountered by General Johnson, consisting, as was afterwards ascertained, of one army corps and part of another, crossed the Rapidan at Jacobs' Ford, and marched thence by a road which enters the Raccoon Ford road near Payne's Farm where the action took place. The usual precautions had been taken by General Johnson to guard against a flank attack, but owing to the character of the country, the presence of the enemy was not discovered until his skirmishers fired upon the ambulance train.

The ground was unfavorable for the use of artillery, but sections of [Captains John C.] Carpenter's and [William F.] Dement's batteries participated in the engagement and rendered efficient and valuable service.

Our total loss in killed, wounded, and missing was five hundred and forty-five. Lieut Colonel [Simeon T.] Walton, commanding 23rd Virginia Regiment, was killed, and Colonel Raleigh T. Colston, commanding 2d Virginia Regiment, severely wounded, while leading their respective commands with conspicuous gallantry. Colonel Colston has since died. General Johnson mentions with well merited praise the conduct of those brave and lamented officers.

The promptness with which this unexpected attack was met and repulsed reflects great credit upon General Johnson and the officers and men of his division.

While these events were transpiring, information was received from Brigadier General [Thomas L.] Rosser, whose brigade of cavalry was guarding the roads leading from Ely's and Germanna Fords to Fredericksburg, that the whole Federal Army, after crossing the Rapidan, had moved up the river in the direction of Orange Court House. General Rosser had attacked a train of wagons near Wilderness Tavern and captured a large number, some of which he brought off, and destroyed the remainder. He also secured two hundred and eighty mules & one hundred and fifty prisoners.

Preparations were made to meet the attack which this information led us to expect, but as the enemy did not advance, the army was withdrawn during the night to the west side of Mine Run, where it took up a more favorable position and proceeded to strengthen it with entrenchments. The next day the enemy appeared on the opposite side of the creek immediately in our front, and skirmishing took place along the whole line, but no attack was made. On the night of the 28th General Stuart was ordered with Hampton's cavalry to endeavor to gain the rear of the enemy and ascertain his purpose. He penetrated as far as Parker's Shop on the Plank road, where he attacked and defeated a body of Federal cavalry, but the pursuit was arrested by the intelligence that the movements of the enemy indicated that a general engagement was imminent. He resumed his position on our right flank during the night, having captured more than one hundred prisoners and a quantity of military stores.

On the morning of the 29th a heavy fire of artillery was opened upon our lines, which was supposed to be preparatory to a general assault, a large force having been previously concentrated opposite our right. Our batteries responded occasionally, but the artillery fire ceased in about an hour, and nothing but the usual skirmishing took place during the remainder of the day.

Believing that the enemy would not abandon an enterprise undertaken with so great a display of force without giving battle, I was unwilling to lose the advantage of our position, and awaited the development of his plans until the night of the 1st December, but finding that he hesitated to bring on an engagement, determined to move against him on the following morning. The troops were disposed for the purpose before dawn, but as soon as it became light enough to distinguish objects, his pickets were found to have disappeared, and on advancing our skirmishers it was discovered that his whole army had retreated under cover of the night.

Pursuit was immediately commenced, but on arriving near the river it was found that the Federal Army had recrossed at Germanna, Culpeper Mine, and Ely's Fords. The withdrawal had no doubt begun the previous afternoon, but was concealed by the dense forest through which the roads of retreat lay. The same cause prevented the efficient use of our cavalry, and rendered it necessary for the infantry to pursue with caution. About five hundred prisoners fell into our hands.

Our casualties were slight with exception of those sustained by Johnson's division in the action at Payne's Farm. They are stated in the accompanying returns. Among them were several valuable officers whose names are appropriately mentioned in the reports of their superiors.

The army returned to its former position on the Rapidan.

The conduct of both officers and men throughout these operations deserves the highest commendation. The promptness with which they marched to meet the enemy, their uncomplaining fortitude while lying in line of battle for five days exposed without shelter to a drenching storm, followed by intense cold, and their steadiness and cheerful resolution in anticipation of an attack, could not have been excelled.

As has been already stated, the country was very unfavorable for cavalry. Hampton's division rendered good service in guarding our right flank. Fitz Lee's division repulsed several efforts of the Federal cavalry under General [Judson] Kilpatrick to gain the south side of the Rapidan at Raccoon and Morton's Fords, in rear of our left.

I cannot conclude without alluding to the wanton destruction of the property of citizens by the enemy. Houses were torn down or rendered uninhabitable, furniture and farming implements broken or destroyed, and many families, most of them in humble circumstances, stripped of all they possessed and left without shelter and without food. I have never witnessed on any previous occasion such entire disregard of the usages of civilized warfare and the dictates of humanity.

I forward herewith the reports of corps, division, and other commanders, and a map of the scene of operations.

Very respectfully, your obt servt

R. E. LEE
Genl

CHAPTER THIRTEEN

Prelude to Campaign of 1864

"The great effort of the enemy . . . will be made in Virginia"

THE LAST FIGHTING of 1863 was barely finished when General Lee was called upon personally to help save the wrecked command in the West. In November, after Davis overruled those general officers in the Army of Tennessee who passed a resolution on Bragg's incompetence, Bragg let the President down by his failures at Missionary Ridge and Lookout Mountain (November 23-25), and, when those decisive Federal victories opened the way to Atlanta, Bragg resigned on November 30. Davis, having removed one third of the infantry and the senior corps commander from the Army of Northern Virginia, then sought to send its commanding general to the West. On December 9, Lee went to Richmond for conferences with the President that lasted until the 21st. According to a letter the President wrote the general in August, 1863, he continued to regard Lee as his "adviser" and "expediter." "I need your counsel," he wrote. "You were required in the field and I deprived myself of the support you gave me here." In December Davis believed another field required Lee's services.

Lee recognized the personal nature of the force which called itself "Lee's army." It was the Army of Northern Virginia only in the records; the men were fighting for Lee. He had built the army, its structure and prestige, given the army the character and cohesiveness and pride with which the men identified themselves. Without him the depleted force would have lost its effectiveness. In Richmond he persuaded the President to send West a general who did not at present command an army: he suggested Beauregard but Davis appointed his ancient enemy, Joseph E. Johnston. Lee returned to Orange to hold his starving army together through the winter, to rebuild morale where it had faded by reorganizing units of his veterans, and to try to increase its declining manpower.

On the wastefulness of dispersing his veteran units, he wrote General Elzey at Richmond in February, "The troops of this army, independent of Longstreet's corps, are scattered from North Carolina to the Valley, which, besides being deleterious to discipline, is injurious to the service and hazardous to the country." Among the veterans at hand he made many shifts in brigadier-generals, largely necessitated by the losses in general officers at Gettysburg. In division command the only change was Wilcox, in Hill's corps, promoted to major-general to replace Pender, killed at Gettysburg. In the cavalry, to provide incentive to promising men, the two divisions of three brigades each were changed to three divisions of two brigades each, with a seventh brigade on paper — the troops for which Lee could not pry out of their innocuous employment in South Carolina.

To increase effectiveness in artillery command, when the want of horses caused him to abandon a number of his guns, he gave up Armistead Long from his staff to become commander of Second Corps artillery. Porter Alexander was given permanent command of First Corps artillery and Lindsay Walker continued with the Third. As Chilton shifted to the adjutant-general's office (in March) shortly after Lee relinquished Long, his personal staff was reduced to three — Venable, Marshall and Walter Taylor — though he drew upon the services of a number of specialists in a larger, informal staff.

In his struggle to victual and equip his men, he corresponded to no purpose with Commissary-General Northrop, a bureaucrat whose inefficiency was accompanied by overpowering self-righteousness, but received all cooperation within the limitations of Quartermaster-General Lawton, one of his former brigadiers. To strengthen the Western frontier from the Valley southwest to Saltville, and to develop coordinating forces on whom he could depend, Lee wrote continuously to Imboden and Samuel Jones. (As Lee's voluminous correspondence with Jones was designed to inspire him, and as it failed of that purpose, it has not been reproduced.) Lee also wrote in detail about the wasteland of command in coastal North Carolina, no longer officially under his authority.

In September, 1863, D. H. Hill, the interim Department commander, had been returned to the field and fought with Bragg at Chickamauga. As he was one of the officers (Longstreet and Forrest were among others) who protested at Bragg's continuation in command, Harvey Hill got into the President's black book and was without command. Davis appointed Bragg as his new "Military Adviser" and he more or less directed the operations on the Carolina coast. Pickett's performance in North Carolina had not satisfied Bragg, and Pickett, removed from the field, was given titular command of a Department with headquarters and no troops at Petersburg. Lee's concern was caused by the employment of troops detached from his army (four of Pickett's scattered brigades and Hoke's brigade from the Second Corps) who, as with Longstreet the year before at Suffolk, might be engaged in peripheral action when he needed them.

On February 22, he went again for conferences in Richmond — which this time included Bragg — to discuss the coming campaign with special reference to the West. A growing apprehension and discouragement in the Confederacy was expressed in a rather desperate demand for offensives to replace the defensive policy, and Davis was sufficiently infected by the air of desperation to direct Joe Johnston to assume an offensive with the bedraggled Army of Tennessee. Naturally defensive-minded (called, by some, "Retreating Joe"), Johnston supported his native aversion to offensive warfare by reasonable requests for manpower, equipment and supplies necessary to undertake such a movement. At the same time Longstreet, whose First Corps survivors were freezing in the mountains where he conducted a futile siege of Knoxville, began to send in fanciful plans for going on the offensive.

Lee was recalled from the conferences over these ill-considered schemes by Dahlgren's cavalry raid on Richmond, which, though doing little damage, created considerable confusion. Through March and April he wrote some of his most powerful letters, revealing his grasp of the enemy's intentions across the whole Confederate front and providing in detail the specific countermeasures. In Lee's broadly comprehensive April 15th letter to Davis, he outlines the desired strategy for his army, in meeting the enemy's total plans in the East, as well as suggesting the strategic employment of troops throughout the Confederacy; also he states the conditions necessary for the success of his strategy and predicts (accurately) the results of failure to establish those conditions. His correspondence, extremely illuminating of his mental processes in shifting and weighing information, availed nothing toward the end of eliminating scattered dispersal in order to concentrate against the enemy's major objectives — either on his front or in the Confederate West.

In March, shortly after U. S. Grant was made general-in-chief of the Federal armies, he attached himself personally to the Army of the Potomac. Lee interpreted this to mean that the enemy's major offensive would be directed at Richmond. He also predicted that Grant would direct secondary offensive operations in Virginia, the most menacing of which would come at the south side of the James River — the vulnerable spot in all of Lee's calculations. He predicted, also correctly, that the secondary army, transported up the James by the United States Navy, would strike between Richmond and Petersburg, the junction point of the capital with the Lower South. This course would threaten Drewry's Bluff from the land side and, if the river fort fell, Richmond would be exposed from the south.

Against this threat, General Lee suggested that the troops not needed in the Carolinas be hurried to the Petersburg area and placed under the command of Beauregard, as the Charleston defenses could function without the presence of a full general. Instead, Beauregard was appointed commander of a formalized Department from the James to Wilmington, with headquarters at Weldon, North Carolina, and no troops were sent to Petersburg, where Pickett's status was reduced from titular department head to district commander. This not only left the back door to Richmond unprotected, but kept general officers and brigades of Lee's army engaged in the siege of New Berne at the time when Grant was preparing to mount his offensive. Lee's correspondence shows the extent to which Davis, with all his respect for Lee, had pre-empted control of Lee's army and the areas of his responsibility. As the campaign approached, Lee literally begged for the return of the troops belonging to his army — Robert Hoke, newly promoted to major-general and Hoke's old brigade, Pickett's four brigades, and R. D. Johnston's brigade detached to guard Hanover Junction. None came.

After a struggle, Lee did effect the return of Longstreet and his two divisions (at the outside, 10,000 total) from their futilities in the Tennessee mountains. The men were in hard case and the corps had been shaken by Longstreet's feuds with general officers while he exercised independent command. McLaws insisted on a court-martial hearing of the charges against him and, though cleared of all save a couple of technicalities, he was transferred out of the army by Lee in the interests of accord. Kershaw succeeded him in division command. Robertson, commander of Hood's old brigade, was dismissed without a hearing but Law, a brigade commander in Hood's old division, fought Longstreet skillfully and deviously all the way to Davis; he not only was reinstated but caused Longstreet to receive a stiff rebuke from the war office and the President.

Longstreet held a grudge against Law because he stood in the way of Longstreet's appointing Micah Jenkins to succeed to the command of Hood's division, when Hood was promoted to lieutenant-general in the Army of Tennessee. The War Department settled the controversy by appointing Field to succeed Hood, and Longstreet got into deeper trouble with the administration by trying to keep Field out of his corps. At least Longstreet's difficulties seemed to have cured him of ambition for independent command, and he returned to Lee without evidencing any desires to impose his strategy on the commanding general.

With Longstreet's two divisions, Lee gathered about 45,000 infantry south of the Rapidan — approximately 57,000 troops with cavalry and artillery, not all of which was present. Out of an "aggregate present for duty" of 127,000, Grant prepared to advance with 75,000 infantry plus something over 20,000 more coming up with Burnside. By enemy infantry and by the enemy's forces of all arms, Lee would be outnumbered a little better than two-to-one when he met the new commander-in-chief.

594   To JEFFERSON DAVIS
                           Richmond, Virginia

Headquarters, Army of Northern Virginia
December 3, 1863

Mr. President:

I have considered with some anxiety the condition of affairs in Georgia & Tennessee. My knowledge of events has been principally derived from the public papers and the impressions I have received may be erroneous, but there appears to me to be grounds to apprehend that the enemy may penetrate Georgia and get possession of our depots of provisions and important manufactories. I see it stated that Genl Bragg has been relieved from command, and that Genl Hardee is only acting until another commander shall be assigned to that army. I know the difficulties that surround this subject, but if Genl Beauregard is considered suitable for the position, I think he can be replaced at Charleston by Genl Gilmer. More force, in my opinion, is required in Georgia, and it can only be had, so far as I know, from Mississippi, Mobile, and the Department of South Carolina, Georgia, and Florida. The occupation of Cleveland [Tennessee] by the enemy cuts off Genl Longstreet from his base, and unless he succeeds quickly in defeating Genl Burnside, he will have to retire either into Virginia or North Carolina. I see no reason why Genl Sam Jones should not be ordered to advance to his support, or at least to divert the attention of the column that is said to be moving on Charleston, Tennessee.

I have ventured to trouble Your Excellency with these suggestions as I know how much your attention is occupied with the general affairs of the country, especially as the session of Congress approaches. I think that every effort should be made to concentrate as large a force as possible under the best commander to insure the discomfiture of Grant's army. To do this and gain the great advantage that would accrue from it, the safety of points practically less important than those endangered by his army must be hazarded.

Upon the defence of the country threatened by Genl Grant depends the safety of the points now held by us on the Atlantic, and they are in as great danger from his successful advance as by the attacks to which they are at present directly subjected.

Very respectfully, your obt servt

R. E. LEE
Genl

595 To JEFFERSON DAVIS
Richmond, Virginia

Headquarters, Army of Northern Virginia
Rapidan
December 7, 1863

Mr. President:

I have had the honor to receive your dispatch, inquiring whether I could go to Dalton [Georgia]. I can if desired, but of the expediency of the measure you can judge better than I can. Unless it is intended that I should take permanent command, I can see no good that will result, even if in that event any could be accomplished. I also fear that I would not receive cordial cooperation, & I think it necessary if I am withdrawn from here that a commander for this army be sent to it. Genl Ewell's condition I fear is too feeble to undergo the fatigue and labor incident to the position. I hope Your Excellency will not suppose that I am offering any obstacles to any measure you may think necessary. I only seek to give you the opportunity to form your opinion after a full consideration of the subject. I have not that confidence either in my strength or ability as would lead me of my own option to undertake the command in question.

I am with great respect, your obt servt

R. E. LEE
Genl

596 To GENERAL J. E. B. STUART
Commanding Cavalry

Camp
December 9, 1863

General:

I am called to Richmond this morning by the President. I presume the rest will follow. My heart and thought will always be with this army. Please look out for positions for the cavalry, where they can be

foraged, and be not too far away from the field of operations. I have set
Colonel Corley to work. I expect to be back.

Very truly

R. E. Lee

597   COLONEL W. H. TAYLOR TO GENERAL
RICHARD S. EWELL
Commanding Second Corps

December 14, 1863

8 A.M.

General:

Upon the receipt of the latest intelligence from the Valley last
night, Maj Genl Fitz Lee was ordered with two brigades of cavalry to
the Valley. Though I only directed General Stuart to send a brigade, so
your wishes in this respect were complied with, I also instructed
General Hill to have a brigade in readiness to move this morning, and
directed the quartermasters at Orange and Gordonsville to be prepared
to transport it. Since the receipt of yours of 4 this morning, I have ordered
the movement of the brigade of infantry, and directed the Quartermaster
Department to arrange the transportation with as little delay as practicable. I have informed the officer in command in the Valley of these movements. Colonel [Edward] Willis is kept informed. I sent him a courier
on yesterday, giving notice of the movements of the enemy up to the
date of my dispatch. He was then near Liberty Mills. I also requested
General Stuart to keep him promptly advised of all movements. Nothing
from the Valley this morning. It is now 9 o'clock. General Hill said last
night he would send General Walker's brigade, that being the most
convenient.

Very respectfully

W. H. Taylor

Assistant Adjutant General

598   To HIS WIFE
Richmond, Virginia

Camp

December 22, 1863

I reached here safely dear Mary yesterday, & though the commencement of my journey seemed unpropitious, having been detained at the

depot at Richmond till after 8 a.m., we got into Orange earlier than usual. I thought a great deal of you during the journey & grieved over your suffering condition. May God grant you speedy alleviation of your pain & restore you to comfort & ease! I fear your proposed change of residence will not bring to you any additional relief, but on the contrary more care, whatever advantages it may give to others. If you could take Custis' room, so far as a dormitory is concerned, it would be very comfortable. But then you would have the inconvenience of the stairs. The back room down stairs would have some advantages. But I hope you will select one most agreable to you irrespective of other considerations. I find all well here so far. All anxious to get away. I can gratify some. I hope you will all have a happy Xmas & that your hearts will expand in love & gratitude to our glorious Creator & Saviour for all His mercies & benefits, more especially for His salvation to which He has opened us a door. I shall be with you in mind though absent in body. May God have you all in His holy keeping!

Truly & sincerely yours

R. E. Lee

599   To HIS WIFE
Richmond, Virginia

Orange
Xmas night, 1863

I am filled with sadness dear Mary at the intelligence conveyed in your letter of last evening. I have been oppressed with sorrowful forebodings since parting with Charlotte. She seemed to me stricken with a prostration I could not understand. Dear child she promised to be better the next morning & I wrote to her in a cheerful & hopeful mood which I could not feel. That you may know my sorrow in all its breadth & depth, as far as I know my own heart, I feel for her all the love I bear Fitzhugh. That is very great. I pray she may be spared to us. Yet God's will be done. The blow so grievous to us is intended I believe in mercy to her. She was so devoted to Fitzhugh. Seemed so bound up in him, that apparently she thought of & cared for nothing else. They seemed so united, that I loved them as one person. I would go down tomorrow, but from your letter have no hope of finding her alive, or of being able to do anything for her. I feel that all will be done for her that human power can, & oh I pray that our Merciful Father will yet spare her, or gently take her to Himself! Telegraph me if I can yet reach there in time.

I received today the two boxes you sent. Distributed the socks & am much obliged for the turkey.

Truly & affly
R. E. LEE

600   To HIS WIFE
                    Richmond, Virginia

Sunday Morning
December 27, 1863

Custis' despatch which I received last night, demolished all the hopes in which I had been indulging during the day of dear Charlotte's recovery. It has pleased God to take from us one exceedingly dear to us & we must be resigned to His holy will. She I trust will enjoy peace & happiness forever, while we must patiently struggle on under all the ills that may be in store for us. What a glorious thought it is that she has joined her little cherubs & our angel Annie in Heaven! Thus dear Mary is link by link of the strong chain broken that binds us to earth, & smooths our passage to another world. Oh that we may at last unite in that haven of rest, where trouble & sorrow never enters, to join in the everlasting chorus of praise & glory to our Lord & Saviour! I grieve for our lost darling as a father can only grieve for a daughter. I loved her with a father's love, & my sorrow is heightened by the thought of the anguish her death will cause our dear son, & the poignancy it will give to the bars of his prison. May God in His mercy enable him to bear the blow He has so suddenly dealt, & sanctify it to his everlasting happiness!

As I can now be of no service to our dear child, & do not know whether I could reach Richmond in time for the funeral, I must leave the payment of the last offices of friendship to those around her, & bear my sorrow in silence alone. May God have mercy upon us all & have you in His holy keeping.

Truly & devotedly yours
R. E. LEE

601   To HIS WIFE
                    Richmond, Virginia

Camp, Orange
December 29, 1863

I received tonight dear Mary your letter of yesterday, & am greatly relieved at learning that our sweet Charlotte suffered so little in her last moments. I am truly grateful to our Merciful God that He removed her from us so gently, & gave to us a sign, in the clasping of her hands in silent prayer, that He was taking her to Himself. I grieve only for ourselves, & particularly for our dear son, whose sorrow under the circumstances will be inexpressibly grievous. I now long to see him more & more & wish I could communicate with him without affording to his jailors the opportunity of rejoicing in his misery. I fear your letters were not received at Hickory Hill. They would have met with some response. Cousin Anne's heart is too loving not to have replied. Although Uncle Williams loved her very dearly, he would have known he could be of no service to her, & might have preferred to be alone in his grief. I am glad to hear your sufferings are less. May God guard & protect you all. Do not send me anything more. We have a plenty of everything & one turkey left. I want less & less every day. Give much love to my dear sons & daughters. Ask Carrie to send the accompanying letter to Margaret when she has an opportunity. It is to tell her of the safe arrival of some things she sent the soldiers.

Very truly & affly yours

R. E. LEE

602   To JEFFERSON DAVIS
Richmond, Virginia

Headquarters
January 2, 1864

Mr. President:

The time is at hand when if an attempt can be made to capture the enemy's forces at New Berne it should be done. I can now spare troops for the purpose, which will not be the case as spring approaches. If I have been correctly informed, a brigade from this army, with [General Seth M.] Barton's brigade (Pickett's division), now near Kinston [North Carolina] will be sufficient if the attack can be secretly & suddenly made. New Berne is defended on the land side by a line of entrenchments from the Neuse to the Trent [Rivers]. A redoubt near the Trent protects that flank, while three or four gunboats are relied upon to defend the flank on the Neuse. The garrison has been so long unmolested & experiences such a feeling of security that it is represented as careless. The gunboats are small & indifferent, & do not keep up a head of steam. A bold party could descend the Neuse in boats at night, capture the gunboats, & drive the enemy by their aid from the works on that side of the river, while a force should attack them in front. A large amount of provisions & other supplies are said to be at New Berne, which are much wanted for this army, besides much that is reported in the country that will thus be rendered accessible to us. The gunboats, aided by the iron clads building on the Neuse & Roanoke, would clear the waters of the enemy & capture their transports, which could be used for transportation. I have not heard what progress is making in the completion of the iron clads or when they will be ready for service. A bold naval officer will be required for the boat expedition, with suitable men & officers to man the boats & serve the gunboats when captured. Can they be had? I have sent Genl Early with two brigades of infantry & two brigades of cavalry, under Fitz Lee, to Hardy & Hampshire Counties to endeavour to get out some cattle that are reported within the enemy's lines. But the weather has been so unfavourable that I fear he will not meet with much success. The heavy rain storm will swell all the streams beyond fording, & the cold weather & snow in the mountains will present other obstacles. Many of the infantry are without shoes, & the cavalry worn down by their pursuit of [General William W.] Averell. We are now issuing to the troops a fourth of a pound of salt meat, & have only three days' supply at that rate. Two droves of cattle from the West that were reported to be for this army have, I am told, been directed to Richmond. I can learn of no supply of meat on the road to the army, & fear I shall be unable to retain it in the field.

I am with great respect, your obt servt

R. E. LEE
Genl

603   To COLONEL LUCIUS B. NORTHROP
Commissary General, Richmond, Virginia

Headquarters, Army of Northern Virginia
January 5, 1864

Colonel:

Your letter of the 7th ultimo reached here during my absence in Richmond and I have not been able to reply to it since my return until now.

I regret very much to learn that the supply of beef for the Army is so nearly exhausted. I have endeavored since first taking command to collect for its use all the provisions I could, and am still making every effort in my power to gather subsistence in front of our line of operations. No beef has been issued to the Cavalry Corps by the Chief Commissary, that I am aware of, for eighteen months. During that time it has supplied itself, and has now I understand sufficient to last it until the middle of February.

The commissaries of the other corps, under orders of the Chief Commissary of the Army, have purchased all the cattle and provisions within their reach. This is the only relief I can afford to the Subsistence Department in supplying the army. I cannot adopt your suggestions to employ the organization of your bureau to impress provisions. Neither the law or regulations of the War Department in my opinion give me that power. I am authorized by the orders of the Department to impress provisions and forage when occasion required, and I have exercised that power under certain emergencies, through the proper officers of this army, but withdrew it when the necessity passed. You wish me to do it continuously, to accumulate supplies for the troops, and to give orders to that effect to the officers and agents of your bureau, over whom I cannot legitimately exercise any control. As I understand the law and regulations on the subject, you can be empowered to do this by the Secretary of War, and I should consider that I was going beyond my province were I to assume that authority.

I have been mortified to find that when any scarcity existed this was the only army in which it is found necessary to reduce the rations. My information not being official, and derived from officers of other armies, I may be mistaken, but I have never heard of any reduction in the meat ration issued to the troops in and about Richmond, Petersburg, Wilmington, Charleston, Savannah, Mobile, or in the Southwest. Many of these troops are in a measure stationary, less exposed to the inclemency of the weather, and undergoing less hardship and danger than the troops of this army. Many of them could with propriety, I think, be placed on lighter diet than troops in the field, and it may have been the case without coming to my knowledge. I understand that at the present time the army of General Johnston is receiving full rations of meat, bread, rice, molasses, and some whisky, while in this army only a quarter of a pound of salt and three-quarters of a pound of fresh meat are being issued. We have also had in addition half rations of sugar and coffee, one day's issue of fruit, and some lard. These latter articles have been of great advantage. I am always glad to hear of troops receiving abundance of provisions at any point, but think all ought to fare alike, if possible. It stops complaint and produces more contentment.

I have the honor to be with great respect, your obedient servant

R. E. LEE
General

604   To HIS WIFE
                           Richmond, Virginia

                                                            Camp
                                                    January 10, 1864
My dear Mary:
    I hope you have not suffered this cold weather. It has been colder
than I have experienced it since the commencement of the war & ice is
very abundant & strong. We have kept very comfortable however & been
able to maintain good fires which I fear the poor people in town have not
been able to do & that there has been much suffering. I received a present from Miss Kitty Stiles of a pair of knit yarn jackets. They are very
elastic & nice, but I do not know whether they are as warm as the
flannel & have not yet put them on. The box also contained some peaches,
rather quince, & cherries. I send you her note that you may see she still
preserves the recollection of dear Annie. I have also received a present
of a fine mutton, of which I send you a leg, as I think it probable you
cannot get such often in Richmond. I have nothing new to relate. All is
quiet along the lines. Our rations are very scant, & shoes, blankets & overcoats few. I trust we shall be able to get along. The last batch of socks you
sent by Genl Chilton have been distributed & the gloves that were with
them. They were very acceptable as are all you send. You must give
much love to the girls, Custis, & Rob, & present me to all friends. The
messenger is waiting to take the mutton to the cars. I hope it will reach
you safely.

                                               Very truly & affly

                                                    R. E. Lee

605   To GENERAL SAMUEL COOPER
                      Adjutant and Inspector General

                                                        Headquarters
                                                    January 10, 1864
General:
    I have received your letter of the 9th instant in reference to the re-
quest of Genl Longstreet to be relieved from his present command and of
his corps. I do not know the reasons that have induced him to take this
step, but hope they are not such as to make it necessary. I do not know
any one to take his place in either position. I do not think it advantageous

that he and Lt Genl Ewell should exchange corps, believing that each corps would be more effective as at present organized. I cannot therefore recommend their exchange.

I am respectfully, your obt servt

R. E. LEE
Genl

606   To JEFFERSON DAVIS
Richmond, Virginia

Headquarters, Army of Northern Virginia
January 13, 1864

Mr. President:

I have the honor to call your attention to some matters affecting the execution of the conscript law in the case of those who have recently been made liable to it, as well as of others.

There is a strong disposition manifested by the men to enlist in commands serving near their homes. This has been the case in several States, but I refer particularly to western Virginia. I am informed that this disposition is encouraged by the officers, who are naturally desirous to increase their forces. The evils of the system have already been experienced. Men who so enlist conceive that they have a kind of right to serve in certain localities, and are averse to being transferred to others. This was illustrated by the numerous desertions that took place last summer from the commands of Genl [Albert G.] Jenkins, Col [Gabriel C.] Wharton, and Lieut Col [J. Lyle] Clarke when they were brought to this army. But another and greater objection arises from the condition of the commands in western Virginia. I regret to say that from all I can learn, those which would probably be most resorted to by such conscripts in that country as avail themselves of the right to volunteer are not as efficient as they should be, and that the men who may go into them will be to a great extent lost to the general service without a thorough reorganization of these forces. I refer particularly to the commands of General [John D.] Imboden, Col William L. Jackson, and Major General Sam Jones.

My own opportunities of observation have not impressed me favorably with regard to the discipline and efficiency of General Imboden's troops, and the accounts I receive represent the others with few exceptions to be no better.

General Early in a recent letter states that his operations were impeded, and in a measure arrested by his inability to get service from General Imboden's men. He says he could get no information about the enemy because he could make no reconnaissances with those troops. I have been disappointed in my expectations of the services of Genl Sam Jones' command also. I think a reorganization of these troops necessary, and a change of commanders desirable.

The department requires a man of judgment and energy, whose discretion can be depended upon without always awaiting orders. The importance of this command will be augmented in view of the occupation by the enemy of East Tennessee, threatening Southwest Virginia, and demanding able, intelligent, and vigorous management on our part. We can afford to lose nothing by want of discipline and efficiency among the troops.

In the mean time, in view of the facts I have alluded to, I think it desirable that no more men should be permitted to enter the organizations I have mentioned than it is impossible to prevent, as I consider that those who do enlist in them will be taken from the efficient strength of the army in a great measure.

I am told that the repeal of the substitute law will bring in about 1,400 men from the counties of Rockingham and Augusta, besides large numbers from the vicinity of Lynchburg. The former will probably elect to volunteer in Imboden's and the others in Jackson's and Jones' commands.

If nothing more can be done, I earnestly recommend that none be permitted so to enlist beyond the number required to fill up existing organizations in those commands. No increase of them from this source should be allowed, but all the men that can be obtained should be used to fill up the depleted regiments of this army.

What I have said of Virginia is equally applicable to other States. The disposition to enlist in organizations somewhat local in their nature and remote from the principal theatres of hostilities should be checked, and the recruits thrown as far as possible into the more important and active armies, which need them most. I respectfully suggest that the enrolling officers be ordered to see that none volunteer in such commands as I have mentioned beyond the legal complement and that no new companies be formed.

With great respect, your obt svt

R. E. Lee
General

607   To HIS WIFE
                     Richmond, Virginia

                                                        Camp
                                               January 15, 1864

My Dear Mary:
    I take advantage of Col Wood's return to Richmond this morning
to acknowledge your letter of the 9th. The socks arrived safely & have
been distributed. Sis Nannie's eight pairs to the Marylanders & yours to
the most needy. I hope others are being received though I hear of great
want in the army. I am glad you are comfortably arranged in your big
house. I have feared that you would suffer in many respects & would
have preferred that you were more retired. In my own case I would
rather be in a hut with my own family than in a palace with others. The
gentlemen too, I suspect feel the encroachment & it will end in their going to Church Hill or some other eminence. I hope that your new doctor
may, if he cannot relieve, at least assuage your affliction. What is his name
& reputation? I pray that God may bless his labours. As regards myself I
am pretty well & comfortable enough in my tent. I should be more so I
know in a house, but I have none to go to. The people are very kind in
giving me invitations to take a room in their house, but they do not
know what they ask. I of course cannot go alone or be alone, as a crowd
is always around me. You must thank that kind lady for the socks she
sent me. An accident befell a pair I have been wearing & I want one to
replace them. Custis can either send me a pair from my trunk which I
had in use last winter or you can send me the one you have. I gave away
three pairs of the new ones I had here.
    I received a kind letter from Mrs. Jones the other day sending me a
field glass. The glass was lost aboard the *Ceres* coming into Wilmington
with Mr. Ward's baggage. Mrs. Jones was Miss Mary Savage of Savannah
& one of the belles of that city in my younger days. But I will enclose her
letter.

        Give much love to all & believe me very truly & affly yours

                                               R. E. LEE

    P.S. Custis can send the socks by Major Taylor or Col Baldwin

                                               R. E. L.

608 To GENERAL ALEXANDER R. LAWTON
Quartermaster General, Richmond, Virginia

Headquarters, Army of Northern Virginia
January 19, 1864

General:

I desire to state more fully to you my views with reference to procuring a supply of shoes for the army, as I fear that unless great efforts are made, the return of the season of active operations will find a large number of the men barefooted.

It is the opinion of the Quartermaster of this army, that if we were supplied with tools and materials, from one-third to one-half of the army could be shod by the system of brigade shoemakers, already brought to your attention. I am satisfied that this system can be made an important auxiliary of the department, and am anxious that some measure may be devised to procure leather in sufficient quantities. I caused a requisition for the least amount that we could get along with, viz, 37,500 pounds to be made, of which we have only received 8,000 or 9,000 pounds. I hope that the rest will be forthcoming. I think there is leather, and enough, in the country concealed by speculators, of which we never hear until the enemy captures and destroys it. Such was the case at Salem, where General Averell reports that he destroyed cords of it. Such was also the case at Luray and Sperryville. That at Luray was in the hands of a speculator named [Peter B.] Borst, I am informed, who had concealed it there.

If this leather cannot be had in any other way it should be impressed. But before resorting to impressment I would much prefer to resort to the system of exchanging hides for leather. This approaches nearer to a purchase on a specie basis, and would certainly draw out the leather from its concealment, and not have that tendency to repress production, which is one of the worst consequences of impressment. I recommend that the prohibition against such exchanges be removed from this army at least, in view of the vital importance of procuring a prompt supply of leather. The result of the experiment would enable you to judge better of its merits, and afford a better idea of the amount of leather in the country than can be otherwise obtained.

Should you resort to impressment I advise that good men be selected to regulate it. Major [H. M.] Bell, Quartermaster at Staunton, or Captain [R. H.] Phillips, Assistant Quartermaster at the same place, would manage the matter so as to prevent hardships, and get as much as can be expected by that system.

I think that we could be more expeditiously and certainly supplied by exchanges however. Whatever is to be done must be done without delay, as it is indispensable to the efficiency of the army in the approaching campaign. The leather will be placed in charge of active and vigilant officers in the brigades who will see that none is wasted and that all is applied to the use of the troops.

Very respectfully, your obt servt

R. E. LEE
General

609   To JEFFERSON DAVIS
Richmond, Virginia

Headquarters, Army of Northern Virginia
January 19, 1864

Mr. President:

I beg leave to bring your attention again to the abuse of the right of volunteering by conscripts and its effects upon the armies in the field.

In this connection I have the honor to submit a letter from Colonel [John S.] Preston, while commandant of the camp of instruction at Columbia, which he sent me in reply to a letter from me on this subject written recently. It will show Your Excellency the difficulties that have attended an equal distribution of conscripts from the State of South Carolina among the various regiments in different armies. The evil still exists, and unless some change is made in the law or its execution there is little chance of recruiting the reduced regiments from that State which are with the armies most actively engaged.

The evil complained of is greater in South Carolina than in any other State, though it exists to some extent in all. The South Carolina regiments in this army are much reduced by hard service, and it has been found impossible to recruit them, principally, if not entirely, on account of the encouragement given to men to volunteer in regiments engaged in the defense of the Department of South Carolina, Georgia, and Florida, and the measures adopted in that department to retain conscripts.

As showing the effect of this system upon the regiments engaged in local defense, many of which have seen no active service, or very little, I call your attention to the strength of the following cavalry regiments now in the State of South Carolina, as represented by General Hampton: Third Regiment ([Colonel Charles J.] Colcock's), about 1,100 men; Fourth ([Colonel B. Huger] Rutledge's), 1,350; Fifth ([Colonel John] Dunovant's), 1,200; Sixth ([Colonel Hugh K.] Aiken's), 1,000. There are other organizations quite as full.

It is a matter of great moment that the recruits for this army should reach it in full time for the coming campaign, and whatever is to be done to bring them out should be done without delay. As I understand the law, the right to volunteer ceases after enrollment, and I respectfully suggest that it be vigorously enforced, and that no more enrolled men be assigned to the regiments in the department, but that they be equally distributed among those in the armies of Virginia and Tennessee.

If the Department of War has not the power to prevent this practice, I think Congress should at once confer it, as otherwise the service will suffer much. If nothing else can be done, I recommend that some of the full regiments in the Department of South Carolina, &c., be ordered to the field, and the reduced regiments sent to Charleston to recruit. This would at least restrain the disposition to volunteer in the former regiments. It is not the least evil that results from the encouragement given to men to enter organizations intended for local service that they acquire the idea that they have a right to remain in such service and desert when ordered to other points. I have already mentioned to Your Excellency the cases of the commands from western Virginia when ordered to this army last summer, as illustrating this fact, and if the reports with reference to the conduct of some of the troops sent from Charleston to Vicksburg last summer be true, it would appear that the same cause has produced a like effect among them.

With great respect, your obedient servant

R. E. LEE
General

610   To JEFFERSON DAVIS
Richmond, Virginia

Headquarters
January 20, 1864

Mr. President:
I have delayed replying to your letter of the 4th until the time arrived for the execution of the attempt on New Berne. I regret very much that the boats on the Neuse & Roanoke are not completed. With their aid I think success would be certain. Without them, though the place may be captured, the fruits of the expedition will be lessened and our maintenance of the command of the waters in North Carolina uncertain. I think every effort ought be made now to get them into service as soon as possible. You will see by the enclosed letters to Genls Pickett &

[W. H. C.] Whiting the arrangements made for the land operations. The water expedition I am willing to trust to Col [John Taylor] Wood. If he can succeed in capturing the gunboats I think success will be certain, as it was by aid from the water that I expected [General Robert F.] Hoke to be mainly assisted.

In view of the opinion expressed in your letter, I would go to North Carolina myself. But I consider my presence here always necessary, especially now when there is such a struggle to keep the army fed & clothed. Genl Early is still in the Valley. The enemy there has been reinforced by troops from Meade's army, and [by] calling down Genl Averell with his cavalry. I do not know what their intentions are. Report from Genl Early yesterday stated that Averell with his cavalry had started for Moorefield. I will, however, go to North Carolina if you think it necessary. Genl Fitz Lee brought out of Hardy 110 prisoners, 250 horses and mules, 27 wagons, & 460 head of cattle. He captured 40 wagons, but 13 turned over on the mountains & had to be abandoned. He had also to leave behind between one & two hundred head of cattle. The difficulties he encountered were very great, owing to the extreme cold, ice, storms, &c. Nearly all his men were frost-bitten, some badly. Many injured by the falling of their horses. He got within six miles of Paddytown, but could not cross the mountains, owing to the icy road & the smoothness of his horses. He could take with him neither artillery nor wagons.

I am with great respect, your obt servt

R. E. Lee
Genl

611   To GENERAL ALEXANDER R. LAWTON
Quartermaster General, Richmond, Virginia

Headquarters, Army of Northern Virginia
January 20, 1864

General:

I design sending Genl Hoke to North Carolina on special service. About one thousand of his men will leave Gordonsville this evening about 7 p.m. for Richmond, & the remainder, about the same number, tomorrow evening, 21st. I have divided them in order that they might take the down freight trains, so as not to interfere with the supply of provisions for this army. I request that you will forward them to Petersburg to Genl Pickett, who will give them further orders. They can march from Richmond to Petersburg if more convenient, but you will have to forward their camp equipage. I shall direct Genl Pickett, in forwarding them on, to employ the empty trains going south & endeavor not to embarrass the transportation of supplies on the road. Please make arrangements to pass them right through Richmond. Each regiment will be in charge of its commanding officer. Genl Hoke will see to their conveyance from Petersburg.

Very respectfully, your obt servt

R. E. LEE
Genl

612   To COLONEL JOHN T. WOOD
Richmond, Virginia

Headquarters
January 20, 1864

Colonel:

Genl Hoke's brigade will leave to-morrow evening. He himself will precede it to Petersburg to arrange for its transportation & for that of the guns, &c. He carries orders for Genl Pickett. I have endeavored to anticipate everything. If you want any help from the military call upon Genl Pickett, and this will be your warrant. If you get possession of the gunboats turn their guns on the batteries on the Neuse, to facilitate Hoke's advance. Should the place fall, secure all the water transportation you can for the movement of troops and supplies. Urge the completion of the gunboats on the Roanoke & Neuse, that they may become available as soon as possible.

Wishing you all success, & commending you to the care of a merciful Providence,

I am very truly yours

R. E. LEE
Genl

613   To GENERAL WILLIAM H. C. WHITING
Commanding at Wilmington, North Carolina

Headquarters
January 20, 1864

General:

An attack on New Berne is contemplated by the forces under command of Genl Pickett. The time will be between the 25th & 30th instant. I request that you will give all the assistance in your power, especially by threatening simultaneously with your troops north of the Cape Fear the enemy's positions at Moorehead City, &c., so as to prevent their reinforcing New Berne. Genl Pickett will telegraph you the day, by which you will know what is meant. Commit nothing to the telegraph on the subject & keep the matter secret.

> Very respectfully, your obt servt
>
> R. E. LEE
> Genl

614   To GENERAL ROBERT F. HOKE
          Commanding Brigade

> Headquarters
> January 20, 1864

General:

I desire you to proceed tomorrow to Petersburg and arrange with Genl Pickett for the transportation of the troops, guns, &c., to Kinston. Your brigade will follow you in the evening, and I desire that it pass through Richmond at once towards its destination. Upon completing the business concerning which you have oral instructions, you will take some convenient position in North Carolina & recruit your regiments. Communicate with the enrolling officers in the State and endeavor to get conscripts and recruits. To cover your movement you will give out that it is for the purpose of arresting deserters and absentees & recruiting your brigade. On arriving at Petersburg you will deliver to Genl Pickett the orders with which you are charged, and explain to him fully the plan of operations. Report to me your progress in collecting troops for your brigade, your position, &c. See strictly to the comfort and health of your men, as well as to their discipline & instruction.

> I am very resply, your obt servt
>
> R. E. LEE
> Genl

615   To GENERAL SAMUEL JONES
          Commanding Department of Western Virginia

> Headquarters, Army of Northern Virginia
> January 21, 1864

General:

Your letter of the 17th instant is received, and I return my thanks for the cattle and beef you have furnished. Our necessity is great, and I hope they will soon arrive.

It is necessary to make every exertion to procure supplies in order to keep our armies in the field.

Everything in the way of subsistence that can be brought out of the enemy's lines by secret means should be procured. But in addition to this, I wish you to try and ascertain where there are cattle, sheep, hogs, &c., that might be obtained by sending a force after them. If I can learn of these in sufficient quantities to justify an expedition, I will send one, if it is in my power. Be cautious in receiving reports on this subject, as they are apt to be exaggerated or made without accurate observation.

Very respectfully, your obt servt

R. E. LEE
General

616   GENERAL ORDERS, NO. 7

Headquarters, Army of Northern Virginia
January 22, 1864

The commanding general considers it due to the army to state that the temporary reduction of rations has been caused by circumstances beyond the control of those charged with its support.

Its welfare and comfort are the objects of his constant and earnest solicitude, and no effort has been spared to provide for its wants.

It is hoped that the exertions now being made will render the necessity of short duration, but the history of the army has shown that the country can require no sacrifice too great for its patriotic devotion.

Soldiers! You tread with no unequal step the road by which your fathers marched through suffering, privations, and blood, to independence. Continue to emulate in the future, as you have in the past, their valor in arms, their patient endurance of hardships, their high resolve to be free, which no trial could shake, no bribe seduce, no danger appal, and be assured that the just God who crowned their efforts with success will, in His own good time, send down His blessing upon yours.

R. E. LEE
Genl

617   To JAMES A. SEDDON
Secretary of War

Headquarters, Army of Northern Virginia
January 22, 1864

Sir:

A regular supply of provisions to the troops in this army is a matter of great importance. Short rations are having a bad effect upon the men, both morally and physically. Desertions to the enemy are becoming more frequent, and the men cannot continue healthy and vigorous if confined to this spare diet for any length of time. Unless there is a change, I fear the army cannot be kept together. I am granting furloughs at the rate of 16 for each company of one hundred men, and eight for every company of fifty men, and other companies in proportion. This alleviates the matter to some extent, but these furloughs cannot be continued with safety longer than the opening of spring, nor increased without embarrassing the railroads in the country. It is absolutely necessary that the army should be properly fed. The present distribution of the supplies purchased by the Commissary Department does not effect the object. I recommend therefore that the portion of the Army Regulations, No. 1127, which authorizes commissaries to sell to officers for the use of their families be rescinded. I am confident that a large amount of supplies will thus be saved for the subsistence of the Army. At Richmond, Petersburg, Wilmington, Charleston, Savannah, Augusta, Atlanta, Mobile, and a multitude of minor posts, many thousand rations are consumed for officers' families. This regulation was copied from the U. S. Army, where it was intended as a measure of necessity for the subsistence of officers and families on the frontier. The privilege was not designed to be used by those officers stationed in cities, where the market was open to all. The regulation is liable to much abuse, especially at the minor posts, which are very numerous, and causes great dissatisfaction among the people, who assert that their tithes instead of going to the support of the Army are consumed by the families of the officers. The posts are now so attractive that there is a constant effort to create new ones, or to accumulate officers at those already established. The change of the regulation would arrest these abuses and place the officers at posts on a nearer equality with those in the field. They should make the same arrangements to provide for their families which their comrades in the field are compelled to make, with less opportunity.

Very respectfully, your obt servt

R. E. LEE
General

618   To HIS WIFE
Richmond, Virginia

Camp
January 24, 1864

I have received two letters from you dear Mary since I last wrote. That of the 16th accompanying the bag of gloves & socks, & one without date enclosing Martha's letter. The likeness you mentioned did not come & according to your desire I return her letter. I also send one from the Quartermaster of a Louisiana brigade to whom some of your socks were given. The socks I think are more useful than the gloves, though all are appreciated. The latter after the next month will not be of much advantage. I also received the pair of socks from Mrs. Radford. They are very nice, but I have not yet worn them. As regards the people at Romancoke, I much prefer their receiving their free papers & seeking their fortune. It has got to be done & it was in accordance with your father's will. I am unable to attend to them & I am afraid they will suffer or come to some harm. I do not see why they can not be freed & hire themselves out as others do, & think it might be accomplished. I am afraid there is some desire on the part of the community to continue them in slavery, which I must resist. I wish you would talk to Mr. Caskie on the subject & Mr. Frank Smith, whom I see is in Richmond. Mr. Collins can hire some of them out at any rate. It will diminish the number to clothe & feed. How are clothes & shoes to be obtained for them? I wish I could hear of your being benefited by your new doctor. It is pleasing at least to learn that his medicines are agreable & that he holds out hopes. Tell Mildred I am glad to hear that she has taken the socks in hand. I shall expect great numbers now. I have given out that my daughter just from a celebrated school is at work & the expectations of the soldiers are raised. I have read Fitzhugh's letter with much interest. Poor fellow he has nothing to draw his thoughts from his deep sorrow & I fear it will wear him down. You must not trouble yourself to send me anything. I want nothing but a little bread & meat, & that thank God I yet awhile get. Try & take care of yourself & get well. That is the greatest benefit you can do me. I have endeavoured to get to Beverly Turner his shirts & have had them put up & properly directed for some days, but as yet have not found an opportunity. I have had to disperse the cavalry as much as possible to obtain forage for their horses, & it is that which causes the trouble. Provisions for the men too are very scarce, & what with light diet & light clothing I fear they suffer. But still they are cheerful & uncomplaining. I received a report from one division the other day, in which it was stated that over 400 men were barefoot & over 1000 without blankets. Give much love to the girls & Custis. I received yesterday a letter from Rob. He was well.

Very truly & affly yours

R. E. LEE

P.S. Since writing, a courier to the cavalry camp has taken Beverly's jackets to him.

R. E. L.

619   To JEFFERSON DAVIS
                          Richmond, Virginia

                                    Headquarters, Orange Court House
                                              January 27, 1864

Mr. President:
    I have not been unmindful of your request expressed in your let-
ter of the 16th instant, desiring my opinion in reference to the reorganization of the troops in West Virginia. It is the difficulty of this subject
& the importance of selecting a proper commander that has caused my
silence. There are many able officers in this army, & many, I have no
doubt, capable of administering that department, could I designate them.
All have done well in their present positions, but to send them to a new
& difficult field would be an experiment. But so important do I consider
the maintenance of western Virginia to the successful conduct of the
war, that I will relinquish any of them you may select for its command,
though I do not know where to replace them. A change I think is necessary, both for the sake of the officers in that department & the interests
of the country. The duties might be more unsuitable to the health of
Genl Ewell than his present position. I have also great confidence in the
ability of Genls Early, [Robert E.] Rodes, Edward Johnson, & [Cad-
mus M.] Wilcox. Of the brigadiers, I think Genl [John B.] Gordon of
Alabama [Georgia] one of the best. I do not know to what duty Genl
[Simon B.] Buckner is assigned, but of the officers that have been serving
in that department I think Genl [Robert] Ransom is the most prominent. If any of these officers are selected, & they should not answer, they
should be removed & another tried.
    If a proper man can be found I think it would be better to include the
Shenandoah Valley in his command, in order that he might concentrate
the troops where most necessary. A better discipline should be instituted
among the troops themselves. Their local character should be abolished
by law. All deserters from other armies [should] be returned to their
proper commands, & all authority to organize companies either within
or without the enemy's lines be revoked. This authority causes desertion
from the general service. Men go within the enemy's lines, either really
or nominally, with the connivance or invitation of the officers, to enter
these organizations. In a word the system should be such as to organize
the men of the country for its defence & not for their convenience or the
benefit of certain individuals. Unless this is done, the resources of that
country will be lost to us, both its mineral wealth & provisions. The

first step to improvement is an energetic active commander, & no time should be lost in his selection.

I have the honour to be, your obt servt

R. E. LEE
Genl

620 To GENERAL JAMES L. KEMPER
Richmond, Virginia

Headquarters, Army of Northern Virginia
January 29, 1864

General:

I have read with great interest your letter of the 22d instant. Its subject is a matter of constant anxiety and consideration with me. I agree with you in believing that the only safe plan for supporting the army is by calling out the full resources of the country, and I am glad to hear that you think these resources ample. The great difficulty is as to the best mode of making them available. Wholesale impressments will give us present relief, but I fear it will injure our future supplies. It will cause concealment and waste, and deter many farmers from exerting all their efforts in producing full and proper crops. Already I hear of land in Virginia lying idle from this cause. It should be made the interest of every one to labour and contribute all he can, and the proper regulation of the currency will best effect this object. But I think the present law and orders on the subject should be so modified as to authorize the Government to impress when necessary a certain proportion of everything produced in the country. This proportion to depend upon the wants of the Government. It should be made equal and as light as possible, and every care taken to deprive the execution of the measure of all harshness. If it requires all the meat in the country to support the army, it should be had, and I believe this could be accomplished by not only showing its necessity, but that all equally contributed, and that it was faithfully applied. Great dissatisfaction is now occasioned by the conduct of the agents and the belief that much of what is collected for the Government is applied to the support of post garrisons and the families of those there stationed, and that it does not reach the armies in the field. Much could be done I think by judicious agents in whom the people have confidence, and it was with this view that I desired you to take charge of the collection of supplies in Virginia.

The other subject referred to in your letter, I believe, has received the attention of Congress and the Department. The prevention of men called into service selecting local organizations, fixed batteries, &c., so as to avoid service in the field, is very beneficial, and the authority given to the President to change a judge from one military court to another, and to commanding officers to assign officers of the army to duty on those courts when necessary, will be attended with good results. The bill empowering commanding officers when separated from the army to call general courts-martial is also good. I think your proposition to empower all general officers to constitute general courts-martial while operating with an army, would create confusion and embarrassment. But if they were authorized to order courts-martial in their brigades or divisions to take cognizance of the class of offences referred by the Articles of War to garrison or regimental courts-martial it would be beneficial. When separated from the army under this new bill, should it pass, they order general courts-martial. You need not apologize for writing to me on any subject. I only wish I could do anything to advance the good of the service or feel that my views sufficiently approximated the truth to make them of value. Hoping that you will be able to join the army at the opening of the campaign,

I am with great respect, your obt servt

R. E. LEE
General

621   To GENERAL ALEXANDER R. LAWTON
Quartermaster General, Richmond, Virginia

Headquarters, Army of Northern Virginia
January 30, 1864

General:

I have sent two Quartermasters over the ridge to purchase leather for the use of this army. The one in the lower Valley reports that he has found 2,880 sides, all in the hands of original manufacturers except 220 sides, which are in the hands of speculators. The officer in the upper Valley had only visited three tanneries when he wrote, and had only found 400 sides ready for use, but many were in course of preparation. Some of this leather could be bought at Government prices, though it was offered in exchange for rawhides. They asked as high in some cases as $10 a pound for upper and $7 for sole. The Chief Quartermaster of the Army brought me this morning a sample of the shoes recently sent from Richmond. One pair was of Richmond manufacture and another from Columbus, Georgia. They were intended to be fair samples of each lot and were selected with that view. Neither could compare with the shoes made in this army. In the Richmond shoe the face of the leather was turned in. That is, the side of the skin next the animal was turned out, which is contrary to the practice of the best makers and contrary to the arrangement of nature. Without knowing the result of experiment in this matter, I should therefore think it wrong. The leather of the Columbus shoe was not half tanned and the shoe was badly made. The soles of both slight and would not stand a week's march in mud and water. If I could get leather I could set 500 shoemakers to work. The scraps would answer for repairs. I have the workmen and tools. Can you get for me the leather I have referred to above, or authorize the Chief Quartermaster of the Army to do so? I am not in favor of exchanging hides for leather at the rates established by the schedule, viz, 45¢ for the hides and $2.80 for the leather. The old rule in Virginia, and I believe it is still practiced, was to receive one-half of the leather produced by the hides. I do not know whether we could exchange at that rate. The army is in great distress for shoes and clothes. Every inspection report painfully shows it, artillery, cavalry, & infantry. The requisitions sent in are unanswered.

I am with great respect, your obt svt

R. E. Lee
General

622   To GENERAL SAMUEL JONES
Commanding Department of Western Virginia

Headquarters, Army of Northern Virginia
February 2, 1864

General:

I have received your dispatch of the 31st ultimo reporting indications of another advance of the enemy from the Kanawha, and your opinion that there should be some troops on the railroad. I have no troops to send; and the facts had better be reported to the Secretary of War, as your department is beyond the limits of my command. General Averell by the last reports of scouts in the Valley, was at Martinsburg with his cavalry. I think it probable however from the success that has hitherto attended his expeditions, that whenever the weather permits they will be renewed, and every preparation ought now to be made to resist them. The main cause of his success appears to me at this distance to be owing to the terror with which he has inspired the troops. As soon as his approach is announced his progress is neither retarded nor watched. A body of select troops should remain constantly in his front, obstructing his advance and reporting his route, that the troops might be concentrated at the desired point. I know the difficulty of guarding a long line. You cannot have sufficient force at every vulnerable point, whereas the enemy can select whatever point he pleases. But I think the main passes through the mountains could be so fortified as to be held by a small force, and the minor ones so obstructed as to greatly embarrass their passage. If the home guards or local organizations could be got to hold the fortified passes, it would leave all your regular force free to move where necessary. But if you could make your arrangements such as to enable you to attack them at some vulnerable point and throw them on the defensive it would lighten your labor exceedingly.

I have sent Capt [Conway R.] Howard, of the Engineers of this army, to examine the routes through the Allegheny range south of Staunton. He will be joined by some young officers who have been occupied in that country for some time, and I hope a serviceable map of the roads, &c., can be formed by the spring, which may aid in future operations. I would recommend, if not already done, that similar examinations in the ranges west be made. I would recommend also that the people be organized for the defence of the country. That all subject to military duty be brought into the regular service, and that existing organizations be filled rather than new ones created. That all deserters be sent to their proper commands and all cowards punished. I wish I could spare you some troops or aid you in any way, but the enemy in my front is active and increasing and I require all I have.

I am with great respect, your obt servt

R. E. LEE
General

623   To JEFFERSON DAVIS
Richmond, Virginia

Headquarters, Orange Court House
February 3, 1864

Mr. President:
The approach of spring causes me to consider with anxiety the probable action of the enemy and the possible operations of ours in the ensuing campaign. If we could take the initiative & fall upon them un-

expectedly we might derange their plans & embarrass them the whole summer. There are only two points east of the Mississippi where it now appears this could be done. If Longstreet could be strengthened or given greater mobility than he now possesses he might penetrate into Kentucky, where he could support himself, cut Grant's communications so as to compel him at least to detach from Johnston's front, & enable him to take the offensive & regain the ground we have lost. I need not dwell upon the advantages of success in that quarter. The whole is apparent to you. Longstreet can be given greater mobility by supplying him with horses & mules to mount his infantry. He can only be strengthened by detaching from Beauregard's, Johnston's, or this army. If I could draw Longstreet secretly & rapidly to me I might succeed in forcing Genl Meade back to Washington, & exciting sufficient apprehension, at least for their own position, to weaken any movement against ours. All the cavalry would have to be left in Longstreet's present front & [General Samuel] Jones would have to be strengthened. If the first plan is adopted, supplies will have at once to be accumulated at Bristol or along the Virginia & Tennessee Railroad, ostensibly for Longstreet's present use. If the latter, provision must be made at Gordonsville & Richmond for this army. We are not in a condition, & never have been, in my opinion, to invade the enemy's country with a prospect of permanent benefit. But we can alarm & embarrass him to some extent & thus prevent his undertaking anything of magnitude against us. I have ventured to suggest these ideas to Your Excellency for consideration, that, viewing the whole subject with your knowledge of the state of things East & West, you may know whether either is feasible, or what else can better be done. Time is an important element to our success.

I am with great respect, your obt servt

R. E. LEE
Genl

624   To HIS WIFE
Richmond, Virginia

Camp
February 6, 1864

I received dear Mary your letter of the 30th some days ago, & last night your note accompanying a bag of gloves & socks & a box of coffee. Mrs. Devereux sent the coffee to you & not me & I shall have to send it back. It is so long since we have had the foreign bean that we no longer desire it. We have a domestic article which we procure by the bushel, that answers very well. You must keep the good things for yourself. We have a plenty. We have had to reduce our allowance of meat one-half, & some days we have none. But I believe our servants complain more of it than anyone else, & Perry on the strength of it has been taken sick. The gloves & socks are very acceptable & I shall give them out this morning. I am glad you have not been discouraged by the notice of the papers. Your plan is to make more gloves & knit more socks. The socks of Mrs. Shepherd are very nice, but I think it is better to give them to the soldiers than to dispose of them as you suggested. The soldiers are much in need. I have got up some shoes lately, & the socks will be a great addition. Tell Life my reliance is on her. I think I hear her needles rattle as they fly though the meshes. I will return your bag after the socks, &c., are distributed. I am sorry to hear that you have been suffering. I fear you took cold in your rides. I hope & pray your present doctor may be able under the blessing of a Merciful God to relieve you. I have no expectation of going to Richmond. I have as much as I can do here & more too. I am very glad that sweet Annie Leigh is there. I think she ought to come up & see her old cousin. Tell her to remember me to her mama & papa & all at Shirley. I sent my thanks to Mrs. Charles Talcott through Mrs. Randolph. I wish I could get Mrs. Nannie Peyton's donation of socks. They would come in very well now. I am very sorry to hear of the destruction of Brandon & the suffering of the old people at the White House. I can do nothing for either. I send you all the Northern stamps I have & return some that were in the envelope transmitting Mrs. Devereux's letter. Why did you send them to me? I am glad Mrs. G. W. has returned to her husband. I hope she is as pretty as ever. You must remember me to all friends. With much love to the girls, I am very affectly & sincerely yours

R. E. Lee

P.S. I send Mildred some songs.

R. E. L.

625   GENERAL ORDERS, NO. 15

Headquarters, Army of Northern Virginia
February 7, 1864

I.   The attention of the army has already been called to the obligation of a proper observance of the Sabbath, but a sense of its importance, not only as a moral and religious duty, but as contributing to the personal health and well being of the troops, induces the commanding general to repeat the orders on that subject.

He has learned with great pleasure that in many brigades convenient houses of worship have been erected, and earnestly desires that every facility consistent with the requirements of discipline shall be afforded the men to assemble themselves together for the purpose of devotion.

II.   To this end he directs that none but duties strictly necessary shall be required to be performed on Sunday, and that all labor, both of men and animals, which it is practicable to anticipate or postpone, or the immediate performance of which is not essential to the safety, health, or comfort of the army, shall be suspended on that day.

III.   Commanding officers will require the usual inspections on Sunday to be held at such time as not to interfere with the attendance of the men on divine service at the customary hour in the morning.

They also will give their attention to the maintenance of order and quiet around the places of worship, and prohibit anything that may tend to disturb or interrupt religious exercises.

R. E. Lee
Genl

626   To JAMES A. SEDDON
Secretary of War

Headquarters, Army of Northern Virginia
February 8, 1864

Sir:

The present decision of the Department on the provisions of the act of Congress approved April 16, 1862, section 10, seems to be that an officer or private can only be promoted for valour and skill to a vacancy in his own company. This limits the promotions for valour & skill to such an extent that it renders the law almost a dead letter. I would earnestly recommend that if this is the true interpretation of the law that it be modified so as to permit promotions on this account to any company or regiment from the same State, or at least to any company in the regiment to which the private or officer belongs. It is very important to increase the number of these promotions and to render them more certain. In the coming campaign we should use every incentive to acts of daring and skillful and brave conduct on the part of officers and men.

I am very respectfully, your obt servt

R. E. Lee
General

627　　　　　　To GENERAL ARNOLD ELZEY
　　　　　　　　Commanding at Richmond, Virginia

　　　　　　　　　　Headquarters, Army of Northern Virginia
　　　　　　　　　　　　　　　　　February 11, 1864
General:
　　As far as I am able to learn, the expedition up the Peninsula has returned to Yorktown. I therefore know of no benefit that the troops sent
to Hanover Junction & Richmond can now accomplish. They were taken
from their huts, and, without adequate clothing, will suffer exposed to
cold weather like the present. I therefore request that you will order
them back. I recommend that their transportation be so arranged as not
to interfere with that of the supplies for this army.

　　　　　　　　　I am very respectfully, your obt servt

　　　　　　　　　　　　　　　　　R. E. LEE
　　　　　　　　　　　　　　　　　Genl

628　　　　　　　　To HIS WIFE
　　　　　　　　　Richmond, Virginia

　　　　　　　　　　　　Camp, Orange Court House
　　　　　　　　　　　　　　　February 14, 1864

　　I have received dear Mary your letter of the 8th. The opinion of
your doctor gives me great hope. I trust the change he perceives in you
may daily increase & grow into perfect health. I beg you will do all in
your power to aid him & be careful not to expose yourself to cold or
anything injurious. I have not sent back the coffee, but I do not know
what we shall do with it as we have so long been without it, that I fear
it will injure us. I received yesterday from Eliza Beverley of Avend, 13
pairs of very nice socks which she has been preparing during the winter
for the soldiers, & which I distributed immediately. I understand the
ladies in that county have 160 pairs, but cannot get them to us. They
would be a great relief. Unless we can get them soon the advantages will
be lost. Now that you have your yarn I hope your supplies will be coming in. I sent back the bag many days ago. I am glad to hear that some
kind people at the North think of poor Fitzhugh. God grant that he
could be released, but I trust He will permit that in His own good time.
There is a report here, which I presume is not true, that Mrs. G. W. her-

self was sent away. She has so many friends everywhere that I hardly think she would be interfered with, & besides could do them no harm. I have no news to tell you. We are all quiet again. This day last week we were prepared for battle, but I believe the advance of the enemy was only intended to see where we were & whether they could injure us. Their loss in comparison with ours was large. Our scouts report they place their entire loss in killed, wounded, & missing at 1200. But I think that is exaggerated. Our old friend [General John] Sedgwick was in command. In reference to Rob, his company would be a great pleasure & comfort to me & he would be extremely useful to me in various ways. I have written to him to that effect. But I am opposed to officers surrounding themselves with their sons & relatives. It is wrong in principle & in that case the selection for offices would be made from private & social relations, rather than for the public good. Rob's case is at present rather peculiar & I do not think under the circumstances, it would be improper for him to serve with me. I have so told him. There is the same objection to his going with Fitz Lee. He has Lees & relatives enough around him. I should prefer Rob's being in the line, in an independent position, where he could rise by his own merit, & not through the recommendation of his relatives. I expect him here soon, when I can better see what he himself thinks. The young men have no fondness for the society of the old Genl. He is too sombre & heavy for them. God bless you all.

Truly & affly yours

R. E. LEE

629   To JAMES A. SEDDON
                Secretary of War

Headquarters, Army of Northern Virginia
February 15, 1864

Sir:

I have caused lists to be prepared of the absentees from this army, with a view to adopt measures to bring back as many of the able bodied as possible before the opening of the spring campaign. The reports from three divisions have been sent in. Early's division, 3,227; Rodes', 4,102; Johnson's, 4,054; and reported by Medical officers as absent from artillery of 2d Corps, 227; giving a total 11,610. Some of these are prisoners, some deserters, others at home permanently disabled, and others properly detailed. Many of them however are absent at the hospitals, either as patients or nurses, ward masters, clerks, &c. Many more detailed as disabled men in conscript camps and Government workshops. I propose to send a commission, consisting of Surgeon R. J. Breckinridge, Medical Inspector Army of Northern Virginia, Surgeon R. T. Coleman, Ewell's corps, and Surgeon S. W. Langton, Hill's corps, to the hospitals in Virginia, South Carolina, North Carolina, and Georgia, with the authority to send back to the army all of these patients or detailed men who are fit for field service, and to report on those detailed on Government works or in conscript camps, whether their places may not be supplied by men now disabled. In order to give due authority to the commission, I respectfully request that it be appointed by an order from the Department. I hope you will take speedy action in this matter, as it is a matter of extreme importance to get every able bodied man back to the field as soon as we can.

I am with great respect, your obt servt

R. E. LEE
General

630   To JAMES A. SEDDON
Secretary of War

Headquarters, Army of Northern Virginia
February 16, 1864

Sir:

The vital importance of the subject of food for the army and my own anxiety induce me to trouble you with a repetition of a suggestion I made some time since, but about which I have not been favored with the views of the Department. I fear that the discipline of the army is suffering from our present scarcity of supplies, and am sure that you will agree with me in the opinion that there is no sacrifice too great to preserve its efficiency. I had the honor to suggest to you that meat and perhaps other articles of necessity could be obtained by offering cotton and tobacco in exchange for them. This is I believe especially true of the border counties of the State. Those people have no currency, and can only supply their necessities by barter. They will not receive Confederate money, because they can do nothing with it, and it is idle to attempt to get their produce from them by impressment. But I feel confident that they would cheerfully bring forward whatever they have in exchange for cotton and tobacco, particularly the former.

They stand in great need of it for making clothing, and it would also serve as a means for buying what they do not make. I do not consider the objection that some of this cotton would find its way to the enemy as worthy of being weighed against the benefits that we would derive from adequate supplies of articles of prime necessity to the army, for it is the latter we should now be satisfied is our only dependence. A letter recently received from a gentleman in the lower Valley, who has our success much at heart, gives assurance that the experiment will succeed there. He represents the want of cotton yarns as very urgent, and says that if the Government will send 100,000 pounds of those yarns to New Market they can readily be exchanged at the rate of one pound of cotton for two of cured bacon. He says that the supplies of that region are now finding their way to the enemy in exchange for what the people absolutely require and have no other means of purchasing. Interest and their own inclinations will induce them to trade more readily with us, and he thinks the moral effect would be good. His suggestions do not purport to be theoretical, but to be the result of observation of the wants of his neighbors, who appear to need cotton as much as we do meat. I respectfully ask that the experiment be made to the extent above mentioned, and we will then be able to form a better opinion of the merits of the plan, and can extend it or put an end to it as circumstances may direct. I shall be very glad to have your views on the subject, as something must be done, and I can suggest no better plan.

Very respectfully, your obt servt

R. E. LEE
General

631   To GENERAL ARNOLD ELZEY
Commanding at Richmond, Virginia

Headquarters, Army of Northern Virginia
February 18, 1864

General:
    General Hampton has written me of the effects of the late hard march to the Peninsula upon his command. The injury done to the troops morally and physically by movements at this season is so great that I beg leave to call your attention again to the importance of having scouts who can be relied upon, and of weighing well the rumors and reports brought in by pickets and citizens before attaching any importance to them or sending them abroad. Pickets or scouts bringing in false or exaggerated rumors should be severely punished. Nothing so shakes the con-

fidence of the people and the troops, nor has a greater tendency to render those on outpost duty careless and inefficient.

I am very respectfully, your obt svt

R. E. Lee
General

632   To JEFFERSON DAVIS
Richmond, Virginia

Headquarters
February 18, 1864

Mr. President:
I have received the dispatch forwarded to me today from Genl Longstreet, requesting ten thousand men to insure the capture of Knoxville. I have no information of the practicability of the plan. I think it may be assumed that its defences are stronger now than when it was last attacked, & an attempt to capture it by assault would not only be hazardous but attended with great loss of life. To reduce it by approaches would require time &, it seems to me at this distance, render necessary an army sufficient to defeat a relieving force that, now the railroad to Chattanooga has been opened, could be quickly sent from Grant's troops. If a movement could be made to cut off supplies from Knoxville it would draw out the garrison, & this appears to me the wiser course. Could supplies be sent if troops were? For without the former the latter would be unavailing. I wrote today to the Secretary of War suggesting that Pickett's division be sent to him in the spring & that a brigade of Buckner's now at Dalton be returned to its division at once. I see by the Northern papers that Genl [Quincy A.] Gillmore and Admiral [John A.] Dahlgren have gone to Florida, carrying three brigades with them. This reduces the force operating against Charleston. Genl Longstreet is under the impression that Sedgwick's corps has been withdrawn from Meade's army & sent to Knoxville. A division of it was sent to Harper's Ferry at the time of Genl Early's descent upon Petersburg [West Virginia], & a brigade was sent to Johnson's Island when the alarm was spread of a congregation of a force at Point Pelee in Canada. I cannot discover that any other troops have been sent from the Rappahannock, & my instructions to the scouts are to be particularly watchful, both here & on the Baltimore & Ohio Railroad. Still they may be deceived. It is reported in the Northern papers that Longstreet has been reinforced. If a portion of Meade's army is sent west a part of this could be withdrawn. I would not think it wise if it is not, as we are now greatly outnumbered.

It is very important to repossess ourselves of Tennessee, as also to take the initiative before our enemies are prepared to open the campaign. My information is restricted entirely to my own front, & I can do nothing for want of proper supplies. With these & effective horses I think I could disturb the quiet of the enemy & drive him to the Potomac.

I am most respectfully, your obt servt

R. E. Lee
Genl

633   MAJOR C. S. VENABLE TO GENERAL RICHARD S. EWELL
Commanding Corps

Headquarters, Army of Northern Virginia
February 22, 1864

General:
The general commanding sets out for Richmond this morning, being called thither on business with His Excellency the President. He will be absent several days. He directs me to say that General [Robert H.] Chilton will remain here in the office, and is instructed to consult with you on all matters of importance connected with the army. Should it become necessary, General Lee desires you either to move up to Orange Court House or to remove the office to your quarters as you may think proper.

I am very respectfully, your obedient servant

C. S. Venable
Major and Aide-de-Camp

634   To GENERAL SAMUEL COOPER
Adjutant and Inspector General
TELEGRAM

Orange Court House
February 29, 1864

AS AT PRESENT ADVISED, ENEMY'S CAVALRY APPEARS TO BE MOVING BY OUR LEFT & RIGHT, ONE COLUMN IN THE DIRECTION OF CHARLOTTESVILLE, THE OTHER TOWARDS FREDERICK'S HALL.

R. E. Lee
Genl

635   COLONEL W. H. TAYLOR TO GENERAL
ARNOLD ELZEY
Commanding at Richmond, Virginia
TELEGRAM

Orange Court House
February 29, 1864

GENL [ARMISTEAD L.] LONG, AT FREDERICK'S HALL, REPORTS THAT EN-
EMY, AFTER CUTTING RAILROAD BELOW THAT POINT, MOVED TO LOUISA COURT
HOUSE & RICHMOND ROAD, & TURNED OFF IN DIRECTION OF THE LATTER
PLACE. HE ALSO REPORTED THAT [GENERAL JUDSON] KILPATRICK HAS GONE
THROUGH SPOTSYLVANIA. PLEASE NOTIFY COL [BRADLEY T.] JOHNSON, AT
HANOVER JUNCTION.

W. H. TAYLOR
A. A. G.

636   To GENERAL SAMUEL COOPER
Adjutant and Inspector General
TELEGRAM

Orange Court House
March 2, 1864

JUST RETURNED FROM MADISON COURT HOUSE. ENEMY INFANTRY &
CAVALRY RECROSSED ROBERTSON RIVER INTO CULPEPER LAST NIGHT WITHOUT
INJURY.

R. E. LEE

637   To GENERAL SAMUEL COOPER
Adjutant and Inspector General
TELEGRAM

Orange Court House
March 2, 1864

ALL QUIET IN FRONT. PLEASE KEEP ME ADVISED OF MOVEMENTS OF KIL-
PATRICK.

R. E. LEE

638   To GENERAL EDWARD JOHNSON
                    Commanding Division

                                    Headquarters, Army of Northern Virginia
                                                          March 2, 1864
General:
    I wish you to move with so much of your division as is not on
picket towards the Wilderness. You can either take the Turnpike or
Plank road. If the former, continue as far as its intersection with Wilderness Run. If the latter, to Wilderness Church, unless you hear of Kilpatrick's returning to the Rapidan west of those points. The object is to
endeavor to intercept him. Go as far as you conveniently can tonight.
General Stuart with Wickham's & Rosser's brigades has gone down the
Plank road, and will be tonight at Parker's Store or Wilderness Church.
He has directions to communicate with you, inform you of movements
of enemy, &c., and I wish you to conform to the information you receive or can obtain. Make arrangements for provisions and forage, and
you may take with you one or two batteries of [Colonel William] Nelson's battalion. I will direct him to be ready, and will notify Genl Ewell.
The pickets on the Rapidan have been instructed to keep you advised
of any movement of enemy in that quarter, and Genl Ewell will be directed to support you if necessary. I have directed a company of couriers
to report to you. Let me know what road you take and where you will
be tonight.

                                        Very respectfully, &c.

                                                          R. E. LEE
                                                          General

639   To GENERAL ARNOLD ELZEY
                  Commanding at Richmond, Virginia
                              TELEGRAM

                                              Orange Court House
                                                  March 3, 1864

    YOUR TELEGRAM OF 12.15 RECEIVED. ON CALL FROM GENERAL COOPER
I HAVE ORDERED TROOPS TO RICHMOND. ARE THEY NEEDED? IF NOT, INFORM
ME PROMPTLY. ARE THERE ANY INDICATIONS OF AN ATTACK BY [GENERAL

BENJAMIN F.] BUTLER, OR DID HE APPARENTLY SIMPLY MOVE TO KILPAT-
RICK'S RELIEF?

R. E. LEE
General

640   To JAMES A. SEDDON
                      Secretary of War

Headquarters
March 6, 1864

Sir:

I have just received your letter of the 5th instant enclosing a slip
from one of the Richmond journals, giving an account of the recent attack upon that city, & a copy of some papers found on the dead body
of Col [Ulric] Dahlgren, disclosing the plan & purpose of the enterprize.

I concur with you in thinking that a formal publication of these papers should be made under official authority, that our people & the world
may know the character of the war our enemies wage against us, & the
unchristian & atrocious acts they plot & perpetrate. But I cannot recommend the execution of the prisoners that have fallen into our hands. Assuming that the address & special orders of Col Dahlgren correctly state
his designs & intentions, they were not executed, & I believe, even in a
legal point of view, acts in addition to intentions are necessary to constitute crime. These papers can only be considered as evidence of his intentions. It does not appear how far his men were cognizant of them, or
that his course was sanctioned by his Government. It is only known that
his plans were frustrated by a merciful Providence, his forces scattered,
& he killed. I do not think it right therefore to visit upon the captives
the guilt of his intentions. I do not pretend to speak the sentiments of
the army, which you seem to desire. I presume that the blood boils with
indignation in the veins of every officer & man as they read the account
of the barbarous & inhuman plot, & under the impulse of the moment
many would counsel extreme measures. But I do not think that reason &
reflection would justify such a course. I think it better to do right, even if
we suffer in so doing, than to incur the reproach of our consciences &
posterity. Nor do I think that under present circumstances policy dictates the execution of these men. It would produce retaliation. How
many & better men have we in the enemy's hands than they have in ours?
But this consideration should have no weight provided the course was in
itself right. Yet history records instances where such considerations have
prevented the execution of marauders & devastators of provinces.

It may be pertinent to this subject to refer to the conduct of some of our men in the Valley. I have heard that a party of [Major Harry W.] Gilmor's battalion, after arresting the progress of a train of cars on the Baltimore & Ohio Railroad, took from the passengers their purses & watches. As far as I know no military object was accomplished after gaining possession of the cars, & the act appears to have been one of plunder. Such conduct is unauthorized & discreditable. Should any of that battalion be captured the enemy might claim to treat them as highway robbers. What would be our course? I have ordered an investigation of the matter & hope the report may be untrue.

I am with great respect, your obt servt

R. E. LEE
Genl

641   To HIS WIFE
Richmond, Virginia

Camp
March 18, 1864

I arrived safely dear Mary yesterday & found all well. I was very sorry to leave you all & especially not to see more of dear Fitzhugh to whom my heart was so full I could say but little. I hope however he will soon come up when I can see more of him. There were 67 pairs of socks in the bag I brought up instead of 64 as you supposed, & I found here three dozen pairs of beautiful white yarn socks sent over by our kind cousin Julia & sweet little Carrie, (I suppose the latter wishes to console me for not having Bertus) making 103 pairs all of which I sent to the Stonewall Brigade. One dozen of the Stuart socks had double heels. Can you not teach Mildred that stitch? Indeed all might have had them, but I did not observe the larger package as closely as the smaller. They sent me also some hams, which I had rather they had eaten, & each wrote me a kind note. Tell Maggie she must thank them for all. I take advantage of Bryan's visit to Richmond to send you a portion of a box some kind people have sent me from the Allegheny. A roll of butter, 10 dozen eggs & a few apples. Have some omelettes made for those poor little girls, to revive them after their repose, & to cheer up the repast of the gentlemen.

You must give my kind regards to your large family & give much love to my children. I pray that you may be preserved & relieved from all your troubles & that we may all be again united here on earth & forever in Heaven.

Most truly & affly

R. E. Lee

642   To HIS WIFE
Richmond, Virginia

Camp
March 20, 1864

I received dear Mary last evening the bag of socks & your note of the 18th. The count held out this time, 43 pairs. I sent them to the Stonewall Brigade which I heard were in need. This contribution with the parcel I brought up & the package from cousin Julia makes 146 pairs to that brigade which is about as much as I send to any brigade. I have sent out to ascertain who are in need to be prepared for the next arrival. I send down the jacket. It is becoming delapidated but I think will answer till warm weather. Enlarge the neck if you can. The one you did enlarge is more comfortable. I have no news. Our enemies seem to be quiet. The storm which menaced us & threatened to be the equinoctial has passed away & the sun this morning is beautifully bright. How good God is to us. Oh that I could praise Him & thank Him as I ought. I pray that He may add to His numerous blessings the healing of you. Give much love to my dear children. I hope Fitzhugh is well & will soon be strong again. Tell him he must come up & see us when he is ready. Stuart wants to see him.

Truly & affly

R. E. Lee

643   To HIS WIFE
Richmond, Virginia

Camp
March 24, 1864

I received this evening dear Mary your note of the 23rd with the bag of socks, &c. I concur with you in wishing that their number had been greater, but they are still a great help this snowy weather. The bag only contained 17 pairs socks & 1 pair gloves. You had better get one of the girls to count them accurately & set down the number. The number of pairs scarcely ever agrees with your statement & it may be that some of them are abstracted. If so I should like to know. I gave the white pair to Bryan to take over to Priv Jones' brother. This made one of the 17 pairs. Bryan was delighted to recover his tobacco, & I am much obliged to you for the jacket. I sent this batch of socks to the Stonewall Brigade, having ascertained that there were about 300 men whose homes are within the enemy's lines, & who are destitute of socks. This will make about 162 pairs that have been sent to that brigade. We had a very deep snow Tuesday. Col Murray said he measured it in several places in the woods around our camp & found it 18 inches deep. But I believe in the neighborhood it is rated at 15 inches. It has also been very cold. Monday I was on Clarke's Mountain & along the Rapidan & to my feelings with the northeaster blowing in my face it was as cold as any day in winter. I hope you have not suffered, but are still progressing favourably. I pray to God hourly to bless & comfort you, & oh may He restore you in His own good time. You must not become weary but arm yourself with patience & resignation. How are those poor little girls. Mildred has it in power now to give them a great treat. Squirrel soup thickened with peanuts. Custis Morgan [a pet squirrel] in such an exit from the stage would cover himself with glory. Tell Rob I have had a present of a very pretty pipe. It is beautifully carved, made by a Mississippian in camp, with his penknife. Ask him if he would recommend my commencing the inspiration at this late day. I hardly think it worth the trouble.

You must give a great deal of love to my children & kind regards to all. God bless you & all with you. May He be always with you & always preserve you.

Very truly & affly

R. E. Lee

P.S. I enclose a note from Dr. McCaw. I have no means of preserving such, do not like to destroy them, & therefore have previously sent some of the same character that they at least may be preserved in your remembrance.

R. E. L.

644   To JEFFERSON DAVIS
                      Richmond, Virginia

                                    Headquarters, Army of Northern Virginia
                                                        March 25, 1864
Mr. President:
   I have the honor to acknowledge the receipt of the letter forwarded
to me by your directions, containing the views of the writer as to the
intentions of the enemy in the approaching campaign.
   I have read the speculations of the Northern papers on the subject,
and the order of Genl Grant published in our papers yesterday, but I
am not disposed to believe from what I now know, that the first important effort will be directed against Richmond.
   The Northern papers, particularly if they derive their information
from official sources, as they profess, do not in all probability represent
the real purpose of the Federal Government, but are used to create false
impressions. The order of Genl Grant, closely considered, is not inconsistent with this idea. There was no apparent occasion for the publication at such a time and place of his intention to take up his headquarters with the Army of the Potomac, and the announcement appears to
me to be made with some hidden purpose. It will be remembered that
Northern papers of the 14th instant represented Genl Grant as en route
for Tennessee to arrange affairs there preparatory to assuming immediate
command of the Army of the Potomac. What those arrangements were,
we do not know, but if of sufficient moment to require Genl Grant's
personal presence in the West just on the eve of his entering upon active
duties with another army, it can not be probable that he had completed
them by the time his order bears date, March 17th, especially as several
of the few days intervening between his departure from Washington
and the publication of the order, must have been consumed in travelling.
The establishment of an office in Washington to which communications
from other armies than that which Genl Grant accompanies shall be addressed, evidently leaves everything to go on under the direction of the
former authorities as before, and allows no room for inferences as to
whether any army will be active or not, merely from the fact of the
presence of Genl Grant. There is to my mind an appearance of design
about the order which makes it of a piece with the publications in the
papers, intended to mislead us as to the enemy's intention, and if possible, induce corresponding preparation on our part. You will remember
that a like ruse was practised at Vicksburg. Just before the Federal Army
went down the river, the indications given out were such, that it was

thought the attempt on Vicksburg would be abandoned, and that it was proper to reinforce Genl Bragg, whose army it was supposed would next be attacked. It is natural that the enemy should try to conceal the point which he intends to assail first, as he may suppose that our armies, being connected by shorter lines than his, can concentrate more rapidly. In confirmation of these views, I cannot learn that the army of Genl Meade has been reinforced by any organized troops, nor can I learn of any coming east over the Baltimore & Ohio Railroad which I have ordered to be closely watched. A dispatch from Genl Imboden dated March 23rd states that it is reported that the enemy was moving troops westwards over that road all last week. The report is vague but if true, the troops referred to may be recruits, convalescents & furloughed men going to the corps from the east now serving in the west, or they may be reinforcements for the Army of Tennessee. I have reiterated my order about watching the road, and directed the rumor above mentioned to be carefully investigated. From present indications, I am inclined to believe that the first efforts of the enemy will be directed against Genl Johnston or Genl Longstreet, most probably the former. If it succeeds, Richmond will no doubt be attacked. The condition of the weather and the roads will probably be more favorable for active operations at an early day in the South than in Virginia where it will be uncertain for more than a month. Although we cannot do more than weigh probabilities, they are useful in stimulating and directing a vigilant observation of the enemy, and suggesting such a policy on our part as may determine his. His object can be ascertained with the greatest certainty by observing the movements of his armies closely. I would advise that we make the best preparations in our power to meet an advance in any quarter, but be careful not to suffer ourselves to be misled by feigned movements into strengthening one point at the expense of others, equally exposed and equally important. We should hold ourselves in constant readiness to concentrate as rapidly as possible wherever it may be necessary, but do nothing without reasonably certain information except prepare. This information I have already said, can be best obtained by unremitting vigilance in observing those armies that will most probably be active in the campaign, and I trust that Your Excellency will impress this fact, and the importance of energy, accuracy, and intelligence in collecting information upon all officers in a position to do so. Should a movement be made against Richmond in large force, its preparation will no doubt be indicated by the withdrawal of troops from other quarters, particularly the Atlantic coast and the West. The officers commanding in these regions should endeavor to get early and accurate information of such withdrawal. Should Genl Johnston or Genl Longstreet find the forces opposed to them reduced sufficiently to justify attacking them, they might entirely frustrate the enemy's plans by defeating him. Energy and activity on our part, with a constant readiness to seize any opportunity to strike a blow, will embarrass, if not entirely thwart the enemy in concentrating his different armies, and compel him to conform his movements to our own. If Genl Johnston could be put in a condition to operate successfully against the army opposed to him, he would effectually prevent a combination against Richmond. In the meantime, to guard against any contingency, everything not immediately required should be sent away from Richmond, and stores of food and other supplies collected in suitable and safe places for the use of the troops that it may become necessary to assemble for its defence. I beg to repeat that the utmost vigilance and circumspection, coupled with active and energetic preparation are of the first moment to us.

With high respect, your obt servt

R. E. LEE
Genl

645   To GENERAL JAMES LONGSTREET
Greeneville, Tennessee

Headquarters
March 28, 1864

My Dear General:

Upon the reception of your letter of the 16th I wrote to Colonel Gorgas, requesting him to send to you the 1,500 saddles and bridles which I was told when I first wrote to inquire about horses, &c., could be furnished at this time (April 1). I inclose his answer. You see what little aid we can calculate on beyond what we can create for ourselves. I very much regret this disappointment, as could you have got these equipments, they might have afforded you valuable assistance. It looks now as if Grant was really going to operate the Army of the Potomac. When it was first communicated in their papers, and even upon the publication of his order assuming command, I considered it a stratagem to attract our attention here, while he was left unmolested in dealing us a blow from the West. It may be so still, but if their papers are to be believed, he returned to Washington City on the 22d instant, and was to repair to the Rappahannock on the 23d. One of our scouts even reports that he did come up in the train of the 24th, all the cross roads, stations, &c., having been strictly guarded to prevent the train being molested. If he is really going to operate here, we may expect a concentration of troops in this region. It is stated that Burnside is collecting his corps at Annapolis. That looks as if a movement on our flank, either by the Peninsula or through North Carolina, was intended. It is stated that the Ninth and Second Corps are assembling under Burnside. I have seen it stated in the *Philadelphia Enquirer* and *Washington Chronicle* that certain Pennsylvania regiments were at Harrisburg and certain Indiana regiments were en route to Annapolis, said to belong to the Ninth Corps. The Second Corps, as far as I know, is in our front. You would know whether the Ninth has been withdrawn from before you. It behooves us to be on the alert, or we will be deceived. You know that is part of Grant's tactics. He deceived Pemberton when he turned him, and in this last move of Sherman threw dust in Polk's eyes. If a good move could be made before they are ready to execute their plans, we would confound their schemes and break them up. I have read attentively your letter to the President. Either of the plans there stated will answer if they can be carried out. You and Johnston can alone judge of their feasibility. If one or the other can be executed, it should be commenced at once. If not, we shall be obliged to conform to their plans and concentrate wherever they are going to attack us. The great obstacle everywhere is scarcity of supplies. That is the controlling element to which everything has to yield. See what you have before you. Endeavor to ascertain plans of enemy, and thwart them. If you can ascertain that any troops from the West are coming East, let me know.

Very truly and sincerely, with earnest aspiration for your welfare

R. E. Lee

646   To G. W. C. LEE
               Richmond, Virginia

Camp, Orange Court House
March 29, 1864

I read tonight, my dear son, your letter of the 25th, returning Col [Walter H. J.] Stevens'. The recommendation of you to succeed Genl Elzey is highly complimentary. No one can predict with certainty with what success you would operate, but I think you will do as well as those at least who have preceded you. I see no reason why you should not be successful. You have intelligence, energy, strength and the independence of the country at heart. The time is coming, indeed has come, when every one must put out their strength. They cannot consult their feelings or individual opinions where to serve, but must take those positions where it is reasonably evident they will be of most value. If you can be of more service in commanding the troops around Richmond than in your present position, I think you ought to accept. The prospect is now stronger, than a week since, that the struggle in Virginia for Richmond will be continued. Grant is now with the Army of the Potomac. The impression in that army is that he will operate it. Burnside is collecting an army at Annapolis. It will probably be thrown on one of our flanks. There are indications that more troops will be sent to the Valley of the Shenandoah. It is said they have commenced to rebuild the railroad from Harper's Ferry to Winchester. Everything at this time is suggestive of another attempt on Richmond. It may be intended to mislead us, but it must not be neglected. The troops around Richmond may have an important part to play. They should be well prepared and well commanded. I would rather have you there than any one I could now select. I hope therefore you will decide wisely. But if you do not accept the position, I think from the fact that it was tendered to you, connected with the former proposition for you to command in the Valley, is evidence that the President thinks your services in the field are desirable. You can therefore signify your desire for it in some other capacity than that suggested. It is necessary that the Corps of Engineers attached to this Army should be reorganized and strengthened. I also want a proper Chief. If you do not take the service now offered, and will accept that of Chief Engineer of this Army, I will apply for you. If you do not take it, I must get some one else. I never had any conversation with the President as to the rank the Chief would hold, and therefore cannot speak on that point. I would prefer to have a general officer on many accounts, as he could take command of troops operating under him. There will be an Engineer regiment under Col Talcott, several companies of Pioneers, under charge of Engineer Officers, Engineer officers with the Staff of the Army &c., and I think it would form a proper command for a Brigadier Genl. You would be of great comfort and assistance to me as Chief of Staff, but I think it probable the position of Chief Engineer would be more agreeable to you. You refuse command because you have no experience in the field. I appreciate the motives. But until you come in the field you never will gain experience. I think now is the time for you to take the field in some capacity. I assure you every one that has capacity will be much needed. If Grant operates the Army in Virginia he will concentrate a large force on one or more lines. Unless we can take the inititative in the West to disturb their plans, we shall have to concentrate to meet him. I shall require all the aid I can get.

Fitzhugh has reached Stuart's Camp this evening, I have not seen him. There is a terrible rain storm raging, and we are pretty much deluged. I have written for him to come over in the morning. I am glad to hear that all are well. Give much love to your mother, the girls, and my cousin Margaret.

God bless, guide and protect you my dear son

Your father
R. E. Lee

647   To HIS WIFE
Richmond, Virginia

Camp
March 30, 1864

My Dear Mary:

Your note of the 29th with the bag of socks arrived this afternoon. The number of pairs as stated by you was correct — 30 pairs good & true. I am glad to find there is arithmetic enough in my family to count 30. I thought if you placed your daughter at work all would go right. With the aid of little Bertus they could hardly go wrong. I have sent this parcel to the Stonewall Brigade which makes over 200 pairs sent to that brigade. I hope it is nearly satisfied. Is the cotton received from Government too, for if so the socks will have to be receipted for? Fitzhugh has gone with Genl Stuart to hear Governor Vance address the North Carolina troops. I could not go. They are to be back to dinner & Fitzhugh says he must return tomorrow. I shall leave him to give you all news. I am glad to hear you are better. Any advance is delightful. Give much love to the girls & remember me to all friends. With constant prayers for yourself,

I am with great affection, truly yours
R. E. Lee

648   To JEFFERSON DAVIS
Richmond, Virginia

Headquarters, Army of Northern Virginia
March 30, 1864

Mr. President:

Since my former letter on the subject the indications that operations in Virginia will be vigorously prosecuted by the enemy are stronger than they then were. Genl Grant has returned from the army in the West. He is at present with the Army of the Potomac, which is being reorganized & recruited. From the reports of our scouts the impression prevails in that army that he will operate it in the coming campaign. Every train brings it recruits, & it is stated that every available regiment at the North is added to it. It is also reported that Genl Burnside is organizing a large army at Annapolis, & it seems probable that additional troops are being sent to the Valley. It is stated that preparations are making to rebuild the railroad from Harper's Ferry to Winchester, which would indicate a reoccupation of the latter place. The Baltimore & Ohio Railroad is very closely guarded along its whole extent. No ingress or egress from their lines is permitted to citizens as heretofore, and everything shows secrecy & preparation. Their plans are not sufficiently developed to discover them, but I think we can assume that if Genl Grant is to direct operations on this frontier he will concentrate a large force on one or more lines, & prudence dictates that we should make such preparations as are in our power. If an aggressive movement can be made in the West it will disconcert their plans & oblige them to conform to ours. But if it cannot, Longstreet should be held in readiness to be thrown rapidly in the Valley if necessary to counteract any movement in that quarter, in accomplishing which I could unite with him, or he unite with me, should circumstances require it on the Rapidan. The time is also near at hand when I shall require all the troops belonging to this army. I have delayed calling for Genl Hoke, who, besides his own brigade, has two regiments of another of this army, under the expectation that the object of his visit to North Carolina may yet be accomplished. I have heard nothing on the subject recently, & if our papers are correct in their information, the enemy has thrown reinforcements into that State, & the Neuse is barricaded just above New Berne. There is another brigade of this army, Genl R. D. Johnston's at Hanover Junction. I should like as soon as possible to get them both back.

I am with great respect, your most obt svt

R. E. Lee
Genl

649   To GENERAL SAMUEL COOPER
Adjutant and Inspector General

Headquarters, Army of Northern Virginia
April 1, 1864

General:

Your circular of March 23rd with reference to Partisan Rangers has been received. The organizations of Partisan Rangers serving with this army are the 4th & 5th North Carolina Cavalry (59th & 63rd Regiments), now absent in North Carolina; Lt Col [John S.] Mosby's battalion, serving in Fauquier; Capt [James C.] Kincheloe's company, serving in Prince William; Capt [John H.] McNeill's company & Maj Gilmor's battalion & Maj [Charles T.] O'Ferrall's battalion, serving in the Valley Department.

Of these, the 4th & 5th North Carolina Regiments have been serving as regular cavalry, and will come under Act No. 19, published in General Orders, No. 29, Adjutant & Inspector General's Office, current series, being continued in their present organizations as regular cavalry. I am making an effort to have Col Mosby's battalion mustered into the regular service. If this cannot be done I recommend that this battalion be retained as partisans for the present. Lt Col Mosby has done excellent service, & from the reports of citizens & others I am inclined to believe that he is strict in discipline & a protection to the country in which he operates. Gilmor's battalion I have already recommended to be disbanded & the companies brought under Section 2 of Act No. 19. I renew the recommendation, & recommend the same course to be pursued with Kincheloe's company, O'Ferrall's battalion, & McNeill's company. Experience has convinced me that it is almost impossible, under the best officers even, to have discipline in these bands of Partisan Rangers, or to prevent them from becoming an injury instead of a benefit to the service, and even where this is accomplished the system gives license to many deserters & marauders, who assume to belong to these authorized companies & commit depredations on friend & foe alike. Another great objection to them is the bad effect upon the discipline of the army from the constant desire of the men to leave their commands & enjoy the great license allowed in these bands. With the single exception mentioned, I hope the order will be issued at once disbanding the companies & battalions serving in this department.

I am very respectfully, your obt servt

R. E. LEE
Genl

650   To MISS AGNES LEE
                   Richmond, Virginia

Camp, Orange Court House
April 3, 1864

My precious little Agnes:
    The storm of yesterday retarded the train so much, that it did not reach Orange till late in the night, & I did not receive your letter of 31 March till this morning. It was a welcome harbinger of a brighter

day & has turned my thoughts much to you & those with you this holy morning. If you have missed me how much more must I have missed you? I wish indeed you could pay me a visit. There are plenty of houses as you say, whose owners no doubt would receive you, but I know their condition, few or no servants, little or nothing to eat, want & devastation around them. How could I ask them to augment their troubles? Besides the time has arrived when we may become actively engaged any day, & for those in the army to leave, not for those out of it to come. It is not a time for reviews or merriment, but for hard & serious work. As there is no place near me where you could obtain accomodation, I should be able to see but little of you, & you would see not more of the army than you do at present. I hope however the time may come when you can see the army as you desire & I can see you as I wish. I shall in that case surely take advantage of it. During winter when we are more apt to be quiet, the weather keeps you housed, & in more favourable weather the army is "not at home." I am very much obliged to you for your attention to my shirts. Those now with me elicit my tenderest care & like the snows of winter are fading from view. I must send you my pipe to keep for me. I infer that Bertus does not recommend my indoctrination into the odorous art, as he has withheld his desired advice. I fear it is rather late for me to learn anything good. Remember me to my cousin Savinia & tell sweet Annie Leigh I want to see her badly. I hope Fitzhugh got down comfortably yesterday. I could see but little of him when here. Give my love to your mother & sisters & kiss Maggie for me. I shall have no cake to give you when you come. We have consumed three large pound cakes, besides smaller choses. All from over the mountains. My staff are all so devoted to the ladies, that it takes a quantity of sweets to satisfy them.

You must give to Miss Mary Lyons my sincere wishes for her happiness.

With earnest prayers my dear child for every blessing to you,

I am as ever your father

R. E. Lee

651   To JEFFERSON DAVIS
Richmond, Virginia

Headquarters
April 5, 1864

Mr. President:

All the information I receive tends to show that the great effort of the enemy in this campaign will be made in Virginia. Nothing as yet has been discovered to develop their plan. Reinforcements are certainly daily arriving to the Army of Potomac. I cannot ascertain whence they come. Information was received on the 3rd from two scouts, derived from citizens along the Orange & Alexandria Railroad, that the troops on the cars said they belonged to Grant's Army of the Tennessee. A resident of Culpeper stated that the 11th & 12th Army Corps had returned there. I telegraphed to Genls Johnston & Longstreet to know if they were still in the West. I enclose their answers. Both seem to think they are in their front, but preparing to leave. The tone of the Northern papers, as well as the impression prevailing in their armies, go to show that Grant with a large force is to move against Richmond. One of their correspondents at Harrisburg stated, upon the occasion of the visit of Genls Burnside & Hancock, that it was certain that the former would go to North Carolina. They cannot collect the large force they mention for their operations against Richmond without reducing their other armies. This ought to be discovered & taken advantage of by our respective commanders. I infer from the information I receive that Longstreet's corps is in the vicinity of Abingdon & Bristol. It is therefore in position to be thrown west or east. Unless it is certain that it can be advantageously employed west for a speedy blow, I would recommend that it be returned to this army. The movements & reports of the enemy may be intended to mislead us, & should therefore be carefully observed. But all the information that reaches me goes to strengthen the belief that Genl Grant is preparing to move against Richmond.

I am with great respect, your obt servt

R. E. Lee
Genl

652   To GENERAL J. E. B. STUART
Commanding Cavalry

April 6, 1864

My Dear General:

I am much obliged to you for the fine watermelon. I tried to tempt General Long to stay to eat it, but he would not. Can't you come over and dine with us?

I will embody your remarks, or rather admonition, to our prisoners in a general order. You know I clip my words very much, and it need not interfere with your promulgating to the cavalry your views. I received from Richmond last evening information concerning enemy's

movements, &c., exaggerated, I think, but to the general effect of what
we know. Grant, it is said, has been to Fort Monroe. You can see them
when you come over.

Truly

R. E. LEE

653   To GENERAL BRAXTON BRAGG
          Commanding Armies of Confederate States
               Richmond, Virginia

Headquarters
April 7, 1864

General:

I have had the honour to receive your letter of the 4th instant, enclosing a note from the Honorable Secretary of War, with the accompanying memoranda, &c. I think it apparent that the enemy is making
large preparations for the approaching campaign in Virginia. The extent or whence the troops are derived are not so evident. The report of
"Potomac," of 1st April, to Maj [William] Norris of 60,000 troops
marching from Washington to Point Lookout I suppose intended for wit.
There are rumors from citizens of troops from the West joining Genl
Meade, but none of my scouts have seen them. I therefore think it doubtful. A self-elected scout in the Valley reports [General George H.]
Thomas' corps having passed over the Baltimore & Ohio Railroad to
Baltimore, & citizens in Culpeper & Fauquier report the arrival of the
11th & 12th Corps on the Rappahannock. These reports are not confirmed. Genl Longstreet has reported the departure from his front of the
9th & 23rd Corps (Burnside's & [General George L.] Hartsuff's). Reports from two scouts north of the Rappahannock received last night
state that great activity prevails on the Orange & Alexandria Railroad.
Troops are constantly passing up from Alexandria. They think they are
recruits & furloughed men. Their clothes are too new & overcoats of
too deep a blue for old troops. They estimate that from 20,000 to 25,000
men have been conveyed on the railroad to the Rappahannock in the
last ten days. The artillery that they have seen appears larger than
ordinary. These men have been on opposite sides of the railroad, with
no communication with each other. All quiet on the Potomac & at Aquia. I
think every preparation should be made to meet the approaching storm,
which will apparently burst on Virginia, & unless its force can be diverted by an attack in the West, that troops should be collected to oppose
it. I desire Hoke's & R. D. Johnston's brigades to be returned to me

from North Carolina & Hanover Junction, & all the recruits that can be obtained. Supplies of all kinds should be collected in Richmond or at points accessible to this army as rapidly as possible. With our present supplies on hand the interruption of the trains on the southern roads would cause the abandonment of Virginia.

I am with great respect, your obt servt

R. E. LEE
Genl

654   CIRCULAR

Headquarters, Army of Northern Virginia
April 7, 1864

I hope that few of the soldiers of this army will find it necessary at any time in the coming campaign to surrender themselves prisoners of war. We cannot spare brave men to fill Federal prisons. Should, however, any be so unfortunate as to fall through unavoidable necessity into the hands of the enemy, it is important that they should preserve entire silence with regard to everything connected with the army, the positions, movements, organizations, or probable strength of any portion of it. I wish the commanding officers of regiments and companies to instruct their men, should they be captured, under any circumstances not to disclose the brigade, division, or corps to which they belong, but to give simply their names, company, and regiment, and not to speak of military matters even among their associates in misfortune. Proper prudence on the part of all will be of great assistance in preserving that secrecy so essential to success.

I am general respectfully, your obedient servant

R. E. LEE
General

655   To JEFFERSON DAVIS
Richmond, Virginia

Headquarters
April 8, 1864

Mr. President:

I received yesterday reports from two of our most reliable scouts, upon whom I have depended for information. One was dated the 4th

& the other the 6th. The writer of the former had been near Alexandria, had communication with persons inside the town every day, & had watched the Alexandria & Orange Railroad four or five days. He states that a large number of recruits are being sent to the Army of Potomac, & expressed surprize at the number of troops conveyed on the road, but that no additional corps had yet passed up. The general impression was that the great battle would take place on the Rapidan & that the Federal Army would advance as soon as the weather is settled. All the white troops had been taken from the intrenchments around Alexandria & ordered to Genl Meade, & their places supplied by negroes. It was reported that the troops from Charleston were to be brought to Fort Monroe. The writer of the latter was in Culpeper in communication with the Court House, watching the enemy movements. Among the reports in circulation was that the 11th & 12th Corps were expected. That may be however to encourage their men who were deserting in expectation of a fight. I think Genl Beauregard had better be notified of the report of the transfer of the troops from Charleston to Fort Monroe, which I think very probable, & that all available reinforcements be sent to this army.

I am with great respect, your obt servt

R. E. LEE
Genl

656   To HIS WIFE
          Richmond, Virginia

Camp
April 9, 1864

The bag of socks arrived last evening my dear Mary with your note of the 6th. Who counted them for you? There were only 23 pairs & not 25 as you stated. I opened the bag & counted them myself twice; then sent them over to Major [E. H.] Janney who also counted them & we both made them 23 pairs. I am anxious to get as many socks now as possible, before active operations commence. As soon as the Stonewall Brigade is supplied I will send to the 61st Regiment. I am glad you have heard from Mary & Edward. Tell the former how rejoiced I am to hear of her improvement, how much I love her & how often I think of her. Everything recalls her to me & I earnestly implore our Heavenly Father that she may soon be restored to us well & happy as we can be in this world. Say to Edward how much I am obliged to him for his affection & remembrance. I want for nothing but independence & peace to our distracted country. The money Fitzhugh has transferred might as well I suppose remain in bonds as they are. If you can take care of them you might as well retain them & use the interest, or give them to Custis as you prefer.

Give much love to all & believe me always yours

R. E. LEE

657   To G. W. C. LEE
                                  Richmond, Virginia

Camp
April 9, 1864

My Dear Custis:

I have delayed replying to your letter of the 5th to see what action would be had upon my application for a Chief Engineer of this army. By the order received last evening directing General [Martin L.] Smith to report to me for engineer duty, I conclude the President has decided against my application for you.

I thought that position presented less objections to your serving with me than any other. Though a member of the General Staff of the Army, your operations, presence etc., would have been with the Corps of Engineers and as independent as any other commander, while your work would have been obvious to all and spoken for itself. As Chief of Staff, your connection with me would be more intimate, your work more a part of my own, your action less distinct and separate, and assumed at least to be by my direction.

This would be very agreeable to me, but more open to all the objections that could be brought against your holding the place of Chief of Engineers. I presume, therefore, it would not be favorably considered. It is a delicate matter to apply for any one on the staff of another. I am not certain that it is proper to ask for one, serving with the President. In addition it is more important that he should have the aid he desires than I should. Although, therefore, anxious to have you, I am at a loss how to proceed. I know the kind feelings of the President toward you, and to me, and to my wants he has always shown the kindest consideration.

I want all the aid I can get now. I feel a marked change in my strength since my attack last spring at Fredericksburg, and am less com-

petent for my duty than ever. I admire the sentiments that induced you
to decline the command around Richmond. But the reasons that operated
in that case will prevail in all similar, and are not likely to be changed by
time, should you continue where you are.

However, it is done, and I believe will turn out for the best. I have a
high opinion of Generals [James L.] Kemper and [William] Mahone in
the positions in which they have been tested. How they would do in
others, it is difficult to say. A single road I believe General M. would
manage admirably. He could attend to it personally and would see to
everything himself. Over a more extended field, the chain through all the
Confederacy, it is also problematic.

Give much love to everybody, and believe me always,

Your devoted father

R. E. LEE

658   To JAMES A. SEDDON
                            Secretary of War

Headquarters, Army of Northern Virginia
April 12, 1864

Sir:

I have the honor to call your attention to the importance of making
the best preparation in our power to meet any possible contingencies
of the campaign that in all probability is now near at hand. No arrangements that our foresight can suggest, or our means accomplish should
be neglected, and while every exertion should, and I doubt not will,
be made to insure our success, we should not be unprepared for unfavorable results, and neglect precautions that may lighten any calamity
that may befall us.

The subject of the greatest immediate importance is the collection
at suitable and safe places of adequate supplies of provisions and forage. I
earnestly recommend that no private interests be allowed to interfere
with the use of all the facilities for transportation that we possess until
the wants of the army are provided for. The railroads should be at
once devoted exclusively to this purpose, even should it be found necessary to suspend all private travel for business or pleasure upon them for
the present.

It is difficult, in view of the conflicting information received, to ascertain what the purpose of the enemy may be, but an investment of
Richmond is one of the possibilities for which we should be prepared.

Even should no actual investment be made, it is not improbable that an accumulation of troops in or near the city may become necessary, and operations may be carried on in its immediate vicinity.

In either case, I think it very desirable that all the population whose presence would impede or endanger our efforts should be removed, especially that part of it which increases the consumption of public stores, without aiding or strengthening the army. Prisoners of the enemy and our own paroled men are of this class, and I think no time should be lost in placing them in some other locality.

Besides these, the presence of Federal deserters and persons with no visible & reputable means of support is not only a burden, but in a critical movement might be attended with danger.

As far as practicable all such should be removed from the city and every encouragement given to the rest of the non-combatant population to retire, except those whose services may be useful or who will not increase the scarcity of supplies.

With reference to the transportation of supplies, &c., I beg leave also to urge that all officers and agents connected with it be required to give their constant personal attention to their duties. They should not only give orders and directions, but as far as practicable see in person to the faithful execution of them. Much that is considered impracticable from the reports of employees & agents has been found to be feasible when intelligent and energetic officers have taken it in hand themselves.

All should be prepared for a degree of effort, self sacrifice, and labor, until the crisis has been safely passed, such as may not be necessary in the performance of duty on ordinary occasions.

You will be able best to determine how the surplus population to which I have referred can be disposed of, but you will perceive the urgent necessity that nothing should be left undone while there is yet time to make our preparations.

I think it advisable also that such public property as is not necessary for the immediate use of the army should be removed to a place of security without delay.

Whatever inconvenience and even hardship may result from a vigorous and thorough preparation for the most complete defence we can make will be speedily forgotten in the event of success or amply repaid by the benefits such a course will confer upon us in case of misfortune.

I am with great respect, your obt servt

R. E. LEE
Genl

659   To JEFFERSON DAVIS
                    Richmond, Virginia

                                        Headquarters
                                        April 12, 1864
Mr. President:
    My anxiety on the subject of provisions for the army is so great that
I cannot refrain from expressing it to Your Excellency. I cannot see how
we can operate with our present supplies. Any derangement in their arrival or disaster to the railroad would render it impossible for me to keep
the army together, & might force a retreat into North Carolina. There is
nothing to be had in this section for man or animals. We have rations for
the troops today & tomorrow. I hope a new supply arrived last night, but
I have not yet had a report. Every exertion should be made to supply the
depots at Richmond & at other points. All pleasure travel should cease,
and everything be devoted to necessary wants.

            I am with great respect, your obt servt

                                        R. E. LEE
                                        Genl

660   To GENERAL BRAXTON BRAGG
            Commanding Armies of Confederate States

                                        Headquarters
                                        April 13, 1864
General:
    From the letters of Genls Pickett & Hoke the completion of the
gunboats seemed so distant & even indefinite that I could see no advantage in retaining the latter longer in North Carolina. All the troops we
can get will be required in Virginia, and as far as I can judge those not
necessary in the Department of Georgia, South Carolina, & Florida should
be moved northward gradually, so as not to interrupt the transportation
of supplies, to the extent at least of replacing Pickett & Hoke. Pickett
should be disengaged so as to join Longstreet. Our scouts report that
the three corps of Genl Meade's army, as at present organized, number
75,000 men, and that he will move with 100,000. This force is said to be
independent of Burnside & that which will be on the Peninsula. I did not
intend to change Johnston's [General R. D. Johnston] position [Hanover
Junction] till I saw further as to the probable plans of the enemy, &

have not yet ordered Hoke to join me. If anything is to be done in North Carolina it should be done quickly.

Very resply, your obt servt

R. E. LEE
Genl

661   To JEFFERSON DAVIS
Richmond, Virginia

Headquarters
April 15, 1864

Mr. President:

The reports of the scouts are still conflicting as to the character of the reinforcements to the Army of the Potomac, & the composition of that at Annapolis under Genl Burnside. I think it probably that the 8th Corps, which embraces the troops who have heretofore guarded the line of the B[altimore] & O[hio] R[ail]r[oad], the entrenchments around Washington, & Alexandria, &c., have been moved up to the Rappahannock, & that an equivalent has been sent to Annapolis from Genl Meade. Lt Col Mosby states that the 11th & 12th Corps, consolidated, have been also sent to Genl Burnside. But whatever doubt there may be on these points, I think it certain that the enemy is organizing a large army on the Rappahannock, & another at Annapolis, & that the former is intended to move directly on Richmond, while the latter is intended to take it in flank or rear. I think we may also reasonably suppose that the Federal troops that have so long besieged Charleston will, with a portion of their iron clad steamers, be transferred to the James River. I consider that the suspension of the attack on that city was virtually declared when Genl Gillmore transferred his operations to the St. John's River. It can only be continued during the summer months by the fleet. The expedition of the enemy up Red River has so diminished his forces about New Orleans & Mobile that I think no attack upon the latter city need be apprehended soon, especially as we have reason to hope that he will return from his expedition in a shattered condition. I have thought therefore that Genl Johnston might draw something from Mobile during the summer to strengthen his hands, & that Genl Beauregard with a portion of his troops might move into North Carolina to oppose Genl Burnside should he resume his old position in that State, or be ready to advance to the James River should that route be taken. I do not know what benefit Genl Buckner can accomplish in his present position. If he is able to advance into Tennessee, reoccupy Knoxville, or unite with Genl Johnston, great good may be accomplished, but if he can only hold Bristol, I think he had better be called for a season to Richmond. We shall have to glean troops from every quarter to oppose the apparent combination of the enemy. If Richmond could be held secure against the attack from the east, I would propose that I draw Longstreet to me & move right against the enemy on the Rappahannock. Should God give us a crowning victory there, all their plans would be dissipated, & their troops now collecting on the waters of the Chesapeake will be recalled to the defence of Washington. But to make this move I must have provisions & forage. I am not yet able to call to me the cavalry or artillery. If I am obliged to retire from this line, either by a flank movement of the enemy or the want of supplies, great injury will befall us. I have ventured to throw out these suggestions to Your Excellency in order that in surveying the whole field of operations you may consider all the circumstances bearing on the question. Should you determine it is better to divide this army & fall back towards Richmond I am ready to do so. I however see no better plan for the defence of Richmond than that I have proposed.

I am with great respect, your obt servt

R. E. LEE
Genl

662   To GENERAL J. E. B. STUART
Commanding Cavalry

April 16, 1864

General:

I have just conversed with Col Corley in reference to Rosser. He says he can get no grain in Albemarle that he is aware of. If located there, his horses will be grazed in all the meadows & thus shorten our crop of hay next year. He wishes to keep all hay grounds intact during the summer. If he is obliged to be furnished with grain by railroad he prefers him to be within reach of Gordonsville or Orange Court House. Is there no place on the Rapidan, or within the fork that he can procure grass?

Very resply

R. E. LEE
Genl

663   To GENERAL BRAXTON BRAGG
           Commanding Armies of Confederate States

Headquarters
April 16, 1864

General:

I received last evening your letter of the 14th instant by the hands of Major [Francis S.] Parker. I trust that the expedition in North Carolina will be attended with success, & that the troops in the Department of South Carolina, Georgia, & Florida may be made available to oppose the combined operations of the enemy in Virginia. No attack of moment can be made upon Charleston or the southern coast during the summer months, & I think Genl Johnston can draw with impunity some troops from Mobile to him. Buckner's force too might be made available in some way; I fear as he stands now it will be lost to us. At present my hands are tied. If I was able to move, with the aid of Longstreet & Pickett, the enemy might be driven from the Rappahannock and be obliged to look to the safety of his own capital instead of the assault upon ours. I cannot even draw to me the cavalry or artillery of the army, and the season has arrived when I may be attacked any day. The scarcity of our supplies gives me the greatest uneasiness. All travel should be suspended on the railroad until a sufficiency is secured. I can have a portion of the corn ground into meal for the army if it is sent to me. I do not know whether all can be furnished. The mills are mostly on the Rapidan, and consequently exposed if any movement takes place. It will also increase the hauling, which at this time I should like to avoid if possible. If the meal can be prepared in Richmond it will be more convenient at this time. If it cannot, we can at least grind part of the corn if sent to us. If we are forced back from our present line the [Virginia] Central Railroad, Charlottesville, & all the upper country will be exposed, and I fear great injury inflicted on us.

Most respy, your obt servt

R. E. LEE
Genl

664   To GENERAL BRAXTON BRAGG
Commanding Armies of Confederate States

Headquarters
April 16, 1864

General:

I have received your letter of the 13th, enclosing a copy of a communication from Col Gorgas in reference to the large proportion of artillery with this army. I have never found it too large in battle, and it has generally been opposed by about 300 pieces of the enemy of larger calibre, longer range, & with more effective ammunition. If however its equipment overtaxes the means of the Ordnance Department, or as you suggest its supply of horses cannot be kept up, that decides the question, and no argument on the subject is necessary. Taking the European standard of three guns for every thousand men, based upon the experience of their wars, not ours, the number of guns in this army will fall short, provided the regiments are filled to the minimum allowed by law. I think Col Gorgas is correct in not adhering to this standard when the organizations recede from their maximum of strength. Taking his own standard, and allowing five guns to each brigade, we ought to have 230 guns. Longstreet has 12 brigades, Ewell 13, Hill fourteen, and the cavalry (including the Carolina brigade being organized) 7 = 46 brigades. Taking Col Gorgas' statement as correct, which I have not time to verify, there are in this army 197 guns; with General Longstreet 27, and in the Washington Artillery (if full) 16 = 238 [240]. The excess is not large, but going back to the European standard, we have 206 regiments. Taking the minimum & not the maximum of strength ($206 \times 640 = 131,840$), and allowing three guns for every thousand men ($131,840 \div 3$) 395 guns. Our aggregate present & absent would give us more. I differ from Col Gorgas in thinking that 20 guns are too much for the cavalry. In my opinion they are not enough. We should have a battery for each brigade and a reserve battery for each division. The 7 brigades would require 7 batteries, and the 3 divisions 3 reserve batteries, making ten.

Very resply, your obt servt

R. E. Lee
Genl

665   To GENERAL BRAXTON BRAGG
Commanding Armies of Confederate States

Headquarters
April 16, 1864

General:

I learn from Genl Longstreet that all of his troops will not reach Charlottesville before the 21st, the railroad not being able to transport over 1,500 a day. For want of good camping ground in the neighborhood of that place, I have directed him to take position in the vicinity of Gordonsville, where he will be more convenient for service here or eastward, & for procurement of supplies. The brigades will march from Charlottesville as they arrive, so as not to embarrass the railroad. Genl Longstreet states that, with the view of equalizing the commands with him in Tennessee, he had attached [General Evander] Law's brigade of Hood's old division to Buckner's division for service, Buckner having with him but two of his brigades, the other being with Genl Johnston's army. He has not ordered Law's brigade to move with his corps. I understood the order of the Department to embrace all of his corps with him. If that was the intention, I request you to order Law's brigade forward. The brigades in motion with Genl Longstreet will amount to about 9,000 men. That of Law's numbers about 1,500.

Very resply, your obt servt

R. E. LEE
Genl

666   To GENERAL JOHN D. IMBODEN
Commanding at Mount Crawford

Headquarters
April 18, 1864

General:

A scout just from the Valley reports that Averell, with all the cavalry that could be spared from that region, left Martinsburg and went up the Baltimore & Ohio Railroad last Tuesday, leaving only a garrison in that city. He also states that there is no force at Harper's Ferry. I think it probable that Averell will make an attempt upon the Virginia & Tennessee Railroad at the time proposed for the combined movement against Richmond from some point beyond the North Mountain. I see no indications of a movement up the Valley. Reports have been industriously spread abroad to that effect. An examination of the Potomac & Winchester Railroad has been made by engineers, &c., but I believe it was with the intention of misleading. I hope you and Genl [John C.] Breckinridge will be prepared to unite and beat him back wherever he may come, & drive him across the Potomac. I shall be so occupied in all probability that I shall be unable to aid you.

Very respectfully, your obt servt

R. E. LEE
Genl

667   To JEFFERSON DAVIS
Richmond, Virginia

Orange Court House
April 19, 1864

Mr. President:

I have read the letter of Lt Col H. D. Capers which you did me the honour to transmit to me. The object of the writer is no doubt praiseworthy, but I do not think it would be well to attempt at this time the reestablishment of the Society of the Cincinnati. I think it important to unite as closely as possible the interests of the army with the interests of the citizens. They are one in reality & all for the Country. It would revive I fear the ancient opposition to the Order, give rise to misconstruction, & furnish themes to the discontented, dissatisfied, & captious. We want harmony, sympathy, & cooperation of all our people. You may recollect before, the design of the Cincinnati was to maintain & perpetuate social feelings & relations, & how it was misrepresented. I believe too greatly by the southern states & the politicians of the Jefferson School. We have now but one thing to do; to establish our independence. We have no time for anything else, & nothing of doubtful bearing on the subject should be risked. I have the honour to return to Your Excellency the letter of Col Capers.

With great respect, your obt servt

R. E. LEE

668   To HIS WIFE
                              Richmond, Virginia

                                                          Camp
                                                     April 23, 1864

I received this morning dear Mary by one of our scouts from north
of the Rappahannock a package addressed to me, containing articles for
you. Later in the day I received a letter from Mrs. Peyton which I
enclose & which explains the matter. You will be interested in the part
relating to dear Anne. It is a great comfort to me to know that she is
relieved from the pain, anxiety, & suffering of this world. I trust she is
in the abode of the blessed who die in the Lord, where I pray we may all
be united. Our life in this world is of no value except to prepare us for
a better. That should be our constant aim & the end of all our efforts. I
hope dear Mary this warm weather is mitigating your pains & relaxing
the hold of your disease. I am much rejoiced at the report of your doctor.
Did he have recourse to the homopathic application to his finger, for the
bite of Custis Morgan, & insist on another grip. I should have recommended squirrel soup for your disease immediately. I fear he will give
some of the family a terrible bite before he is despatched. It is their
nature, & they become more vicious with age. I recommend he be confined to his cage or be dismissed. I suppose next week we shall be occupied in the field. I do not know when I shall be able to write to you
again. I advise you to get into some quiet place for the summer as soon
as you can. Halifax, Charlotte, Liberty, or any place where you can find
security & food. Richmond is not the place for you. Give much love to all
my children. May God guard direct & bless you all here & hereafter, is
my constant & earnest prayer.

                                        Truly & most affly yours

                                                     R. E. LEE

669   To JEFFERSON DAVIS
                              Richmond, Virginia

                                                     Headquarters
                                                     April 25, 1864

Mr. President:
     The advance of the Army of the Potomac seems to be delayed for
some reason. It appears to be prepared for movement but is probably

waiting for its cooperative columns. The signal officer on Clarke's Mountain reported in the forenoon of yesterday that a brigade of cavalry, with a few ambulances was moving on the Germanna Ford road. Genl Fitz Lee who has two brigades of cavalry in the vicinity of Fredericksburg was notified to attend to them, [General John R.] Chambliss' brigade was moved down the Plank road to within four miles of the Wilderness Tavern, & Genl R. Johnston at the Junction placed on his guard. At night the picket at Germanna reported the enemy at Ely's Ford, but did not know in what force. This morning I learn that they had not crossed, but were at the river. Their object is not yet discovered. The delay of the enemy I hope will give us grass sufficient to get our troops together. The cavalry is halted near Fredericksburg for the benefit of grazing on the river lands. I have brought the artillery nearer the front.

I telegraphed to Your Excellency yesterday to know whether if the enemy remained quiet & the weather favourable this week, it would be convenient for you to visit the army. It would be very gratifying to the troops & I hope pleasing to Your Excellency.

With great respect, your obt servt

R. E. LEE
Genl

670   To JEFFERSON DAVIS
Richmond, Virginia

Headquarters
April 29, 1864

Mr. President:
I received this morning a report from a scout just from the vicinity of Washington that Genl Burnside, with 23,000 men, 7,000 of which are negroes, marched through that city on Monday last to Alexandria. He also states that the 11th & 12th Corps have not been sent to Virginia. This report was forwarded by Genl Fitz Lee from Fredericksburg, & I presume the scout to be [Frank] Stringfellow. If so, he has good grounds for his assertion. If true, I think it shows that Burnside's destination is the Rappahannock frontier, and that he will have to be met north of the James River. I would therefore recommend that the troops which you design to oppose him, which are south of that river, be drawn towards it. I think there are sufficient troops in North Carolina for the local operations contemplated there without those sent from this army, and request that Hoke's brigade and the two regiments attached to it be

returned to me. I think it better to keep the organization of the corps complete, and if necessary to detach a corps, than to weaken them & break them up. I have kept Longstreet in reserve for such an emergency, and shall be too weak to oppose Meade's army without Hoke's and R. D. Johnston's brigades. The enemy yesterday made a demonstration on our left with two brigades of cavalry. The supporting force could not be accurately ascertained. He advanced no further than Robertson River, sending about a regiment of cavalry into Madison Court House, & retired at night.

With great respect, your obt svt

R. E. LEE
Genl

671   To G. W. C. LEE
                              Richmond, Virginia

Camp
April 30, 1864

My Dear Custis:

Nothing of much interest has occurred during the past week. The reports of scouts all indicate large preparations on the part of the enemy, and a state of readiness for action. The Ninth Corps is reported to be encamped (or rather was on the 27th) on the Orange & Alexandria Railroad, between Fairfax Court House and Alexandria.

This is corroboration of information sent the President yesterday, but there may be some mistakes as to the fact or number of corps. All their troops north of the Rappahannock have been moved south, their guards called in, &c. The garrisons, provost guards, &c., in Northern cities have been brought forward and replaced by State troops. A battalion of heavy artillery is said to have recently arrived in Culpeper, numbering 3,000.

I presume these are the men stated in their papers to have been drawn from the forts in New York Harbor. I wish we could make corresponding preparations. If I could get back Pickett, Hoke, and B. R. Johnson, I would feel strong enough to operate.

I have been endeavoring for the last eight or ten days to move Imboden against the Baltimore & Ohio Railroad in its unprotected state, but have not been able. I presume he has his difficulties, as well as myself. I am afraid it is too late now. I cannot yet get the troops together for want of forage, and am looking for grass.

Endeavor to get accurate information from the Peninsula, James River, &c. My scouts have not returned from Annapolis, and may get back too late.

Your affectionate father

R. E. LEE

672   To JEFFERSON DAVIS
Richmond, Virginia
TELEGRAM

Orange Court House
April 30, 1864

BURNSIDE'S FORCES WITH ARTILLERY, WAGONS, AMBULANCES, &C., PASSED THROUGH CENTREVILLE 28TH INSTANT. ITS ADVANCE REACHED MANASSAS THAT EVENING. THE REGULAR REGIMENTS FROM BOSTON, NEW YORK & OTHER POINTS ANNOUNCED HAVING REACHED WASHINGTON ON THEIR WAY TO THE FRONT. I AGAIN RECOMMEND TROOPS BE ADVANCED TOWARDS THE RAPPAHANNOCK AND THOSE BELONGING TO THIS ARMY BE RETURNED TO IT.

R. E. LEE

673   To JEFFERSON DAVIS
Richmond, Virginia

Headquarters, Army of Northern Virginia
April 30, 1864

Mr. President:

My dispatch of 1¾ p.m. today announced to you the march of Burnside's forces through Centreville. Citizens report the arrival of his troops at Rappahannock Station. I send you the *Philadelphia Inquirer* of the 26th, from which you will learn that all their available forces are being advanced to the front. They are also apparently drawing troops from Florida & the southern coast. Lt Col Mosby, who was within a mile of Centreville on the 28th, the day that Burnside passed through, learned from prisoners that no troops were left at Annapolis except convalescents. I see no evidence of more troops being brought from Tennessee, and it may be inferred from newspapers sent, and from the *Washington Chronicle* of the 27th, that the 12th Corps is still in that department. As far as I can judge, although there may be a large force in Tennessee, it seems to occupy an extended line, & is not yet concentrated as if for attack. If Genl Johnston could be reinforced from Mobile, or by Genl Polk, he might be able to penetrate their lines, or successfully resist their advance. Our scouts report that the engineer troops, pontoon trains, and all the cavalry of Meade's army have been advanced south of the Rappahannock. The regiments of the (old) 5th Corps, which have been guarding the Orange & Alexandria Railroad, have been brought forward and replaced by negro troops. Everything indicates a concentrated attack on this front, which renders me the more anxious to get back the troops belonging to this army, & causes me to suggest if possible, that others be moved from points at the south, where they can be spared, to Richmond. There will no doubt be a strong demonstration made north or south of the James River, which Beauregard will be able successfully to resist. I judge also from present indications, that Averell & Sigel will move against the Virginia & Tennessee Railroad or Staunton, to resist which Genls Breckinridge and Imboden should act in concert. I have requested them to do so.

With great respect, your obt servt

R. E. Lee
Genl

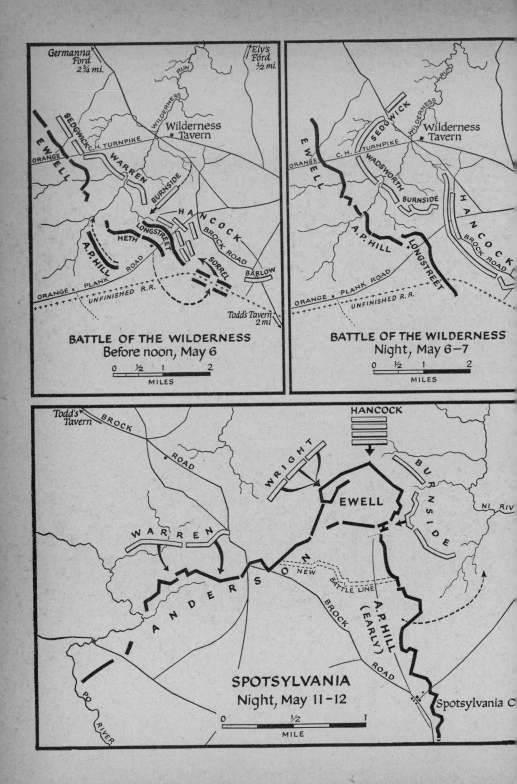

BATTLE OF THE WILDERNESS
Before noon, May 6

0   ½   1   2
MILES

BATTLE OF THE WILDERNESS
Night, May 6–7

0   ½   1   2
MILES

SPOTSYLVANIA
Night, May 11–12

0   ½   1
MILE

CHAPTER FOURTEEN

The Wilderness and Spotsylvania

MAY 1864

"I may be forced to fall back"

DURING THE CONSTANT heavy action from May 5 through May 20, General Lee was given few opportunities to write at length to anyone. Except for his significant May 4 letter to Davis, written on the march the night before the Battle of the Wilderness, his mostly brief messages must be interpreted against the background of (1) his known urgency to concentrate his army in order to sustain maneuver and avoid falling back on Richmond, and (2) the secondary thrusts of the enemy into the Valley and south of Richmond.

As the Valley operations were under his authority, though too remote for his control, he wrote highly generalized directions to Brigadier General Breckinridge. The imposing Kentuckian commanded a scratch force of two infantry brigades, some artillery, and the unreliables of Imboden's cavalry. Due to the ineptitude of the Federal commander, Sigel, and the timely support of the V.M.I. cadets at New Market, on May 15 Breckinridge was able to clear the Valley temporarily of the enemy and offer 2400 troops, after casualties, for Lee's major campaign.

South of the James had been separately departmentalized, with Beauregard formally in command, and Lee had no authority in the emergencies between Richmond and Petersburg, which threatened the capital's connections with the South and indirectly the city itself. As Davis had brought up no troops in response to Lee's warnings and advice, Drewry's Bluff and the railroad between Richmond and Petersburg were saved by a series of hair-raising last-ditch stands commanded jointly and informally by Pickett, D. H. Hill (who came as a volunteer) and Robert Ransom, Lee's former division commander who had succeeded Elzey in command of the Department of Richmond. The troops they rushed onto the field by regiments would have availed nothing unless the Federal army, approaching 40,000 aggregate in all arms, had been commanded by Butler, probably the worst political general then still active in the war. After Butler had been halted by Pickett's hodgepodge of troops and guns (including a battalion from Lee's army, which happened to be in the area fattening the gaunt horses on spring grass), Beauregard then came on to assume command and the troops from the Carolina coasts were hurried northward from their garrisons and sieges. Among these more than 20,000 troops were Pickett's four separated brigades (none under his command) and Hoke's old brigade. General Lee's concern was with the return of these troops belonging to his army, since manifestly the assembled number was more than necessary to contain the likes of Butler, while he did not have enough to maintain maneuver against Grant.

With these concurrent actions on his flank and rear, General Lee was forced to concentrate against Grant's major offensive by dismissing from his mind the possibility that Richmond might fall behind him. (General Meade remained officially in command of the Army of the Potomac, which he had reorganized, and Lee frequently refers to "Meade's army," but Grant was *de facto* commander in that the policy and decisions were his, and it is simpler to follow history's designation of the Federal force as "Grant's army.") Before Grant moved out, Lee had boldly determined to meet him with a counteroffensive, though this must be deduced from his actions and known preferences (as in the April 15th letter to Davis) rather than from his scant correspondence.

On May 2, Lee became convinced that Grant, at Culpeper, would thrust across the Germanna and Ely Fords in the Rapidan in the most direct line toward Richmond. The well-fed, well-led Federal army was equipped and supplied as no armed force ever before on earth, with sixty-five miles of wagon train including such items as mobile telegraphic stations, and from the beginning Lee considered the effect on Grant's movements of the dependence on supply. This effect would cause his southern movement to be easterly, within reach of the tidal rivers, from which he could be supplied from naval bases. However, until Grant committed himself Lee could not eliminate the possibility of a southwesterly swing which would threaten the Virginia Central. For this reason Longstreet remained in camp at Gordonsville, a day's march farther on than the corps of Ewell and A. P. Hill.

Grant moved out on the night of May 3, crossed the river at the fords and bivouacked his army on the night of the 4th in the densest part of the Wilderness. As soon as Lee learned that Grant had committed himself, he put Ewell's corps in motion to the east along the Old Turnpike, nearest the river, and two divisions of Hill's corps on the Plank Road which ran its haphazard course to the south of and loosely parallel with the Turnpike. Hill's Third Division, R. H. Anderson, remained at Orange as rear guard until the wagon train had gone forward. (The worn cavalry could not be used for this purpose because the physical superiority of the Federal cavalry required the presence of Stuart's troopers on the flank. Newly under Sheridan, the cavalry with Grant numbered 12,500 men, armed with new repeating carbines and superbly mounted.) Longstreet was ordered to move on a third east-west route, the Catharpin Road, covered by Stuart. All three roads bisected the north-south Brock Road, the main passageway for Grant's army.

Grant had moved aggressively, without feints or maneuver, in the apparent intention of overwhelming Lee. Since Lee did not defend the river crossings, Grant headed south on the assumption that Lee was retreating. Lee's strategy was to catch in flank Grant's heavily encumbered army in passage over the narrow, vine-enclosed roads. Tactics were something else.

When Grant discovered the presence of the Confederates approaching his flank on the Old Turnpike, he ordered his strung-out columns to turn about and attack, without waiting for the proper disposition of the troops. Though Ewell's men were rocked by the suddenness of the assault, then pinned down by the weight of numbers, the Second Corps veterans stabilized their front and threw back Warren's corps, and part of Sedgwick's, with heavy losses.

While this fight was in full progress from the forenoon until after three, Hill's corps, moving up on the Plank Road, was offered a fine opportunity of striking between Grant's scattered units, but the Confederates were unaware of the weakly held intersection of the Plank Road and Brock Road. It developed that the Old Turnpike, where Ewell was engaged, and the Plank Road were separated by two and three-quarters miles of obscuring jungle near the Brock Road, and Lee found himself fighting two separate battles with a blind gap between his corps.

While Wilcox's division was exploring this gap, another hastily organized Federal assault was delivered at Heth's division astride the Plank Road. Before the day was over, most of Hancock's corps and part of Sedgwick's (more than 30,000) assailed first Heth, then Heth and Wilcox, who was recalled to support Heth. Again the piecemeal nature of the Federal assaults made it possible for Lee's infantry to throw them back with heavy losses — though both Heth and Wilcox were fought almost into the ground before night came.

For the next morning, May 6, Lee planned to relieve Heth and Wilcox with Anderson's division and Longstreet, and counterattack the poorly anchored Federal left flank. Longstreet's divisions were brought up from the Catharpin Road across country in a night march. Before they came up, the Federals renewed their attacks on Hill's exhausted men, who had not re-formed their lines from the evening before. Hill's two divisions fell back in growing disorder, and were saved from rout by the terrain and the guns of Poague's battalion placed in the clearing at the Tapp farm. Before these guns could be overrun, Longstreet's men arrived. Catching the Federals in the disorder inevitable in troops advancing through the Wilderness, Longstreet first halted and then forced back the enemy.

Before noon, Lee reverted to the counterattack plan around the unanchored Federal left. Longstreet quickly organized a force from several divisions, led by his own chief of staff, young Moxley Sorrel, and sent them forward secreted in the bed of an unfinished railroad. Their attack from south to north was highly successful and opened the Plank Road for a general advance.

In the confusion, Longstreet was shot by some of his own men, and removed in an ambulance to the rear. Micah Jenkins was killed in the same volley. Lee and Charles Field, the unwanted division commander in Longstreet's corps, needed several hours to straighten out the Confederate lines, which were perpendicular to each other when Longstreet fell. By the time the general advance was resumed, around four, some of Hancock's men had re-formed behind log breastworks along the Brock Road, and Burnside's corps, after wandering all over the Wilderness, had come up in support.

During the seesaw action on the Plank Road, Ewell, from his strong position, had an opportunity on the Federal right flank, which was also exposed; but, away from Lee's direct supervision, he was absolutely supine. When Lee rode over to the Old Turnpike at the end of the day, he ordered the flanking movement to be attempted. Though it achieved some local success, and added to the bag of Federal prisoners, it was too late to affect the total battle.

Grant had fought an extremely unskillful battle. Perhaps made overconfident by victories over the poor Confederate command situations in the West, he simply came in swinging, and the army he inherited was badly mauled, losing more than 15,000 men and finishing the second day on the defensive. But Lee, with his army divided by the gap between his two wings and hurt by Ewell's fighting his competent tactical action in no relation whatsoever to the rest of the army, lacked the manpower to overcome the handicaps of terrain and personnel inadequacy. In terms of the physically weaker opponent fighting his powerful enemy to a standstill — quite literally halting his movement and forcing him to throw up defensive works — the victory would be Lee's. In terms of strategy, the battle was a stalemate. Grant's army had not been punished too severely to prevent its resuming movement and Lee was still in position to maneuver.

After one day's pause, Grant moved southward during the night of May 7, crossing Lee's front and aiming for the crossroads town of Spotsylvania Court House. There he would be between Lee's army and Richmond. Foreseeing this move, Lee directed a road, or trace, constructed through the woods roughly paralleling the Brock Road south, and ordered a night movement by R. H. Anderson, who had temporarily succeeded Longstreet in corps command. Mahone succeeded to command of Anderson's division in Hill's corps. (A. P. Hill fell ill, and Jubal Early temporarily assumed command of the Third Corps.)

The race to the courthouse crossroads was close, narrowly won by Kershaw's division on the morning of May 8 through the magnificent cooperation of Jeb Stuart and the hard fighting of Fitz Lee's cavalry brigades in obstructing the march of Warren's corps on the Brock Road. Grant's intention was thwarted before either commanding general came onto the field, and for all strategic purposes the Battle of Spotsylvania Court House was won right there. Lee was in front of Grant, across his line of march.

Grant then attempted power movements to crush Lee's roadblock to Richmond, and these were not successful. Except for a projecting salient, called the "Mule Shoe," which Ewell's corps had fortified where the chance of battle placed them, Lee utilized the terrain to form powerful angled lines with well-covered flanks, and put his weary men to digging the most intricate and complete field fortifications yet seen in warfare. After all other lines were erected, Lee planned to withdraw Edward Johnson's division of Ewell's corps from the projecting Mule Shoe, and build a new line nearer the base. Before he did this, on the foggy, rainy night of the 11th to 12th, Hancock's corps assaulted the point in a pre-dawn attack.

For a complexity of reasons, Johnson's men offered scarcely any defense and the once proud division of Stonewall Jackson was wrecked as the enemy crowded inside the salient. Partly through the confusion of the attacking masses in the wet woods and largely through the counteraction directed by Lee in field command, inspired performances of individual leaders (especially Rodes, and Ramseur in his division, and Gordon in temporary command of Early's division) drove the Federals back outside the salient, which that day became "Bloody Angle." At Spotsylvania, as earlier at Sharpsburg, Lee showed himself to be as great a combat tactician as a strategist, though no hint of his personal participation is given in his correspondence. With only enfeebled, inadequate Ewell on hand as a veteran permanent corps commander, Lee had directed the three corps as a single force, interchanging units without regard to channels of command.

Then the new line was drawn across the base of the salient and a subsequent mass attack was repulsed with heavy casualties. Though the lines were impregnable, Grant remained at Spotsylvania until the 21st of May, waiting for reinforcements as replacements for his losses which passed 30,000. During his inaction, Beauregard bottled up Butler between two arms of water at Bermuda Hundred, at last freeing for Lee Pickett's division and Hoke's brigade. R. D. Johnston, released from Hanover Junction, joined him during the Wilderness. These troops belonged to his army. In some computations of Lee's strength, these troops have been counted twice — on the roster and when they joined him. His only replacements for losses, then at least 17,000, were Breckinridge's 2400, which arrived from the Valley at Hanover Junction. None of these troops, except Johnston's brigade, were available at Spotsylvania and Lee, growing desperate at the necessity of falling back toward Richmond, began to try to arouse the President to the urgency of concentration.

Also during Spotsylvania, the army suffered a grievous blow and Lee a personal loss when Jeb Stuart took a mortal wound at Yellow Tavern, where he was leading part of his cavalry in a field fight to keep Sheridan's mounted columns out of Richmond. None of Grant's multi-pronged offensive had succeeded, but Lee's army was being bled of its capacity to sustain maneuver.

674   To GENERAL JOHN C. BRECKINRIDGE
Commanding Department of Southwestern Virginia

Headquarters, Army of Northern Virginia
May 1, 1864

General:

I gather from the reports of scouts recently from the Valley that [General William W.] Averell has set out on an expedition, the design of which is either to reach some point on the Virginia & Tennessee Railroad, or to effect the capture of Staunton. The general impression is that he will pursue the route which he took on his last raid. I think it would be well to have everything prepared to meet him, & in conjunction with Genl Imboden to destroy him if possible. The enemy will probably make a diversion from the Kanawha Valley to keep your forces occupied while he accomplishes his main design. I am inclined to think that his object is to move on Staunton. If so, you might move against his line of communications while Imboden holds him in front, or concoct some other plan of defeating him. These movements in the Western Department will probably be simultaneous with the attack by Grant here, who has recently been reinforced by Burnside's army from Annapolis, so it will be impossible to send any reinforcements to the Valley from this army. I have instructed Genl Imboden to communicate with you. A late report from a citizen places Genl [Franz] Sigel at Martinsburg, but this conflicts with former reports.

I am very respectfully, your obt servt

R. E. LEE
Genl

P.S. I doubt the intelligence of Averell's arrival at Charleston, & think that he is nearer some point on his old route.

R. E. LEE

675   To GENERAL BRAXTON BRAGG
           Commanding Armies of the Confederate States
                          TELEGRAM

Orange Court House
May 2, 1864

YOUR DISPATCH RECEIVED. THE TWENTY-FIRST GEORGIA REGIMENT, FORTY-THIRD NORTH CAROLINA REGIMENT, HOKE'S BRIGADE, AND [ROBERT D.] JOHNSTON'S BRIGADE ARE ABSENT FROM THEIR DIVISIONS — FORMER IN NORTH CAROLINA, LATTER AT HANOVER JUNCTION. PLEASE RELIEVE AND SEND THEM ON.

R. E. LEE

676   To HIS WIFE
                  Richmond, Virginia

Camp, Orange Court House
May 2, 1864

Your note of Saturday dear Mary with the bag of socks arrived yesterday. I distributed the socks to the Stonewall Brigade which makes 392 sent to those troops. I am much obliged to you for the shirt & collars. They look very nice. I hope I have enough to answer for the present. I send down the flannel shirts you made for me which I have not required, also my winter boots, to be put in my trunks. I also send the embroidered collar & cuffs sent me by the Misses Semons. Please ask Custis to send up my summer boots, the long pair I sent down last fall, also my blue pants of summer cloth, without stripes. You must thank Cousin George for the gauntlets & give them to Custis if he wants them, if not, & you will send them up, I will give them to Fitzhugh or Rob. Tell Custis he must help himself to any gloves, socks, or boots he wants out of my stock. I believe there is nothing of value in my trunks that he would fancy. If there is, to take them. I should like to have a pair of suspenders in my trunk, new pair. I have a pair of pants on that require them. Fitzhugh & Beverly Turner dined with me yesterday. Both well. They came back with me from church. Mr. Wilmer gave us a beautiful sermon. I saw Mrs. Wilmer with him.

I have no time for more. Give a great deal of love to Custis, Rob & the girls & kind regards to all friends.

With a heart full for you & constant prayers for your restoration & preservation,

I remain most truly

R. E. LEE

677   To GENERAL BRAXTON BRAGG
Commanding Armies of Confederate States
TELEGRAM

Orange Court House
May 4, 1864

ENEMY HAS STRUCK HIS TENTS. INFANTRY, ARTILLERY, AND CAVALRY ARE MOVING TOWARD GERMANNA AND ELY'S FORDS. THIS ARMY IN MOTION TOWARD MINE RUN. CAN PICKETT'S DIVISION MOVE TOWARD SPOTSYLVANIA COURT HOUSE?

R. E. LEE

678   To GENERAL JOHN C. BRECKINRIDGE
Commanding Department of Southwestern Virginia
TELEGRAM

Orange Court House
May 4, 1864

THE PRESIDENT INFORMS ME THAT YOU WILL REPORT TO ME. FOR THE PRESENT YOU WILL TAKE THE GENERAL DIRECTION OF AFFAIRS AND USE GEN-

ERAL IMBODEN'S FORCE AS YOU THINK BEST. HE HAS BEEN ORDERED TO REPORT
TO YOU. I TRUST YOU WILL DRIVE THE ENEMY BACK.

R. E. LEE

679 To GENERAL JOHN C. BRECKINRIDGE
Commanding Department of Southwestern Virginia
TELEGRAM

Orange Court House
May 4, 1864

I DO NOT KNOW WHETHER STAUNTON IS THE THREATENED POINT, BUT
ALL THE FORCE SENT WEST SEEM TO HAVE RETURNED EAST, AND ARE NOW
COMING UP BY FRONT ROYAL OR THE VALLEY. THESE ARE THE FORCES I WISH
YOU TO MEET, OR BY SOME MOVEMENT TO DRAW BACK BEFORE THEY GET ON
MY LEFT. IMBODEN REPORTS SIGEL WITH 7,000 MEN APPROACHING FRONT
ROYAL. COMMUNICATE WITH HIM, AND TRY AND CHECK THIS VALLEY MOVE-
MENT AS SOON AS POSSIBLE.

R. E. LEE

680 To JEFFERSON DAVIS
Richmond, Virginia

Headquarters, New Verdiersville
May 4, 1864

Mr. President:
I have the honor to acknowledge the receipt of your letter of the
2nd instant.
You will already have learned that the army of Genl Meade is in
motion, and is crossing the Rapidan on our right, whether with the intention of attacking, or moving towards Fredericksburg, I am not able to
say. But it is apparent that the long threatened effort to take Richmond
has begun, and that the enemy has collected all his available force to accomplish it. The column on the Peninsula if not already moving, will
doubtless now cooperate with Genl Meade, and we may assume is as
strong as the enemy can make it.
Under these circumstances I regret that there is to be any further
delay in concentrating our own troops. I fully appreciate the advantages

of capturing New Berne, but they will not compensate us for a disaster in Virginia or Georgia. Success in resisting the chief armies of the enemy will enable us more easily to recover the country now occupied by him, if indeed he do not voluntarily relinquish it. We are inferior in numbers, and as I have before stated to Your Excellency the absence of the troops belonging to this army weakens it more than by the mere number of men. Unless the force that it will be necessary to leave in North Carolina is able to reduce New Berne, I would recommend that the attempt be postponed, and the troops in N. C. belonging to this army be at once returned to it, and that Genl Beauregard with all the force available for the purpose, be brought without delay to Richmond. Your opportunities of deciding this question are superior to my own, my advice being based upon such lights as I possess. It seems to me that the great efforts of the enemy here and in Georgia have begun, and that the necessity of our concentration at both points is immediate and imperative.

I submit my views with great deference to the better judgment of Your Excellency, and am satisfied that you will do what the best interests of the country require. The army was put in motion today, and our advance already occupies our former position on Mine Run. The enemy's cavalry is reported advancing both towards Fredericksburg and in this direction, evidently with the intention of ascertaining the disposition of our forces.

With great respect, your obt servt

R. E. LEE
Genl

681   To GENERAL RICHARD S. EWELL
Commanding Corps
TELEGRAM

May 5, 1864

GENERAL EWELL:

CAPTAIN [R. E.] WILBOURN REPORTS EVERYTHING MOVING TO OUR RIGHT EXCEPT CAVALRY. IF SO, BETTER MOVE THE DIVISIONS TO OCCUPY LINES AT MINE RUN, AND BE PREPARED FOR ACTION.

R. E. LEE
General

682 MAJOR C. MARSHALL TO GENERAL RICHARD
S. EWELL
Commanding Corps

Headquarters
Mrs. Capps' [Tapps'] House,
between Parker's Store and Brock Road
May 5, 1864
[6 P.M.]

General:

The general commanding directs me to say that the enemy have made no headway in their attack on General [Henry] Heth, who is near the intersection of the Brock and Plank roads. He hopes to have General [Richard H.] Anderson tomorrow morning, and General Longstreet also, and he wants you to get General [S. Dodson] Ramseur and be ready to act early in the morning. The enemy appear to be on the Wilderness Tavern ridge, and if you see no chance to operate on their right, the general proposes to endeavor to crush their left. He wishes you to send back and care for all your wounded, fill up your ammunition, and be ready to act early in the morning. General [Cadmus M.] Wilcox has just reported that the enemy, who was drawn up on Wilderness Tavern ridge, is all moving up to our right. Should that be the case the General suggests to you the practicability of moving over and taking that ridge, thus severing the enemy from his base, but if this cannot be done without too great a sacrifice, you must be prepared to reenforce our right and make your arrangements accordingly.

Very respectfully, your obedient servant

C. MARSHALL
Aide-de-Camp

683   To JAMES A. SEDDON
Secretary of War
TELEGRAM

Headquarters, Army of Northern Virginia
May 5, 1864
11 P.M.

THE ENEMY CROSSED THE RAPIDAN YESTERDAY AT ELY'S AND GERMANNA FORDS. TWO (2) CORPS OF THIS ARMY MOVED TO OPPOSE HIM. EWELL'S, BY

THE OLD TURNPIKE, & HILL'S, BY THE PLANK ROAD. THEY ARRIVED THIS MORN-
ING IN CLOSE PROXIMITY TO THE ENEMY'S LINE OF MARCH. A STRONG ATTACK
WAS MADE UPON EWELL, WHO REPULSED IT, CAPTURING MANY PRISONERS &
FOUR (4) PIECES OF ARTILLERY. THE ENEMY SUBSEQUENTLY CONCENTRATED
UPON GENL HILL, WHO, WITH HETH'S & WILCOX'S DIVISIONS, SUCCESSFULLY
RESISTED REPEATED & DESPERATE ASSAULTS. A LARGE FORCE OF CAVALRY & AR-
TILLERY ON OUR RIGHT FLANK WAS DRIVEN BACK BY [GENERAL THOMAS L.]
ROSSER'S BRIGADE. BY THE BLESSING OF GOD WE MAINTAINED OUR POSITION
AGAINST EVERY EFFORT UNTIL NIGHT, WHEN THE CONTEST CLOSED. WE HAVE
TO MOURN THE LOSS OF MANY BRAVE OFFICERS & MEN. THE GALLANT BRIG GENL
J. M. JONES WAS KILLED, & BRIG GENL [LEROY A.] STAFFORD, I FEAR, MOR-
TALLY WOUNDED WHILE LEADING HIS COMMAND WITH CONSPICUOUS VALOR.

R. E. LEE

684   To JAMES A. SEDDON
Secretary of War
TELEGRAM

Headquarters, Army of Northern Virginia
Near Orange Court House
May 6, 1864

EARLY THIS MORNING, AS THE DIVISIONS OF GENL HILL ENGAGED ON YES-
TERDAY WERE BEING RELIEVED, THE ENEMY ADVANCED AND CREATED SOME
CONFUSION. THE GROUND LOST WAS RECOVERED AS SOON AS THE FRESH TROOPS
GOT INTO POSITION, AND THE ENEMY DRIVEN BACK TO HIS ORIGINAL LINE.
AFTERWARDS WE TURNED THE LEFT OF HIS FRONT LINE AND DROVE IT FROM
THE FIELD, LEAVING A LARGE NUMBER OF HIS DEAD AND WOUNDED IN OUR
HANDS, AMONG THEM GENL [JAMES S.] WADSWORTH. A SUBSEQUENT AT-
TACK FORCED THE ENEMY INTO HIS ENTRENCHED LINES ON THE BROCK ROAD,
EXTENDING FROM WILDERNESS TAVERN ON THE RIGHT TO TRIGG'S MILL. EVERY
ADVANCE ON HIS PART, THANKS TO A MERCIFUL GOD, HAS BEEN REPULSED. OUR
LOSS IN KILLED IS NOT LARGE, BUT WE HAVE MANY WOUNDED, MOST OF THEM
SLIGHTLY, ARTILLERY BEING LITTLE USED ON EITHER SIDE. I GRIEVE TO AN-
NOUNCE THAT LIEUT GENL LONGSTREET WAS SEVERELY WOUNDED, AND GENL
[MICAH] JENKINS KILLED. GENERAL [JOHN] PEGRAM WAS BADLY WOUNDED
YESTERDAY. GENL STAFFORD, IT IS HOPED, WILL RECOVER.

R. E. LEE

685
To JAMES A. SEDDON
Secretary of War
TELEGRAM

Headquarters, Army of Northern Virginia
May 7, 1864

GENL [JOHN B.] GORDON TURNED THE ENEMY'S EXTREME RIGHT YESTER-
DAY EVENING, & DROVE HIM FROM HIS RIFLE PITS. AMONG THE PRISONERS
CAPTURED WERE GENLS [TRUMAN] SEYMOUR & [ALEXANDER] SHALER. A NUM-
BER OF ARMS WERE ALSO TAKEN. THE ENEMY HAS ABANDONED THE GERMANNA
FORD ROAD, & REMOVED HIS PONTOON BRIDGE TOWARDS ELY'S. THERE HAS BEEN
NO ATTACK TODAY. ONLY SLIGHT SKIRMISHING ALONG THE LINES.

R. E. LEE

686
MAJOR W. H. TAYLOR TO GENERAL J. E. B. STUART
Commanding Cavalry

Headquarters, Army of Northern Virginia
May 7, 1864

General:
General Lee directs me to say that he wishes you would make an
examination and thoroughly inform yourself about the roads on our
right, which it would be advisable or necessary for us to follow should
the enemy continue his movement toward Spotsylvania Court House, or
should we desire to move on his flank in that direction. Find out about
the roads which the infantry would take, and upon which our artillery,
&c., could be thrown around. The enemy now and then advance and feel
our lines, and the general thinks there is nothing to indicate an intention
on his part to retire, but rather that appearances would indicate an intention to move toward Spotsylvania Court House. Your note of 12 received. General Ewell reports that they (the enemy) have abandoned
the Germanna road, and the general thinks they may move toward
Fredericksburg or Spotsylvania Court House and must open some new
way of communication. The general is now about starting to visit General Ewell's lines. He relies upon you to keep him accurately informed
of the enemy's movements should they be in the direction above indicated.

I am most respectfully, your obedient servant
W. H. TAYLOR
Assistant Adjutant General

Fitz Lee's note, indorsed by you at 1.30 p.m., just received. The general says that if what is reported therein is true, it confirms his suspicions. He desires you to ascertain what is going on in the direction alluded to.

Respectfully

W. H. T.

687 MAJOR W. H. TAYLOR TO GENERAL RICHARD S. EWELL
Commanding Corps

Headquarters, Army of Northern Virginia
May 7, 1864
7 P.M.

General:

General Lee directs me to say that he has instructed General Anderson to put Longstreet's corps in motion for Spotsylvania Court House as soon as he can withdraw it from its present position. He will proceed either by Todd's Tavern or Shady Grove Church as circumstances may determine. The general desires you to be prepared to follow with your command should it be discovered that the enemy is moving in that direction, or should any change in his position render it advisable.

I am most respectfully, your obedient servant

W. H. TAYLOR
Assistant Adjutant General

P.S. General Lee will be at Parker's Store tonight. Rodes is closing in to Hill.

688   To JAMES A. SEDDON
Secretary of War
TELEGRAM

Headquarters, Army of Northern Virginia
Via Orange Court House
May 8, 1864

THE ENEMY HAS ABANDONED HIS POSITION AND IS MOVING TOWARDS FREDERICKSBURG.

THIS ARMY IS IN MOTION ON HIS RIGHT FLANK, AND OUR ADVANCE IS NOW
AT SPOTSYLVANIA COURT HOUSE.

R. E. LEE

689   To GENERAL RICHARD S. EWELL
                   Commanding Corps

Headquarters, Army of Northern Virginia
May 8, 1864

I desire you to move on with your corps as rapidly as you can, without injuring the men, to Shady Grove Church. Anderson by this time
is at Spotsylvania Court House and may need your support. The best
route that I know of is the road from Chewning's house to the field in
which my headquarters were, and from which a road has been cut
through the pines in rear of the artillery battalion, crossing the Plank
road to White Hall Mill, where you will fall into Anderson's route to
Shady Grove Church. I will proceed to Shady Grove Church, and wish
you to follow me on to that point.

I am most respectfully, your obedient servant

R. E. LEE
General

690   To GENERAL RICHARD S. EWELL
                  Commanding Corps

Headquarters, Army of Northern Virginia
May 8, 1864

General:
General Hill has reported to me that he is so much indisposed that
he fears he must relinquish the command of his corps. In that case, I
shall be obliged to put General Early in command of it. I wish you to
transfer [General Harry T.] Hays' brigade to [General Robert D.]
Johnston's division, so that the two Louisiana brigades may be together,
they being so much reduced and General Stafford being disabled. In
order to equalize your divisions, you will then transfer R. D. Johnston's
brigade, or some other of Rodes' brigades, whose command is junior to
General Gordon, to General Early's division, so that General Gordon
may take command of the latter.

Very respectfully

R. E. LEE
General

691   To JAMES A. SEDDON
                 Secretary of War
                    TELEGRAM

                                          Near Spotsylvania Court House
                                                      May [8], 1864
                                                         2½ P.M.

AFTER A SHARP ENCOUNTER WITH THE FIFTH ARMY CORPS, [GENERAL GOUVERNEUR K.] WARREN'S, AND [GENERAL ALFRED T.] TORBERT'S DIVISION OF CAVALRY, GENERAL R. H. ANDERSON, WITH THE ADVANCE OF THE ARMY, REPULSED THE ENEMY WITH HEAVY SLAUGHTER AND TOOK POSSESSION OF THE COURT HOUSE. I AM THE MORE GRATEFUL TO THE GIVER OF ALL VICTORY THAT OUR LOSS IS SMALL.

                                                      R. E. LEE
                                                      General

692   To JAMES A. SEDDON
                 Secretary of War
                    TELEGRAM

                                 Headquarters, Army of Northern Virginia
                                                      May 8, 1864
                                                         9 P.M.

AFTER THE REPULSE OF THE ENEMY FROM SPOTSYLVANIA COURT HOUSE THIS MORNING, RECEIVING REINFORCEMENTS, HE RENEWED THE ATTACK ON OUR POSITION, BUT WAS AGAIN HANDSOMELY DRIVEN BACK.

                                                      R. E. LEE

693   To JAMES A. SEDDON
                 Secretary of War
                    TELEGRAM

                                          Spotsylvania Court House
                                                      May 10, 1864

GENL GRANT'S ARMY IS ENTRENCHED NEAR THIS PLACE ON BOTH SIDES OF THE BROCK ROAD. FREQUENT SKIRMISHING OCCURRED YESTERDAY AND TODAY, EACH ARMY ENDEAVORING TO DISCOVER THE POSITION OF THE OTHER. TODAY THE ENEMY SHELLED OUR LINES AND MADE SEVERAL ASSAULTS WITH INFANTRY AGAINST DIFFERENT POINTS, PARTICULARLY ON OUR LEFT, HELD BY GENL R. H. ANDERSON. THE LAST, WHICH OCCURRED AFTER SUNSET, WAS

THE MOST OBSTINATE, SOME OF THE ENEMY LEAPING OVER THE BREAST-
WORKS. THEY WERE EASILY REPULSED, EXCEPT IN FRONT OF [GENERAL GEORGE
P.] DOLES' BRIGADE, WHERE THEY DROVE OUR MEN FROM THEIR POSITION
AND FROM A FOUR-GUN BATTERY THERE POSTED. THE MEN WERE SOON RAL-
LIED, AND BY DARK OUR LINE WAS REESTABLISHED AND THE BATTERY RECOV-
ERED. A LARGE BODY OF THE ENEMY MOVED AROUND OUR LEFT ON THE EVE-
NING OF THE 9TH AND TOOK POSSESSION OF THE ROAD ABOUT MIDWAY
BETWEEN SHADY GROVE CHURCH AND THE COURT HOUSE. GENL EARLY WITH
A PART OF HILL'S CORPS DROVE THEM BACK THIS EVENING, TAKING ONE GUN
AND A FEW PRISONERS. THANKS TO A MERCIFUL PROVIDENCE OUR CASUALTIES
HAVE BEEN SMALL. AMONG THE WOUNDED ARE BRIG GENLS [HARRY T.] HAYS
AND HENRY H. WALKER.

R. E. LEE

694   To GENERAL RICHARD S. EWELL
             Commanding Corps

Headquarters, Army of Northern Virginia
May 10, 1864
8.15 P.M.

General:
    It will be necessary for you to reestablish your whole line tonight.
Set the officers to work to collect & refresh their men and have everything ready for the renewal of the conflict at daylight tomorrow. I wish
Genl Rodes to rectify his line & improve its defences, especially that part
which seemed so easily overcome this afternoon. If no flanking arrangement, a ditch had better be dug on the outside, & an abatis made in front.
Perhaps Genl Grant will make a night attack as it was a favorite amuse-
ment of his at Vicksburg. See that ammunition is provided & every man
supplied.

Very respectfully, your obt servt
R. E. LEE
Genl

695   To JAMES A. SEDDON
               Secretary of War
               TELEGRAM

Headquarters
May 12, 1864

THIS MORNING AT DAWN THE ENEMY BROKE THROUGH THAT PART OF
OUR LINE OCCUPIED BY [GENERAL EDWARD] JOHNSON'S DIVISION AND GAINED

POSSESSION OF A PORTION OF OUR BREASTWORKS, WHICH HE STILL HOLDS. A NUMBER OF PIECES OF ARTILLERY FELL INTO HIS HANDS. THE ENGAGEMENT HAS CONTINUED ALL DAY, AND WITH THE EXCEPTION INDICATED WE HAVE MAINTAINED OUR GROUND. IN THE BEGINNING OF THE ACTION WE LOST A LARGE NUMBER OF PRISONERS, BUT THANKS TO A MERCIFUL PROVIDENCE OUR SUBSEQUENT CASUALTIES WERE NOT LARGE. MAJOR GENL JOHNSON AND BRIG GENL [GEORGE H.] STEUART WERE TAKEN PRISONERS. THE BRAVE GENL [ABNER] PERRIN WAS KILLED AND GENLS [JAMES A.] WALKER OF THE STONEWALL BRIGADE AND [JUNIUS] DANIEL SEVERELY WOUNDED.

R. E. LEE

696   To JEFFERSON DAVIS
Richmond, Virginia
TELEGRAM

Spotsylvania Court House
May 12, 1864

IN BUTLER'S OFFICIAL REPORT TO GRANT, MAY 5TH, HE STATES THAT THE EIGHTEENTH AND TENTH ARMY CORPS HAVE ARRIVED IN HIS DEPARTMENT. THESE CORPS CAME FROM NORTH & SOUTH CAROLINA, GEORGIA, AND FLORIDA, & CONSTITUTE MOST OF THE FEDERAL TROOPS IN THOSE STATES. CANNOT WE NOW DRAW MORE TROOPS FROM THOSE DEPARTMENTS?

R. E. LEE

697   To JAMES A. SEDDON
Secretary of War
TELEGRAM

Headquarters, Army of Northern Virginia
May 13, 1864

THE ENEMY TODAY HAS APPARENTLY BEEN ENGAGED IN BURYING HIS DEAD & CARING FOR HIS WOUNDED. HE HAS MADE NO ATTACK ON OUR LINES. THE LOSS OF ARTILLERY YESTERDAY IS ASCERTAINED TO HAVE BEEN TWENTY PIECES.

R. E. LEE

698   To JEFFERSON DAVIS
                    Richmond, Virginia
                    TELEGRAM

Spotsylvania Court House
May 13, 1864

IF GENL HOKE WITH FRESH TROOPS CAN BE SPARED FROM RICHMOND IT
WOULD BE OF GREAT ASSISTANCE. WE ARE OUTNUMBERED AND CONSTANT
LABOR IS IMPAIRING THE EFFICIENCY OF THE MEN.

R. E. LEE

699   MAJOR C. S. VENABLE TO GENERAL RICHARD
                    S. EWELL
                    Commanding Corps

Headquarters, Army of Northern Virginia
May 14, 1864
12.30 P.M.

General:
    General Lee bids me say that he has received the reports of your
scouts and skirmishers. The enemy is making movements here which
are not yet to be fully understood. He seems to be extending to our
right, having occupied the position at the Beverly house and the Gayle
house (on this side the river). The force at the Beverly house this morning was heavy, and General William H. F. Lee thinks the force at Gayle
house was merely to cover a movement up a bottom leading into the Ny.

I am very respectfully, your obedient servant

C. S. VENABLE
Assistant Adjutant General

700   To GENERAL JOHN C. BRECKINRIDGE
                Commanding Department of Southwestern Virginia
                    TELEGRAM

Headquarters, Army of Northern Virginia
May 14, 1864

IF YOU CAN DRIVE BACK THE DIFFERENT EXPEDITIONS THREATENING THE
VALLEY IT WOULD BE VERY DESIRABLE FOR YOU TO JOIN ME WITH YOUR
WHOLE FORCE.

R. E. LEE
Genl

701   To JEFFERSON DAVIS
Richmond, Virginia
TELEGRAM

Headquarters, Spotsylvania Court House
May 14, 1864

BRECKINRIDGE IS CALLING FOR REINFORCEMENTS TO DEFEND VALLEY. IF
WITHDRAWN THERE WILL BE NO OPPOSITION TO [GENERAL FRANZ] SIGEL.
GENL GRANT IS REOPENING ROUTE BY AQUIA CREEK AND RECEIVING REIN-
FORCEMENTS AND SUPPLIES.

R. E. LEE

702   To JEFFERSON DAVIS
Richmond, Virginia
TELEGRAM

Spotsylvania Court House
May 15, 1864

YESTERDAY AFTERNOON THE ENEMY ASSAULTED A PORTION OF WILCOX'S
LINE & WAS HANDSOMELY REPULSED. MAHONE'S AND LANE'S BRIGADES AT-
TACKED HIS LEFT & CAPTURED ABOUT THREE HUNDRED PRISONERS & FOUR
STANDS OF COLORS. DURING THE FORENOON OF TODAY THERE HAS BEEN
LIGHT SKIRMISHING ALONG THE LINES. THE ENEMY SEEMS TO BE SHIFTING
HIS POSITION TO OUR RIGHT. ANOTHER ATTACK WAS MADE THIS AFTERNOON
ON HIS LEFT BY [GENERALS AMBROSE R.] WRIGHT'S & [NATHANIEL H.] HARRIS'
BRIGADES RESULTING IN THE CAPTURE OF SOME PRISONERS & A STAND OF
COLORS.

R. E. LEE

703   To HIS WIFE
Richmond, Virginia

Spotsylvania Court House
May 16, 1864

My Dearest Mary:
    I received your note with the 20 pairs socks. The latter I have
distributed. Just before leaving Orange the Quartermaster received thirty

thousand pairs which are sufficient. The ladies had better therefore retain for the present the socks they manufacture. I have thought of you very often in these last eventful days & have wished to write to you, but have found it impossible. As I write I am expecting the sound of the guns every moment. I grieve the loss of our gallant officers & men, & miss their aid & sympathy. A more zealous, ardent, brave & devoted soldier, than Stuart, the Confederacy cannot have.

Praise be to God for having sustained us so far. May His blessing be continued to us. I return the bag, napkins & towel. Give much love to all. God bless & preserve you.

Truly & affly

R. E. Lee

704 To JAMES A. SEDDON
Secretary of War
TELEGRAM

Guiney's
May 16, 1864

THE ENEMY REMAINED QUIET IN OUR FRONT TODAY. LATE THIS AFTERNOON HE IS REPORTED MOVING IN FORCE TO OUR RIGHT ON THE TELEGRAPH ROAD. HIS TRAINS HAVE BEEN PASSING BACK TOWARDS FREDERICKSBURG, APPARENTLY TO PROCURE FRESH SUPPLIES.

R. E. Lee

705 To GENERAL JOHN C. BRECKINRIDGE
Commanding Valley District
TELEGRAM

Spotsylvania Court House
May 16, 1864
12¼ P.M.

I OFFER YOU THE THANKS OF THIS ARMY FOR YOUR VICTORY OVER GENL SIGEL. PRESS HIM DOWN THE VALLEY, & IF PRACTICABLE FOLLOW HIM INTO MARYLAND.

R. E. Lee

706   To GENERAL JOHN C. BRECKINRIDGE
Commanding Valley District
TELEGRAM

Guiney's Station
May 16, 1864

IF YOU [DO NOT DEEM] IT PRACTICABLE TO CARRY OUT THE SUGGESTION OF MY DISPATCH OF THIS MORNING TO DRIVE THE ENEMY FROM THE VALLEY & PURSUE HIM INTO MARYLAND, YOU CAN BE OF GREAT SERVICE WITH THIS ARMY. IF YOU CAN FOLLOW SIGEL INTO MARYLAND, YOU WILL DO MORE GOOD THAN BY JOINING US. IF YOU CANNOT, & YOUR COMMAND IS NOT OTHERWISE NEEDED IN THE VALLEY OR IN YOUR DEPARTMENT, I DESIRE YOU TO PREPARE TO JOIN ME. ADVISE ME WHETHER THE CONDITION OF AFFAIRS IN YOUR DEPARTMENT WILL ADMIT OF THIS MOVEMENT SAFELY, & IF SO, I WILL NOTIFY YOU OF THE TIME & ROUTE.

R. E. LEE

707   To JAMES A. SEDDON
Secretary of War
TELEGRAM

Spotsylvania Court House
May 17, 1864

THE ENEMY HAS MADE NO DEMONSTRATION AGAINST OUR POSITION TODAY. HIS ARMY STILL LIES IN THE VALLEY OF THE NY, EXTENDING ACROSS THE ROAD FROM THIS PLACE TO FREDERICKSBURG. FOR SOME REASON THERE SEEMS TO BE A PAUSE IN HIS MOVEMENTS. THE ARMY RECEIVED WITH JOY THE NEWS OF GENL BEAUREGARD'S SUCCESS SOUTH OF JAMES RIVER, AS REPORTED IN THE PAPERS OF TODAY.

R. E. LEE

708   To GENERAL JOHN C. BRECKINRIDGE
Commanding Valley District
TELEGRAM

Spotsylvania Court House
May 17, 1864

DISPATCH OF TODAY RECEIVED. IT IS REPORTED THAT AVERELL & [GENERAL GEORGE] CROOK HAVE RETIRED. IF YOU CAN ORGANIZE A GUARD FOR VALLEY

AND BE SPARED FROM IT, PROCEED WITH INFANTRY TO HANOVER JUNCTION
BY RAILROAD. CAVALRY, IF AVAILABLE, CAN MARCH.

R. E. LEE
Genl

709   To JEFFERSON DAVIS
                      Richmond, Virginia
                      TELEGRAM

Spotsylvania Court House
May 18, 1864

IF THE CHANGED CIRCUMSTANCES AS AROUND RICHMOND WILL PERMIT,
I RECOMMEND THAT SUCH TROOPS AS CAN BE SPARED BE SENT TO ME AT ONCE.
REPORTS FROM OUR SCOUTS UNITE IN STATING THAT REINFORCEMENTS TO
GENL GRANT ARE ARRIVING. THE 22ND CORPS IN WHOLE OR PART HAS PASSED
THROUGH FREDERICKSBURG AND DRAFTED MEN ARE ARRIVING FROM THE NORTH.

R. E. LEE

710   To JEFFERSON DAVIS
                      Richmond, Virginia
                      TELEGRAM

Spotsylvania Court House
May 18, 1864

I THINK GENL GRANT IS WAITING FOR REINFORCEMENTS. THE 22ND, A
CORPS UNDER [GENERAL CHRISTOPHER C.] AUGUR, & SOME ARTILLERY SERVING
AS INFANTRY ARE ARRIVING. THE "CHRONICLE" OF THE 13TH STATES THAT THE
10TH & 18TH CORPS . . . (EFFECTIVE) RICHMOND WHERE THEY DO NO GOOD
TO GENL GRANT. THE FORTS AROUND WASHINGTON & THE NORTHERN CITIES
ARE BEING STRIPPED OF TROOPS. THE QUESTION IS WHETHER WE SHALL FIGHT
THE BATTLE HERE OR AROUND RICHMOND. IF THE TROOPS ARE OBLIGED TO BE
RETAINED AT RICHMOND I MAY BE FORCED BACK.

R. E. LEE

711   To JAMES A. SEDDON
                           Secretary of War
                           TELEGRAM

                                          Spotsylvania Court House
                                                   May 18, 1864
                                                      7 P.M.

THE ENEMY OPENED HIS BATTERIES AT SUNRISE ON A PORTION OF EWELL'S
LINES, ATTEMPTED AN ASSAULT, BUT FAILED. HE WAS EASILY REPULSED. SUBSE-
QUENTLY HE CANNONADED A PORTION OF HILL'S LINES UNDER EARLY. CASUAL-
TIES ON OUR SIDE VERY FEW.

                                                      R. E. LEE

712   To JEFFERSON DAVIS
                           Richmond, Virginia
                           TELEGRAM

                                          Spotsylvania Court House
                                                   May 20, 1864

TELEGRAM OF 19TH RECEIVED. AM FULLY ALIVE TO IMPORTANCE OF CON-
CENTRATION AND BEING NEAR BASE. THE LATTER CONSIDERATION MAY IMPEL
ME TO FALL BACK EVENTUALLY. WILL DO SO AT ONCE IF DEEMED BEST. MY
LETTERS GAVE YOU MY VIEWS. THE TROOPS PROMISED WILL BE ADVANTAGEOUS
IN EITHER EVENT. I HAVE POSTED BRECKINRIDGE AT [HANOVER] JUNCTION TO
GUARD COMMUNICATION, WHENCE HE CAN SPEEDILY RETURN TO VALLEY IF
NECESSARY. HIS INFANTRY NUMBERS TWENTY-FOUR HUNDRED.

                                                      R. E. LEE
                                                         Genl

713 MAJOR C. MARSHALL TO GENERAL RICHARD
                           S. EWELL
                      Commanding Corps

                                                   [May 20, 1864]
General:
     General Lee directs me to say that Maj Genl W. H. F. Lee reports
at 2.30 p.m. that his pickets were driven in at Smith's Mill, where the

Telegraph road crosses the Ny River. They report that the enemy has a line of dismounted skirmishers, followed by infantry.

Very respectfully, your obedient servant

C. MARSHALL
Aide-de-Camp

P.S. The enemy seems to be lengthening out his line down the Ny, offering us an opportunity to strike at him. The general wishes to know whether you discover any movement of the enemy in your front, and whether his rear is weak enough for you to strike at?

C. M.

714 MAJOR C. S. VENABLE TO GENERAL RICHARD S. EWELL
Commanding Corps

Headquarters, Army of Northern Virginia
May 20, 1864
8.30 P.M.

General:

General Lee bids me say that the enemy seems now, by the reports of our reconnoitering officers, to have extended his left to the Po in front of Anderson's. He has heard nothing from you of the enemy in your front, or of the necessity of your retaining your present position. He desires you to have your troops in readiness to move at daybreak tomorrow to take position on the right. He desires you to move at that time without further orders, provided you find nothing to detain you in your present position. Your troops can move by the road in rear of the lines out of view, and cross the Po at Crutchfield's. Your wagons can move by the old Spotsylvania Court House road. He desires to hear from you.

Yours very respectfully

C. S. VENABLE
Aide-de-Camp

715   GENERAL ORDERS, NO. 44

Headquarters, Army of Northern Virginia
May 20, 1864

The commanding general announces to the army with heartfelt sorrow the death of Maj Genl J. E. B. Stuart, late commander of the Cavalry Corps of the Army of Northern Virginia. Among the gallant soldiers who have fallen in this war General Stuart was second to none in valor, in zeal, and in unfaltering devotion to his country. His achievements form a conspicuous part of the history of this army, with which his name and services will be forever associated. To military capacity of a high order and all the nobler virtues of the soldier he added the brighter graces of a pure life, guided and sustained by the Christian's faith and hope. The mysterious hand of an all wise God has removed him from the scene of his usefulness and fame. His grateful countrymen will mourn his loss and cherish his memory. To his comrades in arms he has left the proud recollection of his deeds, and the inspiring influence of his example.

R. E. Lee
General

CHAPTER FIFTEEN

North Anna to Petersburg

"Our best policy . . . to unite"

G RANT'S CAMPAIGN has usually been described as a series of crablike flanking movements, but this is not strictly accurate. Grant began his operations by crossing the Rapidan, heading nearly due south with the intention of rolling over Lee's army. After Lee struck against his flank at the Wilderness, Grant resumed a southward movement, crossing Lee's front in a night march. When Lee won the race for Spotsylvania and stood astride Grant's passage, then Grant tried and failed to overrun him. After Spotsylvania, Grant moved (May 21) in a wide semicircle, beginning southeastward, where he utilized the naval base at Port Royal, and swinging back southwestward to the Telegraph Road (approximately the present Route 1), where he again pointed due south to Richmond. In this semicircular movement his intention was, as at Spotsylvania, to get between Lee and Richmond on the most direct north-south route to the capital. As Lee anticipated the movement by way of the naval base, and as Grant (with Sheridan off on his raid) lacked sufficient cavalry to screen his operations, Lee was waiting for him at the North Anna River, again squarely across his path.

Two miles south of the North Anna was Hanover Junction, where the Virginia Central crossed the Richmond, Fredericksburg & Potomac. Lee seemed not to expect another straight-on attack from Grant, with the Federals so close to the vulnerable railroads, and placed his army for movement rather than to contest a river crossing. However, Grant pushed Warren's corps across upriver, at Jericho Mills, and revealed the intention of crossing Hancock the next day at the bridges. When Hancock came over on May 24 and Warren was strengthened, Lee had devised one of the most ingenious defensive tactics of the war to receive them. By ar-

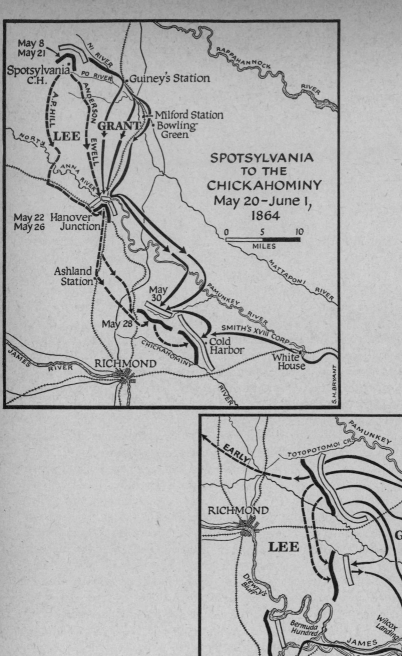

May 8
May 21

Spotsylvania C.H.

NI RIVER

PO RIVER

Guiney's Station

RAPPAHANNOCK

RIVER

A.P. HILL

ANDERSON

Milford Station
Bowling-
Green

LEE

GRANT

EWELL

NORTH

ANNA RIVER

SPOTSYLVANIA
TO THE
CHICKAHOMINY
May 20–June 1,
1864

May 22
May 26

Hanover
Junction

0   5   10
MILES

MATTAPONI RIVER

Ashland
Station

PAMUNKEY RIVER

May
30

May 28

CHICKAHOMINY

SMITH'S XVIII CORPS

Cold
Harbor

JAMES
RIVER

RICHMOND

White
House

RIVER

S.H.BRYANT

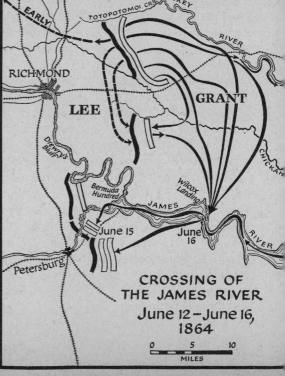

EARLY

PAMUNKEY

TOTOPOTOMOI CR.

RIVER

RICHMOND

LEE

GRANT

CHICKAH

Drewry's
Bluff

Bermuda
Hundred

Wilcox
Landing

JAMES

June 15

June
16

RIVER

Petersburg

CROSSING OF
THE JAMES RIVER
June 12–June 16,
1864

0   5   10
MILES

ranging heavily fortified lines in a triangle, the apex resting on high
ground on the river, he had Grant's army divided and Hancock's corps
isolated from support on the same side of the river with Lee's army.

But on that day Lee fell ill with an acute intestinal disorder which
disabled him for more than a week, and there was no one to direct an
assault on the exposed Hancock. When Grant withdrew the troops back
to the north bank of the river, Lee grew extremely agitated at missing
the opportunities earned by his brilliant tactics, even though no repulse
could have been more decisive than the bloodless victory of the North
Anna.

It was after the great unfought battle of the North Anna, when Grant
found that he could neither move around nor over Lee's army, that he
made his wide swing to his left, southeast, and tried to turn Lee's flank
and come at Richmond from another direction. Each move, however unsuccessful, brought him nearer to Richmond, and brought Lee nearer to
immobilization in works, and his correspondence from Spotsylvania on-
ward was directed at effecting a concentration of troops which would enable him to maintain maneuver. Before leaving the North Anna, Lee
learned that Grant would reinforce his already huge army by drawing
Smith's XVIII Corps from Butler, trapped in his works at Bermuda Hundred. Since this made it obvious that Grant planned no offensive south
of the James, Lee suggested that Beauregard, leaving only enough men
to contain Butler, collaborate with him in a countermove against Grant.

Unknown to Lee, Beauregard had made the same suggestion to the
President. Davis revealed to Beauregard that he regarded him as fixed in
his own Department (as Lee was in his) and regarded Beauregard's
troops as potential feeders for Lee's support — not for concentration in
a countermaneuver but only for possible emergencies. With this knowledge, Beauregard determined to relinquish no troops at all to Lee. Against
this unknown background Lee began his movement to meet Grant's
swing to the southeast.

Grant's army moved on May 26 along the north bank of the North
Anna, which soon became the Pamunkey, and crossed to the south bank
at and in the area of the abandoned river port of Hanovertown. Here, by
a patchwork of cross-country roads, Grant could move to the Old Church
Road, which entered Richmond by way of Mechanicsville, or swing
westward to the Virginia Central. Lee's continuing brief reports indicate
little of the heavy skirmishing along Totopotomoi Creek and the hard
cavalry engagement at Haw's Shop (where parts of the South Carolina
mounted regiments first joined him) by which Lee grew convinced
that Grant was shifting for a thrust at Richmond in the region of the
Old Church Road.

Because of Lee's continuing shift to the right across the Federal front, Grant strove to turn Lee's right to the east of the Old Church Road at the road intersection at Cold Harbor Tavern, throwing in Smith's recently arrived XVIII Corps beyond Lee's flank. It was to counter this danger that Lee, receiving no cooperation from Beauregard, sent his May 30 night telegram to Davis calling for Hoke's division. (Robert Hoke was the former brigadier with Lee who, after a successful winter action at Plymouth, North Carolina, had been occupied with the ineffectual siege of New Berne at the opening of Grant's Virginia campaign. Coming up to the Bermuda Hundred area with the various brigades which arrived after Butler had been checked, Hoke, then major general, was given command of a division formed of four North Carolina brigades, numbering about 7000 after casualties.)

Before Grant concentrated at Cold Harbor, Lee — still sick — from his headquarters ordered a joint attack by Hoke and Anderson on the morning of June 1 to capture the intersection from Sheridan's cavalry while the Federal infantry columns were in motion. In Lee's absence, the coordination was so poor and the assault so ill managed that General Lee did not even mention the abortive attempt at counteroffensive in his messages. Late on the 1st the Federals struck between Hoke and Anderson, where they were contained after effecting a breach. On June 2 Grant, finding Lee again across his front, determined once more to try to drive over the depleted army in his path. This misguided effort, beginning at daylight June 3, resulted in the highest casualties in the war for a period of time — 7000 in little more than fifteen minutes for the main assault, when most of the damage was done to the Army of the Potomac.

With upwards of 50,000 casualties by then, the army Grant inherited was shaken in morale and lowered in effectiveness, with a heavy proportion of its veterans lost. While stalemated before Lee's works at Cold Harbor, Grant reverted to the employment of secondary offensives designed to disrupt Lee's supplies. Hunter, who succeeded Milroy in the Valley as arsonist and pillager, drove toward Lynchburg, while Sheridan was sent off with two cavalry divisions to wreck the Virginia Central from the west and join Hunter.

To prevent the juncture of these two enemy forces, Lee was forced to send off most of his cavalry. Under Wade Hampton the Confederate troopers turned back Sheridan at Trevilian's Station and he returned to Grant without accomplishing anything. For Hunter, Lee wanted to go beyond a mere counter. He wanted this force, which (in Lee's words) "infested the Valley," to be destroyed, and he wanted to clear the Valley for the gathering of supplies. To accomplish this he relinquished Jackson's old Second Corps, then reduced to 8000 infantry newly under

Jubal Early. Lee had used an illness of Ewell's to retire him from the army; to salvage his pride and to employ his limited usefulness, Ewell was to succeed Robert Ransom in command of the Richmond defenses. With Early went Breckinridge. Hunter fled before their approach back into the mountains and saved his army, but left the Valley clear. To prevent Hunter's return, Lee ordered Early northward down the Valley to gather supplies and to present such threat as possible to Washington that might draw off troops from Grant.

While Lee had saved his supply sources and kept open Richmond's communications north of the James, he had reduced his own army to 28,000 infantry (plus Hoke's unattached division) and two lean cavalry brigades, when Grant made his next move. This was a shift of the operations to south of the James designed, by taking lightly held Petersburg, to cut off Richmond and Lee from the Lower South. A capture of the junction city across Lee's lines of communication would force him out of his works and into the open.

The Army of the Potomac moved out of the Cold Harbor lines on the night of June 12-13, marching eastward along the north bank of the Chickahominy to a pontoon crossing at Long Bridge, then south through the damp heat of the low country to the James River at the wharf of Dr. Wilcox. Here, with the help of ferries from Fort Monroe, the Federal army's engineering corps built a stout pontoon bridge across the 700-yard-wide James, with tidal waves reaching four feet, to Windmill Point, sixteen miles by road from Petersburg. Hancock's Corps crossed to the south bank of the James during the night of the 14th-15th.

Simultaneously with this movement, Smith's XVIII Corps was returned by naval transport to Butler's army and, crossing on pontoons to the south side of the Appomattox River, made a direct assault on the fortifications at Petersburg in the afternoon of the 15th. Hancock arrived on the field late in the afternoon but did not become engaged, and Smith failed to exploit the breach he made in the works manned then by only one infantry brigade, supported by considerable artillery — or, rather, the 2200 infantrymen supported the guns.

During this action the Confederate departmental system collapsed. At the clearinghouse for the separate Departments, Braxton Bragg, Lee's successor as expediter, failed to expedite. As Beauregard, in his jealousy of Lee, had communicated meticulously through the war office, he did not turn to Lee until Bragg's incompetence made his situation desperate; then he explained nothing, provided only fragmentary and mostly inaccurate information, and simply demanded that the general (with whom he had refused to cooperate) now send him units from his own army. Beauregard, understandably under severe strain, failed to analyze the situation on his front and never tried to clarify the situation to Lee.

After it was all over, Beauregard wrote a persuasive myth about the "urgent reports" he sent to Lee for help in meeting "Grant's whole army" on his front, and, despite all the existing records, this myth has created an impression of Lee's army idly occupying an empty section in front of Richmond while the general bemusedly refused to credit Beauregard's intelligence. Beauregard's myth was built on a skillful, and quite conscienceless, arrangement of quotations out of context from both Lee's messages and his, combined with omissions from the correspondence, especially where Lee asked him point blank if he knew that Grant had crossed the James and Beauregard wired in answer that he did not know. Lee's letters and telegrams, in full, trace his course through the confusion caused by Beauregard's erratic behavior and the breakdown in the departmental system within which both he and Beauregard operated.

On the 13th, the day when his pickets found Grant's army gone from Cold Harbor, Lee crossed to the south side of the Chickahominy and moved eastward from Richmond (in the area of the second part of the Seven Days) until his cavalry made contact with Grant's cavalry and Warren's V Corps. On the first day, he knew Grant's approximate location and on the next day, the 14th, his two letters to Davis show that he knew Grant was at the James, that Lee expected him to cross over, and that he had detached Hoke to be in readiness to return to Beauregard. In the morning of June 15, Colonel Paul, of Beauregard's staff, visited Lee's camp to petition for the return of Hoke and all troops belonging in the south-side Department, and Lee's messages to Davis and Bragg show that this request was met promptly in detail. (At that time Hancock was marching in Beauregard's Department from Windmill Point, but Beauregard did not then know this.)

The complications, which are ignored in the myth and by all repeaters of the myth, began at half-past two in the morning of the 16th. After trying vainly to obtain advice from Bragg, Beauregard abandoned his lines across Bermuda Hundred during the night of the 15th-16th and moved all his force to Petersburg. The first Lee heard of this was in the wire which awakened him in the middle of the night announcing that the lines containing Butler *had* been abandoned and rather casually suggesting that he might restore them.

To this first indirect call from Beauregard for the use of troops from the Army of Northern Virginia in his Department, Lee immediately put Pickett's division in motion and followed it by Field, both under command of Anderson, and then himself crossed the river on the morning of the 16th. Beauregard's action, done without informing Lee in advance, had exposed the railroad connecting Richmond and Petersburg to But-

ler's troops, who were tearing up the tracks and in position astride the
highway when Pickett's first brigades crossed to the south side. At that
stage Beauregard (who passed lightly over this crisis) was isolated at
Petersburg, with Lee and one third of Lee's army fighting in his Department to reopen communications between the two cities. Grant saw
such opportunity in the wedge between the cities that he diverted divisions from the VI Corps and part of the XVIII Corps to support Butler.

Lee's first message on arriving at Drewry's Bluff on the morning of the
16th reveals that he had received no information from Beauregard. But
one of the suppressed messages showed that Beauregard knew nothing
of the situation at the lines he had abandoned and, blithely assuming that
all had been taken care of, asked for "more" reinforcements with which
to open a counteroffensive against the "enemy." Far from mentioning
that Grant's whole army was in his front, he implied such a small number as could be driven away. This is the message that Lee answered at
half-past ten in the morning of the 16th, while his own troops were
deploying for action against Butler. At that time, Burnside's corps had
marched from Windmill Point to Petersburg and Warren's V Corps
made the march during the day and evening, nearing Petersburg at midnight. It was not Lee who could not be convinced of this, but Beauregard who did not know of the enemy activity on his own front. Lee's
4 P.M. wire asks the direct question if Grant's army had been seen crossing the James. Beauregard's answer on the afternoon of the 16th was:
"No information yet received of Grant's crossing James River." He
mentioned that Hancock was with Smith in his front.

One corps from Grant's army did not mean that Grant had crossed
his whole army to the south side. All during the 16th, as during the 15th,
Grant's cavalry north of the James had remained active on A. P. Hill's
front near Riddell's shop, and Rooney Lee's two brigades were too thin
to break through the screen. With Pickett and Field on the south side,
Lee had left barely 20,000 infantry in front of Richmond, and Grant
had an army of more than 100,000, exclusive of Butler's smaller army.
There was nothing to prevent Grant's dividing his army, sending Hancock to support Butler at Petersburg. The pontoon bridge from Wilcox's
Landing to Windmill Point was beyond the point of observation from
north of the James or by the Confederate gunboats, and the only information Lee — isolated at Drewry's Bluff — could obtain of Grant's
movements south of the James must come from Beauregard.

The last Federal infantry crossed the James at the end of the day of
the 16th, followed by the cavalry at midnight, and it was not until the
17th that the north side of the James was free of enemy action. And it
was not until the afternoon of the 17th that Pickett and Field retook

Beauregard's abandoned lines, reopening the passage between the capital and Petersburg. By then, only then, Beauregard's messages did grow urgent and more detailed, though still indefinite and inaccurate. (He asked Lee for information of Warren's V Corps, when that corps was fighting on his own front.) After receiving this report on the 17th, Lee ordered Kershaw, already at the crossing over the James, to move to Petersburg, and ordered A. P. Hill to cross at 3 A.M.

On the morning of the 18th Kershaw moved into the lines at Petersburg, followed shortly by Field's then 3000-man division, leaving only Pickett to contain Butler. Lee rode into Petersburg after Kershaw and Field, and Hill's corps began arriving at the end of the day.

Despite Beauregard's unhelpful, contradictory messages to Lee (in which he tried to get Lee's troops without their general), his approximately 14,000 infantry made a magnificent stand during the 16th and 17th against repeated assaults delivered by three corps of Grant's army and one of Butler's. The heroic defense was made possible by the disconnected, clumsy attacks mounted by an army which had, for the time being, been drained of offensive strength. With the Petersburg action, Grant lost more men than Lee had, in all arms, to begin with, and the fought-out men had little taste for further attacks against breastworks. After Lee's two divisions got into position, the last Federal assaults petered out, and by the time Lee himself rode onto the field it was all over.

June 18th marked the end of Grant's campaign against Richmond, and it also marked the end of Lee's capacity to maintain maneuver. In achieving a stalemate against Grant's hosts, Lee had been forced into static fortifications, the one eventuality he most dreaded. As he told Early before the Second Corps left for the Valley, once his army was placed in the position to withstand a siege, "it will be a mere question of time."

716   To JAMES A. SEDDON
Secretary of War
TELEGRAM

Spotsylvania Court House
May 21, 1864
8.40 A.M.

THE ENEMY IS APPARENTLY AGAIN CHANGING HIS BASE. THREE GUNBOATS CAME UP TO PORT ROYAL TWO DAYS SINCE. THIS MORNING AN INFANTRY FORCE APPEARED AT GUINEY'S. HIS CAVALRY ADVANCED AT DOWNER'S BRIDGE, ON BOWLING GREEN ROAD. HE IS APPARENTLY PLACING THE MATTAPONY BETWEEN

US, AND WILL PROBABLY OPEN COMMUNICATION WITH PORT ROYAL. I AM
EXTENDING ON THE TELEGRAPH ROAD, AND WILL REGULATE MY MOVEMENTS
BY THE INFORMATION [RECEIVED. THE CHARACTER] OF HIS ROUTE I FEAR WILL
SECURE HIM FROM ATTACK TILL HE CROSSES PAMUNKEY.

R. E. LEE

717   To GENERAL RICHARD H. ANDERSON
Commanding Corps

Headquarters, Army of Northern Virginia
May 21, 1864
3 P.M.

General:
  Genl Early reports that he has swept his front & finds nothing but a
line of skirmishers. I have directed Genl Field to sweep his front, & if
he finds enemy gone, to prepare his troops to march & report result to
you. I wish you, if he reports enemy gone, to put your troops in motion
at once on the route which I have designated to you.

I am very respectfully, your obt servt

R. E. LEE
Genl

718   To GENERAL JOHN C. BRECKINRIDGE
Commanding at Hanover Junction

Spotsylvania Court House
May 21, 1864

  Remain at Junction. Defend the position. Get up your transportation and be prepared to move. Fitz Lee is following cavalry.

R. E. LEE

719   To JEFFERSON DAVIS
Richmond, Virginia

Headquarters, Army of Northern Virginia
May 22, 1864
Dickinson's Mill
Telegraph Road
5 A.M.

Mr. President:
  I have had the honor to receive this morning your letters of the 19th
& 20th instant. Part of the troops you were so kind as to order to me

have joined, viz, Hoke's & Barton's brigades. Corse's & Kemper's reached Milford yesterday evening, but I have not been able as yet to get them to me, I hope to do so today. The enemy night before last commenced to withdraw from his position & to move towards Bowling Green. The movement was not discovered until after daylight, & in a wooded country like that in which we have been operating, where nothing is known beyond what can be ascertained by feeling, a day's march can always be gained. The enemy left in his trenches the usual amount of force generally visible, & the reports of his movement were so vague & conflicting that it required some time to sift the truth. It appeared however that he was endeavoring to place the Mattapony River between him & our army, which secured his flank, & by rapid movements to join his cavalry under [General Philip] Sheridan to attack Richmond. I therefore thought it safest to move to the Annas [North Anna and South Anna Rivers] to intercept his march, and to be within easy reach of Richmond. As soon therefore as his forces in my front could be disposed of, I withdrew the army from its position, & with two corps arrived here this morning. The 3d Corps (Hill's) is moving on my right & I hope by noon to have the whole army behind the Annas. I should have preferred contesting the enemy's approach inch by inch; but my solicitude for Richmond caused me to abandon that plan. The enemy's whole force with the exception of the 9th Corps had left their former positions before dark yesterday. I have not heard of their infantry beyond Bowling Green. I have thought it probable that he might from that point open communication with Port Royal on the Rappahannock; but I learned yesterday from a scout returned from the north of that river, that they had commenced to rebuild the railroad from Acquia Creek to Fredericksburg. As soon as I can get more positive information concerning the movements of the enemy, I will forward it to you.

I am with great respect, your obt servant

R. E. LEE
Genl

720   To JAMES A. SEDDON
                Secretary of War

Hanover Junction
May 22, 1864
9.30 A.M.

I have arrived at this place with the head of Ewell's corps. Longstreet is close up. Hill I expect to come in on my right but have not heard from him since I left him last night. I have learned as yet nothing of the movements of the enemy east of the Mattapony.

R. E. LEE
Genl

721   To JEFFERSON DAVIS
Richmond, Virginia

Headquarters, Army of Northern Virginia
May 23, 1864

Mr. President:
Your letter of the 19th instant giving me a general account of the condition of military affairs has been received. This army is now lying south of the North Anna. I have moved General Breckinridge's command in front of Hanover Court House to guard the main route from Richmond. I will add to it Col Bradley T. Johnson's, which I think will be sufficient to check any movement in that direction if made. At present all my information indicates that the movement of General Grant's army is in the direction of Milford Station, and General Hampton who is in front of that place is of the opinion that it will march upon Hanover Junction by that route. If that is its course, I think it is for the purpose of adhering to the railroad which, as I informed you yesterday, I hear is being repaired north of the Rappahannock. During its reconstruction, General Grant will have time to recruit and reorganize his army, which as far as I am able to judge, has been very much shaken. I think it is on that account that he interposed the Mattapony between us. Whatever route he pursues I am in a position to move against him, and shall endeavor to engage him while in motion. I shall also be near enough Richmond I think, to combine the operations of this army with that under General Beauregard and shall be as ready to reinforce him if occasion requires, as to receive his assistance. As far as I can understand, General Butler is in a position from which he can only be driven by assault, and which I have no doubt, has been made as strong as possible. Whether it would be proper or advantageous to attack it, General Beauregard can determine, but if not, no more troops are necessary there than to retain the enemy in his entrenchments. On the contrary General Grant's army will be in the field, strengthened by all available troops from the north, and it seems to me our best policy to unite upon it and endeavor to crush it. I should be very glad to have the aid of General Beauregard in such a blow, and if it is possible to combine, I think it will succeed. The courage

of this army was never better, and I fear no injury to it from any retrograde movement that may be dictated by sound military policy, I do not think it would be well to permit the enemy to approach the Chickahominy, if it can be prevented, and do not see why we could not combine against him after he has crossed the Pamunkey as on the Chickahominy. His difficulties will be increased as he advances, and ours diminished, and I think it would be a great disadvantage to us to uncover our railroads to the west, and injurious to open to him more country than we can avoid.

I am with great respect, your obt servt

R. E. Lee
Genl

722   To HIS WIFE
Richmond, Virginia

Hanover Junction
May 23, 1864

On my arrival here yesterday dear Mary I received your note & Agnes'. Genl Grant having apparently become tired of forcing his passage through us, on the night of the 20th began to move around our right towards Bowling Green, placing the Mattapony River between us. Fearing he might unite with Sheridan & make a sudden & rapid move upon Richmond I determined to march to this point so as to be within striking distance of Richmond & be able to intercept him. He has however as far as I can judge not passed beyond Bowling Green on the route east of Mattapony. The army is now south of the North Anna. We have the advantage of being nearer our supplies & less liable to have our communication, trains, &c., cut by his cavalry & he is getting farther from his base. Still I begrudge every step he makes towards Richmond. I hope you are all well & that my dear Daughter has recovered entirely. Tell Agnes all is done that can be done in reference to the daughters of her correspondent.

Ask Custis to send me my cotton drawers & socks. My present ones are becoming too warm. Yesterday was hot. But this morning the wind is easterly & cool. With prayers for your health & happiness & much love to all, I am as ever fondly yours

R. E. Lee

723
To JAMES A. SEDDON
Secretary of War
TELEGRAM

Hanover Junction
May 23, 1864

ABOUT NOON TODAY THE ENEMY APPROACHED THE TELEGRAPH BRIDGE OVER THE NORTH ANNA. IN THE AFTERNOON HE ATTACKED THE GUARD AT THE BRIDGE AND DROVE IT TO THIS SIDE. ABOUT THE SAME TIME THE 5TH CORPS, GENL WARREN, CROSSED AT JERICHO FORD ON OUR LEFT. WAS ATTACKED BY A. P. HILL & HIS ADVANCE CHECKED.

R. E. LEE

724
MAJOR W. H. TAYLOR TO GENERAL RICHARD H. ANDERSON
Commanding Corps

Headquarters, Army of Northern Virginia
May 23, 1864
11.30 P.M.

Major General Anderson:
The general commanding directs that you have the wagons of your corps packed and everything in readiness by daybreak tomorrow to move in any direction.

Most respectfully,
W. H. TAYLOR
Assistant Adjutant General

725
To GENERAL BRAXTON BRAGG
Commanding Armies of Confederate States
TELEGRAM

Hanover Junction
May 24, 1864
6 A.M.

IT IS REPORTED THAT THE SIXTH NORTH CAROLINA REGIMENT AND FIRST NORTH CAROLINA BATTALION, HOKE'S BRIGADE, AND THIRD VIRGINIA REGIMENT, KEMPER'S BRIGADE, DID NOT ACCOMPANY THEIR BRIGADES. PLEASE SEND THEM IF PRACTICABLE.

R. E. LEE

726   To JAMES A. SEDDON
                                 Secretary of War
                                 TELEGRAM

                                                          Taylorsville
                                                          May 24, 1864
                                                          9.30 P.M.

THE ENEMY HAS BEEN MAKING FEEBLE ATTACKS UPON OUR LINES
TODAY, PROBABLY WITH A VIEW OF ASCERTAINING OUR POSITION. THEY WERE
EASILY REPULSED. GENL MAHONE DROVE THREE REGIMENTS ACROSS THE RIVER,
CAPTURING A STAND OF COLORS & SOME PRISONERS, AMONG THEM ONE AIDE-
DE-CAMP OF GENL [JAMES H.] LEDLIE.

                                                          R. E. LEE

727   To JEFFERSON DAVIS
                                 Richmond, Virginia

                                 Headquarters, Army of Northern Virginia
                                                          May 25, 1864
                                                          4¾ A.M.

Mr. President:
    I have the honor to enclose a dispatch of the 16th instant from Lieut
Genl Grant to Major Genl Burnside, captured on the person of the
A. A. A. G. 1st Brigade, 1st Division, 9th Army Corps giving an account
of certain successes of the Federal arms, and of the amount of reinforcements sent to the Army of the Potomac. I understand that all the forts
and posts have been stripped of their garrisons. Norfolk, Fort Monroe,
Washington, &c., are left with but small guards, and every available man
has been brought to the front. This makes it necessary for us to do likewise, and I have no doubt that Your Excellency will do all in your power
to meet the present emergency. If Genl Beauregard is in condition to
unite with me in any operation against Genl Grant, I should like to know
it, and at what point a combination of the troops could be made most
advantageously to him. We have been obliged to withdraw from the
banks of the North Anna, in consequence of the ground being favorable
to the enemy, and the stage of the water such that he can cross at any
point.
    Our lines cover Hanover Junction, extending up the river to An-
derson's Ford, and thence south to Little River. The enemy yesterday
moved around us in all directions, examining our position, and entrench-

ing as he came, until he reached the Central Road above Verdirn. I presume he has destroyed all within his reach. In the evening he fell back towards the North Anna.

With great respect, your obt servt

R. E. LEE
Genl

**728   MAJOR W. H. TAYLOR TO GENERAL
RICHARD S. EWELL
Commanding Corps**

Headquarters, Army of Northern Virginia
May 26, 1864
10.45 A.M.

General:

General Lee directs me to say that General Kershaw has reported that the enemy was moving up the river all night, infantry, cavalry, and artillery, crossing from this to the other side. At the same time they were working in his (Kershaw's) front, apparently intrenching. It is very important to know what is on this side of the river. General Anderson has been instructed to advance his skirmishers cautiously, with a view of ascertaining what is in his front. You are desired to do the same.

Respectfully,

W. H. TAYLOR
Assistant Adjutant General

**729   MAJOR W. H. TAYLOR TO GENERAL
RICHARD H. ANDERSON
Commanding Corps**

Headquarters
May 27, 1864
4.20 A.M.

General:

General Lee wishes you to ascertain what is in your front, and if you discover that the enemy is leaving you to be prepared to move your command promptly to the south side of the South Anna River.

W. H. TAYLOR
Assistant Adjutant General

730   To JAMES A. SEDDON
                            Secretary of War
                            TELEGRAM

                                                    Taylorsville
                                                    May 27, 1864
                                                    6.45 A.M.

THE ENEMY RETIRED TO THE NORTH ANNA LAST NIGHT. A PORTION OF HIS
FORCE IS STILL VISIBLE ON THE NORTH BANK, BUT CAVALRY & INFANTRY HAVE
CROSSED AT HANOVERTOWN. I HAVE SENT THE CAVALRY IN THAT DIRECTION TO
CHECK THE MOVEMENT, AND WILL MOVE THE ARMY TO ASHLAND.

                                                    R. E. LEE

731   MAJOR W. H. TAYLOR TO GENERAL
                    RICHARD S. EWELL
                    Commanding Corps

                                        Headquarters, Hanover Junction
                                                    May 27, 1864
                                                    8.30 A.M.

General:
    General [Lunsford L.] Lomax states that Colonel [John A.] Baker,
commanding [James B.] Gordon's brigade of cavalry, reports the enemy's infantry and cavalry as having crossed at Hanovertown, on the
Pamunkey. The general commanding desires you to begin to withdraw
your troops quietly and so as not to be seen, and to move back to the
south side of the South Anna. Please direct General Breckinridge to put
his column in motion at once.

                                        Respectfully,

                                            W. H. TAYLOR
                                        Assistant Adjutant General

732   MAJOR W. H. TAYLOR TO GENERAL
RICHARD H. ANDERSON
Commanding Corps

Headquarters, Army of Northern Virginia
Jenkins' House, near Hughes' Shop
May 27, 1864
7.30 P.M.

General:

General Lee directs me to inform you that he will stop for the night at the above place. He wishes you to have your troops made as comfortable as possible for the night, and to move at 3 o'clock in the morning for Atlee's Station. General Ewell's corps is now near Hughes' Shop and will move at the same hour in the same direction. The object of the general is to get possession of the ridge between Totopotomoi and Beaver Dam Creek, upon which stands Pole Green Church. You will give General Pickett all necessary instructions to join you in the morning. General Ewell's corps is just east of you and General Hill west of Pickett.

W. H. TAYLOR
Assistant Adjutant General

733   To JEFFERSON DAVIS
Richmond, Virginia

Headquarters, Near Hughes' Shop
On the road to Atlee's
May 28, 1864

Mr. President:

Information I received yesterday at noon led me to believe that the enemy was proceeding from near Hanovertown by Haw's Shop towards the Mechanicsville road, and induced me to take position on the ridge between the Totopotomoi and Beaver Dam Creeks, so as to intercept his march to Richmond. On reaching this point I could only learn that cavalry had been seen as far as Haw's Shop, and that a column of infantry was seen from Hanover Court House passing down what is called the River road, which I understand to be the road from Hanover Court House to Hanovertown. The want of information leads me to doubt whether the enemy is pursuing the route just described, or whether, now that he finds the road open by Ashland, he may not prefer to take it. This causes me to pause for a while, but should he proceed on the road to

Mechanicsville, the army will be placed on the Totopotomoi Ridge.

Should he on the other hand take the Telegraph road, I shall try to intercept him as near Ashland as I can. In either event I shall endeavor to engage him as soon as possible, and will be near enough to Richmond for General Beauregard to unite with me if practicable. Should any field nearer to Richmond be more convenient to him, and he will designate it, I will endeavor to deliver battle there.

I am with great respect, your obt servt

R. E. Lee
Genl

734   MAJOR W. H. TAYLOR TO GENERAL
            JOHN C. BRECKINRIDGE
            Commanding Valley Troops

On Road Near Atlee's
May 28, 1864
10.30 A.M.

General:

General Early is near Pole Green Church, in line of battle. Anderson is well closed up in his rear. Early wrote from Hundley's at 8 a.m. Keep your troops well closed up on Anderson. The troops ahead of you marched at times alongside of the wagons. You might expedite your march by pursuing the same course. General Hill is following you.

W. H. Taylor
Assistant Adjutant General

735   To GENERAL JOHN C. BRECKINRIDGE
            Commanding Valley Troops

Atlee's
May 28, 1864
5 P.M.

General:

I wish you would place your troops on the road from this place to Haw's Shop (or Salem [Enon] Church), to guard that road. The enemy is at Haw's Shop, & may take our troops in reverse. After crossing the Hanover Court House & Mechanicsville road, about 3/4 mile, you reach a road leading to a Mrs. Tinsley's, & running parallel to the Hanover Court

House road. Opposite Mrs. Tinsley's gate, there is Mrs. Hill. On either side I understand you can obtain water. Send forward officers to explore.

Vry resply

R. E. Lee
Genl

736   To JAMES A. SEDDON
                        Secretary of War

Headquarters, Army of Northern Virginia
Atlee's
May 28, 1864
6 P.M.

Sir:

The army is in front of this position extending towards Totopotomoi Creek. As far as I can ascertain none of the enemy have advanced south of that creek. I believe that he is assembling his army behind it. Genl Fitz Lee's division of cavalry engaged the enemy's cavalry near Haw's Shop about noon today and drove them back upon their infantry, which prisoners stated to be the 5th and 6th Corps. I have not however received very definite information as yet either as regards their position or numbers.

I am with respect, your obdt servt

R. E. Lee

737   To GENERAL BRAXTON BRAGG
                 Commanding Armies of Confederate States
                          TELEGRAM

Headquarters, Army of Northern Virginia
May 29, 1864

I TELEGRAPHED GENL BEAUREGARD THIS MORNING THAT I WOULD BE HAPPY TO SEE HIM HERE TODAY. I CANNOT SAY WHERE I WILL BE TOMORROW.

R. E. Lee

738   To JEFFERSON DAVIS
Richmond, Virginia
TELEGRAM

Atlee's
May 29, 1864
9 o'clock P.M.

IN CONFERENCE WITH GENL BEAUREGARD HE STATES THAT HE HAS ONLY
TWELVE THOUSAND INFANTRY AND CAN SPARE NONE. IF GENL GRANT ADVANCES
TOMORROW I WILL ENGAGE HIM WITH MY PRESENT FORCE.

R. E. LEE
General

739   To HIS WIFE
Richmond, Virginia

Atlee's
May 29, 1864

I received this morning dear Mary your note of yesterday & the
basket of provisions. You must thank Mrs. Tucker, Mrs. Stannard & Mrs.
Randolph for their kindness & consideration. I have not been very sick,
but could not keep my horse for some days back. I am better now & hope
to be well tomorrow. It is the more aggravating from the work I have
to do. I trust God will give me strength for all He wishes me to do. I
had hoped dear Daughter was well. Give her much love & tell her how
much I sympathize with her. I am glad you have got Precious Life
back. You had all better keep together & go somewhere where you can
get peace & quiet. I think of you very often & wish I could be with
you. May God keep & preserve you all. Do not send any of the whiskey.
Some kind gentleman has sent me some brandy which I am using. I
want for nothing. Everybody is so kind that I am overwhelmed by it.
The enemy is moving again this afternoon, apparently to our left on the
line which they came from.

Give much love to Smith, Carter, Custis, all the girls & our kind
friends. Fitzhugh, Rob, Fitz & all the boys are well. I am writing in the
midst of many things. God bless you all.

Truly & affly yours
R. E. LEE

740   To JEFFERSON DAVIS
Richmond, Virginia

Headquarters, Army of Northern Virginia
May 30, 1864

Mr. President:

As I informed you by telegraph, my conference with Genl Beauregard resulted in the conclusion on his part, that he cannot spare any troops to reinforce this army. He thinks the enemy in his front superior to him in numbers. Of this I am unable to judge, but suppose of course that with his means of information, his opinion is correct. I think it very important to strengthen this army as much as possible, and it has occurred to me that the presence of the two armies north and south of James River, may render it possible to spare with safety some of the troops in Richmond or its defences. It is immaterial to what State the troops may belong, as I can place them in brigades from the same, and even if they be few in numbers, they will add something to our strength. I submit this proposition to your judgment and hope you may be able to find means to increase our numbers without endangering the safety of Richmond. I think it important that troops enough should be retained to man the works at Drewry's & Chaffin's Bluffs and to support the batteries around the city, in order to guard against a sudden attack by cavalry or otherwise. If this army is unable to resist Grant, the troops under Genl Beauregard and in the city will be unable to defend it.

Very respectfully, your obt servt

R. E. LEE
Genl

741   To GENERAL RICHARD H. ANDERSON
Commanding Corps

Headquarters, Army of Northern Virginia
May 30, 1864
11 A.M.

General:

As far as I can judge from the information I have received, I think the enemy will take a line for their right up Crump's Creek to Taliaferro's Mill, & thence along up to Smith's Store, & thence to the Totopotomoi Creek, embracing McKenzie's Corner, then down the north side of the Totopotomoi & cross over to the head waters of the Matadequin, near Bethesda Church. After fortifying this line they will probably make another move by their left flank over towards the Chickahominy. This is just a repetition of their former movements. It can only be arrested by striking at once at that part of their force which has crossed the Toto-potomoi in Genl Early's front. I have desired him to do this if he thought it could be done advantageously, & have written to him that you will support him. Please communicate with him at once. Whatever is determined on should be done as soon as practicable.

I am very respectfully, your obt servt

R. E. LEE
Genl

742 To GENERAL BRAXTON BRAGG
Commanding Armies of the Confederate States
TELEGRAM

Atlee's
May 30, 1864
3.15 P.M.

SCOUT FROM DOWN PAMUNKEY REPORTS THAT GENL [GEORGE A.] CUSTER & JUNIOR OFFICERS OF ENEMY'S CAVALRY NEAR OLD CHURCH STATE THAT BUTLER'S FLEET WOULD BE AT WEST POINT TODAY. THIS MAY BE THE FLEET REPORTED GOING DOWN THE JAMES YESTERDAY & PROBABLY CONVEYING [GENERAL WILLIAM F.] SMITH'S CORPS TO GRANT. THE IDEA IS GENERAL AMONGST THEM THAT BUTLER IS TO REINFORCE THEM. ONE STEAMER WAS AT WHITE HOUSE YESTERDAY & WAS COMMUNICATED WITH BY OFFICER & DETACHMENT FROM GRANT'S ARMY. SCOUT LEFT VICINITY OF WHITE HOUSE AT 8 THIS MORNING. AT THAT TIME HAD HEARD NOTHING OF APPEARANCE OF FLEET. CITIZENS REPORTED BOATS AT BRICK HOUSE.

R. E. LEE

743 To JEFFERSON DAVIS
Richmond, Virginia
TELEGRAM

Atlee's
May 30, 1864
7.30 P.M.

GENERAL BEAUREGARD SAYS THE DEPARTMENT MUST DETERMINE WHAT TROOPS TO SEND FOR HIM. HE GIVES IT ALL NECESSARY INFORMATION. THE

RESULT OF THIS DELAY WILL BE DISASTER. BUTLER'S TROOPS (SMITH'S CORPS) WILL BE WITH GRANT TOMORROW. HOKE'S DIVISION, AT LEAST, SHOULD BE WITH ME BY LIGHT TOMORROW.

R. E. LEE

744   MAJOR W. H. TAYLOR
        TO GENERAL RICHARD H. ANDERSON
               Commanding Corps

Headquarters, Near Coleman's
On road from Shady Grove Church to Mechanicsville
May 31, 1864

General:

I am directed by General Lee to say that he wishes you to get every available man in the ranks by tomorrow. Gather in all stragglers and men absent without proper authority. Send to the field hospitals and have every man capable of performing the duties of a soldier returned to his command. Send back your inspectors with instructions to see that the wishes of the general commanding are carried out. Let every man fit for duty be present.

I am most respectfully, your obedient servant

W. H. TAYLOR
Assistant Adjutant General

745   To GENERAL AMBROSE P. HILL
               Commanding Corps

Headquarters, Army of Northern Virginia
June —, 1864
12.30 P.M.

General:

I have received your note of 11 a.m. I am glad that you are able to make the disposition of the troops you propose, as it meets my views, as expressed in a former note to you. Now that you have your troops in a line, I hope you will strengthen it as much as possible and hold it. I have little fear of your ability to maintain your position if our men do as they generally do. The time has arrived, in my opinion, when something more is necessary than adhering to lines and defensive positions. We shall be obliged to go out and prevent the enemy from selecting such positions as he chooses. If he is allowed to continue that course we shall at last be obliged to take refuge behind the works of Richmond and stand a siege, which would be but a work of time. You must be prepared to fight him in the field, to prevent him taking positions such as he desires, and I expect the co-operation of all the corps commanders in the course which necessity now will oblige us to pursue. It is for this purpose that I desire the corps to be kept together and as strong as possible, and that our absentees will be brought forward and every attention given to refreshing and preparing the men for battle. Their arms and ammunition should be looked to and cooked provisions provided ahead.

R. E. LEE
General

P.S. I am anxious to get recommendations to fill the vacancies in the different commands in your corps.

R. E. L.

746   To JAMES A. SEDDON
Secretary of War

Headquarters, Army of Northern Virginia
June 1, 1864

There has been skirmishing along the lines today.

General Anderson and Genl Hoke attacked the enemy in their front this forenoon and drove them to their entrenchments.

This afternoon the enemy attacked Genl Heth and were handsomely repulsed by [Generals John R.] Cooke's and [William W.] Kirkland's brigades. Genls Breckinridge and Mahone drove the enemy from their front, taking about 150 prisoners.

A force of infantry is reported to have arrived at Tunstall's Station from the White House and to be extending up the York River Railroad. They state that they belong to Butler's forces.

Very resply

R. E. LEE
Genl

747   To GENERAL P. G. T. BEAUREGARD
           Commanding Department South of James River
                          TELEGRAM

                                Headquarters, Army of Northern Virginia
                                                        June 1, 1864
                                                        12.45 P.M.

   IT WOULD BE DISADVANTAGEOUS TO ABANDON THE LINE BETWEEN RICH-
MOND AND PETERSBURG, BUT AS TWO-THIRDS OF BUTLER'S FORCE HAS JOINED
GRANT CAN YOU NOT LEAVE SUFFICIENT GUARD TO MOVE WITH THE BALANCE
OF YOUR COMMAND TO NORTH SIDE OF JAMES RIVER AND TAKE COMMAND OF
RIGHT WING OF ARMY?

                                               R. E. LEE
                                               General

748   To GENERAL P. G. T. BEAUREGARD
           Commanding Department South of James River
                          TELEGRAM

                                        Shady Grove Church
                                              June 1, 1864
                                              4 P.M.

   GENERAL GRANT APPEARS TO BE GRADUALLY APPROACHING THE YORK
RIVER RAILROAD. WHETHER WITH A VIEW OF TOUCHING THE JAMES RIVER OR
NOT I CANNOT ASCERTAIN. I AM IGNORANT OF THE MOVEMENTS OF THE ENEMY
IN YOUR FRONT, OR WHETHER IT WOULD BE IN YOUR POWER TO TAKE POSITION
NORTH OF JAMES RIVER.

                                               R. E. LEE
                                               General

749   To JAMES A. SEDDON
                    Secretary of War

                                Headquarters, Army of Northern Virginia
                                                        June 2, 1864
                                                        8 P.M.

Sir:
   Yesterday afternoon the enemy's cavalry were reported to be advancing by the left of our line towards Hanover Court House and Ash-

land. General Hampton, with Rosser's brigade, proceeded to meet them. Rosser fell upon their rear, charged down the road towards Ashland bearing everything before him. His progress was arrested at Ashland by the entrenchments of the enemy, when he changed his direction and advanced up the Fredericksburg Railroad. General William H. F. Lee came up at this time with a part of his division and a joint attack was made. The enemy was quickly driven from the place and pursued towards Hanover Court House until dark.

During the afternoon [of May 31st] General Fitz Lee was forced to retire from Old Cold Harbor on our extreme right, and as it was evident that the enemy was moving in that direction our own line was extended accordingly, General Hoke occupying the extreme right. The enemy attacked [on June 1st] in heavy force and succeeded in penetrating between Hoke and Anderson, where there was an interval in our line, causing the right of Anderson and the left of Hoke to fall back a short distance. General Hoke subsequently recovered his position and General Anderson's right assumed one a short distance in rear of that it first occupied. This morning the enemy's movement to our right continuing, corresponding changes were made in our line, Breckinridge's command and two divisions of General Hill being placed on the right. General Early with Ewell's corps and Heth's division occupied our left, and was directed to endeavor to get upon the enemy's right flank and drive down in front of our line. General Early made the movement in the afternoon and drove the enemy from his entrenchments, following him until dark.

While this attack was progressing Genl Hill reinforced Breckinridge with two brigades of Wilcox's division and dislodged the enemy from Turkey Hill in front of our extreme right.

Very respectfully, your obt servant

R. E. LEE
Genl

750   CIRCULAR

Headquarters, Army of Northern Virginia
June 3, 1864

Commanding officers will thoroughly examine their lines this afternoon, and cause them to be strengthened as far as possible with abatis & otherwise. They will see that the men are provided with rations and ammunition, & issue instructions that one-third of the officers and men in the trenches be awake and on duty throughout the night, and on the alert against night or early morning attacks. This can be accomplished by judicious reliefs without too much fatigue to the men.

R. E. Lee
Genl

751   To JEFFERSON DAVIS
Richmond, Virginia

Headquarters, Near Gaines' Mill
June 3, 1864
1 P.M.

Mr. President:

Your letter of 4 p.m. yesterday is just received. My letter to the Honorable Secretary of War of 5 a.m. this morning, will have informed Your Excellency of the events of yesterday & the day before, and your aide Col Johnston conveyed to you those of today. The right of our line extends to Turkey Hill, which is the last hill on this side of the Chickahominy, and covers McClellan's Bridge. I do not know how the report of the advance of the enemy's cavalry to that point originated. It is not correct. I sent Genl Fitz Lee with his division over the Chickahominy to Bottom's Bridge yesterday. He reports this morning that he has the river strongly guarded to that point, with pickets over to the James.

So far every attack of the enemy has been repulsed. His assaults [at Cold Harbor] began early this morning, and continued until about 9 o'clock. The only impression made on our line was at a salient of Genl Breckinridge's position, where the enemy broke through and captured part of a battalion. He was immediately driven out with severe loss by Genl [Joseph] Finegan's brigade & the Maryland Battalion, and the line restored.

I am gratified to learn of the efforts made by Your Excellency to bring out troops. I think it very important that those men engaged in preparing ammunition should remain, as Your Excellency has directed.

Genl Hoke reports that the troops in his front are said to belong to Butler's forces, and it is said that prisoners have been captured from the 18th Corps. I hope that Genl Beauregard will be able to find out the strength of the enemy in his front, and that he can spare additional reinforcements for this army at once. No time should be lost if reinforcements can be had.

Very respy, your obt servt

R. E. Lee
Genl

752   To JAMES A. SEDDON
                          Secretary of War

                                    Headquarters, Army of Northern Virginia
                                                          June 3, 1864
                                                          8-¾ P.M.

Sir:

About 4½ a.m. today the enemy made an attack upon the right of our line. In front of General Hoke's and part of General Breckinridge's line he was repulsed without difficulty. He succeeded in penetrating a salient on General Breckinridge's line and captured a portion of the battalion there posted. General Finegan's brigade of Mahone's division and the Maryland Battalion of Breckinridge's command immediately drove the enemy out with severe loss. Repeated attacks were made upon General Anderson's position, chiefly against his right under General Kershaw. They were met with great steadiness and repulsed in every instance.

The attack extended to our extreme left under General Early, with like results. Later in the day it was twice renewed against General Heth who occupies Early's left, but was repulsed with loss.

General Hampton encountered the enemy's cavalry near Haw's Shop, and a part of Genl William H. F. Lee's division drove them from their entrenchments.

General Fitz Lee's division occupies the south side of the Chickahominy as far as Long Bridge, with pickets extending across to the James.

Our loss today has been small, and our success, under the blessing of God, all that we could expect.

                              Very respectfully, your obt servt

                                                          R. E. LEE
                                                          Genl

753   To HIS WIFE
                          Richmond, Virginia

                                                          Gaines' Mill
                                                          June 4, 1864

On returning to camp last evening dear Mary I found your note & basket. Thank Mrs. Stannard for the bread which is a great comfort to me. I am getting so well that I do not think I require the blackberry wine. I have enough of port for the present. I think Mary had better use it. It will strengthen her. I am in hopes she will soon be well. I am glad to hear that you contemplate a visit to Fluvanna. I think you had better go as soon as you can. We are all in the hands of our Merciful God, whom I know will order all things for our good, but we do not know what that is or what He may determine, & it behooves us to use the perception & judgement He has given us for our guidance & well being. It is evident that great danger is impending over us, & therefore those not required to meet it, or who might be overwhelmed by it should it fall upon us, should get out of harm's way in time. I trust & believe He will save us in His own good time, & upon Him is my whole faith & reliance. Give much love to my dear daughters & Custis. Our boys in the field are well. Fitzhugh with his division was engaged at Ashland evening before last, & last evening near Old Church. On both occasions doing well.

Very truly & affly
R. E. LEE

754   To GENERAL RICHARD H. ANDERSON
Commanding Corps

Headquarters, Army of Northern Virginia
June 4, 1864
6 P.M.

General:

I apprehend from the quietude the enemy has preserved today that he is preparing to leave us tonight, and I fear will cross the Chickahominy. In that event the best course for us to pursue in my opinion, would be to move down and attack him with our whole force, provided we could catch him in the act of crossing. I wish you would keep your pickets on the alert tonight and endeavor to detect any movement in your front, and should you discover that he is abandoning his position be prepared to move your whole corps on the direct road from Gaines' Mill by Parker's Mill towards Dispatch Station. A report from Fitz Lee dated 3:30 p.m. today, from the south side of the Chickahominy says he can discover as yet no indications of a move of the enemy by his left flank.

Very resply, your obt servt
R. E. LEE
Genl

755　　　　　　To JAMES A. SEDDON
　　　　　　　　　　Secretary of War
　　　　　　　　　　　　TELEGRAM

　　　　　　　　　　　Headquarters, Army of Northern Virginia
　　　　　　　　　　　　　　　　　　　　　　　June 4, 1864
　　　　　　　　　　　　　　　　　　　　　　　8.30 P.M.

SIR:

　　LAST NIGHT, AFTER THE DATE OF MY DISPATCH, GENERALS BRECKINRIDGE
AND FINEGAN WERE ATTACKED BY THE ENEMY AS THEY WERE PREPARING TO
REESTABLISH THEIR SKIRMISH LINE. THE ENEMY WAS SOON REPULSED. IMME-
DIATELY AFTERWARDS AN ATTACK WAS MADE UPON GENERAL HOKE'S FRONT
WITH A LIKE RESULT.

　　UP TO THE TIME OF WRITING NOTHING HAS OCCURRED ALONG THE LINES
TODAY EXCEPT SKIRMISHING AT VARIOUS POINTS. THE POSITION OF THE ARMY
IS SUBSTANTIALLY UNCHANGED.

　　　　　　　　　　　　VERY RESPECTFULLY, YOUR OBT SERVT

　　　　　　　　　　　　　　　　　　　　R. E. LEE
　　　　　　　　　　　　　　　　　　　　Genl

756　　　　　　To JAMES A. SEDDON
　　　　　　　　　　Secretary of War
　　　　　　　　　　　　TELEGRAM

　　　　　　　　　　　Headquarters, Army of Northern Virginia
　　　　　　　　　　　　　　　　　　　　　　　June 5, 1864
　　　　　　　　　　　　　　　　　　　　　　　8.30 P.M.

　　NOTHING HAS OCCURRED ON THE LINES TODAY EXCEPT SLIGHT SKIRMISH-
ING. THERE IS NO APPARENT CHANGE IN THE POSITION OF THE ENEMY. NO
MOVEMENT ON HIS PART HAS BEEN DISCOVERED.

　　　　　　　　　　　　VERY RESPECTFULLY, YOUR OBT SERVT

　　　　　　　　　　　　　　　　　　　　R. E. LEE
　　　　　　　　　　　　　　　　　　　　Genl

757   To JEFFERSON DAVIS
                                      Richmond, Virginia

                                               Headquarters, Army of Northern Virginia
                                                                        on the field
                                                                        June 6, 1864
                                                                        7½ A.M.

Mr. President:

I think some good officer should be sent into the Valley at once to
take command there and collect all the forces, regulars, locals, and reserves, & endeavour to drive the enemy out. I do not know Genl
[George C.] Vaughan who seems to be now in command. Genl [John]
Echols has gone home sick and I think from the nature of his disease is
incapacitated for field service though a most excellent officer. Genl
Breckinridge is at present disabled by the fall of his horse & has gone to
Richmond. From the representations made to me I think he will be well
in a day or two. I recommend that he be sent out to the Valley to take
command & do what is practicable in rousing the inhabitants & defending
the country. Other persons of influence in that country should be sent
on the same mission. Genl W. E. Jones wrote to me before reaching
Staunton that he had with him 4000 infantry & dismounted cavalry, 1000
mounted men & plenty of artillery following. Genl Imboden who was at
that time below Staunton wrote to me that he had 3000 men. I was in
hopes their united forces would have defeated Genl [David] Hunter.
The only assistance I can give from this army as I wrote you last night
would be to send back Wharton's & Echols' brigades [Breckinridge's
force] numbering now about 2100 muskets. They are now in reserve &
I have ordered them to be provisioned for two days. I have also sent into
Richmond to ascertain whether they could be transported by rail to
Staunton & in what time. These are elements necessary to a proper decision in the case. It is apparent that if Grant cannot be successfully resisted here we cannot hold the Valley. If he is defeated it can be recovered. But unless a sufficient force can be had in that country to restrain
the movements of the enemy, he will do us great evil & in that event I
think it would be better to restore to Genl Breckinridge the troops drawn
from him. The enemy is now moving in my front. He is withdrawing
from our left, but I have not yet been able to discover what is his purpose
or intention. I fear he may have, during the night thrown a force across
the Chickahominy below us. Prisoners taken in front of Longstreet's &
Ewell's corps day before yesterday stated that they belonged to Gilmore's
corps & that the whole of that corps had united with Genl Grant & that

Gilmore was here in person. That there was nothing left at Bermuda Hundred except negro troops & some cavalry. Their statements must always be taken with hesitation, but the officers who examined them say that they were apparently telling what they believed to be true.

I am very respectfully, your obt servt

R. E. LEE
Genl

758   To HIS WIFE
Richmond, Virginia

Gaines' Mill
June 7, 1864

I received last night dear Mary your letter of the 5th & the nice bread sent me by Mrs. Haxall & Barton. You must tell the kind ladies they must not send me so many things. I fear they will deprive themselves of what is not necessary to me & may be to them. I am well now & have all that is needful to me. Tell Mrs. Randolph I have taken some of the blackberry today & find it very nice. I think though the sight of her would be more beneficial to me. You must take from the box sent by Hattie Harrison what you want & send me the balance. The tea & soap may be of use to you. I saw Fitzhugh yesterday. He was very well. I am full of gratitude to our Heavenly Father for His preservation of all of our sons & nephews & especially for the safety of our dear Rob. May they all be, preserved & feel to whom they owe it. You must give much love to Mary I. when you write, & if you have an opportunity thank Hattie Harrison for me. I had an interesting visit from Dr. Hughes yesterday & am delighted to hear that all your symptoms are so favourable. He agrees with me in believing that you had better leave Richmond as soon as you can. I hope you will do so. I am glad to hear that Mary is so much better. Give much love to her, Agnes, Life, & all friends. May God preserve you all.

Truly & sincerely

R. E. LEE

759   To JAMES A. SEDDON
                          Secretary of War

                                Headquarters, Army of Northern Virginia
                                                June 8, 1864
                                                8 P.M.

Sir:
     The enemy has been unusually quiet today along the whole extent
of his lines, and nothing of importance has occurred. Two divisions of
his cavalry under Genl Sheridan are reported to have crossed the
Pamunkey yesterday at New Castle Ferry and to have encamped last
night at Dunkirk and Aylett's on the Mattapony. They were accompanied by artillery, ambulances, wagons, and beef cattle.

                          Very respectfully, your obt servt

                                                R. E. LEE
                                                Genl

760   To HIS WIFE
                       Richmond, Virginia

                                                Gaines' Mill
                                                June 8, 1864

     I received today your note without date. It is useless for us to grieve
for the calamity at Staunton or elsewhere. We must bear everything with
patience that is inflicted on us. It will be impossible to remove the silver,
&c., from Lexington. It will incur more danger in removal than in remaining. It must bide its fate. I hope you are all well. Give love to the
girls & may God bless & preserve you all.

                                Truly & sincerely

                                                R. E. LEE

761   To JAMES A. SEDDON
                    Secretary of War
                    TELEGRAM

                                        Headquarters, Army of Northern Virginia
                                                                June 9, 1864
                                                                  9.30 P.M.

SIR:

THE ENEMY HAS BEEN QUIET TODAY, APPARENTLY ENGAGED IN STRENGTH-
ENING HIS ENTRENCHMENTS. SKIRMISHING ON THE LINES HAS BEEN VERY
LIGHT.

            VERY RESPECTFULLY, YOUR OBEDIENT SERVANT

                                                            R. E. LEE
                                                            General

762   To GENERAL BRAXTON BRAGG
                Commanding Armies of the Confederate States

                                        Headquarters, Army of Northern Virginia
                                                                June 9, 1864
                                                                  2½ P.M.

Telegrams of Genl Beauregard received. I am aware of no troops
having left Genl Grant's army. The regiment of cavalry and infantry
seen by Genl Ware [*for* Henry A. Wise] is a small force. Genl Hoke's
troops are now in the trenches, and cannot be withdrawn until night under
any circumstances. Genl Ransom's brigade is on the right bank of the
Chickahominy protecting the batteries there posted. I know no necessity
for the removal of these troops, but if directed will send them. No troops
have left Genl Grant's army to my knowledge, and none could have
crossed James River without being discovered. I think it very improbable
that he would weaken himself under existing circumstances. Stanton's
dispatches state that all available troops had been drawn from Butler except enough to hold his lines. It is further stated in a letter apparently
from some one connected with Genl Butler, that certain troops collected
at Point Lookout to reinforce Butler, were diverted to Grant.

Couriers seem to reach me from Richmond more promptly than
telegrams.

                                                            R. E. LEE

P.S. I intended the foregoing for the telegraph, but send it by courier to save time.

R. E. L.

763   To JEFFERSON DAVIS
                      Richmond, Virginia

Headquarters, Army of Northern Virginia
June 9, 1864

Mr. President:

In my report to the Honorable Secretary of War yesterday evening, I stated that Genl Sheridan with a large force of cavalry had crossed the Pamunkey in the afternoon of the 7th at New Castle Ferry, and encamped that night about Dunkirk and Aylett's on the Mattapony. He was accompanied by artillery, wagons, ambulances, and beef cattle. I have received no definite information as to his purpose, but conjecture that his object is to cooperate with Genl Hunter, and endeavor to reach the James, breaking the railroads &c., as he passes, and probably to descend on the south side of that river. I think it necessary to be on our guard and make every arrangement in our power to thwart his purpose and protect our communications and country. I have directed Genls Hampton and Fitz Lee with their divisions to proceed in the direction of Hanover Junction, and thence, if the information they receive justifies it, along the Central Railroad, keeping the enemy on their right, and shape their course according to his. The pause in the operations of Genl Grant induces me to believe that he is awaiting the effect of movements in some other quarter to make us change our position, and renders the suggestion I make with reference to the intention and destination of Genl Sheridan more probable. It was stated by a prisoner captured yesterday belonging to Genl Sheridan's command, that they had heard that Genl [John H.] Morgan was in Pennsylvania and that they were going in pursuit. I mention this improbable story as you may know whether there is any truth in the statement with reference to Genl Morgan. A negro servant belonging to our army who had been captured by the enemy, made his escape from Genl Sheridan yesterday at 10 a.m. near Mangonick Church, and was under the impression that they would encamp that night at Bowling Green. Three prisoners brought in to Genl Hampton confirm in part the statement of the servant.

An extract from the *Philadelphia Inquirer* published in our papers reports that the army of the Northwest under Genl [John] Pope was on its way to reinforce that of the Potomac, and a gentleman from the Valley says that a force of two or three thousand men, believed to be under Genl Pope was moving to join Genl Hunter, and should have reached Staunton by this time. There may be therefore some probability in the story. I do not know whence reinforcements can be drawn to our armies unless Genl Kirby Smith can cross a part of his force to join Genl Johnston and enable him to assume the offensive.

Very respectfully, your obt servt

R. E. LEE
Genl

764   To GENERAL RICHARD H. ANDERSON
Commanding Corps

Headquarters, Army of Northern Virginia
June 9, 1864
4:15 P.M.

General:

I have been compelled to draw Genl Early down from the left to a position near Gaines' Mill in order to relieve Genl Hoke's troops from the trenches, as the latter may be needed on other duty. I wish you to make your dispositions to protect your left on his withdrawal.

I am very respectfully, your obt servt

R. E. LEE
Genl

765   To GENERAL BRAXTON BRAGG
Commanding Armies of the Confederate States
TELEGRAM

Mechanicsville
June 9, 1864
4:45 P.M.

YOUR DISPATCH OF ONE O'CLOCK JUST RECEIVED. HAVE ORDERED RANSOM'S BRIGADE TO MARCH BY ROUTE IT CAME TO GENL BEAUREGARD. IF NOT NECESSARY PLEASE COUNTERMAND ORDER.

R. E. LEE

766   To JAMES A. SEDDON
                                    Secretary of War

                                                 Headquarters, Gaines' Mill
                                                 June 10, 1864

Sir:

I have the honor to acknowledge the receipt of your letter of yesterday. With my present information as to the movements of the enemy's
cavalry I am unable to determine their destination. The last dispatch from
General Hampton, dated at Frederick's Hall today, states that they encamped last night at New Market, which is on the road from Chilesburg
to Waller's Church, General Hampton's own command being nearly west
of them at Frederick's Hall. My first impression was that the object of
the expedition was to cooperate with the forces under General Hunter in
the Valley, and there is nothing as yet in their movements inconsistent
with this idea. They may intend to strike for the James River above
Richmond, and cross to the south side to destroy the Danville road. I
think it very important that we should be on our guard against such an
attempt, and that parties should be held in readiness to burn the bridges
over the river upon their approach. These parties should be under the
direction of intelligent and cool men, for fear the bridges might be pre-
maturely fired, and good scouts be sent out on the roads to give timely
notice of the approach of the enemy. I suppose you will be able to obtain men of the character indicated among the reserve forces of that section.

I will keep you advised as far as I can of the enemy's movements,
and should he turn towards the river our cavalry under General Hampton
will endeavor to protect the bridges, and if unable to do so, will aid the
parties charged with burning them.

Under existing circumstances I think it would be best to make every
preparation to repair the railroad and the bridges to be in readiness for a
more favorable opportunity to restore travel, but it would not be prudent
to begin the work now.

I am glad to learn that you are exerting yourself to accumulate stores
for the army. No effort should be spared to provide against such interruption of our transportation as the enemy's superiority in cavalry may
enable him to effect. If practicable, I hope that provision will be made
to continue the supply of vegetables. It greatly promotes the health and
comfort of the men.

                                    Very respectfully, your obt servt

                                                 R. E. LEE
                                                 Genl

767   To JAMES A. SEDDON
                                Secretary of War
                                     TELEGRAM

                                        Headquarters, Army of Northern Virginia
                                                              June 10, 1864
                                                                  8½ P.M.

SIR:

    THE ENEMY HAS MADE NO MOVEMENT TODAY. THE SKIRMISHING ALONG
THE LINES HAS BEEN SOMEWHAT MORE ACTIVE AND SYSTEMATIC THAN DURING
THE LAST TWO DAYS.

                                        VERY RESPLY, YOUR OBT SERVT

                                                        R. E. LEE
                                                        Genl

768   To JAMES A. SEDDON
                                Secretary of War
                                     TELEGRAM

                                        Headquarters, Army of Northern Virginia
                                                              June 11, 1864
                                                                  6½ P.M.

SIR:

    THE ENEMY HAS BEEN QUIET TODAY, WITH THE USUAL SKIRMISHING
ALONG THE LINES.

                              VERY RESPECTFULLY, YOUR OBT SERVT

                                                        R. E. LEE
                                                        Genl

769   To JEFFERSON DAVIS
                                Richmond, Virginia
                                   INDORSEMENT

                                                        Headquarters
                                                        June 11, 1864

Respectfully returned [to President Davis].
    I acknowledge the advantage of expelling enemy from the Valley.
The only difficulty with me is the means. It would [take] one corps of

this army. If it is deemed prudent to hazard the defense of Richmond, the interests involved by thus diminishing the force here, I will do so. I think this is what the enemy would desire. A victory over General Grant would also relieve our difficulties. I see no indications of his attacking me in his present position. Think he is strengthening his defenses to withdraw a portion of his force, and with the other move to the James River. To attack him here I must assault a very strong line of intrenchments and run great risk to the safety of the army.

R. E. LEE

770   To HIS WIFE
Richmond, Virginia

June 12, 1864

My dear Mary:

I have received your several notes, but have not had an opportunity to reply to them. I am glad you have William Carter with you. I hope you will take good care of him & soon make him well. We require everyone in the field we can get. I presume they have suffered everything at Hickory Hill & Uncle Williams'. Indeed I have heard that the enemy has taken everything from them. It is lamentable in the extreme. You must thank the kind ladies for the nice bread. Tell them their remembrance of me is more comforting than their rolls & loaves. Little Sallie I understand had to run off to North Carolina to get rid of her beaux. What is she going to do now? I must write & thank Mr. Jackson for the pieces of cotton. I do not require night shirts. You had better keep them for day shirts, which I may require after awhile. I saw Fitzhugh & Rob yesterday on their way from one wing of the army to the other. My pen will not mark & I must stop. Give love to my daughters. How are the dear little cormorants? I hear they eat everything before them. I am glad their appetites are good. I hope you are doing well. I am well again, thank God. May He in His infinite mercy keep you all under the shadow of His wings.

Truly & constantly

R. E. LEE

771   To GENERAL SAMUEL COOPER
Adjutant and Inspector General

Headquarters, Army of Northern Virginia
June 12, 1864

General:

During the late movements of the army, the condition of General Ewell's health rendered it proper that he should be relieved temporarily from the command of his corps. Although now restored to his usual health, I think the labor and exposure to which he would be inevitably exposed would at this time again incapacitate him for field service. The general, who has all the feelings of a good soldier, differs from me in this opinion, and is not only willing but anxious to resume his command. I, however, think in the present emergency it would jeopardize his life, and should his strength fail, it would prove disadvantageous to the service. I therefore propose that he be placed on some duty attended with less labor and exposure. It has occurred to me that the command of the defenses of Richmond would be more in accordance with his state of health, and give him a position where he could perform valuable service. I cordially recommend that he be placed on this duty unless circumstances exist of which I am unaware which render it improper. This arrangement is intended to be temporary, as it is proposed to replace him in command of his corps after the present occasion for extraordinary exertion shall have passed.

I am, very respectfully, your obedient servant

R. E. LEE
General

772   To JAMES A. SEDDON
Secretary of War

Headquarters, Army of Northern Virginia
June 13, 1864
10 P.M.

Sir:

A dispatch just received from Maj Genl Hampton states that he defeated the enemy's cavalry near Trevilian with heavy loss, capturing 500 prisoners, besides the wounded. The enemy retreated in confusion, apparently by the route he came, leaving his dead and wounded on the field.

At daybreak this morning it was discovered that the army of Genl Grant had left our front. Our skirmishers were advanced between one and two miles, but failing to discover the enemy were withdrawn, and the army was moved to conform to the route taken by him. He advanced a body of cavalry and some infantry from Long Bridge to Riddell's Shop, which were driven back this evening nearly two miles, after some sharp skirmishing.

Very resply, your obt servt

R. E. LEE
Genl

773   To JEFFERSON DAVIS
                Richmond, Virginia

Headquarters, Army of Northern Virginia
June 14, 1864
12:10 P.M.

Mr. President:

I have just received your note of 11½ p.m. yesterday. I regret very much that I did not see you yesterday afternoon, and especially after your having taken so long a ride. If the movement of Early meets with your approval, I am sure it is the best that can be made, though I know how difficult it is with my limited knowledge to perceive what is best.

I think the enemy must be preparing to move south of James River. Our scouts and pickets yesterday stated that Genl Grant's whole army was in motion for the fords of the Chickahominy from Long Bridge down, from which I inferred that he was making his way to the James River as his new base. I cannot however learn positively that more than a small part of his army has crossed the Chickahominy. Our contest last evening, as far as I am able to judge was with a heavy force of cavalry and the 5th Corps of his army. They were driven back until dark as I informed you, by a part of Hill's corps. Presuming that this force was either the advance of his army, or the cover behind which it would move to James River, I prepared to attack it again this morning, but it disappeared from before us during the night, and as far as we can judge from the statements of prisoners, it has gone to Harrison's landing. The force of cavalry here was pressed forward early this morning, but as yet no satisfactory information has been obtained. It may be Genl Grant's intention to place his army within the fortifications around Harrison's landing, which I believe still stand, and where by the aid of his gunboats, he could offer a strong defence. I do not think it would be advantageous to attack him in that position. He could then either refresh it or transfer it to the other side of the river without our being able to molest it, unless our ironclads are stronger than his. It is reported by some of our scouts that a portion of his troops marched to the White House, and from information derived from citizens, were there embarked. I thought it probable that these might have been their discharged men, especially as a scout reported under date of the 9th instant that transports loaded with troops have been going up the Potomac for three days and nights, passing above Alexandria. On the night of the 8th, upwards of thirty steamers went up, supposed to be filled with troops, no doubt many of these were wounded and sick men. Still I apprehend that he may be sending troops up the James River with the view of getting possession of Petersburg before we can reinforce it. We ought therefore to be extremely watchful & guarded. Unless I hear something satisfactory by evening, I shall move Hoke's division back to the vicinity of the pontoon bridge across James River, in order that he may cross if necessary. The rest of this army can follow should circumstances require it.

The victories of Forrest [at Brice's Crossroads, Mississippi] and Hampton are very grateful at this time, and show that we are not forsaken by a gracious Providence. We have only to do our whole duty, and everything will be well. A scout in Prince William reports that the enemy are rebuilding the bridges on the Orange & Alexandria Railroad adjacent to Alexandria. This may be with the view of opening the Manassas Gap Railroad to communicate with the Valley, their tenure of which I trust will not be permanent.

Most respectfully, your obt servt

R. E. Lee
Genl

774   To JEFFERSON DAVIS
Richmond, Virginia

Headquarters, Army of Northern Virginia
June 14, 1864
3¾ P.M.

Mr. President:
As far as I can judge from the information I have received, Genl Grant has moved his army to James River in the vicinity of Westover. A

portion of it I am told moved to Wilcox's landing, a short distance below. I see no indications of his attacking me on this side of the river, though of course I cannot know positively. As his facilities for crossing the river and taking possession of Petersburg are great, and as I think it will more probably be his plan, I have sent Genl Hoke with his command to a point above Drewry's Bluff in easy distance of the first pontoon bridge above that place. He will execute any orders you may send to him there. I cannot judge now whether he should move at once to the other side of the river, but think it prudent that he should be in position to do so when required. From my present information Genl Grant crossed his army at several points below Long Bridge, and moved directly towards James River, sending a force in this direction to guard the roads so as to make it impracticable for us to reach him.

Very respectfully, your obt servt

R. E. LEE
Genl

775   To GENERAL BRAXTON BRAGG
            Commanding Armies of the Confederate States

Headquarters, Army of Northern Virginia
June 14, 1864
4 P.M.

General:
    I have directed Genl Hoke's command to proceed this afternoon to the vicinity of the first pontoon bridge above Drewry's Bluff. I have deemed it prudent that he should be within reach of Petersburg. For as far as I am able to judge of the movements of the army of Genl Grant I think it probable that he will cross James River. He has moved his army across Long Bridge & the bridges below that point to James River apparently striking for Harrison's & Wilcox's Landing. He shows no indication of operating on this side & has broken up his depot at the White House.

I am with great respect, your obt servt

R. E. LEE
Genl

776   To JAMES A. SEDDON
Secretary of War

Headquarters, Army of Northern Virginia
June 14, 1864
9 P.M.

Sir:

The force of the enemy mentioned in my last dispatch as being on the Long Bridge road disappeared during the night. It was probably advanced to cover the movement of the main body, most of which, as far as I can learn, crossed the Chickahominy at Long Bridge and below, and has reached James River at Westover and Wilcox's Landing. A portion of Genl Grant's army upon leaving our front at Cold Harbor is reported to have proceeded to the White House and embarked at that place. Everything is said to have been removed and the depot at the White House broken up. The cars, engine, railroad iron, and bridge timber that had been brought to that point have also been reshipped.

Very respectfully, your obt servt

R. E. LEE
Genl

777   To JEFFERSON DAVIS
Richmond, Virginia

Headquarters, Army of Northern Virginia
June 15, 1864
12 ¾ P.M.

Mr. President:

As I informed you last evening I had intended to move the troops nearer the exterior lines of defences around Richmond, but from the movements of the enemy's cavalry and the reports that have reached me this morning, his plans do not appear to be settled. Unless therefore I hear something more satisfactory, they will remain where they are. Should I move my camp, it will be somewhere on Cornelius Creek in the cleanest wood I can find near the New Market road or Osborne turnpike.

Most resply, your obt servt

R. E. LEE
Genl

778   To GENERAL BRAXTON BRAGG
            Commanding Armies of the Confederate States

Headquarters, Army of Northern Virginia
June 15, 1864
12:20 P.M.

General:
     Your letter of 8.45 a.m. enclosing various dispatches from Genl
Beauregard, is just received. I directed Genl Hoke this morning, unless
he should receive contrary orders from you, to cross the James River and
report to Genl Beauregard. I had a visit this morning from Col [Samuel
R.] Paul aide-de-camp of Genl Beauregard, who stated among other
things that the General was of opinion that if he had his original force,
he would be able to hold his present lines in front of Genl Butler and at
Petersburg. He is however particularly anxious to have Ransom's brigade,
which I believe is now at Chaffin's Bluff, and I doubt whether he will be
satisfied or consider himself strong enough until he is ordered to him. I
think therefore it had better be done. If [General Archibald] Gracie's
brigade cannot be returned to that place, perhaps the locals under Genl
Custis Lee might be able to hold it. But as long as this army remains in
its front, I will endeavor to make it safe. I had determined to move this
army back near the exterior line of defences near Richmond, but from
the movements of the enemy's cavalry this morning, and reports that
have reached me, I do not wish to draw too far back. Unless therefore I
am better satisfied, I shall remain where I am today, as the enemy's
plans do not seem to be settled. I am much grieved to hear of the death
of Lt Genl [Leonidas] Polk.

Very respectfully, your obt servt

R. E. LEE
Genl

779   To JAMES A. SEDDON
              Secretary of War

Headquarters, Army of Northern Virginia
June 15, 1864
6 P.M.

Sir:
     After the withdrawal of our cavalry yesterday evening from in front
of the enemy's works at Harrison's Landing his cavalry again advanced

on the Salem Church road, and this morning were reported in some force on that road and at Malvern Hill.

General William H. F. Lee easily drove back the force at the latter point, which retreated down the River road beyond Carter's Mill. A brigade of infantry was sent to support the cavalry on the road to Smith's Store and drove the enemy to that point without difficulty.

Nothing else of importance has occurred today.

Very respectfully, your obt servt

R. E. LEE
Genl

780   To JEFFERSON DAVIS
Richmond, Virginia

Riddell's Shop, Charles City Road
June 15, 1864
6:50 P.M.

Mr. President:

Your note of 1:20 p.m. today has just been received. As soon as I heard of the enemy's crossing the Chickahominy at Long Bridge I moved Heth's division across the river to White Oak Swamp bridge, and prepared the other troops for motion. Our skirmishers at daylight were moved forward, and finding no enemy in front of our lines for between one and two miles were recalled, and the army moved over the Chickahominy. Genl Heth's division holds the White Oak Swamp bridge, the rest of Hill's corps is at Riddell's Shop at the intersection of the Long Bridge and Charles City roads. Longstreet's corps is to his right on the Long Bridge road, and Hoke's division at the intersection of the Darbytown and Long Bridge roads. Our cavalry occupy the Willis Church road and Malvern Hill. The only enemy we have yet seen is that that has come up from the Long Bridge, and is opposed to Genl Heth at White Oak Swamp bridge and extends to this point. We have driven him from this position down the Long Bridge road, but I have not yet heard that White Oak Swamp bridge is uncovered. Genl Early was in motion this morning at 3 o'clock & by daylight was clear of our camps. He proceeded on the mountain road direct to Charlottesville, and arrangements have been made to give him 15 days supplies. If you think it better to recall him, please send a trusty messenger to overtake him tonight. I do not know that the necessity for his presence today is greater than it was yesterday. His troops would make us more secure here, but success in the Valley would relieve our difficulties that at present press heavily upon us. As I write, Wilcox's division is pressing the enemy down the Long Bridge road.

Most respectfully, your obt servt

R. E. LEE
Genl

781   To JEFFERSON DAVIS
Richmond, Virginia

June 15, 1864
8:20 P.M.

Mr. President:
I have just received your note of today. I directed Ransom's brigade this afternoon, if no contrary orders had been received, to report to Genl Beauregard, & replaced it for the night by one of Longstreet's. Genl G. W. C. Lee will repair to Chaffin's tomorrow at 3 a.m. with a portion of his command, leaving the Virginia reserves to support the batteries at Bottoms Bridge.

I am much grieved at the death of Genl Polk. I am unable to recommend a successor. As much as I esteem & admire Genl [William N.] Pendleton, I would not select him to command a corps in this army. I do not mean to say by that he is not competent, but from what I have seen of him, I do not know that he is. I can spare him, if in your good judgment, you decide he is the best available. I know nothing of the character of those officers you designate. As far as I do know some, I should think they would not answer. Major Genl [Alexander P.] Stewart I do not know. I regret I am unable to aid you, for I know the importance of selecting a proper officer.

Only the enemy's cavalry opposed us today & they were driven back on all the roads. If Genl Johnston would like Genl Ewell I would spare him. My own opinion is that Genl E's health is unequal to his duties, but he does not agree with me. Johnston knows & likes him, & I do the same.

Most truly & resply yours

R. E. LEE
Genl

782   To GENERAL P. G. T. BEAUREGARD
                    Petersburg, Virginia
                        TELEGRAM

                                              Drewry's Bluff
                                              June 16, 1864
                                               9.40 A.M.

PLEASE INFORM ME OF CONDITION OF AFFAIRS. PICKETT'S DIVISION IS IN
VICINITY OF YOUR LINES FRONT OF BERMUDA [HUNDRED].

                                              R. E. LEE

783   To GENERAL BRAXTON BRAGG
          Commanding Armies of the Confederate States
                        TELEGRAM

                                              Drewry's Bluff
                                              June 16, 1864
                                               9.40 A.M.

JUST ARRIVED AT THIS POINT WITH PICKETT'S DIVISION. HAVE INFORMED
GENERAL BEAUREGARD. DIRECT TO ME HERE.

                                              R. E. LEE

784   To GENERAL P. G. T. BEAUREGARD
                    Petersburg, Virginia
                        TELEGRAM

                                              Drewry's Bluff
                                              June 16, 1864
                                               10.30 A.M.

YOUR DISPATCH OF 9.45 RECEIVED. IT IS THE FIRST THAT HAS COME TO
HAND. I DO NOT KNOW THE POSITION OF GRANT'S ARMY, AND CANNOT STRIP
NORTH BANK OF JAMES RIVER. HAVE YOU NOT FORCE SUFFICIENT?

                                              R. E. LEE

785   To GENERAL P. G. T. BEAUREGARD
                    Petersburg, Virginia
                        TELEGRAM

                                              Drewry's Bluff
                                              June 16, 1864
                                                   3 P.M.

GENERAL:

DISPATCH OF 12.45 RECEIVED. PICKETT HAD PASSED THIS PLACE AT DATE
OF MY FIRST DISPATCH. I DID NOT RECEIVE YOUR NOTICE OF INTENDED EVACUA-
TION TILL 2 A.M. TROOPS WERE THEN AT MALVERN HILL, FOUR MILES FROM
ME. AM GLAD TO HEAR YOU CAN HOLD PETERSBURG. HOPE YOU WILL DRIVE
THE ENEMY. HAVE NOT HEARD OF GRANT'S CROSSING JAMES RIVER.

                                              R. E. LEE

786   To GENERAL P. G. T. BEAUREGARD
                    Petersburg, Virginia
                        TELEGRAM

                                              June 16, 1864
                                                   4 P.M.

THE TRANSPORTS YOU MENTION HAVE PROBABLY RETURNED BUTLER'S
TROOPS. HAS GRANT BEEN SEEN CROSSING JAMES RIVER?

                                              R. E. LEE

787   To JEFFERSON DAVIS
                    Richmond, Virginia

                        Headquarters, Army of Northern Virginia
                                              Drewry's Bluff
                                              June 16, 1864
                                                   7½ P.M.

Mr. President:
    I received this morning at 2 a.m. a dispatch from Genl Beauregard,
stating that he had abandoned his line on Bermuda Neck and would concentrate all his force on Petersburg. He also said that his skirmishers and
pickets would be withdrawn at daylight. I immediately ordered General Pickett's division to proceed across James River and occupy the lines,
directing Genl Anderson to move another division to the river and pro-

ceed in person to Bermuda and take direction of affairs. I requested Genl Beauregard not to withdraw his skirmishers and pickets until the arrival of those troops, though I feared from the lateness of the hour that he would not receive my message in time. Genl Anderson's troops were in the vicinity of Malvern Hill, and it was 9 o'clock a.m. today before the division crossed the river at Drewry's Bluff. One brigade with Genls Anderson & Pickett at its head preceded the division more than an hour; but before it could reach the lines, they had been occupied by the enemy, who advanced a force as far as the Petersburg turnpike. On learning this condition of affairs, I ordered over a second division to the support of the first, and a third to the vicinity of the bridge. The enemy was easily driven back, and General Anderson soon regained our second line of entrenchments. At last accounts the enemy in force occupied our first line, extending from Howlett's house on the river by Ware Bottom Church, from which I fear it will be difficult and costly to dislodge him. I have not learned from Genl Beauregard what force is opposed to him in Petersburg, or received any definite account of operations there, nor have I been able to learn whether any portion of Grant's army is opposed to him. Taking advantage of his occupation of the bluff at Howlett's house the enemy brought up five vessels and prepared to sink them in Trent's Reach. Two had been sunk with torpedoes in their bows when the officer who reported it to Captain Pegram left. I suppose the object is to prevent our gunboats from descending the river.

A dispatch just received from General Beauregard states that he countermanded the order for the withdrawal of his pickets and skirmishers, and that they occupied our second line at 10¼ a.m. today, but that they were afterwards forced to retire upon Petersburg.

I am with great respect, your obt servt

R. E. Lee
Genl

788   To JAMES A. SEDDON
Secretary of War
TELEGRAM

Headquarters, Army of Northern Virginia
June 17, 1864

SIR:

GENL BEAUREGARD TELEGRAPHS THAT LAST NIGHT THE ENEMY ASSAULTED HIS LINES TWICE AND WERE REPULSED, LEAVING 400 PRISONERS, INCLUDING

ELEVEN COMMISSIONED OFFICERS, IN OUR HANDS. TODAY THE ENEMY CARRIED
A WEAK POINT IN HIS LINES. OUR TROOPS ASSAULTED AND CARRIED OUR ORIG-
INAL LINES NEAR BERMUDA HUNDRED WITH SLIGHT LOSS ON OUR PART.

VERY RESPECTFULLY, YOUR OBT SERVT

R. E. LEE
Genl

789   To GENERAL P. G. T. BEAUREGARD
Petersburg, Virginia
TELEGRAM

Drewry's Bluff
June 17, 1864
6 A.M.

I AM DELIGHTED AT YOUR REPULSE OF THE ENEMY. ENDEAVOR TO RECOVER
YOUR LINES. CAN YOU ASCERTAIN ANYTHING OF GRANT'S MOVEMENTS? I AM
CUT OFF NOW FROM ALL INFORMATION. AT 11 P.M. LAST NIGHT WE TOOK
THE ORIGINAL LINE OF BREAST-WORKS AT HOWLETT'S HOUSE, AND THE REST OF
THE LINE IS BEING RECOVERED. I HAVE DIRECTED THAT THE BATTERY OF HEAVY
ARTILLERY BE REESTABLISHED, AND THE RAILS AT WALTHALL JUNCTION BE
REPLACED AND THE ROAD REOPENED.

R. E. LEE

790   To JEFFERSON DAVIS
Richmond, Virginia
TELEGRAM

Headquarters, Clay's House
June 17, 1864
10.30 A.M.

AT 11 LAST NIGHT TOOK BREAST-WORKS AT HOWLETT'S HOUSE. OTHER
PORTIONS OF THE SAME LINE WERE TAKEN. PICKETT'S DIVISION NOW OCCUPIES
TRENCHES FROM HOWLETT'S TO FRONT OF CLAY'S. FIELD'S DIVISION IS ON THE

RIGHT, BUT I BELIEVE [WHOLE] OF FRONT LINE NOT OCCUPIED. BATTERY AT HOWLETT'S IS BEING REESTABLISHED. SAW FIVE VESSELS SUNK BY ENEMY IN TRENT'S REACH. BEHIND LIE THE MONITORS. COUNTED 10 STEAMERS WITHIN THE REACH. ENEMY MADE TWO ATTEMPTS ON BEAUREGARD LAST NIGHT, BUT WERE REPULSED, WITH LOSS. FOUR HUNDRED PRISONERS, INCLUDING 11 COMMISSIONED OFFICERS CAPTURED. HE HAS NOT ENTRENCHED HIS ORIGINAL POSITION. SOME FIGHTING HAS OCCURRED THERE THIS MORNING WITHOUT RESULT. HAVE ORDERED RAILROAD AT PORT WALTHALL, DESTROYED BY ENEMY YESTERDAY, REPAIRED & REOPENED.

R. E. LEE

791 To GENERAL P. G. T. BEAUREGARD
Petersburg, Virginia
TELEGRAM

Clay's House
June 17, 1864
10.45 A.M.

BATTERY AT HOWLETT'S IS BEING REESTABLISHED. HOPE YOUR NEW LINE WILL PROTECT THE CITY. I WOULD RECOMMEND IT BEING ESTABLISHED SUFFICIENTLY IN ADVANCE. YOUR LINE FROM HOWLETT'S TO CLAY'S IS REOCCUPIED. ENEMY STILL HOLD SOME PORTION ON RIGHT OF CLAY'S.

R. E. LEE

792 To GENERAL P. G. T. BEAUREGARD
Petersburg, Virginia
TELEGRAM

Clay's House
June 17, 1864
12 M.

TELEGRAM OF 9 A.M. RECEIVED. UNTIL I CAN GET MORE DEFINITE INFORMATION OF GRANT'S MOVEMENTS I DO NOT THINK IT PRUDENT TO DRAW MORE TROOPS TO THIS SIDE OF THE RIVER.

R. E. LEE

793   To GENERAL W. H. F. LEE
Malvern Hill
TELEGRAM

Clay's House
June 17, 1864
3.30 P.M.

PUSH AFTER ENEMY AND ENDEAVOR TO ASCERTAIN WHAT HAS BECOME
OF GRANT'S ARMY. INFORM GENERAL HILL.

R. E. LEE

794   To GENERAL AMBROSE P. HILL
Riddell's Shop
TELEGRAM

Clay's House
June 17, 1864

GENERAL BEAUREGARD REPORTS LARGE NUMBER OF GRANT'S TROOPS CROSSED
JAMES RIVER ABOVE FORT POWHATAN YESTERDAY. IF YOU HAVE NOTHING CON-
TRADICTORY OF THIS MOVE TO CHAFFIN'S BLUFF.

R. E. LEE

795   To GENERAL P. G. T. BEAUREGARD
Petersburg, Virginia
TELEGRAM

Clay's House
June 17, 1864
4.30 P.M.

HAVE NO INFORMATION OF GRANT'S CROSSING JAMES RIVER, BUT UPON
YOUR REPORT HAVE ORDERED TROOPS UP TO CHAFFIN'S BLUFF.

R. E. LEE

796   To GENERAL P. G. T. BEAUREGARD
Petersburg, Virginia
TELEGRAM

Clay's House
June 17, 1864
5 P.M.

AT 4 P.M. WAS COMPELLED TO ASSAULT CENTER OF OUR FORMER LINE
HELD BY ENEMY. WE NOW HOLD ENTIRE LINE FROM HOWLETT'S TO DUNN'S
HILL. ALL PRISONERS FROM TENTH CORPS.

R. E. LEE

797   To GENERAL AMBROSE P. HILL
Riddell's Shop
TELEGRAM

Headquarters, Drewry's Bluff
June 17, 1864
10 P.M.

MOVE YOUR COMMAND PROMPTLY AT 3 A.M. TOMORROW FOR CHAFFIN'S
BLUFF. CROSS THE RIVER AND MOVE TO THE PETERSBURG TURNPIKE; THERE
AWAIT FURTHER ORDERS. SEND TO EXAMINE ABOUT BRIDGES.

R. E. LEE

798   To GENERAL P. G. T. BEAUREGARD
Petersburg, Virginia
TELEGRAM

Headquarters, Drewry's Bluff
June 17, 1864
10 P.M.

GENERAL KERSHAW'S DIVISION, WHICH WILL CAMP TONIGHT ON RED-
WATER CREEK, IS ORDERED TO CONTINUE ITS MARCH TOMORROW TO PETERS-
BURG.

R. E. LEE

799   To E. H. GILL
                Superintendent, Richmond and Petersburg Railroad
                              TELEGRAM

                                                    Drewry's Bluff
                                                    June 18, 1864
                                                    3.30 A.M.

CAN TRAINS RUN THROUGH TO PETERSBURG? IF SO, SEND ALL CARS AVAIL-
ABLE TO RICE'S TURNOUT. IF THEY CANNOT RUN THROUGH, CAN ANY BE SENT
FROM PETERSBURG TO THE POINT WHERE THE ROAD IS BROKEN. IT IS IMPOR-
TANT TO GET TROOPS TO PETERSBURG WITHOUT DELAY.

                                                    R. E. LEE

800   To GENERAL JUBAL A. EARLY
                              Lynchburg, Virginia
                                 TELEGRAM

                          Headquarters, Army of Northern Virginia
                                                    June 18, 1864

GRANT IS IN FRONT OF PETERSBURG. WILL BE OPPOSED THERE. STRIKE AS
QUICK AS YOU CAN, AND, IF CIRCUMSTANCES AUTHORIZE, CARRY OUT THE
ORIGINAL PLAN, OR MOVE UPON PETERSBURG WITHOUT DELAY.

                                                    R. E. LEE

801   To JEFFERSON DAVIS
                              Richmond, Virginia

                          Headquarters, Army of Northern Virginia
                                                    June 18, 1864

Mr. President:
     From information received last night it is pretty certain that Grant's
whole force has crossed to the south side of the James River. [General
James H.] Wilson's division of cavalry crossed yesterday. I have ordered
all the troops over towards Petersburg, leaving the outer defences of

Richmond in charge of Genl G. W. C. Lee to whom I have ordered
Col [Martin W.] Gary's command and several light batteries to report.
Genl William [H.] F. Lee I have ordered to Petersburg with [General
Rufus] Barringer's N[orth] C[arolina] brigade, leaving [General John
R.] Chambliss to cooperate with Hampton if practicable in striking at
Sheridan, who is apparently making for the White House. If he cannot
cooperate with Hampton I have ordered him to follow Genl William
[H.] F. Lee to Petersburg. Genl Hampton will continue to watch Sheri-
dan and endeavor to strike at him, but if the latter escapes & takes transport at the White House, Hampton is ordered to move as rapidly as possible for Petersburg. The enemy having transferred Wilson's division of
cavalry to the south side obliges me to call over Genl W. H. F. Lee.

Most resply, your obt servt

R. E. Lee
Genl

P.S. I go to Petersburg.

R. E. L.

802   To GENERAL BRAXTON BRAGG
Commanding Armies of Confederate States
TELEGRAM

Petersburg
June 18, 1864

PLEASE CAUSE ALL INFORMATION TO BE ADDRESSED TO ME HERE. KER-
SHAW'S & FIELD'S DIVISIONS PRECEDED ME.

R. E. Lee

803   To GENERAL WADE HAMPTON
Aenon Church
TELEGRAM

Headquarters, Army of Northern Virginia
June 18, 1864

IF SHERIDAN ESCAPES AND GETS TO HIS TRANSPORTS AT THE WHITE HOUSE
YOU MUST LOSE NO TIME IN MOVING YOUR ENTIRE COMMAND TO OUR RIGHT

NEAR PETERSBURG. KEEP YOURSELF THOROUGHLY ADVISED OF HIS MOVEMENTS
AND INTENTIONS AS FAR AS PRACTICABLE.

R. E. LEE
General

804   To JAMES A. SEDDON
                      Secretary of War
                         TELEGRAM

Petersburg
June 19, 1864

A DISPATCH JUST RECEIVED FROM NEW LONDON STATES THAT AN ASSAULT
WAS MADE ON OUR LINES AT LYNCHBURG LAST NIGHT & REPULSED BY TROOPS
THAT HAD ARRIVED. WHEN REST OF OUR FORCE CAME UP, PREPARATIONS WERE
MADE TO ATTACK THIS MORNING, BUT ENEMY RETREATED IN CONFUSION. OUR
TROOPS IN PURSUIT.

R. E. LEE

805   To HIS WIFE
                    Richmond, Virginia

Petersburg
June 19, 1864

I have received dear Mary your little missives & the bread for which
take many thanks. I asked Custis yesterday to write to you & say I had
not time. I am much obliged to the kind people for the clothes, but if
they are not gray as I understand from Major Ferguson's note, they are
of no use to me in the field. You will therefore have to keep them. I
hope to go to church this blessed day & shall remember you all in my
poor prayers. Never forget me or our suffering country. I saw Fitzhugh
& Rob yesterday. All well. Give much love to my daughters & my little
sweetheart. God bless you all.

Truly & affly
R. E. LEE

806   To JEFFERSON DAVIS
Richmond, Virginia

Headquarters, Army of Northern Virginia
Near Petersburg, Virginia
June 19, 1864

Mr. President:

I have received your letter of the 18th. I was able to leave with General G. W. C. Lee only the forces which belong to Richmond. I placed at his disposal two battalions of artillery under Colonel [Thomas H.] Carter in addition to what he originally had, which I thought might be advantageously employed in connection with Gary's cavalry and such infantry support as General Lee could furnish, in operating on the James River against any parties that might be landed, or in embarrassing its navigation. I wished him to display as much force as possible, and to be active and vigilant in warding off any threatened blow. His force is not more than sufficient for this purpose, but if we can get early intelligence, and especially maintain the road from Petersburg to Richmond in running order, I think we shall be able to meet any attack the enemy may make upon the latter place.

Night before last he apparently reduced the force on his lines in front of Bermuda Hundred, and from the reports received during the night, matters seemed to be so threatening in Petersburg, that I directed General Anderson to march at once with Kershaw's and Field's divisions, Pickett's division being left to guard our lines from Howlett's to Ashton Creek. I halted one division of Hill's on the north side of the Appomattox, in supporting distance of both places. General Beauregard had felt constrained to contract his lines on the east side of Petersburg before my arrival, and I found his troops in their new position. I am unable to judge of the comparative strength of the two lines, but as far as I can see, the only disadvantage is the proximity of the new line to the city. No attack has been made by the enemy since my arrival, though sharp skirmishing and cannonading has been kept up. My greatest apprehension at present is the maintenance of our communications south. It will be difficult, and I fear impracticable to preserve it uninterrupted. The enemy's left now rests on the Jerusalem road, and I fear it would be impossible to arrest a sudden attack aimed at a distant point. In addition, the enemy's cavalry, in spite of all our efforts, can burn the bridges over the Nottoway and its branches, the Meherrin & even the Southside [Rail]road is very much exposed, and our only dependence seems to

me to be on the Danville. Every effort should be made to secure to that
road sufficient rolling stock by transferring that of other roads, and to
accumulate supplies of all kinds in Richmond in anticipation of temporary interruptions. When roads are broken every aid should be given
to the companies to enable them to restore them immediately. Duplicate
timbers for all the bridges should be prepared in safe places to be used in
an emergency, and every other arrangement made to keep the roads in
running order.

Most respectfully and truly yours

R. E. Lee
Genl

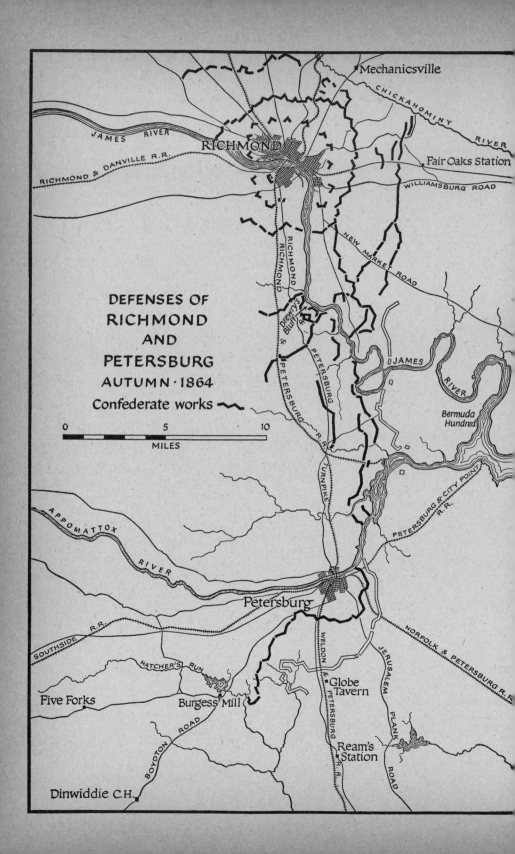

Mechanicsville

CHICKAHOMINY RIVER

JAMES RIVER

RICHMOND

RICHMOND & DANVILLE R.R.

Fair Oaks Station

WILLIAMSBURG ROAD

NEW MARKET ROAD

RICHMOND & PETERSBURG

Drewry's Bluff

JAMES RIVER

PETERSBURG R.R.

Bermuda Hundred

DEFENSES OF
RICHMOND
AND
PETERSBURG
AUTUMN · 1864
Confederate works ∿

0   5   10
MILES

TURNPIKE

PETERSBURG & CITY POINT R.R.

APPOMATTOX RIVER

Petersburg

SOUTHSIDE R.R.

NORFOLK & PETERSBURG R.R.

HATCHER'S RUN

Five Forks

Burgess Mill

WELDON & PETERSBURG R.R.

Globe Tavern

JERUSALEM PLANK ROAD

BOYDTON ROAD

Ream's Station

Dinwiddie C.H.

CHAPTER SIXTEEN

The Siege of Petersburg

"The result must be calamitous"

THE DEFENSE OF THE CITY of Petersburg was only one item in the siege which began, in effect, June 19. At Petersburg the fortifications outside the city facing east, with the northern flank on the Appomattox River, ran south about three miles and then bent back to the west, facing south. Though these works were subjected to continual fire from sharpshooters, artillery and the new trench mortars, Grant used the superiority of his numbers for whipsaw operations to the south of Petersburg, to cut the lifeline railroads, and to the north of the James, to threaten Richmond or to break the Virginia Central.

To indicate the flow of replacements Grant drew upon, in only four engagements from June 22 to August 24, his losses in prisoners alone approached 8000 in the infantry (the size of Kershaw's and Field's troops combined). Such losses to relatively small numbers of Confederates also indicated the below-standard performance of the veterans in the bled Army of the Potomac and the heavy proportion of raw recruits. These attacks began on June 21 on the Weldon Railroad.

Simultaneously with this first infantry foray, two columns of cavalry (Wilson's division, which were the last troops to cross the James on the night of the 16th, and Kautz's smaller force, which had operated with Butler) moved west to other railroads. The Southside Railroad ran east-west to Lynchburg and on to Tennessee, and the Richmond & Danville, which ran southwest from Richmond to connections with central North Carolina, crossed the Southside at Burkeville. Followed by Rooney Lee, and engaged by companies of farmers' reserves, the Federal cavalry did no extensive damage, and their loitering to rob caused them to run into a trap set across their return course by infantry and the main cavalry force returning from shepherding Sheridan back from his abortive raid. Wilson lost 1000 prisoners, thirteen guns, all his wagons, and most of the personal loot.

On July 28 Grant sent a strong force to the north of the James. Outside the artillerists on the fixed guns in the fortifications, there were scarcely any troops east of Richmond except Gary's weak cavalry brigade, another of the South Carolina units released to the field too late for seasoning. The small units of veterans which Lee rushed back across the river were hard put to contain the assault.

Then on July 30, with the Petersburg works thus thinned by Lee's emergency dispersals, Burnside's IX Corps exploded 8000 pounds of powder under a segment of lines southwest of the city. This publicized Battle of the Crater was particularly sanguinary and gruesome for the period of time it lasted and the relatively small numbers involved. The attacking forces crowded or were pressed into the pit of shifting, loose earth, littered with the dismembered parts of the Confederate soldiers who had been in line over the blast, and the crater was turned into a slaughter pen by Lee's enraged troops. Again the Federal assault was poorly coordinated.

On August 14-16, Federals were back on the north side of the James, where Field's 3000-man division was then stationed at Chaffin's Bluff. At the Battles of Charles City Road and New Market Road, again the troops which Lee hurried back across the river — each time a little fewer, a little tireder — struggled to contain the weight hurled at them. Lee felt it necessary to go to the river fort himself and, while he was there, on August 19, the Federals were back on the Weldon Railroad, at Globe Tavern, something over three miles south of Lee's right flank. Grant's infantry was shaken by A. P. Hill, giving up 2700 prisoners, but they permanently destroyed a section of the railroad. Five days later, August 24, five miles south of Globe Tavern, two Federal corps started destroying the tracks at Ream's Station. A. P. Hill and Wade Hampton drove the enemy, bagging 2000 prisoners from Hancock's previously formidable corps, but more of the railroad was gone for good.

Having given up something like 10,000 prisoners of all arms, in addition to heavy casualties, Grant could still detach two divisions of Sheridan's cavalry (down to 6465) to follow the VI Corps (at 12,674 down to half its original strength) for a concentration against Early in the Valley. Combined with the XIX Corps and the remnants of Hunter's army, Sheridan fielded more than 32,000 infantry, to bring his total effective force to better than 40,000 plus 5000 at Harper's Ferry.

Jubal Early, with little more than 10,000 infantry and 3000 cavalry to begin with, from mid-June to early August had diverted considerable

Federal strength. In addition to Grant's VI Corps, Hunter's old army and troops from around Washington, he had occupied the cavalry forces of Averell and Crook, who would otherwise have been engaged in destructive raids. Yet, though he kept the Valley safe, his operations accomplished nothing directly for Lee militarily. Lee had hoped that Grant would attack his lines at Petersburg instead of sending off troops to be used against Early, but Grant at that phase began to apply those techniques of attrition which his admirers, in retrospect, claim was his policy all along. He only turned systematically against Lee's supplies, in avoidance of fixed positions, after his army proved unequal to defeating Lee in battle and he could not maneuver Lee out of the works which compensated for the inferior numbers of his wretchedly conditioned men.

When Grant sent Sheridan west in August, Lee on August 6 tried the desperate counter of sending Dick Anderson, with a force composed of Kershaw's division and Fitz Lee's cavalry division, back to middle Virginia, to cooperate with Early on the other side of the Blue Ridge. It was a pathetic return to the great days when Lee was in middle Virginia and Jackson in the Valley. Before Lee could build this force with Wade Hampton's division or it could cooperate effectively with Early, the slowly grinding actions on his flanks prevented Lee from reinforcing Anderson and continuing freedom of movement. Except for the addition of Fitz Lee's attenuated brigades to support the depleted regiments of the unreliable Valley cavalry, Early alone had to take on Sheridan's new army.

Early had performed minor miracles with his small force, crossing the Potomac in early July and threatening Washington. Back in Virginia on July 14, he again maneuvered the enemy north of the Potomac and on July 28 was situated near Winchester. When Sheridan came with the newly organized army on August 10, a series of maneuverings and skirmishes went on between the two forces until September 18. By then Sheridan was ready to come to battle and so was Early, and they met at Winchester on September 19. Early, essentially a combat fighter, had been superb at division command but, like so many others, he lacked the tactical grasp for handling several divisions and the cavalry. Even with his limitations, and the disparity between the forces (three to one in infantry), the fine division leaders — Rodes, Ramseur and Gordon — made it an even fight. Then Rodes was killed, Fitz Lee went out with a heavy wound, the poorly disciplined Valley cavalry grew unsteady, and coordination began to go.

Driven from the field, Early, not feeling defeated, re-formed to the south at Fisher's Hill and received Sheridan's attack on the 22nd. Against the odds, Early needed to be a genius; instead, all of his limitations were revealed. Coordination went quickly, the cavalry broke and the small army was routed. Even the famed artillery, pride of the old Second Corps, lost guns in the rush.

Early retreated up to the middle Valley, and Sheridan was free to turn the fertile area into a wasteland. But Old Jube still did not give up. Lee sent him Kershaw and a cavalry brigade (regiment size) and Early came back at the Federals again. In a surprise morning attack at Cedar Creek, October 19, his men drove the enemy back to a second line and then a third, and only one more push was needed for a decisive victory. At the moment of decision, his will faltered in the final commitment: the enemy was given time to rally, some of his underfed men were quickly exhausted and others were diverted by the enemy's supply wagons. With the disparity of numbers, no margin was allowed for error; once the tide turned, it was all over. Young Ramseur was mortally wounded and, for effective purposes, Early's command was wrecked. Kershaw's diminished division was returned to Lee.

Early's finish in the Shenandoah Valley, the scene of great Confederate victories, was a dramatic turn to both sides. The smallness of Early's force was not made known and, as Grant believed it to be 40,000, the victories redounded to Sheridan's fame as Old Jube's star waned. In all truth, Sheridan had sustained 16,962 casualties (5000-odd at Cedar Creek), more troops than Early had ever had with him. But it was too late in the day for extenuations. Defeats were irreversible and the loss of the Valley was a finality. Lee, even though he had underestimated the forces with Sheridan, withheld censure from Early.

By then, disasters were enclosing him from all sides. Back in middle July, Jefferson Davis, irrationally determined that an offensive should be opened against Sherman's numerically superior army, decided to remove Joe Johnston from command. Lee wrote an extremely strong letter, for him, advising against the change of commanders, but Davis placed Hood in command. In six weeks the offensive which Hood was ordered to mount half-wrecked his army and removed it from Sherman's path; on September 3, Atlanta was entered.

Lee also wrote strong letters to the President on the urgent need of building a reserve to occupy the works outside Richmond; he pointed out that the exertions of his physically weakened men in running back and forth from south of Petersburg to north of the James were depleting his army. Many were out ill, many more stole off during the night: their wasted bodies could no longer support their spirits. In the desperate remedies he suggested for the support of his men, Lee, with a far grimmer tone than he had ever used before, gave prophetic warnings of the consequences of the continuation of his present situation. These warnings went unheeded, while the pendulum continued to swing from north to south of Petersburg, whittling away at his army.

On September 29, the garrison troops lost Fort Harrison, a key position in the network of fortifications designed by Lee east of Richmond, and two slim brigades of veterans barely saved the break from spreading to Fort Gilmer — rupturing the whole line north from the river fort at Chaffin's Bluff and opening the way to Richmond. On the 30th, Lee recrossed the river and personally directed an attack designed to retake Fort Harrison, but his exhausted men and worn leaders effected no more coordination on offense than did the enemy.

Then in October, back to south of Petersburg, the Federals began to stretch westward, threatening to enclose the city in a semicircle. To meet the extension, Lee could only thin his lines in the fortifications — which, after running three miles south of the Appomattox, ran three miles west to Battery 45 — and start extending entrenchments to the southwest. More of the weakened men went to the hospital, over to the enemy or home, under the strain of the manual labor of digging new lines in front of the Boydton Plank Road for eight miles to Burgess's Mill on Hatcher's Run.

On October 27 two Federal corps crossed Hatcher's Run in a move on the Plank Road, and were engaged by A. P. Hill, supported by the cavalry with Wade Hampton, which was then fighting mostly as dismounted infantry. The enemy retired. On the same day, Federals east of Richmond struck beyond the heavy fortifications, which extended northward from the river fort, along the Charles City and New Market Roads. By then (October 19) Longstreet, returned to duty with his right arm partially paralyzed, had been established in command north of the James, with the divisions of Hoke and Field permanently stationed there.

During this period, except in Hill's Third Corps, the old corps structure of the army gave way to Lee's makeshift extemporizations. Hoke, with Longstreet, was not organized with the First Corps, while Pickett, who was, was detached with a declining division in the Bermuda Hundred lines which he had retaken in June. Anderson, who had been promoted to lieutenant-general while in command of the First Corps, had so lost spirit and competence that he was given command of a scratch force composed of Bushrod Johnson's small division (formed during the May emergency at Bermuda Hundred), with a few oddments and the artillery in a section of the line, the whole dignified with the name of the Fourth Corps as commensurate with his rank. On December 5, when the VI Corps was brought back to Grant from the Valley, Lee recalled

the remnants of Early's corps — Gordon's division, Ramseur's old division commanded by John Pegram, and Rodes's old division — all three
scarcely equal in size to an 1863 division. This left Early with no more
than a discouraged observation force at Waynesboro.

Beauregard had been transferred West to assume command of still
another Department, this one composed of the ravaged regions through
which Hood's army wandered until it was destroyed as an effective force
in front of Nashville, December 16. As Sherman had then marched across
Georgia from Atlanta to Savannah, evacuated on December 21, and a
great amphibious armada was threatening Fort Fisher, which guarded
the last open port of Wilmington, Lee's army was once again turned to
as a source of manpower to prop up the last crumbling walls of the
Confederacy falling around him. In December Hoke was sent back to
North Carolina where Braxton Bragg had been established as Department commander, with the Department again (now that it no longer
mattered) under Lee's authority. Hampton and his division, commanded
by Calbraith Butler, went to South Carolina in January.

On January 15, Fort Fisher fell, followed by the capture of Wilmington. With the end rapidly approaching, Congress defied the President by
creating an office of general-in-chief, and Davis — whose relations with
Lee were strained at that point — appointed Lee to the meaningless
office.

807   To JAMES A. SEDDON
                              Secretary of War

                                        Headquarters, Army of Northern Virginia
                                                              June 22, 1864

Sir:
        Since Friday last there has been skirmishing along the lines in front
of Bermuda Hundred and around Petersburg. The Federal army appears
to be concentrated at these two places and is strongly entrenched. Yesterday a movement of infantry, cavalry, and artillery was made towards
the right of our forces at Petersburg in the direction of the Weldon Railroad. The enemy was driven back, and his infantry is reported to have
halted. His cavalry have continued to advance upon the road by a route
farther removed from our position.

        The enemy's infantry was attacked this afternoon on the west side
of the Jerusalem Plank road and driven from his first line of works to
his second on that road by General Mahone with a part of his division.

About sixteen hundred prisoners, four pieces of artillery, eight stands of colors, and a large number of small arms were captured.

Very respectfully, your obt servt

R. E. Lee
Genl

808   MAJOR W. H. TAYLOR TO GENERAL G. W. C. LEE
Commanding Richmond Local Defence Troops
TELEGRAM

[June 22, 1864]

COLONEL GORGAS TELEGRAPHS AMMUNITION FOR HEAVY GUNS AND MORTARS WILL BE VERY SCARCE AS LONG AS WORKMEN ARE KEPT IN THE FIELD. HOW MANY MEN OF THIS CLASS ARE WITH THE LOCAL TROOPS, AND CAN THEY NOT BE ALLOWED TO RETURN TO THE ARSENAL?

W. H. Taylor
Assistant Adjutant General

809   To GENERAL BRAXTON BRAGG
Commanding Armies of the Confederate States
TELEGRAM

Petersburg
June 22, 1864
2 P.M.

FROM ALL I CAN LEARN THE ENEMY'S CAVALRY, [GENERALS JAMES H.] WILSON'S, [SAMUEL P.] SPEAR'S, & [AUGUST V.] KAUTZ'S, ARE MOVING THROUGH DINWIDDIE INQUIRING THE ROAD TO BURKEVILLE & THE HIGH BRIDGE ON THE SOUTH SIDE RAILROAD. THEY ARE FOLLOWED BY ONE BRIGADE FROM THIS ARMY. LET GENL KEMPER COLLECT WHAT RESERVES HE CAN AT THE THREATENED POINTS AT ONCE.

R. E. Lee

810   To HIS WIFE
                           Richmond, Virginia

                                              Camp near Petersburg
                                              June 24, 1864

   I have received dearest Mary your note of Sunday & the nice bread
from Mrs. Conway. Thank her for it. The cheese is very acceptable. I
am glad to hear the clothes given me by those kind gentlemen are such
as I can wear. I do not require them at present, having as many as I can
transport. I received yesterday your note of Wednesday evening. I am
glad to hear that you have appointed a time for leaving Richmond. As
sorry as I shall be to be farther separated from you, I shall take great
comfort in your safer & more pleasant situation. Do not delay your departure. I will endeavour to see you if possible. I fear your kind friends
in Bedford have suffered from the inroads of [General David] Hunter. I
trust a kind Providence has protected them. I am very well & kind friends
present themselves every where. Give much love to my dear children. I
am always thinking of you & them.

                                              Very truly & sincerely

                                                      R. E. LEE

811   To JAMES A. SEDDON
                           Secretary of War

                                   Headquarters, Army of Northern Virginia
                                              June 24, 1864
                                                  9 P.M.

Sir:
       Yesterday the enemy made a demonstration with infantry upon the
Weldon Railroad, but before he had done much damage ,was driven back
by General Mahone with a portion of his command. About six hundred
prisoners and twenty-eight commissioned officers were taken, most of
whom were captured by [General Edward A.] Perry's Florida brigade.
   This morning the enemy was felt on both flanks, and a part of one
of General Hoke's brigades entered his works. Not being supported,
they were unable to hold the position and retired with few casualties,
but losing the advance line, which had succeeded in entering the enemy's

entrenchments. A small number of prisoners was taken, but the enemy's loss is supposed to have been slight.

Very respectfully, your obt servt

R. E. LEE
Genl

812   To GENERAL WADE HAMPTON
Care of General Braxton Bragg
TELEGRAM

Hancock's
June 25, 1864
7 A.M.

FOR WANT OF CAVALRY OUR RAILROAD COMMUNICATIONS SOUTH HAVE BEEN CUT. IF YOU CANNOT ENGAGE SHERIDAN TO ADVANTAGE HE CAN BE WATCHED WITH A SMALLER FORCE. SEND TO ME CHAMBLISS' BRIGADE AND ANY OTHER BRIGADE WHICH CAN BE SPARED.

R. E. LEE

813   To JAMES A. SEDDON
Secretary of War

Headquarters, Army of Northern Virginia
June 25, 1864

Sir:

General W. H. F. Lee pursued the enemy's cavalry which advanced along the South Side Railroad. He had a skirmish on the 22d near Dinwiddie Court House, and the next day struck their column in flank near Black's and White's, cutting in two and getting possession of the road by which they were moving towards Nottoway Court House. The road was held after an engagement which continued from 12 m. until dark, the enemy making repeated attempts to break through and rejoin his advance. He withdrew from General Lee's front at daylight on the 24th, leaving his dead and wounded on the field, taking the road to Hungarytown and Keysville. General Lee is still following them.

Very respectfully, your obt servt

R. E. LEE
Genl

814

MAJOR W. H. TAYLOR TO
GENERAL FITZHUGH LEE
Commanding Cavalry Division
TELEGRAM

June 26, 1864

TELEGRAM RECEIVED. IF THERE IS NOTHING TO DETAIN YOUR COMMAND
ON NORTH SIDE JAMES, THE GENERAL COMMANDING DESIRES YOUR DIVISION
TO COME ON THIS WAY, FOLLOWING HAMPTON'S.

W. H. TAYLOR
Assistant Adjutant General

815

To JAMES A. SEDDON
Secretary of War

Headquarters, Army of Northern Virginia
June 26, 1864

Sir:
  The enemy has been quiet today in our front. A dispatch dated
25th was received this morning from Captain [Benjamin L.] Farinholt,
commanding at Staunton River Bridge, expressing his confidence of being able to protect it.
  This afternoon General W. H. F. Lee reports that he attacked the
enemy near Staunton River Bridge yesterday afternoon and drove him
until dark. He also states that the enemy was signally repulsed at the
bridge the same evening and retreated this morning, leaving about thirty
of his dead on the field.

Very respectfully, your obt servt

R. E. LEE
Genl

816

To JEFFERSON DAVIS
Richmond, Virginia

Headquarters, Army of Northern Virginia
June 26, 1864

Mr. President:
  I have the honor to acknowledge the receipt of your letter of the
25th instant. Genl [David] Hunter has escaped Early, and will make

good his retreat, as far as I can understand, to Lewisburg. Although his expedition has been partially interrupted, I fear he has not been much punished, except by the demoralization of his troops and the loss of some artillery. From his present position he can easily be reorganized and re-equipped, and unless we have sufficient force to resist him, will repeat his expedition. This would necessitate the return of Early at Staunton. I think it better that he should move down the Valley, if he can obtain provisions, which would draw Hunter after him, and may enable him to strike [General John] Pope before he can effect a junction with Hunter. If circumstances favor, I should also recommend his crossing the Potomac. I think I can maintain our lines here against Genl Grant. He does not seem disposed to attack, and has thrown himself strictly on the defensive. I am less uneasy about holding our position than about our ability to procure supplies for the army. I fear the latter difficulty will oblige me to attack Genl Grant in his entrenchments, which I should not hesitate to do but for the loss it will inevitably entail. A want of success would in my opinion be almost fatal, and this causes me to hesitate in the hope that some relief may be procured without running such great hazard.

I should like much to have the benefit of Your Excellency's good judgment and views upon this subject.

Great benefit might be drawn from the release of our prisoners at Point Lookout if it can be accomplished. The number of men employed for this purpose would necessarily be small, as the whole would have to be transported secretly across the Potomac where it is very broad, the means of doing which must first be procured. I can devote to this purpose the whole of the Marylanders of this army, which would afford a sufficient number of men of excellent material and much experience, but I am at a loss where to find a proper leader. As he would command Maryland troops and operate upon Maryland soil it would be well that he should be a Marylander. Of those connected with this army I consider Col Bradley T. Johnson the most suitable. He is bold & intelligent, ardent & true, and yet I am unable to say whether he possesses all the requisite qualities. Everything in an expedition of the kind would depend upon the leader. I have understood that most of the garrison at Point Lookout was composed of negroes. I should suppose that the commander of such troops would be poor & feeble. A stubborn resistance, therefore, may not reasonably be expected. By taking a company of the Maryland artillery, armed as infantry, the dismounted cavalry and their infantry organization, as many men would be supplied as transportation could be procured for. By throwing them suddenly on the beach with some concert of action among the prisoners, I think the guard might be overpowered, the prisoners liberated & organized, and marched immediately on the route to Washington.

The artillery company could operate the guns captured at the Point. The dismounted cavalry with the released prisoners of that arm could mount themselves on the march, and the infantry would form a respectable force. Such a body of men under an able leader, although they might not be able without assistance to capture Washington, could march around it and cross the upper Potomac where fordable. I do not think they could cross the river in a body at any point below Washington, unless possibly at Alexandria. Provisions, &c., would have to be collected in the country through which they pass. The operations on the river must be confided to an able naval officer, who I know will be found in Col [John Taylor] Wood. The subject is one worthy of consideration, and can only be matured by reflection.

The sooner it is put in execution the better, if it be deemed practicable.

At this time, as far as I can learn, all the troops in the control of the United States are being sent to Grant, and little or no opposition could be made by those at Washington.

With relation to the project of Marshal Kane, if the matter can be kept secret, which I fear is impossible, should Genl Early cross the Potomac, he might be sent to join him.

Very respectfully, Your Excellency's obdt servt

R. E. LEE
Genl

817   To HIS WIFE
                    Richmond, Virginia

Camp, Petersburg
June 26, 1864

I received today dear Mary your note of yesterday with the clothes. I return in the bag my flannel drawers which please have put in my trunk. I have plenty of socks for the present. I hope it is not as hot in Richmond as here. It is perfectly stifling & then the dust is so dense that the atmosphere is distressing. The men suffer a great deal in the trenches, & this condition of things with the extreme heat of the sun nearly puts an end to military operations. I received a kind letter from Dr. Peyton today saying they were all well in his neighborhood. A despatch from

Fitzhugh today states he had attacked the enemy's cavalry near Staunton River on the Danville road & driven them till dark. They had been repulsed at the river & turned down the stream. I hope all was well with him. This makes the third attack he has made upon them since they started on this raid.

I shall continue to hope to see you before your departure. If I do not I shall with confidence commit you & my dear daughters to the hands of our Merciful Father in Heaven, with the firm belief that He will order all things for the best for us, both in this world & the next. May He have mercy on us all & specially guard & protect you. Give much love to the girls & believe me always & as ever yours

R. E. Lee

P.S. All that I can do for Mr. Williams is to represent his case to Col Ould, which I will do.

R. E. L.

818   To JAMES A. SEDDON
               Secretary of War

Headquarters, Army of Northern Virginia
June 28, 1864

Sir:

The enemy has been engaged today apparently in strengthening his lines in front of Petersburg, advancing them at some points.

His cavalry, after being repulsed at Staunton River Bridge on the afternoon of the 26th [25th] retired in the direction of Christianville, where they encamped that night. The next morning they continued their march towards Lawrenceville by way of Brentsville, and a part of them encamped last night about eight miles northwest of the former place. They appear to be making their way back to the main body of the army.

Very respectfully, your obt servt

R. E. Lee
Genl

819   To MISS MILDRED LEE
                          Richmond, Virginia

                                                    Camp, Petersburg
                                                    June 28, 1864

My precious Life:
    I have received your note & grieve at the sickness of your poor
mother. It is cooler today & I trust the change of temperature may be
beneficial to her. You must give her a great deal of love & say I wish I
could see her & cure her. I fear both are beyond my power. It is impossible for me to leave here at this time, & I do not know when I shall
be able. Her day of departure from Richmond must not be postponed
on my account. I trust she will have a safe & prosperous journey & be
much benefited by her visit to the country. The sooner she leaves Richmond in my opinion the better. May God guard her & you all. I hope
Mary is well again & that Agnes enjoys good health. Give my love to
both & say I wish I could bid them farewell. I trust we may meet in
more happy times. For yourself accept my thanks for your remembrance
of me & think of me always. I have no news. I would recommend you
to restore Custis Morgan to his native woods. I admire his taste in going
to see Miss Mary Triplett, but fear he will bite some of you very severely before you make up your mind to part with him. Good bye my
precious child. Take good care of your mother & let me know how she
is.

        With kind regards to all friends, I am truly your father

                                                    R. E. LEE

820   To JAMES A. SEDDON
                          Secretary of War
                          TELEGRAM

                                                Dunn's Hill, near Petersburg
                                                    June 29, 1864
                                                    8.30 P.M.

SIR:

    GENL HAMPTON REPORTS THAT HE ATTACKED THE ENEMY'S [WILSON'S]
CAVALRY YESTERDAY AFTERNOON ON THEIR RETURN FROM STAUNTON RIVER
BRIDGE THIS SIDE OF SAPPONY CHURCH, AND DROVE THEM BEYOND THAT POINT.
THE FIGHT CONTINUED DURING THE NIGHT, AND AT DAYLIGHT THIS MORNING
HE TURNED THEIR LEFT AND ROUTED THEM. WHEN THEY REACHED REAMS'

STATION THEY WERE CONFRONTED BY A PORTION OF MAHONE'S DIVISION, WHO
ATTACKED THEM IN FRONT, WHILE THEIR LEFT FLANK WAS TURNED BY GENL
FITZ LEE'S CAVALRY. THE ENEMY WAS COMPLETELY ROUTED AND SEVERAL
PIECES OF ARTILLERY, WITH A NUMBER OF PRISONERS, WAGONS, AMBULANCES,
&C., CAPTURED. THE CAVALRY ARE IN PURSUIT.

R. E. LEE

821   To JEFFERSON DAVIS
                         Richmond, Virginia

Headquarters, Petersburg
June 29, 1864

Mr. President:
      I enclose for your perusal a letter received today from Genl Early.
His general plan of action is in conformity to my original instructions &
conversation with him before his departure. I still think it is our policy
to draw the attention of the enemy to his own territory. It may force
Grant to attack me, or weaken his force. It will also I think oblige Hunter
to cross the Potomac or expose himself to attack. From either of these
events I anticipate good results. The success of Genl J. E. Johnston,
announced in this morning's journals, besides its general good effect,
will favor Early's movement. If it could be united with a release of the
prisoners at Point Lookout the advantages would be great. I believe the
latter only requires a proper leader. Can one be found? There will be
time to shape Early's course or terminate it when he reaches the Potomac, as circumstances require. He could not be withdrawn from the
Valley without inviting a return of Hunter's expedition. To retain him
there inactive would not be advantageous. As before stated, my greatest
present anxiety is to secure regular and constant supplies. At this time I
am doing well, but I must look to the future. I have started today a
train of wagons, via Dinwiddie Court House to Stony Creek Station,
Petersburg and Weldon Railroad, for corn to be brought there from
Weldon. This, with the standing crop of clover & oats, will subsist our
horses for the present. The enemy's cavalry having been turned away
from the High Bridge and repulsed at the Staunton River bridge, are returning. Hampton encountered them last night at Sappony Church and
arrested their progress. Fitz Lee will today reach Reams' Station, but I
fear he will not be able to prevent their getting east of the railroad.

With great respect, your obt servt

R. E. LEE
Genl

822   To HIS WIFE
                            Richmond, Virginia

                                              Camp, Petersburg
                                                 June 30, 1864

   I was very glad dear Mary to receive your note yesterday & to hear
that you were better. I trust you will continue to improve & soon be
well as usual. God grant that you may be entirely restored in His own
good time. Do you recollect what a happy day thirty three years ago
this was? How many hopes & pleasures it gave birth to? God has been
very merciful & kind to us & how thankless & sinful I have been. I pray
that He may continue His mercies & blessings to us & give us a little
peace & rest together in this world & finally gather us & all He has
given us around His throne in the world to come. I am encamped in
the yard of a Mrs. Shippen, formerly Miss Gilliam. She has been for
three years suffering with rheumatism in her joints similar to yourself.
Last winter I think she was seized with a violent attack of pneumonia.
As she grew better, her rheumatism diminished. It seemed to discend &
the swelling of her joints settled in her feet. She now walks about, having once been obliged to be carried. Her feet are still somewhat swollen
I believe, at any rate very tender & sensitive & her only pain is now
there. You can see yet, in the lineaments of her face traces of great
suffering. She is very kind. Sends me rolls, vegetables, & milk, & on two
occasions at our dinner at sunset has sent us a tureen of delightful calf's
head soup. I hope your attack will pass off in the same way. The President has just arrived & I must bring my letter to a close. Give much
love to my dear daughters. Custis I hope will see you this evening. God
bless you all.

                                       Truly & sincerely as ever

                                                 R. E. LEE

823   To JAMES A. SEDDON
                              Secretary of War
                                 TELEGRAM

                                         Headquarters, Near Petersburg
                                                   July 1, 1864

GENL BEAUREGARD REPORTS A FEEBLE DEMONSTRATION MADE BY ENEMY
ON A PORTION OF GENL JOHNSON'S LINES ABOUT 5 P.M. YESTERDAY. HIS

SKIRMISHERS, SUPPORTED BY TWO LINES OF TROOPS, DROVE IN OUR SKIRMISH-
ERS, WHICH WERE REESTABLISHED AT DARK. IN VARIOUS CONFLICTS WITH THE
ENEMY'S CAVALRY IN THEIR LATE EXPEDITION AGAINST THE RAILROADS, BE-
SIDES THEIR KILLED AND WOUNDED LEFT ON THE FIELD, OVER A THOUSAND
PRISONERS, THIRTEEN PIECES OF ARTILLERY, THIRTY WAGONS AND AMBU-
LANCES, MANY SMALL ARMS, HORSES, ORDNANCE STORES, AND SEVERAL HUN-
DRED NEGROES TAKEN FROM THE PLANTATIONS ON THEIR ROUTE WERE CAP-
TURED.

R. E. LEE
General

824   To JEFFERSON DAVIS
                     Richmond, Virginia

Headquarters, Army of Northern Virginia
July 2, 1864

Mr. President:

As far as my judgment and experience enable me to decide, I am
convinced that the cavalry service will be benefitted by having one
officer to control its operations, and to be held responsible for its condition. Since the death of Genl Stuart, I have placed each division under
the charge of its division commander, and when two or more have operated together, have directed the senior officer to assume command. The
disadvantage of this arrangement in my opinion is that he neither feels
nor exercises that authority which is required by the responsibility of his
position. It is taken up one day and laid aside the next, and is not as effective as if exercised by one who is permanently and solely responsible.
You know the high opinion I entertain of Genl Hampton, and my appreciation of his character and services. In his late expedition he has displayed both energy and good conduct, and although I have feared that
he might not have that activity and endurance so necessary in a cavalry
commander, and so eminently possessed by Genl Stuart, yet should you
be unable to assign anyone to the command of the cavalry in this army
whom you deem possessed of higher qualifications, I request authority
to place him in the command. If this be done, it will necessitate appointing a commander for his division, and I will hereafter recommend to you
some person for that position.

With high respect, your obt servt

R. E. LEE
Genl

825   To MISS MILDRED LEE
                      Richmond, Virginia

                                                    Camp, Petersburg
                                                    July 5, 1864
My precious Life:
    I received this morning by your brother your note of the 3rd & am
very glad to hear that your mother is better. I sent out immediately to
try & find some lemons, but could only procure two, sent to me by a
kind lady, Mrs. Kirkland, in Petersburg. These were gathered from
her own trees. There are none to be purchased. I found one in my
valise, dried up, which I also send as it may prove to some value. I also
put up some early apples which you can roast for your mother & one
pear. This is all the fruit I can get. You must go to market every morning & see if you cannot find some fruit for her. There are no lemons
to be had. Tell her lemonade is not as palatable or digestible as buttermilk. Try & get some good buttermilk for her. With ice it is delicious &
very nutritious. I hope she will continue to improve & be soon well &
leave that heated city. It must be roasting now. The sight of sweet Mary
T[riplett] would be refreshing. Take her to see your poor mother.
    Tell her I can only think of her & pray for her recovery. I wish I
could be with her to nurse her & care for her. Keep Custis Morgan out of
her sight & if you would immerse his head under the water for five minutes in one of his daily baths, it would relieve him & you of infinite
trouble. Good-bye my dear daughter. Give much love to precious
Agnes. I am glad your dear sister is well enough to be out. Tell her
she must get strong & take care of your mother. I want to see you all
very much, but cannot now see the day when. I think of you, long for
you, pray for you. It is all I can do. Think sometimes of your devoted
father.

                                                    R. E. LEE

826   To JEFFERSON DAVIS
                      Richmond, Virginia

                              Headquarters, Army of Northern Virginia
                                                    July 5, 1864
Mr. President:
    The subject of recruiting and keeping up our cavalry force, has
occupied much of my thoughts, especially since the opening of the

present campaign. The enemy is numerically superior to us in this arm, and possesses greater facilities for recruiting his horses and keeping them in serviceable condition. In the several engagements that have taken place between the cavalry of the two armies, I think great loss has been inflicted upon him, but it has been attended with a diminution of our force which we were less able to bear. Could I sweep his cavalry from the field, or preserve a fair proportion between its numbers and our own, I should feel that our present situation was in a measure secure. But in view of the disparity that exists, and the difficulty of increasing or even maintaining our force, I cannot but entertain serious apprehensions about the safety of our southern communications. Should we be unable to preserve them, I need not point out the consequences. I do not know from what quarter reinforcements can be had. There is one regiment of Georgia cavalry under Col Anderson which I believe is desirous of joining this army. The War Department can best decide whether it can be spared but if it can be, I beg that it may be ordered to me without delay. You will know whether any can be drawn from Genl Johnston's department. That which is in western Virginia is needed there and I am aware of no other source of supply.

I think that horses might be obtained from Texas, as we have now access to the Mississippi at various points. Those horses would make very serviceable animals for cavalry, and could be brought across the river by swimming, as cattle are higher up the stream, and on the Missouri. Even if only a few can be obtained in this way it would be of great assistance. It has also occurred to me that horses at least for artillery service could be obtained on the northern and western borders of Virginia by the system of exchange which is now being successfully carried on for subsistence. If good agents were selected and sent to the western and northwestern parts of the State, with authority to exchange cotton and tobacco for horses, the facilities for carrying on the traffic would be greater than that in articles of more difficult transportation, and at the present prices of those commodities in the North, the profits would be a great temptation, and insure the success of the experiment. I think if anything is to be done, now is our most favorable opportunity. I hope Your Excellency will be able to devise some means of obtaining an increase of our supply of horses, and recruiting our cavalry, as upon that in a great measure I believe, depends the issue of the campaign in Virginia.

Very respectfully, your obt servt

R. E. Lee
Genl

827   To JEFFERSON DAVIS
                        Richmond, Virginia

                                                Camp, Petersburg
                                                July 6, 1864

Mr. President:
    I am very much obliged to you for the perusal of the letters from
Mr. Mason & Genl Williams. I hope that the favourable anticipations of
the former may be realized. As far as I have been able to judge, this war
presents to the European world but two aspects. A contest in which one
party is contending for abstract slavery & the other against it. The existence of vital rights involved does not seem to be understood or appreciated. As long as this lasts, we can expect neither sympathy or aid. Nor
can we expect the policy of any Government towards us to be governed
by any other consideration than that of self interest. Our safety depends
upon ourselves alone. If we can defeat or drive the armies of the enemy
from the field, we shall have peace. All our efforts & energies should be
devoted to that object. I return the letters you did me the honour to
enclose & am

                    With great respect, your obt servt

                                                R. E. Lee
                                                Genl

828   To HIS WIFE
                        Richmond, Virginia

                                                Camp
                                                July 7, 1864

    I was very glad dear Mary this morning to receive your note, & to
learn that you were better. The absence of all fever I hope is indicative
of absence of disease & that now your strength will soon return to
you. You must try & find something you like to eat. I have been able to
procure no more lemons as yet though I hope some may be found. The
doctors here prescribe buttermilk, vegetables, fruit, &c., or anything
palatable to the patient, but in small quantities. How would you like
a little squirrel soup? Custis Morgan would shew in such a position. If
not required by you, I know it would be beneficial to the poor sick &
wounded in the hospitals & it would be most grateful to his feelings to

be converted into nutritious aliment for them & devote his life to the good of the country. I know his mother will take the hint. The drought & heat still continues & the dust is almost intolerable to man & beast. But God will send us a sweet rain in time, to refresh us & save the vegetables, corn, &c. Custis has gone to Wilmington & does not want Billy. I pray you may soon be well & not delay in that hot city, that was insupportable even to Mr. Soule. You must not write while you are unwell, but depute one of the girls. Good-bye & may God bless you all.

Truly & devotedly

R. E. LEE

829   To GENERAL RICHARD S. EWELL
               Commanding Richmond Defences

Headquarters, Army of Northern Virginia
July 9, 1864

General:
    Your note of July 7, in reply to my communication of 4th instant, has been received. The object of my inquiries in that note was to know whether you could not make some arrangement with the Richmond defense troops under your command to hold the front lines near Deep Bottom, so that the brigades detached from this army to Chaffin's farm might be held in reserve, in order that they may be moved readily and rapidly to any part of our line which may be threatened. At this distance I cannot judge what should be the disposition of our troops, and wish to learn from you as soon as possible whether you can make the arrangement desired.

Very respectfully

R. E. LEE
General

830   To JEFFERSON DAVIS
               Richmond, Virginia

Camp
July 10, 1864

Mr. President:
    I have the honour to send you a *N. Y. Herald* of the 8th containing some items of interest. You will see the people in the U. S. are mystified

about our forces [Early's expedition] on the Potomac. The expedition will have the effect I think at least of teaching them they must keep some of their troops at home & that they cannot denude their frontier with impunity. It seems also to have put them in bad temper as well as bad humour. Gold you will see has gone as high as 271 & closed at 266¾. Provisions, &c., are rising. I see also they are removing the prisoners from Point Lookout.

I trust that you & your family are in good health & wish you every happiness.

Very resply, your obt servt

R. E. LEE

831   To HIS WIFE
Richmond, Virginia

Camp
July 10, 1864

I was much pleased dear Mary on the arrival of my little courier this morning to hear that you were better & that Custis Morgan was still among the missing. I think the farther he gets from you the better you will be. Tomatoes are ripening now & ought to be had in the Richmond market. Have some of them got & put them in the sun till ripe. They will make delicious food for you & the acid will be very agreable. I can get no lemons here. I trust you will soon be well enough to leave the city. I am very thankful that rheumatism is diminishing & I hope by fall you will be walking all about again. I saw some gentlemen from Fredericksburg today who say that every one is delighted that Grant is down here & that things in that upper country are flourishing & people reviving. Grant seems so pleased with his present position that I fear he will never move again. Give much love to the girls & remember me to all friends. The shells have scattered the poor inhabitants in Petersburg so that many of the churches are closed, & indeed they have been visited by the enemy's shells. Mr. Platt, pastor of the principal E. church had service at my headquarters today. We had a respectable audience. Some ladies, many officers & soldiers. The service was under the trees, & the discourse on the subject of salvation. My prayers are always offered up for you.

Truly & affly

R. E. LEE

P.S. You must not write while you are so sick. Let one of the girls write for you.

R. E. L.

832   To GENERAL JUBAL A. EARLY
                    Commanding Valley District

Headquarters, Army of Northern Virginia
July 11, 1864

General:

Your letter of the 7th was received this morning. Your movements and arrangements appear to me to have been judicious, and I am glad you did not delay to storm the works at Maryland Heights. It was better to turn them and endeavor to draw the enemy from them. I hope you get the Northern papers, as they will keep you advised of their preparations to oppose you. They rely greatly upon Genl Hunter's force coming in your rear. About the 4th instant, as far as I can judge, he was in the vicinity of Charleston, on the Kanawha, with his own, [Generals William W.] Averell's & [George] Crook's commands. To encounter you in your present position he must either ascend the Ohio to Parkersburg & take the railroad to Grafton, thence by the Baltimore & Ohio Railroad, if that is left practicable, or go up to Pittsburg, and thence by the Central Pennsylvania. You will be able to judge of the time that either of these routes will require to bring him in position, and I think that even his whole force, aided by such troops as might join him, would be unable to oppose you successfully. I ascertained some days ago that on the 6th instant Genl Grant sent off a portion of his troops, and as far as I am able to judge, they consisted of [General James B.] Ricketts' division, of the 6th Corps, and their destination was Washington City. I think it probable that about a brigade of cavalry, without their horses, were sent on the night of the 6th to the same point. I learn this morning from our scouts on James River that about the same number of troops judging from the transports descended the river yesterday, and I presume they are bound for Washington City. Whether these belong to the 6th Corps or have been taken from other corps of his army, which I think more probable, I have not yet ascertained. We may however assume that a corps or its equivalent has been sent by Genl Grant to Washington, and I send a special messenger to apprise you of this fact that you may be on your guard and take this force into consideration with others that may be brought to oppose you. In your further operations you must of course be guided by the circumstances by which you are surrounded, and the information you may be able to collect, and must not consider yourself committed to any particular line of conduct, but be governed by your good judgment. Should you find yourself obliged, in consequence of the forces opposed to you, to return to the south side of the Potomac, you can take advantage of the fords east of the Blue Ridge, keeping your cavalry well to your front and causing them to retire by fords between you and Washington. In the event of your recrossing the Potomac, your route through Loudoun will facilitate the procurement of provisions, forage, &c., for your command, and will be otherwise most advantageous, giving you a strong country through which to pass, and enabling you if pressed to retire into the Valley and threaten and hang upon the enemy's flank should he push on towards Richmond.

I recommend that you have the fords of the Potomac examined by a competent officer, and held by a small force of cavalry or infantry, as you may deem most advisable.

I can tell you nothing further of the expedition mentioned to you in my letter of the 3d instant than was stated in that letter, having heard nothing from it since, except that the subject was a matter of general conversation in Richmond, which may tend to frustrate it.

You can retain the special messenger until you may wish to send him back for any purpose.

I need not state to you the advantage of striking at the bodies of troops that may be collected to oppose you in detail before they are enabled to unite. None of the forces that I have mentioned, nor any reported in the Northern papers as being likely to oppose you, will be able in my opinion to resist you, provided you can strike them before they are strengthened by others. Should you hear of the near approach of Genl Hunter, and can strike at him before he is reinforced by troops from the east, you can easily remove that obstacle from your path in my opinion. Trusting you and our cause to the care of a merciful Providence,

I remain very resply, your obt servt

R. E. LEE
Genl

833   To JEFFERSON DAVIS
                         Richmond, Virginia
                            TELEGRAM

                                        Headquarters, Near Petersburg
                                                   July 12, 1864

TELEGRAM OF TODAY RECEIVED. I REGRET THE FACT STATED. IT IS A BAD
TIME TO RELEASE THE COMMANDER OF AN ARMY SITUATED AS THAT OF TEN-
NESSEE. WE MAY LOSE ATLANTA AND THE ARMY TOO.

  HOOD IS A BOLD FIGHTER.

  I AM DOUBTFUL AS TO OTHER QUALITIES NECESSARY.

                                                    R. E. LEE

834   To JEFFERSON DAVIS
                         Richmond, Virginia

                                                     Camp
                                                July 12, 1864
                                                   9½ P.M.

Mr. President:

  I send you a paper of the 10th instant containing Mr. Secretary
Stanton's bulletin to Genl [John A] Dix, acknowledging a defeat of
Genl [Lew] Wallace at Monocacy by Genl Early. I have also received a
dispatch from Genl Fitz Lee this evening reporting that he met Genl
[David] Gregg with his division advancing towards Reams' Station,
charged him with three of his regiments & drove him back, capturing
some 30 men & two officers. His loss small. The enemy's not known. He
thinks he was moving against the railroad. We have only had it in operation two days, but have got through several trains of corn & provisions.

  I am distressed at the intelligence conveyed in your telegram of
today. It is a grievous thing to change commander of an army situated
as is that of the Tennessee. Still if necessary it ought to be done. I know
nothing of the necessity. I had hoped that Johnston was strong enough
to deliver battle. We must risk much to save Alabama, Mobile & communication with the Trans Mississippi. It would be better to concentrate
all the cavalry in Mississippi & Tennessee on Sherman's communications.
If Johnston abandons Atlanta I suppose he will fall back on Augusta. This
loses us Mississippi & communication with Trans Mississippi. We had
better therefore hazard that communication to retain the country. Hood

is a good fighter, very industrious on the battle field, careless off, & I have had no opportunity of judging of his action, when the whole responsibility rested upon him. I have a high opinion of his gallantry, earnestness & zeal. Genl [William J.] Hardee has more experience in managing an army.

May God give you wisdom to decide in this momentous matter.

Truly & resply yours

R. E. LEE

P.S. Today we could get no papers from the enemy, from which I inferred there was some good news they wished to withhold. The one sent was captured. You must excuse its condition.

R. E. LEE

835   To JAMES A. SEDDON
Secretary of War

Headquarters, Army of Northern Virginia
July 19, 1864

Sir:

I have the honor to transmit herewith the report of Genl Early of his late operations in the Valley and in Maryland.

In forwarding this report I deem it proper to state briefly for the information of the Department the object of detaching the force under Genl Early. I think, however, that it would not be prudent to give publicity to this statement at the present time.

Finding that it would be necessary to detach some troops to repel the force under Genl Hunter, which was threatening Lynchburg, I resolved to send one that would be adequate to accomplish that purpose effectually, and if possible strike a decisive blow. At the same time Genl Early was instructed, if his success justified it, and the enemy retreated down the Valley, to pursue him, and, if opportunity offered, to follow him into Maryland. It was believed that the Valley could then be effectually freed from the presence of the enemy, and it was hoped that by threatening Washington and Baltimore Genl Grant would be compelled either to weaken himself so much for their protection as to afford us an opportunity to attack him, or that he might be induced to attack us.

After the retreat of Genl Hunter towards western Virginia his pursuit by Genl Early was attended with great difficulty, owing to the obstacles in the way of supplying our troops. At the same time the presence of Genl Hunter's forces in the Kanawha Valley endangered important interests in southwestern Virginia. It was thought that the readiest way to draw him from that region would be to push down the Valley and enter Maryland, and at the same time it was hoped that the other advantages of such an invasion before alluded to might be secured. In addition to these considerations there were other collateral results, such as obtaining military stores and supplies, that were deemed of sufficient importance to warrant the attempt.

Genl Early's report will explain his operations, and the value of the results obtained need not be further stated at present, as there are yet some to be expected in the future. I may, however, say that so far as the movement was intended to relieve our territory in that section of the enemy, it has up to the present time been successful.

With great respect, your obt servt

R. E. LEE
Genl

836   To JEFFERSON DAVIS
Richmond, Virginia

Petersburg
July 23, 1864

Mr. President:
I have had the honour to receive your letter of the 22 instant enclosing a memorandum of information obtained of the probable movements of Genl Grant's army. I am aware of the ease with which the troops sent for the protection of Washington can be returned to this point. I, however, think it very doubtful whether President Lincoln will permit this to be done as long as Genl Early is so close to the Potomac. Should he be able to obtain a large militia or volunteer force on the north bank of the Potomac, it might be hazarded, but I have not discovered any alacrity exhibited by such troops to take the field. Genl Early supposed the force which engaged him on the 18th at the Shenandoah to be composed of the 6th Corps, Hunter's troops, & two divisions of the 19th Corps. I had previously heard of the arrival in Washington of the latter corps from New Orleans, & that it had been originally destined for Grant's army, but was diverted to meet that emergency. Its presence in Washington is confirmed by the enclosed letter, which seems to be from Mr. Baxter, member of Congress from Vermont. I have

written to Genl Early to inquire what has become of the force he drove across the Shenandoah, & to say that if he cannot detain it on that frontier, it will be necessary for him to return. I have thought much upon the subject of interrupting the enemy's communications on James River, & have written to Genl Ewell that I would spare troops for the purpose if it could be accomplished. I am aware of the difficulties & of the enemy's facilities for cutting off a small force, & our inability to apply a large one. Still I hope something can be obtained. I have no idea that Grant will evacuate his position unless forced. It is one from which he can attack us at three points, as he may select, & our success will depend upon our early information & celerity of movement, as we have not troops sufficient to guard all points. I believe the troops reported to have crossed James River this morning are for the purpose of preventing our operations on the river. I have sent Kershaw's division to Chaffin's Bluff to reinforce Genl [James] Conner. A mounted force with long range guns might, by a secret & rapid march, penetrate the lines south of the Potomac, & excite the alarms of the authorities at Washington, but if its approach was known, I fear the defences south of the river could be manned in time to prevent it. Wishing you all health & prosperity,

I am with great respect, your obt servt

R. E. LEE
Genl

837   To GENERAL RICHARD S. EWELL
Commanding Richmond Defences

Headquarters, Army of Northern Virginia
Petersburg
July 24, 1864

General:

Upon hearing that the enemy were reinforcing their troops on the north side of the James River yesterday morning General Kershaw's division was ordered to Chaffin's Bluff. I directed him to assume command of the troops under General Conner, reconnoiter the enemy and ascertain his position, intentions, &c. He informs me that about two brigades entrenched themselves on Tilghman's farm last night and are still working; that it is reported that a second pontoon bridge has been constructed south of Bailey's Run, and that the enemy is apparently making a permanent lodgment on both banks of Bailey's Run with a view to future operations. He states that he has disposed of his troops so as to defend the Varina, New Market, and Darbytown roads. My object in sending troops there was to endeavor to dislodge the enemy, drive them across the river, and destroy the bridges, and if practicable I wish this done, and have sent a dispatch to General Kershaw to that effect. We cannot afford to sit down in front of the enemy and allow him to entrench himself wherever he pleases, and I wish you to see if you cannot break him up on the north side of the James River.

I am with great respect, your obedient servant

R. E. LEE
General

838   To G. W. C. LEE
Richmond, Virginia

Camp
July 24, 1864

My Dear Son:

I have received your letter of the 20th. Col Carter's report of his operations was very satisfactory as far as they went, but they are not sufficient to arrest the navigation of the river. Nothing less in my opinion will produce the result desired. I have written to Genl Ewell on the subject, & I wish if in your power you would help him to a conclusion. I sent yesterday Genl Kershaw's division to Chaffin's, which I can ill spare, & which I fear I shall be obliged soon to recall. Genl Early telegraphs that the 6th & 19th Corps, he learned on the 23rd, were moving back through Leesburg towards Alexandria. I presume it is for the purpose of returning to Grant, when I shall require all the troops I can get. If anything can therefore be done it must be done quickly. I directed Genl Kershaw to take command of the brigades under Conner, examine the enemy's position at Deep Bottom, & see what could be done. I have not heard from him yet. The 60th Alabama has been returned to Gracie's brigade, & B. R. Johnson's old brigade has been sent in its place. The latter seemed much worn down, & I was in hopes a little relief would bring it up. Genl Gary does not seem yet to have his cavalry well in hand, & perhaps on its present duties it is impossible to give it that instruction & discipline it requires. But until he does get it in that condition, it will never possess steadiness or reliability. Where are we to get sufficient troops to oppose Grant? He is bringing to him now the 19th Corps, & will bring every man he can get. His talent & strategy consists in accumulating overwhelming numbers. I see it stated in the papers that the enemy has abandoned the Trans Mississippi country. Is it so? They must be very weak, & unless Kirby Smith can operate to advantage in Missouri he had better cross to this side. There must be but few troops in [General Edward] Canby's department, now that the 19th Corps has been withdrawn. I received the package of clothes. They are very nice, & suit admirably. They are so much admired that I fear I shall have many applicants for their loan from the beaux. I saw Fitzhugh & Robt yesterday. Both well. Please send the accompanying letter to your mother if you can. I am glad to learn she is improving.

Your devoted father

R. E. LEE

839   To GENERAL RICHARD H. ANDERSON
Commanding Corps

Headquarters
July 27, 1864

General:

A dispatch just received from Genl Kershaw has determined me to send Genl Heth's division to reinforce him. I wish you to proceed to Deep Bottom & take command of the troops belonging to this army there. Examine the enemy's position, endeavor to ascertain his strength, and if practicable drive him away and destroy his bridges.

Turn over to Genl Field the orders recently issued as regards strengthening his lines, &c., and direct him to make his daily reports to me.

Very respectfully, your obt servt

R. E. LEE
Genl

840   To GENERAL RICHARD S. EWELL
Commanding Richmond Defences
TELEGRAM

Dunn's Hill
July 28, 1864

WHAT IS THE ENEMY'S FORCE OF CAVALRY? WHAT DO YOU PROPOSE TO DO? ARE YOU DIRECTING OPERATIONS?

R. E. LEE

841
To JAMES A. SEDDON
Secretary of War
TELEGRAM

Dunn's Hill
July 30, 1864
3.25 P.M.

AT FIVE A.M. THE ENEMY SPRUNG A MINE UNDER ONE OF THE SALIENTS
ON GENL B. R. JOHNSON'S FRONT & OPENED HIS BATTERIES UPON OUR LINES &
THE CITY OF PETERSBURG. IN THE CONFUSION CAUSED BY THE EXPLOSION OF
THE MINE HE GOT POSSESSION OF THE SALIENT. WE HAVE RETAKEN THE SA-
LIENT & DRIVEN THE ENEMY BACK TO HIS LINES WITH LOSS.

R. E. LEE

842
To JAMES A. SEDDON
Secretary of War
TELEGRAM

Headquarters, Near Petersburg
July 30, 1864
6.30 P.M.

GENL A. P. HILL REPORTS THAT GENERAL MAHONE IN RETAKING THE
SALIENT POSSESSED BY THE ENEMY THIS MORNING RECOVERED THE FOUR (4)
GUNS WITH WHICH IT WAS ARMED, CAPTURED TWELVE (12) STAND OF COLORS,
SEVENTY-FOUR (74) OFFICERS, INCLUDING BRIG GENL [JOSEPH J.] BARTLETT
& STAFF, & EIGHT HUNDRED & FIFTY-FIVE (855) ENLISTED MEN. UPWARDS
OF FIVE HUNDRED (500) OF THE ENEMY'S DEAD ARE LYING UNBURIED IN
THE TRENCHES. HIS LOSS SLIGHT.

R. E. LEE

843
To HIS WIFE
"Bremo," Virginia

Camp
July 31, 1864

I have received your letter of the 27th dear Mary, & am glad you are
recovering from your fall. It must have been a great shock to you, & I

fear injury in your condition. I commend you greatly for adhering to the prescription & regulations of your physician, & I would not have you to depart from them. In your letter written just before leaving Richmond you stated he directed that you should lie on your back for the following three weeks & keep quiet, doing nothing. How came you to be walking about on polished floors & making me drawers? I am much obliged to you for the latter, but I should greatly have preferred them to have been made by other hands than yours. Your daughters you know have very nimble fingers & my Agnes considers herself a great cutter & fitter. Why did you not let her try her hand upon some masculine garments? It is time she was learning, for my hopes in a certain quarter are not yet relinquished. There is Precious Life too, can sew beautifully. The drawers have come since I commenced writing. I have not had an opportunity yet of trying them on, nor do I expect to require them before the weather gets cooler. I hope my present garments will carry me through the summer. You can therefore have a third pair made as suits your convenience. I am charmed with your description of the family at Bremo. I have always heard their hospitality & charity extolled. Genl Cocke has been proverbial for it all his life. What a pity it would be for our enemies to get within reach of it. How many happy homes have they destroyed, & turned the occupants adrift in the world with nothing. From how many hearts have they expelled all hopes of happiness forever. Planting darkness & despair where flourished love & happiness before. Yesterday morning they sprung a mine under one of our batteries on the line, & got possession of a portion of our entrenchments. It was the part defended by Genl Beauregard's troops. I sent Genl Mahone with two brigades of Hill's corps, who charged into them handsomely, recapturing the entrenchments, the guns, 12 stand of colours, 73 officers including Genl Bartlett, his staff & three cols & 855 enlisted men. There were upwards of 500 of his dead unburied in the trenches, among them many officers & blacks. He suffered severely. He has withdrawn his troops from the north side of the James. I do not know what he will attempt next. He is mining at other points along our line. I trust he will succeed no better in his next than his last attempt. Give my love to Miss Silia & kind regards to Genl Cocke, the Dr., Mrs. C. & all the family. You must also give much love to Markie & Kate & great sympathy for the latter. Kiss my dear daughters for me & believe me always yours

R. E. Lee

844   To HIS WIFE
                        "Bremo," Virginia

                                              Camp
                                        August 7, 1864

I have received dear Mary your letter of the 4th & those of Dr. Hughes & Miss Manly. I do not know what you must do about the former. Although I highly appreciate the kindness that prompts his actions yet it is difficult to express it & in this & similar cases impossible to return it except in feeling. That is very unprofitable to the recipients & in present times I fear destructive. I trust God will restore you & enable you to devise some material mode of shewing the appreciation of both of us of his unselfish & untiring attentions. As regards Miss Manly you ought not to have let her undertaken such a labour. I am however extremely obliged to her & her kind colabourers, & impressively touched by the sad thoughts which must have been interwoven with their stitches. May God lighten their sorrows & gladden their hearts by good works. I went up to Richmond Friday evening to see the President on matters of business, intending to return Saturday evening as my time was very limited, & business pressing. On going to the depot I found there was no train & I came down early this morning leaving the whole household asleep. I was very glad to get a glimpse at Mary, Custis, Smith, & indeed all the occupants of the house, & was sorry you & your fellow travellers were not there. I only had a glimpse of them though, for I was all the time with the President. Little Annie was sick & I only saw her on my first arrival. I was saddened too to hear of the death of our good old Uncle Williams. It was however a great relief to think he was now beyond the reach of his cowardly persecutors the Yankees, & enjoying the mercy of an everloving God, & I trust his pardon & forgiveness. It has been revolting to my feelings when I have thought of his destitute position & the indignities to which he was subjected. He died Saturday morning & was to be buried Sunday evening in Richmond by the side of his wife. With the exception of Mrs. Fitzhugh he was the last connecting link to the persons whom I enjoyed in my boyhood & who made my days so happy. I found Mary pretty well. She complained of being weak, was very thin, but in her usual spirits. She seemed to enjoy little Lizzie Wickham as much as Mildred did Custis Morgan. She is indeed a dear little child. I do not think Mary will leave Richmond. I think she prefers it. She sees more people, &c. I hope she will keep well. Do not make yourself uneasy. Custis is very well & very kind & affectionate. I was glad to be with Smith too. He looks very badly I think. I hope you have recovered from your fall. It must have been a dreadful blow in your condition. Present my kind regards & warm thanks to the kind people around you. Tell my precious Agnes I will reply to her kind letter. Kiss Life for me.

With true affc

R. E. Lee

845   To GENERAL GEORGE E. PICKETT
Hancock's House
TELEGRAM

Petersburg
August 9, 1864
9.30 P.M.

ORDER [WILLIAM T.] POAGUE'S BATTERY TO TAKE POSITION AGAINST DUTCH GAP. TURN EVERY ONE OF YOUR HEAVY GUNS AT HOWLETT'S ON THEM. SEND A COURIER TO CAPTAIN [JOHN K.] MITCHELL FOR ASSISTANCE FROM THE FLEET.

R. E. Lee

846   To JEFFERSON DAVIS
Richmond, Virginia

Headquarters, Army of Northern Virginia
August 9, 1864

Mr. President:

The soap ration for this army has become a serious question. Since leaving Orange Court House the Commissary, Lt Col [Robert G.] Cole, has only been able to make three issues of three days rations each. The great want of cleanliness which is a necessary consequence of these very limited issues is now producing sickness among the men in the trenches, and must effect their self respect & morale. The importance of the subject and the general complaints which have arisen must be my excuse for troubling you with the matter. An offer of 24000 pounds at $3.75/100 has been made to the Commissary of the Army but the Commissary General declined to authorize the purchase at that price. He speaks of the purchase of several lots at a smaller price $2.50/100 per pound, but holds

out no definite prospect of sending an adequate supply. Such is the
condition of the troops & their immediate necessities in regard to soap are
so great that I hope the purchase of the 24000 pounds at even the advanced price of $3.75/100 will be authorized & that contracts will be
entered into at once for the future regular and adequate supply of the
soap ration to the troops. Their health, comfort & respectability cannot
otherwise be secured.

With great respect, your obt servt

R. E. LEE
Genl

847 To GENERAL RICHARD S. EWELL
Chaffin's Bluff
TELEGRAM

Petersburg
August 10, 1864

I THINK THAT THE CAMP AT DUTCH GAP IS PROBABLY THE MARINES.
COULD NOT CAPTAIN MITCHELL SHELL IT WHILE PICKETT OPENED ON LAND
BATTERIES AND YOU ATTACKED IT? THEY WILL SOON BE FORTIFIED.

R. E. LEE

848 To JAMES A. SEDDON
Secretary of War
TELEGRAM

Headquarters
August 11, 1864

YOUR DESPATCH OF TODAY RECEIVED. GENL GRANT HAS BEEN AT HARPER'S
FERRY. GENL SHERIDAN HAS BEEN PLACED IN COMMAND OF THAT DEPART-
MENT, THE GREATER PART OF HIS CAVALRY HAS GONE WITH HIM. THE PART
OF THE 19TH CORPS THAT HAS BEEN SERVING HERE, & PROBABLY THE 18TH
CORPS, ARE THE ONLY INFANTRY I BELIEVE THAT HAVE LEFT GENL MEADE.

R. E. LEE

849   To GENERAL RICHARD H. ANDERSON
Culpeper Court House

Headquarters
August 11, 1864

General:

The *Washington Chronicle* of the 8th states that Genl Sheridan has superseded Genl Hunter in command of the troops on the upper Potomac, and I believe that the greater part of his cavalry has been detached by Genl Grant and sent to Washington and Baltimore. This morning Genl Hampton commences his march for Culpeper with his division to report to you. It is desirable that the presence of our troops be felt beyond the Rappahannock. You had better take position north of Culpeper Court House and let the cavalry operate north of Rappahannock River. Should the enemy's forces move west of the Blue Ridge range, leaving Washington uncovered, the cavalry might cross the Potomac east of the mountains and demonstrate against that city. Should he concentrate all his cavalry in the Valley, unless it can be withdrawn by other operations, ours must meet it, and Genl Hampton must take command of all the cavalry when united. Any enterprise that can be undertaken to injure the enemy, distract or separate his forces, embarrass his communications on the Potomac or on land is desirable. If you can learn what troops have been detached from Grant's army let me know. Prisoners and deserters state the 18th Corps and the portion of the 19th operating here have left.

Very respectly, your obdt servt

R. E. LEE
Genl

850   To GENERAL WADE HAMPTON
Commanding Cavalry Division

Headquarters
August 11, 1864

General:

I desire you to proceed with your division to Culpeper. On arrival you will report to Lt Genl R. H. Anderson, commanding in that quarter. The object is to threaten the enemy's flank and rear should he move across the Blue Ridge into the Valley, and to retain his forces about

Washington for its protection. It is desirable that the presence of the troops in that region be felt, and should the enemy move up the Potomac, leaving his capital uncovered, that the cavalry cross the Potomac if practicable east of the Blue Ridge. Should the enemy's cavalry be concentrated in the Valley, ours must meet it, if it cannot cause its withdrawal by other operations. Specific instructions will be given you by Genl Anderson.

Very respectfully, your obt servt

R. E. LEE
Genl

851   To GENERAL RICHARD S. EWELL
Chaffin's Bluff
TELEGRAM

Headquarters, Army of Northern Virginia
August 12, 1864

DESERTER REPORTS THAT MEN AT DUTCH GAP ARE VOLUNTEERS, PAID 40 CENTS EXTRA FOR DIGGING, THEIR PURPOSE BEING TO DIG A CANAL. IF THEY CANNOT BE STOPPED ARRANGEMENTS MUST BE MADE TO MAKE THE CANAL USELESS BY CHOOSING POSITIONS AND ERECTING BATTERIES, &C. SEE WHAT CAN BE DONE.

R. E. LEE

852   To JEFFERSON DAVIS
Richmond, Virginia

Headquarters
August 12, 1864

Mr. President:

I received last night your dispatch of the 11th giving information of the enemy's movements. I was aware of the departure of a large part of Sheridan's cavalry, and that he had taken command of the Federal forces in the Valley. [General Alfred] Torbert's division is the only one that has yet reached that region, and I am not positive whether the whole of the other divisions have gone or not, though it is so reported. I thought it best, however, to move Hampton's division to Culpeper, and it commenced its march yesterday. W. H. F. Lee's division is retained, and I hope it will be sufficient for the protection of the railroad. If I find that the enemy's cavalry here is superior to ours I will recall some of Hampton's. I have assigned General H[ampton] to the command of the cavalry. Genl [Matthew Calbraith] Butler, he thinks, is best qualified to command his division. As he does so now by right of seniority I have recommended no change. The forces opposed to Genl Early consist of the 6th, 8th, two divisions of the 19th & the 13th Corps. The latter recently arrived from New Orleans. Genl Early was at Newtown on the 11th, and the enemy, who for the two previous days had been endeavoring to approach his rear, was apparently moving towards Front Royal. I have directed Genl Anderson to move towards Thornton's Gap and be governed by circumstances. Genl Early reports that Genl Bradley Johnson's brigade had been surprised in camp near Moorefield & routed, losing four guns. I have directed that if Genl J[ohnson] is to blame he must be relieved from command.

I went up to Howlett's Thursday morning, having heard that the enemy had thrown a body of troops on the neck at Dutch Gap, with a view of endeavoring to drive them off. Their position was about 2½ miles from the battery, & Maj [Francis W.] Smith reported from his experience on former occasions, owing to inferior powder, he could not be certain of throwing his shot more than 1,200 yards. I signaled to Genl Ewell to attack them from his side & to arrange with Capt Mitchell to shell them from his gunboats. This I hoped would have been done that afternoon, but he could not complete his arrangements until yesterday afternoon, and then had to suspend the attack for an exchange of prisoners previously arranged. The force I understand is composed partly of negroes, & that they are engaged in cutting a canal through the neck. What use they will make of it I do not see, unless their object is to turn Pickett's left. I have posted Lt Col Poague's battalion of artillery on the heights of Proctor's Creek, west of Howlett's farm, & will commence a heavy battery on the river in that vicinity as soon as possible. Perhaps it is thought the James River can be so reduced as to prevent the navigation of our naval boats.

With great respect, your obt servt

R. E. Lee
Genl

P.S. Genl Grant is reported to have returned from Harper's Ferry. He was at Old Point on the 8th, & a deserter states he & Butler were at Dutch Gap yesterday.

R. E. L.

853   To GENERAL RICHARD H. ANDERSON
Culpeper Court House
TELEGRAM

Headquarters, Army of Northern Virginia
August 12, 1864

GENERAL EARLY, AT NEWTOWN, STATES THE ENEMY TO BE MOVING UP
THE SHENANDOAH WITH A VIEW OF REACHING HIS REAR, APPARENTLY TOWARD
FRONT ROYAL. IT MAY BE HIS PURPOSE TO MOVE UP LURAY VALLEY. YOU
HAD BETTER MOVE UP TO SPERRYVILLE AND BE GOVERNED BY CIRCUMSTANCES.
HAMPTON SHOULD REACH YOU THE 15TH. KEEP HIM APPRISED AND KEEP IN
COMMUNICATION WITH EARLY.

R. E. LEE

854   To GENERAL WADE HAMPTON
Beaver Dam, Virginia
TELEGRAM

Headquarters, Army of Northern Virginia
August 14, 1864

HALT YOUR COMMAND AND RETURN TOWARD RICHMOND. GREGG'S DI-
VISION [OF CAVALRY] IS CROSSING AT DEEP BOTTOM. SEND BACK AN OFFICER
TO ASCERTAIN POSITION.

R. E. LEE

855   To GENERAL CHARLES W. FIELD
Chaffin's Bluff
TELEGRAM

Headquarters, Army of Northern Virginia
August 14, 1864

HAVE SENT TO HALT HAMPTON AND ORDERED CAVALRY FROM THIS SIDE.
IF UNNECESSARY LET ME KNOW. AID THE CAVALRY ALL YOU CAN AND DRIVE
BACK ENEMY.

R. E. LEE

856   To GENERAL RICHARD S. EWELL
                  Commanding Richmond Defences
                          TELEGRAM

                                              Headquarters
                                           August 14, 1864
                                              6.15 P.M.

I WISH HAMPTON TO RETURN TO RICHMOND AS SOON AS PRACTICABLE
WITH HIS WHOLE COMMAND. YOU MUST REINFORCE FIELD FROM RICHMOND.
WHERE DO YOU EXPECT THEM FROM THIS SIDE?

                                              R. E. LEE
                                              General

857   To GENERAL CHARLES W. FIELD
                         Chaffin's Bluff
                          TELEGRAM

                          Headquarters, Army of Northern Virginia
                                           August 14, 1864

HAMPTON WILL BE WITH YOU THIS EVENING. TWO BRIGADES GO FROM
HERE. MAJOR [EDWARD C.] ANDERSON, WITH 500 CAVALRY, ORDERED FROM
RICHMOND. THIS MAY BE A FEINT TO DRAW TROOPS FROM HERE. WATCH
CLOSELY AND RETURN THE TROOPS HERE AT THE EARLIEST MOMENT.

                                              R. E. LEE

858   To HIS WIFE
                       "Bremo," Virginia

                                                   Camp
                                           August 14, 1864
My Dear Mary:
    Although I have not heard from you since I last wrote about a
week ago, I will take advantage of the quiet of this evening to express
the hope that the non arrival of your usual weekly letter has been occasioned by the irregularity of the mails, & not by increased indisposition on your part. I wrote to Agnes the other day, & have heard from
Mary the past week, so you will not be without information of me, & I
have heard of you. I have been kept from church today by the enemy's
crossing to the north side of the James River & the necessity of moving

troops to meet him. I do not know what his intentions are. He is said to be cutting a canal across the "Dutch Gap," a point in the river, but I can as yet not discover it. I was up there yesterday & saw nothing to indicate it. He may not however have progressed farther than his preliminary operations. We shall ascertain in a day or two. I received today a kind letter from the Reverend Mr. Cole of Culpeper Court House. He is a most excellent man in all relations of life. He says there is not a church standing in all that country within the lines formerly occupied by the enemy. All are razed to the ground & the materials used, often for the vilest purposes. Two of the churches at the Court House barely escaped destruction. The pews were all taken out to make seats for the theatre. The fact was reported to the commanding officer, Genl Newton, from Norfolk, by their own men of the Christian Commission, but he took no steps to rebuke or arrest it. We must suffer patiently to the end, when all things will be made right. I send you a letter from Mr. Wickham which has been sent to me. Although the intelligence it conveys has already reached you, it will be interesting, & will serve to shew the attention of Mr. Wickham. I trust our dear uncle is happy & at peace. In a letter to Fitzhugh Mr. Wickham states that he left his property to his son Williams, Mr. Wickham & Williams Wickham. I hope they will be able to save some of it. I believe everything is gone except the land. I also send you a very just tribute to the worth of Genl Stuart, taken from an English paper, the *Index*. You may not have seen it, & it is worth preserving. We have had a sweet rain this afternoon & it still continues. More water has fallen than at any point I have been since I left Orange. I trust it will revive vegetation. Give much love to the girls & kind regards to Dr. & Mrs. Cocke & the Genl, & all the family.

Very truly & sincerely

R. E. Lee

859   MAJOR W. H. TAYLOR TO
GENERAL CHARLES W. FIELD
Chaffin's Bluff
TELEGRAM

Headquarters, Army of Northern Virginia
August 15, 1864
12.36 A.M.

YOUR TELEGRAM OF 9 P.M. RECEIVED. TWO BRIGADES AND TWO REGIMENTS OF INFANTRY AND W. H. F. LEE'S DIVISION OF CAVALRY ARE ON THEIR

WAY TO YOU. THE INFANTRY LEFT BY RAIL AT 7.30 & 9.30 P.M. THE CAVALRY
WILL MOVE RIGHT ON. SEND AN OFFICER TO MEET IT WITH INSTRUCTIONS TO
GENL W. H. F. LEE WHERE HE IS MOST REQUIRED. HAMPTON IS MOVING DOWN
FROM OTHER SIDE. KEEP RICHMOND ADVISED OF MOVEMENTS OF ENEMY'S
CAVALRY.

W. H. TAYLOR
A. A. G.

860   To JEFFERSON DAVIS
Richmond, Virginia
TELEGRAM

Chaffin's Bluff
August 16, 1864
10.35 A.M.

GENL FIELD, ON THE DARBYTOWN ROAD, REPORTS THAT GENL [W. H. F.]
LEE'S PICKETS AT THE SWAMP HAVE BEEN DRIVEN BACK, AND THAT THE EN-
EMY IN HEAVY FORCE ARE ADVANCING UP THE CHARLES CITY ROAD AND ARE
NEARLY AT WHITE'S TAVERN. ENEMY IS IN REAR OF FIELD'S FORCE, AND IT
WILL BE THROWN OVER ON THE LEFT TO ATTACK ENEMY IN FLANK. I REC-
OMMEND THE WORKS AT RICHMOND BE MANNED. IF HAMPTON'S FORCE IS
ACCESSIBLE, PLEASE ORDER IT AT ONCE DOWN CHARLES CITY ROAD.

R. E. LEE

861   To JAMES A. SEDDON
Secretary of War
TELEGRAM

Chaffin's Bluff
August 16, 1864
4 P.M.

THE ENEMY HAS MADE A DETERMINED ATTACK ON OUR LINE BETWEEN
THE DARBYTOWN AND CHARLES CITY ROADS. AT ONE TIME HE BROKE THROUGH
BUT WAS REPULSED, AND WE NOW OCCUPY OUR ORIGINAL POSITIONS.

R. E. LEE

862

To JAMES A. SEDDON
Secretary of War
TELEGRAM

Chaffin's Bluff
August 16, 1864
8.30 P.M.

THE ENEMY DID NOT RENEW THE ATTACK AFTER HIS REPULSE MENTIONED IN MY FIRST DISPATCH. HIS FORCE ON THE CHARLES CITY ROAD, AFTER ADVANCING TO WITHIN TWO (2) MILES OF WHITE'S TAVERN, WAS DRIVEN BACK ACROSS WHITE OAK SWAMP. OUR LOSS WAS SMALL.

R. E. LEE

863

MAJOR W. H. TAYLOR TO GENERAL CADMUS M. WILCOX
Dunlop's
TELEGRAM

August 18, 1864

THE CAMP OF ARMY HEADQUARTERS IS BEING MOVED TO THE NORTH SIDE OF JAMES RIVER. COMMUNICATIONS FOR THE COMMANDING GENERAL SHOULD BE ADDRESSED TO CHAFFIN'S BLUFF UNTIL OTHERWISE DIRECTED.

W. H. TAYLOR
Assistant Adjutant General

864

To JAMES A. SEDDON
Secretary of War
TELEGRAM

Chaffin's Bluff
August 18, 1864

THIS MORNING OUR SKIRMISHERS REOCCUPIED THE HILL NORTH OF DUTCH GAP, FROM WHICH THE ENEMY HAD BEEN DRIVEN BY OUR GUNBOATS.

THIS AFTERNOON THE LEFT OF OUR LINE NORTH OF JAMES RIVER AD-

VANCED AGAINST THE ENEMY'S RIGHT TO DISCOVER HIS STRENGTH AND POSI-
TION; DROVE IN HIS SKIRMISH LINE, AND FINDING HIM STRONGLY ENTRENCHED
WITHDREW.

ABOUT NOON THE ENEMY IN FRONT OF PETERSBURG MOVED HIS FIFTH
CORPS TOWARDS THE WELDON RAILROAD, WHEN HE WAS MET BY GENL HETH,
WHO DROVE HIM A MILE, CAPTURING ONE HUNDRED AND FIFTY PRISONERS.

R. E. LEE

865   To JAMES A. SEDDON
Secretary of War
TELEGRAM

Chaffin's Bluff
August 20, 1864

GENL HILL ATTACKED THE ENEMY'S FIFTH CORPS YESTERDAY AFTERNOON
AT DAVIS' HOUSE THREE (3) MILES FROM PETERSBURG ON WELDON RAILROAD.
DEFEATED AND CAPTURED ABOUT TWENTY-SEVEN HUNDRED (2,700) PRISON-
ERS, INCLUDING ONE (1) BRIG GENL AND SEVERAL FIELD OFFICERS. LOSS ON
OUR SIDE BELIEVED TO BE SMALLER THAN THAT OF THE ENEMY.

R. E. LEE

866   To JAMES A. SEDDON
Secretary of War
TELEGRAM

Chaffin's Bluff
August 20, 1864

A PORTION OF OUR FORCE IN THE VALLEY CROSSED SHENANDOAH AT FRONT
ROYAL ON THE 16TH AND DROVE THE ENEMY'S CAVALRY, WHICH RETREATED
TOWARDS WINCHESTER, BURNING THE HAY AND WHEAT STACKS IN THEIR
ROUTE. ON THE 17TH SHERIDAN BEGAN TO RETIRE FROM HIS POSITION, WAS
PURSUED BY GENL EARLY, WHO OVERTOOK TWO (2) DIVISIONS OF THE SIXTH
(6) CORPS AND LARGE FORCE OF CAVALRY AT WINCHESTER; DROVE THEM
THROUGH THE TOWN AND CAPTURED OVER TWO HUNDRED (200) PRISONERS,
SOME OF WHOM BELONGED TO WILSON'S CAVALRY DIVISION. ENEMY HAS
FALLEN BACK TOWARDS HARPER'S FERRY.

R. E. LEE

867   To GENERAL WADE HAMPTON
                   Commanding Cavalry Division
                          TELEGRAM

                                            Petersburg
                                         August 21, 1864
                                            4.45 P.M.

YOUR TELEGRAM RECEIVED. IF ENEMY'S CAVALRY HAS LEFT NORTH SIDE
I DESIRE YOU TO MOVE WITH HAMPTON'S DIVISION TO THIS POINT AS SOON AS
PRACTICABLE.

                                            R. E. LEE

868   MAJOR W. H. TAYLOR TO CHARLES G. TALCOTT
                   Superintendent Danville Railroad
                          TELEGRAM

                     Headquarters, Army of Northern Virginia
                                         August 21, 1864
                                            11 P.M.

IT IS REPORTED THAT ENEMY'S CAVALRY CROSSED WELDON RAILROAD AT
REAMS' THIS EVENING AND TOOK DIRECTION OF DINWIDDIE COURT HOUSE. RAID
ON SOUTH SIDE AND DANVILLE ROAD MAY BE CONTEMPLATED. BE ON THE
LOOKOUT FOR THEM.

                                       W. H. TAYLOR
                                  Assistant Adjutant General

869   To JAMES A. SEDDON
                   Secretary of War
                          TELEGRAM

                                            Dunn's Hill
                                         August 21, 1864

THE ENEMY ABANDONED LAST EVENING HIS POSITION NORTH OF JAMES
RIVER & RETURNED TO THE SOUTH SIDE. THIS MORNING GENL HILL ATTACKED
HIS POSITION ON WELDON RAILROAD. DROVE HIM FROM HIS ADVANCED LINES

TO HIS MAIN ENTRENCHMENTS FROM WHICH HE WAS NOT DISLODGED. OVER
THREE HUNDRED PRISONERS EXCLUSIVE OF WOUNDED WERE CAPTURED. OUR
LOSS WAS PRINCIPALLY IN [GENERAL JOHNSON] HAGOOD'S BRIGADE WHICH
MOUNTED ENEMY'S ENTRENCHMENTS. SUPPORTS FAILING, MANY WERE CAP-
TURED.

R. E. LEE

870   To JEFFERSON DAVIS
                 Richmond, Virginia

Headquarters, Army of Northern Virginia
August 22, 1864

Mr. President:

The enemy availed himself of the withdrawal of troops from Petersburg to the north side of James River, to take a position on the Weldon
Railroad. He was twice attacked on his first approach to the road, and
worsted both times, but the attacking force was too small to drive him
off.

Before the troops could be brought back from north of James River,
he had strengthened his position so much, that the effort made yesterday
to dislodge him was unsuccessful, and it was apparent that it could not
be accomplished even with additional troops, without a greater sacrifice
of life than we can afford to make, or than the advantages of success
would compensate for. As I informed Your Excellency when we first
reached Petersburg, I was doubtful of our ability to hold the Weldon
road so as to use it. The proximity of the enemy and his superiority of
numbers rendered it possible for him to break the road at any time, and
even if we could drive him from the position he now holds, we could
not prevent him from returning to it or to some other point, as our
strength is inadequate to guard the whole road. These considerations
induced me to abandon the prosecution of the effort to dislodge the
enemy.

I think it is his purpose to endeavor to compel the evacuation of
our present position by cutting off our supplies, and that he will not renew the attempt to drive us away by force.

His late demonstration on the north side of the James was designed
I think in part, to cause the withdrawal of troops from here to favor his
movement against the road, but also to endeavor if possible to force his
way to Richmond. Being foiled in the attempt, he has brought back all
the troops engaged in it, except those at Dutch Gap, and it is possible
that they too will be withdrawn to this side of the James. It behooves

us to do everything in our power to thwart his new plan of reducing us by starvation, and all our energies should be directed to using to its utmost capacity our remaining line of communication with the south. The best officers of the Quartermaster Department should be selected to superintend the transportation of supplies by the Danville road and its Piedmont connections and all the roads south of it.

I shall do all in my power to procure some supplies by the Weldon road, bringing them by rail to Stony Creek, and thence by wagons. One train has already been sent out, and others are prepared to go. I think by energy and intelligence on the part of those charged with the duty, we will be able to maintain ourselves until the corn crop in Virginia comes to our relief, which it will begin to do to some extent in about a month. It should be our effort to provide not only for current wants but if practicable, to accumulate a surplus to provide against those occasional interruptions of the roads which the enemy's policy justifies us in anticipating. I think this can be done with proper effort, and by the full use of all the rolling stock we can accumulate.

Our supply of corn is exhausted today, the small reserve accumulated in Richmond having been used. I am informed that all the corn that was brought from the south was transported to this place and Richmond, but the supply was not sufficient to enable the Quartermaster Department to accumulate a larger reserve. If this be true, it is desirable that steps be at once taken to increase the quantity brought over the southern roads, and if practicable, corn should be brought into Wilmington until our crop becomes available.

I trust that Your Excellency will see that the most vigorous and intelligent efforts be made to keep up our supplies, and that all officers concerned in the work, be required to give their unremitting personal attention to their duty.

With great respect, your obt servt

R. E. LEE
Genl

871   To JAMES A. SEDDON
                            Secretary of War

Headquarters, Army of Northern Virginia
August 23, 1864

Sir:

The subject of recruiting the ranks of our army is growing in importance and has occupied much of my attention. Unless some measures can be devised to replace our losses, the consequences may be disastrous. I think that there must be more men in the country liable to military duty than the small number of recruits received would seem to indicate. It has been several months since the passage of the last conscript law, and a large number of able bodied men and officers are engaged in enforcing it. They should by this time, if they have not been remiss, have brought out most of the men liable to conscription, and should have no duty to perform, except to send to the army those who arrive at the legal age of service.

I recommend that the facts of the case be investigated, and that if the officers and men engaged in enrolling have finished their work, with the exception indicated, they be returned to the army, where their presence is much needed. It is evidently inexpedient to keep a larger number out of service in order to get a smaller. I would also respectfully recommend that the list of detailed men be revised, and that all details of arms bearing men be revoked, except in cases of absolute necessity. I have myself seen numbers of men claiming to be detailed in different parts of the country who it seemed to me might well be in service. The corps are generally secured or beyond the necessity of further labor, and I hope some of the agricultural details may be revoked. Our numbers are daily decreasing, and the time has arrived in my opinion when no man should be excused from service, except for the purpose of doing work absolutely necessary for the support of the army. If we had here a few thousand men more to hold the stronger parts of our lines where an attack is least likely to be made, it would enable us to employ with good effect our veteran troops. Without some increase of our strength, I cannot see how we are to escape the natural military consequences of the enemy's numerical superiority.

Very respectfully, your obt servt

R. E. LEE
Genl

872   To GENERAL WADE HAMPTON
Commanding Cavalry Division

Headquarters
August 24, 1864
2.45 P.M.

General:

Your note of 2.30 is received. General Heth's division will also move down the railroad, and General Hill will go in command. I wish you to report to him, and do all in your power to punish the enemy. You ought to have out your scouts to ascertain their position and the best point to attack them.

Very respectfully

R. E. LEE
General

873   To JAMES A. SEDDON
Secretary of War
TELEGRAM

Headquarters
August 26, 1864

GENL A. P. HILL ATTACKED THE ENEMY IN HIS ENTRENCHMENTS AT REAMS' STATION YESTERDAY EVENING, AND AT THE SECOND ASSAULT CARRIED HIS ENTIRE LINE. COOKE'S & MACRAE'S NORTH CAROLINA BRIGADES, UNDER GENL HETH, AND LANE'S NORTH CAROLINA BRIGADE, OF WILCOX'S DIVISION, UNDER GENL CONNER, WITH PEGRAM'S ARTILLERY, COMPOSED THE ASSAULTING COLUMN. ONE LINE OF BREAST WORKS WAS CARRIED BY THE CAVALRY UNDER GENL HAMPTON WITH GREAT GALLANTRY, WHO CONTRIBUTED LARGELY TO THE SUCCESS OF THE DAY. SEVEN (7) STAND OF COLORS, TWO THOUSAND PRISONERS, AND NINE PIECES OF ARTILLERY ARE IN OUR POSSESSION. THE LOSS OF THE ENEMY IN KILLED AND WOUNDED IS REPORTED TO BE HEAVY, OURS RELATIVELY SMALL. OUR PROFOUND GRATITUDE IS DUE TO THE GIVER OF ALL VICTORY, & OUR THANKS TO THE BRAVE MEN & OFFICERS ENGAGED.

R. E. LEE

874   To GENERAL JUBAL A. EARLY
Commanding Valley District

Headquarters, Army of Northern Virginia
August 26, 1864

General:
Your letter of the 23rd has been received, & I am much pleased at your having forced the enemy back to Harper's Ferry. This will give protection to the Valley and arrest the travel on the Baltimore & Ohio Railroad. It will however have little or no effect upon Grant's operations, or prevent reinforcements being sent to him. If Sheridan's force is as

large as you suppose, I do not know that you could operate to advantage north of the Potomac. Either Anderson's troops or a portion of yours might, however, be detached to destroy the railroad west of Charlestown, and Fitz Lee might send a portion of his cavalry to cross the Potomac east of the Blue Ridge, as you propose. I cannot detach at present more cavalry from this army, the enemy is too strong in that arm. I am aware that Anderson is the ranking officer, but I apprehend no difficulty on that score. I first intended him to threaten the enemy east of the Blue Ridge, so as to retain near Washington a portion of the enemy's forces. He crossed the mountains at your suggestion, & I think properly. If his troops are not wanted there he could cross into Loudoun or Fauquier & return to Culpeper. It would add force to the movement of cavalry east of the Blue Ridge. I am in great need of his troops, and if they can be spared from the Valley, or cannot operate to advantage there, I will order them back to Richmond. Let me know.

Very resply

R. E. LEE
Genl

875   To HIS WIFE
"Bremo," Virginia

Camp, Petersburg
August 28, 1864

I received yesterday dear Mary your letter of the 18th & am rejoiced to hear of your improvement in health. I trust your particular disease will in time yield to the influence of your general strength, & if your difficulty to locomotion at present arises from the effects of your fall, that with time that will vanish. You must however be very careful of yourself, & though I am very glad you are able to ride, which will prove a pleasure as well as benefit if properly regulated, still unless you are very prudent in the beginning, may lead to colds & injury. I enclose a kind letter from Miss Mary Tinsley, the purport of which you will perceive. I thanked her for her father & mother's kind invitation, told her of the distress which travelling occasioned you, &c., &c., but if you can, you had better write to them yourself. A letter from Custis yesterday reported the invalids doing well & that Mary & Annie Leigh were to go to the country tomorrow but did not state where. I hope their trip may benefit both. I am very grateful that Rob's injury was slight

& Fitzhugh unhurt. Bev's wound was more serious, but I trust his youth under the favour of a kind Providence will soon restore him. We have had two quite sharp conflicts during the past week. The 14th & 25th. Although the enemy was punished, still we were unable to drive him within his original lines. His position however has been so near the Weldon Railroad that we could not operate it with safety, & unless we can drive him away entirely, his present position is but little more disadvantageous for us than his former. His attempt is now to starve us out, which I trust he will be unable to accomplish, nor will it be possible as long [as] our farmers maintain their present patriotism. In the battle of the 14th Mr. Bernard Taylor was killed while gallantly serving his gun. He was the nephew of Mr. William Taylor & he & his brother his principal heirs. I am very sorry for his death. On the 25th Fitzhugh's division behaved splendidly, charging on foot the enemy's works on the right, & capturing the men at their posts with their arms, &c. The North Carolina brigades signalized themselves, & behaved most handsomely. As usual we have to mourn the loss of brave men & officers, worth more to me than the whole Federal nation. But we must bear all that an ever loving God inflicts upon us, until He is graciously pleased to pardon our sins & to relieve us from the heavy punishment they have brought upon us. You must give much love to my dear daughters. Present my kind regards to Dr. & Mrs. Cocke & all the family. With unchanged love for yourself, I am most truly

R. E. LEE

876   To JEFFERSON DAVIS
                                    Richmond, Virginia

Headquarters, Army of Northern Virginia
September 2, 1864

Mr. President:

I beg leave to call your attention to the importance of immediate and vigorous measures to increase the strength of our armies, and to some suggestions as to the mode of doing it. The necessity is now great, and will soon be augmented by the results of the coming draft in the United States. As matters now stand, we have no troops disposable to meet movements of the enemy or strike where opportunity presents, without taking them from the trenches and exposing some important point. The enemy's position enables him to move his troops to the right or left without our knowledge, until he has reached the point at which he aims, and we are then compelled to hurry our men to meet him, incurring the risk of being too late to check his progress and the additional risk of the advantage he may derive from their absence. This was fully illustrated in the late demonstration north of James River, which called troops from our lines here, who if present might have prevented the occupation of the Weldon Railroad. These rapid and distant movements also fatigue and exhaust our men, greatly impairing their efficiency in battle. It is not necessary, however, to enumerate all the reasons for recruiting our ranks. The necessity is as well known to Your Excellency as to myself and as much the object of your solicitude. The means of obtaining men for field duty, as far as I can see, are only three.

A considerable number could be placed in the ranks by relieving all able bodied white men employed as teamsters, cooks, mechanics, and laborers, and supplying their places with negroes. I think measures should be taken at once to substitute negroes for whites in every place in the army, or connected with it, where the former can be used. It seems to me that we must choose between employing negroes ourselves, and having them employed against us.

A thorough and vigorous inspection of the rolls of exempted and detailed men is in my opinion of immediate importance. I think you will agree with me that no man should be excused from service for any reason not deemed sufficient to entitle one already in service to his discharge.

I do not think that the decision of such questions can be made so well by any as by those whose experience with troops has made them acquainted with those urgent claims to relief, which are constantly brought to the attention of commanding officers, but which they are forced to deny. For this reason I would recommend that the rolls of exempts and details in each State be inspected by officers of character and influence who have had experience in the field and have had nothing to do with the exemptions and details. If all that I have heard be true, I think it will be found that very different rules of action have been pursued towards men in service and those liable to it in the matter of exemptions and details, and I respectfully recommend that Your Excellency cause reports to be made by the Enrolling Bureau of the number of men enrolled in each State, the number sent to the field, and the number exempted or detailed. I regard this matter as of the utmost moment. Our ranks are constantly diminishing by battle and disease, and few recruits are received. The consequences are inevitable, and I feel confident that the time has come when no man capable of bearing arms should be excused, unless it be for some controlling reason of public necessity. The safety of the country requires this in my judgment, and hardship to individuals must be disregarded in view of the calamity that would follow to the whole people if our armies meet with disaster. No detail of an arms bearing man should be continued or granted, except for the performance of duty that is indispensable to the army, and that cannot be performed by one not liable to or fit for service. Agricultural details take numbers from the army without any corresponding advantage. I think that the interest of land owners and cultivators may be relied upon to induce them to provide means for saving their crops, if they be sent to the field. If they remain at home their produce will only benefit the enemy, as our armies will be insufficient to defend them. If the officers and men detailed in the Conscript Bureau have performed their duties faithfully, they must have already brought out the chief part of those liable to duty, and have nothing to do now except to get such as from time to time reach military age. If this be true many of these officers and men can now be spared for the army. If not, they have been derelict, and should be sent back to the ranks, & their places supplied by others who will be more active. Such a policy will stimulate the energy of this class of men. The last resource is the reserve force. Men of this class can render great service in connection with regular troops, by taking their places in trenches, forts, &c., and leaving them free for active operations.

I think no time should be lost in bringing out the entire strength of this class, particularly in Virginia & North Carolina. If I had the reserves of Virginia to hold the trenches here, or even enough to man those below Richmond on the north side of the river, they would render greater service than they can in any other way. They would give me a force to act with on the defensive or offensive, as might be necessary, without weakening any part of our lines. Their mere presence in the works below Richmond would prevent the enemy from making feints in that quarter to draw troops from here, except in such force as to endanger his own lines around Petersburg. But I feel confident that with vigorous effort, and an understanding on the part of the people of the necessity of the case, we could get more of this class than enough for the purpose last indicated. We could make our regular troops here available in the field.

The same remarks are applicable to the reserves of North Carolina, who could render similar services at Wilmington, and allow the regular troops to take the field against any force that might land there. I need not remind Your Excellency that the reserves are of great value in connection with our regular troops to prevent disaster, but would be of little avail to retrieve it. For this reason they should be put in service before the numerical superiority of the enemy enables him to inflict a damaging blow upon the regular forces opposed to him. In my opinion the necessity for them will never be more urgent, or their services of greater value than now. And I entertain the same views as to the importance of immediately bringing into the regular service every man liable to military duty. It will be too late to do so after our armies meet with disaster, should such unfortunately be the case.

I trust Your Excellency will excuse the length and earnestness of this letter, in view of the vital importance of its subject, and am confident that you will do all in your power to accomplish the objects I have in view.

With great respect, your obt servt

R. E. Lee
Genl

877   To HIS WIFE
"Bremo," Virginia

Richmond
September 5, 1864

My Dear Mary:

I received by Robt yesterday your letter of the 3rd. I am glad to learn from him that your general health is improving & that you are enabled to continue your rides without pain. I hope your general health will produce at least some relaxation of your particular complaint & that the approaching fall will entirely renovate your strength. As to your future residence it is difficult to speak with any degree of certainty as to what will be best. The usual uncertainty attending all things in this world is increased by the condition of the war. Our enemies say they will certainly have Richmond before long, in which event it will be better for you to be away. I enclose a check on the Confederate States Treasury for $800. which you can get when you desire. Beverley Coderise is not with me at present. He & some of his comrades went to the Valley some time since to procure horses to remount themselves & I have heard they were all captured. I do not know that it is true. I called to see the Caskies yesterday on my way to the President's & saw Mr. C. & Miss Norvell. Mrs. C. was in her room unwell. Nearly every one is said to be out of town. I miss you all very much when I come to Richmond & thus lose my only pleasure attending my visit. It is excessively hot. Miss Annie & Lizzie are very well & the former very sweet. The father of the latter came to see her yesterday & in consideration of a candy douceur she received him very graciously. She is as interesting as ever. Mrs. Davis shewed me her baby yesterday, which is a remarkably fine one. I hope Mary will fatten up now under the generous feeding which Robt describes as practised at Bremo & that Precious Life will find the means of assuaging her appetite. Tell her she must write sometimes to her papa. Tell Agnes Miss Sallie Warwick is not very well, so she says, & that she can not see me. Custis is remarkably well & so is Rob. The sight of them is a great comfort to me. I return to my camp today. I came up on some business which I fear I cannot accomplish. The fall of Atlanta is a blow to us, which is not very grievous & which I hope we will soon recover from. Present my kind regards to Dr. & Mrs. Cocke & all the family. Give much love to the girls & believe me always yours

R. E. LEE

878   To GENERAL BRAXTON BRAGG
Commanding Armies of the Confederate States

Headquarters, Army of Northern Virginia
September 10, 1864

General:

I have the honor to acknowledge the receipt of your letter of the 7th instant, and the accompanying report of the result of an inspection of the conscript service in Georgia. The facts presented by the last named document are not calculated to give much encouragement. The very small number of men sent to the field by the conscript law had already attracted my attention, and I have made some suggestions to the President which I thought calculated to make the law more effectual in its operation. Among them I advised that none but reserves and disabled soldiers should be employed to collect conscripts, and that all able bodied men and officers now detailed on that duty, who are of the proper age, be sent to the field. The reserves I think will be likely to do the work more thoroughly, as they will know that the increase of the regular armies diminishes the probability of a call upon their own class. I also advised the enrolling officers be not allowed to grant furloughs to conscripts pending the application of the latter for exemption or detail. I think it a sound principle that the enrolling & conscript officers should be restricted entirely to the duty of putting men in the field. I think we may safely leave it to the conscripts themselves to make out their claims to relief from active service. As the system of exemptions and details is now conducted, I do not expect any material increase of our strength. I was informed by Genl [James L.] Kemper [commanding the Virginia reserves] that in this state alone there were no less than forty thousand exempts, details and applications for detail yet undecided. Of the applicants I suppose the greater part have furloughs. Another point that I regard as very essential to the thorough enforcement of the law, is that no officer be put on enrolling duty at his own home. I recommended to the President to have an inspection made of the conscription service with a view to obtain accurate information as to its working. To me it now seems a very imperfect system of recruiting our armies. It is possible that nothing better can be done, but it is certain that in no department of the service are energy, intelligence and practical ability more vitally important to our success. I think the Department should be filled by the best capacity and the greatest vigor and industry that can be obtained, and should be confined to the single duty of putting men in the army.

Very respectfully, your obt servt

R. E. LEE
Genl

879 To GENERAL BRAXTON BRAGG
Commanding Armies of the Confederate States

Petersburg
September 12, 1864

In reply to Genl Hood's despatch I regret to state, that in my opinion it would be disadvantageous to reduce this army, & that no men can be spared without great hazard. If however the Department think otherwise, I will hold my position as long as I can retain the men in it.

Very resply

R. E. LEE
Genl

880 To GENERAL RICHARD H. ANDERSON
Commanding First Corps

Headquarters
September 17, 1864

General:
I have been desirous for some time of recalling you to me. But my unwillingness to diminish the force in the Valley has prevented. A victory over Sheridan would materially change the aspect of affairs & I

fear Genl Early's force without Kershaw's division would be insufficient. Upon the receipt of this therefore should circumstances permit, I wish you would with your staff return here & take command of the other divisions of your corps, & direct Genl Kershaw to report with his division to Genl Early for the present. Should you & Genl Early agree that the presence of Kershaw's division in the Valley is unnecessary you can bring it to Gordonsville with you. Otherwise let it remain until I can see further. Let me know what is your determination.

Very resply

R. E. LEE
Genl

881   To JAMES A. SEDDON
Secretary of War
TELEGRAM

Dunn's Hill
September 17, 1864

AT DAYLIGHT YESTERDAY THE ENEMY'S SKIRMISH LINE WEST OF THE JERUSALEM PLANK ROAD WAS DRIVEN BACK UPON HIS ENTRENCHMENTS ALONG THEIR WHOLE EXTENT & HIS LOCATION ASCERTAINED. NINETY PRISONERS TAKEN IN THE OPERATION. AT THE SAME HOUR GENL HAMPTON ATTACKED HIS POSITION, NORTH OF NORFOLK RAILROAD, NEAR SYCAMORE CHURCH. CAPTURED ABOUT THREE HUNDRED PRISONERS, SOME ARMS, WAGONS, LARGE NUMBER OF HORSES, & TWENTY-FIVE HUNDRED CATTLE. GENL GREGG ATTACKED GENL HAMPTON ON HIS RETURN IN THE AFTERNOON AT BELCHES' MILL, ON THE JERUSALEM PLANK ROAD, BUT WAS REPULSED & DRIVEN BACK. EVERYTHING WAS BROUGHT OFF SAFELY. OUR ENTIRE LOSS DOES NOT EXCEED FIFTY MEN.

R. E. LEE

882   To JAMES A. SEDDON
Secretary of War

Headquarters, Army of Northern Virginia
September 17, 1864

Sir:

There is immediate necessity for the services of five thousand negroes for thirty days to labor on the fortifications at this place, those on James River, around Richmond, at Danville, and at several points on the South Side and Danville Railroads. The amount of labor to be done, and the importance of having it done promptly, make it impossible to exact it of the troops without impairing their efficiency and requiring their absence from exposed positions. Much of the work is to be performed at places where there are few or no troops at present, but where it is deemed proper to prepare for possible future operations. I think the necessity sufficiently urgent to justify calling for this labor at once. From your endorsement upon the applications of Genl Stevens for negroes, I understand that you think that the act of Congress of February 17, 1864, does not empower you to order the impressment of slaves engaged in raising grain or provisions, but that the general commanding the department where their services are needed has the power to do so. I am willing to exercise such powers as I possess in the premises, but have no instruments to put them in execution.

I cannot consistently with the exigencies of the service detail officers and soldiers from the army for this duty, nor if I could, would that agency be suitable in my judgment. The impressments would not be made equally and justly, as the officers would necessarily be ignorant of the comparative resources and wants of the districts in which they would have to operate. If the agents of the Conscript Bureau can be employed for the purpose I am prepared to give them such authority to act as I lawfully may. They could consult with the local authorities and arrange for the prompt execution of the impressment in such manner as to be least injurious to the agricultural interests. I enclose a tabular statement of the quotas of the counties from which it is proposed to draw the negroes, showing the credits to which each is entitled. The number called for is large, but allowance must be made for failure in some quarters, and as the negroes will be sent on at different times, there will not be as great a number as the call embraces taken from the farms at any one time. I respectfully ask instructions how to proceed at your earliest convenience.

Very resply, your obt servt

R. E. LEE
Genl

883
To HIS WIFE
"Bremo," Virginia

Camp, Petersburg
September 18, 1864

My Dear Mary:
I have been again called to Richmond & while there received your letter of the 9th. It reached me however just as I was preparing to take

the cars for Petersburg Thursday & I have not been able to reply till now. I am glad that you are all enjoying your accustomed health & hope that more permanent benefit will be felt by all from the enjoyment of the pure country air & the association of such kind friends. I breakfasted one morning at Mr. Warwick's where I met Mr. Galt, who had seen the girls at church the preceding Sunday. Tell Mary I have been unable as yet to ascertain what can be done for her client Isaiah Patterson. I presume his term of service is nearly expired, if it is not already terminated, for I think they are only called out for 30 days at a time. I have great consideration for my African fellow citizens, but must have some for their white brethren. All must do their part in this great emergency. I am as sensible as you & Fitzhugh can be of my failing strength & approaching infirmities & am as careful to shield myself from exciting causes as I can be. But what care can a man give to himself in a time of war? It is from no desire of exposure or hazard that I live in a tent, but from necessity. I must be where I can speedily & at all times attend to the duties of my position & be near or accessible to the officers with whom I have to act. What house could I get to hold all the staff? Our citizens are very kind in offering me a room or rooms in their houses, in which I could be sheltered, but it would separate me from the staff officers, delay the transaction of business, & turn the residence of my kind landlords into a barrack where officers, couriers, distressed women, &c., would be entering day & night. I shall be very glad this winter to get a house if practicable. You must thank Mildred for her letter. I will answer it when I can. At my former visit to Richmond I found one of Miss Kirkland's domestic shirts & being without a night shirt used it for that purpose. I have it now. It is very comfortable but I am told by Robt that it washes badly. He gave up the two he had on that account. I am sorry for it, as the material is very nice. I shall retain the one I have to sleep in. If daughter wants the balance of the prise let her have it. I saw Miss Howell in a dress exactly like it, but it had never been washed. I am not yet wearing my new drawers & you need not send the third pair. We shall want for the army all the socks we can get, so you need not fear having too many. Put the girls to knitting. They must be hungry for work. Has Miss Bettie Brandon finished her pair yet? Tell her her soldier shall not marry her until she can clothe him. Sickness is decreasing in the army & I hope next month to have it well. Tell the young women to send me all their beaux. I want them at once. Love to all.

Very truly

R. E. LEE

884

To JAMES A. SEDDON
Secretary of War
TELEGRAM

Dunn's Hill
September 20, 1864

GENL EARLY REPORTS THAT ON THE MORNING OF THE 19TH THE ENEMY
ADVANCED ON WINCHESTER NEAR WHICH PLACE HE MET HIS ATTACK, WHICH
WAS RESISTED FROM EARLY IN THE DAY TILL NEAR NIGHT, WHEN HE WAS
COMPELLED TO RETIRE. AFTER NIGHT HE FELL BACK TO NEWTOWN & THIS
MORNING TO FISHER'S HILL. OUR LOSS IS REPORTED SEVERE. MAJ GENL [ROB-
ERT E.] RODES & BRIG GENL [ARCHIBALD C.] GODWIN WERE KILLED NOBLY DO-
ING THEIR DUTY. THREE (3) PIECES OF ARTILLERY OF [LIEUTENANT COLONEL
J. FLOYD] KING'S BATTALION WERE LOST. THE TRAINS & SUPPLIES WERE
BROUGHT OFF SAFELY.

R. E. LEE

885

To JAMES A. SEDDON
Secretary of War
TELEGRAM

Dunn's Hill
September 23, 1864

GENL EARLY REPORTS THAT LATE YESTERDAY THE ENEMY ATTACKED HIS
POSITION AT FISHER'S HILL & SUCCEEDED IN DRIVING BACK THE LEFT OF HIS
LINE & THROWING A FORCE IN HIS REAR, WHEN THE WHOLE OF HIS TROOPS
GAVE WAY. THIS RESULTED IN A LOSS OF 12 PIECES OF ARTILLERY, THOUGH
BUT FEW MEN.

R. E. LEE

886

To GENERAL RICHARD H. ANDERSON
Orange Court House
TELEGRAM

Headquarters, Army of Northern Virginia
Dunn's Hill
September 23, 1864

EARLY HAS AGAIN MET WITH A REVERSE, FALLING BACK TO NEW MARKET.
SEND KERSHAW'S DIVISION WITH BATTALION OF ARTILLERY THROUGH SWIFT

RUN GAP TO REPORT TO HIM AT ONCE. YOU WILL REPORT HERE IN PERSON
WITH YOUR STAFF ACCORDING TO PREVIOUS ORDERS.

R. E. LEE

887   To GENERAL JUBAL A. EARLY
New Market, Virginia
TELEGRAM

Headquarters, Army of Northern Virginia
September 23, 1864

KERSHAW'S DIVISION WITH A BATTALION OF ARTILLERY HAS BEEN OR-
DERED TO YOU THROUGH SWIFT RUN GAP. CALL OUT ALL THE TROOPS IN THE
VALLEY TO REINFORCE YOU. SEND TO MEET KERSHAW. ENCOURAGE YOUR
TROOPS, AND DO NOT BRING ON BATTLE UNTIL KERSHAW JOINS YOU AND YOUR
TROOPS ARE RALLIED.

R. E. LEE

888   To WILLIAM SMITH
Governor of Virginia

Headquarters, Army of Northern Virginia
September 24, 1864

Governor:
    I have the honor to ask your aid to relieve us in the Valley as far
as may be in your power. Genl Early has again met with a reverse and
has fallen back to New Market. I have written to him to call to his aid
all the local troops, and have thought that there may be some who are
not within reach of the Confederate authorities. I hope you will do all
in your power to increase his strength, as it is not possible in the present
condition of affairs for me to spare any reinforcements for him. I need
not remind Your Excellency of the importance of holding the Valley,
and the local troops can render great assistance.

Very respectfully, your obt servt

R. E. LEE
Genl

889   To GENERAL JOHN ECHOLS
Abingdon, Virginia
TELEGRAM

Headquarters, Army of Northern Virginia
September 24, 1864

DISPATCH OF TODAY RECEIVED. GLAD YOU ARE MAKING ARRANGEMENTS
TO MEET ADVANCE OF ENEMY. CALL OUT EVERY MAN. YOU MUST RELY UPON
THE FORCE AROUND YOU AND RESIST TO THE LAST.

R. E. LEE
Genl

890   To JAMES A. SEDDON
Secretary of War
TELEGRAM

Headquarters
September 26, 1864

GENL EARLY REPORTS ENEMY ADVANCED AGAINST HIM ON 24TH AT NEW
MARKET, WHEN HE FELL BACK TO PORT REPUBLIC TO UNITE WITH KERSHAW.
ON THE 25TH THE ENEMY ADVANCED TOWARDS HARRISONBURG, HIS CAVALRY
HAVING PROBABLY PASSED THAT PLACE.

R. E. LEE

891   To JAMES A. SEDDON
Secretary of War
TELEGRAM

Headquarters, Army of Northern Virginia
September 29, 1864

GENL EARLY REPORTS THAT AFTER DRIVING THE ENEMY'S CAVALRY FROM
HIS FRONT NEAR PORT REPUBLIC HE MOVED TO WAYNESBORO AND DROVE TWO
2 DIVISIONS OF CAVALRY FROM THAT PLACE. THIS LAST FORCE RETREATED
THROUGH STAUNTON, AND A PORTION OF OUR CAVALRY ENTERED THAT PLACE
TODAY. NO ENEMY SOUTH OF STAUNTON. HIS MAIN FORCE IS ABOUT HARRISON-
BURG.

R. E. LEE

892   To GENERAL BRAXTON BRAGG
          Commanding Armies of the Confederate States
                        TELEGRAM

                                        Headquarters
                                    September 29, 1864

GENL EWELL REPORTS THE ENEMY HAVE POSSESSION OF FORT HARRISON.
ORDER OUT THE LOCALS AND ALL THE OTHER TROOPS TO HIS ASSISTANCE.

                                        R. E. LEE

893   To JAMES A. SEDDON
                    Secretary of War
                        TELEGRAM

                    Headquarters, Army of Northern Virginia
                                      Chaffin's Bluff
                                    September 29, 1864
                                          9.30 P.M.

GENL [JOHN] GREGG REPORTS THAT HE REPULSED THE SEVERAL ATTACKS
OF THE ENEMY MADE AGAINST THE INTERMEDIATE LINE OF DEFENCES, CAP-
TURING MANY PRISONERS. THE ENEMY STILL HOLD BATTERY HARRISON ON THE
EXTERIOR LINE. OUR LOSS IS VERY SMALL.

                                        R. E. LEE

894   To GENERAL RICHARD S. EWELL
                     Chaffin's Bluff
                        TELEGRAM

                                    [September 29, 1864]

HAVE TELEGRAPHED GENL BRAGG TO ORDER OUT LOCALS. ENDEAVOR TO
RETAKE FORT HARRISON.

                                        R. E. LEE

895   To GENERAL RICHARD S. EWELL
                              Chaffin's Bluff
                              TELEGRAM

                              Headquarters, Army of Northern Virginia
                                             September 29, 1864

CAN YOU NOT DRAW SOME TROOPS FROM YOUR LEFT TO RETAKE FORT
HARRISON? IT WILL TAKE TIME FOR TROOPS FROM HERE TO REACH NORTH
SIDE. DON'T WAIT FOR THEM, ENDEAVOR TO RETAKE THE SALIENT AT ONCE.
PICKETT HAS BEEN ORDERED TO SEND A BRIGADE TO NORTH SIDE.

                                                    R. E. LEE

896   MAJOR W. H. TAYLOR TO GENERAL
                          SAMUEL COOPER
                    Adjutant and Inspector General
                              TELEGRAM

                              Headquarters, Army of Northern Virginia
                                             September 29, 1864

GENL LEE HAS MOVED TO CHAFFIN'S BLUFF, WHERE HE CAN BE COM-
MUNICATED WITH. PLEASE INFORM THE HONORABLE SECRETARY OF WAR &
GENL BRAGG.

                                                    W. H. TAYLOR
                                                    A. A. G.

897   To JAMES A. SEDDON
                          Secretary of War
                              TELEGRAM

                                             Chaffin's Bluff
                                             September 30, 1864
                                             8.10 P.M.

AN ATTEMPT WAS MADE THIS AFTERNOON TO RETAKE BATTERY HAR-
RISON WHICH, THOUGH PARTLY SUCCESSFUL, FAILED.

                                                    R. E. LEE

898   To JAMES A. SEDDON
                         Secretary of War
                            TELEGRAM

                                              Chaffin's Bluff
                                              October 1, 1864

GENERAL EARLY REPORTS THAT ALL THE ENEMY'S CAVALRY HAD RETIRED
TOWARDS HARRISONBURG, & THERE IS NO FORCE OF ENEMY SOUTH OF NORTH
RIVER.

                                              R. E. LEE

899   To JAMES A. SEDDON
                         Secretary of War
                            TELEGRAM

                                              Chaffin's Bluff
                                              October 4, 1864

GENL BRECKINRIDGE REPORTS THAT THE ENEMY ATTACKED SALTVILLE
ON THE 2ND INSTANT & RECEIVED A BLOODY REPULSE. THEY RETIRED DURING
THE NIGHT IN CONFUSION, APPARENTLY IN THE DIRECTION OF SANDY RIVER,
LEAVING MOST OF THEIR DEAD AND WOUNDED IN OUR HANDS. HE IS PURSUING
THEM. ALL OUR TROOPS BEHAVED WELL.

                                              R. E. LEE

900   To JAMES A. SEDDON
                         Secretary of War
                            TELEGRAM

                           Headquarters, Army of Northern Virginia
                                              Chaffin's Bluff
                                              October 7, 1864

GENL ANDERSON TODAY DROVE THE ENEMY FROM HIS POSITION NEAR EX-
TERIOR LINE OF DEFENCES AT CHARLES CITY ROAD TO VICINITY OF NEW
MARKET ROAD, WHERE HE WAS FOUND STRONGLY ENTRENCHED, AND WAS
NOT DISLODGED. TEN (10) PIECES OF ARTILLERY, WITH THEIR CAISSONS, SOME
HORSES, & PRISONERS WERE CAPTURED. OUR LOSS SAID TO BE SMALL; ENEMY'S

NOT KNOWN. THE BRAVE GENL GREGG, OF THE TEXAN BRIGADE, FELL DEAD AT
THE HEAD OF HIS MEN.

R. E. LEE

901   To JAMES A. SEDDON
             Secretary of War
             TELEGRAM

Chaffin's Bluff
October 7, 1864

GENL EARLY REPORTS SHERIDAN'S WHOLE FORCE COMMENCED RETIRING
DOWN THE VALLEY THE NIGHT OF THE FIFTH (5TH). OUR TROOPS FOLLOWED
THEM THROUGH HARRISONBURG THE NEXT DAY.

R. E. LEE

902   To JAMES A. SEDDON
             Secretary of War
             TELEGRAM

Chaffin's Bluff
October 9, 1864

GENL EARLY REPORTS THAT SHERIDAN IS STILL MOVING RAPIDLY DOWN
THE VALLEY. ROSSER ATTACKED A LARGE FORCE OF ENEMY'S CAVALRY ON THE
7TH AND DROVE IT HANDSOMELY, CAPTURING SEVERAL WAGONS, AMBULANCES,
AND NINE (9) FORGES WITH THEIR TEAMS, A NUMBER OF HORSES, ABOUT
FIFTY (50) PRISONERS, BESIDES KILLING AND WOUNDING A CONSIDERABLE
NUMBER OF ENEMY.

R. E. LEE

903   To GENERAL AMBROSE P. HILL
             Commanding Corps

Headquarters
Chaffin's
October 10, 1864

General:
    Grant is bringing to him all the reinforcements he can get. I have
heard those that were collected around Washington are being brought

down. I think reinforcements were received this side last night. There was crossing on the bridge and much commotion on his lines to the right. Probably they were new troops. I have also received information that on getting his reinforcements he intended to move by his right flank, approaching from the Chickahominy, and by his left to the South Side road. I wish you would see that all extra duty men in all the departments — wagoners, cooks, clerks, couriers, &c. — that can possibly be spared be placed in the ranks; that all the reserves, militia, &c., around Petersburg be put in the trenches, and that as many of your old troops as you think it safe to take out be held in readiness for field service. Tell Hampton to have his scouts on the alert and all his men prepared for action. The time stated for this movement is said to be from 10th to 15th instant. We must drive them back at all costs.

Very truly

R. E. LEE

904   To JAMES A. SEDDON
                    Secretary of War
                      TELEGRAM

Chaffin's Bluff
October 13, 1864

AT SEVEN (7) A.M. THIS MORNING ENEMY ENDEAVORED TO ADVANCE BE-
TWEEN THE DARBYTOWN AND CHARLES CITY ROADS, BUT WAS REPULSED IN
EVERY ATTEMPT. THE MOST STRENUOUS EFFORT WAS MADE ABOUT 4 P.M.,
AFTER WHICH HE WITHDREW, LEAVING MANY DEAD. OUR LOSS VERY SLIGHT.

GENL BRECKINRIDGE REPORTS THAT A FORCE OF THE ENEMY CAME TO
GREENEVILLE ON THE 12TH, AND WAS DEFEATED BY BRIG GENL [JOHN C.]
VAUGHN. SOME PRISONERS, TWO STAND OF COLORS, MANY HORSES AND ARMS,
WERE CAPTURED. THE ENEMY LOST MANY KILLED AND WOUNDED. OUR LOSS
SLIGHT.

R. E. LEE
Genl

905　　　To GENERAL JOHN C. BRECKINRIDGE
　　　　　　　Commanding in Southwestern Virginia
　　　　　　　　　　　TELEGRAM

Chaffin's Bluff
October 20, 1864

GENL EARLY HAS MET WITH ANOTHER REVERSE AND HAS LOST LARGELY
IN ARTILLERY. IF YOU CAN SPARE THE BATTERY YOU MENTIONED SEND IT TO
HIM, AS ALSO THE TROOPS WITHOUT DELAY.

R. E. LEE

906　　　　　　To JAMES A. SEDDON
　　　　　　　　　　Secretary of War
　　　　　　　　　　TELEGRAM

Chaffin's Bluff
October 20, 1864

GENL EARLY REPORTS THAT BEFORE DAY ON THE 19TH HE ATTACKED
SHERIDAN'S CAMP ON CEDAR CREEK, SURPRISED AND ROUTED THE 8TH AND
19TH CORPS, AND DROVE THE 6TH CORPS BEYOND MIDDLETOWN, CAPTURING
EIGHTEEN (18) PIECES OF ARTILLERY AND THIRTEEN HUNDRED (1,300) PRIS-
ONERS. THE ENEMY SUBSEQUENTLY MADE A STAND ON THE PIKE AND IN TURN
ATTACKED HIM, WHEN HIS LEFT GAVE WAY AND HIS TROOPS RETREATED. THE
ENEMY ON THE RETREAT CAPTURED THIRTY (30) PIECES OF ARTILLERY AND
WAGONS AND AMBULANCES. THE PRISONERS WERE BROUGHT OFF AND HIS LOSS
IN MEN WAS NOT GREAT. THE GALLANT GENL [S. DODSON] RAMSEUR WAS
SERIOUSLY WOUNDED AND FELL INTO THE HANDS OF THE ENEMY.

R. E. LEE

907　　　　　　To JAMES A. SEDDON
　　　　　　　　　　Secretary of War
　　　　　　　　　　TELEGRAM

Chaffin's Bluff
October 21, 1864

DISPATCH FROM GENL EARLY JUST RECEIVED STATES THAT HE LOST
TWENTY-THREE (23) PIECES OF ARTILLERY ON THE 19TH. HIS LOSS IN KILLED

& WOUNDED IN THE EARLY PART OF THE DAY WAS NOT MORE THAN ONE HUNDRED (100). HIS LOSS IN PRISONERS NOT KNOWN. ENEMY'S LOSS BE-LIEVED TO BE SEVERE. HE HAS SECURED OVER THIRTEEN HUNDRED (1,300) PRISONERS.

R. E. LEE

908   To HIS WIFE
                              "Bremo," Virginia

Chaffin's
October 25, 1864

My Dear Mary:
   I received Sunday evening your letter of the 18th. I had gone into church in the morning & had some hope of finding you in Richmond. Though disappointed at not seeing you I still felt relieved at your be-ing in a quiet safe place. I still think it better for you to find some other abode than Richmond, though as you have decided to return I trust it will be for the best. The question now is not what is most agre-able, but what is best. If the girls prefer the town which it seems they do, they can take the risk, but in your helpless condition I think it very hazardous in the present uncertainty of events. Everyone too who has no business in Richmond, or who cannot do the State some good by being there ought to be away. It adds to the number to be fed, & otherwise may increase our difficulties. I heard Mr. Patterson preach a very good sermon on the subject of the forgiveness of our enemies. It is a hard lesson to learn now, but still it is true & requires corresponding efforts. I received a letter from Nannie Peyton yesterday saying that the Federals had arrested the principal citizens in that neighborhood, & placed them on the cars running to Alexandria to prevent the trains be-ing attacked by our men. Among them she mentioned her husband, the only physician in the neighborhood, & Mr. Foster of the Plains, who is in wretched health & subject to cough & hemorhages. I am glad Mr. Wilmar has been to see you & that you had the opportunity of partaking of the blessed communion. May it serve constantly to keep our Redeemer in our hearts & minds & enable us to follow His holy precept & exam-ple. Custis has not been very well. He is annoyed with boils. I have not heard from Fitzhugh or Robt lately. I trust they are well. Give much love to my dear daughters. I have not time to write to them. My feeble prayers are constantly offered up for you & them. May a Merciful God watch over us all.
   You must give my affectionate regards to the kind family where

you are. I wish I could give to them my thanks in person for their kindness to you.

With much love, affly yours

R. E. LEE

909   To JAMES A. SEDDON
Secretary of War

Headquarters, Army of Northern Virginia
October 27, 1864

Sir:

Genl Hill reports that the enemy crossed Hatcher's Run this morning at Armstrong's Mill and Monk's Neck Bridge, force unknown. Genl Longstreet reports that the enemy is moving to our left and that cavalry and infantry have appeared on the Nine Mile road. There thus appears to be a simultaneous movement on both flanks. Our troops have made corresponding movements.

Very respectfully, your obt servt

R. E. LEE
Genl

910   To JAMES A. SEDDON
Secretary of War
TELEGRAM

Chaffin's Bluff
October 27, 1864

THE MOVEMENT OF THE ENEMY AGAINST OUR LEFT TODAY WAS REPULSED. TWO ATTACKS UPON OUR LINES WERE MADE — ONE BETWEEN THE HENRICO POOR HOUSE AND CHARLES CITY ROAD, THE OTHER ON THE WILLIAMSBURG ROAD. SEVERAL HUNDRED PRISONERS AND FOUR STANDS OF COLOURS WERE CAPTURED. OUR LOSS VERY SLIGHT. ON THE 25TH COL MOSBY, NEAR BUNKER HILL, CAPTURED BRIG GENL [ALFRED N.] DUFFIE, SEVERAL OTHER PRISONERS, A NUMBER OF HORSES, AND KILLED A NUMBER OF THE ENEMY. HE SUSTAINED NO LOSS.

R. E. LEE

911   To JAMES A. SEDDON
                               Secretary of War
                                   TELEGRAM

                                                        Chaffin's Bluff
                                                     October 27, 1864
                                                           11 P.M.

GENL HILL REPORTS THAT THE ENEMY CROSSED ROWANTY CREEK BELOW
BURGESS' MILL AND FORCED BACK THE CAVALRY. IN THE AFTERNOON GENL
HETH ATTACKED AND AT FIRST DROVE THEM, BUT FOUND THEM IN TOO STRONG
FORCE. AFTERWARDS THE ENEMY ATTACKED AND WERE REPULSED. THEY STILL
HOLD THE PLANK ROAD AT BURGESS' MILL. HETH TOOK COLORS AND SOME
PRISONERS.

                                                        R. E. LEE
                                                            Genl

912   To JAMES A. SEDDON
                               Secretary of War
                                   TELEGRAM

                                                        Chaffin's Bluff
                                                     October 28, 1864

GENL HILL REPORTS THAT THE ATTACK OF GENL HETH UPON THE EN-
EMY ON THE BOYDTON PLANK ROAD, MENTIONED IN MY DISPATCH LAST
EVENING, WAS MADE BY THREE (3) BRIGADES UNDER GENL MAHONE IN FRONT,
AND GENL HAMPTON IN THE REAR. MAHONE CAPTURED FOUR HUNDRED (400)
PRISONERS, THREE (3) STANDS OF COLORS, AND SIX (6) PIECES OF ARTILLERY.
THE LATTER COULD NOT BE BROUGHT OFF, THE ENEMY HAVING POSSESSION OF
THE BRIDGE. IN THE ATTACK SUBSEQUENTLY MADE BY THE ENEMY GENL MA-
HONE BROKE THREE (3) LINES OF BATTLE, AND DURING THE NIGHT THE ENEMY
RETIRED FROM THE BOYDTON ROAD, LEAVING HIS WOUNDED AND MORE THAN
TWO HUNDRED AND FIFTY (250) DEAD ON THE FIELD. ABOUT NINE (9)
O'CLOCK P.M. A SMALL FORCE ASSAULTED AND TOOK POSSESSION OF OUR WORKS
ON THE BAXTER ROAD IN FRONT OF PETERSBURG, BUT WAS SOON DRIVEN OUT.
    ON THE WILLIAMSBURG ROAD YESTERDAY GENL FIELD CAPTURED UP-
WARDS OF FOUR HUNDRED (400) PRISONERS AND SEVEN (7) STANDS OF COLORS.
THE ENEMY LEFT A NUMBER OF DEAD IN FRONT OF OUR WORKS AND RETURNED
TO HIS FORMER POSITION TODAY.

                                                        R. E. LEE

913
To JEFFERSON DAVIS
Richmond, Virginia

Petersburg
November 2, 1864

Mr. President:

I had the honour to receive last evening your letter of the 31st. I am sorry to hear that Genl Law anticipates injustice at the hands of Genl Longstreet. I do not, & think that Genl Law has nothing to do but his whole duty, & he need fear nothing. I know of no objection to making the transfer of his brigade to Hoke's division, provided the change is acceptable to the brigades themselves. It is neither right or politic to consult the wishes of the commander alone.

The information contained in the notes you enclosed me, I hope is exaggerated as regards to numbers. Grant will get every man he can, & 150,000 men is the number generally assumed by Northern papers & reports. Unless we can obtain a reasonable approximation to his force I fear a great calamity will befall us. On last Thursday at Burgess' Mill we had three brigades to oppose six divisions. On our left two divisions to oppose two corps. The inequality is too great. Our cavalry at Burgess' Mill I think saved the day. I came along our whole line yesterday from Chaffin's Bluff to this place. Today I shall visit the lines here & tomorrow go down to the right. I always find something to correct on the lines, but the great necessity I observed yesterday, was the want of men.

With great respect, your obt servt

R. E. LEE
Genl

914
To HIS WIFE
Richmond, Virginia

Petersburg
November 15, 1864

My Dear Mary:

I send up an old shirt which you thought might be useful to some of our poor wounded soldiers. I have another if you desire it. I also send the pillow case you gave me last year. You will see its forlorn condition. I want another one badly, of any material you have. You can guess at the size by the one returned. Please mend my pair of drawers herewith sent & if no sick or wounded soldier requires them, ask Daughter to put them in my trunk. I hope you are all well. Love to every body.

Very truly

R. E. LEE

915   To HIS WIFE
                              Richmond, Virginia

Petersburg
November 16, 1864

My Dear Mary:

After writing last night the accompanying note, yours of the 15th arrived. I am very sorry to hear of the death of little Abe, for I know the sorrow it will give the Warwicks, & especially to sweet little Sallie. You must give them my sincere sympathy. Surely in this instance the dead are the happier. Please thank Miss Eliza Woodward for me & give her my grateful thanks for her remembrance of me. You must keep the comfort. You may recollect they were the friends of Mrs. Hackley & Talcott & formerly lived in Norfolk with them I believe. They were residing in Fredericksburg at the time of Genl Burnside's attack on that place, & I think remained there till forced away by circumstances. I am glad to hear of Miss Carrie Mason again. I feared the Philistines had her. It is a little singular however that she & Col Jenifer should visit Richmond always at the same time. I fear it is ominous. Has she any superstition on the subject? Tell her to put away her idols. This is no time for manship. She must devote herself to her country. If she wants to do a good thing, let her come & see me. I hope she is as fair as ever & carries weight equal to Miss Jennie Fairfax. I am glad to hear that Custis is better. I have not heard from him since I left Chaffin's. I was down with the cavalry Monday. Heard of Fitzhugh, but did not see him. It gives me a ride of over 30 miles when I visit that part of the line, & I cannot go out of my way. My horse is dreadfully rough & I am very stiff & heavy. I do not require my flannels yet. I am wearing the jackets Miss Kitty Stiles knit for me, which are very pleasant, & the cotton drawers you sent me. They are abundantly warm yet awhile. You can send me the other pair & the check shirts, when convenient. Give much love to every body & believe me always yours

R. E. LEE

916 To MISS AGNES LEE
Richmond, Virginia

Petersburg
November 20, 1864

My precious little Agnes:

I was not able to reply to your last letter. The one in which you put so speedily in execution your "good intentions." It reached me on the field north of James River at the time of Genl Grant's movement against our left, previous to the last. I tore in bits & consigned it to the winds, lest it might adorn the pages of some of the veracious sheets of our Northern bretheren. But I read it Agnes, every word, & it brought me pleasant thoughts in our struggle, & softened the asperities of the day. Every day is marked with sorrow & every field has its grief, the death of some brave man! We have had more days of quiet since Grant's last lateral move, & beautiful weather to enjoy it in. I suppose he is preparing some great blow with which he intends to demolish us, but from which I trust a Merciful Providence will shield us. I got a letter from your Uncle Carter the other day. He was contemplating a visit to Richmond, where he said Mrs. Taylor was going for a milder atmosphere. I was sorry to hear she was quite feeble. The rest of the family were well. I have not heard of your brothers for some days. They are all at some distance from me now & I presume each is engrossed in his occupations. On my last visit to the right I saw Mrs. Hampton who had come on to see the Genl. Miss Sallie had left that very day for Abingdon to visit her aunt, much to the disappointment of some young gentlemen who accompanied me. Miss Jennie Pegram is at present agitating the thoughts of that class of soldiers in this city. I see her bright face occasionally as she flashes it on her beaux, but in pity she turns it away from me, for it is almost dazzling. How is my wounded nephew? No wonder he covers his breast with his beard, which he hopes like the shield of Achilles will turn aside the darts of such fair archers. Cupid is always busy when Mars is quiet & our young heroes think it necessary to be killed in some way. It matters little to them which. I hope your poor mother has some relief from her suffering. You must do everything to compose & comfort her. I was so sorry to hear of the affliction of the Warwicks. I know how it will grieve sweet little Sallie. But what a gain to the dear child. Release from the sin & sorrow of this world! Give my love & sincere sympathy to her, & her father. You must also give much love to your mama & sisters. I hope to see you all again some of these days, but cannot say when.

Your affectionate father

R. E. Lee

917   To GENERAL WADE HAMPTON
Commanding Cavalry Division

[November 21, 1864]

General:

I shall not be able to meet you today. What I wished to see you about was the practicability of striking Grant a blow, either this side or the north side of James River, on the supposition I could draw Early down to aid. Can a vulnerable point be found without having to pass over their breast-works, which as far as I can judge are well arranged and strongly fortified, and composed of several lines and batteries? You must not mention this to anybody. Give me your views and try to ascertain the way to strike.

Very truly

R. E. Lee
General

918   To HIS WIFE
Richmond, Virginia

Petersburg
November 25, 1864

My Dear Mary:

I find that Col Corley has no socks, you had better therefore send down yours. To save you all trouble write to Major Ferguson to send up & get them, weigh & pack them & send them to Col Corley. I will ask Major Janney to distribute them. I suppose the yarn was furnished by Government & the price of the wool must be charged to the men. On arriving here on the evening of the 23rd I found we had changed our camp. The house that we were occupying was wanted, indeed had been rented by a newly married couple, & they had ejected Col Taylor that day. We have however a very good abode about 1½ miles from

Petersburg, south of the Appomattox, belonging to a Mr. Turnbull, who had sent his family off for fear of Genl Grant & his missiles. It is dreadfully cold. I wish I had a good wood to encamp in, where I could pitch my tent. But there is none convenient. My door will not shut, so that I have a goodly company of cats & puppies around my hearth. But I shall rectify that. I hope my poor little Agnes is relieved. Write me word. It made me very sad to leave her suffering. I send to Mildred the notification from the Cliosophic Society, to get her advice on the subject. The only benefit that I could be to the oratory of the fair members would be to exhort them to practice saying "yes," so as to be prepared for an emergency. I return Miss Ruffin's note which you promised to answer. Tell her the socks fit exactly & are very nice. I am extremely obliged to her. Miss Carrie has been so far away that she has had no opportunity of enjoying Confederate poetry. I therefore send her Mr. Caylat's last production. Tell her she must omit the poetry but accept the intention. I hope daughter is well. She must tell Miss Bettie Brander that Col Marshall is busy having his photograph taken. I do not see what she wants with the original & copy too. Remember me to all the household & give much love to my children. I hope you are better & that your pains will soon leave you.

With much affection, very truly yours

R. E. LEE

919   To HIS WIFE
Richmond, Virginia

Petersburg
November 30, 1864

I received yesterday dear Mary your letter of the 27th & am glad to learn that your supply of socks is so large. If two or three hundred would send an equal number, we should have a sufficiency. I will endeavour to have them distributed to the most needy. I enclose $30 for the repairs of my overcoat. Please ask Major Coxe to add to my obligations to him to paying for it. If it is more, will you make up the deficiency. I am anxious to get it & will send for it, for although the weather is delicious now, it will change soon, & if the army moves, I shall be at a loss, as it is my house & bed when in the field. I wish you could go out & enjoy this charming weather. You can however appreciate it in the house. The bright sun & balmy atmosphere pervades every where. I am

delighted to hear that my poor little Agnes is well. Tell her she must
not get sick again. It makes me too sad. Robt will tell you of everything.
He is going to try to get to Romankoke. I hope he will be able to regulate
matters satisfactorily. Tell him he must go to Chelsea & remember me
to Mrs. Moore & Mrs. Robinson, &c. The latter has some pretty daughters. Thank her for the gloves & socks which I wish you would [*letter
cut*] first opportunity. Whenever you desire to send anything to me,
put it up securely, direct it clearly, & send it to Major Wood's office,
Quartermaster in charge of transportation. My couriers always go there
& start from there. In fact that is their abiding place in Richmond. Ask
the girls to recollect it. I should be glad to gratify Mr. Eaches, but you
know I am the worst sitter in the world & am a very poor subject to
take. I am not in my quarters longer than necessary to transact the business of the office, when I go on the lines. If he chooses to come down
& take the chances of catching me disengaged, I have no objection, but
I can make no promises or engagement, & perhaps the very day he might
come, I should be obliged to be in the field. He had better wait until the
weather is less favourable for out door operations. Give much love to
every body & believe me always yours

R. E. LEE

P.S. I send a letter which I received a long time ago, & have preserved that I might retain the writer's name. I think it will be safer with
you or one of the girls.

R. E. L.

920   To JEFFERSON DAVIS
                          Richmond, Virginia

Headquarters
Turnbull's
December 5, 1864

Mr. President:
      General Early reports that his scouts stated the Sixth Corps had
broken camp on the 2d and taken the cars at Stephenson's Depot, said to
be going to City Point. From reports received from Longstreet and
Ewell last night, I think this corps or a part of it may have reached the
north side of James River last night. My last report from scouts on the
James was to the 2d. There has been great activity on the river in
transportation of supplies, but no troops had passed in any numbers

since the 17th ultimo. Reports of Early and Longstreet have not yet been corroborated, but the whole preparations of the enemy indicate some movement against us. All we want to resist them is men.

With great respect, your obedient servant

R. E. LEE
General

921   To JAMES A. SEDDON
Secretary of War
TELEGRAM

Petersburg
December 7, 1864

A SCOUT JUST IN REPORTS ENEMY, CAVALRY, INFANTRY, & ARTILLERY, MOVING DOWN JERUSALEM PLANK ROAD; HAD PASSED CAPT PROCTOR'S THIS MORNING. GENL PICKETT REPORTS ENEMY CROSSING TO SOUTH SIDE AT COX'S LANDING. NOTHING TO INDICATE INTENTION OF ENEMY ON OUR RIGHT. HAVE DIRECTED GENL LONGSTREET TO REINFORCE PICKETT, & INSTRUCTED CAPT MITCHELL TO COOPERATE. THE SIXTH CORPS ARRIVED LAST NIGHT. REPORTED ON THIS FRONT. PLEASE EXPEDITE MOVEMENT OF TROOPS FROM WAYNESBORO.

R. E. LEE

922   To JAMES A. SEDDON
Secretary of War
TELEGRAM

Petersburg
December 8, 1864

SECOND & FIFTH CORPS OF ENEMY, WITH GREGG'S DIVISION OF CAVALRY, ARE MOVING SOUTH ON JERUSALEM PLANK ROAD. CAVALRY REACHED SUSSEX COURT HOUSE AT SEVEN P.M. YESTERDAY. HILL & HAMPTON ARE FOLLOWING.

APPEARANCES INDICATE THEY ARE MOVING AGAINST WELDON, WHERE I AM CONCENTRATING ALL THE DEPOT GUARDS I CAN.

R. E. LEE

923

To JAMES A. SEDDON
Secretary of War
TELEGRAM

Petersburg
December 10, 1864
11 o'clock

HAMPTON, AFTER DRIVING ENEMY'S CAVALRY UPON HIS INFANTRY, ON
AFTERNOON OF 8TH RECROSSED THE NOTTOWAY & REACHED BELFIELD AT DAY-
LIGHT YESTERDAY. IN THE AFTERNOON ENEMY ATTACKED THE POSITION, BUT
WERE SUCCESSFULLY RESISTED. THIS MORNING ENEMY IS REPORTED RETIRING
& HAMPTON FOLLOWING. THE BRIDGE OVER THE MEHERRIN WAS SAVED. OUR
LOSS, AS FAR AS KNOWN, SMALL. THE GARRISON, UNDER [JOHN J.] GARNETT,
& THE RESERVES BEHAVED WELL.

R. E. LEE

924

To JAMES A. SEDDON
Secretary of War
TELEGRAM

Petersburg
December 10, 1864

ABOUT NOON YESTERDAY THE 1ST DIVISION OF 2ND CORPS OF ENEMY,
SUPPORTING THEIR CAVALRY, FORCED BACK OUR CAVALRY PICKETS ON THE
VAUGHAN ROAD SOUTH OF THE APPOMATTOX & ADVANCED TOWARDS DINWIDDIE
COURT HOUSE. TODAY OUR CAVALRY, REINFORCED BY INFANTRY, DROVE THEM
BACK ACROSS HATCHER'S RUN, CAPTURING A FEW PRISONERS, AND REESTAB-
LISHED OUR LINES. GENL LONGSTREET MADE A RECONNAISSANCE OF ENEMY'S
LINES TODAY ON NORTH SIDE OF JAMES RIVER AS FAR AS NEW MARKET
HEIGHTS, DRIVING IN THEIR PICKETS, & FOUND THEM FORTIFIED ALONG THE
WHOLE DISTANCE.

R. E. LEE

925   To G. W. C. LEE
                                  Richmond, Virginia

Near Petersburg
December 13, 1864

My Dear Son:
    I have been expecting to see you for some weeks, but each day that I have appointed to return to the north side of the James River, some movement of the enemy has occurred, or some rumour of a projected movement has reached me, to prevent. Yesterday week I had directed our caravan to be prepared to move the next morning, but during the night, or rather before day this day week, I heard of their last move down the Plank road, & had to put our troops in motion. We succeeded in arresting them at the Meherrin & turning them back. Their route of retreat was due east in direction of Jerusalem & Sussex Court House, & thus their infantry got out of our way, & we could only strike their rear guard of cavalry. The weather was wretched, & I fear our men & animals suffered much. The enemy reached their camps last night & our men are coming in this morning. Their prisoners stated they were going to Weldon, & I suppose were bound on a distant mission as they carried beef cattle & a long train of wagons. Their trains, &c., were all east of their route of march. We did them little harm I fear. They destroyed about six miles of railroad, so the superintendent reports, & burned some small bridges. During this operation they attempted to turn our right flank, & to reach Dinwiddie Court House. In this they also failed. I do not know what they will attempt next.
    I have a nice pair of woolen gloves, gauntlet shaped, which may keep you warm this cold weather. If you want them will send them up. If you do not, let me know. I am afraid you will ruin my character with the young ladies, & may cause that of the family for fidelity to be suspected. Several of them wishing, I suppose, to see how they would like me as a father-in-law, have requested my photograph, which I have promised, & have relied on those you were to have sent me. Not one has ever reached me, & I am taxed with breach of promise. See what a strait you have placed me in. Robt got here Tuesday & I had to forward him next day on Ajax. He had, I fear, a disagreable ride as it rained all day. I hope you & your men are comfortable & that every thing is well with you. Have you been able to pole your road through that slushy wood?
    God bless & keep you my dear son, is the daily prayer of your affectionate father

R. E. LEE

926   To GENERAL SAMUEL COOPER
Adjutant and Inspector General
TELEGRAM

Headquarters, Army of Northern Virginia
December 13, 1864

YOUR DISPATCH OF TODAY RECEIVED. EVERY AVAILABLE MAN AT THE
SOUTH SHOULD NOW BE SENT TO SAVANNAH. AS LONG AS GRANT RETAINS HIS
PRESENT FORCE HERE I DO NOT THINK THIS ARMY CAN BE WEAKENED. IF HE
WITHDRAWS ANY PART, I CAN DETACH PROPORTIONALLY. IF THE DEPARTMENT
THINKS OTHERWISE I WILL SEND WHATEVER IT DIRECTS.

R. E. LEE

927   To JEFFERSON DAVIS
Richmond, Virginia
TELEGRAM

Petersburg
December 14, 1864

CHIEF COMMISSARY OF THIS ARMY RECEIVED NOTICE YESTERDAY FROM
RICHMOND THAT THERE WAS NO SALT MEAT THERE TO SEND HIM, BUT WOULD
FORWARD PRESERVED MEAT. HE THINKS HE MAY GET ENOUGH TO LAST TO-
MORROW. NEITHER MEAT NOR CORN ARE NOW COMING OVER THE SOUTHERN
ROADS, AND I HAVE HEARD THERE WAS MEAT IN WILMINGTON.

R. E. LEE

928   To HIS WIFE
Richmond, Virginia

Near Petersburg
December 17, 1864

My Dear Mary:
    I received day before yesterday the box with the hat, gloves & socks
& also the bushel of apples. You had better have kept the latter, as it would
have been more useful to you than to me, & I should have enjoyed its
consumption by yourself & the girls, more than by me. The gloves

brought by Mrs. Grinnell are very nice. You must thank her for them &
express my sympathy for her loss & present distress. I hope however
her husband is in a fair way to recover. I can do very well without the
boots. You must also thank Mrs. Lyons for the furs, & beg the kind
people to send me nothing more. I fear the furs will be more needed
by Mr. Lyons than by me & that he may consequently suffer. Send
them down when convenient. The reason you were troubled by visits of
the courier about the box, in your first note, the 12th, apprising me of
having sent it, you did not state it was through Major Wood. I was out
when the courier brought the note & asking for the box, no one could
give any explanation. We are a dull people in the army, & it is requisite
you should be very explicit. You had better send the socks to Major
Ferguson, to be forwarded as the bundle appears to be large. I am some
distance from the railroad depot now, & our little couriers have as much
as they can carry ordinarily.

Robt can select any of my hats he prefers. I have offered them repeatedly, but he declines. Custis has the same privilege, also Fitzhugh.
When last here Robt had a nice black hat with cord, &c., new. He said
he wanted no other.

Give much love to every body.

Very truly & affly

R. E. LEE

929   To JEFFERSON DAVIS
Richmond, Virginia
TELEGRAM

Headquarters, Army of Northern Virginia
December 19, 1864

DISPATCH OF TODAY RECEIVED. BEAUREGARD AND HARDEE MUST JUDGE
OF NECESSITY OF EVACUATING SAVANNAH. IF DONE TROOPS CAN BE SAVED, AND
BY UNITING ALL IN DIRECTION OF BRANCHVILLE ANY COLUMN MARCHING ON
CHARLESTON WOULD BE THREATENED AND COMMUNICATION PRESERVED. I
CANNOT FIND THAT ANY TROOPS HAVE LEFT GRANT. HE HAS UNITED TO HIM
THE SIXTH AND NINETEENTH CORPS. IF HOKE AND JOHNSON ARE SENT SOUTH
IT WILL NECESSITATE THE ABANDONMENT OF RICHMOND WITH THE PRESENT
OPPOSING FORCE.

R. E. LEE

930   To JAMES A. SEDDON
                                Secretary of War

                                        Headquarters, Army of Northern Virginia
                                                        December 26, 1864

Sir:
    Your telegraph today has been received. I shall be very glad to re-
lieve all the local troops now in the trenches in front of Richmond, but
I don't know where to get troops to replace them with. Genl Ewell
writes that he has now only eight hundred men to guard a line formerly
manned by two thousand. Since the departure of Genl Hoke the extreme left of our line has had to be in a measure abandoned and the rest
very thinly manned. I do not know whether they can be stretched out
any farther. I will however communicate with Genl Longstreet and
see what can be done. Reports from Genl Early state that the 8th Corps
had been called from the Valley to Genl Grant, and it is certain that the
enemy's camps in the Valley are much diminished. I have drawn from the
Valley all the troops I can, and by his concentration Grant may be
meditating an attack. If so, I do not see where I am to get troops to meet
him, as ours seem rather to diminish than to increase.

                            Very respectfully, your obt servt

                                            R. E. LEE
                                            Genl

931   To HIS WIFE
                                Richmond, Virginia

                                                        Petersburg
                                                December 30, 1864

My Dear Mary:
    I have received your note of Monday, & am glad to hear that you
were all well. The Lyons' furs & the fur robe have also arrived safely,
but I can learn nothing of the saddle of mutton. Bryan, of whom I inquired as to its arrival, is greatly alarmed lest it has been sent to the
soldier's dinner. If the soldiers get it I shall be content. We can do very
well without it. In fact I would rather they should have it, than I. My
little couriers say they have seen or heard nothing of it at Major Wood's.
If it was sent there it could not have been properly directed, or they
think they would certainly have seen it. I shall be glad if Major Wood

misunderstood the directions & supposed it was your contribution for the soldier's dinner. I shall be equally grateful to Mr. Mason for his fine saddle. I enclose Mrs. Well's note which I find on my table, that you may see who sent you the ginger. You had better send me the socks presented by Mrs. Harwood of Gloucester. If they do not suit me, they will some officers near me. I am sorry I could not see Becky but I had not time to call. The collar you sent me of Custis' fits very well, but I prefer the other kind you made me, if I could only get them to fit the shirt. I am glad you were able to have some of your friends with you Xmas. I am unable to have any enjoyment of that kind now. I was very grateful to be able to attend church on that day & offer my feeble praise to our Merciful Father for the precious gift of his Holy Son. I brought with me from church Col Talcott to dinner. My young family had gone to more pleasant feasts. We however had a nice turkey & potatoes. Tell Daughter the boots arrived safely today. I have had the pleasure of Mr. Eaches' company this morning. Do advise all artists to amuse themselves with the photographs & give wide range to their fancy.

Love to all.

Very truly & affly

R. E. Lee

932   To GENERAL JOHN C. BRECKINRIDGE
Commanding in Southwestern Virginia

Headquarters
January 10, 1865

General:

I have previously stated to you the importance of clearing the mountains & country in your department of deserters, absentees, &c. I hope you will now be able to accomplish it. No time should be lost in setting on foot the complete organization of your command & the regulation of all matters pertaining to your department.

A letter has recently been referred to me by the Secretary of War, from the Honorable C. G. Memminger, who is now residing at Flat Rock, North Carolina, giving a lamentable account of the sufferings of the citizens in that section of country, from the conduct of deserters, traitors, &c. I had previously instructed Genl Martin to employ all the force under his command, Cols Palmer's & Thomas' troops, in destroying these bandetti & their haunts. I have now repeated these instructions & suggested that a combined movement might be made to advantage by the reserves in South Carolina, his own troops in North Carolina & a portion of yours, & directed him to communicate with you on the subject. If nothing should prevent & the plan be practicable, I request that you will cooperate with him.

Very resply

R. E. Lee
Genl

933   To JAMES A. SEDDON
Secretary of War
TELEGRAM

Headquarters, Army of Northern Virginia
January 11, 1865

THERE IS NOTHING WITHIN REACH OF THIS ARMY TO BE IMPRESSED. THE COUNTRY IS SWEPT CLEAR. OUR ONLY RELIANCE IS UPON THE RAILROADS. WE HAVE BUT TWO DAYS' SUPPLIES.

R. E. Lee

934   To JEFFERSON DAVIS
Richmond, Virginia

Headquarters near Petersburg
January 15, 1865

Mr. President:
I have seen Genl Hampton & concluded under the discretion given me in your letter of the 11th to detach Genl [Matthew Calbraith] Butler's division of cavalry to S. C. for service there this winter, but it is with the understanding that it is to return to me in the spring in time for the opening of the campaign. Without this condition, I think it would be disadvantageous to send it. May I ask you to impose this condition & let me know. In the meantime I will get the men ready to start. Genl Hampton thinks he can mount the men in S. C. & will telegraph to the Governor to collect horses, which the men will buy if placed at reasonable prices. The horses here will be placed in camp in N. C. or with Major Paxton at Lancaster, & the men transported by rail. If the Governor can give no assurance of their procuring mounts, or if Hampton cannot make arrangements for subsistence of the horses, I will not send them. I think Hampton will be of service in mounting his men & arousing the spirit

& strength of the State & otherwise do good. I will therefore send him. He will report the state of affairs on his arrival & then you can determine, whether it will be necessary to take any steps in reference to him. He will take immediate measures to place Butler in the field & I desire Young's brigade to be ordered to join Butler. I understand Young prefers commanding his brigade to a division under [General Joseph] Wheeler.

Genl Bragg [commanding in North Carolina] telegraphs at 8 p.m. yesterday from Sugar Loaf, that the enemy succeeded on the night of the 13th in extending a line across the Peninsula between him & Fort Fisher. That upon close examination he thought it too strong to attack with his inferior force. Fisher has been reinforced with sufficient veterans to make it safe & that the width of the river is such that the enemy cannot controul it even with artillery of which he has as yet landed none. Bombardment of Fisher on the 14th light. Weather continues fine & sea smooth. I have telegraphed in reply to concentrate his forces & endeavour to dislodge him. That he will land his cannon & besiege Fisher. He gives no estimate of strength of enemy, & makes no call for reinforcements.

With great respect, your obt servt

R. E. LEE
Genl

935   To JAMES A. SEDDON
Secretary of War

Headquarters, Army of Northern Virginia
January 16, 1865

Sir:

I have the honor to acknowledge the receipt of your letter of the 12th instant, with its enclosures. I thank you for your prompt and energetic measures for the relief of the army.

As soon as I was informed of the breach in our railroad connections I issued the enclosed appeal to the farmers and others in the country accessible by our remaining communications, and sent Maj Tannahill to them to obtain all the supplies that could be procured. I am glad to say that so far as I know the crisis in relation to this matter is now past.

Very respectfully, your obt servt

R. E. LEE
Genl

(ENCLOSURE)

Headquarters, Army of Northern Virginia
January 12, 1865

To the Farmers East of the Blue Ridge
and South of James River:

The recent heavy freshet having destroyed a portion of the railroad from Danville to Goldsboro, and thereby cut off temporarily necessary supplies for the Army of Northern Virginia, an appeal is respectfully made to the farmers, millers, and other citizens to furnish, with all possible promptness, whatever breadstuffs, meat (fresh or salt), and molasses, they can spare. Such citizens as Major Robt Tannahill may select are asked to act as agents in purchasing and collecting supplies through the various officers connected with the Commissary Department on the lines of railroad.

Arrangements have been made to pay promptly for all supplies delivered under this appeal, or to return the same in kind as soon as practicable.

R. E. LEE

936   To GENERAL WILLIAM TERRY
Commanding Stonewall Brigade

Turnbull's
January 16, 1865

General:

I enclose you $100 sent by a friend to the Stonewall Brigade, who desires it to be laid out by you in procuring for it some substantial benefit. He does not wish his name disclosed, & has been prompted to this step by seeing in the papers that the brigade was suffering.

From its conduct & association this brigade has acquired the affection of the whole country & stands high in the esteem of the army. I should very much regret that it should suffer for anything that could be legitimately provided. I had not heard that it was in want, & had hoped it had not been called on to undergo more than what all must suffer in a cause such as we are engaged in. I know that & more will be cheerfully borne by it in accomplishing our purpose. I would however be glad if you would inform me if any suffering exists that I can relieve.

With great respect, your obt servt

R. E. LEE
Genl

937   To HIS WIFE
                 Richmond, Virginia

                                                    Petersburg
                                                January 17, 1865
My Dear Mary:
    I send Major Janney's statement of the socks & gloves received. He
seems to have gone back to the commencement of the contribution this
fall. Before distribution he has to see in what brigades the men are in
most need. This takes some time in the beginning, but goes on rapidly
when commenced. I return the bag. I am glad to see Custis for a little
while & to learn that you are all well. Give much love to the girls. I am
very glad that little Annie is improving. I hope she will soon be well
again & never be sick more. Tell Mildred that I felt quite flattered at
Custis' visit, but I learned about 10 o'clock last night that Miss Jenny
Fairfax & a bevy of young damsels came down in the same train, to attend some festival at an artillery camp. That is the way children hum-
bug their fathers.

                                                    [R. E. LEE]

938   To JEFFERSON DAVIS
                 Richmond, Virginia

                            Headquarters, Army of Northern Virginia
                                                January 19, 1865
Mr. President:
    I received tonight your letter of the 18th instant stating that it had
been reported to you that I had changed my opinion in regard to the extension of my duties, while retaining command of the Army of Northern
Virginia. I do not know how such a report originated, nor am I aware of
having said anything to have authorized it. I do not think that while
charged with my present command embracing Virginia & N. C. & the
immediate controul of this army I could direct the operations of the
armies in the S. Atlantic States. If I had the ability I would not have
the time. The arrangement of the details of this army extended as it is,
providing for its necessities & directing its operations engrosses all my
time & still I am unable to accomplish what I desire & see to be necessary.
I could not therefore propose to undertake more.
    I am greatly gratified by the expression of your confidence in offer-
ing me the extensive command proposed in your letter, but I must state

that with the addition of the immediate command of this army I do not think I could accomplish any good. I am willing to undertake any service to which you think proper to assign me, but I do not wish you to be misled as to the extent of my capacity.

I am with great respect, your obt servt

R. E. LEE
Genl

939   To WILLIAM P. MILES
Richmond, Virginia

Headquarters, Army of Northern Virginia
January 19, 1865

Sir:

I received tonight your letter of the 18th instant enclosing a telegram from the Governor of South Carolina requesting me to use my influence to send troops to that State. As far as I know the views of the Government, no representations will be necessary to cause troops to be transferred to South Carolina, if any could be obtained. I can only say I shall be most happy to do everything in my power to defend the State, but I do not know where to obtain the troops. Concurring in all you state with reference to the importance of preserving the port of Charleston, defeating the army of Sherman, and cheering the spirits of the people, I do not think that this would be accomplished by so weakening this army as to enable the enemy to disperse it, and achieve what he has been struggling to obtain the whole campaign. It seems to me it would only aggravate our disasters by adding the loss of Richmond to that of Charleston, should it fall. Although as you state, the ground is unfavorable in this region for military operations at this time, yet the two armies are in such close proximity to each other, that a hard frost would make the ground practicable for the movement of artillery if necessary, and enable Genl Grant to move his whole army against us. I have been obliged to detach troops to Wilmington to resist the movement against that place, and in addition to the brigade sent to South Carolina, have ordered Butler's division of cavalry to Genl Hardee. It will be impossible for me to send sufficient troops from this army to oppose Sherman's, and at the same time resist Grant.

Sherman's army alone is equal to this, and I can see no benefit from inviting disaster at both places. If the people in South Carolina & Georgia would turn out in all their strength, aided by the troops now in that department, the advance of Sherman ought to be checked. Unless they do, or troops from Hood's army can be got there in time, I do not see how his progress can be arrested. Should Charleston fall, as painful as the thought is to me, I cannot concur in the opinion of Governor Magrath that our cause would be lost or the contest ended. Should the force you propose be detached from this army, it would take half its strength. You can judge then, as well as myself, what would be our prospect of success in either State. Nor in my opinion would it be possible to conceal the movement from the enemy. If he did not learn it through spies and traitors, it would be published in the papers & thus reach him. It was through the Savannah papers that he ascertained the movement of Bragg to Georgia, and was induced to precipitate the attack upon Wilmington. I have given my opinion upon the matters presented in your letter, but I need not tell you, that the transfer of troops from this army to any part of the country does not depend upon me, but rests with the War Department. Any troops it may order I will cheerfully send. I return to you Governor Magrath's telegram.

I have the honor to be with great respect, your obt servt

R. E. LEE
Genl

940   To JAMES A. SEDDON
Secretary of War

Headquarters, Army of Northern Virginia
January 27, 1865

Sir:

I have the honor to call your attention to the alarming frequency of desertions from this army. You will perceive, from the accompanying papers, that fifty-six deserted from Hill's corps in three days. I have endeavored to ascertain the causes, and think that the insufficiency of food and non-payment of the troops have more to do with the dissatisfaction among the troops than anything else. All commanding officers concur in this opinion. I have no doubt that there is suffering for want of food. The ration is too small for men who have to undergo so much exposure and labor as ours.

I know there are great difficulties in procuring supplies, but I cannot help thinking that with proper energy, intelligence, & experience on the part of the Commissary Department a great deal more could be accomplished. There is enough in the country, I believe, if it was properly sought for. I do not see why the supplies that are collected from day to day could not, by intelligent effort, be collected in such a manner as to have more on hand at a given time. The fact that they are collected at all is proof that they exist, and it must be possible to gather more in a given time than is now done. It will not answer to reduce the ration in order to make up for deficiencies in the Subsistence Department. The proper remedy is increased effort, greater experience in business, and intelligent management. It may be that all is done that can be, but I am not satisfied that we cannot do more. I think the efficiency of the army demands an increase of the ration, and I trust that no measure will be neglected that offers a chance of improvement.

Very respectfully, your obt servt

R. E. LEE
Genl

941   To HIS WIFE
Richmond, Virginia

Turnbull's
January 29, 1865

My Dear Mary:

You will see by Major Janney's acknowledgements that both of your bags have arrived safely & that all the socks previously received have been distributed. The bag containing the 60 pairs, jacket, shoes, &c., was sent by express which caused its delay. I return the bags. The straw bag has pretty much come to grass & is no longer reliable. I have no photographs. Daughter forgot them. We are enjoying ice water in abundance. Our neighbours also possess the same luxury. The Patapsco is frozen, I understand so that steamers cannot ply between Baltimore & Norfolk. The Potomac must also be frozen, if it is true that the James is closed. If our men had only clothes & abundant food, I should not care for the cold. Give much love to the girls & all the household. I heard from Fitzhugh recently. All well. Tell Margaret & Carrie when tired of their beaux they had better come to see me.

With much affection, truly yours

R. E. LEE

942
To HIS WIFE
Richmond, Virginia

Near Petersburg
February 3, 1865

My Dear Mary:

I have received your note of the 1st. I am very much obliged to Mr. Mead for the trouble he has taken in relation to the Lee genealogy. I have no desire to have it published & do not think it would afford sufficient interest beyond the immediate family, to compensate for the expense. I think the money had better be applied to relieve the poor.

I send you the memo of socks received by Major Janney. There was one pair less than you stated. The bag was returned yesterday during my absence or I should have written. I return the photographs as you desire. I do not see the advantage, however, of sending to me to be returned. I heard from Fitzhugh & Rob yesterday, all well. I grieve over the death of my darling little niece. How our pleasures in life go out. A bright joyous & affectionate spirit has left us. May God have mercy on us & make us ready & anxious to follow her. I did not write the sad news to the boys or impart it to Mrs. Pegram whom I met yesterday at a review of Pegram's division. I had not the heart. She looked very happy & said she was having splendid times. Long may it last. I can hardly see. Give much to my dear daughters.

Very affly & truly

R. E. LEE

943
To GENERAL SAMUEL COOPER
Adjutant and Inspector General

Headquarters
Petersburg
February 4, 1865

General:

I received your telegram of the 1st instant announcing my confirmation by the Senate as General-in-Chief of the Armies of the Confederate States. I am indebted alone to the kindness of His Excellency the President for my nomination to this high and arduous office, and wish I had the ability to fill it to advantage. As I have received no in-

structions as to my duties, I do not know what he desires me to undertake.

I am respectfully, your obedient servant

R. E. LEE
General

944   To GENERAL SAMUEL COOPER
Adjutant and Inspector General
TELEGRAM

Headquarters, Army of Northern Virginia
February 6, 1865

THE ENEMY MOVED IN STRONG FORCE YESTERDAY TO HATCHER'S RUN.
PART OF HIS INFANTRY, WITH GREGG'S CAVALRY, CROSSED & PROCEEDED ON
THE VAUGHAN ROAD, THE INFANTRY TO CAT TAIL CREEK, THE CAVALRY TO DIN-
WIDDIE COURT HOUSE, WHERE ITS ADVANCE ENCOUNTERED A PORTION OF OUR
CAVALRY & RETIRED. IN THE AFTERNOON PARTS OF HILL'S & GORDON'S TROOPS
DEMONSTRATED AGAINST THE ENEMY ON THE LEFT OF HATCHER'S RUN, NEAR
ARMSTRONG'S MILL. FINDING HIM ENTRENCHED THEY WERE WITHDRAWN
AFTER DARK. DURING THE NIGHT THE FORCE THAT HAD ADVANCED BEYOND
THE CREEK RETURNED TO IT & WERE REPORTED TO BE RECROSSING.

THIS MORNING [GENERAL WILLIAM J.] PEGRAM'S DIVISION MOVED DOWN
THE RIGHT BANK OF THE CREEK TO RECONNOITER, WHEN IT WAS VIGOROUSLY
ATTACKED. THE BATTLE WAS OBSTINATELY CONTESTED SEVERAL HOURS, BUT
GENL PEGRAM BEING KILLED, WHILE BRAVELY ENCOURAGING HIS MEN, & COL
[JOHN S.] HOFFMAN WOUNDED, SOME CONFUSION OCCURRED, & THE DIVISION
WAS PRESSED BACK TO ITS ORIGINAL POSITION. EVANS' DIVISION, ORDERED BY
GENL GORDON TO SUPPORT PEGRAM'S, CHARGED THE ENEMY & FORCED HIM
BACK, BUT WAS IN TURN COMPELLED TO RETIRE. MAHONE'S DIVISION ARRIV-
ING, ENEMY WAS DRIVEN RAPIDLY TO HIS DEFENCES ON HATCHER'S RUN. OUR
LOSS IS REPORTED TO BE SMALL, THAT OF THE ENEMY NOT SUPPOSED GREAT.

R. E. LEE
Genl

945 To JAMES A. SEDDON
Secretary of War

Headquarters, Army of Northern Virginia
February 8, 1865

Sir:

All the disposable force of the right wing of the army has been operating against the enemy beyond Hatcher's Run since Sunday. Yesterday, the most inclement day of the winter, they had to be retained in line of battle, having been in the same condition the two previous days and nights. I regret to be obliged to state that under these circumstances, heightened by assaults and fire of the enemy, some of the men had been without meat for three days, and all were suffering from reduced rations and scant clothing, exposed to battle, cold, hail, and sleet. I have directed Colonel Cole, Chief Commissary, who reports that he has not a pound of meat at his disposal, to visit Richmond and see if nothing can be done. If some change is not made and the Commissary Department reorganized, I apprehend dire results. The physical strength of the men, if their courage survives, must fail under this treatment. Our cavalry has to be dispersed for want of forage. Fitz Lee's and Lomax's divisions are scattered because supplies cannot be transported where their services are required. I had to bring William H. F. Lee's division forty miles Sunday night to get him in position. Taking these facts in connection with the paucity of our numbers, you must not be surprised if calamity befalls us. According to reports of prisoners we were opposed on Hatcher's Run by the Second and Fifth Corps, part of the Ninth, one division of the Sixth, and Gregg's division (three brigades) of cavalry. It was also reported that the Twenty-third Corps (Schofield's) reached City Point the 5th, and that it was present; but this is not confirmed by other reports. At last accounts it was stated to be on the Potomac, delayed by ice. A scout near Alexandria reports it is to march on Gordonsville, General Baker on Kinston. I think it more probable it will join Grant here.

With great respect, your obedient servant

R. E. LEE
General

946　　GENERAL ORDERS, NO. 1

Headquarters, Confederate Army
February 9, 1865

In obedience to General Orders, No. 3, Adjutant and Inspector General's Office, February 6, 1865, I assume command of the military forces of the Confederate States. Deeply impressed with the difficulties and responsibility of the position, and humbly invoking the guidance of Almighty God, I rely for success upon the courage and fortitude of the army, sustained by the patriotism and firmness of the people, confident that their united efforts, under the blessing of Heaven, will secure peace and independence. The headquarters of the army, to which all special reports and communications will be addressed, will be, for the present, with the Army of Northern Virginia. The stated and regular returns and reports of each army and department will be forwarded, as heretofore, to the office of the Adjutant and Inspector General.

R. E. LEE
General

947　　To WILLIAM P. MILES
Richmond, Virginia

Headquarters
February 9, 1865

My Dear Sir:
I regret I cannot furnish you with a copy of your letter enclosing the telegram from Governor Magrath. My position is so uncertain & means of preserving papers so insecure that for fear of confidential letters falling into wrong hands, I am in the habit of destroying them after acting on them. Supposing you had retained a copy of your letter, it & the telegram was thus treated. I hope that another copy is accessible to you & that you will suffer no inconvenience.

Very resply, your obt servt

R. E. LEE
Genl

948   To JEFFERSON DAVIS
Richmond, Virginia

Headquarters
Petersburg
February 9, 1865

Mr. President:

I have today, in obedience to orders issued from the Adjutant and Inspector General's Office, entered upon the duties of the office of General-in-Chief. I know I am indebted entirely to your indulgence and kind consideration for this honorable position. I must beg you to continue these same feelings to me in the future and allow me to refer to you at all times for counsel and advice. I cannot otherwise hope to be of service to you or the country. If I can relieve you from a portion of the constant labor and anxiety which now presses upon you, and maintain a harmonious action between the great armies, I shall be more than compensated for the addition to my present burdens. I must, however, rely upon the several commanders for the conduct of the military operations with which they are charged, and hold them responsible. In the event of their neglect or failure I must ask for their removal. As it is necessary to bring every man back to the ranks that we can, I beg leave to submit for your approval the following proposition: To allow me to proclaim by your authority a pardon to all deserters and absentees who will return to their regiments or companies within thirty days from the date of its publication at the headquarters of the military departments, with the assurance that this will be the last act of amnesty extended for such offenses, and with the promise that hereafter all such offenders will receive the full sentence of the courts upon their conviction, without suspension, remission, or delay, from which there need be no appeal for clemency. I propose to except from this act of forgiveness those who, having been once pardoned, have repeated the offense, and all those who have entered the service of the enemy. All who may desert after the publication of the order shall receive quick and merited punishment. This may be of some service and do some good. It is the only method that I can propose to cause the return of our absentees, and perhaps if done at this time, when we may expect a reaction of public sentiment, the people at home may force them out. The reason why I think it better to issue such an order under my name and by your authority is that you having before proclaimed a pardon, should you repeat it many might hereafter persuade themselves that it would again be offered them, and be again tempted to desert. I would go up to consult with you in person in this and other matters, but I do not feel at liberty to leave at this time. May I request you to give me an early answer to this proposition, as there is no time to be lost.

With great respect, your obedient servant

R. E. LEE
General

949   To HIS WIFE
                     Richmond, Virginia

Petersburg
February 11, 1865

My Dear Mary:
    I send Major Janney's receipt for the socks & am glad that the count is correct. I also return the bag. You must keep the turkey & eat it when you desire. I wish to come up as soon as I can but cannot say when. You can then tell me if it was good, which will suit me as well. Fitz Lee came down this morning & returns this evening. He will give you accounts of us. Give love to the girls & Margaret.

Truly yours
R. E. LEE

950   To HIS WIFE
                     Richmond, Virginia

Turnbull's
February 12, 1865

My Dear Mary:
    After writing to you yesterday by the bag, your note (without date) about the dog arrived. I know nothing about him except that he would be very out of place following me in a campaign. He would be exposed to danger, hunger & thirst, & I think he would be equally miserable cooped up in Richmond. I therefore propose, if you think it would be agreable to him, to send him to Dr. Cocke, where he could roam in the country & sport in the James. Has the doctor any dogs, or does he like them? If you can do nothing else with him I will take him here & let him take his chance. I enclose a note received from kind Kitty Stiles, who has sent me another set of jackets, some catsup & other things

which I have not yet examined. It will give you some information of our friends in Savannah. I also send for your perusal a letter from a Mrs. Yatman whom I do not know, that you may know what brave patriotic women are in the Confederacy. The latter part of her letter is a pure mistake into which she has been good naturedly led by some quizzing soldiers. Burn the letter after perusal. Love to all.

Affly & truly yours

R. E. LEE

951   To ALEXANDER H. STEVENS, ET AL.
Richmond, Virginia

Headquarters, Armies of the Confederate States
February 13, 1865

Gentlemen:

I had yesterday the honour to receive your letter of the 4th instant recommending the assignment of Genl Joseph E. Johnston to the command of the Army of Tennessee. The three corps of that army have been ordered to South Carolina & are now under the command of Genl Beauregard, two of them having already arrived in that department. I entertain a high opinion of Genl Johnston's capacity, but think a continual change of commanders is very injurious to any troops & tends greatly to their disorganization. At this time as far as I understand the condition of affairs, an engagement with the enemy may be expected any day & a change now would be particularly hazardous. Genl Beauregard is well known to the citizens of South Carolina as well as to the troops of the Army of Tennessee, & I would recommend that it be certainly ascertained that a change was necessary before it was made.

I do not consider that my appointment as Genl in Chief of the Armies of the Confederate States confers the right which you assume belongs to it, nor is it proper that it should. I can only employ such troops & officers as may be placed at my disposal by the War Department. Those withheld or relieved from service are not at my disposal.

I have the honour to be your most obt servt

R. E. LEE
Genl

952   CIRCULAR

Headquarters, Army of Northern Virginia
February 18, 1865

General:
All leaves of absence and furloughs to go south of North Carolina
are suspended, and you are desired not to forward any applications for
such leaves or furloughs until further orders.
By command of General R. E. Lee:

W. H. TAYLOR
Assistant Adjutant General

953   To HIS WIFE
Richmond, Virginia

Petersburg
February 18, 1865

My Dear Mary:
I enclose Major Janney's count of the socks & return the bag. You
will see that your count is right. I arrived safely with all my property &
find my table as usual filled with letters, which I must try & work off.
I enclose a note to Miss Norma.
Give much love to every body. Tell Margaret I am very uneasy.

Truly & affly

R. E. LEE

P.S. The other bag which you sent by express has not arrived.

R. E. L.

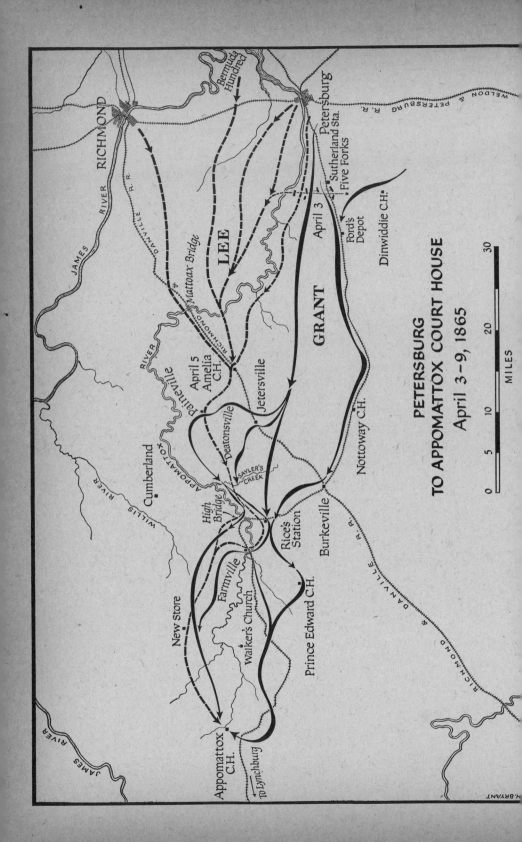

PETERSBURG
TO APPOMATTOX COURT HOUSE
April 3–9, 1865

MILES

0   5   10   20   30

H. BRYANT

RICHMOND

JAMES RIVER

Bermuda Hundred

Petersburg
Sutherland Sta.
Five Forks
Ford's Depot
Dinwiddie C.H.

WELDON & PETERSBURG R.R.

DANVILLE R.R.

Mattoax Bridge

LEE

April 3

GRANT

April 5
Amelia C.H.

Jetersville

Deatonsville

SAYLER'S
CREEK

Nottoway C.H.

Burkeville

Rice's Station

Prince Edward C.H.

RICHMOND & DANVILLE R.R.

Paineville

APPOMATTOX RIVER

WILLIS RIVER

Cumberland

High Bridge

Farmville

New Store

Walker's Church

Appomattox C.H.

to Lynchburg

JAMES RIVER

CHAPTER SEVENTEEN

Appomattox

FEBRUARY—APRIL 1865

"I shall endeavour . . . to fight to the end"

BEGINNING FEBRUARY 19, Lee's revealing letters reflect the assertion of his sense of duty over his realistic appraisal. In this division, his correspondence also reflects a desperation in military thinking quite unlike his thoughts upon his personal life. By his February 22 letter to Longstreet, it is clear he accepted the impossibility of maintaining defensive lines which had stretched to more than thirty miles. Longstreet, also accepting the inevitable, talked with Major General Ord on the subject of arranging terms for the cessation of hostilities. Upon Ord's encouragement, Lee wrote Grant on March 2 to propose a meeting for discussing means of ending the war. Grant, on the grounds that only the President of the United States possessed the authority for conducting a conference, declined to meet Lee.

Previously Lincoln had revealed in the Hampton Roads Peace Conference (February 3) that no peace terms would be discussed with the states in rebellion until Confederate forces laid down their arms: the South must first surrender. With this knowledge, prior to his letter to Grant, Lee had held a private conversation with Virginia's Senator R. M. T. Hunter, who had been a member of the peace conference. Lee urged him to offer a resolution in the Senate that would obtain better terms than, as Hunter reported Lee as saying, "were likely to be given after a surrender." Hunter claimed that Davis had already impugned his motives for seeking peace terms, and told Lee, "if he thought the chances for success desperate, I thought he ought to say so to the President." Though Lee held frequent conversations with Davis during February, it is unlikely that he ever brought himself to introduce a subject which would be so distasteful to the President.

During the same period, Secretary of War Seddon, despairing of the cause, resigned on February 5, and the next day Breckinridge was appointed to the office. Almost immediately, he went to Hunter with the same advice as Lee's. Hunter reported that he told Breckinridge, "I saw no hope of peace unless the President would pledge himself to co-operate, which I hardly thought he would do." As Lee's attitude, then, was supported by Longstreet, the army's senior general officer, by Breckinridge, a former general in the War Department, and Hunter, a powerful Senate leader (the latter two of whom stood to lose heavily), the crux of the matter was that men in a position to know recognized that the South was defeated, but no one was willing to assume the responsibility of trying to convince Davis of this.

Against this background, Lee received Grant's negative reply of March 4, and all the forlorn stratagems he considered from late February must be interpreted within his acceptance of the hopelessness of their position. On February 1, Sherman's army started northward from Savannah, moved through South Carolina against little organized opposition (taking Charleston from the landslide on the 17th), and in March entered North Carolina. With Wilmington gone, the Federal forces on the Carolina coast combined with the army that had finished Hood in Tennessee to form a new army, commanded by Schofield, and moved westward from the coast to the line of the Weldon Railroad. Against these two armies, a small force under Hardee and survivors of the Army of Tennessee were collected, along with oddments of militia. Lee, in one of his few acts as general-in-chief, appointed Joe Johnston commanding general.

As Johnston fell back before Sherman, his force diminished steadily, with men dropping out along the way, and by March 23 Johnston estimated that he had no more than 13,500 men in the field. On that day, Sherman and Schofield met at Goldsboro, North Carolina, uniting 80,000 troops only 120 miles south of Lee. Lee's returns for March 1 showed 56,000 men of all arms, including the garrison gunners on the stationary artillery in the fortifications outside Richmond, but the desertions and the absent-sick after March 1 are not computable, and this drain was heavy. Grant fielded 100,000. For Lee and Johnston (who admitted that he could "do no more than annoy" Sherman) to attempt to carry on the foredoomed struggle, the only logical plan was a junction of their armies.

For practical purposes the Confederacy was reduced to the 120 miles between Grant and Sherman, with Sherman moving northward in the slow closing of the vise. Since Grant was held outside Lee's fortified lines, the obvious course was for Lee to move south away from Grant and unite with Johnston against Sherman before Grant came up. This scheme was logical only in the abstract of strategy. Tactically it was impossible. Lee's men and horses could not conceivably outdistance Grant's well-conditioned army, and under any forced marching the army would physically disintegrate.

Yet, in the thinking of desperation, where realities became ignored, Lee attempted an even more far-fetched stratagem. He planned an attack on what Gordon believed to be a vulnerable sector of the Federal works, with the purpose of striking a blow at the northern end of Grant's lines sufficiently decisive to cause him to contract at the southern end. With Grant's lines shortened, Lee might hold his own works with fewer men and send some picked troops to Johnston. The attack on Hare's Hill (Fort Stedman) March 25 culminated all previous futilities on the offensive. Gordon's men entered the Federal lines well enough in the surprise assault but, overwhelmed within the works, the troops could only surrender or try to make it back to their own lines. Between 3000 and 4000 did not make it back, losing Lee about 10 per cent of his infantry. General Lee was not forthright in writing Breckinridge of this costly failure, and his letter to Davis was in the realm of strategy unrelated to actualities, as the nearness of the enemy to his headquarters and the imminence of disaster caused him to be very guarded about putting details of numbers on paper.

After Fort Stedman, he could only hope to retire his army from the thirty miles of works before the enemy stormed the weakly held lines. However, Grant started to move on March 29, stretching farther to the southwest beyond the heavy fortifications. Sheridan's cavalry had returned from the Valley, leaving a swath of destruction, and combined with Warren's V Corps in the movement. On March 30, Lee stretched his thin lines thinner and, beyond the last light works, collected a force of about 10,500 infantry and cavalry at Five Forks — an intersection of five roads. Pickett was in command, with three of his brigades, filled up with last-ditch conscripts, and two brigades from Bushrod Johnson's battered division.

On March 31 Pickett moved out boldly enough, and drove Sheridan back to Dinwiddie Court House. That night, in a driving rain, Pickett retired to Five Forks and placed the men in an indifferent defensive position. On the 31st coordination had failed between Sheridan and Warren, but on April 1 the combined force moved against Five Forks while Pickett and Fitz Lee, then chief of cavalry, were away from the lines eating some freshly caught shad which Tom Rosser had baked. Had the three generals been present, they could not have contained the weight hurled at the lines of physically weak men, with segments demoralized by conscripts and absence of company officers. However, had the general officers been on the field, alert and determined, Lee's right need not have caved in so quickly and completely as in the disorder at Five Forks, where most of the infantry with Pickett was captured.

With his right turned, for Lee the issue was reduced to immediate escape. His withdrawal was complicated by the enemy's early morning push on Sunday, April 2, which broke his lines west of Petersburg, separating the troops beyond Hatcher's Run. A. P. Hill left a sickbed to ride to the point of the break for a personal reconnaissance, and, calling on two Federal stragglers to surrender, was shot dead from his horse. Lee's telegrams to Richmond advised the authorities to evacuate the capital. As this eventuality had not been properly prepared for, the President and his cabinet fled south in a rush for the last trains out on the Richmond & Danville, leaving the city to the mobs and the flames that resulted from the foolish order to burn the government warehouses.

Lee's problem was to hold the Petersburg lines during the day of the 2nd until he could cross his survivors that night north of the Appomattox. This was achieved, with Longstreet having joined him with Field's division from north of the James. During the night of the 2nd-3rd, Lee led the main force, of less than 15,000 infantry, with the guns and breaking-down wagons, westward, with detailed plans for uniting his other scattered forces. Mahone, who had replaced Pickett at Bermuda Hundred (called the Howlett Line), withdrew during the early morning of the 3rd and pushed westward. Ewell, with Kershaw's division, Gary's little cavalry brigade, and the oddments in the Richmond defenses under Custis Lee, crossed south of the James and angled southwest toward Amelia Court House. Fragments of Heth's and Wilcox's divisions of Hill's corps, of Pickett's division and Anderson's command — all those isolated west of the break — escaped westward mostly as individuals and, with the cavalry, gradually fell in with the converging units on the way to Amelia.

Lee was dutifully holding to the strategic line of joining Joe Johnston. Amelia was a station on the Richmond & Danville where Lee expected to find supplies, and from which he planned to follow the railroad to Danville. Longstreet's van, which then included Gordon in command of the Second Corps remnants, reached Amelia on the morning of the 4th, and that night Ewell arrived. But no supplies had been sent from Richmond; instead, the waiting boxes contained ammunition for the guns. A frantic scouring of the surrounding countryside brought in practically nothing, and lost Lee the day he had gained on Grant.

With the army facing starvation, Lee planned to move southwest along the railroad, ordering supplies sent up from Danville. However, because of his delay during the 5th, the Federal cavalry crossed his line of march, with infantry coming up in support. His men were too feeble and his scattered units too disorganized (brigades reported at 150 strength) to consider trying to drive the enemy aside. Improvising, he turned west from Amelia, aiming for Farmville on the Southside Railroad to Lynchburg, from where supplies might be sent. His last order on the retreat, sent to Gordon at four in the morning of the 6th, outlined the line of the new march in as exact detail as on any day in the life of the army. Though there was no correspondence to show it, Lee's decisions, which had always been based on a consideration of supplies, were at last motivated entirely by a need to save his army from starvation. The emaciated men fell steadily from the ranks and guns were abandoned as the poor horses collapsed.

As the columns crawled westward on the 6th, Longstreet led the van with Field's division, then the skeletal divisions of Heth and Wilcox, followed by Mahone's division, which had not been engaged in any of the last days' calamities. The middle of the column, with the bulk of the wagons, was led by Anderson, with the few survivors of Pickett's and Bushrod Johnson's divisions. Next came Ewell, with Kershaw's division at 1600 and Custis Lee's so-called division — the Richmond local defense troops, the artillerists from the stationary guns and a naval "battalion." After the last of the wagons, Gordon followed as rear guard. In one of those breakdowns in coordination inevitable among beaten, exhausted troops, the middle column cut itself off from the van and the rear guard. Attacked from three sides in the shallow valley through which ran Sayler's Creek, Anderson's and Ewell's forces were obliterated as organized units. Most of the men surrendered, including one-legged Ewell and Lee's oldest son. Isolated Gordon fought his way through with heavy losses to fall in on Mahone, and the army consisted only of a van and rear guard.

On the 7th, the disintegrating force staggered through Farmville where, on recrossing the Appomattox River, negligence at the bridges caused more casualties, confusion and loss of time. That night came Grant's first letter to Lee, written at five o'clock but delivered several hours later.

General:
    The results of the last week must convince you of the hopelessness of further resistance on the part of the Army of Northern Virginia in this struggle. I feel that it is so, and regard it as my duty to shift from myself the responsibility of any further effusion of blood, by asking of you the surrender of that portion of the C. S. Army known as the Army of Northern Virginia.

Lee showed the letter to Longstreet, who quoted himself as saying "Not yet." Apparently in agreement with Longstreet, Lee wrote to Grant and inquired about the terms for a possible end of hostilities. The next day, the 8th, the ghost of an army stumbled ahead through the warm day, heading for Appomattox Station, where supplies might be expected from Lynchburg. During the afternoon, Gordon, then in advance, camped one mile away from Appomattox Court House, two miles north of the railroad station. Wagons and artillery stretched ahead of him to the area of the courthouse. Behind Gordon, the column of troops and guns stretched only five miles to the end of Longstreet's rear guard.

Early that night came another letter from Grant. Graciously phrased, Grant's message said, in effect, that the only terms were for Lee's troops to lay down their arms and be paroled. He added: "I will meet you, or will designate any officers to meet any officers you may name for the same purpose, at any point agreeable to you, for the purpose of arranging definitely the terms upon which the surrender of the Army of Northern Virginia will be received."

Again Lee said, "Not yet." He replied to Grant that he would meet him at ten o'clock the next morning, but not "with a view to surrender the Army of Northern Virginia."

Shortly after Lee wrote his April 8 letter to Grant, he learned that the enemy was across his front. Moving by the more direct route south of the Appomattox, which Lee had used to protect his left flank, the well-conditioned Federals had reached Appomattox Station before his men. Those in front were only part of Grant's army. The rest was pressing on his rear.

As never when he made decisions of grand strategy, of maneuver and major battles, he called in Longstreet and Gordon, of the infantry, and his nephew Fitz Lee, of the cavalry, for a council. Earlier in the day he had been told by his old friend Pendleton that a group of officers had authorized him to advise Lee that they believed he should open negotiations for surrender, and perhaps the general wished to know if his ranking subordinates shared this attitude. They did not. The group decision was to try to break through at daylight. If that failed — then there would be no alternative.

Fittingly, Lee's army ended its career with an attack. For a while, the cavalry and Gordon's small force of infantry drove the enemy. Then, west of the courthouse, the desperate assault force was enclosed on three sides by an ever-growing enemy. Gordon sent an urgent message to Lee that unless he could get help from Longstreet he was done. As Longstreet was at that point holding off two corps, if redoubtable Gordon admitted that he could not continue without help, it was all over.

At eight-thirty Lee rode toward his picket line behind a flag-of-truce party, intending to keep what he regarded as his ten o'clock engagement with Grant. Instead, he met a messenger from Grant, who had called off the meeting under the terms presented in Lee's note of the night before. Again writing most considerately, Grant said, "As I have no authority to treat on the subject of peace, the meeting proposed for 10 A.M. today could lead to no good."

Then Lee dictated his April 9 note of capitulation, signed it, and a little later wrote another note asking for a suspension of hostilities. For a Federal attack order had not been rescinded and there were some generals, particularly men with Sheridan, like Custer, who were eager to build their own glory record as long as the hostilities were not officially ended.

After an anxious and anguished wait, Lee received shortly after noon Grant's note arranging a new meeting in the parlor of the house of the McLean family, a little way north of the courthouse. For the second time that Sunday, General Lee moved ahead toward the enemy lines, accompanied only by bespectacled Colonel Marshall (Walter Taylor begged off) and Sergeant Tucker, the courier who one week before had been the sole companion of A. P. Hill when he was killed. At the end of the ride he suffered, in front of a gathering of Federal general officers, the ordeal of surrender. Grant, a stranger to Lee, did everything possible to spare him humiliation.

The following day, April 10, Lee told Marshall what he wanted written as General Order 9. After he edited Marshall's draft, making several changes, the order which became famous as "Lee's Farewell Address" was given to clerks to copy and Lee to sign.

Having signed his own parole, Lee waited until the 12th for his men to sign theirs and, in front of the enemy, stack their arms and furl their flags. The total number paroled at Appomattox in the days following the surrender were 28,231, but, as Lee wrote Davis in his April 12 letter, only 7892 organized infantry with arms were present on April 9, when the army ceased to fight. The other men of all arms who drifted in during the following days were mostly those who had been physically unable to keep up with the march from Petersburg. At least a few were men who had been absent sick and came to Appomattox to receive their official paroles.

On April 15 Lee rode between the blackened walls of gutted buildings through the streets of Richmond to the red-brick house where his family was living a half block west of Capitol Square. Over the Capitol, in which he had accepted command of Virginia's forces, the United States flag was flying and Federal soldiers patrolled the streets. The war was not yet officially ended. Jefferson Davis, with a dwindling band of followers, was fleeing southward, hoping to escape to the West and continue the war "indefinitely." On April 20, lacking only two days of being a full four years since he had come to Richmond as a private citizen, Lee, as a paroled prisoner of war, at last wrote Jefferson Davis (then at Charlotte, North Carolina) that he recommended a "suspension of hostilities and the restoration of peace." For Lee the struggle for independence was over.

954   To JOHN C. BRECKINRIDGE
                              Secretary of War

                                                    Headquarters, Petersburg
                                                    February 19, 1865

Sir:
    The accounts received today from South & North Carolina are unfavourable. Genl Beauregard reports from Winnsboro that four corps of the enemy are advancing on that place, tearing up the Charlotte Railroad, & that they will probably reach Charlotte by the 24th & before he can concentrate his troops there. He states Genl Sherman will doubtless move thence on Greensboro, Danville, & Petersburg, or unite with Genl Schofield at Raleigh or Weldon.

    Genl Bragg reports that Genl Schofield is now preparing to advance from New Berne to Goldsboro, & that a strong expedition is moving against the Weldon Railroad at Rocky Mount. He says that little or no assistance can be received from the State of North Carolina. That exemptions & reorganizations under late laws have disbanded the State forces, & that they will not be ready for the field for some time.

    I do not see how Sherman can make the march anticipated by Genl Beauregard. But he seems to have everything his own way, which is calculated to cause apprehension. Genl Beauregard does not say what he proposes, or what he can do. I do not know where his troops are, or on what lines they are moving. His despatches only give movements of the enemy. He has a difficult task to perform under present circumstances, & one of his best officers, Genl Hardee, is incapacitated by sickness. I have also heard that his own health is indifferent, though he has never so stated. Should his strength give way, there is no one on duty in the department that could replace him, nor have I any one to send there. Genl J. E. Johnston is the only officer whom I know who has the confidence of the army & people, & if he was ordered to report to me I would place him there on duty. It is necessary to bring out all our strength, & I fear to unite our armies, as separately they do not seem able to make head against the enemy. Everything should be destroyed that cannot be removed out of the reach of Genls Sherman & Schofield.

Provisions must be accumulated in Virginia, & every man in all the States must be brought out. I fear it may be necessary to abandon all our cities, & preparation should be made for this contingency.

I have the honour to be, your obt servt

R. E. LEE
Genl

955   To JEFFERSON DAVIS
Richmond, Virginia

Headquarters
Petersburg
February 19, 1865

Mr. President:
Your despatch of yesterday suggesting that I repair to Genl Beauregard's headquarters to confer with him is received. He reports today from Winnsboro that four corps of the enemy are advancing on that place from Columbia & Alston, tearing up the Charlotte Railroad, & that they will probably reach Charlotte on the 24th, before his forces can concentrate there. He thinks Genl Sherman will thence move on Greensboro, Danville, & Petersburg, or, if short of supplies, on Raleigh & Weldon, to form a junction with Genl Schofield.

Genl Bragg reports a strong expedition moving on Weldon Railroad at Rocky Mount, & continued preparations for the advance from New Berne to Goldsboro & Raleigh. He says little or no assistance can be had from the State of N. C., that exemptions & reorganizations under late laws have disbanded the State forces, & that they will not be ready for some time.

From this condition of things there is nothing to intercept Sherman's or Schofield's march through the country except the want of supplies, nor, unless our troops can be concentrated, anything to oppose them but this army which will be unable to cope with the armies of Genls Grant, Sherman, & Schofield. I however cannot believe that Genl Sherman can make the march anticipated by Genl Beauregard if our troops can do anything. They can at least destroy or remove all provisions in his route, which I have again directed Genl Beauregard to do, & requested the cooperation of Governor Vance. Everything on his route & Schofield's should be removed. I am unacquainted with the local officers on the route & request proper instructions be given by the Adjutant & Inspector General. At the present rate of Beauregard's retreat, he will soon be within striking distance of the Roanoke, where from present appearances it seems is the first point at which the enemy can be brought to a stand. I fear Wilmington will have to be evacuated & Bragg fall back in the same direction, nor unless the enemy can be beaten, can Richmond be held. I think it prudent that preparations be made at all these points in anticipation of what may be necessary to be done. The cotton & tobacco in Richmond & Petersburg not necessary should be quietly removed also.

Genl Beauregard makes no mention of what he proposes or what he can do, or where his troops are. He does not appear from his despatches to be able to do much.

With great respect, your obt servt

R. E. LEE
Genl

956   To JOHN C. BRECKINRIDGE
Secretary of War

Headquarters, Petersburg
February 21, 1865

I have had the honour to receive your letter of yesterday's date. I have repeated the orders to the commanding officers to remove & destroy everything in enemy's route. In the event of the necessity of abandoning our position on the James River, I shall endeavour to unite the corps of the army about Burkeville (junction of South Side & Danville Railroads), so as to retain communication with the north & south as long as practicable, & also with the west. I should think Lynchburg, or some point west, the most advantageous place to which to remove stores from Richmond. This however is a most difficult point at this time to decide, & the place may have to be changed by circumstances.

It was my intention in my former letter to apply for Genl J. E. Johnston, that I might assign him to duty, should circumstances permit. I have had no official report of the condition of Genl Beauregard's health. It is stated from many sources to be bad. If he should break entirely down, it might be fatal. In that event I should have no one with whom to supply his place. I therefore respectfully request Genl Johnston may be ordered to report to me & that I may be informed where he is.

With great respect, your obt servt

R. E. LEE
Genl

957   To HIS WIFE
                                   Richmond, Virginia

                                                            Petersburg
                                                        February 21, 1865
My Dear Mary:
   After sending my note this morning I received from the Express
Office the bag of socks, the acknowledgement of which by Major Janney, I herewith enclose. You will see that your count was correct. You
will have to send down your offerings as soon as you can & bring your
works to a close, for I think Genl Grant will move against us soon,
within a week if nothing prevents, & no man can tell what may be the
result. Sherman & Schofield are both advancing & seem to have every
thing their own way, but trusting in a Merciful God, who does not always give the battle to the strong, I pray we may not be overwhelmed.
I shall however endeavour to do my duty & fight to the last. Should it
be necessary to abandon our position to prevent being surrounded, what
will you do? Will you remain or leave the city? You must consider the
question & make up your mind. You will be able to retain nothing in
the house, & I do not see how you can live, or where go. It is a fearful
condition & we must rely for guidance & protection upon a kind Providence. May it guard & comfort you. Give much love to all. Tell Daughter to give Lizzie the bag of cakes for her doll. They are all hearts. I
return the bag, which contained the socks.

                                                  Very truly & affly

                                                     R. E. LEE

958   To GENERAL JAMES LONGSTREET
                    Commanding North of James River

                                Headquarters, Confederate States Armies
                                                        February 22, 1865
General:
   Your letter of the 14th instant is received. It arrived during my
absence in Richmond, and has not been overlooked. I agree with you
entirely in believing that if we had gold we could get sufficient supplies for our army, but the great difficulty is to obtain the gold. It is not
in the coffers of the Government or the banks, but is principally
hoarded by individuals throughout the country, and is inaccessible to us.

I hope under the reorganization of the Commissary Department, if we can maintain possession of our communications, that the army will be better supplied than heretofore, and that we can accumulate some provisions ahead. As regards the concentration of our troops near the capital, the effect would be to produce a like concentration of the enemy, and an increase of our difficulties in obtaining food and forage. But this, whether for good or evil, is now being accomplished by the enemy, who seems to be forcing Genls Beauregard & Bragg in this direction. If Sherman marches his army to Richmond, as Genl Beauregard reports it is his intention to do, and Genl Schofield is able to unite with him, we shall have to abandon our position on the James River, as lamentable as it is on every account. The want of supplies alone would force us to withdraw when the enemy reaches the Roanoke. Our line is so long, extending nearly from the Chickahominy to the Nottoway, and the enemy is so close upon us that if we are obliged to withdraw, we cannot concentrate all our troops nearer than some point on the line of railroad between Richmond and Danville. Should a necessity therefore arise, I propose to concentrate at or near Burkeville. The route for the troops north of James River would have to be through Richmond, on the road to Amelia Court House, the cavalry passing up the north branch of the river and crossing at some point above Richmond. Pickett's division would take the route through Chesterfield Court House, crossing the Appomattox at Goode's Bridge. With the army concentrated at or near Burkeville, our communications north and south would be by that railroad and west by the South Side Railroad. We might also seize the opportunity of striking at Grant, should he pursue us rapidly, or at Sherman, before they could unite. I wish you to consider this subject, and give me your views. I desire you also to make every preparation to take the field at a moment's notice, and to accumulate all the supplies you can. Genl Grant seems to be preparing to move out by his left flank. He is accumulating near Hatcher's Run depots of supplies, and apparently concentrating a strong force in that quarter. Yesterday & today trains have passed from his right to his left loaded with troops, which may be the body of 8,000 which you report having left Signal Hill yesterday. I cannot tell whether it is his intention to maintain his position until his other columns approach nearer, or to anticipate any movement by us which he might suppose would then become necessary. I wish you would watch closely his movements on the north side of the river, and try and ascertain whether he is diminishing his force. If he makes the move which appearances now indicate, he may draw out his whole force, abandoning his lines of defense, or hold them partially and move with the remainder of his troops.

I should like very much to confer with you on these subjects, but I fear it will be impossible for me to go north of James River, and I do not know that it will be convenient for you to come here.

Very respectfully, your obt servt

R. E. LEE
Genl

P.S. Can you not return Pickett's brigade to him in order that I may withdraw Grimes' brigade from his line, its division having been ordered to our right.

R. E. L.

959   To JEFFERSON DAVIS
Richmond, Virginia

Headquarters
February 23, 1865

Mr. President:

I have received the copy of Genl Beauregard's despatch of 21st instant, & wish it was in our power to carry out his plan. The idea is good, but the means are lacking. I have directed all the available troops in the Southern Department to be concentrated, with a view to embarrass if they cannot arrest Sherman's progress, & still hope that he cannot make the march contemplated by Genl Beauregard. I think it probable he may turn east by Camden towards the coast. It seems to me he ought not to be allowed to gather sufficient supplies for his journey, & indeed I do not know where they can be obtained. Our troops seem to be much scattered, but by diligence & boldness they can be united. I am much obliged to Your Excellency for ordering Genl Johnston to report to me. I have placed him in command of the army operating against Sherman, & directed him to assign Genl Beauregard to duty with him. Genl Beauregard is a good soldier, & I know will cheerfully & heartily cooperate with him. I hope for favourable results from their union & that Sherman may still be driven back. I have heard from many sources that Genl Beauregard's health was very feeble & feared he might entirely give way before he was willing to announce it. I know of no one who had so much the confidence of the troops & people as Genl Johnston, & believe he has capacity for the command. I shall do all in my power to strengthen him, & should he be forced across the Roanoke, unite with him in a blow against Sherman before the latter can join Genl Grant.

This will necessitate the abandonment of our position on James River, for which contingency every preparation should be made.

Genl Gilmer has arrived at Genl Beauregard's headquarters, Charlotte, & will be of much service to him.

I am with great respect, your obt servt

R. E. LEE
Genl

960   To JOHN C. BRECKINRIDGE
Secretary of War

Headquarters, Confederate States Armies
February 24, 1865

Sir:

I regret to be obliged to call your attention to the alarming number of desertions that are now occurring in the army. Since the 12th instant they amount in two divisions of Hill's corps, those of Wilcox and Heth, to about four hundred. There are a good many from other commands. The desertions are chiefly from the North Carolina regiments, and especially those from the western part of that State. It seems that the men are influenced very much by the representations of their friends at home, who appear to have become very despondent as to our success. They think the cause desperate and write to the soldiers, advising them to take care of themselves, assuring them that if they will return home the bands of deserters so far outnumber the home guards that they will be in no danger of arrest. I do not know what can be done to prevent this evil, unless some change can be wrought in the state of public sentiment by the influence of prominent citizens of the State. The deserters generally take their arms with them. I shall do all in my power to remedy the evil by a stern enforcement of the law, but that alone will not suffice. I have thought that you might be able to enlist the aid of prominent citizens of North Carolina, who might do something to cheer and stimulate the people. These desertions have a very bad effect upon the troops who remain and give rise to painful apprehension.

I submit the matter to your judgment, hoping that you will be able to devise some remedy.

Very respectfully, your obt servt

R. E. LEE
Genl

961   To JEFFERSON DAVIS
                                  Richmond, Virginia

                                                            Near Petersburg
                                                            March 2, 1865

Mr. President:
    I received today the letter from Genl Longstreet to which you
referred in your note of the 28th ultimo. I have proposed to Genl Grant
an interview, in the hope that some good may result, but I must confess
that I am not sanguine. My belief is that he will consent to no terms,
unless coupled with the condition of our return to the Union. Whether
this will be acceptable to our people yet awhile I cannot say. I shall go
to Richmond tomorrow or next day to see you, & hope you will grant
me an hour's conversation on the subject. Genl Longstreet proposed that
I should meet Genl Grant at the point where he met Genl [Ed-
ward O. C.] Ord, & desired to have two or three days' notice. I have
therefore appointed Monday next for the interview with Genl Grant.

                                    With great respect, your obt sevt

                                                            R. E. Lee
                                                            Genl

962   To GENERAL U. S. GRANT
                              Commanding United States Army

                                  Headquarters, Confederate States Armies
                                                            March 2, 1865
General:
    Lieutenant General Longstreet has informed me that in a recent
conversation between himself and Major General Ord as to the possibility
of arriving at a satisfactory adjustment of the present unhappy difficulties by means of a military convention, General Ord stated that if I desired to have an interview with you on the subject you would not decline, provided I had authority to act. Sincerely desiring to leave nothing
untried which may put an end to the calamities of war, I propose to
meet you at such convenient time and place as you may designate, with
the hope that upon an interchange of views it may be found practicable
to submit the subjects of controversy between the belligerents to a convention of the kind mentioned. In such event I am authorized to do whatever the result of the proposed interview may render necessary or advisable. Should you accede to this proposition I would suggest that, if

agreeable to you, we meet at the place selected by Generals Ord and Longstreet for their interview at 11 a.m. on Monday next.

Very respectfully, your obedient servant

R. E. LEE
General

963   To JOHN C. BRECKINRIDGE
                    Secretary of War
                    TELEGRAM

Headquarters
March 3, 1865

FITZ LEE WILL ASSEMBLE HIS CAVALRY NEAR MECHANICSVILLE & GORDONS-VILLE. BETTER SUSPEND TRANSPORTATION OF ARTICLES TO LYNCHBURG. COL CHILDS, AT FAYETTEVILLE, HAS APPROVED PRESS DISPATCH GIVING SHERMAN'S POSITION. I SUGGEST PAPERS IN RICHMOND BE REQUIRED NOT TO PUBLISH.

R. E. LEE

964   To JOHN C. BRECKINRIDGE
                    Secretary of War

Headquarters, Confederate States Armies
March 9, 1865

Sir:

I have received tonight your letter of this date requesting my opinion upon the military condition of the country.

It must be apparent to every one that it is full of peril and requires prompt action.

My correspondence with the Department will show the extreme difficulties under which we have labored during the past year to keep this army furnished with necessary supplies. This difficulty is increased, and it seems almost impossible to maintain our present position with the means at the disposal of the Government. In our former operations in this State a large portion of our forage and subsistence was collected by the staff officers connected with the army by the use of transportation, and we were not confined to what the several departments could supply. The country within reach of our present position has been nearly or quite exhausted, and we are now dependent upon what those departments can provide. Their respective chiefs can best inform you of the means at their command, but from all the information I possess, the only practicable relief is in the generous contribution of the people to our necessities, and that is limited by the difficulties of transportation, whatever may be the extent of their willingness and ability, of which I am unable to form an accurate opinion.

Unless the men and animals can be subsisted, the army cannot be kept together, and our present lines must be abandoned. Nor can it be moved to any other position where it can operate to advantage without provisions to enable it to move in a body.

The difficulties attending the payment and clothing of the troops, though great, are not so pressing, and would be relieved in a measure by military success. The same is true of the ordnance supplies, and I therefore confine my remarks chiefly to those wants which must be met now, in order to maintain a force adequate to justify a reasonable hope of such success. If the army can be maintained in an efficient condition, I do not regard the abandonment of our present position as necessarily fatal to our success.

The army operating under Genl Johnston has not yet been concentrated, and its strength is not accurately known. It is believed, however, to be inferior to that of the enemy, and its condition gives no strong prospect of a marked success.

In the most southern portions of the country, east of the Mississippi, our forces are numerically inferior to those of the enemy, nor do I see any prospect, from my present information, of putting them on a footing adequate to the performance of the services that they will probably be called upon to render during the approaching campaign.

While the military situation is not favorable, it is not worse than the superior numbers and resources of the enemy justified us in expecting from the beginning. Indeed, the legitimate military consequences of that superiority have been postponed longer than we had reason to anticipate.

Everything in my opinion has depended and still depends upon the disposition and feelings of the people. Their representatives can best decide how they will bear the difficulties and sufferings of their condition and how they will respond to the demands which the public safety requires.

The necessity of replying promptly to your letter, to enable you to make the use of my answer, which you desire, prevents me going into detail and compels me to be brief.

With sentiments of great respect, your obt svt

R. E. LEE
Genl

965   To JEFFERSON DAVIS
                              Richmond, Virginia

                              Headquarters, Armies of the Confederate States
                                                      March 10, 1865

Mr. President:

I do not know whether the law authorising the use of negro troops has received your sanction, but if it has, I respectfully recommend that measures be taken to carry it into effect as soon as practicable.

It will probably be impossible to get a large force of this kind in condition to be of service during the present campaign, but I think no time should be lost in trying to collect all we can. I attach great importance to the result of the first experiment with these troops, and think that if it prove successful, it will greatly lessen the difficulty of putting the law into operation.

I understand that the Governor of Virginia is prepared to do all that may be required of him under the authority he possesses. I hope it will be found practicable to raise some negro companies in Richmond, and have written to Genl Ewell to do all in his power to get them, as soon as he shall be informed in what manner to proceed. In the beginning it would be well to do everything to make the enlistment entirely voluntary on the part of the negroes, and those owners who are willing to furnish some of their slaves for the purpose, can do a great deal to inspire them with the right feeling to prepare them to become soldiers, and to be satisfied with their new condition. I have received letters from persons offering to select the most suitable among their slaves, as soon as Congress should give the authority, and think that a considerable number would be forthcoming for the purpose if called for.

I hope that if you have approved the law, you will cause the necessary steps to carry it into effect to be taken as soon as possible.

                              With great respect, your obt servt

                                                      R. E. LEE
                                                      Genl

966   To JEFFERSON DAVIS
                              Richmond, Virginia

                                          Headquarters, Petersburg
                                                      March 14, 1865

Mr. President:

In reply to your despatch of the 13th instant, relative to the orders given by Genl Johnston for the removal of the supplies from Raleigh, I will state that on the 12th instant I received the following despatch from him in cipher. "Is it so important to prevent the interruption of the road by Raleigh, by which you are supplied, as to make it proper to fight with the chance of winning against us? I would not fight Sherman's united army unless your situation makes it necessary." I replied on the same day, "I fear I cannot hold my position if road by Raleigh is interrupted. Should you be forced back in this direction both armies would certainly starve. You must judge what the probability will be of arresting Sherman by a battle. If there is a reasonable probability I would recommend it. A bold & unexpected attack might relieve us." I do not think more specific instructions can be given. A defeat would not improve our condition, & the officer on the spot can alone judge as to the propriety of delivering battle. The army under Genl Johnston is about being united at Raleigh. It is inferior in number to the enemy, & I fear its tone is not yet restored. It is in great part without field transportation, & labours under other disadvantages. I think it would be better at this time if practicable to avoid a general engagement & endeavour to strike the enemy in detail. This is Genl Johnston's plan, in which I hope he may succeed, & he may then recover all the ground he may be obliged to relinquish in accomplishing it. The greatest calamity that can befall us is the destruction of our armies. If they can be maintained, we may recover from our reverses, but if lost we have no resource. I will endeavour to keep Your Excellency advised of Genl Johnston's intentions, but from his despatches & reports of the condition of his army I fear it may be necessary to relinquish Raleigh.

With great respect, your obt servt

R. E. Lee
Genl

967   To JOHN C. BRECKINRIDGE
                      Secretary of War
                          TELEGRAM

Headquarters
March 21, 1865

GENL VAUGHAN REPORTS THIS MORNING "THAT THOMAS IS AT KNOXVILLE, THAT THREE (3) REGIMENTS & SOME NEGRO TROOPS ARE REPAIRING THE EAST TENNESSEE RAILROAD, & THAT ENEMY HAVE COMMENCED THEIR ADVANCE." GENL J. E. JOHNSTON, AT 9.20 A.M., AT BENTONVILLE, REPORTS "THAT HE

IS REMOVING HIS WOUNDED TO SMITHFIELD, THE ENEMY'S ENTRENCHED POSI-
TION AND GREATLY SUPERIOR NUMBERS, SHERMAN'S ARMY BEING IN OUR
FRONT, MAKE FURTHER OFFENSIVE MOVEMENTS IMPRACTICABLE."

R. E. LEE

968   To JOHN C. BRECKINRIDGE
Secretary of War
TELEGRAM

Headquarters
March 25, 1865

AT DAYLIGHT THIS MORNING GENL GORDON ASSAULTED & CARRIED ENEMY'S
WORKS AT HARE'S HILL, CAPTURED NINE (9) PIECES OF ARTILLERY, EIGHT (8)
MORTARS, BETWEEN FIVE & SIX HUNDRED PRISONERS, AMONG THEM ONE BRIG
GENERAL AND NUMBER OF OFFICERS OF LOWER GRADE. ENEMY'S LINES WERE
SWEPT AWAY FOR DISTANCE OF FOUR OR FIVE HUNDRED YARDS TO RIGHT &
LEFT, AND TWO EFFORTS MADE TO RECOVER CAPTURED WORKS WERE HAND-
SOMELY REPULSED; BUT IT WAS FOUND THAT THE ENCLOSED WORKS IN REAR,
COMMANDING ENEMY'S MAIN LINE, COULD ONLY BE TAKEN AT GREAT SACRI-
FICE, & TROOPS WERE WITHDRAWN TO ORIGINAL POSITION. IT BEING IMPRACTI-
CABLE TO BRING OFF CAPTURED GUNS, OWING TO NATURE OF GROUND, THEY
WERE DISABLED AND LEFT. OUR LOSS REPORTED IS NOT HEAVY. AMONG WOUNDED
IS BRIG GENL [WILLIAM] TERRY FLESH WOUND AND BRIG GENL PHIL COOK IN
ARM. ALL THE TROOPS ENGAGED, INCLUDING TWO BRIGADES UNDER BRIG GENL
RANSOM, BEHAVED MOST HANDSOMELY. THE CONDUCT OF THE SHARPSHOOTERS
OF GORDON'S CORPS, WHO LED ASSAULT, DESERVES THE HIGHEST COMMENDA-
TION. THIS AFTERNOON THERE WAS SKIRMISHING ON THE RIGHT BETWEEN THE
PICKET LINES, WITH VARIED SUCCESS. AT DARK ENEMY HELD CONSIDERABLE
PORTION OF THE LINE FURTHEST IN ADVANCE OF OUR MAIN WORKS.

R. E. LEE

969   To JEFFERSON DAVIS
Richmond, Virginia

Headquarters, Confederate States Armies
March 26, 1865

Mr. President:
    My despatch of yesterday to the Secretary of War will have in-
formed you of the attack made upon a portion of the enemy's lines

around Petersburg, and the result which attended it. I have been unwilling to hazard any portion of the troops in an assault upon fortified positions, preferring to reserve their strength for the struggle which must soon commence, but I was induced to assume the offensive from the belief that the point assailed could be carried without much loss, and the hope that by the seizure of the redoubts in the rear of the enemy's main line, I could sweep along his entrenchments to the south, so that if I could not cause their abandonment, Genl Grant would at least be obliged so to curtail his lines, that upon the approach of Genl Sherman, I might be able to hold our position with a portion of the troops, and with a select body unite with Genl Johnston and give him battle. If successful, I would then be able to return to my position, and if unsuccessful I should be in no worse condition, as I should be compelled to withdraw from James River if I quietly awaited his approach. But although the assault upon the fortified works at Hare's Hill was bravely accomplished, the redoubts commanding the line of entrenchments were found enclosed and strongly manned, so that an attempt to carry them must have been attended with great hazards, and even if accomplished, would have caused a great sacrifice of life in the presence of the large reserves which the enemy was hurrying into position. I therefore determined to withdraw the troops, and it was in retiring that they suffered the greatest loss, the extent of which has not yet been reported.

I fear now it will be impossible to prevent a junction between Grant and Sherman, nor do I deem it prudent that this army should maintain its position until the latter shall approach too near. Genl Johnston reports that the returns of his force of the 24th instant gave his effective infantry thirteen thousand five hundred. He must therefore have lost. after his concentration at Smithfield about eight thousand men. This could hardly have resulted from the casualties of battle, and I fear must be the effect of desertion. Should this prove to be the case, I can not reasonably expect him to bring across the Roanoke more than ten thousand infantry, a force that would add so little strength to this army as not to make it more than a match for Sherman, with whom to risk a battle in the presence of Grant's army, would hardly seem justifiable. Genl Johnston estimates Genl Sherman's army, since its union with Schofield and the troops that were previously in N. Carolina, at sixty thousand. I have no correct data upon which to form an estimate of the strength of Genl Grant's army. Taking their own account, it would exceed a hundred thousand, and I fear it is not under eighty thousand. Their two armies united would therefore exceed ours by nearly a hundred thousand. If Genl Grant wishes to unite Sherman with him without a battle, the latter after crossing the Roanoke has only to take an easterly direction towards Sussex, while the former moving two days march towards Weldon, provided I moved out to intercept Sherman, would render it impossible for me to strike him without fighting both armies.

I have thought it proper to make the above statement to Your Excellency of the condition of affairs, knowing that you will do whatever may be in your power to give relief.

I am with great respect, your obt servt

R. E. Lee
Genl

970 GENERAL ORDERS, NO. 8

Headquarters, Army of Northern Virginia
March 27, 1865

It having been reported that the evil habit prevails with some in this army of proposing to their comrades in jest to desert and go home, the commanding general earnestly warns those guilty of this practice against the danger they incur. The penalty for advising or persuading a soldier to desert is death; and those indulging in such jests will find it difficult on a trial to rebut the presumption of guilt arising from their words.

This order and the 23d Article of War will be forthwith read to each company in the army once a day for three days, and to every regiment at dress parade once a week for a month; and at such other times hereafter, in addition to those prescribed for the Articles of War, as commanding officers may deem proper.

By command of General R. E. Lee:

W. H. Taylor
Assistant Adjutant General

971 To HIS WIFE
Richmond, Virginia

Petersburg
March 28, 1865

My Dear Mary:

I have received your note with the bag of socks & return the bag & receipt. The count is all right this time. I have put in the bag Genl Scott's autobiography, which I thought you might like to read. The Genl of course stands out very prominently & does not hide his light under a bushel, but he appears the bold sagacious truthful man as he is. I saw Fitzhugh & Rob yesterday. They dined with me. I had been on the lines & returned late & found them here. They returned to their bivouac last night & this morning will resume their former position. I enclose a note for little Agnes. I shall be very glad to see her tomorrow, but cannot recommend pleasure trips now.

Love to all.

Very truly & affly

R. E. LEE

972   To MISS AGNES LEE
                Richmond, Virginia

Petersburg
March 28, 1865

My Dear Agnes:

I received last night your letter of the 26th & I felt great pleasure at the thought of seeing you & wishing I could enjoy that pleasure. The Meade's have more than once proposed to me to bring you to see them & I should like you very much to do so. I do not know that there is any objection on the score you mention, provisions, for every one seems to have a sufficiency of food, but I cannot say what a day may bring forth. I fear you have put off your visit too late. Genl Grant is evidently preparing for something & is marshalling & preparing his troops for some movement, which is not yet disclosed. Yesterday he was collecting troops on his left & this morning it continues. It would be very dreadful if you should be caught in a battle when the road would have to be used for military purposes & you cut off. I think it necessary to inform you that you may be prepared. If you do come you must let me know by military telegraph that I may send a conveyance for you at the appointed hour. You must wish a great deal of happiness to Miss Bierne & I wish I could see her & Miss Sally too. I do not like to hear of the latter going to weddings. I fear it is premonitory.

Give much love to your mother, sisters & friends.

Your affectionate father

R. E. LEE

973   To MISS AGNES LEE
                              Petersburg, Virginia

                                                              March 29, 1865
My dear little Agnes:
    I have just heard of your arrival in Petersburg. I am too sorry I
cannot go in to see you, but I must go to the right. The enemy in strong
force is operating in that direction. I do not yet know to what extent
or when I can visit you.

                                              Very affly your father

                                                              R. E. Lee

974   To JOHN C. BRECKINRIDGE
                                Secretary of War
                                   TELEGRAM

                                                              Headquarters
                                                            March 29, 1865

    ENEMY ARE REPORTED TO HAVE CROSSED HATCHER'S RUN AT MONK'S NECK
BRIDGE WITH INFANTRY & CAVALRY, MOVING TOWARDS DINWIDDIE COURT
HOUSE.

                                                              R. E. Lee

975   To JOHN C. BRECKINRIDGE
                                Secretary of War
                                   TELEGRAM

                          Headquarters, Armies of the Confederate States
                                                            March 29, 1865

    THE ENEMY CROSSED HATCHER'S RUN THIS MORNING AT MONK'S NECK
BRIDGE WITH A LARGE FORCE OF CAVALRY, INFANTRY, & ARTILLERY, AND TO-
NIGHT HIS LEFT EXTENDED TO DINWIDDIE COURT HOUSE. GREGG'S CAVALRY
ADVANCED A MILE AND A HALF ON FORD'S ROAD TOWARD THE SOUTH SIDE RAIL-
ROAD. GENERAL ANDERSON MOVED OUT FROM HIS POSITION AND STRUCK HIS
COLUMN NEAR THE INTERSECTION OF THE QUAKER ROAD AND BOYDTON PLANK
ROAD, BUT DID NOT SUCCEED IN DRIVING HIM BACK.

                                                              R. E. Lee

976 To JOHN C. BRECKINRIDGE
Secretary of War
TELEGRAM

Headquarters
March 30, 1865

GENL GORDON REPORTS THAT THE ENEMY, AT 11 P.M. YESTERDAY, AD-
VANCED AGAINST A PART OF HIS LINE DEFENDED BY BRIG GENL [WILLIAM G.]
LEWIS, BUT WAS REPULSED. THE FIRE OF ARTILLERY AND MORTARS CONTINUED
FOR SEVERAL HOURS WITH CONSIDERABLE ACTIVITY. NO DAMAGE ON OUR LINES
REPORTED.

THE ENEMY STILL MAINTAINS HIS POSITION WEST OF HATCHER'S RUN, OC-
CUPYING DINWIDDIE COURT HOUSE WITH SHERIDAN'S CAVALRY. SKIRMISHING
WAS FREQUENT ALONG THE LINES TODAY, BUT NO SERIOUS ATTACK. PART OF
[GENERAL WESLEY] MERRITT'S DIVISION UNDER GENL [ALFRED] GIBBS AT-
TACKED GENL FITZ LEE TWICE THIS MORNING AT FIVE FORKS, BUT WAS
REPULSED. ABOUT 3 P.M., FITZ LEE ATTACKED HIM AND DROVE HIM FROM
HIS POSITION, CAPTURING A FEW PRISONERS. THE FORCE OF THE ENEMY WEST
OF HATCHER'S RUN CONSISTS OF THE FIFTH CORPS, PART OF THE SECOND AND
PART OF THE SIXTH, WITH GREGG'S AND SHERIDAN'S CAVALRY.

R. E. LEE

977 To MISS AGNES LEE
Petersburg, Virginia

March 31, 1865

My precious little Agnes:
I was so sorry I was not here to see you yesterday. I might have
persuaded you to have remained with me. If you had have staid or
come out at 4 o'clock this morning I could have seen you with my weary
sleepy eyes. Now I have to go to the right of our lines again, & do not
know when I shall have the pleasure of seeing you.
May God bless & guard you.

Your affectionate father

R. E. LEE

P.S. Let me know what I can do for you. I can send for you when
you desire.

R. E. L.

978   To JOHN C. BRECKINRIDGE
                              Secretary of War
                                  TELEGRAM

                                                           Headquarters
                                                        March 31, 1865

FINDING THIS MORNING THAT THE ENEMY WAS EXTENDING HIS LEFT TO
EMBRACE THE WHITE OAK ROAD, GENL ANDERSON PLACED THREE BRIGADES IN
POSITION TO REPEL HIM. BEFORE THE DISPOSITION WAS COMPLETED, THE
ENEMY ADVANCED AND WAS FIRMLY MET BY OUR TROOPS AND DRIVEN BACK
WITH LOSS TO HIS POSITION NEAR THE BOYDTON PLANK ROAD. OUR TROOPS
WERE THEN WITHDRAWN, AND WERE FOLLOWED BY THE ENEMY, WHO IN
TURN DROVE US BACK TO OUR LINES. OUR LOSS WAS NOT LARGE, AND WE CAP-
TURED OVER FOUR HUNDRED PRISONERS.

                                                              R. E. LEE

979   To JEFFERSON DAVIS
                              Richmond, Virginia

                                 Headquarters, Confederate States Armies
                                                          April 1, 1865
Mr. President:
    The movement of Genl Grant to Dinwiddie Court House seriously
threatens our position, and diminishes our ability to maintain our present lines in front of Richmond and Petersburg. In the first place it cuts
us off from our depot at Stony Creek at which point forage for the
cavalry was delivered by the Weldon Railroad and upon which we relied to maintain it. It also renders it more difficult to withdraw from our
position, cuts us off from the White Oak road, and gives the enemy an
advantageous point on our right and rear. From this point I fear he
can readily cut both the South Side & the Danville Railroads being far
superior to us in cavalry. This in my opinion obliged us to prepare for
the necessity of evacuating our position on James River at once, and also
to consider the best means of accomplishing it, and our future course. I
should like very much to have the views of Your Excellency upon this
matter as well as counsel, and would repair to Richmond for the purpose,
did I not feel that my presence here is necessary. Should I find it practicable I will do so, but should it be convenient for Your Excellency or
the Secretary of War to visit headquarters, I should be glad to see you.

The reported advance of Stoneman from the west, and the movement of the enemy upon the Roanoke, add to our difficulties.

Very respectfully, your obt serv't

R. E. LEE
Genl

980   To JOHN C. BRECKINRIDGE
Secretary of War

Headquarters, Army of Northern Virginia
April 1, 1865

Sir:

After my dispatch of last night I received a report from Genl Pickett, who, with three of his own brigades and two of Genl [Bushrod R.] Johnson's, supported the cavalry under Genl Fitz Lee near Five Forks, on the road from Dinwiddie Court House to the South Side road. After considerable difficulty, and meeting resistance from the enemy at all points, Genl Pickett forced his way to within less than a mile of Dinwiddie Court House. By this time it was too dark for further operations, and Genl Pickett resolved to return to Five Forks to protect his communication with the railroad. He inflicted considerable damage upon the enemy and took some prisoners. His own loss was severe, including a good many officers. Genl Terry had his horse killed by a shell and was disabled himself. Genl Fitz Lee's & Rosser's divisions were heavily engaged, but their loss was slight. Genl W. H. F. Lee lost some valuable officers. Genl Pickett did not retire from the vicinity of Dinwiddie Court House until early this morning, when his left flank being threatened by a heavy force, he withdrew to Five Forks, where he took position with Genl W. H. F. Lee on his right, Fitz Lee and Rosser on his left, with [General William P.] Roberts' brigade on the White Oak road connecting with Genl Anderson. The enemy attacked Genl Roberts with a large force of cavalry, and after being once repulsed finally drove him back across Hatcher's Run. A large force of infantry, believed to be the 5th Corps with other troops, turned Genl Pickett's left and drove him back on the White Oak road, separating him from Genl Fitz Lee, who was compelled to fall back across Hatcher's Run. Genl Pickett's present position is not known. Genl Fitz Lee reports that the enemy is massing his infantry heavily behind the cavalry in his front. The infantry that engaged Genl Anderson yesterday has moved from his front towards our right, and is supposed to participate in the operations above described.

Prisoners have been taken today from the 24th Corps, and it is believed that most of that corps is now south of the James. Our loss today is not known. A report from Staunton represents that the 8th Corps passed over the Baltimore & Ohio Railroad from the 20th to the 25th ultimo. Genl Hancock is at Harper's Ferry with two thousand men. One division of the 19th Corps is at Winchester, with about a thousand cavalry. The infantry at Winchester have marching orders, and all these troops are said to be destined for Genl Grant's army.

The enemy is also reported to have withdrawn all his troops from Wolf Run Shoals & Fairfax Station, and to be concentrating them at Winchester.

Very respectfully, your obt servt

R. E. LEE
Genl

981   To MISS AGNES LEE
Petersburg, Virginia

April 1, 1865

My precious little Agnes:

I received your kind note last night. I am obliged to go to the right today & will be compelled to visit Richmond the first moment I can. I do not know when I shall see you. You must therefore make your arrangements to return irrespective of me. Thank Mrs. Meade & Mrs. P. for their kindness to you in my name, for I fear I shall not be able. Bryan will do for you anything you desire. Let me know what I can do.

Truly & affly your father

R. E. LEE

982   To JOHN C. BRECKINRIDGE
Secretary of War
TELEGRAM

Headquarters
April 2, 1865

I SEE NO PROSPECT OF DOING MORE THAN HOLDING OUR POSITION HERE TILL NIGHT. I AM NOT CERTAIN THAT I CAN DO THAT. IF I CAN I SHALL WITHDRAW TONIGHT NORTH OF THE APPOMATTOX, AND IF POSSIBLE IT WILL BE BETTER TO WITHDRAW THE WHOLE LINE TONIGHT FROM JAMES RIVER. THE

BRIGADES ON HATCHER'S RUN ARE CUT OFF FROM US. ENEMY HAVE BROKEN THROUGH OUR LINES AND INTERCEPTED BETWEEN US AND THEM, AND THERE IS NO BRIDGE OVER WHICH THEY CAN CROSS THE APPOMATTOX THIS SIDE OF GOODE'S OR BEAVER'S, WHICH ARE NOT VERY FAR FROM THE DANVILLE RAIL- ROAD. OUR ONLY CHANCE, THEN, OF CONCENTRATING OUR FORCES, IS TO DO SO NEAR DANVILLE RAILROAD, WHICH I SHALL ENDEAVOR TO DO AT ONCE. I ADVISE THAT ALL PREPARATION BE MADE FOR LEAVING RICHMOND TONIGHT. I WILL ADVISE YOU LATER, ACCORDING TO CIRCUMSTANCES.

R. E. LEE

983 To JOHN C. BRECKINRIDGE
Secretary of War
TELEGRAM

Headquarters
April 2, 1865

I THINK THE DANVILLE ROAD WILL BE SAFE UNTIL TOMORROW.

R. E. LEE

984 To GENERAL HENRY HETH
Commanding Division
TELEGRAM

April 2, 1865

MOVE UP TO THE LEFT WITH YOUR WHOLE FORCE AND ENDEAVOR TO REESTABLISH LINES. GORDON HAS SUCCEEDED IN REOCCUPYING MOST OF HIS.

R. E. LEE

985 To JEFFERSON DAVIS
Richmond, Virginia
TELEGRAM

Petersburg
April 2, 1865

I THINK IT IS ABSOLUTELY NECESSARY THAT WE SHOULD ABANDON OUR POSITION TONIGHT. I HAVE GIVEN ALL THE NECESSARY ORDERS ON THE SUBJECT

TO THE TROOPS, AND THE OPERATION, THOUGH DIFFICULT, I HOPE WILL BE
PERFORMED SUCCESSFULLY. I HAVE DIRECTED GENERAL STEVENS TO SEND AN
OFFICER TO YOUR EXCELLENCY TO EXPLAIN THE ROUTES TO YOU BY WHICH
THE TROOPS WILL BE MOVED TO AMELIA COURT HOUSE, AND FURNISH YOU WITH
A GUIDE AND ANY ASSISTANCE THAT YOU MAY REQUIRE FOR YOURSELF.

R. E. LEE

986   To JOHN C. BRECKINRIDGE
Secretary of War
TELEGRAM

Petersburg
April 2, 1865

IT IS ABSOLUTELY NECESSARY THAT WE SHOULD ABANDON OUR POSITION
TONIGHT, OR RUN THE RISK OF BEING CUT OFF IN THE MORNING. I HAVE GIVEN
ALL THE ORDERS TO OFFICERS ON BOTH SIDES OF THE RIVER, & HAVE TAKEN
EVERY PRECAUTION THAT I CAN TO MAKE THE MOVEMENT SUCCESSFUL. IT
WILL BE A DIFFICULT OPERATION, BUT I HOPE NOT IMPRACTICABLE. PLEASE
GIVE ALL ORDERS THAT YOU FIND NECESSARY IN & ABOUT RICHMOND. THE
TROOPS WILL ALL BE DIRECTED TO AMELIA COURT HOUSE.

R. E. LEE

987   To GENERAL RICHARD S. EWELL
Commanding North of James River
TELEGRAM

Headquarters, Confederate States Army
April 2, 1865

I WISH YOU TO MAKE ALL PREPARATIONS QUIETLY AND RAPIDLY TO ABAN-
DON YOUR POSITION TONIGHT IF NECESSARY. SEND BACK ON THE LINE OF
DANVILLE RAILROAD ALL SUPPLIES, AMMUNITION, &C., THAT IS POSSIBLE. HAVE
YOUR FIELD TRANSPORTATION READY AND YOUR TROOPS PREPARED FOR BATTLE
OR MARCHING ORDERS, AS CIRCUMSTANCES MAY REQUIRE. ENDEAVOR TO AVOID
ALL ALARM OR NOTICE OF YOUR PREPARATIONS FROM GETTING TO ENEMY.
SAVE ALL PUBLIC PROPERTY. IF YOUR ARTILLERY OR TRANSPORTATION REQUIRES
HORSES YOU MUST TAKE THEM IN THE CITY.

R. E. LEE

988   To GENERAL RICHARD S. EWELL
            Commanding North of James River
                    TELEGRAM

                                        Petersburg
                                        April 2, 1865
                                        3 P.M.

IT WILL BE NECESSARY FOR US TO ABANDON OUR POSITION IF POSSIBLE
TONIGHT. WILL YOU BE ABLE TO DO SO? ANSWER AS SOON AS POSSIBLE.

                                        R. E. LEE

989   To JEFFERSON DAVIS
                Richmond, Virginia

                                        Petersburg, Virginia
                                        April 2, 1865
                                        3 P.M.

Mr. President:
    Your letter of the 1st is just received. I have been willing to detach
officers to recruit negro troops, and have sent in the names of many
who are desirous of recruiting companies, battalions, or regiments to the
War Department. After receiving the General Orders on that subject,
establishing recruiting depots in the several States, I supposed that this
mode of raising the troops was preferred. I will continue to submit the
names of those who offer for the service, and whom I deem competent,
to the War Department; but among the numerous applications which are
presented, it is difficult for me to decide who are suitable for the duty. I
am glad Your Excellency has made an appeal to the Governors of the
States, and hope it will have a good effect. I have had a great desire
to confer with you upon our condition, and would have been to Richmond before this; but anticipating movements of the enemy, which have
occurred, I felt unwilling to be absent. I have considered our position
very critical, but have hoped that the enemy might expose himself in
some way that we might take advantage of, and cripple him.
    Knowing when Sheridan moved on our right that our cavalry
would be unable to resist successfully his advance upon our communications, I detached Pickett's division to support it. At first Pickett succeeded in driving the enemy, who fought stubbornly, and after being
reinforced by the 5th Corps (U. S.), obliged Pickett to recede to the Five

Forks on the Dinwiddie Court House and Ford's road, where unfortunately he was yesterday defeated. To relieve him, I had to again draw out three brigades under Genl Anderson, which so weakened our front line that the enemy last night and this morning succeeded in penetrating it near the Church road, separating our troops around the town from those on Hatcher's Run. This has enabled him to extend to the Appomattox, thus enclosing and obliging us to contract our lines to the city. I have directed the troops from the lines on Hatcher's Run, thus severed from us, to fall back towards Amelia Court House, and I do not see how I can possibly help withdrawing from the city to the north side of the Appomattox tonight. There is no bridge over the Appomattox above this point nearer than Goode's and Bevill's over which the troops above mentioned could cross to the north side and be made available to us. Otherwise I might hold this position for a day or two longer; but would have to evacuate it eventually, and I think it better for us to abandon the whole line on James River tonight if practicable. I have sent preparatory orders to all the officers, and will be able to tell by night whether or not we can remain here another day, but I think every hour now adds to our difficulties. I regret to be obliged to write such a hurried letter to Your Excellency, but I am in the presence of the enemy endeavoring to resist his advance.

I am most respectfully & truly yrs

R. E. LEE
Genl

990   To JEFFERSON DAVIS
                         Richmond, Virginia
                              TELEGRAM

Petersburg
April 2, 1865

YOUR TELEGRAM RECEIVED. I THINK IT WILL BE NECESSARY TO MOVE TONIGHT. I SHALL CAMP THE TROOPS HERE NORTH OF THE APPOMATTOX. THE ENEMY IS SO STRONG THAT THEY WILL CROSS ABOVE US & CLOSE US IN BETWEEN THE JAMES & APPOMATTOX RIVERS, IF WE REMAIN.

R. E. LEE

991   To GENERAL RICHARD S. EWELL
Commanding Richmond Defence Troops

Headquarters, Army of Northern Virginia
Hebron Church, 6 Miles from Goode's Ford
April 3, 1865
6½ P.M.

Lieutenant General Ewell:
When you were directed to cross the Appomattox at Genito Bridge
it was supposed that a pontoon bridge had been laid at that point as ordered. But I learn today from Mr. Haxall that such is not the case.
Should you not be able to cross at that point or at some bridge higher up,
you must take the best road to Rudd's Store on the Goode's Bridge road,
and cross the Appomattox on the bridge at that point, and then conform
to your original instructions. This portion of the army is now on its way
to Goode's Bridge, the flats at Bevill's Bridge being flooded by high water. Notify me of your approach to the bridge & passage of the Appomattox by courier to Amelia Court House, or wherever I may be.

I am very respectfully, your obt sevt

R. E. LEE
Genl

7½ A.M. April 4th

P.S. The courier has returned with this note, having been able to
learn nothing of you. I am about to cross the river. Get to Amelia Court
House as soon as possible & let me hear from you.

R. E. L.

992   To GENERAL RICHARD S. EWELL
Commanding Richmond Defence Troops

Headquarters, Army of Northern Virginia
April 4, 1865
9 P.M.

General:
I am very much gratified by your letter of today to learn there is
such a favourable prospect of your crossing at Mattoax Bridge. I hope
your anticipations may be realized, & that you may be safely over by this

time. Notify Genl Mahone of your crossing, who is preserving the bridge at Goode's Ferry only until he shall hear you do not require it. He has orders to destroy the bridge as soon as he hears you do not need it. I wish you to give him the earliest intelligence. Genl Gordon will remain at his present position at Scott's Shop, on the Goode's Bridge road, until he hears of your approach, & then he has orders to join me here. I wish you to notify him of the probable time of your arrival at Scott's Shop.

Very respectfully, your obt servt

R. E. LEE
Genl

993   MAJOR W. H. TAYLOR TO GENERAL
RICHARD H. ANDERSON
Commanding Corps

April 5, 1865

Lieutenant General Anderson:
The general commanding directs me to say that the troops (Mahone's and Pickett's) took the wrong road from the first. They were pursuing the Paineville road and deviating every step from the railroad. They are now retracing their steps, and will turn in and march parallel with the railroad toward Jetersville. He gives you this information that you may avoid a similar mistake. The wagon train is on the Paineville road. The troops should turn off near railroad and take direction of Jetersville. There may be no plain wagon road, but you can ascertain, for Pickett and Mahone are now moving, and regulate your march accordingly.

Respectfully

W. H. TAYLOR

994   To GENERAL JOHN B. GORDON
Commanding Corps

Amelia Springs
April 6, 1865
4 A.M.

General:
I have seen the dispatches (intercepted) you sent me. It was from my expectation of an attack being made from Jetersville that I was anxious that the rear of the column should reach Deatonsville as soon as

possible. I hope the rear will get out of harm's way, and I rely greatly upon your exertions and good judgment for its safety. I know that men and animals are much exhausted, but it is necessary to tax their strength. I wish after the cavalry crosses the bridge at Flat Creek that it be thoroughly destroyed so as to prevent pursuit in that direction. The bridge over the same stream on the road to Jetersville I have had destroyed. By holding the position at Amelia Springs with our cavalry, which can retire by Deatonsville or up the road toward Paineville, we can secure the rear of the column from interruption. About two miles from Amelia Springs on the Deatonsville road a road leads off to the right to Chapman's into the Ligontown road, by which Farmville may be reached provided there is a bridge over the Appomattox at Ligontown. I hear there is none; therefore I see no way of relieving the column of the wagons, and they must be brought along. You must, of course, keep everything ahead of you, wagons, stragglers, &c. I will try to get the head of the column on, and to get provisions at Rice's Station or Farmville.

Very respectfully, &c.

R. E. LEE
General

995   To JEFFERSON DAVIS
Danville, Virginia
TELEGRAM

Headquarters
Rice's Station, South Side Railroad
April 6, 1865

I SHALL BE TONIGHT AT FARMVILLE. YOU CAN COMMUNICATE BY TELEGRAPH TO MEHERRIN AND BY COURIER TO LYNCHBURG.

VERY RESPECTFULLY AND TRULY YOURS

R. E. LEE

996   To GENERAL U. S. GRANT
Commanding Armies of the United States

April 7, 1865

General:

I have received your note of this date. Though not entertaining the opinion you express of the hopelessness of further resistance on the part of the Army of Northern Virginia, I reciprocate your desire to

avoid useless effusion of blood, and therefore, before considering your
proposition, ask the terms you will offer on condition of its surrender.

Very respectfully, your obt servt

R. E. Lee
Genl

997   To GENERAL U. S. GRANT
Commanding Armies of the United States

April 8, 1865

General:
    I received at a late hour your note of today. In mine of yesterday I
did not intend to propose the surrender of the Army of Northern Virginia, but to ask the terms of your proposition. To be frank, I do not
think the emergency has arisen to call for the surrender of this army;
but as the restoration of peace should be the sole object of all, I desired
to know whether your proposals would lead to that end. I cannot, therefore, meet you with a view to surrender the Army of Northern Virginia;
but as far as your proposal may affect the C. S. forces under my command, & tend to the restoration of peace, I should be pleased to meet you
at 10 a.m. tomorrow, on the old stage road to Richmond, between the
picket lines of the two armies.

Very resply, your obt servt

R. E. Lee
Genl

998   To GENERAL U. S. GRANT
Commanding Armies of the United States

April 9, 1865

General:
    I received your note of this morning on the picket line, whither I
had come to meet you and ascertain definitely what terms were embraced in your proposal of yesterday with reference to the surrender of
this army. I now request an interview in accordance with the offer contained in your letter of yesterday for that purpose.

Very respectfully, your obt servt

R. E. Lee
Genl

999   To GENERAL U. S. GRANT
                Commanding Armies of the United States

                                Headquarters, Army of Northern Virginia
                                                April 9, 1865
General:
    I sent a communication to you today from the picket line, whither
I had gone in hopes of meeting you in pursuance of the request contained in my letter of yesterday. Maj Genl Meade informs me that it
would probably expedite matters to send a duplicate through some
other part of your lines. I therefore request an interview, at such time
and place as you may designate, to discuss the terms of the surrender of
this army in accordance with your offer to have such an interview, contained in your letter of yesterday.

                        Very resply, your obt servt

                                        R. E. LEE
                                        Genl

1000   To GENERAL U. S. GRANT
                Commanding Armies of the United States

                                                April 9, 1865
General:
    I ask a suspension of hostilities pending the adjustment of the terms
of the surrender of this army, in the interview requested in my former
communication today.

                        Very respectfully, your obt servt

                                        R. E. LEE
                                        Genl

1001   To GENERAL U. S. GRANT
                Commanding Armies of the United States

                                Headquarters, Army of Northern Virginia
                                                April 9, 1865
General:
    I have received your letter of this date containing the terms of sur-
render of the Army of Northern Virginia as proposed by you. As they

are substantially the same as those expressed in your letter of the 8th instant, they are accepted. I will proceed to designate the proper officers to carry the stipulations into effect.

Very respectfully, your obt servt

R. E. LEE
General

1002   SPECIAL ORDERS, NO. ——

Headquarters, Armies of the Confederate States
April 9, 1865

Lieut Genl James Longstreet, Maj Genl John B. Gordon, and Brig Genl William N. Pendleton are hereby designated to carry into effect the stipulations this day entered into between Lieut Genl U. S. Grant, commanding Armies of the United States, and General R. E. Lee, commanding Armies of the Confederate States, in which General Lee surrendered to General Grant the Army of Northern Virginia.

By command of General R. E. Lee:

W. H. TAYLOR
Lieutenant Colonel and Assistant Adjutant General

1003   GENERAL ORDER, NO. 9

Headquarters, Army of Northern Virginia
April 10, 1865

After four years of arduous service, marked by unsurpassed courage and fortitude, the Army of Northern Virginia has been compelled to yield to overwhelming numbers and resources.

I need not tell the brave survivors of so many hard fought battles, who have remained steadfast to the last, that I have consented to the result from no distrust of them.

But feeling that valor and devotion could accomplish nothing that would compensate for the loss that must have attended the continuance of the contest, I determined to avoid the useless sacrifice of those whose past services have endeared them to their countrymen.

By the terms of the agreement officers and men can return to their homes and remain until exchanged. You will take with you the satisfaction that proceeds from the consciousness of duty faithfully performed, and I earnestly pray that a Merciful God will extend to you His blessing and protection.

With an increasing admiration of your constancy and devotion to your country, and a grateful remembrance of your kind and generous considerations for myself, I bid you all an affectionate farewell.

R. E. LEE
Genl

1004 PAROLE OF GENERAL ROBERT E. LEE AND STAFF

We, the undersigned prisoners of war belonging to the Army of Northern Virginia, having been this day surrendered by General Robert E. Lee, C. S. A., commanding said army, to Lieut Genl U. S. Grant, commanding Armies of the United States, do hereby give our solemn parole of honor that we will not hereafter serve in the armies of the Confederate States, or in any military capacity whatever, against the United States of America, or render aid to the enemies of the latter, until properly exchanged, in such manner as shall be mutually approved by the respective authorities.

Done at Appomattox Court House, Virginia, this 9th day of April, 1865.

> R. E. LEE, Genl
> W. H. TAYLOR, Lt Col A A G
> CHARLES S. VENABLE, Lt Col & A A G
> CHARLES MARSHALL, Lt Col & A A G
> H. E. PEYTON, Lt Col & A & Inspt Genl
> GILES B. COOKE, Maj & A A & I G
> H. E. YOUNG, Maj A A G. Judge Adv

1005   To JEFFERSON DAVIS

Near Appomattox Court House, Virginia
April 12, 1865

Mr. President:

It is with pain that I announce to Your Excellency the surrender of the Army of Northern Virginia. The operations which preceded this result will be reported in full. I will therefore only now state that upon arriving at Amelia Court House on the morning of the 4th with the advance of the army, on its retreat from the lines in front of Richmond

and Petersburg, and not finding the supplies ordered to be placed there,
nearly twenty-four hours were lost in endeavoring to collect in the
country subsistence for men and horses. This delay was fatal, and could
not be retrieved. The troops, wearied by continued fighting and marching for several days and nights, obtained neither rest nor refreshment;
and on moving on the 5th on the Richmond and Danville Railroad, I
found at Jetersville the enemy's cavalry, and learned the approach of his
infantry and the general advance of his army towards Burkeville. This
deprived us of the use of the railroad, and rendered it impracticable to
procure from Danville the supplies ordered to meet us at points of our
march. Nothing could be obtained from the adjacent country. Our
route to the Roanoke was therefore changed, and the march directed
upon Farmville, where supplies were ordered from Lynchburg. The
change of route threw the troops on the roads pursued by the artillery
and wagon trains west of the railroad, which impeded our advance and
embarrassed our movements. On the morning of the 6th Genl Longstreet's corps reached Rice's Station on the Lynchburg Railroad. It was
followed by the commands of Genls R. H. Anderson, Ewell, and Gordon,
with orders to close upon it as fast as the progress of the trains would
permit or as they could be directed (diverted) on roads farther west.
Genl Anderson, commanding Pickett's and B. R. Johnson's divisions, became disconnected with Mahone's division, forming the rear of Longstreet. The enemy's cavalry penetrated the line of march through the
interval thus left and attacked the wagon train moving towards Farmville. This caused serious delay in the march of the center and rear of the
column, and enabled the enemy to mass upon their flank. After successive attacks Anderson's and Ewell's corps were captured or driven from
their position. The latter general, with both of his division commanders, Kershaw and Custis Lee, and his brigadiers, were taken prisoners.
Gordon, who all the morning, aided by Genl W. H. F. Lee's cavalry, had
checked the advance of the enemy on the road from Amelia Springs and
protected the trains, became exposed to his combined assaults, which he
bravely resisted and twice repulsed; but the cavalry having been withdrawn to another part of the line of march, and the enemy massing heavily on his front and both flanks, renewed the attack about 6 p.m., and
drove him from the field in much confusion. The army continued its
march during the night, and every effort was made to reorganize the
divisions which had been shattered by the day's operations. But the men
depressed by fatigue and hunger, many threw away their arms, while
others followed the wagon trains and embarrassed their progress. On the
morning of the 7th rations were issued to the troops as they passed
Farmville, but the safety of the trains requiring their removal upon the

approach of the enemy, all could not be supplied. The army reduced to two corps under Longstreet and Gordon, moved steadily on the road to Appomattox Court House. Thence its march was ordered by Campbell Court House through Pittsylvania towards Danville. The roads were wretched and the progress of the trains slow. By great efforts the head of the column reached Appomattox Court House on the evening of the 8th, and the troops were halted for rest. The march was ordered to be resumed at one (1) a.m. on the 9th. Fitz Lee with the cavalry, supported by Gordon, was ordered to drive the enemy from his front, wheel to the left, and cover the passage of the trains, while Longstreet, who from Rice's Station had formed the rear guard, should close up and hold the position. Two battalions of artillery and the ammunition wagons were directed to accompany the army. The rest of the artillery and wagons to move towards Lynchburg. In the early part of the night the enemy attacked Walker's artillery train near Appomattox Station on the Lynchburg Railroad, and were repelled. Shortly afterwards their cavalry dashed towards the Court House till halted by our line. During the night there were indications of a large force massing on our left and front. Fitz Lee was directed to ascertain its strength, and to suspend his advance till daylight if necessary. About five (5) a.m. on the 9th, with Gordon on his left, he moved forward and opened the way. A heavy force of the enemy was discovered opposite Gordon's right, which, moving in the direction of Appomattox Court House, drove back the left of the cavalry and threatened to cut off Gordon from Longstreet. His cavalry at the same time threatening to envelop his left flank, Gordon withdrew across the Appomattox River, and the cavalry advanced on the Lynchburg road and became separated from the army. Learning the condition of affairs on the lines, where I had gone under the expectation of meeting Genl Grant to learn definitely the terms he proposed in a communication received from him on the 8th, in the event of the surrender of the army, I requested a suspension of hostilities until these terms could be arranged. In the interview which occurred with Genl Grant in compliance with my request, terms having been agreed on, I surrendered that portion of the Army of Northern Virginia which was on the field, with its arms, artillery, and wagon trains; the officers and men to be paroled, retaining their side arms and private effects. I deemed this course the best under all the circumstances by which we were surrounded. On the morning of the 9th, according to the reports of the ordnance officers, there were seven thousand eight hundred and ninety-two (7892) organized infantry with arms, with an average of seventy-five (75) rounds of ammunition per man. The artillery, though reduced to sixty-three (63) pieces, with ninety-three (93) rounds of ammunition, was sufficient. These comprised all the supplies of ordnance that could be relied on in the State of Virginia. I have no accurate report of the cavalry, but believe it did not exceed two thousand and one hundred (2100) effective men. The enemy was more than five times our numbers. If we could have forced our way one day longer it would have been at a great sacrifice of life; at its end, I did not see how a surrender could have been avoided. We had no subsistence for man or horse, and it could not be gathered in the country. The supplies ordered to Pamplin's Station from Lynchburg could not reach us, and the men deprived of food and sleep for many days, were worn out and exhausted.

With great respect, yr obdt svt

R. E. LEE
Genl

1006　　　　　　　To JEFFERSON DAVIS

Richmond, Virginia
April 20, 1865

Mr. President:

The apprehensions I expressed during the winter, of the moral condition of the Army of Northern Virginia, have been realized. The operations which occurred while the troops were in the entrenchments in front of Richmond and Petersburg were not marked by the boldness and decision which formerly characterized them. Except in particular instances, they were feeble; and a want of confidence seemed to possess officers and men. This condition, I think, was produced by the state of feeling in the country, and the communications received by the men from their homes, urging their return and the abandonment of the field. The movement of the enemy on the 30th March to Dinwiddie Court House was consequently not as strongly met as similar ones had been. Advantages were gained by him which discouraged the troops, so that on the morning of the 2d April, when our lines between the Appomattox and Hatcher's Run were assaulted, the resistance was not effectual: several points were penetrated and large captures made. At the commencement of the withdrawal of the army from the lines on the night of the 2d, it began to disintegrate, and straggling from the ranks increased up to the surrender on the 9th. On that day, as previously reported, there were only seven thousand eight hundred and ninety-two (7892) effective infantry. During the night, when the surrender became known, more than ten thousand men came in, as reported to me by the

Chief Commissary of the Army. During the succeeding days stragglers continued to give themselves up, so that on the 12th April, according to the rolls of those paroled, twenty-six thousand and eighteen (26,018) officers and men had surrendered. Men who had left the ranks on the march, and crossed James River, returned and gave themselves up, and many have since come to Richmond and surrendered. I have given these details that Your Excellency might know the state of feeling which existed in the army, and judge of that in the country. From what I have seen and learned, I believe an army cannot be organized or supported in Virginia, and as far as I know the condition of affairs, the country east of the Mississippi is morally and physically unable to maintain the contest unaided with any hope of ultimate success. A partisan war may be continued, and hostilities protracted, causing individual suffering and the devastation of the country, but I see no prospect by that means of achieving a separate independence. It is for Your Excellency to decide, should you agree with me in opinion, what is proper to be done. To save useless effusion of blood, I would recommend measures be taken for suspension of hostilities and the restoration of peace.

I am with great respect, yr obdt svt

R. E. LEE
Genl

Editor's Note

THE LETTERS in this volume are reproduced basically as General Lee wrote them. His divisions into paragraphs and other sections are retained and his spelling and grammar are preserved, without benefit of *sic*, as they appear in the original manuscripts. Spelling and grammar have, however, been corrected in the letters and dispatches not written by General Lee. Punctuation has been inserted where necessary for clarity in all the letters; periods have been inserted without the use of brackets in place of dashes at the end of sentences, unnecessary capitals have been shifted to lower case letters.

All information inserted by the editors is enclosed in brackets; material in parentheses is General Lee's, as in the original manuscript. Proper names, the terms meant by confusing contractions, dates and additional information necessary to identify an individual, place or specific situation, and words necessary for coherence have been inserted in brackets.

When a printed source was used, the typographical or printing errors were corrected without the use of brackets.

All abbreviations have been expanded, except military ranks and contractions for proper names. To add some flavor of the period, ampersands have been retained, and the complimentary close has been retained in its abbreviated form as it appears in the manuscript. Unimportant, scratched out portions of a letter, along with slips of the pen, have not been reproduced. Where the canceled passage was deemed important it has been included in the Notes. Any gap in the text due to mutilation or damage to the manuscript is indicated by brackets. Whenever possible, missing words have been supplied by conjecture and enclosed in brackets, and a question mark has been inserted within the brackets when the reading is doubtful.

Figures, numbers, monetary designations and units of measure and weight are retained as written.

Due to the nature of the connecting narratives, there are no explanatory footnotes in the text. The identification of each document — its character and location as well as any notes that appear on the original which are not part of the letter — appears in the Notes section. Symbols used to describe the character of the documents are:

AL	Autographed Letter
ALS	Autographed Letter Signed
AD	Autographed Document
ADS	Autographed Document Signed
DS	Document Signed
FC	File Copy
LS	Letter Signed
RC	Recipient Copy
Lbc	Letterbook Copy
Copy	Contemporary Copy

Depositories where the original manuscripts are located are designated by the following National Union Catalogue symbols:

DLC	Library of Congress
DNA	National Archives
NcD	Duke University
NcU	University of North Carolina
Vi	Virginia State Library
ViHi	Virginia Historical Society

Where the institution holding the original has requested that the collection be cited and the full name given, we have done so. Letters from private collections, whose owners graciously consented to let us publish them, are identified as to the character of the manuscript and the owner's name and residence.

LOUIS H. MANARIN
Associate Editor

Notes

CHAPTER 1

ALS (DLC).
2. ALS (DNA).
3. CC (DLC).
4. Robert E. Lee, Jr., *Recollections and Letters of General Robert E. Lee* (New York, 1904), pp. 26-27. Hereafter cited as Lee, Jr., *Recollections*.
5. AD (DLC).
6. *War of the Rebellion: Official Records of the Union and Confederate Armies* (Washington, 1880-1901), Series I, II, 775-776. Hereafter cited as *O. R.*
7. *Ibid.*, pp. 777-778.
8. A. L. Long, *Memoirs of Robert E. Lee* (New York, 1886), p. 102. Hereafter cited as Long, *Memoirs*.
9. Copy (DLC) marked "Copy of a mouldy letter."
10. *O. R.*, Series I, II, 784-785.
11. *Ibid.*
12. Lbc (DNA).
13. Copy (DLC) marked "Copy."
14. Lbc (DNA).
15. Lbc (DNA).
16. ALS (DLC).
17. *O. R.*, Series I, LI, pt. 2, 67-68. Governor's proclamation in *O. R.*, Series I, II, 797.
18. Lbc (DNA).
19. Lbc (DNA).
20. *O. R.*, Series I, LI, pt. 2, 69.
21. Lbc (DNA).
22. Lbc (DNA).
23. Lbc (DNA).
24. Lbc (DNA).
25. Lbc (DNA). Special Orders, No. 39, in *O. R.*, Series I, II, 828.
26. *O. R.*, Series I, LI, pt. 2, 79.
27. ALS (DLC).
28. Lbc (DNA).
29. Lbc (DNA). Jackson's of 11th in *O. R.*, Series I, II, 832-833.
30. Lbc (DNA).
31. Lbc (DNA).
32. Lbc (DNA).
33. Lbc (DNA). Cocke's of 14th in *O. R.*, Series I, II, 841-842.

34. ALS (DLC). Convention referred to is the Episcopal Convention of the Diocese of Virginia.
35. Lbc (DNA). Taliaferro's of 14th in *O. R.*, Series I, II, 843-844.
36. Lbc (DNA). Mason's of 15th in *O. R.*, Series I, II, 848-850.
37. Lbc (DNA).
38. LS (DLC).
39. *O. R.*, Series I, II, 872.
40. Lbc (DNA).
41. Lbc (DNA).
42. ALS (DLC).
43. Lbc (DNA).
44. Lbc (DNA).
45. Lbc (DNA).
46. Lbc (DNA). Jackson's of 21st in *O. R.*, Series I, II, 863-864.
47. ALS (DLC). See letter of May 25th to his wife.
48. Lbc (DNA).
49. Lbc (DNA).
50. Lbc (DNA).
51. Lbc (DNA).
52. *O. R.*, Series I, II, 911-912.
53. ALS (DLC).
54. Lbc (DNA).
55. ALS (DLC).
56. Lbc (DNA).
57. Lbc (DNA). Magruder's of 10th is Battle Report of Big Bethel, *O. R.*, Series I, II, 91-92.
58. Lbc (DNA).
59. FC (Vi).
60. *O. R.*, Series I, II, 930. Hill's of 15th in *O. R.*, Series I, II, 927.
61. ALS (DLC).
62. ALS (DLC).
63. ALS (DLC) Signature cut off and part of the body of the letter on reverse also cut.
64. *O. R.*, Series I, III, 689-690.
65. *Ibid.*, p. 963. Magruder's of 30th in *O. R.*, Series I, II, 960-961.

CHAPTER 2

66. ALS (DLC). Signature cut off.
67. LC (DNA).
68. ALS (DLC). Signature cut off.
69. Lbc (DNA).
70. Lbc (DNA). Wise's of 24th in *O. R.*, Series I, V, 804-805.
71. ALS (DLC).
72. ALS (DLC).
73. J. William Jones, *Life and Letters of Robert E. Lee, Soldier and Man*

(New York, 1906), pp. 146-147. Hereafter cited as Jones, *Life and Letters.*

74. ALS (DLC).
75. Lbc (DNA).
76. *O. R.*, Series I, V, 192. The original order has no number.
77. ALS (DLC).
78. Lee, Jr., *Recollections*, pp. 46-47. Long, *Memoirs*, pp. 125-127.
79. Lbc (DNA).
80. Lbc (DNA). Wise's letter is quoted from *O. R.*, Series I, V, 879.
81. ALS (DLC).
82. ALS (DLC).

CHAPTER 3

83. ALS (DLC).
84. *O. R.*, Series I, VI, 309.
85. *Ibid.*, p. 312.
86. *Ibid.*, pp. 312-313.
87. ALS (DLC).
88. ALS (DLC). See preceding letter.
89. Lbc (DNA).
90. ALS (DLC).
91. Lee, Jr., *Recollections*, pp. 57-58. This letter is the printed version; the original was not found.
92. LS, University of South Carolina.
93. ALS (DLC).
94. Lbc (DNA). Gist's of 12th in *O. R.*, Series I, VI, 345.
95. Lbc (DNA).
96. Lbc (DNA).
97. ALS (DLC).
98. ALS (NcD).
99. LS. Mrs. Miles F. Storm, Winter Haven, Florida.
100. ALS (NcD).
101. Lbc (DNA).
102. Lbc (DNA).
103. ALS (DLC). Lee's father died at Dungeness on March 15, 1818. The plantation was given to General Nathanael Greene by the state of Georgia for services rendered her during the Revolutionary War.
104. ALS (NcD). See preceding letter.
105. ALS (DLC). See preceding letter.
106. Lbc (DNA).
107. Lbc (DNA).
108. Lbc (DNA).
109. ALS (DLC).
110. Lbc (DNA).
111. Lbc (DNA).

112. Lbc (DNA). For Evans's letter on charges against the officers of the Lyles Rifles, see *O. R.*, Series I, VI, 382-383.
113. Lbc (DNA). Wayne's letter of the 14th is in *O. R.*, Series I, VI, 381-382.
114. Lbc (DNA).
115. Lbc (DNA).
116. Lbc (DNA).
117. Lbc (DNA).
118. ALS (DLC).
119. Lbc (DNA).
120. Lbc (DNA).
121. ALS (DLC).
122. *O. R.*, Series I, LIII, 221. Lee's telegram is in reply to one from Davis, *O. R.*, Series I, VI, 400.

CHAPTER 4

123. *O. R.*, Series I, V, 1099.
124. ALS (DLC).
125. ALS (DLC).
126. Lbc (DNA). Holmes's letters of the 15th and 16th are in *O. R.*, Series I, V, 1100-1101. His letter of the 14th is in the same volume, page 1106.
127. Lbc (DNA). Holmes's letter of the 14th is in *O. R.*, Series I, V, 1106.
128. *O. R.*, Series I, XI, pt. 3, 385-386. Cabell's letter is in *O. R.*, Series I, IX, 69-70.
129. Lbc (DNA). Johnson's letter of the 18th is in *O. R.*, Series I, XII, pt. 2, 827-828.
130. ALS (DLC).
131. ALS (NcD).
132. LC (DNA).
133. *O. R.*, Series, XI, pt. 3, 398-399. Magruder's letters of the previous dates are in *O. R.*, Series I, XI, pt. 3, 392-393, 395, 396.
134. Lbc (DNA). Johnston's letter and Stoddert's and Stuart's reports are in *O. R.*, Series I, XI, pt. 3, 400-402. Lee's of the 25th to Johnston is in the same volume, page 397.
135. Lbc (DNA). Johnston's letter of the 27th is in *O. R.*, Series I, XI, pt. 3, 405.
136. Lbc (DNA).
137. Lbc (DNA). Lee's of the 26th to Magruder is in *O. R.*, Series I, XI, pt. 3, 398-399.
138. Lbc (DNA).
139. ALS (DLC).
140. Lbc (DNA).
141. Lbc (DNA).
142. *O. R.*, Series I, XVI, 432. Beauregard was in command of the Army of Tennessee. After the Battle of Shiloh on April 6th, he fell back to Corinth and was being pressed by a large Union force under General Halleck.
143. *Ibid.*, XII, pt. 3, 846.

144. ALS (NcU-SHC #605). Ewell's letter of the 16th is in *O. R.*, Series I, XII, pt. 3, 850-851.
145. Lbc (DNA). See next letter.
146. Lbc (DNA). See preceding letter.
147. Lbc (DNA).
148. Lbc (DNA). Lee's letter to Field on the morning of the 19th is in *O. R.*, Series I, XII, pt. 3, 855-856.
149. Lbc (DNA).
150. LS. Confederate Museum, Richmond, Virginia.
151. Lbc (DNA). Field's letter of the 20th is in *O. R.*, Series I, XII, pt. 1, 436.
152. Lbc (DNA).
153. *O. R.*, Series I, XII, pt. 3, 858-859. Ewell's letter of the 20th is in *O. R.*, Series I, XII, pt. 3, 857.
154. Lbc (DNA).
155. ALS (DLC).
156. Lbc (DNA).
157. *O. R.*, Series I, XII, pt. 3, 866-867. Ewell had moved his headquarters to Somerset. His division was located approximately seven miles from Gordonsville and consequently could move either to Fredericksburg or the Valley, when needed.
158. LS (NcU-SHC #1412). Jackson's letter of the 23rd is in *O. R.*, Series I, XII, pt. 3, 863-864.
159. Lbc (DNA).
160. ALS (DLC).
161. LS (DLC). Ewell's letter of the 26th is in *O. R.*, Series I, XII, pt. 3, 867-868.
162. Lbc (DNA). Lee's letter of the 26th to Holmes is in *O. R.*, Series I, IX, 464-465.
163. LS (NcU-SHC #1412).
164. Lbc (DNA). Johnston's letter of the 27th is in *O. R.*, Series I, XI, pt. 3, 469.
165. Lbc (DNA).
166. LS (NcU-SHC #1412). Jackson's letter of the 29th is in *O. R.*, Series I, XII, pt. 3, 872.
167. Lbc (DNA). Ewell's letter of the 30th is in *O. R.*, Series I, XII, pt. 3, 876. For Jackson's letter of the 29th, see preceding note.
168. Lbc (DNA).
169. *O. R.*, Series I, XII, pt. 3, 881.
170. Lbc (DNA). Lee had previously recommended that Colonel Clarke's regiment be retained in North Carolina and report to General Holmes.
171. Lbc (DNA). Johnston's letter of the 8th is in *O. R.*, Series I, XI, pt. 3, 499-500. Johnston referred to three letters signed "R. E. Lee, Genl, by W. H. Taylor, A. A. G." Only one appears in *O. R.* (XI, pt. 3, 497).
172. LS. Washington and Lee University. Lee's telegram of the 6th is in *O. R.*, Series I, XII, pt. 3, 881.

173. Lbc (DNA).
174. Lbc (DNA). Johnston's two letters of the 9th are in *O. R.*, Series I, XI, pt. 3, 502-504.
175. Lbc (DNA).
176. *O. R.*, Series I, XII, pt. 3, 510-511. Johnston's letter of the 10th is in *O. R.*, Series I, XII, pt. 3, 506.
177. ALS (DLC).
178. Lbc (DNA).
179. Lbc (DNA).
180. *O. R.*, Series I, XII, pt. 3, 892-893.
181. Lbc (DNA).
182. *O. R.*, Series I, XI, pt. 3, 526.
183. Lbc (DNA).
184. Lbc (DNA).

CHAPTER 5

185. *O. R.*, Series I, XI, pt. 3, 569.
186. Lbc (DNA).
187. Lbc (DNA).
188. Douglas Southall Freeman, *Lee's Dispatches: Unpublished Letters of General Robert E. Lee, C. S. A. to Jefferson Davis and the War Department of the Confederate States of America 1862-1865* (New York, 1915), pp. 5-10. Hereafter cited as Freeman, *Lee's Dispatches.*
189. Lbc (DNA).
190. *O. R.*, Series I, XII, pt. 3, 905-906.
191. *Ibid.*, XI, pt. 3, 576.
192. Lbc (DNA). Jackson's letter of the 6th is in *O. R.*, Series I, XII, pt. 3, 906-907.
193. Lbc (DNA).
194. *O. R.*, Series I, XI, pt. 3, 584.
195. *Ibid.*, LI, pt. 2, 1074.
196. Lbc (DNA).
197. ALS (DLC).
198. ALS (DLC).
199. Lbc (DNA).
200. Lbc (DNA).
201. *O. R.*, Series I, XI pt. 3, 590.
202. Lbc (DNA). Stuart's report of his ride around McClellan is in *O. R.*, Series I, XI, pt. 1, 1036-1040.
203. ALS (NcD). D. S. Freeman refers to this as the "missing link" in the correspondence that preceded Jackson's move from the Valley.
204. Lbc (DNA). Lee's letter of the 8th to Jackson is in *O. R.*, Series I, XI, pt. 3, 582-583. His letter of the 11th to Jackson is on pages 589-590 of the same volume.
205. Lbc (DNA).
206. ALS (NcD).

207. ALS (DNA).
208. Jones, *Life and Letters*, pp. 184-185.
209. *O. R.*, Series I, XI, pt. 1, 1042.
210. DS Confederate Museum, Richmond, Virginia. This document bears the signature of R. H. Chilton, Lee's Assistant Adjutant General.
211. LS (Vi).
212. ALS (DLC).
213. Freeman, *Lee's Dispatches*, pp. 15-17.
214. *O. R.*, Series I, XI, pt. 3, 617.
215. RC (NcD).
216. *O. R.*, Series I, XI, pt. 3, 622.
217. RC (NcD).
218. *O. R.*, Series I, XI, pt. 2, 675.
219. LS (NcU-SHC).
220. *O. R.*, Series I, XI, pt. 2, 685.
221. *Ibid.*, p. 687.
222. LS (Vi).
223. LS (Vi).
224. LS (Vi).
225. LS (Vi).
226. LS (Vi).
227. Lbc (DNA).
228. Lbc (DNA).
229. Lbc (DNA). Actual number of guns captured at Frazier's Farm is not known.

Chapter 6

230. LS (Vi).
231. ALS (DLC).
232. *O. R.*, Series I, XI, pt. 3, 638.
233. *Ibid.*, p. 640.
234. Jones, *Life and Letters*, pp. 185-186.
235. *O. R.*, Series I, LI, pt. 2, 1074-1075.
236. Lbc (DNA).
237. Lbc (DNA).
238. Lbc (DNA).
239. Lbc (DNA).
240. Lbc (DNA).
241. ALS (NcD).
242. LS (Vi).
243. Freeman, *Lee's Dispatches*, pp. 38-40.
244. Lbc (DNA).
245. Lbc (DNA). General Adolph von Steinwehr had arrested five citizens of Luray and threatened to execute one for every one of his soldiers killed by guerrillas unless the guerrilla was delivered up by the people.
246. ALS (DLC).

247. Lbc (DNA).
248. Jones, *Life and Letters*, p. 188.
249. Lbc (DNA).
250. ALS (DLC).
251. LS (Vi).
252. Lbc (DNA).
253. Lbc (DNA).
254. LS (Vi).
255. LS (NcD).
256. Lbc (DNA).
257. Lbc (DNA).
258. ALS (DLC).
259. Lbc (DNA).
260. Lbc (DNA).
261. *O. R.*, Series I, XII, pt. 3, 929.
262. Lbc (DNA).
263. ALS (Vi).
264. Lbc (DNA).
265. ALS (NcD).
266. *O. R.*, Series I, XI, pt. 3, 678.
267. ALS (Vi).
268. ALS (DLC).
269. *O. R.*, Series I, LI, pt. 2, 1075-1076.
270. FC Confederate Museum, Richmond, Virginia.
271. ALS (DNA).
272. RC (DNA).
273. *O. R.*, Series I, LI, pt. 2, 609. Davis's reply is in *O. R.*, Series I, XII, pt. 3, 938.
274. Lbc (DNA).
275. ALS Washington and Lee University. Pope's letter to McClellan of July 4, 1862, is in *O. R.*, Series I, XI, pt. 3, 295-297. His letter of August 20, 1862, to Halleck is in *O. R.*, Series I, XII, pt. 3, 603.
276. Freeman, *Lee's Dispatches*, p. 52.
277. ALS (DLC).
278. Lbc (DNA).
279. RC (NcD).
280. RC (NcD).
281. LS (Vi).
282. *O. R.*, Series I, XII, pt. 2, 562-563.
283. RC (NcD).
284. LS Washington and Lee University.
285. Lbc (DNA) Jackson's report on Cedar Mountain is in *O. R.*, Series I, XII, pt. 2, 181-185.
286. Lbc (DNA). Jackson's report on Second Manassas is in *O. R.*, Series I, XII, pt. 2, 181-185. Longstreet's is in the same volume, pages 563-568. Stuart's is also in the same volume, pages 733-738.

CHAPTER 7

287. Lbc (DNA).
288. FC (Vi).
289. FC (DNA).
290. RC (NcD).
291. Lbc (DNA).
292. FC (Vi).
293. Confederate Imprint (DNA). Marked "Received A. & I. G. O., September 16, 62."
294. FC (Vi).
295. FC (Vi).
296. DS (Vi).
297. FC (Vi).
298. FC (Vi).
299. FC (Vi).
300. O. R., Series I, XIX, pt. 2, 606.
301. FC (Vi).
302. O. R., Series I, LI, pt. 2, 618-619.
303. ALS (NcU-SHC #472).
304. O. R., Series I, XIX, pt. 2, 609-610.
305. Lbc (DNA).
306. FC (DNA). Letter marked "An extract truly copied from the original. Sept. 24, 1862. Burton N. Harrison Private Secretary." Burton Harrison was Jefferson Davis's private secretary.
307. ALS, DS (DNA).

CHAPTER 8

308. LS (DNA).
309. Lbc (DNA).
310. Lbc (DNA).
311. Lbc (DNA).
312. LS (DNA).
313. ALS (NcD).
314. Lbc (DNA).
315. O. R., Series I, XIX, pt. 2, 720-721.
316. Lbc (DNA).
317. O. R., Series I, XXI, 1013.
318. LS (DNA).
319. LS (DNA).
320. LS (DNA).
321. Lbc (DNA).
322. FC (NcD).
323. LS (DNA).
324. ALS (DLC).
325. LS (NcU-SHC #1412).

326. LS (DNA).
327. Lbc (DNA).
328. Lbc (DNA).
329. LS (DNA).
330. Lbc (DNA).
331. ALS (NcD).
332. LS (NcU-SHC #1412).
333. Lbc (DNA).
334. ALS (DLC).
335. LS (DNA).
336. Jones, *Life and Letters*, p. 202.
337. ALS (DLC).
338. RC (DNA).
339. RC (DNA).
340. RC (DNA).
341. RC (DNA).
342. Lbc (DNA).
343. RC (DNA).
344. RC (DNA).
345. LS (DNA).
346. RC (DNA).
347. LS (DNA).
348. ALS (DLC).
349. RC (DNA).
350. DS (DNA).

CHAPTER 9

351. ALS (DLC).
352. ALS (DLC).
353. ALS (DLC).
354. ALS (DLC).
355. *O. R.*, Series I, XXI, 1079.
356. Lbc (DNA).
357. ALS (NcD).
358. Lbc (DNA).
359. ALS (Vi).
360. RC (DNA).
361. LS (DNA).
362. Lbc (DNA).
363. RC (DNA). Letter marked "General Lee left before this copy was ready for his signature. T. M. R. Talcott Maj & A. D. C."
364. *O. R.*, Series I, XXI, 1101.
365. Lbc (DNA).
366. LS (DNA).
367. Lbc (DNA).
368. ALS (DLC).

369. ALS (DNA).
370. Lbc (DNA).
371. Lbc (DNA). Davis's letter of the 4th is in *O. R.*, Series I, XIV, 1019-1020.
372. ALS (DLC).
373. ALS (DLC).
374. Lbc (DNA).
375. Lbc (DNA).
376. Lbc (DNA).
377. Lbc (DNA).
378. Lbc (DNA). The last paragraph is marked "P. S." in letterbook copy.
379. ALS (DLC).
380. ALS (DLC).
381. Lbc (DNA).
382. ALS (NcD).
383. Jones, *Life and Letters*, p. 286.
384. ALS (DLC).
385. Lbc (DNA).
386. ALS (DLC).
387. Lbc (DLC). Longstreet's letter of the 19th is in *O. R.*, Series I, XVIII, 926-927.
388. ALS (DLC).
389. Lbc (DNA). Longstreet's letter of the 24th is in *O. R.*, Series I, XVIII, 942.
390. LS (DNA).
391. ALS (DLC).
392. Lbc (DNA).

CHAPTER 10

393. ALS (DLC).
394. ALS Mr. W. J. Driver, Sarasota, Florida.
395. Lbc (DNA).
396. LS (DNA). Seddon's letter of the 6th is in *O. R.*, Series I, XXV, pt. 2, 708-709.
397. ALS (DLC).
398. ALS (DLC).
399. LS (DNA). Cooper's letter of the 14th is in *O. R.*, Series I, XXV, pt. 2, 720.
400. LS (NcD).
401. Lbc (DNA).
402. *O. R.*, Series I, XXV, pt. 2, 731.
403. ALS (DLC).
404. *O. R.*, Series I, XXV, pt. 2, 859.
405. LS (DNA).
406. ALS (DLC).
407. Lbc (DNA).

408. RC (NcD).
409. RC (NcD).
410. RC (NcD).
411. RC (NcD).
412. *O. R.*, Series I, LI, pt. 2, 699.
413. Lbc (DNA).
414. Lbc (DNA).
415. RC (DNA).
416. Lbc (DNA).
417. Lbc (DNA).
418. LS (NcU-SHC #472).
419. LS (NcU-SHC #472).
420. RC (NcD).
421. *O. R.*, Series I, XXV, pt. 2, 764.
422. Lbc (DNA).
423. *O. R.*, Series I, XXV, pt. 2, 769.
424. *Ibid.*
425. RC (NcD).
426. LS. Lee Letters, Emory University.
427. FC (DNA).
428. Lbc (DNA).
429. LS (NcU-SHC #472).
430. LS (DNA).
431. RC (DNA).
432. RC (DNA).
433. RC (DNA).
434. RC (NcD).
435. RC (DNA).
436. Lbc (DNA).
437. LS (DNA), Lbc (DNA).

CHAPTER 11

438. Lbc (DNA).
439. RC (DNA).
440. LS (Vi).
441. Jones, *Life and Letters*, pp. 287-288.
442. *O. R.*, Series I, XXV, pt. 2, 792.
443. ALS (Vi).
444. ALS (DLC).
445. ALS (NcD).
446. ALS (DNA).
447. Jones, *Life and Letters*, p. 247. Omissions in the copy used are indicated by ellipses.
448. ALS (DLC).
449. ALS (DLC).
450. ALS (Vi).

451. Lbc (DNA).
452. RC (NcD).
453. Lbc (DNA).
454. LS (Vi).
455. FC (Vi).
456. ALS (DLC).
457. LS (DNA).
458. ALS (DLC).
459. Lbc (DNA).
460. Lbc (DNA).
461. LS (Vi).
462. Lbc (DNA).
463. Lbc (ViHi).
464. FC (DNA).
465. RC (DNA).
466. ALS (DLC).
467. *O. R.*, Series I, XXVII, pt. 3, 880-882.
468. Jones, *Life and Letters*, p. 245. Lee's son, W. H. F. Lee, was wounded during the Battle of Brandy Station.
469. Lbc (ViHi).
470. Lbc (ViHi).
471. ALS (DLC).
472. Jones, *Life and Letters*, pp. 245-246. Omissions in the copy used are indicated by ellipses.
473. Lbc (ViHi). Seddon's letters of the 9th and 10th are in *O. R.*, Series I, XXVII, pt. 3, 874-876, 882.
474. ALS (NcD).
475. Lbc (ViHi).
476. RC (NcD).
477. Lbc (DNA).
478. Lbc (ViHi).
479. *O. R.*, Series I, XXVII, pt. 3, 896.
480. Lbc (ViHi). A note in the letterbook states: "Copy from memory; draught mislaid."
481. Lbc (ViHi).
482. RC (DNA).
483. Lbc (ViHi).
484. Lbc (ViHi).
485. Lbc (ViHi).
486. Lbc (ViHi).
487. Lbc (DNA).
488. Lbc (ViHi).
489. Lbc (ViHi). General Orders, No. 72, is in *O. R.*, Series I, XXVII, pt. 3, 912-913.
490. Lbc (ViHi).
491. *O. R.*, Series I, LI, pt. 2, 726.

492. Lbc (ViHi).
493. LS (Vi).
494. Lbc (DNA).
495. LS (Vi).
496. Lbc (ViHi).
497. Lbc (ViHi).
498. *O. R.*, Series I, XXVII, pt. 3, 942-943.
499. Lbc (ViHi). A note in the letterbook states: "(From Memory) sketch of letter."
500. Lbc (DNA). Pickett's letter of the 21st is in *O. R.*, Series I, XXVII, pt. 3, 910.
501. ALS (DLC). Mrs. Lee was in Union-occupied territory, hence the reason for secrecy. Since the letter was going behind Federal lines, Lee did not sign it.
502. Lbc (ViHi).
503. Lbc (ViHi).
504. Lbc (ViHi).
505. Lbc (ViHi).
506. *O. R.*, Series I, XXVII, pt. 2, 311.
507. Lbc (ViHi).
508. ALS (DLC).
509. Lbc (DNA). Pickett is on duty escorting prisoners.
510. Lbc (ViHi).
511. *O. R.*, Series I, XXVII, pt. 3, 985.
512. LS (Vi).
513. RC (NcD).
514. *O. R.*, Series I, XXVII, pt. 3, 995.
515. *Ibid.*, p. 998.
516. ALS (DLC).
517. LS (Vi).
518. Lbc (DNA).
519. *O. R.*, Series I, XXVII, pt. 3, 1001.
520. RC (NcD).
521. *O. R.*, Series I, XXVII, pt. 3, 1006.
522. ALS (DLC).
523. Lbc (ViHi).
524. ALS (DNA).
525. *O. R.*, Series I, XXVII, pt. 3, 1020.
526. Lbc (ViHi).
527. LS (DNA).
528. Lbc (DNA).
529. Lbc (DNA).
530. Lbc (DNA).
531. Lbc (ViHi).
532. ALS (DLC).
533. ALS. Mr. W. J. Driver, Sarasota, Florida.

534. ALS (DLC).
535. Lbc (ViHi). Davis's letter of the 21st is in *O. R.*, Series I, XXVII, pt. 3, 1030-1031.
536. ALS (Vi).
537. RC (NcD).
538. RC (NcD).
539. ALS (DLC).
540. LS (DNA).
541. *O. R.*, Series I, XXVII, pt. 3, 1075.
542. FC (DNA). The preliminary report on the Battle of Gettysburg is in *O. R.*, Series I, XXVII, pt. 2, 305-311.

CHAPTER 12

543. *O. R.*, Series I, LI, pt. 2, 752-753.
544. Lbc (DNA).
545. LS (Vi).
546. Jones, *Life and Letters*, pp. 288-289.
547. *O. R.*, Series I, LI, pt. 2, 1076. Davis's reply is in *O. R.*, Series I, XXIX pt. 2, 639-640.
548. Lbc (ViHi).
549. *O. R.*, Series I, LI, pt. 2, 761.
550. ALS (DLC).
551. LS (Vi).
552. ALS (Vi).
553. ALS (DLC).
554. Lbc (ViHi). See Lee to Davis, September 11, 1863, *O. R.*, Series I, XXIX, pt. 2, 710.
555. LS (Vi).
556. LS (Vi).
557. ALS (NcD). Actually, neither Hood nor Wofford was killed; Hood lost a leg.
558. Lbc (ViHi).
559. Lbc (ViHi).
560. Lbc (ViHi).
561. ALS (Vi).
562. Lbc (DNA).
563. *O. R.*, Series I, XXIX, pt. 1, 405-406.
564. LS (DNA).
565. LS (Vi).
566. Lbc (DNA). Lawton's letter of the 12th is in *O. R*, Series I, XXIX, pt. 2, 784-785.
567. ALS (DLC).
568. RC (DNA).
569. LS (DNA).
570. *O. R.*, Series I, XXX, pt. 2, 69. Polk's letter of the 27th is in *O. R.*, Series I, XXX, pt. 4, 708.

571. ALS (DLC).
572. Lbc (DNA).
573. Lbc (DNA). Jones's letter of the 22nd was to Seddon and is in *O. R.*, Series I, XXIX, pt. 2, 799.
574. ALS (DLC).
575. LS (DNA).
576. Lbc (DNA).
577. ALS (DLC).
578. LS (DNA).
579. ALS (DLC).
580. ALS (DLC).
581. RC (DNA).
582. RC (DNA).
583. *O. R.*, Series I, LI, pt. 2, 788.
584. RC (DNA).
585. RC (DNA).
586. *O. R.*, Series I, XXIX, pt. 1, 824.
587. RC (DNA).
588. RC (DNA).
589. *O. R.*, Series I, XXIX, pt. 1, 825.
590. Lbc (DNA).
591. LS (DNA).
592. ALS (DLC).
593. DLS (DNA).

CHAPTER 13

594. Lbc (ViHi).
595. Lbc (ViHi).
596. *O. R.*, Series I, XXIX, pt. 2, 866.
597. *Ibid.*, LI, pt. 2, 796-797.
598. ALS (NcD).
599. ALS (DLC).
600. ALS (DLC).
601. ALS (DLC).
602. ALS (NcD).
603. *O. R.*, Series I, XXXIII, 1064-1065.
604. ALS (DLC).
605. Lbc (ViHi). Cooper's letter of the 9th is in *O. R.*, Series I, XXXII, pt. 2, 539.
606. Lbc (ViHi).
607. ALS (DLC).
608. Lbc (DNA).
609. *O. R.*, Series I, XXXIII, 1097-1098.
610. Lbc (ViHi).
611. Lbc (ViHi).

612. Lbc (ViHi).
613. Lbc (ViHi).
614. Lbc (ViHi).
615. Lbc (DNA). Jones's letter of the 17th is in O. R., Series I, XXXIII, 1093.
616. DS (DLC).
617. Lbc (DNA).
618. ALS (DLC).
619. ALS (Vi). For Davis's of the 16th, see G. W. C. Lee to R. E. Lee, O. R., Series I, XXXIII, 1091-1092.
620. Lbc (DNA).
621. Lbc (DNA).
622. Lbc (DNA). Jones's letter of the 31st is in O. R., Series I, XXXIII, 1135.
623. Lbc (ViHi).
624. ALS (DLC).
625. DS (DLC).
626. Lbc (DNA).
627. Lbc (DNA).
628. ALS (DLC).
629. LS (DNA).
630. Lbc (DNA).
631. Lbc (DNA).
632. ALS (Vi). Longstreet's letter to Cooper is in O. R., Series I, XXXII, pt. 2, 759.
633. O. R., Series I, XXXIII, 1192-1193.
634. RC (DNA).
635. RC (DNA).
636. RC (DNA).
637. RC (DNA).
638. Lbc (DNA).
639. O. R., Series I, XXXIII, 1206.
640. ALS (DNA).
641. ALS (DLC).
642. ALS (DLC).
643. ALS (DLC).
644. LS (Vi).
645. O. R., Series I, LII, pt. 2, 648-649. Longstreet's letter of the 16th is in
646. Typed copy (NcD).
647. ALS (DLC).
648. Lbc (ViHi).
649. LS (DNA).
650. ALS (DLC).
651. ALS. Lee Letters, Emory University.
652. O. R., Series I, XXXIII, 1265.
653. Lbc (ViHi).
     O. R., Series I, XXXII, pt. 3, 641. Longstreet's letter to Davis is on page 637 of the same volume.

654. *O. R.*, Series I, XXXIII, 1266-1267.
655. ALS (Vi).
656. ALS (DLC).
657. Jones, *Life and Letters*, p. 304.
658. LS (Vi).
659. Lbc (ViHi).
660. Lbc (ViHi).
661. ALS. Dr. Harry Warthen, Richmond, Virginia.
662. Lbc (ViHi).
663. ALS. Washington and Lee University.
664. Lbc (ViHi).
665. Lbc (ViHi).
666. Lbc (ViHi). A notation in the letterbook states: "Official copy of substance of letter as given to me by Lt Col Taylor on the 18th April. C. Marshall A. D. C."
667. ALS (Vi).
668. ALS (DLC).
669. ALS (Vi).
670. Lbc (ViHi).
671. Jones, *Life and Letters*, p. 305.
672. RC (NcD).
673. Lbc (DNA).

Chapter 14

674. LS (DNA).
675. *O. R.*, Series I, LI, pt. 2, 885.
676. ALS (DLC).
677. *O. R.*, Series I, LI, pt. 2, 887.
678. *Ibid.*, XXXVII, pt. 1, 712.
679. *Ibid.*, XXXVII, pt. 1, 713.
680. LS (Vi).
681. *O. R.*, Series I, XXXVI, pt. 2, 952.
682. *Ibid.*
683. RC (DNA).
684. RC (NcD).
685. RC (DNA).
686. *O. R.*, Series I, XXXVI, pt. 2, 969-970.
687. *Ibid.*, p. 968.
688. RC (DNA). Lee's notion that the enemy was moving to Fredericksburg was based on insufficient information and was held by him very briefly. Anderson was at Spotsylvania Court House when Lee sent this message.
689. *O. R.*, Series I, LI, pt. 2, 902.
690. *Ibid.*, pp. 902-903.
691. RC (NcD).
692. RC (NcD).
693. RC (NcD). Same sent to Davis and Bragg.

694. LS (DLC).
695. RC (NcD).
696. RC (NcD).
697. RC (DNA).
698. RC (NcD).
699. *O. R.*, Series I, LI, pt. 2, 929-930.
700. RC (DNA).
701. RC (NcD).
702. RC (NcD).
703. ALS (DLC).
704. RC (DNA).
705. LS (DLC).
706. RC (DNA).
707. RC (DNA).
708. RC (DNA).
709. RC (NcD).
710. RC (NcD). The portion left out was also left out in the original, probably through faulty transmission.
711. RC (DNA).
712. RC (NcD).
713. *O. R.*, Series I, XXXVI, pt. 3, 801.
714. *Ibid.*
715. *Ibid.*, p. 800.

Chapter 15

716. RC (DNA). Words inserted are on a file copy of the telegram at Duke University and not on the original. They were unintelligible at the time of deciphering.
717. LS (NcU-SHC # 7).
718. RC (DNA).
719. LS (Vi).
720. RC (DNA).
721. LS (Vi).
722. ALS (DLC).
723. RC (DNA).
724. *O. R.*, Series I, XXXVI, pt. 3, 826.
725. *Ibid.*, LI, pt. 2, 957.
726. RC (DNA). Taylorsville was where telegraphed from, not Lee's headquarters.
727. LS (Vi).
728. *O. R.*, Series I, LI, pt. 2, 960.
729. *Ibid.*, XXXVI, pt. 3, 837.
730. RC (DNA). Only cavalry crossed at Hanovertown.
731. *O. R.*, Series I, LI, pt. 2, 962.
732. *Ibid.*, XXXVI, pt. 3, 838.
733. LS (Vi).

734. *O. R.*, Series I, XXXVI, pt. 3, 844.
735. ALS (DNA).
736. FC (NcD).
737. RC (NcD).
738. RC (NcD).
739. ALS (DLC).
740. LS (Vi).
741. LS (NcU-SHC # 7).
742. RC (NcD).
743. *O. R.*, Series I, XXXVI, pt. 3, 850.
744. *Ibid.*, p. 858.
745. *Ibid.*, XL, pt. 2, 702-703. The recipient is unknown but appears to be General A. P. Hill.
746. LS (DNA).
747. *O. R.*, Series I, XXXVI, pt. 3, 864.
748. *Ibid.*, p. 865.
749. FC (DNA).
750. LS (NcU-SHC # 7). This copy of the circular was sent to General Anderson.
751. LS (Vi).
752. LS (DNA).
753. ALS (DLC).
754. LS (NcU-SHC # 7).
755. FC (DNA).
756. RC (NcD).
757. LS (Vi).
758. ALS (DLC).
759. ALS (DNA).
760. ALS (DLC).
761. *O. R.*, Series I, XXXVI, pt. 1, 1034.
762. LS. Confederate Museum, Richmond, Virginia. Lee is evidently referring to Beauregard's telegram to Bragg which was forwarded to Lee. See *O. R.*, Series I, XXXVI, pt. 3, 884.
763. Freeman, *Lee's Dispatches*, pp. 221-223.
764. LS (NcU-SHC # 7).
765. RC (NcD).
766. FC (DNA).
767. LS (DNA).
768. LS (DNA).
769. *O. R.*, Series I, LI, pt. 2, 1003.
770. ALS (DLC).
771. *O. R.*, Series I, XXXVI, pt. 3, 897-898.
772. LS (DNA).
773. LS (Vi).
774. LS (Vi).
775. LS (Vi).

776. FC (DNA).
777. LS (Vi).
778. LS (Vi).
779. LS (DNA).
780. LS (Vi).
781. ALS (Vi).
782. *O. R.*, Series I, XL, pt. 2, 659.
783. *Ibid.*, XL, pt. 1, 749.
784. *Ibid.*, XL, pt. 2, 659.
785. *Ibid.*
786. *Ibid.*
787. LS (Vi).
788. RC (NcD).
789. *O. R.*, Series I, XL, pt. 2, 664.
790. RC (DNA).
791. *O. R.*, Series I, XL, pt. 2, 664.
792. *Ibid.*
793. *Ibid.*, p. 663.
794. *Ibid.*, p. 662.
795. *Ibid.*, p. 665.
796. *Ibid.*
797. *Ibid.*, p. 663.
798. *Ibid.*, p. 665.
799. *Ibid.*, p. 668.
800. *Ibid.*, XXXVI, pt. 1, 766.
801. LS (Vi).
802. RC (DNA).
803. *O. R.*, Series I, XL, pt. 2, 667.
804. RC (DNA).
805. ALS (DLC).
806. LS (Vi).

CHAPTER 16

807. FC (DNA).
808. *O. R.*, Series I, XL, pt. 2, 679.
809. RC (DNA).
810. ALS (DLC).
811. LS (DNA).
812. RC (NcD).
813. LS (DNA).
814. *O. R.*, Series I, XXXVI, pt. 3, 903.
815. LS (DNA).
816. Lbc (ViHi).
817. ALS (DLC).
818. LS (DNA).
819. ALS (DLC).

820. RC (DNA).
821. Lbc (ViHi).
822. ALS (DLC).
823. RC (DNA).
824. LS (Vi).
825. ALS (DLC).
826. LS (Vi).
827. Typed copy (NcD).
828. ALS (DLC).
829. *O. R.*, Series I, XL, pt. 3, 755-756.
830. ALS (Vi).
831. ALS (DLC).
832. Lbc (ViHi).
833. RC (NcD).
834. ALS (Vi).
835. FC (DNA).
836. ALS (NcD).
837. *O. R.*, Series I, XL, pt. 3, 796.
838. ALS (NcD).
839. LS (NcU-SHC # 7).
840. *O. R.*, Series I, XL, pt. 3, 813.
841. RC (DNA).
842. RC (DNA).
843. ALS (DLC).
844. ALS (DLC).
845. *O. R.*, Series I, XLII, pt. 2, 1168.
846. LS (Vi) Last line written by Lee.
847. *O. R.*, Series I, XLII, pt. 2, 1169.
848. RC (DNA).
849. Lbc (ViHi).
850. Lbc (ViHi).
851. *O. R.*, Series I, XLII, pt. 2, 1173.
852. Lbc (ViHi).
853. *O. R.*, Series I, XLIII, pt. 1, 997.
854. *Ibid.*, XLII, pt. 2, 1177.
855. *Ibid.*
856. *Ibid.*, LI, pt. 2, 1035.
857. *Ibid.*, XLII, pt. 2, 1177.
858. ALS (DLC).
859. ALS Confederate Museum, Richmond, Virginia.
860. RC (NcD).
861. RC (DNA).
862. RC (DNA).
863. *O. R.*, Series I, XLII, pt. 2, 1186.
864. RC (DNA).
865. RC (DNA).

866. RC (DNA).
867. *O. R.*, Series I, XLII, pt. 2, 1193.
868. *Ibid.*, p. 1192. The same telegram was sent to Colonel Sanford, Superintendent of the South Side Railroad.
869. RC (DNA).
870. LS (Vi).
871. LS (DNA).
872. *O. R.*, Series I, XLII, pt. 2, 1202.
873. RC (DNA).
874. Lbc (ViHi).
875. ALS (DLC).
876. LS (Vi).
877. ALS (DLC).
878. Freeman, *Lee's Dispatches*, pp. 296-298.
879. ALS (NcD).
880. ALS (NcU-SHC # 7).
881. RC (DNA).
882. LS (DNA).
883. ALS (DNA).
884. RC (DNA).
885. RC (DNA).
886. FC. Confederate Museum, Richmond, Virginia.
887. FC. Confederate Museum, Richmond, Virginia.
888. LS. Mr. Howard Lehman, New York City.
889. FC. Confederate Museum, Richmond, Virginia.
890. RC (DNA).
891. RC (DNA).
892. FC. Confederate Museum, Richmond, Virginia.
893. RC (DNA).
894. FC. Confederate Museum, Richmond, Virginia.
895. FC. Confederate Museum, Richmond, Virginia.
896. RC (DNA).
897. FC (DNA).
898. RC (DNA).
899. RC (DNA).
900. RC (DNA).
901. RC (DNA).
902. RC (DNA).
903. *O. R.*, Series I, XLII, pt. 3, 1144-1145.
904. RC (DNA).
905. RC (DNA).
906. RC (DNA).
907. RC (DNA).
908. ALS (DLC).
909. ALS (DNA). A notation on the letter states: "By Charles Marshall, aide-de-camp, for and in the absence of General Lee."

910. RC (DNA).
911. RC (DNA).
912. RC (DNA).
913. ALS (Vi). It is obvious from this letter that Lee did not know all the facts on the Law-Longstreet controversy.
914. ALS (DLC).
915. ALS (DLC).
916. ALS (DLC).
917. *O. R.*, Series I, XLII, pt. 3, 1223.
918. ALS (DLC).
919. ALS (DLC). The omitted portion is cut off in the original.
920. *O. R.*, Series I, XLIII, pt. 2, 936.
921. RC (DNA).
922. RC (DNA).
923. RC (DNA).
924. RC (DNA).
925. ALS (NcD).
926. RC (DNA).
927. RC (NcD).
928. ALS (DLC).
929. *O. R.*, Series I, XLIV, 966.
930. LS (DNA).
931. ALS (DLC).
932. ALS (DLC).
933. RC (DNA).
934. ALS (NcD).
935. LS (DNA), FC (DNA).
936. ALS. Confederate Museum, Richmond, Virginia.
937. ALS (DNA).
938. ALS (Vi).
939. LS (NcU-SHC # 508).
940. LS (DNA).
941. ALS (DLC).
942. ALS (DLC).
943. *O. R.*, Series I, XLVI, pt. 2, 1199.
944. RC (DNA).
945. *O. R.*, Series I, XLVI, pt. 1, 381-382. Lee addressed Seddon as Secretary of War; actually Seddon was out and John C. Breckinridge was now Secretary of War.
946. *Ibid.*, pt. 2, 1226-1227.
947. ALS (NcU-SHC # 508).
948. *O. R.*, Series I, LI, pt. 2, 1082-1083.
949. ALS (DLC).
950. ALS (DLC).
951. ALS (DLC). This letter was also addressed to Senators A. E. Maxwell, J. M. Baker, R. W. Walker, A. T. Caperton, S. C. Haynes, W. P. Johnson,

A. H. Garland, J. W C. Watson, H. C. Burnett, J. L. Orr, G. G. Vest, W. E. Simms, W. A. Graham, W. S. Oldham, W. T. Dortch, A. G. Brown, L T. Wigfall.

952. *O. R.*, Series I, XLVI, pt. 2, 1240.
953. ALS (DLC).

CHAPTER 17

954. ALS (DNA).
955. ALS. Justin G. Turner, Los Angeles, California.
956. ALS (DNA).
957. ALS (DLC).
958. LS. Washington and Lee University.
959. ALS. Lee Letters, Emory University.
960. LS (DNA).
961. ALS (NcD).
962. *O. R.*, Series I, XLVI, pt. 2, 824. Grant's reply is on page 825 of the same volume.
963. RC (DNA).
964. FC (DNA).
965. LS (NcD).
966. ALS. Lee Letters, Emory University.
967. RC (DNA).
968. RC (DNA).
969. LS (Vi).
970. *O. R.*, Series I, XLVI, pt. 3, 1357.
971. ALS (DLC).
972. ALS (DLC).
973. ALS (DLC).
974. RC (DNA).
975. RC (DNA).
976. RC (NcD).
977. ALS (DLC).
978. RC (NcD).
979. Freeman, *Lee's Dispatches*, pp. 358-360.
980. LS (DNA).
981. ALS (DLC).
982. RC (DNA).
983. RC (DNA).
984. RC. Washington and Lee University.
985. RC (DNA).
986. *O. R.*, Series I, XLVI, pt. 3, 1378.
987. *O. R.*, Series I, XLVI, pt. 3, 1380.
988. RC (DNA).
989. Lbc (DLC).
990. RC (NcD).
991. LS (DNA).

992. LS (DNA).
993. *O. R.*, Series I, XLVI, pt. 3, 1385. The same was sent to General Ewell and Gordon.
994. *Ibid.*, p. 1387.
995. *Ibid.*, p. 1386.
996. ALS (DNA).
997. ALS (DNA).
998. LS (DNA).
999. LS (DNA).
1000. LS (DNA).
1001. FC (DNA).
1002. *O. R.*, Series I, XLVI, pt. 3, 666-667.
1003. ADS. Washington and Lee University.
1004. DS (DNA).
1005. Lbc (DLC).
1006. Lbc (DLC).

Index of Addressees

General Index

ABSENTEES, 671-672. *See also* Desertions

Aiken, Col. Hugh K., 654

Alexander, Col. Edward Porter, 54, 222, 255; at Fredericksburg, 362, 368, 369, 372; at Chancellorsville, 454, 464, 470; given command of First Corps artillery, 638

Amelia Court House, Lee orders all troops to, 900, 925-926, 928, 929

Amelia Island, defenses of, 89

Anderson, Maj. Edward C., 113, 834

Anderson, Gen. G. B., 316, 320

Anderson, Gen. G. T., at Second Manassas, 281; in Sharpsburg campaign, 316, 319; wounded at Gettysburg, 541, 578

Anderson, Gen. J. R., at Fredericksburg, 154, 156, 157, 159, 169, 170; in command at Fredericksburg, 166, 171

Anderson, Maj. Robert and Mrs., 118

Andrews, Col. R. Snowden, 470

Apalachicola River, Lee orders defenses improved, 121

Appomattox, Lee's army withdraws to, 901-902, 924-929

Archer, Gen. James J., ordered to join A. P. Hill, 190, 191; at Second Manassas, 282; in Maryland campaign, 317, 321; at Fredericksburg, 369, 370, 371; regiment at Chancellorsville, 463; taken prisoner at Gettysburg, 541, 575

Arlington, 7, 108; slaves to be freed, 100, 105, 350, 354. *See also* Slaves

Armistead, Gen. Lewis A., 539, 580, 585

Artillery, Lee's ideas on, 704

Ashby, Capt. Turner, 40

Ashton, Private Lewis, 198

Atlanta, Sherman enters, 800; fall of, 851

Augur, Gen. Christopher C., occupies Falmouth, 151, 152; opposite Fredericksburg, 154, 156; joins Grant at Spotsylvania, 733

Augusta and Savannah Railroad, 117

Averell, Gen. William W., 556; Lee does not expect advance of, 618; cavalry pursues, 647; destroys stocks of leather, 653; in the Valley, 656, 665; believed to be heading for Richmond, 703; on expedition toward Staunton, 716-717; at Spotsylvania, 732; Early keeps occupied, 799; with Hunter near Charleston, 819

Avery, Col. Isaac E., 578

Anderson, Gen. Richard H., 244, 255, 325; to be withdrawn from Drewry's Bluff, 252, 254; ordered to Louisa Court House, 256; division joins Lee at Groveton, 267; in Second Manassas campaign, 276, 281, 283; in Sharpsburg campaign, 302, 311, 314, 320; at Fredericksburg, 369, 372; in Chancellorsville campaign, 424, 425, 438, 444, 445, 446, 447, 448-449, 454, 457, 459, 460, 462, 463, 465, 468, 470; Lee's high opinion of, 489; in Gettysburg campaign, 513, 516, 517, 521, 525, 563, 577; after Gettysburg, 621; in the Wilderness, 713, 721; at Spotsylvania, 715, 724, 725, 726; ordered to attack Cold Harbor, 740; in campaign, North Anna to Petersburg, 742, 749, 751, 760, 762, 786, 794; sent back to middle Virginia, 799; commands scratch force, 801; Hampton sent to join at Culpeper, 832-833, 835; ordered to move in the Valley, 834, 835; at the siege of Petersburg, 846, 861; ordered to return to Lee, 852-853; in retreat, 901, 936; skirmishes near Boydton Plank Road, 920, 921; at Five Forks, 923

BAKER, COL. JOHN A., 752

Baker, Gen. Lawrence S., 567, 890

Baldwin, Col. Briscoe G., 374; at Chancellorsville, 442, 448; at Gettysburg, 526; sent to Gorgas to procure arms, 590

Ball, Col. William B., 338, 339

Baltimore and Ohio Railroad, 16, 20, 32, 34, 43, 257, 296, 521, 522, 574, 618, 843; closely watched, 683, 688; unprotected, 707

Banks, Gen. Nathaniel P., 391; Lee suggests attack on, 151, 152, 156, 163; Lee believes he may join McDowell, 166-167, 168; falls back on Strasburg, 174; Lee favors delaying blow against, 174; advanced to Darnestown, 298; troops assemble at Staten Island, 355; Hunter reported to be reinforcing, 527

Barbour, Maj. Alfred M., 183

Barksdale, Gen. William, 315, 368; in Chancellorsville campaign, 447, 461, 465, 466, 467; killed, 539, 578, 585

Barringer, Gen. Rufus, 791

Barter, Lee suggests system of, 672-673

Bartlett, Gen. Joseph J., 827, 828

Bartlett, Capt. Joseph L., report of Second Manassas, 267-268

Barton, Gen. Seth M., 646, 745

Battle reports, Lee's: the Seven Days, 211-222; Cedar Mountain, 270-275; Second Manassas, 275-285; Sharpsburg, 312-324; Fredericksburg, 366-374; Chancellorsville, 458-472; Gettysburg, 569-585; Mine Run, 632-636

Bayard, Gen. George D., 364

Baylor, Col. William S. H., 269

Beale, Col. Richard L. T., 354

Beaufort, steamer, 153

Beaufort, S. C., gunboats threaten, 86

Beauregard, Gen. P. G. T., 430; sent to Manassas, 8; sent to Alexandria, 41; shifted to the West, 125; Pemberton ordered to send troops to, 145; to be prepared to defend Wilmington, 388, 391; A. P. Hill to reinforce, 434; jealous of Lee, 473; Lee suggests he reinforce Johnston in the West, 503; Lee suggests he assemble army at Culpeper Court House, 527, 528, 529, 531; appointed commander of new department, 640; Lee favors moving into N. C., 699; commands south of the James, 709, 711; comes north to assume command, 712; holds Butler at Bermuda Hundred, 716, 732; determined to relinquish no troops to Lee, 738; demands units from Lee's army, 741-742, 744; refuses to cooperate with Lee, 741-743, 744; Lee hopes to be reinforced by, 720, 747, 750, 754, 755, 763; can spare Lee no troops, 756, 757; in campaign, North Anna to Petersburg, 758; anxious

to have Ransom's brigade, 781; fails to inform Lee of his leaving Bermuda Hundred, 785-786; at Petersburg, 785, 786, 789, 794; transferred West, 802; at the Battle of the Crater, 828; to decide about evacuating Savannah, 878; in South Carolina, 894; reports Sherman on the move, 904, 905; health reported to be bad, 906, 909; assigned to Johnston, 909

Bell, Maj. H. M., 653

Bennett, Col. Johnathan M., 27

Berkeley plantation, 181, 225

Best, Col. Emory F., 462

Big Bethel, "Battle" of, 7

Birney, Gen. David B., 247

Black, Col. John L., 567

Blair, Francis P., 4

Bonham, General Milledge L., 33

Borst, Peter B., 653

Boswell, Capt. James K., 463

Boteler, Hon. A. R., 194

Bowman, Lt. Col. Samuel, 57

Boyce, Capt. Robert, 320

Boydton Plank Road, 801, 867, 920, 921

Boykin Rangers, 198

Bragg, Gen. Braxton, 293; reinforcement considered, 378; victory at Stone's River, 387; reinforcements sent to, 398; embattled at Chattanooga, 586-587, 600-601, 602; in Tenn., 605, 606; resigns, 637; proves incompetent as expediter, 741; Lee requests troops from, 749; as Department commander in N. C., 802, 882; ordered to call out local troops, 859; reports Schofield preparing to advance, 904

Branch, Col. John L., 94

Branch, Gen. L. O'Bryan, 168, 198; Lee reluctant to entrust A. P. Hill's division to, 238; in the Maryland campaign, 317, 321

Breckinridge, Gen. John C., directed to be prepared for raid by Averell, 704, 716; to aid Imboden, 709; clears enemy from the Valley, 711; to take general direction of Valley operations, 718-719; Lee asks aid of, at Spotsylvania, 729; asks for reinforcements to defend the Valley, 730; requested to pursue Sigel or join Lee at Spotsylvania, 731, 732; posted at Hanover Junction, 734; with Early in the Valley, 741; to guard main route from Richmond, 747; in campaign, North Anna to Petersburg, 752, 754, 756, 760, 762, 764; temporarily disabled, 767; reports on enemy actions, 861, 863; ordered to clear mountains of deserters, 880; appointed Secretary of War, 898

Breckinridge, Surgeon R. J., 672

Brent, Private J. R. A., 198

Bristoe Station, Meade escapes Lee at, 613

Brockenbrough, Col. John M., 284, 317, 369

Brown, Col. John T., 462, 470

Brown, Joseph E., 37, 81, 117-118

Brunswick, Ga., 112, 113; Lee proposes to destroy, 115

Buchanan, Capt. Franklin, 88

Buckner, Gen. Simon B., 531, 662, 699-700, 701; forces of, 601; in Tenn., 602; Law assigned to, 703

Buell, Gen. Don Carlos, 293

Buford, Capt., 611

Buford, Gen. John, 603

Burnside, Gen. Ambrose E., 207; Lee uncertain of movements of, 141, 225; reinforces McClellan, 194, 195; lands at Fredericksburg, 226; said to have withdrawn from S. C., 236; believed transferred to Va., 249; reported to have left Fredericksburg, 253; strength at Fredericksburg, 254; pushed back by A. P. Hill, 290-291; believed to have joined Pope, 256, 258, 275, 293; reported to be advancing up Potomac, 304; replaces McClellan and moves toward Fredericksburg, 326, 327, 338, 341, 344, 345, 346, 348, 351, 352, 355, 356, 367; at Fredericksburg, 363; "Mud March" of, 375-376; Lee speculates as to intentions of, 384, 386, 389, 390-393, 395, 397, 398; army increasing, 386; goes to Washington, 396; Lee eager to learn whereabouts of troops of, 420; rumored recalled from Ky., 531; marches on Knoxville, 600; to join Rosecrans, 601; said to be collecting army at Annapolis, 685, 686, 688, 699; said to be going to N. C., 691; marches to Alexandria, 706; marches through Centreville, 708; in the Wilderness, 714; reinforces Grant, 717; at Petersburg, 743, 798

Butler, Gen. Benjamin F., 678; in command at Fort Monroe, 625; halted by Pickett, 712; trapped by Beauregard at Bermuda Hundred, 716, 738, 747; Beauregard abandons "siege" of, 742-743; forces join Grant, 758, 760, 761, 763; with Grant at Dutch Gap, 834

Butler, Edward, 37, 68, 97

Butler, Gen. Matthew Calbraith, commands Hampton's division, 802, 834; sent to S. C., 881; Young's brigade ordered to join, 882; division sent to Hardee, 885

CABELL, COL. HENRY C., 132, 368

Camp life, Lee's descriptions of, 64, 67, 69, 70, 78, 400

Campbell, Gen. John A., 273, 274

Canby, Gen. Edward, 826

Capers, Lt. Col. H. D., 704

Carolina, steamer, 120

Carpenter, Capt. John C., 634

Carrington, Lt. A. C., 432

Carter, Col. Hill, 144

Carter, Col. Thomas H., at Chancellorsville, 465, 470; at Gettysburg, 575; with Custis Lee at Richmond, 793

Casualties: in the Seven Days, 222; at Second Manassas, 307; at Chancellorsville, 426, 471; at Gettysburg, 481, 563; at Winchester, 572; at Mine Run, 634, 635; at Cold Harbor, 740; Sheridan's, 800

Catlett's Station, 227, 253, 262, 277

Cavalry, Lee promoted to command of 1st, 3-4; Lee concerned about, 812, 814-815

Cedar Creek, 800, 864-865

Cedar Mountain, Jackson attacks at, 226; battle report of, 270-275

Cedar Run, Jackson victorious at, 251. See also Cedar Mountain

Central Railroad. See Virginia Central Railroad

Chambliss, Col. John R., in Gettysburg campaign, 573, 583; Rob Lee serves with, 616; on watch for Army of Potomac, 706; to strike at Sheridan, 791; Lee asks for brigade of, 805

Chancellorsville, 423-426, 450-458; battle report, 458-472

Charles City Road, Battle of, 798, 838-839

Charleston, Union fleet off, 92, 107; Lee expects attack on, 397-398, 399; besieged, 586; Sherman takes, 898

Charleston and Savannah Railroad, 102, 115, 117

Charleston Light Dragoons, 94

Charleston Mercury, 564

Charlotte Railroad, 904, 905

Chase, Capt. Edward, 57

Chattanooga, fighting at, 600, 601

Cheat Mountain, assault on fails, 73, 752; Jackson and Johnson drive toward, 170

fers with, 586, 637; directs Johnston to take offensive in Tenn., 639; pre-empts control of Lee's army and responsibility, 640; removes Johnston from command, 800; appoints Lee general-in-chief, 802; Lee hesitant to suggest peace talks to, 897; flees south, 900, 903, 904

Davis, Gen. Joseph R., 476, 496, 563

Davis, Surgeon W. B., 411

Delony, Lt. Col. William G., 603

Dement, Capt. William F., 634

De Saussure, Col. Wilmot G., 94, 95

Desertions, problem of, 587, 591, 886, 892, 910, 918. *See also* Absentees

Deshler, Gen. James, 604

Dimmock, Col. Charles, 27, 51

Dix, Gen. John A., 559, 821; to negotiate re exchange of prisoners, 232; at West Point, 496, 497

Dole, Gen. George P., 728

Donelson, Gen. Daniel S., 63, 145

Dowd, Col. William F., 120

Drayton, Gen. Thomas F., 85, 109, 316

Dreux, Lt. Col. Charles D., 57

Drewry's Bluff, defenses of, 126, 169, 177; gunboats fire on, 173; reinforcements to be sent to, 187; McClellan expected to take battery at, 195; fortifications strengthened, 225; R. H. Anderson to be withdrawn from, 252

Duffie, Gen. Alfred N., 866

Dulany, Lt. Col. Richard H., 339

Dungeness, Lee visits, 103-104, 106

Dunovant, Col. John, 654

Dunovant, Col. Richard G. M., 85, 95

DuPont, Admiral Samuel F., 527

Dutch Gap, 830, 831; canal across, 833, 837

EACHES, MR., photographer, 873, 880

Early, Gen. Jubal, 325; at Cedar Mountain, 273; at Second Manassas, 282; in Sharpsburg campaign, 319, 320; at Fredericksburg, 361, 370, 371; at Chancellorsville, 424, 447-448, 449, 450, 453, 454, 455, 461, 465-466, 467, 468, 470; moves to York, 478; in Gettysburg campaign, 502, 514, 521, 525, 570, 573, 574, 575, 577, 578, 584; victorious at Winchester, 515, 516, 517; and fighting near Orange Court House, 629; at Mine Run, 630, 631, 633; sent to get cattle, 647; complains of Imboden's men, 651; operations in Shenandoah Valley, 656, 741, 799, 806-807, 811, 819, 822-823, 824, 825, 834, 835, 840, 845, 856, 858, 861,

862, 864, 879; Lee has confidence in, 662; absentees from division of, 671; at Spotsylvania, 715, 727; assumes command of Hill's corps, 715, 725; operates against Hunter in the Valley, 741; in campaign, North Anna to Petersburg, 745, 754, 762, 764, 772, 782; at siege of Petersburg, 798-799, 873; opposes Sheridan in the Valley, 799; forces withdrawn from, 802; at Cedar Creek, 864-865

Echols, Gen. John, 768

Echols, Capt. William H., 106

Edmundson, Col. H. A., 42

Edwards, Col. Oliver E., 85, 95

XVIII Corps, 738, 740, 741

Elford, Col. Charles J., 95

Elizabeth River, defenses of, 52

Elkhorn, Battle of, 129

Ellis, John W., Governor of North Carolina, 38

Elzey, Gen. Arnold, 39, 383, 493, 513, 531

Emory, Gen. William H., 247

Evans, Gen. Nathan G. ("Shank"), at Cedar Mountain, 272; at Second Manassas, 281; Lee wants aid of, at Gettysburg, 476, 484, 496

Ewell, Gen. Richard S., authorized to strike at enemy, 146; Lee suggests he reinforce Field, 151, 159; Lee suggests he move on Culpeper Court House, 165; at Swift Run Gap, 166; ordered to Gordonsville, 168, 169, 171; moves down the Valley, 172, 174; in the defense of Richmond, 204; in the Seven Days, 211, 215, 216, 219, 220; wounded at Second Manassas, 227, 266, 269, 280; ordered toward Gordonsville, 271; at Cedar Mountain, 273, 274; Lawton commands division in Sharpsburg campaign, 319; resumes command, 477; takes Winchester, 477; moves toward Harrisburg, 478; Lee favors promotion of, 488; Federal troops escape, 556; in Gettysburg campaign, 479, 481, 503, 506, 510, 514, 518, 519, 520, 523, 530, 534, 538, 540, 541, 550, 558, 564, 568, 570, 571, 573, 574, 577, 581, 582, 584; pursues Meade, 613; sick, 633; considered too feeble for Ga. command, 642; Lee considers W. Va. command unsuitable for, 662; to support Johnson, 677; commands 13 brigades, 702; in the Wilderness, 713, 714, 722, 723; at Spotsylvania, 715, 716; to command Richmond defenses, 741, 776; in campaign, North

the "Longstreet controversy," 480; wants troops from Hill, 485-486, 489-490, 493-494, 495, 496, 500; reorganizes, 487-490, 496; on encouraging peace feelers of the North, 507-509; begins march north, 502-503, 505, 515-516; Gettysburg campaign, 516-585; withdraws from Gettysburg, 538-551; consolidates troops, 563; on the criticism of the Gettysburg campaign, 564-565; Battle Report, 569-585; pursued by Meade, 588; outlines strategy, 639, 666-667, 674, 682-684, 685, 688, 699; confers with Jefferson Davis, 586, 637; taken ill again, 587, 595, 616; offers to resign, 589-590; declines command of Army of Tennessee, 587, 596, 614; Battle Report of Mine Run, 632-636

DEC. 1863–APR. 1865: reorganizes units, 638; gathers forces south of the Rapidan, 641; prefers not to go to Dalton, Ga., 642; reluctant to go to N. C., 656; on the observance of Sunday, 668-669; on officers' sons living with them, 671; concentrates against Grant's major offensive, 712; Wilderness campaign, 712-714, 718-723; at Spotsylvania, 715-716, 723-736, 737; ingenious defensive tactics at North Anna, 737-738; ill with intestinal disorder, 738; counter-offensive against Grant, 738, 747-748; difficulties with Beauregard, 741-743; forced into static fortifications, 744; campaigns from North Anna to Petersburg, 749-794; and the siege of Petersburg, 798-802, 809-838, 840, 841-895; appointed general-in-chief, 802, 888; concerned about cavalry force, 813, 814-815; concerned about replacements, 847-850, 851-852; on his own failing strength, 855; needs reinforcements, 888; declines extension of command to include South Atlantic states, 884-885; assumes command as general-in-chief, 891, 892, 894; works toward arranging cessation of hostilities, 897; writes to Grant, 897, 901, 902, 911-912, 931-934; sees hopelessness of his situation, 897, 898, 912-913; strength vs. that of Federal forces, 898; futile offensive at Fort Stedman, 899; evacuates Petersburg and moves southwest, 900-901, 925-926, 928; note of capitulation, 903; meets Grant, 903; "Farewell Address," 903, 934-935; returns to Richmond, 903; writes Davis and recommends suspension of hostilities, 904, 935-939; proposes interview with Grant, 911; parole, 935

Lee, Robert E., Jr., xii; father asks that he remain at college, 15; undecided whether to join army or continue schooling, 48, 70-71; decides to go in army, 129; goes off to war, 134; with Jackson's army, 153; aide de camp to his brother, 381; father would like to have him with him, 671

Lee, Col. Stephen D., 259, 276, 283

Lee, Capt. Sydney Smith, 164

Lee, Gen. W. H. F. (Fitzhugh, Rooney), son of R. E. Lee, xii; in western Va., 61, 79; promoted, 63, 105; Lee's hopes for, 89; Stuart praises, 196-197; meets mishap on reconnoitering expedition, 74; marriage, 83; inherits White House, 180; makes charge at Catlett's Station, 265; at Port Royal with Stuart, 272, 353, 354, 368; cavalry ordered to march to Fredericksburg, 339, 366; engages gunboats near Tappahannock, 409; in Chancellorsville campaign, 436, 459, 461, 471; wounded, 511, 512; prisoner of war, 542, 547, 567, 598, 615, 625; rejoins Stuart, 687; at Spotsylvania, 729, 734; and fighting, North Anna to Petersburg, 743, 762, 764, 782; ordered to Petersburg, 792; follows Federal cavalry near Petersburg, 797, 805, 806, 809; at siege of Petersburg, 833, 837, 838, 847, 890; at Five Forks, 923; repulses enemy, with Gordon, 936

Letcher, John, appoints Lee to command Virginia forces, 4; appoints Jackson colonel, 6; Lee requests funds and supplies of, 14; proclamation transferring Virginia forces to the Confederacy, 44-45; requested to organize defense of Richmond, 50

Letterman, Surgeon Jonathan, 482

Lewis, Capt. J. W., 367

Lewis, Gen. William G., 921

Liddell, Col. P. F., 236

Lincoln, Abraham, signs Lee's commission, 4; Emancipation Proclamation, 292; reported at Aquia Creek, 351; Burnside talks with, 396; calls for troops to defend Pa. frontier, 531; terms for discussion of peace, 897

Lomax, Gen. Lunsford L., 752, 890

Long, Gen. Armistead L., with Lee as Chief of Ordnance, 98; in the Seven Days, 222; acts as Lee's Military Secretary, 306, 309; at Fredericksburg, 374;

Stuart, Gen. J. E. B. (*Continued*)
the Seven Days, 212-213, 216, 220-221;
captures Pope's papers, 227; ordered to
watch enemy movements, 233; moves
toward Fredericksburg, 245, 272; cuts
enemy communications at Catlett's Station, 253, 262; to move toward Culpeper
Court House, 259-260; at Second Manassas, 276, 277, 279, 282, 285; in the
Sharpsburg campaign, 290, 302, 308, 309,
314, 322, 323, 324; Chambersburg raid,
291; ordered to observe McClellan
closely, 331, 334, 336, 339, 340, 342, 444;
at Fredericksburg, 361, 370, 373-374; re-
pels enemy crossing of Rappahannock,
388; ordered to attack Milroy in the
Shenandoah, 402-403; largest command,
477; observes Hooker's movements, 435,
436, 437, 460; in Chancellorsville campaign, 424, 425, 441, 442, 444, 445-446,
448, 451, 459, 461, 462, 464, 470, 471; in-
discreet execution of orders at Gettysburg, 478, 481, 516, 518; during Gettysburg campaign, 519, 520, 521, 524, 529,
540, 546-547, 555, 570, 572, 573, 574, 580-
581, 582; after Gettysburg, 603, 608, 611,
612, 613; and the fighting on the Rapidan, 630; at Mine Run, 635; directed
to send brigade to Valley, 643; to communicate with Johnson, 677; in the
Wilderness campaign, 713; in Spotsylvania campaign, 715, 723; killed, 716,
736; Lee praises, 731, 736; tribute to in
English paper, 837
Stuart Horse Artillery, 198
Stump, Capt. George W., 410
Suffolk, Lee urges reinforcement of, 38
Sumner, Gen. Edwin V., 247, 304, 310;
offers ultimatum to citizens of Fredericksburg, 327, 367; moves toward
Fredericksburg, 339, 340-341, 366; at
Fredericksburg, 363; death of, 420
Sunday, Lee's orders on the observance
of, 668-669
Supplies, Lee's difficulties in obtaining,
647-648, 653-654, 658-660, 663, 664-665,
672-673, 698, 700, 843, 877, 883, 890
Swift Run Gap, Ewell at, 166, 168-169,
170, 171

Talcott, Col. Andrew, 14, 686, 880
Talcott, Maj. Thomas M. R., 222; at
Fredericksburg, 351, 368, 374; at Chan-
cellorsville, 448, 472
Taliaferro, Col. William B., 325; directed
to fire on enemy ships, 21; urged to in-

crease his forces, 31-32; wounded, 266,
269; at Cedar Mountain, 273, 274; at
Second Manassas, 277, 280; at Fred-
ericksburg, 370, 371
Tannahill, Maj. Robert, 882, 883
Tatnall, Flag Officer Josiah, 153, 161, 164
Taylor, Gen. George W., 279
Taylor, Gen. Richard, 239
Taylor, Col. Walter H., on Lee's per-
manent personal staff, 6, 61, 63, 70, 84,
100, 166, 180, 182, 186, 222, 302, 303, 374,
447, 472, 535, 549, 643, 676, 723, 724, 749,
751, 752, 753, 754, 803, 806, 838, 839, 841,
860, 895, 903, 930, 934, 935
Taylor, William F., 333
Teazer, steamer, 153
Tennessee Regiment, First, 42
Tents, Lee requests for men, 189
Terrett, Col. George H., 30
Terry, Gen. William, 914
Thomas, Gen. Edward L., at Second
Manassas, 273, 282, 284; at Fredericks-
burg, 370, 371
Thomas, Gen. George H., 692, 915
Tomlin, Col. Harrison B., 173
Tompkins, Col. Christopher Q., 65
Toombs, Gen. Robert A., 311, 321
Torbert, Gen. Alfred T., 726, 833
Trapier, Gen. James, 120
Traveler, Lee's horse, 229
Tredegar Iron Works, 4, 6, 7, 297
Trimble, Gen. Isaac R., at Second Man-
assas, 273, 277, 279, 283; wounded, 266,
269, 283; in Sharpsburg campaign, 319;
at Chancellorsville, 463; in Gettysburg
campaign, 488, 579, 580; wounded at
Gettysburg, 539, 580
Tucker, Sgt. George W., 903
Tucker, Capt. John R., 153
Turney, Col. Peter, 42

United States, frigate, 52
U. S. Navy, threatens Lee's defenses, 6-7

Van Dorn, Gen. Earl, 129
Vance, Gov. Zebulon (N. C.), 687, 905
Vaughan, Gen. George C., 767
Vaughn, Gen. John C., 863, 915
Venable, Maj. Charles S., on Lee's per-
manent personal staff, 180, 222, 374, 472,
500, 505, 546, 729, 735, 935
Vicksburg, Lee unable to send assistance
to, 473; fall of, 552, 586; Union strategy
at, 682-683
Virginia: votes to secede, 4; forms alli-
ance with Confederacy, 5, 12, 13; trans-

fers military forces to Confederacy, 44-45; summary of preparations for defense of, 50-52; Union prepares offensive against, 125; invading forces cleared from, 228

Virginia, ironclad, 7, 125, 126, 132, 143, 152, 161, 164, 165, 172

Virginia and Tennessee Railroad, 60, 62, 146, 618, 703

Virginia Armory, 7

Virginia Army, composition of, 6

Virginia Cavalry, 198

Virginia Central Railroad, 60, 61, 139, 198, 224, 226, 232, 271-272, 423, 622-623

Volunteers, Lee complains about, 650-651, 654-655

WADSWORTH, GEN. JAMES S., 722

Walker, Gen. Henry H., 105, 118, 317, 563; wounded at Spotsylvania, 727

Walker, Gen. James A., 487; at Fredericksburg, 237, 370, 371; wounded at Spotsylvania, 728

Walker, Gen. John G., 297; in Sharpsburg campaign, 302, 311, 314, 317, 318, 319, 320

Walker, Leroy Pope, 35

Walker, Col. R. Lindsay, 316; at Fredericksburg, 369, 370; at Chancellorsville, 470; at Gettysburg, 577; commands Third Corps artillery, 638

Wallace, Gen. Lew, 821

Waller, Maj. Richard P., 385

Waller, Maj. Thomas, 354

Walton, Col. James B., 487-488; in Second Manassas campaign, 277-278, 282, 283; at Fredericksburg, 362

Walton, Lt. Col. Simeon T., 634

Warren, Gen. Gouverneur K., in the Wilderness, 713; at Spotsylvania, 715, 726; at Petersburg, 743, 744; at Jericho Mills, 737, 749; combines with Sheridan, 899

Washington, George, 3, 5

Washington, Lt. J. Barroll, 139

Washington, Lt. Col. John A., 61, 63, 64, 71, 74, 75, 78

Washington, Martha, 3, 180

Washington, Capt. T. A., 84

Washington Chronicle, 420, 685, 708, 832

Wayne, Gen. Henry C., 114-115

Weldon Railroad, 798, 804, 840, 841, 842, 847, 848, 874, 876, 904, 905, 922

West Virginia, formation of, 7; Lee discusses choice of commander for, 662

Wharton, Col. Gabriel C., 556, 557, 650

Wheeler, Gen. Joseph, 882

Wheeling, defense of, 32

White, Maj. Elijah V., 331, 332, 574

White, Gen. Julius, 297

White House, 100, 105, 108, 128, 180

Whiting, Maj. Jasper S., 177

Whiting, Gen. William H. C., 237, 656; reinforces Jackson, 190, 211; at Gaines' Mill, 215; at Malvern Hill, 219; commands Wilmington defenses, 376, 410, 504-505

Wickham, Col. Williams C., 380, 512, 595; at Second Manassas, 279; reconnoiters at Rappahannock, 409; at Chancellorsville, 462; in Gettysburg campaign, 502

Wigfall, Gen. Louis T., 412

Wilbourn, Capt. R. D., 425, 720

Wilcox, Gen. Cadmus M., 140; at Second Manassas, 281, 282, 284; at Chancellorsville, 459, 461, 466, 467, 470; at Gettysburg, 480, 481, 577, 580; promoted, 638; Lee has confidence in, 662; in the Wilderness, 713, 721, 722, 730; from North Anna to Petersburg, 783; desertions in corps of, 910

Wilderness campaign, 424, 712-714, 721-723, 737

Wilkes, Capt. Charles, 98

Williams, Col. J. J., 119

Williams, Seth, 487

Willis, Col. Edward, 488, 643

Willis, Dr. Francis T., 117, 118

Wilmington, 388, 391; capture of, 802

Wilson, Gen. James H., 791; at siege of Petersburg, 797, 798, 803, 810

Winchester, Jackson congratulated on march to, 187; Ewell takes, 477; Early victorious at, 515, 516, 517; devastation at, 562; Battle of, 570-572; capture of, 840; troops for Grant concentrate at, 924

Winder, Gen. Charles S., 251, 273

Winder, Gen. John H., 57

Wingfield, Captain, 209

Wise, Gen. Henry A., 202; rivalry with Floyd, 60; ordered to join Floyd, 62; ordered to confine command to "Wise Legion," 64; asks to be detached from Floyd's command, 66; congratulated by Lee, 72; Lee asks advice of, 77; brigade attached to Longstreet's command, 234

Wise Legion, 64, 65

Withers, John, 84

Wofford, Gen. William T., 455, 467, 603

Wood, Maj. D. H., 878, 879